THE NEW WORLD

IDEA INDEX

TO

THE HOLY BIBLE

Edited by

The Reverend Harvey K. Griffith

WORLD PUBLISHING

TIMES MIRROR

NEW YORK

Library of Congress Card Number: 72–77416

WORLD PUBLISHING
TIMES MIRROR

PRINTED IN THE UNITED STATES OF AMERICA

TABLE OF CONTENTS

ACKNOWLEDGEMENTS

LOGIC

This Index is the product of over seventeen years of research. The logic for concept (idea) indexing was developed by Professor William H. Russell of the U.S. Naval Academy and Major Charles M. Bowling (USAF retired) founder, Casyndekan, Inc., Colorado Springs, Colorado. The logic is based on a philosophy of Predefined Unity (developed by the same two gentlemen) wherein an Idea Set is created prior to indexing the subject matter.

CONCEPT SET DEVELOPMENT AND PRELIMINARY CLASSIFICATION

The Idea Set was compiled and refined over an eighteen month period by the Reverend Harvey K. Griffith, Dr. Lowell King, Sister Annette Boudreau, Dr. Robert Lester, the Reverend Edward Everding, Father Patrick O'Donnell, Dr. Lawrence Lacour, Dr. Allen J. Allen, Dr. E. R. Therkelsen, Miss Karen Anderson, and Mr. Lawrence M. Gress.

The preliminary classification was completed by seminarians: Mr. Gary L. Armstrong, Mr. Donald Purvis, Mr. Phillip Meredith and Mr. James Fox.

CLASSIFICATION AND EDITING

The Texts of the Bible were classified for Casyndekan, Inc., by the above named seminarians under the guidance of Dr. Edward Everding, professor of New Testament Studies at Iliff School of Theology, Denver, Colorado, and Father Patrick O'Donnell, professor of Old Testament Studies at St. Thomas Seminary, Denver, Colorado. Their work was supervised, edited and compiled by the Reverend Harvey K. Griffith, B.A., B.D., M.S., Casyndekan staff consultant on Religious studies with the assistance of Miss Karen Anderson, B.Th. and members of the Casyndekan Staff.

To insure exhaustive accurate classification, a separate board of editorial consultants was established by Dr. Michael J. Grady, Jr., Director of Educational Research, Casyndekan, Inc. The Editorial Board represents an ecumenical cross section of religious persuasion, and their experience ranges from literary scholarship in colleges and universities to active clerical work in churches and parishes.

They are:

Ralph T. Barnes, Ph. L.
Asst. Prof. of Philosophy
Metropolitan State College
Denver, Colorado
(Lay scholar)

Michael S. Birchenall, Ph.D.
Teacher, Comparative Religion
Mitchell High School
Colorado Springs, Colorado
(Episcopalian)

Dr. Lawrence Bixler
Professor of Philosophy & Religion
Northwest Christian College
Eugene, Oregon
(Christian Church)

Monsignor John F. Cox, Ph.D.
Vicar General Diocese of Providence
Warwick, R.I.
(Roman Catholic)

Dr. Edward Everding
Iliff School of Theology
Denver, Colorado
(Methodist)

Rev. Dr. Shepard S. Johnson
Sudbury, Mass.
(Methodist)

Charles A. Meyer, M.A.
Professor of Old Testament Literature
University of Northern Colorado
Greeley, Colorado
(Lay scholar)

Rev. Dr. E. H. Westmoreland
Houston, Texas
(Southern Baptist)

The composite findings of the total editorial board were statistically validated by Dr. Grady and indicated an 85.8% agreement with the Casyndekan classification.

TECHNICAL DESIGN AND FORMAT

The overall indexing project was coordinated by Lawrence M. Gress, B.A., M.A., Casyndekan Staff Coordinator and Technical Editor.

The design and format are the joint project of the Casyndekan Staff and Mr. Daniel E. Soyka, Vice President, Bible and Religious Division, World Publishing Company.

The layout and composition of the index were completed by the production department of Casyndekan, Inc.

INSTRUCTIONS ON THE USE OF THE IDEA INDEX

THE LOGIC FOR IDEA INDEXING

We read for ideas, not words. If man's natural thinking process encompasses block of words — ideas — then it is logical to classify material according to concepts or idea relationships, instead of the individual words that make up the concepts. The first step in idea (or concept) indexing, therefore, is to determine which ideas are to be classified, to develop a concept set. Once the set of concepts is developed, each passage or text can be classified against the set of concepts to determine the location of individual ideas within the overall text.

This provides for easy cross-referencing of ideas from one text to another because all texts are classified according to a predefined set of ideas rather than the actual words contained in the text.

Idea indexing also eliminates the mechanical problems of word indices by identifying themes in contexts where synonyms are used in place of the actual theme in question. In other words, in a given passage, the theme of "resurrection" may be discussed at great length in such terms as "raised up," "live again" or "raised from the dead," without the actual word, "resurrection," ever appearing. Where the traditional word concordance might not cite "resurrection" as a theme in that particular passage, the Idea Index highlights it.

THE NATURE OF THE IDEA INDEX

The Idea Index is designed to reference concepts and concept relationships, just as a concordance is designed to reference key words, names, or biographical listings. The Index further provides a complete listing of the principal Biblical personalities arranged in alphabetical order, under each of the ideas cited. The citations are listed in Biblical order by chapter and verse, including the Apocrypha, making this index usable for any edition of the Bible.

HOW TO USE THE IDEA INDEX

A Thesaurus of Related Ideas is provided to equate the concepts in the index to your particular frame of reference. The ideas in the set are also defined to insure consistent semantic application of all terms. Whether you are concerned with a specific theme or only vaguely remember a topic in the Bible, by using the Thesaurus and idea definitions, you can find all the references to your idea, in context. This is achieved by referring to the term in the Thesaurus which is most closely synonymous with your own. For example, if you are interested in locating the text or texts where banishment is used as a form of punishment for false worship, look up "banishment" in the Thesaurus, and it will refer you to the ideas ALIENATION and PUNISHMENT in the index. Under ALIENATION you will find several related ideas, one of which is "as PUNISHMENT for FALSE BELIEF." Enter the index as you would a dictionary, locating the main idea above the left hand column.

In the example below the main idea is ALIENATION. The primary sub-idea is PUNISHMENT, and the secondary sub-idea is FALSE BELIEF. The personalities involved in the texts containing this triple intersection of ideas are the author or narrator and the Israelites. The actual texts are Hebrews 6:1-8 and Jeremiah 18:13-17. The words in lower case medium type indicate the nature of the idea relationship. In this reference the context of these ideas indicates that ALIENATION, in both Hebrews 6:1-8 and Jeremiah 18:13-17, was used as a form of punishment for the specific transgression of false belief.

EXAMPLE: 1

ALIENATION

as **PUNISHMENT**
      for **FALSE BELIEF**
          Author   Heb 6:1-8
          Israelites   Jer 18:13-17

In some cases, only two ideas are identified in a given relationship. Although these references are more general than the combinations of three (like example 1), they are still sufficiently specific to provide the context of the idea (see example 2). This reference gives a general listing of ALIENATION as a form of punishment for any transgression.

EXAMPLE: 2

ALIENATION

as **PUNISHMENT**
      Israelites   Lev 26:1-46
      Moses   Lev 17:1-9;
                    10-14;
                    18:1-30;
                    19:1-37;
                    Num 15:22-31

If, however, you are concerned with a more general idea "Honesty" for example, you can go directly to the Index section on HONESTY, find all of the related ideas under HONESTY, and select the idea relationships which identify the exact context of "Honesty" most closely related to your area of interest.

Notice that in both examples, the ideas are printed in bold face type, and the connectives and modifiers are printed in medium face. This facilitates rapid recognition of the primary ideas in alphabetical order and indicates their relationships.

NOTE: an asterisk denotes an apocryphal listing.

DEFINITIONS OF IDEAS

ACCEPTANCE — the state of approval or endorsement.

ALIENATION — a condition of estrangement or separation caused by a hostile act.

ANGER — an emotion revealing hostility or displeasure resulting from mistreatment.

ANXIETY — a state of uneasiness revealing apprehension and mental suffering.

AUTHORITY — the right and power to enforce, influence or rule.

BEHAVIOR — the manner in which an individual conducts himself.

BELIEF — knowledge that a person or a group holds with conviction.

BLASPHEMY — an irreverent statement or act directed toward God or something sacred.

BLESSING — an act of approval or favor.

BROTHERHOOD — a fraternal relationship of persons united under a common creed.

CAPTIVITY — the state of restraint or bondage.

CHAOS — a condition of extreme disorder or confusion.

COMMITMENT — a pledge of intention.

COMMUNITY — persons living together in a common environment for the purpose of providing for their mutual needs.

COMPASSION — sympathic identification with another's situation.

COMPULSION — a force that causes an involuntary reaction.

CONDEMNATION — the state of censure, conviction or strong disapproval.

CONFRONTATION — a face-to-face encounter.

CONVERSION — a transformation that causes change.

COURAGE — the quality of bravery or self-reliance.

COVENANT — an agreement or promise between two parties with an awareness of a divine presence.

COVETOUSNESS — a strong desire for something that belongs to another.

CREATION — bringing in to being; the universe.

DEATH — the state of lifelessness or an ending.

DEFEAT — the state of utter frustration or being completely overcome by a hostile force.

DEITY — a divine being having omnipotent, omniscient and omnipresent qualities.

DESIRE — a wish for.

DESPAIR – the state of complete hopelessness.

DESTRUCTION – the state of obliteration or ruin.

DIGNITY – the quality of individual prestige and stateliness.

DISCIPLESHIP – following a teacher or charismatic leader with devotion.

DISOBEDIENCE – a refusal or failure to follow commands.

DOUBT – a condition of wavering uncertainty regarding an opinion or belief.

ELECTION – an act of divine selection.

ENEMY – one party or force hostile to another.

ENVIRONMENT – the natural, physical, social, cultural or religious surroundings of an individual or group; the world.

EQUALITY – having like qualities.

ETERNITY – the characteristic of being infinite.

EVIL – a quality revealing immorality or wickedness.

FAITH – a state of complete trust or confidence.

FALSE BELIEF – beliefs differing from the established norms.

FAMILY – a group of persons related by blood or marriage through several generations.

FEAR – the emotion caused by the presence of danger, suffering or authority.

FIDELITY – faithful devotion.

FOLLOWER – one who pursues and adheres to the teachings of a religious leader.

FREEDOM – the state of being without restraint.

FRIENDSHIP – the state of a close acquaintanceship between parties.

FULFILLMENT – the state of completion or satisfaction.

GIFT – a natural ability.

GOOD – the quality of being desirable or valid.

GRACE – an act of unmerited favor.

GRATITUDE – a feeling of thankful appreciation.

GREED – an excessive desire to have or acquire more than one needs.

GRIEF – the state of intense emotional suffering.

GUILT – a state or feeling of having transgressed or committed an offense.

HATE – the emotion expressing an intense dislike or animosity toward someone or something.

HEALING — the act of curing, renewing, or making whole again.

HERESY — an unorthodox religious belief opposing established views or doctrines.

HONESTY — the quality of trustworthiness and integrity.

HOPE — a feeling of anticipation for the fulfillment of what is desired.

HUMILITY — the quality of being submissive or humble.

IDOLATRY — the excessive worship or devotion to idols or persons.

IGNORANCE — the state of being uninformed or unknowing.

INDIFFERENCE — the attitude of apathy or unconcern.

INNOCENCE — the state of being free from sin, evil or guilt.

INSTRUCTION — a means of teaching.

JEALOUSY — a feeling of distrust and envy.

JOY — a feeling of delight and happiness.

JUDGMENT — a determination of the degree of imperfection or fault.

JUSTICE — an act of fairness to an offender in relation to the laws and customs of a community.

KILLING — an act causing death.

KNOWLEDGE — the comprehension of a body of information.

LAW — a code of conduct for a given community or group.

LEADERSHIP — a quality in a person or a position of authority that permits him to command, guide or direct others.

LIFE — the essence of being or existing.

LOVE — an act of devotion or strong affection.

LUST — an intense desire for personal satisfaction.

MARRIAGE — persons united in the intimate state of matrimony.

MEDIATION — the act of intercession between two parties to arbitrate differences.

MEDITATION — an act of contemplation.

MESSIANIC FIGURE — a leader by divine choice.

MIRACLE — an unusual event that seems to contradict the known laws of nature.

MISSION — propagating one's religious beliefs.

MOTIVATION — the stimulus or incentive that is the prime cause for a particular pattern of behavior.

NEW AGE — a view of an end with a promise of a new beginning.

OBEDIENCE — the act of complying with what is required.

OLD AGE — the state of maturity.

ONENESS — the quality of unity or homogeneity.

OPPRESSION — the state of physical or mental distress caused by persecution or overbearance.

ORDER — the condition of a uniform arrangement of things or events based upon some plan or system.

PARADOX — a statement or act that seems to be a contradiction of facts revealing an absurd inconsistency.

PATIENCE — the ability to persevere or endure without complaint.

PEACE — the state of harmony or freedom from war or strife.

PIETY — the quality of reverent devotion to one's religious duties.

POLITICS — the science of strategy and tactics in the political affairs of government.

POVERTY — the condition of being poor or in need.

PRAISE — an act of glorification or a compliment resulting from a feeling of gratitude.

PRAYER — an act in which there is communion with a deity.

PRESENCE — the state where the all-pervading presence of God is experienced.

PRIDE — an attitude of high self-esteem or satisfaction in one's achievements.

PROMISE — a pledge assuring future action.

PROPHECY — a foretelling as revealed by the prophets through divine inspiration.

PROVIDENCE — the benevolent guidance of God in His creation.

PRUDENCE — a quality revealing sound judgment, discretion and sensible conduct.

PUNISHMENT — a disciplinary action imposed upon an offender.

PURIFICATION — a ceremony of cleansing or regeneration, such as baptism.

QUALITY OF LIFE — the spiritual and physical attributes in a person's life.

RATIONALIZATION — a process of logical reasoning.

RECONCILIATION — the act of restoring harmony.

REJECTION — the act of refusing to accept or believe.

REPENTANCE — a feeling of regret or remorse for wrong deeds or intentions.

RESPECT — a quality of reverence and esteem for someone or something.

RESURRECTION — the act of rising from death into life eternal.

REVELATION — a manifestation revealing the divine will.

REVENGE — an act of vengeance or retaliation.

REWARD — a special acknowledgement or compensation given for some deed.

RITE — a ceremonial act or observance.

SACREDNESS — the condition of being consecrated to a deity or set apart as a religious rite.

SACRIFICE — an offering or giving up of something of high value in homage to a deity or as a selfless gift to one's fellow man.

SADNESS — an emotion expressing unhappiness or sorrow.

SALVATION — an act of divine deliverance.

SCRIPTURES — the sacred writings containing the beliefs of a religious group.

SECURITY — the assurance of one's present or future freedom from fear or doubt.

SELF-REALIZATION — the discovery or understanding of the component realities in one's life.

SELFISHNESS — concern only for one's own self-interest.

SERVICE — an act of contribution to the welfare of others.

SEX — the attraction of one sex to the other.

SHARING — the act of giving a portion or participating with others.

SIGNS — manifestations in the life of man indicative of divine will.

SIN — rejection of the divine plan for good in total or in part.

SPIRIT — the immaterial entity making up the will, intellect and emotions.

STEALING — an act of taking something that belongs to another; dishonesty.

STEWARDSHIP — the act of managing one's life or resources in accord with the divine purpose.

SUFFERING — the state of enduring unpleasantness or pain.

TEMPERANCE — the quality of abstaining from, or acting in moderation.

TEMPTATION — an act of enticement or strong attraction which provokes a risk.

TRADITION — established behavior and belief patterns based on continuous cultural practices.

TRUTH — the quality of correctness in relation to an established or verified fact; religious truth.

VICTORY – a successful end to a struggle involving the defeat of some form of opposition.

VIOLENCE – an intense use of force causing fury or disorder.

VIRTUE – the quality of moral excellence.

WEALTH – a state of abundant resources suggesting prosperity.

WILL – the quality of a person's inclination and determination in a situation.

WISDOM – the quality of comprehending and using good judgment with profound discretion.

WITNESS – the state of holding evidence or being an observer in a particular situation.

WORSHIP – an act showing reverence for a deity through religious rites and ceremonies.

YOUTH – the state of being young and in the maturing process.

THESAURUS OF RELATED IDEAS

Term	see IDEA
Abhorrence	HATE
Ability	GIFT
Abolish	ALIENATION
	DESTRUCTION
	REJECTION
Abomination	HATE
Abstinence	TEMPERANCE
Absurdity	PARADOX
	RATIONALIZATION
Abundance	WEALTH
Acceptance	ACCEPTANCE
Acclamation	PRAISE
Accomplishment	FULFILLMENT
Accuracy	TRUTH
Accusations	JUDGMENT
	WITNESS
Achievement	FULFILLMENT
Acknowledgement	ACCEPTANCE
	REWARD
Acquaintanceship	FRIENDSHIP
Acquittal	GRACE
Act	BEHAVIOR
	SIGNS
Adaptation	RECONCILIATION
Adherent	FOLLOWER
Adjustment	RECONCILIATION
Admonition	INSTRUCTION
Adolescence	YOUTH
Adoption	ELECTION
	FAMILY
Adoration	LOVE
	PRAISE
	WORSHIP
Adultery	MARRIAGE-FIDELITY
	(inFIDELITY)
	SEX-FIDELITY
	(inFIDELITY)
Adversary	ENEMY
Adversity	POVERTY
Advice	INSTRUCTION
Advocate	DISCIPLESHIP
	FOLLOWER
	MEDIATION
Affairs	POLITICS
Affection	LOVE
Affliction	SUFFERING
Affluence	WEALTH
Aged	OLD AGE
Agnosticism	DOUBT
Agony	SUFFERING
Agreement	ACCEPTANCE
	COMMITMENT
	COVENANT
	ONENESS
Aid	SERVICE
Alarm	FEAR
Alienation	ALIENATION
Allegiance	FIDELITY
	OBEDIENCE
Allegory	INSTRUCTION
	PARADOX
	SIGNS
Alliance	COVENANT
Allocation	SHARING
Allurement	TEMPTATION
Altar	RITE
	SACREDNESS
	WORSHIP

Term	see IDEA
Amnesty	GRACE
Ancestors	FAMILY
Ancient	OLD AGE
Anger	ANGER
Anguish	ANXIETY
	QUALITY OF LIFE
	SUFFERING
Animosity	HATE
Annihilation	DESTRUCTION
Anointed leadership	ELECTION
	MESSIANIC FIGURE
Anticipation	HOPE
Anxiety	ANXIETY
Apathy	INDIFFERENCE
Apologetics	INSTRUCTION
	MISSION
Apostasy	HERESY
Apostle	DISCIPLESHIP
	FOLLOWER
Appoint	ELECTION
Apportionment	SHARING
Appreciation	GRATITUDE
Apprehension	ANXIETY
	DOUBT
Approval	ACCEPTANCE
	BLESSING
Aptitude	GIFT
Arbitration	MEDIATION
Arrogance	PRIDE
Ashamed	GUILT
Assassination	KILLING
Assault	CONFRONTATION
	VIOLENCE
Assent	ACCEPTANCE
Assistance	SERVICE
Assurance	BELIEF
	PROMISE
	SECURITY
Atheism	FALSE BELIEF
	REJECTION-DEITY
Atmosphere	ENVIRONMENT
Atonement	RECONCILIATION
	SALVATION
Attitude	BEHAVIOR
Attraction	COMPULSION
	TEMPTATION
Attribute	QUALITY OF LIFE
Authenticity	TRUTH
Authority	AUTHORITY
Avarice	GREED
Avenge	REVENGE
Aversion	HATE
Awareness	KNOWLEDGE
	SELF-REALIZATION
Awe	FEAR
	RESPECT
Bad	EVIL
	SIN
Balance	EQUALITY
Banishment	ALIENATION
	PUNISHMENT
Banquet	RITE
Baptism	PURIFICATION
Battle	CONFRONTATION-VIOLENCE
Beat	DEFEAT
Beauty	QUALITY OF LIFE
Beginning	CREATION
	NEW AGE

THESAURUS

Term	see IDEA	Term	see IDEA
Beguile	HONESTY (disHONESTY)	Changing	CONVERSION
	TEMPTATION	Chaos	CHAOS
Behavior	BEHAVIOR	Characteristic	QUALITY OF LIFE
Being	SPIRIT	Charge	COMMITMENT
Belief	BELIEF		MISSION
Believer	FOLLOWER	Charismatic leader	MESSIANIC FIGURE
Benediction	PRAYER	Charity	LOVE
Benefit	GOOD	Chastisement	PUNISHMENT
Benevolence	LOVE	Chastity	VIRTUE
Bereavement	DEATH	Childhood	YOUTH
	SADNESS	Choice	FREEDOM
Beseech	DESIRE		WILL
	PRAYER	Chosen	ELECTION
	WILL	Circumcision	PURIFICATION
Bestow	BLESSING		RITE
Betrayal	FIDELITY (inFIDELITY)	Clan	COMMUNITY
Betrothal	MARRIAGE	Cleansing	PURIFICATION
	PROMISE	Clemency	GRACE
Beware	PROPHECY	Codes	LAW
	SIGNS	Coercion	COMPULSION
Beyond death	RESURRECTION		OPPRESSION
Bigamy	MARRIAGE	Comfort	COMPASSION
Bigotry	JUDGMENT		PEACE
	OPPRESSION	Command	INSTRUCTION
Birth	CREATION-LIFE	Commandments	LAW
Birthright	TRADITION-FAMILY	Commandership	LEADERSHIP
Bitterness	HATE	Commendation	BLESSING
Blameworthiness	GUILT		GRATITUDE
Blasphemy	BLASPHEMY		PRAISE
Blessing	BLESSING	Commitment	COMMITMENT
Blood	LIFE		COVENANT
Boast	PRIDE		PROMISE
Bondage	CAPTIVITY	Common sense	PRUDENCE
Bountiful	WEALTH		WISDOM
Bounty	BLESSING	Communion	PRAYER
	REWARD	Communion, Holy	RITE
	SHARING	Community	COMMUNITY
Bravery	COURAGE		FAMILY
Brethren	BROTHERHOOD	Compact	COVENANT
Brotherhood	BROTHERHOOD	Companionship	FRIENDSHIP
Build	CREATION	Compassion	COMPASSION
Burden	OPPRESSION	Competence	GIFT
Calamity	DESTRUCTION	Completeness	ONENESS
	PUNISHMENT	Completion	FULFILLMENT
Call	ELECTION	Compliance	OBEDIENCE
Callousness	INDIFFERENCE	Compliment	PRAISE
Calm	PEACE	Composure	PATIENCE
Capability	GIFT	Comprehension	KNOWLEDGE
	QUALITY OF LIFE		WISDOM
Captivity	CAPTIVITY	Compulsion	COMPULSION
Care	PROVIDENCE	Concealment	HONESTY (disHONESTY)
	PRUDENCE	Conceit	PRIDE
Carnal	LIFE	Conception	CREATION
	QUALITY OF LIFE	Concern	COMPASSION
Castaway	ALIENATION		FEAR
	REJECTION		STEWARDSHIP
Caught	CAPTIVITY	Condemnation	CONDEMNATION
Causation	CREATION	Condolence	COMPASSION
Cause	PROVIDENCE	Conduct	BEHAVIOR
Caution	PRUDENCE	Confederate	COMMUNITY-COVENANT
Celebration	RITE		POLITICS
Celestial	NEW AGE	Confession	COMMITMENT
Celibacy	TEMPERANCE		PRAYER
Censure	CONDEMNATION		SELF-REALIZATION
Census	COMMUNITY-ORDER	Confidence	BELIEF
Ceremony	PURIFICATION		COURAGE
	RITE		FAITH
Certainty	SECURITY		HOPE
	TRUTH		

THESAURUS

THESAURUS

Term	see IDEA
Disaster	DEFEAT
	DESTRUCTION
Disbelief	BELIEF (unBELIEF)
Discard	REJECTION
Discernment	JUDGMENT
	PRUDENCE
	RATIONALIZATION
	WILL
Disciple	DISCIPLESHIP
	FOLLOWER
Discipleship	DISCIPLESHIP
	FOLLOWER
Discipline	PUNISHMENT
Disclosure	REVELATION
Discouragement	DESPAIR
Discourtesy	RESPECT (disRESPECT)
Discretion	PRUDENCE
	WILL
Disgrace	HUMILITY
	RESPECT (disRESPECT)
Dishonesty	HONESTY (disHONESTY)
Dishonor	RESPECT (disRESPECT)
Disinherit	REJECTION
Disloyalty	FIDELITY (inFIDELITY)
Disobedience	DISOBEDIENCE
Disorder	CHAOS
	VIOLENCE
Displeasure	ANGER
Dispute	CONFRONTATION
	REJECTION
Disrespect	RESPECT (disRESPECT)
Dissension	CONFRONTATION
	REJECTION
Distinction	DIGNITY
	QUALITY OF LIFE
Distress	SUFFERING
Distribution	SHARING
Distrust	DOUBT
	JEALOUSY
Diversity	EQUALITY (inEQUALITY)
Divine Being	DEITY
Divine deliverance	SALVATION
Divine favor	BLESSING
Divine foretelling	REVELATION
Divine guidance	PROPHECY
	PROVIDENCE
	REVELATION
Divine influence	PROVIDENCE
	REVELATION
Divine instruction	REVELATION
Divine selection	ELECTION
Divinity	DEITY
Divorce	MARRIAGE-FREEDOM
Doctrinal	BELIEF
	INSTRUCTION
Doctrine	BELIEF
	SCRIPTURES
Domination	CAPTIVITY
	OPPRESSION
Doubt	BELIEF (unBELIEF)
	DOUBT
Dread	FEAR
Dreams	REVELATION
Drunkenness	LUST
Duty	MISSION
Earth	CREATION
	ENVIRONMENT
Edification	INSTRUCTION

Term	see IDEA
Egoism	PRIDE
	SELFISHNESS
Election	ELECTION
Emancipation	FREEDOM
Embarkation	NEW AGE
Emotion	BEHAVIOR
	SPIRIT
Emulation	DESIRE-EQUALITY
Encountering	CONFRONTATION
Encouragement	HOPE
	MOTIVATION
Endeavour	COMMITMENT
Ending	DEATH
	FULFILLMENT
Endorsement	ACCEPTANCE
Endowment	GIFT
Endurance	PATIENCE
	SUFFERING
Enemy	ENEMY
Enjoyment	JOY
Enlightenment	KNOWLEDGE
	SELF-REALIZATION
Enmity	HATE
Entanglement	CONFRONTATION
Enticement	TEMPTATION
Environment	ENVIRONMENT
Envy	COVETOUSNESS
	JEALOUSY
Equality	EQUALITY
Equity	JUSTICE
Equivalence	EQUALITY
Eroticism	SEX
Error	IGNORANCE
	RATIONALIZATION
	TRUTH (unTRUTH)
Escape	CAPTIVITY-FREEDOM
Eschatology	FULFILLMENT
	HOPE
	JUDGMENT
	NEW AGE
	PROMISE
	PROPHECY
Essence	LIFE
Establishment	TRADITION
Esteem	RESPECT
Estrangement	ALIENATION
Eternal life	LIFE-ETERNITY
	RESURRECTION
Eternity	ETERNITY
Ethics	VIRTUE
Etymology	KNOWLEDGE
Eucharist	RITE
Evangelism	MISSION
Everlasting	ETERNITY
Evidence	WITNESS
Evil	EVIL
	SIN
Exaltation	PRAISE
Excellence	GOOD
Excessive desire	COVETOUSNESS
	GREED
	LUST
Exclusion	REJECTION
Excommunication	ALIENATION
	REJECTION
Excuse	GRACE
Execution	KILLING
Exhortation	INSTRUCTION

THESAURUS

THESAURUS

THESAURUS

xxi

THESAURUS

Term	see IDEA
Omnipresence	DEITY
	PRESENCE
Omniscience	DEITY
	WISDOM
Oneness	ONENESS
Opinion	BELIEF
	JUDGMENT
Opposition	CONFRONTATION
	REJECTION
Oppression	OPPRESSION
Order	ORDER
Ordination	RITE-SACREDNESS
Organization	ORDER
Origination	CREATION-ORDER
Ostentation	PRIDE
Overbearing	OPPRESSION
Overseer	AUTHORITY
	LEADERSHIP
Overthrown	DEFEAT
Pain	SUFFERING
Paradox	PARADOX
Pardon	GRACE
Parentage	FAMILY
Passion	DESIRE
	LUST
	SUFFERING
Passover	RITE
Patience	PATIENCE
Peace	PEACE
Penalty	CONDEMNATION
	PUNISHMENT
Penitence	REPENTANCE
Perceive	KNOWLEDGE
	PRUDENCE
	WISDOM
Perdition	CONDEMNATION
	NEW AGE
Perfection	VIRTUE
Persecution	OPPRESSION
Perseverance	PATIENCE
Personal revelation	REVELATION
Petition	PRAYER
Phenomenon	MIRACLE
	SIGNS
Physical surroundings	ENVIRONMENT
Piety	PIETY
Pillage	STEALING
Pity	COMPASSION
Plan	ORDER
Plea	DESIRE
	PRAYER
Plead	MEDITATION
Pleasure	JOY
Pledge	COMMITMENT
	PROMISE
Plenty	WEALTH
Political	POLITICS
Politics	POLITICS
Ponder	MEDITATION
Poor	POVERTY
Possession	WEALTH
Posterity	NEW AGE
Potential	GIFT
	QUALITY OF LIFE
Poverty	POVERTY
Power	AUTHORITY
Practice	TRADITION
Praise	PRAISE

Term	see IDEA
Prayer	PRAYER
Preaching	INSTRUCTION
Precept	LAW
Predestination	ELECTION
Prediction	PROPHECY
Prejudice	JUDGMENT
Presence	PRESENCE
Preservation	PROVIDENCE
Prestige	DIGNITY
Pride	PRIDE
Principles	LAW
Prize	REWARD
Procedure	ORDER
Procession	ORDER
	RITE
Proclamation	INSTRUCTION
Prodigy	MIRACLE
	SIGNS
Profanity	BLASPHEMY
Profundity	WISDOM
Prohibition	TEMPERANCE
Promise	PROMISE
Proper	GOOD
Prophecy	PROPHECY
Propitation	MEDIATION
Prospect	HOPE
Prosperity	WEALTH
Prostitution	LUST
	SEX-SIN
Protection	SECURITY
Proud	PRIDE
Providence	PROVIDENCE
Provocation	MOTIVATION
Prudence	PRUDENCE
Punishment	PUNISHMENT
Purge	PURIFICATION
Purification	PURIFICATION
Purity	INNOCENCE
	VIRTUE
Pursuing	DISCIPLESHIP
Quality of life	QUALITY OF LIFE
Question	DOUBT
Quietness	PEACE
Race	COMMUNITY-FAMILY
Rage	ANGER
	VIOLENCE
Rationality	QUALITY OF LIFE
	WISDOM
Rationalization	RATIONALIZATION
Reality	TRUTH
Reason	MOTIVATION
Reasoning	RATIONALIZATION
Rebellion	REJECTION
	VIOLENCE
Rebirth	PURIFICATION
	RESURRECTION
Rebuke	INSTRUCTION
	PUNISHMENT
Recompense	REWARD
Reconciliation	RECONCILIATION
Recovering	HEALING
Redeemer	MESSIANIC FIGURE
Redemption	RECONCILIATION
	SALVATION
Reflection	MEDITATION
Refuge	SECURITY
Refusing	REJECTION
Regard	RESPECT
Regeneration	CONVERSION

THESAURUS

Term	see IDEA
Regeneration (cont'd)	PURIFICATION
	SALVATION
Regret	REPENTANCE
Regularity	ORDER
Regulation	LAW
Rehabilitation	HEALING
Reign	AUTHORITY
	LEADERSHIP
Reincarnation	RESURRECTION
Rejection	REJECTION
Rejoice	JOY
Reliance	FAITH
Religiousness	PIETY
	SACREDNESS
Religious surroundings	ENVIRONMENT
Relinquishment	SACRIFICE
Remedy	HEALING
Remembrance	RITE
	SIGNS
Remorse	GUILT
	REPENTANCE
Renewal	CONVERSION
	HEALING
Repay	JUSTICE
	REVENGE
Repentance	REPENTANCE
Representation	SIGNS
Reproach	OPPRESSION
	PUNISHMENT
Repudiation	REJECTION
Reputation	QUALITY OF LIFE
Request	DESIRE
	PRAYER
Require	COMPULSION
	INSTRUCTION
Resentment	ANGER
	JEALOUSY
Resources	WEALTH
Respect	RESPECT
Rest	PEACE
Restoration	RECONCILIATION
Restraint	CAPTIVITY
	OPPRESSION
Resurrection	RESURRECTION
Retaliation	REVENGE
Retribution	PUNISHMENT
	REVENGE
Revelation	REVELATION
Revenge	REVENGE
Revere	FEAR
	WORSHIP
Reverence	PIETY
	RESPECT
	WORSHIP
Revolt	DISOBEDIENCE
Reward	REWARD
Richness	WEALTH
Ridicule	RESPECT (disRESPECT)
Right	GOOD
Righteousness	VIRTUE
Riot	CONFRONTATION
	VIOLENCE
Rite	RITE
Ritual	RITE
Robbery	STEALING
Role	BEHAVIOR
Rudeness	RESPECT (disRESPECT)
Ruin	DESTRUCTION

Term	see IDEA
Rule	AUTHORITY
Rulership	LEADERSHIP
Rules	LAW
Sabbath	RITE
	SACREDNESS
Sacrament	RITE
Sacredness	SACREDNESS
Sacred writings	SCRIPTURES
Sacrifice	SACRIFICE
Sacrilege	BLASPHEMY
Sadness	SADNESS
Safety	SECURITY
Saint	SACREDNESS
Salvation	SALVATION
Sameness	EQUALITY
Sanctify	RITE-SACREDNESS
Sanctity	SACREDNESS
Sanctuary	SACREDNESS-SIGNS
Satiate	GREED
Satisfaction	FULFILLMENT
Save	SALVATION
Savior	MESSIANIC FIGURE
Scandal	EVIL
	HONESTY (disHONESTY)
Scorn	HATE
Scourge	PUNISHMENT
	REVENGE
Scriptures	SCRIPTURES
Secret	IGNORANCE
Security	SECURITY
Seduction	TEMPTATION
Self-abasement	HUMILITY
Self-admiration	PRIDE
Self-centeredness	SELFISHNESS
Self-condemnation	GUILT
	SELF-REALIZATION
Self-control	TEMPERANCE
Self-deception	FALSE BELIEF
Self-esteem	DIGNITY
	PRIDE
Self-indulgence	SELFISHNESS
Selfishness	SELFISHNESS
Self-realization	SELF-REALIZATION
Self-reliance	COURAGE
Self-reproach	REPENTANCE
Self-restraint	TEMPERANCE
Self-righteous	PIETY
Senility	OLD AGE
Senseless	RATIONALIZATION
Sensualism	SEX
Sensuality	LUST
Sentence	JUDGMENT
Separation	ALIENATION
	REJECTION
Serenity	PEACE
Servant	FOLLOWER
	STEWARDSHIP
Service	SERVICE
	STEWARDSHIP
Sex	SEX
Sexual gratification	LUST
	SEX
Shame	GUILT
	HUMILITY
Sharing	SHARING
Shun	ALIENATION
	REJECTION
Signal	SIGNS

THESAURUS

Term	see IDEA	Term	see IDEA
Signs & symbols	SIGNS	Testimony	WITNESS
Silence	PEACE	Thankfulness	GRATITUDE
Sin	EVIL	Thanksgiving	GRATITUDE
	SIN	Theft	STEALING
Sincerity	HONESTY	Threaten	MOTIVATION
Singing	PRAISE		SECURITY (inSECURITY)
	RITE	Timeless	ETERNITY
Skepticism	DOUBT	Timidity	FEAR
Skill	GIFT	Tolerance	PATIENCE
Slaughter	KILLING	Tongues	GIFT
Slothful	QUALITY OF LIFE	Torment	ANXIETY
Sober	QUALITY OF LIFE		OPPRESSION
	TEMPERANCE	Tradition	LAW
Social surroundings	ENVIRONMENT		TRADITION
Society	COMMUNITY	Traitor	ENEMY
Sodomy	SEX		FIDELITY (inFIDELITY)
Solemnity	SACREDNESS	Tranquillity	PEACE
Sorrow	GRIEF	Transforming	CONVERSION
	SADNESS	Transgression	EVIL
Soul	SPIRIT		GUILT
Sound judgment	PRUDENCE		SIN
Sovereignty	AUTHORITY	Translation	NEW AGE-LIFE
Spirit	SPIRIT	Treachery	FIDELITY (inFIDELITY)
Stateliness	DIGNITY		HONESTY (disHONESTY)
Statesmanship	POLITICS	Trepidation	ANXIETY
Steadfastness	FIDELITY		FEAR
Stealing	STEALING	Tribes	COMMUNITY
Stewardship	OBEDIENCE	Tribulation	OPPRESSION
	SERVICE	Triumph	VICTORY
	STEWARDSHIP	Trouble	SECURITY (inSECURITY)
Stimulus	MOTIVATION		SUFFERING
Straightforwardness	HONESTY	Truce	COVENANT
Strategy	ORDER		PEACE
	POLITICS	Trust	FAITH
Strength	AUTHORITY	Trustworthiness	HONESTY
Strife	CONFRONTATION	Truth	TRUTH
Submission	HUMILITY	Truthfulness	HONESTY
	OBEDIENCE	Turbulence	VIOLENCE
Success	VICTORY	Turmoil	CHAOS
Suffering	SUFFERING	Tyranny	OPPRESSION
Suicide	KILLING	Ulterior motive	MOTIVATION
Superstition	FALSE BELIEF	Unaware	IGNORANCE
	TRADITION	Unbelief	BELIEF (unBELIEF)
Supplication	DESIRE		DOUBT
	PRAYER	Uncertainty	DOUBT
	WILL	Unclean	CONDEMNATION
Supporting	DISCIPLESHIP	Unconcern	INDIFFERENCE
Supreme	AUTHORITY	Understand	KNOWLEDGE
	DEITY		SELF-REALIZATION
	LEADERSHIP		WISDOM
Surroundings	ENVIRONMENT	Uneasiness	ANXIETY
Suspicion	DOUBT	Uneducated	IGNORANCE
	JEALOUSY	Unfaithfulness	FIDELITY (inFIDELITY)
Symbolism	SIGNS		HERESY
Symmetry	ORDER		IDOLATRY
Sympathy	COMPASSION	Ungodliness	EVIL
Tabernacle	SACREDNESS-SIGNS		SIN
Tactics	POLITICS	Unhappiness	SADNESS
Talent	GIFT	Uniformity	EQUALITY
Teaching	INSTRUCTION		ORDER
Teachings	SCRIPTURES	Uninformed	IGNORANCE
Temperance	TEMPERANCE	Unity	ONENESS
Temple	SACREDNESS-SIGNS	Universe	CREATION
Temptation	TEMPTATION		ENVIRONMENT
Tenderness	COMPASSION	Unknowing	IGNORANCE
Tenet	BELIEF	Unlawful	DISOBEDIENCE
Terror	FEAR	Unmerited	GRACE
Testament	COVENANT	Unorthodox	HERESY
	LAW	Unreasonable	RATIONALIZATION

THESAURUS

Term	see IDEA
Unrestricted	FREEDOM
Unusualness	MIRACLE
Unwise	IGNORANCE
Unwritten law	TRADITION
Upright	VIRTUE
Urge	DESIRE
Urgency	COMPULSION
Valid	GOOD
	TRUTH
Valor	COURAGE
Value	GOOD
	WEALTH
Vanity	PRIDE
Veneration	PIETY
	WORSHIP
Vengeance	REVENGE
Verdict	JUDGMENT
Vice	EVIL
	SIN
Victory	VICTORY
Violation	DISOBEDIENCE
	SIN
Violence	VIOLENCE
Virtue	VIRTUE
Visions	REVELATION
Vitality	LIFE
Volition	ELECTION
	FREEDOM
	WILL
Vow	COMMITMENT
	PROMISE
Want	COVETOUSNESS
	DESIRE
	POVERTY
War	CONFRONTATION
Waste	DESTRUCTION
Wavering	DOUBT
Weakness	DESIRE
	TEMPTATION
Wealth	WEALTH
Wedding	MARRIAGE
	RITE
	TRADITION
Welfare	QUALITY OF LIFE
Wickedness	EVIL
	SIN
Will	DESIRE
	WILL
Win	VICTORY
Wisdom	KNOWLEDGE
	WISDOM
Wish	DESIRE
	WILL
Witness	WITNESS
Woe	GRIEF
	SADNESS
Word of God	SCRIPTURES
	TRUTH
World	ENVIRONMENT
Worry	ANXIETY
Worship	WORSHIP
Worth	GOOD
	VIRTUE
	WEALTH
Worthiness	DIGNITY
Wrath	ANGER
Wrong	EVIL
	SIN
Wrong belief	FALSE BELIEF

Term	see IDEA
Wrongdoing	EVIL
	SIN
Youth	YOUTH
Zeal	QUALITY OF LIFE

ACCEPTANCE

of **AUTHORITY**
Joshua — Josh 4:9-19
of **DEITY**
Blind — Jn 9:1-41
David — Ps 101:1-2b
Elihu — Job 34:29-33
Jesus — Mt 11:27;
Phil 2:5-11
Job — Job 42:1-6
Joseph — Gen 41:1-57
Mankind — Ps 86:8-10
Nebuchadnezzar — Dan 4:1-3;
34-35
of **MESSIANIC FIGURE**
Canaanite Woman — Mt 15:21-28;
Mk 7:24-30

of God's **AUTHORITY**
INSTRUCTION on
God — Is 33:7-16
REVELATION of
Isaiah — Is 51:17-52:12
John — Rev 5:1-14
Nebuchadnezzar — Dan 4:28-33
through **SELF-REALIZATION**
Centurion — Mt 8:5-13;
Lk 7:1-10
Jesus — Mt 28:16-20
Paul — Rom 13:1-7

of **BEHAVIOR**
INSTRUCTION on
Paul — 2 Cor 11:16-20
before the **KING**
Esther — Esth 5:1-8
of **BELIEF**
in **DEITY**
Believers — Heb 11:1-40
David — Ps 6:8-10
Israelites — Zech 13:7-9
of **FOLLOWERs**
Believers — Acts 11:19-21
Disciples — Jn 1:19-51
People — Jn 12:36b-43;
Acts 17:10-15
INSTRUCTION on
Jesus — Mk 11:20-26;
Jn 3:1-21;
6:25-59;
Heb 3:1-6a
Jews — Acts 28:17-31
in **MESSIANIC FIGURE**
Blind — Jn 9:1-41
Crowd — Mt 21:1-11;
Mk 11:1-10;
Lk 19:28-38
Jews — Jn 11:1-57
People — Jn 7:25-31;
37-52
Samaritans — Jn 4:27-42
in the **SCRIPTURES**
Jesus — Jn 5:19-47
through **WORSHIP**
Mary — Mt 28:9-10

of **BROTHERHOOD**
by **FOLLOWERs**
Paul — Philm 1:15-20
INSTRUCTION on
Jesus — Mt 18:5-6;
Mk 9:42-48;

INSTRUCTION on (cont'd)
Jesus — Lk 17:1-6
Moses — Deut 23:1-8
Paul — Rom 14:1-23;
16:1-23;
1 Cor 16:5-12;
13-24;
2 Cor 7:2-4;
Phil 2:19-30;
4:21-23;
1 Tim 5:1-2

of **COMMITMENT**
to **COVENANT**
Israelites — Ezra 10:1-6
by **DEITY**
Moses — Ex 33:12-23
INSTRUCTION on
Jesus — Mt 10:26-39

of **COMPULSION** to serve
INSTRUCTION on
Servants — 1 Pet 2:18-20
REVELATION of
Jeremiah — Jer 25:15-29

of **CONFRONTATION**
David — 2 Sam 18:1-19:8a
Jesus — 1 Pet 2:21-25
with **DEITY**
Moses — Ex 33:7-11;
Num 12:4-10;
Deut 34:1-12
with **ENVIRONMENT**
Esau — Gen 33:1-16
Esther — *Esth 15:1-16
Judith — *Jdt 11:1-23
INSTRUCTION on
Paul — 2 Cor 6:11-13

of **CONVERSION**
through **REVELATION**
Paul — Gal 1:11-17
through **SELF-REALIZATION**
Gentiles — Acts 10:1-11:18

of **COVENANT**
DESIREd
Moses — Deut 29:1-15
with **FIDELITY**
Chiefs — Neh 10:14-27
Israelites — Neh 9:38;
10:1;
2-8;
28-30
Levites — Neh 10:9-13
by the **PEOPLE**
Israelites — Ex 24:1-18
by giving **SIGNS**
Abraham — Gen 21:22-34
of **TRUTH**
Jesus — 2 Cor 3:12-18

through **COVENANT**
of **RECONCILIATION**
Gentiles — Eph 2:11-22

of **CREATION**
of **DEITY**
Believers — 1 Tim 4:1-5
Jesus — Jn 1:1-18

of **DEITY**
　desired for **PRAYER**
　　Agur　　　　　　Prov 30:1-14
　　Asaph　　　　　Ps 74:1-2
　　Azariah　　　　*Azar 1:11-22
　　Believers　　　1 Pet 3:8-12
　　David　　　　　Ps 6:8-10;
　　　　　　　　　　19:11-14;
　　　　　　　　　　141:1-2
　　Israelites　　　Hos 5:15-6:3;
　　　　　　　　　　*Bar 2:11-23
　　Judahites　　　Lam 5:1-22
　　Psalmist　　　　Ps 44:23-26;
　　　　　　　　　　84:8-9
　provides **RESURRECTION**
　　Israelites　　　Rom 11:7-24

DESIRE for
　　Esther　　　　　Esth 8:3-8
　　Jacob　　　　　Gen 32:1-23
　　Jonathan　　　*1 Mc 11:20-37
　of **COVENANT**
　　Moses　　　　　Deut 29:1-15
　INSTRUCTION on
　　Paul　　　　　　2 Cor 5:9-10
　of the **REVELATION**
　　Daniel　　　　　Dan 4:19-27
　　Isaiah　　　　　Is 65:1-25

of **DESIRE**
　to **WORSHIP**
　　Wise Men　　　Mt 2:1-12

DESIREd by
　DEITY
　　Isaiah　　　　　Is 55:1-13

of **ELECTION**
　by **DEITY**
　　Jesus　　　　　Mt 3:13-17;
　　　　　　　　　　17:1-8;
　　　　　　　　　　Mk 1:9-11;
　　　　　　　　　　9:2-8;
　　　　　　　　　　Lk 3:21-22;
　　　　　　　　　　9:28-36
　by **FOLLOWER**
　　Matthew　　　　Mt 9:9;
　　　　　　　　　　Lk 5:27-28
　INSTRUCTION on
　　Jesus　　　　　Mt 15:12-14;
　　　　　　　　　　20:1-16;
　　　　　　　　　　22:1-14
　　Peter　　　　　2 Pet 1:8-11
　by **MESSIANIC FIGURE**
　　Noah　　　　　Gen 6:5-22
　to **MISSION**
　　Jesus　　　　　Jn 12:27-36a
　　God　　　　　　Gen 2:21-25

of **EQUALITY** of men
　by **DEITY**
　　Mankind　　　Gal 1:18-2:10
　INSTRUCTION on
　　Believers　　　Jas 2:1-13
　in **WORSHIP**
　　Mankind　　　Is 66:17-24

of **ETERNAL**
　COVENANT
　　Believers　　　Is 56:1-8

of **FIDELITY**
　of **FOLLOWER**s
　　Jesus　　　　　Lk 14:25-27
　　Peter　　　　　Jn 21:15-23
　INSTRUCTION on
　　Jesus　　　　　Lk 12:1-12
　　Moses　　　　　Deut 26:16-19
　　Sardis　　　　　Rev 3:1-6
　　Solomon　　　Prov 19:1-29

by **FOLLOWER**s
　in **CONFRONTATION**
　　Jesus　　　　　Lk 24:13-35

of **FOLLOWER**s
　　Crowd　　　　　Jn 12:12-19
　　People　　　　Lk 19:47-48
　through **ELECTION**
　　Matthew　　　　Mt 9:9;
　　　　　　　　　　Lk 5:27-28

through dis**HONESTY**
　　Holofernes　　　*Jdt 11:1-23

INSTRUCTION on
　　Holy Spirit　　Jn 20:1-29
　　Jesus　　　　　Mt 5:43-47;
　　　　　　　　　　Lk 6:27-35
　　People　　　　Lk 7:24-30
　of God's **AUTHORITY**
　　God　　　　　　Is 33:7-16
　　Isaiah　　　　　Is 51:17-52:12
　　Jesus　　　　　Mt 28:16-20
　　Paul　　　　　　Rom 13:1-7
　of **BELIEF**
　　Jesus　　　　　Mk 11:20-26;
　　　　　　　　　　Jn 3:1-21;
　　　　　　　　　　6:25-59;
　　　　　　　　　　Heb 3:1-6a
　　Jews　　　　　Acts 28:17-31
　of **BROTHERHOOD**
　　Jesus　　　　　Mt 18:5-6;
　　　　　　　　　　Mk 9:42-48;
　　　　　　　　　　Lk 17:1-6
　　Moses　　　　　Deut 23:1-8
　　Paul　　　　　　Rom 14:1-23;
　　　　　　　　　　16:1-23;
　　　　　　　　　　1 Cor 16:5-12;
　　　　　　　　　　13-24;
　　　　　　　　　　2 Cor 7:2-4;
　　　　　　　　　　Phil 2:19-30;
　　　　　　　　　　4:21-23;
　　　　　　　　　　1 Tim 5:1-2
　of **COMMITMENT**
　　Jesus　　　　　Mt 10:26-39
　of **COMPULSION** to serve
　　Servants　　　1 Pet 2:18-20
　of **ELECTION**
　　Jesus　　　　　Mt 15:12-14;
　　　　　　　　　　20:1-16;
　　　　　　　　　　22:1-14
　　Peter　　　　　2 Pet 1:8-11
　of **EQUALITY** of men
　　Believers　　　Jas 2:1-13
　of **FIDELITY**
　　Jesus　　　　　Lk 12:1-12
　　Moses　　　　　Deut 26:16-19
　　Sardis　　　　　Rev 3:1-6
　　Solomon　　　Prov 19:1-29
　of **JUDGMENT**
　　God　　　　　　Is 41:1-42:4

of JUDGMENT (cont'd)	
Jesus	Mk 9:38-41; Lk 9:49-50
of KNOWLEDGE	
Father	Prov 4:1-9; 10-19; 20-27
Solomon	Prov 1:8-9; 5:1-14; 9:1-6; 13:1-25; 19:1-29
Uriel	*2 Esd 4:13-21
of LAW	
Moses	Deut 4:1-14
Paul	Acts 24:1-27; 26:1-32
of NEW AGE	
Apollos	Acts 18:24-28
Jesus	Mt 9:16-17; 18:1-4; 22:1-14; Mk 2:18-22; Lk 5:36-39; 14:15-24
Paul	1 Cor 15:1-11; Gal 2:17-19; Eph 4:17-24; Col 2:6-15; 3:1-4; 5-17; 1 Tim 6:11-16
of PRAYER	
Jesus	Mt 6:9-13; Lk 18:9-14
Men	1 Pet 3:1-7
Paul	Rom 15:25-33
of PROVIDENCE	
God	Is 46:1-13
James	Jas 4:13-16
Preacher	Eccl 5:8-20
of PUNISHMENT	
Author	Heb 12:3-11
Eliphaz	Job 5:8-17
God	Ezek 6:11-14
Solomon	Prov 3:1-35
as QUALITY OF LIFE	
Jesus	Mk 9:33-37
Maiden	Song 1:5-6
Paul	1 Cor 7:17-24; 25-35
through RECONCILIATION	
Jesus	Mt 18:15-17
Paul	2 Cor 5:20-6:2
of RESPECT	
Jesus	Mt 26:6-13; Mk 14:3-9; Jn 5:19-47
of the RESURRECTION	
Paul	Acts 17:1-9; 24:1-27; 1 Cor 15:29-34
Women	Lk 24:1-12
of SALVATION	
God	Is 46:1-13
Jesus	Jn 6:25-59
Paul	Rom 5:12-21; 9:30-10:21; 1 Cor 1:18-25
Peter	2 Pet 3:14-18a

of STEWARDSHIP	
Jesus	Mt 10:40-42; 21:33-43; Mk 12:1-12; Lk 15:11-32; 20:9-18
of SYMBOLISM	
Paul	Phil 2:5-11
of TRUTH	
Author	Heb 2:1-4
Hosea	Hos 14:9
James	Jas 1:19-21
Jesus	Mt 4:23-25; 9:16-17; 13:3b-9; 10-17; 18-23; 23:1-3; Mk 2:18-22; 4:1-9; 10-20; 21-25; 26-29; Lk 5:36-39; 8:4-8; 11-15; 16-18; 14:34-35; Jn 15:18-25
John	2 Jn 1:7-11; Jude 1:3-4
John the Baptist	Jn 3:31-36
Laodicea	Rev 3:14-22
Nebuchadnezzar	Dan 3:28-30
Paul	1 Cor 4:14-21; Gal 3:1-5; 2 Thes 1:7b-10; 2 Tim 2:14-19
Peter	2 Pet 1:19b-21
Thyatira	Rev 2:18-29
Women	Lk 24:1-12
of VIRTUE	
God	Gen 4:1-16
Paul	1 Tim 4:6-10
of JUDGMENT	
of DEITY	
David	Ps 141:5-7
Psalmist	Ps 82:8; 119:73-80
INSTRUCTION on	
God	Is 41:1-42:4
Jesus	Mk 9:38-41; Lk 9:49-50
PROPHECY of	
Isaiah	Is 52:13-53:12
REVELATION of	
Eli	1 Sam 3:1-4:1a
through WORSHIP	
Priests	Ezra 10:16-19
of the KNOWLEDGE	
of DEITY	
Ahab	1 Kgs 20:1-43
Believers	1 Jn 4:4-6
David	Ps 41:11-12
Elihu	Job 37:14-22
Israelites	Jer 31:31-34

concerning the **MESSIANIC FIGURE**
Jesus	Jn 2:23-25; 6:60-71
Peter	Mt 16:13-20

of **KNOWLEDGE** as Enlightenment
    PROPHECY of
Isaiah	Is 29:17-24
Zedekiah	Jer 32:1-8

    SELF-REALIZATION on
Jesus	Mt 3:13-17

of the **LAW**
    of **DEITY**
Peter	2 Pet 3:1-2
Psalmist	Ps 93:5

    INSTRUCTION on
Moses	Deut 4:1-14
Paul	Acts 24:1-27; 26:1-32

    PROPHECY of
Isaiah	Is 2:1-5

    SCRIPTURES on
John	Rev 22:6-21

of **MEDIATION**
    in **MISSION**
John the Baptist	Mt 3:1-12; Mk 1:2-8; Lk 3:1-6

    PROPHECY of
Elijah	Mal 4:4-6

MEDITATION on
    of **PUNISHMENT**
Jeremiah	Jer 10:17-22; Lam 3:1-66

of **MESSIANIC FIGURE**
Blind	Jn 9:1-41
Crowd	Mt 21:1-11; Mk 11:1-10; Lk 19:28-38
Jews	Jn 11:1-57
People	Jn 7:25-31; 37-52
Samaritans	Jn 4:27-42

    in **CONFRONTATION**
Nathanael	Jn 1:19-51

    through **CONVERSION**
Centurion	Mt 27:45-56

    in **NEW AGE**
God	*2 Esd 2:33-41

    with **RESPECT**
Jesus	Heb 1:5-14
Jews	Mt 21:12-17

    as way of **SALVATION**
Jesus	Jn 10:1-18

    through **SIGNS**
Jonah	Mt 16:1-4
Nicodemus	Jn 3:1-21

of **MISSION**
    through **ELECTION**
Jesus	Jn 12:27-36a

    of **MEDIATION**
John the Baptist	Mt 3:1-12; Mk 1:2-8; Lk 3:1-6

because of the **RESURRECTION**

because of the **RESURRECTION** (cont'd)
Paul	1 Cor 15:1-11

of **TRUTH**
Galatians	Gal 4:12-20
Thessalonians	1 Thes 1:2-10; 2:13-16

as **MOTIVATION**
    for **WORSHIP**
Shepherds	Lk 2:1-20

of the **NEW AGE**
    INSTRUCTION on
Apollos	Acts 18:24-28
Jesus	Mt 9:16-17; 18:1-4; 22:1-14; Mk 2:18-22; Lk 5:36-39; 14:15-24
Paul	1 Cor 15:1-11; Gal 2:17-19; Eph 4:17-24; 2:6-15; 3:1-4; 5-17; 1 Tim 6:11-16

    with **MESSIANIC FIGURE**
Ezra	*2 Esd 2:33-41

    PROPHECY of
Believers	Lk 10:17-20

    REVELATION of
Isaiah	Is 57:14-21
Israelites	Mal 2:17-3:5

    through **SELF-REALIZATION**
Criminal	Lk 23:39-43
John the Baptist	Jn 3:22-30

PRAYER for
Jesus	Jn 17:6-19; 20-26
Moses	Ex 33:12-23
Nehemiah	Neh 1:5-11a .

of **PRAYER**
    INSTRUCTION on
Jesus	Mt 6:9-13; Lk 18:9-14
Men	1 Pet 3:1-7
Paul	Rom 15:25-33

of the **PRESENCE**
    of **DEITY**
Abraham	Gen 18:1-8
Holy Spirit	Lk 3:21-22
Isaiah	Is 8:8b-10
Israelites	Lev 9:1-24
Lot	Gen 19:1-3

    REVELATION of
Moses	Ex 33:12-23

of **PROMISE**
    REVELATION of
Ezekiel	Ezek 43:18-27
Jesus	Mt 11:7-15
Mary	Lk 1:26-38

of the **PROMISE** of order
    by **DEITY**
Israelites	Jer 31:35-37

PROPHECY of
  of **JUDGMENT**
    Isaiah   Is 52:13-53:12
  of **KNOWLEDGE**
    Isaiah   Is 2:1-5
    Zedekiah   Jer 32:1-8
  of the **LAW**
    Isaiah   Is 2:1-5
  of **MEDIATION**
    Elijah   Mal 4:4-6
  of **NEW AGE**
    Believers   Lk 10:17-20
  of **PROVIDENCE**
    Zedekiah   Jer 27:12-15
  of the **RESURRECTION**
    Jesus   Mt 26:31-35;
                    Mk 14:27-31
  of **SALVATION**
    Jesus   Mt 24:37-41;
                    Lk 23:39-43
    Joel   Acts 2:14-36
  of **SIGNS**
    Joseph   Gen 40:1-23
  of **TRUTH**
    Jesus   Lk 16:19-31
    Paul   1 Thes 5:12-22
    Peter   2 Pet 3:1-2
    Zedekiah   Jer 27:12-15
  of **VIRTUE**
    Isaiah   Is 52:13-53:12

of **PROPHECY**
  concerning **CONFRONTATION**
    Hezekiah   Is 39:1-8

of **PROVIDENCE**
  of **DEITY**
    Cyrus   Is 45:14-25
    Jacob   Gen 28:10-22
    Job   Job 1:20-21;
                    2:9-10
  INSTRUCTION on
    God   Is 46:1-13
    James   Jas 4:13-16
    Preacher   Eccl 5:8-20
  through **MESSIANIC FIGURE**
    Jesus   Jn 18:1-11
  PROPHECY of
    Zedekiah   Jer 27:12-15
  REVELATION of
    People   Jer 27:1-11
  through **SELF-REALIZATION**
    Magicians   Ex 8:16-19

desired for **PUNISHMENT**
  of **DEITY**
    Daniel   Dan 9:4-19
    Elihu   Job 36:16-25
    Micah   Mic 7:7-20

of **PUNISHMENT**
  INSTRUCTION on
    Author   Heb 12:3-11
    Eliphaz   Job 5:8-17
    God   Ezek 6:11-14
    Solomon   Prov 3:1-35
  MEDITATION on
    Jeremiah   Jer 10:17-22;
                    Lam 3:1-66

as **QUALITY OF LIFE**

as **QUALITY OF LIFE** (cont'd)
  required by **DEITY**
    God   Mic 6:6-8
    Sirach   *Sir 41:1-4
  INSTRUCTION on
    Jesus   Mk 9:33-37
    Maiden   Song 1:5-6
    Paul   1 Cor 7:17-24;
                    25-35

of **RATIONALIZATION**
  required by **DEITY**
    James   Jas 3:13-18

of **RECONCILIATION**
  by **DEITY**
    God   2 Cor 5:14-19
    Jesus   Gal 4:4-7

through **RECONCILIATION**
  INSTRUCTION on
    Jesus   Mt 18:15-17
    Paul   2 Cor 5:20-6:2
  REVELATION of
    Israelites   Ezek 20:40-44;
                    Hos 2:14-15
    Moses   Lev 1:1-17

lack of **RESPECT**
  by **FOLLOWERs**
    Paul   Gal 1:18-2:10

of **RESPECT**
  for **DEITY**
    Jesus   Lk 2:21-40;
                    41-52
  INSTRUCTION on
    Jesus   Mt 26:6-13;
                    Mk 14:3-9;
                    Jn 5:19-47
  for **MESSIANIC FIGURE**
    Jesus   Heb 1:5-14
    Jews   Mt 21:12-17
  REVELATION of
    Eli   1 Sam 2:27-36
  in **WORSHIP**
    Believers   Heb 12:12-29

of the **RESURRECTION**
  INSTRUCTION on
    Paul   Acts 17:1-9;
                  24:1-27;
                  1 Cor 15:29-34
    Women   Lk 24:1-12
  for **MISSION**
    Paul   1 Cor 15:1-11
  PROPHECY of
    Jesus   Mt 26:31-35;
                    Mk 14:27-31

REVELATION of
  of **AUTHORITY**
    John   Rev 5:1-14
    Nebuchadnezzar Dan 4:28-33
  of the **COMPULSION** to serve
    Jeremiah   Jer 25:15-29
  through **CONVERSION**
    Nations   Zeph 3:9-10
    Paul   Gal 1:11-17
  of **JUDGMENT**
    Eli   1 Sam 3:1-4:1a

of **NEW AGE**
　Isaiah　　　　　　　Is 57:14-21
　Israelites　　　　　Mal 2:17-3:5
of **PRESENCE**
　Moses　　　　　　　Ex 33:12-23
of **PROMISE**
　Ezekiel　　　　　　Ezek 43:18-27
　Jesus　　　　　　　Mt 11:7-15
　Mary　　　　　　　Lk 1:26-38
of **PROVIDENCE**
　People　　　　　　Jer 27:1-11
of **RECONCILIATION**
　Israelites　　　　　Ezek 20:40-44;
　　　　　　　　　　Hos 2:14-15
　Moses　　　　　　　Lev 1:1-17
of **RESPECT**
　Eli　　　　　　　　1 Sam 2:27-36
of **RITE**
　Believers　　　　　Is 56:1-8
　Moses　　　　　　　Lev 21:1-22:33
of **TRUTH**
　Jeremiah　　　　　Jer 11:1-14
　John　　　　　　　Rev 22:6-21

of **REVELATION**
　in **CONFRONTATION**
　　Jesus　　　　　　Lk 24:13-35
　DESIREd
　　Daniel　　　　　　Dan 4:19-27
　　Isaiah　　　　　　Is 65:1-25

of **RITE**
　by **DEITY**
　　God　　　　　　　Ps 51:18-19
　REVELATION of
　　Believers　　　　Is 56:1-8
　　Moses　　　　　　Lev 21:1-22:33
　as **TRADITION**
　　Joseph　　　　　Gen 43:16-34

of **SALVATION**
　from **DEITY**
　　God　　　　　　　Ps 118:22-27
　INSTRUCTION on
　　God　　　　　　　Is 46:1-13
　　Jesus　　　　　　Jn 6:25-59
　　Paul　　　　　　Rom 5:12-21;
　　　　　　　　　　9:30-10:21;
　　　　　　　　　　1 Cor 1:18-25
　　Peter　　　　　　2 Pet 3:14-18a
　through **MESSIANIC FIGURE**
　　Jesus　　　　　　Jn 10:1-18
　PROPHECY of
　　Jesus　　　　　　Mt 24:37-41;
　　　　　　　　　　Lk 23:39-43
　　Joel　　　　　　Acts 2:14-36

SCRIPTURES on
　through **CONVERSION**
　　James　　　　　Acts 15:6-29
　of **LAW**
　　John　　　　　　Rev 22:6-21
　of **SIGNS**
　　Jonah　　　　　Lk 11:29-32

SIGNS of
　Rebekah　　　　　Gen 24:11-27
　Servant　　　　　Gen 24:11-27
of **SIGNS**

of **SIGNS** (cont'd)
　by **FOLLOWERs**
　　Believers　　　　Acts 9:32-43
　from **MESSIANIC FIGURE**
　　Jonah　　　　　　Mt 16:1-4
　　Nicodemus　　　　Jn 3:1-21
　PROPHECY of
　　Joseph　　　　　Gen 40:1-23
　REVELATION of
　　Ezekiel　　　　　Ezek 17:1-10
　　Jesus　　　　　　Mt 17:1-8;
　　　　　　　　　　Mk 9:2-8;
　　　　　　　　　　Lk 9:28-36
　　John　　　　　　Rev 17:6b-18
　　Jonah　　　　　　Mt 12:38-42
　SCRIPTURES on
　　Jonah　　　　　　Lk 11:29-32

of **SINlessness**
　Jesus　　　　　　　2 Cor 5:20-6:2

of **STEWARDSHIP**
　INSTRUCTION on
　　Jesus　　　　　　Mt 10:40-42;
　　　　　　　　　　21:33-43;
　　　　　　　　　　Mk 12:1-12;
　　　　　　　　　　Lk 15:11-32;
　　　　　　　　　　20:9-18

of **STEWARDSHIP** responsibilities
　Moses　　　　　　Lev 23:9-14
　by **FOLLOWERs**
　　Apostles　　　　Mt 10:26-39

of **SYMBOLISM**
　INSTRUCTION on
　　Paul　　　　　　Phil 2:5-11

of the **TRUTH**
　by **DEITY**
　　David　　　　　Ps 17:1-2
　　Jesus　　　　　Jn 7:15-24
　　Nebuchadnezzar　Dan 3:28-30
　by **FOLLOWERs**
　　Believers　　　Acts 13:4-12;
　　　　　　　　　1 Jn 4:4-6
　　Gentiles　　　Acts 13:14-52
　　Jesus　　　　　Jn 10:1-18;
　　　　　　　　　1 Jn 4:1-3

　INSTRUCTION on
　　Author　　　　Heb 2:1-4
　　Hosea　　　　　Hos 14:9
　　James　　　　　Jas 1:19-21
　　Jesus　　　　　Mt 4:23-25;
　　　　　　　　　9:16-17;
　　　　　　　　　13:3b-9;
　　　　　　　　　10-17;
　　　　　　　　　18-23;
　　　　　　　　　23:1-3;
　　　　　　　　　Mk 2:18-22;
　　　　　　　　　4:1-9;
　　　　　　　　　10-20;
　　　　　　　　　21-25;
　　　　　　　　　26-29;
　　　　　　　　　Lk 5:36-39;
　　　　　　　　　4-8;
　　　　　　　　　11-15;
　　　　　　　　　16-18;
　　　　　　　　　14:34-35;
　　　　　　　　　Jn 15:18-25
　　John　　　　　2 Jn 1:7-11;

INSTRUCTION on (cont'd)
John	Jude 1:3-4
John the Baptist	Jn 3:31-36
Laodicea	Rev 3:14-22
Nebuchadnezzar	Dan 3:28-30
Paul	1 Cor 4:14-21;
	Gal 3:1-5;
	2 Thes 1:7b-10;
	2 Tim 2:14-19
Peter	2 Pet 1:19b-21
Thyatira	Rev 2:18-29
Women	Lk 24:1-12

from **MESSIANIC FIGURE**
Jesus	Jn 4:1-26

in **MISSION**
Galatians	Gal 4:12-20
Thessalonians	1 Thes 1:2-10;
	2:13-16

PROPHECY of
Jesus	Lk 16:19-31
Paul	1 Thes 5:12-22
Peter	2 Pet 3:1-2
Zedekiah	Jer 27:12-15

REVELATION of
Jeremiah	Jer 11:1-14
John	Rev 22:6-21

through **SELF-REALIZATION**
Disciples	Lk 24:50-51

through the **TRUTH**
Joseph	Gen 45:1-28
People	Acts 2:37-41

of **VIRTUE**
by **DEITY**
Believers	Ps 34:15-22;
	Heb 12:12-29
God	Prov 21:1-31;
	Is 45:14-25
Mankind	Ps 15:1-5b

INSTRUCTION on
God	Gen 4:1-16
Paul	1 Tim 4:6-10

PROPHECY of
Isaiah	Is 52:13-53:12

through **SELF-REALIZATION**
Centurion	Lk 23:46-49

ALIENATION

before the **AUTHORITY**
of **MESSIANIC FIGURE**
Demon	Mt 9:32-34;
	Mk 1:21-28;
	Lk 4:31-37

of **AUTHORITY**
PROPHECY of
King	Hos 10:9-15

REVELATION of
Belshazzar	Dan 5:26-28

BEHAVIOR causing
in **MISSION**
Barnabas	Acts 15:30-41
Paul	Acts 15:30-41

through **BEHAVIOR**
in the **ENVIRONMENT**

in the **ENVIRONMENT** (cont'd)
Israelites	*1 Esd 9:16-36

of **FOLLOWER**
Judas	Mt 26:47-56;
	Mk 14:43-50
	Lk 22:47-54a;

of **MESSIANIC FIGURE**
Jesus	Mt 21:12-17;
	Mk 11:15-19;
	Lk 19:45-46

through un**BELIEF**
in **DEITY**
Israelites	Rom 11:25-32

of the **BROTHERHOOD**
Israelites	Zech 11:4-14

INSTRUCTION on
Jesus	Mt 18:15-17
Paul	1 Cor 5:9-13

of **COMMUNITY**
Gentiles	Eph 2:11-22
Israelites	1 Kgs 12:1-20
Rehoboam	2 Chr 10:1-12:16

from **ENVIRONMENT**
Israelites	*1 Mc 1:36-40

PROPHECY of
Ahijah	1 Kgs 11:26-40

SELF-REALIZATION on
Job	Job 19:13-19

through **CONFRONTATION**
Abraham	Gen 13:2-9;
	10-13
Edomites	2 Chr 21:1-23:21
Isaac	Gen 26:12-31
Jephthah	Judg 11:1-3

with **MESSIANIC FIGURE**
Jesus	Jn 2:12-22

PROPHECY of
Jerusalemites	Zech 14:1-21

REVELATION of
Israelites	Ezek 21:1-7

with **TRADITION**
Hagar	Gen 16:1-6

from **DEITY**
through un**BELIEF**
Israelites	Rom 11:25-32

through in**FIDELITY**
Israelites	Heb 4:1-13

as **PUNISHMENT**
Babylonians	Is 14:1-23
Bethelites	Zech 7:4-8:23
Edomites	Ezek 35:1-15
God	Gen 11:1-9;
	Ps 37:12-22;
	53:4-5;
	2 Thes 1:7b-10
Israelites	Num 14:39-45;
	2 Chr 10:1-12:16;
	Is 9:8-10:4;
	Ezek 20:9-26
Jonah	Jon 1:1-17
Judahites	2 Kgs 23:25b-30;
	24:18-25:7
Priests	Mal 1:6-2:9

through **SIN**
Gentiles	Rom 1:24-32
God	Ps 34:15-22;

of **DEITY** (cont'd)
Israelites   21:1-18;
  Ps 74:1-2;
  78:21-31;
  Ezek 20:9-26;
  Hos 8:4-7
Moses   Ex 4:10-16;
  Deut 3:23-29

caused by **FALSE BELIEF**
Herod   Lk 3:18-20
INSTRUCTION on
James   Jas 1:19-21
Preacher   Eccl 7:1-22
of **MESSIANIC FIGURE**
Jesus   Mt 21:12-17;
  Mk 10:13-16;
  11:15-19;
  Lk 9:51-56

against **TRADITION**
Moses   Lev 10:1-20

revealed to **COMMUNITY**
by **DEITY**
Edomites   Mal 1:2-5
Judahites   Jer 7:29-8:3

COMPULSION through
of **DEITY**
Babylonians   Rev 16:17-21
in **MISSION**
Ezekiel   Ezek 3:12-15

CONFRONTATION with the
of **DEITY**
David   Ps 7:6-8
God   2 Sam 22:1-51;
  Ps 2:4-6;
  18:7-15;
  Rev 15:1-16:1
Israelites   Num 16:36-50

CONFRONTATION with
Ephraimites   Judg 8:1-3
Hiram   1 Kgs 9:10-14
through **FALSE BELIEF**
Pharisees   Lk 6:6-11
INSTRUCTION on
Bildad   Job 18:1-4
of **MESSIANIC FIGURE**
Jesus   Mk 3:1-6
PROPHECY of
Zephaniah   Zeph 2:1-2
REVELATION of
Aaron   Num 12:4-10
Gog   Ezek 38:17-23

of **DEITY**
Bethelites   Zech 7:4-8:23
God   Ps 30:1-5;
  89:38-51;
  106:32-33;
  Jer 4:23-26
Israelites   Num 11:4-10;
  25:1-5;
  Josh 7:1-5;
  Judg 2:20-23;
  2 Kgs 13:1-9;
  21:1-18;
  Ezek 20:9-26;
  Hos 8:4-7

of **DEITY** (cont'd)
Moses   Ex 4:10-16;
  Deut 3:23-29
revealed to **COMMUNITY**
Edomites   Mal 1:2-5
Judahites   Jer 7:29-8:3
COMPELs action
Babylonians   Rev 16:17-21
resulting from in**FIDELITY**
Elihu   Job 32:2b-5
God   Eph 5:3-14
Israelites   Judg 10:6-18
Judahites   Jer 25:1-7
as **JUDGMENT**
God   Ps 95:7d-11;
  Is 9:8-10:4;
  Rev 11:15-19
Jonah   Jon 4:1-11
Judahites   2 Kgs 23:25b-30
as **PUNISHMENT**
David   Ps 21:8-13
God   Jer 12:7-13;
  Nah 1:1-9;
  1 Thes 2:13-16
Isaiah   Is 63:1-6
Israelites   Judg 2:11-19;
  3:7-11;
  Is 42:18-43:7;
  Ezek 43:6-12
Jeremiah   Jer 18:18-23;
  Lam 3:1-66
Judahites   Lam 4:1-22;
  Hos 5:8-14
Zedekiah   Jer 52:1-3
Zephaniah   Zeph 1:14-16
against **SIN**
God   Job 36:26-33;
  Is 5:24b-30;
  Rom 1:18;
  Col 3:5-17
Isaiah   Is 63:7-64:12
Israelites   Num 11:31-35;
  Deut 9:7-24;
  29:16-29;
  1 Kgs 16:8-14;
  2 Kgs 17:7-23;
  Ps 78:56-66
Judahites   Jer 44:1-14
Manasseh   2 Chr 33:1-25
Solomon   1 Kgs 11:1-13
against un**TRUTH**
God   Job 42:7-9

ETERNAL
PROPHECY of
Judahites   Jer 17:1-4
REVELATION of
Jeremiah   Jer 15:10-21

against in**FIDELITY**
PROPHECY of
God   2 Chr 36:1-23

resulting from dis**HONESTY**
Samson   Judg 14:10-20
REVELATION of
Ammonites   Ezek 21:28-32

INSTRUCTION on
in **JUDGMENT**

INSTRUCTION on
  in JUDGMENT (cont'd)

    Job   Job 19:25-29
  KNOWLEDGE of
    Sirach   *Sir 1:22-30
    Solomon   Prov 14:1-35
  in LAW
    Jesus   Mt 5:21-26
  as MOTIVATION
    Sirach   *Sir 20:1-8
  as PUNISHMENT
    Job   Job 19:25-29
    Solomon   Prov 19:1-29
  as QUALITY OF LIFE
    Solomon   Prov 19:1-29
  in SALVATION
    Zephaniah   Zeph 2:3
  in SIN
    David   Ps 4:2-5
    Paul   Eph 4:25-5:2
    Sirach   *Sir 27:30-28:12
    Solomon   Prov 22:22-23:14;
                 29:1-27
  not as a VIRTUE
    Sirach   *Sir 10:6-11

in JUDGMENT
  of DEITY
    God   Ps 95:7d-11;
                 Is 9:8-10:4;
                 Rev 11:15-19
    Jonah   Jon 4:1-11
    Judahites   2 Kgs 23:25b-30
  INSTRUCTION on
    Job   Job 19:25-29
  PROPHECY of
    Isaiah   Is 34:1-17;
                 59:1-21;
                 66:1-16

KNOWLEDGE of
  of DEITY
    Israelites   Ezek 22:17-22
  INSTRUCTION on
    Sirach   *Sir 1:22-30
    Solomon   Prov 14:1-35

in LAW
  INSTRUCTION on
    Jesus   Mt 5:21-26

MEDIATION with the
  of DEITY
    Moses   Ps 106:19-23

MEDITATION on
  as Divine PUNISHMENT
    Jeremiah   Lam 2:1-22

of MESSIANIC FIGURE
    Jesus   Mt 21:12-17;
                 Mk 3:1-6;
                 10:13-16;
                 11:15-19;
                 Lk 9:51-56

as MOTIVATION
    Ephraimites   Hos 7:3-7
    Satan   Rev 12:13-17
  of DEITY

of DEITY (cont'd)
    God   Zeph 1:17-18
    Israelites   2 Sam 24:1-25;
                 1 Chr 21:1-22:1;
                 Is 10:24-27c;
                 Ezek 16:15-34;
                 21:8-17;
                 Zech 1:7-17
  INSTRUCTION on
    Sirach   *Sir 20:1-8
  PROPHECY of
    Israelites   Ezek 16:35-43
  REVELATION of
    Daniel   Dan 11:5-20
    God   Zeph 3:8

MOTIVATION for
  is FALSE BELIEF
    Herod   Mt 2:16-18

PRAYER concerning
  of DEITY
    Asaph   Ps 79:5-13
    Followers   Ps 80:4-7
  MEDITATION on
    Jeremiah   Jer 10:23-25

PRESENCE of the
  of DEITY
    God   Is 30:27-33
    Saul   1 Sam 11:1-15

PROPHECY of
  CONFRONTATION with
    Zephaniah   Zeph 2:1-2
  that is ETERNAL
    Judahites   Jer 17:1-4
  against inFIDELITY
    God   2 Chr 36:1-23
  in JUDGMENT
    Isaiah   Is 34:1-17;
                 59:1-21;
                 66:1-16
  as MOTIVATION
    Israelites   Ezek 16:35-43
  in PROVIDENCE
    Elamites   Jer 49:34-39
  as PUNISHMENT
    God   Mic 5:7-15
    Isaiah   Is 13:1-22
    Israelites   Hos 13:9-11
    Jeremiah   Jer 6:9-15
    Judahites   Jer 4:5-8;
                 42:7-22
    Prophets   Jer 23:16-22

in PROVIDENCE
  PROPHECY of
    Elamites   Jer 49:34-39
  REVELATION of
    Israelites   Ezek 20:32-39

as Divine PUNISHMENT
    David   Ps 21:8-13
    God   Jer 12:7-13;
                 Nah 1:1-9;
                 1 Thes 2:13-16
    Isaiah   Is 63:1-6
    Israelites   Judg 2:11-19;
                 3:7-11;

as Divine **PUNISHMENT** (cont'd)

Israelites	Is 42:18-43:7; Ezek 43:6-12
Jeremiah	Jer 18:18-23; Lam 3:1-66
Judahites	Lam 4:1-22; Hos 5:8-14
Zedekiah	Jer 52:1-3
Zephaniah	Zeph 1:14-16

for **FALSE BELIEF**

God	Rev 14:9-12

INSTRUCTION on

Job	Job 19:25-29
Solomon	Prov 19:1-29

MEDITATION on

Jeremiah	Lam 2:1-22

PROPHECY of

God	Mic 5:7-15
Isaiah	Is 13:1-22
Israelites	Hos 13:9-11
Jeremiah	Jer 6:9-15
Judahites	Jer 4:5-8; 42:7-22
Prophets	Jer 23:16-22

REVELATION of

Edomites	Ezek 25:12-14; 35:1-15
Egyptians	Ezek 30:13-19
Ezekiel	Ezek 8:16-18; 13:1-16; 36:1-7
Israelites	Num 11:1-3; Ezek 5:5-17; 6:11-14; 7:1-27; 19:10-14; 22:17-22; 23-31; 36:16-21
Jeremiah	Jer 7:16-20; 25:30-38; 30:23-31:1; 33:1-9
John	Rev 14:17-20
Judahites	Ezek 23:22-35; 24:1-14
Philistines	Ezek 25:15-17
Rulers	Zech 10:3-12

PUNISHMENT out of

Nebuchadnezzar	Dan 3:19-23

as **QUALITY OF LIFE**
　INSTRUCTION on

Solomon	Prov 19:1-29

resulting from **disRESPECT**

Sanballat	Neh 4:1-3

REVELATION of
　CONFRONTATION with

Aaron	Num 12:4-10
Gog	Ezek 38:17-23

　that is **ETERNAL**

Jeremiah	Jer 15:10-21

　resulting from **disHONESTY**

Ammonites	Ezek 21:28-32

as **MOTIVATION**

Daniel	Dan 11:5-20
God	Zeph 3:8

in **PROVIDENCE**

Israelites	Ezek 20:32-39

as Divine **PUNÍSHMENT**

Edomites	Ezek 25:12-14; 35:1-15
Egyptians	Ezek 30:13-19
Ezekiel	Ezek 8:16-18; 13:1-16; 36:1-7
Israelites	Num 11:1-3; Ezek 5:5-17; 6:11-14; 7:1-27; 19:10-14; 22:17-22; 23-31; 36:16-21
Jeremiah	Jer 7:16-20; 25:30-38; 30:23-31:1; 33:1-9
John	Rev 14:17-20
Judahites	Ezek 23:22-35; 24:1-14
Philistines	Ezek 25:15-17
Rulers	Zech 10:3-12

resulting in **SECURITY**

Israelites	Is 51:17-52:12

caused by **SIN**

Isaiah	Is 57:14-21
Solomon	1 Kgs 11:1-13

in **SALVATION**
　INSTRUCTION on

Zephaniah	Zeph 2:3

SECURITY resulting from
　REVELATION of

Israelites	Is 51:17-52:12

as **SIGNS**
　of **FALSE BELIEF**

Babylonians	*Bel 1:28-30

SIN causing Divine
　REVELATION of

Isaiah	Is 57:14-21
Solomon	1 Kgs 11:1-13

in **SIN**
　INSTRUCTION on

David	Ps 4:2-5
Paul	Eph 4:25-5:2
Sirach	*Sir 27:30-28:12
Solomon	Prov 22:22-23:14; 29:1-27

over **SIN**

Moses	Ps 106:32-33

resulting from **SIN**

Edomites	Amos 1:11-12
Nehemiah	Neh 5:6-13; 13:4-9

VIRTUE in
　INSTRUCTION on

Sirach	*Sir 10:6-11

　of **FALSE BELIEF**

God	Ex 32:7-14
Moses	Ex 32:15-24

concerning the **PROVIDENCE** (cont'd)
  of **DEITY**
    Habakkuk   Hab 1:12-17

caused by **PUNISHMENT**
  PROPHECY of
    Isaiah   Is 13:1-22
    Jeremiah   Jer 4:19-22
    Zephaniah   Zeph 1:14-16

concerning **PUNISHMENT**
  SELF-REALIZATION of
    Judahites   Jer 26:7-19

in **PUNISHMENT**
  INSTRUCTION on
    Moses   Deut 28:15-68
  MEDITATION on
    Jeremiah   Jer 10:17-22

as **QUALITY OF LIFE**
    Daughters   Song 8:8-9
    David   Ps 69:13-21
    Jeremiah   Jer 20:7-18
  MEDITATION on
    Jeremiah   Jer 15:10-21
  SELF-REALIZATION of
    David   Ps 55:1-3a;
                        3b-8

RATIONALIZATION caused by
  SELF-REALIZATION of
    Paul   2 Cor 12:19-21

concerning the **RESURRECTION**
  through **FALSE BELIEF**
    Priest   Acts 4:1-22

REVELATION of
  in **BEHAVIOR**
    Nebuchadnezzar   Dan 2:1-13
  KNOWLEDGE of
    Daniel   Dan 7:28
    Ethiopians   Ezek 30:6-9
  as **MOTIVATION**
    Daniel   Dan 7:15-16;
                        8:26-27

concerning **SECURITY**
  in the **ENVIRONMENT**
    Jacob   Gen 34:1-31
  INSTRUCTION on
    Paul   2 Cor 5:1-5
  MEDITATION on
    Jesus   Mt 6:25-34
  PROPHECY of
    People   Is 20:1-6

SELF-REALIZATION of
  in **BEHAVIOR**
    Jesus   Mt 26:36-46;
                        Mk 14:32-42;
                        Lk 22:39-46
  in **COMMITMENT**
    Paul   Rom 9:1-5
  concerning **PUNISHMENT**
    Judahites   Jer 26:7-19
  as **QUALITY OF LIFE**
    David   Ps 55:1-3a;
                        3b-8
  caused by **SIN**

caused by **SIN** (cont'd)
    Paul   Rom 7:14-25

SIGNS of
  INSTRUCTION on
    John   Rev 12:10-12

caused by **SIN**
  MEDITATION on
    God   Jer 9:2-9
  SELF-REALIZATION of
    Paul   Rom 7:14-25

concerning **SIN**
  against **DEITY**
    Psalmist   Ps 119:129-136;
                        137-144

in the **STEWARDSHIP**
  of **FOLLOWER**
    Martha   Lk 10:38-42

AUTHORITY

ACCEPTANCE of
  by the **PEOPLE**
    Joshua   Josh 4:9-19
  of **DEITY**
    Blind   Jn 9:1-41
    David   Ps 101:1-2b
    Elihu   Job 34:29-33
    Jesus   Mt 11:27;
                        Phil 2:5-11
    Job   Job 42:1-6
    Joseph   Gen 41:1-57
    Mankind   Ps 86:8-10
    Nebuchadnezzar   Dan 4:1-3;
                        34-35

  in **POLITICS**
    Absalom   2 Sam 15:1-12
    Adonijah   1 Kgs 1:5-10
    David   1 Chr 18:1-20:8
    Haman   Esth 3:1-6
    Rehoboam   1 Kgs 12:1-20;
                        2 Chr 10:1-12:16
    Saul   1 Sam 13:1-23
    Solomon   1 Kgs 1:41-53;
                        9:15-23

  INSTRUCTION on
    God   Is 33:7-16
    Isaiah   Is 51:17-52:12
    Jesus   Mt 28:16-20
    Paul   Rom 13:1-7
  of **MESSIANIC FIGURE**
    Canaanite Woman   Mt 15:21-28;
                        Mk 7:24-30
  REVELATION on
    John   Rev 5:1-14
    Nebuchadnezzar   Dan 4:28-33
  SELF-REALIZATION of
    Centurion   Mt 8:5-13;
                        Lk 7:1-10

ALIENATION by
  of **MESSIANIC FIGURE**
    Demon   Mt 9:32-34;
                        Mk 1:21-28;
                        Lk 4:31-37

PROPHECY of
King   Hos 10:9-15
REVELATION on
Balshazzar   Dan 5:26-28

ANGER in the
of DEITY
Job   Job 9:8-13
Mankind   Ps 76:7-9

ANGER of
King   Prov 20:1-30

BLASPHEMY against
of MESSIANIC FIGURE
Pharisees   Mt 9:32-34

BLESSING in the
of DEITY
Jesus   Jn 5:19-47

over CHAOS
in the ENVIRONMENT
God   Gen 1:1-2

COMPASSION of
Jesus   Mt 8:5-13;
     Lk 7:1-10
Nehemiah   Neh 5:14-19
CONDEMNATION by
of MESSIANIC FIGURE
Jesus   Mt 21:18-22;
     Mk 11:20-26
Pharisees   Mt 12:22-32
REVELATION of
Job   Job 38:12-15;
     40:6-14

COURAGE in the
of DEITY
Believers   Eph 6:10-18

COVENANT of
in DISCIPLESHIP
God   2 Cor 3:4-6
in LEADERSHIP
David   2 Sam 5:1-5;
     1 Chr 11:1-12:40
brings PEACE
David   2 Sam 3:17-39
in POLITICS
David   1 Chr 11:1-12:40
Jonathan   *1 Mc 10:15-44
Maccabeus   *2 Mc 14:18-25
Simon   *1 Mc 14:16-24;
     15:15-24
REJECTION of
Israelites   Zech 11:4-14
Ptolemy   *1 Mc 11:1-19
SACREDNESS of
Jonathan   *1 Mc 10:15-44

of DEATH
INSTRUCTION on
Preacher   Eccl 8:1-9
REVELATION of
John   Rev 6:7-8

DEFEAT of
Kings   Hos 7:3-7
REVELATION of
Daniel   Dan 11:5-20

of DEITY
God   Mt 26:36-46;
     Mk 14:32-42
ACCEPTANCE of
Blind   Jn 9:1-41
David   Ps 101:1-2b
Elihu   Job 34:29-33
Jesus   Mt 11:27;
     Phil 2:5-11
Job   Job 42:1-6
Joseph   Gen 41:1-57
Mankind   Ps 86:8-10
Nebuchadnezzar   Dan 4:1-3;
     34-35

ANGER in
Job   Job 9:8-13
Mankind   Ps 76:7-9
BLESSING in
Jesus   Jn 5:19-47
in DISCIPLESHIP
God   2 Tim 1:3-7
over the ENEMY
David   Ps 18:31-42
God   Is 42:5-17
Judith   *Jdt 16:1-17
Solomon   Ps 72:8-14
over EVIL
God   Ps 59:6-8
FAITH in
Jesus   Eph 1:15-2:10
Jethro   Ex 18:1-12
Paul   1 Cor 2:1-5
in FAMILY
Joshua   Josh 19:49-51
FEAR of the
Adversaries   Ex 15:1-18
God   Job 37:23-24
Kings   Ps 48:4-8
Mankind   Ps 102:12-22
revealed through GRACE
Mary   Lk 1:39-56
IGNORANCE of
Elihu   Job 36:26-33
Job   Job 37:14-22
Pharaoh   Ex 5:1-5
JOY in
Israelites   Neh 8:9-12
JUSTICE in
God   Job 37:23-24;
     Ps 62:8-12
Israelites   Deut 10:12-22
Psalmist   Ps 82:8
Solomon   *Wis 16:15-29
LEADERSHIP in
Aaron   Ex 4:10-16
David   2 Sam 22:1-51;
     1 Chr 28:1-29:30;
     Ps 18:43-45
Gideon   Judg 8:22-23
God   Ps 47:5-9;
     66:5-7;
     93:1-2;
     103:19-22;
     Is 40:1-11;
     51:1-16;
     Rev 11:15-19;
     19:6-10
Israelites   Ex 15:1-18;
     Ps 77:11-20;
     Jer 31:31-34
Jesus   Mt 28:16-20;

of **MESSIANIC FIGURE** (cont'd)
                              Mk 2:23-28;
                              Lk 6:1-5
PROPHECY of
  Jesus   Mt 24:29-31;
                              Mk 13:24-27
REVELATION on
  Ezekiel   Ezek 1:4-28;
                              10:1-22
  Isaiah   Is 49:1-26
  Moses   Ex 7:1-7

for **DISCIPLESHIP**
  in **COVENANT**
    God   2 Cor 3:4-6
  through **DEITY**
    God   2 Tim 1:3-7
  of **FOLLOWER**s
    Jesus   Mt 10:1;
                              Mk 6:7-13;
                              Lk 9:1-6

INSTRUCTION on
  Jesus   Mt 18:18-20
  in **MISSION**
    Holy Spirit   1 Thes 1:2-10
    Jesus   Mk 3:13-19

DISOBEDIENCE to
  Mattathias   *1 Mc 2:15-22
INSTRUCTION on
  Jesus   Mt 7:24-27;
                              Lk 6:46-49

DOUBT concerning
  of **MESSIANIC FIGURE**
    Crowd   Mt 9:18-26;
                              Mk 5:35-43;
                              Lk 8:40-56
    Elders   Mk 11:27-33;
                              Lk 20:1-8
    Pharisees   Lk 5:17-26
    Priests   Mt 21:23-27;
                              Mk 11:27-33;
                              Lk 20:1-8

of **EVIL**
  over **ENVIRONMENT**
    Ungodly Men   *Wis 2:6-11
  in **FALSE BELIEF**
    Satan   2 Thes 2:3b-10
  INSTRUCTION on
    Paul   2 Cor 10:1-6
    Solomon   *Wis 5:15-23
  REVELATION of
    John   Rev 13:1-4

FAITH in
  of **DEITY**
    Jesus   Eph 1:15-2:10
    Jethro   Ex 18:1-12
    Paul   1 Cor 2:1-5
  by **FOLLOWER**
    Leper   Mt 8:2-4;
                              Mk 1:40-45;
                              Lk 5:12-16

INSTRUCTION on
  Jesus   Mt 17:14-20;
                              21:18-22;
                              Mk 11:20-26;
                              Lk 17:1-6;
                              Jn 12:44-50;

INSTRUCTION on (cont'd)
  Jesus   14:1-14
  Paul   1 Cor 12:27-31a
of **MESSIANIC FIGURE**
  Jesus   Mt 8:23-27;
                              9:27-31;
                              Mk 4:35-41;
                              Lk 8:22-25
  in **MISSION**
    Disciples   Mk 6:7-13;
                              Lk 9:1-6
    Paul   Eph 3:1-13
  PROPHECY on
    Isaiah   Is 30:8-17

in **FAMILY**
  PROPHECY on
    Jacob   Gen 47:27-48:22
  REVELATION on
    Jehu   2 Kgs 10:29-31

FEAR of
  Adonijah   1 Kgs 1:41-53
  God   Job 37:23-24
  Kings   Ps 48:4-8
  Mankind   Ps 102:12-22
  INSTRUCTION on
    Moses   Deut 6:4-19;
                              12:32-13:18;
                              17:14-20
  REVELATION on
    Amos   Amos 3:3-8

of **FOLLOWER**s
  in **DISCIPLESHIP**
    Jesus   Mt 10:1;
                              Mk 6:7-13;
                              Lk 9:1-6
  FAITH in
    Leper   Mt 8:2-4;
                              Mk 1:40-45;
                              Lk 5:12-16
  over **GOOD**
    James   Jas 5:14-18
  over **HEALING**
    Disciples   Mk 6:7-13;
                              Lk 9:1-6
    Jesus   Mt 10:1
  JOY over
    Believers   Lk 10:17-20
  over **MIRACLE**
    Demons   Mk 6:7-13;
                              Lk 9:1-6
    Jesus   Mt 10:1
  in **SERVICE**
    Jesus   Mt 10:1
  through the **SPIRIT**
    Holy Spirit   Eph 3:14-19

FRIENDSHIP with
  TRADITION of
    Daniel   *Bel 1:1-2

FULFILLMENT of the
  of **DEITY**
    Believers   Eph 3:20-21
    God   Num 11:14-24a;
                              Is 14:24-27;
                              50:1-11
    Jesus   Jn 3:31-36

OBEDIENCE to (cont'd)

Women	1 Cor 14:34-40; Eph 5:21-33; 1 Tim 2:8-15; Tit 2:1-10; 1 Pet 3:1-7

ORDER in

God	Gen 1:20-23

through PARADOX

Jesus	Mt 11:7-15; Lk 7:24-30

in POLITICS

Jesus	Mt 22:15-22; Mk 12:13-17; Lk 20:19-26
Mordecai	Esth 8:9-14
Paul	Rom 13:1-7

PRAISE of

David	Ps 29:1-2
Psalmist	Ps 99:4-5; 150:2

PRUDENCE of

Moses	Deut 17:14-20

concerning SACREDNESS

Esther	Esth 9:29-32
Jesus	Jn 7:15-24

SERVICE to

Jesus	Mt 22:15-22; Mk 12:13-17; Lk 20:19-26

SPIRIT of

Jesus	Jn 7:15-24

VICTORY in

Believers	Rev 2:18-29

WISDOM in

Jesus	Mt 7:28-29
Preacher	Eccl 7:1-22; 9:1-16
Sirach	*Sir 10:1-5

WITNESS to

Asaph	Ps 78:1-8
Holy Spirit	Acts 1:6-11
Paul	2 Cor 10:1-6

of YOUTH

Preacher	Eccl 9:17-10:20

JOY in

Joash	2 Chr 21:1-23:21
Princess	Ps 45:13-15

of DEITY

Israelites	Neh 8:9-12

of FOLLOWERs

Believers	Lk 10:17-20

in WORSHIP

David	1 Chr 15:1-16:43

JUSTICE in

of DEITY

God	Job 37:23-24; Ps 62:8-12
Israelites	Deut 10:12-22
Psalmist	Ps 82:8
Solomon	*Wis 16:15-29

INSTRUCTION on

Paul	2 Cor 13:1-4
Solomon	Prov 29:1-27; *Wis 6:1-11

of MESSIANIC FIGURE

Pilate	Mt 27:11-26; Mk 15:6-15

JUSTICE (cont'd)

of MISSION

Paul	2 Cor 13:5-10

PROPHECY of

Isaiah	Is 9:2-7; 32:1-8

in KILLING

Hazael	2 Kgs 8:7-15
Joab	2 Sam 20:1-26

through FALSE BELIEF

Herod	Mt 2:16-18

for LEADERSHIP

in COVENANT

David	2 Sam 5:1-5; 1 Chr 11:1-12:40

from DEITY

Aaron	Ex 4:10-16
David	2 Sam 22:1-51; 1 Chr 28:1-29:30; Ps 18:43-45
Gideon	Judg 8:22-23
Jesus	Mt 28:16-20; Acts 2:14-36; Eph 1:15-2:10; Phil 2:5-11
Judah	Judg 1:1-21
King	Prov 21:1-31
Maccabeus	*2 Mc 15:6-10
Mankind	Jer 32:26-44; Zech 14:1-21
Moses	Ex 32:30-35
Paul	Gal 1:1-5
Solomon	Ps 72:8-14

in LEADERSHIP

of DEITY

God	Ps 47:5-9; 66:5-7; 93:1-2; 103:19-22; Is 40:1-11; 51:1-16 Rev 11:15-19; 19:6-10
Israelites	Ex 15:1-18; Ps 77:11-20; Jer 31:31-34

over FOLLOWERs

Jesus	Mt 4:23-25; 1 Cor 11:2-16
Paul	Eph 1:1-2; Col 1:1-2

INSTRUCTION on

David	1 Kgs 2:1-4
Elisha	2 Kgs 9:1-13
Ezra	Ezra 7:25-26
Jesus	Mt 7:28-29
Joshua	Josh 1:12-18
Jotham	Judg 9:7-15
Moses	Deut 1:9-18; 16:18-20; 17:14-20
Nehemiah	Neh 7:1-3
Paul	1 Cor 11:2-16
Samuel	1 Sam 12:1-25
Solomon	1 Kgs 1:28-40

of MESSIANIC FIGURE

David	2 Sam 2:1-7; 5:1-15;

over **POLITICS**
Psalmist — Ps 2:7-9
over **PURIFICATION**
Holy Spirit — Jn 1:19-51
SACREDNESS in
Jesus — Mt 12:1-8;
Mk 2:23-28;
Lk 6:1-5
VICTORY in
Jesus — Mt 8:28-34;
Mk 5:1-20;
Lk 8:26-39
WISDOM in
Jesus — Mt 22:41-46;
Mk 12:35-37a;
Lk 20:41-44
WITNESS to
Peter — 2 Pet 1:16-19a
MIRACLE by
Israelites — Ex 15:1-18
of **DEITY**
God — Mic 1:2-4;
Nah 1:1-9;
2 Cor 4:7-12
Jesus — Lk 11:14-23
of **FOLLOWERs**
Demons — Mk 6:7-13;
Lk 9:1-6
Jesus — Mt 10:1
of **MESSIANIC FIGURE**
Demon — Mk 1:21-28;
Lk 4:31-37
in **MISSION**
Holy Spirit — Rom 15:14-24
PROPHECY of
Moses — Deut 34:1-12
REVELATION on
Israelites — Deut 11:1-25
in **MISSION**
for **DISCIPLESHIP**
Holy Spirit — 1 Thes 1:2-10
Jesus — Mk 3:13-19
FAITH in
Disciples — Mk 6:7-13;
Lk 9:1-6
Paul — Eph 3:1-13
for **HEALING**
Apostles — Mt 10:7-8
JUSTICE in
Paul — 2 Cor 13:5-10
of **LEADERSHIP**
Paul — 1 Tim 1:1-2
MIRACLE by
Holy Spirit — Rom 15:14-24
OBEDIENCE to
Titus — Tit 3:1-7
SERVICE to
Apostles — Mt 10:7-8
Elders — 1 Pet 5:1-5
Paul — Tit 1:1-4
WILL of
Paul — 1 Cor 1:1-3
WITNESS to
Israelites — Ps 106:6-12
Paul — 2 Cor 2:14-17
Pharaoh — Ex 9:13-35;
Rom 9:14-29
Titus — Tit 2:11-15

OBEDIENCE to
by **FOLLOWERs**
God — 2 Chr 14:1-16:14
INSTRUCTION on
Demon — Mk 1:21-28;
Lk 4:31-37
Jesus — Mt 7:24-27;
Lk 6:46-49;
24:44-49
Paul — Rom 13:1-7;
2 Cor 10:1-6;
Tit 3:8-11
Peter — Lk 5:1-11;
1 Pet 2:13-17;
5:1-5
Preacher — Eccl 8:1-9
Servants — 1 Pet 2:18-20
Solomon — Prov 23:15-24:22
Women — 1 Cor 14:34-40;
Eph 5:21-33;
1 Tim 2:8-15;
Tit 2:1-10;
1 Pet 3:1-7
in **MISSION**
Titus — Tit 3:1-7
PROPHECY of
Israelites — *Bar 2:11-23
ONENESS with the
of **DEITY**
God — Deut 6:4-19;
Is 44:6-8; 21-23;
46:1-13
Jesus — Jn 1:1-18;
5:19-47;
14:1-14;
Col 1:18-20
REVELATION on
God — Is 43:8-13
OPPRESSION by
Psalmist — Ps 119:161-168
in the **ENVIRONMENT**
Pharaoh — Ex 5:6-14
PROPHECY on
Israelites — Is 14:1-23
Samuel — 1 Sam 8:1-22
REVELATION on
John — Rev 7:1-8
Levites — 2 Chr 30:1-31:21
ORDER by
INSTRUCTION on
God — Gen 1:20-23
REVELATION on
God — *2 Esd 16:51-78
Job — Job 38:12-15
ORDER created by
of **DEITY**
David — Ps 19:1-4b
Ezra — *2 Esd 8:4-36
God — Ps 19:4c-6;
33:4-9;
50:1-6;
65:5-8;
74:12-17;
77:11-20;
89:5-18;
93:3-4;
95:1-7c;

of **DEITY** (cont'd)
God   97:1-5;
                      104:1-4;
                      5-9;
                      135:5-7;
                      147:12-20
Jeremiah   *Jer 6:60-73
Manasseh   *Mana 1:1-5
Mankind   Ps 8:3-8
Sirach   *Sir 16:24-30;
                      17:15-32;
                      18:1-14;
                      33:7-15;
                      39:17-27;
                      42:15-43:33
Solomon   *Wis 7:15-8:1;
                      9:1-18;
                      11:21-12:2;
                      13:1-9

puts **ORDER**
in the **ENVIRONMENT**
God   Gen 1:1-2;
                      3-5;
                      6-8;
                      9-13;
                      14-19;
                      24-31;
                      2 Sam 22:1-51;
                      Ps 18:7-15

revealed by **PARADOX**
INSTRUCTION on
Jesus   Mt 11:7-15;
                      Lk 7:24-30

PEACE through
REVELATION on
John   Rev 6:3-4

in **POLITICS**
in the **ENVIRONMENT**
Abner   2 Sam 2:8-32
David   2 Sam 8:1-18;
                      20:1-26
Demetrius   *1 Mc 11:1-19;
                      38-53
Ehud   Judg 3:15-23
Simon   *1 Mc 14:25-49

INSTRUCTION on
Jesus   Mt 22:15-22;
                      Mk 12:13-17;
                      Lk 20:19-26
Mordecai   Esth 8:9-14
Paul   Rom 13:1-7
PROPHECY of
Deborah   Judg 4:4-5
Jesus   Mt 2:1-12
REVELATION of
God   Is 41:1-42:4
Moses   Ex 3:11-22
as **TRADITION**
Israelites   2 Sam 23:8-39;
                      1 Chr 11:1-12:40
Jeconiah   *1 Esd 1:34-36
Jehoiachin   *1 Esd 1:43-45
Jehoiakim   *1 Esd 1:37-42
John   *1 Mc 16:18-24
Josiah   *1 Esd 1:33

as **TRADITON** (cont'd)
Zedekiah   *1 Esd 1:46-58

PRAISE of
Bodyguard   *1 Esd 4:1-12
Israelites   Ex 15:1-18
INSTRUCTION on
David   Ps 29:1-2
Psalmist   Ps 99:4-5;
                      150:2

REVELATION of
Isaiah   Is 6:1-13
Jeremiah   Jer 9:23-24
in **WORSHIP**
David   Ps 24:7-10;
                      138:4-6
Psalmist   Ps 150:2

PROPHECY on
FAITH in
Isaiah   Is 30:8-17
in **FAMILY**
Jacob   Gen 47:27-48:22
FULFILLMENT of
Elisha   2 Kgs 8:7-15
Jehu   2 Kgs 15:8-12
in **LEADERSHIP**
Balaam   Num 23:27-24:13
Believers   Rev 2:18-29
Deborah   Judg 4:4-5
Eliakim   Is 22:15-25
God   Jer 30:18-22
Isaiah   Is 15:1-16:14
Israelites   Hos 8:8-10
Jesus   Lk 1:26-38
Obadiah   Obad 1:17-21
Samuel   1 Sam 13:1-23
in **MIRACLE**
Moses   Deut 34:1-12
in **POLITICS**
Deborah   Judg 4:4-5
Jesus   Mt 2:1-12
WISDOM of
Holy Spirit   Jn 16:12-15
WITNESS to
John   Rev 11:1-14

PRUDENCE of
INSTRUCTION on
Moses   Deut 17:14-20

PURIFICATION by the
of **DEITY**
Holy Spirit   Mt 3:1-12;
                      Mk 1:2-8;
                      Lk 3:15-17;
                      Acts 1:1-5
of **MESSIANIC FIGURE**
Holy Spirit   Jn 1:19-51

REJECTION of
Israelites   1 Kgs 12:1-20;
                      2 Chr 10:1-12:16
Queen of Sheba   2 Sam 20:1-26
through **FALSE BELIEF**
Diotrephes   3 Jn 1:9-11
Sinners   Jude 1:8-10
REVELATION of
Pharaoh   Ex 7:1-7
REPENTANCE by the
Heliodorus   *2 Mc 3:1-40

REPENTANCE by the (cont'd)
    Israelites   Rom 11:7-24

REVELATION on
  ACCEPTANCE of
    John   Rev 5:1-14
    Nebuchadnezzar   Dan 4:28-33
  of DEATH
    John   Rev 6:7-8
  of EVIL
    John   Rev 13:1-4
  in FAMILY
    Jehu   2 Kgs 10:29-31
  FULFILLMENT of
    Jesus   Lk 21:25-28
  in LEADERSHIP
    Daniel   Dan 7:17-27;
        8:15-25;
        11:1-4;
        5-20;
        21-45
    God   Jer 30:23-31:1
    Isaiah   Is 6:1-13
    Jeremiah   Jer 1:4-10;
        16:19-21;
        33:14-26
    John   Rev 4:1-11;
        12:1-6;
        17:6b-18;
        19:11-16
    Moses   Num 27:12-23
    Samuel   1 Sam 8:1-22
  over LIFE
    Ezekiel   Ezek 18:1-4
    Isaiah   Is 54:1-17
    Job   Job 39:5-8;
        9-12;
        13-18;
        19-25;
        40:15-24;
        41:1-12;
        13-34
    John   Rev 13:11-18
  in MIRACLE
    Israelites   Deut 11:1-25
  in POLITICS
    God   Is 41:1-42:4
    Moses   Ex 3:11-22
  WISDOM in
    Holy Spirit   1 Cor 2:10-16
    Isaiah   Is 55:1-13
    Job   Job 38:4-7;
        16-18;
        19-21;
        22-24;
        25-30;
        31-38;
        39-41;
        39:1-4;
        5-8;
        13-18;
        26-30

REWARD by
  Daniel   Dan 6:1-3
  David   1 Sam 17:1-18:5
  Mordecai   Esth 8:1-2
  for FOLLOWERs
    Paul   1 Cor 9:7-14

SACREDNESS in
  INSTRUCTION on

INSTRUCTION on (cont'd)
    Esther   Esth 9:29-32
    Jesus   Jn 7:15-24
  of MESSIANIC FIGURE
    Jesus   Mt 12:1-8;
        Mk 2:23-28;
        Lk 6:1-5
  REVELATION on
    Levites   Num 1:47-54
  SCRIPTURES on
    Paul   2 Tim 3:14-17

SCRIPTURES on
  over LIFE
    Hosea   Rom 9:14-29
  WITNESS to
    David   Mt 22:41-46;
        Mk 12:35-37a;
        Lk 20:41-44
    Paul   2 Tim 3:14-17

SELF-REALIZATION on
    Paul   Phil 3:4-16
  of LEADERSHIP
    David   2 Sam 5:6-16;
        1 Chr 14:1-17
    Solomon   Prov 8:1-21
  over LIFE
    Jesus   Jn 17:1-5

SERVICE to
    David   1 Sam 16:14-23
    Hiram   1 Kgs 5:1-18;
        2 Chr 2:1-4:22
    Job   Job 28:1-13
    Melchizedek   Heb 7:1-28
    Solomon   1 Kgs 4:7-19
  of DEITY
    Israelites   Ex 31:1-11
    Jesus   Jn 10:19-40
  INSTRUCTION on
    Jesus   Mt 22:15-22;
        Mk 12:13-17;
        Lk 20:19-26
  by MESSIANIC FIGURE
    Jesus   Heb 7:1-28
  in MISSION
    Apostles   Mt 10:7-8
    Elders   1 Pet 5:1-5
    Paul   Tit 1:1-4
  in WORSHIP
    Satan   Rev 13:1-4

SHARING of
    Moses   Num 11:14-24a

SPIRIT of
  INSTRUCTION on
    Jesus   Jn 7:15-24

SUFFERING by
  of DEITY
    Elisha   2 Kgs 8:1-6
    Israelites   Ps 106:19-23
  REVELATION on
    Israelites   Hag 1:1-11
    John   Rev 6:7-8
  SELF-REALIZATION on
    Paul   Phil 3:4-16

TRADITION in

PRAISE of (cont'd)

David　138:4-6
Psalmist　Ps 150:2

SERVICE to

Satan　Rev 13:1-4

of YOUTH

INSTRUCTION on

Preacher　Eccl 9:17-10:20

BEHAVIOR

CONDEMNATION of

caused by FALSE BELIEF

Paul　2 Tim 3:1-9
Pharisees　Mt 23:23-24

of MESSIANIC FIGURE

Crowd　Lk 11:14-23
Scribes　Mk 3:20-30

COVENANT on

in MARRIAGE

Alexander　*1 Mc 10:51-58

of OBEDIENCE

Noah　Gen 6:5-22

in POLITICS

Jonathan　*1 Mc 12:1-23

of ENEMY

in the ENVIRONMENT

Israelites　Josh 9:1-2

through FALSE BELIEF

ANGER

Herod　Lk 3:18-20

ANXIETY

Pharisees　Lk 19:47-48;
　　　　Jn 11:1-57
Priests　Jn 11:1-57

BLASPHEMY

Adversaries　Ps 79:1-4

CONDEMNATION

Paul　2 Tim 3:1-9
Pharisees　Mt 23:23-24

DESTRUCTION

Assyrians　2 Kgs 19:9b-37
Paul　Gal 5:7-12

DOUBT

Simon　Lk 7:36-50

EVIL

Jews　Acts 19:13-20

FEAR

Herod　Mk 6:14-16;
　　　　Lk 9:7-9

HATE

Pharisees　Lk 11:53-54

IDOLATRY

Demetrius　Acts 19:23-41
Ephesians　Acts 19:23-41
People　Is 46:1-13
Solomon　*Wis 13:10-19

IGNORANCE

Pharisees　Mt 15:12-14;
　　　　Lk 19:39-40
Sinners　2 Pet 3:3-7

JEALOUSY

Priest　Acts 5:17-42
Sadducees　Acts 5:17-42

KILLING

KILLING (cont'd)

Herod　Mt 14:1-12;
　　　　Mk 6:17-29
Pharaoh　Ex 1:15-22

PARADOX

Israelites　Is 48:1-22
Pharisees　Mt 23:29-33

REJECTION

Pharisees　Lk 11:53-54;
　　　　19:39-40

REPENTANCE

Magicians　Acts 19:13-20

REVELATION

Herodias　Mk 6:17-29

SELFISHNESS

Demetrius　Acts 19:23-41
Pharisees　Lk 11:37-44

SEX

Jeremiah　*Jer 6:41-44

SPIRIT

Pharisees　Mt 16:5-12

WEALTH

Jason　*2 Mc 4:18-20

of FOLLOWERs

ACCEPTANCE

Crowd　Jn 12:12-19
People　Lk 19:47-48

ALIENATION

Disciples　Mt 26:47-56;
　　　　Mk 14:43-50
Judas　Mt 26:47-56;
　　　　Lk 22:47-54a;
　　　　Mk 14:43-50

ANXIETY

Epaphroditus　Phil 2:19-30
Paul　Gal 4:8-11;
　　　　12-20

BLESSING

Crowd　Jn 12:12-19
Jesus　Lk 24:50-51

DISCIPLESHIP

Crowd　Mt 8:1

FAITH

Apostles　Mt 10:26-39
Crowd　Mt 15:29-31
Thessalonians　1 Thes 3:1-10

FEAR

Disciples　Mt 8:23-27;
　　　　Mk 4:35-41;
　　　　Lk 8:22-25

GREED

Judas　Mt 26:14-16;
　　　　Mk 14:10-11;
　　　　Lk 22:3-6

GRIEF

Paul　2 Cor 1:23-2:4

HEALING

Jesus　Mt 12:15-21;
　　　　17:14-20

INDIFFERENCE

Disciples　Mt 26:36-46;
　　　　Mk 14:32-42;
　　　　Lk 22:39-46

JEALOUSY

Jews　Acts 17:1-9;
　　　　10-15

JOY

People　Lk 13:10-17

LOVE

LOVE (cont'd)
Thessalonians   1 Thes 3:1-10
OBEDIENCE
Abraham   Gen 12:1-8;
                     13:14-18
Disciples   Mt 21:1-11;
                     Mk 11:1-10;
                     Lk 19:28-38

OPPRESSION
Jews   Acts 17:1-9
Saul   Acts 9:1-19
ORDER
Israelites   Num 10:11-28
PRAISE
Blind   Lk 18:35-43
Crowd   Jn 12:12-19
Jesus   1 Pet 4:12-19
PRIDE
Thessalonians   1 Thes 2:17-20
PRUDENCE
Paul   Tit 3:1-7
PURIFICATION
Cornelius   Acts 10:1-11:18
Holy Spirit   Acts 1:1-5
Jesus   Mk 1:9-11;
                     Lk 3:21-22
People   Acts 2:37-41
REJECTION
Gentiles   Acts 14:1-7
Jews   Acts 14:1-7;
                     17:10-15;
                     18:1-17
Judas   Mt 26:47-56;
                     Mk 14:43-50;
                     Lk 22:47-54a
Peter   Mt 26:69-75;
                     Mk 14:66-72;
                     Lk 22:54b-62;
                     Jn 18:12-27

SACRIFICE
Paul   1 Cor 9:1-6
SADNESS
Disciples   Jn 16:5-11
SELFISHNESS
Disciples   Mt 26:36-46;
                     Mk 14:32-42;
                     Lk 22:39-46

SERVICE
Paul   1 Cor 9:1-6

INSTRUCTION on
ACCEPTANCE of
Holy Spirit   Jn 20:1-29
Jesus   Mt 5:43-47;
                     Lk 6:27-35
Paul   2 Cor 11:16-20
People   Lk 7:24-30
ANGER
James   Jas 1:19-21
Preacher   Eccl 7:1-22
ANXIETY
Jesus   Mt 6:25-34;
                     Lk 12:22-31

BLASPHEMY
Wife   Job 2:9-10
CAPTIVITY
Antiochus   *2 Mc 14:26-27
Believers   Eph 6:5-9
Paul   Phil 1:12-30
Sirach   *Sir 33:24-31

COMPASSION
God   *2 Esd 2:15-32
Sirach   *Sir 4:1-10
CONDEMNATION
Bildad   Job 8:1-7
Jesus   Mt 5:21-26;
                     12:33-37;
                     23:27-28
Job   Job 19:1-6
Paul   Gal 2:11-14
Preacher   Eccl 9:17-10:20
Zophar   Job 11:1-6
COURAGE
Paul   1 Cor 16:13-24

COVETOUSNESS
Jesus   Lk 14:7-11
DESTRUCTION
Preacher   Eccl 3:1-8
DIGNITY
Paul   Rom 13:11-14
DISCIPLESHIP
Jesus   Mt 5:13-16;
                     10:9-15;
                     16-22;
                     23;
                     26-39;
                     Mk 2:13-14;
                     6:7-13;
                     Lk 9:1-6;
                     14:34-35
Paul   1 Cor 9:1-6;
                     1 Tim 3:14-16

DISOBEDIENCE
God   Gen 3:9-13
Serpent   Gen 3:1-8
Vashti   Esth 1:10-22
DOUBT
Jesus   Mt 14:28-33
with ENEMY
Jesus   Mt 5:43-47;
                     Lk 6:27-35
Sirach   *Sir 12:8-18
EVIL
Sirach   *Sir 20:18-23;
                     22:1-6;
                     25:1-2

FAITH
Author   Heb 12:12-29
God   Is 44:6-8;
                     21-23
James   Jas 2:14-26
Paul   Col 2:6-15;
                     2 Tim 2:1-7

in FAMILY
Paul   Col 3:18-4:1
Sirach   *Sir 7:1-36;
                     11:29-34;
                     29:21-28;
                     33:16-23;
                     42:9-14
Tobit   *Tb 4:1-21
FEAR
Agur   Prov 30:15-33
Jude   Jude 1:21-23
FRIENDSHIP
Paul   2 Cor 6:14-7:1;
                     Col 4:15-18
Sirach   *Sir 12:8-18
Solomon   Prov 25:1-28

ORDER (cont'd)

Joshua	Josh 1:10-11

PARADOX in

Jesus	Mt 10:26-39;
	11:16-19;
	19:27-30;
	23:27-28;
	Mk 10:28-31;
	Lk 7:31-35;
	13:22-30
Paul	Gal 2:11-14
Pharisees	Mt 23:1-3

PATIENCE

Paul	1 Thes 5:12-22

PEACE

Author	Heb 12:12-29
Preacher	Eccl 3:1-8

PIETY

Jesus	Mt 6:1

in POLITICS

Demetrius	*1 Mc 11:20-37

in POVERTY

Sirach	*Sir 29:8-13
Solomon	Prov 22:22-23:14

PRIDE

Preacher	Eccl 7:1-22
Solomon	Prov 27:1-27

PRUDENCE

Amos	Amos 5:7-13
God	Gen 6:5-22
Isaiah	Is 8:8b-10
James	Jas 3:1-12
Jesus	Mt 5:21-26;
	33-37;
	7:15-20;
	Lk 10:38-42;
	21:34-36
Maiden	Song 3:1-5
Paul	1 Cor 10:23-11:1;
	Eph 5:15-20;
	Col 4:5-6;
	1 Thes 5:1-11;
	1 Tim 5:3-16;
	17-25
Preacher	Eccl 5:1-7
Sirach	*Sir 8:1-19;
	13:1-13;
	18:19-26;
	27-33;
	31:12-24
Solomon	Prov 1:2-6;
	5:1-14;
	10:1-32;
	22:1-16;
	22-23:14

PURIFICATION

God	Is 1:10-17
John the Baptist	Jn 1:19-51

REPENTANCE

John the Baptist	Lk 3:7-9;
	10-14
Paul	2 Cor 13:11-13

as REWARD

Paul	Rom 2:1-24
Sirach	*Sir 4:1-10

SACREDNESS

Cyrus	*1 Esd 2:1-7
Moses	Deut 22:1-12

SADNESS

Preacher	Eccl 7:1-22

SERVICE

SERVICE (cont'd)

Isaac	Gen 27:1-40
Jesus	Mt 5:38-42;
	Lk 14:1-6
John	3 Jn 1:3-8
Paul	Phil 2:1-4;
	Col 3:18-4:1;
	1 Thes 5:1-11;
	12-22;
	Tit 3:12-15

SEX

Lemuel	Prov 31:1-9
Paul	1 Cor 7:1-7;
	8-16;
	1 Thes 4:1-12
Sirach	*Sir 9:1-9;
	19:1-3;
	26:5-12;
	42:9-14

SHARING

Moses	Deut 15:1-11
Paul	Col 4:15-18;
	Tit 3:12-15
Preacher	Eccl 4:4-12

SUFFERING

Holy Spirit	Acts 20:17-38
Preacher	Eccl 11:9-12:7

TEMPERANCE

James	Jas 3:1-12
Jesus	Mt 6:16-18
Lemuel	Prov 31:1-9
Paul	1 Cor 7:1-7;
	8-16;
	36-38;
	Col 2:16-23
Sirach	*Sir 19:1-3;
	37:27-31
Tobit	*Tb 4:1-21

TEMPTATION

Jesus	Mt 4:1-11
Paul	1 Cor 7:8-16;
	36-38
Solomon	Prov 23:15-24:22

VIOLENCE

Preacher	Eccl 3:1-8

concerning WEALTH

Artaxerxes	*1 Esd 8:8-24
Darius	*1 Esd 6:27-34
Demetrius	*1 Mc 11:20-37
Preacher	Eccl 5:8-20
Sirach	*Sir 13:1-13;
	18:27-33;
	42:6-7
Solomon	Prov 12:1-28;
	14:1-35
Tobit	*Tb 4:1-21

concerning WILL in

David	Ps 32:8-11
John the Baptist	Lk 3:7-9

WISDOM of

Agur	Prov 30:15-33
Daughters	Song 1:8
Jesus	Mt 5:31-32
Solomon	Prov 6:6-11

as WITNESS

Jesus	Mt 5:13-16
Paul	Acts 24:1-27;
	2 Cor 3:1-3

of YOUTH

Jesus	Mt 19:13-15;
	Mk 10:13-16

MEDITATION on
  in COMPASSION
    Jeremiah   Lam 3:1-66
  in DEATH
    Job   Job 7:7-11
  in INNOCENCE
    Job   Job 16:12-17
  in OBEDIENCE
    Paul   2 Thes 3:3-5

in MESSIANIC FIGURE
  ACCEPTANCE of
    Blind   Jn 9:1-41
    Crowd   Mt 21:1-11;
                 Mk 11:1-10;
                 Lk 19:28-38
    Jews   Jn 11:1-57
    People   Jn 7:25-31;
                 37-52
    Samaritans Jn 4:27-42
  CONDEMNATION of
    Jews   Jn 8:21-59
  through FAITH
    Blind   Lk 18:35-43;
                 Jn 9:1-41
    Jews   Jn 12:9-11
    Martha   Jn 11:1-57
    Mary   Jn 2:1-11
    Official   Jn 4:43-54
  results in HEALING
    Blind   Mk 10:46-52;
                 Lk 18:35-43;
                 Jn 9:1-41
    Jesus   Mt 9:18-26;
                 27-31;
                 14:34-36
    Martha   Jn 11:1-57
    Mary   Jn 11:1-57
    Official   Jn 4:43-54
    Woman   Mk 5:25-34;
                 Lk 8:40-56
  IGNORANCE of
    People   Jn 7:1-14
  MIRACLE of
    Disciples   Jn 2:1-11
    Jesus   Mt 9:27-31
    Woman   Mk 5:25-34;
                 Lk 8:40-56
  REJECTION of
    People   Jn 7:37-52;
                 12:36b-43
  WITNESS to
    Blind   Jn 9:1-41
    Crowd   Mt 21:1-11;
                 Mk 11:1-10;
                 Lk 19:28-38
    Disciples   Jn 2:1-11
    Peter   Mt 16:13-20

in MIRACLE
  by FOLLOWER
    Peter   Mt 14:28-33
  INSTRUCTION on
    God   Ex 4:1-9
    Jesus   Mk 9:14-29
  of MESSIANIC FIGURE
    Disciples   Jn 2:1-11
    Jesus   Mt 9:27-31
    Woman   Mk 5:25-34;
                 Lk 8:40-56
  in MISSION

in MISSION (cont'd)
    Jesus   Mt 15:21-28
  in WORSHIP
    Israelites   1 Kgs 18:1-46

through MIRACLE
    Israelites   Josh 4:20-5:1
  of DEITY
    Israelites   Ex 4:27-31;
                 Ps 78:40-55
    Joshua   Josh 10:1-15
    People   Lk 1:57-80

in MISSION
  of LOVE
    Men   Tit 2:1-10
  of MIRACLE
    Jesus   Mt 15:21-28
  of ONENESS
    Believers   Eph 4:7-16

in OBEDIENCE
    Believers   Heb 11:1-40
  of FOLLOWERs
    Paul   Philm 1:21-25
  MEDITATION on
    Paul   2 Thes 3:3-5

in ONENESS
  of FOLLOWERs
    Believers   Acts 2:42-47
  in MISSION
    Believers   Eph 4:7-16

in PATIENCE
  with FOLLOWERs
    Jesus   1 Tim 1:12-17

PEACE in
  INSTRUCTION on
    Jesus   Jn 14:1-14

PRAISE of
  in MISSION
    Believers   Eph 1:3-14

PRAISE through
  INSTRUCTION on
    Peter   1 Pet 1:3-9

PROPHECY of
  BLESSING in
    Elizabeth   Lk 1:39-56
    Jeremiah   Jer 17:5-8
  through HOPE
    Holy Spirit Jn 7:37-52

in PURIFICATION
  of FOLLOWERs
    Holy Spirit 2 Thes 2:13-15
  in MISSION
    John the Baptist Mt 3:1-12;
                 Lk 3:1-6
causing REJECTION
  of FALSE BELIEF
    Daniel   *Bel 1:3-7
    Jews   Jn 10:19-40
REJECTION of
  in MESSIANIC FIGURE
    People   Jn 7:37-52;
                 12:36b-43

BELIEF (cont'd)

REWARDs of
  in **DEITY**
    Believers   Heb 11:1-40
  INSTRUCTION on
    Author   Heb 10:32-39
    Jesus   Jn 11:1-57;
                     12:27-36a
    Paul   Rom 9:30-10:21;
                     11:7-24;
                     2 Thes 1:7b-10
    Solomon   Prov 28:1-28
  PROPHECY of
    Jesus   Jn 7:37-52
  SCRIPTURES on
    People   1 Pet 2:4-10

SCRIPTURES on
  ACCEPTANCE of
    Jesus   John 5:19-47
  concerning **LIFE**
    Jesus   Jn 7:37-52

SELF-REALIZATION of
  through **FAITH**
    Centurion   Lk 23:46-49
  through **SUFFERING**
    Paul   2 Tim 1:8-14

SUFFERING for
  INSTRUCTION on
    Paul   Phil 1:12-30
  SELF-REALIZATION of
    Paul   2 Tim 1:8-14

in VICTORY
  of **DEITY**
    David   Ps 56:6b-9;
                     59:9-10
    Jeremiah   Jer 20:7-18
    Jesus   1 Jn 4:19-5:5
  INSTRUCTION on
    Jehoshaphat   2 Chr 17:1-20:37

in WILL
  INSTRUCTION on
    Paul   Rom 14:1-23

WITNESS to
  by **FOLLOWER**s
    Jesus   1 Jn 5:8-12
    Samaritan   Jn 4:1-26;
                     27-42
  in **MESSIANIC FIGURE**
    Blind   Jn 9:1-41
    Crowd   Mt 21:1-11;
                     Mk 11:1-10;
                     Lk 19:28-38
    Disciples   Jn 2:1-11
    Peter   Mt 16:13-20
  in **MISSION**
    Paul   2 Cor 4:13-15
  SCRIPTURES on
    Jesus   Jn 20:30-31

unBELIEF

ANGER concerning
  Israelites   Ps 74:1-2;

unBELIEF

BLASPHEMY through
  People   Acts 2:1-13

CONDEMNATION of
  INSTRUCTION on
    Jesus   Jn 3:1-21
    Paul   1 Tim 5:3-16
  in **MESSIANIC FIGURE**
    Jews   Jn 8:21-59

DEFEAT through
  Judahites   Lam 4:1-22

in DEITY
  DOUBT in
    Israelites   Rom 11:7-24
  REJECTION of
    Israelites   Is 49:1-26;
                     Ezek 9:1-11
  in **SACREDNESS**
    Moses   Num 20:2-13

DESTRUCTION through
  INSTRUCTION on
    John   Jude 1:5-7
  PROPHECY of
    Jonah   Jon 3:1-10
    Tobit   *Tb 14:1-15

DOUBT through
  concerning **DEITY**
    Israelites   Rom 11:7-24
    Jeremiah   Jer 1:4-10
    Moses   Ex 4:1-9;
                     10-16;
                     5:6-14
    People   Acts 2:1-13
  caused by **FALSE BELIEF**
    Jews   Jn 6:25-59;
                     10:19-40
    Pharisees   Jn 9:1-41
  INSTRUCTION on
    Jesus   Mt 21:28-32
  in **MESSIANIC FIGURE**
    People   Jn 7:25-31;
                     12:36b-43

causing **HERESY**
  through **FALSE BELIEF**
    Sinners   2 Pet 3:3-7

causing **IDOLATRY**
  through **FALSE BELIEF**
    Crowds   Acts 14:8-18

in JUSTICE
  of **DEITY**
    Israelites   Ezek 18:25-29;
                     33:10-20

causing **KILLING**
  through **FALSE BELIEF**
    Sarah   *Tb 3:7-15

in MESSIANIC FIGURE
  causing **DOUBT**
    People   Jn 7:25-31;
                     12:36b-43
in MIRACLE
  through **FALSE BELIEF**
    Jesus   Mt 13:53-58

unBELIEF (cont'd)

PROPHECY of
  FULFILLMENT of
    Isaiah   Mt 15:3-9;
            Mk 7:1-23
    Mary   Lk 1:39-56

REJECTION of
  in **DEITY**
    Israelites   Is 49:1-26;
            Ezek 9:1-11
  by **FOLLOWERs**
    Jews   Acts 13:14-52
  INSTRUCTION on
    Achior   *Jdt 5:22-6:13
    Elihu   Job 35:1-4
    Jesus   Mt 7:6;
            Lk 10:1-16
    Jews   Acts 28:17-31
    Paul   2 Cor 6:14-7:1

REPENTANCE from
  INSTRUCTION on
    Paul   Acts 17:16-34

REVENGE for
  Moses   Num 11:14-24a

in **SACREDNESS**
  of **DEITY**
    Moses   Num 20:2-13

in **VICTORY**
    Caleb   Num 13:26b-33
    Danites   Judg 18:7-10

in **WORSHIP**
  causing **KILLING**
    John   Rev 13:11-18

BLASPHEMY

against **AUTHORITY**
  of **MESSIANIC FIGURE**
    Pharisees   Mt 9:32-34

BEHAVIOR revealing
    Belshazzar   Dan 5:18-25
    Israelites   Neh 13:15-22
    Jehoiakim   *1 Esd 1:37-42
  through **FALSE BELIEF**
    Adversaries   Ps 79:1-4
  INSTRUCTION on
    Wife   Job 2:9-10
  against **MESSIANIC FIGURE**
    Jews   Jn 8:21-59
    People   Lk 22:63-65
    Scribes   Mk 3:20-30
    Soldiers   Mt 27:27-31;
            Mk 15:16-20
  REVELATION of
    Daniel   Dan 11:21-45
  in **WORSHIP**
    Antiochus   *2 Mc 5:11-7;
            6:1-11

through **unBELIEF**
    People   Acts 2:1-13

CONFRONTATION with
    Antiochus   *2 Mc 9:1-4
    Babylonians   Jer 52:4-27
  through **FALSE BELIEF**
    Pharisees   Lk 16:14-15
  by **MESSIANIC FIGURE**
    Crowd   Lk 11:14-23
    Herod   Lk 23:6-16
    Pharisees   Mt 12:22-32
    Priests   Lk 23:33-38
    Scribes   Mt 9:1-8;
            Mk 2:1-12;
            Lk 5:17-26
    Soldiers   Lk 23:33-38

against **COVENANT**
  through **inFIDELITY**
    Israelites   Mal 2:10-16
against **DEITY**
  PUNISHMENT for
    Antiochus   *2 Mc 9:5-29
  through **disRESPECT**
    Priests   Mal 1:6-2:9
  SIGNS of
    Israelites   Neh 9:16-18
  SIN of
    Adversaries   Ps 74:3-9
    Israelites   Amos 2:6-8
    Mankind   Ps 10:3-11
  through **unTRUTH**
    Mankind   Rev 16:8-9;
            10-11;
            17-21

through **inFIDELITY**
  of **FOLLOWER**
    Judas   Mt 26:47-56;
            Mk 14:43-50;
            Lk 22:47-54a
  PROPHECY of
    Paul   1 Tim 4:1-5

INSTRUCTION on
    Paul   1 Cor 11:17-22
  against **LAW**
    God   Ex 20:1-17
    Moses   Deut 5:1-21
  in **RITE**
    Paul   1 Cor 11:27-34

JUDGMENT of
    Rulers   Acts 6:8-8:3
  through **FALSE BELIEF**
    Caiaphas   Mt 26:57-68;
            Mk 14:53-65
    Jews   Jn 10:19-40;
            18:28-19:16
  INSTRUCTION on
    Jesus   Lk 16:14-15
    Paul   1 Cor 11:17-22
  against **MESSIANIC FIGURE**
    Jesus   Mt 21:12-17;
            Mk 11:15-19;
            Lk 19:45-46
    People   Lk 23:1-5
    Priests   Lk 22:66-71
  PROPHECY of
    Isaiah   Is 5:8-24a
  REVELATION on
    Ezekiel   Ezek 9:1-11
    Israelites   Mal 2:17-3:5

SCRIPTURES on
Paul   Rom 2:1-24

against LAW
Moses   Ex 22:21-31;
                        Lev 19:1-37
through FALSE BELIEF
Israelites   Deut 18:9-22
INSTRUCTION on
God   Ex 20:1-17
Moses   Deut 5:1-21
REVELATION on
Moses   Lev 18:1-30;
                        24:10-23

against MESSIANIC FIGURE
BEHAVIOR revealing
Jews   Jn 8:21-59
People   Lk 22:63-65
Scribes   Mk 3:20-30
Soldiers   Mt 27:27-31;
                        Mk 15:16-20
CONFRONTATION with
Crowd   Lk 11:14-23
Herod   Lk 23:6-16
Pharisees   Mt 12:22-32
Priests   Lk 23:33-38
Scribes   Mt 9:1-8;
                        Mk 2:1-12;
                        Lk 5:17-26
Soldiers   Lk 23:33-38
JUDGMENT of
Jesus   Mt 21:12-17;
                        Mk 11:15-19;
                        Lk 19:45-46
People   Lk 23:1-5
Priests   Lk 22:66-71
RECONCILIATION overcomes
Paul   1 Tim 1:12-17
SIN of
Crowd   Mt 27:33-44;
                        Mk 15:21-32

in PRAYER
Priest   *1 Mc 7:36-38

PROPHECY of
through inFIDELITY
Paul   1 Tim 4:1-5
KNOWLEDGE of
Gentiles   Mk 10:32-34
as disRESPECT
Ezekiel   Ezek 24:15-24
SIGNS of
Jesus   Mt 24:9-14;
                        15-22;
                        23-28;
                        Mk 13:14-23;
                        Lk 21:7-19

PUNISHMENT for
by DEITY
Antiochus   *2 Mc 9:5-29
caused by FALSE BELIEF
Author   Heb 6:1-8
INSTRUCTION on
Paul   1 Tim 1:18-20
PROPHECY of
Jeremiah   Jer 32:26-44
Moabites   Jer 48:1-47

REVELATION on
Israelites   Ezek 5:5-17
Jeremiah   Jer 19:1-15
Samuel   1 Sam 3:1-4:1a
Zechariah   Zech 5:1-4

as QUALITY OF LIFE
Pharisees   Mk 7:1-23

RECONCILIATION overcomes
against MESSIANIC FIGURE
Paul   1 Tim 1:12-17
REVELATION of
Israelites   Ezek 36:16-21;
                        22-32

disRESPECT through
against DEITY
Priests   Mal 1:6-2:9
PROPHECY of
Ezekiel   Ezek 24:15-24
in WORSHIP
Judahites   Jer 7:29-8:3

REVELATION on
Ezekiel   Ezek 8:16-18
Isaiah   Is 65:1-25
Israelites   Ezek 5:5-17;
                        8:5-6;
                        20:27-29;
                        22:1-16;
                        36:16-21;
                        22-32;
                        Mal 3:13-4:3
Jeremiah   Jer 19:1-15
Prophetesses   Ezek 13:17-23
Samuel   1 Sam 3:1-4:1a
Zechariah   Zech 5:1-4
against LAW
Moses   Lev 18:1-30;
                        24:10-23
in RITE
Israelites   Ezek 44:6-9
SIGNS of
Daniel   Dan 8:9-12;
                        13-14;
                        9:24-27;
                        12:5-13
John   Rev 13:1-4;
                        5-10

in RITE
through FALSE BELIEF
Israelites   Ezek 23:36-49
INSTRUCTION on
Paul   1 Cor 11:27-34
REVELATION on
Israelites   Ezek 44:6-9

SCRIPTURES on
Paul   Rom 2:1-24

SIGNS of
against DEITY
Israelites   Neh 9:16-18
INSTRUCTION on
Paul   2 Thes 2:3b-10;
                        2 Tim 3:1-9

PROPHECY of
Jesus   Mt 24:9-14;
                        15-22;

BLASPHEMY (cont'd)

PROPHECY of (cont'd)
Jesus   23-28;
  Mk 13:14-23;
  Lk 21:7-19
REVELATION on
Daniel   Dan 8:9-12;
  13-14;
  9:24-27;
  12:5-13
John   Rev 13:1-4;
  5-10
in **WORSHIP**
Antiochus   *1 Mc 1:54-61

SIN of
Holy Spirit   Mk 3:20-30
Zedekiah   2 Chr 36:1-23

against **DEITY**
Adversaries   Ps 74:3-9
Israelites   Amos 2:6-8
Mankind   Ps 10:3-11
through **FALSE BELIEF**
Israelites   Ezek 16:15-34;
  20:9-26;
  22:23-31
Prophets   Jer 23:9-12;
  13-15;
  2 Pet 2:1-3
INSTRUCTION on
Holy Spirit   Mt 12:22-32;
  Lk 12:1-12
James   Jas 5:12
Jesus   Mk 12:37b-40;
  Lk 20:45-47
against **MESSIANIC FIGURE**
Crowd   Mt 27:33-44;
  Mk 15:21-32
PROPHECY of
Isaiah   Is 3:8-12
Jerusalemites   Zeph 3:1-5
Sennacherib   Is 37:22-29
REVELATION of
Ezekiel   Ezek 8:16-18
Isaiah   Is 65:1-25
Israelites   Ezek 8:5-6;
  20:27-29;
  22:1-16;
  Mal 3:13-4:3
Prophetesses   Ezek 13:17-23

against **TRUTH**
through **FALSE BELIEF**
Sinners   Jude 1:3-4
INSTRUCTION on
Pharisees   Mt 23:15

unTRUTH in
against **DEITY**
Mankind   Rev 16:8-9;
  10-11;
  17-21

BLESSING

in **AUTHORITY**
of **DEITY**
Jesus   Jn 5:19-47

BLESSING (cont'd)

BEHAVIOR revealing
of **DEITY**
Midwives   Ex 1:15-22
of **FOLLOWERs**
Crowd   Jn 12:12-19
Jesus   Lk 24:50-51
of **MESSIANIC FIGURE**
Peter   Mt 16:13-20
PROPHECY of
Jesus   Lk 13:34-35

of **BELIEF**
in **DEITY**
Israelites   Ps 84:10-12
by **FOLLOWERs**
Jesus   Gal 3:19-25
INSTRUCTION on
Paul   Gal 3:6-9
PROPHECY of
Elizabeth   Lk 1:39-56
Jeremiah   Jer 17:5-8

in **BROTHERHOOD**
for **FOLLOWERs**
Believers   1 Cor 14:1-12

of **COMMUNITY**
Israelites   Neh 11:1-2
Joshua   Josh 22:1-8
Solomon   1 Kgs 8:14-21;
  2 Chr 5:1-7:10
INSTRUCTION on
Moses   Deut 33:1-29
through **WORSHIP**
Aaron   Lev 9:1-24
Solomon   1 Kgs 8:54-61

COMPULSION of
by **DEITY**
Balaam   Num 23:13-26

CONFRONTATION with
INSTRUCTION on
Jesus   Lk 6:27-35
Joab   2 Sam 18:1-19:8a

CONVERSION through
REVELATION of
Isaiah   Is 58:1-14
Judahites   Jer 24:1-10

of **CREATION**
God   Ps 145:10-13a
by **DEITY**
Psalmist   Ps 115:12-18
God   Gen 1:20-23;
  24-31

from **DEITY**
for **VIRTUE**
Believers   Ps 55:22
God   Ps 73:1-3;
  112:2-4;
  Prov 3:1-35;
  14:1-35
Hosea   Hos 14:9
Israelites   Ps 84:10-12
Mankind   Ps 5:11-12
People   Rom 3:21-30

of **DEITY**
    in **AUTHORITY**
      Jesus   Jn 5:19-47
    BEHAVIOR revealing
      Midwives   Ex 1:15-22
    BELIEF in
      Israelites   Ps 84:10-12
    COMPULSION of
      Balaam   Num 23:13-26
    in **CREATION**
      Psalmist   Ps 115:12-18
    DESIRE for
      Bethelites   Zech 7:1-3
      Job   Job 29:1-6
    in **ELECTION**
      God   Ps 65:1-4
    is **ETERNAL**
      David   Ps 41:13;
                     145:1-3
      Ethan   Ps 89:52
      God   Ps 30:1-5;
                     133:1-3
      Israelites   Ps 132:11-18
      King   Ps 45:2-9
      Psalmist   Ps 113:2-4

through **FIDELITY**
    Believers   Ps 40:4-5
    Caleb   Josh 14:6-15
    David   Ps 63:1-8
    God   Ps 24:3-6;
                   37:23-40
    Isaiah   Is 63:7-64:12
    Job   Job 1:20-21
    Mankind   Ps 1:1-3;
                   25:8-15
    Psalmist   Ps 119:1-8
through **HONESTY**
    David   Ps 32:1-2
through **JUDGMENT**
    Japheth   Gen 9:26-27
    Shem   Gen 9:26-27
PRAYER for
    David   1 Chr 17:1-27;
                   Ps 4:1;
                   29:10-11;
                   72:18-20;
                   103:1-5;
                   122:6-9;
                   144:12-15
    Ezra   Ezra 7:27-28
    Isaac   Gen 27:41-28:5
    Israelites   *Bar 1:5-14
    Jews   *2 Mc 1:1-9
    Job   Job 42:10-17
    John   3 Jn 1:1-2
    Moses   Ps 90:13-17
    Peter   1 Pet 1:3-9
    Psalmist   Ps 44:23-26;
                   67:1-7;
                   115:12-18;
                   126:4-6;
                   128:5-6;
                   132:6-10
    Sirach   *Sir 50:22-24
    Solomon   2 Chr 5:1-7:10;
                   Ps 72:5-7;
                   15-17
through **PRESENCE**
    God   Is 43:14-44:5
    Israelites   Ezek 34:25-31:

through **PRESENCE** (cont'd)
    Israelites   36:8-15
    Zechariah   Lk 1:57-80
through **PROMISE**
    Abraham   Gen 22:1-19
    Caleb   Num 14:11-24;
                   Deut 1:19-46
    Isaac   Gen 26:1-11
    Jacob   Gen 28:10-22
through **PROVIDENCE**
    Assyrians   Is 19:18-25
    Baruch   *Bar 5:1-4
    Believers   Ps 97:10-12
    David   Ps 13:5-6;
                   16:5-8;
                   18:31-42;
                   22:6-11;
                   23:1-4;
                   5-6;
                   89:19-37
    Egyptians   Is 19:18-25
    God   Ps 67:1-7;
                   68:4-14;
                   107:33-38;
                   113:5-9;
                   127:1-2;
                   147:12-20
    Isaac   Gen 25:7-11
    Israelites   Deut 4:32-40;
                   2 Chr 30:1-31:21
                   Ps 78:40-55;
                   105:23-25;
                   Is 19:18-25;
                   Hos 2:16-20;
                   13:4-6;
                   Amos 2:9-12
    Joseph   Gen 39:1-23
    Judahites   2 Chr 17:1-20:37
    Mankind   Ps 8:3-8;
                   Zech 10:1-2
    Melchizedek   Gen 14:17-20
    Nebuchadnezzar *Bar 1:5-14
    Psalmist   Ps 66:8-12;
                   85:1-3;
                   92:5-11
    Solomon   1 Chr 28:1-29:30
through **PUNISHMENT**
    Psalmist   Ps 94:12-15
as **QUALITY OF LIFE**
    Isaac   Gen 26:12-31
SALVATION through
    David   Ps 28:8-9;
                   68:19-23
    God   Ps 103:1-5
    Psalmist   Ps 80:14-19
SECURITY in
    David   Ps 61:4-5;
                   144:1-2
    Eliphaz   Job 5:18-27
    Israelites   Ps 84:5-7;
                   Joel 3:16b-21
    Mankind   Ps 2:10-11
SIGNS of
    David   Ps 86:14-17
    Obededom   1 Chr 13:1-14;
                   2 Sam 6:1-23
SIN against
    Job   Job 24:1-12;
                   13-25
for **STEWARDSHIP**
    David   Ps 41:1-3

in **WORSHIP**
    David   Ps 26:8-12

SALVATION through
  by **DEITY**
    David   Ps 28:8-9;
                68:19-23
    God   Ps 103:1-5
    Psalmist   Ps 80:14-19

SCRIPTURES on
  in **RECONCILIATION**
    Jesus   Gal 3:10-14
  as **VIRTUE**
    David   Rom 3:31-4:25

in **SECURITY**
    Mephibosheth   2 Sam 9:1-13
  of **DEITY**
    David   Ps 61:4-5;
                144:1-2
    Eliphaz   Job 5:18-27
    Israelites   Ps 84:5-7
                Joel 3:16b-21
    Mankind   Ps 2:10-11
  PROPHECY of
    Isaiah   Is 54:1-17
    Israelites   Zech 9:13-17
  REVELATION on
    Israelites   Ezek 34:11-16;
                25-31
    Jeremiah   Jer 33:1-9

SIGNS of
  by **DEITY**
    David   Ps 86:14-17
    Obededom   1 Chr 13:1-14
                2 Sam 6:1-23
  REVELATION on
    God   Mt 3:13-17
                Mk 1:9-11
    Isaiah   Is 55:1-13
    Jesus   Lk 3:21-22

for **SIN** against
  by **DEITY**
    Job   Job 21:14-18;
                24:1-12;
                13-25

in **SIN**
  INSTRUCTION on
    Job   Job 21:7-13;
                28-34
  MEDITATION on
    Asaph   Ps 73:1-3;
                4-12
    Jeremiah   Jer 11:18-12:6
in **STEWARDSHIP**
    Moses   Ex 39:32-43
  INSTRUCTION on
    Jesus   Mt 19:27-30;
                Mk 10:28-31;
                Lk 18:28-30
    Paul   Rom 12:14-21
  of **MESSIANIC FIGURE**
    Jesus   Mt 14:13-21;
                Mk 6:30-44;
                8:1-10
                Lk 9:12-17
                Jn 6:1-15

REVELATION on
    Israelites   Ezek 44:15-31;
                Mal 3:6-12

as **VIRTUE**
  of **DEITY**
    Hosea   Hos 14:9
    People   Rom 3:21-30
for **VIRTUE**
  from **DEITY**
    Believers   Ps 55:22
    God   Ps 73:1-3;
                112:2-4;
                Prov 3:1-35;
                14:1-35
    Israelites   Ps 84:10-12
    Mankind   Ps 5:11-12
  INSTRUCTION on
    David   Ps 15:5c
    Peter   1 Pet 3:13-17
    Sirach   *Sir 14:1-2;
                26:1-4
    Wife   Prov 31:10-31
  PROPHECY of
    Isaiah   Is 3:8-12
  SCRIPTURES on
    David   Rom 3:31-4:25

BROTHERHOOD

ACCEPTANCE in
  of **FOLLOWER**
    Paul   Philm 1:15-20
  INSTRUCTION on
    Jesus   Mt 18:5-6;
                Mk 9:42-48;
                Lk 17:1-6
    Moses   Deut 23:1-8
    Paul   Rom 14:1-23;
                16:1-23;
                1 Cor 16:5-12;
                13-24;
                2 Cor 7:2-4;
                Phil 2:19-30;
                4:21-23;
                1 Tim 5:1-2

ALIENATION from
    Israelites   Zech 11:4-14
  INSTRUCTION on
    Jesus   Mt 18:15-17
    Paul   1 Cor 5:9-13
BLESSING in
  by **FOLLOWER**
    Believers   1 Cor 14:1-12
COMPASSION in
    Israelites   Judg 21:1-7;
                13-15
  REVELATION on
    Israelites   Is 49:1-26
COVENANT of
  REJECTION of
    Tyre   Amos 1:9-10
DIGNITY in
  INSTRUCTION on
    Paul   2 Cor 3:1-3

VICTORY in
   PROPHECY of
      Jesus   Mt 16:13-20

WEALTH of
   Nehemiah   Neh 5:14-19

through **WILL**
   of **DEITY**
      Jesus   Mt 12:46-50;
                  Mk 3:31-35;
                  Lk 8:19-21

WISDOM given to
   INSTRUCTION on
      Holy Spirit   Neh 9:19-21

revealed through **WITNESS**
   to **DEITY**
      Holy Spirit   Rom 8:14-25
   in **MISSION**
      Holy Spirit   2 Cor 3:1-3

CAPTIVITY

through **AUTHORITY**
   Solomon   1 Kgs 9:15-23
   of **DEITY**
      Adversaries   Ps 78:56-66

COMMUNITY in
   Amorites   Judg 1:22-36
   Canaanites   Josh 16:9-10;
                  17:7-13;
                  Judg 1:22-36
   Psalmist   Ps 137:1-3
   INSTRUCTION on
      Baruch   *Bar 1:1-4
by **COMPULSION**
   Chaldeans   Hab 1:5-11
   Ishmael   Jer 41:10
   Israel   Ex 2:23b-25
   Israelites   Ex 1:8-14
   Nebuchadnezzar   Jer 52:28-30
   REVELATION on
      Ezekiel   Ezek 3:22-27

CONFRONTATION with
   Apostles   Acts 5:17-42
   Damascenes   2 Kgs 16:5-9
   Israelites   2 Kgs 15:27-31;
                  17:1-6;
                  18:9-12;
                  *1 Esd 1:46-58
   Jehoahaz   2 Kgs 23:31-35
   Jehoiachin   2 Chr 36:1-23;
                  *1 Esd 1:43-45
   Jehoiakim   2 Kgs 24:8-17;
                  2 Chr 36:1-23;
                  *1 Esd 1:37-42
   Jeremiah   Jer 37:11-15;
                  16-21
   John   Acts 4:1-22
   Jonathan   *1 Mc 12:39-53
   Joseph   Gen 37:12-28;
                  42:7-17
   Judah   Dan 1:1-7
   Judahites   2 Kgs 24:8-17;
                  25:8-17;

CONFRONTATION with (cont'd)
   Judahites   18-22;
                  2 Chr 36:1-23;
                  Jer 39:1-14;
                  52:4-27
   Lot   Gen 14:1-16
   Paul   Acts 16:16-24
   Peter   Acts 4:1-22
   Samson   Judg 15:9-20
   Silas   Acts 16:16-24
   Zedekiah   2 Kgs 24:18-25:7;
                  Jer 52:4-27
   through **FALSE BELIEF**
      Herod   Lk 3:18-20
      People   Is 46:1-13
   INSTRUCTION on
      John The Baptist   Lk 3:18-20
   PROPHECY of
      Babylonians   Jer 50:1-46
      Isaiah   2 Kgs 20:12-21;
                  Is 39:1-8
      Jeremiah   Jer 32:26-44
      Jerusalemites   Zech 14:1-21
      Jesus   Lk 9:43b-45
      Judahites   Jer 37:16-21
      Smyrna   Rev 2:8-11
      Zedekiah   Jer 34:1-7
   REVELATION on
      Babylonians   Jer 27:1-11
      Satan   Rev 20:1-3

DESIRE for
   of **MESSIANIC FIGURE**
      People   Jn 7:25-31

ELECTION to
   by **DEITY**
      Kings   2 Kgs 3:1-27

FALSE BELIEF concerning
   promises **FREEDOM**
      Hananiah   Jer 28:1-17
      Israelites   Ex 32:1-6;
                  7-14
   SIGNS of
      Prophets   Rev 19:17-21
   caused by in**FIDELITY**
      Judahites   1 Chr 9:1-16
   INSTRUCTION on
      Paul   Gal 5:1
   PROPHECY of
      Jesus   Mt 26:36-46;
                  Mk 14:32-42
      Judahites   Jer 38:14-28

of **FOLLOWER**s
   as **PUNISHMENT**
      Peter   Acts 12:1-25

FREEDOM from
   Ezra   Ezra 7:6-10
   Israelites   Ezra 2:1-2a
   Jeremiah   Jer 40:1-6
   Johanan   Jer 41:11-18
   Pharaoh   Ex 12:29-32
   Samson   Judg 15:9-20
   Timothy   *2 Mc 12:24-25
   through **COVENANT**
      Zechariah   Zech 9:1-12
      Zedekiah   Jer 34:8-12

REVELATION on (cont'd)
   Moses   Ex 6:2-9
TRADITION revealing
   Israelites   Deut 6:20-25

SECURITY from
  by **DEITY**
    Isaiah   Is 62:1-12
  TRADITION revealing
    Egyptians   Gen 47:13-26

SELF-REALIZATION of
  caused by **SIN**
    Paul   Rom 7:14-25

SIGNS of
  Philistines   1 Sam 4:1b-22
  FALSE BELIEF concerning
    Prophets   Rev 19:17-21
  PROPHECY of
    Egyptians   Is 20:1-6
  REVELATION on
    Ezekiel   Ezek 12:1-16;
                  17:1-10
    Israelites   Ezek 17:11-21;
                  19:1-4;
                  5-9
    Jeremiah   Jer 24:1-10
    John   Rev 13:5-10
    Zechariah   Zech 5:5-11

caused by **SIN**
    Edomites   Obad 1:10-14
    Israelites   Ps 107:10-16;
                  Amos 2:6-8;
                  8:4-7
    Philistines   Amos 1:6-8
    Tyre   Amos 1:9-10
  SELF-REALIZATION of
    Paul   Rom 7:14-25

STEWARDSHIP through
  in **MISSION**
    Paul   Philm 1:1-3

TRADITION revealing
  KNOWLEDGE of
    Jeremiah   *Jer 6:1
  as **PUNISHMENT**
    Israelites   *Sir 48:15-16;
                  49:4-7
  in **RITE**
    Israelites   Ex 13:11-16

CHAOS

AUTHORITY over
  in the **ENVIRONMENT**
    God   Gen 1:1-2

in the **COMMUNITY**
  Ephesians   Acts 19:23-41
  PROPHECY of
    Isaiah   Is 3:1-7

CONFRONTATION with
  in the **ENVIRONMENT**
    Israelites   Judg 7:16-22

REVELATION on
  John   Rev 11:15-19
CREATION out of
  in the **ENVIRONMENT**
    God   Gen 1:1-2
  REVELATION on
    Jeremiah   Jer 4:23-26
    John   Rev 8:1-6

in the **ENVIRONMENT**
  AUTHORITY over
    God   Gen 1:1-2
    Jews   Acts 21:27-22:29
  CONFRONTATION with
    Israelites   Judg 7:16-22
  CREATION out of
    God   Gen 1:1-2
  SIGNS of
    Jesus   Mt 27:45-56;
                Lk 23:44-45

through **FALSE BELIEF**
  PUNISHMENT for
    Israelites   Jer 18:13-17

through **FIDELITY**
  to the **MISSION**
    Jesus   Mt 10:26-39;
                Lk 12:51-53

in the **NEW AGE**
  PROPHECY of
    Jesus   Mt 24:29-31;
                Mk 13:24-27

PROMISE of
  PROPHECY of
    Jesus   Mk 13:1-2

PROPHECY of
  in the **COMMUNITY**
    Isaiah   Is 3:1-7
  in the **NEW AGE**
    Jesus   Mt 24:29-31;
                Mk 13:24-27
  as **PUNISHMENT**
    Isaiah   Is 13:1-22;
                22:1-14;
                24:1-12;
                34:1-17
    Jeremiah   Jer 13:12-14;
                  23:1-8
    Jesus   Lk 19:41-44;
                23:27-32
  SIGNS of
    Isaiah   Is 24:18c-23
    Jesus   Mt 24:4-8;
                15-22;
                Mk 13:3-8;
                14-23;
                Lk 17:22-37;
                21:7-19;
                25-28

PROVIDENCE over
  by **DEITY**
    Philistines   1 Sam 7:2-17

PUNISHMENT for
  caused by **FALSE BELIEF**
    Israelites   Jer 18:13-17

SACREDNESS of (cont'd)
  INSTRUCTION on
    Paul   2 Cor 6:14-7:1
  REVELATION on
    Moses   Num 6:1-21
  concerning WORSHIP
    Israelites   Neh 10:39b

SACRIFICE in
  to DEITY
    Jephthah   Judg 11:29-33
    Jonah   Jon 1:1-17
  INSTRUCTION on
    Jesus   Mt 13:44-46
    Paul   Rom 13:11-14;
                        1 Cor 9:24-27
  to MISSION
    Paul   1 Cor 9:15-23
  PROPHECY of
    Jesus   Mt 16:21-28;
                        Mk 8:34-9:1;
                        Lk 9:23-27
  through WORSHIP
    Hannah   1 Sam 1:1-28
    Israelites   Neh 10:32-33;
                        35-36

SELF-REALIZATION of
  ANXIETY from
    Paul   Rom 9:1-5
  through FAITH
    Paul   Gal 2:20-21
  GUILT overcome through
    Nehemiah   Neh 1:5-11a

in SERVICE
  to DEITY
    Isaiah   Is 19:18-25
    Judah   Gen 44:1-34
  of FOLLOWER
    Titus   2 Cor 8:16-24
  INSTRUCTION on
    Joshua   Josh 24:14-15
  to MISSION
    Paul   1 Cor 9:15-23;
                      Gal 6:11-18;
                      Col 2:1-5
  PROPHECY of
    Zedekiah   Jer 27:12-15
  REVELATION on
    Moses   Num 8:23-26
    People   Jer 27:1-11

to SPIRIT
  INSTRUCTION on
    Paul   Rom 8:5-13

through SUFFERING
  of FOLLOWER
    Paul   2 Cor 1:3-7

to TRADITION
  in MARRIAGE
    Jehoshaphat   2 Chr 17:1-20:37

to VIOLENCE
    Mattathias   *1 Mc 2:39-48
to providing WEALTH
  for WORSHIP
    Israelites   Neh 10:37a;
                      37b-39a

through WITNESS
  of FOLLOWER
    John   Acts 4:1-22
    Peter   Acts 4:1-22
  INSTRUCTION on
    Paul   2 Cor 5:11-13
  to MISSION
    Paul   Acts 19:21-22

WITNESS to
  to DEITY
    Israelites   Josh 24:16-24

COMMUNITY

ALIENATION from
    Gentiles   Eph 2:11-22
    Israelites   1 Kgs 12:1-20
                      *1 Mc 1:36-40
    Rehoboam   2 Chr 10:1-12:16
  PROPHECY of
    Ahijah   1 Kgs 11:26-40
  SELF-REALIZATION of
    Job   Job 19:13-19

ANGER against
  by DEITY
    Edomites   Mal 1:2-5
    Judahites   Jer 7:29-8:3

BLESSING of
    Israelites   Neh 11:1-2
    Joshua   Josh 22:1-8
    Solomon   1 Kgs 8:14-21;
                      2 Chr 5:1-7:10
  INSTRUCTION on
    Moses   Deut 33:1-29
  through WORSHIP
    Aaron   Lev 9:1-24
    Solomon   1 Kgs 8:54-61

CAPTIVITY of
    Amorites   Judg 1:22-36
    Canaanites   Josh 16:9-10;
                      17:7-13;
                      Judg 1:22-36
    Psalmist   Ps 137:1-3
  INSTRUCTION on
    Baruch   *Bar 1:1-4

CHAOS in
    Ephesians   Acts 19:23-41
  PROPHECY of
    Isaiah   Is 3:1-7
COMPASSION of
    Ezra   *2 Esd 12:40-51
CONDEMNATION of
    Sirach   *Sir 50:25-26
  PROPHECY of
    Joshua   Josh 6:22-27
                      7:6-26

COVENANT with
  for FAMILY
    Aaron   *Sir 45:25-26
    David   *Sir 45:25-26
  FULFILLMENT of
    Israelites   Josh 22:1-8
  for PEACE

for **PEACE** (cont'd)	
Solomon	1 Kgs 5:1-18
DESTRUCTION of	
REVELATION on	
Psalmist	Ps 2:7-9
DISOBEDIENCE of	
Jeremiah	Jer 43:4-7
DOUBT of	
concerning **MISSION**	
Jesus	Mt 13:53-58;
	Mk 6:1-6;
	Lk 4:16-30
REVELATION on	
Judahites	Jer 9:2-9
as **ENEMY**	
of **DEITY**	
Mankind	Ps 2:1-3
EVIL in	
Israelites	Is 1:4-9
against **DEITY**	
Jason	*2 Mc 4:7-17
Judahites	Jer 3:6-11
Mankind	Ps 2:1-3
FAMILY in	
Asherites	Josh 19:24-31
Benjaminites	Josh 18:11-28
Caleb	Josh 14:6-15
Danites	Josh 19:40-48
Ephraimites	Josh 16:6-8;
	9-10
Gadites	Josh 13:24-28
Israelites	Josh 13:8-14;
	14:1-5;
	18:1-10;
	Jer 40:11-12
Issachar	Josh 19:17-23
Josephites	Josh 16:1-5;
	17:14-18
Joshua	Josh 19:49-51
Judahites	Josh 15:1-12;
	20-63
Levites	Josh 13:29-33;
	21:1-7;
	8-45
Manassites	Josh 13:29-33;
	17:1-6:7-13
Naphtalites	Josh 19:32-39
Reubenites	Josh 13:15-23
Simeonites	Josh 19:1-9
Zebulunites	Josh 19:10-16
with **COVENANT**	
Aaron	*Sir 45:25-26
David	*Sir 45:25-26
REVELATION on	
Joshua	Josh 13:1-7
TRADITION of	
Israelites	Ps 114:1-2
	*1 Esd 5:44-46
recognizes **FAMILY**	
Benjaminites	Neh 11:31-36
Judahites	Neh 11:25-30
FEAR in	

FEAR in (cont'd)	
Israelites	Deut 2:1-25;
	Josh 2:8-14
of **DEITY**	
God	Ps 2:4-6
GOOD in	
from **DEITY**	
David	Ps 51:18-19
GRIEF in	
from **DEITY**	
Ezra	*2 Esd 5:31-42
HATE in	
through **FALSE BELIEF**	
God	*Wis 12:3-11
JEALOUSY in	
Moses	Ps 106:13-18
JOY of	
INSTRUCTION on	
Solomon	1 Kgs 1:28-40
JUSTICE to	
from **DEITY**	
David	Ps 9:17-20
Macron	*2 Mc 10:10-13
REVELATION on	
God	Ps 9:15-16
LEADERSHIP in	
Deborah	Judg 5:6-9
Moses	Ex 15:22-27
PROPHECY of	
Isaiah	Is 3:1-7
REVELATION on	
Israelites	Jer 30:18-22;
	Ezek 37:15-28
Priests	Ezek 44:15-31
receives **LOVE**	
of **DEITY**	
God	Ps 87:1-3
MARRIAGE in	
INSTRUCTION on	
Joshua	Josh 23:1-16
OBEDIENCE to	
INSTRUCTION on	
Ezra	*1 Esd 9:1-15
Joshua	Josh 1:12-18
Moses	Lev 24:10-23
ONENESS in	
Canaanites	Judg 1:22-36
Israelites	Ezra 3:1-3a;
	Neh 7:33b-8:2
Jebusites	Josh 15:20-63;
	Judg 1:1-21
Psalmist	Ps 133:1-3
of **FOLLOWER**s	
Believers	Acts 4:32-5:10
INSTRUCTION on	
Paul	Rom 15:1-13
REVELATION on	
Israelites	Ezek 37:15-28
OPPRESSION of	
Israelites	Neh 1:1-4;

OPPRESSION of (cont'd)
Israelites	5:1-5
Rehoboam	1 Kgs 12:1-20; 2 Chr 10:1-12:16

ORDER in
Gatekeepers	Ezra 2:42
Israelites	Num 33:1-4; Ezra 2:2b-20; 21-35; 64:65-67; Neh 7:4-33a; 11:3-6
Levites	Ezra 2:40; Neh 12:1-7
Moses	Num 3:14-39; 4:34-49; 34:1-15; 16-29; 35:1-8
Priests	Ezra 2:36-39; 59-63
Servants	Ezra 2:43-54; 55-58
Singers	Ezra 2:41
Isaac	Gen 26:32-33
Israelites	Num 1:20-46; 26:5-51; 32:34-38; 39-42; Deut 3:12-22; Neh 7:33b-8:2

INSTRUCTION on
Jesus	Mt 10:24-25

REVELATION on
Moses	Num 1:1-19; 2:1-34; 3:40-51; 26:1-4; 52-56; 27:1-11; 36:1-13

PEACE in
Psalmist	Ps 133:1-3
Israelites	Josh 11:16-23

INSTRUCTION on
Paul	Rom 12:14-21; 15:1-13

PROPHECY of
Isaiah	Is 11:10-16

POLITICS in
Levites	Neh 11:19-24

INSTRUCTION on
Moses	Deut 16:18-20

PRAISE of
Psalmist	Ps 87:1-3

INSTRUCTION on
David	Ps 34:1-3

PROPHECY of
Isaiah	Is 60:1-22

PROPHECY concerning
ALIENATION from
Ahijah	1 Kgs 11:26-40

CHAOS in
Isaiah	Is 3:1-7

CONDEMNATION of
Joshua	Josh 6:22-27;

CONDEMNATION of (cont'd)
Joshua	7:6-26

FULFILLMENT of
Jeremiah	*1 Esd 1:46-58; 2:1-7
Jesus	Mt 2:19-23

LEADERSHIP in
Isaiah	Is 3:1-7

PEACE in
Isaiah	Is 11:10-16

PRAISE of
Isaiah	Is 60:1-22

REJECTION by
Moses	Num 16:3-11

of DEITY
Israelites	2 Kgs 17:7-23
Mankind	Ps 2:1-3
Psalmist	Ps 44:9-16
Jesus	Mt 13:53-58; Mk 6:1-6; Lk 4:16-30

of MISSION
Jesus	Lk 13:34-35

SELF-REALIZATION on
Job	Job 19:13-19

REJECTION of
by FOLLOWERs
Jesus	Mt 19:27-30; Mk 10:28-31; Lk 18:28-30

REVELATION on
DOUBT concerning
Judahites	Jer 9:2-9

WITNESS of
Ezekiel	Ezek 40:1-5

REVENGE on
INSTRUCTION on
Mordecai	Esth 8:9-14

REWARDs of
INSTRUCTION on
Darius	*1 Esd 4:42-57

SACREDNESS of
INSTRUCTION on
Attharates	*1 Esd 9:49-55

in WORSHIP
Levites	Ezra 8:15-20

SACRIFICE to
by FOLLOWERs
Believers	Acts 4:32-5:10

SERVICE to
Simon	Lk 23:26

INSTRUCTION on
Gedaliah	Jer 40:7-10

SHARING in
by FOLLOWERs
Believers	Acts 4:32-5:10

WEALTH in
Abraham	Gen 13:2-9
Jacob	Gen 47:27-48:22
Levites	Num 35:1-8

WEALTH in (cont'd)	
Lot	Gen 13:2-9
Moses	Num 34:16-29
INSTRUCTION on	
Moses	Deut 21:15-17
WILL of	
REVELATION on	
Ezra	*2 Esd 9:38-10:59
WITNESS to	
REVELATION on	
Ezekiel	Ezek 40:1-5
WORSHIP in	
BLESSING of	
Aaron	Lev 9:1-24
Solomon	1 Kgs 8:54-61
SACREDNESS of	
Levites	Ezra 8:15-20

COMPASSION

of **AUTHORITY**	
Jesus	Mt 8:5-13; Lk 7:1-10
Nehemiah	Neh 5:14-19
BEHAVIOR revealing	
Boaz	Ruth 2:1-23
David	2 Sam 9:1-13
INSTRUCTION on	
God	*2 Esd 2:15-32
Sirach	*Sir 4:1-10
MEDITATION on	
Jesus	Lk 13:34-35
by **MESSIANIC FIGURE**	
Crowd	Mk 8:1-10
Jesus	Mk 1:40-45; 5:21-24; Lk 7:11-17; 8:40-56; Jn 11:1-57
BELIEF concerning	
MEDITATION on	
Jeremiah	Lam 3:1-66
of **BROTHERHOOD**	
Israelites	Judg 21:1-7; 13-15
REVELATION on	
Israelites	Is 49:1-26
COMMITMENT with	
of **FOLLOWERs**	
Paul	2 Cor 1:3-7
of **COMMUNITY**	
Ezra	*2 Esd 12:40-51
CONFRONTATION with	
Ahab	1 Kgs 20:1-43
Joseph	Gen 43:16-34
of **MESSIANIC FIGURE**	
Crowd	Mk 6:30-44
Jesus	Mt 14:13-21; 15:32-39

of **DEITY**	
David	2 Sam 12:1-31
Israelites	Judg 2:11-19
for **CREATION**	
God	Ps 145:8-9
DESIRE for	
Asaph	Ps 77:1-10
God	Mic 6:6-8
Job	Job 14:13-17
FIDELITY of	
Israelites	Neh 9:26-31; Ps 106:40-46
Psalmist	Ps 119:73-80
in **JUDGMENT**	
Solomon	*Wis 12:3-11
as **MOTIVATION**	
God	Gen 2:18-20
PRAYER for	
Asaph	Ps 83:1
Daniel	Dan 2:14-19
David	Ps 4:1; 6:1-5; 28:1-5; 30:6-10; 38:1-2
Ethan	Ps 89:38-51
Ezekiel	Ezek 4:12-15
Isaiah	Is 63:7-64:12
Israelites	Jer 14:19-22
Jeremiah	Jer 11:18-12:6; 15:10-21
Job	Job 10:8-12
Joel	Joel 1:2-20
Judahites	Lam 5:1-22
Maccabeus	*2 Mc 8:1-7; 10:1-9
Moses	Ps 90:13-17
Psalmist	Ps 102:12-22; 106:1-5; 123:3-4
Sirach	*Sir 36:1-10; 11-17
PROVIDENCE by	
God	Gen 3:20-24; Ps 103:6-13
Jonah	Jon 4:1-11
Solomon	*Wis 18:20-25
as **QUALITY OF LIFE**	
God	Ex 22:21-31
RECONCILIATION by	
Followers	Ps 80:4-7
God	Mic 7:7-20
Israelites	Deut 30:1-10
RESPECT for	
David	Ps 69:13-21
SALVATION through	
Psalmist	Ps 85:4-7
SIGN of	
Cain	Gen 4:1-16
SIN forgiven through	
Sirach	*Sir 18:1-14
through **STEWARDSHIP**	
Solomon	Ps 72:8-14
as **VIRTUE**	
Abraham	Gen 18:23-33
DESIRE for	
Israel	Ex 5:15-21
Jeremiah	Jer 37:16-21
Job	Job 19:20-24

of **DEITY**
Asaph	Ps 77:1-10
God	Mic 6:6-8
Job	Job 14:13-17

in **WORSHIP**
Ezra	Neh 9:32-37

ELECTION through
    SCRIPTURES on
God	Rom 9:14-29
Israelites	Judg 21:13-15

ETERNAL
    PROPHECY of
Isaiah	Is 54:1-17

through **FIDELITY**
    to **COVENANT**
Azariah	*Azar 1:11-22

for **FOLLOWERs**
    KNOWLEDGE of
Jesus	Heb 4:14-16

    PROVIDENCE through
God	Ps 135:13-14

    SIN forgiven through
Paul	2 Cor 2:5-11

FREEDOM through
Evilmerodach	2 Kgs 25:27-30

INSTRUCTION on
    in **JUDGMENT**
God	*Wis 12:19-22

    in **LAW**
Jesus	Mt 12:9-14
Moses	Deut 23:15-25:19

    as **QUALITY OF LIFE**
Jesus	Mt 18:23-35
Paul	Col 3:5-17

    in **STEWARDSHIP**
Jesus	Lk 15:11-32

    as **VIRTUE**
God	Ps 82:2-7;
	*Wis 12:19-22
Sirach	*Sir 12:1-7

in **JUDGMENT**
    of **DEITY**
Solomon	*Wis 12:3-11

    INSTRUCTION on
God	*Wis 12:19-22

KNOWLEDGE of
    of **FOLLOWERs**
Jesus	Heb 4:14-16

in **LAW**
    INSTRUCTION on
Jesus	Mt 12:9-14
Moses	Deut 23:15-25:19

MEDITATION on
Jesus	Lk 13:34-35
Israelites	Jer 14:7-9
Jeremiah	Lam 3:1-66

of **MESSIANIC FIGURE**
Crowd	Mk 8:1-10
Jesus	Mk 1:40-45;
	5:21-24;

of **MESSIANIC FIGURE** (cont'd)
Jesus	Lk 7:11-17;
	8:40-56;
	Jn 11:1-57

    CONFRONTATION with
Crowd	Mk 6:30-44
Jesus	Mt 14:13-21;
	15:32-39

    as **MOTIVATION**
Jesus	Mt 20:29-34

    PRAYER for
Jesus	Heb 5:1-10

    RESPECT for
David	1 Sam 23:14-24:22;
	26:1-25

as **MOTIVATION**
    of **DEITY**
God	Gen 2:18-20
Reuben	Gen 37:12-28

    of **MESSIANIC FIGURE**
Jesus	Mt 20:29-34

PRAYER for
    of **DEITY**
Asaph	Ps 83:1
Daniel	Dan 2:14-19
David	Ps 4:1;
	6:1-5;
	28:1-5;
	30:6-10;
	38:1-2
Ethan	Ps 89:38-51
Ezekiel	Ezek 4:12-15
Isaiah	Is 63:7-64:12
Israelites	Jer 14:19-22
Jeremiah	Jer 11:18-12:6;
	15:10-21
Job	Job 10:8-12
Joel	Joel 1:2-20
Judahites	Lam 5:1-22
Maccabeus	*2 Mc 8:1-7;
	10:1-9
Moses	Ps 90:13-17
Psalmist	Ps 102:12-22;
	106:1-5;
	123:3-4
Sirach	*Sir 36:1-10;
	11-17

    MEDITATION on
Israelites	Jer 14:7-9
Jeremiah	Lam 3:1-66

    of **MESSIANIC FIGURE**
Jesus	Heb 5:1-10

    SELF-REALIZATION of
Israelites	Jer 14:7-9
Jesus	Mt 26:36-46;
	Mk 14:32-42

    in **WORSHIP**
Israelites	*Jdt 6:14-20
Manasseh	*Mana 1:6-7
Moses	Deut 3:23-29;
	9:25-29

PROPHECY of
    ETERNAL
Isaiah	Is 54:1-17

    PROVIDENCE through
Isaiah	Is 14:1-23
Jerusalemites	Zech 12:1-13:6

RECONCILIATION through
  Israelites   Hos 11:8-9
  Judahites   Jer 12:14-17
SALVATION through
  Isaiah   Is 40:1-11

PROVIDENCE by
  of DEITY
    God   Gen 3:20-24;
                     Ps 103:6-13
    Jonah   Jon 4:1-11
    Solomon   *Wis 18:20-25
  for FOLLOWER
    God   Ps 135:13-14
  PROPHECY of
    Isaiah   Is 14:1-23
    Jerusalemites   Zech 12:1-13:6

as QUALITY OF LIFE
  of DEITY
    God   Ex 22:21-31
  INSTRUCTION on
    Jesus   Mt 18:23-35
    Paul   Col 3:5-17

RECONCILIATION through
  of DEITY
    Followers   Ps 80:4-7
    God   Mic 7:7-20
    Israelites   Deut 30:1-10
  PROPHECY of
    Israelites   Hos 11:8-9
    Judahites   Jer 12:14-17
  REVELATION on
    Israelites   Jer 30:18-22;
                     Zech 1:7-17

RESPECT for
  of DEITY
    David   Ps 69:13-21

through RESPECT
  for MESSIANIC FIGURE
    David   1 Sam 23:14-24:22;
                     26:1-25

REVELATION on
  of BROTHERHOOD
    Israelites   Is 49:1-26
  SIGNS of
    John   Rev 8:13
    Jonah   Jon 4:1-11

SALVATION through
  of DEITY
    Psalmist   Ps 85:4-7
    Moses   Ex 2:1-10
  PROPHECY of
    Isaiah   Is 40:1-11
  REVELATION on
    Israelites   Zech 10:3-12

SCRIPTURES on
  God   Rom 9:14-29

SECURITY in
  Cain   Gen 4:1-16
  David   1 Sam 22:1-23
  REVELATION on
    Isaiah   Is 51:1-16

SELF-REALIZATION of
  PRAYER for
    Israelites   Jer 14:7-9
    Jesus   Mt 26:36-46;
                     Mk 14:32-42

SIGN of
  of DEITY
    Cain   Gen 4:1-16
  REVELATION on
    John   Rev 8:13
    Jonah   Jon 4:1-11

SIN forgiven through
  of DEITY
    Sirach   *Sir 18:1-14
  for FOLLOWERs
    Paul   2 Cor 2:5-11
  INSTRUCTION on
    Paul   Gal 5:25-6:6;
                     2 Tim 2:20-26

through STEWARDSHIP
    Solomon   Ps 72:8-14
  INSTRUCTION on
    Jesus   Lk 15:11-32
  in MISSION
    Isaiah   Is 61:1-11

as VIRTUE
  of DEITY
    Abraham   Gen 18:23-33
  INSTRUCTION on
    God   Ps 82:2-7;
                     *Wis 12:19-22
    Sirach   *Sir 12:1-7

in WORSHIP
  DESIRE for
    Ezra   Neh 9:32-37
  PRAYER for
    Israelites   *Jdt 6:14-20
    Manasseh   *Mana 1:6-7
    Moses   Deut 3:23-29;
                     9:25-29

COMPULSION

ACCEPTANCE of
  INSTRUCTION on
    Servants   1 Pet 2:18-20
  REVELATION on
    Jeremiah   Jer 25:15-29
in ANGER
  of DEITY
    Babylonians   Rev 16:17-21
  of MISSION
    Ezekiel   Ezek 3:12-15

to ANXIETY
  Darius   Dan 6:10-15;
                   16-23

for BLESSING
  of DEITY
    Balaam   Num 23:13-26

in CAPTIVITY

SELF-REALIZATION of
  of **EVIL**
    Eliphaz   Job 15:12-16
  to **SACRIFICE**
    Jesus   Mt 26:36-46;
                     Mk 14:32-42;
                     Lk 22:39-46

  to **SERVICE**
    Solomon   2 Chr 8:1-18
  in **ENVIRONMENT**
    Solomon   1 Kgs 9:15-23
  by **FOLLOWER**
    Jesus   Jn 12:20-26
  of **MESSIANIC FIGURE**
    Simon   Mt 27:32;
                     Mk 15:21-32;
                     Lk 23:26

  in **SEX**
    Dinah   Gen 34:1-31
    Elders   *Susa 1:19-27

  in **SUFFERING**
    MEDITATION on
      Jeremiah   Lam 3:1-66

  in **TEMPERANCE**
    INSTRUCTION on
      Paul   Rom 14:1-23

  in **WISDOM**
    INSTRUCTION on
      Daniel   Dan 1:1-7

  to **WITNESS**
    PROPHECY of
      God   Amos 3:3-8

  in **WORSHIP**
    for **IDOLATRY**
      John   Rev 13:11-18

CONDEMNATION

by **AUTHORITY**
  of **MESSIANIC FIGURE**
    Jesus   Mt 21:18-22;
                     Mk 11:20-26

of **AUTHORITY**
  of **MESSIANIC FIGURE**
    Pharisees   Mt 12:22-32
  REVELATION on
    Job   Job 38:12-15;
                     40:6-14

of **BELIEF**
  in **DEITY**
    Job   Job 13:13-19
  INSTRUCTION on
    Elihu   Job 33:8-12
    Jesus   Jn 3:1-21
    Paul   1 Tim 5:3-16
  in **MESSIANIC FIGURE**
    Jews   Jn 8:21-59

of **COMMUNITY**
  Sirach   *Sir 50:25-26

PROPHECY of
  Joshua   Josh 6:22-27;
                     7:6-26

CONFRONTATION with
    David   2 Sam 15:13-16:14
    Nehemiah   Neh 2:19-20
  INSTRUCTION on
    John the Baptist   Lk 3:18-20
  by **MESSIANIC FIGURE**
    Jesus   Lk 13:10-17;
                     Jn 2:12-22
    Jews   Jn 5:1-18
    Pharisees   Mt 12:1-8;
                     Mk 2:23-28;
                     Lk 6:1-5
    Soldiers   Lk 23:33-38
  PROPHECY of
    Priests   Mk 10:32-34
    Shemaiah   1 Kgs 12:21-24;
                     2 Chr 10:1-12:16

of **CREATION**
  MEDITATION on
    Job   Job 3:1-10
  REVELATION on
    God   Gen 3:14-19

by **DEITY**
  of in**FIDELITY**
    Ephraimites   Hos 7:13-16
    Isaiah   Is 17:9-11

DESIRE for
    Officials   Dan 6:4-9
  by **DEITY**
    Balak   Num 22:5-14;
                     15-21;
                     23:13-26;
                     23:27-24:13
    Habakkuk   Hab 1:12-17
    Israel   Ex 5:15-21
  through **FALSE BELIEF**
    Pharisees   Lk 11:53-54
  of **MESSIANIC FIGURE**
    Pharisees   Mt 12:9-14;
                     22:15-22;
                     Mk 3:1-6;
                     12:13-17;
                     Lk 6:6-11
    Priests   Mt 27:1-2;
                     Lk 20:19-26

ETERNAL
  through **FALSE BELIEF**
    Holy Spirit   Mt 12:22-32;
                     Mk 3:20-30
    John   Jude 1:5-7
  INSTRUCTION on
    Jesus   Mt 25:31-46;
                     Lk 16:19-31
  REVELATION on
    Mankind   Is 66:17-24

through **FALSE BELIEF**
    Paul   2 Tim 3:1-9
    Pharisees   Mt 23:23-24

of in**FIDELITY**
  by **DEITY**
    Ephraimites   Hos 7:13-16

by **DEITY** (cont'd)
  Isaiah   Is 17:9-11
caused by **FALSE BELIEF**
  Author   Heb 6:1-8
  God   Rev 14:9-12
of **FOLLOWERs**
  Author   Heb 6:1-8;
                        10:19-31;
                        12:12-29
  Peter   2 Pet 2:17-22
INSTRUCTION on
  Jesus   Mt 7:21-23;
                        26:17-30;
                        Mk 14:17-21;
                        Lk 13:22-30
PROPHECY of
  Isaiah   Is 8:19-22
  Jeremiah   Jer 17:5-8
REVELATION on
  Israelites   Jer 3:1-5
  Jeremiah   Jer 26:1-6

of **FOLLOWERs**
  through **in**FIDELITY
    Author   Heb 6:1-8;
                        10:19-31;
                        12:12-29
    Peter   2 Pet 2:17-22
  as **JUDGMENT**
    Jews   Acts 24:1-27;
                        25:1-12
    Mankind   Jas 4:11-12
  in **NEW AGE**
    Pharisees   Mt 23:13

of **dis**HONESTY
  by **DEITY**
    God   Prov 12:1-28
    Job   Job 13:1-12
  through **FALSE BELIEF**
    Paul   Acts 13:4-12
    Rulers   Acts 6:8-8:3
  MEDITATION on
    Jeremiah   Jer 4:9-10
  REVELATION on
    Prophetesses   Ezek 13:17-23
    Prophets   Jer 23:23-32;
                        Ezek 13:1-16

INSTRUCTION on
  Bildad   Job 8:1-7
  Jesus   Mt 5:21-26;
                        12:33-37;
                        23:27-28
  Job   Job 19:1-6
  Paul   Gal 2:11-14
  Preacher   Eccl 9:17-10:20
  Zophar   Job 11:1-6
  of **BELIEF**
    Elihu   Job 33:8-12
    Jesus   Jn 3:1-21
    Paul   1 Tim 5:3-16
  for **ETERNITY**
    Jesus   Mt 25:31-46;
                        Lk 16:19-31
  of **in**FIDELITY
    Jesus   Mt 7:21-23;
                        26:17-30;
                        Mk 14:17-21;
                        Lk 13:22-30
  as **JUDGMENT**

as **JUDGMENT** (cont'd)
  Author   Heb 5:11-14
  God   Is 1:24-26
  Jesus   Mt 12:33-37;
                        18:15-17;
                        23:13;
                        15;
                        Lk 11:37-44;
                        16:14-15
  Job   Job 12:1-6;
                        21:28-34
  Jotham   Judg 9:16-21
  Paul   Rom 2:1-24;
                        5:12-21;
                        14:1-23;
                        1 Cor 5:1-5
  Peter   Acts 8:14-25
KNOWLEDGE of
  Eliphaz   Job 15:7-11
  God   *Wis 12:23-27
of **LAW**
  Moses   Deut 11:26-32;
                        27:11-26
  Paul   Rom 3:31-4:25;
                        Gal 3:10-14
in **NEW AGE**
  Paul   Gal 5:16-21
as **PUNISHMENT**
  David   1 Kgs 2:5-12
as **QUALITY OF LIFE**
  Bildad   Job 18:5-7;
                        8-11
  Jesus   Lk 6:24-26
  Laodicea   Rev 3:14-22
of **RESURRECTION**
  Jesus   Jn 5:19-47
of **RITE**
  Moses   Deut 27:11-26
  Paul   1 Cor 11:27-34
SIGNS of
  Jesus   Mk 8:11-13
of **SIN**
  Author   Heb 6:1-8;
                        10:19-31
  God   Is 1:10-17
  Isaiah   Is 56:9-57:13
  James   Jas 4:1-10
  Jesus   Mt 12:43-45;
                        18:5-6;
                        7-9;
                        21:33-43;
                        22:1-14;
                        Mk 9:42-48;
                        12:1-12;
                        37b-40;
                        Lk 11:24-26;
                        13:1-5;
                        14:15-24;
                        17:1-6;
                        19:11-27;
                        20:9-18;
                        45-47
  John   1 Jn 5:13-21;
                        Jude 1:5-7
  Paul   Rom 8:1-4;
                        1 Cor 6:9-11;
                        2 Cor 13:1-4;
                        Eph 5:3-14;
                        Col 3:5-17;
                        1 Tim 5:17-25
  Sirach   *Sir 41:5-13

of **SIN** (cont'd)

Solomon	Prov 8:1-21; 19:1-29; 20:1-30

of **STEWARDSHIP**

Jesus	Mt 25:14-30

of **TRUTH**

Eliphaz	Job 15:1-6
Jesus	Mt 23:29-33
Paul	Gal 1:6-10; 2:11-14

as **JUDGMENT**

Daniel	Dan 5:18-25
Israelites	Lev 26:1-46
Moabites	Num 21:21-32
Women	Amos 4:1-3

by **DEITY**

Chaldeans	Hab 1:5-11
Egyptians	Ezek 29:9b-16
Ephraimites	Hos 9:10-17; 13:12-14
God	Ps 50:16-21
Israelites	Is 9:8-10:4; Hos 6:7-9; 10:9-15; Amos 6:8-11
Man	Ex 21:33-22:17
Satan	Zech 3:1-10

for **FALSE BELIEF**

Apostles	Mt 10:9-15
Disciples	Mk 6:7-13; Lk 9:1-6
Israelites	Ezek 23:36-49
James	Jas 5:1-6
Jews	Jn 18:28-19:16
Jezebel	Rev 2:18-29
People	Lk 23:1-5
Prophets	2 Pet 2:1-3
Sinners	Jude 1:11-13

of **FOLLOWERs**

Jews	Acts 24:1-27; 25:1-12
Mankind	Jas 4:11-12

INSTRUCTION on

Author	Heb 5:11-14
God	Is 1:24-26
Jesus	Mt 12:33-37; 18:15-17; 23:13; 15; Lk 11:37-44; 16:14-15
Job	Job 12:1-6; 21:28-34
Jotham	Judg 9:16-21
Paul	Rom 2:1-24; 5:12-21; 14:1-23; 1 Cor 5:1-5
Peter	Acts 8:14-25

against **MESSIANIC FIGURE**

Caiaphas	Mt 26:57-68; Mk 14:53-65
People	Lk 23:1-5
Priests	Lk 22:66-71
Satan	Jn 16:5-11

PROPHECY of

Amos	Amos 3:13-15
Ephraimites	Hos 7:8-12
Ezekiel	Ezek 16:44-52

PROPHECY of (cont'd)

Habakkuk	Hab 2:9-11; 12-14; 15-16; 17; 18-20
Isaiah	Is 30:1-7; 27-33; 31:1-3; 33:1-6; 34:1-17
Israelites	Ezek 16:53-63; Hos 5:1-2; 10:1-8; 12:10-14; Amos 4:4-5; 5:7-13; 6:1-7
Jeremiah	Jer 4:13-18; 21:13-14
Jerusalemites	Zeph 3:1-5
Jesus	Mt 11:20-24
Micah	Mic 3:1-12
Moabites	Jer 48:1-47
Nineveh	Nah 3:1 4́; 5-19
Priests	Mal 1:6-2:9
Prophets	Jer 23:13-15
Shemaiah	Jer 29:24-32
Zephaniah	Zeph 2:4-7

REVELATION on

Chaldeans	Is 47:1-15
Edomites	Ezek 35:1-15
Egyptians	Ezek 29:1-5; 30:20-26; 32:17-32
Ezekiel	Ezek 14:12-23; 36:1-7
God	Is 41:1-42:4
Gog	Ezek 38:3-9; 39:1-16
Habakkuk	Hab 2:5-6a
Isaiah	Is 5:1-7; 65:1-25
Israelites	Ezek 5:5-17; 17:11-21; 20:27-29; 22:17-22; 34:1-10; 36:16-21; Hos 2:9-13; Mal 2:17-3:5
Jeremiah	Jer 1:13-16; 25:30-38
Jesus	Mt 11:20-24
Judahites	Ezek 23:22-35; 24:1-14
Moabites	Ezek 25:8-11
Rulers	Zech 11:15-17
Zedekiah	Jer 24:1-10

SCRIPTURES on

Jesus	Mt 12:38-42: Lk 11:29-32

SELF-REALIZATION of

Hypocrite	Mt 7:1-5; Lk 6:36-45

of **WORSHIP**

Paul	1 Cor 11:17-22

KNOWLEDGE of

Eliphaz	Job 15:7-11

as **PUNISHMENT**
    from **DEITY**
        Israelites　　　　　　Is 9:8-10:4
    for **FALSE BELIEF**
        Israelites　　　　　　Deut 29:16-29
    INSTRUCTION on
        David　　　　　　　　1 Kgs 2:5-12
    of **MESSIANIC FIGURE**
        Crowd　　　　　　　　Mk 15:6-15;
        　　　　　　　　　　　Lk 23:18-25
    PROPHECY of
        Shebna　　　　　　　Is 22:15-25
    REVELATION on
        Zedekiah　　　　　　Jer 24:1-10

as **QUALITY OF LIFE**
    of **DEITY**
        Judahites　　　　　　Jer 9:2-9
    INSTRUCTION on
        Bildad　　　　　　　Job 18:5-7;
        　　　　　　　　　　　8-11
        Jesus　　　　　　　　Lk 6:24-26
        Laodicea　　　　　　Rev 3:14-22

through **disRESPECT**
    David　　　　　　　　Ps 31:9-12
    of **DEITY**
        Job　　　　　　　　　Job 17:6-10
    REVELATION on
        God　　　　　　　　　Is 44:24-45:13

of **RESURRECTION**
    INSTRUCTION on
        Jesus　　　　　　　　Jn 5:19-47

REVELATION on
    by **AUTHORITY**
        Job　　　　　　　　　Job 38:12-15;
        　　　　　　　　　　　40:6-14
    of **CREATION**
        God　　　　　　　　　Gen 3:14-19
    for **ETERNITY**
        Mankind　　　　　　Is 66:17-24
    of **inFIDELITY**
        Israelites　　　　　　Jer 3:1-5
        Jeremiah　　　　　　Jer 26:1-6
    of **disHONESTY**
        Prophetesses　　　　Ezek 13:17-23
        Prophets　　　　　　Jer 23:23-32;
        　　　　　　　　　　　Ezek 13:1-16
    as **JUDGMENT**
        Chaldeans　　　　　Is 47:1-15
        Edomites　　　　　　Ezek 35:1-15
        Egyptians　　　　　　Ezek 29:1-5;
        　　　　　　　　　　　30:20-26;
        　　　　　　　　　　　32:17-32
        Ezekiel　　　　　　　Ezek 14:12-23;
        　　　　　　　　　　　36:1-7
        God　　　　　　　　　Is 41:1-42:4
        Gog　　　　　　　　　Ezek 38:3-9;
        　　　　　　　　　　　39:1-16
        Habakkuk　　　　　Hab 2:5-6a
        Isaiah　　　　　　　Is 5:1-7;
        　　　　　　　　　　　65:1-25
        Israelites　　　　　　Ezek 5:5-17;
        　　　　　　　　　　　17:11-21;
        　　　　　　　　　　　20:27-29;
        　　　　　　　　　　　22:17-22;
        　　　　　　　　　　　34:1-10;
        　　　　　　　　　　　36:16-21;
        　　　　　　　　　　　Hos 2:9-13;

as **JUDGMENT** (cont'd)
    Israelites　　　　　　Mal 2:17-3:5
    Jeremiah　　　　　　Jer 1:13-16;
    　　　　　　　　　　　25:30-38
    Jesus　　　　　　　　Mt 11:20-24
    Judahites　　　　　　Ezek 23:22-35;
    　　　　　　　　　　　24:1-14
    Moabites　　　　　　Ezek 25:8-11
    Rulers　　　　　　　Zech 11:15-17
    Zedekiah　　　　　　Jer 24:1-10
    in **NEW AGE**
        Jesus　　　　　　　　Lk 17:22-37
    as **PUNISHMENT**
        Zedekiah　　　　　　Jer 24:1-10
    of **disRESPECT**
        God　　　　　　　　　Is 44:24-45:13
    SIGNS of
        Israelites　　　　　　Hos 1:6-7
        John　　　　　　　　Rev 17:6b-18
        Zechariah　　　　　　Zech 5:1-4
    of **SIN**
        Ezekiel　　　　　　　Ezek 11:1-13
        Israelites　　　　　　Is 43:14-44:5;
        　　　　　　　　　　　Hos 1:6-7
        Job　　　　　　　　　Job 40:1-2

of **RITE**
    by **DEITY**
        Israelites　　　　　　Amos 5:21-25
    revealing **FALSE BELIEF**
        Israelites　　　　　　Deut 18:9-22
    INSTRUCTION on
        Moses　　　　　　　Deut 27:11-26
        Paul　　　　　　　　1 Cor 11:27-34
    PROPHECY of
        Haggai　　　　　　　Hag 2:10-14

SALVATION from
    by **DEITY**
        Jesus　　　　　　　　Rom 5:6-11

SCRIPTURES on
    as **JUDGMENT**
        Jesus　　　　　　　　Mt 12:38-42;
        　　　　　　　　　　　Lk 11:29-32
    of **SIN**
        Paul　　　　　　　　Gal 3:19-25

SELF-REALIZATION of
    as **JUDGMENT**
        Hypocrite　　　　　Mt 7:1-5;
        　　　　　　　　　　　Lk 6:36-45

SIGNS of
    INSTRUCTION on
        Jesus　　　　　　　　Mk 8:11-13
    PROPHECY of
        Haggai　　　　　　　Hag 2:10-14
    REVELATION on
        Israelites　　　　　　Hos 1:6-7
        John　　　　　　　　Rev 17:6b-18
        Zechariah　　　　　　Zech 5:1-4
of **SIN**
    David　　　　　　　2 Sam 3:17-39
    Job　　　　　　　　　Job 22:6-11
    Moses　　　　　　　Num 16:3-11
    Nehemiah　　　　　Neh 13:23-29
    by **DEITY**
        Believer　　　　　　Heb 10:19-31;
        　　　　　　　　　　　1 Pet 3:8-12

by **DEITY** (cont'd)

God	Prov 3:1-35; 6:16-19; 12:1-28; 14:1-35; Jn 3:31-36; 1 Thes 4:1-12; 2 Thes 2:11-12
Israelites	1 Sam 12:1-25; Neh 9:26-31; Ezek 16:15-34
Job	Job 19:1-6
Mankind	1 Sam 2:11-26; 2 Sam 22:1-51; Ps 1:4-6; 18:25-30
Zophar	Job 20:4-29

revealing **FALSE BELIEF**

Isaiah	Is 1:21-23
Paul	2 Tim 3:10-13; Tit 3:8-11
Scribes	Mk 12:37b-40; Lk 20:45-47

INSTRUCTION on

Author	Heb 6:1-8; 10:19-31
God	Is 1:10-17
Isaiah	Is 56:9-57:13
James	Jas 4:1-10
Jesus	Mt 12:43-45; 18:5-6; 7-9; 21:33-43; 22:1-14; Mk 9:42-48; 12:1-12; 37b-40; Lk 11:24-26; 13:1-5; 14:15-24; 17:1-6; 19:11-27; 20:9-18; 45-47
John	1 Jn 5:13-21; Jude 1:5-7
Paul	Rom 8:1-4; 1 Cor 6:9-11; 2 Cor 13:1-4; Eph 5:3-14; Col 3:5-17; 1 Tim 5:17-25
Sirach	*Sir 41:5-13
Solomon	Prov 19:1-29; 20:1-30
Wisdom	Prov 8:1-21

MEDITATION on

David	Ps 52:1-4

by **MESSIANIC FIGURE**

Crowd	Mt 27:33-44; Mk 15:21-32
Jesus	Mk 11:15-19

MISSION for

Jonah	Jon 1:1-17

PROPHECY of

Enoch	Jude 1:14-16
Isaiah	Is 2:6-11; 5:8-24a
Jeremiah	Jer 22:13-19; 23:1-8
Judahites	Jer 25:8-14

PROPHECY of (cont'd)

Micah	Mic 2:1-10
Nathan	2 Sam 12:1-31
Sennacherib	Is 37:22-29

REVELATION on

Ezekiel	Ezek 11:1-13
Israelites	Is 43:14-44:5; Hos 1:6-7
Job	Job 40:1-2

SCRIPTURES on

Paul	Gal 3:19-25

of **STEWARDSHIP**

INSTRUCTION on

Jesus	Mt 25:14-30

of **TRUTH**

through **FALSE BELIEF**

Cephas	Gal 2:11-14
Paul	2 Cor 11:7-15; 2 Thes 2:11-12; 1 Tim 6:2c-5

INSTRUCTION on

Eliphaz	Job 15:1-6
Jesus	Mt 23:29-33
Paul	Gal 1:6-10; 2:11-14

of **WORSHIP**

Josiah	2 Kgs 23:4-15

as **JUDGMENT**

Paul	1 Cor 11:17-22

CONFRONTATION

ACCEPTANCE in

with **DEITY**

Moses	Ex 33:7-11; Num 12:4-10; Deut 34:1-12
Esther	*Esth 15:1-16
Judith	*Jdt 11:1-23

with **FOLLOWERs**

Jesus	Lk 24:13-35

INSTRUCTION on

Paul	2 Cor 6:11-13

with **MESSIANIC FIGURE**

Nathanael	Jn 1:19-51

PROPHECY of

Hezekiah	Is 39:1-8

REVELATION on

Jesus	Lk 24:13-35

ALIENATION through

Edomites	2 Chr 21:1-23:21

in **ENVIRONMENT**

Abraham	Gen 13:2-9; 10-13
Isaac	Gen 26:12-31
Jephthah	Judg 11:1-3
Lot	Gen 13:2-9; 10-13

with **MESSIANIC FIGURE**

Jesus	Jn 2:12-22

PROPHECY of

Jerusalemites	Zech 14:1-21

REVELATION on

Israelites	Ezek 21:1-7

with **TRADITION**
Hagar　　　　　　　Gen 16:1-6

with **ANGER**
of **DEITY**
David　　　　　　　Ps 7:6-8
God　　　　　　　2 Sam 22:1-51;
　　　　　　　　　Ps 2:4-6;
　　　　　　　　　18:7-15;
　　　　　　　　　Rev 15:1-16:1
Israelites　　　　　Num 16:36-50
through **FALSE BELIEF**
Pharisees　　　　　Lk 6:6-11
INSTRUCTION on
Bildad　　　　　　Job 18:1-4
by **MESSIANIC FIGURE**
Jesus　　　　　　　Mk 3:1-6
PROPHECY of
Zephaniah　　　　　Zeph 2:1-2
REVELATION on
Aaron　　　　　　　Num 12:4-10
Gog　　　　　　　Ezek 38:17-23

with **ANXIETY**
Hezekiah　　　　　Is 36:1-37:4c
Isaac　　　　　　　Gen 26:34-35
Rebekah　　　　　Gen 26:34-35
through **FALSE BELIEF**
Demetrius　　　　　Acts 19:23-41
of **FOLLOWERs**
Jesus　　　　　　　Mt 17:22-23
PROPHECY of
Babylonians　　　　Jer 50:1-46
Zechariah　　　　　Zech 9:1-12

with **BLASPHEMY**
Antiochus　　　　　*2 Mc 9:1-4
Babylonians　　　　Jer 52:4-27
through **FALSE BELIEF**
Pharisees　　　　　Lk 16:14-15
by **MESSIANIC FIGURE**
Crowd　　　　　　Lk 11:14-23
Herod　　　　　　Lk 23:6-16
Pharisees　　　　　Mt 12:22-32
Priests　　　　　　Lk 23:33-38
Scribes　　　　　　Mt 9:1-8;
　　　　　　　　　Mk 2:1-12;
　　　　　　　　　Lk 5:17-26
Soldiers　　　　　　Lk 23:33-38

with **BLESSING**
INSTRUCTION on
Jesus　　　　　　　Lk 6:27-35
Joab　　　　　　　2 Sam 18:1-19:8a

with **CAPTIVITY**
Damascenes　　　　2 Kgs 16:5-9
Israelites　　　　　2 Kgs 15:27-31;
　　　　　　　　　17:1-6;
　　　　　　　　　18:9-12
Jehoahaz　　　　　2 Kgs 23:31-35
Jehoiachin　　　　　2 Chr 36:1-23
Jehoiakim　　　　　2 Kgs 24:8-17;
　　　　　　　　　2 Chr 36:1-23
Jeremiah　　　　　Jer 37:11-15;
　　　　　　　　　16-21
Judah　　　　　　Dan 1:1-7
Judahites　　　　　2 Kgs 24:8-17;
　　　　　　　　　25:8-17;
　　　　　　　　　18-22;
　　　　　　　　　2 Chr 36:1-23;

with **CAPTIVITY** (cont'd)
Judahites　　　　　Jer 52:4-27
Zedekiah　　　　　2 Kgs 24:18-25:7;
　　　　　　　　　Jer 52:4-27
through **FALSE BELIEF**
Herod　　　　　　Lk 3:18-20
People　　　　　　Is 46:1-13

INSTRUCTION on
John the Baptist　　Lk 3:18-20
by **MESSIANIC FIGURE**
Annas　　　　　　Jn 18:12-27
Caiaphas　　　　　Mt 26:57-68;
　　　　　　　　　Mk 14:53-65;
　　　　　　　　　Jn 18:12-27
Jesus　　　　　　　Mt 26:47-56;
　　　　　　　　　Mk 14:43-50;
　　　　　　　　　Lk 22:47-54a
Pilate　　　　　　Mt 27:1-2;
　　　　　　　　　Mk 15:1-5
PROPHECY of
Babylonians　　　　Jer 50:1-46
Isaiah　　　　　　2 Kgs 20:12-21;
　　　　　　　　　Is 39:1-8
Jeremiah　　　　　Jer 32:26-44
Jerusalemites　　　Zech 14:1-21
Jesus　　　　　　　Lk 9:43b-45
Judahites　　　　　Jer 37:16-21
Smyrna　　　　　　Rev 2:8-11
Zedekiah　　　　　Jer 34:1-7
REVELATION on
Babylonians　　　　Jer 27:1-11
Satan　　　　　　Rev 20:1-3

with **CHAOS**
in the **ENVIRONMENT**
Israelites　　　　　Judg 7:16-22
REVELATION on
John　　　　　　　Rev 11:15-19

with **COMPASSION**
Ahab　　　　　　　1 Kgs 20:1-43
Joseph　　　　　　Gen 43:16-34
of **MESSIANIC FIGURE**
Crowd　　　　　　Mk 6:30-44
Jesus　　　　　　　Mt 14:13-21;
　　　　　　　　　15:32-39

with **CONDEMNATION**
David　　　　　　2 Sam 15:13-16:14
Nehemiah　　　　　Neh 2:19-20
INSTRUCTION on
John the Baptist　　Lk 3:18-20
of **MESSIANIC FIGURE**
Jesus　　　　　　　Lk 13:10-17;
　　　　　　　　　Jn 2:12-22
Jews　　　　　　　Jn 5:1-18
Pharisees　　　　　Mt 12:1-8;
　　　　　　　　　Mk 2:23-28;
　　　　　　　　　Lk 6:1-5
Priests　　　　　　Lk 23:33-38
Soldiers　　　　　Lk 23:33-38
PROPHECY of
Priests　　　　　　Mk 10:32-34
Scribes　　　　　　Mk 10:32-34
Shemaiah　　　　　1 Kgs 12:21-24;
　　　　　　　　　2 Chr 10:1-12:16

with **COURAGE**
from **DEITY**
Joshua　　　　　　Josh 11:1-15

of FOLLOWERs
Joseph	Mt 27:57-61; Mk 15:42-47

INSTRUCTION on
Elisha	2 Kgs 6:8-23
Moses	Deut 20:1-9; 31:1-8
Smyrna	Rev 2:8-11

REVELATION on
John	Rev 1:4-20

bringing COVENANT
of PEACE
Maccabeus	*2 Mc 12:10-12

with DEATH
Antiochus	*2 Mc 1:10-17
Gedaliah	Jer 41:1-3
Israelites	*1 Mc 2:29-38
Jews	*2 Mc 12:1-9
Josiah	*1 Esd 1:25-32
Maccabeus	*1 Mc 9:1-22
Simon	*1 Mc 16:11-17
Timothy	*2 Mc 10:24-38

PROPHECY of
Ethiopians	Zeph 2:8-12
Isaiah	Is 52:13-53:12
Jeroboam	Amos 7:10-17
Tyre	Ezek 26:7-14

REVELATION on
Egyptians	Ezek 30:10-12; 31:10-18
Ezekiel	Ezek 30:1-5; 33:23-29
Gog	Ezek 39:1-16
Israelites	Amos 9:8-10

with DEFEAT
Abimelech	Judg 9:50-55
Ahab	1 Kgs 22:1-40
Ahaz	2 Chr 26:1-28:27
Amaziah	2 Kgs 14:8-14
Goliath	1 Sam 17:1-18:5
Hoshea	2 Kgs 17:1-6
Israelites	2 Kgs 10:32-33; 13:1-9; 15:27-31; 18:9-12; 1 Chr 10:1-14; 2 Chr 10:1-12:16
Jehoahaz	2 Chr 36:1-23
Jehoiakim	2 Kgs 24:8-17
Jehoram	2 Kgs 8:16-24; 2 Chr 21:2-23:21
Jeroboam	2 Chr 13:1-22
Joash	2 Chr 24:1-27
Judahites	2 Kgs 18:13-16; 2 Chr 25:1-28; Jer 39:1-14; 52:4-27
Nineveh	Nah 2:6-10
Rehoboam	1 Kgs 14:25-28
Saul	1 Sam 31:1-13
Tibni	1 Kgs 16:15-22
Zedekiah	2 Kgs 24:18-25:7
Zimri	1 Kgs 16:15-22

caused by DEITY
David	Ps 89:38-51
Israelites	Ps 44:9-16
Solomon	1 Kgs 8:22-53; 2 Chr 5:1-7:10

through FALSE BELIEF
Prophets	Rev 19:17-21

INSTRUCTION on
Moses	Deut 28:15-68

PROPHECY of
Ammonites	Jer 49:1-6
Assyrians	Is 31:4-9
Babylonians	Jer 50:1-46; 51:1-64
Edomites	Jer 49:7-22
Egyptians	Is 20:1-6; Jer 46:2-12; 13-26
Isaiah	Is 9:8-10:4
Israelites	Jer 5:15-17; 6:9-15
Jeremiah	Jer 6:1-8; 8:14-17; 20:1-6; 21:1-10; 32:1-8; 26-44; 43:8-13
Jerusalemites	Zech 14:1-21
Judahites	Jer 37:3-10
Micaiah	1 Kgs 22:1-40; 2 Chr 17:1-20:37
Moabites	Jer 48:1-47
Nineveh	Nah 3:5-19
Philistines	Jer 47:1-7
Samaritans	Amos 3:11-12
Tyre	Ezek 26:7-14
Zedekiah	Jer 34:1-7

REVELATION on
Ammonites	Ezek 21:28-32
Babylonians	Rev 18:21-24
Egyptians	Ezek 29:17-21; 30:10-12; 13-19; 20-26; 32:1-16; 17-32
Ezekiel	Ezek 33:23-29
Gog	Ezek 39:1-16
Israelites	Ezek 21:18-24
Jeremiah	Jer 19:1-15
Judahites	Ezek 23:22-35
Prophets	Rev 11:1-14
Satan	Rev 12:7-9
Tyre	Ezek 26:1-6; 28:1-10

with DEITY
ACCEPTANCE in
Moses	Ex 33:7-11

beyond DEATH
Job	Job 19:25-29
Mankind	Ex 33:12-23

through DISOBEDIENCE
Israelites	Num 16:16-24

in FEAR
Adam	Gen 3:9-13

concerning GOOD
Satan	Job 1:6-8; 2:1-3

through GRACE
Jesus	Mt 5:3-12

in HUMILITY
Job	Job 40:3-5; 42:1-6

in INNOCENCE

in INNOCENCE (cont'd)
Israelites   Deut 18:9-22
through MIRACLE
Balaam   Num 22:22-35
Ezekiel   Ezek 3:12-15
Samaritans   2 Kgs 7:3-20
in REPENTANCE
Job   Job 42:1-6
as WITNESS
Israelites   Num 14:11-24;
  Deut 5:1-21
Moses   Num 12:4-10;
  Deut 34:1-12

with DESTRUCTION
Abimelech   Judg 9:42-45
Benjaminites   Judg 20:45-48
Habakkuk   Hab 1:2-4
Israelites   Judg 4:23-24;
  Josh 6:15-21;
  22-27;
  11:16-23;
  Judg 20:45 48
Joshua   Josh 8:1-29;
  10:28-43;
  11:1-15
Judahites   2 Kgs 23:36-24:7;
  Jer 39:1-14;
  52:4-27
Nebuchadnezzar   2 Kgs 25:8-17
through FALSE BELIEF
Gideon   Judg 6:11-32
Israelites   Deut 7:6-16
INSTRUCTION on
Moab   Is 15:1-16:14
Moses   Deut 7:1-5
PROPHECY of
Adversaries   Zech 12:1-13:6
Ammonites   Jer 49:1-6
Babylonians   Is 13:1-22;
  21:1-10;
  Jer 50:1-46;
  51:1-64
Canaanites   Is 23:1-14
Edomites   Jer 49:7-22
Egyptians   Jer 46:2-12;
  13-26
Elamites   Jer 49:34-39
Hazorites   Jer 49:28-33
Isaiah   Is 8:5-8a;
  30:8-17
Israelites   Hos 10:9-15;
  11:5-7
Jeremiah   Jer 6:22-26;
  10:17-22;
  21:1-10
Judahites   Jer 25:8-14;
  37:3-10
Moabites   Jer 48:1-47
Philistines   Jer 47:1-7
Tyre   Ezek 26:7-14
Zedekiah   Jer 34:1-7
REVELATION on
Babylonians   Rev 18:21-24
Daniel   Dan 9:24-27;
  11:21-45
Egyptians   Ezek 30:6-9;
  10-12;
  20-26
Ezekiel   Ezek 30:1-5;
  33:23-29

REVELATION on (cont'd)
Satan   Rev 20:7-10

with DISCIPLESHIP
to MESSIANIC FIGURE
Andrew   Jn 1:19-51
Peter   Jn 1:19-51

with DISOBEDIENCE
INSTRUCTION on
Jesus   Mt 18:15-17
Nebuchadnezzar   *Jdt 1:1-2:20
PROPHECY of
Ahab   1 Kgs 22:1-40;
  2 Chr 17:1-20:37
Josiah   *1 Esd 1:25-32

with DOUBT
Disciples   Lk 24:36-43
Gideon   Judg 8:4-9
MEDITATION on
Ezekiel   Ezek 20:45-49
concerning MESSIANIC FIGURE
Jews   Jn 5:1-18
in MISSION
Disciples   Mt 17:14-20;
  Mk 9:14-29;
  Lk 9:37-43a
PROPHECY of
Zedekiah   Jer 32:1-8
REVELATION on
Ananias   Acts 9:1-19
Disciples   Lk 24:36-43
with ENEMY
Assyrians   Is 10:27d-32
Esther   Esth 7:1-10
Israelites   Ezra 5:3-5;
  Neh 4:7-12;
  6:17-19
Joram   2 Kgs 8:25-29
Moses   Deut 2:1-25
Nehemiah   Neh 2:9-11
through violated COVENANT
David   Ps 55:20-21
by DEITY
David   1 Sam 17:1-18:5
Esther   *Esth 14:1-19
Solomon   *Wis 5:15-23
INSTRUCTION on
Antiochus   *1 Mc 3:27-37
PROPHECY of
Isaiah   Is 8:8b-10
Israelites   Nah 2:1-5
Jeremiah   Jer 6:22-26
REVELATION on
Aaron   *Sir 45:6-22
Michael   Rev 12:7-9
Prophets   Rev 11:1-14

with EVIL
through FALSE BELIEF
Diotrephes   3 Jn 1:9-11
of FOLLOWERs
Paul   2 Cor 10:7-11
by MESSIANIC FIGURE
Priests   Mk 11:15-19
PROPHECY of
Judahites   Jer 4:5-8
REVELATION on
Jeremiah   Jer 1:13-16

with **FAITH**
  in **MESSIANIC FIGURE**
    Criminal   Lk 23:39-43
    Crowd   Lk 6:17-19
    Jesus   Mt 9:18-26
    Lepers   Lk 17:11-19
    Woman   Mk 5:25-34;
        Lk 8:40-56
  SELF-REALIZATION of
    Jairus   Mk 5:21-24;
        Lk 8:40-56

with **FAMILY**
    Moses   Ex 18:1-12;
        Num 10:29-32
    Esau   Gen 26:34-35
    Israelites   Josh 22:9-34;
        Judg 20:12-17
    Jacob   Gen 29:1-14
    Joseph   Gen 42:1-6
    Menelaus   *2 Mc 4:23-29
    Simon   *2 Mc 3:1-40;
        4:1-6

with **FEAR**
    Assyrians   Is 10:27d-32;
        *Jdt 15:1-7
    Disciples   Lk 24:36-43
    Esther   *Esth 15:1-16
    Israelites   Ezra 4:4-5;
        *Jdt 7:1-22
    Joseph   Gen 44:1-34;
        50:1-21
    Moab   Num 22:2-4
    Philistines   1 Sam 29:1-11
  of **DEITY**
    Adam   Gen 3:9-13
  through **FALSE BELIEF**
    Priests   Lk 22:1-2
  INSTRUCTION on
    Moses   Deut 20:1-9
  of **MESSIANIC FIGURE**
    Demon   Mk 1:21-28;
        Lk 4:31-37
  PROPHECY of
    Damascenes   Jer 49:23-27
    Saul   1 Sam 28:3-25
    Zechariah   Zech 9:1-12
  REVELATION on
    Disciples   Lk 24:36-43
    John   Rev 6:12-17
    Prophets   Rev 11:1-14

with **FOLLOWERs**
  ACCEPTANCE in
    Jesus   Lk 24:13-35

with **FRIENDSHIP**
    Micah   Judg 17:7-13

with **GOOD**
    Ungodly men   *Wis 2:12-20
    Satan   Job 1:6-8;
        2:1-3

through **GRACE**
    David   2 Sam 19:8b-43
  of **DEITY**
    Jesus   Mt 5:3-12
  INSTRUCTION on
    Elisha   2 Kgs 6:8-23

INSTRUCTION on (cont'd)
    Jesus   Lk 10:29-37
  of **MESSIANIC FIGURE**
    David   1 Sam 23:14-24:22;
        26:1-25

with **GRIEF**
    Jehoram   2 Kgs 6:24-31
  PROPHECY of
    Jerusalemites   Zech 12:1-13:6

with **GUILT**
    Judah   Gen 38:24-30

with **HATE**
  INSTRUCTION on
    Sirach   *Sir 25:12-15
  PROPHECY of
    Jeremiah   Jer 4:30-31

with **HEALING**
    David   1 Sam 16:14-23
  REVELATION on
    Daniel   Dan 10:10-21

with **HERESY**
  INSTRUCTION on
    Moses   Deut 29:16-29

through **HUMILITY**
  in **WORSHIP**
    Joshua   Josh 5:13-15

with **IDOLATRY**
    Josiah   *Sir 49:1-3
  through **FALSE BELIEF**
    Elijah   1 Kgs 18:1-46
  REVELATION on
    Ezekiel   Ezek 6:1-7

with **INDIFFERENCE**
  by **MESSIANIC FIGURE**
    Pharisees   Mk 3:1-6

through **INNOCENCE**
  in **MISSION**
    Apostles   Mt 10:16-22

INSTRUCTION on
  with **ANGER**
    Bildad   Job 18:1-4
  with **BLESSING**
    Jesus   Lk 6:27-35
    Joab   2 Sam 18:1-19:8a
  with **CAPTIVITY**
    John the Baptist   Lk 3:18-20
  with **CONDEMNATION**
    John the Baptist   Lk 3:18-20
  with **COURAGE**
    Elisha   2 Kgs 6:8-23
    Moses   Deut 20:1-9;
        31:1-8
    Smyrna   Rev 2:8-11
  with **DEFEAT**
    Moses   Deut 28:15-68
  with **DESTRUCTION**
    Moab   Is 15:1-16:14
    Moses   Deut 7:1-5
  with **DISOBEDIENCE**
    Jesus   Mt 18:15-17
    Nebuchadnezzar   *Jdt 1:1-2:20

with **DEFEAT** (cont'd)

Babylonians	51:1-64
Edomites	Jer 49:7-22
Egyptians	Is 20:1-6; Jer 46:2-12; 13-26
Isaiah	Is 9:8-10:4
Israelites	Jer 5:15-17; 6:9-15
Jeremiah	Jer 6:1-8; 8:14-17; 20:1-6; 21:1-10; 32:1-8; 26-44; 43:8-13
Jerusalemites	Zech 14:1-21
Judahites	Jer 37:3-10
Micaiah	1 Kgs 22:1-40; 2 Chr 17:1-20:37
Moabites	Jer 48:1-47
Nineveh	Nah 3:5-19
Philistines	Jer 47:1-7
Samaritans	Amos 3:11-12
Tyre	Ezek 26:7-14
Zedekiah	Jer 34:1-7

with **DESTRUCTION**

Adversaries	Zech 12:1-13:6
Ammonites	Jer 49:1-6
Babylonians	Is 13:1-22; 21:1-10; Jer 50:1-46; 51:1-64
Canaanites	Is 23:1-14
Edomites	Jer 49:7-22
Egyptians	Jer 46:2-12; 13-26
Elamites	Jer 49:34-39
Hazorites	Jer 49:28-33
Isaiah	Is 8:5-8a; 30:8-17
Israelites	Hos 10:9-15; 11:5-7
Jeremiah	Jer 6:22-26; 10:17-22; 21:1-10
Judahites	Jer 25:8-14; 37:3-10
Moabites	Jer 48:1-47
Philistines	Jer 47:1-7
Tyre	Ezek 26:7-14
Zedekiah	Jer 34:1-7

with dis**OBEDIENCE**

Ahab	1 Kgs 22:1-40; 2 Chr 17:1-20:37
Josiah	*1 Esd 1:25-32

with **DOUBT**

Zedekiah	Jer 32:1-8

with **ENEMY**

Isaiah	Is 8:8b-10
Israelites	Nah 2:1-5
Jeremiah	Jer 6:22-26

with **EVIL**

Judahites	Jer 4:5-8

with **FEAR**

Damascenes	Jer 49:23-27
Saul	1 Sam 28:3-25
Zechariah	Zech 9:1-12

FULFILLMENT of

FULFILLMENT of (cont'd)

Elisha	2 Kgs 3:1-27
Israelites	Judg 20:29-36
Jeremiah	Jer 39:1-14
Jesus	Mt 26:47-56; Mk 14:12-16; 43-50; Lk 22:7-13
Joash	2 Kgs 13:22-25
Micaiah	1 Kgs 22:1-40; 2 Chr 17:1-20:37

with **GRIEF**

Jerusalemites	Zech 12:1-13:6

with **HATE**

Jeremiah	Jer 4:30-31

with **KILLING**

Gentiles	Mk 10:32-34
Jesus	Mt 16:21-28; 17:22-23; 20:17-19; 26:1-2; Mk 8:31-33; 9:30-32; Lk 9:18-22; 43b-45; 18:31-34

with **MIRACLE**

Assyrians	Is 31:4-9

with **OPPRESSION**

Gog	Ezek 38:10-13
Isaiah	Is 24:16b-18b

with **POLITICS**

Shemaiah	1 Kgs 12:21-24; 2 Chr 10:1-12:16

with **SACREDNESS**

Saul	1 Sam 19:18-24

with **VICTORY**

Ahithophel	2 Sam 16:15-17:2!
Babylonians	Jer 46:13-26
Balaam	Num 24:14-25
Deborah	Judg 4:6-9
Elisha	2 Kgs 3:1-27; 13:14-19
Hezekiah	Is 38:1-22
Isaiah	Is 29:1-8
Israelites	Zech 9:13-17
Jerusalemites	Zech 14:1-21
Joshua	Josh 17:14-18
Samuel	1 Sam 15:1-35

with **VIOLENCE**

Ammonites	Jer 49:1-6
Babylonians	Jer 43:8-13; 50:1-46; 51:1-64
Damascenes	Jer 49:23-27
Edomites	Jer 49:7-22
Egyptians	Jer 46:2-12; 13-26
Ephraimites	Hos 7:13-16
Gog	Ezek 38:10-13
Hazorites	Jer 49:28-33
Israelites	Deut 28:15-68; Hos 10:9-15; 11:5-7; Amos 6:12-14; Nah 2:1-5
Jeremiah	Jer 6:1-8; 21:1-10
Jerusalemites	Zech 12:1-13:6; 14:1-21
Joel	Joel 1:2-20

with **VICTORY** (cont'd)

Asa	1 Kgs 15:16-22
Baasha	1 Kgs 15:25-32
Babylonians	Jer 39:1-14; 52:4-27
David	1 Sam 17:1-18:5; 6-30; 27:1-28:2; 30:1-31; 2 Sam 5:17-25; 8:1-18; 12:1-31; 18:1-19:8a; 21:15-22; 1 Chr 11:1-12:40; 14:1-17; 18:1-20:8
Gideon	Judg 8:10-12
Hezekiah	2 Kgs 18:4-8; 2 Chr 32:1-33
Israelites	Num 21:1-3; Deut 11:26-32; Judg 3:26-30; 4:10-16; 23-24; 20:37-44; 1 Sam 11:1-15; 2 Sam 10:1-19; 2 Kgs 3:1-27; 1 Chr 5:1-26; Esth 9:1-10; 11-15
Jehoram	2 Chr 21:1-23:21
Joab	2 Sam 2:8-32
Joash	2 Kgs 13:22-25
Jonathan	1 Sam 13:1-23; 14:1-46
Jotham	2 Chr 26:1-28:27
King	Ps 45:2-9
Nebuchadnezzar	2 Kgs 24:18-25:7; 2 Chr 36:1-23
Saul	1 Sam 15:1-35
Sennacherib	Is 36:1-37:4c
Simeonites	1 Chr 4:24-43

through help of **DEITY**

David	2 Sam 22:1-51; Ps 17:13-14; 18:31-42; 41:11-12
God	Ps 76:1-3; 144:1-2
Israelites	Neh 9:22-25
Jacob	Hos 12:2-6
Judith	*Jdt 16:1-17
Maccabeus	*1 Mc 3:10-26; *2 Mc 8:24-33; 12:13-23; 26-28; 15:20-27
Psalmist	Ps 118:10-14

INSTRUCTION on

Judith	*Jdt 14:1-5
Moses	Deut 7:1-5; 21:10-14; 28:1-14; 31:1-8

by **MESSIANIC FIGURE**

Psalmist	Ps 2:7-9

PROPHECY of

Ahithophel	2 Sam 16:15-17:29
Babylonians	Jer 46:13-26

PROPHECY of (cont'd)

Balaam	Num 24:14-25
Deborah	Judg 4:6-9
Elisha	2 Kgs 3:1-27; 13:14-19
Hezekiah	Is 38:1-22
Isaiah	Is 29:1-8
Israelites	Zech 9:13-17
Jerusalemites	Zech 14:1-21
Joshua	Josh 17:14-18
Samuel	1 Sam 15:1-35

REVELATION on

Babylonians	Ezek 32:1-16
Gideon	Judg 6:11-32
Isaiah	Is 54:1-17
Israelites	Gen 32:24-32; Judg 20:24-28; Ezek 39:1-16; Zeph 2:8-12
Jeremiah	Jer 1:17-19
John	Rev 12:10-12; 13-17; 15:1-16:1; 17:6b-18; 19:17-21
Joshua	Josh 8:1-29 10:1-15
Judahites	Is 7:1-9
Maccabeus	*2 Mc 15:11-19
Michael	Rev 12:7-9
Moses	Num 33:50-56
Nebuchadnezzar	Ezek 29:17-21

with **VIOLENCE**

Abijam	1 Kgs 15:1-8
Babylonians	Jer 52:4-27
Chaldeans	Hab 1:5-11
Gideon	Judg 8:10-12
Habakkuk	Hab 1:2-4
Israelites	Judg 3:26-30; 4:10-16; 1 Chr 10:1-14; Esth 9:1-10
Joshua	Josh 8:1-29
Judahites	Jer 39:1-14
Nebuchadnezzar	Dan 1:1-7
Satan	Rev 12:13-17
Zedekiah	Jer 34:1-7

of **DEITY**

Nations	Zech 14:1-21

in the **ENVIRONMENT**

Abimelech	Judg 9:34-41; 42-45
Caleb	Josh 15:13-19
Danites	Judg 18:27-31
Israelites	Judg 1:22-36; Ex 17:8-16; Num 21:21-32; 33-35; 31:7-12; Deut 2:26-3:11; Josh 10:1-15; 16-27; 11:1-15; 16-23; Judg 3:12-14; 5:19-22; 7:23-25; 20:19-23; 24-28; 29-36

CONFRONTATION (cont'd)

with **YOUTH** (cont'd)
        INSTRUCTION on
           Jesus   Mk 9:42-48
           Paul   2 Cor 6:11-13

CONVERSION

through **ACCEPTANCE** ✓
    of **MESSIANIC FIGURE**
        Centurion   Mt 27:45-56
    REVELATION on
        Nations   Zeph 3:9-10
        Paul   Gal 1:11-17
    SCRIPTURES on
        James   Acts 15:6-29
    SELF-REALIZATION of
        Gentiles   Acts 10:1-11:18

BLESSING in ✓
    REVELATION on
        Isaiah   Is 58:1-14
        Judahites   Jer 24:1-10

CONDEMNATION through
    of **WORSHIP**
        Josiah   2 Kgs 23:4-15

in **DEATH**
    INSTRUCTION on
        Paul   1 Cor 15:51-58

through **FAITH** ✓
    in **DEITY**
        Achior   *Jdt 14:6-10
        Israelites   Jer 3:21-4:4
    of **FOLLOWERs**
        Believers   Acts 9:32-43
        Corinthians Acts 18:1-17
        Lydia   Acts 16:11-15
        Simon   Acts 8:4-13
        Zacchaeus   Lk 19:1-10
    PROPHECY of
        Isaiah   Is 2:1-5;
                      17:7-8
    REVELATION on
        Believers   Is 56:1-8
        Saul   Acts 9:1-19

of **FOLLOWERs** ✓
    through **FAITH**
        Believers   Acts 9:32-43
        Corinthians Acts 18:1-17
        Lydia   Acts 16:11-15
        Simon   Acts 8:4-13
        Zacchaeus   Lk 19:1-10
    with **JOY**
        Barnabas   Acts 15:1-5
        Ethiopian   Acts 8:26-40
        Paul   Acts 15:1-5
    through **JUSTICE**
        Zacchaeus   Lk 19:1-10
    through **LOVE**
        Zacchaeus   Lk 19:1-10
    through **REPENTANCE**
        Jailer   Acts 16:25-40
        Thessalonians 1 Thes 1:2-10
        Zacchaeus   Lk 19:1-10

through **GRACE**
    of **DEITY**
        Israelites   Num 14:11-24
    INSTRUCTION on
        Hezekiah   2 Chr 30:1-31:21
        Paul   1 Cor 15:1-11
        Peter   Acts 3:1-26
    REVELATION on
        Ezekiel   Ezek 33:10-20
        Isaiah   Is 55:1-13
        Israelites   Ezek 18:30-32

through **HEALING**
    by **MESSIANIC FIGURE**
        Jesus   Mt 9:1-8
    in **MISSION**
        Jesus   Mt 9:10-13

through **HOPE**
    INSTRUCTION on
        Paul   2 Cor 3:12-18

from **IDOLATRY**
    PROPHECY of
        Israelites   Is 31:4-9

INSTRUCTION on
    in **DEATH**
        Paul   1 Cor 15:51-58
    through **GRACE**
        Hezekiah   2 Chr 30:1-31:21
        Paul   1 Cor 15:1-11
        Peter   Acts 3:1-26
    through **HOPE**
        Paul   2 Cor 3:12-18
    through **PURIFICATION**
        Jesus   Lk 12:49-50
    through **REJECTION**
        Paul   Gal 2:17-19
    through **REPENTANCE**
        Daniel   Dan 4:19-27
        David   Ps 51:13-17
        Ezekiel   Ezek 14:1-11
        God   Is 46:1-13
        Hosea   Hos 12:2-6;
                      14:1-3
        Isaiah   Is 51:17-52:12
        James   Jas 4:1-10
        Jeremiah   Jer 13:15-17;
                      Lam 3:1-66
        Joel   Joel 2:12-17
        Joshua   Josh 24:16-24
        Laodicea   Rev 3:14-22
        Paul   Acts 21:27-22:29;
                      Eph 4:25-5:2
        Pergamum Rev 2:12-17
        Sardis   Rev 3:1-6

with **JOY**
    of **FOLLOWERs**
    REWARDs of
        Peter   1 Pet 3:8-12
        Zophar   Job 11:13-20
    SPIRIT of
        Paul   Rom 12:1-2
    WISDOM in
        Paul   2 Cor 3:12-18
    WITNESS to
        Paul   Acts 26:1-32

of FOLLOWERs (cont'd)

Barnabas	Acts 15:1-5
Ethiopian	Acts 8:26-40
Paul	Acts 15:1-5

through JUSTICE
  of FOLLOWER

Zacchaeus	Lk 19:1-10

to LIFE
  REVELATION on

Ezekiel	Ezek 18:21-24; 25-29
Israelites	Ezek 18:30-32

through LOVE
  of FOLLOWER

Zacchaeus	Lk 19:1-10

through MIRACLE
  by MESSIANIC FIGURE

Jesus	Mt 9:1-8

  REVELATION of

Saul	Acts 9:1-19

through MISSION
  of HEALING

Jesus	Mt 9:10-13

  of PURIFICATION

Disciples	Mt 28:16-20

  of REPENTANCE

Jesus	Mt 4:17; 9:10-13

through OBEDIENCE
  REVELATION on

Paul	Acts 26:1-32

revealed in PRAISE
  of DEITY

Mankind	Rev 11:1-14

revealed in PRIDE
  before DEITY

Mankind	Ps 22:27-31

PROPHECY of
  through FAITH

Isaiah	Is 2:1-5; 17:7-8

  from IDOLATRY

Israelites	Is 31:4-9

  through REPENTANCE

Isaiah	Is 10:20-23
Israelites	Ezek 16:53-63; Hos 14:4-8
Jeremiah	Jer 12:14-17

through PURIFICATION
  INSTRUCTION on

Jesus	Lk 12:49-50

  MISSION of

Disciples	Mt 28:16-20

through REJECTION
  INSTRUCTION on

Paul	Gal 2:17-19

  MEDITATION on

Jeremiah	Jer 5:1-14

through REPENTANCE

Israelites	Num 21:4-9
People	Acts 2:37-41

  before DEITY

David	Ps 32:3-7; 51:3-12
Ephraim	Jer 31:15-22

  of DEITY

God	Num 23:13-26; 1 Sam 15:1-35; 1 Chr 21:1-22:1; Ezek 24:1-14; Joel 2:12-17; Jon 3:1-10
Israelites	Hos 3:1-5; 5:15-6:3

  of FOLLOWER

Jailer	Acts 16:25-40
Thessalonians	1 Thes 1:2-10
Zacchaeus	Lk 19:1-10

  INSTRUCTION on

Daniel	Dan 4:19-27
David	Ps 51:13-17
Ezekiel	Ezek 14:1-11
God	Is 46:1-13
Hosea	Hos 12:2-6; 14:1-3
Isaiah	Is 51:17-52:12
James	Jas 4:1-10
Jeremiah	Jer 13:15-17; Lam 3:1-66
Joel	Joel 2:12-17
Joshua	Josh 24:16-24
Laodicea	Rev 3:14-22
Paul	Acts 21:27-22:29 Eph 4:25-5:2
Pergamum	Rev 2:12-17
Sardis	Rev 3:1-6

  MISSION of

Jesus	Mt 4:17; 9:10-13

  PROPHECY of

Isaiah	Is 10:20-23
Israelites	Ezek 16:53-63; Hos 14:4-8
Jeremiah	Jer 12:14-17

  REVELATION on

Daniel	Dan 4:19-27
Ezekiel	Ezek 18:25-29; 33:10-20
Isaiah	Is 55:1-13; 58:1-14
Israelites	Ezek 18:30-32; 20:40-44; 44:6-9; Hos 2:14-15
Jeremiah	Jer 3:12-14a; 31:2-6
Prophets	Jer 23:16-22
Zechariah	Zech 1:1-6

  SELF-REALIZATION of

Criminal	Lk 23:39-43
Nebuchadnezzar	Dan 4:34-35

REVELATION on
  through FAITH

Believers	Is 56:1-8
Saul	Acts 9:1-19

  through GRACE

Ezekiel	Ezek 33:10-20
Isaiah	Is 55:1-13

through **GRACE** (cont'd)
    Israelites   Ezek 18:30-32
to **LIFE**
    Ezekiel   Ezek 18:21-24;
        25-29
    Israelites   Ezek 18:30-32
through **MIRACLE**
    Saul   Acts 9:1-19
through **OBEDIENCE**
    Paul   Acts 26:1-32
through **REPENTANCE**
    Daniel   Dan 4:19-27
    Ezekiel   Ezek 18:25-29;
        33:10-20
    Isaiah   Is 55:1-13;
        58:1-14
    Israelites   Ezek 18:30-32;
        20:40-44;
        44:6-9;
        Hos 2:14-15
    Jeremiah   Jer 3:12-14a;
        31:2-6
    Prophets   Jer 23:16-22
    Zechariah   Zech 1:1-6

REWARDs of
    by **DEITY**
        Eliphaz   Job 22:21-30
    INSTRUCTION on
        Peter   1 Pet 3:8-12
        Zophar   Job 11:13-20
    REVELATION on
        Zechariah   Zech 1:1-6
    SELF-REALIZATION of
        Gentiles   Acts 10:1-11:18
    through **REPENTANCE**
        Criminal   Lk 23:39-43
        Nebuchadnezzar   Dan 4:34-35

SPIRIT of
    INSTRUCTION on
        Paul   Rom 12:1-2

WISDOM in
    INSTRUCTION on
        Paul   2 Cor 3:12-18

WITNESS to
    INSTRUCTION on
        Paul   Acts 26:1-32
    by **MESSIANIC FIGURE**
        Centurion   Mk 15:33-41

in **WORSHIP**
    through **CONDEMNATION**
        Josiah   2 Kgs 23:4-15

COURAGE

through **AUTHORITY**
    of **DEITY**
        Believers   Eph 6:10-18
    given to **FOLLOWER**s
        Paul   2 Cor 10:7-11

through **BELIEF**
    INSTRUCTION on
        David   1 Chr 28:1-29:30

INSTRUCTION on (cont'd)
    God   Is 44:6-8;
        21-23
    Paul   2 Cor 5:6-8
in **CONFRONTATION**
    INSTRUCTION on
        Elisha   2 Kgs 6:8-23
        Moses   Deut 20:1-9;
        31:1-8
        Smyrna   Rev 2:8-11
    REVELATION on
        John   Rev 1:4-20

from **DEITY**
    in **CONFRONTATION**
        Joshua   Josh 11:1-15
    DESIRE for
        Job   Job 13:20-27
    FIDELITY of
        Jehoshaphat   2 Chr 17:1-20:37
    PRESENCE of
        Believers   Acts 4:23-31
        Ezra   Ezra 7:27-28
        Israelites   Hag 1:15b-2:9
        Joshua   Josh 1:1-9
    PROVIDENCE through
        David   Ps 27:1-3;
        56:10-13
        God   Ps 91:1-13
    through **RECONCILIATION**
        Israelites   Is 42:18-43:7

DESIRE for
    from **DEITY**
        Job   Job 13:20-27

through **FIDELITY**
    of **DEITY**
        Jehoshaphat   2 Chr 17:1-20:37
    INSTRUCTION on
        David   Ps 27:13-14;
        31:19-24

of **FOLLOWER**s
    through **AUTHORITY**
        Paul   2 Cor 10:7-11
    in **CONFRONTATION**
        Joseph   Mt 27:57-61;
        Mk 15:42-47
    through **PRESENCE**
        Holy Spirit   Acts 4:23-31
    as **VIRTUE**
        Mankind   Ps 112:5-9

INSTRUCTION on
    Paul   1 Cor 16:13-24
    through **BELIEF**
        David   1 Chr 28:1-29:30
        God   Is 44:6-8;
        21-23
        Paul   2 Cor 5:6-8
    in **CONFRONTATION**
        Elisha   2 Kgs 6:8-23
        Moses   Deut 20:1-9;
        31:1-8
        Smyrna   Rev 2:8-11
    through **FIDELITY**
        David   Ps 27:13-14;
        31:19-24

through **KNOWLEDGE**
Solomon — Prov 3:1-35
through **PROVIDENCE**
Hezekiah — 2 Chr 32:1-33
through **SECURITY**
God — Is 41:1-42:4
Solomon — Prov 3:1-35
Zophar — Job 11:13-20
in **STEWARDSHIP**
Isaiah — Is 35:1-10
in **TRUTH**
Paul — Phil 1:12-30
as **VIRTUE**
Solomon — Prov 28:1-28
through **KNOWLEDGE**
INSTRUCTION on
Solomon — Prov 3:1-35

in **MISSION**
Paul — 1 Thes 2:1-12

in **NEW AGE**
PROPHECY of
Isaiah — Is 35:1-10

PRAYER for
Believers — Acts 4:23-31

in **PRESENCE**
of **DEITY**
Believers — Acts 4:23-31
Ezra — Ezra 7:27-28
Israelites — Hag 1:15b-2:9
Joshua — Josh 1:1-9
REVELATION on
Paul — Acts 18:1-17

PROPHECY of
in **NEW AGE**
Isaiah — Is 35:1-10
in **SECURITY**
Isaiah — Is 37:4d-7; 54:1-17
Israelites — Jer 46:27-28
Micah — Mic 4:1-8

through **PROVIDENCE**
of **DEITY**
David — Ps 27:1-3; 56:10-13
God — Ps 91:1-13
INSTRUCTION on
Hezekiah — 2 Chr 32:1-33
REVELATION on
Paul — Acts 22:30-23:11

through **RECONCILIATION**
by **DEITY**
Israelites — Is 42:18-43:7

RESPECT for
Maccabeus — *2 Mc 8:1-7
of **MESSIANIC FIGURE**
Paul — Phil 1:12-30

REVELATION on
in **CONFRONTATION**
John — Rev 1:4-20
in **PRESENCE**
Paul — Acts 18:1-17
through **PROVIDENCE**
Paul — Acts 22:30-23:11
in **SECURITY**
Ezekiel — Ezek 2:1-8a; 3:4-9

in **SECURITY** (cont'd)
Isaiah — Is 7:1-9
Israelites — Zeph 3:11-13
Joshua — Deut 31:14-23
Paul — Acts 27:1-28:16

in **SECURITY**
in **DEITY**
David — Ps 56:1-4
God — Ps 91:1-13
Nehemiah — Neh 4:13-23
Psalmist — Ps 118:5-9
INSTRUCTION on
God — Is 41:1-42:4
Solomon — Prov 3:1-35
Zophar — Job 11:13-20
PROPHECY of
Isaiah — Is 37:4d-7; 54:1-17
Israelites — Jer 46:27-28
Micah — Mic 4:1-8
REVELATION on
Ezekiel — Ezek 2:1-8a; 3:4-9
Isaiah — Is 7:1-9
Israelites — Zeph 3:11-13
Joshua — Deut 31:14-23
Paul — Acts 27:1-28:16

in **STEWARDSHIP**
INSTRUCTION on
Isaiah — Is 35:1-10

in **TRUTH**
INSTRUCTION on
Paul — Phil 1:12-30

as **VIRTUE**
of **FOLLOWER**s
Mankind — Ps 112:5-9
INSTRUCTION on
Solomon — Prov 28:1-28

COVENANT

ACCEPTANCE of
Israelites — Ex 24:1-18
DESIRE for
Moses — Deut 29:1-15
through **RECONCILIATION**
Gentiles — Eph 2:11-22
of **TRUTH**
Jesus — 2 Cor 3:12-18
ALIENATION from
as **PUNISHMENT**
Israelites — Zech 11:4-14
AUTHORITY of
in **DISCIPLESHIP**
God — 2 Cor 3:4-6
in **LEADERSHIP**
David — 2 Sam 5:1-5; 1 Chr 11:1-12:40
provides **PEACE**
David — 2 Sam 3:17-39
in **POLITICS**
David — 1 Chr 11:1-12:40
Jonathan — *1 Mc 10:15-44
Maccabeus — *2 Mc 14:18-25
Simon — *1 Mc 14:16-24; 15:15-24

REJECTION of	
Israelites	Zech 11:4-14
Ptolemy	*1 Mc 11:1-19
SACREDNESS in	
Jonathan	*1 Mc 10:15-44
BEHAVIOR required by	
Isaiah	Is 33:7-16
Israelites	Ex 24:1-18
in **MARRIAGE**	
Alexander	*1 Mc 10:51-58
is **OBEDIENCE**	
Noah	Gen 6:5-22
in **POLITICS**	
Jonathan	*1 Mc 12:1-23
BLASPHEMY against	
through in**FIDELITY**	
Israelites	Mal 2:10-16
BLESSING in	
of **ELECTION**	
Author	Heb 9:15-22
Israelites	Deut 5:1-21
as **ETERNAL**	
Isaiah	Is 61:1-11
Jeremiah	Jer 32:26-44
through **FIDELITY**	
Isaiah	Is 61:1-11
Israelites	1 Chr 15:1-16:43;
	Ps 105:7-15
PROMISE of	
Abraham	Gen 13:14-18;
	17:1-8;
	*Sir 44:19-21;
	Gal 3:15-18
God	Gen 12:1-8;
	Acts 3:1-26
Israelites	Deut 7:6-16
Moses	Deut 29:1-15
of **BROTHERHOOD**	
REJECTION of	
Tyre	Amos 1:9-10
concerning **CAPTIVITY**	
FREEDOM from	
Zechariah	Zech 9:1-12
Zedekiah	Jer 34:8-12
COMMITMENT to	
Israelites	Jer 50:1-46
ACCEPTANCE of	
Israelites	Ezra 10:1-6
with **COMMUNITY**	
David	*Sir 45:25-26
FULFILLMENT of	
Israelites	Josh 22:1-8
of **PEACE**	
Solomon	1 Kgs 5:1-18
concerning **DEATH**	
SALVATION from	
Noah	*Sir 44:16-18
caused by **SIN**	
Ungodly Men	*Wis 1:16-2:5
of **DEATH**	
RECONCILIATION through	
Jesus	Heb 9:15-22

DESIRE for	
in **POLITICS**	
Abner	2 Sam 3:1-16
of **DESTRUCTION**	
caused by **SIN**	
Isaiah	Is 28:14-22
of **DISCIPLESHIP**	
ETERNAL	
Israelites	*Bar 2:27-35
FIDELITY to	
Jehoiada	2 Chr 21:1-23:21
DISOBEDIENCE to	
through in**FIDELITY**	
Israelites	Judg 2:20-23;
	Jer 11:1-14;
	Hos 6:7-9
Priests	Mal 1:6-2:9
providing **FREEDOM**	
People	Jer 34:8-12
of **LAW**	
Ephraimites	Ps 78:9-20
Isaiah	Is 24:1-12
Israelites	Deut 29:16-29;
	Ezek 44:6-9;
	Hos 8:1-3
PUNISHMENT for	
Israelites	Judg 2:1-5
caused by **SIN**	
Israelites	*2 Esd 2:1-7
of **ELECTION**	
of **FAMILY**	
David	Ps 89:1-4
by **GRACE**	
Israelites	Rom 9:1-5
of **LIFE**	
Ezekiel	Ezek 16:8-14
through **OBEDIENCE**	
Moses	Ex 19:1-8;
	Deut 29:1-15
PRAISE of	
Ezra	Neh 9:7-8
REJECTION of	
Israelites	Rom 9:1-5
ELECTION to	
BLESSING through	
Author	Heb 9:15-22
Israelites	Deut 5:1-21
ENEMY of	
CONFRONTATION with	
David	Ps 55:20-21
ETERNAL	
ACCEPTANCE of	
Believers	Is 56:1-8
BLESSING in	
Isaiah	Is 61:1-11
Jeremiah	Jer 32:26-44
of **DISCIPLESHIP**	
Israelites	*Bar 2:27-35
with **FAMILY**	
Israelites	1 Chr 15:1-16:43;
	Ps 105:7-15
FULFILLMENT of	
God	Ps 111:5-9

MEDITATION of (cont'd)
    through **DEATH**
        Jesus   Heb 9:15-22
    for **LIFE**
        Jesus   Heb 12:12-29
    through **SACRIFICE**
        Aaron   Lev 24:5-9
    through **SERVICE**
        Jesus   Heb 8:6-13

of **NEW AGE**
    FULFILLMENT of
        Jesus   2 Cor 3:12-18;
                       Heb 8:6-13
    through **GRACE**
        Paul   Gal 4:21-26
    WITNESS to
        Paul   1 Cor 11:23-26

OBEDIENCE to
    BEHAVIOR required by
        Noah   Gen 6:5-22
    of **LAW**
        Josiah   2 Kgs 23:1-3;
                       2 Chr 34:1-35:27
        Judahites   2 Kgs 23:1-3
    PROVIDENCE through
        Believers   Is 56:1-8
        Israelites   Ex 15:22-27
    SIGNS of
        Abraham   Gen 17:9-14
        Moses   1 Cor 10:1-13

ONENESS in
    RECONCILIATION through
        Gentiles   Eph 2:11-22

OPPRESSION in
    SIGNS of
        Paul   Gal 4:21-26

ORDER in
    SECURITY through
        Noah   Gen 9:8-19
    SIGNS of
        God   Gen 9:8-19
of **PEACE**
        Israelites   Ezek 37:15-28
    with **COMMUNITY**
        Solomon   1 Kgs 5:1-18
    through **CONFRONTATION**
        Maccabeus   *2 Mc 12:10-12
    FIDELITY through
        Levi   Mal 1:6-2:9
        Phinehas   *Sir 45:23-24
    dis**HONESTY** in
        Gibeon   Josh 9:3-15
    PROMISE in
        Isaiah   Is 54:1-17
    RECONCILIATION through
        Gentiles   Eph 2:11-22
        Phinehas   Num 25:6-18
    SECURITY in
        Isaac   Gen 26:12-31
        Israelites   Ezek 34:25-31;
                       Hos 2:16-20

PIETY in
    of **STEWARDSHIP**
        Paul   Acts 18:18-23

of **POLITICS**
    DESIRE for
        Abner   2 Sam 3:1-16
    SECURITY in
        Maccabeus   *1 Mc 8:1-32

PROMISE in
    with **FAMILY**
        Abraham   Gen 13:14-18;
                       15:1-21;
                       17:1-8
        Azariah   *Azar 1:11-22
        David   1 Sam 23:14-24:22
        God   Gen 17:15-22
        Jacob   *Sir 44:23
    of **FRIENDSHIP**
        Jonathan   1 Sam 17:1-18:5;
                       23:14-24:22
    FULFILLMENT of
        Abraham   Gal 3:15-18;
                       Heb 6:13-20
        God   Ex 6:2-9;
                       Lev 26:1-46;
                       Deut 4:15-31;
                       Ps 89:19-37
        Israelites   Deut 7:6-16
        Jeremiah   Jer 33:14-26
        Jesus   Gal 3:26-29
        Solomon   1 Kgs 8:22-53
    of **GRACE**
        Zechariah   Lk 1:57-80
    HOPE through
        Paul   Gal 4:21-26;
                       27-31
    of **JUSTICE**
        Israelites   Hos 2:16-20
    for **LEADERSHIP**
        Jehoiada   2 Kgs 11:4-20;
                       2 Chr 21:1-23:21
    of **MARRIAGE**
        Abraham   Gen 24:1-10
    of **MIRACLE**
        Moses   Ex 34:10-11
    for **ORDER**
        God   Gen 9:8-19
    for **PATIENCE**
        Abraham   Heb 6:13-20
    of **PEACE**
        Isaiah   Is 54:1-17
    REJECTION of
        God   Ps 89:38-51
    for **VICTORY**
        Moses   Ex 34:10-11

PROVIDENCE through
    of **LIFE**
        God   Gen 1:24-31
    OBEDIENCE to
        Believers   Is 56:1-8
        Israelites   Ex 15:22-27
    SACREDNESS in
        Aaron   Num 18:8-20
    WEALTH in
        Moses   Ex 34:12-28
    WITNESS to
        God   Ps 78:1-8

of **PURIFICATION**
    RECONCILIATION through
        Jesus   Heb 9:15-22

of **RECONCILIATION**
  through **DEATH**
    Jesus   Heb 9:15-22
  through **FAITH**
    Jesus   Gal 3:19-25
  FULFILLMENT of
    Jesus   Heb 9:15-22
  through **JUSTICE**
    Abimelech   Gen 21:22-34
    Abraham   Gen 21:22-34
  through **PURIFICATION**
    Jesus   Heb 9:15-22
  through **REPENTANCE**
    Israelites   Lev 26:1-46
  through **SACRIFICE**
    Jesus   Mt 26:17-30;
                   Mk 14:22-26
  WITNESS to
    Holy Spirit   Heb 10:1-18
    Jacob   Gen 31:44-55

RECONCILIATION through
  of **LIFE**
    Author   Heb 9:15-22;
                   10:19-31
    Jesus   Mt 26:17-30;
                   Mk 14:22-26
    Moses   Ex 24:1-18
  ONENESS in
    Gentiles   Eph 2:11-22
  of **PEACE**
    Gentiles   Eph 2:11-22
    Phinehas   Num 25:6-18

REJECTION of
    Isaiah   Is 33:7-16
  of **BROTHERHOOD**
    Tyre   Amos 1:9-10
  of **ELECTION**
    Israelites   Rom 9:1-5
  through **in**FIDELITY
    Israelites   Ps 106:19-23;
                   Ezek 16:53-63;
                   17:11-21
  of **FREEDOM**
    People   Jer 34:13-22
  of **LAW**
    God   Heb 8:6-13
    Israelites   Ezek 20:9-26
    Jesus   Eph 2:11-22
    Paul   Gal 4:21-26
  of **PROMISE**
    God   Ps 89:38-51
  through **dis**RESPECT
    Zechariah   Zech 11:4-14

SACREDNESS of
    Aaron   *Sir 45:6-22
    Jonathan   *1 Mc 10:15-44
  of **LAW**
    Moses   Ex 34:12-28
  of **PROVIDENCE**
    Aaron   Num 18:8-20
  in **RITE**
    Disciples   Mt 26:17-30
    Jesus   Mk 14:22-26
    Moses   Ex 34:12-28
  SIGNS of
    Israelites   Ex 31:12-17;
                   Ezek 20:9-26

SACRIFICE as
  through **MEDIATION**
    Aaron   Lev 24:5-9

SACRIFICE in
  SIGNS of
    Moses   Ex 12:1-14

of **SALVATION**
  from **DEATH**
    Noah   *Sir 44:16-18

SALVATION through
  of **GRACE**
    Jesus   Heb 10:1-18

SECURITY through
  with **FAMILY**
    David   2 Sam 23:1-7
  FULFILLMENT of
    God   2 Chr 21:1-23:21
  LOVE in
    David   1 Sam 20:1-42
  ORDER in
    Noah   Gen 9:8-19
  of **PEACE**
    Isaac   Gen 26:12-31
    Israelites   Ezek 34:25-31;
                   Hos 2:16-20
  of **POLITICS**
    Maccabeus   *1 Mc 8:1-32
  of **SERVICE**
    Jesus   Heb 7:1-28

of **SERVICE**
  SECURITY in
    Jesus   Heb 7:1-28

of **SEX**
  VIRTUE in
    Job   Job 31:1-4

SIN against
  through **DISOBEDIENCE**
    Israelites   *2 Esd 2:1-7
  through **EVIL**
    Israelites   *1 Mc 1:8-15
  REVELATION on
    Habakkuk   Hab 2:5-6a

of **STEWARDSHIP**
  PIETY in
    Paul   Acts 18:18-23

of **TRUTH**
  ACCEPTANCE of
    Jesus   2 Cor 3:12-18

VIRTUE of
  of **GRACE**
    Israelites   Hos 2:16-20
  INSTRUCTION on
    Jesus   Mt 6:25-34

WEALTH in
  of **PROVIDENCE**
    Moses   Ex 34:12-28

WISDOM in
  of **LAW**
    Sirach   *Sir 24:1-34

WITNESS to
　　Isaiah　　　　　　Is 59:1-21
　of FREEDOM
　　God　　　　　　　Is 42:5-17
　of LAW
　　Israelites　　　　Jer 31:31-34
　of NEW AGE
　　Paul　　　　　　　1 Cor 11:23-26
　of PROVIDENCE
　　God　　　　　　　Ps 78:1-8
　of RECONCILIATION
　　Holy Spirit　　　Heb 10:1-18
　　Jacob　　　　　　Gen 31:44-55

COVETOUSNESS

of GIFT
　INSTRUCTION on
　　Paul　　　　　　　1 Cor 12:27-31a;
　　　　　　　　　　　14:1-12

INSTRUCTION on
　Jesus　　　　　　　Lk 14:7-11
　of GIFT
　　Paul　　　　　　　1 Cor 12:27-31a;
　　　　　　　　　　　14:1-12
　in NEW AGE
　　Jesus　　　　　　Lk 12:22-31
　in STEWARDSHIP
　　Paul　　　　　　　1 Tim 6:6-10

JUDGMENT against
　INSTRUCTION on
　　Jesus　　　　　　Lk 12:13-15

LAW concerning
　INSTRUCTION on
　　God　　　　　　　Ex 20:1-17
　　Moses　　　　　　Deut 5:1-21;
　　　　　　　　　　　7:17-26
　　Paul　　　　　　　Rom 7:7-13;
　　　　　　　　　　　13:8-10

in NEW AGE
　INSTRUCTION on
　　Jesus　　　　　　Lk 12:22-31

PROMISE of
　by DEITY
　　Abraham　　　　Gen 26:1-11

PUNISHMENT for
　PROPHECY of
　　Habakkuk　　　Hab 2:6b-8

SIN of
　Levites　　　　　Num 16:3-11
　INSTRUCTION on
　　Jesus　　　　　　Mt 21:33-43;
　　　　　　　　　　　Mk 12:1-12;
　　　　　　　　　　　Lk 20:9-18
　　Paul　　　　　　　Rom 7:7-13;
　　　　　　　　　　　Eph 5:3-14
　PROPHECY of
　　Micah　　　　　　Mic 2:1-10

in STEWARDSHIP
　INSTRUCTION on
　　Paul　　　　　　　1 Tim 6:6-10

in TRADITION

in TRADITION (cont'd)
　　Jacob　　　　　　Gen 25:27-34

CREATION

ACCEPTANCE of
　by DEITY
　　Believers　　　　1 Tim 4:1-5
　　Jesus　　　　　　Jn 1:1-18

BLESSING of
　by DIETY
　　Psalmist　　　　Ps 115:12-18
　by FOLLOWERs
　　God　　　　　　　Ps 145:10-13a;
　　　　　　　　　　　Gen 2:1-4a

CHAOS in
　God　　　　　　　　Gen 1:1-2
　REVELATION on
　　Jeremiah　　　　Jer 4:23-26
　　John　　　　　　　Rev 8:1-6

COMPASSION for
　by DEITY
　　God　　　　　　　Ps 145:8-9

CONDEMNATION of
　INSTRUCTION on
　　Artaxerxes　　　Ezra 4:17-22
　MEDITATION on
　　Job　　　　　　　Job 3:1-10
　REVELATION on
　　God　　　　　　　Gen 3:14-19

DEATH in the
　Devil　　　　　　　*Wis 2:21-24

by DEITY
　God　　　　　　　　Ps 65:5-8;
　　　　　　　　　　　Amos 5:7-13
　ACCEPTANCE of
　　Believers　　　　1 Tim 4:1-5
　　Jesus　　　　　　Jn 1:1-18
　BLESSING of
　　Psalmist　　　　Ps 115:12-18
　COMPASSION for
　　God　　　　　　　Ps 145:8-9
　DESTRUCTION of
　　God　　　　　　　2 Pet 3:11-13
　　Job　　　　　　　Job 10:8-12
　DOUBT concerning
　　Abraham　　　　Gen 17:15-22
　　Sinners　　　　　2 Pet 3:3-7
　FAITH in
　　Believers　　　　Heb 11:1-40
　FULFILLMENT of
　　God　　　　　　　Jn 1:1-18;
　　　　　　　　　　　Rev 21:1-8
　　Jesus　　　　　　Jn 1:1-18
　as GOOD
　　God　　　　　　　1 Tim 4:1-5
　　Mankind　　　　Eccl 7:23-29;
　　　　　　　　　　　*Wis 2:21-24
　PRAISE of
　　Azariah　　　　　*Azar 1:28-68
　　David　　　　　　Ps 8:1-2;
　　　　　　　　　　　19:1-4b;
　　　　　　　　　　　65:9-13;
　　　　　　　　　　　124:6-8

PRAISE of (cont'd)
Ethan	Ps 89:5-18
Ezra	Neh 9:6
Psalmist	Ps 98:7-9; 104:24-26
Sirach	*Sir 42:15-43:33
through His SPIRIT	
Mankind	Ps 104:27-30

SUFFERING in
Job	Job 16:7-11; 30:16-23

WEALTH in
God	Deut 10:12-22

WITNESS to
David	Ps 19:1-4b
God	Ps 97:6-9

DESTRUCTION of the
by DEITY
God	2 Pet 3:11-13
Job	Job 10:8-12

PROPHECY of
Jeremiah	Jer 4:23-26

REVELATION on
Isaiah	Is 51:1-16
John	Rev 6:12-17

of DISCIPLESHIP
in MISSION
Disciples	Mt 28:16-20

DOUBT of
Abraham	Gen 17:15-22
Sinners	2 Pet 3:3-7

ENEMY of the
through FALSE BELIEF
Satan	Mt 13:36-43

FAITH in the
Believers	Heb 11:1-40

of FAMILY
in the ENVIRONMENT
Lot	Gen 19:30-38
Noah	Gen 9:8-19

INSTRUCTION on
Paul	Gal 4:27-31

REVELATION on
Israel	Gen 35:1-15

TRADITION of
Abraham	Gen 25:1-6
Adam	Gen 4:25-26; 5:1-28
Cain	Gen 4:17-19; 20-24
Isaac	Gen 25:19-26
Ishmael	Gen 25:12-18
Jacob	Gen 29:31-30:24
Joseph	Gen 41:1-57
Moses	Ex 2:16-23a
Nahor	Gen 22:20-24
Nephilim	Gen 6:1-4
Tamar	Gen 38:24-30

FULFILLMENT of
God	Gen 2:1-4a
Israelites	Neh 6:15-16
Solomon	2 Chr 8:1-18

by DEITY
God	Jn 1:1-18;

by DEITY (cont'd)
God	Rev 21:1-8
Jesus	Jn 1:1-18

INSTRUCTION on
Israelites	Ex 39:32-43

PROPHECY of
Jesus	Lk 2:1-20
Prophet	Mt 1:18-25
Samson	Judg 13:24-25

REVELATION on
Zerubbabel	Zech 4:6b-10a

of Sanctuary
Israelites	Ezra 6:13-18

GOOD in
by DEITY
God	1 Tim 4:1-5
Mankind	Eccl 7:23-29; *Wis 2:21-24

REVELATION on
Egyptians	Ezek 31:1-9

GRATITUDE for
by FOLLOWERs
God	Ps 145:10-13a

GRIEF in the
MEDITATION on
Job	Job 3:1-10

HOPE in the
INSTRUCTION on
Paul	Rom 8:14-25

SCRIPTURES on
Jeremiah	Jer 30:1-3

HUMILITY of the
before DEITY
David	Ps 8:3-8
God	Is 2:12-17

IDOLATRY in the
through FALSE BELIEF
Nebuchadnezzar	Dan 3:1-6

IGNORANCE
INSTRUCTION on
Isaiah	Is 40:12-31

REVELATION on
Israelites	Is 49:1-26

INSTRUCTION on
of FAMILY
Paul	Gal 4:27-31

of LIFE
Angel	Lk 2:1-20
Gabriel	Lk 1:5-25; 26-38
God	Gen 1:20-23; 24-31; 8:13-22; 9:1-7
Jesus	Jn 3:1-21
Manoah	Judg 13:2-7
Mary	Lk 1:26-38

of MIRACLE
Joseph	Mt 1:18-25
Joshua	Josh 10:16-27

of SANCTUARY
Cyrus	2 Chr 36:1-23; Ezra 1:2-4

of the SANCTUARY (cont'd)
Israelites   25-28;
                    29;
                    38:1-7;
                    8;
                    9-20;
                    39:1;
                    2-7;
                    8-21;
                    22-26;
                    27-31
Moses   Ex 25:10-22;
                    23-30;
                    31-40;
                    26:1-14;
                    15-30;
                    31-37;
                    27:1-8;
                    9-19;
                    20-21;
                    28:1-5;
                    6-12;
                    13-30;
                    31-35;
                    36-39;
                    40-43;
                    30:1-10;
                    17-21;
                    Lev 24:1-4
INSTRUCTION on
Cyrus   2 Chr 36:1-23;
                    Ezra 1:2-4
Darius   Ezra 6:1-12
David   1 Chr 22:2-19;
                    28:1-29:30
Hezekiah   2 Chr 29:1-36
Jesus   Mt 16:13-20
Joash   2 Kgs 12:4-16
Moses   Ex 35:4-29
Paul   1 Cor 3:10-17;
                    1 Tim 4:1-5
Solomon   2 Chr 2:1-4:22
Tattenai   Ezra 5:6-17
PROPHECY of
Haggai   Ezra 5:1-2;
                    Hag 1:1-11
Jeremiah   Jer 31:38-40
Zechariah   Ezra 5:1-2
REVELATION on
Ezekiel   Ezek 45:1-9
Moses   Ex 25:1-9;
                    40:1-33
Zechariah   Zech 6:9-15
for WORSHIP
Israelites   Ezra 3:1-3a;
                    7-9;
                    10-11;
                    5:1-2;
                    Hag 1:12-14
Levites   2 Chr 34:1 35:27

SERVICE of the
to DEITY
God   Ps 104:1-4
Israelites   Is 44:6-8;
                    21-23
in WORSHIP
Jeroboam   1 Kgs 12:25-33

by SPIRIT
of DEITY

of DEITY (cont'd)
Mankind   Ps 104:27-30
SCRIPTURES on
Adam   1 Cor 15:42-50

SUFFERING in the
by DEITY
Job   Job 16:7-11;
                    30:16-23

TRADITION of
of FAMILY
Abraham   Gen 25:1-6
Adam   Gen 4:25-26;
                    5:1-28
Cain   Gen 4:17-19;
                    20-24
Isaac   Gen 25:19-26
Ishmael   Gen 25:12-18
Jacob   Gen 29:31-30:24
Joseph   Gen 41:1-57
Moses   Ex 2:16-23a
Nahor   Gen 22:20-24
Nephilim   Gen 6:1-4
Tamar   Gen 38:24-30
of LIFE
Esau   Gen 25:19-26
Jacob   Gen 25:19-26
Jesus   Lk 2:1-20;
                    Jn 1:1-18
John the Baptist   Lk 1:57-80
Noah   Gen 5:29-32
Samson   Judg 13:24-25
of TRADITION
with SACREDNESS
Esther   Esth 9:29-32
God   Gen 2:1-4a;
                    Ex 20:1-17
Israelites   Esth 9:16-19
Mordecai   Esth 9:20-28

VICTORY in the
REVELATION on
Isaiah   Is 54:1-17

VIOLENCE in the
REVELATION on
John   Rev 19:11-16

WEALTH in the
Solomon   1 Kgs 7:1-12
by DEITY
God   Deut 10:12-22

reveals WILL
God   Rev 4:1-11
of DEITY
Believers   Jn 1:1-18
God   Is 40:12-31

WISDOM in the
by DEITY
God   Ps 104:24-26;
                    136:4-9;
                    Prov 3:1-35;
                    8:22-31;
                    Jer 10:1-16;
                    51:1-64
Job   Job 9:8-13

by **DEITY** (cont'd)
Sirach   *Sir 1:1-10;
  17:1-14

INSTRUCTION on
Solomon   Prov 23:15-24:22
REVELATION on
Job   Job 38:8-11

WITNESS to the
Angel   Judg 13:2-7
by **DEITY**
David   Ps 19:1-4b
God   Ps 97:6-9
SCRIPTURES on
Jeremiah   Jer 36:1-7;
  27-32

DEATH

TIME of

Aaron	Num 20:22-29
Abdon	Judg 12:13-15
Abijah	2 Chr 14:1-16:14
Abijam	1 Kgs 15:1-8
Abimelech	Judg 9:50-55
Abraham	Gen 25:7-11
Adonijah	1 Kgs 2:13-25
Ahab	1 Kgs 16:29-34
Ahaz	2 Kgs 16:10-20;
	2 Chr 26:1-28:27
Ahaziah	2 Kgs 9:14-29;
	2 Chr 21:1-23:21
Alexander	*1 Mc 1:1-7
Amaziah	2 Kgs 13:17-22;
	2 Chr 25:1-28
Amon	2 Kgs 21:19-26
Antiochus	*1 Mc 6:1-17
Asa	1 Kgs 15:23-24;
	2 Chr 14:1-16:14
Athaliah	2 Kgs 11:4-20;
	2 Chr 21:1-23:21
Baasha	1 Kgs 15:33-16:7
Belshazzar	Dan 5:30-31
David	1 Kgs 2:5-12
Eglon	Judg 3:24-25
Egyptians	Ex 14:23-31
Elah	1 Kgs 16:8-14
Eleazar	Josh 24:33
Eli	1 Sam 4:1b-22
Elimelech	Ruth 1:1-18
Elisha	2 Kgs 13:20-21
Elon	Judg 12:11-12
Gedaliah	2 Kgs 25:23-26
Gideon	Judg 8:29-32
Herod	Mt 2:19-23;
	Acts 12:1-25
Hezekiah	2 Kgs 20:12-21
Ibzan	Judg 12:8-10
Isaac	Gen 35:27-29
Ishbosheth	2 Sam 4:1-12
Jacob	Gen 49:29-33
Jair	Judg 10:3-5
Jason	*2 Mc 5:5-10
Jehoahaz	2 Kgs 13:1-9;
	23:31-35
Jehoash	2 Kgs 13:10-13
Jehoiada	2 Chr 24:1-27
Jehoiakim	2 Kgs 23:36-24:7

TIME of (cont'd)

Jehoram	2 Chr 21:1-23:21
Jehoshaphat	1 Kgs 22:41-50;
	2 Chr 21:1-23:21
Jehu	2 Kgs 10:34-36
Jephthah	Judg 12:1-7
Jeroboam	1 Kgs 14:19-20;
	2 Chr 13:1-22
Jesus	Mk 15:33-41;
	Lk 23:46-49
Jezebel	2 Kgs 9:30-37
Joab	1 Kgs 2:28-35
Joash	2 Kgs 12:19-21
Job	Job 42:10-17
John the Baptist	Mt 14:1-12
Jonathan	1 Sam 31:1-13;
	*1 Mc 13:12-24
Joram	2 Kgs 9:14-29
Joseph	Gen 50:22-26
Joshua	Josh 24:29-31
Josiah	2 Kgs 23:25b-30
Jotham	2 Kgs 15:32-38
Judas	Mt 27:3-10
Judith	*Jdt 16:21-25
Macron	*2 Mc 10:10-13
Manasseh	2 Kgs 21:1-18
Mattathias	*1 Mc 2:49-70
Miriam	Num 20:1
Moses	Deut 34:1-12
Naboth	1 Kgs 21:13-16
Noah	Gen 9:28-29
Omri	1 Kgs 16:23-28
Onias	*2 Mc 4:30-38
Othniel	Judg 3:7-11
Pekah	2 Kgs 15:27-31
Pekahiah	2 Kgs 15:23-26
Ptolemy	*1 Mc 11:1-19
Rachel	Gen 35:16-20
Rehoboam	1 Kgs 14:29-31;
	2 Chr 10:1-12:16
Samson	Judg 16:23-31
Samuel	1 Sam 25:1-44
Saul	1 Sam 31:1-13
Shallum	2 Kgs 15:13-15
Sheba	2 Sam 20:1-26
Shimei	1 Kgs 2:36-46
Sisera	Judg 4:17-22;
	5:23-27
Solomon	1 Kgs 11:41-43
Stephen	Acts 6:8-8:3
Tibni	1 Kgs 16:15-22
Tobiah	*Tb 14:1-15
Tobit	*Tb 14:1-15
Tola	Judg 10:1-2
Uzziah	2 Chr 26:1-28:27
Zechariah	2 Kgs 15:8-12
Zimri	1 Kgs 16:15-22

AUTHORITY over
by **MESSIANIC FIGURE**
Lazarus   Jn 11:1-57
Satan   Heb 2:5-18
REVELATION of
John   Rev 6:7-8

BELIEF concerning
MEDITATION on
Job   Job 7:7-11

COMPULSION regarding
Darius   Dan 6:10-15

PROPHECY concerning (cont'd)

Jeremiah	Jer 7:29-8:3
Jeroboam	Amos 7:10-17
Jesus	Mt 16:21-28;
	Mk 8:31-33;
	10:32-34;
	Lk 5:33-35;
	9:18-22;
	13:31-33;
	Jn 12:1-8;
	13:31-35:21:15-23
Moses	Ex 11:1-10
Shallum	Jer 22:10-12
Tyre	Ezek 26:7-14
Zedekiah	Jer 34:1-7

PROPHECY of
  as **PUNISHMENT**

Ahab	1 Kgs 21:17-29
Ahijah	1 Kgs 14:1-18
Amaziah	Amos 7:10-17
Coniah	Jer 22:24-30
Edomites	Obad 1:5-9
Elijah	2 Kgs 1:1-18
Ephraimites	Hos 7:13-16;
	9:10-17
Isaiah	Is 3:16-4:1
Israelites	Ezek 16:35-43;
	Amos 2:13-16;
	5:1-3;
	6:8-11
Jehoiakim	Jer 22:13-19
Jeremiah	Jer 16:1-13;
	20:1-6;
	21:1-10;
	29:1-23;
	42:7-22;
	43:8-13;
	44:20-28
Jezebei	Rev 2:18-29
Judahites	Jer 9:10-22;
	42:7-22;
	44:1-14
Obadiah	Obad 1:17-21
Samaria	Hos 13:15-16
Samuel	1 Sam 28:3-25
Shebna	Is 22:15-25

  as **QUALITY OF LIFE**

Isaiah	Is 40:1-11

resulting from **SIN**

Jeremiah	Jer 31:29-30

PROVIDENCE in

Elihu	Job 34:16-20
God	1 Sam 2:11-26
Jesus	Lk 23:46-49
Psalmist	Ps 88:10-12
Solomon	*Wis 18:5-19

  of **MESSIANIC FIGURE**

Jesus	Mt 27:45-56

PROPHECY of

Jesus	Jn 12:1-8

as **PUNISHMENT**

Andronicus	*2 Mc 4:30-38
Antiochus	*1 Mc 1:54-61
Criminals	Lk 23:27-32
Cyrus	*Bel 1:40-42
Elders	*Susa 1:60-64
Ephraimites	Hos 13:1-3
Eunuchs	Esth 2:19-23

as **PUNISHMENT** (cont'd)

Gideon	Judg 8:18-21
Haman	Esth 7:1-10
Israelites	Deut 1:19-46;
	Josh 7:6-26
Joshua	Josh 10:16-27
Menelaus	*2 Mc 13:3-8
Moses	Ex 21:12-17;
	18-32;
	22:18-20;
	21-31;
	Lev 24:10-23
Officials	Dan 6:24
Prophet	1 Kgs 13:1-34
Sennacherib	Is 37:36-38
Shadrach	Dan 3:19-23

  from **DEITY**

Ahaziah	2 Chr 21:1-23:2?
David	1 Chr 21:1-22:1;
	Ps 55:15-19
Elihu	Job 36:5-15
God	1 Sam 25:1-44;
	Ps 55:23
Israelites	Num 11:31-35;
	16:36-50;
	21:4-9;
	2 Sam 24:1-25;
	Ps 78:21-31;
	*1 Esd 1:46-58
Judahites	2 Chr 26:1-28:2?
Onan	Gen 38:1-11
Solomon	1 Kgs 1:41-53

  for **FALSE BELIEF**

Ahaziah	2 Kgs 1:1-18
Ananias	Acts 4:32-5:10
Cyrus	*Bel 1:8-9;
	21-22
Darius	Dan 6:4-9
Elijah	1 Kgs 18:1-46
False Prophet	Rev 19:17-21
God	Num 3:1-4;
	25:1-5
Hananiah	Jer 28:1-17
Jews	*2 Mc 12:38-45
John	1 Jn 3:11-18
Moses	Ex 21:33-22:17;
	Lev 20:1-27;
	Deut 12:32-13:18
Sapphira	Acts 4:32-5:10
Sinners	2 Pet 2:10b-16

  of **FOLLOWERs**

Rulers	Acts 6:8-8:3

INSTRUCTION on

Angel	*2 Esd 7:75-87
Antiochus	*1 Mc 1:41-53
Darius	Dan 6:24;
	*1 Esd 6:27-34
God	Ps 82:2-7
Israelites	Judg 20:12-17
Jesus	Mt 15:3-9;
	Mk 7:1-23
Moses	Ex 32:25-29;
	35:1-3;
	Lev 20:1-27;
	Deut 16:21-17:7;
	8-13;
	21:18-21;
	22-23;
	23:15-25:19;
	28:15-68
Nebuchadnezzar	Dan 3:1-6;

as **QUALITY OF LIFE** (cont'd)	
Moses	Ps 90:1-12
Ungodly men	*Wis 1:16-2:5
SIGNS of	
Elijah	2 Kgs 2:1-18
Uzzah	1 Chr 13:1-14
by **DEITY**	
Egyptians	Ex 12:29-32
Uzzah	2 Sam 6:1-23
through **FALSE BELIEF**	
Israelites	1 Sam 6:1-7:1
Moses	Deut 12:32-13:18
PROPHECY of	
Ezekiel	Ezek 24:15-24
Joseph	Gen 40:1-23
REVELATION on	
Israelites	Ezek 15:1-8
John	Rev 5:1-14;
	8-9;
	10-11;
	14:17-20
resulting from **SIN**	
Aaron	Num 18:1-7
Jesus	Rom 5:6-11
Man	Gen 7:1-24
Moses	Lev 20:1-27
INSTRUCTION on	
James	Jas 1:13-15
Jesus	Jn 8:21-59
Moses	Ex 19:9-15;
	Deut 22:13-30
Paul	Rom 5:12-21;
	6:1-14;
	15-23;
	7:7-13;
	8:5-13;
	1 Cor 15:51-58
Peter	1 Pet 2:21-25
Solomon	Prov 12:1-28
PROPHECY of	
Jeremiah	Jer 31:29-30
REVELATION on	
Ezekiel	Ezek 18:1-4
	10-13;
	14-20;
	21-24;
	25-29;
	33:1-9;
	10-20
Moses	Num 1:47-54
to **SIN**	
through **MESSIANIC FIGURE**	
Believers	Gal 5:22-24
STEWARDSHIP concerning	
PROPHECY of	
Isaiah	2 Kgs 20:1-11
TRADITION concerning	
PROVIDENCE in	
Solomon	*Wis 18:5-19
as **PUNISHMENT**	
Pharisees	Jn 7:53-8:11
TRUTH concerning	
INSTRUCTION on	
Jesus	1 Pet 4:1-6
VIRTUE in	
Jesus	1 Pet 3:18-22

DEFEAT	
of **AUTHORITY**	
Kings	Hos 7:3-7
REVELATION of	
Babylonians	Rev 18:1-3
Daniel	Dan 11:5-20
through **unBELIEF**	
Judahites	Lam 4:1-22
CONFRONTATION with	
Abimelech	Judg 9:50-55
Ahab	1 Kgs 22:1-40;
	2 Chr 17:1-20:37
Ahaz	2 Chr 26:1-28:27
Amaziah	2 Kgs 14:8-14
Antiochus	*1 Mc 6:1-17;
	*2 Mc 9:1-4
Azariah	*1 Mc 5:55-62
Benjaminites	Judg 20:37-44
Demetrius	*1 Mc 14:1-3
Gaal	Judg 9:34-41
Goliath	1 Sam 17:1-18:5
Hoshea	2 Kgs 17:1-6
Israelites	Josh 7:1-5;
	Judg 20:19-23;
	24-28;
	1 Sam 4:1b-22;
	2 Kgs 10:32-33;
	13:1-9;
	15:27-31;
	18:9-12;
	1 Chr 10:1-14;
	2 Chr 10:1-12:16;
	Ps 79:1-4
Jason	*2 Mc 5:5-10
Jeconiah	*1 Esd 1:34-36
Jehoahaz	2 Chr 36:1-23
Jehoiakim	2 Kgs 24:8-17
Jehoram	2 Kgs 8:16-24;
	2 Chr 21:1-23:21
Jeroboam	2 Chr 13:1-22
Joash	2 Chr 24:1-27
Jonathan	*1 Mc 12:39-53
Josiah	2 Chr 34:1-35:27
Judahites	Josh 15:20-63;
	2 Kgs 18:13-16;
	2 Chr 25:1-28;
	Jer 39:1-14;
	52:4-27
Maccabeus	*1 Mc 6:18-54
Nineveh	Nah 2:6-10
Rehoboam	1 Kgs 14:25-28
Samson	Judg 16:16-22
Saul	1 Sam 31:1-13
Tibni	1 Kgs 16:15-22
Uzziah	*Jdt 7:23-32
Zedekiah	2 Kgs 24:18-25:7
Zimri	1 Kgs 16:15-22
caused by **DEITY**	
David	Ps 89:38-51
Israelites	Ps 44:9-16
Solomon	1 Kgs 8:22-53;
	2 Chr 5:1-7:10
through **FALSE BELIEF**	
Prophets	Rev 19:17-21
INSTRUCTION on	
Moses	Deut 28:15-68
PROPHECY of	
Ammonites	Jer 49:1-6
Assyrians	Is 31:4-9

LEADERSHIP through (cont'd)	
Aaron	Ex 4:10-16
David	2 Sam 22:1-51;
	1 Chr 28:1-29:30;
	Ps 18:43-45
Gideon	Judg 8:22-23
God	Ps 47:5-9;
	66:5-7;
	93:1-2;
	103:19-22;
	Is 40:1-11;
	51:1-16;
	Rev 11:15-19;
	19:6-10
Israelites	Ex 15:1-18;
	Ps 77:11-20;
	Jer 31:31-34
Jesus	Mt 28:16-20;
	Acts 2:14-36;
	Eph 1:15-2:10;
	Phil 2:5-11
Judah	Judg 1:1-21
King	Prov 21:1-31
Maccabeus	*2 Mc 15:6-10
Mankind	Jer 32:26-44;
	Zech 14:1-21
Moses	Ex 32:30-35
Paul	Gal 1:1-5
Solomon	Ps 72:8-14
over **LIFE**	
Bildad	Job 25:1-6
David	Ps 29:3-9
Elihu	Job 33:8-12;
	34:10-15
Eliphaz	Job 5:8-17
Ezra	*2 Esd 6:35-59
God	Job 26:5-14;
	Ps 24:1-2;
	50:7-15;
	66:1-4;
	90:1-12;
	Is 13:1-22;
	Amos 4:13;
	9:5-6;
	Hab 3:3-15;
	Mt 22:23-33;
	Mk 12:18-27;
	Lk 20:27-40
Hannah	1 Sam 2:1-10
Job	Job 9:1-7;
	8-13;
	12:7-12;
	13-25
Judith	*Jdt 16:1-17
Mankind	Ps 8:3-8
Sirach	*Sir 17:1-14;
	33:7-15
Solomon	*Wis 16:1-14
LOVE in	
Jesus	Jn 5:19-47
MIRACLE by	
God	Mic 1:2-4;
	Nah 1:1-9;
	2 Cor 4:7-12
Jesus	Lk 11:14-23
ONENESS with	
God	Deut 6:4-19;
	Is 44:6-8;
	21-23;
	46:1-13;

ONENESS with (cont'd)	
God	Jn 1:1-18
Jesus	Jn 1:1-18;
	5:19-47;
	14:1-14;
	Col 1:18-20
ORDER through	
David	Ps 19:1-4b
Ezra	*2 Esd 8:4-36
God	Ps 19:4c-6;
	33:4-9;
	50:1-6;
	65:5-8;
	74:12-17;
	77:11-20;
	89:5-18;
	93:3-4;
	95:1-7c;
	97:1-5;
	104:1-4;
	5-9;
	135:5-7;
	147:12-20
Jeremiah	*Jer 6:60-73
Manasseh	*Mana 1:1-5
Mankind	Ps 8:3-8
Sirach	*Sir 16:24-30:
	17:15-32;
	18:1-14;
	33:7-15;
	39:17-27;
	42:15-43:33
Solomon	*Wis 7:15-8:1;
	9:1-18;
	11:21-12:2;
	13:1-9
PATIENCE with	
Isaiah	Is 40:12-31
involved in **POLITICS**	
David	Ps 108:6-13;
	110:1-4
God	Ps 2:4-6;
	33:10-12;
	60:6-8;
	76:10-12;
	113:2-4
Israelites	Ps 68:28-35
Solomon	*Wis 6:1-11;
	12:12-18
PRAISE of	
Crowds	Mt 9:1-8;
	Mk 2:1-12;
	Lk 5:17-26
Darius	Dan 6:25-27
David	Ps 8:1-2;
	9;
	68:28-35
Elihu	Job 36:26-33
Israelites	Mal 1:2-5
Mankind	Ps 22:27-31
Psalmist	Ps 46:8-11;
	48:1-3;
	92:5-11;
	99:1-3;
	106:1-5
Queen of Sheba	2 Chr 9:1-31
Sirach	*Sir 42:15-43:33
Zedekiah	Jer 32:16-25
PURIFICATION through	
Holy Spirit	Mt 3:1-12;
	Mk 1:2-8;

PURIFICATION through (cont'd)
Holy Spirit   Lk 3:15-17;
                           Acts 1:1-5
REJECTION of
Ephraimites   Hos 7:3-7
Saul   1 Sam 15:1-35
VICTORY through
God   Gen 18:9-15;
                           Ps 24:7-10;
                           48:9-14;
                           60:6-8;
                           76:4-6;
                           Jer 32:16-25;
                           Mt 19:23-26;
                           Mk 10:23-27;
                           Lk 1:26-38
Isaiah   Is 63:1-6
Jesus   Lk 18:18-27
Paul   Phil 4:10-20
WEALTH by
God   Deut 10:12-22;
                           Job 41:1-12;
                           Ps 24:1-2;
                           50:7-15;
                           Rom 11:33-36;
                           1 Cor 11:23-26
WISDOM in
Baruch   *Bar 3:24-37
Elihu   Job 36:5-15
God   Job 26:5-14;
                           Ps 147:1-6;
                           Prov 22:1-16
Job   Job 12:13-25
WITNESS to
David   Ps 9:9-12
God   Deut 3:23-29;
                           Is 44:6-8;
                           21-23
Jesus   Jn 8:21-59;
                           12:44-50
Psalmist   Ps 71:1-21

BELIEF in
ACCEPTANCE of
Believers   Heb 11:1-40
David   Ps 6:8-10
Israelites   Zech 13:7-9
is BLESSING
Israelites   Ps 84:10-12
CONDEMNATION of
Job   Job 13:13-19
through DISCIPLESHIP
Jesus   Jn 12:44-50
DOUBT concerning
Israelites   Rom 11:7-24
through FEAR
Israelites   Ex 14:23-31
through HOPE
David   Ps 62:5-7
Jeremiah   Jer 17:13
brings JOY
Believers   Prov 16:1-33;
                           Rom 15:1-13
Psalmist   Ps 33:20-22
JUSTICE in
Israelites   Ezek 18:25-29;
                           33:10-20
through MIRACLE
Israelites   Ex 4:27-31;
                           Ps 78:40-55
Joshua   Josh 10:1-15

through MIRACLE (cont'd)
People   Lk 1:57-80
results in PRAISE
Followers   Ps 106:6-12
REJECTION of
Israelites   Is 49:1-26;
                           Ezek 9:1-11
REWARD of
Believers   Heb 11:1-40
VICTORY through
David   Ps 56:6b-9;
                           59:9-10
Jeremiah   Jer 20:7-18
Jesus   1 Jn 4:19-5:5

unBELIEF in
ALIENATION through
Israelites   Rom 11:25-32
SACREDNESS of
Moses   Num 20:2-13

BLASPHEMY against
PRAYER concerning
Priest   *1 Mc 7:36-38
PUNISHMENT for
Antiochus   *2 Mc 9:5-29
through disRESPECT
Priests   Mal 1:6-2:9
SIGNS of
Israelites   Neh 9:16-18
SIN of
Adversaries   Ps 74:3-9
Israelites   Amos 2:6-8
Mankind   Ps 10:3-11
through unTRUTH
Mankind   Rev 16:8-9;
                           10-11;
                           17-21

BLESSING of
Midwives   Ex 1:15-22
COMPULSION of
Balaam   Num 23:13-26
in CREATION
Psalmist   Ps 115:12-18
DESIRE for
Bethelites   Zech 7:1-3
Job   Job 29:1-6
in ELECTION
God   Ps 65:1-4
is ETERNAL
David   Ps 41:13;
                           145:1-3
Ethan   Ps 89:52
God   Ps 30:1-5;
                           133:1-3
Israelites   Ps 132:11-18
King   Ps 45:2-9
Psalmist   Ps 113:2-4
through FIDELITY
Believers   Ps 40:4-5
Caleb   Josh 14:6-15
David   Ps 63:1-8
God   Ps 24:3-6;
                           37:23-40
Isaiah   Is 63:7-64:12
Job   Job 1:20-21
Mankind   Ps 1:1-3;
                           25:8-15
Psalmist   Ps 119:1-8
through HONESTY

through **LOVE**
Jesus   Jn 14:27-31
through **OBEDIENCE**
Psalmist   Ps 119:9-16;
                               105-112
ONENESS in
Believers   1 Jn 4:13-18
REPENTANCE through
Israelites   Jer 3:21-4:4
SACRIFICE in
Jephthah   Judg 11:29-33
Jonah   Jon 1:1-17
SERVICE to
Isaiah   Is 19:18-25
as **WITNESS**
Israelites   Josh 24:16-24

COMPASSION of
David   2 Sam 12:1-31
Israelites   Judg 2:11-19
for **CREATION**
God   Ps 145:8-9
DESIRE for
Asaph   Ps 77:1-10
God   Mic 6:6-8
Job   Job 14:13-17
FIDELITY of
Israelites   Neh 9:26-31;
                               Ps 106:40-46
Psalmist   Ps 119:73-80
in **JUDGMENT**
Solomon   *Wis 12:3-11
as **MOTIVATION**
God   Gen 2:18-20
PRAYER for
Asaph   Ps 83:1
Daniel   Dan 2:14-19
David   Ps 4:1;
                               6:1-5;
                               28:1-5;
                               30:6-10;
                               38:1-2
Ethan   Ps 89:38-51
Ezekiel   Ezek 4:12-15
Isaiah   Is 63:7-64:12
Israelites   Jer 14:19-22
Jeremiah   Jer 11:18-12:6;
                               15:10-21
Job   Job 10:8-12
Joel   Joel 1:2-20
Judahites   Lam 5:1-22
Maccabeus   *2 Mc 8:1-7;
                               10:1-9
Moses   Ps 90:13-17
Psalmist   Ps 102:12-22;
                               106:1-5;
                               123:3-4
Sirach   *Sir 36:1-10;
                               11-17
in **PROVIDENCE**
God   Gen 3:20-24;
                               Ps 103:6-13
Jonah   Jon 4:1-11
Solomon   *Wis 18:20-25
as **QUALITY OF LIFE**
God   Ex 22:21-31
RECONCILIATION through
Followers   Ps 80:4-7
God   Mic 7:7-20
Israelites   Deut 30:1-10

RESPECT for
David   Ps 69:13-21
SALVATION through
Psalmist   Ps 85:4-7
SIGNS of
Cain   Gen 4:1-16
over **SIN**
Sirach   *Sir 18:1-14
in **STEWARDSHIP**
Solomon   Ps 72:8-14
as **VIRTUE**
Abraham   Gen 18:23-33

COMPELS
action through **ANGER**
Babylonians   Rev 16:17-21
BLESSING
Balaam   Num 23:13-26

COMPULSION of
GRACE through
Lot   Gen 19:12-29
in **JOY**
Israelites   Neh 12:43

CONDEMNATION by
DESIRE for
Habakkuk   Hab 1:12-17
Israel   Ex 5:15-21
for in**FIDELITY**
Ephraimites   Hos 7:13-16
Isaiah   Is 17:9-11

for dis**HONESTY**
God   Prov 12:1-28
Job   Job 13:1-12
as **JUDGMENT**
Chaldeans   Hab 1:5-11
Egyptians   Ezek 29:9b-16
Ephraimites   Hos 9:10-17;
                               13:12-14
God   Ps 50:16-21
Israelites   Is 9:8-10:4;
                               Hos 6:7-9;
                               10:9-15;
                               Amos 6:8-11
Man   Ex 21:33-22:17
Satan   Zech 3:1-10
PRAYER for
David   Ps 109:6-20;
                               21-31
Nehemiah   Neh 4:4-5
as **PUNISHMENT**
Israelites   Is 9:8-10:4
as **QUALITY OF LIFE**
Judahites   Jer 9:2-9
for dis**RESPECT**
Job   Job 17:6-10
of **RITE**
Israelites   Amos 5:21-25
SALVATION from
Jesus   Rom 5:6-11
for **SIN**
Believer   Heb 10:19-31;
                               1 Pet 3:8-12
God   Prov 3:1-35;
                               6:16-19;
                               12:1-28;
                               14:1-35;

for **SIN** (cont'd)

God	Jn 3:31-36; 1 Thes 4:1-12; 2 Thes 2:11-12
Israelites	1 Sam 12:1-25; Neh 9:26-31; Ezek 16:15-34
Job	Job 19:1-6
Mankind	1 Sam 2:11-26; 2 Sam 22:1-51; Ps 1:4-6; 18:25-30
Zophar	Job 20:4-29

CONFRONTATION with
  ACCEPTANCE in

Moses	Ex 33:7-11; Num 12:4-10; Deut 34:1-12

  COURAGE in

Joshua	Josh 11:1-15

  after **DEATH**

Job	Job 19:25-29
Mankind	Ex 33:12-23

  through **DISOBEDIENCE**

Israelites	Num 16:16-24

  FEAR of

Adam	Gen 3:9-13

  GOOD of

Satan	Job 1:6-8; 2:1-3

  GRACE of

Jesus	Mt 5:3-12

  in **HUMILITY**

Job	Job 40:3-5; 42:1-6

  MIRACLE of

Balaam	Num 22:22-35
Ezekiel	Ezek 3:12-15
Samaritans	2 Kgs 7:3-20

  in **REPENTANCE**

Job	Job 42:1-6

  REVENGE of

Moses	Num 31:1-6

  SUFFERING in

David	Ps 9:13-14

  WITNESS to

Israelites	Num 14:11-24; Deut 5:1-21
Moses	Num 12:4-10; Deut 34:1-12

COURAGE before
  DESIRE for

Job	Job 13:20-27

  through **FIDELITY**

Jehoshaphat	2 Chr 17:1-20:37

  through **PRESENCE**

Believers	Acts 4:23-31
Ezra	Ezra 7:27-28
Israelites	Hag 1:15b-2:9
Joshua	Josh 1:1-9

Deity's CREATION

God	Ps 65:5-8; Amos 5:7-13

  ACCEPTANCE of

Believers	1 Tim 4:1-5
Jesus	Jn 1:1-18

  BLESSING in

Psalmist	Ps 115:12-18

COMPASSION for

God	Ps 145:8-9

DESTRUCTION of

God	2 Pet 3:11-13
Job	Job 10:8-12

DOUBT concerning

Abraham	Gen 17:15-22
Sinners	2 Pet 3:3-7

FAITH in

Believers	Heb 11:1-40

FULFILLMENT of

God	Jn 1:1-18; Rev 21:1-8
Jesus	Jn 1:1-18

GOOD in

God	1 Tim 4:1-5
Mankind	Eccl 7:23-29; *Wis 2:21-24

HUMILITY before

David	Ps 8:3-8
God	Is 2:12-17

JOY in

God	1 Chr 15:1-16:43; Ps 96:10-13; 97:1-5

LIFE in

David	Ps 139:13-18
God	Ps 33:4-9; 100:1-3; 146:5-7b; Is 42:5-17; 44:24-45:13; 66:1-16; Amos 4:13; Zech 12:1-13:6; Jn 1:1-18; Heb 3:1-6a
Jesus	Jn 1:1-18
Job	Job 10:8-12
Mankind	Ex 3:11-22
Mary	Mt 1:18-25
Psalmist	Ps 119:73-80
Sirach	*Sir 17:1-14

LOVE in

Solomon	*Wis 11:21-12:2

MIRACLE in

God	Is 50:1-11

ORDER in

God	Job 39:9-12; Ps 24:1-2; 3-6; 33:4-9; 89:5-18; 90:1-12; 102:23-28; 104:5-9; 19-23; 121:2-8; 135:5-7; 136:4-9; Is 42:5-17; 44:24-45:13; Jer 5:20-25; Zech 10:1-2; Jn 1:1-18; Acts 17:16-34; 2 Pet 3:3-7
Israelites	Is 45:14-25

PRAISE of

Azariah	*Azar 1:28-68
David	Ps 8:1-2;

PRAISE of (cont'd)
David 19:1-4b; 65:9-13; 124:6-8
Ethan Ps 89:5-18
Ezra Neh 9:6
Psalmist Ps 98:7-9; 104:24-26
Sirach *Sir 42:15-43:33
PRUDENCE in
God Prov 16:1-33
SERVICE of
God Ps 104:1-4
Israelites Is 44:6-8; 21-23
SPIRIT in
Mankind Ps 104:27-30
SUFFERING in
Job Job 16:7-11; 30:16-23

WEALTH in
God Deut 10:12-22
WISDOM in
God Ps 104:24-26; 136:4-9; Prov 3:1-35; 8:22-31; Jer 10:1-16; 51:1-64
Job Job 9:8-13
Sirach *Sir 1:1-10; 17:1-14

WITNESS to
David Ps 19:1-4b
God Ps 97:6-9

DEFEAT caused by
David Ps 89:38-51
Israelites Ps 44:9-16
Solomon 1 Kgs 8:22-53; 2 Chr 5:1-7:10
PRAYER for
Job Job 7:17-21
PROVIDENCE in
Egyptians Ex 14:23-31
Israelites Deut 28:15-68; Judg 3:12-14; Ps 106:40-46
Psalmist Ps 44:9-16
as PUNISHMENT
Israelites Num 14:39-45

DESIRE for
to allow TEMPTATION
Satan Job 1:9-12; 2:4-6
for WITNESS
God Hos 6:4-6

DESIRE of
for FAITH
God Hos 6:4-6
for HUMILITY
God Ps 51:13-17; Mic 6:6-8
for JOY
Believers Eccl 3:9-15
for JUSTICE
God Mic 6:6-8
Israelites Amos 5:21-25
for KILLING

for KILLING (cont'd)
Moses Ex 4:24-26
for LOVE
God Hos 6:4-6
for OBEDIENCE
God Ps 53:1-3
Psalmist Ps 119:17-24
Samuel 1 Sam 15:1-35
for PEACE
God Is 27:2-6
for PURIFICATION
Jesus Mt 3:13-17
for REPENTANCE
Israelites Ezek 33:10-20
Mankind 2 Pet 3:8-10
for SERVICE
David Ps 35:1-3
God Mic 6:6-8

DESTRUCTION by
DESIRE for
Israelites Ex 32:7-14
ETERNAL
God Ps 52:5-7
of disHONESTY
God Ps 63:11c
Mankind Ps 5:4-7
as JUDGMENT
God Hab 3:3-15
Sodomites Gen 19:12-29
KNOWLEDGE of
God Is 10:5-16; 29:13-14
Isaiah Is 66:17-24
PRAYER for
David Ps 68:28-35; 69:22-28
Isaiah Is 26:7-19
Jeremiah Jer 17:14-18; 18:18-23
through PRESENCE
David Ps 21:8-13
PROMISE of
God Is 5:8-24a; Jer 4:27-29
through PROVIDENCE
David Ps 18:31-42
God Is 10:33-34
Philistia Is 14:28-32
as PUNISHMENT
Asaph Ps 83:9-18
Assyrians Is 10:24-27c; 14:24-27
Babylonians Is 14:1-23
David Ps 21:8-13; 63:9-10; 68:1-3
God 2 Chr 36:1-23; Nah 1:10,12,13, 1 Cor 3:10-17; Rev 11:15-19
Isaiah Is 63:1-6
Israelites Num 16:25-35; Deut 2:1-25; Is 9:8-10:4; 10:17-19; Jer 12:7-13; Jude 1:5-7
Judahites 2 Kgs 23:25b-30
Mankind Ps 64:7-10
Sinners 2 Pet 3:3-7

as **PUNISHMENT** (cont'd)
Zophar	Job 20:4-29

RECONCILIATION through
Isaiah	Is 9:8-10:4

SALVATION from
Rehoboam	2 Chr 10:1-12:16

SIGNS of
Adversaries	Ps 74:3-9
Hezekiah	2 Kgs 18:4-8

resulting from **SIN**
Bildad	Job 8:10-19
David	Ps 9:5-8;
	55:9-11;
	58:6-9;
	59:12-13b
Elihu	Job 34:21-28
God	Ps 37:12-22;
	23-40;
	73:13-20;
	94:20-23;
	145:13b-20;
	Prov 10:1-32
Mankind	Ps 1:4-6;
	9:17-20
Psalmist	Ps 92:5-11;
	104:31-35
Zimri	1 Kgs 16:8-14

DIGNITY of

ETERNAL
God	Is 40:12-31

KNOWLEDGE of
Job	Job 31:5-34

in **PRESENCE**
David	1 Chr 11:1-12:40
Solomon	2 Chr 1:1-17

RESPECT for
David	Ps 18:46-50;
	145:1-3
God	Ps 104:1-4
Mankind	Ps 8:3-8

SECURITY in
David	Ps 25:16-21

as **VIRTUE**
David	Ps 7:6-8
Job	Job 27:1-12

DISOBEDIENCE to
Babylonians	2 Kgs 17:24-41
David	2 Sam 11:1-27
Israelites	Neh 9:16-18;
	26-31;
	Is 1:2-3;
	Dan 9:4-19
Jason	*2 Mc 4:7-17
Judahites	Jer 7:21-28;
	29-8:3
Pharisees	Mt 15:3-9;
	Mk 7:1-23

in **COMMITMENT**
Daniel	Dan 9:4-19

causes **CONFRONTATION**
Israelites	Num 16:16-24

through in**FIDELITY**
Israelites	Ps 106:13-18;
	Rom 9:30-10:21
Mankind	Ps 12:1-4

PROMISE concerning
Zedekiah	*1 Esd 1:46-58

PROVIDENCE overcomes

PROVIDENCE overcomes (cont'd)
Mankind	Rom 11:25-32

PUNISHMENT for
Azariah	*Azar 1:1-10
David	Ps 55:15-19;
	89:19-37
God	Judg 9:56-57;
	Ps 95:7d-11;
	119:17-24
Israelites	Num 16:25-35;
	Josh 7:6-26;
	Judg 10:6-18;
	2 Kgs 18:9-12;
	Neh 9:32-37;
	Ps 106:24-27;
	Jer 32:16-25;
	*Bar 2:1-10;
	24-26;
	Heb 4:1-13
Jehoshaphat	2 Chr 17:1-20:37
Judahites	2 Kgs 23:36-24:7
Moses	Deut 31:30-32:47
Psalmist	Ps 137:4-6
Saul	1 Chr 10:1-14
Uzzah	2 Sam 6:1-23;
	1 Chr 13:1-14

as **SIN**
Eve	Gen 3:1-8
Israelites	Ps 106:6-12;
	*2 Esd 1:4-23

DOUBT in
Israelites	Num 11:1-3
Jehoram	2 Kgs 6:32-7:2

PUNISHMENT for
Princes	Ezek 11:1-13

as **SIN**
Ephraimites	Ps 78:9-20
Israelites	Ps 78:32-39

ELECTION by

ACCEPTANCE of
Jesus	Mt 3:13-17;
	17:1-8;
	Mk 1:9-11;
	9:2-8;
	Lk 3:21-22;
	9:28-36

BLESSING in
God	Ps 65:1-4

for **CAPTIVITY**
Kings	2 Kgs 3:1-27

for **DISCIPLESHIP**
God	Ps 105:1-6
Israelites	Deut 10:12-22
Jesus	Jn 10:19-40;
	17:6-19
Thessalonians	1 Thes 1:2-10

of **ENEMY**
Hadad	1 Kgs 11:14-22
Rezon	1 Kgs 11:23-25
Solomon	1 Kgs 11:14-22;
	23-25

FAITH in
Thessalonians	2 Thes 2:13-15

of **FAMILY**
David	2 Chr 5:1-7:10
God	Ps 33:10-12;
	132:11-18;
	147:12-20

of FAMILY (cont'd)

Israelites	Deut 14:1-2;
	1 Kgs 8:22-53;
	Ps 47:1-4;
	135:1-4;
	Amos 3:1-2

as FULFILLMENT

God	Is 44:24-45:13

GRACE in

Believers	1 Pet 2:4-10
Elizabeth	Lk 1:57-80
Israelites	Rom 11:25-32
Mankind	Ex 33:12-23
Paul	Col 1:25-27

JUSTICE in

Believers	Lk 18:1-8;
	Rom 8:28-39

of LEADERSHIP

Aaron	Ex 6:10-13
David	*Sir 47:1-11
Ehud	Judg 3:15-23
Jesus	1 Pet 2:4-10
Joshua	Deut 3:23-29
Micah	Mic 4:1-8
Moses	Ex 6:10-13
Othniel	Judg 3:7-11
Prophet	Deut 18:9-22
Solomon	*Wis 9:1-18

of LIFE

Jesus	Jn 6:25-59

LOVE in

Israelites	Mal 1:2-5
Judahites	Ps 78:67-72

ELECTION by

OBEDIENCE to

Abraham	Gen 18:16-22

PRAISE of

Israelites	Is 42:18-43:7

REJECTION of

Ephraimites	Ps 78:67-72
Saul	1 Sam 13:1-23

for SACREDNESS

Aaron	Num 17:1-13
Israelites	1 Sam 12:1-25
Jews	Rom 2:25-3:20
Levites	Deut 10:1-11
Solomon	1 Chr 22:2-19

to SERVICE

Aaron	Ex 4:10-16;
	Ps 105:26-36
God	Is 41:1-42:4
High Priest	Heb 5:1-10
Isaiah	Is 49:1-26
Israelites	Is 41:1-42:4;
	43:8-13
Jesus	Heb 5:1-10
Levites	1 Chr 15:1-16:43
Moses	Ps 105:26-36
Priests	Ex 28:1-5

of VICTORY

Assyrians	Is 10:5-16
Israelites	Deut 4:15-31

WISDOM in

Sirach	*Sir 24:1-34

WITNESS to

Jesus	Mt 11:27

ENEMY of

COMMUNITY as

Mankind	Ps 2:1-3

in CONFRONTATION

David	1 Sam 17:1-18:5
Esther	*Esth 14:1-19
Solomon	*Wis 5:15-23

KNOWLEDGE of

David	Ps 3:1-2;
	21:8-13

PROVIDENCE over

Israelites	Ezra 8:31-36;
	Is 9:8-10:4;
	*1 Esd 6:3-6
Mankind	Ps 17:6-7

RESPECT by

David	Ps 18:43-45
God	Ps 132:11-18

EQUALITY with

HUMILITY in

Jesus	Phil 2:5-11

LEADERSHIP revealing

God	Is 46:1-13

REJECTION of

Bildad	Job 25:1-6
Ezra	*2 Esd 4:1-12;
	5:31-42
Job	Job 9:1-7;
	8-13;
	14-19;
	30-35
Zophar	Job 11:7-12

SACREDNESS in

Jesus	Jn 5:1-18

EVIL against

Jehoiachin	*1 Esd 1:43-45
Jehoiakim	*1 Esd 1:37-42
Sodomites	Gen 19:4-11
Zedekiah	*1 Esd 1:46-58

in COMMUNITY

Mankind	Ps 2:1-3

through inFIDELITY

Israelites	Ps 78:40-55
Mankind	Ps 14:1-3

FREEDOM from

Solomon	*Wis 11:21-12:2

through disHONESTY

Elihu	Job 33:26-28
Ezra	*1 Esd 8:71-90
Israelites	*1 Esd 9:1-15;
	*Bar 2:11-23;
	3:1-8
Manasseh	*Mana 1:8-10
Mankind	Ps 12:1-4

JUDGMENT on

Author	Heb 13:1-25
David	Ps 58:6-9
God	Ps 9:5-8;
	15-16;
	14:4-6;
	65:1-4;
	75:6-8;
	Rom 1:18;
	1 Thes 4:1-12;
	Rev 18:4-20
Mankind	Ps 1:4-6;
	64:7-10
Psalmist	Ps 94:1-3
Sodomites	Gen 18:16-22

KNOWLEDGE of

David	Ps 19:11-14;
	21:8-13;

FIDELITY of (cont'd)
  Psalmist   118:5-9;
                           130:5-6
  Razis   *2 Mc 14:37-46
  Solomon   Prov 3:1-35
 JUDGMENT on
  Believers   1 Jn 4:13-18
  Jesus   1 Pet 2:21-25
 PRAYER because of
  Isaiah   Is 26:7-19;
                           33:1-6
  Israelites   Hos 5:15-6:3
 as QUALITY OF LIFE
  David   2 Sam 15:13-16:14
 RECONCILIATION through
  Israelites   Is 10:20-23
 through RESURRECTION
  Maccabeus   *2 Mc 12:38-45
 SALVATION through
  Believers   1 Pet 1:3-9
  David   1 Sam 17:1-18:5;
                           Ps 27:1-3;
                           86:1-7
  Habakkuk   Hab 3:16-19
  Jesus   Heb 7:1-28
  Job   Job 19:25-29
  Micah   Mic 7:7-20
  Psalmist   Ps 119:121-128
  Shadrach   Dan 3:16-18
  Sirach   *Sir 33:1-3
  Thessalonians   2 Thes 2:13-15

 SECURITY in
  Believers   Ps 55:22;
                           Prov 22:17-21
  David   Ps 4:2-5;
                           7:9-11;
                           11:1-3;
                           16:1-4;
                           5-8;
                           23:1-4;
                           25:8-15;
                           27:7-12;
                           28:6-7;
                           56:6b-9;
                           10-13;
                           62:1-2;
                           5-7;
                           143:7-12
  God   Ps 125:1-3;
                           Prov 29:1-27;
                           30:1-14;
                           Is 26:1-6
  Isaiah   Is 25:1-5;
                           50:1-11
  Israelites   Deut 31:1-8
  Jehoshaphat   2 Chr 17:1-20:37
  Jeremiah   Jer 16:19-21
  Mankind   2 Sam 22:1-51;
                           Ps 18:25-30
  Moses   Ps 90:1-12
  Paul   2 Cor 1:8-11;
                           2 Tim 4:9-18
  Psalmist   Ps 10:12-18;
                           33:20-22;
                           46:1-3;
                           71:1-21;
                           94:20-23;
                           118:10-14
 as VIRTUE
  Abraham   Gen 15:1-21

 as VIRTUE (cont'd)
  David   Ps 7:9-11
 FAMILY of
  BELIEF in
   Jesus   1 Jn 4:19-5:5
  DISCIPLINE for
   Believers   Heb 12:3-11
   Israelites   Deut 8:1-10
  ETERNAL
   God   Ps 48:4-8
  FIDELITY of
   Israelites   1 Sam 12:1-25;
                           1 Kgs 6:1-38
   Jesus   Heb 3:1-6a
   Mother   *2 Mc 7:1-42
   Solomon   *Sir 47:12-22
  PRAYER for
   Sirach   *Sir 36:11-17
  PROVIDENCE for
   Believers   Ps 128:3-4;
                           1 Jn 2:28-3:3
   God   Ps 87:4-6;
                           127:3-5
   Jacob   Gen 29:31-30:24
   Noah   Gen 8:1-12
  SALVATION for
   God   Gal 4:4-7
  SECURITY in
   Believers   Is 40:1-11

FEAR of
   Adversaries   Ex 15:1-18
   God   Job 37:23-24
   Israelites   Ex 20:18-20
   Kings   Ps 48:4-8
   Mankind   Ps 102:12-22
   Samaritans   2 Kgs 7:3-20
  results in BELIEF
   Israelites   Ex 14:23-31
  by COMMUNITY
   God   Ps 2:4-6

FIDELITY in
   Israelites   1 Sam 12:1-25
  reveals JUDGMENT
   Author   Heb 10:19-31
   David   Ps 9:17-20
   God   Eccl 12:12-14
   Job   Job 9:25-29
   Mankind   Ps 64:7-10;
                           76:7-9
   Psalmist   Ps 119:113-120
  results in KNOWLEDGE
   Mankind   Ps 111:10;
                           Prov 1:7
  as MOTIVATION
   Abraham   Gen 22:1-19
   Job   Job 9:30-35
  PROMISE through
   Psalmist   Ps 119:33-40
  as RESPECT
   Babylonians   2 Kgs 17:24-41
   Darius   Dan 6:25-27
   David   Ps 19:7-10
   God   Prov 23:15-24:22;
                           Is 33:1-6
   Isaiah   Is 8:11-15;
                           59:1-21
   Israelites   Deut 4:1-14;
                           6:20-25;

as **RESPECT** (cont'd)

Israelites	Hos 3:1-5; Hag 1:12-14
Job	Job 1:1
Jonah	Jon 1:1-17
Kings	Ps 2:10-11
Mankind	Ps 15:1-5b; 33:4-9
Micah	Mic 7:7-20
Moses	Deut 6:4-19
Nehemiah	Neh 1:11b-2:8
Peter	1 Pet 2:13-17
Psalmist	Ps 67:1-7; 99:1-3
Sirach	*Sir 25:7-11; 32:14-24; 40:18-27
Wisdom	Prov 1:20-33

SALVATION through

God	Ps 85:8-13
Sirach	*Sir 34:13-17

SIGNS of

Mankind	Ps 65:5-8

as **VIRTUE**

Sirach	*Sir 15:1-10

FIDELITY of
  FAITH in

Believers	Ps 40:4-5
David	Ps 16:5-8; 25:1-7; 26:1-3; 55:23
Israelites	Josh 22:9-34
Job	Job 1:9-12
King	Ps 21:1-7
Maccabeus	*2 Mc 8:8-23; 15:6-10
Psalmist	Ps 116:1-11; 118:5-9; 130:5-6
Razis	*2 Mc 14:37-46
Solomon	Prov 3:1-35

  GRATITUDE for

David	Ps 108:1-5
Psalmist	Ps 106:1-5; 116:12-19

  HOPE in

Believers	Ps 33:13-19; 147:7-11
Psalmist	Ps 33:20 22

  IGNORANCE of

Asaph	Ps 73:21-28
Israelites	Hos 4:1-3

  INNOCENCE through

David	Ps 69:4-12
Job	Job 23:8-14; 27:1-12

  JOY in

Believers	Ps 128:1-2
David	Ps 144:12-15
God	Prov 12:1-28
King	Ps 63:11b
Psalmist	Ps 119:73-80

  JUSTICE in

God	Ps 111:5-9; Rom 2:25-3:20
Isaiah	Is 61:1-11

  LIFE through

God	Ps 119:89-96

  to **OLD AGE**

to **OLD AGE** (cont'd)

Psalmist	Ps 71:1-21

  PRAISE of

David	Ps 57:7-11; 145:1-3
Ethan	Ps 89:1-4
Psalmist	Ps 71:22-24

FIDELITY to
  BLESSING in

Believers	Ps 40:4-5
Caleb	Josh 14:6-15
David	Ps 63:1-8
God	Ps 24:3-6; 37:23-40
Isaiah	Is 63:7-64:12
Job	Job 1:20-21
Mankind	Ps 1:1-3; 25:8-15
Psalmist	Ps 119:1-8

  brings **DEATH**

Eleazar	*2 Mc 6:18-31
Jews	*2 Mc 7:1-42

  in **DISCIPLESHIP**

David	Ps 27:7-12; 63:1-8
God	2 Thes 3:3-5
Jews	*2 Mc 6:12-17
Paul	1 Cor 1:4-9
Psalmist	Ps 95:1-7c

  by **FAMILY**

Israelites	1 Sam 12:1-25; 1 Kgs 6:1-38
Jesus	Heb 3:1-6a
Mother	*2 Mc 7:1-42
Solomon	*Sir 47:12-22

  through **FEAR**

Israelites	1 Sam 12:1-25

  FULFILLMENT through

God	Heb 10:19-31

  in doing **GOOD**

Elihu	Job 34:10-15
Josiah	*1 Esd 1:23-24
Judith	*Jdt 8:1-8
Sirach	*Sir 2:7-11; 15:11-20

  through **GRACE**

God	Ps 99:6-9; 145:13b-20
Israelites	Neh 9:16-18
Tobit	*Tb 13:1-18

  because of **LEADERSHIP**

Israelites	Deut 31:1-8; Hos 2:16-20; 21-23

  LIFE through

Paul	Gal 2:17-19
Psalmist	Ps 80:14-19

  through **OBEDIENCE**

Apostles	Acts 5:17-42
Asa	1 Kgs 15:9-15
David	Ps 17:3-5; 18:20-24
Ezekiel	Ezek 2:8b-3:3
Ezra	*2 Esd 13:51-58
Isaiah	Is 50:1-11
Job	Job 1:1; 22; 2:9-10
John	1 Jn 1:5-10
Judahites	Hos 11:12-12:1

DESIRE for (cont'd)
Psalmist	130:1-2
by **ELECTION**	
God	Is 44:24-45:13
ETERNAL	
God	Jn 1:1-18
HONESTY of	
Balaam	Num 23:13-26
God	1 Sam 15:1-35;
	Is 55:1-13;
	Tit 1:1-4

KNOWLEDGE of
Egyptians	Ex 7:1-7
of **LAW**	
Israelites	*2 Esd 2:33-41;
	*Bar 2:1-10
of **NEW AGE**	
God	Mt 24:34-36

PRAYER for
Believers	Ps 34:15-22;
	145:13b-20
Daniel	Dan 2:20-23
David	2 Sam 22:1-51;
	Ps 3:3-6;
	5:1-3;
	13:1-4;
	17:1-2;
	6-7;
	18:1-3;
	4-6;
	20:6-9;
	22:1-5;
	25:16-21;
	28:1-5;
	6-7;
	30:1-5;
	31:1-8;
	19-24;
	34:4-10
	40:1-3;
	61:4-5;
	138:1-3
Elijah	1 Kgs 17:1-24
Elisha	2 Kgs 6:8-23
Ezekiel	Ezek 4:12-15
God	Ps 99:6-9;
	Prov 2:1-22
Hannah	1 Sam 1:1-28
Hezekiah	2 Chr 30:1-31:21;
	32:1-33;
	Is 38:1-22
Isaac	Gen 25:19-26
Israelites	Neh 9:26-31;
	Ps 78:21-31;
	107:4-9;
	10-16
Jabez	1 Chr 4:1-23
Jehoahaz	2 Kgs 13:1-9
Job	Job 42:7-9
Jonah	Jon 2:1-10
Manasseh	2 Chr 33:1-25
Manoah	Judg 13:9-14
Moses	Num 14:11-24
People	Ps 107:17-22;
	23-32
Prophet	1 Kgs 13:1-34
Psalmist	Ps 10:12-18;
	66:13-20;

PRAYER for (cont'd)
Psalmist	102:12-22;
	116:1-11;
	118:5-9;
	15-21
Sarah	*Tb 3:16-17
Sirach	*Sir 51:1-12
Solomon	1 Kgs 8:22-53;
	*Wis 7:7-14
Susanna	*Susa 1:42-51
Tobiah	*Tb 3:16-17
by **PRESENCE**	
David	Ps 17:15;
	51:3-12
God	Num 14:11-24;
	Is 6:1-13
Jesus	Col 2:6-15
Nehemiah	Neh 1:11b-2:8
of **PROMISE**	
Abraham	Gen 21:1-7
Believer	Eccl 5:1-7;
	Heb 11:1-40
Egyptians	Ezek 30:1-12
Ezekiel	Ezek 28:1-10
Ezra	Neh 9:7-8
God	Ps 12:5-6;
	18:25-30;
	Is 14:24-27;
	45:14-25;
	46:1-13;
	Jer 4:27-29;
	2 Pet 3:8-10
Hagar	Gen 16:11-16
Israelites	Josh 21:8-45
	Neh 9:22-25;
	Ps 105:37-42;
	Ezek 37:1-14
Jesus	Rom 15:1-13
Joshua	Josh 23:1-16
Moses	Ex 4:27-31;
	23:20-33;
	Deut 23:15-25:19
Solomon	1 Kgs 8:54-61
by **PROVIDENCE**	
David	Ps 22:22-26;
	23:1-4
Ezra	Ezra 7:6-10
God	Prov 16:1-33
Paul	Phil 4:10-20
Rehoboam	1 Kgs 12:1-20;
	2 Chr 10:1-12:16
of **SALVATION**	
Believers	Ps 91:14-16
God	Is 46:1-13;
	Hab 3:3-15
Holy Spirit	Tit 3:1-7
Israelites	Ps 77:11-20;
	Is 31:4-9
Jesus	Eph 1:15-2:10;
	2 Tim 1:8-14
Paul	2 Tim 4:9-18
of **SECURITY**	
Believers	Heb 6:13-20
David	Ps 38:11-16
Israelites	Is 31:4-9
of **TRUTH**	
Agur	Prov 30:1-14

GIFT of
is **LOVE**	
God	2 Tim 1:3-7

is **LOVE** (cont'd)
Holy Spirit   Rom 5:1-5
is **ONENESS**
Holy Spirit   1 Cor 12:4-11
is **TEMPERANCE**
God   2 Tim 1:3-7
is **WISDOM**
Disciples   Acts 2:1-13
James   Jas 3:13-18
Solomon   *Wis 7:15-8:1; 2-21
WITNESS to
Holy Spirit   Heb 2:1-4

GOOD from
PRAYER for
Psalmist   Ps 125:4-5

GOOD of
Asa   1 Kgs 15:9-15
Tobit   *Tb 1:10-22
in **COMMUNITY**
David   Ps 51:18-19
CONFRONTATION with
Satan   Job 1:6-8; 2:1-3
in **CREATION**
God   1 Tim 4:1-5
Mankind   Eccl 7:23-29; *Wis 2:21-24
DESIRE for
Mankind   Ps 4:6-8
ETERNAL
God   Ps 119:137-144; 153-160
for **FIDELITY**
Elihu   Job 34:10-15
Josiah   *1 Esd 1:23-24
Judith   *Jdt 8:1-8
Sirach   *Sir 2:7-11; 15:11-20
in **JUDGMENT**
David   Ps 9:1-4
God   Ps 11:4-7
Sirach   *Sir 39:17-27

KNOWLEDGE of
Job   Job 1:6-8; 2:1-3
Mankind   Ps 1:4-6
PRESENCE of
Mankind   Ps 15:1-5b
PROMISE of
Solomon   *Wis 15:1-6
PROVIDENCE through
Believers   Ps 92:12-15; Rom 8:28-39
God   Ps 85:8-13; 118:15-21
James   Jas 1:16-18
Sirach   *Sir 39:28-35
PUNISHMENT through
Psalmist   Ps 119:65-72
as **QUALITY OF LIFE**
God   Nah 1:1-9
SECURITY in
Believers   Prov 18:1-24
God   Ps 37:12-22
as **VIRTUE**
God   Ps 77:11-20
Job   Job 1:1

GRACE of
COMPULSION by
Lot   Gen 19:12-29
CONFRONTATION with
Jesus   Mt 5:3-12
CONVERSION through
Israelites   Num 14:11-24
DESIRE for
Abraham   Gen 18:23-33
Job   Job 14:13-17
People   Jer 42:1-6
ELECTION by
Believers   1 Pet 2:4-10
Elizabeth   Lk 1:57-80
Israelites   Rom 11:25-32
Mankind   Ex 33:12-23
Paul   Col 1:25-27
strengthens **FIDELITY**
God   Ps 99:6-9; 145:13b-20
Israelites   Neh 9:16-18
Tobit   *Tb 13:1-18
JUDGMENT by
David   1 Chr 21:1-22:1
God   Amos 7:1-3; 4-6
Nineveh   Jon 3:1-10
KNOWLEDGE of
Habakkuk   Hab 2:12-14:17
MEDIATION through
Jesus   Rom 5:1-5
Moses   Ex 32:7-14; Deut 9:7-24; 25-29

PRAYER for
Amos   Amos 7:1-3; 4-6
Author   Heb 13:1-25
Daniel   Dan 9:4-19
David   Ps 9:13-14; 25:8-15; 27:7-12; 39:7-13; 40:11; 41:4-10; 51:1-2; 3-12; 13-17; 57:1-3
Ezekiel   Ezek 9:1-11
Habakkuk   Hab 3:1; 2
Isaiah   Is 33:1-6; 63:7-64:12
Israelites   Neh 9:26-31; Jer 14:19-22; Hos 5:15-6:3; *Bar 2:11-23; 3:1-8
Jeremiah   Jer 17:14-18
Joel   Joel 1:2-20
John   2 Jn 1:1-3; Rev 1:4-20; 22:6-21
Jonah   Jon 1:1-17; 2:1-10
Judahites   Lam 5:1-22
Moses   Num 12:11-16
Nineveh   Jon 3:1-10
Paul   1 Cor 1:4-9; Gal 6:11-18;

PRAYER for (cont'd)
Paul	Col 1:1-2; Tit 1:1-4; Philm 1:1-3; 21-25
Peter	1 Pet 1:1-2
Psalmist	Ps 119:57-64; 73-80; 129-136; 123:1-2; 3-4

PROMISE through
Antiochus	*2 Mc 9:5-29
Manasseh	*Mana 1:6-7
Peter	2 Pet 1:3-4

PROVIDENCE through
David	Ps 23:5-6
God	Ps 147:1-6
Israelites	2 Kgs 13:22-25; Neh 9:19-21; Is 1:4-9
Jesus	2 Thes 2:16-17
Solomon	*Wis 16:1-14

PUNISHMENT by
Job	Job 35:13-16

as **QUALITY OF LIFE**
Believers	Jas 4:1-10
God	Deut 4:15-31; Ps 86:14-17; 111:2-4; 119:153-160; Is 30:18-26; Joel 2:12-17; Jas 5:7-11
Jonah	Jon 4:1-11

RECONCILIATION through
Believers	1 Pet 1:3-9
God	Is 1:24-26; 44:6-8; 21-23; Mic 7:7-20; Mt 6:14-15
Isaiah	Is 63:7-64:12
Psalmist	Ps 85:4-7

SALVATION through
Believers	1 Jn 1:5-10
David	Ps 26:8-12
Epaphroditus	Phil 2:19-30
God	Ps 103:1-5; Mt 19:23-26; Mk 10:23-27
Isaiah	Is 63:7-64:12
Israelites	Neh 9:26-31; Is 42:18-43:7
Jesus	1 Jn 2:1-6
Mankind	Tit 2:11-15; 3:1-7
Paul	2 Cor 5:20-6:2
Sirach	*Sir 51:1-12

SIN forgiven by
Abijam	1 Kgs 15:1-8
Asaph	Ps 79:5-13
David	Ps 25:1-7; 16-21; 32:1-2; 3-7
God	Ps 65:1-4; 103:6-13; 130:3-4
Hezekiah	Is 38:1-22
Israelites	Ps 78:32-39;

SIN forgiven by (cont'd)
Israelites	*Bar 3:1-8
Joshua	Zech 3:1-10
Manasseh	*Mana 1:6-7; 11-15
Psalmist	Ps 85:1-3
Sirach	*Sir 2:7-11; 18:1-14
Solomon	1 Kgs 8:22-53; *Wis 11:21-12:2

in **STEWARDSHIP**
Macedonians	2 Cor 8:1-6

as **VIRTUE**
God	Ex 34:5b-9; Ps 86:1-7; 112:2-4; 116:1-11; 145:8-9
James	Jas 3:13-18

GRATITUDE to
Jesus	Col 3:5-17

ETERNAL
Psalmist	Ps 44:4-8

for **FIDELITY**
David	Ps 108:1-5
Psalmist	Ps 106:1-5; 116:12-19

KNOWLEDGE of
Daniel	Dan 2:20-23

PRAYER of
Asaph	Ps 75:1
Daniel	Dan 6:10-15
David	Ps 9:1-4
Isaiah	Is 25:1-5
Jonah	Jon 2:1-10
Paul	Col 1:9-14; 2 Thes 1:3-4

for **PROMISE**
David	Ps 142:5-7

for **PROVIDENCE**
David	Ps 30:11-12; 40:6-10; 52:8-9; 54:6-7; 86:11-13; 144:1-2
Isaiah	Is 26:7-19

RITE of
David	Ps 26:6b-7; 28:6-7; 56:10-13; 57:7-11

for **SECURITY**
David	Ps 124:6-8
Hezekiah	Is 38:1-22

SIGNS of
Rebekah	Gen 24:28-60

as **VIRTUE**
David	Ps 140:12-13

GRIEF of
concerning **COMMUNITY**
Ezra	*2 Esd 5:31-42

HATE by
Israelites	Amos 6:8-11

for **inFIDELITY**
God	Mal 2:10-16

for **disHONESTY**
God	Prov 6:16-19

DEITY (cont'd)

for wrong **QUALITY OF LIFE**
God	Is 1:10-17
Isaiah	Is 61:1-11

for **SIN**
God	Ps 11:4-7; 31:1-8; Prov 6:16-19; 15:1-33; 16:1-33; 20:1-30
Mankind	Ps 5:4-7
Psalmist	Ps 119:97-104

HEALING by
Jeroboam	1 Kgs 13:1-34
Jesus	Mt 12:22-32; Lk 11:14-23

KNOWLEDGE of
Jesus	Lk 8:40-56

PRAYER for
Abraham	Gen 20:1-18
David	Ps 6:1-5; 41:4-10
Egyptians	Is 19:18-25
Hezekiah	2 Chr 32:1-33; Is 38:1-22
Israelites	Hos 5:15-6:3
Jeremiah	Jer 17:14-18
Moses	Num 12:11-16
Tobiah	*Tb 3:16-17

through **PROVIDENCE**
Abimelech	Gen 20:1-18
David	Ps 41:1-3
God	Ps 103:1-5; 146:7c-9
People	Ps 107:17-22

HONESTY of
DOUBT in
People	1 Jn 5:8-12

FULFILLMENT through
Balaam	Num 23:13-26
God	1 Sam 15:1-35; Is 55:1-13; Tit 1:1-4

HOPE in
Believers	Heb 6:13-20

JUSTICE in
Elihu	Job 34:10-15
Job	Job 31:5-34

PRAISE of
Jesus	Jn 7:15-24

dis**HONESTY** of
SUFFERING through
Jeremiah	Jer 20:7-18

dis**HONESTY** with
through **EVIL**
Elihu	Job 33:26-28
Ezra	*1 Esd 8:71-90
Israelites	*1 Esd 9:1-15; *Bar 2:11-23; 3:1-8
Manasseh	*Mana 1:8-10
Mankind	Ps 12:1-4

HOPE in
Holy Spirit	Rom 15:1-13

results in **BELIEF**
David	Ps 62:5-7

results in **BELIEF** (cont'd)
Jeremiah	Jer 17:13

for **NEW AGE**
Believers	1 Jn 2:28-3:3
Isaiah	Is 28:1-13
Paul	1 Cor 1:4-9

through **RESURRECTION**
Believers	1 Pet 1:13-2:3

HUMILITY before
Eliphaz	Job 22:21-30
Esther	*Esth 14:1-19

IDOLATRY before
through in**FIDELITY**
Israelites	Mal 2:10-16
Jeremiah	*Jer 6:4-7
Solomon	*Wis 15:1-6

JUDGMENT on
Egyptians	Ex 12:1-14
Gentiles	Rom 1:24-32
God	Is 2:18-22; 45:14-25

PROVIDENCE in
Solomon	*Wis 14:1-11

PUNISHMENT for
Israelites	Ps 78:56-66; Ezek 43:6-12
Moses	Deut 31:30-32:47

SIN of
Israelites	Ps 106:19-23

IGNORANCE concerning
PRAYER related to
Job	Job 33:13-14

INDIFFERENCE of
to **PRAYER**
Job	Job 24:1-12; 30:16-23
Psalmist	Ps 88:13-14

INNOCENCE before
BELIEF in
David	Ps 7:3-5

CONFRONTATION with
Israelites	Deut 18:9-22

through **FIDELITY**
David	Ps 69:4-12
Job	Job 23:8-14; 27:1-12

JUDGMENT on
Isaiah	Is 50:1-11
Job	Job 23:1-7

KNOWLEDGE of
Israelites	Ps 44:17-22
Job	Job 10:1-7

MEDIATION with
Jesus	1 Thes 3:11-13

PRAYER for
Jeremiah	Jer 15:10-21

PUNISHMENT for
Job	Job 9:14-19; 20-24

as **QUALITY OF LIFE**
David	Ps 18:20-24

JEALOUSY of
God	Num 25:6-18; Deut 6:4-19

as **MOTIVATION**

in **JUDGMENT** (cont'd)

Job	31:35-37
Mankind	Heb 10:19-31
People	Rom 2:1-24
Sirach	*Sir 35:12-20
Solomon	1 Kgs 8:22-53; 2 Chr 5:1-7:10; Ps 72:1-4

KNOWLEDGE of

Asaph	Ps 73:13-20
Ezra	*2 Esd 4:33-52
Mankind	Ps 58:10-11

in **NEW AGE**

Ezra	*2 Esd 4:33-52

PRAYER for

David	Ps 7:3-5; 6-8; 9:17-20; 17:1-2; 26:1-3; 28:1-5; 35:19-21; 22-28; 55:9-11; 56:6b-9
Ezra	*2 Esd 5:21-30
Jephthah	Judg 11:12-28
Psalmist	Ps 10:1-2; 12-18; 94:1-3
Susanna	*Susa 1:42-51

PRESENCE of

David	2 Sam 23:1-7
God	Is 41:1-42:4
Micah	Mic 3:1-12

through **PROVIDENCE**

God	Ezra 9:6-15; Ps 140:12-13
Hannah	1 Sam 2:1-10

in **PUNISHMENT**

David	Ps 17:13-14
Elihu	Job 36:5-15
Eliphaz	Job 5:8-17
God	Ps 94:20-23
Isaiah	Is 59:1-21
Israelites	Neh 9:32-37; Is 42:18-43:7
Job	Job 27:1-12
Paul	2 Thes 1:5-7a
Sirach	*Sir 39:28-35

as **QUALITY OF LIFE**

God	Is 30:18-26

RESPECT for

God	Ps 33:4-9
Nebuchadnezzar	Dan 4:36-37

SECURITY in

Believers	Ps 37:23-40

concerning **SIN**

David	Ps 7:12-16

as **VIRTUE**

God	Ps 89:5-18; 94:12-15; 97:1-5; 99:4-5; 145:13b-20; Is 5:8-24a; Jer 9:23-24; 11:18-12:6; Dan 9:4-19; Zeph 3:1-5

as **VIRTUE** (cont'd)

Psalmist	Ps 129:1-4

KNOWLEDGE concerning
ACCEPTANCE of

Ahab	1 Kgs 20:1-43
Believers	1 Jn 4:4-6
David	Ps 41:11-12
Elihu	Job 37:14-22
Israelites	Jer 31:31-34

KNOWLEDGE of
concerning **DISCIPLESHIP**

God	2 Tim 2:14-19

concerning **EVIL**

David	Ps 19:11-14; 21:8-13; 69:4-12; 139:23-24
Elihu	Job 36:5-15
Ephraimites	Hos 6:10-7:2
God	Ps 90:1-12; Prov 5:15-23; 15:1-33; 23:15-24:22
Jeremiah	Jer 16:16-18
Jesus	Mt 12:22-32; Lk 11:14-23
Job	Job 13:20-27
Mankind	Ps 53:1-3
Psalmist	Ps 94:4-7
Sirach	*Sir 16:6-23; 17:15-32; 22:27-23:6; 16-27
Solomon	*Wis 17:1-21

of **INNOCENCE**

Israelites	Ps 44:17-22
Job	Job 10:1-7

KNOWLEDGE of
concerning **SUFFERING**

David	Ps 13:1-4; 38:3-10
Israelites	Ex 3:7-10; Neh 9:9-11

LAW of
ACCEPTANCE of

Peter	2 Pet 3:1-2
Psalmist	Ps 93:5

DISCIPLESHIP to

Moses	Deut 10:1-11

DISOBEDIENCE to

Babylonians	2 Kgs 17:24-41
Israelites	Neh 9:16-18; 26-31; Dan 9:4-19
Jason	*2 Mc 4:7-17
Judahites	Jer 7:21-28; 29-8:3
Pharisees	Mt 15:3-9; Mk 7:1-23

FAITH in

Psalmist	Ps 119:41-48; 65-72

FULFILLMENT of

Israelites	*2 Esd 2:33-41; *Bar 2:1-10

GOOD in

GOOD in (cont'd)
David   Ps 19:7-10
God   Ps 119:137-144
Psalmist   Ps 119:169-176
HOPE in
Psalmist   Ps 119:73-80;
                         145-152
JOY in
Mankind   Ps 1:1-3;
                         112:1
Psalmist   Ps 119:161-168
LOVE of
Believers   1 Jn 4:19-5:5
God   1 Jn 3:19-24
Psalmist   Ps 119:33-40;
                         65-72;
                         73-80;
                         89-96;
                         105-112;
                         113-120;
                         121-128;
                         137-144;
                         153-160;
                         161-168
OBEDIENCE to
David   2 Sam 22:1-51;
                         Ps 40:6-10
God   Eccl 12:12-14
Israelites   Ps 105:43-45
Psalmist   Ps 119:41-48;
                         49-56;
                         57-64;
                         65-72;
                         81-88;
                         97-104;
                         105-112;
                         113-120;
                         121-128;
                         129-136;
                         137-144;
                         153-160;
                         161-168;
                         169-176
Sirach   *Sir 1:22-30;
                         17:1-14;
                         32:14-24
PEACE through
Psalmist   Ps 119:161-168
PRAISE of
David   Ps 19:7-10;
                         56:10-13
Ezra   Neh 9:12-15;
                         *2 Esd 9:26-37
Psalmist   Ps 119:9-16;
                         89-96;
                         129-136;
                         161-168;
                         169-176
REJECTION of
Israelites   Jer 6:16-21;
                         *2 Esd 2:33-41
Judahites   Jer 8:8-13;
                         Amos 2:4-5
WISDOM in
Ezra   *1 Esd 8:1-7
Psalmist   Ps 119:73-80;
                         97-104
Sirach   *Sir 6:18-37
WITNESS to
God   Rom 3:21-30
Psalmist   Ps 119:9-16;

WITNESS to (cont'd)
Psalmist   41-48
LEADERSHIP by
AUTHORITY of
God   Ps 47:5-9;
                         66:5-7;
                         93:1-2;
                         103:19-22;
                         Is 40:1-11;
                         51:1-16;
                         Rev 11:15-19;
                         19:6-10
Israelites   Ex 15:1-18;
                         Ps 77:11-20;
                         Jer 31:31-34
LEADERSHIP from
AUTHORITY for
Jesus   Mt 28:16-20;
                         Acts 2:14-36;
                         Eph 1:15-2:10;
                         Phil 2:5-11
Judah   Judg 1:1-21
King   Prov 21:1-31
Maccabeus   *2 Mc 15:6-10
Mankind   Jer 32:26-44;
                         Zech 14:1-21
Moses   Ex 32:30-35
Paul   Gal 1:1-5
Solomon   Ps 72:8-14
AUTHORITY in
Aaron   Ex 4:10-16
David   2 Sam 22:1-51;
                         1 Chr 28:1-29:30
                         Ps 18:43-45
LEADERSHIP of
ETERNAL
David   Ps 110:1-4
God   Ex 15:1-18;
                         Deut 33:1-29;
                         Ps 9:5-8;
                         10:12-18;
                         29:10-11;
                         145:10-13a;
                         146:10;
                         Jer 10:1-16;
                         Lam 5:1-22;
                         Rev 11:15-19
King   Ps 61:6-7
FIDELITY of
Israelites   Deut 31:1-8;
                         Hos 2:16-20;
                         21-23
JUDGMENT on
David   Ps 139:23-24
God   Is 33:17-24
KNOWLEDGE of
Ahab   1 Kgs 20:1-43
Ammonites   Ezek 25:1-7
Edomites   Ezek 35:1-15
Egyptians   Ex 7:1-7;
                         14:1-14;
                         Ezek 29:6-9a;
                         9b-16;
                         17-21;
                         30:6-9;
                         13-19;
                         20-26;

KNOWLEDGE of (cont'd)
Egyptians	32:1-16
Ezekiel	Ezek 11:1-13; 15:1-8; 24:15-24; 25-27; 33:23-29
God	Heb 8:6-13
Israelites	Ex 5:6-14; Ezek 6:1-7; 8-10; 11-14; 7:1-27; 12:1-16; 17-20; 13:17-23; 16:53-63; 17:11-21; 20:9-26; 40-44; 22:1-16; 28:24-26; 34:17-22; 25-31; 36:8-15; 37:1-14; 15-28; Hos 2:16-20; Joel 3:16b-21
Joel	Joel 2:18-27
Mankind	1 Kgs 8:54-61; Ps 59:13c-15; Ezek 36:22-32; 37-38
Moabites	Ezek 25:8-11
Moses	Ex 7:14-25
Prophetesses	Ezek 13:17-23
Sidon	Ezek 28:20-23
Tyre	Ezek 26:1-6

in LAW
Psalmist	Ps 119:105-112

PRAYER for
Agur	Prov 30:1-14
David	Ps 5:8-10

PRESENCE of
David	2 Sam 5:6-16
Ezra	Ezra 7:27-28
Gideon	Judg 6:33-35
Israelites	Lev 25:39-55; Num 23:13-26
Jesus	Lk 4:1-13; Col 1:18-20
Joshua	Josh 6:22-27
Othniel	Judg 3:7-11

PROMISE of
David	1 Kgs 2:1-4

PROVIDENCE in
Adversaries	Ps 83:9-18
David	2 Sam 22:1-51; Ps 18:43-45; 23:1-4; 139:7-12
Ephraimites	Ps 78:9-20
God	Ps 136:10-22; Prov 10:1-32
Isaiah	Is 63:7-64:12
Israelites	Ex 13:17-22; 32:30-35; Deut 8:11-20; Josh 5:13-15; Neh 9:12-15;

PROVIDENCE in (cont'd)
Israelites	Ps 105:43-45; 107:4-9
Paul	2 Cor 3:4-6

as QUALITY OF LIFE
God	Is 40:12-31

RESPECT for
Moses	Deut 31:30-32:47

RESURRECTION through
Jesus	Acts 5:17-42

SALVATION through
God	Is 33:17-24
Israelites	Judg 2:11-19
Psalmist	Ps 80:1-3

SECURITY in
Asaph	Ps 73:21-28

LEADERSHIP through
AUTHORITY of
Gideon	Judg 8:22-23

LIFE from
through ELECTION
Jesus	Jn 6:25-59

EQUALITY in
God	Prov 22:1-16

ETERNAL
Believers	1 Jn 2:24-27; 5:8-12
God	Ps 90:1-12; 93:1-2; 102:23-28; 133:1-3; Is 40:12-31; 41:1-42:4; 44:6-8; 21-23; 48:1-22; Hab 1:12-17; 1 Tim 6:11-16; Rev 1:4-20; 15:1-16:1; 21:1-8
Jesus	Jn 6:25-59
John	1 Jn 1:1-4

through FIDELITY
God	Ps 119:89-96
Paul	Gal 2:17-19
Psalmist	Ps 80:14-19

KNOWLEDGE of
David	Ps 16:9-11; 39:4-6
Israelites	Hos 13:4-6
Jeremiah	Jer 1:4-10

through MEDIATION
Aaron	Num 16:36-50
Jesus	1 Tim 2:1-7

in NEW AGE
Mankind	Rev 21:1-8

PRAYER for
David	Ps 13:1-4; 18:4-6; 30:6-10; 31:13-18; 59:11; 64:1-2; 86:1-7
Hezekiah	Is 38:1-22
Psalmist	Ps 88:3-9; 119:25-32; 33-40;

ETERNAL (cont'd)
God	26;
	138:7-8;
	Jer 31:2-6

FIDELITY of
Asaph	Ps 77:1-10
David	Ps 5:8-10;
	13:5-6;
	18:46-50;
	36:5-9
God	Ex 34:5b-9;
	Deut 7:6-16;
	1 Chr 15:1-16:43;
	2 Chr 17:1-20:37;
	Ps 25:1-7;
	8-15;
	26:1-3;
	31:1-8;
	13-18;
	19-24;
	32:8-11;
	33:4-9;
	13-19;
	20-22;
	36:10-12;
	40:11;
	42:6-11;
	44:23-26;
	48:9-14;
	51:1-2;
	52:8-9;
	57:1-3;
	7-11;
	59:9-10;
	16-17;
	62:8-12;
	63:1-8;
	66:13-20;
	69:13-21;
	85:4-7;
	8-13;
	86:1-7;
	11-13;
	14-17;
	89:1-4;
	5-18;
	19-37;
	90:13-17;
	92:1-4;
	94:16-19;
	100:4-5;
	103:1-5;
	6-13;
	14-18;
	106:1-5;
	107:1-3;
	4-9;
	10-16;
	17-22;
	23-32;
	39-43;
	108:1-5;
	109:21-31;
	115:1-2;
	117:1-2;
	118:1-4;
	28-29;
	119:41-48;
	57-64;
	81-88;
	89-96;

FIDELITY (cont'd)
God	145-152;
	153-160;
	130:7-8;
	136:1-3;
	4-9;
	10-22;
	23-25;
	26;
	138:1-3;
	7-8;
	143:7-12;
	145:8-9;
	147:7-11;
	Jer 9:23-24;
	31:2-6;
	32:16-25;
	33:10-11;
	Lam 3:1-66;
	Dan 9:4-19;
	Joel 2:12-17;
	Mic 7:7-20
Isaiah	Is 63:7-64:12
Israelites	Neh 9:16-18;
	Ps 98:1-3
Jonah	Jon 4:1-11
King	Ps 61:6-7
Mankind	Ps 17:6-7

KNOWLEDGE of
Believers	1 Jn 4:7-12
Jesus	Jn 10:1-18

as **MOTIVATION**
Believers	1 Jn 4:19-5:5
Jesus	Jn 3:1-21;
	Rom 5:6-11;
	Eph 1:15-2:10

in **NEW AGE**
Disciples	Jn 16:25-28

PRAYER for
David	Ps 36:10-12
Psalmist	Ps 33:20-22

PRESENCE of
Believers	1 Jn 4:7-12
Corinthians	2 Cor 13:11-13
David	Ps 26:8-12

PROVIDENCE through
Believers	1 Cor 2:6-9
Ezra	*2 Esd 3:1-36
Israelites	Hos 11:1-4
Jesus	2 Thes 2:16-17
Job	Job 10:8-12
Psalmist	Ps 116:1-11

PUNISHMENT through
Believers	Heb 12:3-11
God	Prov 3:1-35

as **QUALITY OF LIFE**
God	1 Jn 4:7-12;
	13-18
Isaiah	Is 61:1-11

RECONCILIATION through
Israelites	Is 42:18-43:7;
	Zech 10:3-12
Jesus	1 Jn 4:7-12

RESPECT for
God	Ps 147:7-11
Israelites	Ps 103:6-13;
	14-18

SALVATION through
Believer	Jas 1:12;
	Ps 145:13b-20;
	1 Jn 4:7-12

SALVATION through (cont'd)
   David   Ps 6:1-5;
                        31:13-18
   Jesus   Eph 1:15-2:10
   Mankind   Tit 3:1-7
SECURITY in
   David   Ps 18:1-3;
                        31:19-24
   King   Ps 21:1-7
overcomes SIN
   Jesus   Rom 5:6-11
TRUTH in
   Disciples   Lk 24:50-51;
                        Jn 8:21-59
as VIRTUE
   God   Ps 11:4-7;
                        33:4-9;
                        146:7c-9;
                        Prov 15:1-33

LUST against
PUNISHMENT for
   Gentiles   Rom 1:24-32

MEDIATION with
concerning ANGER
   Moses   Ps 106:19-23
on DEATH
   Jesus   Rom 8:28-39
in DISCIPLESHIP
   Jesus   Jn 14:1-14;
                        Rom 8:28-39;
                        Eph 2:11-22;
                        Heb 6:13-20;
                        7:1-28;
                        9:23-28
concerning EVIL
   Mankind   1 Sam 2:11-26
through GRACE
   Jesus   Rom 5:1-5
   Moses   Ex 32:7-14;
                        Deut 9:7-24;
                        25-29
for GUILT
   Aaron   Ex 28:36-39
for INNOCENCE
   Jesus   1 Thes 3:11-13
for LIFE
   Aaron   Num 16:36-50
   Jesus   1 Tim 2:1-7
through MIRACLE
   Aaron   Num 16:36-50
concerning REVENGE
   God   Ps 37:1-11
   Israelites   Jer 51:1-64
SACREDNESS of
   Elihu   Job 33:23-25
concerning SACRIFICE
   Aaron   Ex 30:1-10
   High Priest   Heb 5:1-10
on SERVICE
   Aaron   Ex 28:1-5
   Isaiah   Is 40:1-11
   Job   Job 42:7-9
WISDOM in
   Elihu   Job 36:1-4
WITNESS to
   Israelites   Mal 2:17-3:5

MIRACLE by
through AUTHORITY

---

through AUTHORITY (cont'd)
   God   Mic 1:2-4;
                        Nah 1:1-9;
                        2 Cor 4:7-12
   Jesus   Lk 11:14-23
BELIEF in
   Israel   Ex 4:27-31
   Israelites   Ps 78:40-55
   Joshua   Josh 10:1-15
   People   Lk 1:57-80
CONFRONTATION with
   Balaam   Num 22:22-35
   Ezekiel   Ezek 3:12-15
   Samaritans   2 Kgs 7:3-20
in CREATION
   God   Is 50:1-11
FREEDOM through
   Israelites   Jer 32:16-25
MEDIATION through
   Aaron   Num 16:36-50
PRAYER for
   Sirach   *Sir 36:1-10
through PRESENCE
   David   Ps 29:3-9;
                        144:5-8
   God   2 Sam 22:1-51;
                        Ps 18:7-15;
                        Nah 1:1-9
   Jesus   Jn 14:18-24
PROMISE of
   God   Is 29:13-14
through PROVIDENCE
   Assyrians   2 Kgs 19:9b-37
   Elijah   1 Kgs 17:1-24
   Elisha   2 Kgs 2:19-22;
                        4:42-44
   Ephraimites   Ps 78:9-20
   Ezekiel   Ezek 33:21-22
   God   Ps 66:5-7;
                        135:8-12;
                        136:10-22;
                        Hab 3:3-15
   Isaiah   Is 63:7-64:12
   Israelites   Ex 13:17-22;
                        14:15-22;
                        Num 11:31-35;
                        Josh 6:15-21;
                        Neh 9:9-11;
                        12-15;
                        Ps 78:21-31;
                        106:6-12;
                        Is 42:18-43:7
   Jonah   Jon 4:1-11
   Samson   Judg 15:9-20
RESPECT for
   David   Ps 29:3-9
SALVATION through
   Daniel   Dan 6:16-23;
                        *Bel 1:31-39

SIGNS of
   Believers   Acts 4:23-31
   Elders   Num 11:24b-30
   Elijah   2 Kgs 1:1-18
   Gideon   Judg 6:36-40
   Moses   Ps 105:26-36
   Philistines   1 Sam 5:1-12;
                        6:1-7:1
   Samuel   1 Sam 12:1-25

is MOTIVATION

is **MOTIVATION** (cont'd)
  for **PRAISE**
    David   Ps 40:1-3

MOTIVATION of
  through **ANGER**
    God   Zeph 1:17-18
    Israelites   2 Sam 24:1-25;
         1 Chr 21:1-22:1;
         Is 10:24-27c;
         Ezek 16:15-34;
         21:8-17;
         Zech 1:7-17
  through **ANXIETY**
    Habakkuk   Hab 1:2-4
  through **COMPASSION**
    God   Gen 2:18-20
  through **JEALOUSY**
    God   Zeph 1:17-18;
         Zech 7:4-8:23
    Israelites   Zech 1:7-17
  through **JOY**
    David   Ps 4:6-8
  through **LOVE**
    Believers   1 Jn 4:19-5:5
    Jesus   Jn 3:1-21;
         Rom 5:6-11;
         Eph 1:15-2:10
  REPENTANCE as
    Israelites   Neh 9:26-31
    People   Rom 2:1-24
  through **SPIRIT**
    Cyrus   *1 Esd 2:1-7
    Daniel   *Susa 1:42-51
    Israelites   Ex 35:30-36:7
    Mankind   1 Sam 16:1-13
    Zerubbabel   Zech 4:6b-10a

NEW AGE of
  HOPE in
    Believers   1 Jn 2:28-3:3
    Isaiah   Is 28:1-13
    Paul   1 Cor 1:4-9
  JUSTICE in
    Ezra   *2 Esd 4:33-52
  LIFE in
    Mankind   Rev 21:1-8
  LOVE in
    Disciples   Jn 16:25-28
  REPENTANCE in
    John the Baptist   Mt 3:1-12
  SERVICE in
    Israelites   Is 43:14-44:5
  SPIRIT in
    Believers   1 Cor 2:6-9
  VICTORY in
    Mankind   Rev 21:1-8
  WILL in
    Believers   Lk 12:32-34

OBEDIENCE to
    Balaam   Num 22:5-14;
         15-21
    Benjaminites   Ezra 1:5
    Ezra   *2 Esd 14:19-48
    Joseph   Mt 1:18-25
    Judahites   Ezra 1:5
  through **COMMITMENT**
    Psalmist   Ps 119:9-16;
         105-112
  through **ELECTION**

through **ELECTION** (cont'd)
    Abraham   Gen 18:16-22
  FIDELITY in
    Apostles   Acts 5:17-42
    Asa   1 Kgs 15:9-15
    David   Ps 17:3-5;
         18:20-24
    Ezekiel   Ezek 2:8b-3:3
    Ezra   *2 Esd 13:51-58
    Isaiah   Is 50:1-11
    Job   Job 1:1;
         22;
         2:9-10
    John   1 Jn 1:5-10
    Judahites   Hos 11:12-12:1
    Levites   Ezra 1:5
    Psalmist   Ps 119:49-56
    Tobit   *Tb 1:3-9;
         10-22
  FREEDOM through
    Psalmist   Ps 119:41-48
  HONESTY of
    Sirach   *Sir 1:22-30
  KNOWLEDGE of
    Jesus   Jn 8:21-59;
         14:27-31
    Psalmist   Ps 119:33-40
  PRAYER for
    Author   Heb 13:1-25
    Psalmist   Ps 119:1-8
  results in **PRESENCE**
    Amos   Amos 5:14-15
    Israelites   Ezek 36:22-32
    Jehoshaphat   2 Chr 17:1-20:37
    Jesus   Jn 8:21-59
  through **PROMISE**
    David   Ps 56:10-13
    Israelites   Ex 19:1-8
    Psalmist   Ps 119:145-152
  PROVIDENCE through
    Mankind   Ps 1:1-3
  through **RESPECT**
    God   Prov 23:15-24:22;
         Eccl 12:12-14
  SALVATION through
    Mankind   Ps 15:1-5b
    Psalmist   Ps 119:145-152
  SECURITY in
    Hannah   1 Sam 2:1-10
  SIGNS of
    Abraham   Gen 17:23-27

OLD AGE
  SECURITY in
    Believers   Ps 92:12-15

ONENESS with
    God   Deut 6:4-19;
         Is 44:6-8;
         21-23;
         46:1-13
    Jesus   Jn 1:1-18;
         5:19-47;
         14:1-14;
         Col 1:18-20
  in **BROTHERHOOD**
    Jesus   Jn 8:21-59;
         17:20-26
  COMMITMENT to
    Believers   1 Jn 4:13-18

GIFT of
Holy Spirit   1 Cor 12:4-11
through PRESENCE
    Jesus   Jn 14:1-14;
                         18-24;
                         16:29-33
as QUALITY OF LIFE
    God   Is 44:24-45:13;
                         14-25;
                         Zech 14:1-21;
                         Rom 3:21-30;
                         1 Cor 8:4-6;
                         Gal 3:19-25;
                         1 Tim 2:1-7
    Jesus   Jn 10:19-40
SALVATION through
    God   1 Tim 2:1-7
TRUTH in
    God   Eph 4:1-6

OPPRESSION by
    Isaiah   Is 52:13-53:12
KNOWLEDGE of
    Israelites   Ex 2:23b-25;
                         Acts 6:8-8:3
PROVIDENCE through
    David   Ps 89:38-51
    God   Ps 107:39-43
    Israelites   Ps 107:4-9
as PUNISHMENT
    God   Jer 32:16-25
    Israelites   Judg 4:1-3;
                         10:6-18;
                         13:1;
                         2 Kgs 13:1-9
    Job   Job 10:13-17;
                         19:7-12
as QUALITY OF LIFE
    David   Ps 57:4-6

ORDER made by
through AUTHORITY
    David   Ps 19:1-4b
    Ezra   *2 Esd 8:4-36
    God   Ps 19:4c-6;
                         33:4-9;
                         50:1-6;
                         65:5-8;
                         74:12-17;
                         77:11-20;
                         89:5-18;
                         93:3-4;
                         95:1-7c;
                         97:1-5;
                         104:1-4;
                         5-9;
                         135:5-7;
                         147:12-20
    Jeremiah   *Jer 6:60-73
    Manasseh   *Mana 1:1-5
    Mankind   Ps 8:3-8
    Sirach   *Sir 16:24-30;
                         17:15-32;
                         18:1-14;
                         33:7-15
                         39:17-27;
                         42:15-43:33
    Solomon   *Wis 7:15-8:1;
                         9:1-18;
                         11:21-12:2;

through AUTHORITY (cont'd)
    Solomon   13:1-9
ETERNAL
    God   Eccl 3:9-15
KNOWLEDGE of
    God   Ps 87:4-6
through PRESENCE
    God   Ps 68:4-14
PROMISE of
    God   Gen 8:13-22
PROVIDENCE in
    Amos   Amos 3:3-8
    God   Ps 65:9-13;
                         104:10-13;
                         107:23-32;
                         147:7-11;
                         Jer 31:35-37

PATIENCE of
    Isaiah   Is 40:12-31
in JUDGMENT
    Isaiah   Is 26:7-19
in PRESENCE
    Jesus   Heb 10:1-18
PROVIDENCE through
    Jeremiah   Lam 3:1-66
SALVATION through
    David   Ps 62:1-2;
                         5-7
as VIRTUE
    God   Ex 34:5b-9

PEACE from
    DESIRE for
        Job   Job 10:18-22
    ETERNAL
        Jesus   2 Thes 2:16-17
    through FIDELITY
        God   Is 26:1-6
    through JUDGMENT
        God   Is 2:1-5
    through LAW
        Psalmist   Ps 119:161-168
    PRAYER for
        David   Ps 29:10-11;
                         122:6-9
        John   2 Jn 1:1-3;
                         3 Jn 1:13-15;
                         Rev 1:4-20
        Paul   Col 1:1-2;
                         Tit 1:1-4;
                         Philm 1:1-3
        Peter   1 Pet 1:1-2;
                         5:12-14
        Psalmist   Ps 125:4-5;
                         128:5-6;
                         131:1-3
    PROMISE of
        Solomon   1 Chr 22:2-19
    PROVIDENCE in
        Asa   2 Chr 14:1-16:14
        Believers   Prov 16:1-33
        God   Is 2:1-5
        Isaiah   Is 63:7-64:12
    as QUALITY OF LIFE
        God   1 Cor 14:26-33
    RECONCILIATION through
        Israelites   Nah 1:10,12,13,15
        Jesus   Col 1:18-20
    SECURITY in

RITE of (cont'd)
David   13:5-6;
18:46-50;
26:6b-7;
27:4-6;
30:1-5;
59:9-10;
63:1-8;
65:1-4;
144:9-11;
*Sir 47:1-11
God   Rev 4:1-11
Jeremiah   Jer 20:7-18
Psalmist   Ps 66:8-12;
87:7;
147:1-6
for **SALVATION**
David   Ps 9:13-14;
40:13-17
God   Rev 19:1-5
Psalmist   Ps 67:1-7
for **SECURITY**
David   Ps 59:16-17
Eliphaz   Job 5:8-17
through **STEWARDSHIP**
Psalmist   Ps 116:12-19
through **TRUTH**
Disciples   Lk 24:50-51
as **VIRTUE**
Psalmist   Ps 71:1-21;
111:2-4
in **WORSHIP**
Hilkaiah   *Susa 1:60-64

PRESENCE of
Ezekiel   Ezek 4C:1-5
Jesus   1 Pet 3:18-22
ACCEPTANCE of
Abraham   Gen 18:1-8
Holy Spirit Lk 3:21-22
Isaiah   Is 8:8b-10
Israelites   Lev 9:1-24
Lot   Gen 19:1-3
ALIENATION from
Israelites   Amos 7:7-9;
8:1-3;
11-14
Samson   Judg 16:16-22
Saul   1 Sam 16:14-23
ANGER in
God   Is 30:27-33
Saul   1 Sam 11:1-15
BLESSING through
God   Is 43:14-44:5
Israelites   Ezek 34:25-31;
36:8-15
Zechariah Lk 1:57-80
COURAGE through
Believers   Acts 4:23-31
Ezra   Ezra 7:27-28
Israelites   Hag 1:15b-2:9
Joshua   Josh 1:1-9
DIGNITY in
David   1 Chr 11:1-12:40
Solomon   2 Chr 1:1-17
DISCIPLESHIP in
Believers   Ps 46:4-7;
2 Cor 6:14-7:1;
1 Thes 4:13-18
David   1 Chr 15:1-16:43;
Ps 23:1-4

DISCIPLESHIP in (cont'd)
Holy Spirit Acts 2:1-13;
10:1-11:18;
2 Tim 1:8-14
Jesus   Jn 14:18-24
Psalmist   Ps 105:1-6
FAITH in
Believers   Ps 145:13b-20;
Eph 3:14-19
David   Ps 27:13-14;
139:13-18
Israelites   Is 42:18-43:7;
Zeph 3:14-20
Jeremiah   Jer 42:7-22
in **FAMILY**
Mankind   Rev 21:1-8
FEAR of
Egyptians Is 19:1-15
Elihu   Job 37:1-13;
14-22
Isaiah   Is 63:7-64:12
Israelites   Deut 5:22-33
Jacob   Gen 28:10-22
Job   Job 23:15-17
Saul   1 Sam 18:6-30
Tobit   *Tb 12:1-22
FULFILLMENT through
David   Ps 17:15;
51:3-12
God   Num 14:11-24;
Is 6:1-13
Jesus   Col 2:6-15
Nehemiah Neh 1:11b-2:8
GOOD in
Mankind   Ps 15:1-5b
GRIEF in
David   Ps 30:6-10
HOPE in
Believers   Tit 2:11-15
HUMILITY in
God   Is 57:14-21
IGNORANCE of
Elihu   Job 37:23-24
Job   Job 23:8-14;
35:13-16
Psalmist   Ps 10:1-2
JOY in
Believers   Acts 13:14-52
David   Ps 16:9-11
Elihu   Job 33:26-28
God   Ps 48:1-3
Israelites   Zech 2:6-13
King   Ps 21:1-7
JUSTICE in
David   2 Sam 23:1-7
God   Is 41:1-42:4
Micah   Mic 3:1-12
LIFE in
God   Is 66:1-16
Hagar   Gen 16:11-16
Israelites   Jer 30:10-11
Manoah   Judg 13:15-23
Simeon   Lk 2:21-40
Zechariah Zech 4:1-6a;
10b-14
LOVE in
Believers   1 Jn 4:7-12
Corinthians 2 Cor 13:11-13
David   Ps 26:8-12
MIRACLE through
David   Ps 29:3-9;

MIRACLE through (cont'd)
David	144:5-8
God	2 Sam 22:1-51;
	Ps 18:7-15;
	Nah 1:1-9
Jesus	Jn 14:18-24

OBEDIENCE through
Amos	Amos 5:14-15
Israelites	Ezek 36:22-32
Jehoshaphat	2 Chr 17:1-20:37
Jesus	Jn 8:21-59

ONENESS in
Jesus	Jn 14:1-14;
	18-24;
	16:29-33

ORDER in
God	Ps 68:4-14

PATIENCE in
Jesus	Heb 10:1-18

PRAISE in
Asaph	Ps 76:1-3
God	Ps 140:12-13
Psalmist	Ps 84:3-4

PURIFICATION in
Jesus	Jn 1:19-51

REWARDs of
David	Ps 23:5-6;
	41:11-12
God	Ps 24:3-6

SACREDNESS in
David	1 Sam 16:1-13;
	Ps 27:4-6
	63:1-8
God	Num 5:1-4;
	16:36-50;
	Ps 11:4-7;
	Ezek 44:4-5;
	Hab 2:18-20;
	Hag 1:1-11
Israelites	Ex 40:34-38;
	Deut 5:22-33;
	Ezek 43:6-12
Joshua	Josh 5:13-15
Moses	Ex 24:1-18;
	34:29-35;
	2 Cor 3:7-11
Psalmist	Ps 84:1-2
Solomon	2 Chr 5:1-7:10

SERVICE in
Israelites	Ex 31:1-11
Jesus	Heb 8:1-5;
	9:23-28
Nehemiah	Neh 2:16-18
Saul	1 Sam 19:18-24

through SPIRIT
Daniel	Dan 4:18
Eliphaz	Job 4:12-16
Ezekiel	Ezek 2:1-8a;
	3:12-15;
	22-27;
	8:1-4;
	11:1-13;
	22-25;
	43:1-5
God	Gen 1:1-2;
	3:1-8;
	Ps 139:7-12
Holy Spirit	Tit 3:1-7
Isaiah	Is 32:15-20
Israelites	Ezek 37:1-14;
	39:25-29;

through SPIRIT (cont'd)
	Hag 1:12-14
Jerusalemites	Zech 7:4-8:23
Joseph	Gen 41:1-57
Micah	Mic 3:1-12
Moses	Ex 17:1-7
Samson	Judg 13:24-25;
	14:5-9
Saul	1 Sam 9:1-10:16

SUFFERING in
David	Ps 38:1-2;
	39:7-13

VICTORY through
David	2 Sam 7:1-29;
	1 Chr 17:1-27
Israelites	Deut 20:1-9;
	Jer 46:27-28;
	Zech 10:3-12
Jephthah	Judg 11:29-33
Jeremiah	Jer 1:4-10;
	17-19
Samson	Judg 14:10-20;
	15:9-20

VIOLENCE in
Deborah	Judg 5:2-5

WEALTH in
Hezekiah	2 Kgs 18:4-8

WILL in
Believers	Phil 2:12-18

WISDOM in
Believers	1 Jn 4:13-18
Daniel	Dan 5:10-17
Elihu	Job 32:6-10
Elizabeth	Lk 1:39-56
God	Jer 23:23-32
Isaiah	Is 11:1-9
Moses	Ex 4:10-16
Stephen	Acts 6:8-8:3

WITNESS to
Azariah	2 Chr 14:1-16:14
Balaam	Num 23:27-24:13
Barnabas	Acts 11:22-24
David	2 Sam 23:1-7
Holy Spirit	1 Jn 4:13-18
Isaiah	Is 61:1-11
Israelites	Num 14:10;
	16:16-24
Moses	Num 20:2-13
Peter	Acts 4:1-22
Prophets	Num 11:24b-30
Zechariah	2 Chr 24:1-27

PROMISE of
ACCEPTANCE of
Israelites	Jer 31:35-37

ALIENATION through
Israelites	*1 Esd 8:91-96;
	9:1-15

BLESSING through
Abraham	Gen 22:1-19
Caleb	Num 14:11-24;
	Deut 1:19-46
Isaac	Gen 26:1-11
Jacob	Gen 28:10-22

for DESTRUCTION
God	Is 5:8-24a;
	Jer 4:27-29

concerning DISOBEDIENCE
Zedekiah	*1 Esd 1:46-58

DOUBT in
Israelites	Ps 106:24-27

DOUBT in (cont'd)

| Sarah | Gen 16:1-6; 18:9-15 |

concerning the ENEMY

| Uzziah | *Jdt 7:23-32 |

to FAMILY

Abraham	Gen 17:15-22; 22:1-19
Believers	Rom 9:6-13
David	2 Sam 7:1-29; 1 Chr 17:1-27; Ps 132:11-18
Isaac	Gen 26:12-31
Ishmael	Gen 21:15-21
Sarah	Gen 17:15-22

FULFILLMENT of

Abraham	Gen 21:1-7
Believer	Eccl 5:1-7; Heb 11:1-40
Egyptians	Ezek 30:10-12
Ezekiel	Ezek 28:1-10
Ezra	Neh 9:7-8
God	Ps 12:5-6; 18:25-30; Is 14:24-27; 45:14-25; 46:1-13; Jer 4:27-29; 2 Pet 3:8-10
Hagar	Gen 16:11-16
Israelites	Josh 21:8-45; Neh 9:22-25; Ps 105:37-42; Ezek 37:1-14
Jesus	Rom 15:1-13
Joshua	Josh 23:1-16
Moses	Ex 4:27-31; 23:20-33; Deut 23:15-25:19
Solomon	1 Kgs 8:54-61

for GOOD

| Solomon | *Wis 15:1-6 |

through GRACE

Antiochus	*2 Mc 9:5-29
Manasseh	*Mana 1:6-7
Peter	2 Pet 1:3-4

GRATITUDE for

| David | Ps 142:5-7 |

HUMILITY in

| God | Ps 37:1-11 |

LEADERSHIP through

| David | 1 Kgs 2:1-4 |

for LIFE

| Psalmist | Ps 119:49-56; 113-120; 153-160 |

concerning MARRIAGE

| Sarah | *Tb 3:16-17 |

concerning ORDER

| God | Gen 8:13-22 |

for PEACE

| Solomon | 1 Chr 22:2-19 |

PRAISE of

Asaph	Ps 79:5-13
David	Ps 69:29-36; 109:21-31
Manasseh	*Mana 1:11-15

of REWARDs

| Abraham | Gen 18:16-22 |
| Israelites | Deut 26:16-19 |

of VICTORY

of VICTORY (cont'd)

David	Ps 110:1-4
God	Ps 50:7-15
Peter	2 Pet 1:3-4

of WILL

| Solomon | 1 Kgs 3:1-15 |

WITNESS to

| Holy Spirit | Jn 15:26-27 |

PROMISE to

OBEDIENCE to

David	Ps 56:10-13
Israelites	Ex 19:1-8
Psalmist	Ps 119:145-152

of SACRIFICE

| Jonah | Jon 2:1-10 |

PROVIDENCE of

ACCEPTANCE of

Cyrus	Is 45:14-25
Jacob	Gen 28:10-22
Job	Job 1:20-21; 2:9-10

ALIENATION from

| Israelites | 2 Kgs 10:32-33 |

ANXIETY concerning

| Habakkuk | Hab 1:12-17 |

BLESSING through

Assyrians	Is 19:18-25
Baruch	*Bar 5:1-4
Believers	Ps 97:10-12
David	Ps 13:5-6; 16:5-8; 18:31-42; 22:6-11; 23:1-4; 5-6; 89:19-37
Egyptians	Is 19:18-25
God	Ps 67:1-7; 68:4-14; 107:33-38; 113:5-9; 127:1-2; 147:12-20
Isaac	Gen 25:7-11
Israelites	Deut 4:32-40; 2 Chr 30:1-31:21; Ps 78:40-55; 105:23-25; Is 19:18-25; Hos 2:16-20; 13:4-6; Amos 2:9-12
Joseph	Gen 39:1-23
Judahites	2 Chr 17:1-20:37
Mankind	Ps 8:3-8; Zech 10:1-2
Melchizedek	Gen 14:17-20
Nebuchadnezzar	*Bar 1:5-14
Psalmist	Ps 66:8-12; 85:1-3; 92:5-11
Solomon	1 Chr 28:1-29:30

in CAPTIVITY

| God | Ps 107:10-16 |
| Joseph | Ps 105:16-22 |

through CHAOS

| Philistines | 1 Sam 7:2-17 |

COMPASSION in

| God | Gen 3:20-24; |

COMPASSION in (cont'd)

	Ps 103:6-13
Jonah	Jon 4:1-11
Solomon	*Wis 18:20-25

COURAGE through

David	Ps 27:1-3;
	56:10-13
God	Ps 91:1-13

in DEATH

Elihu	Job 34:16-20
God	1 Sam 2:11-26
Jesus	Lk 23:46-49
Psalmist	Ps 88:10-12

in DEFEAT

Egyptians	Ex 14:23-31
Israelites	Deut 28:15-68;
	Judg 3:12-14;
	Ps 106:40-46
Psalmist	Ps 44:9-16

revealed in DESTRUCTION

David	Ps 18:31-42
God	Is 10:33-34
Philistia	Is 14:28-32

in DISCIPLESHIP

Believers	Acts 11:19-21;
	2 Pet 2:4-10a
David	Ps 28:8-9
Solomon	*Wis 19:18-22

overcomes DISOBEDIENCE

Mankind	Rom 11:25-32

DOUBT in

David	Ps 22:1-5
Ethan	Ps 89:38-51
Israelites	Ex 16:1-21;
	17:1-7;
	Num 14:1-2;
	Deut 6:4-19;
	Ps 95:7d-11
Mankind	Ps 3:1-2

PROVIDENCE of
DOUBT in

Psalmist	Ps 88:10-12;
	13-14

over ENEMY

David	Ps 18:1-3;
	23:5-6;
	25:1-7;
	27:7-12;
	31:13-18;
	35:17-18;
	59:1-5;
	108:6-13
Israelites	Ezra 8:31-36;
	Is 9:8-10:4;
	*1 Esd 6:3-6
Mankind	Ps 17:6-7

over EVIL

Absalom	2 Sam 16:15-17:29
Believers	Ps 125:1-3
God	Amos 3:3-8
Job	Job 24:13-25
Psalmist	Ps 119:17-24
Saul	1 Sam 16:14-23
Shechemites	Judg 9:22-25

FAITH in

Asaph	Ps 73:21-28
Believers	Ps 55:22;
	1 Pet 5:6-11
David	Ps 3:3-6;

FAITH in (cont'd)

David	13:5-6;
	20:6-9;
	22:1-5;
	6-11;
	23:5-6;
	27:4-6;
	28:6-7;
	32:8-11;
	55:15-19;
	56:1-4;
	57:1-3;
	60:9-12;
	62:8-12;
	142:5-7
God	Ps 86:1-7
Jeremiah	Jer 20:7-18
Jonah	Jon 2:1-10
Moses	Ex 19:9-15
Psalmist	Ps 71:1-21

over FAMILY

Believers	Ps 128:3-4;
	1 Jn 2:28-3:3
God	Ps 87:4-6;
	127:3-5
Jacob	Gen 29:31-30:24
Noah	Gen 8:1-12

through FEAR

Amorites	Josh 4:20-5:1
David	Ps 25:8-15
Egyptians	Is 19:16-17
Habakkuk	Hab 3:2
People	Ps 107:23-32
Sanballat	Neh 6:15-16

FULFILLMENT through

David	Ps 22:22-26;
	23:1-4
Ezra	Ezra 7:6-10
God	Prov 16:1-33
Paul	Phil 4:10-20
Rehoboam	1 Kgs 12:1-20;
	2 Chr 10:1-12:16

for GOOD

Believers	Ps 92:12-15;
	Rom 8:28-39
God	Ps 85:8-13;
	118:15-21
James	Jas 1:16-18
Sirach	*Sir 39:28-35

through GRACE

David	Ps 23:5-6
God	Ps 147:1-6
Israelites	2 Kgs 13:22-25;
	Neh 9:19-21;
	Is 1:4-9
Jesus	2 Thes 2:16-17
Solomon	*Wis 16:1-14

GRATITUDE for

David	Ps 30:11-12;
	40:6-10;
	52:8-9;
	54:6-7;
	86:11-13;
	144:1-2
Isaiah	Is 26:7-19

over GRIEF

Psalmist	Ps 119:25-32

HEALING through

Abimelech	Gen 20:1-18
David	Ps 41:1-3
God	Ps 103:1-5;

DEITY (cont'd)

in VICTORY (cont'd)

God	89:5-18; 118:15-21; 136:10-22; 149:1-4; Prov 21:1-31
Hezekiah	2 Kgs 20:1-11
Isaiah	Is 59:1-21
Israelites	Ex 3:7-10; Num 21:33-35; Deut 1:19-46; 2:26-3:11; 12-22; 9:1-6; 12:1-31; 31:1-8; Josh 11:16-23; Judg 4:10-16; 7:16-22; 1 Sam 19:1-10; 1 Chr 15:1-16:43; Neh 4:13-23; Ps 44:1-3; 4-8; 105:7-15; 23-25; 106:6-12; Is 43:14-44:5
Jacob	Gen 46:1-7
Jephthah	Judg 11:29-33
Jeroboam	2 Kgs 14:23-29
Jesus	Rom 8:1-4; Col 2:6-15
Joshua	Num 14:8-9; Josh 23:1-16
Judah	Judg 1:1-21
Maccabeus	*1 Mc 4:1-35
Mankind	Ps 18:25-30
Paul	2 Tim 3:10-13
Psalmist	Ps 92:5-11; 94:16-19
Uzziah	2 Chr 26:1-28:27

in VIOLENCE

David	2 Sam 22:1-51; Ps 18:31-42
God	2 Chr 17:1-20:37
Hezekiah	2 Chr 32:1-33
Israelites	Ex 14:1-14; Deut 1:19-46
Jonah	Jon 1:1-17

WEALTH by

Cyrus	Is 44:24-45:13
David	Ps 30:6-10
God	Ps 112:2-4; Eccl 6:1-12; 1 Tim 6:17-19
Israelites	Ex 11:1-10; 12:33-36; Deut 8:11-20; 17:14-20; Josh 5:10-12; 2 Chr 17:1-20:37; Neh 9:22-25; Ps 105:37-42; Hos 2:2-8
Job	Job 42:10-17
King	Ps 45:2-9
Psalmist	Ps 72:1-4
Solomon	1 Kgs 3:1-15; 2 Chr 1:1-17

WILL in

WILL in (cont'd)

God	Ps 135:5-7; Mt 10:26-39
James	Jas 1:16-18
Job	Job 12:13-25

WISDOM through

Believers	1 Jn 2:24-27
Cyrus	Is 44:24-45:13
God	Eccl 1:12-2:26; Is 44:24-45:13
Isaiah	Is 50:1-11
James	Jas 1:5-8
Solomon	2 Chr 1:1-17

WITNESS to

David	Ps 145:4-7
God	1 Jn 5:8-12
Holy Spirit	Gal 4:4-7
Israelites	Deut 10:12-22
Jesus	Jn 3:31-36
Mankind	Ps 64:7-10
Paul	2 Tim 4:9-18
Psalmist	Ps 66:13-20; 71:22-24

PRUDENCE of
in CREATION

God	Prov 16:1-33

PUNISHMENT by
ACCEPTANCE of

Daniel	Dan 9:4-19
Elihu	Job 36:16-25
Micah	Mic 7:7-20

ALIENATION as

Babylonians	Is 14:1-23
Bethelites	Zech 7:4-8:23
Edomites	Ezek 35:1-15
God	Gen 11:1-9; Ps 37:12-22; 53:4-5; 2 Thes 1:7b-10
Israelites	Num 14:39-45; 2 Chr 10:1-12:16; Is 9:8-10:4; Ezek 20:9-26
Jonah	Jon 1:1-17
Judahites	2 Kgs 23:25b-30; 24:18-25:7
Priests	Mal 1:6-2:9

through ANGER

David	Ps 21:8-13
God	Jer 12:7-13; Nah 1:1-9; 1 Thes 2:13-16
Isaiah	Is 63:1-6
Israelites	Judg 2:11-19; 3:7-11; Is 42:18-43:7; Ezek 43:6-12
Jeremiah	Jer 18:18-23; Lam 3:1-66
Judahites	Lam 4:1-22; Hos 5:8-14
Zedekiah	Jer 52:1-3
Zephaniah	Zeph 1:14-16

for BLASPHEMY

Antiochus	*2 Mc 9:5-29

BLESSING through

Psalmist	Ps 94:12-15

CAPTIVITY as

Israelites	2 Kgs 17:7-23;

CAPTIVITY as (cont'd)
Israelites	Neh 9:32-37; Ps 106:40-46; *Bar 2:1-10

CONDEMNATION as
Israelites	Is 9:8-10:4

DEATH as
Ahaziah	2 Chr 21:1-23:21
David	1 Chr 21:1-22:1; Ps 55:15-19
Elihu	Job 36:5-15
God	1 Sam 25:1-44; Ps 55:23
Israelites	Num 11:31-35; 16:36-50; 21:4-9; 2 Sam 24:1-25; Ps 78:21-31; *1 Esd 1:46-58
Judahites	2 Chr 26:1-28:27
Onan	Gen 38:1-11
Solomon	1 Kgs 1:41-53

DEFEAT as
Israelites	Num 14:39-45

in **DESTRUCTION**
Asaph	Ps 83:9-18
Assyrians	Is 10:24-27c; 14:24-27
Babylonians	Is 14:1-23
David	Ps 21:8-13; 63:9-10; 68:1-3
God	2 Chr 36:1-23; Nah 1:10,12,13, 15-2:2; 1 Cor 3:10-17; Rev 11:15-19
Isaiah	Is 63:1-6
Israelites	Num 16:25-35; Deut 2:1-25; Is 9:8-10:4; 17-19; Jer 12:7-13; Jude 1:5-7
Judahites	2 Kgs 23:25b-30
Mankind	Ps 64:7-10
Sinners	2 Pet 3:3-7
Zophar	Job 20:4-29

DISCIPLESHIP through
Psalmist	Ps 118:15-21

for **DISOBEDIENCE**
Azariah	*Azar 1:1-10
David	Ps 55:15-19; 89:19-37
God	Judg 9:56-57; Ps 95:7d-11; 119:17-24
Israelites	Num 16:25-35; Josh 7:6-26; Judg 10:6-18; 2 Kgs 18:9-12; Neh 9:32-37; Ps 106:24-27; Jer 32:16-25; *Bar 2:1-10; 24-26; Heb 4:1-13
Jehoshaphat	2 Chr 17:1-20:37
Judahites	2 Kgs 23:36-24:7
Moses	Deut 31:30-32:47
Psalmist	Ps 137:4-6

for **DISOBEDIENCE** (cont'd)
Saul	1 Chr 10:1-14
Uzzah	2 Sam 6:1-23; 1 Chr 13:1-14

for **DOUBT**
Princes	Ezek 11:1-13

of **ENEMY**
Asaph	Ps 79:5-13
Azariah	*Azar 1:1-10
David	Ps 5:8-10; 6:8-10; 31:13-18; 35:19-21; 40:13-17; 41:4-10; 54:4-5; 59:11; 63:9-10; 69:22-28; 109:6-20; 21-31; 143:7-12
God	Ps 97:1-5; Nah 1:1-9; 10,12,13,15-2:2
Isaiah	Is 25:1-5; 63:7-64:12
Psalmist	Ps 71:1-21; 80:14-19; 129:5-8

for **EVIL**
Angels	2 Pet 2:4-10a
Asaph	Ps 83:2-8
Babylonians	Is 14:1-23
Bildad	Job 8:10-19
Chaldeans	Hab 1:12-17
David	Ps 3:7-8; 7:3-5; 9-11; 12-16; 12:1-4; 28:1-5; 31:13-18; 35:4-8; 39:7-13; 59:1-5; 12-13b; 139:19-22; 140:9-11; 141:5-7; 8-10
Ephraimites	Hos 9:10-17
Gentiles	Rom 1:24-32
God	Ps 11:4-7; 31:19-24; 34:15-22; 37:1-11; 23-40; 50:16-21; 52:5-7; 53:4-5; 68:19-23; 73:13-20; 125:4-5; 146:7c-9; 147:1-6; Prov 10:1-32; 16:1-33; 22:22-23:14; Hab 3:3-15
Isaiah	Is 26:7-19;

for **EVIL** (cont'd)

Isaiah	63:7-64:12
Israelites	Deut 31:30-32:47; Judg 2:11-19; 6:1-6; 2 Kgs 17:7-23; Ps 78:56-66; 106:13-18; Is 9:8-10:4; 42:18-43:7; Ezek 43:6-12; Hos 8:4-7; 11-14; 9:7-9; 10:9-15; *2 Esd 1:24-40
Jews	*2 Mc 5:11-7:42
Job	Job 13:1-12; 27:1-12; 13-23; 31:5-34
Judahites	Lam 4:1-22
Mankind	Ps 5:4-7; 2 Pet 2:4-10a
Paul	2 Thes 1:5-7a
Psalmist	Ps 10:12-18; 92:5-11; 119:73-80; 129:1-4
Sirach	*Sir 17:15-32; 23:16-27
Sodomites	Gen 19:4-11
Zimri	1 Kgs 16:15-22
Zophar	Job 20:4-29

through **FEAR**

God	Ps 14:4-6
Israelites	Num 16:25-35

FULFILLMENT through

God	Rev 15:1-16:1

through **GOOD**

Psalmist	Ps 119:65-72

through **GRACE**

Job	Job 35:13-16

for **GUILT**

God	Nah 1:1-9

is **HUMILITY**

Jeremiah	Jer 17:13

for **IDOLATRY**

Israelites	Ps 78:56-66; Ezek 43:6-12
Moses	Deut 31:30-32:47

for **INDIFFERENCE**

God	Is 29:13-14
Israelites	Is 42:18-43:7; Amos 4:6-12

for **INNOCENCE**

Job	Job 9:14-19; 20-24

through **JEALOUSY**

God	Nah 1:1-9
Israelites	Deut 29:16-29

JOY in

Believers	Ps 58:10-11

JUSTICE in

David	Ps 17:13-14
Elihu	Job 36:5-15
Eliphaz	Job 5:8-17
God	Ps 94:20-23
Isaiah	Is 59:1-21
Israelites	Neh 9:32-37; Is 42:18-43:7

JUSTICE in (cont'd)

Job	Job 27:1-12
Paul	2 Thes 1:5-7a
Sirach	*Sir 39:28-35

for **KILLING**

Cain	Gen 4:1-16

through **LOVE**

Believers	Heb 12:3-11
God	Prov 3:1-35

for **LUST**

Gentiles	Rom 1:24-32

through **OPPRESSION**

God	Jer 32:16-25
Israelites	Judg 4:1-3; 10:6-18; 13:1; 2 Kgs 13:1-9
Job	Job 10:13-17; 19:7-12

for **PRIDE**

Assyrians	Is 10:5-16
Eliphaz	Job 22:21-30
God	Is 2:12-17
Hezekiah	2 Chr 32:1-33

in spite of **PURIFICATION**

Job	Job 9:30-35; 23:8-14

is **REJECTION**

God	Ps 68:4-14; Hos 6:4-6
Israelites	Neh 9:26-31; Ps 95:7d-11; Is 9:8-10:4; 30:8-17; Heb 3:12-19
Jeremiah	Jer 17:13
Judahites	Jer 7:29-8:3
Psalmist	Ps 119:113-120

REPENTANCE of

David	1 Chr 21:1-22:1
God	Ex 32:7-14; Jer 42:7-22; Amos 7:1-3; 4-6; Jon 3:1-10
Israelites	2 Sam 24:1-25; 1 Chr 21:1-22:1
Rehoboam	2 Chr 10:1-12:16

REVENGE as

David	Ps 56:6b-9
God	Nah 1:1-9; Rev 19:1-5
Solomon	*Wis 18:5-19
Unbelievers	2 Thes 2:11-12

SUFFERING through

Antiochus	*2 Mc 9:5-29
Azariah	2 Kgs 15:1-7
God	Rev 16:4-7
Israelites	Ex 32:30-35; Neh 9:26-31; Is 1:4-9
Job	Job 10:13-17; 19:7-12
Uzziah	2 Chr 26:1-28:27

WILL in

Tyre	Is 23:1-14

WISDOM in

Sirach	*Sir 32:14-24

PURIFICATION by
AUTHORITY of

as PUNISHMENT (cont'd)

Israelites	Neh 9:26-31; Ps 95:7d-11; Is 9:8-10:4; 30:8-17; Heb 3:12-19
Jeremiah	Jer 17:13
Judahites	Jer 7:29-8:3
Psalmist	Ps 119:113-120

resulting from SIN

Believers	Heb 6:1-8; 10:19-31
David	Ps 140:6-8
Elihu	Job 34:34-37
Gentiles	Rom 1:24-32
Israelites	Ps 78:56-66; Jer 2:1-13; 6:27-30; Hos 10:1-8; 13:4-6; *2 Esd 1:24-40
Mankind	Ps 14:1-3
Sinners	Jn 9:1-41
Sirach	*Sir 15:11-20

of STEWARDSHIP

Cain	Gen 4:1-16

REJECTION of

Ephraimites	Hos 7:3-7
Israelites	Is 1:2-3; 4-9
Saul	1 Sam 15:1-35

unBELIEF in

Israelites	Is 49:1-26; Ezek 9:1-11

by COMMUNITY

Israelites	2 Kgs 17:7-23
Mankind	Ps 2:1-3
Psalmist	Ps 44:9-16

CONFRONTATION with

Jesus	Lk 10:1-16

through inFIDELITY

Ephraimites	Hos 7:8-12
Job	Job 21:14-18; 34:5-9

through KNOWLEDGE

Galatian	Gal 4:8-11
Israelites	Ex 16:1-21; Num 14:26-38
Mankind	Ps 10:3-11

through disRESPECT

Israelites	Jer 6:9-15

of RITE

Israelites	Amos 5:21-25; Mal 2:10-16
Priests	Mal 1:6-2:9

SIGNS of

Israelites	Ps 78:40-55
Jesus	Jn 15:18-25

REPENTANCE to

in CONFRONTATION

Job	Job 42:1-6

results in CONVERSION

David	Ps 32:3-7; 51:3-12
Ephraim	Jer 31:15-22
God	Num 23:13-26; 1 Sam 15:1-35; 1 Chr 21:1-22:1; Ezek 24:1-14;

results in CONVERSION (cont'd)

God	Joel 2:12-17; Jon 3:1-10
Israelites	Hos 3:1-5; 5:15-6:3

PRAYER of

Daniel	Dan 9:4-19
Israelites	1 Sam 12:1-25; Hos 5:15-6:3

concerning PUNISHMENT

David	1 Chr 21:1-22:1
God	Ex 32:7-14; Jer 42:7-22; Amos 7:1-3; 4-6; Jon 3:1-10
Israelites	2 Sam 24:1-25; 1 Chr 21:1-22:1
Rehoboam	2 Chr 10:1-12:16

RESPECT for

People	Mic 7:7-20

RESPECT for

BLESSING in

Believers	Ps 33:13-19; 128:1-2; 3-4; Eccl 8:10-17
David	Ps 31:19-24
God	Ps 115:12-18; Prov 28:1-28
King	Ps 21:1-7
Mankind	Ps 112:1
Psalmist	Ps 71:1-21

through FAITH

David	2 Sam 22:1-51; Ps 18:1-3

through FEAR

Babylonians	2 Kgs 17:24-41
Darius	Dan 6:25-27
David	Ps 19:7-10
God	Prov 23:15-24:22; Is 33:1-6
Isaiah	Is 8:11-15; 59:1-21
Israelites	Deut 4:1-14; 6:20-25; Hos 3:1-5; Hag 1:12-14
Job	Job 1:1
Jonah	Jon 1:1-17
Kings	Ps 2:10-11
Mankind	Ps 15:1-5b; 33:4-9
Micah	Mic 7:7-20
Moses	Deut 6:4-19
Nehemiah	Neh 1:11b-2:8
Peter	1 Pet 2:13-17
Psalmist	Ps 67:1-7; 99:1-3
Sirach	*Sir 25:7-11; 32:14-24; 40:18-27
Wisdom	Prov 1:20-33

FULFILLMENT through

Believers	Ps 145:13b-20

HUMILITY in

God	Ps 138:4-6
Job	Job 30:9-15

JOY in

as **QUALITY** of life (cont'd)
   God   2 Cor 5:9-10
   Israelites   Ezek 33:10-20
   Jesus   Mt 16:21-28
   Paul   2 Thes 1:5-7a
RECONCILIATION through
   Isaiah   Is 40:1-11
for **RESPECT**
   God   Ps 112:2-4
   Israelites   Mal 3:13-4:3
for **SIN**
   Zophar   Job 20:4-29
for **STEWARDSHIP**
   God   Prov 25:1-28
   Isaiah   Is 49:1-26
   Israelites   2 Chr 30:1-31:21
for **VIRTUE**
   Believers   Ps 58:10-11;
                   92:12-15;
                   Eph 6:5-9;
                   Jas 4:1-10;
                   2 Pet 2:4-10a
   David   2 Sam 22:1-51;
                   Ps 18:20-24;
                   41:11-12
   Eliphaz   Job 22:1-5
   God   Ps 24:3-6;
                   37:12-22;
                   23-40;
                   75:9-10;
                   Prov 12:1-28
   Psalmist   Ps 125:4-5
REWARDs of
   David   Ps 23:5-6;
                   41:11-12
   God   Prov 19:1-29
                   Jer 32:16-25
   Jesus   Mt 7:7-11

CONVERSION through
   Eliphaz   Job 22:21-30
DESIRE for
   Israelites   Amos 5:4-6
   Psalmist   Ps 116:12-19
for **FIDELITY**
   Asa   2 Chr 14:1-16:14
   Believers   Ps 91:1-13;
                   14-16;
                   128:1-2;
                   3-4;
                   Dan 9:4-19;
                   Jn 9:1-41;
                   Col 3:18-4:1;
                   Heb 6:9-12;
                   1 Pet 5:6-11
   Bildad   Job 8:10-19;
                   20-22
   David   Ps 19:11-14
   Elihu   Job 36:5-15
   Ezra   *2 Esd 13:51-58
   God   Ps 25:8-15;
                   Prov 3:1-35;
                   Rev 11:15-19
   Israelites   Ex 19:1-8
   Mankind   Ps 15:1-5b;
                   18:25-30
   Psalmist   Ps 119:25-32
   Sirach   *Sir 2:12-18

KNOWLEDGE of
   Hannah   1 Sam 2:1-10
   Solomon   1 Kgs 8:22-53
PRAYER for
   David   Ps 25:1-7
   Nehemiah   Neh 5:14-19;
                   13:10-14;
                   15-22;
                   23-29;
                   30-31

RITE to
   ACCEPTANCE of
      God   Ps 51:18-19
   CONDEMNATION of
      Israelites   Amos 5:21-25
   JOY in
      David   Ps 63:1-8
      Isaiah   Is 26:7-19
      Psalmist   Ps 67:1-7
   revealing **PIETY**
      Daniel   Dan 9:1-3
   PRAISE of
      Asaph   Ps 75:9-10
      David   Ps 9:1-4;
                 13:5-6;
                18:46-50;
                26:6b-7;
                27:4-6;
                30:1-5;
                59:9-10;
                63:1-8;
                65:1-4;
                144:9-11;
                *Sir 47:1-11
      God   Rev 4:1-11
      Jeremiah   Jer 20:7-18
      Psalmist   Ps 66:8-12;
                87:7;
                147:1-6
   REJECTION of
      Israelites   Amos 5:21-25
                   Mal 2:10-16
      Priests   Mal 1:6-2:9
   SACREDNESS in
      Nineveh   Jon 3:1-10
   SACRIFICE as
      David   Ps 27:4-6;
                40:6-10;
                51:18-19
      God   Ps 51:13-17
      Israelites   Amos 5:21-25
      Nineveh   Jon 3:1-10
   WITNESS to
      David   Ps 26:6b-7

SACREDNESS of
   AUTHORITY of
      Jesus   Lk 22:66-71;
                   Jon 10:19-40
   un**BELIEF** in
      Moses   Num 20:2-13
   EQUALITY in
      Jesus   Jn 5:1-18
   ETERNAL
      God   Ps 93:5
   PRESENCE of
      David   1 Sam 16:1-13;
                   Ps 27:4-6;
                   63:1-8

PRESENCE of (cont'd)

God	Num 5:1-4;
	16:36-50;
	Ps 11:4-7;
	Ezek 44:4-5;
	Hab 2:18-20;
	Hag 1:1-11
Israelites	Ex 40:34-38;
	Deut 5:22-33;
	Ezek 43:6-12
Joshua	Josh 5:13-15
Moses	Ex 24:1-18;
	34:29-35;
	2 Cor 3:7-11
Psalmist	Ps 84:1-2
Solomon	2 Chr 5:1-7:10

PROMISE concerning

David	Ps 132:1-5

RESPECT for

Israelites	Is 29:17-24

in RITE

Nineveh	Jon 3:1-10

SIGNS of

Moses	Ex 31:18;
	32:15-24

in STEWARDSHIP

Aaron	Ex 29:42b-46

SACRIFICE to

COMMITMENT to

Jephthah	Judg 11:29-33
Jonah	Jon 1:1-17

MEDIATION concerning

Aaron	Ex 30:1-10
High Priest	Heb 5:1-10

PRAYER concerning

Jesus	Jn 12:27-36a

PROMISE to

Jonah	Jon 2:1-10

PROVIDENCE in

Abraham	Gen 22:1-19

RECONCILIATION through

High Priest	Heb 5:1-10

RESPECT for

David	Ps 20:1-5

as RITE

David	Ps 27:4-6;
	40:6-10;
	51:18-19
God	Ps 51:13-17
Israelites	Amos 5:21-25
Nineveh	Jon 3:1-10

SECURITY through

Lot	Gen 19:4-11

as SIN

God	Prov 15:1-33

through STEWARDSHIP

David	Ps 54:6-7

SALVATION by

ACCEPTANCE of

God	Ps 118:22-27

BLESSING in

David	Ps 28:8-9;
	68:19-23
God	Ps 103:1-5
Psalmist	Ps 80:14-19

from CAPTIVITY

God	Ps 136:10-22
Israelites	Ex 12:37-42;
	50-51;

from CAPTIVITY (cont'd)

Israelites	13:3-10;
	11-16;
	16:1-21;
	18:1-12;
	19:1-8;
	Deut 5:1-21;
	6:4-19;
	Ps 105:37-42;
	43-45;
	135:8-12;
	Acts 13:14-52

through COMPASSION

Psalmist	Ps 85:4-7

from CONDEMNATION

Jesus	Rom 5:6-11

from DEATH

Azariah	*Azar 1:28-68
Daniel	*Bel 1:31-39
Esther	*Esth 14:1-19
Mordecai	*Esth 13:8-18

from DESTRUCTION

Rehoboam	2 Chr 10:1-12:16

in DISCIPLESHIP

David	Ps 69:29-36
God	Ps 34:15-22;
	85:8-13

DOUBT in

Israelites	Ps 78:21-31
Moses	Ex 5:22-6:1

from ENEMY

Baruch	*Bar 4:21-37
David	2 Sam 3:17-39;
	1 Chr 15:1-16:43;
	Ps 3:7-8;
	55:15-19;
	69:13-21;
	86:14-17;
	109:21-31;
	124:1-5;
	144:5-8;
	9-11
Hezekiah	*Sir 48:17-25
Jews	*2 Mc 1:10-17
Judith	*Jdt 8:28-36
Mordecai	*Esth 10:4-13
Psalmist	Ps 44:4-8;
	106:47-48
Sirach	*Sir 51:1-12

from EVIL

David	Ps 28:1-5;
	39:7-13
Israelites	Ps 130:7-8
Psalmist	Ps 71:1-21

through FAITH

Believers	1 Pet 1:3-9
David	1 Sam 17:1-18:5;
	Ps 27:1-3;
	86:1-7
Habakkuk	Hab 3:16-19
Jesus	Heb 7:1-28
Job	Job 19:25-29
Micah	Mic 7:7-20
Psalmist	Ps 119:121-128
Shadrach	Dan 3:16-18
Sirach	*Sir 33:1-3
Thessalonians	2 Thes 2:13-15

for FAMILY

God	Gal 4:4-7

through FEAR

God	Ps 85:8-13

FULFILLMENT of

Sirach	*Sir 34:13-17
Believers	Ps 91:14-16
God	Is 46:1-13;
	Hab 3:3-15
Holy Spirit	Tit 3:1-7
Israelites	Ps 77:11-20;
	Is 31:4-9
Jesus	Eph 1:15-2:10;
	2 Tim 1:8-14
Paul	2 Tim 4:9-18

through GRACE

Believers	1 Jn 1:5-10
David	Ps 26:8-12
Epaphroditus	Phil 2:19-30
God	Ps 103:1-5;
	Mt 19:23-26;
	Mk 10:23-27
Isaiah	Is 63:7-64:12
Israelites	Neh 9:26-31;
	Is 42:18-43:7
Jesus	1 Jn 2:1-6
Mankind	Tit 2:11-15;
	3:1-7
Paul	2 Cor 5:20-6:2
Sirach	*Sir 51:1-12

HOPE in

Believers	1 Tim 4:6-10
David	Ps 38:17-22;
	39:7-13
God	Ps 65:5-8
Psalmist	Ps 119:81-88;
	161-168;
	169-176;
	123:1-2

through HUMILITY

Eliphaz	Job 22:21-30

JOY in

David	Ps 13:5-6;
	51:3-12
God	Ps 132:11-18
Israelites	Ps 14:7;
	53:6
Jethro	Ex 18:1-12

through LEADERSHIP

God	Is 33:17-24
Israelites	Judg 2:11-19
Psalmist	Ps 80:1-3

through LIFE

Asaph	Ps 73:21-28
Believers	Ps 91:1-13;
	97:10-12
Daniel	Dan 6:16-23
David	Ps 56:10-13;
	70:1-5;
	86:11-13;
	138:7-8;
	143:7-12
Elihu	Job 33:29-30
God	Ps 68:19-23
Peter	Acts 12:1-25
Psalmist	Ps 66:8-12;
	116:1-11;
	118:15-21;
	119:81-88;
	89-96

through LOVE

Believer	Jas 1:12;
	Ps 145:13b-20;
	1 Jn 4:7-12
David	Ps 6:1-5;

through LOVE (cont'd)

David	Ps 31:13-18
Jesus	Eph 1:15-2:10
Mankind	Tit 3:1-7

through MIRACLE

Daniel	Dan 6:16-23;
	*Bel 1:31-39

through OBEDIENCE

Mankind	Ps 15:1-5b
Psalmist	Ps 119:145-152

through ONENESS

God	1 Tim 2:1-7

from OPPRESSION

God	Ps 76:7-9;
	Rev 7:9-17
Psalmist	Ps 118:10-14;
	119:121-128;
	129-136;
	153-160;
	120:1-2

PARADOX in

God	Ps 118:22-27

through PATIENCE

David	Ps 62:1-2;
	5-7

PRAISE for

David	Ps 9:13-14;
	40:13-17
God	Rev 19:1-5
Psalmist	Ps 67:1-7

through PURIFICATION

Believers	Tit 3:1-7

through REPENTANCE

Israelites	Judg 3:15-23

through REVENGE

David	Ps 54:1-2

through SHARING

Peter	2 Pet 1:3-4

through SPIRIT

David	Ps 31:1-8

through SUFFERING

Believer	Jas 1:12
David	Ps 34:4-10
	41:1-3;
	69:1-3
Eliphaz	Job 5:18-27
Israelites	*Bar 2:11-23
Paul	2 Cor 1:8-11
People	Ps 107:17-22
Psalmist	Ps 126:4-6
Sirach	*Sir 51:1-12

through VICTORY

Believers	1 Jn 4:4-6
David	1 Sam 17:1-18:5;
	Ps 54:6-7
God	Ps 3:7-8;
	Mt 24:23-28;
	Mk 13:14-23
Isaiah	Is 63:1-6
Israelites	Deut 33:1-29
Jesus	1 Cor 15:51-58
Judith	*Jdt 9:1-14

from VIOLENCE

Israelites	Ex 14:23-31

through WILL

God	Ps 106:6-12;
	Mt 18:12-14;
	Rev 7:9-17
Mankind	2 Pet 3:8-10

through WISDOM

God	Is 33:1-6

WITNESS to
David	Ps 40:6-10; 51:13-17
Elihu	Job 33:26-28
Israelites	Is 43:8-13
Jesus	2 Cor 5:14-19
Mankind	Ps 22:27-31
Psalmist	Ps 102:12-22

SECURITY in
  BLESSING in
David	Ps 61:4-5; 144:1-2
Eliphaz	Job 5:18-27
Israelites	Ps 84:5-7; Joel 3:16b-21
Mankind	Ps 2:10-11

  from **CAPTIVITY**
Isaiah	Is 62:1-12

  COURAGE in
David	Ps 56:1-4
God	Ps 91:1-13
Nehemiah	Neh 4:13-23
Psalmist	Ps 118:5-9

  over **DEATH**
David	Ps 16:9-11

  DESPAIR concerning
Psalmist	Ps 42:1-5; 6-11

  in the face of **DESTRUCTION**
David	Ps 57:1-3

  DIGNITY of
David	Ps 25:16-21

  in **DISCIPLESHIP**
David	Ps 28:8-9
God	Ps 34:15-22; 91:1-13; 102:23-28

  from **ENEMY**
David	2 Sam 22:1-51; Ps 7:1-2; 11:1-3; 17:8-12; 18:16-19; 46:50; 23:5-6; 31:1-8; 13-18; 54:4-5; 57:4-6; 61:1-3; 64:1-2; 70:1-5; 138:7-8; 141:8-10; 142:5-7; 143:7-12
God	Ps 136:23-25
Habakkuk	Hab 3:3-15

  from **EVIL**
David	Ps 11:1-3; 12:7-8; 19:11-14; 26:8-12; 36:10-12; 59:1-5; 62:8-12; 64:1-2; 139:19-22; 140:1-5; 141:3-4

from **EVIL** (cont'd)
God	2 Thes 3:3-5
Jesus	Jn 17:6-19
Job	Job 21:7-13; 14-18; 24:13-25
Psalmist	Ps 43:1-5; 121:2-8

through **FAITH**
Believers	Ps 55:22; Prov 22:17-21
David	Ps 4:2-5; 7:9-11; 11:1-3; 16:1-4; 5-8; 23:1-4; 25:8-15; 27:7-12; 28:6-7; 56:6b-9; 10-13; 62:1-2; 5-7; 143:7-12
God	Ps 125:1-3; Prov 29:1-27; 30:1-14; Is 26:1-6
Isaiah	Is 25:1-5; 50:1-11
Israelites	Deut 31:1-8
Jehoshaphat	2 Chr 17:1-20:37
Jeremiah	Jer 16:19-21
Mankind	2 Sam 22:1-51; Ps 18:25-30
Moses	Ps 90:1-12
Paul	2 Cor 1:8-11; 2 Tim 4:9-18
Psalmist	Ps 10:12-18; 33:20-22; 46:1-3; 71:1-21; 94:20-23; 118:10-14

in **FAMILY**
Believers	Is 40:1-11

over **FEAR**
Believers	Prov 16:1-33
David	Ps 27:1-3
Job	Job 4:1-6

by **FULFILLMENT**
Believers	Heb 6:13-20
David	Ps 38:11-16
Israelites	Is 31:4-9

GOOD of
Believers	Prov 18:1-24
God	Ps 37:12-22

GRATITUDE for
David	Ps 124:6-8
Hezekiah	Is 38:1-22

HOPE in
Believers	Ps 146:5-7b
David	Ps 22:12-21; 40:13-17
Habakkuk	Hab 3:16-19
Isaiah	Is 8:16-18
Jeremiah	Lam 3:1-66
Psalmist	Ps 42:1-5; 6-11; 43:1-5;

HOPE in (cont'd)
Psalmist	71:1-21;
	94:16-19;
	116:1-11;
	119:49-56;
	113-120

JOY through
Believers	Ps 146:5-7b
David	Ps 16:9-11;
	35:9-10
Followers	Ps 64:7-10
Mankind	Ps 55:11-12

JUSTICE of
Believers	Ps 37:23-40

through **LEADERSHIP**
Asaph	Ps 73:21-28

through **LIFE**
Baruch	Jer 36:20-26
Believers	Ps 46:1-3;
	91:14-16
David	Ps 25:16-21;
	36:5-9;
	41:1-3
Israelites	Neh 9:12-15;
	19-21
Jeremiah	Jer 11:18-12:6;
	36:20-26
Job	Job 2:4-6
Levites	Num 18:8-20;
	Deut 10:1-11;
	18:1-8;
	Josh 13:29-33
	Ezek 44:15-31
Solomon	Ps 72:8-14

through **LOVE**
David	Ps 18:1-3;
	31:19-24
King	Ps 21:1-7

through **OBEDIENCE**
Hannah	1 Sam 2:1-10

for **OLD AGE**
Believers	Ps 92:12-15

from **OPPRESSION**
Hezekiah	Is 38:1-22
Isaiah	Is 19:18-25
Israelites	1 Chr 15:1-16:43;
	Ps 105:7-15

through **PEACE**
David	Ps 4:6-8
God	Ps 147:12-20

through **POLITICS**
Israelites	Judg 2:11-19

for **POVERTY**
God	Ps 12:5-6;
	14:4-6;
	132:11-18
Isaiah	Is 25:1-5

PRAISE of
David	Ps 59:16-17
Eliphaz	Job 5:8-17

through **SACRIFICE**
Lot	Gen 19:4-11

through **SERVICE**
Believers	Ps 46:4-7
David	Ps 124:6-8
God	Ps 127:1-2;
	Rev 7:9-17
Psalmist	Ps 121:2-8

for **SUFFERING**
Believers	Ps 33:13-19;
	145:13b-20;

for **SUFFERING** (cont'd)
Believers	2 Pet 2:4-10a
David	Ps 22:22-26;
	27:4-6;
	32:3-7;
	35:17-18;
	38:17-22;
	40:1-3;
	54:6-7
Ezra	*2 Esd 7:1-18
God	Ps 91:1-13
Mankind	Ps 9:9-12;
	Rev 21:1-8

through **VICTORY**
Believers	Ps 46:8-11

through **VIOLENCE**
David	Ps 3:3-6;
	140:1-5
Ezra	Ezra 8:21-23
God	Ps 48:1-3

through **WISDOM**
God	Prov 2:1-22

WITNESS to
Asaph	Ps 73:21-28
Paul	1 Cor 1:4-9;
	2 Cor 3:4-6

SERVICE to
COMMITMENT to
Isaiah	Is 19:18-25

CREATION as
God	Ps 104:1-4
Israelites	Is 44:6-8;
	21-23

through **ELECTION**
Aaron	Ex 4:10-16;
	Ps 105:26-36
God	Is 41:1-42:4
High Priest	Heb 5:1-10
Isaiah	Is 49:1-26
Israelites	Is 41:1-42:4;
	43:8-13
Jesus	Heb 5:1-10
Levites	1 Chr 15:1-16:43
Moses	Ps 105:26-36
Priests	Ex 28:1-5

ETERNAL
God	Ps 121:2-8

FIDELITY of
Believers	Ps 125:1-3
God	Hos 5:15-6:3
Isaiah	Is 63:7-64:12
Israelites	Josh 24:29-31
Job	Job 31:5-34

MEDIATION concerning
Aaron	Ex 28:1-5
Isaiah	Is 40:1-11
Job	Job 42:7-9

in **NEW AGE**
Israelites	Is 43:14-44:5

revealing **RESPECT**
God	Jn 12:20-26
Kings	Ps 2:10-11

through **STEWARDSHIP**
Samuel	1 Sam 2:11-26

as **VIRTUE**
Elihu	Job 35:5-8

SIN against
results in **ALIENATION**
Gentiles	Rom 1:24-32

results in **ALIENATION** (cont'd)
   God   Ps 34:15-22;
                         37:23-40;
                         Prov 15:1-33;
                         Mic 7:7-20;
                         Eph 5:3-14
   Israelites   Ex 32:30-35;
                         Deut 29:16-29;
                         31:30-32:47

causes **ANGER**
   God   Job 36:26-33;
                         Is 5:24b-30;
                         Rom 1:18;
                         Col 3:5-17
   Isaiah   Is 63:7-64:12
   Israelites   Num 11:31-35;
                         Deut 9:7-24;
                         29:16-29;
                         1 Kgs 16:8-14;
                         2 Kgs 17:7-23;
                         Ps 78:56-66
   Judahites   Jer 44:1-14
   Manasseh   2 Chr 33:1-25
   Solomon   1 Kgs 11:1-13

through **BLASPHEMY**
   Adversaries   Ps 74:3-9
   Israelites   Amos 2:6-8
   Mankind   Ps 10:3-11

BLESSING for
   Job   Job 24:1-12;
                         13-25

causing **CHAOS**
   God   Is 48:1-22

COMPASSION over
   Sirach   *Sir 18:1-14

CONDEMNATION for
   Believer   Heb 10:19-31;
                         1 Pet 3:8-12
   God   Prov 3:1-35;
                         6:16-19;
                         12:1-28;
                         14:1-35;
                         Jn 3:31-36;
                         1 Thes 4:1-12;
                         2 Thes 2:11-12
   Israelites   1 Sam 12:1-25;
                         Neh 9:26-31;
                         Ezek 16:15-34
   Job   Job 19:1-6
   Mankind   1 Sam 2:11-26;
                         2 Sam 22:1-51;
                         Ps 1:4-6;
                         18:25-30
   Zophar   Job 20:4-29

of **COVETOUSNESS**
   Levites   Num 16:3-11

DEATH for
   Jesus   Rom 5:6-11

resulting **DESTRUCTION**
   Bildad   Job 8:10-19
   David   Ps 9:5-8;
                         55:9-11;
                         58:6-9;
                         59:12-13b
   Elihu   Job 34:21-28
   God   Ps 37:12-22;
                         23-40;
                         73:13-20;
                         94:20-23;
                         145:13b-20;
                         Prov 10:1-32

resulting **DESTRUCTION** (cont'd)
   Mankind   Ps 1:4-6;
                         9:17-20
   Psalmist   Ps 92:5-11;
                         104:31-35
   Zimri   1 Kgs 16:8-14

through **DISOBEDIENCE**
   Eve   Gen 3:1-8
   Israelites   Ps 106:6-12;
                         *2 Esd 1:4-23

DOUBT as
   Ephraimites   Ps 78:9-20
   Israelites   Ps 78:32-39

of **ENEMY**
   David   Ps 17:8-12;
                         59:13c-15

as **EVIL**
   Mankind   Ps 10:3-11
   Sodomite   Gen 13:10-13

GOOD of
   Elihu   Job 35:5-8

forgiven through **GRACE**
   Abijam   1 Kgs 15:1-8
   Asaph   Ps 79:5-13
   David   Ps 25:1-7;
                         16-21;
                         32:1-2;
                         3-7
   God   Ps 65:1-4;
                         103:6-13;
                         130:3-4
   Hezekiah   Is 38:1-22
   Israelites   Ps 78:32-39;
                         *Bar 3:1-8
   Joshua   Zech 3:1-10
   Manasseh   *Mana 1:6-7;
                         1:11-15
   Psalmist   Ps 85:1-3
   Sirach   *Sir 2:7-11;
                         18:1-14
   Solomon   1 Kgs 8:22-53;
                         *Wis 11:21-12:2

causes **GRIEF**
   Ezra   *1 Esd 8:71-90
   Israelites   *1 Esd 8:91-96

IDOLATRY as
   Israelites   Ps 106:19-23

IGNORANCE concerning
   Mankind   Ps 14:4-6

INDIFFERENCE as
   Israelites   Neh 9:26-31;
                         Ps 81:5c-16

causing **JEALOUSY**
   Israelites   Deut 31:30-32:47
   Judahites   1 Kgs 14:21-24

JUSTICE in
   David   Ps 7:12-16

KILLING as
   Er   Gen 38:1-11
   God   Prov 6:16-19

LOVE overcomes
   Jesus   Rom 5:6-11

through **MARRIAGE**
   Israelites   *1 Esd 8:91-96

through **OPPRESSION**
   Mankind   Ps 10:3-11
   Psalmist   Ps 10:1-2

REJECTION of
   Believers   Heb 6:1-8;
                         10:19-31
   David   Ps 140:6-8

REJECTION of (cont'd)

Elihu	Job 34:34-37
Gentiles	Rom 1:24-32
Israelites	Ps 78:56-66; Jer 2:1-13; 6:27-30; Hos 10:1-8; 13:4-6; *2 Esd 1:24-40
Mankind	Ps 14:1-3
Sinners	Jn 9:1-41
Sirach	*Sir 15:11-20

REPENTANCE of

David	Ps 7:12-16; 19:11-14; 51:1-2
Israelites	Num 14:39-45; *Bar 2:27-35
Sirach	*Sir 17:15-32

REVENGE for

God	Ps 9:9-12; Prov 20:1-30
Isaiah	Is 59:1-21; 63:1-6

REWARDs for

Zophar	Job 20:4-29

SACRIFICE as

God	Prov 15:1-33

cause of SUFFERING

Solomon	2 Chr 5:1-7:10

SPIRIT of
  in CREATION

Mankind	Ps 104:27-30

KNOWLEDGE of

God	Prov 17:1-28
Jesus	Lk 10:21-22
Mankind	1 Sam 16:1-13; 1 Kgs 8:22-53; 1 Chr 28:1-29:30; 2 Chr 5:1-7:10

as MOTIVATION

Cyrus	*1 Esd 2:1-7
Daniel	*Susa 1:42-51
Israelites	Ex 35:30-36:7
Mankind	1 Sam 16:1-13
Zerubbabel	Zech 4:6b-10a

in NEW AGE

Believers	1 Cor 2:6-9

PRESENCE of

Daniel	Dan 4:18
Eliphaz	Job 4:12-16
Ezekiel	Ezek 2:1-8a; 3:12-15; 22-27; 8:1-4; 11:1-13; 22-25; 43:1-5
God	Gen 1:1-2; 3:1-8; Ps 139:7-12
Holy Spirit	Tit 3:1-7
Isaiah	Is 32:15-20
Israelites	Ezek 37:1-14; 39:25-29; Hag 1:12-14
Jerusalemites	Zech 7:4-8:23
Joseph	Gen 41:1-57
Micah	Mic 3:1-12

PRESENCE of (cont'd)

Moses	Ex 17:1-7
Samson	Judg 13:24-25; 14:5-9
Saul	1 Sam 9:1-10:16

as QUALITY OF LIFE

God	2 Kgs 19:9b-37

SALVATION through

David	Ps 31:1-8

STEWARDSHIP to
  BLESSING in

David	Ps 41:1-3

COMPASSION in

Solomon	Ps 72:8-14

over POVERTY

David	Ps 41:1-3

SACREDNESS in

Aaron	Ex 29:42b-46

SUFFERING attributed to

Israelites	Ps 106:19-23
Job	Job 16:12-17

KNOWLEDGE of

David	Ps 13:1-4; 38:3-10
Israelites	Ex 3:7-10; Neh 9:9-11

PRAYER concerning

David	Ps 38:1-2; 39:7-13

PROVIDENCE concerning

Asaph	Ps 77:1-10
David	Ps 20:1-5; 31:1-8; 32:3-7; 34:4-10; 60:1-5
Elihu	Job 36:5-15; 16-25
Followers	Ps 80:4-7
God	Ps 107:33-38; 39-43; 140:12-13; 146:7c-9; 147:1-6
Israelites	Ps 78:32-39
Psalmist	Ps 88:3-9; 15-18; 119:49-56
Sirach	*Sir 35:12-20
Solomon	*Wis 16:1-14

as PUNISHMENT

Antiochus	*2 Mc 9:5-29
Azariah	2 Kgs 15:1-7
God	Rev 16:4-7
Israelites	Ex 32:30-35; Neh 9:26-31; Is 1:4-9
Job	Job 10:13-17; 19:7-12
Uzziah	2 Chr 26:1-28:27

SUFFERING attributed to
RATIONALIZATION for

Job	Job 6:1-7

RECONCILIATION with

Aaron	Num 16:36-50

SIGNS of

Philistines	1 Sam 5:1-12

resulting from SIN

PROVIDENCE in (cont'd)
God	Prov 21:1-31
Hezekiah	2 Kgs 20:1-11
Isaiah	Is 59:1-21
Israelites	Ex 3:7-10;
	Num 21:33-35;
	Deut 1:19-46;
	2:26-3:11;
	12-22;
	9:1-6;
	12:1-31;
	31:1-8;
	Josh 11:16-23;
	Judg 4:10-16;
	7:16-22;
	1 Sam 19:1-10;
	1 Chr 15:1-16:43;
	Neh 4:13-23;
	Ps 44:1-3;
	4-8;
	105:7-15;
	23-25;
	106:6-12;
	Is 43:14-44:5
Jacob	Gen 46:1-7
Jephthah	Judg 11:29-33
Jeroboam	2 Kgs 14:23-29
Jesus	Rom 8:1-4;
	Col 2:6-15
Joshua	Num 14:8-9;
	Josh 23:1-16
Judah	Judg 1:1-21
Maccabeus	*1 Mc 4:1-35
Mankind	Ps 18:25-30
Paul	2 Tim 3:10-13
Psalmist	Ps 92:5-11;
	94:16-19
Uzziah	2 Chr 26:1-28:27

RECONCILIATION in
Isaiah	Is 63:1-6
Israelites	Nah 1:10,12,13.

in RESURRECTION
Jesus	Acts 2:14-36

SALVATION in
Believers	1 Jn 4:4-6
David	1 Sam 17:1-18:5;
	Ps 54:6-7
God	Ps 3:7-8;
	Mt 24:23-28;
	Mk 13:14-23
Isaiah	Is 63:1-6
Israelites	Deut 33:1-29
Jesus	1 Cor 15:51-58
Judith	*Jdt 9:1-14

SECURITY in
Believers	Ps 46:8-11

VIRTUE of
God	Ps 98:1-3

VIOLENCE by
CONFRONTATION with
Nations	Zech 14:1-21

KNOWLEDGE of
Israelites	Judg 3:1-6

PROVIDENCE in
David	2 Sam 22:1-51;
	Ps 18:31-42
God	2 Chr 17:1-20:37
Hezekiah	2 Chr 32:1-33
Israelites	Ex 14:1-14;
	Deut 1:19-46

PROVIDENCE in (cont'd)
Jonah	Jon 1:1-17
Judahites	2 Kgs 15:32-38

VIRTUE of
ACCEPTANCE as
Believers	Ps 34:15-22;
	Heb 12:12-29
God	Prov 21:1-31;
	Is 45:14-25
Mankind	Ps 15:1-5b

COMPASSION as
Abraham	Gen 18:23-33

DIGNITY as
David	Ps 7:6-8
Job	Job 27:1-12

GOOD as
God	Ps 77:11-20;
	86:1-7

GRACE as
God	Ex 34:5b-9;
	Ps 86:1-7;
	112:2-4;
	116:1-11;
	145:8-9
James	Jas 3:13-18

JUSTICE as
God	Ps 89:5-18;
	94:12-15;
	97:1-5;
	99:4-5;
	145:13b-20;
	Is 5:8-24a;
	Jer 9:23-24;
	11:18-12:6;
	Dan 9:4-19;
	Zeph 3:1-5
Psalmist	Ps 129:1-4

LOVE as
God	Ps 11:4-7;
	33:4-9;
	146:7c-9;
	Prov 15:1-33

PATIENCE as
God	Ex 34:5b-9

PEACE as
James	Jas 3:13-18
Solomon	Ps 72:5-7

VICTORY as
God	Ps 98:1-3

WISDOM as
Believers	Ps 37:23-40

WILL of
AUTHORITY of
God	Ps 115:3-8;
	Is 40:12-31;
	44:24-45:13
Jesus	Jn 10:1-18;
	Acts 2:14-36

BROTHERHOOD through
Jesus	Mt 12:46-50;
	Mk 3:31-35;
	Lk 8:19-21

CONFRONTATION with
Abraham	Gen 22:1-19
Job	Job 23:1-7;
	31:35-37
Pharaoh	Ex 5:1-5

TRUTH in (cont'd)
Elihu	Job 36:1-4
God	Ps 19:7-10

VIRTUE through
Believers	Ps 37:23-40

WITNESS of
to **KNOWLEDGE**
David	2 Sam 23:1-7
God	Gen 31:44-55;
	Jer 29:24-32;
	Amos 4:13
Hezekiah	Is 37:8-20
Holy Spirit	Jn 16:12-15
Israelites	Deut 4:32-40
Jesus	Jn 8:12-20;
	14:1-14

WITNESS to
David	Ps 9:9-12
God	Deut 3:23-29;
	Is 44:6-8;
	21-23
Jesus	Jn 8:21-59;
	12:44-50
Psalmist	Ps 71:1-21

through **BROTHERHOOD**
Holy Spirit	Rom 8:14-25

COMMITMENT to
Israelites	Josh 24:16-24

CONFRONTATION with
Israelites	Num 14:11-24;
	Deut 5:1-21
Moses	Num 12:4-10;
	Deut 34:1-12

in **CREATION**
David	Ps 19:1-4b
God	Ps 97:6-9

DESIRE for
God	Hos 6:4-6

ETERNAL
God	Ps 135:13-14
Israelites	Ps 48:9-14

GIFT of
Holy Spirit	Heb 2:1-4

JUDGMENT of
Aaron	Ex 28:13-30

through **MEDIATION**
Israelites	Mal 2:17-3:5

RESPECT in
Ezekiel	Ezek 44:4-5

as **RITE**
David	Ps 26:6b-7

SIGNS of
Isaiah	Is 19:18-25
Jesus	Jn 10:19-40;
	Acts 2:14-36

as **TRUTH**
God	Is 45:14-25
Israelites	Is 49:1-26
Jeremiah	Jer 10:1-16
Jesus	Jn 8:21-59
John	1 Jn 1:5-10

VIRTUE in
Mankind	Ezek 38:14-16
Psalmist	Ps 71:22-24

DESIRE

for **ACCEPTANCE**
Esther	Esth 8:3-8
Jacob	Gen 32:1-23
Jonathan	*1 Mc 11:20-37

of **COVENANT**
Moses	Deut 29:1-15

by **DEITY**
Isaiah	Is 55:1-13

INSTRUCTION on
Paul	2 Cor 5:9-10

of **REVELATION**
Daniel	Dan 4:19-27
Isaiah	Is 65:1-25

ACCEPTANCE of
to **WORSHIP**
Wise Men	Mt 2:1-12

for **BLESSING**
of **DEITY**
Bethelites	Zech 7:1-3
Job	Job 29:1-6

REVELATION of
People	Zech 7:4-8:23

for **CAPTIVITY**
of **MESSIANIC FIGURE**
People	Jn 7:25-31

for **COMPASSION**
Israel	Ex 5:15-21
Jeremiah	Jer 37:16-21
Job	Job 19:20-24

of **DEITY**
Asaph	Ps 77:1-10
God	Mic 6:6-8
Job	Job 14:13-17

in **WORSHIP**
Ezra	Neh 9:32-37

for **CONDEMNATION**
Balak	Num 22:5-14;
	15-21;
	23:13-26,
	27-24:13
Officials	Dan 6:4-9

by **DEITY**
Habakkuk	Hab 1:12-17
Israel	Ex 5:15-21

through **FALSE BELIEF**
Pharisees	Lk 11:53-54

of **MESSIANIC FIGURE**
Pharisees	Mt 12:9-14;
	22:15-22;
	Mk 3:1-6;
	12:13-17;
	Lk 6:6-11
Priests	Mt 27:1-2;
	Lk 20:19-26
Scribes	Lk 20:19-26

for **COURAGE**
from **DEITY**
Job	Job 13:20-27

for **COVENANT**
ACCEPTANCE of
Moses	Deut 29:1-15

in **POLITICS**
Abner	2 Sam 3:1-16

for FUFILLMENT (cont'd)

Maiden	Song 3:1-5
Nehemiah	Neh 1:11b-2:8
Preacher	Eccl 1:12-2:26

by **DEITY**

Asa	2 Chr 14:1-16:14
Believers	Ps 145:13b-20
Daniel	Dan 9:4-19
David	Ps 4:1;
	20:1-5;
	39:7-13;
	54:1-2;
	55:1-3a;
	61:1-3;
	69:13-21;
	86:1-7;
	108:6-13;
	109:1-5;
	21-31;
	140:6-8;
	141:1-2;
	142:5-7;
	143:1-2;
	7-12
God	1 Chr 28:1-29:30;
	Ps 37:1-11;
	Jer 29:1-23
Holy Spirit	Lk 11:9-13
King	Ps 21:1-7
Psalmist	Ps 84:8-9;
	88:1-2;
	102:1-11;
	119:145-152;
	130:1-2

INSTRUCTION on

Solomon	Prov 2:1-22;
	13:1-25

by **MESSIANIC FIGURE**

Jesus	Mt 14:13-21;
	15:32-39;
	Mk 6:30-44;
	8:1-10;
	Lk 9:12-17;
	Jn 6:1-15
John the Baptist	Mt 11:2-6;
	Lk 7:18-23
Queen of Sheba	1 Kgs 10:1-13;
	2 Chr 9:1-31

REVELATION on

Solomon	1 Kgs 3:1-15

in **WORSHIP**

David	Ps 28:1-5
Ezra	*1 Esd 8:41-44

for GOOD

from **DEITY**

Mankind	Ps 4:6-8

INSTRUCTION on

Amos	Amos 5:14-15
Sirach	*Sir 16:1-5

for GRACE

from **DEITY**

Abraham	Gen 18:23-33
Job	Job 14:13-17
People	Jer 42:1-6

concerning **FALSE BELIEF**

Paul	2 Tim 4:9-18

of **MESSIANIC FIGURE**

Demons	Lk 8:26-39
Jesus	Mt 9:10-13

in WORSHIP

Demons	Mk 5:1-20
Nehemiah	Neh 1:5-11a

for GRATITUDE

INSTRUCTION on

God	Ps 50:22-23
Psalmist	Ps 105:1-6

for HEALING

by **FOLLOWERs**

Crowd	Mt 15:29-31;
	Lk 6:17-19
Jesus	Mk 3:7-12;
	6:53-56

INSTRUCTION on

Crowds	Mt 4:23-25

for HERESY

Israelites	Is 2:6-11

for HOPE

INSTRUCTION on

Solomon	Prov 13:1-25

for HUMILITY

by **DEITY**

God	Ps 51:13-17;
	Mic 6:6-8

INSTRUCTION on

Zephaniah	Zeph 2:3

SELF-REALIZATION of

Paul	2 Cor 12:19-21

for INNOCENCE

of **MESSIANIC FIGURE**

Pilate	Mt 27:11-26

INSTRUCTION on

for **ACCEPTANCE**

Paul	2 Cor 5:9-10

for **EVIL**

Jesus	Jn 8:21-59

for **FAMILY**

David	2 Sam 3:1-16
Sirach	*Sir 16:1-5

for **FULFILLMENT**

Solomon	Prov 2:1-22;
	13:1-25

for **GOOD**

Amos	Amos 5:14-15
Sirach	*Sir 16:1-5

for **GRATITUDE**

God	Ps 50:22-23
Psalmist	Ps 105:1-6

for **HEALING**

Crowds	Mt 4:23-25

for **HOPE**

Solomon	Prov 13:1-25

for **HUMILITY**

Zephaniah	Zeph 2:3

for **JUSTICE**

Elihu	Job 33:31-33
Job	Job 31:38-40
Sirach	*Sir 27:8-15

for **LEADERSHIP**

Zechariah	Zech 10:1-2

for **LOVE**

Paul	1 Cor 14:1-12

for **LUST**

Preacher	Eccl 6:1-12

for **MARRIAGE**
    Naomi   Ruth 3:1-18
for **OBEDIENCE**
    Artaxerxes   Ezra 7:20-24
for **OLD AGE**
    Peter   1 Pet 1:13-2:3
PARADOX in
    Paul   Gal 5:16-21
for **PEACE**
    David   Ps 34:11-14
for **PRIDE**
    Preacher   Eccl 6:1-12
for **REPENTANCE**
    Paul   2 Cor 12:19-21;
                        Gal 4:12-20
for **REWARD**
    Paul   Phil 1:12-30
for **SACREDNESS**
    God   Is 51:1-16
for **SERVICE**
    Paul   2 Tim 4:9-18
for **SEX**
    Psalmist   Ps 45:10-12
for **TEMPTATION**
    Paul   1 Tim 6:6-10
for **WEALTH**
    Jesus   Mt 6:19-24
for **WISDOM**
    Elihu   Job 33:31-33
    Father   Prov 4:1-9
    Jesus   Mt 9:10-13
    Job   Job 6:21-27
    Solomon   Prov 5:1-14;
                        6:20-7:27;
                        9:1-6;
                        *Wis 6:12-25
    Wisdom   Prov 1:20-33

for **JOY**
    by **DEITY**
        Believers   Eccl 3:9-15
    in **MISSION**
        John   2 Jn 1:12-13

for **JUSTICE**
    Elihu   Job 32:15-22
    by **DEITY**
        God   Mic 6:6-8
        Habakkuk   Hab 1:2-4;
                         12-17
        Israelites   Amos 5:21-25
        Job   Job 13:20-27;
                         21:19-27;
                         31:5-34
    by **FOLLOWERs**
        Festus   Acts 25:13-27
        Paul   Acts 25:1-12
    INSTRUCTION on
        Elihu   Job 33:31-33
        Job   Job 31:38-40
        Sirach   *Sir 27:8-15

for **KILLING**
    Esau   Gen 27:41-28:5
    Eunuchs   Esth 2:19-23
    Haman   Esth 3:7-15
    Herodias   Mt 14:1-12;
                     Mk 6:17-29
    Jeremiah   Jer 38:1-13
    Jezebel   1 Kgs 19:1-21
    Priests   Mt 26:3-5;

for **KILLING** (cont'd)
    Priests   Mk 14:1-2
    Saul   1 Sam 19:1-10;
                   11-17;
                   26:1-25

    by **DEITY**
        Moses   Ex 4:24-26
    through **FALSE BELIEF**
        Jeremiah   Jer 26:7-19
        Jews   Acts 9:20-31
    of **MESSIANIC FIGURE**
        Jews   Jn 5:1-18
        Priests   Lk 22:1-2
    PROPHECY of
        Israelites   Jer 18:18-23
    REVELATION on
        David   1 Sam 23:1-13

for **LEADERSHIP**
    Absalom   2 Sam 15:1-12
    Adonijah   1 Kgs 1:5-10
    Gaal   Judg 9:26-29
    Israelites   Judg 8:22-23;
                   10:6-18;
                   1 Sam 8:1-22
    Solomon   1 Kgs 1:15-21;
                   22-27

    INSTRUCTION on
        Zechariah   Zech 10:1-2

for **LIFE**
    MEDITATION on
        Paul   Phil 3:4-16
    SELF-REALIZATION of
        Jesus   Mt 26:36-46;
                   Mk 14:32-42

for **LOVE**
    Maiden   Song 1:2-4;
                   3:1-5;
                   8:1-4;
                   5b-7;
                   14
    Young Man   Song 8:13
    by **DEITY**
        God   Hos 6:4-6
    INSTRUCTION on
        Paul   1 Cor 14:1-12

for **LUST**
    INSTRUCTION on
        Preacher   Eccl 6:1-12

for **MARRIAGE**
    Adonijah   1 Kgs 2:13-25
    Ahasuerus   Esth 2:1-4
    Samson   Judg 14:1-4
    INSTRUCTION on
        Naomi   Ruth 3:1-18

MEDITATION on
for **DEATH**
    Job   Job 3:11-19;
                   20-26;
                   7:12-16

for **LIFE**
    Paul   Phil 3:4-16
for **PEACE**
    David   Ps 55:3b-8

for **PEACE** (cont'd)
  Job — Job 3:11-19
for **REWARD**
  Paul — Phil 3:4-16
for **WISDOM**
  Preacher — Eccl 7:23-29

by **MESSIANIC FIGURE**
  for **FULFILLMENT**
  Jesus — Mt 14:13-21; 15:32-39; Mk 6:30-44; 8:1-10; Lk 9:12-17; Jn 6:1-15
  John the Baptist — Mt 11:2-6; Lk 7:18-23
  Queen of Sheba — 1 Kgs 10:1-13; 2 Chr 9:1-31
  for **GRACE**
  Demons — Lk 8:26-39
  Jesus — Mt 9:10-13
  for **WISDOM**
  Jesus — Mt 16:13-20
  to **WITNESS**
  Jesus — Lk 2:41-52

for **MIRACLE**
  by **MESSIANIC FIGURE**
  Pharisees — Mk 8:11-13

for **OBEDIENCE**
  by **DEITY**
  God — Ps 53:1-3
  Psalmist — Ps 119:17-24
  Samuel — 1 Sam 15:1-35
  INSTRUCTION on
  Artaxerxes — Ezra 7:20-24
  PROPHECY of
  Isaiah — Is 2:1-5
  REVELATION on
  Balaam — Num 22:22-35
  SELF-REALIZATION of
  Paul — Rom 7:14-25

for **OLD AGE**
  INSTRUCTION on
  Peter — 1 Pet 1:13-2:3

for **OPPRESSION**
  of **FOLLOWERs**
  Gentiles — Acts 14:1-7
  Jews — Acts 14:1-7

for **ORDER**
  PROPHECY of
  Believers — 1 Cor 14:34-40

PARADOX in
  INSTRUCTION on
  Paul — Gal 5:16-21

for **PEACE**
  Nebuchadnezzar — Dan 4:1-3
  Psalmist — Ps 120:5-7
  by **DEITY**
  God — Is 27:2-6
  Job — Job 10:18-22
  INSTRUCTION on
  David — Ps 34:11-14
  MEDITATION on

MEDITATION on (cont'd)
  David — Ps 55:3b-8
  Job — Job 3:11-19
  PROPHECY of
  Isaiah — Is 28:1-13

for **POLITICS**
  Tobiah — Neh 6:17-19
  COVENANT of
  Abner — 2 Sam 3:1-16

for **PRIDE**
  by **DEITY**
  Mankind — Ps 10:3-11
  INSTRUCTION on
  Preacher — Eccl 6:1-12

PROPHECY of
  for **DEATH**
  Jeremiah — Jer 7:29-8:3
  for **DESTRUCTION**
  Israelites — Hos 10:1-8
  for **KILLING**
  Israelites — Jer 18:18-23
  for **OBEDIENCE**
  Isaiah — Is 2:1-5
  for **ORDER**
  Believers — 1 Cor 14:34-40
  for **PEACE**
  Isaiah — Is 28:1-13
  for **VICTORY**
  Zedekiah — Jer 21:1-10
  for **WEALTH**
  Gog — Ezek 38:10-13
  for **WISDOM**
  Isaiah — Is 21:11-12

for **PRUDENCE**
  in **WORSHIP**
  Herod — Mt 2:1-12

for **PURIFICATION**
  by **DEITY**
  Jesus — Mt 3:13-17

for **REJECTION**
  Ahab — 1 Kgs 21:1-4

for **REPENTANCE**
  by **DEITY**
  Israelites — Ezek 33:10-20
  Mankind — 2 Pet 3:8-10
  INSTRUCTION on
  Paul — 2 Cor 12:19-21; Gal 4:12-20
  REVELATION on
  Ezekiel — Ezek 18:21-24
  Jeremiah — Jer 26:1-6; 36:1-7

REVELATION of
  for **BLESSING**
  People — Zech 7:4-8:23

REVELATION on
  for **DEATH**
  Mankind — Rev 9:1-12
  for **FULFILLMENT**
  Solomon — 1 Kgs 3:1-15
  for **KILLING**
  David — 1 Sam 23:1-13

by **FOLLOWER** (cont'd)
  Ezekiel   Ezek 14:1-11
INSTRUCTION on
  Elihu   Job 33:31-33
  Father   Prov 4:1-9
  Jesus   Mt 9:10-13
  Job   Job 6:21-27
  Solomon   Prov 5:1-14;
                  6:20-7:27;
                  9:1-6;
                  *Wis 6:12-25
  Wisdom   Prov 1:20-33
MEDITATION on
  Preacher   Eccl 7:23-29
by **MESSIANIC FIGURE**
  Jesus   Mt 16:13-20
in **MISSION**
  Paul   Col 2:1-5
PROPHECY of
  Isaiah   Is 21:11-12
REVELATION on
  Belshazzar   Dan 5:7-9;
                  10-17
  Daniel   Dan 7:15-16;
                  8:15-25
  Nebuchadnezzar Dan 2:1-13;
                  4:4-9
  Pharaoh   Gen 41:1-57
SELF-REALIZATION of
  Solomon   2 Chr 1:1-17

to **WITNESS**
by **DEITY**
  God   Hos 6:4-6
by **MESSIANIC FIGURE**
  Jesus   Lk 2:41-52

to **WORSHIP**
  Wise men   Mt 2:1-12
PRUDENCE in
  Herod   Mt 2:1-12
SERVICE in
  Israelites   Josh 24:16-24

DESPAIR

BEHAVIOR revealing
  Esau   Gen 27:1-40
  Hagar   Gen 21:15-21
  Job   Job 30:24-31
  MEDITATION on
    Jeremiah   Jer 12:7-13
    Job   Job 7:7-11;
                  9:30-35;
                  14:18-22

over **JUDGMENT**
of **DEITY**
  Job   Job 9:14-19;
                  25-29
  MEDITATION on
    Job   Job 19:7-12

MEDITATION on
  Jeremiah   Jer 8:18-9:1;
                  12:7-13
  Job   Job 7:7-11;
               9:30-35;
               14:18-22

as **QUALITY OF LIFE**
  David   Ps 38:3-10
  Job   Job 7:1-6;
              14:7-12;
              17:1-5;
              11-16

in **NEW AGE**
PROPHECY of
  Amos   Amos 5:18-20

PRAYER concerning
  Psalmist   Ps 43:1-5
by **MESSIANIC FIGURE**
  Jesus   Mt 27:45-56

PROPHECY of
in **NEW AGE**
  Amos   Amos 5:18-20;
              21:1-10
as **QUALITY OF LIFE**
  Isaiah   Is 51:17-52:12

PUNISHMENT causing
INSTRUCTION on
  Isaiah   Is 59:1-21
  Jeremiah   Jer 6:22-26
PROPHECY of
  Egyptians   Is 19:1-15
  Isaiah   Is 8:19-22;
              21:1-10

as **QUALITY OF LIFE**
  David   Ps 22:12-21;
              143:3-4
  Job   Job 6:1-7;
              21:1-6
  Psalmist   Ps 88:15-18
MEDITATION on
  David   Ps 38:3-10
  Job   Job 7:1-6;
              14:7-12;
              17:1-5;
              11-16
PROPHECY of
  Isaiah   Is 51:17-52:12
SELF-REALIZATION of
  Job   Job 19:13-19

SECURITY from
by **DEITY**
  Psalmist   Ps 42:1-5;
              6-11

SELF-REALIZATION of
as **QUALITY OF LIFE**
  Job   Job 19:13-19

SIGNS of
PROPHECY of
  Isaiah   Is 7:18-25
REVELATION on
  John   Rev 6:12-17

SIN causing
MEDITATION on
  Jeremiah   Jer 8:18-9:1

DESTRUCTION

RECONCILIATION through
  Isaiah   Is 9:8-10:4
SALVATION from
  Rehoboam   2 Chr 10:1-12:16
SECURITY in
  David   Ps 57:1-3
SIGNS of
  Adversaries   Ps 74:3-9
  Hezekiah   2 Kgs 18:4-8
SIN resulting in
  Bildad   Job 8:10-19
  David   Ps 9:5-8;
                55:9-11;
                58:6-9;
                59:12-13b
  Elihu   Job 34:21-28
  God   Ps 37:12-22;
                23-40;
                73:13-20;
                94:20-23;
                145:13b-20;
                Prov 10:1-32
  Mankind   Ps 1:4-6;
                9:17-20
  Psalmist   Ps 92:5-11;
                104:31-35
  Zimri   1 Kgs 16:8-14

DESIRE for
  Assyrians   Is 10:5-16
  Haman   Esth 3:1-6
  Sanballat   Neh 4:7-12;
                6:1-4;
                5-9
  Satan   1 Pet 5:6-11;
                Rev 12:13-17
  by DEITY
    Israelites   Ex 32:7-14;
                Deut 9:7-24
  MESSIANIC FIGURE
    Pharisees   Mk 3:1-6;
                Lk 6:6-11
    Priests   Mk 11:15-19;
                Lk 19:47-48
  PROPHECY of
    Israelites   Hos 10:1-8

ETERNAL
  by DEITY
    God   Ps 52:5-7
  PROPHECY of
    Damascus   Is 17:1-6
    Isaiah   Is 34:1-17
  REVELATION on
    Edomites   Ezek 35:1-15
    Tyre   Ezek 27:25b-36;
                28:11-19

of FALSE BELIEF
  SIGNS of
    Daniel   *Bel 1:21-22

through FALSE BELIEF
  Assyrians   2 Kgs 19:9b-37
  Paul   Gal 5:7-12
results from inFIDELITY
  to COVENANT
    Jeremiah   Jer 22:1-9
  of FOLLOWERs
    Author   Heb 10:32-39

PROPHECY of
  Jeremiah   Jer 12:14-17
  Judahites   Jer 9:10-22;
                38:14-28
REVELATION on
  Isaiah   Is 8:11-15

FREEDOM from
  INSTRUCTION on
    Jesus   Mt 7:13-14

of disHONESTY
  by DEITY
    God   Ps 63:11c
    Mankind   Ps 5:4-7

INSTRUCTION on
  Preacher   Eccl 3:1-8
  through unBELIEF
    John   Jude 1:5-7
  through CONFRONTATION
    Moab   Is 15:1-16:14
    Moses   Deut 7:1-5
  as JUDGMENT
    Moses   Ex 23:20-33;
                Num 33:16-36;
                Deut 7:1-5
  as MOTIVATION
    Psalmist   Ps 146:3-4
  as PUNISHMENT
    Eliphaz   Job 15:17-35
    God   Is 1:18-20;
                *2 Esd 2:8-9
    Joshua   Josh 23:1-16
    Moses   Deut 6:4-19;
                8:11-20;
                28:15-68
  as QUALITY OF LIFE
    Jesus   Mt 7:15-20
  of TRUTH
    Baruch   Jer 36:20-26

as JUDGMENT
  by DEITY
    God   Hab 3:3-15
    Sodomites   Gen 19:12-29
  through FALSE BELIEF
    Moses   Ex 23:20-33;
                34:12-28;
                Num 33:16-36;
                Deut 7:1-5;
                12:1-31
  INSTRUCTION on
    Moses   Ex 23:20-33;
                Num 33:16-36;
                Deut 7:1-5
  PROPHECY of
    Israelites   Amos 9:1-4
    Joel   Joel 2:1-11
  REVELATION on
    Amos   Amos 7:1-3;
                4-6
    Daniel   Dan 7:2-14

KNOWLEDGE of
  Job   Job 1:13-19
  Nehemiah   Neh 2:12-15
  by DEITY
    God   Is 10:5-16;
                29:13-14
    Isaiah   Is 66:17-24

PROPHECY of (cont'd)

Baasha	1 Kgs 15:33-16:7
Edomites	Jer 49:7-22;
	Amos 1:11-12
Ephraimites	Is 28:1-13;
	Hos 5:3-7;
	8-14;
	13:15-16
Habakkuk	Hab 2:12-14:17
Isaiah	Is 10:20-23;
	33-34;
	17:12-14;
	19:1-15;
	21:1-10;
	22:1-14;
	24:1-12;
	26:20-27:1;
	28:14-22;
	30:27-33;
	31:1-3;
	32:9-14;
	33:1-6;
	7-16;
	34:1-17;
	66:1-16
Israelites	Jer 5:15-17;
	6:16-21;
	11:15-17;
	Ezek 16:35-43;
	Hos 8:4-7;
	11-14;
	10:1-8;
	13:7-8;
	9-11;
	Amos 3:13-15;
	5:4-6;
	6:8-11;
	7:10-17
Jeremiah	Jer 4:13-18;
	19-22;
	23-26;
	5:1-14;
	6:1-8;
	7:29-8:3;
	14-17;
	13:12-14;
	14:10-12;
	17-18;
	16:1-13;
	17:19-27;
	21:13-14;
	22:1-9;
	20-23;
	29:1-23;
	32:26-44;
	34:13-22;
	43:8-13;
	44:20-28;
	45:1-5
Jeroboam	1 Kgs 13:1-34
Jesus	Lk 19:41-44
Joel	Joel 3:16b-21
John the Baptist	Mt 3:1-12;
	Lk 3:7-9;
	15-17
Judahites	Jer 4:5-8;
	8:8-13;
	9:10-22;
	44:1-14;
	Hos 5:3-7;
	Amos 2:4-5

PROPHECY of (cont'd)

Micah	Mic 1:5-9;
	2:1-10;
	3:1-12;
	5:7-15
Moabites	Is 25:10-12;
	Amos 2:1-3
Nineveh	Nah 1:11;
	14;
	2:11-13;
	3:5-19;
	Zeph 2:13-14;
	15
Philistines	Amos 1:6-8
Shebna	Is 22:15-25
Tyre	Is 23:1-14;
	Ezek 26:7-14;
	19-21;
	Amos 1:9-10;
	Zech 9:1-12
Women	Amos 4:1-3
Zechariah	Zech 9:13-17;
	11:1-3
Zedekiah	Jer 27:12-15
Zephaniah	Zeph 1:14-16;
	17-18;
	2:4-7

REVELATION on

Ammonites	Ezek 21:28-32;
	25:1-7;
	Zeph 2:8-12
Belshazzar	Dan 5:26-28
Chaldeans	Is 47:1-15
Edomites	Ezek 25:12-14;
	35:1-15
Egyptians	Ezek 29:1-5;
	6-9a;
	9b-16;
	30:13-19;
	31:10-18;
	32:1-16
Ezekiel	Ezek 6:1-7;
	13:1-16;
	14:1-11;
	20:45-49;
	21:25-27
God	Is 41:1-42:4
Gog	Ezek 39:1-16
Isaiah	Is 5:1-7;
	6:1-13;
	56:9-57:13;
	65:1-25
Israelites	Jer 2:14-19;
	5:1-14;
	Ezek 5:5-17;
	6:11-14;
	7:1-27;
	21:1-7;
	8-17;
	22:1-16;
	23:5-10;
	36-49;
	Hos 1:4-5;
	2:9-13;
	Amos 7:7-9;
	8:8-10;
	9:1-4;
	Zech 13:7-9
Jacobites	Amos 9:8-10
Jehu	1 Kgs 15:33-16:7
Jeremiah	Jer 15:1-4;

as **PUNISHMENT** (cont'd)
Nations 8
People Jer 27:1-11
Philistines Ezek 25:15-17
Prophets 2 Kgs 21:1-18;
Jer 14:13-16
Solomon 2 Chr 7:11-22
Tyre Ezek 26:1-6;
27:25b-36;
28:1-10
Zechariah Zech 5:1-4
Zedekiah Jer 24:1-10
Zephaniah Zeph 1:2-6;
10-11;
12-13

SALVATION from
by **DEITY**
Rehoboam 2 Chr 10:1-12:16

SECURITY from
Joash 2 Kgs 12:17-18
Moses Lev 13:1-59
by **DEITY**
David Ps 57:1-3
PROPHECY of
Benjaminites Jer 6:1-8
Israelites Amos 3:11-12

SELF-REALIZATION of
in **NEW AGE**
Jesus Lk 12:49-50

SIGNS of
Asa 1 Kgs 15:9-15
Jehoiada 2 Chr 21:1-23:21
by **DEITY**
Adversaries Ps 74:3-9
Hezekiah 2 Kgs 18:4-8
in **ENVIRONMENT**
God Ex 7:14-25;
8:1-15;
20-32;
9:1-7;
8-12;
13-35;
10:1-20
Jehoiada 2 Kgs 11:4-20
through **FALSE BELIEF**
Daniel *Bel 1:21-22
INSTRUCTION on
Hezekiah 2 Chr 29:1-36
Paul 1 Thes 5:1-11;
2 Thes 2:3b-10
PROPHECY of
Ezekiel Ezek 24:15-24
Isaiah Is 7:18-25;
30:18-26
Jeremiah Jer 44:29-30
Jesus Mt 24:4-8;
Mk 13:3-8;
14-23;
Lk 21:7-19;
20-24
Joel Joel 2:1-11
REVELATION on
Daniel Dan 7:2-14
Ezekiel Ezek 5:1-4;
17:1-10
Israelites Ezek 15:1-8;
19:10-14

REVELATION on (cont'd)
John Rev 8:7;
8-9;
12:1-6;
16:12-16;
17-21;
17:6b-18
Zechariah Zech 5:1-4
of **Sanctuary**
Alcimus *1 Mc 9:54-57
Israelites 2 Chr 30:1-31:21
Josiah 2 Kgs 23:4-15;
2 Chr 34:1-35:27
Manasseh 2 Chr 33:1-25

SIN causing
Asa 2 Chr 14:1-16:14
Jehu 2 Kgs 10:18-28
COVENANT of
Isaiah Is 28:14-22
by **DEITY**
Bildad Job 8:10-19
David Ps 9:5-8;
55:9-11;
58:6-9;
59:12-13b
Elihu Job 34:21-28
God Ps 37:12-22;
23-40;
73:13-20;
94:20-23;
145:13b-20;
Prov 10:1-32
Mankind Ps 1:4-6;
9:17-20
Psalmist Ps 92:5-11;
104:31-35
Zimri 1 Kgs 16:8-14
through **FALSE BELIEF**
Israelites Ezek 22:23-31
Moses Deut 12:1-31;
20:10-18
Sinners Jude 1:8-10;
11-13
INSTRUCTION on
Isaiah Is 59:1-21
Jesus Mt 7:24-27;
13:36-43;
47-50;
Lk 6:46-49
Paul Rom 6:1-14;
Phil 3:17-21
Solomon Prov 1:10-19;
11:1-31;
12:1-28;
13:1-25;
14:1-35
MEDITATION on
David Ps 101:5-7;
8
by **MESSIANIC FIGURE**
Isaiah Is 11:1-9
PROPHECY of
Eliezer 2 Chr 17:1-20:37
Isaiah Is 1:27-31
Moses Num 32:6-15
REVELATION on
Believers Mal 3:13-4:3
Daniel Dan 8:15-25
Isaiah Is 66:17-24
SELF-REALIZATION of

as QUALITY OF LIFE (cont'd)
Jesus   Lk 14:7-11
in RESPECT
Paul   Rom 12:9-13;
                        13:1-7
Preacher   Eccl 7:1-22
Solomon   Prov 26:1-28
Wife   Prov 31:10-31
in STEWARDSHIP
Jesus   Lk 22:24-27
of TRUTH
Jesus   Jn 18:28-19:16

KNOWLEDGE of
of DEITY
Job   Job 31:5-34
REVELATION on
King   Ezek 28:11-19

PRAYER for
PROPHECY of
Beliver   1 Cor 11:2-16

in PRESENCE
of DEITY
David   1 Chr 11:1-12:40
Solomon   2 Chr 1:1-17

PROPHECY of
in AUTHORITY
Jesus   Mt 24:29-31;
                        Mk 13:24-27

in PROVIDENCE
REVELATION on
Egyptians   Ezek 31:1-9

as QUALITY OF LIFE
Believers   Acts 15:6-29
Paul   2 Cor 11:21-29
INSTRUCTION on
Jesus   Lk 14:7-11

RESPECT for
Uzziah   2 Chr 26:1-28:27
of DEITY
David   Ps 18:46-50;
                        145:1-3
God   Ps 104:1-4
Mankind   Ps 8:3-8
in ENVIRONMENT
Tyre   Ezek 27:1-9a;
                        9b-11
INSTRUCTION on
Paul   Rom 12:9-13;
                        13:1-7
Preacher   Eccl 7:1-22
Solomon   Prov 26:1-28
Wife   Prov 31:10-31
of MESSIANIC FIGURE
Jesus   Heb 2:5-18
in WORSHIP
Women   1 Cor 11:2-16

REVELATION on
in AUTHORITY
Ezekiel   Ezek 1:4-28;
                        10:1-22
Isaiah   Is 49:1-26
Moses   Ex 7:1-7

in PROVIDENCE
Egyptians   Ezek 31:1-9

of RITE
in WORSHIP
Believers   1 Cor 11:27-34

SECURITY in
of DEITY
David   Ps 25:16-21
INSTRUCTION on
Solomon   Prov 10:1-32;
                        28:1-28

SELF-REALIZATION of
as VIRTUE
David   Ps 26:8-12

in STEWARDSHIP
INSTRUCTION on
Jesus   Lk 22:24-27

of TRUTH
INSTRUCTION on
Jesus   Jn 18:28-19:16
in MISSION
Paul   2 Cor 12:14-18
Titus   2 Cor 12:14-18

as VIRTUE
Job   Job 17:6-10
of DEITY
David   Ps 7:6-8
Job   Job 27:1-12
in MISSION
Men   Tit 2:1-10
SELF-REALIZATION of
David   Ps 26:8-12

in WORSHIP
Believers   1 Cor 11:27-34
Women   1 Cor 14:34-40
through RESPECT
Women   1 Cor 11:2-16

DISCIPLESHIP
AUTHORITY for
in COVENANT
God   2 Cor 3:4-6
through DEITY
God   2 Tim 1:3-7
of FOLLOWERs
Jesus   Mt 10:1;
                        Mk 6:7-13;
                        Lk 9:1-6

INSTRUCTION on
Jesus   Mt 18:18-20
in MISSION
Holy Spirit   1 Thes 1:2-10
Jesus   Mk 3:13-19

BEHAVIOR in
of FOLLOWERs
Crowd   Mt 8:1
INSTRUCTION on
Jesus   Mt 5:13-16;
                        10:9-15;
                        16-22;23;
                        26-39;

through **PUNISHMENT** (cont'd)
by **DEITY**
   Psalmist   Ps 118:15-21

as **QUALITY OF LIFE**
INSTRUCTION on
   Jesus   Mt 8:18-22;
                       Lk 9:57-62
   Paul   Phil 2:5-11;
                       3:4-16

RECONCILIATION through
to **DEITY**
   God   Ps 111:5-9

RITE of
in **WORSHIP**
   Abraham   Gen 12:1-8;
                       13:2-9;
                       14-18
   Isaac   Gen 26:12-31

SALVATION through
to **DEITY**
   David   Ps 69:29-36
   God   Ps 34:15-22;
                       85:8-13
in **MISSION**
   Gentiles   Acts 13:14-52
REVELATION on
   Heliodorus   *2 Mc 3:1-40
SCRIPTURES on
   Paul   Eph 6:10-18

SECURITY through
to **DEITY**
   David   Ps 28:8-9
   God   Ps 34:15-22;
                       91:1-13;
                       102:23-28
REVELATION on
   John   Rev 7:1-8

STEWARDSHIP in
INSTRUCTION on
   Jesus   Mt 10:7-8;
                       26:39;
                     28:16-20;
                     Mk 4:21-25;
                     10:35-45;
                     Lk 8:16-18;
                     14:25-27
   John the Baptist Lk 3:10-14
   Paul   Tit 2:1-10

TRUTH in
to **DEITY**
   James   Jas 1:16-18
INSTRUCTION on
   Jesus   Mt 5:1-2;
                     13:3b-9;
                     10-17;
                     18-23;
                     Mk 4:1-9;
                     10-20;
                     33-34;
                     8:1-3;
                     4-8;
                     9-10;
                     11-15;
                     9:10-11

VIRTUE in
of **FOLLOWERs**
   Paul   2 Thes 1:11-12
REVELATION on
   Abraham   Gen 17:1-8

DISOBEDIENCE

to **AUTHORITY**
   Mattathias   *1 Mc 2:15-22
INSTRUCTION on
   Jesus   Mt 7:24-27;
                     Lk 6:46-49

BEHAVIOR revealing
   Midwives   Ex 1:15-22
to **DEITY**
   David   2 Sam 11:1-27
   Israelites   Is 1:2-3
INSTRUCTION on
   God   Gen 3:9-13
   Serpent   Gen 3:1-8
   Vashti   Esth 1:10-22
in **MISSION**
   Jonah   Jon 1:1-17
PROPHECY of
   Jeremiah   Jer 22:20-23
   Zedekiah   *1 Esd 1:46-58
to **TRADITION**
   Ham   Gen 9:21-25

in **COMMITMENT**
   Shimei   1 Kgs 2:36-46
to **DEITY**
   Daniel   Dan 9:4-19

of **COMMUNITY**
   Jeremiah   Jer 43:4-7

COMPULSION to
   God   Gen 3:20-24

CONFRONTATION with
   Israelites   Num 16:16-24
INSTRUCTION on
   Jesus   Mt 18:15-17
   Nebuchadnezzar *Jdt 1:1-2:20
PROPHECY of
   Ahab   1 Kgs 22:1-40;
                     2 Chr 17:1-20:37
   Josiah   *1 Esd 1:25-32

to **COVENANT**
through in**FIDELITY**
   Israelites   Judg 2:20-23;
                     Jer 11:1-14;
                     Hos 6:7-9
   Priests   Mal 1:6-2:9
providing **FREEDOM**
   People   Jer 34:8-12
of **LAW**
   Ephraimites   Ps 78:9-20
   Isaiah   Is 24:1-12
   Israelites   Deut 29:16-29;
                     Ezek 44:6-9;
                     Hos 8:1-3

PUNISHMENT for
   Israelites   Judg 2:1-5

to **LAW** (cont'd)

Israelites	Num 15:32-36; Deut 9:7-24; Ezra 9:1-2; Mal 3:6-12
Sinners	1 Tim 1:8-11

of **DEITY**

Babylonians	2 Kgs 17:24-41
Israelites	Neh 9:16-18; 26-31; Dan 9:4-19
Jason	*2 Mc 4:7-17
Judahites	Jer 7:21-28; 29-8:3
Pharisees	Mt 15:3-9; Mk 7:1-23

caused by **FALSE BELIEF**

Israelites	Ex 32:1-6; 2 Kgs 17:7-23; Ezek 20:9-26; 22:23-31
Judahites	2 Kgs 17:7-23

INSTRUCTION on

Antiochus	*2 Mc 6:1-11
Israelites	Ex 16:22-30
Moses	Deut 21:18-21; 28:15-68
Paul	Rom 5:12-21
Shadrach	Dan 3:8-12; 16-18

MEDITATION on

Chaldeans	Dan 3:8-12

by **MESSIANIC FIGURE**

Jesus	Jn 5:1-18

PROPHECY of

Jerusalemites	Zeph 3:1-5

REVELATION on

Israelites	Ezek 5:5-17

SELF-REALIZATION of

Ezra	Ezra 9:6-15
Nehemiah	Neh 1:5-11a

of **WORSHIP**

Israelites	Neh 13:10-14

by **MESSIANIC FIGURE**
to **LAW**

Jesus	Jn 5:1-18

in **MISSION**

Jonah	Jon 1:1-17

PROMISE concerning
to **DEITY**

Zedekiah	*1 Esd 1:46-58

PROPHECY of
through in**FIDELITY**

Ahijah	1 Kgs 14:1-18
Jeremiah	Jer 42:7-22
Moses	Deut 31:24-29

to **LAW**

Jerusalemites	Zeph 3:1-5

to **TRUTH**

Johanan	Jer 43:4-7
Judahites	Jer 25:1-7; 42:7-22

PROVIDENCE overcomes
to **DEITY**

Mankind	Rom 11:25-32

PUNISHMENT for

Moses	Lev 26:1-46
Nebuchadnezzar	*Jdt 1:1-2:20
Shadrach	Dan 3:19-23
Solomon	*Wis 11:1-20

to **COVENANT**

Israelites	Judg 2:1-5

to **DEITY**

Azariah	*Azar 1:1-10
David	Ps 55:15-19; 89:19-37
God	Judg 9:56-57; Ps 95:7d-11; 119:17-24
Israelites	Num 16:25-35; Josh 7:6-26; Judg 10:6-18; 2 Kgs 18:9-12; Neh 9:32-37; Ps 106:24-27; Jer 32:16-25; *Bar 2:1-10; 24-26; Heb 4:1-13
Jehoshaphat	2 Chr 17:1-20:37
Judahites	2 Kgs 23:36-24:7
Moses	Deut 31:30-32:47
Psalmist	Ps 137:4-6
Saul	1 Chr 10:1-14
Uzzah	2 Sam 6:1-23; 1 Chr 13:1-14

caused by **FALSE BELIEF**

Author	Heb 6:1-8

INSTRUCTION on

Achior	*Jdt 5:1-21
Agur	Prov 30:15-33
Artaxerxes	Ezra 7:25-26; *1 Esd 8:8-24
Ezra	*1 Esd 9:1-15
God	Gen 2:16-17; 3:14-19
Jeremiah	Jer 44:20-28
Jesus	Lk 12:41-46; 47-48
Joshua	Josh 23:1-16; 24:16-24
Lot	Gen 19:12-29
Moses	Deut 28:15-68; 29:16-29
Nebuchadnezzar	Dan 3:1-6; 13-15
Paul	Rom 2:1-24; 2 Cor 10:1-6; 13:1-4; 2 Thes 3:6-15
Solomon	Prov 5:1-14; *Wis 6:1-11

PROPHECY of

Ahijah	1 Kgs 11:26-40
Amaziah	2 Chr 25:1-28
Asa	2 Chr 14:1-16:14
God	Mic 5:7-15
Huldah	2 Kgs 22:3-20
Jeremiah	Jer 17:19-27; 29:1-23; 34:13-22
Jeroboam	1 Kgs 13:1-34; 14:1-18
Judahites	Jer 44:1-14
Samuel	1 Sam 13:1-23;

PROPHECY of (cont'd)
Samuel	28:3-25
Zedekiah	Jer 22:1-9

REVELATION on
Ezekiel	Ezek 3:16-21; 11:1-13
Holy Spirit	Heb 3:6b-11
Isaiah	Is 31:4-9
Israelites	Num 14:26-38; Is 48:1-22; Jer 9:25-26
Jeremiah	Jer 16:1-13; 23:33-40
Judahites	Jer 13:1-11
Moses	Num 16:36-50
Nathan	2 Sam 7:1-29; 1 Chr 17:1-27
Solomon	1 Kgs 9:1-9; 11:1-13

through disRESPECT
Mordecai	Esth 3:1-6

REVELATION on
through inFIDELITY
Ezekiel	Ezek 3:22-27
Isaiah	Is 65:1-25
Israelites	Jer 2:14-19; 20-29; 5:1-14; Ezek 15:1-8
Moses	Deut 31:14-23
Samuel	1 Sam 8:1-22

to LAW
Israelites	Ezek 5:5-17

to TRUTH
Ezekiel	Ezek 33:30-33

in RITE
INSTRUCTION on
Aaron	Lev 10:1-20

of WORSHIP
Naphtali	*Tb 1:3-9
Nicanor	*2 Mc 15:1-5

SALVATION from
of FOLLOWERs
Gentiles	Rom 11:7-24

INSTRUCTION on
Paul	Rom 11:25-32

SIGNS of
INSTRUCTION on
Paul	2 Tim 3:1-9

as SIN
Israelites	Num 14:39-45; 1 Sam 14:1-46; Hos 4:1-3
Joab	2 Sam 18:1-19:8a
Judahites	Jer 7:1-15
Saul	1 Sam 15:1-35

to COVENANT
Israelites	*2 Esd 2:1-7

to DEITY
Eve	Gen 3:1-8
Israelites	Ps 106:6-12; *2 Esd 1:4-23

through FALSE BELIEF
Judahites	Amos 2:4-5
Satan	1 Jn 3:4-10

INSTRUCTION on
James	Jas 4:17
Jesus	Mt 15:15-20; 21:33-43; Mk 7:1-23; 12:1-12; Lk 20:9-18
Paul	Rom 8:5-13; 2 Thes 1:7b-10

PROPHECY of
Isaiah	Is 3:8-12

REVELATION on
Ezekiel	Ezek 12:1-16
Jehu	1 Kgs 15:33-16:7

SELF-REALIZATION of
Jonah	Jon 1:1-17

against TRADITION
Ezra	*2 Esd 3:1-36
Israelites	*Sir 48:15-16; 49:4-7; *Bar 2:27-35

in WORSHIP
Israelites	2 Kgs 14:1-4; 15:1-7
Judahites	2 Kgs 11:21-12:3 15:32-38

against TRADITION
of LAW
Disciples	Mt 15:1-2; Mk 7:1-23
Sinners	1 Tim 1:8-11

PUNISHMENT for
Solomon	*Wis 11:1-20

as SIN
Ezra	*2 Esd 3:1-36
Israelites	*Sir 48:15-16; 49:4-7; *Bar 2:27-35

against TRUTH
through FALSE BELIEF
Judahites	Jer 8:4-7

INSTRUCTION on
John the Baptist	Jn 3:31-36

PROPHECY of
Johanan	Jer 43:4-7
Judahites	Jer 25:1-7; 42:7-22

REVELATION on
Ezekiel	Ezek 33:30-33

DOUBT

concerning AUTHORITY
of DEITY
Jehoram	2 Kgs 6:32-7:2

of MESSIANIC FIGURE
Crowd	Mt 9:18-26; Mk 5:35-43; Lk 8:40-56
Elders	Mk 11:27-33; Lk 20:1-8
Pharisees	Lk 5:17-26
Priests	Mt 21:23-27; Mk 11:27-33; Lk 20:1-8

BEHAVIOR revealing
Aaron	Num 12:1-2

DOUBT (cont'd)

caused by **FALSE BELIEF**
James   Jas 1:5-8
INSTRUCTION on
Jesus   Jn 5:19-47
PROPHECY of
Jerusalemites   Zeph 3:1-5
REVELATION on
Ezekiel   Ezek 33:23-29

of **TRUTH**
caused by **FALSE BELIEF**
Pharisees   Jn 7:32-36
by **FOLLOWERs**
Apostles   Acts 9:20-31
INSTRUCTION on
Jesus   Lk 22:66-71
in **MESSIANIC FIGURE**
Jews   Jn 8:21-59
Nicodemus   Jn 3:1-21
People   Jn 7:1-14
PROPHECY of
Jeremiah   Jer 38:1-13

in **VIRTUE**
of **MESSIANIC FIGURE**
Pharisees   Mt 9:10-13;
    Mk 2:15-17;
    Lk 5:29-32

in **WORSHIP**
Disciples   Mt 28:16-20

ELECTION

ACCEPTANCE of
Jesus   Mt 3:13-17;
    17:1-8;
    Mk 1:9-11;
    9:2-8;
    Lk 3:21-22;
    9:28-36
by **FOLLOWER**
Matthew   Mt 9:9;
    Lk 5:27-28
INSTRUCTION on
Jesus   Mt 15:12-14;
    20:1-16;
    22:1-14
Peter   2 Pet 1:8-11
by **MESSIANIC FIGURE**
Noah   Gen 6:5-22
to **MISSION**
Jesus   Jn 12:27-36a

BLESSING through
to **COVENANT**
Author   Heb 9:15-22
Israelites   Deut 5:1-21
by **DEITY**
God   Ps 65:1-4
PROPHECY of
Gabriel   Lk 1:5-25
Prophet   Judg 6:7-10
REVELATION of
Abraham   Gen 12:1-8
Israelites   Ezek 20:5-8

to **CAPTIVITY**
by **DEITY**

177 ELECTION (cont'd)

by **DEITY** (cont'd)
Kings   2 Kgs 3:1-27
COMPASSION through
SCRIPTURES on
God   Rom 9:14-29
COVENANT of
of **FAMILY**
David   Ps 89:1-4
to **COVENANT**
BLESSING through
Author   Heb 9:15-22
Israelites   Deut 5:1-21
by **GRACE**
Israelites   Rom 9:1-5
of **LIFE**
Ezekiel   Ezek 16:8-14
through **OBEDIENCE**
Moses   Ex 19:1-8;
    Deut 29:1-15
PRAISE of
Ezra   Neh 9:7-8
REJECTION of
Israelites   Rom 9:1-5
for **DEATH**
PROPHECY of
Jesus   Jn 13:31-35
by **DEITY**
ACCEPTANCE of
Jesus   Mt 3:13-17;
    17:1-8;
    Mk 1:9-11;
    9:2-8;
    Lk 3:21-22;
    9:28-36
BLESSING through
God   Ps 65:1-4
to **CAPTIVITY**
Kings   2 Kgs 3:1-27
for **DISCIPLESHIP**
God   Ps 105:1-6
Israelites   Deut 10:12-22
Jesus   Jn 10:19-40;
    17:6-19
Thessalonians   1 Thes 1:2-10
of **ENEMY**
Hadad   1 Kgs 11:14-22
Rezon   1 Kgs 11:23-25
Solomon   1 Kgs 11:14-22;
    23-25
FAITH in
Thessalonians   2 Thes 2:13-15
of **FAMILY**
David   2 Chr 5:1-7:10
God   Ps 33:10-12;
    132:11-18;
    147:12-20
Israelites   Deut 14:1-2;
    1 Kgs 8:22-53;
    Ps 47:1-4;
    135:1-4;
    Amos 3:1-2
as **FULFILLMENT**
God   Is 44:24-45:13
GRACE in
Believers   1 Pet 2:4-19
Elizabeth   Lk 1:57-80
Israelites   Rom 11:25-32
Mankind   Ex 33:12-23

GRACE in (cont'd)
Paul	Col 1:25-27

JUSTICE in
Believers	Lk 18:1-8;
	Rom 8:28-39

of **LEADERSHIP**
Aaron	Ex 6:10-13
David	*Sir 47:1-11
Ehud	Judg 3:15-23
Jesus	1 Pet 2:4-10
Joshua	Deut 3:23-29
Micah	Mic 4:1-8
Moses	Ex 6:10-13
Othniel	Judg 3:7-11
Prophet	Deut 18:9-22
Solomon	*Wis 9:1-18

of **LIFE**
Jesus	Jn 6:25-59

LOVE in
Israelites	Mal 1:2-5
Judahites	Ps 78:67-72

OBEDIENCE to
Abraham	Gen 18:16-22

PRAISE of
Israelites	Is 42:18-43:7

REJECTION of
Ephraimites	Ps 78:67-72
Saul	1 Sam 13:1-23

for **SACREDNESS**
Aaron	Num 17:1-13
Israelites	1 Sam 12:1-25
Jews	Rom 2:25-3:20
Levites	Deut 10:1-11
Solomon	1 Chr 22:2-19

to **SERVICE**
Aaron	Ex 4:10-16;
	Ps 105:26-36
God	Is 41:1-42:4
High Priest	Heb 5:1-10
Isaiah	Is 49:1-26
Israelites	Is 41:1-42:4;
	43:8-13
Jesus	Heb 5:1-10
Levites	1 Chr 15:1-16:43
Moses	Ps 105:26-36
Priests	Ex 28:1-5

of **VICTORY**
Assyrians	Is 10:5-16
Israelites	Deut 4:15-31

WISDOM in
Sirach	*Sir 24:1-34

WITNESS to
Jesus	Mt 11:27

to **DISCIPLESHIP**
to **DEITY**
God	Ps 105:1-6
Israelites	Deut 10:12-22
Jesus	Jn 10:19-40;
	17:6-19
Thessalonians	1 Thes 1:2-10

of **FOLLOWERs**
Andrew	Mt 4:18-22;
	Mk 1:16-20
God	1 Pet 1:1-2
James	Mt 4:18-22;
	Mk 1:16-20;
	Lk 5:1-11
Jesus	Jn 21:15-23
John	Mt 4:18-22;
	Mk 1:16-20;

of **FOLLOWERs** (cont'd)
John	Lk 5:1-11
Matthew	Mk 2:13-14
Matthias	Acts 1:12-26
Peter	Mt 4:18-22;
	Mk 1:16-20;
	Lk 5:1-11
Philip	Jn 1:19-51

INSTRUCTION on
Jesus	Mt 13:10-17;
	Mk 4:10-20;
	Lk 8:9-10
Paul	1 Cor 12:27-31a
Peter	Acts 15:6-29;
	1 Pet 2:4-10

of **MESSIANIC FIGURE**
Believers	Lk 10:1-16
Jesus	Mk 10:17-22;
	Lk 18:18-27
Man	Mt 19:16-22

in **MISSION**
Holy Spirit	2 Cor 1:15-22
Jesus	Mk 3:13-19;
	Lk 6:12-16
Paul	1 Cor 1:1-3;
	Gal 1:11-17

REVELATION on
Saul	Acts 9:1-19

DISOBEDIENCE to
SCRIPTURES on
People	1 Pet 2:4-10

of **ENEMY**
by **DEITY**
Hadad	1 Kgs 11:14-22
Rezon	1 Kgs 11:23-25
Solomon	1 Kgs 11:14-22;
	23-25

FAITH in
by **DEITY**
Thessalonians	2 Thes 2:13-15

of **FOLLOWERs**
Believers	Acts 13:14-52
Jesus	Lk 5:1-11

INSTRUCTION on
Paul	Rom 8:28-39

REVELATION on
Believers	Is 56:1-8

SELF-REALIZATION of
Paul	1 Tim 1:12-17

of **FAMILY**
COVENANT of
David	Ps 89:1-4

by **DEITY**
David	2 Chr 5:1-7:10
God	Ps 33:10-12;
	132:11-18;
	147:12-20
Israelites	Deut 14:1-2;
	1 Kgs 8:22-53;
	Ps 47:1-4;
	135:1-4;
	Amos 3:1-2

of **FOLLOWERs**
Holy Spirit	Rom 8:14-25
Jesus	Eph 1:3-14

INSTRUCTION on
Moses	Deut 31:30-32:47

REJECTION of
  to **COVENANT**
    Israelites   Rom 9:1-5
  by **DEITY**
    Ephraimites   Ps 78:67-72
    Saul   1 Sam 13:1-23
  of **FOLLOWER**
    Judas   Jn 6:60-71
  REVELATION on
    Eli   1 Sam 2:27-36
  TRADITION of
    Esau   Gen 27:1-40

REVELATION on
  to **DISCIPLESHIP**
    Saul   Acts 9:1-19
  through **FAITH**
    Believers   Is 56:1-8
  of **FAMILY**
    Israelites   Zech 13:7-9
    Solomon   1 Kgs 11:1-13
  of **LEADERSHIP**
    Babylonians   Jer 27:1-11
    Cyrus   Is 48:1-22
    Elijah   1 Kgs 19:1-21
    God   1 Sam 2:27-36
    Israelites   1 Kgs 11:1-13;
                              Is 49:1-26
    Joshua   Deut 31:14-23;
                              Josh 1:1-9;
                              Zech 3:1-10;
                              6:9-15
    Samuel   1 Sam 16:1-13
    Zechariah   Zech 11:4-14
    Zerubbabel   Hag 2:20-23
  through **OBEDIENCE**
    Amos   Amos 7:10-17
    Jeremiah   Jer 1:4-10
    Joshua   Zech 3:1-10
  for **SERVICE**
    Elisha   1 Kgs 19:1-21
    Isaiah   Is 66:17-24
    Israelites   Is 43:14-44:5;
                              Jer 30:4-9
    Jeremiah   Jer 1:13-16
    Levites   Num 18:1-7;
                              Ezek 44:10-14
    Moses   Ex 28:40-43
    Samuel   1 Sam 3:1-4:1a

REWARDs of
  of **FOLLOWERs**
    Jesus   Lk 22:28-30
  INSTRUCTION on
    God   *2 Esd 2:15-32
    Paul   Rom 11:7-24
  REVELATION on
    Isaiah   Is 65:1-25

SACREDNESS of
    Moses   Num 16:3-11
  by **DEITY**
    Aaron   Num 17:1-13
    Israelites   1 Sam 12:1-25
    Jews   Rom 2:25-3:20
    Levites   Deut 10:1-11
    Solomon   1 Chr 22:2-19
  over **FALSE BELIEF**
    Moses   Lev 20:1-27
  of **FOLLOWERs**
    Paul   Rom 1:1-7

INSTRUCTION on
    Believers   1 Pet 2:4-10
    Moses   Deut 7:6-16;
                              14:1-2;
                              26:16-19;
                              28:1-14
  of **MESSIANIC FIGURE**
    Jesus   Jn 7:25-31
  PROPHECY of
    Israelites   Zech 2:6-13
  REVELATION on
    Jesus   Mk 9:2-8

    John   Rev 7:1-8
    Manoah   Judg 13:2-7
    Moses   Num 3:11-13
  TRADITION of
    Levites   Num 3:11-13
  for **WORSHIP**
    Aaron   Ex 28:40-43

of **SACRIFICE**
  PROPHECY of
    Jesus   Mt 16:21-28

SCRIPTURES on
  through **COMPASSION**
    God   Rom 9:14-29
  by **GRACE**
    Mankind   Rom 9:14-29
  of **LEADERSHIP**
    Prophet   Acts 3:1-26

SELF-REALIZATION of
  through **FAITH**
    Paul   1 Tim 1:12-17
  of **LEADERSHIP**
    Paul   1 Tim 1:12-17
  through **LOVE**
    Paul   1 Tim 1:12-17

to **SERVICE**
    Levites   Num 3:5-10;
                              8:5-22;
                              Deut 10:1-11;
                              18:1-8
    Moses   Num 4:1-20
  by **DEITY**
    Aaron   Ex 4:10-16;
                              Ps 105:26-36
    God   Is 41:1-42:4
    High Priest   Heb 5:1-10
    Isaiah   Is 49:1-26
    Israelites   Is 41:1-42:4;
                              43:8-13
    Jesus   Heb 5:1-10
    Levites   1 Chr 15:1-16:43
    Moses   Ps 105:26-36
    Priests   Ex 28:1-5
  of **FOLLOWER**
    Jesus   Mk 3:13-19
  in **MISSION**
    Believers   Eph 1:15-2:10
    Jesus   Mt 15:21-28
  PROPHECY of
    Elisha   1 Kgs 19:1-21
    Jeremiah   Jer 1:4-10
  REVELATION on
    Elisha   1 Kgs 19:1-21

ELECTION (cont'd)

REVELATION on (cont'd)
- Isaiah — Is 66:17-24
- Israelites — Is 43:14-44:5; Jer 30:4-9
- Jeremiah — Jer 1:13-16
- Levites — Num 18:1-7; Ezek 44:10-14
- Moses — Ex 28:40-43
- Samuel — 1 Sam 3:1-4:1a

as TRADITION
- Levites — Num 3:40-51
- Merari — Num 4:29-33

in WORSHIP
- Aaron — Ex 29:1-9

for VICTORY
- by DEITY
  - Assyrians — Is 10:5-16
  - Israelites — Deut 4:15-31
- PROPHECY of
  - Israelites — Is 27:12-13
  - Jesus — Mt 24:29-31; Mk 13:24-27

of WILL
- REVELATION on
  - Jesus — Jn 21:15-23
  - Moses — Num 12:4-10

WISDOM in
- by DEITY
  - Sirach — *Sir 24:1-34

of WITNESS
- by DEITY
  - Jesus — Mt 11:27
- in MISSION
  - Barnabas — Acts 13:1-3
  - Ezekiel — Ezek 3:4-9
  - Gentiles — Gal 1:18-2:10
  - Jesus — Jn 8:21-59
  - John the Baptist — Jn 1:1-18
  - Paul — 2 Cor 1:1-2
  - Saul — Acts 13:1-3
- REVELATION on
  - Ezekiel — Ezek 2:1-8a; 3:10-11; 16-21
  - Isaiah — Is 6:1-13

ENEMY

BEHAVIOR of
- in the ENVIRONMENT
  - Israelites — Josh 9:1-2
- MEDITATION on
  - David — Ps 56:5-6a; 62:3-4

BEHAVIOR with
- INSTRUCTION on
  - Jesus — Mt 5:43-47; Lk 6:27-35
  - Sirach — *Sir 12:8-18

COMMUNITY as
- of DEITY
  - Mankind — Ps 2:1-3

ENEMY (cont'd)

CONFRONTATION with
- Aaron — *Sir 45:6-22
- Antiochus — *1 Mc 15:1-14; 25-41; *2 Mc 4:21-22
- Assyrians — Is 10:27d-32
- Esther — Esth 7:1-10
- Israelites — Num 20:14-21; Ezra 4:6-16; 5:3-5; Neh 4:7-12; 6:17-19
- Jephthah — Judg 11:12-28
- Jews — *2 Mc 4:39-50
- Jonathan — *1 Mc 9:58-73
- Joram — 2 Kgs 8:25-29
- Judas — *1 Mc 3:38-44
- Judith — *Jdt 10:1-23
- Kings — Josh 9:1-2
- Maccabeus — *1 Mc 3:46-60; 7:5-35; *2 Mc 8:8-23; 13:1-2; 14:1-2; 3-17
- Moses — Deut 2:1-25
- Nehemiah — Neh 2:9-11
- Samson — Judg 16:1-3
- Simon — *1 Mc 13:12-24; 15:25-41

through violated COVENANT
- David — Ps 55:20-21

by DEITY
- David — 1 Sam 17:1-18:5
- Esther — *Esth 14:1-19
- Solomon — *Wis 5:15-23

INSTRUCTION on
- Antiochus — *1 Mc 3:27-37

PROPHECY of
- Isaiah — Is 8:8b-10
- Israelites — Nah 2:1-5
- Jeremiah — Jer 6:22-26

REVELATION on
- Michael — Rev 12:7-9
- Prophets — Rev 11:1-14

of DEITY
- is COMMUNITY
  - Mankind — Ps 2:1-3
- CONFRONTATION with
  - David — 1 Sam 17:1-18:5
  - Esther — *Esth 14:1-19
  - Solomon — *Wis 5:15-23
- ELECTION of
  - Hadad — 1 Kgs 11:14-22
  - Rezon — 1 Kgs 11:23-25
  - Solomon — 1 Kgs 11:14-22; 23-25
- KNOWLEDGE of
  - David — Ps 3:1-2; 21:8-13
- PROVIDENCE over
  - Israelites — Ezra 8:31-36; Is 9:8-10:4; *1 Esd 6:3-6
  - Mankind — Ps 17:6-7

ELECTION of
- by DEITY
  - Hadad — 1 Kgs 11:14-22

of **DEATH**	
Azariah	*Azar 1:23-27
DOUBT in	
Israelites	Ex 14:1-14
FULFILLMENT of	
Rahab	Josh 6:22-27
of **INNOCENCE**	
Daniel	*Susa 1:60-64
through **JEALOUSY**	
Phinehas	Num 25:6-18
JOY in	
Cyrus	*Bel 1:40-42
LIFE	
David	Ps 54:3
through **MIRACLE**	
Azariah	*Azar 1:23-27
through **OBEDIENCE**	
God	Gen 8:1-12
through **SEX**	
Israelites	Judg 21:8-12
through **VICTORY**	
Othniel	Judg 3:7-11

SECURITY in

through **ALIENATION**	
David	2 Sam 15:13-16:14
ANXIETY concerning	
Jacob	Gen 34:1-31
through **COMPASSION**	
Cain	Gen 4:1-16
David	1 Sam 22:1-23
from **ENEMY**	
Maccabeus	*2 Mc 14:28-30
Rahab	Josh 2:1-7
from **EVIL**	
Tobiah	*Tb 8:1-21
from **FEAR**	
David	1 Sam 21:10-15;
	23:1-13;
	27:1-28:2
Israelites	*Jdt 16:21-25
Nicanor	*2 Mc 8:34-36
through **GRACE**	
David	1 Sam 25:1-44
Joseph	Gen 50:1-21
from **KILLING**	
David	1 Sam 21:1-9
Jonathan	*1 Mc 9:32-42
Maccabeus	*2 Mc 5:11-27
Moses	Deut 4:41-43
through **LEADERSHIP**	
Raphael	*Tb 5:1-21
through **LOVE**	
Isaac	Gen 24:61-67
through **PEACE**	
Israelites	Judg 8:24-28
through **SACRIFICE**	
Reuben	Gen 42:26-38
through **SERVICE**	
Ebedmelech	Jer 38:1-13
from **VIOLENCE**	
Bacchides	*1 Mc 9:43-53
David	2 Sam 16:15-17:29
Jonathan	*1 Mc 12:35-38
Maccabeus	*2 Mc 12:29-31
Rahab	Josh 2:8-14
Simon	*1 Mc 13:31-41
through **WEALTH**	
Jacob	Gen 33:17-20;
	46:28-47:12
Levites	Deut 18:1-8

SERVICE to	
through **BROTHERHOOD**	
Levite	Judg 19:16-21
COMMITMENT to	
Judah	Gen 44:1-34
by **COMMUNITY**	
Simon	Lk 23:26
COMPULSION of	
Solomon	1 Kgs 9:15-23
ELECTION of	
Levites	Deut 18:1-8
FIDELITY in	
Ruth	Ruth 2:1-23
as **PUNISHMENT**	
Gibeon	Josh 9:16-27
SECURITY through	
Ebedmelech	Jer 38:1-13

SIN in

causes **ANGER**	
Edomites	Amos 1:11-12
Nehemiah	Neh 5:6-13
is **BLASPHEMY**	
Holy Spirit	Mk 3:20-30
against **BLESSING**	
Job	Job 21:14-18
in **CAPTIVITY**	
Philistines	Amos 1:6-8
CONDEMNATION of	
David	2 Sam 3:17-39
Moses	Num 16:3-11
DEATH caused by	
Man	Gen 7:1-24
DEFEAT caused by	
Israelites	Josh 7:6-26
is **DISOBEDIENCE**	
Israelites	Num 14:39-45;
	Hos 4:1-3
Saul	1 Sam 15:1-35
is **EVIL**	
Antiochus	*1 Mc 1:8-15
Israelites	Judg 13:1
Man	Gen 6:5-22
Ungodly Men	*Wis 2:6-11
is **IDOLATRY**	
Israelites	Deut 9:7-24
in**JUSTICE**	
Elders	*Susa 1:5-18
is **KILLING**	
Andronicus	*2 Mc 4:30-38
Israelites	Hos 4:1-3
is **LEADERSHIP**	
Israelites	Ezek 34:1-10
is **LUST**	
Benjaminites	Judg 19:22-26
in **MARRIAGE**	
Israelites	*1 Esd 8:68-70
in **ORDER**	
David	2 Sam 24:1-25;
	1 Chr 21:1-22:1
is **PRIDE**	
Ephraimites	Hos 12:7-9
PRUDENCE in	
Ungodly Men	*Wis 2:6-11
REJECTION of	
Israelites	Hos 4:1-3
Joseph	Gen 39:1-23
Susanna	*Susa 1:19-27
REPENTANCE of	
Israelites	Judg 10:6-18
Saul	1 Sam 15:1-35

eternal **BLESSING** (cont'd)
   COVENANT of
      Isaiah   Is 61:1-11
      Jeremiah   Jer 32:26-44
   by **DEITY**
      David   Ps 41:13;
                      145:1-3
      Ethan   Ps 89:52
      God   Ps 30:1-5;
                      133:1-3
      Israelites   Ps 132:11-18
      King   Ps 45:2-9
      Psalmist   Ps 113:2-4

eternal **COMPASSION**
   PROPHECY of
      Isaiah   Is 54:1-17

eternal **CONDEMNATION**
   through **FALSE BELIEF**
      Holy Spirit   Mt 12:22-32;
                      Mk 3:20-30
      John   Jude 1:5-7
   INSTRUCTION on
      Jesus   Mt 25:31-46;
                      Lk 16:19-31
   REVELATION on
      Mankind   Is 66:17-24

eternal **COVENANT**
   ACCEPTANCE of
      Believers   Is 56:1-8
   BLESSING of
      Isaiah   Is 61:1-11
      Jeremiah   Jer 32:26-44
   of **DISCIPLESHIP**
      Israelites   *Bar 2:27-35
   with **FAMILY**
      Israelites   1 Chr 15:1-16:43;
                      Ps 105:7-15
   FULFILLMENT of
      God   Ps 111:5-9
      Israelites   Ezek 16:53-63
   JUSTICE in
      Sirach   *Sir 17:1-14
   LEADERSHIP through
      David   2 Sam 7:1-29;
                      Ps 89:19-37
   Divine **LOVE** revealed in
      Isaiah   Is 55:1-13
   PEACE through
      Israelites   Ezek 37:15-28
   SACREDNESS of
      Aaron   *Sir 45:6-22
   WITNESS to
      Isaiah   Is 59:1-21

eternal **DESTRUCTION**
   by **DEITY**
      God   Ps 52:5-7
   PROPHECY of
      Damascenes   Is 17:1-6
      Isaiah   Is 34:1-17
   REVELATION on
      Edomites   Ezek 35:1-15
      Tyre   Ezek 27:25b-36;
                      28:11-19
eternal **DIGNITY**
   of **DEITY**
      God   Is 40:12-31

eternal **DISCIPLESHIP**
   COVENANT of
      Israelites   *Bar 2:27-35
eternal **FAITH**
   in **DEITY**
      God   Ps 146:5-7b
   INSTRUCTION on
      Isaiah   Is 26:1-6
   PROPHECY of
      Isaiah   Is 32:15-20
eternal **FAMILY**
   of **DEITY**
      God   Ps 48:4-8

FRIENDSHIP
   INSTRUCTION on
      Jesus   Lk 16:1-9

eternal **FULFILLMENT**
   by **DEITY**
      God   Jn 1:1-18
      Jesus   Jn 1:1-18
   PROPHECY of
      Jeremiah   Jer 31:38-40
   REVELATION on
      Isaiah   Is 51:1-16

eternal **GOOD**
   of **DEITY**
      God   Ps 119:137-144
                      153-160
   SCRIPTURES on
      Psalmist   2 Cor 9:6-11
eternal **GRATITUDE**
   to **DEITY**
      Psalmist   Ps 44:4-8
eternal **HOPE**
   INSTRUCTION on
      Psalmist   Ps 131:1-3
eternal **HUMILITY**
   REVELATION on
      Sinners   Jer 23:33-40
eternal **JOY**
   PROPHECY of
      Isaiah   Is 51:1-16;
                      61:1-11
eternal **JUSTICE**
   COVENANT of
      Sirach   *Sir 17:1-14
eternal **LEADERSHIP**
   COVENANT of
      David   2 Sam 7:1-29;
                      Ps 89:19-37
   of **DEITY**
      David   Ps 110:1-4
      God   Ex 15:1-18;
                      Deut 33:1-29
                      Ps 9:5-8;
                      10:12-18;
                      29:10-11;
                      145:10-13a;
                      146:10;

in **WORSHIP** (cont'd)
God   Rev 4:1-11

eternal **PURIFICATION**
TRADITION of
Moses   Num 19:14-22

eternal **REJECTION**
MEDITATION on
Job   Job 7:12-16

eternal **REWARDs**
INSTRUCTION on
Paul   2 Cor 4:16-18;
                             1 Tim 6:11-16
REVELATION on
Isaiah   Is 51:1-16
TRADITION of
Levites   Num 18:21-24

eternal **SACREDNESS**
COVENANT of
Aaron   *Sir 45:6-22
to **DEITY**
God   Ps 93:5
TRADITION of
Israelites   Ex 27:20-21
Moses   Lev 23:26-32;
                             33-44;
                             24:1-4
in **WORSHIP**
Jeremiah   Jer 17:12

eternal **SACRIFICE**
INSTRUCTION on
Jesus   Heb 10:1-18
of **MESSIANIC FIGURE**
Jesus   Heb 9:1-14
TRADITION of
Israelites   Lev 23:9-14;
                             Num 15:1-16
Levites   Num 18:8-20

eternal **SERVICE**
Melchizedek   Heb 7:1-28
to **DEITY**
God   Ps 121:2-8
of **MESSIANIC FIGURE**
Jesus   Heb 7:1-28
TRADITION of
Israelites   Num 10:1-10

eternal **SUFFERING**
through **FALSE BELIEF**
God   Rev 14:9-12
Sinners   Rev 20:7-10

eternal **TRADITION**
of **OBEDIENCE**
Moses   Lev 16:29-34;
                             17:1-9
of **PURIFICATION**
Moses   Num 19:14-22
of **REWARD**
Levites   Num 18:21-24
of **SACREDNESS**
Israelites   Ex 27:20-21
Moses   Lev 23:26-32;
                             33-44;
                             23-14

of **SACRIFICE**
Israelites   Lev 23:9-14;
                             Num 15:1-16
Levites   Num 18:8-20
of **SERVICE**
Israelites   Num 10:1-10

eternal **VICTORY**
REVELATION on
Israelites   Is 45:14-25

eternal **WISDOM**
of **DEITY**
God   Ps 33:10-12
Sirach   *Sir 24:1-34

eternal **WITNESS**
to **DEITY**
God   Ps 135:13-14
Israelites   Ps 48:9-14
INSTRUCTION on
Isaiah   Is 30:8-17
SCRIPTURES on
Isaiah   Is 40:1-11

EVIL

AUTHORITY over
Zedekiah   Jer 52:1-3
by **DEITY**
God   Ps 59:6-8
over **ENVIRONMENT**
Ungodly Men   *Wis 2:6-11
in **FALSE BELIEF**
Satan   2 Thes 2:3b-10
INSTRUCTION on
Paul   2 Cor 10:1-6
Solomon   *Wis 5:15-23
REVELATION on
John   Rev 13:1-4

BEHAVIOR revealing
Ephraimites   Hos 7:3-7
Nations   Zeph 3:6-7
against **DEITY**
Jehoiachin   *1 Esd 1:43-45
Jehoiakim   *1 Esd 1:37-42
Sodomites   Gen 19:4-11
Zedekiah   *1 Esd 1:46-58
against the **ENVIRONMENT**
Antiochus   *1 Mc 1:29-35
through **FALSE BELIEF**
Jews   Acts 19:13-20
INSTRUCTION on
Sirach   *Sir 20:18-23;
                             22:1-6;
                             25:1-2

in **BROTHERHOOD**
INSTRUCTION on
James   Jas 4:11-12

in **COMMUNITY**
Israelites   Is 1:4-9
Jason   *2 Mc 4:7-17
Judahites   Jer 3:6-11
against **DEITY**
Mankind   Ps 2:1-3

through inFIDELITY (cont'd)

Jehoram	2 Kgs 8:16-24; 2 Chr 21:1-23:21
Jehu	2 Kgs 10:29-31
Jeroboam	2 Kgs 14:23-29; 2 Chr 13:1-22
Manasseh	2 Kgs 21:1-18; 2 Chr 33:1-25
Menahem	2 Kgs 15:16-22
Nadab	1 Kgs 15:25-32;
Omri	1 Kgs 16:15-22; 23-28
Pekah	2 Kgs 15:27-31
Pekahiah	2 Kgs 15:23-26
Rehoboam	2 Chr 10:1-12:16
Zechariah	2 Kgs 15:8-12
Zedekiah	2 Kgs 24:18-25:7; 2 Chr 36:1-23
Zimri	1 Kgs 16:15-22

to COVENANT

Israelites	Ps 78:32-39

to DEITY

Israelites	Ps 78:40-55
Mankind	Ps 14:1-3

in ENVIRONMENT

Israelites	Judg 3:7-11; 12-14; 4:1-3

caused by FALSE BELIEF

Isaiah	Is 1:21-23

of FOLLOWERs

Judas	Mt 26:14-16; Mk 14:10-11; Lk 22:3-6

PROPHECY of

Jesus	Mt 26:17-30; Mk 14:17-21

REVELATION on

Ezekiel	Ezek 23:1-4

of FOLLOWERs
CONFRONTATION with

Paul	2 Cor 10:7-11

through inFIDELITY

Judas	Mt 26:14-16; Mk 14:10-11; Lk 22:3-6

FREEDOM from

Disciples	Jn 8:21-59

RECONCILIATION with

Believers	Gal 5:25-6:6

FREEDOM from
against DEITY

Solomon	*Wis 11:21-12:2

of FOLLOWERs

Disciples	Jn 8:21-59

INSTRUCTION on

Paul	Rom 6:1-14

REVELATION on

Ezekiel	Ezek 13:17-23

through disHONESTY

Adversaries	Ps 120:3-4
Jerusalemites	Mic 6:9-16
Mankind	Ps 64:3-6
Prophet	1 Kgs 13:1-34

with DEITY

Elihu	Job 33:26-27
Ezra	*1 Esd 8:71-90
Israelites	*1 Esd 9:1-15;

with DEITY (cont'd)

Israelites	*Bar 2:11-23; 3:1-8
Manasseh	*Mana 1:8-10
Mankind	Ps 12:1-4

in ENVIRONMENT

Delilah	Judg 16:4-9; 10-12; 13-15; 16-22
Elders	*Susa 1:19-27
Jacob	Gen 37:29-36

caused by FALSE BELIEF

Abraham	Gen 12:9-13:1
Ananias	Acts 4:32-5:10
Israelites	Hos 10:1-8
Jesus	Mt 7:15-20
Judahites	Jer 3:6-11
Sapphira	Acts 4:32-5:10

INSTRUCTION on

Isaiah	Is 59:1-21
Rehum	Ezra 4:6-16
Sirach	*Sir 4:20-31; 5:1-6:1; 19:25-30; 20:24-31; 21:1-7; 27:22-29; 28:13-26
Solomon	Prov 6:12-15; 19:1-29

PROPHECY of

Prophets	Jer 5:30-31

INSTRUCTION on
in BROTHERHOOD

James	Jas 4:11-12

through COMPULSION

Jesus	Mt 18:5-6; Mk 9:42-48; Lk 17:1-6

in LAW

Paul	Rom 2:25-3:20; 7:7-13

as MOTIVATION

David	1 Sam 23:14-24:22

in NEW AGE

God	*2 Esd 14:1-18

as QUALITY OF LIFE

Angel	*2 Esd 4:26-32; 7:45-61

JUDGMENT on

David	Ps 58:1-2
Israelites	Judg 20:1-7

by DEITY

Author	Heb 13:1-25
David	Ps 58:6-9
God	Ps 9:5-8; 15-16; 14:4-6; 65:1-4; 75:6-8; Rom 1:18; 1 Thes 4:1-12; Rev 18:4-20
Mankind	Ps 1:4-6; 64:7-10
Psalmist	Ps 94:1-3
Sodomites	Gen 18:16-22

in **AUTHORITY**
  of **DEITY**
    Jesus   Eph 1:15-2:10
    Jethro   Ex 18:1-12
    Paul   1 Cor 2:1-5
  by **FOLLOWER**
    Leper   Mt 8:2-4;
                     Mk 1:40-45;
                     Lk 5:12-16
  INSTRUCTION on
    Jesus   Mt 17:14-20;
                     21:18-22;
                     Mk 11:20-26;
                     Lk 17:1-6;
                     Jn 12:44-50;
                     14:1-14
    Paul   1 Cor 12:27-31a
  of **MESSIANIC FIGURE**
    Jesus   Mt 8:23-27;
                     9:27-31;
                     Mk 4:35-41;
                     Lk 8:22-25
  in **MISSION**
    Disciples   Mk 6:7-13;
                     Lk 9:1-6
    Paul   Eph 3:1-13
  PROPHECY on
    Isaiah   Is 30:8-17

BEHAVIOR revealing
    Believers   Heb 11:1-40
  of **FOLLOWERs**
    Apostles   Mt 10:26-39
    Crowd   Mt 15:29-31
    Thessalonians 1 Thes 3:1-10
  INSTRUCTION on
    Author   Heb 12:12-29
    God   Is 44:6-8;
                     21-23
    James   Jas 2:14-26
    Paul   Col 2:6-15;
                     2 Tim 2:1-7
  in **MESSIANIC FIGURE**
    Blind   Mk 8:22-26
    Crowd   Mk 6:53-56

through **BELIEF**
  of **FOLLOWERs**
    Blind   Mk 10:46-52
    Centurion   Mt 8:5-13;
                     Lk 7:1-10
    Peter   Jn 6:60-71
    Samaritans   Jn 4:27-42
  INSTRUCTION on
    Jesus   Jn 6:25-59;
                     7:37-52;
                     11:1-57
    John   1 Jn 5:13-21
  in **MESSIANIC FIGURE**
    Blind   Lk 18:35-43;
                     Jn 9:1-41
    Jews   Jn 12:9-11
    Martha   Jn 11:1-57
    Mary   Jn 2:1-11
    Official   Jn 4:43-54
  SELF-REALIZATION of
    Centurion   Lk 23:46-49

in **BROTHERHOOD**
  by **FOLLOWERs**

by **FOLLOWERs** (cont'd)
    Believers   Acts 16:1-5
  PROPHECY of
    Jesus   Mt 16:13-20

in **COMMITMENT**
  to **DEITY**
    Abraham   Gen 22:1-19
    Psalmist   Ps 137:4-6
  of **FOLLOWERs**
    Believers   Acts 19:13-20
  INSTRUCTION on
    Paul   2 Tim 2:20-26
  MEDITATION on
    Daniel   Dan 1:8-16
  SELF-REALIZATION of
    Paul   Gal 2:20-21

CONFRONTATION with
  in **MESSIANIC FIGURE**
    Criminal   Lk 23:39-43
    Crowd   Lk 6:17-19
    Jesus   Mt 9:18-26
    Lepers   Lk 17:11-19
    Woman   Mk 5:25-34;
                     Lk 8:40-56
  SELF-REALIZATION of
    Jairus   Mk 5:21-24;
                     Lk 8:40-56

CONVERSION through
  in **DEITY**
    Achior   *Jdt 14:6-10
    Israelites   Jer 3:21-4:4
  of **FOLLOWERs**
    Believers   Acts 9:32-43
    Corinthians   Acts 18:1-17
    Lydia   Acts 16:11-15
    Simon   Acts 8:4-13
    Zacchaeus   Lk 19:1-10
  PROPHECY of
    Isaiah   Is 2:1-5;
                     17:7-8
  REVELATION on
    Believers   Is 56:1-8
    Saul   Acts 9:1-19

COVENANT of
  FIDELITY to
    Israelites   *1 Mc 2:29-38
    Mattathias   *1 Mc 2:15-22;
                     23-28
  JUDGMENT in
    God   Ps 50:1-6
  RECONCILIATION through
    Jesus   Gal 3:19-25

in the **CREATION**
    Believers   Heb 11:1-40
  by **DEITY**
    Believers   Heb 11:1-40

in **DEITY**
  CONVERSION through
    Achior   *Jdt 14:6-10
    Israelites   Jer 3:21-4:4
  DESIRE for
    God   Hos 6:4-6
  ELECTION through
    Thessalonians 2 Thes 2:13-15

JUDGMENT on	
Believers	1 Jn 4:13-18
Jesus	1 Pet 2:21-25

PRAYER because of
Isaiah	Is 26:7-19; 33:1-6
Israelites	Hos 5:15-6:3

as **QUALITY OF LIFE**
David	2 Sam 15:13-16:14

RECONCILIATION through
Israelites	Is 10:20-23

RESPECT for
David	2 Sam 22:1-51; Ps 18:1-3

through **RESURRECTION**
Maccabeus	*2 Mc 12:38-45

SALVATION through
Believers	1 Pet 1:3-9
David	1 Sam 17:1-18:5; Ps 27:1-3; 86:1-7
Habakkuk	Hab 3:16-19
Jesus	Heb 7:1-28
Job	Job 19:25-29
Micah	Mic 7:7-20
Psalmist	Ps 119:121-128
Shadrach	Dan 3:16-18
Sirach	*Sir 33:1-3
Thessalonians	2 Thes 2:13-15

SECURITY through
Believers	Ps 55:22; Prov 22:17-21
David	Ps 4:2-5; 7:9-11; 11:1-3; 16:1-4; 5-8; 23:1-4; 25:8-15; 27:7-12; 28:6-7; 56:6b-9; 10-13; 62:1-2; 5-7; 143:7-12
God	Ps 125:1-3; Prov 29:1-27; 30:1-14; Is 26:1-6
Isaiah	Is 25:1-5; 50:1-11
Israelites	Deut 31:1-8
Jehoshaphat	2 Chr 17:1-20:37
Jeremiah	Jer 16:19-21
Mankind	2 Sam 22:1-51; Ps 18:25-30
Moses	Ps 90:1-12
Paul	2 Cor 1:8-11; 2 Tim 4:9-18
Psalmist	Ps 10:12-18; 33:20-22; 46:1-3; 71:1-21; 94:20-23; 118:10-14

as **VIRTUE**
Abraham	Gen 15:1-21
David	Ps 7:9-11

DESIRE for
　in **DEITY**
God	Hos 6:4-6

ELECTION through
　in **DEITY**
Thessalonians	2 Thes 2:13-15

of **FOLLOWERs**
Believers	Acts 13:14-52
Jesus	Lk 5:1-11

INSTRUCTION on
Paul	Rom 8:28-39

REVELATION on
Believers	Is 56:1-8

SELF-REALIZATION of
Paul	1 Tim 1:12-17

EQUALITY in
　INSTRUCTION on
Peter	Acts 15:6-29

ETERNAL
　in **DEITY**
God	Ps 146:5-7b

INSTRUCTION on
Isaiah	Is 26:1-6

PROPHECY of
Isaiah	Is 32:15-20

FIDELITY in
　INSTRUCTION on
Author	Heb 3:12-19; 4:14-16
Barnabas	Acts 11:22-24
Believers	Rev 14:9-12
David	Ps 37:1-11
Jesus	Lk 12:41-46; Jn 10:1-18
John	Rev 13:5-10
Judith	*Jdt 8:9-27
Paul	1 Cor 16:13-24; 2 Cor 4:16-18; Phil 1:12-30; Col 1:21-23; 2 Thes 2:13-15; 1 Tim 6:20-21; 2 Tim 2:14-19; 3:14-17
Sirach	*Sir 2:7-11; 12-18
Women	1 Tim 3:8-13; 1 Pet 3:1-7

in **MISSION**
Timothy	1 Tim 1:18-20

REVELATION on
Cornelius	Acts 10:1-11:18
Israelites	Zeph 3:11-13

SELF-REALIZATION of
Paul	2 Tim 4:6-8

in the **FIDELITY**
Hezekiah	2 Kgs 18:4-8

to **COVENANT**
Israelites	*1 Mc 2:29-38
Mattathias	*1 Mc 2:15-22; 23-28

of **DEITY**
Believers	Ps 40:4-5
David	Ps 16:5-8;

of **DEITY** (cont'd)
    David   25:1-7;
                           26:1-3;
                           55:23
    Israelites   Josh 22:9-34
    Job   Job 1:9-12
    King   Ps 21:1-7
    Maccabeus   *2 Mc 8:8-23;
                           15:6-10
    Psalmist   Ps 116:1-11;
                           118:5-9;
                           130:5-6
    Razis   *2 Mc 14:37-46
    Solomon   Prov 3:1-35
of **FOLLOWERs**
    God   Ps 9:9-12
    Mankind   Ps 112:5-9
    Thessalonians   1 Thes 1:2-10;
                           2 Thes 1:3-4
    Timothy   2 Tim 1:3-7

of **FOLLOWER**
  BEHAVIOR revealing
    Apostles   Mt 10:26-39
    Crowd   Mt 15:29-31
    Thessalonians   1 Thes 3:1-10
  through **BELIEF**
    Blind   Mk 10:46-52
    Centurion   Mt 8:5-13;
                         Lk 7:1-10
    Peter   Jn 6:60-71
    Samaritans   Jn 4:27-42

of **FOLLOWERs**
  in **BROTHERHOOD**
    Believers   Acts 16:1-5
  in **COMMITMENT**
    Believers   Acts 19:13-20
  through **CONVERSION**
    Believers   Acts 9:32-43
    Corinthians   Acts 18:1-17
    Lydia   Acts 16:11-15
    Simon   Acts 8:4-13
    Zacchaeus   Lk 19:1-10
  ELECTION through
    Believers   Acts 13:14-52
    Jesus   Lk 5:1-11
  FIDELITY in
    God   Ps 9:9-12
    Mankind   Ps 112:5-9
    Thessalonians   1 Thes 1:2-10;
                           2 Thes 1:3-4
    Timothy   2 Tim 1:3-7
  FREEDOM in
    Holy Spirit   2 Cor 3:12-18
  GIFTs through
    Holy Spirit   1 Cor 12:4-11
  KNOWLEDGE of
    Timothy   1 Thes 3:1-10
  PRAYER for
    Believers   Acts 2:42-47
    Paul   1 Thes 3:11-13
  PROMISE of
    Holy Spirit   Gal 3:10-14
    Peter   Mt 26:31-35;
                         Mk 14:27-31;
                         Lk 22:33-34
as **QUALITY OF LIFE**
    Author   Heb 10:32-39

RECONCILIATION through
    Jesus   Gal 3:26-29
in **RESURRECTION**
    Disciples   Jn 20:1-29
    Mary   Jn 20:1-29
    Thomas   Jn 20:1-29
SALVATION through
    Jailer   Acts 16:25-40
    Jesus   1 Jn 5:8-12
    Woman   Lk 7:36-50
SIGNS of
    Believers   Acts 13:4-12
in **TRUTH**
    Believers   Jn 12:44-50;
                         Acts 5:11-16;
                         8:4-13
    People   Acts 17:1-9;
                         10-15;
                         16-34
VIRTUE in
    Abraham   Rom 3:31-4:25

in **FREEDOM**
  of **FOLLOWERs**
    Holy Spirit   2 Cor 3:12-18

in **GIFTs**
  of **FOLLOWERs**
    Holy Spirit   1 Cor 12:4-11
  INSTRUCTION on
    Holy Spirit   Gal 3:1-5

in **HONESTY**
  INSTRUCTION on
    Jesus   Lk 16:10-12
  in **WORSHIP**
    Author   Heb 10:19-31

INSTRUCTION on
  in **AUTHORITY**
    Jesus   Mt 17:14-20;
                         21:18-22;
                         Mk 11:20-26;
                         Lk 17:1-6;
                         Jn 12:44-50;
                         14:1-14
    Paul   1 Cor 12:27-31a
  in **COMMITMENT**
    Paul   2 Tim 2:20-26
  in **GIFTs**
    Holy Spirit   Gal 3:1-5
  in **HONESTY**
    Jesus   Lk 16:10-12
  in **LAW**
    Paul   Rom 3:21-30
  as **MOTIVATION**
    Jesus   Lk 13:6-9
  in **NEW AGE**
    Author   Heb 11:1-40
  in **PRESENCE**
    Jesus   Mt 28:16-20
  in **PROVIDENCE**
    God   Is 41:1-42:4
  as **QUALITY OF LIFE**
    Jesus   Mt 15:12-14;
                         16:5-12;
                         21:18-22;
                         Mk 8:14-21;
                         11:20-26
    Paul   2 Cor 5:6-8;

of FOLLOWERs (cont'd)
    Author — Heb 10:32-39
INSTRUCTION on
    Jesus — Mt 15:12-14;
        16:5-12;
        21:18-22;
        Mk 8:14-21;
        11:20-26
    Paul — 2 Cor 5:6-8;
        Gal 3:6-9;
        1 Thes 5:1-11;
        1 Tim 4:6-10
    Peter — Acts 3:1-26
in MISSION
    Timothy — 1 Tim 1:3-7

RECONCILIATION through
in COVENANT
    Jesus — Gal 3:19-25
in DEITY
    Israelites — Is 10:20-23
of FOLLOWERs
    Jesus — Gal 3:26-29
INSTRUCTION on
    Paul — Rom 3:21-30;
        31-4:25;
        5:1-5;
        9:30-10:21;
        Gal 2:15-16;
        3:6-9;
        10-14;
        5:2-6
PROPHECY of
    Tyre — Is 23:15-18
REVELATION on
    Israelites — Is 50:1-11

RESPECT through
in DEITY
    David — 2 Sam 22:1-51;
        Ps 18:1-3
INSTRUCTION on
    Bishops — 1 Tim 3:1-7
    God — Rev 14:6-7
    Paul — Rom 14:1-23

in RESURRECTION
    Believers — Heb 11:1-40
through DEITY
    Maccabeus — *2 Mc 12:38-45
by FOLLOWERs
    Disciples — Jn 20:1-29
    Mary — Jn 20:1-29
    Thomas — Jn 20:1-29
INSTRUCTION on
    Jesus — Jn 11:1-57
    Paul — 1 Cor 15:12-19;
        29-34;
        35-41;
        2 Cor 4:13-15;
        Col 2:6-15;
        2 Tim 2:8-13
of MESSIANIC FIGURE
    Disciples — Jn 21:1-14

REVELATION on
in PRESENCE
    Jesus — Mt 28:16-20
in PROVIDENCE
    Paul — Acts 18:1-17

in TRUTH
    Peter — Mt 16:13-20
as VIRTUE
    Habakkuk — Hab 2:1-4
    Isaiah — Is 54:1-17

SALVATION through
in DEITY
    Believers — 1 Pet 1:3-9
    David — 1 Sam 17:1-18:5;
        Ps 27:1-3;
        86:1-7
    Habakkuk — Hab 3:16-19
    Jesus — Heb 7:1-28
    Job — Job 19:25-29
    Micah — Mic 7:7-20
    Psalmist — Ps 119:121-128
    Shadrach — Dan 3:16-18
    Sirach — *Sir 33:1-3
    Thessalonians — 2 Thes 2:13-15
of FOLLOWERs
    Jailer — Acts 16:25-40
    Jesus — 1 Jn 5:8-12
    Woman — Lk 7:36-50
INSTRUCTION on
    Author — Heb 4:1-13;
        6:9-12
    James — Jas 2:14-26
    Jesus — Mt 21:28-32;
        22:1-14;
        Lk 7:36-50;
        12:32-34;
        Jn 3:1-21;
        8:12-20;
        21-59;
        12:27-36a
    John the Baptist — Jn 3:31-36
    Paul — Acts 13:14-52;
        Rom 1:16-17;
        3:21-30;
        9:30-10:21;
        11:1-6;
        7-24;
        1 Cor 1:18-25;
        2 Cor 4:13-15;
        Gal 3:10-14;
        5:2-6;
        Eph 1:15-2:10;
        Col 1:21-23;
        1 Thes 4:13-18
in MESSIANIC FIGURE
    Jesus — Jn 1:1-18
PROPHECY of ,
    Isaiah — Is 12:1-6;
        28:14-22;
        33:7-16
    Jesus — Mt 24:9-14;
        Mk 13:9-13;
        Lk 21:7-19
REVELATION on
    God — Is 45:14-25
    Israelites — Jer 30:10-11
    Joel — Joel 2:30-32
SCRIPTURES on
    Jesus — Jn 20:30-31
    Paul — 2 Tim 3:14-17
SELF-REALIZATION of
    Jesus — Jn 17:1-5

SCRIPTURES on

SCRIPTURES on (cont'd)
  as **VIRTUE**
    Abraham   Gal 3:6-9;
                            Jas 2:14-26
SECURITY in
    Believers   Heb 11:1-40
    Daniel   Dan 6:16-23
  in **DEITY**
    Believers   Ps 55:22;
                            Prov 22:17-21
    David   Ps 4:2-5;
                            7:9-11;
                            11:1-3;
                            16:1-4;
                            5-8;
                            23:1-4;
                            25:8-15;
                            27:7-12;
                            28:6-7;
                            56:6b-9;
                            10-13;
                            62:1-2;
                            5-7;
                            143:7-12
    God   Ps 125:1-3;
                            Prov 29:1-27;
                            30:1-14;
                            Is 26:1-6
    Isaiah   Is 25:1-5;
                            50:1-11
    Israelites   Deut 31:1-8
    Jehoshaphat   2 Chr 17:1-20:37
    Jeremiah   Jer 16:19-21
    Mankind   2 Sam 22:1-51;
                            Ps 18:25-30
    Moses   Ps 90:1-12
    Paul   2 Cor 1:8-11;
                            2 Tim 4:9-18
    Psalmist   Ps 10:12-18;
                            33:20-22;
                            46:1-3;
                            71:1-21;
                            94:20-23;
                            118:10-14
  not **FALSE BELIEF**
    Israelites   Mic 3:1-12
  INSTRUCTION on
    God   Is 43:14-44:5
    Isaiah   Is 51:1-16
    Jesus   Mt 6:25-34;
                            Lk 12:1-12;
                            22:35-38;
                            1 Pet 3:13-17
    Moses   Deut 7:17-26
    Peter   1 Pet 1:3-9
    Psalmist   Ps 115:9-11;
                            146:3-4
  PROPHECY of
    Edomites   Jer 49:7-22
    Isaiah   Is 54:1-17
    Jeremiah   Jer 17:5-8
  REVELATION on
    Elijah   2 Kgs 1:1-18
    Ezekiel   Ezek 2:1-8a;
                            3:4-9
    God   Is 46:1-13
    Isaiah   Is 7:1-9;
                            51:1-16;
                            56:9-57:13
    Israelites   Zeph 3:11-13;
                            Zech 7:4-8:23

REVELATION on (cont'd)
    Jeremiah   Jer 1:4-10
  SELF-REALIZATION of
    Paul   2 Tim 1:8-14

SELF-REALIZATION of
  through **BELIEF**
    Centurion   Lk 23:46-49
  in **COMMITMENT**
    Paul   Gal 2:20-21
  as **MOTIVATION**
    Jesus   Mt 26:36-46;
                            Mk 14:32-42;
                            Lk 22:39-46
  as **VIRTUE**
    Paul   Phil 3:4-16

SIGNS of
  of **FOLLOWERs**
    Believers   Acts 13:4-12
  INSTRUCTION on
    Jesus   Jn 14:1-14
  in **MESSIANIC FIGURE**
    Centurion   Mt 27:45-56
    Jesus   Jn 2:23-25;
                            6:1-15
  SCRIPTURES on
    Jesus   Jn 20:30-31

overcomes **SIN**
  by **MESSIANIC FIGURE**
    Paralytic   Mt 9:1-8;
                            Mk 2:1-12;
                            Lk 5:17-26

STEWARDSHIP of
  INSTRUCTION on
    Jesus   Mt 24:42-44;
                            Mk 13:28-37;
                            Lk 8:16-18
    Paul   2 Cor 9:1-5
  in **MISSION**
    Believers   Acts 11:19-21

in **TRUTH**
  of **DEITY**
    Unbelievers   2 Thes 2:11-12
  by **FOLLOWERs**
    Believers   Jn 12:44-50;
                            Acts 5:11-16;
                            8:4-13
    People   Acts 17:1-9;
                            10-15;
                            16-34
  INSTRUCTION on
    Author   Heb 4:1-13
    Deacons   1 Tim 3:8-13
    Jesus   Mt 13:18-23;
                            Mk 1:14-15;
                            4:10-20;
                            9:49-50;
                            Lk 8:11-15
    Paul   Acts 13:4-12;
                            Rom 1:16-17;
                            1 Tim 3:14-16;
                            Tit 1:9-16
  MEDITATION on
    Paul   Eph 1:3-14
  of **MESSIANIC FIGURE**
    Disciples   Lk 24:50-51
    Jesus   Jn 4:1-26

in **NEW AGE** (cont'd)

Pharisees	Jn 7:32-36

in **PROVIDENCE**

Isaiah	Is 44:9-20

in **SIN**

Solomon	*Wis 15:7-19

in **TRUTH**

Gentiles	Eph 4:17-24

INDIFFERENCE through

in **TRUTH**

Gentiles	Eph 4:17-24

JEALOUSY through

Priest	Acts 5:17-42
Sadducees	Acts 5:17-42

caused by **HONESTY**

James	Jas 3:13-18
Officials	Dan 6:4-9
Rulers	Acts 6:8-8:3

JOY through

in **SIN**

Ammonites	Ezek 25:1-7

JUDGMENT on

as **BLASPHEMY**

Caiaphas	Mt 26:57-68; Mk 14:53-65
Jews	Jn 10:19-40; 18:28-19:16

CONDEMNATION as

Apostles	Mt 10:9-15
Disciples	Mk 6:7-13; Lk 9:1-6
Israelites	Ezek 23:36-49
James	Jas 5:1-6
Jews	Jn 18:28-19:16
Jezebel	Rev 2:18-29
People	Lk 23:1-5
Prophets	2 Pet 2:1-3
Sinners	Jude 1:11-13

DEATH as

Priest	Jn 12:9-11

DESTRUCTION as

Moses	Ex 23:20-33; 34:12-28; Num 33:16-36; Deut 7:1-5; 12:1-31

GRACE in

Jesus	Mt 12:22-32; Mk 3:20-30

in **KILLING**

Jews	Jn 18:28-19:16
Pharisees	Jn 11:1-57
Pilate	Mk 15:6-15; Lk 23:18-25
Priests	Jn 11:1-57

in **POLITICS**

Pilate	Mk 15:6-15; Lk 23:18-25

REJECTION as

Jews	Jn 18:28-19:16
Priests	Jn 12:9-11

REVENGE as

Priests	Jn 12:9-11

WITNESS to

Author	Heb 10:19-31

JUSTICE through

PUNISHMENT for

God	*Wis 12:23-27
Sinners	2 Pet 2:10b-16

KILLING through

Herod	Mt 14:1-12; Mk 6:17-29
Pharaoh	Ex 1:15-22
Sarah	*Tb 3:7-15

by **AUTHORITY**

Herod	Mt 2:16-18

DESIRE for

Jeremiah	Jer 26:7-19
Jews	Acts 9:20-31

dis**HONESTY** in

Babylonians	Rev 18:21-24

JUDGMENT on

Jews	Jn 18:28-19:16
Pharisees	Jn 11:1-57
Pilate	Mk 15:6-15; Lk 23:18-25
Priests	Jn 11:1-57

SIGNS of

Daniel	*Bel 1:23-27

SIN of

Israelites	Ezek 22:23-31

KNOWLEDGE of

in **DISCIPLESHIP**

Paul	2 Tim 3:1-9

revealing **HERESY**

Jesus	Jn 16:1-4

revealing **IDOLATRY**

Daniel	*Bel 1:10-20
Jeremiah	*Jer 6:45-59

revealing **IGNORANCE**

Mankind	*Wis 13:1-9
Solomon	*Wis 13:10-19

REJECTION of

Paul	Col 2:1-5; 1 Tim 6:20-21
Sirach	*Sir 34:1-8

concerning **STEALING**

Lawyers	Lk 11:45-52

in the **LAW**

ALIENATION because of

Jesus	Gal 5:2-6

causing **BLASPHEMY**

Israelites	Deut 18:9-22

causing **CONDEMNATION**

Moses	Lev 20:1-27
Paul	Col 2:16-23

causing **DEATH**

Author	Heb 10:19-31

causing **DISOBEDIENCE**

Israelites	Ex 32:1-6; 2 Kgs 17:7-23; Ezek 20:9-26; 22:23-31
Judahites	2 Kgs 17:7-23

causing **HERESY**

Israelites	Jer 27:1-11
Moses	Lev 19:1-37; 20:1-27; Deut 18:9-22
Paul	Col 2:16-23

causing **IDOLATRY**

causes **HERESY**
 Unbelievers 1 Cor 15:12-19

REVELATION concerning
 Herodias Mk 6:17-29

concerning **REVENGE**
 Herodias Mk 6:17-29
 CONFRONTATION with
  Edomites Ezek 25:12-14

REVENGE through
 CONFRONTATION with
  Philistines Ezek 25:15-17
 JUDGMENT on
  Priests Jn 12:9-11

in **RITE**
 cause **BLASPHEMY**
  Israelites Ezek 23:36-49
 causes **CONDEMNATION**
  Israelites Deut 18:9-22
 cause **IDOLATRY**
  Babylonians Dan 3:7
  Belshazzar Dan 5:1-4
 cause **JOY**
  Moses Deut 12:1-31
 concerning **SACREDNESS**
  Moses Deut 12:1-31
 concerning **SACRIFICE**
  Israelites Ezek 23:36-49

concerning **SACREDNESS**
 of **ELECTION**
  Moses Lev 20:1-27
 in **RITE**
  Moses Deut 12:1-31

concerning **SACRIFICE**
 as **MOTIVATION**
  Paul Col 2:16-23
 in **RITE**
  Israelites Ezek 23:36-49
 for **SIN**
  Israelites 2 Kgs 17:7-23
  Judahites Jer 7:29-8:3
  Priests Mal 1:6-2:9

concerning **SALVATION**
 through **PURIFICATION**
  Judeans Acts 15:1-5
 REJECTION of
  Pharisees Mt 23:13

causing in**SECURITY**
 concerning **DEATH**
  Priests Mt 27:62-66
 because of false **FAITH**
  Israelites Mic 3:1-12
 concerning **HOPE**
  Solomon *Wis 13:10-19
 concerning **PEACE**
  Moses Deut 12:1-31

causing **SELFISHNESS**
 Demetrius Acts 19:23-41
 Pharisees Lk 11:37-44
 through dis**HONESTY**
  James Jas 3:13-18
as **MOTIVATION**

as **MOTIVATION** (cont'd)
 Herod Mt 14:1-12;
    Mk 6:17-29
as **SIN**
 James Jas 5:1-6
 Lawyers Lk 11:45-52

concerning **SEX**
 Jeremiah *Jer 6:41-44
 in**FIDELITY** through
  Ephraimites Hos 5:3-7
  Israelites Ezek 23:36-49;
    Hos 9:1-6
 SIN of
  Ephraimites Hos 4:17-19;
    6:10-7:2
  Israelites Ezek 16:15-34;
    23:5-10;
    Hos 4:4-15
  Judahites Ezek 23:11-21
  Prophets Jer 23:9-12
  Sinners 2 Pet 2:10b-16

SIGNS of
 causing **ANGER**
  Babylonians *Bel 1:28-30
 concerning **CAPTIVITY**
  Prophets Rev 19:17-21
 concerning **DEATH**
  Israelites 1 Sam 6:1-7:1
  Moses Deut 12:32-13:1
 causing **DESTRUCTION**
  Daniel *Bel 1:21-22
 causing **EVIL**
  John Rev 16:12-16
 causing **IDOLATRY**
  Babylonians *Bel 1:3-7
  Israelites Ex 32:1-6
 causing **KILLING**
  Daniel *Bel 1:23-27
 concerning **LIFE**
  Moses Deut 12:1-31
 concerning **MIRACLE**
  Jesus Lk 4:16-30
 REJECTION of
  Daniel *Bel 1:23-27

causing **SIN**
 Satan 1 Jn 3:4-10
 of **DISOBEDIENCE**
  Judahites Amos 2:4-5
  Satan 1 Jn 3:4-10
 of **DOUBT**
  James Jas 1:5-8
 of **GREED**
  Tyre Ezek 26:1-6
 revealing **GUILT**
  Herod Mk 6:17-29
  Lawyers Lk 11:45-52
 revealing **HATE**
  Psalmist Ps 119:113-120
 of **HERESY**
  Jezebel Rev 2:18-29
  Pharisees Mt 23:15
 of **IDOLATRY**
  Ephraimites Hos 4:17-19;
    7:13-16;
    8:11-14;
    9:10-17;
    11:1-4;

in **DOUBT** (cont'd)
    Pharisees   Jn 7:32-36
in **HERESY**
    Holy Spirit   1 Tim 4:1-5
    Paul   1 Tim 6:2c-5
    Peter   2 Pet 3:14-18a
in **IDOLATRY**
    Cyrus   *Bel 1:8-9
    Daniel   *Bel 1:10-20
through **IGNORANCE**
    Gentiles   Eph 4:17-24
results in **INDIFFERENCE**
    Gentiles   Eph 4:17-24
results in **PRIDE**
    Paul   1 Tim 6:2c-5
results in **REJECTION**
    Galatians   Gal 4:12-20
    Israelites   Is 48:1-22
    Jezebel   Rev 2:18-29
    John   2 Jn 1:7-11
    Pharisees   Jn 7:32-36;
        9:1-41
    Priests   Mt 28:11-15
    Sinners   Jude 1:3-4
results in **STEALING**
    Satan   Mt 13:18-23;
        Mk 4:10-20;
        Lk 8:11-15

causing **VIOLENCE**
as **MOTIVATION**
    Satan   Rev 20:7-10

concerning **WEALTH**
    Jason   *2 Mc 4:18-20

WITNESS to
revealing dis**HONESTY**
    Ephraimites   Hos 11:12-12:1
in **JUDGMENT**
    Author   Heb 10:19-31
revealing **RATIONALIZATION**
    Micah   Mic 2:1-10
revealing **SIN**
    James   Jas 5:1-6

FAMILY

(genealogy)
    Aaron   Ex 6:14-27;
        1 Chr 6:49-53
    Adam   1 Chr 1:1-54
    Benjamin   1 Chr 7:6-12;
        8:1-40;
        Neh 11:7-9
    David   2 Sam 5:6-16;
        1 Chr 3:1-24
    Edomites   1 Chr 1:1-54
    Ephraim   1 Chr 7:20-40
    Esther   Esth 2:5-7
    Ezra   Ezra 7:1-5
    Gibeon   1 Chr 9:35-44
    God   1 Chr 5:1-26
    Hadad   1 Kgs 11:14-22
    Israelites   Ezra 2:2b-20;
        21-35;
        8:1-14;
        Neh 7:4-33a

(genealogy) (cont'd)
    Issachar   1 Chr 7:1-5
    Jacob   1 Chr 2:1-55
    Jeshua   Neh 12:10-11
    Jethro   Ex 18:27
    Judah   1 Chr 4:1-23
    Levi   1 Chr 6:1-15;
        16-30
    Levites   Neh 11:15-18
    Manasseh   1 Chr 5:1-26;
        7:13-19
    Moses   Ex 6:14-27
    Musicians   1 Chr 6:31-48
    Naphtali   1 Chr 7:13-19
    Priests   Neh 11:10-14
    Reuben   1 Chr 5:1-26
    Saul   1 Chr 9:35-44
    Simeon   1 Chr 4:24-43
    Solomon   1 Chr 3:1-24

AUTHORITY in
by **DEITY**
    Joshua   Josh 19:49-51
PROPHECY on
    Jacob   Gen 47:27-48:2?
REVELATION on
    Jehu   2 Kgs 10:29-31

BEHAVIOR in
INSTRUCTION on
    Paul   Col 3:18-4:1
    Sirach   *Sir 7:1-36;
        11:29-34;
        29:21-28;
        33:16-23;
        42:9-14
    Tobit   *Tb 4:1-21

BELIEF results in
of **DEITY**
    Jesus   1 Jn 4:19-5:5

BROTHERHOOD as
INSTRUCTION on
    Jesus   Mt 12:46-50;
        Mk 3:31-35;
        Lk 8:19-21
    Paul   1 Tim 5:1-2

COMMITMENT in
INSTRUCTION on
    Paul   1 Tim 5:3-16

in **COMMUNITY**
    Asherites   Josh 19:24-31
    Benjaminites   Josh 18:11-28
    Caleb   Josh 14:6-15
    Danites   Josh 19:40-48
    Ephraimites   Josh 16:6-8;
        9-10
    Gadites   Josh 13:24-28
    Israelites   Josh 13:8-14;
        14:1-5;
        18:1-10;
        Jer 40:11-12
    Issachar   Josh 19:17-23
    Joseph   Josh 16:1-5
    Josephites   Josh 17:14-18
    Joshua   Josh 19:49-51
    Judahites   Josh 15:1-12;

FAMILY (cont'd)

in COMMUNITY (cont'd)

Judahites	20-63
Levites	Josh 13:29-33; 21:1-7; 8-45
Manassites	Josh 13:29-33; 17:1-6; 7-13
Naphtalites	Josh 19:32-39
Reubenites	Josh 13:15-23
Simeonites	Josh 19:1-9
Zebulunites	Josh 19:10-16
REVELATION on	
Joshua	Josh 13:1-7

COMMUNITY recognizes

Benjaminites	Neh 11:31-36
Judahites	Neh 11:25-30
with COVENANT	
Aaron	*Sir 45:25-26
David	*Sir 45:25-26

CONFRONTATION with

Esau	Gen 26:34-35
Israelites	Josh 22:9-34; Judg 20:12-17
Jacob	Gen 29:1-14
Joseph	Gen 42:1-6
Menelaus	*2 Mc 4:23-29
Moses	Ex 18:1-12; Num 10:29-32
Simon	*2 Mc 3:1-40; 4:1-6

COVENANT with
for COMMUNITY

Aaron	*Sir 45:25-26
David	*Sir 45:25-26
through ELECTION	
David	Ps 89:1-4
as ETERNAL	
Israelites	1 Chr 15:1-16:43; Ps 105:7-15
KNOWLEDGE of	
God	Ex 2:23b-25
PROMISE in	
Abraham	Gen 13:14-18; 15:1-21; 17:1-8
Azariah	*Azar 1:11-22
David	1 Sam 23:14-24:22
God	Gen 17:15-22
Jacob	*Sir 44:23
SECURITY in	
David	2 Sam 23:1-7

CREATION of

Abraham	Gen 25:1-6
Adam	Gen 4:25-26; 5:1-28
Cain	Gen 4:17-19; 20-24
Isaac	Gen 25:19-26
Ishmael	Gen 25:12-18
Jacob	Gen 29:31-30:24
Joseph	Gen 41:1-57
Lot	Gen 19:30-38
Moses	Ex 2:16-23a
Nahor	Gen 22:20 24
Nephilim	Gen 6:1-4
Noah	Gen 9:8-19

CREATION of (cont'd)

Tamar	Gen 38:24-30
INSTRUCTION on	
Paul	Gal 4:27-31
REVELATION on	
Israel	Gen 35:1-15

of DEITY
through BELIEF

Jesus	1 Jn 4:19-5:5
DISCIPLINE for	
Believers	Heb 12:3-11
Israelites	Deut 8:1-10
is ETERNAL	
God	Ps 48:4-8
FIDELITY of	
Israelites	1 Sam 12:1-25; 1 Kgs 6:1-38
Jesus	Heb 3:1-6a
Mother	*2 Mc 7:1-42
Solomon	*Sir 47:12-22
PRAYER for	
Elijah	1 Kgs 19:1-21
Sirach	*Sir 36:11-17
SALVATION for	
God	Gal 4:4-7
SECURITY in	
Believers	Is 40:1-11

DESIRE for

Lot	Gen 19:30-38
INSTRUCTION on	
David	2 Sam 3:1-16
Sirach	*Sir 16:1-5

DISCIPLINE for
by DEITY

Believers	Heb 12:3-11
Israelites	Deut 8:1-10
INSTRUCTION on	
Sirach	*Sir 30:1-13; 42:1-5
Solomon	Prov 19:1-29

ELECTION of
through COVENANT

David	Ps 89:1-4
by DEITY	
David	2 Chr 5:1-7:10
God	Ps 33:10-12; 132:11-18; 147:12-20
Israelites	Deut 14:1-2; 1 Kgs 8:22-53; Ps 47:1-4; 135:1-4; Amos 3:1-2
of FOLLOWERs	
Holy Spirit	Rom 8:14-25
Jesus	Eph 1:3-14
INSTRUCTION on	
Moses	Deut 31:30-32:47
REVELATION on	
Israelites	Zech 13:7-9
Solomon	1 Kgs 11:1-13

FIDELITY of

Esther	Esth 2:19-23
to DEITY	
Israelites	1 Sam 12:1-25;

to **DEITY** (cont'd)

Israelites	1 Kgs 6:1-38
Jesus	Heb 3:1-6a
Mother	*2 Mc 7:1-42
Solomon	*Sir 47:12-22

in **MISSION**

Jesus	Lk 12:51-53
Women	Tit 2:1-10

of**FOLLOWER**s
  ELECTION of

Holy Spirit	Rom 8:14-25
Jesus	Eph 1:3-14

  PROMISE to

Jesus	Gal 3:26-29

  VIRTUE of

God	1 Jn 3:4-10

FREEDOM of

Moses	Lev 25:39-55

JUDGMENT on
  through **SELF-REALIZATION**

Jacob	Gen 31:1-16

KNOWLEDGE of

Abraham	Gen 11:27-32
Asher	1 Chr 7:20-40
Baruch	*Bar 1:1-4
Danites	Judg 18:27-31
David	Ruth 4:13-22;
	2 Sam 3:1-16;
	1 Chr 14:1-16
Elimech	Ruth 1:1-18
Esau	Gen 36:1-19
Ezra	*2 Esd 1:1-3
Isaac	Gen 25:19-26
Israel	Ex 1:1-7
Jacob	Gen 35:22b-26;
	46:8-27
Jesus	Lk 3:23-38
Job	Job 1:2-3
Joseph	Gen 42:7-17
Judah	Gen 38:1-11
Judahites	1 Chr 9:1-16
Judith	*Jdt 8:1-8
Levites	Num 26:57-62;
	1 Chr 6:54-81;
	Neh 12:22-23
Mattathias	*1 Mc 2:1-5
Moses	Num 1:20-46;
	3:1-4
Noah	Gen 10:1-32
Pharaoh	1 Kgs 9:24
Priests	Neh 12:12-21
Rehoboam	2 Chr 10:1-12:16
Saul	1 Sam 14:47-52
Seir	Gen 36:20-30
Shem	Gen 11:10-26
Tobit	*Tb 1:1-2

  INSTRUCTION on

God	Gen 25:19-26
Solomon	Prov 1:8-9

  of **MESSIANIC FIGURE**

Jesus	Mt 1:1-17

LAW concerning

Moses	Ex 21:12-17;
	Num 36:1-13

  INSTRUCTION on

Moses	Deut 21:15-17;

INSTRUCTION on (cont'd)

Moses	18-21;
	23:15-25:19

REVELATION on

Moses	Ex 21:1;
	Lev 18:1-30;
	Num 27:1-11;
	30:1-16

  TRADITION of

Boaz	Ruth 3:1-18;
	4:1-12
Judah	Gen 38:1-11

of **MESSIANIC FIGURE**
  KNOWLEDGE of

Jesus	Mt 1:1-17

  SALVATION through

Jesus	Mt 1:18-25

MISSION to
  causes in**FIDELITY**

Jesus	Lk 12:51-53

  urging **FIDELITY**

Women	Tit 2:1-10

PRAYER for

Elijah	1 Kgs 19:1-21
Psalmist	Ps 128:5-6
Sirach	*Sir 36:11-17

  SCRIPTURES on

Elijah	Rom 11:1-6

  in **WORSHIP**

Hannah	1 Sam 1:1-28
Isaac	Gen 25:19-26

PRESENCE in
  by **DEITY**

Mankind	Rev 21:1-8

  REVELATION on

Moses	Ex 6:2-9

PROMISE to

Psalmist	Ps 45:16-17

  through **COVENANT**

Abraham	Gen 13:14-18;
	15:1-21;
	17:1-8
Azariah	*Azar 1:11-22
David	1 Sam 23:14-24:1
God	Gen 17:15-22
Jacob	*Sir 44:23

  by **DEITY**

Abraham	Gen 17:15-22;
	22:1-19
Believers	Rom 9:6-13
David	2 Sam 7:1-29;
	1 Chr 17:1-27;
	Ps 132:11-18
Isaac	Gen 26:12-31
Ishmael	Gen 21:15-21
Sarah	Gen 17:15-22

  of **FOLLOWER**s

Jesus	Gal 3:26-29

  INSTRUCTION on

God	*2 Esd 2:10-14
Paul	Gal 4:27-31

PROPHECY of

Angel	Gen 16:7-10
God	Gen 18:9-15

REVELATION on

REVELATION on (cont'd)
Abraham	Gen 12:1-8; 15:1-21
Hagar	Gen 21:11-14
Jacob	Gen 35:1-15

SCRIPTURES on
Abraham	Acts 6:8-8:3; Gal 3:15-18

PROVIDENCE for
by **DEITY**
Believers	Ps 128:3-4; 1 Jn 2:28-3:3
God	Ps 87:4-6; 127:3-5
Jacob	Gen 29:31-30:24
Noah	Gen 8:1-12

INSTRUCTION on
Moses	Deut 31:30-32:47

PROPHECY of
Joseph	Gen 50:22-26

REVELATION on
Isaiah	Is 51:1-16; 66:17-24

RECONCILIATION in
Benjaminites	Judg 21:13-15
David	1 Sam 30:1-31; 2 Sam 13:21-14:33
Israelites	Judg 21:13-15
Tobiah	*Tb 10:1-11:6

PROPHECY of
Baruch	*Bar 5:5-9

through **WORSHIP**
Jews	*2 Mc 1:18-36; 2:16-18

RESPECT for
Daniel	*Susa 1:60-64
Joakim	*Susa 1:1-4
Moses	Ex 21:12-17; Lev 19:1-37

INSTRUCTION on
God	Ex 20:1-17
Jesus	Mt 15:3-9; 19:16-22; Mk 7:1-23; 10:17-22
Moses	Ex 21:12-17; Lev 20:1-27; Deut 5:1-21; 27:11-26
Paul	Eph 6:1-4
Sirach	*Sir 3:1-16; 22:1-6; 30:1-13; 33:16-23; 41:14-23

REVELATION on
Israelites	Ezek 22:1-16

REVELATION on
in **COMMUNITY**
Joshua	Josh 13:1-7

RITE of
REVELATION on
Israelites	Ex 12:43-49

in **WORSHIP**
Job	Job 1:4-5

SALVATION for
of **DEITY**
God	Gal 4:4-7

SALVATION through
of **MESSIANIC FIGURE**
Jesus	Mt 1:18-25

REVELATION on
Israelites	Is 49:1-26
Jesus	Mt 1:18-25
Noah	Gen 7:1-24

SECURITY in
Esther	Esth 8:3-8

through **COVENANT**
David	2 Sam 23:1-7

of **DEITY**
Believers	Is 40:1-11

INSTRUCTION on
Paul	1 Tim 5:3-16

REVELATION on
Israelites	Ezek 34:1-10
Jacob	Gen 46:1-7
Jeremiah	Jer 33:14-26

SIGNS of
PROPHECY of
Angel	*2 Esd 9:38-10:59

SIN in
through **FALSE BELIEF**
Satan	1 Jn 3:4-10

INSTRUCTION on
Micah	Mic 7:1-6
Sirach	*Sir 41:5-13

STEWARDSHIP toward
INSTRUCTION on
Bishops	1 Tim 3:1-7
Deacons	1 Tim 3:8-13

PROPHECY of
Isaiah	Is 54:1-17

REVELATION on
Moses	Lev 25:25-28

TRADITION of
in **COMMUNITY**
Israelites	Ps 114:1-2; *1 Esd 5:44-46

LAW concerning
Boaz	Ruth 3:1-18; 4:1-12
Judah	Gen 38:1-11

VIRTUE in
of **FOLLOWERs**
God	1 Jn 3:4-10

WORSHIP by
through **PRAYER**
Hannah	1 Sam 1:1-28
Isaac	Gen 25:19-26

brings **RECONCILIATION**
Jews	*2 Mc 1:18-36; 2:16-18

in **RITE**
Job	Job 1:4-5

of **AUTHORITY**
    Adonijah   1 Kgs 1:41-53
of **DEITY**
    Adversaries   Ex 15:1-18
    God   Job 37:23-24
    Kings   Ps 48:4-8
    Mankind   Ps 102:12-22
INSTRUCTION on
    Moses   Deut 6:4-19;
                   12:32-13:18;
                   17:14-20
REVELATION on
    Amos   Amos 3:3-8

BEHAVIOR revealing
of **DEITY**
    Samaritans   2 Kgs 7:3-20
of **ENVIRONMENT**
    Jotham   Judg 9:16-21
through **FALSE BELIEF**
    Herod   Mk 6:14-16;
                 Lk 9:7-9
of **FOLLOWERs**
    Disciples   Mt 8:23-27;
                 Mk 4:35-41;
                 Lk 8:22-25
INSTRUCTION on
    Agur   Prov 30:15-33
    Jude   Jude 1:21-23
MEDITATION on
    Pilate   Jn 18:28-19:16
of **MESSIANIC FIGURE**
    Disciples   Mt 14:22-27;
                 Mk 6:45-52;
                 Jn 6:16-24
REVELATION on
    Isaiah   Is 7:1-9

BELIEF through
of **DEITY**
    Israelites   Ex 14:23-31
of **FOLLOWERs**
    People   Jn 12:36b-43

in **COMMITMENT**
MEDITATION on
    Pharisees   Mt 21:45-46

in **COMMUNITY**
    Israelites   Deut 2:1-25;
                 Josh 2:8-14
of **DEITY**
    God   Ps 2:4-6

CONFRONTATION with
    Assyrians   Is 10:27d-32;
                 *Jdt 15:1-7
    Disciples   Lk 24:36-43
    Esther   *Esth 15:1-16
    Israelites   Ezra 4:4-5;
                 *Jdt 7:1-22
    Joseph   Gen 44:1-34;
                 50:1-21
    Moab   Num 22:2-4
    Philistines   1 Sam 29:1-11
of **DEITY**
    Adam   Gen 3:9-13
through **FALSE BELIEF**
    Priests   Lk 22:1-2
INSTRUCTION on
    Moses   Deut 20:1-9

of **MESSIANIC FIGURE**
    Demon   Mk 1:21-28;
                 Lk 4:31-37
PROPHECY of
    Damascenes   Jer 49:23-27
    Saul   1 Sam 28:3-25
    Zechariah   Zech 9:1-12
REVELATION on
    Disciples   Lk 24:36-43
    John   Rev 6:12-17
    Prophets   Rev 11:1-14

of the **DEITY**
    Adam   Gen 3:9-13
    Israelites   Ex 20:18-20
BEHAVIOR revealing
    Samaritans   2 Kgs 7:3-20
causing **BELIEF**
    Israelites   Ex 14:23-31
in **COMMUNITY**
    God   Ps 2:4-6
FIDELITY through
    Israelites   1 Sam 12:1-25
reveals **JUDGMENT**
    Author   Heb 10:19-31
    David   Ps 9:17-20
    God   Eccl 12:12-14
    Job   Job 9:25-29
    Mankind   Ps 64:7-10;
                 76:7-9
    Psalmist   Ps 119:113-120
KNOWLEDGE concerning
    God   Prov 2:1-22
    Mankind   Ps 111:10;
                 Prov 1:7
    Sirach   *Sir 1:11-20;
                 2:7-11;
                 19:20-24
as **MOTIVATION**
    Abraham   Gen 22:1-19
    Job   Job 9:30-35
PROMISE through
    Psalmist   Ps 119:33-40
PROVIDENCE because of
    Amorites   Josh 4:20-5:1
    David   Ps 25:8-15
    Egyptians   Is 19:16-17
    Habakkuk   Hab 3:2
    People   Ps 107:23-32
    Sanballat   Neh 6:15-16
as **PUNISHMENT**
    God   Ps 14:4-6
    Israelites   Num 16:25-35
revealing **RESPECT**
    Babylonians   2 Kgs 17:24-41
    Darius   Dan 6:25-27
    David   Ps 19:7-10
    God   Prov 23:15-24:2
                 Is 33:1-6
    Isaiah   Is 8:11-15;
                 59:1-21
    Israelites   Deut 4:1-14;
                 6:20-25;
                 Hos 3:1-5;
                 Hag 1:12-14
    Job   Job 1:1
    Jonah   Jon 1:1-17
    Kings   Ps 2:10-11
    Mankind   Ps 15:1-5b;
                 33:4-9
    Micah   Mic 7:7-20

of **DEITY** (cont'd)
  Psalmist
INSTRUCTION on
  Jesus

  PROPHECY of
    Joel
  REVELATION on
    John

KNOWLEDGE of
  of DEITY
    God
    Mankind

    Sirach

  of ENVIRONMENT
    Israelites

    Moses
  INSTRUCTION on
    David

of the LAW
  INSTRUCTION on
    God
    Jehoshaphat

MEDITATION on
  in COMMITMENT
    Pharisees
  as QUALITY OF LIFE
    Job

of MESSIANIC FIGURE
  BEHAVIOR revealing
    Disciples

  through CONFRONTATION
    Demon

  FREEDOM from
    Jesus
  as MOTIVATION
    Pharisees
  revealing RESPECT
    Crowd

    Disciples

    God

as MOTIVATION
  Abraham

  Israelites

  Jacob

  Micah
  Nations
  Pharaoh

  Rebekah
of FOLLOWERs
  Disciples

Ps 119:113-120
Lk 12:1-12; 19:11-27
Joel 2:1-11
Rev 18:4-20
Prov 2:1-22
Ps 111:10; Prov 1:7
*Sir 1:11-20; 2:7-11; 19:20-24
Num 13:26b-33; Deut 1:19-46
Ex 2:11-15
Ps 34:11-14
Ps 25:8-15
2 Chr 17:1-20:37
Mt 21:45-46
Job 7:12-16
Mt 14:22-27; Mk 6:45-52; Jn 6:16-24
Mk 1:21-28; Lk 4:31-37
Heb 2:5-18
Mt 22:41-46
Mt 9:1-8; 32-34
Mt 17:1-8; Lk 9:28-36
Is 11:1-9
Gen 12:9-13:1; 20:1-18
Num 14:1-2; 3-4
Gen 33:1-16; 42:26-38; 43:1-15
Judg 18:21-26
Ps 2:4-6
Ex 1:8-14; 15-22
Gen 27:41-28:5
Mt 26:47-56

INSTRUCTION on
  Moses
concerning MESSIANIC FIGURE
  Pharisees
PROPHECY of
  Disciples
  Tyre
REVELATION on
  Elihu

PRAYER concerning
  David
  Jacob

in PRESENCE
  of DEITY
    Egyptians
    Elihu

    Isaiah
    Israelites

    Jacob
    Job
    Saul
    Tobit

in Divine PRESENCE
  INSTRUCTION on
    Psalmist
  PROPHECY of
    Isaiah
  REVELATION on
    Israelites

    Moses
    Zechariah

PROMISE through
  of DEITY
    Psalmist

PROPHECY of
  of JUDGMENT
    Joel
  as MOTIVATION
    Disciples
    Tyre
  of Divine PRESENCE
    Isaiah
  of PUNISHMENT
    Isaiah

PROVIDENCE because of
  of DEITY
    Amorites
    David
    Egyptians
    Habakkuk
    People
    Sanballat
  PROPHECY of
    Elamites
    Isaiah
    Jeremiah
  REVELATION on
    God
    Jeremiah

Ex 4:10-16
Mt 22:41-46
Mk 14:43-50
Ezek 26:15-18
Job 33:15-18
1 Sam 23:1-13
Gen 32:1-23
Is 19:1-15
Job 37:1-13; 14-22
Is 63:7-64:12
Deut 5:22-33; 6:1-3
Gen 28:10-22
Job 23:15-17
1 Sam 18:6-30
*Tb 12:1-22
Ps 114:7-8
Is 2:18-22
Ex 20:18-20; Deut 4:1-14
Ex 3:1-6
Lk 1:5-25
Ps 119:33-40
Joel 2:1-11
Mk 14:43-50
Ezek 26:15-18
Is 2:18-22
Is 2:18-22; 30:27-33
Josh 4:20-5:1
Ps 25:8-15
Is 19:16-17
Hab 3:2
Ps 107:23-32
Neh 6:15-16
Jer 49:34-39
Is 19:16-17
Jer 32:26-44
Is 41:1-42:4
Jer 4:9-10

FEAR (cont'd)

of PUNISHMENT
Israelites	Lev 26:1-46

by DEITY
God	Ps 14:4-6
Israelites	Num 16:25-35

of FOLLOWERs
Magistrates	Acts 16:25-40

INSTRUCTION on
Moses	Deut 19:15-21

PROPHECY of
Isaiah	Is 2:18-22; 30:27-33

REVELATION on
Egyptians	Ezek 30:13-19
Israelites	Ezek 4:16-17

as QUALITY OF LIFE
MEDITATION on
Job	Job 7:12-16

RECONCILIATION through
PROPHECY of
Israelites	Hos 11:10-11

revealing RESPECT
Moses	Lev 19:1-37

of DEITY
Babylonians	2 Kgs 17:24-41
Darius	Dan 6:25-27
David	Ps 19:7-10
God	Prov 23:15-24:22; Is 33:1-6
Isaiah	Is 8:11-15; 59:1-21
Israelites	Deut 4:1-14; 6:20-25; Hos 3:1-5; Hag 1:12-14
Job	Job 1:1
Jonah	Jon 1:1-17
Kings	Ps 2:10-11
Mankind	Ps 15:1-5b; 33:4-9
Micah	Mic 7:7-20
Moses	Deut 6:4-19
Nehemiah	Neh 1:11b-2:8
Peter	1 Pet 2:13-17
Psalmist	Ps 67:1-7; 99:1-3
Sirach	*Sir 25:7-11; 32:14-24; 40:18-27
Wisdom	Prov 1:20-33

INSTRUCTION on
David	1 Chr 15:1-16:43
God	Rev 14:6-7
Jeremiah	Jer 5:20-25
Moses	Deut 8:1-10; 10:12-22; 17:8-13
Princes	Jer 36:11-19
Psalmist	Ps 96:7-9

of MESSIANIC FIGURE
Crowd	Mt 9:1-8; 32-34
Disciples	Mt 17:1-8; Lk 9:28-36
God	Is 11:1-9

REVELATION on
Disciples	Mk 9:2-8

REVELATION on (cont'd)
Isaiah	Is 66:1-16
Jeremiah	Jer 33:1-9

in WORSHIP
David	1 Chr 15:1-16:43; Ps 5:8-10

REVELATION on
of AUTHORITY
Amos	Amos 3:3-8

of JUDGMENT
John	Rev 18:4-20

as MOTIVATION
Elihu	Job 33:15-18

of Divine PRESENCE
Israelites	Ex 20:18-20; Deut 4:1-14
Moses	Ex 3:1-6
Zechariah	Lk 1:5-25

of PUNISHMENT
Egyptians	Ezek 30:13-19
Israelites	Ezek 4:16-17

revealing RESPECT
Disciples	Mk 9:2-8
Isaiah	Is 66:1-16
Jeremiah	Jer 33:1-9

in RITE
INSTRUCTION on
Moses	Deut 31:9-13

SALVATION through
of DEITY
God	Ps 85:8-13
Sirach	*Sir 34:13-17

INSTRUCTION on
Paul	Phil 2:12-18

REVELATION on
Believers	Mal 3:13-4:3

for SECURITY
Elijah	1 Kgs 19:1-21
Israelites	Ex 14:1-14
Obadiah	1 Kgs 18:1-46
People	2 Kgs 25:23-26; Jer 41:11-18
Rehoboam	1 Kgs 12:1-20; 2 Chr 10:1-12:16

SECURITY from
by DEITY
Believers	Prov 16:1-33
David	Ps 27:1-3

SECURITY through
of DEITY
Job	Job 4:1-6

INSTRUCTION on
David	Ps 34:4-10
Elihu	Job 33:1-7
Solomon	Prov 14:1-35

MEDITATION on
David	Ps 55:3b-8

inSECURITY through
of ENVIRONMENT
David	1 Sam 21:10-15; 23:1-13; 27:1-28:2
Israelites	*Jdt 16:21-25

of ENVIRONMENT (cont'd)
Nicanor   *2 Mc 8:34-36

SIGNS of
  of DEITY
    Mankind   Ps 65:5-8
  PROPHECY of
    Jesus   Lk 21:25-28
  REVELATION on
    Ezekiel   Ezek 12:17-20

of SIN
  INSTRUCTION on
    Solomon   *Wis 17:1-21

of TRUTH
  INSTRUCTION on
    Jesus   Mt 10:26-39

VIRTUE in
  of DEITY
    Sirach   *Sir 15:1-10
  INSTRUCTION on
    Sirach   *Sir 10:12-25

FIDELITY

ACCEPTANCE of
  to COVENANT
    Chiefs   Neh 10:14-27
    Israelites   Neh 9:38;
       10:1;
       2-8;
       28-30
    Levites   Neh 10:9-13
  of FOLLOWERs
    Jesus   Lk 14:25-27 ✓
    Peter   Jn 21:15-23 ✓
  INSTRUCTION on
    Jesus   Lk 12:1-12 ✓
    Moses   Deut 26:16-19 ✓
    Sardis   Rev 3:1-6
    Solomon   Prov 19:1-29

BLESSING through
  to COVENANT
    Isaiah   Is 61:1-11
    Israelites   1 Chr 15:1-16:43;
       Ps 105:7-15
  to DEITY
    Believers   Ps 40:4-5
    Caleb   Josh 14:6-15
    David   Ps 63:1-8
    God   Ps 24:3-6;
       37:23-40
    Isaiah   Is 63:7-64:12
    Job   Job 1:20-21
    Mankind   Ps 1:1-3;
       25:8-15
    Psalmist   Ps 119:1-8
  of FOLLOWERs
    John   Rev 1:1-3
  INSTRUCTION on
    Author   Heb 6:1-8
    David   1 Kgs 2:1-4
    Gedaliah   Jer 40:7-10
    James   Jas 1:12;
       22-25
    Jesus   Lk 11:27-28

INSTRUCTION on (cont'd)
    Moses   Deut 6:1-3;
       11:1-25;
       28:1-14;
       30:15-20
    Solomon   Prov 2:1-22;
       28:1-28;
       *Wis 3:10-19
  PROPHECY of
    Jeremiah   Jer 7:21-28;
       12:14-17
  REVELATION on
    Isaiah   Is 56:1-8
    Israelites   Jer 3:21-4:4
    Joshua   Josh 1:1-9
    Moses   Deut 5:22-33
    Solomon   1 Kgs 9:1-9

CHAOS through
  to MISSION
    Jesus   Mt 10:26-39;
       Lk 12:51-53

COMPASSION through
  to COVENANT
    Azariah   *Azar 1:11-22
  to DEITY
    Israelites   Neh 9:26-31;
       Ps 106:40-46
    Psalmist   Ps 119:73-80

COURAGE through
  to DEITY
    Jehoshaphat   2 Chr 17:1-20:3
  INSTRUCTION on
    David   Ps 27:13-14;
       31:19-24

to COVENANT
  ACCEPTANCE of
    Chiefs   Neh 10:14-27
    Israelites   Neh 9:38;
       10:1;
       2-8;
       28-30
    Levites   Neh 10:9-13
  BLESSING through
    Isaiah   Is 61:1-11
    Israelites   1 Chr 15:1-16:4.
       Ps 105:7-15
  COMPASSION through
    Azariah   *Azar 1:11-22
  until DEATH
    Israelites   *1 Mc 1:62-64
  of DISCIPLESHIP
    Jehoiada   2 Chr 21:1-23:2
  by LEADERSHIP
    Jehoiada   2 Kgs 11:4-20
  through LOVE
    God   Neh 9:32-37
    Israelites   1 Kgs 8:22-53;
       2 Chr 5:1-7:10;

SUFFERING through (cont'd)
Psalmist	Ps 119:65-72; 81-88; 105-112; 137-144

VICTORY through
Believers	Ps 149:5-9
Mattathias	*1 Mc 2:39-48

WEALTH through
Job	Job 31:5-34
Uzziah	2 Chr 26:1-28:27

WISDOM in
Ezra	*2 Esd 13:51-58

in YOUTH
God	Eccl 11:9-12:7

DIGNITY of
Job	Job 29:7-13

of FOLLOWERs
Mankind	Ps 112:5-9

INSTRUCTION on
Jesus	Lk 16:10-12

in MISSION
Paul	2 Cor 1:15-22

in DISCIPLESHIP
Elisha	2 Kgs 2:1-18

to DEITY
David	Ps 27:7-12; 63:1-8
God	2 Thes 3:3-5
Jews	*2 Mc 6:12-17
Paul	1 Cor 1:4-9
Psalmist	Ps 95:1-7c

of FOLLOWERs
Blind Men	Mt 20:29-34

INSTRUCTION on
Jesus	Mt 9:14-15; Mk 2:18-22; Lk 5:33-35; 14:25-27; 28-33; Jn 15:1-11; 21:15-23
Paul	Eph 6:10-18
Psalmist	Ps 100:1-3

in MISSION
Paul	2 Cor 1:15-22

DOUBT of
Israelites	Num 20:2-13
Satan	Job 2:4-6

of DEITY
Israelites	Mal 3:13-4:3

of ENEMY
David	1 Sam 27:1-28:2
Sheba	2 Sam 20:1-26

FAITH in
Hezekiah	2 Kgs 18:4-8

to COVENANT
Israelites	*1 Mc 2:29-38
Mattathias	*1 Mc 2:15-22; 23-28

of DEITY
Believers	Ps 40:4-5
David	Ps 16:5-8; 25:1-7; 26:1-3; 55:23

of DEITY (cont'd)
Israelites	Josh 22:9-34
Job	Job 1:9-12
King	Ps 21:1-7
Maccabeus	*2 Mc 8:8-23; 15:6-10
Psalmist	Ps 116:1-11; 118:5-9; 130:5-6
Razis	*2 Mc 14:37-46
Solomon	Prov 3:1-35

of FOLLOWERs
God	Ps 9:9-12
Mankind	Ps 112:5-9
Thessalonians	1 Thes 1:2-10; 2 Thes 1:3-4
Timothy	2 Tim 1:3-7

INSTRUCTION on
Author	Heb 3:12-19; 4:14-16
Barnabas	Acts 11:22-24
Believers	Rev 14:9-12
David	Ps 37:1-11
Jesus	Lk 12:41-46; Jn 10:1-18
John	Rev 13:5-10
Judith	*Jdt 8:9-27
Paul	1 Cor 16:13-24; 2 Cor 4:16-18; Phil 1:12-30; Col 1:21-23; 2 Thes 2:13-15; 1 Tim 6:20-21; 2 Tim 2:14-19; 3:14-17
Sirach	*Sir 2:7-11; 12-18
Women	1 Tim 3:8-13; 1 Pet 3:1-7

in MISSION
Timothy	1 Tim 1:18-20

REVELATION on
Cornelius	Acts 10:1-11:18
Israelites	Zeph 3:11-13

SELF-REALIZATION of
Paul	2 Tim 4:6-8

by FAMILY
Esther	Esth 2:19-23

to DEITY
Israelites	1 Sam 12:1-25; 1 Kgs 6:1-38
Jesus	Heb 3:1-6a
Mother	*2 Mc 7:1-42
Solomon	*Sir 47:12-22

to MESSIANIC FIGURE
Psalmist	Ps 132:6-10

in MISSION
Jesus	Lk 12:51-53
Women	Tit 2:1-10

TRADITION of
Naboth	1 Kgs 21:1-4

through FEAR
of DEITY
Israelites	1 Sam 12:1-25

of FOLLOWER
Peter	Mt 14:28-33

INSTRUCTION on
Mary	Mk 16:1-8
Moses	Ex 20:18-20

INSTRUCTION on (cont'd)
Paul   2 Cor 11:1-6
PROPHECY of
Israelites   Hos 11:10-11

of FOLLOWER
BLESSING through
John   Rev 1:1-3
results in DEATH
Peter   Mt 26:31-35;
                        Mk 14:27-31;
                        Lk 22:33-34;
                        Jn 13:36-38

of FOLLOWERs
ACCEPTANCE of
Jesus   Lk 14:25-27
DIGNITY in
Mankind   Ps 112:5-9
in DISCIPLESHIP
Blind Men   Mt 20:29-34
FAITH in
God   Ps 9:9-12
Mankind   Ps 112:5-9
Thessalonians   1 Thes 1:2-10;
                        2 Thes 1:3-4
Timothy   2 Tim 1:3-7
through FEAR
Peter   Mt 14:28-33
through FRIENDSHIP
Galatians   Gal 4:12-20
through GRACE
Jesus   Eph 4:25-5:2
Onesiphorus   2 Tim 1:15-18
GRATITUDE for
Paul   Phil 4:10-20
in KILLING
Believers   Rev 6:9-11
Levites   Ex 32:25-29
in LEADERSHIP
Holy Spirit   Gal 5:25-6:6
through LOVE
Jesus   Jn 14:18-24
Macedonians   2 Cor 8:1-6
Peter   Jn 6:60-71
through MIRACLE
People   Mk 1:40-45
through OBEDIENCE
Master   Mt 6:19-24
Philippians   Phil 2:12-18
in OPPRESSION
Thessalonians   2 Thes 1:3-4
PRAISE of
Timothy   1 Thes 3:1-10
REWARD for
Jesus   Lk 22:28-30
SACREDNESS in
Holy Spirit   1 Pet 1:1-2
in SACRIFICE
Peter   Mk 14:27-31;
                        Lk 22:33-34;
                        Jn 13:36-38
in SERVICE
Onesimus   Col 4:7-9
Philippians   Phil 4:10-20
Tychicus   Col 4:7-9
in SHARING
Paul   2 Cor 9:1-5
in SUFFERING
Author   Heb 10:32-39

WITNESS to
Jesus   Jn 15:26-27
Timothy   1 Cor 4:14-21

in FRIENDSHIP
Job   Job 6:21-27
of FOLLOWERs
Galatians   Gal 4:12-20
INSTRUCTION on
Paul   2 Tim 4:19-22
Sirach   *Sir 6:2-17;
                        9:10;
                        19:4-12;
                        22:19-26;
                        27:16-21;
                        37:1-6
Solomon   Prov 18:1-24;
                        27:1-27
MEDITATION on
Job   Job 6:14-20

FULFILLMENT through
to DEITY
God   Heb 10:19-31
INSTRUCTION on
Peter   2 Pet 1:8-11
in MISSION
Jesus   Jn 10:1-18
PROPHECY of
Peter   Mt 26:69-75;
                        Mk 14:66-72;
                        Lk 22:54b-62;
                        Jn 18:12-27
REVELATION on
Zechariah   Zech 6:9-15
SCRIPTURES on
Jesus   Mt 26:31-35;
                        Mk 14:27-31

to the GOOD
of DEITY
Elihu   Job 34:10-15
Josiah   *1 Esd 1:23-24
Judith   *Jdt 8:1-8
Sirach   *Sir 2:7-11;
                        15:11-20
INSTRUCTION on
Paul   1 Thes 5:12-22
in WORSHIP
Sirach   *Sir 7:1-36

of GRACE
of DEITY
God   Ps 99:6-9;
                        145:13b-20
Israelites   Neh 9:16-18
Tobit   *Tb 13:1-18
of FOLLOWERs
Jesus   Eph 4:25-5:2
Onesiphorus   2 Tim 1:15-18
INSTRUCTION on
Jesus   Lk 7:36-50
Paul   1 Thes 5:23-24;
                        2 Tim 2:1-7
in MISSION
Paul   2 Cor 4:1-6
REVELATION on
God   Is 42:5-17

SUFFERING through (cont'd)
Paul	6:3-10

TEMPERANCE in
Men	Tit 2:1-10

WITNESS to
Epaphras	Col 1:3-8

to the **MISSION**
causes **CHAOS**
Jesus	Mt 10:26-39;
	Lk 12:51-53

through **OBEDIENCE**
Abijah	2 Chr 13:1-22
Amaziah	2 Kgs 14:1-4;
	2 Chr 25:1-28
Asa	1 Kgs 15:9-15;
	2 Chr 14:1-16:14
Azariah	2 Kgs 15:1-7
David	1 Sam 29:1-11
Hezekiah	2 Kgs 18:1-3;
	4-8;
	2 Chr 29:1-36
Jehoiada	2 Chr 24:1-27
Jehoshaphat	1 Kgs 22:41-50;
	2 Chr 17:1-20:37
Joash	2 Kgs 11:21-12:3;
	2 Chr 24:1-27
Josiah	2 Kgs 22:1-2;
	23:24-25a;
	2 Chr 34:1-35:27
Jotham	2 Kgs 15:32-38;
	2 Chr 26:1-28:27
Uzziah	2 Chr 26:1-28:27

to **COVENANT**
God	Judg 2:1-5;
	Ps 25:8-15;
	103:14-18;
	132:11-18
Joshua	Josh 9:16-27;
	23:1-16

to **DEITY**
Apostles	Acts 5:17-42
Asa	1 Kgs 15:9-15
David	Ps 17:3-5;
	18:20-24
Ezekiel	Ezek 2:8b-3:3
Ezra	*2 Esd 13:51-58
Isaiah	Is 50:1-11
Job	Job 1:1;
	22;
	2:9-10
John	1 Jn 1:5-10
Judahites	Hos 11:12-12:1
Levites	Ezra 1:5
Psalmist	Ps 119:49-56
Tobit	*Tb 1:3-9;
	10-22

of **FOLLOWERs**
Master	Mt 6:19-24
Philippians	Phil 2:12-18

INSTRUCTION on
Aaron	Ex 7:14-25
Abraham	Gen 22:1-19
Author	Heb 2:1-4;
	3:6b-11;
	12-19;
	4:1-13
Barnabas	Acts 11:22-24
Believers	Rev 14:9-12
David	Ps 15:5c

INSTRUCTION on (cont'd)
Father	Prov 4:20-27
God	Ps 95:7d-11
James	Jas 1:22-25
Jesus	Mt 21:28-32;
	23:5-12;
	24:45-51;
	Lk 14:25-27;
	28-33;
	19:11-27;
	Jn 7:53-8:11;
	10:1-18;
	16:1-4
Joshua	Josh 24:14-15
Malachi	Mal 2:10-16
Mattathias	*1 Mc 2:49-70
Moses	Ex 8:1-15;
	9:8-12;
	13-35;
	10:1-20;
	21-23;
	11:1-10;
	14:15-22;
	23-31
Paul	Eph 5:3-14;
	6:5-9;
	Phil 2:12-18;
	4:1-9;
	Col 1:21-23
Peter	1 Pet 5:12-14
Samuel	1 Sam 12:1-25
Solomon	Prov 6:20-7:27;
	8:32-36

PROPHECY of
Micah	Mic 4:1-8
People	Rev 22:6-21

REVELATION on
Isaiah	Is 58:1-14
Israelites	Jer 3:14b-18;
	Ezek 37:15-28
Judahites	Zech 7:4-8:23

SCRIPTURES on
God	2 Cor 6:14-7:1
Jesus	Mt 4:1-11;
	Lk 4:1-13

in **WORSHIP**
Asa	1 Kgs 15:9-15
Israelites	Josh 24:16-24

to **OLD AGE**
by **DEITY**
Psalmist	Ps 71:1-21

to **ONENESS**
INSTRUCTION on
Jesus	Lk 16:13;
	Jn 15:1-11
Paul	1 Cor 10:14-22

REVELATION on
Ezekiel	Ezek 11:14-21

OPPRESSION because of
to **DEITY**
Psalmist	Ps 119:57-64;
	129-136;
	153-160

of **FOLLOWERs**
Thessalonians	2 Thes 1:3-4

INSTRUCTION on
Jesus	Mt 5:38-42

SCRIPTURES on
  through **OBEDIENCE**
    God   2 Cor 6:14-7:1
    Jesus   Mt 4:1-11;
                   Lk 4:1-13

SELF-REALIZATION of
  in **FAITH**
    Paul   2 Tim 4:6-8
  in **LOVE**
    Jesus   Mt 26:36-46;
                   Mk 14:32-42;
                   Lk 22:39-46
  to **WILL**
    Paul   Rom 7:14-25

  in **SERVICE**
    Mordecai   Esth 6:1-5
    Ruth   Ruth 2:1-23
    to **DEITY**
      Believers   Ps 125:1-3
      God   Hos 5:15-6:3
      Isaiah   Is 63:7-64:12
      Israelites   Josh 24:29-31
      Job   Job 31:5-34
    of **FOLLOWERs**
      Onesimus   Col 4:7-9
      Philippians Phil 4:10-20
      Tychicus   Col 4:7-9
    INSTRUCTION on
      Jesus   Lk 16:13
      John   1 Jn 3:11-18
      Moses   Deut 10:12-22
      Paul   Eph 6:5-9;
                 1 Tim 6:1-2b
    in **MISSION**
      Paul   2 Cor 6:3-10
      Servants   1 Tim 6:1-2b
      Slaves   Tit 2:1-10
    PROPHECY of
      Ezekiel   Ezek 16:44-52
    in **WORSHIP**
      Israelites   Neh 10:39b

  in **SEX**
    Ephraimites Hos 7:3-7
    Job   Job 31:5-34
    Nineveh   Nah 3:1-4
    INSTRUCTION on
      Jesus   Mt 19:3-9;
                 Mk 10:1-12;
                 Lk 16:16-18

    REVELATION on
      Ezekiel   Ezek 33:23-29

  in **SHARING**
    of **FOLLOWERs**
      Paul   2 Cor 9:1-5
SPIRIT of
  INSTRUCTION on
    Jesus   Mk 12:28-34
  in **SUFFERING**
    by **MESSIANIC FIGURE**
      Jesus   Heb 5:1-10
    in **MISSION**
      Paul   2 Cor 4:7-12;
                 6:3-10

    REVELATION on
      John   Rev 13:5-10;
                 11-18

SELF-REALIZATION of
  Paul   Col 1:24
SUFFERING through
  Philadelphians Rev 3:7-13
  to **DEITY**
    Israelites   Ps 44:17-22
    Job   Job 2:1-3;
                 6:8-13
    Mother   *2 Mc 7:1-42
    Psalmist   Ps 119:65-72;
                 81-88;
                 105-112;
                 137-144
  of **FOLLOWERs**
    Author   Heb 10:32-39
  INSTRUCTION on
    Author   Heb 12:1-2;
                 3-11
    Believers   Rev 14:9-12
    Elihu   Job 36:16-25
    James   Jas 1:2-4
    Paul   2 Tim 2:1-7;
                 3:10-13;
                 4:1-5
    Peter   1 Pet 1:3-9

  in **TEMPERANCE**
    in **MISSION**
      Men   Tit 2:1-10
    TRADITION of
      Judahites   Jer 35:6-17

  through **TEMPTATION**
    INSTRUCTION on
      Paul   1 Cor 7:1-7;
                 2 Cor 11:1-6;
                 Gal 5:7-12;
                 Col 2:6-15
      Sirach   *Sir 2:1-6
      Solomon   Prov 1:10-19

TRADITION of
  in **FAMILY**
    Naboth   1 Kgs 21:1-4
  against **IDOLATRY**
    Judges   *Sir 46:11-12
  in **JUSTICE**
    Samuel   *Sir 46:13-20
  through **OBEDIENCE**
    Mattathias *1 Mc 2:49-70
  in **TEMPERANCE**
    Judahites   Jer 35:6-17

VICTORY through
  to **DEITY**
    Believers   Ps 149:5-9
    Mattathias *1 Mc 2:39-48
  in the **ENVIRONMENT**
    Jesus   Mt 4:1-11;
                 Lk 4:1-13

  INSTRUCTION on
    Paul   1 Tim 6:11-16
  REVELATION on
    John   Rev 14:13

WEALTH through
  to **DEITY**
    Job   Job 31:5-34
    Uzziah   2 Chr 26:1-28:27
  INSTRUCTION on
    Paul   1 Tim 6:17-19

to **WILL**
  of **DEITY**
    Believer   1 Pet 4:1-6
    Daniel   Dan 11:21-45
  SELF-REALIZATION of
    Paul   Rom 7:14-25

WISDOM in
  to **DEITY**
    Ezra   *2 Esd 13:51-58
  INSTRUCTION on
    Baruch   *Bar 4:1-4
    Father   Prov 4:1-9
    Moses   Deut 4:1-14

WITNESS to
  of **DEITY**
    David   Ps 40:6-10;
           52:8-9
    Ethan   Ps 89:1-4
    Mary   Lk 1:39-56
    Moses   Heb 3:1-6a
  of **FOLLOWERs**
    Jesus   Jn 15:26-27
    Timothy   1 Cor 4:14-21
  INSTRUCTION on
    Isaiah   Is 48:1-22
    Paul   Phil 3:4-16;
           2 Tim 3:10-13
  concerning **MESSIANIC FIGURE**
    Ezra   *2 Esd 2:42-48
  in **MISSION**
    Epaphras   Col 1:3-8

in **WORSHIP**
  of **GOOD**
    Sirach   *Sir 7:1-36
  of **JUSTICE**
    David   Ps 101:1-2b
  through **OBEDIENCE**
    Asa   1 Kgs 15:9-15
    Israelites   Josh 24:16-24
  PRAISE of
    David   Ps 22:22-26
    Psalmist   Ps 146:1-2
  through **SACREDNESS**
    Josiah   2 Kgs 23:21-23
    Simon   *Sir 50:1-21
  through **SACRIFICE**
    Widow   Lk 21:1-4
    Widows   Mk 12:41-44
  through **SERVICE**
    Israelites   Neh 10:39b

of **YOUTH**
  to **DEITY**
    God   Eccl 11:9-12:7

inFIDELITY

ALIENATION through
    Abiathar   1 Kgs 2:26-27
  to **DEITY**
    Israelites   Heb 4:1-13
  INSTRUCTION on
    Jesus   Mt 7:21-23;
           Lk 13:22-30
  in **MISSION**
    Jesus   Lk 12:51-53

ANGER against
  PROPHECY on
    God   2 Chr 36:1-23

causes **ANGER**
  of **DEITY**
    Elihu   Job 32:2b-5
    God   Eph 5:3-14
    Israelites   Judg 10:6-18
    Judahites   Jer 25:1-7

ANXIETY concerning
  of **FOLLOWERs**
    Paul   Gal 1:6-10
  PROPHECY of
    Jesus   Jn 13:21-30

revealing **BLASPHEMY**
  against **COVENANT**
    Israelites   Mal 2:10-16

BLASPHEMY through
  of **FOLLOWER**
    Judas   Mt 26:47-56;
           Mk 14:43-50;
           Lk 22:47-54a
  PROPHECY of
    Paul   1 Tim 4:1-5

CAPTIVITY caused by
    Judahites   1 Chr 9:1-16
  INSTRUCTION on
    Paul   Gal 5:1
  PROPHECY of
    Jesus   Mt 26:36-46;
           Mk 14:32-42
    Judahites   Jer 38:14-28

CONDEMNATION of
  by **DEITY**
    Ephraimites   Hos 7:13-16
    Isaiah   Is 17:9-11
  caused by **FALSE BELIEF**
    Author   Heb 6:1-8
    God   Rev 14:9-12
  of **FOLLOWERs**
    Author   Heb 6:1-8;
           10:19-31;
           12:12-29
    Peter   2 Pet 2:17-22
  INSTRUCTION on
    Jesus   Mt 7:21-23;
           26:17-30;
           Mk 14:17-21;
           Lk 13:22-30
  PROPHECY of
    Isaiah   Is 8:19-22
    Jeremiah   Jer 17:5-8
  REVELATION on
    Israelites   Jer 3:1-5
    Jeremiah   Jer 26:1-6

to **COVENANT**
  as **BLASPHEMY**
    Israelites   Mal 2:10-16
  resulting in **DESTRUCTION**
    Jeremiah   Jer 22:1-9
  through **DISOBEDIENCE**
    Israelites   Judg 2:20-23;
           Jer 11:1-14;
           Hos 6:7-9

through **DISOBEDIENCE** (cont'd)
  Priests   Mal 1:6-2:9
through **EVIL**
  Israelites   Ps 78:32-39
of **FAITH**
  Israelites   *1 Mc 2:29-38
  Mattathias   *1 Mc 2:15-22;
                  23-28

to **DEITY**
  causing **ALIENATION**
    Israelites   Heb 4:1-13
  causing **ANGER**
    Elihu   Job 32:2b-5
    God   Eph 5:3-14
    Israelites   Judg 10:6-18
    Judahites   Jer 25:1-7
  causing **CONDEMNATION**
    Ephraimites Hos 7:13-16
    Isaiah   Is 17:9-11
  brings **DEATH**
    Eleazar   *2 Mc 6:18-31
    Jews   *2 Mc 7:1-42
  through **DISOBEDIENCE**
    Israelites   Ps 106:13-18;
                  Rom 9:30-10:21
    Mankind   Ps 12:1-4
  DOUBT of
    Israelites   Mal 3:13-4:3
  through **EVIL**
    Israelites   Ps 78:40-55
    Mankind   Ps 14:1-3
  HATE of
    God   Mal 2:10-16
  IDOLATRY as
    Israelites   Mal 2:10-16
    Jeremiah   *Jer 6:4-7
    Solomon   *Wis 15:1-6

resulting in **DESTRUCTION**
  Jeremiah   Jer 22:1-9
of **FOLLOWERs**
  Author   Heb 10:32-39
PROPHECY of
  Jeremiah   Jer 12:14-17
  Judahites   Jer 9:10-22;
                38:14-28

REVELATION on
  Isaiah   Is 8:11-15

through **DISOBEDIENCE**
to **COVENANT**
  Israelites   Judg 2:20-23;
                Jer 11:1-14;
                Hos 6:7-9
  Priests   Mal 1:6-2:9
to **DEITY**
  Israelites   Ps 106:13-18;
                Rom 9:30-10:21
  Mankind   Ps 12:1-4
caused by **FALSE BELIEF**
  Israelites   Judg 6:7-10
INSTRUCTION on
  Mary   Mk 16:1-8
PROPHECY of
  Ahijah   1 Kgs 14:1-18
  Jeremiah   Jer 42:7-22
  Moses   Deut 31:24-29
REVELATION on
  Ezekiel   Ezek 3:22-27

REVELATION on (cont'd)
  Isaiah   Is 65:1-25
  Israelites   Jer 2:14-19;
                20-29;
                5:1-14;
                Ezek 15:1-8
  Moses   Deut 31:14-23
  Samuel   1 Sam 8:1-22

as **ENEMY**
  by **FOLLOWER**
    Judas   Mt 26:14-16;
                17-30;
                Mk 14:10-11;
                Lk 22:3-6
  PROPHECY of
    Jesus   Mt 26:17-30;
                Mk 14:17-21;
                Lk 22:14-23;
                Jn 13:21-30
  SCRIPTURES on
    Jesus   Mt 26:17-30;
                Mk 14:17-21

through **EVIL**
  Abijam   1 Kgs 15:1-8
  Ahab   1 Kgs 16:29-34
  Ahaz   2 Kgs 16:1-4;
                2 Chr 26:1-28:27
  Ahaziah   1 Kgs 22:51-53;
                2 Kgs 8:25-29;
                2 Chr 17:1-20:37
                21:1-23:21
  Amon   2 Kgs 21:19-26;
                2 Chr 33:1-25
  Baasha   1 Kgs 15:33-16:7
  Hoshea   2 Kgs 17:1-6
  Israelites   Judg 3:7-11;
                12-14;
                4:1-3
  Jehoahaz   2 Kgs 13:1-9;
                23:31-35
  Jehoash   2 Kgs 13:10-13
  Jehoiachin 2 Chr 36:1-23
  Jehoiakim   2 Kgs 24:8-17;
                2 Chr 36:1-23
  Jehoram   2 Kgs 8:16-24;
                2 Chr 21:1-23:21
  Jehu   2 Kgs 10:29-31
  Jeroboam   2 Kgs 14:23-29;
                2 Chr 13:1-22
  Manasseh   2 Kgs 21:1-18;
                2 Chr 33:1-25
  Menahem   2 Kgs 15:16-22
  Nadab   1 Kgs 15:25-32
  Omri   1 Kgs 16:15-22;
                23-28
  Pekah   2 Kgs 15:27-31
  Pekahiah   2 Kgs 15:23-26
  Rehoboam   2 Chr 10:1-12:16
  Zechariah   2 Kgs 15:8-12
  Zedekiah   2 Kgs 24:18-25:7
                2 Chr 36:1-23
  Zimri   1 Kgs 16:15-22
to **DEITY**
  Israelites   Ps 78:40-55
  Mankind   Ps 14:1-3
caused by **FALSE BELIEF**
  Isaiah   Is 1:21-23

INSTRUCTION on (cont'd)
Jesus   Lk 9:49-50

PROPHECY of
causing ANGER
God   2 Chr 36:1-23
causing ANXIETY
Jesus   Jn 13:21-30
causing BLASPHEMY
Paul   1 Tim 4:1-5
cause for CAPTIVITY
Jesus   Mt 26:36-46;
                        Mk 14:32-42
Judahites   Jer 38:14-28
resulting in DESTRUCTION
Jeremiah   Jer 12:14-17
Judahites   Jer 9:10-22;
                        38:14-28
by DISOBEDIENCE
Ahijah   1 Kgs 14:1-18
Jeremiah   Jer 42:7-22
Moses   Deut 31:24-29
by ENEMY
Jesus   Mt 26:17-30;
                        Mk 14:17-21;
                        Lk 22:14-23;
                        Jn 13:21-30
through EVIL
Jesus   Mt 26:17-30;
                        Mk 14:17-21

REJECTION of
of FOLLOWERs
Jesus   2 Tim 2:8-13
Paul   2 Tim 1:15-18
INSTRUCTION on
Author   Heb 3:12-19
Jesus   Mt 8:18-22;
                        23:34-39;
                        Lk 9:57-62;
                        12:1-12

REJECTION through
PROPHECY of
Isaiah   Is 29:15-16
Jesus   Mt 26:31-35;
                        Mk 14:27-31;
                        Lk 22:14-23;
                        31-32;
                        33-34;
                        Jn 13:1-20;
                        21-30;
                        36-38;
                        16:29-33
Judahites   2 Chr 24:1-27
Peter   Mt 26:69-75;
                        Mk 14:66-72;
                        Lk 22:54b-62;
                        Jn 18:12-27
REVELATION on
Ezekiel   Ezek 3:4-9
Israelites   Jer 3:6-11;
                        19-20;
                        Ezek 20:5-8
Judahites   Jer 3:6-11

REPENTANCE for
through SELF-REALIZATION
Peter   Mt 26:69-75;
                        Mk 14:66-72;
                        Lk 22:54b-62

REVELATION on
results in DESTRUCTION
Isaiah   Is 8:11-15
through DISOBEDIENCE
Ezekiel   Ezek 3:22-27
Isaiah   Is 65:1-25
Israelites   Jer 2:14-19;
                        20-29;
                        5:1-14;
                        Ezek 15:1-8
Moses   Deut 31:14-23
Samuel   1 Sam 8:1-22
through EVIL
Ezekiel   Ezek 23:1-4
causing HERESY
Israelites   Jer 2:14-19
causing IDOLATRY
Israelites   Ezek 20:5-8
Judahites   Ezek 23:11-21

SADNESS through
SELF-REALIZATION of
Peter   Mt 26:69-75;
                        Mk 14:66-72;
                        Lk 22:54b-62

SCRIPTURES on
of ENEMY
Jesus   Mt 26:17-30;
                        Mk 14:17-21

in SEX
FALSE BELIEF concerning
Ephraimites   Hos 5:3-7
Israelites   Ezek 23:36-49;
                        Hos 9:1-6

SUFFERING through
caused by FALSE BELIEF
Mankind   Ps 16:1-4

FOLLOWER

ACCEPTANCE by
in CONFRONTATION
Jesus   Lk 24:13-35

ACCEPTANCE of
Crowd   Jn 12:12-19
People   Lk 19:47-48
in BROTHERHOOD
Paul   Philm 1:15-20
through ELECTION
Matthew   Mt 9:9;
                        Lk 5:27-28
with RESPECT
Apostles   Gal 1:18-2:10
SIGNS of
Believers   Acts 9:32-43

ALIENATION of
resulting from BEHAVIOR
Disciples   Mt 26:47-56;
                        Mk 14:43-50
Judas   Mt 26:47-56;
                        Mk 14:43-50;
                        Lk 22:47-54a

through **BELIEF**
  Jesus   Gal 3:19-25
through **BROTHERHOOD**
  Believers   1 Cor 14:1-12
in **CREATION**
  God   Ps 145:10-13a
through **FIDELITY**
  John   Rev 1:1-3
PRAYER for
  Paul   2 Cor 1:1-2;
                            2 Thes 2:16-17
through **RESPECT**
  Peter   1 Pet 4:12-19

BROTHERHOOD of
ACCEPTANCE of
  Paul   Philm 1:15-20
BLESSING through
  Believers   1 Cor 14:1-12
FAITH in
  Believers   Acts 16:1-5
JUSTICE in
  Paul   1 Cor 6:1-8
LOVE in
  Colossians   Col 1:3-8
  God   1 Jn 3:4-10
  Thessalonians   2 Thes 1:3-4
ONENESS in
  Believers   Acts 4:32-5:10;
                            1 Cor 12:12-26;
                            2 Cor 12:11-13;
                            Eph 2:11-22
  Holy Spirit   Eph 4:1-6
SERVICE of
  Paul   Col 4:10-14;
                            Philm 1:8-14
SHARING of
  Believers   Acts 2:42-47

CAPTIVITY of
FREEDOM from
  Man   Mk 14:51-52
as **PUNISHMENT**
  Peter   Acts 12:1-25

COMMITMENT of
in **DISCIPLESHIP**
  People   Lk 9:57-62
  Scribe   Mt 8:18-22
through **FAITH**
  Believers   Acts 19:13-20
through **HOPE**
  Jesus   Heb 3:6b-11
in **KILLING**
  Jews   Acts 23:12-35
through **LOVE**
  Titus   2 Cor 8:16-24
to **SERVICE**
  Titus   2 Cor 8:16-24
to **SUFFERING**
  Paul   2 Cor 1:3-7
to **WITNESS**
  John   Acts 4:1-22
  Peter   Acts 4:1-22

COMMITMENT to
reveals **COMPASSION**
  Paul   2 Cor 1:3-7

COMMUNITY of
ONENESS in

ONENESS in (cont'd)
  Believers   Acts 4:32-5:10
SACRIFICE for
  Believers   Acts 4:32-5:10
SHARING with
  Believers   Acts 4:32-5:10

COMPASSION for
KNOWLEDGE of
  Jesus   Heb 4:14-16
PROVIDENCE through
  God   Ps 135:13-14
SIN forgiven through
  Paul   2 Cor 2:5-11

COMPASSION of
through **COMMITMENT**
  Paul   2 Cor 1:3-7

COMPULSION of
to **SERVICE**
  Jesus   Jn 12:20-26

CONDEMNATION of
through in**FIDELITY**
  Author   Heb 6:1-8;
                            10:19-31;
                            12:12-29
  Peter   2 Pet 2:17-22
as **JUDGMENT**
  Jews   Acts 24:1-27;
                            25:1-12
  Mankind   Jas 4:11-12
in **NEW AGE**
  Pharisees   Mt 23:13

in **CONFRONTATION**
ACCEPTANCE by
  Jesus   Lk 24:13-35
reveals **ANXIETY**
  Jesus   Mt 17:22-23
reveals **COURAGE**
  Joseph   Mt 27:57-61;
                            Mk 15:42-47
reveals **EVIL**
  Paul   2 Cor 10:7-11
reveals **JOY**
  Believers   Acts 15:30-41
  Titus   2 Cor 7:5-13a
with **KILLING**
  Herod   Acts 12:1-25
with **OPPRESSION**
  Herod   Acts 12:1-25
with **REJECTION**
  Apostles   1 Cor 4:6-13

CONVERSION of
through **FAITH**
  Believers   Acts 9:32-43
  Corinthians   Acts 18:1-17
  Lydia   Acts 16:11-15
  Simon   Acts 8:4-13
  Zacchaeus   Lk 19:1-10
with **JOY**
  Barnabas   Acts 15:1-5
  Ethiopian   Acts 8:26-40
  Paul   Acts 15:1-5
through **JUSTICE**
  Zacchaeus   Lk 19:1-10
through **LOVE**
  Zacchaeus   Lk 19:1-10

through **REPENTANCE**
    Jailer   Acts 16:25-40
    Thessalonians   1 Thes 1:2-10
    Zacchaeus   Lk 19:1-10

COURAGE of
  through **AUTHORITY**
    Paul   2 Cor 10:7-11
  in **CONFRONTATION**
    Joseph   Mt 27:57-61;
                   Mk 15:42-47
  through **PRESENCE**
    Holy Spirit   Acts 4:23-31
  as **VIRTUE**
    Mankind   Ps 112:5-9

DEATH of
  through **FIDELITY**
    Peter   Mt 26:31-35;
                   Mk 14:27-31;
                   Lk 22:33-34;
                   Jn 13:36-38
  as **PUNISHMENT**
    Rulers   Acts 6:8-8:3
  RITE performed at
    Joseph   Mt 27:57-61;
                   Mk 15:42-47;
                   Lk 23:50-53

DESIRE of
  for **HEALING**
    Crowd   Mt 15:29-31;
                   Lk 6:17-19
    Jesus   Mk 3:7-12;
                   6:53-56
  for **JUSTICE**
    Festus   Acts 25:13-27
    Paul   Acts 25:1-12
  for **REVENGE**
    Believers   Rev 6:9-11
  for **REWARD**
    Paul   Philm 1:15-20
  for **WISDOM**
    Ezekiel   Ezek 14:1-11

DESTRUCTION of
  through in**FIDELITY**
    Author   Heb 10:32-39

DIGNITY of
  through **AUTHORITY**
    Paul   1 Cor 9:1-6;
                2 Cor 10:7-11
  FIDELITY of
    Mankind   Ps 112:5-9

in **DISCIPLESHIP**
  AUTHORITY of
    Jesus   Mt 10:1;
               Mk 6:7-13;
               Lk 9:1-6
  BEHAVIOR of
    Crowd   Mt 8:1
  BELIEF of
    Disciples   Jn 1:19-51
  COMMITMENT through
    People   Lk 9:57-62
    Scribe   Mt 8:18-22

DISCIPLESHIP of
  ELECTION to
    Andrew   Mt 4:18-22;
              Mk 1:16-20
    God   1 Pet 1:1-2
    James   Mt 4:18-22;
              Mk 1:16-20;
              Lk 5:1-11
    Jesus   Jn 21:15-23
    John   Mt 4:18-22;
              Mk 1:16-20;
              Lk 5:1-11
    Matthew   Mk 2:13-14
    Matthias   Acts 1:12-26
    Peter   Mt 4:18-22;
              Mk 1:16-20;
              Lk 5:1-11
    Philip   Jn 1:19-51
  FIDELITY in
    Blind Men   Mt 20:29-34
  JUDGMENT in
    Paul   1 Cor 6:1-8
  KNOWLEDGE of
    Apostles   Mt 10:2-4;
              Mk 3:13-19;
              Lk 6:12-16
    Jesus   Jn 13:31-35
  MOTIVATION in
    Jesus   Mt 9:36-38
  VIRTUE in
    Paul   2 Thes 1:11-12

DISOBEDIENCE of
  SALVATION through
    Gentiles   Rom 11:7-24

DOUBT of
  in **FREEDOM**
    Peter   Acts 12:1-25
  in **RESURRECTION**
    Thomas   Jn 20:1-29
  in **TRUTH**
    Apostles   Acts 9:20-31

ELECTION of
    Matthew   Mt 9:9;
              Lk 5:27-28
  to **DISCIPLESHIP**
    Andrew   Mt 4:18-22;
              Mk 1:16-20
    God   1 Pet 1:1-2
    James   Mt 4:18-22;
              Mk 1:16-20;
              Lk 5:1-11
    Jesus   Jn 21:15-23
    John   Mt 4:18-22;
              Mk 1:16-20;
              Lk 5:1-11
    Matthew   Mk 2:13-14
    Matthias   Acts 1:12-26
    Peter   Mt 4:18-22;
              Mk 1:16-20;
              Lk 5:1-11
    Philip   Jn 1:19-51
  FAITH in
    Believers   Acts 13:14-52
    Jesus   Lk 5:1-11
  to **FAMILY**
    Holy Spirit   Rom 8:14-25
    Jesus   Eph 1:3-14

through GRACE
 God   Eph 1:3-14
HATE of
 People   Jn 15:18-25
HOPE in
 Believers   Eph 4:1-6
LEADERSHIP in
 Joshua   Deut 31:1-8
REJECTION of
 Judas   Jn 6:60-71
REWARDs of
 Jesus   Lk 22:28-30
SACREDNESS in
 Paul   Rom 1:1-7
SERVICE in
 Jesus   Mk 3:13-19

as ENEMY
 through inFIDELITY
  Judas   Mt 26:14-16;
       17-30;
       Mk 14:10-11;
       Lk 22:3-6
 of TRUTH
  Israelites Rom 11:25-32

EQUALITY of
 in LEADERSHIP
  Jesus   Jn 13:1-20;
       15:18-25
  Paul   2 Cor 12:11-13
 ONENESS in
  Jesus   Gal 3:26-29
 to TEMPTATION
  Jesus   Heb 4:14-16
 in VICTORY
  Jesus   Lk 20:27-40

EVIL of
 CONFRONTATION with
  Paul   2 Cor 10:7-11
 through inFIDELITY
  Judas   Mt 26:14-16;
       Mk 14:10-11;
       Lk 22:3-6
 FREEDOM from
  Disciples Jn 8:21-59
 RECONCILIATION with
  Believers Gal 5:25-6:6

FAITH in
 AUTHORITY of
  Leper   Mt 8:2-4;
       Mk 1:40-45;
       Lk 5:12-16

FAITH of
 BEHAVIOR revealing
  Apostles Mt 10:26-39
  Crowd   Mt 15:29-31
  Thessalonians 1 Thes 3:1-10
 through BELIEF
  Blind   Mk 10:46-52
  Centurion Mt 8:5-13;
       Lk 7:1-10
  Peter   Jn 6:60-71
  Samaritans Jn 4:27-42
 in BROTHERHOOD
  Believers Acts 16:1-5
 in COMMITMENT
  Believers Acts 19:13-20

results in CONVERSION
 Believers   Acts 9:32-43
 Corinthians Acts 18:1-17
 Lydia   Acts 16:11-15
 Simon   Acts 8:4-13
 Zacchaeus   Lk 19:1-10
ELECTION through
 Believers   Acts 13:14-52
 Jesus   Lk 5:1-11
FIDELITY in
 God   Ps 9:9-12
 Mankind   Ps 112:5-9
 Thessalonians 1 Thes 1:2-10;
       2 Thes 1:3-4
 Timothy   2 Tim 1:3-7
FREEDOM in
 Holy Spirit 2 Cor 3:12-18
GIFTs through
 Holy Spirit 1 Cor 12:4-11
KNOWLEDGE of
 Timothy   1 Thes 3:1-10
PRAYER for
 Believers   Acts 2:42-47
 Paul   1 Thes 3:11-13
PROMISE of
 Holy Spirit Gal 3:10-14
 Peter   Mt 26:31-35;
       Mk 14:27-31;
       Lk 22:33-34
as QUALITY OF LIFE
 Author   Heb 10:32-39
RECONCILIATION through
 Jesus   Gal 3:26-29
in RESURRECTION
 Disciples   Jn 20:1-29
 Mary   Jn 20:1-29
 Thomas   Jn 20:1-29
SALVATION through
 Jailer   Acts 16:25-40
 Jesus   1 Jn 5:8-12
 Woman   Lk 7:36-50
SIGNS of
 Believers   Acts 13:4-12
in TRUTH
 Believers   Jn 12:44-50;
       Acts 5:11-16;
       8:4-13
 People   Acts 17:1-9;
       10-15;
       16-34
as VIRTUE
 Abraham   Rom 3:31-4:25

FAMILY of
 ELECTION
  Holy Spirit Rom 8:14-25
  Jesus   Eph 1:3-14
 PROMISE to
  Jesus   Gal 3:26-29
 VIRTUE in
  God   1 Jn 3:4-10

FEAR of
 BEHAVIOR revealing
  Disciples Mt 8:23-27;
       Mk 4:35-41;
       Lk 8:22-25
 concerning BELIEF
  People   Jn 12:36b-43
 causes inFIDELITY
  Peter   Mt 14:28-33

as **MOTIVATION**
    Disciples   Mt 26:47-56
as **PUNISHMENT**
    Magistrates   Acts 16:25-40

FIDELITY of
  ACCEPTANCE of
    Jesus   Lk 14:25-27
    Peter   Jn 21:15-23
  BLESSING through
    John   Rev 1:1-3
  until **DEATH**
    Peter   Mt 26:31-35;
                   Mk 14:27-31;
                   Lk 22:33-34;
                   Jn 13:36-38
  DIGNITY through
    Mankind   Ps 112:5-9
  in **DISCIPLESHIP**
    Blind Men   Mt 20:29-34
  through **FAITH**
    God   Ps 9:9-12
    Mankind   Ps 112:5-9
    Thessalonians   1 Thes 1:2-10;
                   2 Thes 1:3-4
    Timothy   2 Tim 1:3-7
  in **FRIENDSHIP**
    Galatians   Gal 4:12-20
  through **GRACE**
    Jesus   Eph 4:25-5:2
    Onesiphorus   2 Tim 1:15-18
  GRATITUDE for
    Paul   Phil 4:10-20
  in **KILLING**
    Believers   Rev 6:9-11
    Levites   Ex 32:25-29
  in **LEADERSHIP**
    Holy Spirit   Gal 5:25-6:6
  in **LOVE**
    Jesus   Jn 14:18-24
    Macedonians   2 Cor 8:1-6
    Peter   Jn 6:60-71
  through **OBEDIENCE**
    Master   Mt 6:19-24
    Philippians   Phil 2:12-18
  causes **OPPRESSION**
    Thessalonians   2 Thes 1:3-4
  PRAISE of
    Timothy   1 Thes 3:1-10
  REWARDs for
    Jesus   Lk 22:28-30
  in **SACREDNESS**
    Holy Spirit   1 Pet 1:1-2
  in **SACRIFICE**
    Peter   Mk 14:27-31;
                   Lk 22:33-34;
                   Jn 13:36-38
  in **SERVICE**
    Onesimus   Col 4:7-9
    Philippians   Phil 4:10-20
    Tychicus   Col 4:7-9
  in **SHARING**
    Paul   2 Cor 9:1-5
  SUFFERING through
    Author   Heb 10:32-39
  WITNESS to
    Jesus   Jn 15:26-27
    Timothy   1 Cor 4:14-21

inFIDELITY of

---

inFIDELITY of (cont'd)
  causes **ANXIETY**
    Paul   Gal 1:6-10
  causes **BLASPHEMY**
    Judas   Mt 26:47-56;
                   Mk 14:43-50;
                   Lk 22:47-54a
  CONDEMNATION of
    Author   Heb 6:1-8;
                   10:19-31;
                   12:12-29
    Peter   2 Pet 2:17-22
  causes **DESTRUCTION**
    Author   Heb 10:32-39
  as **ENEMY**
    Judas   Mt 26:14-16;
                   17-30;
                   Mk 14:10-11;
                   Lk 22:3-6
  through **EVIL**
    Judas   Mt 26:14-16;
                   Mk 14:10-11;
                   Lk 22:3-6
  through **FEAR**
    Peter   Mt 14:28-33
  caused by **MIRACLE**
    People   Mk 1:40-45
  REJECTION of
    Jesus   2 Tim 2:8-13
    Paul   2 Tim 1:15-18

FREEDOM of
    Holy Spirit   1 Cor 3:10-17
  from **CAPTIVITY**
    Man   Mk 14:51-52
  from **DOUBT**
    Peter   Acts 12:1-25
  from **EVIL**
    Disciples   Jn 8:21-59
  through **FAITH**
    Holy Spirit   2 Cor 3:12-18
  by **GRACE**
    Jesus   Gal 5:1
  through **REJECTION**
    Satan   Jas 4:1-10
  in **SERVICE**
    Paul   Gal 5:13-15
  in **WEALTH**
    Macedonians   2 Cor 8:1-6

FRIENDSHIP of
  through **FIDELITY**
    Galatians   Gal 4:12-20
  PRAYER for
    Paul   1 Thes 3:1-10

FULFILLMENT by
  of **LAW**
    Jesus   Gal 5:25-6:6

GIFT to
  GRACE as
    Holy Spirit   1 Cor 12:4-11
    Jesus   Eph 4:7-16
  HEALING as
    Holy Spirit   1 Cor 12:4-11
  MIRACLE as
    Holy Spirit   Acts 2:1-13;
                   1 Cor 12:4-11

SERVICE as
  Apostles — Eph 4:7-16
  Evangelists — Eph 4:7-16
  Holy Spirit — 1 Cor 12:4-11
  Pastors — Eph 4:7-16
  Prophet — Eph 4:7-16
  Teachers — Eph 4:7-16
  by SHARING
    Paul — Rom 1:8-15
  SPIRIT as
    Jesus — 1 Cor 2:10-16
  WISDOM as
    Holy Spirit — 1 Cor 2:10-16; 12:4-11
    Unbelievers — 1 Cor 14:13-25
  WITNESS of
    Holy Spirit — 1 Cor 12:4-11

GRATITUDE for
  PRAYER of
    Paul — Col 1:3-8; 1 Thes 1:2-10; 2:13-16; 2 Thes 2:13-15; 2 Tim 1:3-7; Philm 1:4-7

GRATITUDE of
  for BELIEF
    Paul — Rom 1:8-15
  for CREATION
    God — Ps 145:10-13a
  through FIDELITY
    Paul — Phil 4:10-20

GREED of
  BEHAVIOR revealing
    Judas — Mt 26:14-16; Mk 14:10-11; Lk 22:3-6

GRIEF of
  BEHAVIOR revealing
    Paul — 2 Cor 1:23-2:4

GUILT of
  JUDGMENT on
    Sadducees — Acts 22:30-23:11

HATE of
  in ELECTION
    People — Jn 15:18-25

HEALING by
  Jesus — Mt 12:15-21; 17:14-20
  through AUTHORITY
    Disciples — Mk 6:7-13; Lk 9:1-6
    Jesus — Mt 10:1
  as GIFT
    Holy Spirit — 1 Cor 12:4-11

HEALING of
  BELIEF in
    Canaanite — Mt 15:21-28
    Leper — Mt 8:2-4; Mk 1:40-45; Lk 5:12-16
    Woman — Mk 7:24-30

DESIRE for
  Crowd — Mt 15:29-31; Lk 6:17-19
  Jesus — Mk 3:7-12; 6:53-56

HOPE of
  through BELIEF
    Abraham — Rom 3:31-4:25
    Holy Spirit — Gal 5:2-6
  COMMITMENT to
    Jesus — Heb 3:6b-11
  for ELECTION
    Believers — Eph 4:1-6
  in NEW AGE
    Paul — Tit 3:1-7
  in RESURRECTION
    Jesus — 1 Pet 1:3-9
  for SALVATION
    Thessalonians — 1 Thes 1:2-10
  in TRUTH
    Colossians — Col 1:3-8
    Jesus — Col 1:25-27

HUMILITY of
  Apostles — 1 Cor 4:6-13

IGNORANCE of
  in NEW AGE
    Apostles — Acts 1:6-11
  PRAYER concerning
    Believers — Rom 8:26-27
  SIGNS of
    Jesus — Mk 8:14-21

INDIFFERENCE of
  Disciples — Mt 26:36-46; Mk 14:32-42; Lk 22:39-46
  to TRUTH
    Jesus — Mk 8:14-21

INNOCENCE of
  JUDGMENT on
    Claudius — Acts 23:12-35
    Festus — Acts 25:14-27; 26:1-32
    Pharisees — Acts 22:30-23:1
  MEDIATION on
    Jesus — 1 Cor 1:4-9

JEALOUSY of
  Jews — Acts 17:1-9; 10-15
  concerning TRUTH
    Paul — 2 Cor 11:1-6

JOY by
  because of AUTHORITY
    Believers — Lk 10:17-20

JOY of
  People — Lk 14:10-17
  in CONFRONTATION
    Believers — Acts 15:30-41
    Titus — 2 Cor 7:5-13a
  as MOTIVATION
    Holy Spirit — 1 Thes 1:2-10
    Paul — Philm 1:4-7

as **QUALITY OF LIFE**
  Holy Spirit   Gal 5:22-24
in **TRUTH**
  John   2 Jn 1:4-6;
           3 Jn 1:3-8

JUDGMENT of
  is **CONDEMNATION**
    Jews   Acts 24:1-27;
          25:1-12
    Mankind   Jas 4:11-12
  in **DISCIPLESHIP**
    Paul   1 Cor 6:1-8
  as **GUILT**
    Sadducees   Acts 22:30-23:11
  as **INNOCENCE**
    Claudius   Acts 23:12-35
    Festus   Acts 25:13-27;
         26:1-32
    Pharisees   Acts 22:30-23:11
  through **JUSTICE**
    Festus   Acts 25:1-12
  concerning **OBEDIENCE**
    Peter   1 Pet 4:12-19
  through **WISDOM**
    Paul   1 Cor 4:6-13;
        6:1-8
  concerning **YOUTH**
    Corinthians   1 Cor 3:1-4

JUSTICE of
  in **BROTHERHOOD**
    Paul   1 Cor 6:1-8
  CONVERSION through
    Zacchaeus   Lk 13:10-17
  DESIRE for
    Festus   Acts 25:13-27
    Paul   Acts 25:1-12
  in **JUDGMENT**
    Festus   Acts 25:1-12
  SECURITY in
    Claudius   Acts 23:12-35

KILLING of
  COMMITMENT to
    Jews   Acts 23:12-35
  CONFRONTATION with
    Herod   Acts 12:1-25
  revealing **FIDELITY**
    Believers   Rev 6:9-11
    Levites   Ex 32:25-29

KNOWLEDGE of
  through **COMPASSION**
    Jesus   Heb 4:14-16
  in **DISCIPLESHIP**
    Apostles   Mt 10:2-4;
        Mk 3:13-19;
        Lk 6:12-16
    Jesus   Jn 13:31-35
  through **FAITH**
    Timothy   1 Thes 3:1-10
  through **LEADERSHIP**
    Jesus   Jn 10:1-18
  in **LIFE**
    Jesus   2 Cor 4:7-12
  through **LOVE**
    God   1 Cor 8:1-3
    Timothy   1 Thes 3:1-10
  through **OBEDIENCE**
    Jesus   1 Jn 2:1-6

through **SUFFERING**
  God   *2 Esd 16:51-78
in **VICTORY**
  Disciples   Jn 8:21-59
through **WISDOM**
  Holy Spirit   1 Cor 12:4-11
WITNESS to
  Onesimus   Col 4:7-9
  Paul   2 Thes 3:17-18
  Tychicus   Col 4:7-9

LEADERSHIP of
  through **AUTHORITY**
    Jesus   Mt 4:23-25;
        1 Cor 11:2-16
    Paul   Eph 1:1-2;
        Col 1:1-2
  by **ELECTION**
    Joshua   Deut 31:1-8
  EQUALITY in
    Jesus   Jn 13:1-20;
        15:18-25
    Paul   2 Cor 12:11-13
  FIDELITY of
    Holy Spirit   Gal 5:25-6:6
  KNOWLEDGE of
    Jesus   Jn 10:1-18
  concerning **LAW**
    Holy Spirit   Gal 5:16-21
  MOTIVATION for
    Paul   1 Cor 10:23-11:1
  PROMISE of
    Jesus   Mt 16:13-20
  PROVIDENCE through
    Israelites   Num 10:11-28;
        33-36
  RITE by
    Paul   Acts 14:19-28
  SIGNS of
    Ezekiel   Ezek 1:4-28
  TRUTH in
    Paul   1 Cor 4:14-21

LIFE of
  KNOWLEDGE of
    Jesus   2 Cor 4:7-12
  in **NEW AGE**
    Jesus   Jn 13:36-38
  PROMISE of
    God   Eph 6:1-4
  through **RECONCILIATION**
    Jesus   Rom 5:6-11;
        7:1-6;
        Eph 1:3-14
    Peter   1 Pet 1:13-2:3
  through **SALVATION**
    Jesus   2 Tim 2:8-13
  SECURITY in
    Holy Spirit   2 Cor 5:1-5

LOVE of
  Thessalonians   1 Thes 3:1-10
  BELIEF in
    Jesus   Jn 16:25-28;
        1 Jn 3:19-24
    Paul   Philm 1:4-7
  in **BROTHERHOOD**
    Colossians   Col 1:3-8
    God   1 Jn 3:4-10
    Thessalonians   2 Thes 1:3-4

PARADOX of
  in giving **RESPECT**
    John the Baptist   Mt 3:13-17
  SALVATION through
    Jesus   2 Tim 2:8-13

PATIENCE of
  Apostles   1 Cor 4:6-13
  in **BELIEF**
    Jesus   1 Tim 1:12-17
  PRAYER for
    Paul   Col 1:9-14
  as **QUALITY OF LIFE**
    Holy Spirit   Gal 5:22-24

PEACE for
  PRAYER for
    Paul   1 Cor 1:1-3; Gal 1:1-5; Eph 1:1-2; 1 Thes 1:1; 2 Thes 1:1-2; 3:16; 1 Tim 1:1-2; 2 Tim 1:1-2

PEACE of
  as **QUALITY OF LIFE**
    Holy Spirit   Gal 5:22-24
  through **RECONCILIATION**
    Jesus   Eph 2:11-22
  through **SALVATION**
    Women   1 Tim 2:8-15
  in **TRUTH**
    John   1 Jn 3:19-24

PRAISE by
  Blind   Lk 18:35-43
  Crowd   Jn 12:12-19
  Jesus   1 Pet 4:12-19
  ETERNAL
    Jesus   Heb 13:1-25
  FIDELITY of
    Timothy   1 Thes 3:1-10
  PRAYER of
    Paul   2 Thes 1:11-12

PRAISE of
  for **QUALITY OF LIFE**
    Demetrius   3 Jn 1:12
    John   3 Jn 1:3-8
  RECONCILIATION through
    Titus   2 Cor 7:13b-16
  in **RITE**
    King   Ps 45:1
  for **STEWARDSHIP**
    Paul   2 Cor 8:1-6

PRAYER by
  for **BLESSING**
    Paul   2 Cor 1:1-2; 2 Thes 2:16-17
  for **FAITH**
    Believers   Acts 2:42-47
    Paul   1 Thes 3:11-13
  for **FRIENDSHIP**
    Paul   1 Thes 3:1-10
  FULFILLMENT of
    John   1 Jn 3:19-24
    Paul   2 Thes 1:11-12
    Servant   Gen 24:11-27

  for **GRACE**
    Paul   1 Cor 16:13-24; Gal 1:1-5; Eph 1:1-2; Col 4:15-18; 1 Thes 1:1; 3:11-13; 5:25-28; 2 Thes 1:1-2; 11-12; 3:17-18; 1 Tim 1:1-2; 6:20-21; 2 Tim 1:1-2; 15-18; 4:19-22
  of **GRATITUDE**
    Paul   Col 1:3-8; 1 Thes 1:2-10; 2:13-16; 2 Thes 2:13-15; 2 Tim 1:3-7; Philm 1:4-7
  concerning **IGNORANCE**
    Believers   Rom 8:26-27
  for **LOVE**
    Paul   Phil 1:3-11; 1 Thes 3:11-13
  for **PATIENCE**
    Paul   Col 1:9-14
  for **PEACE**
    Paul   1 Cor 1:1-3; Gal 1:1-5; Eph 1:1-2; 1 Thes 1:1; 2 Thes 1:1-2; 3:16; 1 Tim 1:1-2; 2 Tim 1:1-2
  of **PRAISE**
    Paul   2 Thes 1:11-12
  for **SERVICE**
    Paul   Col 4:2-4
  for **WISDOM**
    Paul   Phil 1:3-11; Col 1:9-14
  for **WITNESS**
    Paul   Philm 1:4-7

PRIDE of
  BEHAVIOR revealing
    Thessalonians   1 Thes 2:17-20

PROMISE of
  through **FAITH**
    Holy Spirit   Gal 3:10-14
    Peter   Mt 26:31-35; Mk 14:27-31; Lk 22:33-34

PROMISE to
  for **FULFILLMENT**
    Holy Spirit   Eph 1:3-14
    Jesus   2 Cor 1:15-22
  for **LEADERSHIP**
    Jesus   Mt 16:13-20
  for **LIFE**
    God   Eph 6:1-4
  for **REWARD**
    Jesus   Mt 19:27-30; Mk 10:28-31; Lk 18:28-30

PROVIDENCE of
  through **COMPASSION**
    God   Ps 135:13-14
  through **LEADERSHIP**
    Israelites   Num 10:11-28;
                       33-36
  through **LOVE**
    God   Eph 1:3-14
  through **MIRACLE**
    Jesus   Lk 24:50-51
  through **SUFFERING**
    God   *Wis 16:15-29
  through **WISDOM**
    Holy Spirit   Mt 10:16-22;
                       Lk 12:1-12;
                       Jn 14:25-26;
                       1 Cor 2:1-5

PRUDENCE of
  Paul   Tit 3:1-7
  in **NEW AGE**
    Scribe   Mt 13:51-52
  in **STEWARDSHIP**
    Mary   Lk 10:38-42

PUNISHMENT of
  is **CAPTIVITY**
    Peter   Acts 12:1-25
  is **DEATH**
    Rulers   Acts 6:8-8:3
  FEAR of
    Magistrates   Acts 16:25-40
  is **OPPRESSION**
    Jews   Acts 13:14-52
    Paul   Acts 14:19-28
    Saul   Acts 6:8-8:3
  is **REJECTION**
    Jesus   Heb 10:19-31
  SADNESS in
    Jesus   Lk 23:27-32
  through **SUFFERING**
    Paul   Acts 14:19-28
  WITNESS to
    Women   Lk 23:46-49

PURIFICATION of
  Cornelius   Acts 10:1-11:18
  Holy Spirit   Acts 1:1-5
  Jesus   Mk 1:9-11;
                     Lk 3:21-22
  People   Acts 2:37-41
  BELIEF in
    Holy Spirit   2 Thes 2:13-15
  in **NEW AGE**
    Jesus   Gal 3:26-29
  through **RECONCILIATION**
    Jesus   Eph 5:21-33;
                     Tit 2:11-15
  RITE of
    Believers   Acts 8:4-13
    Corinthians   Acts 18:1-17
    Ephesians   Acts 19:1-12
    Jailer   Acts 16:25-40
    Lydia   Acts 16:11-15
    Saul   Acts 9:1-19
    Timothy   Acts 16:1-5

QUALITY OF LIFE of
  FAITH as
    Author   Heb 10:32-39

JOY as
  Holy Spirit   Gal 5:22-24
LOVE as
  Holy Spirit   Gal 5:22-24
OBEDIENCE as
  Disciples   Mk 14:12-16;
                     Lk 22:7-13
  Paul   Phil 3:17-21
ONENESS as
  Jesus   1 Cor 6:12-20
PATIENCE as
  Holy Spirit   Gal 5:22-24
PEACE as
  Holy Spirit   Gal 5:22-24
PRAISE as
  Demetrius   3 Jn 1:12
  John   3 Jn 1:3-8
SACREDNESS as
  Holy Spirit   1 Cor 3:10-17;
                     6:12-20
SERVICE as
  Holy Spirit   Gal 5:22-24
  Women   Mt 27:45-56
SPIRIT as
  Holy Spirit   Rom 12:9-13
SUFFERING as
  Jesus   1 Pet 2:21-25
  Peter   1 Pet 4:12-19;
                     5:6-11
TEMPERANCE as
  Holy Spirit   Gal 5:22-24
WITNESS as
  Demetrius   3 Jn 1:12

RECONCILIATION of
  through **DEATH**
    Jesus   Eph 2:11-22
  from **EVIL**
    Believers   Gal 5:25-6:6
  through **FAITH**
    Jesus   Gal 3:26-29
  as **FULFILLMENT**
    Holy Spirit   Eph 4:25-5:2
  in **LIFE**
    Jesus   Rom 5:6-11;
                     7:1-6;
                     Eph 1:3-14
    Peter   1 Pet 1:13-2:3
  through **LOVE**
    Jesus   Eph 5:21-33
    Woman   Lk 7:36-50
  through **OBEDIENCE**
    Jesus   Rom 5:12-21
  through **ONENESS** in
    Jesus   Eph 2:11-22
  PEACE in
    Jesus   Eph 2:11-22
  PRAISE of
    Titus   2 Cor 7:13b-16
  PURIFICATION through
    Jesus   Eph 5:21-33;
                     Tit 2:11-15
  SACREDNESS in
    Jesus   1 Cor 1:26-31
                     6:9-11;
                     Eph 5:21-33

REJECTION by
  Judas   Mt 26:47-56;
                     Mk 14:43-50;

SACREDNESS of	
Holy Spirit	Rom 15:14-24
SACRIFICE in	
Believers	Acts 2:42-47
Macedonians	2 Cor 8:1-6
in SERVICE	
Joseph	Mt 27:57-61;
	Mk 15:42-47;
	Lk 23:50-53
Macedonians	2 Cor 8:1-6
Paul	2 Cor 1:3-7
in SHARING	
Paul	1 Cor 9:7-14
WILL of	
Macedonians	2 Cor 8:1-6
WITNESS to	
Paul	1 Cor 1:1-3

SUFFERING of	
Apostles	1 Cor 4:6-13
COMMITMENT to	
Paul	2 Cor 1:3-7
through FIDELITY	
Author	Heb 10:32-39
KNOWLEDGE of	
God	*2 Esd 16:51-78
in PRESENCE	
Jesus	Heb 12:1-2
PROVIDENCE through	
God	*Wis 16:15-29
as PUNISHMENT	
Paul	Acts 14:19-28
as QUALITY OF LIFE	
Jesus	1 Pet 2:21-25
Peter	1 Pet 4:12-19;
	5:6-11
for TRUTH	
Paul	1 Cor 9:7-14

TEMPERANCE of	
as QUALITY OF LIFE	
Holy Spirit	Gal 5:22-24
SALVATION through	
Women	1 Tim 2:8-15

TEMPTATION of	
EQUALITY in	
Jesus	Heb 4:14-16

VICTORY of	
EQUALITY in	
Jesus	Lk 20:27-40
KNOWLEDGE of	
Disciples	Jn 8:21-59
MEDIATION for	
Jesus	Rom 8:28-39
SECURITY in	
Jesus	2 Cor 2:14-17

VIRTUE of	
God	1 Jn 3:4-10
COURAGE as	
Mankind	Ps 112:5-9
DISCIPLESHIP as	
Paul	2 Thes 1:11-12
FAITH as	
Abraham	Rom 3:31-4:25
GOOD as	
Believers	Tit 2:11-15
Noah	Gen 6:5-22

OBEDIENCE as	
Noah	Gen 7:1-24
REWARD for	
Mankind	Ps 112:5-9
WILL as	
Paul	Philm 1:8-14
WISDOM in	
Jesus	1 Cor 1:26-31

WEALTH of	
FREEDOM in	
Macedonians	2 Cor 8:1-6

WILL of	
MEDIATION with	
Holy Spirit	Rom 8:26-27
in STEWARDSHIP	
Macedonians	2 Cor 8:1-6
as VIRTUE	
Paul	Philm 1:8-14

WISDOM of	
as GIFT	
Holy Spirit	1 Cor 2:10-16;
	12:4-11
Unbelievers	1 Cor 14:13-25
in JUDGMENT	
Paul	1 Cor 4:6-13;
	6:1-8
KNOWLEDGE of	
Holy Spirit	1 Cor 12:4-11
MEDIATION through	
Holy Spirit	Rom 8:26-27
through PROVIDENCE	
Holy Spirit	Mt 10:16-22;
	Lk 12:1-12;
	Jn 14:25-26;
	1 Cor 2:1-5
through TRUTH	
Disciples	Mt 13:10-17;
	51-52
John	1 Jn 2:18-23
VIRTUE in	
Jesus	1 Cor 1:26-31

WITNESS of	
AUTHORITY of	
God	Ps 145:10-13a
Holy Spirit	1 Cor 2:1-5
Jesus	Mt 10:1
BELIEF in	
Jesus	1 Jn 5:8-12
Samaritan	Jn 4:1-26;
	27-42
COMMITMENT to	
John	Acts 4:1-22
Peter	Acts 4:1-22
FIDELITY in	
Jesus	Jn 15:26-27
Timothy	1 Cor 4:14-21
as GIFT	
Holy Spirit	1 Cor 12:4-11
KNOWLEDGE of	
Onesimus	Col 4:7-9
Paul	2 Thes 3:17-18
Tychicus	Col 4:7-9
to NEW AGE	
Stephen	Acts 6:8-8:3
PRAYER for	
Paul	Philm 1:4-7

FOLLOWER (cont'd)

in PRESENCE
  Holy Spirit   1 Jn 3:19-24
to PUNISHMENT
  Women   Lk 23:46-49
as QUALITY OF LIFE
  Demetrius   3 Jn 1:12
RESPECT for
  Mary   Mk 15:33-41
  Salome   Mk 15:33-41
to RESURRECTION
  Apostles   Acts 1:6-11
  Disciples   Jn 20:1-29
  Mary   Jn 20:1-29
  Matthias   Acts 1:12-26
  Thomas   Jn 20:1-29
to SALVATION
  Holy Spirit   Rom 8:14-25
to SIGNS
  Crowd   Jn 12:12-19
  Unbelievers   1 Cor 14:13-25
in STEWARDSHIP
  Paul   1 Cor 1:1-3
to TRUTH
  Barnabas   Acts 9:20-31
  Holy Spirit   Rom 9:1-5;
                     1 Cor 2:10-16
  Jesus   Jn 15:26-27
  John   Jn 21:24-25

YOUTH of
  JUDGMENT on
    Corinthians   1 Cor 3:1-4

FREEDOM

from ANXIETY
  INSTRUCTION on
    Paul   1 Cor 7:25-35

BLESSING in
  REVELATION of
    Moses   Ex 11:1-10

from CAPTIVITY
  Ezra   Ezra 7:6-10
  Israelites   Ezra 2:1-2a
  Jeremiah   Jer 40:1-6
  Johanan   Jer 41:11-18
  through COVENANT
    Zechariah   Zech 9:1-12
    Zedekiah   Jer 34:8-12

  through DEITY
    God   Ps 146:7c-9
    Israelites   Jer 11:1-14;
                     Hos 12:10-14;
                     Amos 2:9-12
    Jonah   Jon 2:1-10
    Prophet   Hos 12:10-14
    Solomon   1 Kgs 8:22-53;
                     2 Chr 5:1-7:10
  in ENVIRONMENT
    Pharaoh   Ex 12:29-32
    Samson   Judg 15:9-20
    Timothy   *2 Mc 12:24-25
  FALSE BELIEF concerning
    Hananiah   Jer 28:1-17
    Israelites   Ex 32:1-6;
                     7-14

FREEDOM (cont'd)

INSTRUCTION on
  Artaxerxes   *1 Esd 8:8-24
  Cyrus   *1 Esd 2:1-7
  Isaiah   Is 51:17-52:12
  Moses   Deut 15:12-18;
                     21:10-14
MISSION to bring
  Jesus   Lk 4:16-30
PROPHECY of
  Israelites   Is 14:1-23
  Jacobites   Mic 5:7-15
  Jeremiah   *Jer 6:2-3
  Obadiah   Obad 1:17-21
REVELATION on
  Israelites   Ex 5:22-6:1;
                     Ezek 34:25-31;
                     Joel 3:4-8;
                     Amos 9:7;
                     Mic 6:1-5
  John   Rev 9:13-21
  Moses   Ex 3:7-10;
                     11-22
  Satan   Rev 20:7-10
TRADITION of
  Israelites   *1 Esd 5:9-23;
                     36-43;
                     8:28-40
  Judahites   *1 Esd 5:7-8
  Levites   *1 Esd 5:26-28
  Priests   *1 Esd 5:4-6;
                     24-25
  Servants   *1 Esd 5:29-35
  Solomon   *Wis 19:1-12

through COMPASSION
  Evilmerodach   2 Kgs 25:27-30

COVENANT of
  DISOBEDIENCE to
    People   Jer 34:8-12
  FULFILLMENT of
    Paul   Gal 4:21-26
  REJECTION of
    People   Jer 34:13-22
  WITNESS to
    God   Is 42:5-17

through COVENANT
  from CAPTIVITY
    Zechariah   Zech 9:1-12
    Zedekiah   Jer 34:8-12

through DEATH
  INSTRUCTION on
    Paul   1 Cor 7:39-40

through DEITY
  from CAPTIVITY
    God   Ps 146:7c-9
    Israelites   Jer 11:1-14;
                     Hos 12:10-14;
                     Amos 2:9-12
    Jonah   Jon 2:1-10
    Prophet   Hos 12:10-14
    Solomon   1 Kgs 8:22-53;
                     2 Chr 5:1-7:10
  MIRACLE of
    Israelites   Jer 32:16-25
  VICTORY of
    Israelites   2 Kgs 13:1-9

LIFE of

Jehoiachin	Jer 52:31-34
INSTRUCTION on	
Paul	1 Cor 7:17-24;
	Gal 4:27-31

in MARRIAGE

INSTRUCTION on	
Jesus	Mt 5:31-32;
	19:3-9;
	Mk 10:1-12
Moses	Deut 23:15-25:19
Paul	1 Cor 7:8-16;
	25-35;
	39-40

through MESSIANIC FIGURE

FEAR	
Jesus	Heb 2:5-18
WITNESS to	
Isaiah	Is 61:1-11

through MIRACLE

by DEITY	
Israelites	Jer 32:16-25
INSTRUCTION on	
Peter	Acts 12:1-25
REVELATION on	
Peter	Acts 12:1-25

in MISSION

from CAPTIVITY	
Jesus	Lk 4:16-30

of MISSION

REWARD is	
Paul	1 Cor 9:15-23

through OBEDIENCE

to DEITY	
Psalmist	Ps 119:41-48
INSTRUCTION on	
God	Ex 6:10-13
Paul	Rom 6:15-23
PROPHECY of	
Israelites	2 Chr 26:1-28:27
Judahites	Jer 7:1-15

from OPPRESSION

in ENVIRONMENT	
Paul	Gal 4:1-3
INSTRUCTION on	
Manoah	Judg 13:2-7
Solomon	Prov 6:1-5
REVELATION on	
Israelites	Ezek 45:1-9
Manoah	Judg 13:2-7
Zechariah	Zech 1:18-21

through PEACE

PROPHECY of	
Judahites	Jer 42:7-22

from POLITICS

Edomites	2 Kgs 8:16-24
in ENVIRONMENT	
Benjaminites	Judg 21:16-25
Israelites	Judg 17:1-6

PROPHECY of

PROPHECY of (cont'd)

from CAPTIVITY	
Israelites	Is 14:1-23
Jacobites	Mic 5:7-15
Jeremiah	*Jer 6:2-3
Obadiah	Obad 1:17-21
through GRACE	
Obed	2 Chr 26:1-28:27
through OBEDIENCE	
Israelites	2 Chr 26:1-28:27
Judahites	Jer 7:1-15
through PEACE	
Judahites	Jer 42:7-22

through PRUDENCE

INSTRUCTION on	
Gamaliel	Acts 5:17-42
Peter	1 Pet 2:13-17

through REJECTION

by FOLLOWERs	
Satan	Jas 4:1-10

REVELATION on

from CAPTIVITY	
Israelites	Ex 5:22-6:1;
	Ezek 34:25-31;
	Joel 3:4-8;
	Amos 9:7;
	Mic 6:1-5
John	Rev 9:13-21
Moses	Ex 3:7-10;
	11-22
Satan	Rev 20:7-10
from EVIL	
Ezekiel	Ezek 13:17-23
through LEADERSHIP	
Cyrus	Is 44:24-45:13
through MIRACLE	
Peter	Acts 12:1-25
from OPPRESSION	
Israelites	Ezek 45:1-9
Manoah	Judg 13:2-7
Zechariah	Zech 1:18-21
to WITNESS	
Apostles	Acts 5:17-42

REWARDs of

INSTRUCTION on	
Moses	Deut 15:12-18
in MISSION	
Paul	1 Cor 9:15-23

SACREDNESS of

PROPHECY of	
Jeremiah	2 Chr 36:1-23

in SERVICE

of FOLLOWERs	
Paul	Gal 5:13-15

of SPIRIT

INSTRUCTION on	
Paul	Rom 8:1-4;
	Gal 4:1-3

from TEMPTATION

INSTRUCTION on	
Paul	1 Cor 8:7-13

TRADITION of
    from **CAPTIVITY**

Israelites	*1 Esd 5:9-23; 36-43; 8:28-40
Judahites	*1 Esd 5:7-8
Levites	*1 Esd 5:26-28
Priests	*1 Esd 5:4-6; 24-25
Servants	*1 Esd 5:29-35
Solomon	*Wis 19:1-12

    through **GRACE**

Barabbas	Mt 27:11-26; Mk 15:6-15
Pilate	Mt 27:11-26; Mk 15:6-15

through **VICTORY**
    provided by **DEITY**

Israelites	2 Kgs 13:1-9

    in **ENVIRONMENT**

Lot	Gen 14:1-16

WEALTH in
    of **FOLLOWERs**

Macedonians	2 Cor 8:1-6

of **WILL**
    INSTRUCTION on

Artaxerxes	Ezra 7:13-14
Joshua	Josh 24:14-15
Moses	Deut 30:15-20

to **WITNESS**
    INSTRUCTION on

Apostles	Acts 5:17-42
Paul	Gal 1:18-2:10

    to **MESSIANIC FIGURE**

Isaiah	Is 61:1-11

    REVELATION on

Apostles	Acts 5:17-42

FRIENDSHIP

with **AUTHORITY**
    TRADITION of

Daniel	*Bel 1:1-2

BEHAVIOR concerning
    in **ENVIRONMENT**

Maccabeus	*2 Mc 14:18-25

    INSTRUCTION on

Paul	2 Cor 6:14-7:1; Col 4:15-18
Sirach	*Sir 12:8-18
Solomon	Prov 25:1-28

in **BROTHERHOOD**
    INSTRUCTION on

Paul	Rom 16:1-23

CONFRONTATION with

Micah	Judg 17:7-13

COVENANT of

Jonathan	1 Sam 17:1-18:5; 23:14-24:22

    disHONESTY in

David	Ps 55:20-21

DESIRE for
    in **MISSION**

Paul	1 Thes 2:17-20

ELECTION of
    INSTRUCTION on

Jesus	Jn 15:12-17

in **ENVIRONMENT**
    PROMISE of

Jonathan	*1 Mc 10:15-44

    through **PROVIDENCE**

God	Gen 2:18-20

    RECONCILIATION through

Naomi	Ruth 1:19-22

ETERNAL
    INSTRUCTION on

Jesus	Lk 16:1-9

FALSE BELIEF through
    causes in**FIDELITY**

Paul	2 Tim 4:9-18

FIDELITY in

Job	Job 6:21-27

    of **FOLLOWERs**

Galatians	Gal 4:12-20

    INSTRUCTION on

Paul	2 Tim 4:19-22
Sirach	*Sir 6:2-17; 9:10; 19:4-12; 22:19-26; 27:16-21; 37:1-6
Solomon	Prov 18:1-24; 27:1-27

    MEDITATION on

Job	Job 6:14-20

in**FIDELITY** to
    through **FALSE BELIEF**

Paul	2 Tim 4:9-18

of **FOLLOWERs**
    FIDELITY in

Galatians	Gal 4:12-20

    PRAYER for

Paul	1 Thes 3:1-10

disHONESTY in
    in **ENVIRONMENT**

Simon	*1 Mc 16:11-17

    INSTRUCTION on
        in **BROTHERHOOD**

Paul	Rom 16:1-23

JUDGMENT on
    INSTRUCTION on

James	Jas 4:11-12

in **MISSION**
    DESIRE for

Paul	1 Thes 2:17-20

PRAYER for
    of **FOLLOWERs**

Paul	1 Thes 3:1-10

PROMISE of
  in **COVENANT**
    Jonathan   1 Sam 17:1-18:5;
                   23:14-24:22
  in **ENVIRONMENT**
    Jonathan   *1 Mc 10:15-44

PROVIDENCE through
  in **ENVIRONMENT**
    God   Gen 2:18-20

RECONCILIATION through
  in **ENVIRONMENT**
    Naomi   Ruth 1:19-22

RESPECT for
    Mankind   Ps 15:1-5b
  MEDITATION on
    David   Ps 38:11-16

SALVATION through
  INSTRUCTION on
    Jesus   Lk 16:1-9

SECURITY in
    Jonathan   1 Sam 19:1-10;
                   20:1-42

SIN destroys
  MEDITATION on
    David   Ps 55:12-14

STEWARDSHIP of
  INSTRUCTION on
    Jesus   Lk 10:29-37

TRADITION of
  with **AUTHORITY**
    Daniel   *Bel 1:1-2

TRUTH in
  INSTRUCTION on
    Sirach   *Sir 19:13-17

FULFILLMENT

of the **AUTHORITY**
  of **DEITY**
    Believers   Eph 3:20-21
    God   Num 11:14-24a;
                 Is 14:24-27;
                 50:1-11
    Jesus   Jn 3:31-36
  of **MESSIANIC FIGURE**
    God   Rev 12:10-12
  PROPHECY of
    Elisha   2 Kgs 8:7-15
    Jehu   2 Kgs 15:8-12
  REVELATION on
    Jesus   Lk 21:25-28

BEHAVIOR revealing
  of **MISSION**
    Jesus   Eph 4:7-16
  of **PROPHECY**
    Isaiah   Is 37:36-38;
                 Mt 4:12-16;
                 12:15-21

of **PROPHECY** (cont'd)
    Jeremiah   Mt 2:16-18;
                 27:3-10
    Jesus   Mt 8:14-17;
                 Lk 18:31-34;
                 Jn 12:12-19;
                 Acts 3:1-26
    Jonah   2 Kgs 14:23-29
  of **REVELATION**
    Ezekiel   Ezek 24:15-24
    Joseph   Gen 42:7-17
  SCRIPTURES on
    Isaiah   Jn 12:36b-43
    Jesus   Jn 19:17-42
    Judas   Jn 13:1-20

of **BELIEF**
  INSTRUCTION on
    Jesus   Jn 6:25-59

of un**BELIEF**
  PROPHECY of
    Isaiah   Mt 15:3-9;
                 Mk 7:1-23
    Mary   Lk 1:39-56

of **COMMITMENT**
    Jephthah   Judg 11:34-40
  to **DEITY**
    Believers   Prov 16:1-33
    Egyptians   Is 19:18-25
    Hannah   1 Sam 1:1-28
  INSTRUCTION on
    David   1 Kgs 1:28-40
  REVELATION on
    Isaiah   Is 55:1-13

COMPULSION for
  of **MISSION**
    Ezekiel   Ezek 3:12-15
  SCRIPTURES on
    Judas   Acts 1:12-26

of **COVENANT**
  with **COMMUNITY**
    Israelites   Josh 22:1-8
  ETERNAL
    God   Ps 111:5-9
    Israelites   Ezek 16:53-63
  of **FREEDOM**
    Paul   Gal 4:21-26
  of **NEW AGE**
    Jesus   2 Cor 3:12-18;
                 Heb 8:6-13

  PRAYER for
    Asaph   Ps 74:18-23
  PROMISE in
    Abraham   Gal 3:15-18;
                 Heb 6:13-20
    God   Ex 6:2-9;
                 Lev 26:1-46;
                 Deut 4:15-31;
                 Ps 89:19-37
    Israelites   Deut 7:6-16
    Jeremiah   Jer 33:14-26
    Jesus   Gal 3:26-29
    Solomon   1 Kgs 8:22-53
  through **RECONCILIATION**
    Jesus   Heb 9:15-22
  SECURITY in
    God   2 Chr 21:1-23:2

SIGNS of	
Abraham	Gen 21:1-7
of **CREATION**	
God	Gen 2:1-4a
Israelites	Neh 6:15-16
Solomon	2 Chr 8:1-18
by **DEITY**	
God	Jn 1:1-18;
	Rev 21:1-8
Jesus	Jn 1:1-18
INSTRUCTION on	
Israelites	Ex 39:32-43
PROPHECY of	
Jesus	Lk 2:1-20
Prophet	Mt 1:18-25
Samson	Judg 13:24-25
REVELATION on	
Zerubbabel	Zech 4:6b-10a
of **SANCTUARY**	
Israelites	Ezra 6:13-18
by **DEITY**	
DESIRE for	
Believers	Ps 145:13b-20
Daniel	Dan 9:4-19
David	Ps 4:1;
	20:1-5;
	39:7-13;
	54:1-2;
	55:1-3a;
	61:1-3;
	69:13-21;
	86:1-7;
	108:6-13;
	109:1-5;
	21-31;
	140:6-8;
	141:1-2;
	142:5-7;
	143:1-2;
	7-12
God	1 Chr 28:1-29:30;
	Ps 37:1-11;
	Jer 29:1-23
Holy Spirit	Lk 11:9-13
King	Ps 21:1-7
Psalmist	Ps 84:8-9;
	88:1-2;
	102:1-11;
	119:145-152;
	130:1-2
of **ELECTION**	
God	Is 44:24-45:13
HONESTY of	
Balaam	Num 23:13-26
God	1 Sam 15:1-35;
	Is 55:1-13;
	Tit 1:1-4
KNOWLEDGE of	
Egyptians	Ex 7:1-7
of **LAW**	
Israelites	*2 Esd 2:33-41;
	*Bar 2:1-10
of **NEW AGE**	
God	Mt 24:34-36
of **PRAYER**	
Believers	Ps 34:15-22;
	145:13b-20
Daniel	Dan 2:20-23

of **PRAYER** (cont'd)	
David	2 Sam 22:1-51;
	Ps 3:3-6;
	5:1-3;
	13:1-4;
	17:1-2;
	6-7;
	18:1-3;
	4-6;
	20:6-9;
	22:1-5;
	25:16-21;
	28:1-5;
	6-7;
	30:1-5;
	31:1-8;
	19-24;
	34:4-10;
	40:1-3;
	61:4-5;
	138:1-3
Elijah	1 Kgs 17:1-24
Elisha	2 Kgs 6:8-23
Ezekiel	Ezek 4:12-15
God	Ps 99:6-9;
	Prov 2:1-22
Hannah	1 Sam 1:1-28
Hezekiah	2 Chr 30:1-31:21;
	32:1-33;
	Is 38:1-22
Isaac	Gen 25:19-26
Israelites	Neh 9:26-31;
	Ps 78:21-31;
	107:4-9;
	10-16
Jabez	1 Chr 4:1-23
Jehoahaz	2 Kgs 13:1-9
Job	Job 42:7-9
Jonah	Jon 2:1-10
Manasseh	2 Chr 33:1-25
Manoah	Judg 13:9-14
Moses	Num 14:11-24
People	Ps 107:17-22;
	23-32
Prophet	1 Kgs 13:1-34
Psalmist	Ps 10:12-18;
	66:13-20;
	102:12-22;
	116:1-11;
	118:5-9;
	15-21
Sarah	*Tb 3:16-17
Sirach	*Sir 51:1-12
Solomon	1 Kgs 8:22-53;
	*Wis 7:7-14
Susanna	*Susa 1:42-51
Tobiah	*Tb 3:16-17
through **PRESENCE**	
David	Ps 17:15;
	51:3-12
God	Num 14:11-24;
	Is 6:1-13
Jesus	Col 2:6-15
Nehemiah	Neh 1:11b-2:8
PROMISE of	
Abraham	Gen 21:1-7
Believer	Eccl 5:1-7;
	Heb 11:1-40
Egyptians	Ezek 30:10-12
Ezekiel	Ezek 28:1-10

PROMISE of (cont'd)
Ezra	Neh 9:7-8
God	Ps 12:5-6;
	18:25-30;
	Is 14:24-27;
	45:14-25;
	46:1-13;
	Jer 4:27-29;
	2 Pet 3:8-10
Hagar	Gen 16:11-16
Israelites	Josh 21:8-45;
	Neh 9:22-25;
	Ps 105:37-42;
	Ezek 37:1-14
Jesus	Rom 15:1-13
Joshua	Josh 23:1-16
Moses	Ex 4:27-31;
	23:20-33;
	Deut 23:15-25:19
Solomon	1 Kgs 8:54-61

of **SALVATION**
Believers	Ps 91:14-16
God	Is 46:1-13;
	Hab 3:3-15
Holy Spirit	Tit 3:1-7
Israelites	Ps 77:11-20;
	Is 31:4-9
Jesus	Eph 1:15-2:10;
	2 Tim 1:8-14
Paul	2 Tim 4:9-18

SECURITY in
Believers	Heb 6:13-20
David	Ps 38:11-16
Israelites	Is 31:4-9

of **TRUTH**
Agur	Prov 30:1-14

DESIRE for
Ahab	1 Kgs 21:13-16
Esther	Esth 9:11-15
Maiden	Song 3:1-5
Nehemiah	Neh 1:11b-2:8
Preacher	Eccl 1:12-2:26

by **DEITY**
Asa	2 Chr 14:1-16:14
Believers	Ps 145:13b-20
Daniel	Dan 9:4-19
David	Ps 4:1;
	20:1-5;
	39:7-13;
	54:1-2;
	55:1-3a;
	61:1-3;
	69:13-21;
	86:1-7;
	108:6-13;
	109:1-5;
	21-31;
	140:6-8;
	141:1-2;
	142:5-7;
	143:1-2;
	7-12
God	1 Chr 28:1-29:30;
	Ps 37:1-11;
	Jer 29:1-23
Holy Spirit	Lk 11:9-13
King	Ps 21:1-7
Psalmist	Ps 84:8-9;
	88:1-2;

by **DEITY** (cont'd)
Psalmist	102:1-11;
	119:145-152;
	130:1-2

in **ENVIRONMENT**
Young Man	Song 5:1
Zerubbabel	*1 Esd 4:42-57

INSTRUCTION on
Solomon	Prov 2:1-22;
	13:1-25

by **MESSIANIC FIGURE**
Jesus	Mt 14:13-21;
	15:32-39;
	Mk 6:30-44;
	8:1-10;
	Lk 9:12-17;
	Jn 6:1-15
John the Baptist	Mt 11:2-6;
	Lk 7:18-23
Queen of Sheba	1 Kgs 10:1-13;
	2 Chr 9:1-31

REVELATION on
Solomon	1 Kgs 3:1-15

in **WORSHIP**
David	Ps 28:1-5
Ezra	*1 Esd 8:41-44

of **ELECTION**
　by **DEITY**
God	Is 44:24-45:13

　INSTRUCTION on
Paul	1 Cor 7:17-24

　by **MESSIANIC FIGURE**
Jesus	1 Pet 1:13-2:3

　PROPHECY of
Jesus	Lk 4:16-30
John the Baptist	Lk 1:57-80

　SCRIPTURES on
Jesus	Lk 4:16-30;
	Jn 13:1-20

ETERNAL
　by **DEITY**
God	Jn 1:1-18
Jesus	Jn 1:1-18

　PROPHECY of
Jeremiah	Jer 31:38-40

　REVELATION on
Isaiah	Is 51:1-16

through **FIDELITY**
　of **DEITY**
God	Heb 10:19-31

　INSTRUCTION on
Peter	2 Pet 1:8-11

　in **MISSION**
Jesus	Jn 10:1-18

　PROPHECY of
Peter	Mt 26:69-75;
	Mk 14:66-72;
	Lk 22:54b-62;
	Jn 18:12-17

　REVELATION on
Zechariah	Zech 6:9-15

　SCRIPTURES on
Jesus	Mt 26:31-35;
	Mk 14:27-31

of FREEDOM
  in COVENANT
    Paul   Gal 4:21-26

GIFT of
  by FOLLOWERs
    Holy Spirit   Acts 8:14-25;
                          10:1-11:18;
                          19:1-12

  INSTRUCTION on
    Jesus   Lk 12:47-48
  PROPHECY of
    Joel   Acts 2:14-36

through HONESTY
  of DEITY
    Balaam   Num 23:13-26
    God   1 Sam 15:1-35;
                          Is 55:1-13;
                          Tit 1:1-4

INSTRUCTION on
  of BELIEF
    Jesus   Jn 6:25-59
  of COMMITMENT
    David   1 Kgs 1:28-40
  of CREATION
    Israelites   Ex 39:32-43
  of ELECTION
    Paul   1 Cor 7:17-24
  through FIDELITY
    Peter   2 Pet 1:8-11
  as GIFT
    Jesus   Lk 12:47-48
  of JUDGMENT
    Jesus   Lk 6:24-26
    John   Rev 14:6-7
  of KNOWLEDGE
    Holy Spirit   Jn 14:25-26
  of LAW
    Angel   *2 Esd 7:19-32
    Jesus   Mt 5:17-20;
                          Lk 16:16-18
    Moses   Deut 4:44-49
    Paul   Rom 8:1-4;
                          13:8-10

  of NEW AGE
    Author   Heb 12:12-29
    Jesus   Mt 10:23;
                          13:31-33;
                          47-50;
                          22:1-14;
                          25:31-46;
                          26:17-30;
                          Mk 4:26-29;
                          30-32;
                          10:23-27;
                          Lk 12:49-50;
                          13:18-19;
                          20-21;
                          16:16-18;
                          17:20-21;
                          Jn 12:20-26
    Paul   Acts 17:1-9;
                          Rom 13:11-14;
                          1 Cor 15:20-28;
                          42-50;
                          51-58;
                          2 Cor 5:20-6:2;
                          Eph 1:15-2:10;
                          1 Thes 5:1-11

of PRAYER
    Eliphaz   Job 22:21-30
    James   Jas 1:5-8;
                          5:14-18
    Jesus   Mt 6:9-13;
                          7:7-11;
                          18:18-20;
                          21:18-22;
                          Mk 11:20-26;
                          Lk 11:9-13;
                          18:1-8;
                          Jn 14:1-14;
                          15:1-11;
                          12-17;
                          16:16-24
    John   1 Jn 5:13-21

of PROMISE
    God   Num 30:1-16
    Jesus   Mt 5:3-12;
                          33-37;
                          10:23;
                          16:13-20;
                          18:18-20;
                          Lk 6:20-23
    Paul   Acts 13:14-52
    Sirach   *Sir 18:19-26
  through PROVIDENCE
    Jesus   Mt 13:31-33;
                          Mk 4:30-32;
                          Lk 13:18-19;
                          20-21
  as QUALITY OF LIFE
    Paul   1 Cor 7:17-24;
                          25-35
  of the RESURRECTION
    Men   Lk 24:1-12
    Paul   1 Cor 15:12-19;
                          20-28
    Peter   Acts 2:14-36
  of RITE
    Jacob   Gen 50:1-21
    Moses   Lev 8:1-36
  of SALVATION
    Jesus   Acts 13:14-52
    John the Baptist   Acts 13:14-52
    Paul   Rom 13:11-14;
                          Phil 1:12-30;
                          Col 1:9-14
    Peter   Acts 4:1-22
  through STEWARDSHIP
    Jesus   Lk 17:7-10
    Moses   Ex 40:1-33
    Paul   Col 4:15-18
  of TRUTH
    Holy Spirit   Jn 16:12-15

of JUDGMENT
  INSTRUCTION on
    Jesus   Lk 6:24-26
    John   Rev 14:6-7
  as PROPHESIED
    God   1 Sam 4:1b-22
  REVELATION on
    Jeremiah   Jer 25:30-38
  SCRIPTURES on
    People   Acts 13:14-52

KNOWLEDGE of
  through DEITY
    Egyptians   Ex 7:1-7

by **FOLLOWER**s
Holy Spirit	Eph 1:3-14

INSTRUCTION on
Author	Heb 12:12-29
Jesus	Mt 10:23;
	13:31-33;
	47-50;
	22:1-14;
	25:31-46;
	26:17-30;
	Mk 4:26-29;
	30-32;
	10:23-27;
	Lk 12:49-50;
	13:18-19;
	20-21;
	16:16-18;
	17:20-21;
	Jn 12:20-26
Paul	Acts 17:1-9;
	Rom 13:11-14;
	1 Cor 15:20-28;
	42-50;
	51-58;
	2 Cor 5:20-6:2;
	Eph 1:15-2:10;
	1 Thes 5:1-11

MEDITATION on
Paul	Phil 1:3-11

by **MESSIANIC FIGURE**
Angel	*2 Esd 7:19-32
Jesus	Lk 13:34-35;
	Jn 20:1-29;
	Acts 1:6-11

MISSION of
Jesus	Lk 13:31-33

PROPHECY of
Angel	*2 Esd 7:19-32
Angels	Lk 2:1-20
Isaiah	Is 11:1-9;
	24:18c-23;
	32:15-20;
	33:17-24;
	51:17-52:12;
	60:1-22
Jesus	Mt 16:21-28;
	24:1-3;
	4-8;
	9-14;
	15-22;
	23-28;
	29-31;
	32-33;
	34-36;
	37-41;
	42-44;
	Mk 1:14-15;
	8:34-9:1;
	13:3-8;
	9-13;
	14-23;
	24-27;
	28-37;
	14:22-26;
	Lk 9:23-27;
	21:7-19;
	20-24;
	25-28;

PROPHECY of (cont'd)
Jesus	29-31;
	32-33;
	22:14-23;
	Jn 16:16-24
Joel	Joel 1:2-20
Zechariah	Zech 14:1-21
Zephaniah	Zeph 1:7

REVELATION on
Angels	Lk 2:1-20
Daniel	Dan 9:24-27;
	11:21-45;
	12:1-4;
	5-13
Isaiah	Is 66:17-24
Joel	Joel 2:30-32
John	Rev 11:15-19;
	14:14-16;
	17-20;
	21:1-8;
	9-14;
	22:6-21

SCRIPTURES on
Jesus	Lk 21:20-24

PRAYER concerning
through **DEITY**
Believers	Ps 34:15-22;
	145:13b-20
Daniel	Dan 2:20-23
David	2 Sam 22:1-51;
	Ps 3:3-6;
	5:1-3;
	13:1-4;
	17:1-2;
	6-7;
	18:1-3;
	4-6;
	20:6-9;
	22:1-5;
	25:16-21;
	28:1-5;
	6-7;
	30:1-5;
	31:1-8;
	19-24;
	34:4-10;
	40:1-3;
	61:4-5;
	138:1-3
Elijah	1 Kgs 17:1-24
Elisha	2 Kgs 6:8-23
Ezekiel	Ezek 4:12-15
God	Ps 99:6-9;
	Prov 2:1-22
Hannah	1 Sam 1:1-28
Hezekiah	2 Chr 30:1-31:21;
	32:1-33;
	Is 38:1-22
Isaac	Gen 25:19-26
Israelites	Neh 9:26-31;
	Ps 78:21-31;
	107:4-9;
	10-16
Jabez	1 Chr 4:1-23
Jehoahaz	2 Kgs 13:1-9
Job	Job 42:7-9
Jonah	Jon 2:1-10
Manasseh	2 Chr 33:1-25
Manoah	Judg 13:9-14

of **LAW**
Jesus	Lk 24:44-49; Jn 18:28-19:16

through **PRESENCE**
Saul	1 Sam 9:1-10:16

of **PROMISE**
Belshazzar	Dan 5:30-31
Holy Spirit	Acts 2:1-13
Isaiah	Is 21:1-10
Tyre	Ezek 26:7-14

through **PROVIDENCE**
Babylonians	Jer 51:1-64
Elijah	1 Kgs 18:1-46
Elisha	2 Kgs 7:3-20
Isaiah	Is 9:2-7
Israelites	Ezra 6:13-18
Jahaziel	2 Chr 17:1-20:37
Jeremiah	Ezra 1:1
Prophet	Mt 2:13-15

of **PUNISHMENT**
Ahijah	1 Kgs 14:1-18; 15:25-32
Elijah	2 Kgs 1:1-18; 9:30-37; 10:1-14
God	1 Kgs 2:26-27
Israelites	Num 26:63-65
Jehoram	2 Chr 21:1-23:21
Jehu	1 Kgs 16:8-14; 2 Kgs 9:14-29
Jeremiah	2 Chr 36:1-23; Jer 28:1-17; *Sir 49:4-7
Joshua	1 Kgs 16:29-34
Josiah	2 Kgs 23:16-20
Judahites	2 Kgs 23:36-24:7
Paul	Acts 13:4-12
Tobiah	*Tb 14:1-15

through **RECONCILIATION**
Israelites	Mic 4:9-5:6
Jeremiah	Jer 31:38-40

through **RESURRECTION**
Jesus	Mt 28:1-8

through **RITE**
Jesus	Mt 26:17-30

through **STEWARDSHIP**
Isaiah	Is 52:13-53:12

of **TRUTH**
Jeremiah	Jer 44:20-28

through **PROVIDENCE**
of **DEITY**
David	Ps 22:22-26; 23:1-4
Ezra	Ezra 7:6-10
God	Prov 16:1-33
Paul	Phil 4:10-20
Rehoboam	1 Kgs 12:1-20; 2 Chr 10:1-12:16

in **ENVIRONMENT**
God	Mt 6:25-34
Joseph	Mt 2:19-23

INSTRUCTION on
Jesus	Mt 13:31-33; Mk 4:30-32; Lk 13:18-19; 20-21

MEDITATION on
David	Ps 143:5-6
Jeremiah	Lam 2:1-22

PROPHECY of
Babylonians	Jer 51:1-64
Elijah	1 Kgs 18:1-46
Elisha	2 Kgs 7:3-20
Isaiah	Is 9:2-7
Israelites	Ezra 6:13-18
Jahaziel	2 Chr 17:1-20:37
Jeremiah	Ezra 1:1
Prophet	Mt 2:13-15

REVELATION on
Isaiah	Is 55:1-13
Israelites	Is 49:1-26
Jeremiah	Jer 1:11-12; 31:7-14
Jesus	Jn 12:20-26

of **PUNISHMENT**
Gideon	Judg 8:13-17

by **DEITY**
God	Rev 15:1-16:1

as **PROPHESIED**
Ahijah	1 Kgs 14:1-18; 15:25-32
Elijah	2 Kgs 1:1-18; 9:30-37; 10:1-14
God	1 Kgs 2:26-27
Israelites	Num 26:63-65
Jehoram	2 Chr 21:1-23:21
Jehu	1 Kgs 16:8-14; 2 Kgs 9:14-29
Jeremiah	2 Chr 36:1-23; Jer 28:1-17; *Sir 49:4-7
Joshua	1 Kgs 16:29-34
Josiah	2 Kgs 23:16-20
Judahites	2 Kgs 23:36-24:7
Paul	Acts 13:4-12
Tobiah	*Tb 14:1-15

REVELATION on
Ezekiel	Ezek 12:21-28; 33:21-22
Israelites	Ezek 6:8-10
Nebuchadnezzar	Dan 4:28-33

as **QUALITY OF LIFE**
INSTRUCTION on
Paul	1 Cor 7:17-24; 25-35

through **RECONCILIATION**
of **FOLLOWERs**
Holy Spirit	Eph 4:25-5:2

INSTRUCTION on
Jesus	Heb 10:1-18

PROPHECY of
Israelites	Mic 4:9-5:6
Jeremiah	Jer 31:38-40

REVELATION on
Jeremiah	Jer 31:23-26

SCRIPTURES on
Jesus	1 Cor 15:1-11

through **RESPECT**
for **DEITY**
Believers	Ps 145:13b-20

for **MESSIANIC FIGURE**
Jesus	Heb 1:5-14

of the **RESURRECTION**
  as **PROPHESIED**
    Jesus   Mt 28:1-8

through the **RESURRECTION**
  INSTRUCTION on
    Men   Lk 24:1-12
    Paul   1 Cor 15:12-19;
                  20-28
    Peter   Acts 2:14-36
  of **MESSIANIC FIGURE**
    Jesus   Jn 20:1-29
  SCRIPTURES concerning
    David   Acts 2:14-36

of **REVELATION**
  of **CONFRONTATION**
    Joshua   Josh 8:1-29
  of **SALVATION**
    God   Rev 12:10-12
    Isaiah   Is 51:1-16
    Israelites   Is 49:1-26
    John   Rev 7:1-8
  of **TRUTH**
    Ezekiel   Ezek 12:21-28

REVELATION on
  Ezekiel   Ezek 24:15-24
  Joseph   Gen 42:7-17
  by **AUTHORITY**
    Jesus   Lk 21:25-28
  of **COMMITMENT**
    Isaiah   Is 55:1-13
  of **CREATION**
    Zerubbabel Zech 4:6b-10a
  ETERNAL
    Isaiah   Is 51:1-16
  through **FIDELITY**
    Zechariah   Zech 6:9-15
  of **JUDGMENT**
    Jeremiah   Jer 25:30-38
  of **LAW**
    Jesus   Gal 4:4-7
  of **NEW AGE**
    Angels   Lk 2:1-20
    Daniel   Dan 9:24-27;
                  11:21-45;
                  12:1-4;
                  5-13
    Isaiah   Is 66:17-24
    Joel   Joel 2:30-32
    John   Rev 11:15-19;
                  14:14-16;
                  17-20;
                  21:1-8;
                  9-14;
                  22:6-21
  through **PRAYER**
    Daniel   Dan 10:10-21
    David   2 Sam 5:17-25;
                  1 Chr 14:1-17
    Gabriel   Lk 1:5-25
    God   Is 41:1-42:4
    Isaiah   2 Kgs 20:1-11;
                  Is 58:1-14;
                  65:1-25
    Israelites   Zech 10:3-12;
                  13:7-9
    Jeremiah   Jer 11:18-12:6;
                  15:10-21;

through **PRAYER** (cont'd)
  Jeremiah   31:15-22;
                  33:1-9
  Psalmist   Ps 2:7-9
  Solomon   2 Chr 7:11-22
through **PRESENCE**
  Jesus   Lk 24:13-35
of **PROMISE**
  Ammonites   Ezek 21:28-32
  Daniel   Dan 11:21-45
  Ezekiel   Ezek 12:21-28;
                  17:22-24;
                  21:8-17;
                  34:23-24
  God   Jer 32:16-25;
                  2 Pet 3:11-13
  Israelites   Ezek 22:1-16;
                  36:33-36;
                  47:13-20
  Jeremiah   Jer 33:14-26
  Judahites   Ezek 23:22-35;
                  24:1-14
  Samuel   1 Sam 3:1-4:1a
  Simeon   Lk 2:21-40
through **PROVIDENCE**
  Isaiah   Is 55:1-13
  Israelites   Is 49:1-26
  Jeremiah   Jer 1:11-12;
                  31:7-14
  Jesus   Jn 12:20-26
of **PUNISHMENT**
  Ezekiel   Ezek 12:21-28;
                  33:21-22
  Israelites   Ezek 6:8-10
  Nebuchadnezzar Dan 4:28-33
through **RECONCILIATION**
  Jeremiah   Jer 31:23-26

of **RITE**
  INSTRUCTION on
    Jacob   Gen 50:1-21
    Moses   Lev 8:1-36
  PROPHECY of
    Jesus   Mt 26:17-30

of **SALVATION**
  Jesus   Acts 2:14-36;
                1 Pet 2:21-25
  Jews   Jn 4:1-26
  Rahab   Heb 11:1-40
  through **DEITY**
    Believers   Ps 91:14-16
    God   Is 46:1-13;
                  Hab 3:3-15
    Holy Spirit   Tit 3:1-7
    Israelites   Ps 77:11-20;
                  Is 31:4-9
    Jesus   Eph 1:15-2:10;
                  2 Tim 1:8-14
    Paul   2 Tim 4:9-18
  in **ENVIRONMENT**
    Rahab   Josh 6:22-27
  INSTRUCTION on
    Jesus   Acts 13:14-52
    John the Baptist Acts 13:14-52
    Paul   Rom 13:11-14;
                  Phil 1:12-30;
                  Col 1:9-14
    Peter   Acts 4:1-22

PROPHECY of
  Isaiah   Is 35:1-10
  Jesus   Lk 21:25-28;
                    29-31
REVELATION on
  God   Rev 12:10-12
  Isaiah   Is 51:1-16
  Israelites   Is 49:1-26
  John   Rev 7:1-8

of SCRIPTURES
  through COMPULSION
    Judas   Acts 1:12-26
  on CONFRONTATION
    Jesus   Mt 26:47-56;
                Mk 14:43-50
  through inFIDELITY
    Jesus   Mt 26:31-35;
                Mk 14:27-31
  on JUDGMENT
    People   Acts 13:14-52
  on LAW
    Jesus   Lk 24:44-49;
                Jn 15:18-25
  on NEW AGE
    Jesus   Lk 21:20-24
  concerning PROMISE
    Jesus   Lk 22:35-38
    Paul   Acts 26:1-32;
                1 Cor 2:6-9;
                Gal 4:27-31
  through RECONCILIATION
    Jesus   1 Cor 15:1-11
  on the RESURRECTION
    David   Acts 2:14-36
  on SECURITY
    Jesus   Jn 17:6-19;
                18:1-11
  SIGNS of
    Jesus   Heb 2:5-18
  on TRUTH
    Believers   Acts 10:1-11:18

SCRIPTURES on
  of ELECTION
    Jesus   Lk 4:16-30;
                Jn 13:1-20

SECURITY in
  Levites   Ezra 8:31-36
  of COVENANT
    God   2 Chr 21:1-23:21
  through DEITY
    Believers   Heb 6:13-20
    David   Ps 38:11-16
    Israelites   Is 31:4-9

of SECURITY
  as PROPHESIED
    Isaiah   2 Kgs 19:9b-37
  REVELATION on
    Paul   Acts 27:1-28:16
  SCRIPTURES on
    Jesus   Jn 17:6-19;
                18:1-11

SELF-REALIZATION of
  of KNOWLEDGE
    Paul   1 Cor 13:8-13

SIGNS of
  of COVENANT
    Abraham   Gen 21:1-7
  INSTRUCTION on
    Angel   *2 Esd 7:19-32
  of MISSION
    Israelites   *1 Esd 7:1-9
  of PROPHECY
    Elijah   Mk 9:9-13
    Isaiah   Is 27:7-11;
                38:1-22;
                48:1-22;
                Mt 13:34-35
    Jesus   Mt 21:1-11;
                24:1-3;
                29-31;
                32-33;
                37-41;
                Mk 13:24-27;
                28-37;
                Lk 21:29-31
    Joel   Acts 2:14-36
    John the Baptist Mt 17:9-13
    Joseph   Gen 40:1-23;
                41:1-57
    Prophet   1 Kgs 13:1-34
    Samuel   1 Sam 9:1-10:16
  of REVELATION
    Joel   Joel 3:12-16a
    John   Rev 6:9-11;
                7:1-8;
                10:1-11;
                14:14-16;
                16:17-21
    Mordecai   *Esth 10:4-13
  of SCRIPTURES
    Jesus   Heb 2:5-18
  in WORSHIP
    Solomon   1 Kgs 6:1-38

through STEWARDSHIP
  INSTRUCTION on
    Jesus   Lk 17:7-10
    Moses   Ex 40:1-33
    Paul   Col 4:15-18
  PROPHECY of
    Isaiah   Is 52:13-53:12

of TRUTH
  through DEITY
    Agur   Prov 30:1-14
  INSTRUCTION on
    Holy Spirit   Jn 16:12-15
  in MISSION
    Paul   2 Tim 4:1-5
  PROPHECY of
    Jeremiah   Jer 44:20-28
  REVELATION on
    Ezekiel   Ezek 12:21-28
  SCRIPTURES on
    Believers   Acts 10:1-11:18

of VIRTUE
  INSTRUCTION on
    Jesus   Mt 3:13-17;
                5:3-12;
                48;
                Lk 6:20-23
    Paul   1 Tim 6:6-10

in **WORSHIP**
    DESIRE for
        David   Ps 28:1-5
        Ezra   *1 Esd 8:41-44
    PRAYER for
        Eli   1 Sam 1:1-28
        Ezra   Ezra 8:21-23;
                        Neh 9:9-11
        Samuel   1 Sam 7:2-17
    PROMISE of
        God   1 Kgs 8:14-21;
                        2 Chr 5:1-7:10
    SIGNS of
        Solomon   1 Kgs 6:1-38

GIFT

BLESSING of
    for **MISSION**
        Believers   1 Cor 14:1-12

COVETOUSNESS of
    INSTRUCTION on
        Paul   1 Cor 12:27-31a;
                        14:1-12

of **DEITY**
    is **LOVE**
        God   2 Tim 1:3-7
        Holy Spirit   Rom 5:1-5
    ONENESS with
        Holy Spirit   1 Cor 12:4-11
    is **TEMPERANCE**
        God   2 Tim 1:3-7
    is **WISDOM**
        Disciples   Acts 2:1-13
        James   Jas 3:13-18
        Solomon   *Wis 7:15-8:1;
                        2-21
    WITNESS to
        Holy Spirit   Heb 2:1-4

DIGNITY of
    INSTRUCTION on
        Paul   2 Cor 8:16-24

in **DISCIPLESHIP**
    INSTRUCTION on
        Paul   1 Cor 12:27-31a

FAITH in
    of **FOLLOWERs**
        Holy Spirit   1 Cor 12:4-11
    INSTRUCTION on
        Holy Spirit   Gal 3:1-5

FALSE BELIEF in
    causes **GREED**
        Simon   Acts 8:14-25

of **FOLLOWERs**
    FAITH as
        Holy Spirit   1 Cor 12:4-11
    FULFILLMENT as
        Holy Spirit   Acts 8:14-25;
                        10:1-11:18;
                        19:1-12

GRACE as
    Holy Spirit   1 Cor 12:4-11
    Jesus   Eph 4:7-16
HEALING as
    Holy Spirit   1 Cor 12:4-11
MIRACLE as
    Holy Spirit   Acts 2:1-13;
                        1 Cor 12:4-11
SERVICE as
    Apostles   Eph 4:7-16
    Evangelists   Eph 4:7-16
    Holy Spirit   1 Cor 12:4-11
    Pastors   Eph 4:7-16
    Prophet   Eph 4:7-16
    Teachers   Eph 4:7-16
SHARING of
    Paul   Rom 1:8-15
SPIRIT as
    Jesus   1 Cor 2:10-16
WISDOM as
    Holy Spirit   1 Cor 2:10-16;
                        12:4-11
    Unbelievers   1 Cor 14:13-25
WITNESS to
    Holy Spirit   1 Cor 12:4-11

FULFILLMENT as
    of **FOLLOWERs**
        Holy Spirit   Acts 8:14-25;
                        10:1-11:18;
                        19:1-12
    INSTRUCTION on
        Jesus   Lk 12:47-48
    PROPHECY of
        Joel   Acts 2:14-36

GOOD as
    PROPHECY of
        Believers   1 Cor 14:1-12

GRACE as
    of **FOLLOWERs**
        Holy Spirit   1 Cor 12:4-11
        Jesus   Eph 4:7-16
    INSTRUCTION on
        Paul   Rom 3:21-30;
                        12:3-8

causes **GREED**
    FALSE BELIEF in
        Simon   Acts 8:14-25

HEALING as
    of **FOLLOWERs**
        Holy Spirit   1 Cor 12:4-11

HOPE as
    MEDITATION on
        Paul   1 Cor 1:4-9

INSTRUCTION on
    in **DISCIPLESHIP**
        Paul   1 Cor 12:27-31a
    of **FAITH**
        Holy Spirit   Gal 3:1-5
    of **FULFILLMENT**
        Jesus   Lk 12:47-48
    of **GRACE**
        Paul   Rom 3:21-30;
                        12:3-8

of **WISDOM**
      Hiram   1 Kgs 7:13-14
    from **DEITY**
      Disciples   Acts 2:1-13
      James   Jas 3:13-18
      Solomon   *Wis 7:15-8:1;
                         2-21
    for **FOLLOWER**s
      Holy Spirit   1 Cor 2:10-16;
                         12:4-11
      Unbelievers   1 Cor 14:13-25
    INSTRUCTION on
      Paul   1 Cor 2:6-9;
                         12:1-3;
                         14:1-12;
                         13-25

WITNESS through
    to **DEITY**
      Holy Spirit   Heb 2:1-4
    for **FOLLOWER**s
      Holy Spirit   1 Cor 12:4-11
    of **PROPHECY**
      Believers   1 Cor 14:1-12

to **WITNESS**
    INSTRUCTION on
      Paul   1 Cor 12:27-31a
    SCRIPTURES on
      Paul   1 Cor 1:26-31

in **WORSHIP**
    ORDER for
      Believers   1 Cor 14:26-33
    for **SERVICE**
      Believers   1 Cor 14:26-33
    for **SHARING**
      Believers   1 Cor 14:26-33

GOOD

AUTHORITY over
    of **FOLLOWER**s
      James   Jas 5:14-18

BEHAVIOR revealing
    of **DEITY**
      Asa   1 Kgs 15:9-15
      Tobit   *Tb 1:10-22
    INSTRUCTION on
      Jesus   Mt 5:13-16;
                         Lk 6:27-35
      Sirach   *Sir 4:20-31;
                         18:19-26;
                         23:12-15;
                         25:1-2
      Tobit   *Tb 4:1-21

in **BROTHERHOOD**
    INSTRUCTION on
      Paul   1 Cor 10:23-11:1

in **COMMUNITY**
    from **DEITY**
      David   Ps 51:18-19

CONFRONTATION with
    Satan   Job 1:6-8;
                     2:1-3

CONFRONTATION with (cont'd)
    Ungodly Men   *Wis 2:12-20
in **COVENANT**
    of **LAW**
      Sirach   *Sir 42:1-5
in **CREATION**
    by **DEITY**
      God   1 Tim 4:1-5
      Mankind   Eccl 7:23-29;
                       *Wis 2:21-24
    REVELATION on
      Egyptians   Ezek 31:1-9
before **DEITY**
    BEHAVIOR revealing
      Asa   1 Kgs 15:9-15
      Tobit   *Tb 1:10-22
from **DEITY**
    in **COMMUNITY**
      David   Ps 51:18-19
    PRAYER for
      Psalmist   Ps 125:4-5
of **DEITY**
    CONFRONTATION with
      Satan   Job 1:6-8;
                     2:1-3
    in **CREATION**
      God   1 Tim 4:1-5
      Mankind   Eccl 7:23-29;
                       *Wis 2:21-24
    DESIRE for
      Mankind   Ps 4:6-8
    FIDELITY of
      Elihu   Job 34:10-15
      Josiah   *1 Esd 1:23-24
      Judith   *Jdt 8:1-8
      Sirach   *Sir 2:7-11;
                       15:11-20
    JUDGMENT on
      David   Ps 9:1-4
      God   Ps 11:4-7
      Sirach   *Sir 39:17-27
    KNOWLEDGE of
      Job   Job 1:6-8;
                     2:1-3
      Mankind   Ps 1:4-6
    PRESENCE of
      Mankind   Ps 15:1-5b
    PROMISE of
      Solomon   *Wis 15:1-6
    PROVIDENCE through
      Believers   Ps 92:12-15;
                       Rom 8:28-39
      God   Ps 85:8-13;
                       118:15-21
      James   Jas 1:16-18
      Sirach   *Sir 39:28-35
    PUNISHMENT through
      Psalmist   Ps 119:65-72
    as **QUALITY OF LIFE**
      God   Nah 1:1-9
    SECURITY in
      Believers   Prov 18:1-24
      God   Ps 37:12-22
    as **VIRTUE**
      God   Ps 77:11-20
      Job   Job 1:1

DESIRE for
  from DEITY
    Mankind   Ps 4:6-8
  INSTRUCTION on
    Amos   Amos 5:14-15
    Sirach   *Sir 16:1-5

in ENVIRONMENT
  CONFRONTATION with
    Ungodly Men   *Wis 2:12-20
  JUDGMENT on
    God   Gen 1:3-5;
                       9-13;
                       14-19;
                       24-31
  KNOWLEDGE of
    Ungodly Men   *Wis 2:12-20

ETERNAL
  of DEITY
    God   Ps 119:137-144;
                       153-160
  SCRIPTURES on
    Psalmist   2 Cor 9:6-11

FIDELITY in
  of DEITY
    Elihu   Job 34:10-15
    Josiah   *1 Esd 1:23-24
    Judith   *Jdt 8:1-8
    Sirach   *Sir 2:7-11;
                       15:11-20
  INSTRUCTION on
    Paul   1 Thes 5:12-22
  in WORSHIP
    Sirach   *Sir 7:1-36

of FOLLOWERs
  AUTHORITY of
    James   Jas 5:14-18
  SALVATION through
    Peter   1 Pet 4:12-19
  VIRTUE in
    Believers   Tit 2:11-15
    Noah   Gen 6:5-22

as GIFT
  PROPHECY of
    Believers   1 Cor 14:1-12

HONESTY as
  INSTRUCTION on
    Sirach   *Sir 7:1-36

INSTRUCTION on
  in BROTHERHOOD
    Paul   1 Cor 10:23-11:1
  in LAW
    David   Ps 19:11-14
    Jesus   Mt 7:12;
                       Mk 3:1-6;
                       Lk 6:6-11
    Paul   Rom 7:7-13;
                       1 Tim 1:8-11
  as QUALITY OF LIFE
    David   Ps 34:11-14
    Jesus   Mt 7:15-20;
                       12:33-37;
                       Lk 6:36-45
    John   3 Jn 1:12

in RESURRECTION
    Solomon   *Wis 4:1-9;
                       5:15-23
in SALVATION
    Angel   *2 Esd 7:45-61
    Jesus   Mt 13:24-30;
                       47-50
over SIN
    God   Ps 25:8-15
in STEWARDSHIP
    Paul   Rom 14:1-23
    Solomon   Prov 3:1-35
as VIRTUE
    Author   Heb 13:1-25
    Sirach   *Sir 5:1-6:1;
                       7:1-36;
                       18:15-18

JUDGMENT of
  of DEITY
    David   Ps 9:1-4
    God   Ps 11:4-7
    Sirach   *Sir 39:17-27

  in ENVIRONMENT
    God   Gen 1:3-5;
                       9-13;
                       14-19;
                       24-31

  INSTRUCTION on
    Elihu   Job 34:1-4
    God   Gen 1:20-23
    Jesus   Mt 13:24-30;
                       36-43;
                       47-50

KNOWLEDGE of
  of DEITY
    Job   Job 1:6-8;
                       2:1-3
    Mankind   Ps 1:4-6
  in ENVIRONMENT
    Ungodly Men   *Wis 2:12-20

in the LAW
  COVENANT of
    Sirach   *Sir 42:1-5
  of DEITY
    David   Ps 19:7-10
    God   Ps 119:137-144
    Psalmist   Ps 119:169-176
  INSTRUCTION on
    David   Ps 19:11-14
    Jesus   Mt 7:12;
                       Mk 3:1-6;
                       Lk 6:6-11
    Paul   Rom 7:7-13;
                       1 Tim 1:8-11
  SELF-REALIZATION of
    Paul   Rom 7:14-25

in MISSION
  as VIRTUE
    Bishop   Tit 1:5-8

in NEW AGE
  REVELATION on
    God   *2 Esd 2:10-14;
                       15-32

PRAYER for
    Ezra   Neh 9:7-8
   from **DEITY**
    Psalmist   Ps 125:4-5

PRESENCE of
   of **DEITY**
    Mankind   Ps 15:1-5b

PROMISE of
   of **DEITY**
    Solomon   *Wis 15:1-6

PROPHECY of
   as **GIFT**
    Believers   1 Cor 14:1-12

   as **QUALITY OF LIFE**
    Isaiah   Is 32:1-8

PROVIDENCE through
   of **DEITY**
    Believers   Ps 92:12-15;
         Rom 8:28-39
    God   Ps 85:8-13;
         118:15-21
    James   Jas 1:16-18
    Sirach   *Sir 39:28-35
   INSTRUCTION on
    Eliphaz   Job 5:18-27

PUNISHMENT through
   of **DEITY**
    Psalmist   Ps 119:65-72

as **QUALITY OF LIFE**
   of **DEITY**
    God   Nah 1:1-9
   INSTRUCTION on
    David   Ps 34:11-14
    Jesus   Mt 7:15-20;
         12:33-37;
         Lk 6:36-45
    John   3 Jn 1:12
   PROPHECY of
    Isaiah   Is 32:1-8

RESPECT for
   INSTRUCTION on
    Sirach   *Sir 42:1-5

in **RESURRECTION**
   INSTRUCTION on
    Solomon   *Wis 4:1-9;
         5:15-23

REVELATION on
   in **CREATION**
    Egyptians   Ezek 31:1-9
   in **NEW AGE**
    God   *2 Esd 2:10-14;
         15-32

in **SALVATION**
   of **FOLLOWERs**
    Peter   1 Pet 4:12-19
   INSTRUCTION on
    Angel   *2 Esd 7:45-61
    Jesus   Mt 13:24-30;
         47-50

SECURITY in
   of **DEITY**
    Believers   Prov 18:1-24
    God   Ps 37:12-22
   INSTRUCTION on
    Solomon   Prov 12:1-28

SELF-REALIZATION of
   in **LAW**
    Paul   Rom 7:14-25

SIN against
   of **DEITY**
    Elihu   Job 35:5-8

in **STEWARDSHIP**
   INSTRUCTION on
    Paul   Rom 14:1-23
    Solomon   Prov 3:1-35

as **VIRTUE**
   of **DEITY**
    God   Ps 77:11-20
    Job   Job 1:1
   of **FOLLOWERs**
    Believers   Tit 2:11-15
    Noah   Gen 6:5-22
   INSTRUCTION on
    Author   Heb 13:1-25
    Sirach   *Sir 5:1-6:1;
         7:1-36;
         18:15-18
   in **MISSION**
    Bishop   Tit 1:5-8

in **WORSHIP**
   through **FIDELITY**
    Sirach   *Sir 7:1-36

GRACE

in **AUTHORITY**
   of **DEITY**
    Mary   Lk 1:39-56
   INSTRUCTION on
    Jesus   Jn 20:1-29
   of **MESSIANIC FIGURE**
    Jesus   Mt 9:1-8;
         Mk 2:1-12;
         Lk 5:17-26

BEHAVIOR revealing
   of **DEITY**
    Ahab   1 Kgs 21:17-29
    Israelites   2 Sam 24:1-25
   INSTRUCTION on
    Jude   Jude 1:21-23

BELIEF in
   INSTRUCTION on
    Author   Heb 4:14-16
    John the Baptist   Lk 3:1-6
    Joshua   Num 14:8-9
    Paul   Rom 3:31-4:25;
         2 Cor 4:13-15
    Peter   Acts 10:1-11:18
   SELF-REALIZATION of
    Paul   1 Tim 1:12-17

GRACE (cont'd) 278

in BROTHERHOOD
INSTRUCTION on
Jesus	Mt 18:21-22
Paul	Eph 4:25-5:2
REVELATION on
Zechariah	Zech 7:4-8:23

in COMMITMENT
to DEITY
Believers	1 Jn 1:5-10
Israelites	Ezek 20:9-26
INSTRUCTION on
Solomon	Prov 28:1-28

COMPULSION through
of DEITY
Lot	Gen 19:12-29
CONFRONTATION through
David	2 Sam 19:8b-43
of DEITY
Jesus	Mt 5:3-12
INSTRUCTION on
Elisha	2 Kgs 6:8-23
Jesus	Lk 10:29-37
of MESSIANIC FIGURE
David	1 Sam 23:14-24:22; 26:1-25

CONVERSION through
of DEITY
Israelites	Num 14:11-24
INSTRUCTION on
Hezekiah	2 Chr 30:1-31:21
Paul	1 Cor 15:1-11
Peter	Acts 3:1-26
REVELATION on
Ezekiel	Ezek 33:10-20
Isaiah	Is 55:1-13
Israelites	Ezek 18:30-32

COVENANT of
Israelites	Rom 9:1-5
in NEW AGE
Paul	Gal 4:21-26
PROMISE in
Zechariah	Lk 1:57-80
RITE of
Jesus	Mt 26:17-30; Mk 14:22-26
SALVATION through
Jesus	Heb 10:1-18
forgive SIN
Jesus	Heb 10:1-18
as VIRTUE
Israelites	Hos 2:16-20

from DEITY
DESIRE for
Abraham	Gen 18:23-33
Job	Job 14:13-17
People	Jer 42:1-6

of DEITY
COMMITMENT to
Believers	1 Jn 1:5-10
Israelites	Ezek 20:9-26
COMPULSION through
Lot	Gen 19:12-29

CONFRONTATION through
Jesus	Mt 5:3-12
through CONVERSION
Israelites	Num 14:11-24
ELECTION by
Believers	1 Pet 2:4-10
Elizabeth	Lk 1:57-80
Israelites	Rom 11:25-32
Mankind	Ex 33:12-23
Paul	Col 1:25-27
strengthens FIDELITY
God	Ps 99:6-9; 145:13b-20
Israelites	Neh 9:16-18
Tobit	*Tb 13:1-18
JUDGMENT by
David	1 Chr 21:1-22:1;
God	Amos 7:1-3; 4-6
Nineveh	Jon 3:1-10
KNOWLEDGE of
Habakkuk	Hab 2:12-14; 17
MEDIATION through
Jesus	Rom 5:1-5
Moses	Ex 32:7-14; Deut 9:7-24; 25-29
PRAYER for
Amos	Amos 7:1-3; 4-6
Author	Heb 13:1-25
Daniel	Dan 9:4-19
David	Ps 9:13-14; 25:8-15; 27:7-12; 39:7-13; 40:11; 41:4-10; 51:1-2; 3-12; 13-17; 57:1-3
Ezekiel	Ezek 9:1-11
Habakkuk	Hab 3:1; 2
Isaiah	Is 33:1-6; 63:7-64:12
Israelites	Neh 9:26-31; Jer 14:19-22; Hos 5:15-6:3; *Bar 2:11-23; 3:1-8
Jeremiah	Jer 17:14-18
Joel	Joel 1:2-20
John	2 Jn 1:1-3; Rev 1:4-20; 22:6-21
Jonah	Jon 1:1-17; 2:1-10
Judahites	Lam 5:1-22
Moses	Num 12:11-16
Nineveh	Jon 3:1-10
Paul	1 Cor 1:4-9; Gal 6:11-18; Col 1:1-2; Tit 1:1-4; Philm 1:1-3; 21-25

PRAYER for (cont'd)

Peter	1 Pet 1:1-2
Psalmist	Ps 119:57-64;
	73-80;
	129-136;
	123:1-2;
	3-4

PROMISE through

Antiochus	*2 Mc 9:5-29
Manasseh	*Mana 1:6-7
Peter	2 Pet 1:3-4

PROVIDENCE through

David	Ps 23:5-6
God	Ps 147:1-6
Israelites	2 Kgs 13:22-25;
	Neh 9:19-21;
	Is 1:4-9
Jesus	2 Thes 2:16-17
Solomon	*Wis 16:1-14

PUNISHMENT by

Job	Job 35:13-16

as QUALITY OF LIFE

Believers	Jas 4:1-10
God	Deut 4:15-31;
	Ps 86:14-17;
	111:2-4;
	119:153-160;
	Is 30:18-26;
	Joel 2:12-17;
	Jas 5:7-11
Jonah	Jon 4:1-11

RECONCILIATION through

Believers	1 Pet 1:3-9
God	Is 1:24-26;
	44:6-8;
	21-23;
	Mic 7:7-20;
	Mt 6:14-15
Isaiah	Is 63:7-64:12
Psalmist	Ps 85:4-7

SALVATION through

Believers	1 Jn 1:5-10
David	Ps 26:8-12
Epaphroditus	Phil 2:19-30
God	Ps 103:1-5;
	Mt 19:23-26;
	Mk 10:23-27
Isaiah	Is 63:7-64:12
Israelites	Neh 9:26-31;
	Is 42:18-43:7
Jesus	1 Jn 2:1-6
Mankind	Tit 2:11-15;
	3:1-7
Paul	2 Cor 5:20-6:2
Sirach	*Sir 51:1-12

SIN forgiven by

Abijam	1 Kgs 15:1-8
Asaph	Ps 79:5-13
David	Ps 25:1-7;
	16-21;
	32:1-2;
	3-7
God	Ps 65:1-4;
	103:6-13;
	130:3-4
Hezekiah	Is 38:1-22
Israelites	Ps 78:32-39;
	*Bar 3:1-8
Joshua	Zech 3:1-10

SIN forgiven by (cont'd)

Manasseh	*Mana 1:6-7;
	11-15
Psalmist	Ps 85:1-3
Sirach	*Sir 2:7-11;
	18:1-14
Solomon	1 Kgs 8:22-53;
	*Wis 11:21-12:2

STEWARDSHIP by

Macedonians	2 Cor 8:1-6

as VIRTUE

God	Ex 34:5b-9;
	Ps 86:1-7;
	112:2-4;
	116:1-11;
	145:8-9
James	Jas 3:13-18

DESIRE for
from DEITY

Abraham	Gen 18:23-33
Job	Job 14:13-17
People	Jer 42:1-6

concerning FALSE BELIEF

Paul	2 Tim 4:9-18

of MESSIANIC FIGURE

Demons	Lk 8:26-39
Jesus	Mt 9:10-13

in WORSHIP

Demons	Mk 5:1-20
Nehemiah	Neh 1:5-11a

ELECTION by
through COVENANT

Israelites	Rom 9:1-5

of DEITY

Believers	1 Pet 2:4-10
Elizabeth	Lk 1:57-80
Israelites	Rom 11:25-32
Mankind	Ex 33:12-23
Paul	Col 1:25-27

in ELECTION
of FOLLOWERs

God	Eph 1:3-14

INSTRUCTION on

Jesus	Mt 20:20-28;
	22:1-14;
	Mk 10:35-45
Paul	Rom 9:14-29;
	11:1-6

SCRIPTURES on

Mankind	Rom 9:14-29

over FALSE BELIEF
DESIRE for

Paul	2 Tim 4:9-18

JUDGMENT on

Jesus	Mt 12:22-32;
	Mk 3:20-30

PRAYER for

Moses	Ex 32:30-35

FIDELITY in
of DEITY

God	Ps 99:6-9;
	145:13b-20
Israelites	Neh 9:16-18
Tobit	*Tb 13:1-18

RECONCILIATION through
   Jesus   Rom 5:6-11;
                       Heb 1:2b-4;
                       2:5-18
SALVATION through
   Believers   1 Pet 1:13-2:3
   Jesus   2 Cor 8:7-15
SIN is forgiven by
   Jesus   Jn 1:19-51
   Paralytic   Mt 9:1-8;
                       Mk 2:1-12;
                       Lk 5:17-26
TRUTH by
   Jesus   Jn 1:1-18

in MISSION
   through FIDELITY
     Paul   2 Cor 4:1-6
   PRAYER for
     Jude   Jude 1:1-2
     Peter   2 Pet 1:1-2
   RECONCILIATION through
     Jesus   Rom 3:31-4:25
   SALVATION through
     Jesus   Lk 19:1-10
   STEWARDSHIP by
     Paul   Eph 3:1-13
   TRUTH by
     Paul   Rom 15:14-24;
                     1 Cor 15:1-11

in NEW AGE
   through COVENANT
     Paul   Gal 4:21-26
   INSTRUCTION on
     Jesus   Mt 20:1-16;
                     Mk 4:26-29;
                     Lk 13:18-19
     Paul   Acts 28:17-31;
                     Rom 5:1-5;
                     11:1-6;
                     2 Cor 5:1-5

PRAYER for
   Jehoahaz   2 Kgs 13:1-9
   Moses   Num 11:1-3
   Paul   Tit 3:12-15
of DEITY
   Amos   Amos 7:1-3;
                     4-6
   Author   Heb 13:1-25
   Daniel   Dan 9:4-19
   David   Ps 9:13-14;
                     25:8-15;
                     27:7-12;
                     39:7-13;
                     40:11;
                     41:4-10;
                     51:1-2;
                     3-12;
                     13-17;
                     57:1-3
   Ezekiel   Ezek 9:1-11
   Habakkuk   Hab 3:1;
                     2
   Isaiah   Is 33:1-6;
                     63:7-64:12
   Israelites   Neh 9:26-31;
                     Jer 14:19-22;
                     Hos 5:15-6:3;
                     *Bar 2:11-23;

of DEITY (cont'd)
   Israelites   3:1-8;
   Jeremiah   Jer 17:14-18
   Joel   Joel 1:2-20
   John   2 Jn 1:1-3;
                     Rev 1:4-20;
                     22:6-21
   Jonah   Jon 1:1-17;
                     2:1-10
   Judahites   Lam 5:1-22
   Moses   Num 12:11-16
   Nineveh   Jon 3:1-10
   Paul   1 Cor 1:4-9;
                     Gal 6:11-18;
                     Col 1:1-2;
                     Tit 1:1-4;
                     Philm 1:1-3;
                     21-25
   Peter   1 Pet 1:1-2
   Psalmist   Ps 119:57-64;
                     73-80;
                     129-136;
                     123:1-2;
                     3-4

in FALSE BELIEF
   Moses   Ex 32:30-35
of FOLLOWER
   Paul   1 Cor 16:13-24;
                     Gal 1:1-5;
                     Eph 1:1-2;
                     Col 4:15-18;
                     1 Thes 1:1;
                     3:11-13;
                     5:25-28;
                     2 Thes 1:1-2;
                     11-12;
                     3:17-18;
                     1 Tim 1:1-2;
                     6:20-21;
                     2 Tim 1:1-2;
                     15-18;
                     4:19-22
INSTRUCTION on
   Bildad   Job 8:1-7
   Jeremiah   Jer 10:23-25;
                     Lam 2:1-22
   Jesus   Mt 6:9-13;
                     Mk 11:20-26;
                     Lk 11:1-4;
                     18:9-14
   Joel   Joel 2:12-17
   John   1 Jn 5:13-21
   Malachi   Mal 1:6-2:9
   Paul   1 Thes 5:25-28
   Peter   Acts 8:14-25
MEDITATION on
   Israelites   Jer 14:7-9
of MESSIANIC FIGURE
   People   Lk 23:33-38
in MISSION
   Jude   Jude 1:1-2
   Peter   2 Pet 1:1-2
PROPHECY of
   Israelites   Is 30:18-26
REVELATION on
   Israelites   Jer 3:1-5
SELF-REALIZATION of
   Israelites   Jer 14:7-9
in WORSHIP
   Believers   Acts 4:23-31
   David   2 Sam 12:1-31;

GRACE (cont'd) **284**

INSTRUCTION on
  Author Heb 9:15-22
  God Is 1:18-20;
  *2 Esd 2:1-7
  James Jas 5:14-18;
  19-20
  Jesus Mt 18:21-22;
  Lk 7:36-50;
  12:1-12;
  17:1-6
  John 1 Jn 2:12-17
  Paul Acts 13:14-52;
  Rom 5:12-21;
  6:1-14;
  15-23;
  Col 1:9-14;
  2:6-15
  Sirach *Sir 27:30-28:12
  Solomon Prov 17:1-28
of MESSIANIC FIGURE
  Jesus Jn 1:19-51
  Paralytic Mt 9:1-8;
  Mk 2:1-12;
  Lk 5:17-26
PROPHECY of
  Isaiah Is 33:17-24;
  40:1-11
  Israelites Ezek 16:53-63
REVELATION on
  Isaiah Is 6:1-13
  Israelites Jer 31:31-34
  Jeremiah Jer 33:1-9
  Judahites Hos 1:6-7
  Solomon 2 Chr 7:11-22
TRADITION of
  Solomon 2 Chr 5:1-7:10

STEWARDSHIP by
of DEITY
  Macedonians 2 Cor 8:1-6
INSTRUCTION on
  Jesus Mk 10:28-31;
  Lk 18:28-30
  Peter 1 Pet 4:7-11
in MISSION
  Paul Eph 3:1-13

TRADITION of
FREEDOM through
  Barabbas Mt 27:11-26;
  Mk 15:6-15
  Pilate Mt 27:11-26;
  Mk 15:6-15

SIN forgiven by
  Solomon 2 Chr 5:1-7:10

TRUTH through
of MESSIANIC FIGURE
  Jesus Jn 1:1-18
in MISSION
  Paul Rom 15:14-24;
  1 Cor 15:1-11
REVELATION on
  Paul Gal 1:11-17

as VIRTUE
of DEITY
  God Ex 34:5b-9;
  Ps 86:1-7;

of DEITY (cont'd)
  God 112:2-4;
  116:1-11;
  145:8-9
  James Jas 3:13-18
INSTRUCTION on
  Amos Amos 5:14-15
  Zephaniah Zeph 2:3
SELF-REALIZATION of
  Paul 2 Cor 1:12-14

in WORSHIP
  DESIRE for
  Demons Mk 5:1-20
  Nehemiah Neh 1:5-11a
  MEDIATION through
  Priest Num 15:22-31
  SIGNS of
  Naaman 2 Kgs 5:1-19

GRATITUDE

BEHAVIOR revealing
  to DEITY
  Jesus Col 3:5-17
INSTRUCTION on
  Paul Eph 5:3-14;
  Col 2:6-15

in WORSHIP
  Lepers Lk 17:11-19

for BELIEF
  of FOLLOWERs
  Paul Rom 1:8-15
INSTRUCTION on
  Paul 2 Cor 4:13-15;
  Col 2:6-15

for CREATION
  by FOLLOWERs
  God Ps 145:10-13a
to DEITY
  Jesus Col 3:5-17
  for FIDELITY
  David Ps 108:1-5
  Psalmist Ps 106:1-5;
  116:12-19
  KNOWLEDGE of
  Daniel Dan 2:20-23
  PRAYER of
  Asaph Ps 75:1
  Daniel Dan 6:10-15
  David Ps 9:1-4
  Isaiah Is 25:1-5
  Jonah Jon 2:1-10
  Paul Col 1:9-14;
  2 Thes 1:3-4
  for PROMISE
  David Ps 142:5-7
  for PROVIDENCE
  David Ps 30:11-12;
  40:6-10;
  52:8-9;
  54:6-7;
  86:11-13;
  144:1-2
  Isaiah Is 26:7-19

RITE of
  David   Ps 26:6b-7;
           28:6-7;
           56:10-13;
           57:7-11
for SECURITY
  David   Ps 124:6-8
  Hezekiah   Is 38:1-22
SIGNS of
  Rebekah   Gen 24:28-60
as VIRTUE
  David   Ps 140:12-13

DESIRE for
  INSTRUCTION on
    God   Ps 50:22-23
    Psalmist   Ps 105:1-6

ETERNAL
  to DEITY
    Psalmist   Ps 44:4-8

for FIDELITY
  of DEITY
    David   Ps 108:1-5
    Psalmist   Ps 106:1-5;
           116:12-19
  of FOLLOWERs
    Paul   Phil 4:10-20
  INSTRUCTION on
    Psalmist   Ps 107:1-3;
           118:28-29

for FOLLOWERs
  BELIEF of
    Paul   Rom 1:8-15
  for CREATION
    God   Ps 145:10-13a
  FIDELITY of
    Paul   Phil 4:10-20
  PRAYER of
    Paul   Col 1:3-8;
           1Thes 1:2-10;
           2:13-16;
           2 Thes 2:13-15;
           2 Tim 1:3-7;
           Philm 1:4-7

for FREEDOM
  INSTRUCTION on
    Paul   1 Cor 10:23-11:1

INSTRUCTION on
  for BEHAVIOR
    Paul   Eph 5:3-14;
           Col 2:6-15
  for BELIEF
    Paul   2 Cor 4:13-15;
           Col 2:6-15
  for FIDELITY
    Psalmist   Ps 107:1-3;
           118:28-29
  for FREEDOM
    Paul   1 Cor 10:23-11:1
  for PRESENCE
    Psalmist   Ps 95:1-7c

for PROVIDENCE
  Psalmist   Ps 107:4-9;
           10-16;
           17-22;
           23-32;
           136:4-9;
           10-22;
           23-25;
           26
for SALVATION
  Jeremiah   Jer 31:7-14
for STEWARDSHIP
  Paul   2 Cor 9:12-15

KNOWLEDGE of
  to DEITY
    Daniel   Dan 2:20-23

LAW of
  Moses   Lev 7:11-21

MEDITATION on
  as VIRTUE
    Isaiah   Is 61:1-11

by MESSIANIC FIGURE
  PRAYER of
    Jesus   Mt 15:32-39;
           Jn 11:1-57

PRAYER of
  to DEITY
    Asaph   Ps 75:1
    Daniel   Dan 6:10-15
    David   Ps 9:1-4
    Isaiah   Is 25:1-5
    Jonah   Jon 2:1-10
    Paul   Col 1:9-14;
           2 Thes 1:3-4
  of FOLLOWER
    Paul   Col 1:3-8;
           1 Thes 1:2-10;
           2:13-16;
           2 Thes 2:13-15;
           2 Tim 1:3-7;
           Philm 1:4-7
  INSTRUCTION on
    Jesus   Lk 11:1-4
    Paul   2 Cor 1:8-11;
           Phil 4:1-9;
           Col 4:2-4;
           1 Thes 5:12-22;
           1 Tim 2:1-7
    Psalmist   Ps 136:1-3
  MEDIATION in
    Jesus   Mt 11:25-26
  MEDITATION on
    Jesus   Lk 10:21-22
    Paul   Eph 1:15-2:10
  by MESSIANIC FIGURE
    Jesus   Mt 15:32-39;
           Jn 11:1-57
  PROPHECY of
    Isaiah   Is 12:1-6
  SELF-REALIZATION of
    Paul   1 Tim 1:12-17
  in WORSHIP
    David   1 Chr 17:1-27;
           Ps 7:17;
           138:1-3

in WORSHIP (cont'd)	
Ezra	Ezra 7:27-28
Hannah	1 Sam 2:1-10
Paul	Eph 5:15-20;
	Phil 1:3-11

for PRESENCE
  INSTRUCTION on
| Psalmist | Ps 95:1-7c |

for PROMISE
  of DEITY
| David | Ps 142:5-7 |

for PROVIDENCE
  of DEITY
David	Ps 30:11-12;
	40:6-10;
	52:8-9;
	54:6-7;
	86:11-13;
	144:1-2
Isaiah	Is 26:7-19
INSTRUCTION on
Psalmist	Ps 107:4-9;
	10-16;
	17-22;
	23-32;
	136:4-9;
	10-22;
	23-25;
	26
REVELATION on
Isaiah	Is 51:1-16
in WORSHIP
David	2 Sam 22:1-51

for RECONCILIATION
  REVELATION on
| Israelites | Jer 30:18-22 |
| Jeremiah | Jer 33:10-11 |

for RESPECT
  in WORSHIP
David	1 Chr 15:1-16:43
God	Rev 4:1-11;
	7:9-17;
	11:15-19

REVELATION on
  for PROVIDENCE
| Isaiah | Is 51:1-16 |
  for RECONCILIATION
| Israelites | Jer 30:18-22 |
| Jeremiah | Jer 33:10-11 |

RITE of
  to DEITY
David	Ps 26:6b-7;
	28:6-7;
	56:10-13;
	57:7-11
INSTRUCTION on
Moses	Deut 26:1-11
Psalmist	Ps 97:10-12;
	100:4-5;
	147:7-11
PROPHECY of
Isaiah	Is 26:1-6

in WORSHIP
Hezekiah	2 Chr 30:1-31:21
Israelites	Ezra 3:10-11;
	Ps 122:3-5
Judahites	Neh 12:31a
Levites	Neh 12:44-13:3
Nehemiah	Neh 12:38-42

for SALVATION
  INSTRUCTION on
| Jeremiah | Jer 31:7-14 |

for SECURITY
  of DEITY
| David | Ps 124:6-8 |
| Hezekiah | Is 38:1-22 |

SIGNS of
  to DEITY
| Rebekah | Gen 24:28-60 |

for STEWARDSHIP
  INSTRUCTION on
| Paul | 2 Cor 9:12-15 |

as VIRTUE
  of DEITY
| David | Ps 140:12-13 |
  MEDITATION on
| Isaiah | Is 61:1-11 |

in WORSHIP
  BEHAVIOR revealing
| Lepers | Lk 17:11-19 |
  PRAYER for
David	1 Chr 17:1-27;
	Ps 7:17;
	138:1-3
Ezra	Ezra 7:27-28
Hannah	1 Sam 2:1-10
Paul	Eph 5:15-20;
	Phil 1:3-11
for PROVIDENCE
David	2 Sam 22:1-51
for RESPECT
David	1 Chr 15:1-16:43
God	Rev 4:1-11;
	7:9-17;
	11:15-19
RITE of
Hezekiah	2 Chr 30:1-31:21
Israelites	Ezra 3:10-11;
	Ps 122:3-5
Judahites	Neh 12:31a
Levites	Neh 12:44-13:3
Nehemiah	Neh 12:38-42

GREED

in AUTHORITY
  INSTRUCTION on
| Moses | Deut 17:14-20 |

BEHAVIOR revealing
  of FOLLOWER
Judas	Mt 26:14-16;
	Mk 14:10-11;
	Lk 22:3-6

INSTRUCTION on
  Agur   Prov 30:15-33
  Paul   2 Cor 12:14-18

through **FALSE BELIEF**
  concerning **GIFT**
  Simon   Acts 8:14-25
  causes **disHONESTY**
  Judas   Jn 12:1-8
  as **QUALITY OF LIFE**
  Pharisees   Lk 16:14-15
  as **SIN**
  Tyre   Ezek 26:1-6

of **FOLLOWER**
  BEHAVIOR revealing
  Judas   Mt 26:14-16;
                        Mk 14:10-11;
                        Lk 22:3-6

concerning **GIFT**
  through **FALSE BELIEF**
  Simon   Acts 8:14-25

disHONESTY through
  Israelites   Jer 6:9-15
  Judahites   Jer 8:8-13;
                        Mic 7:1-6
  Laban   Gen 30:25-43
  caused by **FALSE BELIEF**
  Judas   Jn 12:1-8

INSTRUCTION on
  in **AUTHORITY**
  Moses   Deut 17:14-20
  as **QUALITY OF LIFE**
  Solomon   Prov 28:1-28

JUDGMENT on
  INSTRUCTION on
  Jesus   Lk 12:16-21;
                        16:14-15

as **MOTIVATION**
  in **ENVIRONMENT**
  Ptolemy   *1 Mc 11:1-19

PUNISHMENT for
  INSTRUCTION on
  Sirach   *Sir 14:3-19
  REVELATION on
  Eli   1 Sam 2:27-36

as **QUALITY OF LIFE**
  through **FALSE BELIEF**
  ◆ Pharisees   Lk 16:14-15
  INSTRUCTION on
  Solomon   Prov 28:1-28

SECURITY through
  Ishmael   Jer 41:4-9
  INSTRUCTION on
  Jesus   Mt 6:19-24

SIN of
  Ammonites   Amos 1:13-15
  Israelites   Num 11:31-35;
                        Amos 2:6-8;
                        5:7-13;

SIN of (cont'd)
  Israelites   6:1-7;
                        8:4-7
  Mankind   Ps 59:13c-15
  Micah   Mic 2:1-10
  Women   Amos 4:1-3
  through **FALSE BELIEF**
  Tyre   Ezek 26:1-6
  INSTRUCTION on
  Sirach   *Sir 14:3-19
  REVELATION on
  Habakkuk   Hab 2:5-6a

GRIEF

BEHAVIOR revealing
  Antiochus   *1 Mc 6:1-17
  David   1 Sam 30:1-31;
                        2 Sam 1:1-16;
                        3:17-39;
                        13:21-14:33;
                        15:13-16:14;
                        18:1-19:8a
  Ezra   *2 Esd 5:16-20
  Israelites   Judg 2:1-5;
                        2 Sam 1:1-16;
                        Neh 5:1-5;
                        *1 Mc 1:25-28;
                        36-40;
                        3:45;
                        9:1-22
  Jacob   Gen 37:29-36
  Jeremiah   *1 Esd 1:25-32
  Jonathan   *1 Mc 13:25-30
  Mattathias   *1 Mc 2:6-14;
                        39-48
  Mordecai   Esth 4:1-17
  Tobit   *Tb 2:1-8
  of **FOLLOWER**
  Paul   2 Cor 1:23-2:4
  INSTRUCTION on
  Ezekiel   Ezek 24:15-24
  Isaiah   Is 32:9-14
  Preacher   Eccl 3:1-8;
                        7:1-22
  Sirach   *Sir 38:16-23
  MEDITATION on
  Jeremiah   Jer 12:7-13
  PROPHECY of
  Amos   Amos 5:1-3
  Jeremiah   Jer 14:17-18
  REVELATION on
  Tyre   Ezek 27:25b-36
  SELF-REALIZATION of
  Jesus   Mt 26:36-46;
                        Mk 14:32-42
  TRADITION of
  Josiah   *1 Esd 1:25-32
  in **WORSHIP**
  Maccabeus   *1 Mc 4:36-61

in **COMMUNITY**
  from **DEITY**
  Ezra   *2 Esd 5:31-42

COMPULSION of
  MEDITATION on
  Jeremiah   Lam 3:1-66

REVELATION on (cont'd)
  as MOTIVATION
    Ezekiel   Ezek 21:1-7;
                    8-17
  in NEW AGE
    Ezekiel   Exek 30:1-5
  through PUNISHMENT
    Judahites   Ezek 24:1-14
  as QUALITY OF LIFE
    Zephaniah   Zeph 1:10-11

RITE of
    Israelites   1 Sam 25:1-44;
                    28:3-25
  MEDITATION on
    David   2 Sam 1:17-27
  TRADITION of
    Israelites   Judg 11:34-40
  in WORSHIP
    Israelites   *Bar 1:5-14

SELF-REALIZATION of
    Jesus   Mt 26:36-46;
                    Mk 14:32-42
  as QUALITY OF LIFE
    Naomi   Ruth 1:19-22

SIGNS of
  PROPHECY of
    Jeremiah   Mt 2:16-18

SIN causing
    Ezra   Ezra 9:3-5;
                    *1 Esd 8:71-90
    Israelites   *1 Esd 8:91-96
  MEDITATION on
    Jeremiah   Jer 8:18-9:1
in WORSHIP
  as MOTIVATION
    Job   Job 1:20-21
  PRAYER revealing
    Ezra   Ezra 10:1-6
    Israelites   Judg 21:1-7
    Moses   Ex 5:22-6:1 .
    Nehemiah   Neh 1:1-4
  RITE of
    Israelites   *Bar 1:5-14

GUILT

BEHAVIOR revealing
  in ENVIRONMENT
    Adam   Gen 3:1-8
    Eve   Gen 3:1-8
  INSTRUCTION on
    Eliphaz   Job 15:1-6

overcome through COMMITMENT
    Moses   Num 5:5-10
  to DEITY
    David   Ps 32:3-7
  INSTRUCTION on
    Solomon   Prov 28:1-28
  REVELATION on
    Moses   Lev 4:1-35
  SELF-REALIZATION of
    Nehemiah   Neh 1:5-11a

CONFRONTATION with
    Judah   Gen 38:24-30
through FALSE BELIEF
  as SIN
    Herod   Mk 6:17-29
    Lawyers   Lk 11:45-52
inFIDELITY revealing
  SELF-REALIZATION of
    Peter   Mt 26:69-75;
                    Mk 14:66-72;
                    Lk 22:54b-62
of FOLLOWERs
  JUDGMENT on
    Sadducees   Acts 22:30-23:11

INSTRUCTION on
  overcome through COMMITMENT
    Solomon   Prov 28:1-28
  by the LAW
    Moses   Deut 23:15-25:19
  of SIN
    John   1 Jn 3:4-10
    Paul   Rom 7:7-13

JUDGMENT on
    Ephraimites   Hos 13:1-3
    Moses   Ex 21:33-22:17
  by DEITY
    Chaldeans   Hab 1:5-11
    Ephraimites   Hos 13:12-14
    God   Ex 34:5b-9
    Jeremiah   Lam 3:1-66
    Sinners   2 Pet 3:3-7
  of FOLLOWERs
    Sadducees   Acts 22:30-23:11
  INSTRUCTION on
    Jesus   Mt 7:1-5;
                  Lk 6:36-45;
                  Jn 7:53-8:11
    Moses   Deut 17:8-13;
                  19:15-21
    Paul   1 Cor 5:1-5;
                  Gal 5:7-12
  by MESSIANIC FIGURE
    Priests   Lk 22:66-71
  PROPHECY of
    Babylonians   Jer 51:1-64
    Ephraimites   Hos 5:3-7;
                  12:7-9
    Isaiah   Is 13:1-22;
                  24:1-12
    Israelites   Ezek 16:44-52
    Samaria   Hos 13:15-16
  REVELATION on
    Belshazzar   Dan 5:26-28
    Elders   Ezek 20:1-4
    Ezekiel   Ezek 11:1-13;
                  22:1-16
    God   Gen 3:14-19
    Israelites   Jer 2:20-29;
                  30-37;
                  9:1-11;
                  21:18-24;

REVELATION on (cont'd)
    Israelites   22:23-31;
                         36:22-32
    Jeremiah   Jer 30:12-17
    Sidon   Ezek 28:20-23
SELF-REALIZATION of
    Hypocrite   Mt 7:1-5;
                         Lk 6:36-45

KNOWLEDGE of
  INSTRUCTION on
    Jesus   Jn 9:1-41
  SELF-REALIZATION of
    Pharisees   Mt 21:45-46

by LAW
    Moses   Lev 5:1-4
  INSTRUCTION on
    Moses   Deut 23:15-25:19
  REVELATION on
    Moses   Lev 7:1-10

MEDIATION for
  by DEITY
    Aaron   Ex 28:36-39
  INSTRUCTION on
    Moses   Lev 11:1-47
  REVELATION on
    Aaron   Num 18:1-7

MEDITATION on
  of SIN
    Judahites   Lam 5:1-22

of MESSIANIC FIGURE
  JUDGMENT on
    Priests   Lk 22:66-71

PRAYER concerning
    Ezra   Ezra 9:6-15
    Israelites   Jer 14:19-22
  MEDITATION on
    Israelites   Jer 14:7-9

PUNISHMENT for
    Moses   Ex 23:1-9
  by DEITY
    God   Nah 1:1-9
  INSTRUCTION on
    Moses   Deut 27:11-26
    Zophar   Job 11:1-6
  SELF-REALIZATION of
    Joseph   Gen 42:18-25

RECONCILIATION with
    Moses   Lev 16:11-28
  INSTRUCTION on
    Moses   Deut 21:1-9
    Solomon   1 Kgs 2:28-35
  PROPHECY of
    Isaiah   Is 27:7-11
  REVELATION on
    Israelites   Is 43:14-44:5

REVELATION on
  overcome through COMMITMENT
    Moses   Lev 4:1-35
  by the LAW
    Moses   Lev 7:1-10
  of SIN
    Moses   Lev 5:1-4

RITE concerning
  REVELATION on
    Moses   Lev 5:14-6:7;
                         Num 5:5-10

SELF-REALIZATION of
  overcome through COMMITMENT
    Nehemiah   Neh 1:5-11a
  caused by inFIDELITY
    Peter   Mt 26:69-75;
                         Mk 14:66-72;
                         Lk 22:54b-62
  because of SIN
    Ezra   Ezra 9:6-15
    Joseph   Gen 42:18-25
    Judas   Mt 27:3-10
    Pharaoh   Ex 9:13-35;
                         10:1-20

of SIN
    Moses   Num 5:5-10
  through FALSE BELIEF
    Herod   Mk 6:17-29
    Lawyers   Lk 11:45-52
  INSTRUCTION on
    John   1 Jn 3:4-10
    Paul   Rom 7:7-13
  MEDITATION on
    Judahites   Lam 5:1-22
  REVELATION on
    Moses   Lev 5:1-4
  SELF-REALIZATION of
    Ezra   Ezra 9:6-15
    Joseph   Gen 42:18-25
    Judas   Mt 27:3-10
    Pharaoh   Ex 9:13-35;
                         10:1-20

HATE

BEHAVIOR revealing
  of DEITY
    Israelites   Amos 6:8-11
  of FALSE BELIEF
    Pharisees   Lk 11:53-54
  INSTRUCTION on
    John   1 Jn 2:7-11
    Preacher   Eccl 3:1-8
  MEDITATION on
    Job   Job 10:1-7

in COMMUNITY
  through FALSE BELIEF
    God   *Wis 12:3-11

CONFRONTATION with
  INSTRUCTION on
    Sirach   *Sir 25:12-15
  PROPHECY of
    Jeremiah   Jer 4:30-31

by DEITY
    Israelites   Amos 6:8-11
  of inFIDELITY
    God   Mal 2:10-16
  of disHONESTY
    God   Prov 6:16-19

as QUALITY OF LIFE
   God   Is 1:10-17
   Isaiah   Is 61:1-11
of SIN
   God   Ps 11:4-7;
                         31:1-8;
                         Prov 6:16-19;
                         15:1-33;
                         16:1-33;
                         20:1-30
   Mankind   Ps 5:4-7
   Psalmist   Ps 119:97-104

through ELECTION
  of FOLLOWERs
   People   Jn 15:18-25

in ENVIRONMENT
  as MOTIVATION
   Esau   Gen 27:41-28:5

because of FALSE BELIEF
  BEHAVIOR revealing
   Pharisees   Lk 11:53-54
  in COMMUNITY
   God   *Wis 12:3-11

of FALSE BELIEF
  as QUALITY OF LIFE
   Believers   Jude 1:21-23
  concerning SIN
   Psalmist   Ps 119:113-120

of inFIDELITY
  Psalmist   Ps 119:153-160
  by DEITY
   God   Mal 2:10-16
  INSTRUCTION on
   Jesus   Lk 16:13

of FOLLOWERs
  through ELECTION
   People   Jn 15:18-25

of disHONESTY
  by DEITY
   God   Prov 6:16-19
  INSTRUCTION on
   Solomon   Prov 26:1-28

INSTRUCTION on
  of inFIDELITY
   Jesus   Lk 16:13
  of disHONESTY
   Solomon   Prov 26:1-28
  of SIN
   John   1 Jn 3:11-18
   Jude   Jude 1:14-16

KNOWLEDGE of
  of MESSIANIC FIGURE
   People   Jn 7:1-14

MEDITATION on
  as MOTIVATION
   Job   Job 9:20-24
  of SIN
   David   Ps 26:4-6a

of MESSIANIC FIGURE
  KNOWLEDGE of
   People   Jn 7:1-14

as MOTIVATION
  in ENVIRONMENT
   Esau   Gen 27:41-28:5
  MEDITATION on
   Job   Job 9:20-24

PRAYER concerning
  INSTRUCTION on
   Solomon   Prov 28:1-28

PROPHECY of
  of SIN
   Prophet   Hos 9:7-9

PUNISHMENT for
  REVELATION on
   Edomites   Ezek 35:1-15

of QUALITY OF LIFE
  by DEITY
   God   Is 1:10-17
   Isaiah   Is 61:1-11

RATIONALIZATION of
  Moses   Lev 19:1-37

of disRESPECT
  REVELATION on
   Israelites   Ezek 5:5-17
   Judahites   Ezek 23:22-35

REVELATION on
  of disRESPECT
   Israelites   Ezek 5:5-17
   Judahites   Ezek 23:22-35

SIGNS of
  INSTRUCTION on
   Paul   2 Tim 3:1-9
  PROPHECY of
   Jesus   Mt 24:9-14;
                     Mk 13:9-13;
                     Lk 21:7-19

of SIN
   Absalom   2 Sam 13:21-14:33
   David   Ps 139:19-22
  by DEITY
   God   Ps 11:4-7;
                     31:1-8;
                     Prov 6:16-19;
                     15:1-33;
                     16:1-33;
                     20:1-30
   Mankind   Ps 5:4-7
   Psalmist   Ps 119:97-104
  of FALSE BELIEF
   Psalmist   Ps 119:113-120
  INSTRUCTION on
   John   1 Jn 3:11-18
   Jude   Jude 1:14-16
  MEDITATION on
   David   Ps 26:4-6a
  PROPHECY of
   Prophet   Hos 9:7-9

of unTRUTH
 Psalmist   Ps 119:161-168

HEALING

by AUTHORITY
 of DEITY
  Jesus   Mt 12:22-32;
       Lk 11:14-23
 INSTRUCTION on
  Peter   Acts 4:1-22
 of MESSIANIC FIGURE
  Jesus   Mt 9:32-34
 in MISSION
  Apostles Mt 10:7-8

BEHAVIOR revealing
 Jesus   Mt 4:23-25;
       Lk 4:38-39
 Paul   Acts 16:16-24
 Peter   Acts 3:1-26;
       5:11-16;
       9:32-43
 Philip   Acts 8:4-13
 Tobit   *Tb 11:7-19
 by DEITY
  Jeroboam 1 Kgs 13:1-34
 of FOLLOWERs
  Jesus   Mt 12:15-21;
       17:14-20
 INSTRUCTION on
  Jesus   Lk 4:42-44
  Preacher Eccl 3:1-8
 by MESSIANIC FIGURE
  Blind   Mk 8:22-26;
       Lk 18:35-43;
       Jn 9:1-41
  Crowd   Mt 19:1-2;
       Mk 6:53-56
  Deaf   Mk 7:31-37
  Demon   Lk 13:10-17
  Jesus   Mt 8:2-4;
       5-13;
       14-17;
       28-34;
       12:9-14;
       22-32;
       14:13-21;
       15:29-31;
       17:14-20;
       20:29-34;
       Mk 1:29-31;
       32-34;
       40-45;
       2:1-12;
       3:1-6;
       7-12;
       5:1-20;
       35-43;
       9:14-29;
       10:46-52;
       Lk 4:40-41;
       5:12-16;
       17-26;
       6:6-11;
       17-19;
       7:1-10;
       11-17;

by MESSIANIC FIGURE (cont'd)
 Jesus   8:26-39;
       40-56;
       9:10-11;
       37-43a;
       11:14-23;
       14:1-6;
       22:47-54a;
       Jn 5:1-18
 Lazarus   Jn 11:1-57
 Lepers   Lk 17:11-19
 Woman   Mk 7:24-30
 in MISSION
  Jesus   Mt 9:35

BELIEF in
 Lame   Acts 3:1-26
 Paul   Acts 14:8-18
 of FOLLOWERs
  Canaanite Woman Mt 15:21-28;
       Mk 7:24-30
  Leper   Mt 8:2-4;
       Mk 1:40-45;
       Lk 5:12-16
  Woman   Mk 7:24-30
 INSTRUCTION on
  James   Jas 5:14-18
  Jesus   Lk 17:11-19
 by MESSIANIC FIGURE
  Blind   Mk 10:46-52;
       Lk 18:35-43;
       Jn 9:1-41
  Jesus   Mt 9:18-26;
       27-31;
       14:34-36
  Martha   Jn 11:1-57
  Mary   Jn 11:1-57
  Official   Jn 4:43-54
  Woman   Mk 5:25-34;
       Lk 8:40-56
 in MISSION
  Jesus   Mt 15:21-28

COMMITMENT to
 REVELATION on
  Isaiah   Is 57:14-21

CONFRONTATION with
 David   1 Sam 16:14-23
 REVELATION on
  Daniel   Dan 10:10-21

CONVERSION through
 by MESSIANIC FIGURE
  Jesus   Mt 9:1-8
 in MISSION
  Jesus   Mt 9:10-13

by DEITY's
 AUTHORITY
  Jesus   Mt 12:22-32;
       Lk 11:14-23
 BEHAVIOR revealing
  Jeroboam 1 Kgs 13:1-34
 KNOWLEDGE of
  Jesus   Lk 8:40-56
 PRAYER for
  Abraham   Gen 20:1-18
  David   Ps 6:1-5;
       41:4-10

PRAYER for (cont'd)
Egyptians   Is 19:18-25
Hezekiah   2 Chr 32:1-33;
                       Is 38:1-22
Israelites   Hos 5:15-6:3
Jeremiah   Jer 17:14-18
Moses   Num 12:11-16
Tobiah   *Tb 3:16-17
through **PROVIDENCE**
Abimelech   Gen 20:1-18
David   Ps 41:1-3
God   Ps 103:1-5;
                       146:7c-9
People   Ps 107:17-22

DESIRE for
by **FOLLOWERs**
Crowd   Mt 15:29-31;
                       Lk 6:17-19
Jesus   Mk 3:7-12;
                       6:53-56
INSTRUCTION on
Crowds   Mt 4:23-25

through **FIDELITY**
INSTRUCTION on
Author   Heb 12:12-29

by **FOLLOWERs**
with **AUTHORITY**
Disciples   Mk 6:7-13;
                       Lk 9:1-6
Jesus   Mt 10:1
DESIRE for
Crowd   Mt 15:29-31;
                       Lk 6:17-19
Jesus   Mk 3:7-12;
                       6:53-56

of **FOLLOWERs**
BEHAVIOR revealing
Jesus   Mt 12:15-21;
                       17:14-20
through **BELIEF**
Canaanite Woman   Mt 15:21-28;
                       Mk 7:24-30
Leper   Mt 8:2-4;
                       Mk 1:40-45;
                       Lk 5:12-16

as **GIFT**
of **FOLLOWERs**
Holy Spirit   1 Cor 12:4-11

INSTRUCTION on
by **AUTHORITY**
Peter   Acts 4:1-22
through **FIDELITY**
Author   Heb 12:12-29
SIN
Jesus   Jn 9:1-41

KNOWLEDGE of
by **DEITY**
Jesus   Lk 8:40-56
INSTRUCTION on
Father   Prov 4:20-27
by **MESSIANIC FIGURE**
Jesus   Mk 6:25-34

by **MESSIANIC FIGURE**
Jesus   Mt 21:12-17
AUTHORITY of
Jesus   Mt 9:32-34
BEHAVIOR revealing
Blind   Mk 8:22-26;
                       Lk 18:35-43;
                       Jn 9:1-41
Crowd   Mt 19:1-2;
                       Mk 6:53-56
Deaf   Mk 7:31-37
Demon   Lk 13:10-17
Jesus   Mt 8:2-4;
                       5-13;
                       14-17;
                       28-34;
                       12:9-14;
                       22-32;
                       14:13-21;
                       15:29-31;
                       17:14-20;
                       20:29-34;
                       Mk 1:29-31;
                       32-34;
                       40-45;
                       2:1-12;
                       3:1-6;
                       7-12;
                       5:1-20;
                       35-43;
                       9:14-29;
                       10:46-52;
                       Lk 4:40-41;
                       5:12-16;
                       17-26;
                       6:6-11;
                       17-19;
                       7:1-10;
                       11-17;
                       8:26-39;
                       40-56;
                       9:10-11;
                       37-43a;
                       11:14-23;
                       14:1-6;
                       22:47-54a;
                       Jn 5:1-18
Lazarus   Jn 11:1-57
Lepers   Lk 17:11-19
Woman   Mk 7:24-30
through **BELIEF**
Blind   Mk 10:46-52;
                       Lk 18:35-43;
                       Jn 9:1-41
Jesus   Mt 9:18-26;
                       27-31;
                       14:34-36
Martha   Jn 11:1-57
Mary   Jn 11:1-57
Official   Jn 4:43-54
Woman   Mk 5:25-34;
                       Lk 8:40-56
CONVERSION through
Jesus   Mt 9:1-8
KNOWLEDGE of
Jesus   Mk 5:25-34
PRAYER for
Jesus   Mt 21:12-17
through **PRESENCE**
Holy Spirit   Acts 10:1-11:18

as **QUALITY OF LIFE**
  Jesus   1 Pet 2:21-25
SIGNS of
  Jesus   Mt 9:10-13;
                           11:2-6;
                           Mk 2:15-17;
                           Lk 5:29-32;
                           7:18-23;
                           Jn 4:43-54

MISSION of
  Jesus   Mk 1:35-39
  AUTHORITY in
  Apostles   Mt 10:7-8
  BEHAVIOR revealing
  Jesus   Mt 9:35
  BELIEF in
  Jesus   Mt 15:21-28
  CONVERSION through
  Jesus   Mt 9:10-13
  ELECTION to
  Jesus   Lk 4:16-30
  RECONCILIATION through
  Jesus   Mt 9:10-13
  STEWARDSHIP of
  Believers   Lk 10:1-16

PRAYER for
  Abraham   Gen 20:1-18
  David   Ps 6:1-5;
                           41:4-10
  Egyptians   Is 19:18-25
  Hezekiah   2 Chr 32:1-33;
                           Is 38:1-22
  Israelites   Hos 5:15-6:3
  Jeremiah   Jer 17:14-18
  Moses   Num 12:11-16
  Tobiah   *Tb 3:16-17
  INSTRUCTION on
  James   Jas 5:14-18
  Sirach   *Sir 38:1-15
  by **MESSIANIC FIGURE**
  Jesus   Mt 21:12-17

PRESENCE in
  by **MESSIANIC FIGURE**
  Holy Spirit   Acts 10:1-11:18

PROMISE of
  PROPHECY of
  Isaiah   Mt 8:14-17
  as **QUALITY OF LIFE**
  Isaiah   Is 52:13-53:12

through **PROVIDENCE**
  of **DEITY**
  Abimelech   Gen 20:1-18
  David   Ps 41:1-3
  God   Ps 103:1-5;
                           146:7c-9
  People   Ps 107:17-22
  REVELATION on
  Israelites   Ezek 34:11-16
  Jeremiah   Jer 30:12-17

as **QUALITY OF LIFE**
  Naaman   Lk 4:16-30
  by **MESSIANIC FIGURE**
  Jesus   1 Pet 2:21-25
  PROPHECY of
  Isaiah   Is 52:13-53:12

RECONCILIATION through
  PROPHECY of
  Israelites   Hos 6:10-7:2;
                           14:4-8
  REVELATION on
  Jeremiah   Jer 33:1-9

RESPECT for
  INSTRUCTION on
  Sirach   *Sir 38:1-15

REVELATION on
  through **PROVIDENCE**
  Israelites   Ezek 34:11-16
  Jeremiah   Jer 30:12-17

RITE of
  Disciples   Mk 6:7-13
  Moses   Lev 13:1-59;
                           14:1-32
  INSTRUCTION on
  James   Jas 5:14-18

SIGNS of
  by **MESSIANIC FIGURE**
  Jesus   Mt 9:10-13;
                           11:2-6;
                           Mk 2:15-17;
                           Lk 5:29-32;
                           7:18-23;
                           Jn 4:43-54
  REVELATION on
  John   Rev 13:1-4;
                           22:1-5

SIN related to
  Asa   2 Chr 14:1-16:1
  INSTRUCTION on
  Jesus   Jn 9:1-41

STEWARDSHIP of
  in **MISSION**
  Believers   Lk 10:1-16
  REVELATION on
  Isaiah   Is 58:1-14

HERESY

BEHAVIOR revealing
  INSTRUCTION on
  Paul   Rom 16:1-23

unBELIEF causing
  through **FALSE BELIEF**
  Sinners   2 Pet 3:3-7

CONFRONTATION with
  INSTRUCTION on
  Moses   Deut 29:16-29

DESIRE for
  Israelites   Is 2:6-11

through **FALSE BELIEF**
  Sinners   2 Pet 3:3-7

caused by **disHONESTY**
 Prophet   Mic 2:11;
                        2 Pet 2:1-3
 Satan   Jn 8:21-59
 Sinners   1 Jn 2:18-23;
                        4:1-3
 KNOWLEDGE of
 Jesus   Jn 16:1-4
 in **LAW**
 Israelites   Jer 27:1-11
 Moses   Lev 19:1-37;
                        20:1-27;
                        Deut 18:9-22
 Paul   Col 2:16-23
 in **RESURRECTION**
 Unbelievers   1 Cor 15:12-19
 SIN of
 Jezebel   Rev 2:18-29
 Pharisees   Mt 23:15
 in **STEWARDSHIP**
 Pharisees   Mt 23:23-24
 in **TRUTH**
 Holy Spirit   1 Tim 4:1-5
 Paul   1 Tim 6:2c-5
 Peter   2 Pet 3:14-18a

inFIDELITY causing
 Moses   Ex 23:10-13
 REVELATION on
 Israelites   Jer 2:14-19

disHONESTY causing
 through **FALSE BELIEF**
 Prophet   Mic 2:11;
                        2 Pet 2:1-3
 Satan   Jn 8:21-59
 Sinners   1 Jn 2:18-23;
                        4:1-3
 PROPHECY of
 Apostles   Jude 1:17-19
 Jesus   Mt 24:4-8;
                        Mk 13:3-8

INSTRUCTION on
 BEHAVIOR revealing
 Paul   Rom 16:1-23
 concerning **LAW**
 Paul   1 Tim 1:3-7
 concerning **TRUTH**
 Paul   Gal 1:6-10;
                        2 Tim 2:14-19

KNOWLEDGE of
 through **FALSE BELIEF**
 Jesus   Jn 16:1-4
 INSTRUCTION on
 Isaiah   Is 48:1-22
 REVELATION on
 Smyrna   Rev 2:8-11

PROPHECY of
 concerning **TRUTH**
 Paul   1 Tim 4:1-5

PUNISHMENT for
 PROPHECY of
 John   Rev 22:6-21

SIGNS of
 INSTRUCTION on
 Paul   2 Thes 2:3b-10;
                        2 Tim 3:1-9
 PROPHECY of
 False Prophet   Deut 12:1-31
 Jesus   Mt 24:9-14;
                        23-28;
                        Mk 13:14-23

SIN of
 through **FALSE BELIEF**
 Jezebel   Rev 2:18-29
 Pharisees   Mt 23:15
 INSTRUCTION on
 Jeremiah   Jer 5:30-31
 Jesus   Mt 23:16-22
 Pergamum   Rev 2:12-17

 in **STEWARDSHIP**
 through **FALSE BELIEF**
 Pharisees   Mt 23:23-24

 concerning **TRUTH**
 through **FALSE BELIEF**
 Holy Spirit   1 Tim 4:1-5
 Paul   1 Tim 6:2c-5
 Peter   2 Pet 3:14-18a
 INSTRUCTION on
 Paul   Gal 1:6-10;
                        2 Tim 2:14-19

 PROPHECY of
 Paul   1 Tim 4:1-5

HONESTY

brings **BLESSING**
 of **DEITY**
 David   Ps 32:1-2

of **DEITY**
 DOUBT in
 People   1 Jn 5:8-12
 FULFILLMENT through
 Balaam   Num 23:13-26
 God   1 Sam 15:1-35;
                        Is 55:1-13;
                        Tit 1:1-4
 HOPE in
 Believers   Heb 6:13-20
 JUSTICE in
 Elihu   Job 34:10-15
 Job   Job 31:5-34
 OBEDIENCE to
 Sirach   *Sir 1:22-30
 PRAISE of
 Jesus   Jn 7:15-24

with **DEITY**
 concerning **EVIL**
 Elihu   Job 33:26-28
 Ezra   *1 Esd 8:71-90
 Israelites   *1 Esd 9:1-15;
                        *Bar 2:11-23;
                        3:1-8
 Manasseh   *Mana 1:8-10
 Mankind   Ps 12:1-4

DIGNITY in	
INSTRUCTION on	
James	Jas 5:12
Paul	1 Cor 4:1-5
in **DISCIPLESHIP**	
INSTRUCTION on	
Paul	Eph 4:25-5:2
in **MISSION**	
Paul	2 Cor 4:1-6
DOUBT in	
of **DEITY**	
People	1 Jn 5:8-12
concerning **EVIL**	
with **DEITY**	
Elihu	Job 33:26-28
Ezra	*1 Esd 8:71-90
Israelites	*1 Esd 9:1-15;
	*Bar 2:11-23;
	3:1-8
Manasseh	*Mana 1:8-10
Mankind	Ps 12:1-4
in **FAITH**	
INSTRUCTION on	
Jesus	Lk 16:10-12
in **WORSHIP**	
Author	Heb 10:19-31
FEAR of	
in **ENVIRONMENT**	
Abraham	Gen 26:1-11
FULFILLMENT of	
of **DEITY**	
Balaam	Num 23:13-26
God	1 Sam 15:1-35;
	Is 55:1-13;
	Tit 1:1-4
GOOD in	
INSTRUCTION on	
Sirach	*Sir 7:1-36
HOPE in	
of **DEITY**	
Believers	Heb 6:13-20
PROPHECY of	
Hananiah	Jer 28:1-17
HUMILITY in	
INSTRUCTION on	
Paul	2 Cor 11:7-15
INSTRUCTION on	
in **FAITH**	
Jesus	Lk 16:10-12
in **SERVICE**	
John the Baptist	Lk 3:10-14
in **SPIRIT**	
Jesus	Mt 15:10-11;
	Mk 7:1-23
with **WEALTH**	
Jezebel	1 Kgs 21:5-12
Nehemiah	Neh 5:6-13
Solomon	Prov 20:1-30;
	21:1-31

as **WITNESS**	
God	Ex 20:1-17
Moses	Deut 5:1-21;
	19:15-21;
Solomon	Prov 12:1-28;
	14:1-35;
	19:1-29;
	24:23-34;
	25:1-28
JUSTICE in	
of **DEITY**	
Elihu	Job 34:10-15
Job	Job 31:5-34
INSTRUCTION on	
Moses	Deut 23:15-25:1
of **LEADERSHIP**	
in **MISSION**	
Paul	2 Cor 1:15-22
REVELATION on	
Daniel	Dan 11:21-45
in **MISSION**	
of **DISCIPLESHIP**	
Paul	2 Cor 4:1-6
of **LEADERSHIP**	
Paul	2 Cor 1:15-22
of **WITNESS**	
Paul	2 Cor 2:14-17
OBEDIENCE to	
of **DEITY**	
Sirach	*Sir 1:22-30
ENVIRONMENT	
Joseph	Gen 42:18-25
ORDER in	
INSTRUCTION on	
Moses	Deut 19:14
PEACE through	
PROPHECY of	
Isaiah	Is 52:13-53:12
in **POLITICS**	
Alcimus	*2 Mc 14:3-17
Gibeon	Josh 9:3-15
Herod	Acts 12:1-25
PRAISE of	
of **DEITY**	
Jesus	Jn 7:15-24
PRUDENCE in	
INSTRUCTION on	
Jesus	Lk 16:10-12
PURIFICATION of	
in **WORSHIP**	
Author	Heb 10:19-31
REJECTION of	
caused by **FALSE BELIEF**	
Israelites	Jer 5:1-14
James	Jas 1:26
Jesus	1 Jn 2:18-23;
	4:1-3
Paul	Tit 1:9-16
Shemaiah	Jer 29:24-32

PROPHECY of		
Prophets	Jer 27:12-15;	
	16-22	
REVELATION of		
of **LEADERSHIP**		
Daniel	Dan 11:21-45	
REWARDs for		
REVELATION on		
John	Rev 14:1-5	
SACRIFICE for		
REVELATION on		
Isaiah	Is 58:1-14	
SELF-REALIZATION of		
in **LOVE**		
Paul	1 Cor 13:1-3	
through **WISDOM**		
Wisdom	Prov 8:1-21	
in **SERVICE**		
INSTRUCTION on		
John the Baptist	Lk 3:10-14	
SPIRIT of		
INSTRUCTION on		
Jesus	Mt 15:10-11;	
	Mk 7:1-23	
in **TEMPERANCE**		
FALSE BELIEF on		
Jesus	Lk 17:22-37	
with **WEALTH**		
Jehoiada	2 Kgs 12:4-16	
Menelaus	*2 Mc 4:39-50	
INSTRUCTION on		
Jezebel	1 Kgs 21:5-12	
Nehemiah	Neh 5:6-13	
Solomon	Prov 20:1-30;	
	21:1-31	
of **WILL**		
INSTRUCTION on		
James	Jas 5:12	
WISDOM in		
SELF-REALIZATION of		
Wisdom	Prov 8:1-21	
in **WITNESS**		
INSTRUCTION on		
God	Ex 20:1-17	
Moses	Deut 5:1-21;	
	19:15-21	
Solomon	Prov 12:1-28;	
	14:1-35;	
	19:1-29;	
	24:23-34;	
	25:1-28	
in **MISSION**		
Paul	2 Cor 2:14-17	
WITNESS to		
Elihu	Job 33:1-7	
Moses	Ex 23:1-9	

in **WORSHIP**		
FAITH in		
Author	Heb 10:19-31	
through **PURIFICATION**		
Author	Heb 10:19-31	

disHONESTY

ACCEPTANCE through		
Holofernes	*Jdt 11:1-23	
ANGER resulting from		
Samson	Judg 14:10-20	
REVELATION of		
Ammonites	Ezek 21:28-32	
CONDEMNATION of		
by **DEITY**		
God	Prov 12:1-28	
Job	Job 13:1-12	
through **FALSE BELIEF**		
Paul	Acts 13:4-12	
Rulers	Acts 6:8-8:3	
MEDITATION on		
Jeremiah	Jer 4:9-10	
REVELATION on		
Prophetesses	Ezek 13:17-23	
Prophets	Jer 23:23-32;	
	Ezek 13:1-16	
in **COVENANT**		
of **FRIENDSHIP**		
David	Ps 55:20-21	
of **PEACE**		
Gibeon	Josh 9:3-15	
DESTRUCTION caused by		
God	Ps 63:11c	
Mankind	Ps 5:4-7	
DISOBEDIENCE caused by		
in **FALSE BELIEF**		
Prophets	Jer 23:16-22	
DOUBT in		
David	2 Sam 10:1-19;	
	1 Chr 18:1-20:8	
of **ENEMY**		
Alcimus	*2 Mc 14:26-27	
Judith	*Jdt 11:1-23	
Maccabeus	*1 Mc 7:5-35	
PROPHECY of		
Hushai	2 Sam 16:15-17:29	
EVIL through		
Delilah	Judg 16:4-9;	
	10-12;	
	13-15;	
	16-22	
Elders	*Susa 1:19-27	
Jacob	Gen 37:29-36	
caused by **FALSE BELIEF**		
Abraham	Gen 12:9-13:1	
Ananias	Acts 4:32-5:10	
Israelites	Hos 10:1-8	

caused by **FALSE BELIEF** (cont'd)
    Jesus   Mt 7:15-20
    Judahites   Jer 3:6-11
    Sapphira   Acts 4:32-5:10
INSTRUCTION on
    Isaiah   Is 59:1-21
    Rehum   Ezra 4:6-16
    Sirach   *Sir 4:20-31;
        5:1-6:1;
        19:25-30;
        20:24-31;
        21:1-7;
        27:22-29;
        28:13-26
    Solomon   Prov 6:12-15;
        19:1-29
PROPHECY of
    Prophets   Jer 5:30-31

through **EVIL**
    Adversaries   Ps 120:3-4
    Jerusalem   Mic 6:9-16
    Mankind   Ps 64:3-6
    Prophet   1 Kgs 13:1-34

through **FALSE BELIEF**
  CONDEMNATION of
    Paul   Acts 13:4-12
    Rulers   Acts 6:8-8:3
  resulting in **DISOBEDIENCE**
    Prophets   Jer 23:16-22
  caused **EVIL**
    Abraham   Gen 12:9-13:1
    Ananias   Acts 4:32-5:10
    Israelites   Hos 10:1-8
    Jesus   Mt 7:15-20
    Judahites   Jer 3:6-11
    Sapphira   Acts 4:32-5:10
  causes **GREED**
    Judas   Jn 12:1-8
  causes **HERESY**
    Prophet   Mic 2:11;
        2 Pet 2:1-3
    Satan   Jn 8:21-59
    Sinners   1 Jn 2:18-23;
        4:1-3
  causes **IDOLATRY**
    John   Rev 13:11-18
    Prophets   Rev 19:17-21
  causes **JEALOUSY**
    James   Jas 3:13-18
    Officials   Dan 6:4-9
    Rulers   Acts 6:8-8:3
  causes **KILLING**
    Babylonians   Rev 18:21-24
  of **LEADERSHIP**
    Satan   Rev 12:7-9
  of **LOVE**
    John   1 Jn 4:19-5:5
  concerning **PEACE**
    Prophets   Jer 14:13-16
  causes **REJECTION**
    Israelites   Jer 5:1-14
    James   Jas 1:26
    Jesus   1 Jn 2:18-23;
        4:1-3
    Paul   Tit 1:9-16
    Shemaiah   Jer 29:24-32
  causes **SELFISHNESS**
    James   Jas 3:13-18

causes **STEALING**
    Israelites   Ezek 22:23-31
concerning **TEMPERANCE**
    Jesus   Lk 17:22-37
WITNESS to
    Ephraimites   Hos 11:12-12:1

in **FRIENDSHIP**
  COVENANT of
    David   Ps 55:20-21
  in **ENVIRONMENT**
    Simon   *1 Mc 16:11-17

GREED through
    Israelites   Jer 6:9-15
    Judahites   Jer 8:8-13;
        Mic 7:1-6
  in **ENVIRONMENT**
    Laban   Gen 30:25-43
  caused by **FALSE BELIEF**
    Judas   Jn 12:1-8

HATE of
  by **DEITY**
    God   Prov 6:16-19
  INSTRUCTION on
    Solomon   Prov 26:1-28

causing **HERESY**
  through **FALSE BELIEF**
    Prophet   Mic 2:11
    Prophets   2 Pet 2:1-3
    Satan   Jn 8:21-59
    Sinners   1 Jn 2:18-23;
        4:1-3
  PROPHECY of
    Apostles   Jude 1:17-19
    Jesus   Mt 24:4-8;
        Mk 13:3-8

causing **IDOLATRY**
  through **FALSE BELIEF**
    John   Rev 13:11-18
    Prophets   Rev 19:17-21

INSTRUCTION on
  in **DISCIPLESHIP**
    Paul   Eph 4:25-5:2
  through **EVIL**
    Isaiah   Is 59:1-21
    Rehum   Ezra 4:6-16
    Sirach   *Sir 4:20-31;
        5:1-6:1;
        19:25-30;
        20:24-31;
        21:1-7;
        27:22-29;
        28:13-26
    Solomon   Prov 6:12-15;
        19:1-29

through **JEALOUSY**
  FALSE BELIEF causing
    James   Jas 3:13-18
    Officials   Dan 6:4-9
    Rulers   Acts 6:8-8:3

in **KILLING**
    Ishmael   Jer 41:4-9

PROPHECY of
   Isaiah   Is 10:24-27c

PROPHECY of
  in BELIEF
   Holy Spirit   Jn 7:37-52
  in HONESTY
   Hananiah   Jer 28:1-17
  in NEW AGE
   Isaiah   Is 33:17-24;
                      35:1-10
   Malachi   Mal 4:4-6
  in PROMISE
   Isaiah   Is 10:24-27c
  in PROVIDENCE
   Elisha   2 Kgs 6:32-7:2
   Isaiah   Is 29:1-8;
                      30:18-26
  in RECONCILIATION
   Jeremiah   Jer 29:1-23
   Micah   Mic 2:12-13
  in SALVATION
   Isaiah   Is 25:6-9
  in SECURITY
   Isaiah   Is 37:33-35;
                      62:1-12

in PROVIDENCE
  of DEITY
   David   Ps 9:17-20
   Eliphaz   Job 5:8-17
   Jesus   2 Thes 2:16-17
   Psalmist   Ps 130:5-6
  INSTRUCTION on
   Psalmist   Ps 130:7-8
  through MESSIANIC FIGURE
   Gentiles   Mt 12:15-21;
                      Rom 15:1-13
  PROPHECY of
   Elisha   2 Kgs 6:32-7:2
   Isaiah   Is 29:1-8;
                      30:18-26
  REVELATION on
   Ezekiel   Ezek 17:22-24

as QUALITY OF LIFE
  INSTRUCTION on
   Paul   Rom 5:1-5;
                      12:9-13
   Preacher   Eccl 9:1-16

in RECONCILIATION
  through MESSIANIC FIGURE
   Isaiah   Is 11:1-9;
                      10-16
  PROPHECY of
   Jeremiah   Jer 29:1-23
   Micah   Mic 2:12-13
  REVELATION on
   Israelites   Jer 30:4-9
   Jeremiah   Jer 16:14-15;
                      30:1-3
   Rachel   Jer 31:15-22
   Zedekiah   Jer 32:9-15

through RESURRECTION
  Believers   1 Pet 1:13-2:3
  FOLLOWERs have
   Jesus   1 Pet 1:3-9

INSTRUCTION on
  Paul   1 Cor 15:12-19;
                     29-34;
                     51-58;
                     1 Thes 4:13-18
  Peter   Acts 2:14-36
MEDITATION on
  Paul   Phil 3:4-16

REVELATION on
  in ELECTION
   Israelites   Jer 3:19-20
  in PRESENCE
   God   Is 41:1-42:4
  in PROVIDENCE
   Ezekiel   Ezek 17:22-24
  in RECONCILIATION
   Israelites   Jer 30:4-9
   Jeremiah   Jer 16:14-15;
                      30:1-3
   Rachel   Jer 31:15-22
   Zedekiah   Jer 32:9-15
  in SALVATION
   Believers   1 Pet 1:13-2:3
  in SECURITY
   Ezekiel   Ezek 11:14-21

in SALVATION
  by DEITY
   Believers   1 Tim 4:6-10
   David   Ps 38:17-22;
                     39:7-13
   God   Ps 65:5-8
   Psalmist   Ps 119:81-88;
                     161-168;
                     169-176;
                     123:1-2
  by FOLLOWERs
   Thessalonians   1 Thes 1:2-10
  INSTRUCTION on
   Author   Heb 6:9-12
   Baruch   *Bar 4:21-37
   Paul   Rom 8:14-25;
                     Phil 3:17-21;
                     1 Thes 5:1-11
  through MESSIANIC FIGURE
   Believers   1 Pet 1:13-2:3
  PROPHECY of
   Isaiah   Is 25:6-9
  REVELATION on
   Believers   1 Pet 1:13-2:3

SCRIPTURES on
  in the CREATION
   Jeremiah   Jer 30:1-3
  in FIDELITY
   Paul   Rom 15:1-13

in SECURITY
  of DEITY
   Believers   Ps 146:5-7b
   David   Ps 22:12-21;
                     40:13-17
   Habakkuk   Hab 3:16-19
   Isaiah   Is 8:16-18
   Jeremiah   Lam 3:1-66

of **DEITY** (cont'd)
Psalmist   Ps 42:1-5;
6-11;
43:1-5;
71:1-21;
94:16-19;
116:1-11;
119:49-56;
113-120

of **FALSE BELIEF**
Solomon   *Wis 13:10-19
PROPHECY of
Isaiah   Is 37:33-35;
62:1-12

REVELATION on
Ezekiel   Ezek 11:14-21

in **SIGNS**
of **PROPHECY**
Isaiah   Is 7:10-17;
37:30-32

REVELATION on
Daniel   Dan 8:13-14
Ezekiel   Ezek 47:1-12

through **SIGNS**
in **COVENANT**
Paul   1 Cor 11:23-26

in **TRUTH**
of **FOLLOWER**s
Colossians   Col 1:3-8
Jesus   Col 1:25-27
INSTRUCTION on
Jesus   Jn 14:1-14
Paul   Col 1:21-23
in **MISSION**
Paul   Tit 1:1-4

as **VIRTUE**
Job   Job 4:1-6
INSTRUCTION on
Paul   Rom 8:14-25

HUMILITY

before **AUTHORITY**
of **DEITY**
Job   Job 9:1-7
Peter   1 Pet 5:6-11
INSTRUCTION on
Moses   Deut 17:14-20
Paul   2 Cor 10:12-18
Servants   1 Pet 2:18-20
Solomon   Prov 25:1-28
in **MISSION**
Titus   Tit 3:1-7
REVELATION on
Paul   2 Cor 12:1-10
in **WORSHIP**
Mankind   Ps 22:27-31

BEHAVIOR revealing
before **DEITY**
Eliphaz   Job 22:21-30
Esther   *Esth 14:1-19

INSTRUCTION on
Jesus   Lk 14:7-11
Paul   Phil 2:1-4;
Col 3:18-4:1
Sirach   *Sir 32:1-13
of **MESSIANIC FIGURE**
Jesus   Mt 21:1-11;
Mk 11:1-10;
Lk 19:28-38;
Jn 13:1-20
in **WORSHIP**
Women   1 Tim 2:8-15

in **BELIEF**
INSTRUCTION on
Paul   Rom 3:21-30

in **BROTHERHOOD**
INSTRUCTION on
Jesus   Mt 23:5-12
Paul   1 Cor 16:13-24;
Eph 5:21-33
Peter   1 Pet 5:1-5

COMPULSION of
caused by **FALSE BELIEF**
Sinners   Rev 3:7-13
INSTRUCTION on
Women   Esth 1:10-22

CONFRONTATION through
in **WORSHIP**
Joshua   Josh 5:13-15

CONFRONTATION with
before **DEITY**
Job   Job 40:3-5;
42:1-6
of the **CREATION**
before **DEITY**
David   Ps 8:3-8
God   Is 2:12-17

before **DEITY**
Eliphaz   Job 22:21-30
Esther   *Esth 14:1-19
CONFRONTATION with
Job   Job 40:3-5;
42:1-6
of the **CREATION**
David   Ps 8:3-8
God   Is 2:12-17
DESIRE for
God   Ps 51:13-17;
Mic 6:6-8
in **RESPECT**
God   Ps 138:4-6
Job   Job 30:9-15

of **DEITY**
as **VIRTUE**
David   Ps 143:1-2

DESIRE for
God   Ps 51:13-17;
Mic 6:6-8

INSTRUCTION on
Zephaniah   Zeph 2:3

as **QUALITY OF LIFE**
　　Bishop　　　　　　　Tit 1:5-8
　　Women　　　　　　　Tit 2:1-10
　revealing **RESPECT**
　　Slaves　　　　　　　Tit 2:1-10
　STEWARDSHIP of
　　Paul　　　　　　　　Acts 20:17-38
　in **TRUTH**
　　Paul　　　　　　　　1 Cor 2:1-5;
　　　　　　　　　　　　9:15-23

in **NEW AGE**
　INSTRUCTION on
　　Jesus　　　　　　　Mt 18:1-4

PRAYER for
　　Sirach　　　　　　　*Sir 22:27-23:6

in **PRAYER**
　before **DEITY**
　　Azariah　　　　　　*Azar 1:11-22
　　Israelites　　　　　Jer 3:21-4:4
　　Psalmist　　　　　Ps 131:1-3
　INSTRUCTION on
　　Jesus　　　　　　　Mt 6:5-8
　SELF-REALIZATION of
　　Jesus　　　　　　　Mt 26:36-46;
　　　　　　　　　　　　Mk 14:32-42;
　　　　　　　　　　　　Lk 22:39-46

in **PRESENCE**
　of **DEITY**
　　God　　　　　　　Is 57:14-21

PROMISE concerning
　by **DEITY**
　　God　　　　　　　Ps 37:1-11

PROPHECY of
　through **PROVIDENCE**
　　Isaiah　　　　　　　Is 2:6-11;
　　　　　　　　　　　　17:1-6
　as **PUNISHMENT**
　　Babylonians　　　Jer 50:1-46
　　Ezekiel　　　　　Ezek 16:44-52
　　Habakkuk　　　　Hab 2:15-16
　　Isaiah　　　　　　Is 3:16-4:1;
　　　　　　　　　　　　5:8-24a
　　Israelites　　　　Ezek 16:53-63;
　　　　　　　　　　　　Hos 4:4-15;
　　　　　　　　　　　　10:1-8
　　Jeremiah　　　　Jer 13:20-27;
　　　　　　　　　　　　22:20-23
　　Judahites　　　　Jer 13:18-19
　　Moabites　　　　Jer 48:1-47
　　Nineveh　　　　　Nah 3:5-19

in **PROVIDENCE**
　of **DEITY**
　　David　　　　　　　Ps 144:3-4
　　God　　　　　　　Ps 149:1-4
　　Israelites　　　　Deut 8:1-10
　　Mankind　　　　　Ps 18:25-30
　PROPHECY of
　　Isaiah　　　　　　　Is 2:6-11;
　　　　　　　　　　　　17:1-6

　REVELATION on
　　Israelites　　　　Zeph 3:11-13
　　Paul　　　　　　　2 Cor 12:1-10

as **PUNISHMENT**
　　Israelites　　　　Lev 26:1-46
　by **DEITY**
　　Jeremiah　　　　Jer 17:13
　for **FALSE BELIEF**
　　Ephraimites　　　Hos 4:17-19
　　Prophets　　　　Mic 3:1-12
　MEDITATION on
　　Jeremiah　　　　Lam 2:1-22
　PROPHECY of
　　Babylonians　　　Jer 50:1-46
　　Ezekiel　　　　　Ezek 16:44-52
　　Habakkuk　　　　Hab 2:15-16
　　Isaiah　　　　　　Is 3:16-4:1;
　　　　　　　　　　　　5:8-24a
　　Israelites　　　　Ezek 16:53-63;
　　　　　　　　　　　　Hos 4:4-15;
　　　　　　　　　　　　10:1-8
　　Jeremiah　　　　Jer 13:20-27;
　　　　　　　　　　　　22:20-23
　　Judahites　　　　Jer 13:18-19
　　Moabites　　　　Jer 48:1-47
　　Nineveh　　　　　Nah 3:5-19

　REVELATION on
　　Israelites　　　　Jer 2:20-29;
　　　　　　　　　　　　30-37;
　　　　　　　　　　　　Hos 2:9-13
　　Jeremiah　　　　Jer 15:1-4;
　　　　　　　　　　　　5-9
　　Levites　　　　　Ezek 44:10-14

as **QUALITY OF LIFE**
　　James　　　　　　Jas 4:1-10
　INSTRUCTION on
　　Bishops　　　　　1 Tim 3:1-7
　　James　　　　　　Jas 1:9-11
　　Jeremiah　　　　Jer 13:15-17
　　Jesus　　　　　　Mt 5:3-12;
　　　　　　　　　　　　18:1-4;
　　　　　　　　　　　　20:20-28;
　　　　　　　　　　　　Mk 10:35-45;
　　　　　　　　　　　　Lk 6:20-23;
　　　　　　　　　　　　18:9-14
　　Paul　　　　　　　Rom 12:3-8;
　　　　　　　　　　　　1 Cor 3:18-23;
　　　　　　　　　　　　Gal 5:25-6:6;
　　　　　　　　　　　　Col 3:5-17
　of **MESSIANIC FIGURE**
　　Zechariah　　　　Zech 9:1-12
　in **MISSION**
　　Bishop　　　　　Tit 1:5-8
　　Women　　　　　Tit 2:1-10

in **RECONCILIATION**
　INSTRUCTION on
　　Jesus　　　　　　Lk 15:11-32
　　Paul　　　　　　　Rom 3:21-30;
　　　　　　　　　　　　11:7-24
　REVELATION on
　　Egyptians　　　　Ezek 29:9b-16

in **RESPECT**
　before **DEITY**
　　God　　　　　　　Ps 138:4-6
　　Job　　　　　　　Job 30:9-15
　INSTRUCTION on
　　Paul　　　　　　　Rom 12:14-21
　　Solomon　　　　Prov 29:1-27

in **MISSION**
   Slaves   Tit 2:1-10

RESPECT through
  in **WORSHIP**
   Women   1 Cor 11:2-16

dis**RESPECT** causing
  PROPHECY of
   Edomites   Obad 1:1b-4
   God   Zeph 2:8-12
   Isaiah   Is 30:1-7;
                  60:1-22
  REVELATION on
   Isaiah   Is 66:1-16

REVELATION on
  before **AUTHORITY**
   Paul   2 Cor 12:1-10
  ETERNAL
   Sinners   Jer 23:33-40
  in **PROVIDENCE**
   Israelites   Zeph 3:11-13
   Paul   2 Cor 12:1-10
  as **PUNISHMENT**
   Israelites   Jer 2:20-29;
                  30-37;
                  Hos 2:9-13
   Jeremiah   Jer 15:1-4;
                  5-9
   Levites   Ezek 44:10-14

in **RECONCILIATION**
   Egyptians   Ezek 29:9b-16
  in **RESPECT**
   Isaiah   Is 66:1-16

in **RITE**
  INSTRUCTION on
   Jesus   Mt 6:16-18
  in **WORSHIP**
   Ezra   Ezra 8:21-23

SALVATION through
  before **DEITY**
   Eliphaz   Job 22:21-30
  INSTRUCTION on
   Jesus   Mt 18:1-4
   Paul   1 Cor 1:26-31

SELF-REALIZATION of
  as **VIRTUE**
   Jesus   Mt 11:28-30

SIGNS of
   Micah   Mic 1:5-9

in **STEWARDSHIP**
   Paul   Eph 3:14-19
  INSTRUCTION on
   Jesus   Mt 6:2-4;
                  Lk 14:12-14;
                  22:24-27;
                  Jn 13:1-20
  in **MISSION**
   Paul   Acts 20:17-38

in **TRUTH**
  INSTRUCTION on
   Paul   2 Cor 11:30-33
  in **MISSION**
   Paul   1 Cor 2:1-5;
                  9:15-23

as **VIRTUE**
   Moses   Num 12:3
  before **DEITY**
   David   Ps 143:1-2
  INSTRUCTION on
   Sirach   *Sir 3:17-31;
                  6:2-17;
                  7:1-36;
                  10:26-11:1;
                  2-9
   Solomon   Prov 12:1-28;
                  15:1-33;
                  16:1-33;
                  18:1-24;
                  22:1-16
   Women   1 Pet 3:1-7
  SELF-REALIZATION of
   Jesus   Mt 11:28-30

in **WORSHIP**
  BEHAVIOR revealing
   Women   1 Tim 2:8-15
  CONFRONTATION through
   Joshua   Josh 5:13-15
  in **RESPECT**
   Women   1 Cor 11:2-16
  RITE of
   Ezra   Ezra 8:21-23

IDOLATRY

before **AUTHORITY**
  of **DEITY**
   God   Ps 97:6-9
   Jeremiah   *Jer 6:8-40

AUTHORITY over
  in **WORSHIP**
   People   Rev 13:5-10

BEHAVIOR revealing
   Micah   Judg 17:1-6
   Moses   Ex 32:7-14
  in **ENVIRONMENT**
   Danites   Judg 18:27-31
  through **FALSE BELIEF**
   Demetrius   Acts 19:23-41
   Ephesians   Acts 19:23-41
   People   Is 46:1-13
   Solomon   *Wis 13:10-19
  INSTRUCTION on
   Antiochus   *1 Mc 1:41-53
   Isaiah   Is 17:9-11
   Jeremiah   *Jer 6:8-40;
                  45-59
   Samuel   1 Sam 7:2-17
   Solomon   *Wis 14:12-31;
                  15:7-19

unBELIEF causing
  through **FALSE BELIEF**
    Crowds   Acts 14:8-18

COMMITMENT to
  Israelites   Jer 44:15-19

COMPULSION concerning
  INSTRUCTION on
    Nebuchadnezzar Dan 3:1-6
  in **WORSHIP**
    John   Rev 13:11-18

CONFRONTATION with
  Josiah   *Sir 49:1-3
  through **FALSE BELIEF**
    Elijah   1 Kgs 18:1-46
  REVELATION on
    Ezekiel   Ezek 6:1-7

CONVERSION from
  PROPHECY of
    Israelites   Is 31:4-9

revealed in **COVENANT**
  LAW concerning
    Moses   Ex 34:12-28

in the **CREATION**
  through **FALSE BELIEF**
    Nebuchadnezzar Dan 3:1-6

before **DEITY**
  through **inFIDELITY**
    Israelites   Mal 2:10-16
    Jeremiah   *Jer 6:4-7
    Solomon   *Wis 15:1-6
  JUDGMENT on
    Egyptians   Ex 12:1-14
    Gentiles   Rom 1:24-32
    God   Is 2:18-22;
                45:14-25
  PROVIDENCE in
    Solomon   *Wis 14:1-11
  PUNISHMENT for
    Israelites   Ps 78:56-66;
                Ezek 43:6-12
    Moses   Deut 31:30-32:47
  SIN of
    Israelites   Ps 106:19-23

through **FALSE BELIEF**
  Crowds   Acts 14:8-18
  Demetrius   Acts 19:23-41
  Ephesians   Acts 19:23-41
  People   Is 46:1-13
  Solomon   *Wis 13:10-19
  CONFRONTATION with
    Elijah   1 Kgs 18:1-46
  CREATION of
    Nebuchadnezzar Dan 3:1-6
  causing **inFIDELITY**
    Israelites   Judg 2:11-19;
                8:24-28;
                33:35;
                Ezek 23:5-10
  causing **disHONESTY**
    John   Rev 13:11-18
    Prophets   Rev 19:17-21

KNOWLEDGE of
  Daniel   *Bel 1:10-20
  Jeremiah   *Jer 6:45-59
  in **LAW**
    Darius   Dan 6:4-9
PUNISHMENT for
  Baruch   *Bar 4:5-16
  God   Rev 14:9-12
  Israelites   Deut 29:16-29
as **QUALITY OF LIFE**
  Psalmist   Ps 115:3-8;
                135:15-18
RATIONALIZATION of
  Israelites   Ex 32:15-24
RITE of
  Babylonians   Dan 3:7
  Belshazzar   Dan 5:1-4
SIGNS of
  Babylonians   *Bel 1:3-7
  Israelites   Ex 32:1-6
SIN of
  Ephraimites   Hos 4:17-19;
                7:13-16;
                8:11-14;
                9:10-17;
                11:1-4;
                13:1-3
  Israelites   Num 25:1-5;
                2 Kgs 17:7-23;
                Neh 9:16-18;
                Jer 18:13-17;
                Ezek 16:15-34;
                20:9-26;
                23:36-49;
                Hos 2:2-8;
                4:4-15;
                8:4-7;
                10:1-8
  Jeremiah   *Jer 6:4-7;
                60-73
  Jezebel   Rev 2:18-29
  Judahites   Jer 7:29-8:3
  Moses   Num 33:50-56;
                Deut 12:32-13:18
  Prophets   Jer 23:13-15
  Solomon   *Wis 14:1-11
  concerning **TRUTH**
    Cyrus   *Bel 1:8-9
    Daniel   *Bel 1:10-20
  through **inFIDELITY**
    Judges   *Sir 46:11-12
    Solomon   1 Kgs 11:1-13
  before **DEITY**
    Israelites   Mal 2:10-16
    Jeremiah   *Jer 6:4-7
    Solomon   *Wis 15:1-6
  in **ENVIRONMENT**
    Israelites   Judg 3:7-11;
                10:6-18
  caused by **FALSE BELIEF**
    Israelites   Judg 2:11-19;
                8:24-28;
                33-35;
                Ezek 23:5-10
  REVELATION on
    Israelites   Ezek 20:5-8
    Judahites   Ezek 23:11-21

disHONESTY revealing
  through **FALSE BELIEF**

through **FALSE BELIEF** (cont'd)
   John   Rev 13:11-18
   Prophets   Rev 19:17-21

JUDGMENT on
  before **DEITY**
   Egyptians   Ex 12:1-14
   Gentiles   Rom 1:24-32
   God   Is 2:18-22;
                45:14-25
  INSTRUCTION on
   God   Is 41:1-42:4
   Isaiah   Is 44:9-20
   Jeremiah   Jer 5:18-19
   Paul   Acts 17:16-34;
                1 Cor 10:14-22
  PROPHECY of
   Asa   2 Chr 14:1-16:14
   Babylonians Jer 51:1-64
   Israelites   Jer 11:15-17
  REVELATION on
   Chaldeans   Is 47:1-15
   John   Rev 17:1-6a
  in **WORSHIP**
   Josiah   2 Kgs 23:4-15

KNOWLEDGE of
  through **FALSE BELIEF**
   Daniel   *Bel 1:10-20
   Jeremiah   *Jer 6:45-59
  INSTRUCTION on
   Jeremiah   Jer 10:1-16
   Paul   1 Cor 8:4-6;
                7-13

LAW concerning
   Moses   Ex 22:18-20;
                23:20-33;
                Lev 19:1-37
  COVENANT of
   Moses   Ex 34:12-28
  through **FALSE BELIEF**
   Darius   Dan 6:4-9
  INSTRUCTION on
   God   Ex 20:1-17
   Moses   Deut 5:1-21;
                7:1-5;
                17-26;
                27:11-26
  TRADITION of
   Galatian   Gal 4:8-11

as **MOTIVATION**
  INSTRUCTION on
   Paul   1 Cor 10:23-11:1

PROMISE causing
  INSTRUCTION on
   Jesus   Mt 5:33-37

PROVIDENCE in
  before **DEITY**
   Solomon   *Wis 14:1-11

PUNISHMENT for
  before **DEITY**
   Israelites   Ps 78:56-66;
                Ezek 43:6-12
   Moses   Deut 31:30-32:47

through **FALSE BELIEF**
   Baruch   *Bar 4:5-16
   God   Rev 14:9-12
   Israelites   Deut 29:16-29
INSTRUCTION on
   Moses   Deut 4:15-31;
                16:21-17:7
   Solomon   *Wis 14:12-31;
                16:1-14
PROPHECY of
   Babylonians Jer 50:1-46;
                51:1-64
   Egyptians   Jer 46:13-26
   Elijah   1 Kgs 21:17-29
   Habakkuk   Hab 2:18-20
   Isaiah   Is 2:6-11
   Israelites   Ezek 16:35-43;
                Amos 3:13-15;
                5:26-27
   Jeremiah   Jer 32:26-44
   Judahites   Jer 44:1-14
   Micah   Mic 1:5-9
   Moabites   Jer 48:1-47
   Zechariah   Zech 12:1-13:6
REVELATION on
   Egyptians   Ezek 30:13-19
   Ezekiel   Ezek 14:1-11
   God   Is 42:5-17
   Isaiah   Is 56:9-57:13
   Israelites   Ezek 6:8-10;
                Hos 2:9-13
   Jeremiah   Jer 7:16-20;
                11:1-14;
                16:1-13;
                16-18;
                19:1-15
   John   Rev 16:2
   Judahites   Ezek 23:22-35
   Levites   Ezek 44:10-14

as **QUALITY OF LIFE**
  through **FALSE BELIEF**
   Psalmist   Ps 115:3-8;
                135:15-18

RATIONALIZATION of
  through **FALSE BELIEF**
   Israelites   Ex 32:15-24

dis**RESPECT** for
  PROPHECY of
   Isaiah   Is 17:7-8

RITE of
  through **FALSE BELIEF**
   Babylonians Dan 3:7
   Belshazzar   Dan 5:1-4
  INSTRUCTION on
   Jeremiah   *Jer 6:41-44
   Nebuchadnezzar Dan 3:13-15
  in **WORSHIP**
   Ahaziah   1 Kgs 22:51-53;
                2 Chr 17:1-20:37

in**SECURITY** in
  PROPHECY of
   Jeremiah   Jer 10:1-16

SIGNS of

SIGNS of (cont'd)
  in **ENVIRONMENT**
    Danites   Judg 18:14-20
  through **FALSE BELIEF**
    Babylonians   *Bel 1:3-7
    Israelites   Ex 32:1-6

SIN of
    Ahab   1 Kgs 16:29-34
    Belshazzar   Dan 5:18-25
    Israelites   Deut 9:7-24;
                  Ps 106:28-31;
                  34-39
    Jerusalemites Mic 6:9-16
    Judahites   1 Kgs 14:21-24
    Moses   Lev 26:1-46
    Nineveh   Nah 1:11;
                  14
    Omri   1 Kgs 16:23-28
  before **DEITY**
    Israelites   Ps 106:19-23
  through **FALSE BELIEF**
    Ephraimites   Hos 4:17-19;
                  7:13-16;
                  8:11-14;
                  9:10-17;
                  11:1-4;
                  13:1-3
    Israelites   Num 25:1-5;
                  2 Kgs 17:7-23;
                  Neh 9:16-18;
                  Jer 18:13-17;
                  Ezek 16:15-34;
                  20:9-26;
                  23:36-49;
                  Hos 2:2-8;
                  4:4-15;
                  8:4-7;
                  10:1-8
    Jeremiah   *Jer 6:4-7;
                  60-73
    Jezebel   Rev 2:18-29
    Judahites   Jer 7:29-8:3
    Moses   Num 33:50-56;
                  Deut 12:32-13:18
    Prophets   Jer 23:13-15
    Solomon   *Wis 14:1-11
  INSTRUCTION on
    Jesus   Mt 23:16-22
    Moses   Deut 6:4-19
    Paul   Rom 1:19-23;
                  1 Cor 10:1-13
    Solomon   *Wis 14:12-31;
                  15:7-19
  PROPHECY of
    Ahijah   1 Kgs 14:1-18
    Jeremiah   Jer 5:1-14
  REVELATION on
    Ezekiel   Ezek 8:7-13;
                  14-15;
                  16-18;
                  22:1-16
    Israelites   Jer 2:1-13;
                  20-29;
                  Ezek 20:27-29;
                  30-31
    Jeremiah   Jer 1:13-16
    Mankind   Rev 9:13-21
    Moses   Ex 20:21-23

  in **WORSHIP**
    Ahaz   2 Chr 26:1-28:27
    Amaziah   2 Chr 25:1-28
    Amon   2 Chr 33:1-25
    Babylonians   2 Kgs 17:24-41
    Jeroboam   1 Kgs 12:25-33
    Joash   2 Chr 24:1-27
    Manasseh   2 Kgs 21:1-18;
                  2 Chr 33:1-25

STEWARDSHIP involving
  INSTRUCTION on
    Paul   1 Cor 8:1-3

TRADITION of
  CONFRONTATION with
    Josiah   *Sir 49:1-3
  through **FIDELITY**
    Judges   *Sir 46:11-12
  LAW concerning
    Galatian   Gal 4:8-11

in **WORSHIP**
  AUTHORITY over
    People   Rev 13:5-10
  COMPULSION concerning
    John   Rev 13:11-18
  JUDGMENT on
    Josiah   2 Kgs 23:4-15
  RITE of
    Ahaziah   1 Kgs 22:51-53;
                  2 Chr 17:1-20:37
  SIN of
    Ahaz   2 Chr 26:1-28:27
    Amaziah   2 Chr 25:1-28
    Amon   2 Chr 33:1-25
    Babylonians   2 Kgs 17:24-41
    Jeroboam   1 Kgs 12:25-33
    Joash   2 Chr 24:1-27
    Manasseh   2 Kgs 21:1-18;
                  2 Chr 33:1-25

IGNORANCE

of the **AUTHORITY**
  of **DEITY**
    Elihu   Job 36:26-33
    Job   Job 37:14-22
    Pharaoh   Ex 5:1-5
  of **MESSIANIC FIGURE**
    Crowd   Mt 12:22-32;
                  Mk 6:14-16;
                  Lk 11:14-23
    People   Lk 9:7-9

BEHAVIOR revealing
  in **ENVIRONMENT**
    Ephraimites   Hos 7:8-12
  through **FALSE BELIEF**
    Pharisees   Mt 15:12-14;
                  Lk 19:39-40
    Sinners   2 Pet 3:3-7
  INSTRUCTION on
    Agur   Prov 30:15-33
    Deaf   Mk 7:31-37
    Jesus   Mt 8:2-4;
                  9:27-31;

INSTRUCTION on (cont'd)
Jesus   12:15-21;
                         16:13-20;
                         17:9-13;
                         Mk 1:40-45;
                         3:7-12;
                         5:35-43;
                         8:27-30;
                         Lk 5:12-16;
                         8:40-56;
                         9:18-22;
    Preacher   Eccl 4:4-12
    Solomon   Prov 22:1-16
concerning MESSIANIC FIGURE
    Crowd   Lk 11:14-23
in MISSION
    Joseph   Lk 2:41-52
    Mary   Lk 2:41-52

in BELIEF
    regarding MESSIANIC FIGURE
    People   Jn 7:1-14

of COMMITMENT
    Judah   Gen 38:12-23

of CREATION
    INSTRUCTION on
    Isaiah   Is 40:12-31
    REVELATION on
    Israelites   Is 49:1-26

concerning DEITY
    Ephraimites   Hos 5:3-7
    Ezra   *2 Esd 4:1-12
    Jews   Jn 8:21-59
    Psalmist   Ps 42:6-11
    Ungodly Men   *Wis 2:21-24
    Zophar   Job 11:7-12
    PRAYER related to
    Job   Job 33:13-14

concerning DEITY's
    PRESENCE
    Elihu   Job 37:23-24
    Job   Job 23:8-14;
                         35:13-16
    Psalmist   Ps 10:1-2
    PROVIDENCE
    Elihu   Job 34:34-37
    Ephraimites   Hos 11:1-4
    Israelites   Judg 2:6-10;
                         Hos 2:2-8
    Mankind   Prov 20:1-30
    TRUTH
    Unbelievers   2 Cor 4:1-6

through FALSE BELIEF
    BEHAVIOR revealing
    Pharisees   Mt 15:12-14;
                         Lk 19:39-40
    Sinners   2 Pet 3:3-7
    KNOWLEDGE of
    Mankind   *Wis 13:1-9

    Solomon   *Wis 13:10-19

in LAW
    Judahites   Jer 8:4-7
    Pharisees   Mt 12:1-8
in NEW AGE
    Pharisees   Jn 7:32-36
in PROVIDENCE
    Isaiah   Is 44:9-20
in SIN
    Solomon   *Wis 15:7-19
in TRUTH
    Gentiles   Eph 4:17-24

of FIDELITY
    of DEITY
    Asaph   Ps 73:21-28
    Israelites   Hos 4:1-3

of FOLLOWERs
    in NEW AGE
    Apostles   Acts 1:6-11
    in PRAYER
    Believers   Rom 8:26-27
    SIGNS of
    Jesus   Mk 8:14-21

INSTRUCTION on
    of BEHAVIOR
    Agur   Prov 30:15-33
    Deaf   Mk 7:31-37
    Jesus   Mt 8:2-4;
                         9:27-31;
                         12:15-21;
                         16:13-20;
                         17:9-13;
                         Mk 1:40-45;
                         3:7-12;
                         5:35-43;
                         8:27-30;
                         Lk 5:12-16;
                         8:40-56;
                         9:18-22
    Preacher   Eccl 4:4-12
    Solomon   Prov 22:1-16
    of CREATION
    Isaiah   Is 40:12-31
    of JUDGMENT
    Mankind   2 Pet 3:8-10
    Paul   1 Cor 3:1-4
    of KNOWLEDGE
    Baruch   *Bar 3:15-23
    Bildad   Job 18:1-4
    God   Ps 82:2-7
    Jeremiah   Jer 5:20-25
    Jesus   Jn 10:1-18
    Job   Job 28:1-13;
                         14-22
    Paul   Gal 4:8-11
    Preacher   Eccl 11:1-8
    Sirach   *Sir 20:9-17;
                         18-23;
                         21:8-28;
                         22:7-15;
                         16-18;
                         27:8-15;
                         33:4-6;
                         34:1-8;
                         41:14-23;
                         42:8

of **MISSION**
  revealed in **BEHAVIOR**
    Joseph   Lk 2:41-52
    Mary   Lk 2:41-52

of **NEW AGE**
  through **FALSE BELIEF**
    Pharisees   Jn 7:32-36
  by **FOLLOWERs**
    Apostles   Acts 1:6-11
  INSTRUCTION on
    Jesus   Mt 24:42-44;
                        25:1-13;
                        Mk 13:28-37;
                        Lk 12:54-56;
                        21:34-36
    Paul   1 Thes 5:1-11
    Preacher   Eccl 6:1-12
  of **MESSIANIC FIGURE**
    Jesus   Lk 12:39-40
  PROPHECY of
    Jesus   Mt 24:37-41;
                        Jn 8:21-59
  REVELATION on
    Mankind   2 Pet 3:8-10

PRAYER related to
  concerning **DEITY**
    Job   Job 33:13-14
  of **FOLLOWERs**
    Believers   Rom 8:26-27

concerning **PRESENCE**
  of **DEITY**
    Elihu   Job 37:23-24
    Job   Job 23:8-14;
                      35:13-16
    Psalmist   Ps 10:1-2

PROPHECY of
  of **JUDGMENT**
    Isaiah   Is 5:8-24a
  of **KNOWLEDGE**
    Disciples   Lk 18:31-34
    Egyptians   Is 19:1-15
    Isaiah   Is 29:9-12
    Jeremiah   Jer 14:17-18
  of **NEW AGE**
    Jesus   Mt 24:37-41;
                       Jn 8:21-59
  of **SALVATION**
    Caiaphas   Jn 11:1-57
  of **TRUTH**
    Disciples   Lk 9:43b-45

concerning **PROVIDENCE**
  of **DEITY**
    Elihu   Job 34:34-37
    Ephraimites Hos 11:1-4
    Israelites   Judg 2:6-10;
                      Hos 2:2-8
    Mankind   Prov 20:1-30
  through **FALSE BELIEF**
    Isaiah   Is 44:9-20

of **PROVIDENCE**
  INSTRUCTION on
    Preacher   Eccl 9:1-16

PUNISHMENT for
  INSTRUCTION on

INSTRUCTION on (cont'd)
    Jesus   Lk 12:47-48
    Solomon   Pro10:1-32;
                      26:1-28
  PROPHECY of
    Israelites   Hos 4:4-15
    Jesus   Lk 19:41-44
  REVELATION on
    God   Gen 12:9-13:1

as **QUALITY OF LIFE**
  INSTRUCTION on
    Isaiah   Is 56:9-57:13
    Solomon   Prov 9:13-18;
                      18:1-24

of **RECONCILIATION**
  REVELATION on
    Israelites   Ezek 45:18-25

RESPECT of
  INSTRUCTION on
    Solomon   Prov 19:1-29;
                      26:1-28

of **RESURRECTION**
  INSTRUCTION on
    Jesus   Mk 9:9-13
  SCRIPTURES on
    Sadducees   Mt 22:23-33;
                      Mk 12:18-27;
                      Lk 20:27-40

REVELATION on
  of **CREATION**
    Israelites   Is 49:1-26
  of **JUDGMENT**
    Mankind   2 Pet 3:8-10
  of **KNOWLEDGE**
    Daniel   Dan 12:5-13
    Isaiah   Is 6:1-13
    Job   Job 38:1-3
    John   Rev 10:1-11;
                      19:11-16
  of **NEW AGE**
    Mankind   2 Pet 3:8-10
  of **RECONCILIATION**
    Israelites   Ezek 45:18-25
  of **TRUTH**
    Daniel   Dan 8:26-27

of **SALVATION**
  PROPHECY of
    Caiaphas   Jn 11:1-57

SCRIPTURES on
  of **LAW**
    Pharisees   Jn 7:37-52
    Priests   Jn 7:37-52
  of **RESURRECTION**
    Sadducees   Mt 22:23-33;
                      Mk 12:18-27;
                      Lk 20:27-40

SELF-REALIZATION of
  of **KNOWLEDGE**
    Agur   Prov 30:1-14

of **SIGNS**
  by **FOLLOWERs**
    Jesus   Mk 8:14-21

INSTRUCTION on
  Jesus   Lk 12:54-56
REVELATION on
  John   Rev 14:1-5

of SIN

  Jonathan   1 Sam 14:1-46
  Mankind   Ps 14:4-6
  Moses   Lev 5:14-6:7;
                      Num 15:22-31
  through FALSE BELIEF
  Solomon   *Wis 15:7-19
INSTRUCTION on
  Preacher   Eccl 5:1-7
  Sirach   *Sir 19:20-24
  Wisdom   Prov 1:20-33

TRADITION of
  as MOTIVATION
  Abimelech   Gen 20:1-18

concerning TRUTH
  of DEITY
  Unbelievers   2 Cor 4:1-6
  through FALSE BELIEF
  Gentiles   Eph 4:17-24
  INSTRUCTION on
  Author   Heb 5:11-14
  Jesus   Mt 13:10-17;
                      Mk 4:10-20;
                      Lk 8:9-10
  of MESSIANIC FIGURE
  Crowd   Mk 6:1-6
  Nicodemus   Jn 3:1-21
  People   Mt 13:53-58;
                      Lk 4:16-30
  Rulers   1 Cor 2:6-9
  PROPHECY of
  Disciples   Lk 9:43b-45
  REVELATION on
  Daniel   Dan 8:26-27

of VICTORY
  of DEITY
  David   Ps 17:3-5

INDIFFERENCE

BEHAVIOR revealing
  Pharaoh   Ex 7:14-25;
                      8:1-15;
                      20-32;
                      9:1-7;
                      13-35
  of FOLLOWERs
  Disciples   Mt 26:36-46;
                      Mk 14:32-42;
                      Lk 22:39-46
  INSTRUCTION on
  Jesus   Mt 7:6

CONFRONTATION with
  by MESSIANIC FIGURE
  Pharisees   Mk 3:1-6

of DEITY
  to PRAYER
  Job   Job 24:1-12;
                      30:16-23

---

  to PRAYER (cont'd)
  Psalmist   Ps 88:13-14

to DEITY
  as SIN
  Israelites   Neh 9:26-31;
                      Ps 81:5c-16

to ELECTION
  INSTRUCTION on
  Paul   Rom 9:14-29;
                      11:7-24

through FALSE BELIEF
  in TRUTH
  Gentiles   Eph 4:17-24

of FOLLOWERs
  BEHAVIOR revealing
  Disciples   Mt 26:36-46;
                      Mk 14:32-42;
                      Lk 22:39-46
  to TRUTH
  Jesus   Mk 8:14-21

INSTRUCTION on
  to ELECTION
  Paul   Rom 9:14-29;
                      11:7-24
  to LAW
  Jesus   Mt 19:3-9;
                      Mk 10:1-12
  to SIN
  Jesus   Mt 12:43-45;
                      Lk 11:24-26

KNOWLEDGE of
  REVELATION on
  Laodicea   Rev 3:14-22

to LAW
  INSTRUCTION on
  Jesus   Mt 19:3-9;
                      Mk 10:1-12

MEDITATION on
  as MOTIVATION
  Preacher   Eccl 1:12-2:26

concerning MESSIANIC FIGURE
  CONFRONTATION with
  Pharisees   Mk 3:1-6
  SIGNS of
  Disciples   Mk 6:45-52

to MISSION
  SALVATION from
  Jesus   Lk 13:34-35

as MOTIVATION
  MEDITATION on
  Preacher   Eccl 1:12-2:26

to PRAYER
  by DEITY
  Job   Job 24:1-12;
                      30:16-23
  Psalmist   Ps 88:13-14

PROMISE of

PROMISE of (cont'd)
  INSTRUCTION on
    God   Ex 4:18-23
  REVELATION on
    Pharaoh   Ex 7:1-7

PROPHECY of
  as PUNISHMENT
    Isaiah   Is 32:9-14

to PROVIDENCE
  of DEITY
    Isaiah   Is 63:7-64:12
    Pharaoh   Ex 9:8-12;
                   10:1-20;
                   27;
                   11:1-10;
                   14:1-14;
                   15-22

PUNISHMENT for
  by DEITY
    God   Is 29:13-14
    Israelites   Is 42:18-43:7;
                 Amos 4:6-12
  PROPHECY of
    Isaiah   Is 32:9-14
  REVELATION on
    Zephaniah   Zeph 1:12-13

as QUALITY OF LIFE
    Israelites   Hos 4:16
  REVELATION on
    Jeremiah   Jer 7:21-28

REVELATION on
  as QUALITY OF LIFE
    Jeremiah   Jer 7:21-28

SALVATION from
  in MISSION
    Jesus   Lk 13:34-35

SIGNS of
    Pharaoh   Ex 8:16-19
  toward MESSIANIC FIGURE
    Disciples   Mk 6:45-52
  PROPHECY of
    Jesus   Lk 17:22-37

as SIN
    Edomites   Obad 1:10-14
    Israelites   Hag 1:1-11
    Zedekiah   2 Chr 36:1-23
  against DEITY
    Israelites   Neh 9:26-31;
                 Ps 81:5c-16
  INSTRUCTION on
    Jesus   Mt 12:43-45;
               Lk 11:24-26

to TRUTH
  through FALSE BELIEF
    Gentiles   Eph 4:17-24
  of FOLLOWERs
    Jesus   Mk 8:14-21

INNOCENCE

---

of BEHAVIOR
  of MESSIANIC FIGURE
    Jesus   Mt 12:1-8

BELIEF in
  before DEITY
    David   Ps 7:3-5
  MEDITATION on
    Job   Job 16:12-17

CONFRONTATION through
  in MISSION
    Apostles   Mt 10:16-22

CONFRONTATION with
  before DEITY
    Israelites   Deut 18:9-22

before DEITY
  BELIEF in
    David   Ps 7:3-5
  CONFRONTATION with
    Israelites   Deut 18:9-22
  through FIDELITY
    David   Ps 69:4-12
    Job   Job 23:8-14;
               27:1-12
  JUDGMENT on
    Isaiah   Is 50:1-11
    Job   Job 23:1-7
  KNOWLEDGE of
    Israelites   Ps 44:17-22
    Job   Job 10:1-7
  MEDIATION with
    Jesus   1 Thes 3:11-13
  PRAYER for
    Jeremiah   Jer 15:10-21
  PUNISHMENT in
    Job   Job 9:14-19
  as QUALITY OF LIFE
    David   Ps 18:20-24

DESIRE for
  of MESSIANIC FIGURE
    Pilate   Mt 27:11-26

through FIDELITY
  before DEITY
    David   Ps 69:4-12
    Job   Job 23:8-14;
               27:1-12

of FOLLOWERs
  JUDGMENT on
    Claudius   Acts 23:12-35
    Festus   Acts 25:13-27;
               26:1-32
    Pharisees Acts 22:30-23:1
  MEDIATION with
    Jesus   1 Cor 1:4-9

INSTRUCTION on
  in NEW AGE
    Jesus   Lk 18:15-17
  concerning TRUTH
    Jesus   Jn 18:28-19:16
  as VIRTUE
    Jesus   Mt 5:43-47

revealing **ANXIETY**
Jesus   Mt 6:25-34;
                         Lk 12:22-31
revealing **BLASPHEMY**
Wife   Job 2:9-10
revealing **CAPTIVITY**
Antiochus   *2 Mc 14:26-27
Believers   Eph 6:5-9
Paul   Phil 1:12-30
Sirach   *Sir 33:24-31
revealing **COMPASSION**
God   *2 Esd 2:15-32
Sirach   *Sir 4:1-10
revealing **COURAGE**
Paul   1 Cor 16:13-24
revealing **COVETOUSNESS**
Jesus   Lk 14:7-11
revealing **DEATH**
God   *2 Esd 14:1-18
Tobit   *Tb 4:1-21;
                         14:1-15
revealing **DESTRUCTION**
Preacher   Eccl 3:1-8
revealing **DIGNITY**
Paul   Rom 13:11-14
revealing **DISCIPLESHIP**
Jesus   Mt 5:13-16;
                         10:9-15;
                         16-22;
                         23;
                         26-39;
                         Mk 2:13-14;
                         6:7-13;
                         Lk 9:1-6;
                         14:34-35
Paul   1 Cor 9:1-6;
                         1 Tim 3:14-16
concerning **DISOBEDIENCE**
God   Gen 3:9-13
Serpent   Gen 3:1-8
Vashti   Esth 1:10-22
revealing **DOUBT**
Jesus   Mt 14:28-33
with **ENEMY**
Jesus   Mt 5:43-47;
                         Lk 6:27-35
Sirach   *Sir 12:8-18
as **EVIL**
Sirach   *Sir 20:18-23;
                         22:1-6;
                         25:1-2
revealing **FAITH**
Author   Heb 12:12-29
God   Is 44:6-8;
                         21-23
James   Jas 2:14-26
Paul   Col 2:6-15;
                         2 Tim 2:1-7
in **FAMILY**
Paul   Col 3:18-4:1
Sirach   *Sir 7:1-36;
                         11:29-34;
                         29:21-28;
                         33:16-23;
                         42:9-14
Tobit   *Tb 4:1-21
revealing **FEAR**
Agur   Prov 30:15-33
Jude   Jude 1:21-23

revealing **FRIENDSHIP**
Paul   2 Cor 6:14-7:1;
                         Col 4:15-18
Sirach   *Sir 12:8-18
Solomon   Prov 25:1-28
revealing **GOOD**
Jesus   Mt 5:13-16;
                         Lk 6:27-35
Sirach   *Sir 4:20-31;
                         18:19-26;
                         23:12-15;
                         25:1-2
Tobit   *Tb 4:1-21
revealing **GRACE**
Jude   Jude 1:21-23
revealing **GRATITUDE**
Paul   Eph 5:3-14;
                         Col 2:6-15
revealing **GREED**
Agur   Prov 30:15-33
Paul   2 Cor 12:14-18
revealing **GRIEF**
Ezekiel   Ezek 24:15-24
Isaiah   Is 32:9-14
Preacher   Eccl 3:1-8;
                         7:1-22
Sirach   *Sir 38:16-23
revealing **GUILT**
Eliphaz   Job 15:1-6
revealing **HATE**
John   1 Jn 2:7-11
Preacher   Eccl 3:1-8
revealing **HEALING**
Jesus   Lk 4:42-44
Preacher   Eccl 3:1-8
revealing **HERESY**
Paul   Rom 16:1-23
revealing **HUMILITY**
Jesus   Lk 14:7-11
Paul   Phil 2:1-4;
                         Col 3:18-4:1
Sirach   *Sir 32:1-13
revealing **IDOLATRY**
Antiochus   *1 Mc 1:41-53
Isaiah   Is 17:9-11
Jeremiah   *Jer 6:8-40;
                         45-59
Samuel   1 Sam 7:2-17
Solomon   *Wis 14:12-31;
                         15:7-19
revealing **IGNORANCE**
Agur   Prov 30:15-33
Deaf   Mk 7:31-37
Jesus   Mt 8:2-4;
                         9:27-31;
                         12:15-21;
                         16:13-20;
                         17:9-13;
                         Mk 1:40-45;
                         3:7-12;
                         5:35-43;
                         8:27-30;
                         Lk 5:12-16;
                         8:40-56;
                         9:18-22
Preacher   Eccl 4:4-12
Solomon   Prov 22:1-16
revealing **INDIFFERENCE**
Jesus   Mt 7:6

revealing **JEALOUSY**
Eliphaz — Job 5:1-7
Solomon — Prov 27:1-27
revealing **JOY**
Attharates — *1 Esd 9:49-55
Baruch — *Bar 5:1-4
David — Ps 30:1-5
Jesus — Mt 18:12-14
Moses — Deut 16:9-12
Paul — Phil 2:12-18;
3:1-3;
4:1-9;
1 Thes 5:12-22
Preacher — Eccl 3:1-8;
8:10-17;
9:1-16;
11:9-12:7
revealing **JUSTICE**
God — Is 1:10-17
Jesus — Mt 5:38-42
Sirach — *Sir 4:1-10;
20-31
revealing **KILLING**
Abraham — Gen 22:1-19
Ahasuerus — Esth 3:7-15
Artaxerxes — *Esth 13:1-7
Demetrius — *1 Mc 7:1-4
Jehu — 2 Kgs 9:30-37
Jesus — Mt 23:34-39
Preacher — Eccl 3:1-8
of **LEADERSHIP**
Artaxerxes — Ezra 7:11-12
Lemuel — Prov 31:1-9
concerning **LIFE**
Jeremiah — Jer 29:1-23
Maiden — Song 8:14
Preacher — Eccl 3:1-8
concerning **LOVE**
Paul — 1 Cor 16:13-24;
2 Cor 12:14-18;
Eph 4:25-5:2;
Phil 2:1-4;
12-18
Preacher — Eccl 3:1-8
revealing **LUST**
Jesus — Mt 5:27-30
Paul — 1 Cor 7:36-38;
1 Thes 4:1-12
concerning **MARRIAGE**
David — 2 Sam 3:1-16
Isaac — Gen 27:41-28:5
Paul — Eph 5:21-33;
Col 3:18-4:1
Raphael — *Tb 6:1-17
Sirach — *Sir 25:16-26
Tobit — *Tb 4:1-21
revealing **OBEDIENCE**
Abraham — Gen 21:11-14
Angel — Gen 16:7-10
Author — Heb 12:12-29
Esau — Gen 27;1-40
God — Gen 2:16-17
Isaiah — Is 18:1-7
Israelites — Ex 12:50-51;
Josh 4:1-8
Joshua — Num 14:8-9;
Josh 11:1-15
Moses — Ex 34:1-5a
Paul — 1 Cor 4:14-21;
2 Cor 13:11-13;

revealing **OBEDIENCE** (cont'd)
Paul — Eph 5:21-33;
Col 3:18-4:1;
1 Thes 4:1-12
Zedekiah — Jer 32:9-15
concerning **ONENESS**
Jesus — Mt 7:12
revealing **OPPRESSION**
Artaxerxes — *Esth 13:1-7
Pharisees — Mt 23:4
revealing **ORDER**
Jesus — Mt 7:13-14
Joshua — Josh 1:10-11
revealing **PARADOX**
Jesus — Mt 10:26-39;
11:16-19;
19:27-30;
23:27-28;
Mk 10:28-31;
Lk 7:31-35;
13:22-30
Paul — Gal 2:11-14
Pharisees — Mt 23:1-3
revealing **PATIENCE**
Paul — 1 Thes 5:12-22
concerning **PEACE**
Author — Heb 12:12-29
Preacher — Eccl 3:1-8
revealing **PIETY**
Jesus — Mt 6:1
concerning **POLITICS**
Demetrius — *1 Mc 11:20-37
revealing **POVERTY**
Sirach — *Sir 29:8-13
Solomon — Prov 22:22-23:14
revealing **PRIDE**
Preacher — Eccl 7:1-22
Solomon — Prov 27:1-27
revealing **PRUDENCE**
Amos — Amos 5:7-13
God — Gen 6:5-22
Isaiah — Is 8:8b-10
James — Jas 3:1-12
Jesus — Mt 5:21-26;
33-37;
7:15-20;
Lk 10:38-42;
21:34-36
Maiden — Song 3:1-5
Paul — 1 Cor 10:23-11:1;
Eph 5:15-20;
Col 4:5-6;
1 Thes 5:1-11;
1 Tim 5:3-16;
17-25
Preacher — Eccl 5:1-7
Sirach — *Sir 8:1-19;
13:1-13;
18:19-26;
27-33;
31:12-24
Solomon — Prov 1:2-6;
5:1-14;
10:1-32;
22:1-16;
22-23:14

concerning **PURIFICATION**
God — Is 1:10-17
John the Baptist — Jn 1:19-51

revealing **REPENTANCE**
John the Baptist	Lk 3:7-9; 10-14
Paul	2 Cor 13:11-13

concerning **REWARDs**
Paul	Rom 2:1-24
Sirach	*Sir 4:1-10

revealing **SACREDNESS**
Cyrus	*1 Esd 2:1-7
Moses	Deut 22:1-12

revealing **SADNESS**
Preacher	Eccl 7:1-22

revealing **SERVICE**
Isaac	Gen 27:1-40
Jesus	Mt 5:38-42; Lk 14:1-6
John	3 Jn 1:3-8
Paul	Phil 2:1-4; Col 3:18-4:1; 1 Thes 5:1-11; 12-22; Tit 3:12-15

related to **SEX**
Lemuel	Prov 31:1-9
Paul	1 Cor 7:1-7; 8-16; 1 Thes 4:1-12
Sirach	*Sir 9:1-9; 19:1-3; 26:5-12; 42:9-14

revealing **SHARING**
Moses	Deut 15:1-11
Paul	Col 4:15-18; Tit 3:12-15
Preacher	Eccl 4:4-12

revealing **SUFFERING**
Holy Spirit	Acts 20:17-38
Preacher	Eccl 11:9-12:7

revealing **TEMPERANCE**
James	Jas 3:1-12
Jesus	Mt 6:16-18
Lemuel	Prov 31:1-9
Paul	1 Cor 7:1-7; 8-16; 36-38; Col 2:16-23
Sirach	*Sir 19:1-3; 37:27-31
Tobit	*Tb 4:1-21

concerning **TEMPTATION**
Jesus	Mt 4:1-11
Paul	1 Cor 7:8-16; 36-38
Solomon	Prov 23:15-24:22

revealing **VIOLENCE**
Preacher	Eccl 3:1-8

concerning **WEALTH**
Artaxerxes	*1 Esd 8:8-24
Darius	*1 Esd 6:27-34
Demetrius	*1 Mc 11:20-37
Preacher	Eccl 5:8-20
Sirach	*Sir 13:1-13; 18:27-33; 42:6-7
Solomon	Prov 12:1-28; 14:1-35
Tobit	*Tb 4:1-21

revealing **WILL**
David	Ps 32:8-11
John the Baptist	Lk 3:7-9

revealing **WISDOM**
Agur	Prov 30:15-33
Daughters	Song 1:8
Jesus	Mt 5:31-32
Solomon	Prov 6:6-11

as **WITNESS**
Jesus	Mt 5:13-16
Paul	Acts 24:1-27; 2 Cor 3:1-3

of **YOUTH**
Jesus	Mt 19:13-15; Mk 10:13-16
Paul	Eph 6:1-4; Col 3:18-4:1
Solomon	Prov 22:1-16

on **BELIEF**

as **BLESSING**
Paul	Gal 3:6-9

results in **COURAGE**
David	1 Chr 28:1-29:3
God	Is 44:6-8; 21-23
Paul	2 Cor 5:6-8

concerning **DEATH**
James	Jas 2:14-26

in **DISCIPLESHIP**
Holy Spirit	Acts 19:1-12

through **FAITH**
Jesus	Jn 6:25-59; 7:37-52; 11:1-57
John	1 Jn 5:13-21

in **FULFILLMENT**
Jesus	Jn 6:25-59

in **GRACE**
Author	Heb 4:14-16
John the Baptist	Lk 3:1-6
Joshua	Num 14:8-9
Paul	Rom 3:31-4:25; 2 Cor 4:13-15
Peter	Acts 10:1-11:18

in **HEALING**
James	Jas 5:14-18
Jesus	Lk 17:11-19

through **HOPE**
John the Baptist	Jn 3:31-36
Paul	2 Cor 10:12-18

with **HUMILITY**
Paul	Rom 3:21-30

with **JOY**
Paul	2 Cor 7:13b-16
Peter	1 Pet 1:3-9

concerning **LIFE**
Jesus	Jn 8:21-59
Paul	Rom 6:1-14

concerning **LOVE**
Paul	1 Cor 13:4-7; Gal 5:2-6

concerning **MARRIAGE**
Paul	1 Cor 7:8-16

in **MIRACLE**
God	Ex 4:1-9
Jesus	Mk 9:14-29

concerning im**PATIENCE**
Eliphaz	Job 4:1-6

to **PATIENCE**
  Paul   2 Tim 2:20-26
to **PEACE**
  Israelites   Zech 7:4-8:23
  Paul   Rom 8:5-13;
                       14:1-23;
                       2 Tim 2:20-26;
                       Heb 12:12-29
concerning **POVERTY**
  Solomon   Prov 22:22-23:14
concerning **PRIDE**
  Paul   2 Cor 5:11-13
to **PURIFICATION**
  Israelites   Deut 10:12-22
  Paul   2 Tim 2:20-26
through **REPENTANCE**
  James   Jas 5:14-18
  Paul   Rom 2:1-24
  Peter   Acts 8:14-25
  Zephaniah   Zeph 2:1-2
to **SERVICE**
  Joshua   Josh 24:14-15
to **SPIRIT**
  Paul   Rom 8:5-13

on **COMPASSION**
  God   *2 Esd 2:15-32
  Sirach   *Sir 4:1-10
  in **JUDGMENT**
    God   *Wis 12:19-22
  in **LAW**
    Jesus   Mt 12:9-14
    Moses   Deut 23:15-25:19
  as **QUALITY OF LIFE**
    Jesus   Mt 18:23-35
    Paul   Col 3:5-17
  over **SIN**
    Paul   Gal 5:25-6:6;
                   2 Tim 2:20-26
  in **STEWARDSHIP**
    Jesus   Lk 15:11-32
  as **VIRTUE**
    God   Ps 82:2-7;
                   *Wis 12:19-22
    Sirach   *Sir 12:1-7

on **COMPULSION**
  for **EVIL**
    Jesus   Mt 18:5-6;
                 Mk 9:42-48;
                 Lk 17:1-6
  of **HUMILITY**
    Women   Esth 1:10-22
  concerning **IDOLATRY**
    Nebuchadnezzar   Dan 3:1-6
  of **PRAISE**
    Jesus   Lk 19:39-40
  of **TEMPERANCE**
    Paul   Rom 14:1-23
  in **WISDOM**
    Daniel   Dan 1:1-7

on **CONDEMNATION**
  of **BEHAVIOR**
    Bildad   Job 8:1-7
    Jesus   Mt 5:21-26;
                 12:33-37;
                 23:27-28
    Job   Job 19:1-6
    Paul   Gal 2:11-14

of **BEHAVIOR** (cont'd)
  Preacher   Eccl 9:17-10:20
  Zophar   Job 11:1-6
of **unBELIEF**
  Elihu   Job 33:8-12
  Jesus   Jn 3:1-21
  Paul   1 Tim 5:3-16
of **CREATION**
  Artaxerxes   Ezra 4:17-22
for **ETERNITY**
  Jesus   Mt 25:31-46;
                 Lk 16:19-31
of in**FIDELITY**
  Jesus   Mt 7:21-23;
                 26:17-30;
                 Mk 14:17-21;
                 Lk 13:22-30
as **JUDGMENT**
  Author   Heb 5:11-14
  God   Is 1:24-26
  Jesus   Mt 12:33-37;
                 18:15-17;
                 23:13;
                 15;
                 Lk 11:37-44;
                 16:14-15
  Job   Job 12:1-6;
                 21:28-34
  Jotham   Judg 9:16-21
  Paul   Rom 2:1-24;
                 5:12-21;
                 14:1-23;
                 1 Cor 5:1-5
  Peter   Acts 8:14-25
of **LAW**
  Moses   Deut 11:26-32;
                 27:11-26
  Paul   Rom 3:31-4:25;
                 Gal 3:10-14
in **NEW AGE**
  Paul   Gal 5:16-21
as **PUNISHMENT**
  David   1 Kgs 2:5-12
as **QUALITY OF LIFE**
  Bildad   Job 18:5-7;
                 8-11
  Jesus   Lk 6:24-26
  Laodicea   Rev 3:14-22
after **RESURRECTION**
  Jesus   Jn 5:19-47
of **RITE**
  Moses   Deut 27:11-26
  Paul   1 Cor 11:27-34
of **SIN**
  Author   Heb 6:1-8;
                 10:19-31
  God   Is 1:10-17
  Isaiah   Is 56:9-57:13
  James   Jas 4:1-10
  Jesus   Mt 12:43-45;
                 18:5-6;
                 7-9;
                 21:33-43;
                 22:1-14;
                 Mk 9:42-48;
                 12:1-12;
                 37b-40;
                 Lk 11:24-26;
                 13:1-5;
                 14:15-24;

of **SPIRIT**
Paul — Rom 12:1-2
through **WISDOM**
Paul — 2 Cor 3:12-18

on **COURAGE**
in **BEHAVIOR**
Paul — 1 Cor 16:13-24
in **BELIEF**
David — 1 Chr 28:1-29:30
God — Is 44:6-8; 21-23
Paul — 2 Cor 5:6-8
in **CONFRONTATION**
Elisha — 2 Kgs 6:8-23
Moses — Deut 20:1-9; 31:1-8
Smyrna — Rev 2:8-11
through **FIDELITY**
David — Ps 27:13-14; 31:19-24
through **KNOWLEDGE**
Solomon — Prov 3:1-35
through **PROVIDENCE**
Hezekiah — 2 Chr 32:1-33
in **RITE**
Isaiah — Is 40:1-11
in **SECURITY**
God — Is 41:1-42:4
Solomon — Prov 3:1-35
Zophar — Job 11:13-20
in **STEWARDSHIP**
Isaiah — Is 35:1-10
in **TRUTH**
Paul — Phil 1:12-30
as **VIRTUE**
Solomon — Prov 28:1-28

on **COVETOUSNESS**
Jesus — Lk 14:7-11
of **GIFT**
Paul — 1 Cor 12:27-31a; 14:1-12
concerning **NEW AGE**
Jesus — Lk 12:22-31
as **SIN**
Jesus — Mt 21:33-43; Mk 12:1-12; Lk 20:9-18
Paul — Rom 7:7-13; Eph 5:3-14
in **STEWARDSHIP**
Paul — 1 Tim 6:6-10

on **CREATION**
of **FAMILY**
Paul — Gal 4:27-31
of **LIFE**
Angel — Lk 2:1-20
Gabriel — Lk 1:5-25; 26-38
God — Gen 1:20-23; 24-31; 8:13-22; 9:1-7
Jesus — Jn 3:1-21
Manoah — Judg 13:2-7
Mary — Lk 1:26-38
of **MIRACLE**
Joseph — Mt 1:18-25
Joshua — Josh 10:16-27

of **SACREDNESS**
Paul — 1 Cor 3:10-17; 1 Tim 4:1-5
of **SANCTUARY**
Cyrus — 2 Chr 36:1-23; Ezra 1:2-4
Darius — Ezra 6:1-12
David — 1 Chr 22:2-19; 28:1-29:30
Hezekiah — 2 Chr 29:1-36
Jesus — Mt 16:13-20
Joash — 2 Kgs 12:4-16
Moses — Ex 35:4-29
Solomon — 2 Chr 2:1-4:22
Tattenai — Ezra 5:6-17
through **WISDOM**
Solomon — Prov 23:15-24:2

on **DEATH**
Angel — *2 Esd 7:100-11
God — *2 Esd 2:15-32; 14:1-18
Jacob — Gen 49:29-33
James — Jas 2:14-26; 5:19-20
Jesus — Mt 22:23-33; Mk 12:18-27; Lk 20:27-40; Rom 5:12-21; 1 Pet 4:1-6
Job — Job 21:19-27
Moses — Deut 21:22-23
Paul — Rom 6:1-14; 7:1-6; 1 Cor 7:39-40; 13:8-13; 15:12-19; 51-58; 2 Cor 3:7-11; Gal 2:17-19; 20-21; 1 Thes 4:13-18
Preacher — Eccl 8:1-9
Raphael — *Tb 6:1-17
Sirach — *Sir 38:16-23
Solomon — Prov 23:15-24:2; *Wis 1:12-15
Tobit — *Tb 4:1-21; 14:1-15
through **FIDELITY**
Angel — *2 Esd 7:88-99
as **PUNISHMENT**
Angel — *2 Esd 7:75-87
Antiochus — *1 Mc 1:41-53
Darius — Dan 6:24; *1 Esd 6:27-34
God — Ps 82:2-7
Israelites — Judg 20:12-17
Jesus — Mt 15:3-9; Mk 7:1-23
Moses — Ex 32:24-29; 35:1-3; Lev 20:1-27; Deut 16:21-17:7; 8-13; 21:18-21; 22-23; 23:15-25:19; 28:15-68
Nebuchadnezzar — Dan 3:1-6; 13-15

as **PUNISHMENT** (cont'd)

Prophet	1 Kgs 20:1-43
Solomon	Prov 5:15-23;
	9:13-18

as **QUALITY OF LIFE**

James	Jas 4:13-16
Preacher	Eccl 11:9-12:7
Psalmist	Ps 49:16-20
Sirach	*Sir 10:6-11;
	11:14-20;
	14:3-19;
	17:15-32;
	18:1-14;
	41:1-4

through **SIN**

James	Jas 1:13-15
Jesus	Jn 8:21-59
Moses	Ex 19:9-15;
	Deut 22:13-30
Paul	Rom 5:12-21;
	6:1-14;
	15-23;
	7:7-13;
	8:5-13;
	1 Cor 15:51-58
Peter	1 Pet 2:21-25
Solomon	Prov 12:1-28

on **DEFEAT**

in **CONFRONTATION**

Moses	Deut 28:15-68

in **STEWARDSHIP**

Jesus	Mt 13:3b-9;
	Lk 8:4-8

on **DESIRE**

for **EVIL**

Jesus	Jn 8:21-59

for **FAMILY**

David	2 Sam 3:1-16
Sirach	*Sir 16:1-5

for **FULFILLMENT**

Solomon	Prov 2:1-22;
	13:1-25

for **GOOD**

Amos	Amos 5:14-15
Sirach	*Sir 16:1-5

for **GRATITUDE**

God	Ps 50:22-23
Psalmist	Ps 105:1-6

for **HEALING**

Crowds	Mt 4:23-25

for **HOPE**

Solomon	Prov 13:1-25

for **HUMILITY**

Zephaniah	Zeph 2:3

for **JUSTICE**

Elihu	Job 33:31-33
Job	Job 31:38-40
Sirach	*Sir 27:8-15

for **LEADERSHIP**

Zechariah	Zech 10:1-12

for **LOVE**

Paul	1 Cor 14:1-12

for **LUST**

Preacher	Eccl 6:1-12

for **MARRIAGE**

Naomi	Ruth 3:1-18

for **OBEDIENCE**

Artaxerxes	Ezra 7:20-24

for **OLD AGE** (maturity)

Peter	1 Pet1:13-2:3

for **PEACE**

David	Ps 34:11-14

of **PRIDE**

Preacher	Eccl 6:1-12

for **REPENTANCE**

Paul	2 Cor 12:19-21;
	Gal 4:12-20

for **REWARD**

Paul	Phil 1:12-30

for **SACREDNESS**

God	Is 51:1-16

for **SERVICE**

Paul	2 Tim 4:9-18

for **SEX**

Psalmist	Ps 45:10-12

as **TEMPTATION**

Paul	1 Tim 6:6-10

for **WEALTH**

Jesus	Mt 6:19-24

for **WISDOM**

Elihu	Job 33:31-33
Father	Prov 4:1-9
Jesus	Mt 9:10-13
Job	Job 6:21-27
Solomon	Prov 5:1-14;
	6:20-7:27;
	9:1-6;
	*Wis 6:12-25
Wisdom	Prov 1:20-33

on **DESPAIR**

as **PUNISHMENT**

Isaiah	Is 59:1-21
Jeremiah	Jer 6:22-26

on **DESTRUCTION**

Paul	1 Thes 5:1-11;
	2 Thes 2:3b-10
Preacher	Eccl 3:1-8

through **unBELIEF**

John	Jude 1:5-7

in **CONFRONTATION**

Moab	Is 15:1-16:14
Moses	Deut 7:1-5

as **JUDGMENT**

Moses	Ex 23:20-33;
	Num 33:16-36;
	Deut 7:1-5

as **MOTIVATION**

Psalmist	Ps 146:3-4

as **PUNISHMENT**

Eliphaz	Job 15:17-35
God	Is 1:18-20;
	*2 Esd 2:8-9
Joshua	Josh 23:1-16
Moses	Deut 6:4-19;
	8:11-20;
	28:15-68

as **QUALITY OF LIFE**

Jesus	Mt 7:15-20

resulting from **SIN**

Isaiah	Is 59:1-21
Jesus	Mt 7:24-27;
	13:36-43;
	47-50;
	Lk 6:46-49
Paul	Rom 6:1-14;
	Phil 3:17-21

resulting from **SIN** (cont'd)
Solomon	Prov 1:10-19; 11:1-31; 12:1-28; 13:1-25; 14:1-35

of **TRUTH**
Baruch	Jer 36:20-26

as **VIRTUE**
Isaiah	Is 56:9-57:13

on **DIGNITY**
Paul	Rom 13:11-14

in **AUTHORITY**
Agur	Prov 30:15-33
Jesus	Mt 7:28-29; Mk 1:21-28; Lk 4:31-37
Peter	Acts 4:1-22

in **BROTHERHOOD**
Paul	2 Cor 3:1-3

in **FIDELITY**
Jesus	Lk 16:10-12

of **GIFT**
Paul	2 Cor 8:16-24

in **HONESTY**
James	Jas 5:12
Paul	1 Cor 4:1-5

as **QUALITY OF LIFE**
Jesus	Lk 14:7-11

in **RESPECT**
Paul	Rom 12:9-13; 13:1-7
Preacher	Eccl 7:1-22
Solomon	Prov 26:1-28
Wife	Prov 31:10-31

in **STEWARDSHIP**
Jesus	Lk 22:24-27

of **TRUTH**
Jesus	Jn 18:28-19:16

on **DISCIPLESHIP**
Jesus	Mt 5:13-16; 10:9-15; 16-22; 23; 26-39; 18:18-20; Mk 2:13-14; 6:7-13; Lk 9:1-6; 14:34-35
Paul	1 Cor 9:1-6; 1 Tim 3:14-16

concerning **BELIEF**
Holy Spirit	Acts 19:1-12

in **BROTHERHOOD**
Jesus	Mt 12:46-50; Mk 3:31-35; Lk 8:19-21

concerning **COMMITMENT**
Paul	Rom 9:30-10:21

concerning **ELECTION**
Jesus	Mt 13:10-17; Mk 4:10-20; Lk 8:9-10
Paul	1 Cor 12:27-31a
Peter	Acts 15:6-29; 1 Pet 2:4-10

concerning **EQUALITY**
Elihu	Job 33:1-7
Paul	1 Cor 11:2-16

concerning **FIDELITY**
Jesus	Mt 9:14-15; Mk 2:18-22; Lk 5:33-35; 14:25-27; 28-33; Jn 15:1-11; 21:15-23
Paul	Eph 6:10-18
Psalmist	Ps 100:1-3

concerning **GIFT**
Paul	1 Cor 12:27-31a

concerning **HONESTY**
Paul	Eph 4:25-5:2

concerning **LAW**
God	1 Cor 14:34-40
Psalmist	Ps 119:105-112

in **NEW AGE**
Jesus	Lk 9:57-62; 22:28-30
Paul	Gal 6:11-18

concerning **PRAYER**
Author	Heb 13:1-25
Jesus	Mt 9:36-38; Lk 11:1-4

concerning **PRESENCE**
Holy Spirit	Eph 5:15-20
Jesus	Mt 18:18-20

as **QUALITY OF LIFE**
Jesus	Mt 8:18-22; Lk 9:57-62
Paul	Phil 2:5-11; 3:4-16

concerning **STEWARDSHIP**
Jesus	Mt 10:7-8; 26-39; 28:16-20; Mk 4:21-25; 10:35-45; Lk 8:16-18; 14:25-27
John the Baptist	Lk 3:10-14
Paul	Tit 2:1-10

of **TRUTH**
Jesus	Mt 5:1-2; 13:3b-9; 10-17; 18-23; Mk 4:1-9; 10-20; 33-34; Lk 8:1-3; 4-8; 9-10; 11-15; 9:10-11

on **DISOBEDIENCE**
God	Gen 3:9-13
Serpent	Gen 3:1-8
Vashti	Esth 1:10-22

to **AUTHORITY**
Jesus	Mt 7:24-27; Lk 6:46-49

concerning **FIDELITY** (cont'd)

Judith	*Jdt 8:9-27
Paul	1 Cor 16:13-24;
	2 Cor 4:16-18;
	Phil 1:12-30;
	Col 1:21-23;
	2 Thes 2:13-15;
	1 Tim 6:20-21;
	2 Tim 2:14-19;
	3:14-17
Sirach	*Sir 2:7-11;
	12-18
Women	1 Tim 3:8-13;
	1 Pet 3:1-7

in GIFTs

Holy Spirit	Gal 3:1-5

in HONESTY

Jesus	Lk 16:10-12

in JUDGMENT

Elihu	Job 36:16-25
Eliphaz	Job 4:7-11
Jesus	Mt 17:14-20;
	Mk 9:14-29;
	Lk 9:37-43a

in KNOWLEDGE

Jesus	Mt 14:22-27;
	Mk 6:45-52;
	Jn 6:16-24
Paul	1 Cor 13:8-13
Sirach	*Sir 19:4-12

in LAW

Paul	Rom 3:21-30;
	Gal 3:1-5

as MOTIVATION

Jesus	Lk 13:6-9
Paul	Rom 9:30-10:21

in NEW AGE

Author	Heb 11:1-40
Jesus	Mk 4:26-29;
	Lk 13:18-19;
	18:1-8;
	15-17
Paul	Rom 9:30-10:21

in PRAYER

Holy Spirit	Jude 1:20
James	Jas 1:5-8
Jesus	Mt 21:18-22;
	Mk 9:14-29;
	11:20-26;
	Lk 18:1-8;
	Jn 16:25-28

in PRESENCE

Jesus	Mt 28:16-20

in PROVIDENCE

God	Is 41:1-42:4
Jesus	Mt 6:25-34;
	7:7-11;
	10:26-39;
	Lk 12:22-31
Zechariah	Zech 10:1-2

as QUALITY OF LIFE

Jesus	Mt 15:12-14;
	16:5-12;
	21:18-22;
	Mk 8:14-21;
	11:20-26
Paul	2 Cor 5:6-8;
	Gal 3:6-9;
	1 Thes 5:1-11;
	1 Tim 4:6-10
Peter	Acts 3:1-26

in RESURRECTION

Jesus	Jn 11:1-57
Paul	1 Cor 15:12-19;
	29-34;
	35-41;
	2 Cor 4:13-15;
	Col 2:6-15;
	2 Tim 2:8-13

in TRUTH

Author	Heb 4:1-13
Deacons	1 Tim 3:8-13
Jesus	Mt 13:18-23;
	Mk 1:14-15;
	4:10-20;
	9:49-50;
	Lk 8:11-15
Paul	Acts 13:4-12;
	Rom 1:16-17;
	1 Tim 3:14-16;
	Tit 1:9-16

as VIRTUE

Author	Heb 10:32-39
Jesus	Mt 8:5-13;
	25:1-13;
	Lk 7:1-10
Paul	Rom 1:16-17;
	3:31-4:25;
	9:30-10:21;
	Gal 3:10-14;
	Eph 6:10-18;
	1 Tim 6:11-16
Peter	2 Pet 1:5-7

on FAMILY

God	Ex 20:1-17
Jesus	Mt 15:3-9;
	19:16-22;
	Mk 7:1-23;
	10:17-22
Moses	Ex 21:12-17;
	Lev 20:1-27;
	Deut 5:1-21;
	21:15-17;
	18-21;
	23:15-25:19;
	27:11-26
Paul	Eph 6:1-4;
	Col 3:18-4:1
Sirach	*Sir 3:1-16;
	7:1-36;
	11:29-34;
	22:1-6;
	29:21-28;
	30:1-13;
	33:16-23;
	41:14-23;
	42:9-14
Tobit	*Tb 4:1-21

in BROTHERHOOD

Jesus	Mt 12:46-50;
	Mk 3:31-35;
	Lk 8:19-21
Paul	1 Tim 5:1-2

on FEAR

Agur	Prov 30:15-33
Jude	Jude 1:21-23

of AUTHORITY

Moses	Deut 6:4-19;
	12:32-13:18;
	17:14-20

in **MARRIAGE** (cont'd)

Jesus	10:1-12
Moses	Deut 5:1-21
Paul	Rom 7:1-6;
	13:8-10;
	1 Cor 7:1-7;
	8-16;
	25-35;
	39-40;
	1 Thes 4:1-12;
	1 Tim 5:3-16
Solomon	Prov 5:15-23

through **OBEDIENCE**

Aaron	Ex 7:14-25
Abraham	Gen 22:1-19
Author	Heb 2:1-4;
	3:6b-11;
	12-19;
	4:1-13
Barnabas	Acts 11:22-24
Believers	Rev 14:9-12
David	Ps 15:5c
Father	Prov 4:20-27
God	Ps 95:7d-11
James	Jas 1:22-25
Jesus	Mt 21:28-32;
	23:5-12;
	24:45-51;
	Lk 14:25-27;
	28-33;
	19:11-27;
	Jn 7:53-8:11;
	10:1-18;
	16:1-4
Joshua	Josh 24:14-15
Malachi	Mal 2:10-16
Mattathias	*1 Mc 2:49-70
Moses	Ex 8:1-15;
	9:8-12;
	13-35;
	10:1-20;
	21-23;
	11:1-10;
	14:15-22;
	23-31
Paul	Eph 5:3-14;
	6:5-9;
	Phil 2:12-18;
	4:1-9;
	Col 1:21-23
Peter	1 Pet 5:12-14
Samuel	1 Sam 12:1-25
Solomon	Prov 6:20-27
Wisdom	Prov 8:32-36

to **ONENESS**

Jesus	Lk 16:13;
	Jn 15:1-11
Paul	1 Cor 10:14-22

in **OPPRESSION**

Jesus	Mt 5:38-42
Paul	2 Tim 3:10-13

in **ORDER**

Jesus	Mt 24:42-44;
	Mk 13:28-37

through **PATIENCE**

David	Ps 37:23-40
Hosea	Hos 12:2-6
Jesus	Lk 21:34-36
Paul	Eph 4:1-6
Peter	2 Pet 3:14-18a

in **PIETY**

Believers	Acts 2:42-47
Paul	Col 4:2-4;
	1 Tim 4:11-16

through **PURIFICATION**

Elisha	2 Kgs 5:1-19

through **REJECTION**

Author	Heb 3:12-19
Jesus	Mt 8:18-22;
	23:34-39;
	Lk 9:57-62;
	12:1-12

in **REPENTANCE**

Ephesus	Rev 2:1-7
Jeremiah	Jer 6:16-21
Jesus	Lk 16:19-31;
	Jn 7:53-8:11
Samuel	1 Sam 7:2-17
Zephaniah	Zeph 2:3

in **SACREDNESS**

Jesus	Lk 14:34-35

of **SACRIFICE**

Jesus	Lk 14:25-27;
	28-33

in **SERVICE**

Jesus	Lk 16:13
John	1 Jn 3:11-18
Moses	Deut 10:12-22
Paul	Eph 6:5-9;
	1 Tim 6:1-28

in **SEX**

Jesus	Mt 19:3-9;
	Mk 10:1-12;
	Lk 16:16-18

in **SPIRIT**

Jesus	Mk 12:28-34

through **SUFFERING**

Author	Heb 12:1-2;
	3-11
Believers	Rev 14:9-12
Elihu	Job 36:16-25
James	Jas 1:2-4
Paul	2 Tim 2:1-7;
	3:10-13;
	4:1-5
Peter	1 Pet 1:3-9

through **TEMPTATION**

Paul	1 Cor 7:1-7;
	2 Cor 11:1-6;
	Gal 5:7-12;
	Col 2:6-15
Sirach	*Sir 2:1-6
Solomon	Prov 1:10-19

with **WEALTH**

Paul	1 Tim 6:17-19

through **WISDOM**

Baruch	*Bar 4:1-4
Father	Prov 4:1-9
Moses	Deut 4:1-14

in **WITNESS**

Isaiah	Is 48:1-22
Paul	Phil 3:4-16;
	2 Tim 3:10-13

on in**FIDELITY**

resulting in **ALIENATION**

Jesus	Mt 7:21-23;
	Lk 13:22-30

through **FEAR**

Mary	Mk 16:1-8

through **FEAR** (cont'd)

Moses	Ex 20:18-20
Paul	2 Cor 11:1-6

through **PRIDE**

Jesus	Mk 9:38-41;
	Lk 9:49-50

on **FREEDOM**

from **ANXIETY**

Paul	1 Cor 7:25-35

from **CAPTIVITY**

Artaxerxes	*1 Esd 8:8-24
Cyrus	*1 Esd 2:1-7
Isaiah	Is 51:17-52:12
Moses	Deut 15:12-18;
	21:10-14

from **DEATH**

Paul	1 Cor 7:39-40

from **DESTRUCTION**

Jesus	Mt 7:13-14

from **EVIL**

Paul	Rom 6:1-14

through **GRACE**

Paul	Rom 6:1-14;
	Gal 4:4-7

from **MARRIAGE**

Jesus	Mt 5:31-32;
	19:3-9;
	Mk 10:1-12
Moses	Deut 23:15-25:19
Paul	1 Cor 7:8-16;
	25-35;
	39-40

by **MIRACLE**

Peter	Acts 12:1-25

through **OBEDIENCE**

God	Ex 6:10-13
Paul	Rom 6:15-23

from **OPPRESSION**

Manoah	Judg 13:2-7
Solomon	Prov 6:1-5

through **PRUDENCE**

Gamaliel	Acts 5:17-42
Peter	1 Pet 2:13-17

as **REWARD**

Moses	Deut 15:12-18

through **SPIRIT**

Paul	Rom 8:1-4;
	Gal 4:1-3

from **TEMPTATION**

Paul	1 Cor 8:7-13

of **WILL**

Artaxerxes	Ezra 7:13-14
Joshua	Josh 24:14-15
Moses	Deut 30:15-20

to **WITNESS**

Apostles	Acts 5:17-42
Paul	Gal 1:18-2:10

on **FRIENDSHIP**

Paul	2 Cor 6:14-7:1;
	Col 4:15-18
Sirach	*Sir 12:8-18
Solomon	Prov 25:1-28

in **BROTHERHOOD**

Paul	Rom 16:1-23

for **ETERNITY**

Jesus	Lk 16:1-9

concerning **FIDELITY**

Paul	2 Tim 4:19-22
Sirach	*Sir 6:2-17;
	9:10;
	19:4-12;
	22:19-26;
	27:16-21;
	37:1-6
Solomon	Prov 18:1-24;
	27:1-27

on **FULFILLMENT**

of **BELIEF**

Jesus	Jn 6:25-59

of **COMMITMENT**

David	1 Kgs 1:28-40

of **CREATION**

Israelites	Ex 39:32-43

of **ELECTION**

Paul	1 Cor 7:17-24

through **FIDELITY**

Peter	2 Pet 1:8-11

as **GIFT**

Jesus	Lk 12:47-48

of **JUDGMENT**

Jesus	Lk 6:24-26
John	Rev 14:6-7

of **KNOWLEDGE**

Holy Spirit	Jn 14:25-26

of **LAW**

Angel	*2 Esd 7:19-32
Jesus	Mt 5:17-20;
	Lk 16:16-18
Moses	Deut 4:44-49
Paul	Rom 8:1-4;
	13:8-10

as **MOTIVATION**

Jesus	Mt 11:28-30;
	13:44-46

of **NEW AGE**

Author	Heb 12:12-29
Jesus	Mt 10:23;
	13:31-33;
	47-50;
	22:1-14;
	25:31-46;
	26:17-30;
	Mk 4:26-29;
	30-32;
	10:23-27;
	Lk 12:49-50;
	13:18-19;
	20-21;
	16:16-18;
	17:20-21;
	Jn 12:20-26
Paul	Acts 17:1-9;
	Rom 13:11-14;
	1 Cor 15:20-28;
	42-50;
	51-58;
	2 Cor 5:20-6:2;
	Eph 1:15-2:10;
	1 Thes 5:1-11

of **PRAYER**

Eliphaz	Job 22:21-30
James	Jas 1:5-8;
	5:14-18
Jesus	Mt 6:9-13;
	7:7-11;
	18:18-20;

of **PRAYER** (cont'd)

Jesus	21:18-22; Mk 11:20-26; Lk 11:9-13; 18:1-8; Jn 14:1-14; 15:1-11; 12-17; 16:16-24
John	1 Jn 5:13-21

of **PROMISE**

God	Num 30:1-16
Jesus	Mt 5:33-37
Paul	Acts 13:14-52
Sirach	*Sir 18:19-26

through **PROVIDENCE**

Jesus	Mt 13:31-33; Mk 4:30-32; Lk 13:18-19; 20-21

as **QUALITY OF LIFE**

Paul	1 Cor 7:17-24; 25-35

through **RECONCILIATION**

Jesus	Heb 10:1-18

of the **RESURRECTION**

Men	Lk 24:1-12
Paul	1 Cor 15:12-19; 20-28
Peter	Acts 2:14-36

of **RITE**

Jacob	Gen 50:1-21
Moses	Lev 8:1-36

of **SALVATION**

Jesus	Acts 13:14-52
John the Baptist	Acts 13:14-52
Paul	Rom 13:11-14; Phil 1:12-30; Col 1:9-14
Peter	Acts 4:1-22

through **STEWARDSHIP**

Jesus	Lk 17:7-10
Moses	Ex 40:1-33
Paul	Col 4:15-18

of **TRUTH**

Holy Spirit	Jn 16:12-15

of **VIRTUE**

Jesus	Mt 3:13-17; 5:3-12; 48; Lk 6:20-23
Paul	1 Tim 6:6-10

on **GIFT**

Paul	1 Cor 12:27-31a; 14:1-12

of **DIGNITY**

Paul	2 Cor 8:16-24

for **DISCIPLESHIP**

Paul	1 Cor 12:27-31a

of **FAITH**

Holy Spirit	Gal 3:1-5

of **FULFILLMENT**

Jesus	Lk 12:47-48

of **GRACE**

Paul	Rom 3:21-30; 12:3-8

of **MIRACLE**

Peter	Acts 2:14-36

of **PRUDENCE**

Jesus	Mt 25:14-30

through **REPENTANCE**

Holy Spirit	Acts 2:37-41

of **SACREDNESS**

Moses	Ex 35:30-36:7

for **SERVICE**

Paul	Rom 12:3-8; 1 Cor 12:27-31a
Peter	1 Pet 4:7-11

for **SHARING**

Paul	Rom 12:3-8; Eph 4:7-16

of **SPIRIT**

Paul	2 Tim 1:3-7

of **WISDOM**

Paul	1 Cor 2:6-9; 12:1-3; 14:1-12; 13-25

to **WITNESS**

Paul	1 Cor 12:27-31a

on **GOOD**

Jesus	Mt 5:13-16; Lk 6:27-35
Sirach	*Sir 4:20-31; 18:19-26; 23:12-15; 25:1-2
Tobit	*Tb 4:1-21

in **BROTHERHOOD**

Paul	1 Cor 10:23-11:1

in **HONESTY**

Sirach	*Sir 7:1-36

in **LAW**

David	Ps 19:11-14
Jesus	Mt 7:12; Mk 3:1-6; Lk 6:6-11
Paul	Rom 7:7-13; 1 Tim 1:8-11

in **PROVIDENCE**

Eliphaz	Job 5:18-27

as **QUALITY OF LIFE**

David	Ps 34:11-14
Jesus	Mt 7:15-20; 12:33-37; Lk 6:36-45
John	3 Jn 1:12

in **RESURRECTION**

Solomon	*Wis 4:1-9; 5:15-23

in **SALVATION**

Angel	*2 Esd 7:45-61
Jesus	Mt 13:24-30; 47-50

in **SECURITY**

Solomon	Prov 12:1-28

over **SIN**

God	Ps 25:8-15

in **STEWARDSHIP**

Paul	Rom 14:1-23
Solomon	Prov 3:1-35

as **VIRTUE**

Author	Heb 13:1-25
Sirach	*Sir 5:1-6:1; 7:1-36; 18:15-18

on **GRACE**

in **AUTHORITY**

Jesus	Jn 20:1-29

on **GUILT** (cont'd)

Moses	Deut 17:8-13; 19:15-21; 23:15-25:19
Paul	1 Cor 5:1-5; Gal 5:7-12

overcome through **COMMITMENT**

Solomon	Prov 28:1-28

of **SIN**

John	1 Jn 3:4-10
Paul	Rom 7:7-13

on **HATE**

John	1 Jn 2:7-11
Paul	2 Tim 3:1-9
Preacher	Eccl 3:1-8

in **CONFRONTATION**

Sirach	*Sir 25:12-15

of **inFIDELITY**

Jesus	Lk 16:13

of **disHONESTY**

Solomon	Prov 26:1-28

of **SIN**

John	1 Jn 3:11-18
Jude	Jude 1:14-16

on **HEALING**

Crowds	Mt 4:23-25
James	Jas 5:14-18
Jesus	Lk 4:42-44; 17:11-19
Preacher	Eccl 3:1-8

by **AUTHORITY**

Peter	Acts 4:1-22

through **FIDELITY**

Author	Heb 12:12-29

of **SIN**

Jesus	Jn 9:1-41

on **HERESY**

Isaiah	Is 48:1-22
Moses	Deut 29:16-29
Paul	Rom 16:1-23; 2 Thes 2:3b-10; 2 Tim 3:1-9

against **LAW**

Paul	1 Tim 1:3-7

as **SIN**

Jeremiah	Jer 5:30-31
Jesus	Mt 23:16-22
Pergamum	Rev 2:12-17

against **TRUTH**

Paul	Gal 1:6-10; 2 Tim 2:14-19

on **HONESTY**

in **DISCIPLESHIP**

Paul	Eph 4:25-5:2

as **GOOD**

Sirach	*Sir 7:1-36

in **ORDER**

Moses	Deut 19:14

in **SERVICE**

John the Baptist	Lk 3:10-14

of **WILL**

James	Jas 5:12

in **WITNESS**

God	Ex 20:1-17
Moses	Deut 5:1-21; 19:15-21

in **WITNESS** (cont'd)

Solomon	Prov 12:1-28; 14:1-35; 19:1-29; 24:23-34; 25:1-28

on **disHONESTY**

as **EVIL**

Isaiah	Is 59:1-21
Rehum	Ezra 4:6-16
Sirach	*Sir 4:20-31; 5:1-6:1; 19:25-30; 20:24-31; 21:1-7; 27:22-29; 28:13-26
Solomon	Prov 6:12-15; 19:1-29

results in **REJECTION**

Jeremiah	Jer 29:1-23
Jesus	Jn 10:1-18
Paul	2 Thes 2:1-3a

in **STEALING**

Moses	Deut 19:14; 27:11-26

on **HOPE**

in **BELIEF**

John the Baptist	Jn 3:31-36
Paul	2 Cor 10:12-18

in **CONVERSION**

Paul	2 Cor 3:12-18

in the **CREATION**

Paul	Rom 8:14-25

for **ETERNITY**

Psalmist	Ps 131:1-3

through **FIDELITY**

Paul	2 Cor 1:3-7
Solomon	Prov 23:15-24:22

as **MOTIVATION**

Jesus	Mt 13:44-46; Lk 13:6-9

in **NEW AGE**

Jesus	Mt 4:23-25; 10:7-8; Lk 8:1-3; 9:10-11; 12:35-38; 13:18-19
Paul	2 Cor 3:7-11; 4:16-18; 1 Thes 4:13-18; Tit 2:11-15
Peter	1 Pet 1:13-2:3; 2 Pet 3:11-13

in **PROMISE**

John the Baptist	Mt 3:1-12; Mk 1:2-8

in **PROVIDENCE**

Psalmist	Ps 130:7-8

as **QUALITY OF LIFE**

Paul	Rom 5:1-5; 12:9-13
Preacher	Eccl 9:1-16

in **RESURRECTION**

Paul	1 Cor 15:12-19; 29-34; 51-58; 1 Thes 4:13-18

through **JUSTICE** (cont'd)

Moses	Deut 1:9-18; 16:18-20; 19:1-13; 15-21; 23:15-25:19; 27:11-26
Paul	Rom 2:25-3:20; 1 Cor 4:1-5; 1 Tim 5:17-25
Solomon	Prov 24:23-34
Zophar	Job 11:7-12

of **LEADERSHIP**

James	Jas 3:1-12
Moses	Deut 1:9-18; 16:18-20

on **LIFE**

Peter	1 Pet 4:1-6

on **OBEDIENCE**

Moses	Deut 17:8-13

on **ORDER**

Paul	1 Cor 6:1-8

on **POLITICS**

Paul	Rom 13:1-7

on **PRIDE**

Preacher	Eccl 8:10-17

on **PURIFICATION**

Paul	Rom 14:1-23

as **REJECTION**

Jesus	Mt 10:26-39; 12:38-42; 22:1-14; Lk 10:1-16; 11:29-32; 14:15-24; Jn 5:19-47; 12:44-50

on **REWARDs**

Jesus	Mt 12:33-37
Paul	1 Cor 3:10-17; 4:1-5; 2 Cor 5:9-10

on **SELFISHNESS**

Jesus	Lk 11:37-44; 12:13-15; 16-21; 19:11-27

on **SERVICE**

Jesus	Mt 25:31-46

on **SHARING**

Jesus	Mt 25:31-46; Lk 6:36-45

on **SPIRIT**

Jesus	Mt 15:15-20; Mk 7:1-23

on **VIOLENCE**

Jesus	Mt 26:47-56

on **WEALTH**

Jesus	Lk 6:24-26; 16:14-15

of **WILL**

Jesus	Jn 8:12-20

on **WISDOM**

Jesus	Mt 11:16-19; Lk 7:31-35; Jn 7:15-24
Psalmist	Ps 119:65-72

on **WITNESS**

God	Is 43:8-13
Jesus	Mt 18:15-17

on **WITNESS** (cont'd)

John	1 Jn 4:1-3
Moses	Deut 16:21-17:7; 19:15-21
Paul	2 Cor 13:1-4; 1 Tim 5:17-25

on **YOUTH**

Paul	1 Cor 3:1-4

on **JUSTICE**

Angel	*2 Esd 8:63-9:25; 13:1-50
God	Is 1:10-17
Jesus	Mt 5:38-42
Moses	Deut 19:1-13
Sirach	*Sir 4:1-10; 20-31

in **AUTHORITY**

Paul	2 Cor 13:1-4
Solomon	Prov 29:1-27; *Wis 6:1-11

in the **CREATION**

Angel	*2 Esd 5:43-6:6

concerning **FIDELITY**

Jesus	Lk 12:47-48

through **HONESTY**

Moses	Deut 23:15-25:19

through **LAW**

God	Ex 20:1-17
Jesus	Mt 23:23-24
Moses	Deut 5:1-21; 17:8-13; 19:15-21
Paul	Rom 2:1-24

in **NEW AGE**

Angel	*2 Esd 5:43-6:6
Jesus	Mt 20:1-16; 25:31-46

in **PROVIDENCE**

Angel	*2 Esd 5:43-6:6

in **PUNISHMENT**

Author	Heb 2:1-4
Paul	2 Cor 13:1-4
Solomon	1 Kgs 2:28-35

as **QUALITY OF LIFE**

Angel	*2 Esd 7:116-8:3
Wisdom	Prov 8:1-21

in **RECONCILIATION**

Paul	Rom 2:25-3:20

in **SALVATION**

Angel	*2 Esd 7:116-8:3
Jesus	Mt 20:1-16

concerning **SIN**

God	Ps 82:2-7
Isaiah	Is 59:1-21
Solomon	Prov 18:1-24

in **TRUTH**

Elihu	Job 34:1-4
Jesus	Lk 12:1-12

as **VIRTUE**

Bildad	Job 8:1-7
God	Is 56:1-8
Solomon	Prov 12:1-28; 21:1-31

on **KILLING**

Abraham	Gen 22:1-19
Ahasuerus	Esth 3:7-15
Artaxerxes	*Esth 13:1-7
Demetrius	*1 Mc 7:1-4

of **WEALTH**
Moses	Num 13:17b-20
Solomon	*Wis 7:7-14

of **WISDOM**
Baruch	*Bar 3:9-14; 24-37; 4:1-4
Eliphaz	Job 15:7-11
God	Hos 6:4-6
Holy Spirit	Jn 14:25-26
Hosea	Hos 14:9
Jesus	Mt 7:24-27; Lk 6:46-49
Job	Job 28:1-13; 14-22
Nebuchadnezzar	Dan 4:18
Preacher	Eccl 1:2-11; 7:1-22; 8:1-9; 10-17; 12:8-11
Psalmist	Ps 49:1-4
Sirach	*Sir 1:1-10; 11-20; 22-30; 3:17-31; 4:11-19; 5:1-6:1; 18-37; 8:1-19; 9:14-18; 10:26-11:1; 14:20-27; 15:1-10; 18:27-33; 19:20-24; 20:1-8; 9-17; 18-23; 24-31; 21:8-28; 22:16-18; 24:1-34; 25:3-6; 7-11; 27:8-15; 32:14-24; 33:4-6; 16-23; 34:9-12; 37:7-26; 38:24-34; 39:1-11; 40:18-27; 41:14-23; 50:27-29; 51:13-30
Solomon	Prov 1:1; 2-6; 9:7-12; 10:1-32; 11:1-31; 14:1-35; 15:1-33; 17:1-28; 18:1-24; 19:1-29; 20:1-30

of **WISDOM** (cont'd)
Solomon	Prov 21:1-31; 22:17-21; 22-23:14; 15-24:22; 25:1-28; 27:1-27; 29:1-27; *Wis 1:1-5; 6-11; 6:1-11; 12-25; 7:7-14; 15-8:1; 8:2-21
Tobit	*Tb 4:1-21

of **YOUTH**
Paul	Gal 4:1-3

on **LAW**
concerning **ANGER**
Jesus	Mt 5:21-26

concerning **BLASPHEMY**
God	Ex 20:1-17
Moses	Deut 5:1-21

concerning **CAPTIVITY**
Moses	Deut 15:12-18; 23:15-25:19
Paul	Rom 7:1-6

concerning **COMPASSION**
Jesus	Mt 12:9-14
Moses	Deut 23:15-25:19

concerning **CONDEMNATION**
Moses	Deut 11:26-32; 27:11-26
Paul	Rom 3:31-4:25; Gal 3:10-14

of **COVETOUSNESS**
God	Ex 20:1-17
Moses	Deut 5:1-21; 7:17-26
Paul	Rom 7:7-13; 13:8-10

concerning **DEATH**
Moses	Deut 21:22-23
Paul	Rom 7:1-6; 2 Cor 3:7-11; Gal 2:17-19

concerning **DESTRUCTION**
Moses	Deut 20:10-18

concerning **DISCIPLESHIP**
God	1 Cor 14:34-40
Psalmist	Ps 119:105-112

concerning **DISOBEDIENCE**
Antiochus	*2 Mc 6:1-11
Moses	Deut 21:18-21

concerning **EVIL**
Paul	Rom 2:25-3:20; 7:7-13

concerning **FAITH**
Paul	Rom 3:21-30; Gal 3:1-5

concerning **FAMILY**
Moses	Deut 21:15-17; 18-21; 23:15-25:19

through **FEAR**
God	Ps 25:8-15
Jehoshaphat	2 Chr 17:1-20:37

concerning **GOOD**
David — Ps 19:11-14
Jesus — Mt 7:12;
Mk 3:1-6;
Lk 6:6-11
Paul — Rom 7:7-13;
1 Tim 1:8-11
concerning **GRIEF**
Moses — Deut 14:1-2
concerning **GUILT**
Moses — Deut 23:15-25:19
concerning **HERESY**
Paul — 1 Tim 1:3-7
concerning **IDOLATRY**
God — Ex 20:1-17
Moses — Deut 5:1-21;
7:1-5;
17-26;
27:11-26
concerning **KILLING**
God — Gen 9:1-7;
Ex 20:1-17
Jesus — Mt 5:21-26;
19:16-22;
Mk 10:17-22
Moses — Deut 5:1-21;
19:1-13;
21:1-9;
27:11-26
Paul — Rom 13:8-10
concerning **LEADERSHIP**
Moses — Deut 17:14-20
Samuel — 1 Sam 10:17-27
concerning **LIFE**
Baruch — *Bar 3:9-14
Jesus — Lk 10:25-28
Moses — Deut 4:1-14;
14:3-21;
15:19-23;
22:1-12;
30:15-20;
31:30-32:47
Paul — Rom 9:30-10:21;
Gal 3:10-14
Solomon — Prov 19:1-29
concerning **LOVE**
James — Jas 2:1-13
Jesus — Mt 5:43-47;
7:12;
19:16-22;
22:34-40;
Mk 12:28-34;
Lk 10:25-28;
Jn 13:31-35;
14:18-24;
15:1-11;
12-17
John — 1 Jn 2:7-11;
2 Jn 1:4-6
Moses — Deut 6:4-19;
10:12-22
Paul — Rom 13:8-10;
Gal 5:13-15
concerning **LUST**
God — Ex 20:1-17
Moses — Deut 5:1-21
concerning **MARRIAGE**
Ezra — Ezra 9:6-15;
10:7-15
Jesus — Mt 5:31-32

concerning **MARRIAGE** (cont'd)
Moses — Deut 21:10-14;
22:13-30;
23:15-25:19
Paul — Rom 7:1-6
Pharisees — Mk 10:1-12

concerning **OBEDIENCE**
Artaxerxes — Ezra 7:25-26
Asaph — Ps 78:1-8
David — 1 Kgs 2:1-4;
1 Chr 15:1-16:43;
28:1-29:30
Ezra — Ezra 10:7-15
Father — Prov 4:1-9
God — Ex 16:22-30;
Ps 119:1-8
Isaiah — Is 1:10-17
Israelites — Ezek 20:9-26;
Mal 4:4-6
James — Jas 2:1-13
Jesus — Mt 17:24-27;
19:16-22;
22:15-22;
34-40;
23:1-3;
Mk 12:13-17;
28-34;
Lk 10:25-28;
18:18-27;
20:19-26;
Jn 14:15-17;
18-24;
Jn 15:1-11;
12-17
John — 1 Jn 2:7-11;
4:19-5:5;
2 Jn 1:4-6
Joshua — Josh 23:1-16
Moses — Ex 24:1-18;
35:1-3;
Deut 4:1-14;
32-40;
5:1-21;
6:1-3;
4-19;
20-25;
8:1-10;
11-20;
11:1-25;
12:1-31;
32-13:18;
16:9-12;
26:16-19;
27:1-10;
11-26;
28:1-14;
30:1-10;
11-14;
15-20;
31:9-13;
30-32:47
Paul — Rom 2:1-24;
25-3:20;
1 Cor 7:17-24;
1 Tim 6:11-16
Peter — 1 Pet 2:13-17
Psalmist — Ps 119:33-40
Sirach — *Sir 15:11-20
Solomon — 1 Kgs 8:54-61;

concerning **OBEDIENCE** (cont'd)
Solomon	Prov 3:1-35; 6:20-7:27; 19:1-29; 28:1-28; 29:1-27
Tobit	*Tb 4:1-21

concerning **POVERTY**
Moses	Deut 23:15-25:19

concerning **PRAISE**
Asaph	Ps 81:1-5b

concerning **PURIFICATION**
Jesus	Mt 8:2-4; Mk 1:40-45; Lk 5:12-16
Moses	Deut 23:9-14
Paul	Rom 2:25-3:20

concerning **REVENGE**
Jesus	Mt 5:38-42

concerning **SACREDNESS**
Artaxerxes	Ezra 7:20-24
Ezra	Ezra 7:6-10; Neh 7:33b-8:2; 3-8; 13-18; *1 Esd 8:1-7; 8-24; 9:37-48
Jesus	Lk 13:10-17; 16:16-18
Joshua	Josh 8:30-35
Moses	Ex 16:22-30; 34:29-35; 35:1-3; Deut 16:13-15; 31:24-29
Paul	Rom 7:7-13

concerning **SACRIFICE**
Moses	Deut 16:1-8; 26:1-11; 12-15

concerning **SERVICE**
Ezra	Ezra 7:13-14
Moses	Deut 22:1-12; 23:15-25:19
Slaves	Deut 15:12-18

concerning **SEX**
God	Ex 20:1-7
Jesus	Mt 5:27-30; 19:16-22; Mk 10:17-22
Moses	Deut 5:1-21; 22:13-30; 23:15-25:19
Paul	Rom 13:8-10

concerning **STEALING**
God	Ex 20:1-17
Jesus	Mt 19:16-22; Mk 10:17-22
Moses	Deut 5:1-21; 23:15-25:19
Nathan	2 Sam 12:1-31
Paul	Rom 13:8-10

concerning **TEMPERANCE**
God	Lev 10:1-20

concerning **TEMPTATION**
Moses	Deut 27:11-26

concerning **VICTORY**
Jesus	Jn 12:44-50

concerning **VIOLENCE**
Moses	Deut 20:19-20

concerning **WEALTH**
Moses	Deut 15:1-11; 23:15-25:19

concerning **WILL**
David	Ps 27:7-12
God	Ps 147:12-20

concerning **WISDOM**
Baruch	*Bar 4:1-4
Jesus	Mt 5:21-26
Psalmist	Ps 119:25-32; 57-64; 65-72; 121-128; 129-136

on **LEADERSHIP**
    of **AUTHORITY**
David	1 Kgs 2:1-4
Elisha	2 Kgs 9:1-13
Ezra	Ezra 7:25-26
Jesus	Mt 7:28-29
Joshua	Josh 1:12-18
Jotham	Judg 9:7-15
Moses	Deut 1:9-18; 16:18-20; 17:14-20
Nehemiah	Neh 7:1-3
Paul	1 Cor 11:2-16
Samuel	1 Sam 12:1-25
Solomon	1 Kgs 1:28-40

    in **PROVIDENCE**
Joshua	Josh 24:1-13
Moses	Deut 29:1-15

    as **QUALITY OF LIFE**
Elders	1 Pet 5:1-5

    in **RITE**
David	1 Kgs 1:28-40

    as **VIRTUE**
Solomon	Prov 11:1-31

on **LIFE**
    by **AUTHORITY**
God	Gen 1:20-23; Ex 9:13-35; Ps 75:2-5
Solomon	Prov 18:1-24

    as **ETERNAL**
Jesus	Mt 19:16-22; 27-30; 25:31-46; Mk 10:17-22; 28-31; Lk 10:25-28; 18:18-27; 28-30; Jn 3:1-21; 4:27-42; 5:19-47; 8:21-59; 10:19-40; 11:1-57; 12:20-26; 44-50
Paul	Rom 2:1-24; 5:12-21; 6:15-23; 1 Cor 15:42-50;

as **ETERNAL** (cont'd)
Paul   51-58;
                         2 Cor 5:1-5;
                         Gal 6:7-10;
                         1 Tim 6:11-16
Solomon   *Wis 1:12-15
concerning **FIDELITY**
David   Ps 34:11-14
Israelites   Ezek 20:9-26
of **FREEDOM**
Paul   1 Cor 7:17-24;
                         Gal 4:27-31
in **NEW AGE**
Holy Spirit   Jn 3:1-21
Jesus   Mt 7:13-14
Paul   Rom 5:12-21;
                         1 Cor 7:25-35
through **RECONCILIATION**
Author   Heb 9:15-22
Jesus   Heb 13:1-25
through **RESURRECTION**
Jesus   Jn 5:19-47
Paul   Rom 8:5-13;
                         1 Cor 15:35-41;
                         42-50
through **SALVATION**
Jesus   Mt 16:21-28;
                         Mk 8:34-9:1;
                         Lk 9:23-27;
                         Jn 5:19-47
Paul   Rom 1:16-17;
                         6:1-14;
                         8:5-13
over **SIN**
Paul   Rom 6:1-14
Preacher   Eccl 7:1-22
through **TRUTH**
Jesus   Jn 8:12-20;
                         9:1-41;
                         14:1-14
Paul   2 Cor 4:7-12

on **LOVE**
Jesus   Jn 15:12-17
John   1 Jn 3:11-18
in **BROTHERHOOD**
Jesus   Jn 15:12-17
John   1 Jn 2:7-11;
                         4:7-12;
                         19-5:5
Paul   Rom 12:9-13;
                         13:8-10;
                         1 Cor 10:23-11:1;
                         2 Cor 7:2-4;
                         1 Thes 4:1-12;
                         1 Tim 4:11-16
Peter   1 Pet 1:13-2:3;
                         2:13-17;
                         3:8-12;
                         4:7-11;
                         5:12-14
ETERNAL
Paul   1 Cor 13:8-13

as **MOTIVATION**
Author   Heb 10:19-31
James   Jas 4:1-10
Jesus   Mt 5:43-47;

as **MOTIVATION** (cont'd)
Jesus   Lk 6:27-35;
                         13:6-9
Paul   2 Cor 1:23-2:4
in **NEW AGE**
James   Jas 2:1-13
Jesus   Lk 11:9-13
Angel   *2 Esd 5:31-42
as **QUALITY OF LIFE**
Jesus   Mk 9:49-50
Paul   1 Cor 8:7-13;
                         13:8-13;
                         Eph 6:5-9;
                         Col 3:5-17;
                         1 Thes 5:1-11
Wisdom   Prov 8:1-21
as **VIRTUE**
Paul   1 Cor 13:8-13

on **LUST**
Jesus   Mt 5:27-30
Paul   1 Cor 7:36-38;
                         1 Thes 4:1-12
as **MOTIVATION**
Preacher   Eccl 5:8-20
as **QUALITY OF LIFE**
Isaiah   Is 56:9-57:13
as **SIN**
Author   Heb 13:1-25
Jude   Jude 1:14-16
in **STEWARDSHIP**
Paul   1 Tim 6:6-10

on **MARRIAGE**
Jesus   Mt 5:31-32;
                         19:3-9;
                         Mk 10:1-12;
                         Lk 16:16-18
Lemuel   Prov 31:10-31
Moses   Deut 7:1-5
Paul   Rom 7:1-6;
                         1 Cor 7:8-16
Sirach   *Sir 7:1-36;
                         25:16-26;
                         26:1-4;
                         13-18;
                         36:21-26;
                         40:18-27
Solomon   Prov 18:1-24
Women   1 Pet 3:1-7
in **COMMUNITY**
Joshua   Josh 23:1-16
concerning **FIDELITY**
Author   Heb 13:1-25
Bishops   1 Tim 3:1-7
Deacons   1 Tim 3:8-13
God   Ex 20:1-17
Hosea   Hos 3:1-5
Jesus   Mt 5:27-30;
                         31-32;
                         19:3-9;
                         16-22;
                         Mk 10:1-12
Moses   Deut 5:1-21
Paul   Rom 7:1-6;
                         13:8-10;
                         1 Cor 7:1-7;
                         8-16;

concerning **FIDELITY** (cont'd)
　Paul　　　　　25-35;
　　　　　　　　39-40;
　　　　　　　　1 Thes 4:1-12;
　　　　　　　　1 Tim 5:3-16
　Solomon　　　Prov 5:15-23
as **MOTIVATION**
　Paul　　　　　1 Cor 7:36-38
as **QUALITY OF LIFE**
　Solomon　　　Prov 12:1-28
concerning **RESURRECTION**
　Jesus　　　　Mt 22:23-33;
　　　　　　　　Mk 12:18-27

on **MEDIATION**
　of **GUILT**
　　Moses　　　Lev 11:1-47
　for **KILLING**
　　Mordecai　　Esth 4:1-17
　of **LEADERSHIP**
　　Jethro　　　Ex 18:13-26

on **MIRACLE**
　as **GIFT**
　　Peter　　　Acts 2:14-36
　in **RESURRECTION**
　　Paul　　　　1 Cor 15:35-41

on **MOTIVATION**
　concerning **EVIL**
　　David　　　1 Sam 23:14-24:22
　through **FAITH**
　　Jesus　　　Lk 13:6-9
　　Paul　　　　Rom 9:30-10:21
　through **FEAR**
　　Moses　　　Ex 4:10-16
　through **FULFILLMENT**
　　Jesus　　　Mt 11:28-30;
　　　　　　　13:44-46
　in **HOPE**
　　Jesus　　　Mt 13:44-46;
　　　　　　　Lk 13:6-9
　for **IDOLATRY**
　　Paul　　　　1 Cor 10:23-11:1
　for **LIFE**
　　Father　　　Prov 4:20-27
　through **LOVE**
　　Author　　　Heb 10:19-31
　　James　　　Jas 4:1-10
　　Jesus　　　Mt 5:43-47;
　　　　　　　Lk 6:27-35;
　　　　　　　13:6-9
　　Paul　　　　2 Cor 1:23-2:4
　through **LUST**
　　Preacher　　Eccl 5:8-20
　for **MARRIAGE**
　　Paul　　　　1 Cor 7:36-38
　through **OPPRESSION**
　　Jeremiah　　Jer 13:15-17
　for **PURIFICATION**
　　Paul　　　　1 Cor 15:29-34
　through **REWARDs**
　　Jesus　　　Mt 6:1;
　　　　　　　2-4;
　　　　　　　16-18
　for **SACRIFICE**
　　God　　　　Is 1:10-17
　　Zechariah　　Zech 7:4-8:23
　through **SELFISHNESS**
　　Zechariah　　Zech 7:4-8:23

for **SERVICE**
　Author　　　Heb 10:19-31
for **SHARING**
　Jesus　　　Mt 11:28-30
for **SUFFERING**
　Paul　　　　2 Cor 1:23-2:4
for **TEMPTATION**
　James　　　Jas 1:13-15
for **VIOLENCE**
　James　　　Jas 4:1-10

on **NEW AGE**
　concerning **CONDEMNATION**
　　Paul　　　　Gal 5:16-21
　concerning **COVETOUSNESS**
　　Jesus　　　Lk 12:22-31
　concerning **DISCIPLESHIP**
　　Jesus　　　Lk 9:57-62;
　　　　　　　22:28-30
　　Paul　　　　Gal 6:11-18
　concerning **EVIL**
　　God　　　　*2 Esd 14:1-18
　concerning **FAITH**
　　Author　　　Heb 11:1-40
　　Jesus　　　Mk 4:26-29;
　　　　　　　Lk 13:18-19;
　　　　　　　18:1-8;
　　　　　　　15-17
　　Paul　　　　Rom 9:30-10:21
　concerning **FULFILLMENT**
　　Author　　　Heb 12:12-29
　　Jesus　　　Mt 10:23;
　　　　　　　13:31-33;
　　　　　　　47-50;
　　　　　　　22:1-14;
　　　　　　　25:31-46;
　　　　　　　26:17-30;
　　　　　　　Mk 4:26-29;
　　　　　　　30-32;
　　　　　　　10:23-27;
　　　　　　　Lk 12:49-50;
　　　　　　　13:18-19;
　　　　　　　20-21;
　　　　　　　16:16-18;
　　　　　　　17:20-21;
　　　　　　　Jn 12:20-26
　　Paul　　　　Acts 17:1-9;
　　　　　　　Rom 13:11-14;
　　　　　　　1 Cor 15:20-28;
　　　　　　　42-50;
　　　　　　　51-58;
　　　　　　　2 Cor 5:20-6:2;
　　　　　　　Eph 1:15-2:10;
　　　　　　　1 Thes 5:1-11
　concerning **GRACE**
　　Jesus　　　Mt 20:1-16;
　　　　　　　Mk 4:26-29;
　　　　　　　Lk 13:18-19
　　Paul　　　　Acts 28:17-31;
　　　　　　　Rom 5:1-5;
　　　　　　　11:1-6;
　　　　　　　2 Cor 5:1-5
　concerning **HOPE**
　　Jesus　　　Mt 4:23-25;
　　　　　　　10:7-8;
　　　　　　　Lk 8:1-3;
　　　　　　　9:10-11;
　　　　　　　12:35-38;
　　　　　　　13:18-19
　　Paul　　　　2 Cor 3:7-11;

concerning **HOPE** (cont'd)
Paul | 4:16-18;
| 1 Thes 4:13-18;
| Tit 2:11-15
Peter | 1 Pet 1:13-2:3;
| 2 Pet 3:11-13

revealing **JOY**
God | Is 65:1-25
John | Rev 12:10-12
John the Baptist | Jn 3:22-30
Paul | Rom 14:1-23

concerning **LIFE**
Holy Spirit | Jn 3:1-21
Jesus | Mt 7:13-14
Paul | Rom 5:12-21;
| 1 Cor 7:25-35

concerning **LOVE**
James | Jas 2:1-13

concerning **OBEDIENCE**
Jesus | Mt 7:21-23;
| 21:33-43;
| Lk 12:35-38;
| 41-46;
| 13:22-30

concerning **PATIENCE**
James | Jas 5:7-11
Jesus | Lk 12:35-38
Paul | Rom 8:14-25

concerning **PEACE**
Author | Heb 4:1-13
Paul | Rom 14:1-23

concerning **POVERTY**
James | Jas 2:1-13
Jesus | Lk 6:20-23

concerning **PRAISE**
Paul | Rom 14:1-23

concerning **PRUDENCE**
Paul | 2 Thes 2:1-3a

concerning **PURIFICATION**
Holy Spirit | Jn 3:1-21
Paul | Rom 6:1-14;
| 1 Cor 6:9-11

concerning **REPENTANCE**
Jesus | Mt 4:17;
| Mk 1:14-15
Paul | 1 Cor 6:9-11

concerning **REWARDs**
Jesus | Mt 5:3-12;
| 19:27-30;
| 20:1-16;
| 24:45-51;
| 25:1-13;
| Mk 10:28-31;
| Lk 6:20-23;
| 14:12-14;
| 16:1-9;
| 18:28-30;
| Jn 4:27-42;
| 14:1-14
Paul | 2 Cor 4:16-18
Peter | 2 Pet 1:8-11

concerning **SACRIFICE**
Jesus | Mt 9:14-15;
| 13:44-46;
| Mk 2:18-22;
| Lk 5:33-35;
| Heb 10:1-18

concerning **SPIRIT**
Paul | Rom 7:1-6;
| 8:5-13;
| Eph 4:17-24

concerning **SUFFERING**
Paul | Acts 14:19-28;
| Rom 8:14-25;
| 2 Cor 4:16-18;
| 2 Thes 1:5-7a

concerning **VICTORY**
Ephesus | Rev 2:1-7
Jesus | Mt 13:36-43;
| 19:27-30;
| Mk 10:28-31;
| Lk 13:18-19;
| 18:28-30
Laodicea | Rev 3:14-22
Paul | 1 Cor 15:20-28;
| Col 3:1-4
Pergamum | Rev 2:12-17
Philadelphians | Rev 3:7-13
Sardis | Rev 3:1-6
Smyrna | Rev 2:8-11

concerning **WEALTH**
Jesus | Mk 10:17-22;
| 23-27;
| Lk 12:32-34;
| 18:18-27

concerning **WILL**
Jesus | Lk 14:15-24

concerning **WISDOM**
Paul | 1 Cor 2:6-9;
| 2 Cor 3:7-11;
| 2 Thes 2:3b-10

concerning **WITNESS**
Angel | *2 Esd 2:42-48
Jesus | Lk 17:20-21
Paul | Gal 4:27-31
Philip | Acts 8:4-13

concerning **YOUTH**
Jesus | Mt 19:13-15;
| Mk 10:13-16;
| Lk 18:15-17

on **OBEDIENCE**
Abraham | Gen 21:11-14
Angel | Gen 16:7-10
Author | Heb 12:12-29;
| 13:1-25
Esau | Gen 27:1-40
God | Gen 2:16-17
Isaiah | Is 18:1-7
Israelites | Ex 12:50-51;
| Josh 4:1-8
Joshua | Num 14:8-9;
| Josh 11:1-15
Moses | Ex 34:1-5a
Paul | 1 Cor 4:14-21;
| 2 Cor 13:11-13;
| Eph 5:21-33;
| Col 3:18-4:1;
| 1 Thes 4:1-12
Zedekiah | Jer 32:9-15

to **AUTHORITY**
Demon | Mk 1:21-28;
| Lk 4:31-37
Jesus | Mt 7:24-27;
| Lk 6:46-49;
| 24:44-49
Paul | Rom 13:1-7;
| 2 Cor 10:1-6;
| Tit 3:8-11
Peter | Lk 5:1-11;
| 1 Pet 2:13-17;
| 5:1-5

to **AUTHORITY** cont'd)	
Preacher	Eccl 8:1-9
Servants	1 Pet 2:18-20
Solomon	Prov 23:15-24:22
Women	1 Cor 14:34-40;
	Eph 5:21-33;
	1 Tim 2:8-15;
	Tit 2:1-10;
	1 Pet 3:1-7
in **BROTHERHOOD**	
Believers	Acts 15:6-29
to **COMMITMENT**	
Asaph	Ps 76:10-12
Darius	Ezra 6:1-12
Esther	Esth 4:1-17
Paul	Rom 8:5-13;
	2 Cor 2:5-11
Peter	Acts 2:37-41
to **COMMUNITY**	
Ezra	*1 Esd 9:1-15
Joshua	Josh 1:12-18
Moses	Lev 24:10-23
in **CREATION**	
Zerubbabel	Ezra 4:3
for **ETERNITY**	
David	Ps 37:23-40
concerning **FIDELITY**	
Aaron	Ex 7:14-25
Abraham	Gen 22:1-19
Author	Heb 2:1-4;
	3:6b-11;
	12-19;
	4:1-13
Barnabas	Acts 11:22-24
Believers	Rev 14:9-12
David	Ps 15:5c
Father	Prov 4:20-27
God	Ps 95:7d-11
James	Jas 1:22-25
Jesus	Mt 21:28-32;
	23:5-12;
	24:45-51;
	Lk 14:25-27;
	14:28-33;
	19:11-27;
	Jn 7:53-8:11;
	10:1-18;
	16:1-4
Joshua	Josh 24:14-15
Malachi	Mal 2:10-16
Mattathias	*1 Mc 2:49-70
Moses	Ex 8:1-15;
	9:8-12;
	13-35;
	10:1-20;
	21-23;
	11:1-10;
	14:15-22;
	23-31
Paul	Eph 5:3-14;
	6:5-9;
	Phil 2:12-18;
	4:1-9;
	Col 1:21-23
Peter	1 Pet 5:12-14
Samuel	1 Sam 12:1-25
Solomon	Prov 6:20-7:27
Wisdom	Prov 8:32-36
to **KNOWLEDGE**	
Darius	*1 Esd 6:7-26

to **KNOWLEDGE** (cont'd)	
God	Ex 6:28-30
Israelites	Is 50:1-11
Jesus	Jn 13:1-20
Paul	2 Tim 3:14-17
Solomon	Prov 22:17-21
to **LAW**	
Artaxerxes	Ezra 7:25-26
Asaph	Ps 78:1-8
David	1 Kgs 2:1-4;
	1 Chr 15:1-16:43;
	28:1-29:30
Ezra	Ezra 10:7-15
Father	Prov 4:1-9
God	Ex 16:22-30;
	Ps 119:1-8
Isaiah	Is 1:10-17
Israelites	Ezek 20:9-26;
	Mal 4:4-6
James	Jas 2:1-13
Jesus	Mt 17:24-27;
	19:16-22;
	22:15-22;
	34-40;
	23:1-3;
	Mk 12:13-17;
	28-34;
	Lk 10:25-28;
	18:18-27;
	20:19-26;
	Jn 14:15-17;
	18-24;
	15:1-11;
	12-17
John	1 Jn 2:7-11;
	4:19-5:5;
	2 Jn 1:4-6
Joshua	Josh 23:1-16
Moses	Ex 24:1-18;
	35:1-3;
	Deut 4:1-14;
	32-40;
	5:1-21;
	6:1-3;
	4-19;
	20-25;
	8:1-10;
	11-20;
	11:1-25;
	12:1-31;
	12:32-13:18;
	16:9-12;
	26:16-19;
	27:1-10;
	11-26;
	28:1-14;
	30:1-10;
	11-14;
	15-20;
	31:9-13;
	31:30-32:47
Paul	Rom 2:1-24;
	2:25-3:20;
	1 Cor 7:17-24;
	1 Tim 6:11-16
Peter	1 Pet 2:13-17
Psalmist	Ps 119:33-40
Sirach	*Sir 15:11-20
Solomon	1 Kgs 8:54-61;
	Prov 3:1-35;

as **QUALITY OF LIFE**
    Jesus   Mt 10:26-39
concerning **SECURITY**
    Artaxerxes   *Esth 16:1-24
    Isaiah   Is 15:1-16:14
caused by **SIN**
    Bildad   Job 18:12-15
    James   Jas 5:1-6
of **TRUTH**
    Jesus   Mt 23:34-39

on **ORDER**
  in **AUTHORITY**
    God   Gen 1:20-23
  in **COMMUNITY**
    Jesus   Mt 10:24-25
  concerning **CONFRONTATION**
    John   Rev 11:1-14
  in **CREATION**
    Nehemiah   Neh 2:16-18
  for **ETERNITY**
    God   Ps 119:89-96
  as **QUALITY OF LIFE**
    Paul   2 Thes 3:6-15
    Preacher   Eccl 3:1-8
    Solomon   Prov 20:1-30

PARADOX in
  on **DESIRE**
    Paul   Gal 5:16-21

on **PARADOX**
  of **AUTHORITY**
    Jesus   Mt 11:7-15;
                Lk 7:24-30
  in **BEHAVIOR**
    Jesus   Mt 10:26-39;
                11:16-19;
                19:27-30;
                23:27-28;
                Mk 10:28-31;
                Lk 7:31-35;
                13:22-30
    Paul   Gal 2:11-14
    Pharisees   Mt 23:1-3
  in **BROTHERHOOD**
    Jesus   Mt 12:46-50;
                Mk 3:31-35;
                Lk 8:19-21
  concerning **CONFRONTATION**
    Paul   Rom 12:14-21
  in **ELECTION**
    Paul   1 Cor 1:26-31
  in **JUDGMENT**
    Paul   1 Cor 3:1-4
  in **PROMISE**
    Jesus   Mt 10:26-39
  as **QUALITY OF LIFE**
    James   Jas 3:1-12
    Jesus   Mt 19:27-30;
                20:1-16;
                Mk 10:28-31;
                Lk 9:46-48;
                18:9-14
    Paul   1 Cor 4:6-13;
                7:17-24
    Sirach   *Sir 20:9-17
  in **RATIONALIZATION**
    Jesus   Mt 5:38-42
    Paul   1 Cor 6:1-8
    Peter   1 Pet 2:18-20

in **RESURRECTION**
    Paul   1 Cor 15:35-41;
                42-50
in **SALVATION**
    Jesus   Mt 22:1-14;
                Lk 17:22-37;
                Jn 12:20-26
in **SIN**
    Paul   Gal 2:17-19
in **STEWARDSHIP**
    Jesus   Mt 25:31-46;
                Lk 22:24-27
in **TRUTH**
    Jesus   Mk 9:33-37;
                Jn 6:25-59

PATIENCE in
  of **TRUTH**
    Paul   2 Tim 4:1-5

on **PATIENCE**
    Paul   1 Thes 5:12-22
  BELIEF in
    Eliphaz   Job 4:1-6
  to **COMMITMENT**
    Paul   2 Tim 2:20-26
  for **JUDGMENT**
    God   Zeph 3:8
  in **NEW AGE**
    James   Jas 5:7-11
    Jesus   Lk 12:35-38
    Paul   Rom 8:14-25
  in **PRESENCE**
    David   Ps 27:13-14
  with **PROMISE**
    Author   Heb 10:32-39
  in **PROVIDENCE**
    Sirach   *Sir 11:10-13
  as **QUALITY OF LIFE**
    Paul   Rom 12:9-13;
                1 Cor 7:17-24;
                Col 3:5-17
  as **VIRTUE**
    Peter   2 Pet 3:11-13
    Preacher   Eccl 7:1-22
    Sirach   *Sir 11:10-13
    Solomon   Prov 16:1-33

on **PEACE**
    Author   Heb 12:12-29
    Jesus   Jn 14:1-14
    Preacher   Eccl 3:1-8
  in **BROTHERHOOD**
    Paul   1 Thes 5:12-22
  in **COMMUNITY**
    Paul   Rom 12:14-21;
                15:1-13
  through **CONFRONTATION**
    Moses   Deut 20:10-18
  through **FIDELITY**
    Paul   Eph 4:1-6
  in **NEW AGE**
    Author   Heb 4:1-13
    Paul   Rom 14:1-23
  as **QUALITY OF LIFE**
    Jesus   Mt 5:3-12;
                21-26
    Paul   2 Cor 13:11-13;
                Col 3:5-17
    Peter   2 Pet 3:14-18a

through **RECONCILIATION**
Paul   Rom 5:1-5
through **RESURRECTION**
Solomon   *Wis 3:1-9
in **RITE**
Paul   1 Cor 14:34-40
through **SALVATION**
Moses   Ex 14:1-14
in **TRUTH**
Jesus   Mk 9:49-50
Paul   Eph 6:10-18
as **VIRTUE**
Isaiah   Is 56:9-57:13
Sirach   *Sir 6:2-17
on **PIETY**
Jesus   Mt 6:1
in **RITE**
Jesus   Mt 6:16-18

on **PIETY**
in **STEWARDSHIP**
Jesus   Mt 6:2-4
Paul   1 Cor 16:1-4
of **TRUTH**
Paul   1 Cor 5:6-8

on im**PIETY**
as **SIN**
Jesus   Mt 23:27-28;
Mk 12:37b-40;
Lk 20:45-47

on **POLITICS**
concerning **AUTHORITY**
Demetrius   *1 Mc 11:20-37
Jesus   Mt 22:15-22;
Mk 12:13-17;
Lk 20:19-26
Mordecai   Esth 8:9-14
Paul   Rom 13:1-7
in **COMMUNITY**
Moses   Deut 16:18-20

on **POVERTY**
Sirach   *Sir 29:8-13
Solomon   Prov 22:22-23:14
ETERNAL
Jesus   Jn 12:1-8
in **NEW AGE**
James   Jas 2:1-13
Jesus   Lk 6:20-23
as **PUNISHMENT**
Solomon   Prov 6:6-11
as **QUALITY OF LIFE**
James   Jas 1:9-11
Preacher   Eccl 4:13-16
Solomon   Prov 24:23-34;
28:1-28
revealing **RESPECT**
James   Jas 2:1-13
Solomon   Prov 17:1-28
in **STEWARDSHIP**
Jesus   Lk 14:12-14
Moses   Deut 15:1-11
as **VIRTUE**
Solomon   Prov 19:1-29

on **PRAISE**
God   Rev 19:6-10
Psalmist   Ps 113:1
of **AUTHORITY**
David   Ps 29:1-2
Psalmist   Ps 99:4-5;
150-2
through **BELIEF**
Peter   1 Pet 1:3-9
in **BROTHERHOOD**
Paul   Eph 5:15-20
of **COMMUNITY**
David   Ps 34:1-3
of **CREATION**
Psalmist   Ps 148:1-6;
7-14;
150:6
of **JUDGMENT**
Solomon   Prov 27:1-27
of **KNOWLEDGE**
Baruch   *Bar 3:24-37
Jesus   Lk 4:14-15
Preacher   Eccl 9:1-16;
17-10:20
Sirach   *Sir 1:11-20;
4:11-19;
6:18-37;
10:26-11:1;
14:20-27;
15:1-10;
20:24-31;
24:1-34;
37:7-26;
39:1-11
Solomon   *Wis 6:12-25;
7:7-14;
15-8:1;
8:2-21
of **NEW AGE**
Paul   Rom 14:1-23
in **PRAYER**
Jeremiah   Jer 13:15-17
Jesus   Lk 11:1-4
Paul   1 Cor 14:13-25;
Phil 4:1-9
Psalmist   Ps 117:1-2;
150:1
of **PROVIDENCE**
Psalmist   Ps 107:23-32;
147:12-20
of **RECONCILIATION**
Moses   Deut 31:30-32:4
as **RESPECT**
Believers   Rev 19:1-5
David   Ps 22:22-26
God   Rev 14:6-7
through **RITE**
David   1 Chr 15:1-16:43;
Ps 9:9-12;
24:7-10;
68:4-14
Deborah   Judg 5:10-11
God   Is 44:6-8;
21-23
Isaiah   Is 42:5-17
James   Jas 5:13
Jeremiah   Jer 31:7-14
Psalmist   Ps 33:1-3;
47:1-4;

of **TEMPTATION** (cont'd)

Jesus	Mk 14:32-42;
	Lk 22:39-46

for **VICTORY**

Jesus	Mt 6:9-13;
	Lk 21:34-36
Paul	2 Thes 3:1-2

of **WILL**

Jesus	Lk 11:5-8
Paul	Col 4:2-4

for **WISDOM**

Isaiah	Is 8:19-22
James	Jas 1:5-8
Paul	1 Cor 14:13-25
Solomon	Prov 2:1-22

for **WITNESS**

Paul	Rom 15:25-33;
	Eph 6:19-20;
	2 Thes 3:1-2

on **PRESENCE**

in **DISCIPLESHIP**

Holy Spirit	Eph 5:15-20
Jesus	Mt 18:18-20

concerning **PATIENCE**

David	Ps 27:13-14

of **SPIRIT**

Paul	Rom 8:5-13;
	1 Cor 3:10-17;
	6:12-20

on **PRIDE**

Preacher	Eccl 7:1-22
Solomon	Prov 27:1-27

in **BROTHERHOOD**

Paul	2 Cor 1:12-14;
	5:11-13;
	7:2-4

in **COMMITMENT**

Paul	2 Cor 5:11-13

in **CONFRONTATION**

Preacher	Eccl 11:1-8

concerning **DESIRE**

Preacher	Eccl 6:1-12

concerning in**FIDELITY**

Jesus	Mk 9:38-41;
	Lk 9:49-50

of **KNOWLEDGE**

Paul	1 Cor 8:1-3

as **QUALITY OF LIFE**

Preacher	Eccl 1:2-11;
	12-2:26;
	5:8-20;
	9:1-16;
	11:9-12:7;
	12:8-11

as **SIN**

Elihu	Job 35:9-12
James	Jas 4:1-10;
	13-16
Jesus	Lk 18:9-14
Moses	Deut 8:11-20
Sirach	*Sir 3:17-31;
	10:12-15
Solomon	Prov 11:1-31;
	21:1-31

in **STEWARDSHIP**

Jesus	Mt 6:2-4

concerning **TRUTH**

David	Ps 4:2-5

on **PROMISE**

of **ALIENATION**

Ezra	*1 Esd 9:1-15

of **BLESSING**

Darius	Ezra 6:1-12
Jesus	Mt 5:3-12;
	11:28-30;
	Lk 6:20-23;
	Jn 14:18-24
Moses	Deut 15:1-11

concerning **CAPTIVITY**

Baruch	*Bar 4:17-20

of **DISCIPLESHIP**

Holy Spirit	Acts 2:37-41

through **FAITH**

Author	Heb 6:9-12

to **FAMILY**

God	*2 Esd 2:10-14
Paul	Gal 4:27-31

concerning **FULFILLMENT**

Jesus	Mt 5:3-12;
	10:23;
	16:13-20;
	18:18-20;
	Lk 6:20-23
Paul	Acts 13:14-52

of **GRACE**

Jesus	Mt 5:3-12;
	Lk 6:20-23

of **HOPE**

John the Baptist	Mt 3:1-12;
	Mk 1:2-8

as **IDOLATRY**

Jesus	Mt 5:33-37

causing **INDIFFERENCE**

God	Ex 4:18-23

of **JOY**

Bildad	Job 8:20-22
God	*2 Esd 2:15-32

of **KILLING**

God	Ex 4:18-23

of **LIFE**

God	Gen 6:1-4
Jesus	Mt 10:26-39

of **LOVE**

Angel	*2 Esd 5:31-42

of **PEACE**

Jesus	Mt 11:28-30;
	Jn 14:27-31
Paul	Phil 4:1-9

of **SERVICE**

Moses	Num 32:20-33

of **VICTORY**

Bildad	Job 8:20-22
Moses	Deut 7:17-26;
	11:1-25

of **WEALTH**

Artaxerxes	Exra 7:20-24
Moses	Deut 28:1-14;
	30:1-10
Nehemiah	Neh 5:6-13

of **WISDOM**

Angel	*2 Esd 6:29-34
Jesus	Jn 14:25-26

on **PROVIDENCE**

through **DESTRUCTION**

Moses	Deut 7:17-26

through **ENEMY**

God	*2 Esd 1:4-23

as SACREDNESS (cont'd)
Paul	Rom 2:25-3:20; 12:1-2; Col 3:1-4

as SACRIFICE
Paul	Rom 12:1-2
Peter	1 Pet 2:4-10

as SELFISHNESS
Isaiah	Is 56:9-57:13
Job	Job 21:19-27

as SERVICE
God	Is 1:10-17
Jesus	Mt 20:20-28; Mk 9:33-37; 10:35-45; Lk 16:19-31
Paul	Rom 12:9-13; Col 3:5-17; 2 Thes 3:6-15; 1 Tim 6:17-19

as SHARING
Author	Heb 13:1-25
Paul	Rom 12:9-13; 1 Tim 6:17-19
Solomon	Prov 5:15-23

as SPIRIT
Jesus	Mt 15:15-20; Mk 7:1-23

as SUFFERING
Angel	*2 Esd 7:1-18
Jesus	Mt 5:3-12; Lk 6:20-23
Job	Job 16:1-6
Peter	1 Pet 4:1-6
Sirach	*Sir 30:14-25; 40:1-11

as TEMPERANCE
Author	Heb 13:1-25
Believers	Acts 15:6-29
Bishops	1 Tim 3:1-7
Deacons	1 Tim 3:8-13
James	Jas 1:26
Paul	1 Cor 7:25-35; 8:7-13
Solomon	Prov 26:1-28
Women	1 Tim 3:8-13

as TEMPTATION
Jesus	Mt 5:27-30
Solomon	Prov 25:1-28

as WEALTH
James	Jas 1:9-11
Jesus	Mt 19:23-26; Mk 10:23-27
Paul	1 Tim 6:17-19
Solomon	Prov 11:1-31; 13:1-25; 19:1-29; 28:1-28

as WISDOM
Jesus	Mt 6:5-8
Paul	Rom 8:5-13; 1 Cor 3:18-23
Preacher	Eccl 4:13-16
Solomon	Prov 13:1-25
Wisdom	Prov 8:32-36

as WITNESS
Paul	Rom 2:1-24; Phil 1:12-30
Women	1 Pet 3:1-7

as YOUTH
Solomon	Prov 20:1-30

on RATIONALIZATION
   in OLD AGE
Paul	1 Cor 14:13-25

   of ONENESS
Jesus	Mt 12:22-32; Mk 3:20-30

   revealing PARADOX
Jesus	Mt 5:38-42
Paul	1 Cor 6:1-8
Peter	1 Pet 2:18-20

   of POLITICS
Gamaliel	Acts 5:17-42

   of SERVICE
Jesus	Lk 13:10-17

   of WISDOM
Jesus	Mk 12:13-17; Lk 20:19-26

on RECONCILIATION
   through ACCEPTANCE
Jesus	Mt 18:15-17
Paul	2 Cor 5:20-6:2

   concerning ALIENATION
Jesus	Mt 5:21-26

   through DEATH
Jesus	Rom 5:12-21

   from EVIL
Paul	Rom 8:1-4

   through FAITH
Paul	Rom 3:21-30; 3:31-4:25; 5:1-5; 9:30-10:21; Gal 2:15-16; 3:6-9; 10-14; 5:2-6

   through GRACE
Jesus	Mt 6:14-15; 18:21-22
Moses	Deut 30:1-10
Paul	Rom 3:21-30; 5:1-5; 12-21; Gal 2:15-16; 20-21; 3:10-14; Col 1:9-14

   for GUILT
Moses	Deut 21:1-9
Solomon	1 Kgs 2:28-35

   through LOVE
Jesus	Lk 7:36-50
Paul	2 Cor 5:14-19

   through OBEDIENCE
James	Jas 2:14-26
Paul	Rom 2:1-24

   through ONENESS
Jesus	Mt 5:21-26

   through PURIFICATION
Author	Heb 10:19-31
John the Baptist	Lk 3:1-6

   through REPENTANCE
Jesus	Mt 18:15-17; 21:28-32; Lk 12:57-59; 13:1-5; 18:9-14
John the Baptist	Lk 3:1-6
Moses	Deut 30:1-10

causing **CONVERSION** (cont'd)
Joshua	Josh 24:16-24
Laodicea	Rev 3:14-22
Paul	Acts 21:27-22:29; Eph 4:25-5:2
Pergamum	Rev 2:12-17
Sardis	Rev 3:1-6

results in **GIFT**
Holy Spirit	Acts 2:37-41

through **JUDGMENT**
Jesus	Mt 12:38-42; Lk 11:29-32

concerning **NEW AGE**
Jesus	Mt 4:17; Mk 1:14-15
Paul	1 Cor 6:9-11

resulting in **SECURITY**
Zophar	Job 11:13-20

of **SIN**
Eli	1 Sam 2:11-26
Eliphaz	Job 22:21-30
Ezra	Ezra 10:7-15
God	Is 1:10-17
Isaiah	Is 28:14-22
Israelites	Is 31:4-9
Jesus	Lk 17:1-6; 24:44-49
John	1 Jn 1:5-10
John the Baptist	Mk 1:2-8
Paul	Rom 6:1-14; 1 Cor 15:29-34
Peter	Acts 3:1-26; 1 Pet 4:1-6
Sirach	*Sir 34:23-26
Solomon	Prov 28:1-28

through **TRUTH**
Jeremiah	Jer 36:1-7
Paul	Acts 17:16-34

n **RESPECT**
in **BLESSING**
David	1 Chr 15:1-16:43
Psalmist	Ps 96:1-6; 135:19-21

for **DEATH**
Sirach	*Sir 38:16-23

for **FAITH**
Bishops	1 Tim 3:1-7
Paul	Rom 14:1-23

through **FAITH**
God	Rev 14:6-7

for **FAMILY**
God	Ex 20:1-17
Jesus	Mt 15:3-9; 19:16-22; Mk 7:1-23 10:17-22
Moses	Ex 21:12-17; Lev 20:1-27; Deut 5:1-21; 27:11-26
Paul	Eph 6:1-4
Sirach	*Sir 3:1-16; 22:1-6; 30:1-13; 33:16-23; 41:14-23

as **FEAR**
David	1 Chr 15:1-16:43
God	Rev 14:6-7
Jeremiah	Jer 5:20-25

as **FEAR** (cont'd)
Moses	Deut 8:1-10; 10:12-22; 17:8-13
Princes	Jer 36:11-19
Psalmist	Ps 96:7-9

for **GOOD**
Sirach	*Sir 42:1-5

for **HEALING**
Sirach	*Sir 38:1-15

with **HUMILITY**
Paul	Rom 12:14-21
Solomon	Prov 29:1-27

for **LEADERSHIP**
Author	Heb 13:1-25
Paul	2 Cor 8:16-24; 1 Thes 5:12-22; 1 Tim 5:17-25; 6:1-2b
Peter	1 Pet 2:13-17; 5:1-5
Servants	1 Pet 2:18-20

through **LOVE**
Jesus	Mt 5:43-47; Lk 6:27-35; Jn 14:15-17
Paul	1 Cor 13:4-7; Eph 5:21-33; 6:1-4

in **MARRIAGE**
Author	Heb 13:1-25
Men	1 Pet 3:1-7

for **OBEDIENCE**
Paul	Eph 6:1-4; 1 Tim 6:1-2b

for **OLD AGE**
Paul	1 Tim 5:1-2; 3-16
Sirach	*Sir 25:3-6; 32:1-13
Solomon	Prov 23:15-24:22; *Wis 3:10-19; 4:1-9

in **POLITICS**
Peter	1 Pet 2:13-17

for **POVERTY**
James	Jas 2:1-13
Solomon	Prov 17:1-28

through **PRAISE**
Believers	Rev 19:1-5
David	Ps 22:22-26
God	Rev 14:6-7

as **REWARD**
Elders	1 Tim 5:17-25
Solomon	Prov 13:1-25

in **SACREDNESS**
Jesus	Mt 23:16-22

in **SERVICE**
Sirach	*Sir 38:24-34
Solomon	Prov 27:1-27

for **SEX**
Sirach	*Sir 41:14-23

for **WEALTH**
Psalmist	Ps 45:10-12
Sirach	*Sir 40:28-30

for **WISDOM**
Believers	Prov 15:1-33
Father	Prov 4:1-9
Isaiah	Is 29:15-16
Sirach	*Sir 9:14-18; 37:7-26;

for **WISDOM** (cont'd)
Sirach	39:1-11
Solomon	*Wis 8:2-21

for **WITNESS**
Isaiah	Is 51:17-52:12
Peter	1 Pet 2:11-12

for **YOUTH**
Jesus	Mt 18:10
Paul	1 Tim 4:11-16;
	5:1-2

on dis**RESPECT**
results from **EVIL**
Sirach	*Sir 4:20-31;
	41:14-23
Solomon	Prov 18:1-24

on **RESURRECTION**
from **DEATH**
God	*2 Esd 2:15-32
Jesus	Mt 22:23-33;
	Mk 12:18-27;
	Lk 20:27-40
Paul	Rom 6:1-14;
	1 Cor 15:12-19;
	51-58

as **GOOD**
Solomon	*Wis 4:1-9;
	5:15-23

through **GRACE**
Jesus	Lk 24:44-49

of **LIFE**
Jesus	Jn 5:19-47
Paul	Rom 8:5-13;
	1 Cor 15:35-41;
	42-50

concerning **MARRIAGE**
Jesus	Mt 22:23-33;
	Mk 12:18-27;
	Lk 20:27-40

as **MIRACLE**
Paul	1 Cor 15:35-41

on **REVENGE**
by **COMMUNITY**
Mordecai	Esth 8:9-14

as **PUNISHMENT**
Ahasuerus	Esth 1:10-22
Moses	Deut 28:15-68

as **SIN**
Sirach	*Sir 27:30-28:12

on **REWARD**
Jesus	Mt 25:31-46

for **BEHAVIOR**
Paul	Rom 2:1-24
Sirach	*Sir 4:1-10

of **BELIEF**
Author	Heb 10:32-39
Jesus	Jn 11:1-57;
	12:27-36a
Paul	Rom 9:30-10:21;
	11:7-24;
	2 Thes 1:7b-10
Solomon	Prov 28:1-28

of **COMMUNITY**
Darius	*1 Esd 4:42-57

of **CONVERSION**
Peter	1 Pet 3:8-12
Zophar	Job 11:13-20

of **ELECTION**
God	*2 Esd 2:15-32
Paul	Rom 11:7-24

in **ETERNITY**
Paul	2 Cor 4:16-18;
	1 Tim 6:11-16

for **FIDELITY**
Angel	*2 Esd 7:88-99
Believers	Rev 2:18-29
Bildad	Job 8:1-7
David	1 Kgs 2:5-12;
	Ps 37:1-11
Ephesus	Rev 2:1-7
God	Ps 81:5c-16;
	Is 1:18-20
Israelites	Deut 7:6-16
Jesus	Mt 5:43-47;
	7:21-23;
	10:26-39;
	19:27-30;
	21:28-32;
	24:45-51;
	25:14-30;
	Lk 6:27-35;
	12:35-38;
	13:22-30;
	Jn 14:18-24
John	1 Jn 2:1-6;
	12-17;
	24-27;
	2:28-3:3;
	19-24;
	2 Jn 1:7-11
Joshua	Josh 22:1-8
Laodicea	Rev 3:14-22
Moses	Deut 4:15-31
Paul	1 Cor 9:24-27;
	15:51-58;
	Gal 6:7-10;
	2 Tim 4:6-8
Pergamum	Rev 2:12-17
Philadelphians	Rev 3:7-13
Sardis	Rev 3:1-6
Servants	1 Pet 2:18-20
Smyrna	Rev 2:8-11
Solomon	*Wis 3:1-9;
	10-19

is **FREEDOM**
Moses	Deut 15:12-18

of **KNOWLEDGE**
Father	Prov 4:1-9
Preacher	Eccl 9:17-10:20
Sirach	*Sir 51:13-30
Solomon	Prov 19:1-29

as **MOTIVATION**
Jesus	Mt 6:1;
	2-4;
	16-18

in **NEW AGE**
Jesus	Mt 5:3-12;
	19:27-30;
	20:1-16;
	24:45-51;
	25:1-13;
	Mk 10:28-31;
	Lk 6:20-23;
	14:12-14;
	16:1-9;
	18:28-30;

in **NEW AGE** (cont'd)
Jesus	Jn 4:27-42; 14:1-14
Paul	2 Cor 4:16-18
Peter	2 Pet 1:8-11

of **PRAYER**
Jesus	Lk 11:5-8; 9-13

for **QUALITY OF LIFE**
Eliphaz	Job 4:7-11
Jesus	Lk 6:24-26
Paul	Gal 6:7-10
Preacher	Eccl 5:8-20

is **RECONCILIATION**
James	Jas 5:19-20
Jesus	Mt 5:3-12; Lk 6:20-23

as **RESPECT**
Elders	1 Tim 5:17-25
Solomon	Prov 13:1-25

is **RESURRECTION**
Jesus	Lk 14:12-14

is **SALVATION**
Jesus	Mt 5:3-12; 10:26-39; 13:36-43; 19:27-30; 25:31-46; Mk 10:28-31; Lk 6:20-23; 18:28-30; Jn 6:25-59; 12:44-50
John the Baptist	Jn 3:31-36
Paul	Rom 6:15-23; 2 Thes 2:13-15; 2 Tim 4:6-8
Peter	1 Pet 5:1-5; 2 Pet 1:8-11

in**SECURITY**
Jesus	Mt 10:40-42

for **STEWARDSHIP**
Jesus	Mt 10:40-42; 25:14-30; Mk 4:21-25; 26-29; 9:38-41; Lk 8:16-18; 12:41-46; 16:1-9; 19:11-27; Jn 12:20-26
Paul	1 Cor 3:5-9; 2 Cor 9:6-11
Preacher	Eccl 11:1-8
Solomon	Prov 3:1-35
Thyatira	Rev 2:18-29

of **TRUTH**
Paul	1 Cor 3:10-17

for **VIRTUE**
Author	Heb 12:3-11
Believers	Prov 15:1-33
James	Jas 1:12; 5:14-18
Jesus	Mt 5:3-12; Lk 6:20-23; 14:7-11
Paul	1 Cor 6:9-11
Peter	1 Pet 3:8-12; 13-17

for **VIRTUE** (cont'd)
Sirach	*Sir 40:12-17; 41:5-13
Solomon	Prov 3:1-35; 10:1-32; 11:1-31; 14:1-35; 16:1-33; 20:1-30; 22:1-16; *Wis 4:1-9; 5:15-23

on **RITE**
related to **DEATH**
Jacob	Gen 49:29-33

of **GRATITUDE**
Moses	Deut 26:1-11
Psalmist	Ps 97:10-12; 100:4-5; 147:7-11

of **HEALING**
James	Jas 5:14-18

revealing **IDOLATRY**
Jeremiah	*Jer 6:41-44
Nebuchadnezzar	Dan 3:13-15

revealing **JOY**
Asaph	Ps 81:1-5b
Isaiah	Is 49:1-26
James	Jas 5:13
Jeremiah	Jer 31:7-14
Mordecai	Esth 9:20-28
Moses	Deut 16:13-15
Psalmist	Ps 33:1-3; 47:1-4; 66:1-4; 97:10-12; 98:4-6; 100:1-3; 149:5-9
Zephaniah	Zeph 3:14-20

of **LEADERSHIP**
David	1 Kgs 1:28-40

concerning **LIFE**
Moses	Ex 13:3-10

concerning **OBEDIENCE**
Aaron	Lev 9:1-24
Abraham	Gen 17:23-27; 21:1-7
God	Gen 17:9-14
Israelites	*1 Esd 9:1-15

of **PEACE**
Paul	1 Cor 14:34-40

of **PRAISE**
David	1 Chr 15:1-16:43; Ps 9:9-12; 24:7-10; 68:4-14
Deborah	Judg 5:10-11
God	Is 44:6-8; 21-23
Isaiah	Is 42:5-17
James	Jas 5:13
Jeremiah	Jer 31:7-14
Psalmist	Ps 33:1-3; 47:1-4; 5-9; 66:1-4; 95:1-7c; 96:1-6;

through **FAITH** (cont'd)
Paul Eph 1:15-2:10;
 Col 1:21-23;
 1 Thes 4:13-18
with **FEAR**
Paul Phil 2:12-18
through **FRIENDSHIP**
Jesus Lk 16:1-9
through **GOOD**
Angel *2 Esd 7:45-61
Jesus Mt 13:24-30;
 47-50
by **GRACE**
Jesus Mt 20:1-16;
 Jn 3:1-21
Paul Rom 9:6-13;
 11:1-6;
 25-32;
 1 Cor 1:26-31;
 6:12-20;
 Gal 2:15-16;
 4:27-31;
 Eph 1:15-2:10;
 Col 1:9-14;
 1 Thes 5:1-11;
 2 Tim 1:8-14
Peter Acts 2:14-36;
 15:6-29
through **HUMILITY**
Jesus Mt 18:1-4
Paul 1 Cor 1:26-31
of **LIFE**
Jesus Mt 16:21-28;
 Mk 8:34-9:1;
 Lk 9:23-27;
 Jn 5:19-47
Paul Rom 1:16-17;
 6:1-14;
 8:5-13
through **LOVE**
Jesus Lk 15:1-7;
 8-10;
 11-32
through **OBEDIENCE**
Angels Gen 19:12-29
David Ps 37:23-40
God Gen 7:1-24;
 Ps 50:22-23;
 81:5c-16;
 Is 1:18-20
Jesus Mt 7:21-23;
 24-27;
 19:16-22;
 21:33-43;
 Mk 10:17-22;
 12:1-12;
 Lk 6:46-49;
 13:22-30;
 18:18-27;
 20:9-18
John 1 Jn 2:12-17
Paul Rom 2:1-24;
 11:7-24;
 1 Tim 4:11-16
through **ONENESS**
Paul Rom 9:30-10:21
from **OPPRESSION**
Jesus Mt 5:3-12
through **PATIENCE**
Author Heb 6:9-12

through **PATIENCE** (cont'd)
Jude Jude 1:21-23
Paul Rom 2:1-24;
 2 Tim 2:8-13
through **PURIFICATION**
Holy Spirit Jn 3:1-21
Paul 1 Cor 3:10-17;
 6:9-11;
 Col 2:6-15
Peter 1 Pet 3:18-22
through **REPENTANCE**
Israelites Hos 10:9-15
Jesus Mt 21:28-32;
 Lk 15:1-7;
 8-10;
 11-32;
 19:1-10
Paul 2 Cor 7:5-13a
through **SACRIFICE**
God Ps 50:22-23
Jesus Jn 12:20-26
through **SERVICE**
James Jas 2:14-26
Jesus Lk 17:7-10;
 19:1-10
through **SPIRIT**
Paul 1 Cor 5:1-5
through **SUFFERING**
God Ps 50:7-15
Philadelphians Rev 3:7-13
through **TEMPERANCE**
Paul 1 Cor 6:9-11
through **VICTORY**
Paul 1 Thes 4:13-18
concerning **WEALTH**
Jesus Mt 19:16-22;
 23-26;
 Mk 10:23-27;
 Lk 18:18-27
through **WISDOM**
Paul 1 Cor 1:18-25
Solomon Prov 11:1-31
through **WITNESS**
David 1 Chr 15:1-16:4
Isaiah Is 48:1-22
Jesus Mt 10:23
Psalmist Ps 96:1-6
through **YOUTH**
Jesus Mt 19:13-15;
 Mk 10:13-16

on **SECURITY**
in **DEATH**
Raphael *Tb 6:1-17
Solomon Prov 23:15-24:2
in **DIGNITY**
Solomon Prov 10:1-32;
 28:1-28
from **ENEMY**
Romans *1 Mc 8:1-32
from **EVIL**
John 1 Jn 5:13-21
Raphael *Tb 6:1-17
Solomon Prov 2:1-22
through **FAITH**
God Is 43:14-44:5
Isaiah Is 51:1-16

of **DESTRUCTION** (cont'd)
Paul | 1 Thes 5:1-11; 2 Thes 2:3b-10

of **DISOBEDIENCE**
Paul | 2 Tim 3:1-9

of **EVIL**
Jesus | Mt 12:43-45; 16:1-4; Lk 11:24-26
Paul | 2 Tim 3:1-9

of **FAITH**
Jesus | Jn 14:1-14

of **FULFILLMENT**
Angel | *2 Esd 7:19-32

of **HATE**
Paul | 2 Tim 3:1-9

of **HERESY**
Paul | 2 Thes 2:3b-10; 2 Tim 3:1-9

of **IGNORANCE**
Jesus | Lk 12:54-56

of **JOY**
God | Rev 19:6-10

of **JUSTICE**
Angel | *2 Esd 8:63-9:25; 13:1-50

of **MIRACLE**
God | Ex 4:1-9; 17; 7:14-25; 8:1-15; 16-19; 20-32; 9:1-7; 8-12; 13-35; 10:1-20; 21-23
Jesus | Mk 8:11-13
Moses | Num 16:25-35

of **OBEDIENCE**
God | Gen 17:9-14

of **POLITICS**
Angel | *2 Esd 11:1-12:39

of **PRAISE**
God | Rev 19:6-10

of **PRIDE**
Paul | 2 Tim 3:1-9

of **PRUDENCE**
Jesus | Mt 9:16-17; 16:1-4; Mk 2:18-22; Lk 5:36-39; 12:54-56

of **SACREDNESS**
Artaxerxes | *1 Esd 8:8-24
Darius | *1 Esd 6:27-34
Hezekiah | 2 Chr 29:1-36
Joash | 2 Chr 24:1-27
Moses | Deut 6:4-19; 11:1-25; 27:1-10

of **SACRIFICE**
Jesus | Mt 9:14-15; Mk 2:18-22; Lk 5:33-35

of **SELFISHNESS**
Paul | 2 Tim 3:1-9

of **SUFFERING**
Paul | 2 Tim 3:1-9

of **VICTORY**
Elisha | 2 Kgs 13:14-19

of **WITNESS**
Jesus | Mt 11:2-6; 13:34-35; Mk 4:33-34; Lk 7:18-23
Moses | Ex 16:31-36; Deut 31:24-29

on **SIN**
Jesus | Jn 15:18-25
Paul | Gal 5:25-6:6

causing **ALIENATION**
Isaiah | Is 59:1-21
Jeremiah | Jer 5:20-25
Jesus | Mt 5:27-30; 18:7-9; 15-17; Mk 9:42-48
Paul | Rom 6:1-14; 8:5-13; 1 Cor 5:9-13; 6:12-20; Gal 5:16-21; Eph 4:17-24; Col 2:16-23; 3:5-17
Peter | 1 Pet 2:21-25
Solomon | Prov 2:1-22; 17:1-28

of **ANGER**
David | Ps 4:2-5
Paul | Eph 4:25-5:2
Sirach | *Sir 27:30-28:12
Solomon | Prov 22:22-23:14; 29:1-27

of **BLASPHEMY**
Holy Spirit | Mt 12:22-32; Lk 12:1-12
James | Jas 5:12
Jesus | Mk 12:37b-40; Lk 20:45-47

as **BLESSING**
Job | Job 21:7-13; 28-34

of **COVETOUSNESS**
Jesus | Mt 21:33-43; Mk 12:1-12; Lk 20:9-18
Paul | Rom 7:7-13; Eph 5:3-14

causing **DEATH**
James | Jas 1:13-15
Jesus | Jn 8:21-59
Moses | Ex 19:9-15; Deut 22:13-30
Paul | Rom 5:12-21; 6:1-14; 15-23; 7:7-13; 8:5-13; 1 Cor 15:51-58
Peter | 1 Pet 2:21-25
Solomon | Prov 12:1-28

causing **DESTRUCTION**
Isaiah | Is 59:1-21
Jesus | Mt 7:24-27; 13:36-43; 47-50;

causing **DESTRUCTION** (cont'd)

Jesus	Lk 6:46-49
Paul	Rom 6:1-14;
	Phil 3:17-21
Solomon	Prov 1:10-19;
	11:1-31;
	12:1-38;
	13:1-25;
	14:1-35

of **DISOBEDIENCE**

James	Jas 4:17
Jesus	Mt 15:15-20;
	21:33-43;
	Mk 7:1-23;
	12:1-12;
	Lk 20:9-18
Paul	Rom 8:5-13;
	2 Thes 1:7b-10

of **DOUBT**

Jesus	Jn 5:19-47

of **ENEMY**

Paul	Rom 7:7-13

of **EVIL**

Jesus	Mt 12:43-45;
	21:33-43;
	Mk 12:1-12;
	Lk 11:24-26;
	20:9-18

of **FAMILY**

Micah	Mic 7:1-6
Sirach	*Sir 41:5-13

of **GREED**

Sirach	*Sir 14:3-19

of **HERESY**

Jeremiah	Jer 5:30-31
Jesus	Mt 23:16-22
Pergamum	Rev 2:12-17

of **IDOLATRY**

Jesus	Mt 23:16-22
Moses	Deut 6:4-19
Paul	Rom 1:19-23;
	1 Cor 10:1-13
Solomon	*Wis 14:12-31;
	15:7-19

of **JEALOUSY**

David	Ps 37:1-11
Paul	Gal 5:25-6:6
Solomon	Prov 3:1-35;
	23:15-24:22

of **KILLING**

David	2 Sam 11:1-27
Isaiah	Is 56:9-57:13
Jesus	Mt 21:33-43;
	Mk 12:1-12;
	Lk 20:9-18

of **LEADERSHIP**

Solomon	Prov 28:1-28

in **LIFE**

Paul	Rom 6:1-14
Preacher	Eccl 7:1-22

of **LUST**

Author	Heb 13:1-25
Jude	Jude 1:14-16

in **MARRIAGE**

Jesus	Mt 5:31-32;
	19:3-9;
	Mk 10:1-12;
	Lk 16:16-18
Moses	Deut 7:1-5

in **MARRIAGE** (cont'd)

Paul	Rom 7:1-6;
	1 Cor 7:8-16
Sirach	*Sir 25:16-26

concerning **OBEDIENCE**

Paul	Gal 2:17-19

concerning **OPPRESSION**

Bildad	Job 18:12-15
James	Jas 5:1-6

of **PIETY**

Jesus	Mt 23:27-28;
	Mk 12:37b-40;
	Lk 20:45-47

of **PRIDE**

Elihu	Job 35:9-12
James	Jas 4:1-10;
	13-16
Jesus	Lk 18:9-14
Moses	Deut 8:11-20
Sirach	*Sir 3:17-31;
	10:12-25
Solomon	Prov 11:1-31;
	21:1-31

of **REVENGE**

Sirach	*Sir 27:30-28:12

of **SELFISHNESS**

Jesus	Mk 12:37b-40;
	Lk 20:45-47
Jude	Jude 1:14-16

in **SERVICE**

Jesus	Lk 17:1-6

of **SEX**

Agur	Prov 30:15-33
Jesus	Jn 7:53-8:11
Moses	Deut 22:13-30;
	27:11-26
Paul	1 Cor 5:1-5;
	6:12-20;
	Eph 5:3-14
Preacher	Eccl 7:23-29
Sirach	*Sir 23:16-27;
	26:5-12
Solomon	Prov 5:1-14;
	6:20-7:27;
	9:13-18;
	23:15-24:22

causing **SUFFERING**

Eliphaz	Job 15:17-35
Hosea	Hos 14:9
Paul	Rom 2:1-24
Sirach	*Sir 40:1-11

of **TEMPTATION**

Jesus	Mt 18:7-9;
	Lk 17:1-6
Paul	1 Cor 5:9-13;
	8:7-13;
	10:1-13;
	Gal 5:16-21

of **VIOLENCE**

Solomon	Prov 1:10-19

of **WEALTH**

Sirach	*Sir 26:29-27:2;
	29:1-7;
	31:1-11

of **WILL**

James	Jas 1:13-15

concerning **WISDOM**

Solomon	*Wis 1:1-5

of **WITNESS**
    Isaiah   Is 59:1-21
    Paul   Tit 3:8-11

concerning **SPIRIT's**
SALVATION
    Paul   1 Cor 5:1-5

on **SPIRIT**
  of **AUTHORITY**
    Jesus   Jn 7:15-24
  of **CONVERSION**
    Paul   Rom 12:1-2
  as **GIFT**
    Paul   2 Tim 1:3-7
  of **HONESTY**
    Jesus   Mt 15:10-11;
                       Mk 7:1-23
  concerning **KNOWLEDGE**
    Jesus   Lk 8:16-18;
                       12:1-12;
                       Jn 14:25-26
    Paul   Rom 2:1-24;
                       1 Cor 4:1-5
  concerning **LAW**
    Paul   Rom 2:25-3:20
  in **NEW AGE**
    Paul   Rom 7:1-6;
                       8:5-13;
                       Eph 4:17-24
  in **PRAYER**
    Paul   1 Cor 14:13-25
  as **QUALITY OF LIFE**
    Jesus   Mt 15:15-20;
                       Mk 7:1-23
  in **RESURRECTION**
    Paul   1 Cor 15:42-50
  concerning **STEWARDSHIP**
    Jesus   Mt 23:25-26
  concerning **TRUTH**
    Jesus   Jn 14:15-17

on **STEALING**
    God   Ex 20:1-17
    Jesus   Mt 19:16-22;
                       Mk 10:17-22
    Moses   Deut 5:1-21;
                       23:15-25:19
    Nathan   2 Sam 12:1-31
    Paul   Rom 13:8-10
  through **disHONESTY**
    Moses   Deut 19:14;
                       27:11-26
  in **STEWARDSHIP**
    John the Baptist Lk 3:10-14

on **STEWARDSHIP**
    Jesus   Mt 10:40-42;
                       19:27-30;
                     21:33-43;
                     Mk 10:28-31;
                     12:1-12;
                     Lk 15:11-32;
                     18:28-30;
                     20:9-18
    Paul   Rom 12:14-21
  in **DISCIPLESHIP**
    Jesus   Mt 10:7-8;
                     26-39;
                     28:16-20;

in **DISCIPLESHIP** (cont'd)
    Jesus   Mk 4:21-25;
                     10:35-45;
                     Lk 8:16-18;
                     14:25-27
    John the Baptist Lk 3:10-14
    Paul   Tit 2:1-10
  concerning **ENEMY**
    Paul   Rom 12:14-21
    Solomon   Prov 25:1-28
  concerning **EVIL**
    Paul   Rom 12:14-21
  of **FAITH**
    Jesus   Mt 24:42-44;
                     Mk 13:28-37;
                     Lk 8:16-18
    Paul   2 Cor 9:1-5
  of **FAMILY**
    Bishops   1 Tim 3:1-7
    Deacons   1 Tim 3:8-13
  of **FRIENDSHIP**
    Jesus   Lk 10:29-37
  of **GOOD**
    Paul   Rom 14:1-23
    Solomon   Prov 3:1-35
  through **GRACE**
    Jesus   Mk 10:28-31;
                     Lk 18:28-30
    Peter   1 Pet 4:7-11
  of **LIFE**
    John   1 Jn 3:11-18
  through **LOVE**
    Jesus   Mk 12:41-44;
                     Lk 8:16-18;
                     10:29-37;
                     21:1-4;
                     Jn 13:31-35;
                     21:15-23
    Paul   2 Cor 8:7-15;
                     9:1-5;
                     6-11;
                     1 Tim 6:6-10
  concerning **LUST**
    Paul   1 Tim 6:6-10
  concerning **OBEDIENCE**
    Aaron   Ex 7:1-7
    Israelites   Ex 39:1;
                     2-7;
                     8-21;
                     22-26;
                     27-31;
                     32-43
    Jesus   Mt 19:16-22;
                     Mk 10:17-22;
                     Lk 12:41-46;
                     17:7-10;
                     18:18-27;
                     19:11-27
    Moses   Ex 7:1-7;
                     Deut 28:1-14
  concerning **PIETY**
    Jesus   Mt 6:2-4
    Paul   1 Cor 16:1-4
  concerning **POVERTY**
    Jesus   Lk 14:12-14
    Moses   Deut 15:1-11
  of **SACRIFICE**
    God   Ex 20:24-26
    Jesus   Mt 20:20-28;
                     Mk 10:35-45;

as **VIRTUE** (cont'd)
Paul	1 Cor 6:1-8
Peter	1 Pet 3:13-17

on **TEMPERANCE**
James	Jas 3:1-12
Jesus	Mt 6:16-18
Lemuel	Prov 31:1-9
Paul	1 Cor 7:1-7;
	8-16;
	36-38;
	Col 2:16-23
Sirach	*Sir 19:1-3;
	37:27-31
Tobit	*Tb 4:1-21

in **CONFRONTATION**
Joshua	Josh 6:15-21

in **KNOWLEDGE**
Peter	2 Pet 1:5-7
Preacher	Eccl 12:12-14
Sirach	*Sir 4:11-19
Solomon	Prov 29:1-27

in **PRAYER**
Jesus	Lk 11:1-4

as **QUALITY OF LIFE**
Author	Heb 13:1-25
Believers	Acts 15:6-29
Bishops	1 Tim 3:1-7
Deacons	1 Tim 3:8-13
James	Jas 1:26
Paul	1 Cor 7:25-35;
	8:7-13
Solomon	Prov 26:1-28
Women	1 Tim 3:8-13

concerning **SIN**
Jesus	Mk 9:42-48

as **VIRTUE**
Jesus	Mt 19:10-12
Peter	1 Pet 2:11-12
Sirach	*Sir 31:25-31

on **TEMPTATION**
Jesus	Mt 4:1-11
Paul	1 Cor 6:12-20;
	7:8-16;
	36-38
Solomon	Prov 23:15-24:22

in **BROTHERHOOD**
Paul	1 Cor 8:7-13

in **CONFRONTATION**
Solomon	Prov 6:20-7:27

in **DESIRE**
Paul	1 Tim 6:6-10

to in**FIDELITY**
Paul	1 Cor 7:1-7;
	2 Cor 11:1-6;
	Gal 5:7-12;
	Col 2:6-15
Sirach	*Sir 2:1-6
Solomon	Prov 1:10-19

as **MOTIVATION**
James	Jas 1:13-15

in **PROVIDENCE**
Paul	1 Cor 10:1-13

as **QUALITY OF LIFE**
Jesus	Mt 5:27-30
Solomon	Prov 25:1-28

concerning **SECURITY**
Paul	1 Tim 5:3-16

to **SIN**
Jesus	Mt 18:7-9;
	Lk 17:1-6
Paul	1 Cor 5:9-13;
	8:7-13;
	10:1-13;
	Gal 5:16-21

on **TRUTH**
concerning **DEATH**
Jesus	1 Pet 4:1-6

concerning **DEFEAT**
Jesus	Mk 4:1-9

of **FRIENDSHIP**
Sirach	*Sir 19:13-17

concerning **LIFE**
Jesus	Jn 8:12-20;
	9:1-41;
	14:1-14
Paul	2 Cor 4:7-12

concerning **LOVE**
John	1 Jn 2:7-11;
	12-17

concerning **OBEDIENCE**
Corinthians	2 Cor 7:13b-16
David	Ps 143:7-12
Jesus	Mt 13:3b-9;
	18-23;
	Mk 4:1-9;
	10-20;
	21-25;
	Lk 8:4-8;
	11-15;
	16-18;
	11:27-28;
	Jn 3:1-21;
	8:21-59;
	12:44-50
John	1 Jn 2:24-27
Paul	Rom 15:14-24;
	Phil 1:12-30;
	2 Tim 1:8-14
Peter	2 Pet 3:1-2

through **OLD AGE**
Author	Heb 5:11-14;
	6:1-8
Peter	2 Pet 3:14-18a

PATIENCE in
Paul	2 Tim 4:1-5

concerning **REPENTANCE**
Jeremiah	Jer 36:1-7
Paul	Acts 17:16-34

concerning **REWARDs**
Paul	1 Cor 3:10-17

concerning **SACREDNESS**
Holy Spirit	Jn 16:12-15
Paul	2 Tim 1:8-14

concerning **SERVICE**
James	Jas 1:22-25
Jesus	Lk 17:1-6
Paul	Phil 1:12-30

concerning **SHARING**
Jesus	Lk 21:37-38
Paul	Gal 1:18-2:10;
	5:25-6:6;
	2 Tim 2:1-7;
	4:1-5

concerning **SUFFERING**
Paul	2 Tim 1:8-14

concerning **VICTORY**
Jesus   Mk 4:1-9
concerning **WILL**
Jesus   Mk 4:10-20;
                    9:49-50
concerning **YOUTH**
Author   Heb 5:11-14
Paul   Eph 6:1-4

on **VICTORY**
in **AUTHORITY**
Believers   Rev 2:18-29
in **CONFRONTATION**
Judith   *Jdt 14:1-5
Moses   Deut 7:1-5;
                    21:10-14;
                    28:1-14;
                    31:1-8
through **FIDELITY**
Paul   1 Tim 6:11-16
through **KNOWLEDGE**
Solomon   Prov 23:15-24:22
through **LAW**
Jesus   Jn 12:44-50
in **NEW AGE**
Ephesus   Rev 2:1-7
Jesus   Mt 13:36-43;
                    19:27-30;
                    Mk 10:28-31;
                    Lk 13:18-19;
                    18:28-30
Laodicea   Rev 3:14-22
Paul   1 Cor 15:20-28;
                    Col 3:1-4
Pergamum   Rev 2:12-17
Philadelphians   Rev 3:7-13
Sardis   Rev 3:1-6
Smyrna   Rev 2:8-11
through **PROVIDENCE**
Joshua   Josh 24:1-13
in **RESURRECTION**
Paul   Rom 7:1-6
through **SALVATION**
Paul   1 Thes 4:13-18
over **SIN**
God   Gen 4:1-16
in **STEWARDSHIP**
Jesus   Mt 13:3b-9;
                    Lk 8:4-8
through **TRUTH**
Jesus   Mk 4:1-9

on **VIOLENCE**
Preacher   Eccl 3:1-8
in **CONFRONTATION**
Moses   Deut 20:1-9;
                    10-18;
                    19-20
as **MOTIVATION**
James   Jas 4:1-10
as **SIN**
Solomon   Prov 1:10-19

on **VIRTUE**
David   Ps 15:5c
Peter   1 Pet 3:13-17
Sirach   *Sir 14:1-2;
                    26:1-4
Wife   Prov 31:10-31

as **COMPASSION**
God   Ps 82:2-7;
                    *Wis 12:19-22
Sirach   *Sir 12:1-7
as **COURAGE**
Solomon   Prov 28:1-28
in **COVENANT**
Jesus   Mt 6:25-34
concerning **DESTRUCTION**
Isaiah   Is 56:9-57:13
as **FAITH**
Author   Heb 10:32-39
Jesus   Mt 8:5-13;
                    25:1-13;
                    Lk 7:1-10
Paul   Rom 1:16-17;
                    3:31-4:25;
                    9:30-10:21;
                    Gal 3:10-14;
                    Eph 6:10-18;
                    1 Tim 6:11-16
Peter   2 Pet 1:5-7
as **FEAR**
Sirach   *Sir 10:12-25
as **FULFILLMENT** of righteousness
Jesus   Mt 3:13-17;
                    5:3-12;
                    48;
                    Lk 6:20-23
Paul   1 Tim 6:6-10
as **GOOD**
Author   Heb 13:1-25
Sirach   *Sir 5:1-6:1;
                    7:1-36;
                    18:15-18
is **GRACE**
Amos   Amos 5:14-15
Zephaniah   Zeph 2:3
is **HOPE**
Paul   Rom 8:14-25
is **HUMILITY**
Sirach   *Sir 3:17-31;
                    6:2-17;
                    7:1-36;
                    10:26-11:1;
                    2-9
Solomon   Prov 12:1-28;
                    15:1-33;
                    16:1-33;
                    18:1-24;
                    22:1-16
Women   1 Pet 3:1-7
of **INNOCENCE**
Jesus   Mt 5:43-47
is **JOY**
David   Ps 32:8-11
Preacher   Eccl 7:1-22
Solomon   Prov 29:1-27
is **JUSTICE**
Bildad   Job 8:1-7
God   Is 56:1-8
Solomon   Prov 12:1-28;
                    21:1-31
in **LEADERSHIP**
Solomon   Prov 11:1-31
in **LIFE**
Solomon   Prov 10:1-32;
                    12:1-28;
                    15:1-33;

in NEW AGE (cont'd)
Paul   2 Thes 2:3b-10
through PROVIDENCE
Jesus   Mk 4:10-20
Paul   2 Tim 2:1-7
Solomon   Prov 2:1-22
as QUALITY OF LIFE
Jesus   Mt 6:5-8
Paul   Rom 8:5-13;
                    1 Cor 3:18-23
Preacher   Eccl 4:13-16
Solomon   Prov 13:1-25
Wisdom   Prov 8:32-36
through RATIONALIZATION
Jesus   Mk 12:13-17;
                    Lk 20:19-26
in RESURRECTION
Jesus   Mt 22:23-33;
                    Mk 12:18-27;
                    Lk 20:27-40
Solomon   *Wis 8:2-21
in SALVATION
Paul   1 Cor 1:18-25
Solomon   Prov 11:1-31
concerning SIN
Solomon   *Wis 1:1-5
in STEWARDSHIP
Jesus   Lk 16:1-9;
                    10-12
in TRUTH
Apollos   Acts 18:24-28
Jesus   Mt 6:19-24;
                    Mk 4:21-25;
                    Lk 8:16-18;
                    24:44-49
Job   Job 6:28-30
John   1 Jn 2:24-27;
                    5:13-21
Paul   Acts 20:17-38;
                    Rom 16:1-23;
                    1 Cor 1:18-25;
                    2 Cor 1:12-14;
                    Eph 5:3-14;
                    15-20;
                    Col 3:5-17
Preacher   Eccl 12:8-11
Sirach   *Sir 36:18-20

on WITNESS
Jesus   Mt 5:13-16
Paul   Acts 24:1-27;
                    2 Cor 3:1-3
to AUTHORITY
Asaph   Ps 78:1-8
Holy Spirit   Acts 1:6-11
Paul   2 Cor 10:1-6
to COMMITMENT
Paul   2 Cor 5:11-13
to CONVERSION
Paul   Acts 26:1-32
for ETERNITY
Isaiah   Is 30:8-17
to FREEDOM
Apostles   Acts 5:17-42
Paul   Gal 1:18-2:10
as GIFT
Paul   1 Cor 12:27-31a
concerning HONESTY
God   Ex 20:1-17
Moses   Deut 5:1-21;
                    19:15-21

concerning HONESTY (cont'd)
Solomon   Prov 12:1-28;
                    14:1-35;
                    19:1-29;
                    24:23-34;
                    25:1-28
to KNOWLEDGE
Demons   Lk 8:26-39
Holy Spirit   Lk 12:1-12
Isaiah   Is 48:1-22
Jesus   Mk 5:1-20
Joel   Joel 1:2-20
Luke   Acts 1:1-5
Psalmist   Ps 48:9-14
to NEW AGE
Angel   *2 Esd 2:42-48
Jesus   Lk 17:20-21
Paul   Gal 4:27-31
Philip   Acts 8:4-13
as QUALITY OF LIFE
Paul   Rom 2:1-24;
                    Phil 1:12-30
Women   1 Pet 3:1-7
revealing RESPECT
Isaiah   Is 51:17-52:12
Peter   1 Pet 2:11-12
to RESURRECTION
Apostles   Acts 4:32-5:10
Jesus   Mt 28:9-10
Paul   Acts 22:30-23:11;
                    26:1-32;
                    1 Cor 15:1-11;
                    12-19;
                    20-28
Peter   Acts 3:1-26
in RITE
Psalmist   Ps 107:17-22
to SALVATION
David   1 Chr 15:1-16:43
Isaiah   Is 48:1-22
Jesus   Mt 10:23
Psalmist   Ps 96:1-6
to SIN
Isaiah   Is 59:1-21
Paul   Tit 3:8-11
in STEWARDSHIP
Jesus   Lk 24:44-49
to TRUTH
Apollos   Acts 18:24-28
Apostles   Acts 8:14-25
Barnabas   Acts 11:25-26
Baruch   Jer 36:8-10;
                    11-19
Holy Spirit   Jn 16:12-15
Israelites   Zech 7:4-8:23
Jesus   Mk 4:21-25;
                    26-29;
                    Lk 8:16-18;
                    9:57-62;
                    11:33-36;
                    Jn 5:19-47
John   1 Jn 1:1-4
Luke   Lk 1:1-4
Paul   Acts 13:14-52;
                    14:8-18;
                    19:1-12;
                    21:27-22:29;
                    26:1-32;
                    28:17-31;
                    1 Cor 11:23-26;
                    Gal 3:1-5;

INSTRUCTION (cont'd)

to TRUTH (cont'd)
Paul — Eph 4:25-5:2;
1 Tim 3:14-16;
4:6-10;
6:2c-5;
2 Tim 1:8-14;
2:1-7;
14-19;
4:1-5
Peter — Acts 10:1-11:18;
1 Pet 3:13-17;
5:12-14
Philip — Acts 8:4-13;
26-40
Saul — Acts 9:20-31
Women — 1 Pet 3:1-7

on YOUTH
Jesus — Mt 19:13-15;
Mk 10:13-16
Paul — Eph 6:1-4;
Col 3:18-4:1
Solomon — Prov 22:1-16

in AUTHORITY
Preacher — Eccl 9:17-10:20
in CONFRONTATION
Jesus — Mk 9:42-48
Paul — 2 Cor 6:11-13
in NEW AGE
Jesus — Mt 19:13-15;
Mk 10:13-16;
Lk 18:15-17
as QUALITY OF LIFE
Solomon — Prov 20:1-30
concerning TRUTH
Author — Heb 5:11-14
Paul — Eph 6:1-4

JEALOUSY

BEHAVIOR revealing
Israelites — 2 Sam 19:8b-43
Saul — 1 Sam 18:6-30
of DEITY
God — Num 25:6-18;
Deut 6:4-19
in ENVIRONMENT
Sarah — Gen 16:1-6
through FALSE BELIEF
Priests — Acts 5:17-42
Sadducees — Acts 5:17-42
of FOLLOWERs
Jews — Acts 17:1-9;
10-15
INSTRUCTION on
Eliphaz — Job 5:1-7
Solomon — Prov 27:1-27

in COMMUNITY
Moses — Ps 106:13-18

CONFRONTATION with
Joseph — Gen 37:1-11;
12-28
REVELATION on
Gog — Ezek 38:17-23

JEALOUSY (cont'd)

of DEITY
God — Num 25:6-18;
Deut 6:4-19
as MOTIVATION
God — Zeph 1:17-18;
Zech 7:4-8:23
Israelites — Zech 1:7-17
PROVIDENCE in
Israelites — Rom 11:7-24
PUNISHMENT through
God — Nah 1:1-9
Israelites — Deut 29:16-29
as QUALITY OF LIFE
God — Ex 34:12-28;
Deut 4:15-31;
5:1-21
through SIN
Israelites — Deut 31:30-32:4
Judahites — 1 Kgs 14:21-24

in ENVIRONMENT
BEHAVIOR revealing
Sarah — Gen 16:1-6
CONFRONTATION with
Joseph — Gen 37:1-11;
12-28
as MOTIVATION
Sarah — Gen 21:8-10
SALVATION from
Phinehas — Num 25:6-18
through FALSE BELIEF
Priests — Acts 5:17-42
Sadducees — Acts 5:17-42
causing disHONESTY
James — Jas 3:13-18
Officials — Dan 6:4-9
Rulers — Acts 6:8-8:3

in FIDELITY
INSTRUCTION on
God — Ex 20:1-17
Moses — Deut 5:1-21
of FOLLOWERs
Jews — Acts 17:1-9;
10-15
concerning TRUTH
Paul — 2 Cor 11:1-6

causing disHONESTY
through FALSE BELIEF
James — Jas 3:13-18
Officials — Dan 6:4-9
Rulers — Acts 6:8-8:3

INSTRUCTION on
Eliphaz — Job 5:1-7
Solomon — Prov 27:1-27
in FIDELITY
God — Ex 20:1-17
Moses — Deut 5:1-21
as QUALITY OF LIFE
Maiden — Song 8:5b-7
Solomon — Prov 6:20-7:27
of SIN
David — Ps 37:1-11
Paul — Gal 5:25-6:6
Solomon — Prov 3:1-35;
23:15-24:22

LAW concerning	
Moses	Num 5:11-31
as **MOTIVATION**	
of **DEITY**	
God	Zeph 1:17-18;
	Zech 7:4-8:23
Israelites	Zech 1:7-17
REVELATION on	
God	Zeph 3:8
PROVIDENCE in	
of **DEITY**	
Israelites	Rom 11:7-24
PUNISHMENT through	
of **DEITY**	
God	Nah 1:1-9
Israelites	Deut 29:16-29
REVELATION on	
Ezekiel	Ezek 36:1-7
Israelites	Ezek 5:5-17
as **QUALITY OF LIFE**	
Asaph	Ps 73:1-3
of **DEITY**	
God	Ex 34:12-28;
	Deut 4:15-31;
	5:1-21
INSTRUCTION on	
Maiden	Song 8:5b-7
Solomon	Prov 6:20-7:27
REVELATION on	
in **CONFRONTATION**	
Gog	Ezek 38:17-23
as **MOTIVATION**	
God	Zeph 3:8
in **PUNISHMENT**	
Ezekiel	Ezek 36:1-7
Israelites	Ezek 5:5-17
SALVATION from	
in **ENVIRONMENT**	
Phinehas	Num 25:6-18
SIGNS of	
REVELATION on	
Ezekiel	Ezek 8:1-4;
	5-6
of **SIN**	
of **DEITY**	
Israelites	Deut 31:30-32:47
Judahites	1 Kgs 14:21-24
INSTRUCTION on	
David	Ps 37:1-11
Paul	Gal 5:25-6:6
Solomon	Prov 3:1-35;
	23:15-24:22

JOY

in **AUTHORITY**	
Joash	2 Chr 21:1-23:21
Princess	Ps 45:13-15
of **DEITY**	
Israelites	Neh 8:9-12

of **FOLLOWER**s	
Believers	Lk 10:17-20
in **WORSHIP**	
David	1 Chr 15:1-16:43
BEHAVIOR revealing	
of **DEITY**	
Israelites	*1 Esd 9:49-55
in **ENVIRONMENT**	
Israelites	*1 Esd 5:1-3
Joseph	Gen 45:1-28
Simon	*1 Mc 13:42-53
of **FOLLOWER**s	
People	Lk 13:10-17
INSTRUCTION on	
Attharates	*1 Esd 9:49-55
Baruch	*Bar 5:1-4
David	Ps 30:1-5
Jesus	Mt 18:12-14
Moses	Deut 16:9-12
Paul	Phil 2:12-18;
	3:1-3;
	4:1-9;
	1 Thes 5:12-22
Preacher	Eccl 3:1-8;
	8:10-17;
	9:1-16;
	11:9-12:7
PROPHECY of	
Isaiah	Is 24:13-16a
REVELATION on	
Israelites	Zeph 3:14-20
in **BELIEF**	
of **DEITY**	
Believers	Prov 16:1-33;
	Rom 15:1-13
Psalmist	Ps 33:20-22
INSTRUCTION on	
Paul	2 Cor 7:13b-16
Peter	1 Pet 1:3-9
over **BROTHERHOOD**	
PROPHECY of	
Isaiah	Is 62:1-12
of **COMMUNITY**	
INSTRUCTION on	
Solomon	1 Kgs 1:28-40
COMPULSION of	
from **DEITY**	
Israelites	Neh 12:43
CONFRONTATION results in	
Maccabeus	*2 Mc 15:28-36
of **FOLLOWER**s	
Believers	Acts 15:30-41
Titus	2 Cor 7:5-13a
INSTRUCTION on	
Jesus	Mt 5:3-12
CONVERSION with	
of **FOLLOWER**s	
Barnabas	Acts 15:1-5
Ethiopian	Acts 8:26-40
Paul	Acts 15:1-5
in the **CREATION**	
by **DEITY**	

by **DEITY** (cont'd)
    God   1 Chr 15:1-16:43;
                           Ps 96:10-13;
                           97:1-5
INSTRUCTION on
    Psalmist   Ps 118:22-27
REVELATION on
    Isaiah   Is 55:1-13

of **DEITY**
    as **VIRTUE**
        Believers   Ps 68:1-3

DESIRE for
    by **DEITY**
        Believers   Eccl 3:9-15
    in **MISSION**
        John   2 Jn 1:12-13

ETERNAL
    PROPHECY of
        Isaiah   Is 51:1-16;
                      61:1-11

through **FALSE BELIEF**
    in **RITE**
        Moses   Deut 12:1-31
    in **SIN**
        Ammonites   Ezek 25:1-7

through **FIDELITY**
    to **DEITY**
        Believers   Ps 128:1-2
        David   Ps 144:12-15
        God   Prov 12:1-28
        King   Ps 63:11b
        Psalmist   Ps 119:73-80
    INSTRUCTION on
        James   Jas 1:2-4;
                      5:7-11
        Jesus   Jn 15:1-11
        Paul   Phil 2:1-4
        Psalmist   Ps 149:1-4

of **FOLLOWERs**
    results from **CONFRONTATION**
        Believers   Acts 15:30-41
        Titus   2 Cor 7:5-13a
    in **CONVERSION**
        Barnabas   Acts 15:1-5
        Ethiopian   Acts 8:26-40
        Paul   Acts 15:1-5
    as **MOTIVATION**
        Holy Spirit   1 Thes 1:2-10
        Paul   Philm 1:4-7
    as **QUALITY OF LIFE**
        Holy Spirit   Gal 5:22-24
    in **TRUTH**
        John   2 Jn 1:4-6;
                      3 Jn 1:3-8

INSTRUCTION on
    BEHAVIOR revealing
        Attharates   *1 Esd 9:49-55
        Baruch   *Bar 5:1-4
        David   Ps 30:1-5
        Jesus   Mt 18:12-14
        Moses   Deut 16:9-12

BEHAVIOR revealing (cont'd)
    Paul   Phil 2:12-18;
                   3:1-3;
                   4:1-9;
                   1 Thes 5:12-22
    Preacher   Eccl 3:1-8;
                   8:10-17;
                   9:1-16;
                   11:9-12:7
in **BELIEF**
    Paul   2 Cor 7:13b-16
    Peter   1 Pet 1:3-9
of **COMMUNITY**
    Solomon   1 Kgs 1:28-40
in **CONFRONTATION**
    Jesus   Mt 5:3-12
in the **CREATION**
    Psalmist   Ps 118:22-27
in **FIDELITY**
    James   Jas 1:2-4;
                   5:7-11
    Jesus   Jn 15:1-11
    Paul   Phil 2:1-4
    Psalmist   Ps 149:1-4
as **MOTIVATION**
    Paul   2 Cor 1:23-2:4
in **NEW AGE**
    God   Is 65:1-25
    John   Rev 12:10-12
    John the Baptist Jn 3:22-30
    Paul   Rom 14:1-23
in **PROVIDENCE**
    Moses   Deut 26:1-11
as **QUALITY OF LIFE**
    Paul   Rom 5:1-5;
                   12:9-13;
                   2 Cor 7:2-4
    Preacher   Eccl 11:1-8
    Solomon   Prov 17:1-28
in **RESPECT**
    Paul   Phil 2:19-30
in **RITE**
    Asaph   Ps 81:1-5b
    Isaiah   Is 49:1-26
    James   Jas 5:13
    Jeremiah   Jer 31:7-14
    Mordecai   Esth 9:20-28
    Moses   Deut 16:13-15
    Psalmist   Ps 33:1-3;
                   47:1-4;
                   66:1-4;
                   97:10-12;
                   98:4-6;
                   100:1-3;
                   149:5-9
    Zephaniah   Zeph 3:14-20
in **SALVATION**
    Jesus   Lk 10:17-20;
                   15:1-7;
                   8-10;
                   11-32
    Psalmist   Ps 95:1-7c
in **SECURITY**
    Sirach   *Sir 30:14-25
in **STEWARDSHIP**
    Paul   Rom 12:14-21;
                   2 Cor 9:6-11
in **TRUTH**
    John   1 Jn 1:1-4

as **VIRTUE**
  David | Ps 32:8-11
  Preacher | Eccl 7:1-22
  Solomon | Prov 29:1-27

JUDGMENT on
  INSTRUCTION on
    Believers | Rev 18:4-20
    Jesus | Lk 6:24-26

KNOWLEDGE of
  of **DEITY**
    Wisdom | Prov 8:22-31
  in **ENVIRONMENT**
    Jacob | Gen 45:1-28
  INSTRUCTION on
    Paul | 1 Cor 13:4-7
    Solomon | Prov 3:1-35;
             10:1-32;
             23:15-24:22;
             27:1-27;
             29:1-27
  REVELATION on
    Israelites | Is 51:17-52:12

in **LAW**
  of **DEITY**
    Mankind | Ps 1:1-3;
             112:1
    Psalmist | Ps 119:161-168

MEDITATION on
  in **RECONCILIATION**
    Paul | 2 Cor 7:5-13a
  in **SALVATION**
    Isaiah | Is 61:1-11

in **MESSIANIC FIGURE**
  God | *2 Esd 2:33-41
  through **PRESENCE**
    Holy Spirit | Lk 10:21-22

in **MISSION**
  DESIRE for
    John | 2 Jn 1:12-13
  as **MOTIVATION**
    Paul | 1 Thes 2:17-20

as **MOTIVATION**
  of **DEITY**
    David | Ps 4:6-8
  of **FOLLOWER**
    Holy Spirit | 1 Thes 1:2-10
    Paul | Philm 1:4-7
  INSTRUCTION on
    Paul | 2 Cor 1:23-2:4
  in **MISSION**
    Paul | 1 Thes 2:17-20
  REVELATION on
    Jeremiah | Jer 33:1-9

in **NEW AGE**
  INSTRUCTION on
    God | Is 65:1-25
    John | Rev 12:10-12
    John the Baptist | Jn 3:22-30
    Paul | Rom 14:1-23
  PROPHECY of
    Isaiah | Is 35:1-10
    Jesus | Jn 16:16-24

PRAYER for
  from **DEITY**
    David | Ps 40:13-17
    Moses | Ps 90:13-17
    Psalmist | Ps 71:22-24;
              98:7-9;
              126:4-6
  INSTRUCTION on
    Paul | Rom 15:25-33
  MEDITATION on
    Paul | Phil 1:3-11
  in **MESSIANIC FIGURE**
    God | *2 Esd 2:33-41
  REVELATION on
    Believers | Is 56:1-8
  in **WORSHIP**
    Jesus | Jn 17:6-19
    Psalmist | Ps 84:1-2
    Tobit | *Tb 11:7-19

in **PRESENCE**
  of **DEITY**
    Believers | Acts 13:14-52
    David | Ps 16:9-11
    Elihu | Job 33:26-28
    God | Ps 48:1-3
    Israelites | Zech 2:6-13
    King | Ps 21:1-7

through **PRESENCE**
  by **MESSIANIC FIGURE**
    Holy Spirit | Lk 10:21-22

PROMISE of
  INSTRUCTION on
    Bildad | Job 8:20-22
    God | *2 Esd 2:15-32
  REVELATION on
    God | Is 41:1-42:4
    Isaiah | Is 60:1-22
    Jeremiah | Jer 31:2-6

PROPHECY of
  Isaiah | Is 24:13-16a
  over **BROTHERHOOD**
    Isaiah | Is 62:1-12;
  ETERNAL
    Isaiah | Is 51:1-61;
            61:1-11
  in **NEW AGE**
    Isaiah | Is 35:1-10
    Jesus | Jn 16:16-24
  in **PROVIDENCE**
    Isaiah | Is 9:2-7;
            60:1-22
    Jeremiah | Jer 32:26-44
  in **SALVATION**
    Isaiah | Is 12:1-6;
            25:6-9;
            35:1-10
  in **SECURITY**
    Jesus | Jn 16:16-24

in **PROVIDENCE**
  of **DEITY**
    Asaph | Ps 75:9-10
    Baruch | *Bar 5:5-9
    David | Ps 20:1-5;
           30:11-12;
           31:1-8;
           63:1-8

of **DEITY** (cont'd)

Ezra	*1 Esd 8:25-27
God	Ps 127:3-5;
	Eccl 1:12-2:26;
	6:1-12
Habakkuk	Hab 3:16-19
Israelites	1 Kgs 8:62-66;
	Ezra 6:19-22
Preacher	Eccl 5:8-20
Psalmist	Ps 92:1-4;
	126:1-3

INSTRUCTION on

Moses	Deut 26:1-11

PROPHECY of

Isaiah	Is 9:2-7;
	60:1-22
Jeremiah	Jer 32:26-44

REVELATION on

Isaiah	Is 51:1-16
Jeremiah	Jer 33:10-11
Joel	Joel 2:18-27

over **PUNISHMENT**
by **DEITY**

Believers	Ps 58:10-11

as **QUALITY OF LIFE**
of **FOLLOWER**

Holy Spirit	Gal 5:22-24

INSTRUCTION on

Paul	Rom 5:1-5;
	12:9-13;
	2 Cor 7:2-4
Preacher	Eccl 11:1-8
Solomon	Prov 17:1-28

REVELATION on

Isaiah	Is 66:1-16
Jesus	1 Pet 4:12-19

SELF-REALIZATION of

Apostles	Acts 5:17-42
Paul	Phil 4:10-20;
	Col 1:24

in **RECONCILIATION**
by **DEITY**

Jesus	Rom 5:6-11

MEDITATION on

Paul	2 Cor 7:5-13a

in **RESPECT**

Haman	Esth 5:9-14
Israelites	Ex 15:1-18
Mordecai	Esth 8:15-17

of **DEITY**

Believers	Prov 15:1-33
David	Ps 34:4-10

INSTRUCTION on

Paul	Phil 2:19-30

REVELATION on

Isaiah	Is 58:1-14

in **RESURRECTION**

Mary	Mt 28:1-8

REVELATION on

Mary	Mt 28:1-8

REVELATION on

Israelites	Zeph 3:14-20

in the **CREATION**

Isaiah	Is 55:1-13

in **KNOWLEDGE**

Israelites	Is 51:17-52:12

as **MOTIVATION**

Jeremiah	Jer 33:1-9

in **PRAYER**

Believers	Is 56:1-8

in **PROVIDENCE**

Isaiah	Is 51:1-16
Jeremiah	Jer 33:10-11
Joel	Joel 2:18-27

as **QUALITY OF LIFE**

Isaiah	Is 66:1-16
Jesus	1 Pet 4:12-19

in **RESPECT**

Isaiah	Is 58:1-14

in **RESURRECTION**

Mary	Mt 28:1-8

in **RITE**

Moses	Lev 23:33-44;
	25:8-19

RITE of

Israelites	Esth 8:15-17

to **DEITY**

David	Ps 63:1-8
Isaiah	Is 26:7-19
Psalmist	Ps 67:1-7

through **FALSE BELIEF**

Moses	Deut 12:1-31

RITE revealing
INSTRUCTION on

Asaph	Ps 81:1-5b
Isaiah	Is 49:1-26
James	Jas 5:13
Jeremiah	Jer 31:7-14
Mordecai	Esth 9:20-28
Moses	Deut 16:13-15
Psalmist	Ps 33:1-3;
	47:1-4;
	66:1-4;
	97:10-12;
	98:4-6;
	100:1-3;
	149:5-9
Zephaniah	Zeph 3:14-20

REVELATION on

Moses	Lev 23:33-44;
	25:8-19

TRADITION of

Israelites	Esth 9:16-19
Maccabeus	*1 Mc 4:36-61;
	7:39-50;
	*2 Mc 10:1-9
Simon	*1 Mc 13:42-53

in **WORSHIP**

David	2 Sam 6:1-23;
	Ps 122:1-2
Deborah	Judg 5:1
Hezekiah	2 Chr 30:1-31:21
Israelites	Neh 8:13-18;
	*1 Esd 5:59-65
Maccabeus	*2 Mc 10:1-9

in **SALVATION**

Women	Ex 15:19-21

by **DEITY**

David	Ps 13:5-6;
	51:3-12
God	Ps 132:11-18
Israelites	Ps 14:7;
	53:6

by DEITY (cont'd)

Jethro	Ex 18:1-12

in ENVIRONMENT

Cyrus	*Bel 1:40-42

INSTRUCTION on

Jesus	Lk 10:17-20; 15:1-7; 8-10; 11-32
Psalmist	Ps 95:1-7c

MEDITATION on

Isaiah	Is 61:1-11

PROPHECY of

Isaiah	Is 12:1-6; 25:6-9; 35:1-10

in SECURITY

Darius	Dan 6:16-23

of DEITY

Believers	Ps 146:5-7b
David	Ps 16:9-11; 35:9-10
Followers	Ps 64:7-10
Mankind	Ps 5:11-12

INSTRUCTION on

Sirach	*Sir 30:14-25

PROPHECY of

Jesus	Jn 16:16-24

SELF-REALIZATION of
as QUALITY OF LIFE

Apostles	Acts 5:17-42
Paul	Phil 4:10-20; Col 1:24

in TRUTH

Disciples	Lk 24:50-51

SIGNS of
INSTRUCTION on

God	Rev 19:6-10

in WORSHIP

Israelites	Ezra 3:12-13

of SIN
through FALSE BELIEF

Ammonites	Ezek 25:1-7

in STEWARDSHIP
INSTRUCTION on

Paul	Rom 12:14-21; 2 Cor 9:6-11

in WORSHIP

Israelites	1 Chr 28:1-29:30
Levites	Neh 12:27-29

TRADITION of
in RITE

Israelites	Esth 9:16-19
Maccabeus	*1 Mc 4:36-61; 7:39-50; *2 Mc 10:1-9
Simon	*1 Mc 13:42-53

in TRUTH
by FOLLOWERs

John	2 Jn 1:4-6; 3 Jn 1:3-8

INSTRUCTION on

John	1 Jn 1:1-4

SELF-REALIZATION of

Disciples	Lk 24:50-51

as VIRTUE

Believers	Ps 68:1-3

INSTRUCTION on

David	Ps 32:8-11
Preacher	Eccl 7:1-22
Solomon	Prov 29:1-27

in WORSHIP

David	2 Sam 6:1-23; 1 Chr 15:1-16:43; Ps 122:1-2
Deborah	Judg 5:1
Hezekiah	2 Chr 30:1-31:21
Israelites	Neh 8:13-18; *1 Esd 5:59-65
Maccabeus	*2 Mc 10:1-9

PRAYER for

Jesus	Jn 17:6-19
Psalmist	Ps 84:1-2
Tobit	*Tb 11:7-19

reveals SALVATION

Women	Ex 15:19-21

SIGNS of

Israelites	Ezra 3:12-13

STEWARDSHIP in

Israelites	1 Chr 28:1-29:30
Levites	Neh 12:27-29

JUDGMENT

ACCEPTANCE of
from DEITY

David	Ps 141:5-7
Psalmist	Ps 82:8; 119:73-80

INSTRUCTION on

God	Is 41:1-42:4
Jesus	Mk 9:38-41; Lk 9:49-50

PROPHECY of

Isaiah	Is 52:13-53:12

REVELATION of

Eli	1 Sam 3:1-4:1a

concerning WORSHIP

Priests	Ezra 10:16-19

ALIENATION from
INSTRUCTION on

Solomon	Prov 18:1-24

PROPHECY of

Jesus	Jn 12:27-36a

REVELATION of

Hosea	Hos 1:8-9

ANGER in
by DEITY

God	Ps 95:7d-11; Is 9:8-10:4; Rev 11:15-19
Jonah	Jon 4:1-11
Judahites	2 Kgs 23:25b-30

JUDGMENT (cont'd)   **382**

INSTRUCTION on
Job   Job 19:25-29
PROPHECY of
Isaiah   Is 34:1-17;
    59:1-21;
    66:1-16

ANXIETY concerning
by DEITY
Asaph   Ps 74:10-11
of BLASPHEMY
Rulers   Acts 6:8-8:3
through FALSE BELIEF
Caiaphas   Mt 26:57-68;
    Mk 14:53-65
Jews   Jn 10:19-40;
    18:28-19:16
INSTRUCTION on
Jesus   Lk 16:14-15
Paul   1 Cor 11:17-22
against MESSIANIC FIGURE
Jesus   Mt 21:12-17;
    Mk 11:15-19;
    Lk 19:45-46
People   Lk 23:1-5
Priests   Lk 22:66-71
PROPHECY of
Isaiah   Is 5:8-24a
REVELATION on
Ezekiel   Ezek 9:1-11
Israelites   Mal 2:17-3:5
SCRIPTURES on
Paul   Rom 2:1-24

BLESSING through
of DEITY
Japheth   Gen 9:26-27
Shem   Gen 9:26-27
in MISSION
Apostles   Mt 10:9-15

COMPASSION in
by DEITY
Solomon   *Wis 12:3-11
INSTRUCTION on
God   *Wis 12:19-22

of CONDEMNATION
Canaan   Gen 9:21-25
Daniel   Dan 5:18-25
God   Gen 7:1-24
Israelites   Lev 26:1-46
Moabites   Num 21:21-32
Women   Amos 4:1-3
by DEITY
Chaldeans   Hab 1:5-11
Egyptians   Ezek 29:9b-16
Ephraimites   Hos 9:10-17;
    13:12-14
God   Ps 50:16-21
Israelites   Is 9:8-10:4;
    Hos 6:7-9;
    10:9-15;
    Amos 6:8-11
Man   Ex 21:33-22:17
Satan   Zech 3:1-10

for FALSE BELIEF
Apostles   Mt 10:9-15
Disciples   Mk 6:7-13;
    Lk 9:1-6

for FALSE BELIEF (cont'd)
Israelites   Ezek 23:36-49
James   Jas 5:1-6
Jews   Jn 18:28-19:16
Jezebel   Rev 2:18-29
People   Lk 23:1-5
Prophets   2 Pet 2:1-3
Sinners   Jude 1:11-13
of FOLLOWERs
Jews   Acts 24:1-27;
    25:1-12
Mankind   Jas 4:11-12
INSTRUCTION on
Author   Heb 5:11-14
God   Is 1:24-26
Jesus   Mt 12:33-37;
    18:15-17;
    23:13;
    15;
    Lk 11:37-44;
    16:14-15
Job   Job 12:1-6;
    21:28-34
Jotham   Judg 9:16-21
Paul   Rom 2:1-24;
    5:12-21;
    14:1-23;
    1 Cor 5:1-5
Peter   Acts 8:14-25
against MESSIANIC FIGURE
Caiaphas   Mt 26:57-68;
    Mk 14:53-65
People   Lk 23:1-5
Priests   Lk 22:66-71
Satan   Jn 16:5-11
in MISSION
Holy Spirit   Jn 16:5-11
PROPHECY of
Amos   Amos 3:13-15
Ephraimites   Hos 7:8-12
Ezekiel   Ezek 16:44-52
Habakkuk   Hab 2:9-11;
    12-14;
    15-16;
    17;
    18-20
Isaiah   Is 30:1-7;
    27-33;
    31:1-3;
    33:1-6;
    34:1-17
Israelites   Ezek 16:53-63;
    Hos 5:1-2;
    10:1-8;
    12:10-14;
    Amos 4:4-5;
    5:7-13;
    6:1-7
Jeremiah   Jer 4:13-18;
    21:13-14
Jerusalemites   Zeph 3:1-5
Jesus   Mt 11:20-24
Micah   Mic 3:1-12
Moabites   Jer 48:1-47
Nineveh   Nah 3:1-4;
    5-19
Priests   Mal 1:6-2:9
Prophets   Jer 23:13-15
Shemaiah   Jer 29:24-32
Zephaniah   Zeph 2:4-7

REVELATION on
Chaldeans	Is 47:1-15
Edomites	Ezek 35:1-15
Egyptians	Ezek 29:1-5;
	30:20-26;
	32:17-32
Ezekiel	Ezek 14:12-23;
	36:1-7
God	Is 41:1-42:4
Gog	Ezek 38:3-9;
	39:1-16
Habakkuk	Hab 2:5-6a
Isaiah	Is 5:1-7;
	65:1-25
Israelites	Ezek 5:5-17;
	17:11-21;
	20:27-29;
	22:17-22;
	34:1-10;
	36:16-21;
	Hos 2:9-13;
	Mal 2:17-3:5
Jeremiah	Jer 1:13-16;
	25:30-38
Jesus	Mt 11:20-24
Judahites	Ezek 23:22-35;
	24:1-14
Moabites	Ezek 25:8-11
Rulers	Zech 11:15-17
Zedekiah	Jer 24:1-10

SCRIPTURES on
Jesus	Mt 12:38-42;
	Lk 11:29-32

SELF-REALIZATION of
Hypocrite	Mt 7:1-5;
	Lk 6:36-45

of **WORSHIP**
Paul	1 Cor 11:17-22

in **COVENANT**
of **FAITH**
God	Ps 50:1-6

against **COVETOUSNESS**
INSTRUCTION on
Jesus	Lk 12:13-15

of **DEATH**
for **MESSIANIC FIGURE**
Caiaphas	Mt 26:57-68;
	Mk 14:53-65

on **DEATH**
God	Gen 6:5-22
Susanna	*Susa 1:28-41

by **DEITY**
Sirach	*Sir 11:21-28

through **FALSE BELIEF**
Priests	Jn 12:9-11

INSTRUCTION on
Angel	*2 Esd 7:100-115

MEDITATION on
Adam	1 Cor 15:20-28

PROPHECY on
Ezra	*2 Esd 14:19-48

by **DEITY**
Mankind	1 Sam 2:1-10

ACCEPTANCE of
David	Ps 141:5-7
Psalmist	Ps 82:8;
	119:73-80

ANGER in
God	Ps 95:7d-11;
	Is 9:8-10:4;
	Rev 11:15-19
Jonah	Jon 4:1-11
Judahites	2 Kgs 23:25b-30

ANXIETY concerning
Asaph	Ps 74:10-11

BLESSING through
Japheth	Gen 9:26-27
Shem	Gen 9:26-27

COMPASSION in
Solomon	*Wis 12:3-11

DESPAIR from
Job	Job 9:14-19;
	25-29

DESTRUCTION as
God	Hab 3:3-15
Sodomites	Gen 19:12-29

DOUBT concerning
Job	Job 9:20-24

against **ENEMY**
Asaph	Ps 74:18-23;
	83:2-8
David	Ps 70:1-5;
	139:19-22;
	140:9-11
God	Judg 5:31
Psalmist	Ps 137:7-9

on **EVIL**
Author	Heb 13:1-25
David	Ps 58:6-9
God	Ps 9:5-8;
	15-16;
	14:4-6;
	65:1-4;
	75:6-8;
	Rom 1:18;
	1 Thes 4:1-12;
	Rev 18:4-20
Mankind	Ps 1:4-6;
	64:7-10
Psalmist	Ps 94:1-3
Sodomites	Gen 18:16-22

FAITH in
Believers	1 Jn 4:13-18
Jesus	1 Pet 2:21-25

FEAR of
Author	Heb 10:19-31
David	Ps 9:17-20
God	Eccl 12:12-14
Job	Job 9:25-29
Mankind	Ps 64:7-10;
	76:7-9
Psalmist	Ps 119:113-120

as **GOOD**
David	Ps 9:1-4
God	Ps 11:4-7
Sirach	*Sir 39:17-27

through **GRACE**
David	1 Chr 21:1-22:1
God	Amos 7:1-3;
	4-6
Nineveh	Jon 3:1-10

revealing **GUILT**
Chaldeans	Hab 1:5-11
Ephraimites	Hos 13:12-14
God	Ex 34:5b-9
Jeremiah	Lam 3:1-66
Sinners	2 Pet 3:3-7

on **IDOLATRY**

Egyptians	Ex 12:1-14
Gentiles	Rom 1:24-32
God	Is 2:18-22; 45:14-25

INNOCENCE before

Isaiah	Is 50:1-11
Job	Job 23:1-7

JUSTICE in

Azariah	*Azar 1:1-10
Bildad	Job 8:20-22
David	Ps 7:9-11; 51:3-12
Eliphaz	Job 4:7-11; 22:21-30
Ezra	*2 Esd 4:33-52
God	1 Chr 15:1-16:43; Ps 11:4-7; 31:19-24; 37:1-11; 12-22; 23-40; 50:1-6; 67:1-7; 82:1; 96:10-13; 99:4-5; 103:6-13; 119:137-144; 146:5-7b; Prov 16:1-33; 23:15-24:22; 29:1-27; Eccl 3:16-4:3; Jer 17:9-10; Gal 6:7-10; Rev 16:4-7; 19:1-5
Isaiah	Is 28:1-13
Jesus	Mt 16:21-28
Job	Job 21:7-13; 14-18; 24:1-12; 27:13-23; 31:35-37
Mankind	Heb 10:19-31
People	Rom 2:1-24
Sirach	*Sir 35:12-20
Solomon	1 Kgs 8:22-53; 2 Chr 5:1-7:10; Ps 72:1-4

on **LIFE**

God	Eccl 11:9-12:7
Jesus	2 Tim 4:1-5
Mankind	1 Chr 15:1-16:43; Ps 105:7-15

for **PEACE**

God	Is 2:1-5

in **POLITICS**

Believers	Ps 149:5-9
God	Ps 110:5-7

PRAISE of

Psalmist	Ps 97:6-9
Solomon	*Wis 17:1-21

on **PRIDE**

God	Is 2:12-17

REJECTION of

Job	Job 7:17-21

REPENTANCE in

God	Jon 4:1-11

REVENGE as

David	Ps 109:6-20
God	Rev 16:4-7
Mankind	Ps 58:10-11; Heb 10:19-31

of **SPIRIT**

Jesus	Rom 2:1-24; 1 Cor 4:1-5

as **WILL**

Elihu	Job 34:29-33
Mankind	Prov 21:1-31; Jas 4:11-12
Micah	Mic 4:1-8

WISDOM in

Elihu	Job 34:21-28
God	Rom 11:33-36

WITNESS to

Aaron	Ex 28:13-30

DESPAIR from

by **DEITY**

Job	Job 9:14-19; 25-29

MEDITATION on

Job	Job 19:7-12

DESTRUCTION as

by **DEITY**

God	Hab 3:3-15
Sodomites	Gen 19:12-29

caused by **FALSE BELIEF**

Moses	Ex 23:20-33; 34:12-28; Num 33:16-36; Deut 7:1-5; 12:1-31

INSTRUCTION on

Moses	Ex 23:20-33; Num 33:16-36; Deut 7:1-5

PROPHECY of

Israelites	Amos 9:1-4
Joel	Joel 2:1-11

REVELATION on

Amos	Amos 7:1-3; 4-6
Daniel	Dan 7:2-14

in **DISCIPLESHIP**

of **FOLLOWERs**

Paul	1 Cor 6:1-8

MEDITATION on

Paul	1 Cor 11:27-34

on **DISOBEDIENCE**

INSTRUCTION on

Jesus	Lk 13:6-9; 19:11-27

PROPHECY of

Jesus	Mt 11:20-24

REVELATION on

Jesus	Mt 11:20-24

DOUBT concerning

by **DEITY**

Job	Job 9:20-24

DOUBT in

INSTRUCTION on

Paul	Rom 14:1-23

against **ENEMY**
  by **DEITY**
    Asaph   Ps 74:18-23;
                      83:2-8
    David   Ps 70:1-5;
                      139:19-22;
                      140:9-11
    God   Judg 5:31
    Psalmist   Ps 137:7-9
  MEDITATION on
    Psalmist   Ps 120:3-4
  REVELATION on
    Isaiah   Is 66:1-16
    Joel   Joel 3:1-3

on **EVIL**
    David   Ps 58:1-2
    Israelites   Judg 20:1-7
    Joseph   Gen 44:1-34
  by **DEITY**
    Author   Heb 13:1-25
    David   Ps 58:6-9
    God   Ps 9:5-8;
                      15-16;
                      14:4-6;
                      65:1-4;
                      75:6-8;
                      Rom 1:18;
                      1 Thes 4:1-12;
                      Rev 18:4-20
    Mankind   Ps 1:4-6;
                      64:7-10
    Psalmist   Ps 94:1-3
    Sodomites   Gen 18:16-22
  INSTRUCTION on
    Eliphaz   Job 22:12-20
    God   Ps 75:2-5
    Jeremiah   Jer 5:30-31
    Jesus   Mt 13:24-30;
                      36-43;
                      47-50;
                      16:5-12;
                      Jn 3:1-21
    Paul   Rom 2:25-3:20;
                      1 Cor 5:9-13
  by **MESSIANIC FIGURE**
    Satan   Mt 16:21-28;
                      Mk 8:31-33
  PROPHECY of
    Isaiah   Is 3:16-4:1
    Jesus   Mt 11:20-24
  REVELATION on
    God   Ps 9:15-16
    Israelites   Mal 2:17-3:5
    Jesus   Mt 11:20-24
  SCRIPTURES on
    Jesus   Mt 12:38-42;
                      Lk 11:29-32
  SELF-REALIZATION of
    Judahites   Jer 26:7-19

FAITH in
  by **DEITY**
    Believers   1 Jn 4:13-18
    Jesus   1 Pet 2:21-25
  INSTRUCTION on
    Elihu   Job 36:16-25
    Eliphaz   Job 4:7-11
    Jesus   Mt 17:14-20;
                      Mk 9:14-29;

INSTRUCTION on (cont'd)
    Jesus   Lk 9:37-43a

because of **FALSE BELIEF**
  is **REVENGE**
    Priests   Jn 12:9-11

on **FALSE BELIEF**
  as **BLASPHEMY**
    Caiaphas   Mt 26:57-68;
                      Mk 14:53-65
    Jews   Jn 10:19-40;
                      18:28-19:16
  CONDEMNATION as
    Apostles   Mt 10:9-15
    Disciples   Mk 6:7-13;
                      Lk 9:1-6
    Israelites   Ezek 23:36-49
    James   Jas 5:1-6
    Jews   Jn 18:28-19:16
    Jezebel   Rev 2:18-29
    People   Lk 23:1-5
    Prophets   2 Pet 2:1-3
    Sinners   Jude 1:11-13
  DEATH as
    Priests   Jn 12:9-11
  DESTRUCTION as
    Moses   Ex 23:20-33;
                      34:12-28;
                      Num 33:16-36;
                      Deut 7:1-5;
                      12:1-31
  GRACE in
    Jesus   Mt 12:22-32;
                      Mk 3:20-30
  in **KILLING**
    Jews   Jn 18:28-19:16
    Pharisees   Jn 11:1-57
    Pilate   Mk 15:6-15;
                      Lk 23:18-25
    Priests   Jn 11:1-57
  in **POLITICS**
    Pilate   Mk 15:6-15;
                      Lk 23:18-25
  REJECTION as
    Jews   Jn 18:28-19:16
    Priests   Jn 12:9-11
  WITNESS to
    Author   Heb 10:19-31

on **FAMILY**
  through **SELF-REALIZATION**
    Jacob   Gen 31:1-16

FEAR of
  by **DEITY**
    Author   Heb 10:19-31
    David   Ps 9:17-20
    God   Eccl 12:12-14
    Job   Job 9:25-29
    Mankind   Ps 64:7-10;
                      76:7-9
    Psalmist   Ps 119:113-120
  INSTRUCTION on
    Jesus   Lk 12:1-12;
                      19:11-27
  PROPHECY of
    Joel   Joel 2:1-11
  REVELATION on
    John   Rev 18:4-20

of FOLLOWERs
　is CONDEMNATION
　　Jews　　　　　　　Acts 24:1-27;
　　　　　　　　　　　25:1-12
　　Mankind　　　　　Jas 4:11-12
　in DISCIPLESHIP
　　Paul　　　　　　　1 Cor 6:1-8
　as GUILT
　　Sadducees　　　　Acts 22:30-23:11
　as INNOCENCE
　　Claudius　　　　　Acts 23:12-35
　　Festus　　　　　　Acts 25:13-27;
　　　　　　　　　　　26:1-32
　　Pharisees　　　　　Acts 22:30-23:11
　through JUSTICE
　　Festus　　　　　　Acts 25:1-12
　through OBEDIENCE
　　Peter　　　　　　　1 Pet 4:12-19
　through WISDOM
　　Paul　　　　　　　1 Cor 4:6-13;
　　　　　　　　　　　6:1-8
　as YOUTH
　　Corinthians　　　　1 Cor 3:1-4

on FRIENDSHIP
　INSTRUCTION on
　　James　　　　　　Jas 4:11-12

FULFILLMENT of
　INSTRUCTION on
　　Jesus　　　　　　　Lk 6:24-26
　　John　　　　　　　Rev 14:6-7
　PROPHECY of
　　God　　　　　　　1 Sam 4:1b-22
　REVELATION on
　　Jeremiah　　　　　Jer 25:30-38
　SCRIPTURES on
　　People　　　　　　Acts 13:14-52

as GOOD
　by DEITY
　　David　　　　　　Ps 9:1-4
　　God　　　　　　　Ps 11:4-7
　　Sirach　　　　　　*Sir 39:17-27
　concerning ENVIRONMENT
　　God　　　　　　　Gen 1:3-5;
　　　　　　　　　　　9-13;
　　　　　　　　　　　14-19;
　　　　　　　　　　　24-31

of GOOD
　INSTRUCTION on
　　Elihu　　　　　　　Job 34:1-4
　　God　　　　　　　Gen 1:20-23
　　Jesus　　　　　　　Mt 13:24-30;
　　　　　　　　　　　36-43;
　　　　　　　　　　　47-50

GRACE in
　on FALSE BELIEF
　　Jesus　　　　　　　Mt 12:22-32;
　　　　　　　　　　　Mk 3:20-30
　INSTRUCTION on
　　James　　　　　　Jas 2:1-13
　　Jesus　　　　　　　Mt 5:38-42
　　　　　　　　　　　Lk 6:36-45;
　　　　　　　　　　　Jn 7:53-8:11
　　Paul　　　　　　　Rom 2:25-3:20;
　　　　　　　　　　　1 Cor 3:10-17
　　Peter　　　　　　　1 Pet 3:8-12

　PROPHECY of
　　Israelites　　　　　Hos 11:8-9
　REVELATION on
　　Israelites　　　　　Is 43:14-44:5;
　　　　　　　　　　　48:1-22
　through GRACE
　　of DEITY
　　　David　　　　　1 Chr 21:1-22:1
　　　God　　　　　　Amos 7:1-3;
　　　　　　　　　　　4-6
　　　Nineveh　　　　　Jon 3:1-10
　on GREED
　　INSTRUCTION on
　　　Jesus　　　　　　Lk 12:16-21;
　　　　　　　　　　　16:14-15
　of GUILT
　　of FOLLOWERs
　　　Sadducees　　　　Acts 22:30-23:11
　　INSTRUCTION on
　　　Jesus　　　　　　Mt 7:1-5;
　　　　　　　　　　　Lk 6:36-45;
　　　　　　　　　　　Jn 7:53-8:11
　　　Moses　　　　　　Deut 17:8-13;
　　　　　　　　　　　19:15-21
　　　Paul　　　　　　1 Cor 5:1-5;
　　　　　　　　　　　Gal 5:7-12
　　by MESSIANIC FIGURE
　　　Priests　　　　　Lk 22:66-71
　　PROPHECY of
　　　Babylonians　　　Jer 51:1-64
　　　Ephraimites　　　Hos 5:3-7;
　　　　　　　　　　　12:7-9
　　　Isaiah　　　　　Is 13:1-22;
　　　　　　　　　　　24:1-12
　　　Israelites　　　　Ezek 16:44-52
　　　Samaritans　　　Hos 13:15-16
　　REVELATION on
　　　Belshazzar　　　Dan 5:26-28
　　　Elders　　　　　Ezek 20:1-4
　　　Ezekiel　　　　　Ezek 11:1-13;
　　　　　　　　　　　22:1-16
　　　God　　　　　　Gen 3:14-19
　　　Israelites　　　　Jer 2:20-29;
　　　　　　　　　　　30-37;
　　　　　　　　　　　Ezek 9:1-11;
　　　　　　　　　　　21:18-24;
　　　　　　　　　　　22:23-31;
　　　　　　　　　　　36:22-32
　　　Jeremiah　　　　Jer 30:12-17
　　　Sidon　　　　　Ezek 28:20-23
　　SELF-REALIZATION of
　　　Hypocrite　　　　Mt 7:1-5;
　　　　　　　　　　　Lk 6:36-45
　on GUILT
　　Ephraimites　　　　Hos 13:1-3
　　Moses　　　　　　Ex 21:33-22:17
　revealing GUILT
　　by DEITY
　　　Chaldeans　　　Hab 1:5-11
　　　Ephraimites　　　Hos 13:12-14
　　　God　　　　　　Ex 34:5b-9
　　　Jeremiah　　　　Lam 3:1-66
　　　Sinners　　　　　2 Pet 3:3-7
　on IDOLATRY
　　by DEITY
　　　Egyptians　　　Ex 12:1-14

by DEITY (cont'd)

Gentiles	Rom 1:24-32
God	Is 2:18-22; 45:14-25

INSTRUCTION on

God	Is 41:1-42:4
Isaiah	Is 44:9-20
Jeremiah	Jer 5:18-19
Paul	Acts 17:16-34; 1 Cor 10:14-22

PROPHECY of

Asa	2 Chr 14:1-16:14
Babylonians	Jer 51:1-64
Israelites	Jer 11:15-17

REVELATION on

Chaldeans	Is 47:1-15
John	Rev 17:1-6a

in WORSHIP

Josiah	2 Kgs 23:4-15

on IGNORANCE
INSTRUCTION on

Mankind	2 Pet 3:8-10
Paul	1 Cor 3:1-4

PROPHECY of

Isaiah	Is 5:8-24a

REVELATION on

Mankind	2 Pet 3:8-10

of INNOCENCE

Daniel	Dan 6:16-23; *Susa 1:42-51

before DEITY

Isaiah	Is 50:1-11
Job	Job 23:1-7

of FOLLOWERs

Claudius	Acts 23:12-35
Festus	Acts 25:13-27; 26:1-32
Pharisees	Acts 22:30-23:11

MEDITATION on

Job	Job 34:5-9
Pilate	Jn 18:28-19:16

of MESSIANIC FIGURE

Herod	Lk 23:6-16
Pilate	Lk 23:1-5; 6-16; 18-25

INSTRUCTION on

God	Zeph 3:8

in ANGER

Job	Job 19:25-29

of BLASPHEMY

Jesus	Lk 16:14-15
Paul	1 Cor 11:17-22

with COMPASSION

God	*Wis 12:19-22

of CONDEMNATION

Author	Heb 5:11-14
God	Is 1:24-26
Jesus	Mt 12:33-37; 18:15-17; 23:13; 15; Lk 11:37-44; 16:14-15
Job	Job 12:1-6; 21:28-34
Jotham	Judg 9:16-21

of CONDEMNATION (cont'd)

Paul	Rom 2:1-24; 5:12-21; 14:1-23; 1 Cor 5:1-5
Peter	Acts 8:14-25

against COVETOUSNESS

Jesus	Lk 12:13-15

on DEATH

Angel	*2 Esd 7:100-115

of DESTRUCTION

Moses	Ex 23:20-33; Num 33:16-36; Deut 7:1-5

concerning DISOBEDIENCE

Jesus	Lk 13:6-9; Lk 19:11-27

on EVIL

Eliphaz	Job 22:12-20
God	Ps 75:2-5
Jeremiah	Jer 5:30-31
Jesus	Mt 13:24-30; 36-43; 47-50; 16:5-12; Jn 3:1-21
Paul	Rom 2:25-3:20; 1 Cor 5:9-13; Job 36:16-25

of FRIENDSHIP

James	Jas 4:11-12

of GOOD

Elihu	Job 34:1-4
God	Gen 1:20-23
Jesus	Mt 13:24-30; 36-43; 47-50

by GRACE

James	Jas 2:1-13
Jesus	Mt 5:38-42; Lk 6:36-45; Jn 7:53-8:11
Paul	Rom 2:25-3:20; 1 Cor 3:10-17
Peter	1 Pet 3:8-12

on GREED

Jesus	Lk 12:16-21; 16:14-15

of GUILT

Jesus	Mt 7:1-5; Lk 6:36-45; Jn 7:53-8:11
Moses	Deut 17:8-13; 19:15-21
Paul	1 Cor 5:1-5; Gal 5:7-12

of one's HEART

Jesus	Mt 15:15-20; Mk 7:1-23

on IDOLATRY

God	Is 41:1-42:4
Isaiah	Is 44:9-20
Jeremiah	Jer 5:18-19
Paul	Acts 17:16-34; 1 Cor 10:14-22

on IGNORANCE

Mankind	2 Pet 3:8-10
Paul	1 Cor 3:1-4

on JOY

Believers	Rev 18:4-20
Jesus	Lk 6:24-26

with **JUSTICE**
Angel	*2 Esd 5:31-42
Israelites	Zech 7:4-8:23
Jehoshaphat	2 Chr 17:1-20:37
Jesus	Mt 7:1-5;
	12:33-37;
	18:23-35;
	Lk 6:36-45;
	12:57-59;
	Jn 5:19-47
Lemuel	Prov 31:1-9
Moses	Deut 1:9-18;
	16:18-20;
	19:1-13;
	15-21;
	23:15-25:19;
	27:11-26
Paul	Rom 2:25-3:20;
	1 Cor 4:1-5;
	1 Tim 5:17-25
Solomon	Prov 24:23-34
Zophar	Job 11:7-12

on **LEADERSHIP**
James	Jas 3:1-12
Moses	Deut 1:9-18;
	16:18-20

on **LIFE**
Peter	1 Pet 4:1-6

on **OBEDIENCE**
Moses	Deut 17:8-13

on **ORDER**
Paul	1 Cor 6:1-8

on **POLITICS**
Paul	Rom 13:1-7

on **PRIDE**
Preacher	Eccl 8:10-17

on **PRUDENCE**
Jesus	Jn 7:15-24

on **PURIFICATION**
Paul	Rom 14:1-23

concerning **REPENTANCE**
Jesus	Mt 12:38-42;
	Lk 11:29-32

determining **REWARDs**
Jesus	Mt 12:33-37
Paul	1 Cor 3:10-17;
	4:1-5;
	2 Cor 5:9-10

on **SELFISHNESS**
Jesus	Lk 11:37-44;
	12:13-15;
	16-21;
	19:11-27

on **SERVICE**
Jesus	Mt 25:31-46

on **SHARING**
Jesus	Mt 25:31-46;
	Lk 6:36-45

on **VIOLENCE**
Jesus	Mt 26:47-56

on **WEALTH**
Jesus	Lk 6:24-26;
	16:14-15

on **WILL**
Jesus	Jn 8:12-20

on **WISDOM**
Jesus	Mt 11:16-19;
	Lk 7:31-35;
	Jn 7:15-24
Psalmist	Ps 119:65-72

concerning **WITNESS**
God	Is 43:8-13
Jesus	Mt 18:15-17
John	1 Jn 4:1-3
Moses	Deut 16:21-17:7;
	19:15-21
Paul	2 Cor 13:1-4;
	1 Tim 5:17-25

on **YOUTH**
Paul	1 Cor 3:1-4

JOY in
INSTRUCTION on
Believers	Rev 18:4-20
Jesus	Lk 6:24-26

JUSTICE in
Moses	Ex 23:1-9;
	Lev 19:1-37;
	20:1-27
Solomon	1 Kgs 1:41-53

by **DEITY**
Azariah	*Azar 1:1-10
Bildad	Job 8:20-22
David	Ps 7:9-11;
	51:3-12
Eliphaz	Job 4:7-11;
	22:21-30
Ezra	*2 Esd 4:33-52
God	1 Chr 15:1-16:43;
	Ps 11:4-7;
	31:19-24;
	37:1-11;
	12-22;
	23-40;
	50:1-6;
	76:1-7;
	82:1;
	96:10-13;
	99:4-5;
	103:6-13;
	119:137-144;
	146:5-7b;
	Prov 16:1-33;
	23:15-24:22;
	29:1-27;
	Eccl 3:16-4:3;
	Jer 17:9-10;
	Gal 6:7-10;
	Rev 16:4-7;
	19:1-5
Isaiah	Is 28:1-13
Jesus	Mt 16:21-28
Job	Job 21:7-13;
	14-18;
	24:1-12;
	27:13-23;
	31:35-37
Mankind	Heb 10:19-31
People	Rom 2:1-24
Sirach	*Sir 35:12-20
Solomon	1 Kgs 8:22-53;
	2 Chr 5:1-7:10;
	Ps 72:1-4

of **FOLLOWER**
Festus	Acts 25:1-12

INSTRUCTION on
Angel	*2 Esd 5:31-42
Israelites	Zech 7:4-8:23
Jehoshaphat	2 Chr 17:1-20:37

INSTRUCTION on (cont'd)

Jesus	Mt 7:1-5; 12:33-37; 18:23-35; Lk 6:36-45; 12:57-59; Jn 5:19-47
Lemuel	Prov 31:1-9
Moses	Deut 1:9-18; 16:18-20; 19:1-13; 15-21; 23:15-25:19; 27:11-26
Paul	Rom 2:25-3:20; 1 Cor 4:1-5; 1 Tim 5:17-25
Solomon	Prov 24:23-34
Zophar	Job 11:7-12

of MESSIANIC FIGURE

Isaiah	Is 11:1-9

PROPHECY of

Angel	*2 Esd 7:33-44; 8:63-9:25
Isaiah	Is 15:1-16:14
Israelites	Ezek 16:35-43
Jeremiah	Jer 31:31-34
Obadiah	Obad 1:15-16

REVELATION on

Edomites	Ezek 35:1-15
Ezekiel	Ezek 18:14-20; 21-24; 25-29; 33:1-9; 10-20
Isaiah	Is 5:1-7; 65:1-25
Israelites	Ezek 7:1-27; 9:1-11; 18:30-32; 22:23-31
John	Rev 19:11-16; 20:11-15; 22:6-21
Judahites	Ezek 24:1-14
Moses	Num 35:16-25
Zechariah	Zech 7:4-8:23

SCRIPTURES on

Amaziah	2 Kgs 14:7; 2 Chr 25:1-28

SELF-REALIZATION of

Judahites	Jer 26:7-19

on KILLING

through FALSE BELIEF

Jews	Jn 18:28-19:16
Pharisees	Jn 11:1-57
Pilate	Mk 15:6-15; Lk 23:18-25
Priests	Jn 11:1-57

MEDITATION on

Pilate	Jn 18:28-19:16

of MESSIANIC FIGURE

Crowd	Mt 27:11-26; Mk 15:6-15; Lk 23:18-25

on LEADERSHIP

Israelites	Ps 122:3-5

by DEITY

David	Ps 139:23-24
God	Is 33:17-24

INSTRUCTION on

James	Jas 3:1-12
Moses	Deut 1:9-18; 16:18-20

PROPHECY of

Deborah	Judg 4:4-5
Isaiah	Is 24:18c-23; 51:17-52:12

REVELATION on

Egyptians	Ezek 32:1-16
God	Is 41:1-42:4;

on LIFE

by DEITY

God	Eccl 11:9-12:7
Jesus	2 Tim 4:1-5
Mankind	1 Chr 15:1-16:43; Ps 105:7-15

INSTRUCTION on

Peter	1 Pet 4:1-6

MEDITATION on

Jesus	1 Cor 15:20-28

PROPHECY of

Isaiah	Is 51:17-52:12; 66:1-16

REVELATION on

Israelites	Ezek 34:17-22
Joel	Joel 3:12-16a
John	Rev 14:17-20; 20:11-15

on LUST

PROPHECY of

Isaiah	Is 5:8-24a

MEDITATION on

on DEATH

Adam	1 Cor 15:20-28

in DISCIPLESHIP

Paul	1 Cor 11:27-34

against ENEMY

Psalmist	Ps 120:3-4

on INNOCENCE

Job	Job 34:5-9
Pilate	Jn 18:28-19:16

on KILLING

Pilate	Jn 18:28-19:16

on LIFE

Jesus	1 Cor 15:20-28

against MESSIANIC FIGURE

is CONDEMNATION

Caiaphas	Mt 26:57-68; Mk 14:53-65
People	Lk 23:1-5
Priests	Lk 22:66-71
Satan	Jn 16:5-11

is DEATH

Caiaphas	Mt 26:57-68; Mk 14:53-65

KILLING as

Crowd	Mt 27:11-26; Mk 15:6-15; Lk 23:18-25

as **CONDEMNATION**
  Zephaniah   Zeph 2:4-7
on **DEATH**
  Ezra   *2 Esd 14:19-48
as **DESTRUCTION**
  Israelites   Amos 9:1-4
  Joel   Joel 2:1-11
concerning **DISOBEDIENCE**
  Jesus   Mt 11:20-24

on **EVIL**
  Isaiah   Is 3:16-4:1
  Jesus   Mt 11:20-24
by **GRACE**
  Israelites   Hos 11:8-9
of **GUILT**
  Babylonians   Jer 51:1-64
  Ephraimites   Hos 5:3-7;
                 12:7-9
  Isaiah   Is 13:1-22;
                 24:1-12
  Israelites   Ezek 16:44-52
  Samaritans   Hos 13:15-16
on **IDOLATRY**
  Asa   2 Chr 14:1-16:14
  Babylonians   Jer 51:1-64
  Israelites   Jer 11:15-17
on **IGNORANCE**
  Isaiah   Is 5:8-24a
on **JUSTICE**
  Angel   *2 Esd 7:33-44;
                 8:63-9:25
  Isaiah   Is 15:1-16:14
  Israelites   Ezek 16:35-43
  Jeremiah   Jer 31:31-34
  Obadiah   Obad 1:15-16
by **LEADERSHIP**
  Deborah   Judg 4:4-5
  Isaiah   Is 24:18c-23;
                 51:17-52:12
on **LIFE**
  Isaiah   Is 51:17-52:12;
                 66:1-16
on **LUST**
  Isaiah   Is 5:8-24a
on **OPPRESSION**
  Isaiah   Is 3:13-15
on **PRIDE**
  Isaiah   Is 5:8-24a
  Moabites   Jer 48:1-47
on **REJECTION**
  Jesus   Lk 22:14-23
on **REPENTANCE**
  Holy Spirit   Neh 9:26-31
  Jesus   Mt 11:20-24
of **REVENGE**
  Jesus   Lk 21:20-24
  Babylonians   Jer 25:8-14
  Isaiah   Is 34:1-17
  Jeremiah   Jer 4:11-12
on **VIOLENCE**
  Joel   Joel 2:1-11
on **WISDOM**
  Isaiah   Is 32:1-8

PRUDENCE in
  INSTRUCTION on
    Jesus   Jn 7:15-24

on **PURIFICATION**
  INSTRUCTION on
    Paul   Rom 14:1-23
  REVELATION on
    Israelites   Is 48:1-22;
                 Ezek 20:32-39

REJECTION of
  by **DEITY**
    Job   Job 7:17-21

of **REJECTION**
  through **FALSE BELIEF**
    Jews   Jn 18:28-19:16
    Priests   Jn 12:9-11
  INSTRUCTION on
    Jesus   Mt 10:26-39;
                12:38-42;
                22:1-14;
                Lk 10:1-16;
                11:29-32;
                14:15-24;
                Jn 5:19-47;
                12:44-50
  of **MESSIANIC FIGURE**
    Caiaphas   Mt 26:57-68;
                Mk 14:53-65
    People   Lk 23:1-5
    Priests   Lk 22:66-71
  PROPHECY of
    Jesus   Lk 22:14-23
  REVELATION of
    Israelites   Mal 2:17-3:5
  TRADITION of
    Paul   Col 2:16-23

concerning **REPENTANCE**
  INSTRUCTION on
    Jesus   Mt 12:38-42;
                Lk 11:29-32
  PROPHECY of
    Holy Spirit   Neh 9:26-31
    Jesus   Mt 11:20-24
  REVELATION on
    Jesus   Mt 11:20-24

REPENTANCE in
  by **DEITY**
    God   Jon 4:1-11

REVELATION on
  of **BLASPHEMY**
    Ezekiel   Ezek 9:1-11
    Israelites   Mal 2:17-3:5
  as **CONDEMNATION**
    Chaldeans   Is 47:1-15
    Edomites   Ezek 35:1-15
    Egyptians   Ezek 29:1-5;
                30:20-26;
                32:17-32
    Ezekiel   Ezek 14:12-23;
                36:1-7
    God   Is 41:1-42:4
    Gog   Ezek 38:3-9;
                39:1-16
    Habakkuk   Hab 2:5-6a

as CONDEMNATION (cont'd)

Isaiah	Is 5:1-7; 65:1-25
Israelites	Ezek 5:5-17; 17:11-21; 20:27-29; 22:17-22; 34:1-10; 36:16-21; Hos 2:9-13; Mal 2:17-3:5
Jeremiah	Jer 1:13-16; 25:30-38
Jesus	Mt 11:20-24
Judahites	Ezek 23:22-35; 24:1-14
Moabites	Ezek 25:8-11
Rulers	Zech 11:15-17
Zedekiah	Jer 24:1-10

as DESTRUCTION

Amos	Amos 7:1-3; 4-6
Daniel	Dan 7:2-14

concerning DISOBEDIENCE

Jesus	Mt 11:20-24

against ENEMY

Isaiah	Is 66:1-16
Joel	Joel 3:1-3

on EVIL

God	Ps 9:15-16
Israelites	Mal 2:17-3:5
Jesus	Mt 11:20-24

by GRACE

Israelites	Is 43:14-44:5; 48:1-22

as GUILT

Belshazzar	Dan 5:26-28
Elders	Ezek 20:1-4
Ezekiel	Ezek 11:1-13; 22:1-16
God	Gen 3:14-19
Israelites	Jer 2:20-29; 30-37; Ezek 9:1-11; 21:18-24; 22:23-31; 36:22-32
Jeremiah	Jer 30:12-17
Sidon	Ezek 28:20-23

on IDOLATRY

Chaldeans	Is 47:1-15
John	Rev 17:1-6a

on IGNORANCE

Mankind	2 Pet 3:8-10

on JUSTICE

Edomites	Ezek 35:1-15
Ezekiel	Ezek 18:14-20; 21-24; 25-29; 33:1-9; 10-20
Isaiah	Is 5:1-7; 65:1-25
Israelites	Ezek 7:1-27; 9:1-11; 18:30-32; 22:23-31
John	Rev 19:11-16; 20:11-15; 22:6-21

on JUSTICE (cont'd)

Judahites	Ezek 24:1-14
Moses	Num 35:16-24
Zechariah	Zech 7:4-8:23

on LEADERSHIP

Egyptians	Ezek 32:1-16
God	Is 41:1-42:4
Israelites	Ezek 34:17-22
Joel	Joel 3:12-16a
John	Rev 14:17-20; 20:11-15

through MIRACLE

Egyptians	Ex 7:1-7

on OPPRESSION

Israelites	Mal 2:17-3:5

on ORDER

Priests	Ezek 44:15-31

on PURIFICATION

Israelites	Is 48:1-22; Ezek 20:32-39

on REJECTION

Israelites	Mal 2:17-3:5

on REPENTANCE

Jesus	Mt 11:20-24

on REVENGE

Joel	Joel 3:4-8

concerning REWARDs

Daniel	Dan 12:1-4

causing SADNESS

John	Rev 18:4-20

on SEX

Israelites	Ezek 23:36-49; Mal 2:17-3:5

on VICTORY

Daniel	Dan 7:17-27

on WEALTH

John	Rev 18:4-20

on WITNESS

Isaiah	Is 66:17-24
Israelites	Mal 2:17-3:5
John	Rev 20:4-6
Mankind	Ezek 39:17-24

REVENGE as

by DEITY

David	Ps 109:6-20
God	Rev 16:4-7
Mankind	Ps 58:10-11; Heb 10:19-31

on FALSE BELIEF

Priests	Jn 12:9-11

PROPHECY of

Babylonians	Jer 25:8-14
Isaiah	Is 34:1-17
Jeremiah	Jer 4:11-12

REVELATION on

Joel	Joel 3:4-8

concerning REWARDs

INSTRUCTION on

Jesus	Mt 12:33-37
Paul	1 Cor 3:10-17; 4:1-5; 2 Cor 5:9-10

REVELATION on

Daniel	Dan 12:1-4

causing SADNESS

REVELATION on

John	Rev 18:4-20

SCRIPTURES on
  of **BLASPHEMY**
    Paul   Rom 2:1-24
  as **CONDEMNATION**
    Jesus   Mt 12:38-42;
                        Lk 11:29-32
  on **EVIL**
    Jesus   Mt 12:38-42;
                        Lk 11:29-32
  FULFILLMENT of
    People   Acts 13:14-52
  on **JUSTICE**
    Amaziah   2 Kgs 14:7;
                        2 Chr 25:1-28
  concerning **WITNESS**
    Jesus   Jn 8:12-20

on **SELFISHNESS**
  INSTRUCTION on
    Jesus   Lk 11:37-44;
                        12:13-15;
                        16-21;
                        19:11-27

SELF-REALIZATION of
  as **CONDEMNATION**
    Hypocrite   Mt 7:1-5;
                        Lk 6:36-45
  on **EVIL**
    Judahites   Jer 26:7-19
  on **FAMILY**
    Jacob   Gen 31:1-16
  for **GUILT**
    Hypocrite   Mt 7:1-5;
                        Lk 6:36-45
  on **JUSTICE**
    Judahites   Jer 26:7-19

on **SERVICE**
  INSTRUCTION on
    Jesus   Mt 25:31-46

on **SEX**
  REVELATION on
    Israelites   Ezek 23:36-49;
                        Mal 2:17-3:5

on **SHARING**
  INSTRUCTION on
    Jesus   Mt 25:31-46;
                        Lk 6:36-45

of **SPIRIT** as one's heart
  by **DEITY**
    Jesus   Rom 2:1-24;
                        1 Cor 4:1-5
  INSTRUCTION on
    Jesus   Mt 15:15-20;
                        Mk 7:1-23

on **STEALING**
  by **MESSIANIC FIGURE**
    Jesus   Mt 21:12-17;
                        Mk 11:15-19;
                        Lk 19:45-46

in **TRADITION**
  of **ORDER**
    Moses   Ex 18:13-26

on **TRADITION**
  REJECTION of
    Paul   Col 2:16-23

in **VICTORY**
  REVELATION on
    Daniel   Dan 7:17-27

on **VIOLENCE**
  INSTRUCTION on
    Jesus   Mt 26:47-56
  PROPHECY of
    Joel   Joel 2:1-11

on **WEALTH**
    Shunammite   2 Kgs 8:1-6
  INSTRUCTION on
    Jesus   Lk 6:24-26;
                        16:14-15
  REVELATION on
    John   Rev 18:4-20

as **WILL**
  of **DEITY**
    Elihu   Job 34:29-33
    Mankind   Prov 21:1-31;
                        Jas 4:11-12
    Micah   Mic 4:1-8
  INSTRUCTION on
    Jesus   Jn 8:12-20

through **WISDOM**
    Solomon   1 Kgs 3:16-28
  of **DEITY**
    Elihu   Job 34:21-28
    God   Rom 11:33-36
  of **FOLLOWERs**
    Paul   1 Cor 4:6-13;
                        6:1-8
  INSTRUCTION on
    Jesus   Mt 11:16-19;
                        Lk 7:31-35;
                        Jn 7:15-24
    Psalmist   Ps 119:65-72
  PROPHECY of
    Isaiah   Is 32:1-8

concerning **WITNESS**
    Moses   Num 35:26-34
  by **DEITY**
    Aaron   Ex 28:13-30
  on **FALSE BELIEF**
    Author   Heb 10:19-31
  INSTRUCTION on
    God   Is 43:8-13
    Jesus   Mt 18:15-17
    John   1 Jn 4:1-3
    Moses   Deut 16:21-17:7;
                        19:15-21
    Paul   2 Cor 13:1-4;
                        1 Tim 5:17-25
  against **MESSIANIC FIGURE**
    Jesus   Mt 27:11-26;
                      Mk 15:1-5
  in **MISSION**
    Ezekiel   Ezek 33:1-9
  REVELATION on
    Isaiah   Is 66:17-24
    Israelites   Mal 2:17-3:5

REVELATION on (cont'd)
John	Rev 20:4-6
Mankind	Ezek 39:17-24

SCRIPTURES on
Jesus	Jn 8:12-20

of WORSHIP
as CONDEMNATION
Paul	1 Cor 11:17-22

as IDOLATRY
Josiah	2 Kgs 23:4-15

concerning YOUTH
of FOLLOWERs
Corinthians	1 Cor 3:1-4

INSTRUCTION on
Paul	1 Cor 3:1-4

JUSTICE

in AUTHORITY
of DEITY
God	Job 37:23-24; Ps 62:8-12
Israelites	Deut 10:12-22
Psalmist	Ps 82:8
Solomon	*Wis 16:15-29

INSTRUCTION on
Paul	2 Cor 13:1-4
Solomon	Prov 29:1-27; *Wis 6:1-11

PROPHECY of
Isaiah	Is 9:2-7; 32:1-8

through AUTHORITY
to MESSIANIC FIGURE
Pilate	Mt 27:11-26; Mk 15:6-15

of MISSION
Paul	2 Cor 13:5-10

BEHAVIOR revealing
INSTRUCTION on
God	Is 1:10-17
Jesus	Mt 5:38-42
Sirach	*Sir 4:1-10; 20-31

PROPHECY of
Jeremiah	Jer 21:11-12

SCRIPTURES on
Jesus	Mt 12:1-8; Mk 2:23-28; Lk 6:1-5

unBELIEF in
of DEITY
Israelites	Ezek 18:25-29; 33:10-20

in BROTHERHOOD
revealed by FOLLOWER
Paul	1 Cor 6:1-8

COMMITMENT to
INSTRUCTION on
Amos	Amos 5:14-15

in COMMUNITY
Macron	*2 Mc 10:10-13

from DEITY
David	Ps 9:17-20

REVELATION on
God	Ps 9:15-16

CONFRONTATION with
REVELATION on
Job	Job 40:6-14
Mordecai	*Esth 11:2-12

CONVERSION through
of FOLLOWER
Zacchaeus	Lk 19:1-10

in COVENANT
ETERNAL
Sirach	*Sir 17:1-14

PROMISE of
Israelites	Hos 2:16-20

RECONCILIATION through
Abimelech	Gen 21:22-34
Abraham	Gen 21:22-34

in the CREATION
INSTRUCTION on
Angel	*2 Esd 5:43-6:6

of DEITY
concerning AUTHORITY
God	Job 37:23-24; Ps 62:8-12
Israelites	Deut 10:12-22
Psalmist	Ps 82:8
Solomon	*Wis 16:15-29

unBELIEF in
Israelites	Ezek 18:25-29; 33:10-20

in COMMUNITY
David	Ps 9:17-20

DESIRE for
God	Mic 6:6-8
Habakkuk	Hab 1:2-4; 12-17
Israelites	Amos 5:21-25
Job	Job 13:20-27; 21:19-27; 31:5-34

in ELECTION
Believers	Lk 18:1-8; Rom 8:28-39

with EQUALITY
God	1 Chr 15:1-16:43; Ps 9:5-8; 96:10-13; 98:7-9; Acts 10:1-11:18; Gal 1:18-2:10
Mankind	Col 3:18-4:1

FIDELITY in
God	Ps 111:5-9; Rom 2:25-3:20
Isaiah	Is 61:1-11

through HONESTY
Elihu	Job 34:10-15
Job	Job 31:5-34

over **SIN** (cont'd)

Isaiah	Is 59:1-21
Solomon	Prov 18:1-24

in **TRUTH**

Elihu	Job 34:1-4
Jesus	Lk 12:1-12

as **VIRTUE**

Bildad	Job 8:1-7
God	Is 56:1-8
Solomon	Prov 12:1-28; 21:1-31

in **JUDGMENT**

Moses	Ex 23:1-9; Lev 19:1-37; 20:1-27
Solomon	1 Kgs 1:41-53

by **DEITY**

Azariah	*Azar 1:1-10
Bildad	Job 8:20-22
David	Ps 7:9-11; 51:3-12
Eliphaz	Job 4:7-11; 22:21-30
Ezra	*2 Esd 4:33-52
God	1 Chr 15:1-16:43; Ps 11:4-7; 31:19-24; 37:1-11; 12-22; 23-40; 50:1-6; 67:1-7; 82:1; 96:10-13; 99:4-5; 103:6-13; 119:137-144; 146:5-7b; Prov 16:1-33; 23:15-24:22; 29:1-27; Eccl 3:16-4:3; Jer 17:9-10; Gal 6:7-10; Rev 16:4-7; 19:1-5
Isaiah	Is 28:1-13
Jesus	Mt 16:21-28
Job	Job 21:7-13; 14-18; 24:1-12; 27:13-23; 31:35-37
Mankind	Heb 10:19-31
People	Rom 2:1-24
Sirach	*Sir 35:12-20
Solomon	1 Kgs 8:22-53; 2 Chr 5:1-7:10; Ps 72:1-4

INSTRUCTION on

Angel	*2 Esd 5:31-42
Israelites	Zech 7:4-8:23
Jehoshaphat	2 Chr 17:1-20:37
Jesus	Mt 7:1-5; 12:33-37; 18:23-35; Lk 6:36-45; 12:57-59; Jn 5:19-47

INSTRUCTION on (cont'd)

Lemuel	Prov 31:1-9
Moses	Deut 1:9-18; 16:18-20; 19:1-13; 15-21; 23:15-25:19; 27:11-26
Paul	Rom 2:25-3:20; 1 Cor 4:1-5; 1 Tim 5:17-25
Solomon	Prov 24:23-34
Zophar	Job 11:7-12

of **MESSIANIC FIGURE**

Isaiah	Is 11:1-9

PROPHECY of

Angel	*2 Esd 7:33-44; 8:63-9:25
Isaiah	Is 15:1-16:14
Israelites	Ezek 16:35-43
Jeremiah	Jer 31:31-34
Obadiah	Obad 1:15-16

REVELATION on

Edomites	Ezek 35:1-15
Ezekiel	Ezek 18:14-20; 21-24; 25-29; 33:1-9; 10-20
Isaiah	Is 5:1-7; 65:1-25
Israelites	Ezek 7:1-27; 9:1-11; 18:30-32; 22:23-31
John	Rev 19:11-16; 20:11-15; 22:6-21
Judahites	Ezek 24:1-14
Moses	Num 35:16-25
Zechariah	Zech 7:4-8:23

SCRIPTURES on

Amaziah	2 Kgs 14:7; 2 Chr 25:1-28

SELF-REALIZATION of

Judahites	Jer 26:7-19

JUDGMENT on

in **ENVIRONMENT**

Daniel	*Susa 1:52-59
Ezra	*1 Esd 8:8-24
Samuel	1 Sam 7:2-17; 12:1-25

JUDGMENT through

of **FOLLOWER**

Festus	Acts 25:1-12

KNOWLEDGE of

of **DEITY**

Asaph	Ps 73:13-20
Ezra	*2 Esd 4:33-52
Mankind	Ps 58:10-11

INSTRUCTION on

Solomon	Prov 2:1-22; 28:1-28

in **LAW**

Moses	Ex 21:18-32; 23:1-9; Lev 5:14-6:7

INSTRUCTION on
  God   Ex 20:1-17
  Jesus   Mt 23:23-24
  Moses   Deut 5:1-21;
                         17:8-13;
                         19:15-21
  Paul   Rom 2:1-24
REVELATION on
  Israelites   Ezek 45:10-12
  Moses   Lev 24:10-23

MEDITATION on
  in RECONCILIATION
    Jeremiah   Jer 5:1-14
  over SIN
    Preacher   Eccl 3:16-4:3

through MESSIANIC FIGURE
  in JUDGMENT
    Isaiah   Is 11:1-9
  in NEW AGE
    Angel   *2 Esd 11:1-12:39;
                         13:1-50

to MESSIANIC FIGURE
  by AUTHORITY
    Pilate   Mt 27:11-26;
                         Mk 15:6-15

in MISSION
  AUTHORITY of
    Paul   2 Cor 13:5-10

in NEW AGE
  by DEITY
    Ezra   *2 Esd 4:33-52
  INSTRUCTION on
    Angel   *2 Esd 5:43-6:6
    Jesus   Mt 20:1-16;
                         25:31-46
  by MESSIANIC FIGURE
    Angel   *2 Esd 11:1-12:39;
                         13:1-50
  PROPHECY of
    Angel   *2 Esd 8:63-9:25;
                         11:1-12:39
    Isaiah   Is 32:15-20
  REVELATION on
    Angel   *2 Esd 6:7-28

PRAYER for
  of DEITY
    David   Ps 7:3-5;
                         6-8;
                         9:17-20;
                         17:1-2;
                         26:1-3;
                         28:1-5;
                         35:19-21;
                         22-28;
                         55:9-11;
                         56:6b-9
    Ezra   *2 Esd 5:21-30
    Jephthah   Judg 11:12-28
    Psalmist   Ps 10:1-2;
                         12-18;
                         94:1-3
    Susanna   *Susa 1:42-51

MEDITATION on
  Jeremiah   Lam 1:1-22

MEDITATION on (cont'd)
  Job   Job 16:18-22
through PRESENCE
  of DEITY
    David   2 Sam 23:1-7
    God   Is 41:1-42:4
    Micah   Mic 3:1-12

PROMISE of
  in COVENANT
    Israelites   Hos 2:16-20

PROPHECY of
  in AUTHORITY
    Isaiah   Is 9:2-7;
                         32:1-8
  for FIDELITY
    Judahites   Jer 7:1-15
  in JUDGMENT
    Angel   *2 Esd 7:33-44;
                         8:63-9:25
    Isaiah   Is 15:1-16:14
    Israelites   Ezek 16:35-43
    Jeremiah   Jer 31:31-34
    Obadiah   Obad 1:15-16
  in NEW AGE
    Angel   *2 Esd 8:63-9:25
                         11:1-12:39
    Isaiah   Is 32:15-20
  in PUNISHMENT
    Babylonians   Jer 50:1-46
    Edomites   Obad 1:15-16
    Isaiah   Is 3:8-12;
                         27:7-11
    Israelites   Jer 46:27-28;
                         Ezek 16:35-43;
                         Hos 4:4-15;
                         12:2-6
    Jeremiah   Jer 21:13-14;
                         31:29-30
  in RECONCILIATION
    Isaiah   Is 1:27-31
  in SALVATION
    Isaiah   Is 1:27-31
  as VIRTUE
    Isaiah   Is 28:14-22
    Jeremiah   Jer 22:1-9;
                         23:1-8

through PROVIDENCE
  of DEITY
    God   Ezra 9:6-15;
                         Ps 140:12-13
    Hannah   1 Sam 2:1-10
  INSTRUCTION on
    Angel   *2 Esd 5:43-6:6
  REVELATION on
    Israelites   Ezek 34:11-16

in PUNISHMENT
  Moses   Ex 21:12-17;
                         33-22:17;
                         21-31
  by DEITY
    David   Ps 17:13-14
    Elihu   Job 36:5-15
    Eliphaz   Job 5:8-17
    God   Ps 94:20-23
    Isaiah   Is 59:1-21

by **DEITY** (cont'd)
Israelites · Neh 9:32-37;
Is 42:18-43:7
Job · Job 27:1-12
Paul · 2 Thes 1:5-7a
Sirach · *Sir 39:28-35
for **FALSE BELIEF**
God · *Wis 12:23-27
Sinners · 2 Pet 2:10b-16
INSTRUCTION on
Author · Heb 2:1-4
Paul · 2 Cor 13:1-4
Solomon · 1 Kgs 2:28-35
PROPHECY of
Babylonians · Jer 50:1-46
Edomites · Obad 1:15-16
Isaiah · Is 3:8-12;
27:7-11
Israelites · Jer 46:27-28;
Ezek 16:35-43;
Hos 4:4-15;
12:2-6
Jeremiah · Jer 21:13-14;
31:29-30
REVELATION on
Egyptians · Ezek 31:10-18
Ezekiel · Ezek 14:12-23
Israelites · Jer 2:14-19;
Ezek 36:16-21;
39:17-24;
Amos 8:4-7
Jeremiah · Jer 16:16-18
John · Rev 13:5-10;
18:4-20
Moses · Lev 24:10-23
SELF-REALIZATION of
Criminal · Lk 23:39-43

as **QUALITY OF LIFE**
of **DEITY**
God · Is 30:18-26
INSTRUCTION on
Angel · *2 Esd 7:116-8:3
Wisdom · Prov 8:1-21

in **RECONCILIATION**
Moses · Num 5:5-10
in **COVENANT**
Abimelech · Gen 21:22-34
Abraham · Gen 21:22-34
INSTRUCTION on
Paul · Rom 2:25-3:20
MEDITATION on
Jeremiah · Jer 5:1-14
PROPHECY of
Isaiah · Is 1:27-31

RESPECT for
of **DEITY**
God · Ps 33:4-9
Nebuchadnezzar · Dan 4:36-36
through **WORSHIP**
God · Rev 15:1-16:1

REVELATION on
to **COMMUNITY**
God · Ps 9:15-16
CONFRONTATION with
Job · Job 40:6-14
Mordecai · *Esth 11:2-12

in **JUDGMENT**
Edomites · Ezek 35:1-15
Ezekiel · Ezek 18:14-20;
21-24;
25-29;
33:1-9;
10-20
Isaiah · Is 5:1-7;
65:1-25
Israelites · Ezek 7:1-27;
9:1-11;
18:30-32;
22:23-31
John · Rev 19:11-16;
20:11-15;
22:6-21
Judahites · Ezek 24:1-14
Moses · Num 35:16-25
Zechariah · Zech 7:4-8:23
in **LAW**
Israelites · Ezek 45:10-12
Moses · Lev 24:10-23
in **NEW AGE**
Angel · *2 Esd 6:7-28
in **PROVIDENCE**
Israelites · Ezek 34:11-16
in **PUNISHMENT**
Egyptians · Ezek 31:10-18
Ezekiel · Ezek 14:12-23
Israelites · Jer 2:14-19;
Ezek 36:16-21;
39:17-24;
Amos 8:4-7
Jeremiah · Jer 16:16-18
John · Rev 13:5-10;
18:4-20
Moses · Lev 24:10-23
as **VIRTUE**
Israelites · Ezek 45:1-9
Jeremiah · Jer 33:14-26

in **SALVATION**
INSTRUCTION on
Angel · *2 Esd 7:116-8:3
Jesus · Mt 20:1-16
PROPHECY of
Isaiah · Is 1:27-31

SCRIPTURES on
in **JUDGMENT**
Amaziah · 2 Kgs 14:7;
2 Chr 25:1-28

SECURITY in
Joshua · Josh 20:1-9
Moses · Num 35:9-15;
Deut 4:41-43
of **DEITY**
Believers · Ps 37:23-40
of **FOLLOWER**
Claudius · Acts 23:12-35
INSTRUCTION on
Moses · Deut 19:1-13

SELF-REALIZATION of
in **JUDGMENT**
Judahites · Jer 26:7-19
in **PUNISHMENT**
Criminal · Lk 23:39-43

SIGNS of
　INSTRUCTION on
　　Angel　　　　　　*2 Esd 8:63-9:25;
　　　　　　　　　　13:1-50
　PROPHECY of
　　Angel　　　　　　*2 Esd 4:33-52
　REVELATION on
　　Ezra　　　　　　*2 Esd 13:1-50

SIN against
　in ENVIRONMENT
　　Elders　　　　　　*Susa 1:5-18

concerning SIN
　by DEITY
　　David　　　　　　Ps 7:12-16

over SIN
　INSTRUCTION on
　　God　　　　　　　Ps 82:2-7
　　Isaiah　　　　　　Is 59:1-21
　　Solomon　　　　　Prov 18:1-24
　MEDITATION on
　　Preacher　　　　　Eccl 3:16-4:3

in STEWARDSHIP
　　Moses　　　　　　Lev 25:8-19

TRADITION of
　through FIDELITY
　　Samuel　　　　　*Sir 46:13-20

in TRUTH
　INSTRUCTION on
　　Elihu　　　　　　Job 34:1-4
　　Jesus　　　　　　Lk 12:1-12

as VIRTUE
　　Job　　　　　　　Job 29:14-20
　of DEITY
　　God　　　　　　　Ps 89:5-18;
　　　　　　　　　　94:12-15;
　　　　　　　　　　97:1-5;
　　　　　　　　　　99:4-5;
　　　　　　　　　　145:13b-20;
　　　　　　　　　　Is 5:8-24a;
　　　　　　　　　　Jer 9:23-24;
　　　　　　　　　　11:18-12:6;
　　　　　　　　　　Dan 9:4-19;
　　　　　　　　　　Zeph 3:1-5
　　Psalmist　　　　　Ps 129:1-4
　INSTRUCTION on
　　Bildad　　　　　　Job 8:1-7
　　God　　　　　　　Is 56:1-8
　　Solomon　　　　　Prov 12:1-28;
　　　　　　　　　　21:1-31
　PROPHECY of
　　Isaiah　　　　　　Is 28:14-22
　　Jeremiah　　　　　Jer 22:1-9;
　　　　　　　　　　23:1-8
　REVELATION on
　　Israelites　　　　　Ezek 45:1-9
　　Jeremiah　　　　　Jer 33:14-26

WORSHIP of
　through FIDELITY
　　David　　　　　　Ps 101:1-2b
　revealing RESPECT
　　God　　　　　　　Rev 15:1-16:1

KILLING
　of AUTHORITY
　　Hazael　　　　　　2 Kgs 8:7-15
　　Joab　　　　　　　2 Sam 20:1-26
　through FALSE BELIEF
　　Herod　　　　　　Mt 2:16-18

BEHAVIOR revealing
　　Abimelech　　　　Judg 9:1-6
　　Abner　　　　　　2 Sam 2:8-32
　　Athaliah　　　　　2 Kgs 11:1-3
　　Israelites　　　　　Esth 9:1-10;
　　　　　　　　　　11-15;
　　　　　　　　　　16-19
　　Joab　　　　　　　2 Sam 18:1-19:8
　　Samson　　　　　Judg 16:23-31
　in ENVIRONMENT
　　Benjaminites　　　Judg 19:27-30
　　Cain　　　　　　　Gen 4:1-16
　　Ehud　　　　　　Judg 3:15-23
　　Judith　　　　　　*Jdt 13:1-10
　　Lamech　　　　　Gen 4:20-24
　　Mattathias　　　　*1 Mc 2:23-28
　　Samson　　　　　Judg 14:10-20;
　　　　　　　　　　15:1-8;
　　　　　　　　　　9-20
　through FALSE BELIEF
　　Herod　　　　　　Mt 14:1-12;
　　　　　　　　　　Mk 6:17-29
　　Pharaoh　　　　　Ex 1:15-22
　INSTRUCTION on
　　Abraham　　　　　Gen 22:1-19
　　Ahasuerus　　　　Esth 3:7-15
　　Artaxerxes　　　　*Esth 13:1-7
　　Demetrius　　　　*1 Mc 7:1-4
　　Jehu　　　　　　　2 Kgs 9:30-37
　　Jesus　　　　　　Mt 23:34-39
　　Preacher　　　　　Eccl 3:1-8
　MEDITATION on
　　Saul　　　　　　　1 Chr 10:1-14
　SELF-REALIZATION of
　　Judas　　　　　　Mt 27:3-10

unBELIEF causing
　through FALSE BELIEF
　　Sarah　　　　　　*Tb 3:7-15
　for lack of WORSHIP
　　John　　　　　　　Rev 13:11-18

COMMITMENT to
　of FOLLOWER
　　Jews　　　　　　　Acts 23:12-35

CONFRONTATION with
　　Abimelech　　　　Judg 9:46-49
　　Amaziah　　　　　2 Kgs 14:7
　　Angel　　　　　　Is 37:36-38
　　Antiochus　　　　*2 Mc 5:11-27
　　Baasha　　　　　　1 Kgs 15:25-32
　　Babylonians　　　Jer 52:4-27
　　David　　　　　　1 Sam 17:1-18:5
　　Ishmael　　　　　Jer 41:1-3
　　Israelites　　　　　Judg 7:23-25;
　　　　　　　　　　20:37-44;
　　　　　　　　　　45-48;
　　　　　　　　　　1 Kgs 12:1-20;
　　　　　　　　　　21:8-12
　　Jehu　　　　　　　2 Kgs 9:14-29

through disHONESTY (cont'd)

Jael — Judg 4:17-22; 5:23-27
Jehu — 2 Kgs 10:18-28

caused by FALSE BELIEF
Babylonians — Rev 18:21-24
INSTRUCTION on
Jezebel — 1 Kgs 21:5-12

INSTRUCTION on
revealing FIDELITY
Jotham — Judg 9:16-21
through disHONESTY
Jezebel — 1 Kgs 21:5-12
as PUNISHMENT
Jehoiada — 2 Kgs 11:4-20
Jehu — 2 Kgs 10:1-14
Moses — Deut 19:1-13
Solomon — 1 Kgs 2:13-25; 28-35; 36-46; Prov 28:1-28
as SIN
David — 2 Sam 11:1-27
Isaiah — Is 56:9-57:13
Jesus — Mt 21:33-43; Mk 12:1-12; Lk 20:9-18

JUDGMENT on
through FALSE BELIEF
Jews — Jn 18:28-19:16
Pharisees — Jn 11:1-57
Pilate — Mk 15:6-15; Lk 23:18-25
Priests — Jn 11:1-57
MEDITATION on
Pilate — Jn 18:28-19:16
of MESSIANIC FIGURE
Crowd — Mt 27:11-26; Mk 15:6-15; Lk 23:18-25

KNOWLEDGE of
in ENVIRONMENT
Elisha — 2 Kgs 6:32-7:2
PROPHECY of
Jesus — Jn 16:1-4
REVELATION on
Daniel — Dan 11:21-45

LAW concerning
Moses — Ex 21:12-17; 18-32; Lev 17:1-9; 24:10-23
INSTRUCTION on
God — Gen 9:1-7; Ex 20:1-17
Jesus — Mt 5:21-26; 19:16-22; Mk 10:17-22
Moses — Deut 5:1-21; 19:1-13; 21:1-9; 27:11-26
Paul — Rom 13:8-10
REVELATION on
Moses — Num 35:16-25; 26-34

MEDITATION concerning
INSTRUCTION on
Mordecai — Esth 4:1-17
of MESSIANIC FIGURE
DESIRE for
Jews — Jn 5:1-18
Priests — Lk 22:1-2
ELECTION of
Jesus — Acts 2:14-36
JUDGMENT on
Crowd — Mt 27:11-26; Mk 15:6-15; Lk 23:18-25

PROMISE of
INSTRUCTION on
God — Ex 4:18-23

PROPHECY of
concerning CONFRONTATION
Gentiles — Mk 10:32-34
Jesus — Mt 16:21-28; 17:22-23; 20:17-19; 26:1-2; Mk 8:31-33; 9:30-32; Lk 9:18-22; 43b-45; 18:31-34
as PUNISHMENT
Habakkuk — Hab 2:12-14; 17
Jehu — 2 Chr 21:1-23:21
Prophet — 2 Kgs 9:1-13

as PUNISHMENT
INSTRUCTION on
Jehoiada — 2 Kgs 11:4-20
Jehu — 2 Kgs 10:1-14
Moses — Deut 19:1-13
Solomon — 1 Kgs 2:13-25; 28-35; 36-46; Prov 28:1-28

PROPHECY of
Habakkuk — Hab 2:12-14; 17
Jehu — 2 Chr 21:1-23:21
Prophet — 2 Kgs 9:1-13
REVELATION on
Elijah — 1 Kgs 19:1-21
John — Rev 11:1-14
Mankind — Rev 9:13-21
Moses — Num 35:16-25

PUNISHMENT for
Amaziah — 2 Kgs 14:5-6; 2 Chr 25:1-28
Israelites — 1 Kgs 21:19-26
Jehoiada — 2 Chr 21:1-23:21
Jehoram — 2 Kgs 6:24-31
Moses — Lev 26:1-46
Saul — 1 Sam 22:1-23
by DEITY
Cain — Gen 4:1-16
in ENVIRONMENT
David — 2 Sam 1:1-16; 4:1-12

in **ENVIRONMENT** (cont'd)
Josiah	2 Kgs 23:16-20
Phinehas	Num 25:6-18

REVELATION on
concerning **CONFRONTATION**
Prophets	Rev 11:1-14

as **PUNISHMENT**
Elijah	1 Kgs 19:1-21
John	Rev 11:1-14
Mankind	Rev 9:13-21
Moses	Num 35:16-25

as **SIN**
Israelites	Ezek 22:1-16
Mankind	Rev 9:13-21

in**SECURITY** through
David	1 Sam 20:1-42; 21:1-9
Joash	2 Kgs 11:1-3; 2 Chr 21:1-23:21
Jonathan	*1 Mc 9:32-42
Maccabeus	*2 Mc 5:11-27
Moses	Num 35:1-8; Deut 4:41-43

INSTRUCTION on
Moses	Deut 19:1-13
Sirach	*Sir 9:13

REVELATION on
Joshua	Josh 20:1-9
Moses	Num 35:9-15

SELF-REALIZATION of
Judas	Mt 27:3-10

SIGNS of
through **FALSE BELIEF**
Daniel	*Bel 1:23-27

PROPHECY of
Jesus	Mt 24:9-14

REVELATION on
John	Rev 6:3-4; 7-8; 13:11-18
Mankind	Rev 9:13-21

as **SIN**
Absalom	2 Sam 13:21-14:33
Ammonites	Amos 1:13-15
Jezebel	1 Kgs 18:1-46
Manasseh	2 Kgs 21:1-18
Moabites	Amos 2:1-3
Priest	Hos 6:7-9

against **DEITY**
Er	Gen 38:1-11
God	Prov 6:16-19

in **ENVIRONMENT**
Andronicus	*2 Mc 4:30-38
Israelites	Hos 4:1-3

through **FALSE BELIEF**
Israelites	Ezek 22:23-31

INSTRUCTION on
David	2 Sam 11:1-27
Isaiah	Is 56:9-57:13
Jesus	Mt 21:33-43; Mk 12:1-12; Lk 20:9-18

REVELATION on
Israelites	Ezek 22:1-16
Mankind	Rev 9:13-21

in **WORSHIP**
Ahaz	2 Kgs 16:1-4

for lack of **WORSHIP**
John	Rev 13:11-18

in **WORSHIP**
as **SIN**
Ahaz	2 Kgs 16:1-4

KNOWLEDGE

ACCEPTANCE of
of **DEITY**
Ahab	1 Kgs 20:1-43
Believers	1 Jn 4:4-6
David	Ps 41:11-12
Elihu	Job 37:14-22
Israelites	Jer 31:31-34

INSTRUCTION on
Father	Prov 4:1-9; 10-19; 20-27
Solomon	Prov 1:8-9; 5:1-14; 9:1-6; 13:1-25; 19:1-29
Uriel	*2 Esd 4:13-21

concerning **MESSIANIC FIGURE**
Jesus	Jn 2:23-25; 6:60-71
Peter	Mt 16:13-20

PROPHECY of
Isaiah	Is 29:17-24
Zedekiah	Jer 32:1-8

SELF-REALIZATION of
Jesus	Mt 3:13-17

of **ANGER**
of **DEITY**
Israelites	Ezek 22:17-22

INSTRUCTION on
Sirach	*Sir 1:22-30
Solomon	Prov 14:1-35

on **ANXIETY**
REVELATION of
Daniel	Dan 7:28
Ethiopians	Ezek 30:6-9

of **BLASPHEMY**
PROPHECY of
Gentiles	Mk 10:32-34

of **BLESSING**
INSTRUCTION on
Father	Prov 4:10-19
Jesus	Lk 10:23-24
Sirach	*Sir 50:27-29

of **CAPTIVITY**
by **DEITY**
Israelites	Ezek 6:8-10

GRIEF through	
Ezra	*2 Esd 4:1-12
HEALING through	
Jesus	Lk 8:40-56
IGNORANCE of	
Ephraimites	Hos 5:3-7
Ezra	*2 Esd 4:1-12
Jews	Jn 8:21-59
Psalmist	Ps 42:6-11
Ungodly Men	*Wis 2:21-24
Zophar	Job 11:7-12
INNOCENCE in	
Israelites	Ps 44:17-22
Job	Job 10:1-7
JOY in	
Wisdom	Prov 8:22-31
JUSTICE in	
Asaph	Ps 73:13-20
Ezra	*2 Esd 4:33-52
Mankind	Ps 58:10-11
concerning **LIFE**	
David	Ps 16:9-11;
	39:4-6
Israelites	Hos 13:4-6
Jeremiah	Jer 1:4-10
concerning **LOVE**	
Believers	1 Jn 4:7-12
Jesus	Jn 10:1-18
concerning **OPPRESSION**	
Israelites	Ex 2:23b-25;
	Acts 6:8-8:3
concerning **ORDER**	
God	Ps 87:4-6
PRAISE of	
Isaiah	Is 28:23-29
Mankind	Ps 48:9-14
Shepherds	Lk 2:1-20
concerning **REJECTION**	
Galatian	Gal 4:8-11
Israelites	Ex 16:1-21;
	Num 14:26-38
Mankind	Ps 10:3-11
concerning **REPENTANCE**	
Manasseh	2 Chr 33:1-25
Pharaoh	Gen 12:9-13:1
concerning **REWARDs**	
Hannah	1 Sam 2:1-10
Solomon	1 Kgs 8:22-53
WITNESS to	
David	2 Sam 23:1-7
God	Gen 31:44-55;
	Jer 29:24-32;
	Amos 4:13
Hezekiah	Is 37:8-20
Holy Spirit	Jn 16:12-15
Israelites	Deut 4:32-40
Jesus	Jn 8:12-20;
	14:1-14
of **DEITY's**	
LEADERSHIP	
Ahab	1 Kgs 20:1-43
Ammonites	Ezek 25:1-7
Edomites	Ezek 35:1-15
Egyptians	Ex 7:1-7;
	14:1-14;
	Ezek 29:6-9a;
	9b-16;
	17-21;
	30:6-9;

LEADERSHIP	
Egyptians	13-19;
	20-26;
	32:1-16
Ezekiel	Ezek 11:1-13;
	15:1-8;
	24:15-24;
	25-27;
	33:23-29
God	Heb 8:6-13
Israelites	Ex 5:6-14;
	Ezek 6:1-7;
	8-10;
	11-14;
	7:1-27;
	12:1-16;
	17-20;
	13:17-23;
	16:53-63;
	17:11-21;
	20:9-26;
	40-44;
	22:1-16;
	28:24-26;
	34:17-22;
	25-31;
	36:8-15;
	37:1-14;
	15-28;
	Hos 2:16-20;
	Joel 3:16b-21
Joel	Joel 2:18-27
Mankind	1 Kgs 8:54-61;
	Ps 59:13c-15;
	Ezek 36:22-32;
	37-38
Moabites	Ezek 25:8-11
Moses	Ex 7:14-25
Prophetesses	Ezek 13:17-23
Sidon	Ezek 28:20-23
Tyre	Ezek 26:1-6
of **DESTRUCTION**	
Job	Job 1:13-19
Nehemiah	Neh 2:12-15
by **DEITY**	
God	Is 10:5-16;
	29:13-14
Isaiah	Is 66:17-24
PROPHECY of	
Edomites	Obad 1:5-9
REVELATION on	
Daniel	Dan 9:1-3
of **DIGNITY**	
of **DEITY**	
Job	Job 31:5-34
REVELATION on	
King	Ezek 28:11-19
of **DISCIPLESHIP**	
to **DEITY**	
God	2 Tim 2:14-19
FALSE BELIEF in	
Paul	2 Tim 3:1-9
of **FOLLOWERs**	
Apostles	Mt 10:2-4;
	Mk 3:13-19;
	Lk 6:12-16
Jesus	Jn 13:31-35

REVELATION on
   Holy Spirit   1 Cor 2:10-16

of DISOBEDIENCE
  INSTRUCTION on
    James   Jas 4:17
    Rehum   Ezra 4:6-16
  REVELATION on
    Jeremiah   Jer 18:1-12

DOUBT in
  of DEITY
    Israelites   Ezek 8:7-13
  REVELATION on
    Habakkuk   Hab 1:5-11

of ENEMY
    Abimelech   Judg 9:30-33
    David   2 Sam 15:13-16;
                 14:15-17:29
    Hezekiah   2 Kgs 20:12-21
    Israelites   Num 13:21-24;
                 Josh 2:15-24
    John   *1 Mc 16:18-24
    Nehemiah   Neh 6:1-4;
                 5-9;
                 10-14
  by DEITY
    David   Ps 3:1-2;
                 21:8-13
  INSTRUCTION on
    Joshua   Josh 2:1-7
    Moses   Num 13:17b-20
    Paul   Eph 6:10-18;
                 Phil 3:17-21
  REVELATION on
    Moses   Num 13:1-17a
  SELF-REALIZATION of
    Jesus   Mt 26:36-46;
                 Mk 14:32-42

of ENVIRONMENT
  causing FEAR
    Israelites   Num 13:26b-33;
                 Deut 1:19-46
    Moses   Ex 2:11-15

concerning EVIL
  against DEITY
    David   Ps 19:11-14;
                 21:8-13;
                 69:4-12;
                 139:23-24
    Elihu   Job 36:5-15
    Ephraimites   Hos 6:10-7:2
    God   Ps 90:1-12;
                 Prov 5:15-23;
                 15:1-33;
                 23:15-24:22
    Jeremiah   Jer 16:16-18
    Jesus   Mt 12:22-32;
                 Lk 11:14-23
    Job   Job 13:20-27
    Mankind   Ps 53:1-3
    Psalmist   Ps 94:4-7
    Sirach   *Sir 16:6-23;
                 17:15-32;
                 22:27-23:6;
                 16-27
    Solomon   *Wis 17:1-21

in ENVIRONMENT
    Job   Job 21:19-27
  INSTRUCTION on
    God   *2 Esd 1:4-23
    Preacher   Eccl 5:8-20
    Solomon   Prov 26:1-28;
                 *Wis 1:6-11;
                 7:15-8:1
  MEDITATION on
    Jesus   Mt 22:15-22;
                 Mk 12:13-17;
                 Lk 20:19-26
  against MESSIANIC FIGURE
    Pharisees   Lk 5:17-26
    Scribes   Mt 9:1-8;
                 Mk 2:1-12
  PROPHECY of
    Judahites   Jer 17:1-4
  REVELATION on
    God   *2 Esd 16:51-78
    Sardis   Rev 3:1-6
  SELF-REALIZATION of
    David   Ps 51:3-12

of FAITH
  of FOLLOWERs
    Timothy   1 Thes 3:1-10
  INSTRUCTION on
    Jesus   Mt 14:22-27;
                 Mk 6:45-52;
                 Jn 6:16-24
    Paul   1 Cor 13:8-13
    Sirach   *Sir 19:4-12
  in MESSIANIC FIGURE
    Disciples   Jn 16:29-33
    Peter   Mk 8:27-30;
                 Lk 9:18-22
  REVELATION on
    Pergamum   Rev 2:12-17
    Thyatira   Rev 2:18-29

of FALSE BELIEF
  in DISCIPLESHIP
    Paul   2 Tim 3:1-9
  revealing HERESY
    Jesus   Jn 16:1-4
  revealing IDOLATRY
    Daniel   *Bel 1:10-20
    Jeremiah   *Jer 6:45-59
  revealing IGNORANCE
    Mankind   *Wis 13:1-9
    Solomon   *Wis 13:10-19
  REJECTION of
    Paul   Col 2:1-5;
                 1 Tim 6:20-21
    Sirach   *Sir 34:1-8
  concerning STEALING
    Lawyers   Lk 11:45-52
of FAMILY
    Abraham   Gen 11:27-32
    Asher   1 Chr 7:20-40
    Baruch   *Bar 1:1-4
    Danites   Judg 18:27-31
    David   Ruth 4:13-22;
                 2 Sam 3:1-16
    Elimelech   Ruth 1:1-18
    Esau   Gen 36:1-19
    Ezra   *2 Esd 1:1-3
    Isaac   Gen 25:19-26
    Israel   Ex 1:1-7

of FAMILY (cont'd)

Jacob	Gen 35:22b-26; 46:8-27
Jesus	Lk 3:23-38
Job	Job 1:2-3
Joseph	Gen 42:7-17
Judah	Gen 38:1-11
Judahites	1 Chr 9:1-16
Judith	*Jdt 8:1-8
Levites	Neh 12:22-23
Mattathias	*1 Mc 2:1-5
Moses	Num 1:20-46; 3:1-4
Noah	Gen 10:1-32
Pharaoh	1 Kgs 9:24
Priests	Neh 12:12-21
Rehoboam	2 Chr 10:1-12:16
Saul	1 Sam 14:47-52
Seir	Gen 36:20-30
Shem	Gen 11:10-26
Tobit	*Tb 1:1-2

COVENANT with

God	Ex 2:23b-25

INSTRUCTION on

God	Gen 25:19-26
Solomon	Prov 1:8-9

of MESSIANIC FIGURE

Jesus	Mt 1:1-17

of FEAR
  of ENVIRONMENT

Israelites	Num 13:26b-33; Deut 1:19-46
Moses	Ex 2:11-15

  INSTRUCTION on

David	Ps 34:11-14

through FEAR
  of DEITY

God	Prov 2:1-22
Mankind	Ps 111:10; Prov 1:7
Sirach	*Sir 1:11-20; 2:7-11; 19:20-24

of FOLLOWER
  through OBEDIENCE

Jesus	1 Jn 2:1-6

  through SUFFERING

God	*2 Esd 16:51-78

  in VICTORY

Disciples	Jn 8:21-59

  through WISDOM

Holy Spirit	1 Cor 12:4-11

  WITNESS to

Onesimus	Col 4:7-9
Paul	2 Thes 3:17-18
Tychicus	Col 4:7-9

of FULFILLMENT
  through DEITY

Egyptians	Ex 7:1-7

  INSTRUCTION on

Holy Spirit	Jn 14:25-26

  through MESSIANIC FIGURE

Jesus	Mt 17:1-8; Mk 9:2-8; Lk 9:28-36

of PROPHECY

Agabus	Acts 11:27-30
Isaiah	Mt 13:10-17
Jeremiah	Jer 44:29-30
Jesus	Mk 11:1-10; Lk 19:28-38

SCRIPTURES on

Disciples	Jn 2:12-22

SELF-REALIZATION of

Paul	1 Cor 13:8-13

of GOOD
  of DEITY

Job	Job 1:6-8; 2:1-3
Mankind	Ps 1:4-6

  in ENVIRONMENT

Ungodly Men	*Wis 2:12-20

of GRACE
  of DEITY

Habakkuk	Hab 2:12-14; 17

  INSTRUCTION on

Jesus	Lk 10:23-24

GRATITUDE for
  of DEITY

Daniel	Dan 2:20-23

of GUILT
  INSTRUCTION on

Jesus	Jn 9:1-41

  SELF-REALIZATION of

Pharisees	Mt 21:45-46

of HATE
  of MESSIANIC FIGURE

People	Jn 7:1-14

of HEALING
  by DEITY

Jesus	Lk 8:40-56

  INSTRUCTION on

Father	Prov 4:20-27

  by MESSIANIC FIGURE

Jesus	Mk 5:25-34

of HERESY
  through FALSE BELIEF

Jesus	Jn 16:1-4

  INSTRUCTION on

Isaiah	Is 48:1-22

  REVELATION on

Smyrna	Rev 2:8-11

of HOPE
  INSTRUCTION on

Paul	1 Cor 13:4-7
Solomon	Prov 23:15-24:22

HUMILITY in
  INSTRUCTION on

Josiah	2 Kgs 22:3-20
Solomon	Prov 11:1-31

of IDOLATRY
  through FALSE BELIEF

Daniel	*Bel 1:10-20
Jeremiah	*Jer 6:45-59

of **IGNORANCE**
Baruch	*Bar 3:15-23
Bildad	Job 18:1-4
God	Ps 82:2-7
Jeremiah	Jer 5:20-25
Jesus	Jn 10:1-18
Job	Job 28:1-13; 14-22
Paul	Gal 4:8-11
Preacher	Eccl 11:1-8
Sirach	*Sir 20:9-17; 18-23; 21:8-28; 22:7-15; 16-18; 27:8-15; 33:4-6; 34:1-8; 41:14-23; 42:8
Solomon	Prov 15:1-33; 17:1-28; 21:1-31; 22:22-23:14; 26:1-28; 27:1-27; 29:1-27; *Wis 3:10-19; 4:10-20

results in **JOY**
Paul	1 Cor 13:4-7
Solomon	Prov 3:1-35; 10:1-32; 23:15-24:22; 27:1-27; 29:1-27

of **JUSTICE**
Solomon	Prov 2:1-22; 28:1-28

of **LIFE**
John	1 Jn 5:13-21
Preacher	Eccl 7:1-22
Solomon	Prov 9:7-12; 13:1-25
Wisdom	Prov 8:32-36

of **LOVE**
Paul	1 Cor 13:8-13

of **OLD AGE**
Sirach	*Sir 8:1-19; 42:8

of **OPPRESSION**
Solomon	Prov 29:1-27

of **ORDER**
Joshua	Josh 18:1-10

of **PATIENCE**
Paul	1 Cor 13:4-7; Phil 4:1-9
Sirach	*Sir 1:22-30

of **POLITICS**
Jephthah	Judg 11:12-28
Moses	Num 13:17b-20

of **POVERTY**
Solomon	Prov 29:1-27

of **PRIDE**
Paul	1 Cor 8:1-3

concerning **PRUDENCE**
John	1 Jn 2:12-17
Preacher	Eccl 7:1-22
Sirach	*Sir 37:7-26

concerning **PRUDENCE** (cont'd)
Solomon	Prov 13:1-25; 14:1-35; 25:1-28
Wisdom	Prov 8:1-21

of **SADNESS**
Preacher	Eccl 1:12-2:26

of **SHARING**
Paul	1 Thes 5:25-28

SPIRIT (of heart)
Jesus	Lk 8:16-18; 12:1-12; Jn 14:25-26
Paul	Rom 2:1-24; 1 Cor 4:1-5

of **SUFFERING**
Paul	2 Cor 1:8-11

of **TEMPERANCE**
Peter	2 Pet 1:5-7
Preacher	Eccl 12:12-14
Sirach	*Sir 4:11-19
Solomon	Prov 29:1-27

of **VICTORY**
Solomon	Prov 23:15-24:22

of **VIOLENCE**
Esther	Esth 2:19-23
Moses	Num 13:17b-20
Solomon	*Wis 7:7-14

of **WISDOM**
Baruch	*Bar 3:9-14; 24-37; 4:1-4
Eliphaz	Job 15:7-11
God	Hos 6:4-6
Holy Spirit	Jn 14:25-26
Hosea	Hos 14:9
Jesus	Mt 7:24-27; Lk 6:46-49
Job	Job 28:1-13; 14-22
Nebuchadnezzar	Dan 4:18
Preacher	Eccl 1:2-11; 7:1-22; 8:1-9; 10-17; 12:8-11
Psalmist	Ps 49:1-4
Sirach	*Sir 1:1-10; 11-20; 22-30; 3:17-31; 4:11-19; 5:1-6:1; 6:18-37; 8:1-19; 9:14-18; 10:26-11:1; 14:20-27; 15:1-10; 18:27-33; 19:20-24; 20:1-8; 9-17; 18-23; 24-31; 21:8-28; 22:16-18; 24:1-34; 25:3-6;

REVELATION on (cont'd)

	Ezek 39:17-24; 25-29
Mankind	Ezek 38:14-16; 17-23; 39:1-16
Philistines	Ezek 25:15-17

TRADITION of

John	*1 Mc 16:18-24
Moses	Deut 1:1-5

of LIFE
    by DEITY

David	Ps 16:9-11; 39:4-6
Israelites	Hos 13:4-6
Jeremiah	Jer 1:4-10

    in ENVIRONMENT

Danites	Judg 18:1-6
Israelites	Num 21:10-20; 22:1
Moses	Deut 1:19-46

    of FOLLOWER

Jesus	2 Cor 4:7-12

    INSTRUCTION on

John	1 Jn 5:13-21
Preacher	Eccl 7:1-22
Solomon	Prov 9:7-12; 13:1-25
Wisdom	Prov 8:32-36

    MEDITATION on

Jesus	Mk 11:11

    PROPHECY of

Ezekiel	Ezek 11:22-25

    REVELATION on

Jesus	Jn 1:1-18
Job	Job 39:1-4

    TRADITIONs of

Kohath	Num 4:1-20

of LOVE

Maiden	Song 1:7

    of DEITY

Believers	1 Jn 4:7-12
Jesus	Jn 10:1-18

    of FOLLOWERs

God	1 Cor 8:1-3
Timothy	1 Thes 3:1-10

    INSTRUCTION on

Paul	1 Cor 13:8-13

    MEDITATION on

Daughters	Song 5:9

    in MISSION

Jesus	Jn 13:1-20

    REVELATION on

Israelites	Is 49:1-26

of MARRIAGE

Israelites	Ezra 10:20-44
Priests	Ezra 10:16-19

MEDITATION on
    of DEATH

Paul	2 Tim 4:6-8

    of EVIL

Jesus	Mt 22:15-22; Mk 12:13-17; Lk 20:19-26

    of IGNORANCE

Jeremiah	Jer 5:1-14

of LIFE

Jesus	Mk 11:11

of LOVE

Daughters	Song 5:9

of SERVICE

Psalmist	Ps 121:1

of VICTORY

Paul	2 Tim 4:6-8

by MESSIANIC FIGURE

Disciples	Mt 14:28-33
Jesus	Mt 11:27; Jn 2:23-25; 7:1-14; 18:1-11
People	Jn 7:1-14

concerning OPPRESSION

Demons	Mk 1:32-24; Lk 4:40-41

of MESSIANIC FIGURE
    ACCEPTANCE of

Jesus	Jn 2:23-25; 6:60-71
Peter	Mt 16:13-20

    of EVIL

Pharisees	Lk 5:17-26
Scribes	Mt 9:1-8; Mk 2:1-12

    FAITH in

Disciples	Jn 16:29-33
Peter	Mk 8:27-30; Lk 9:18-22

    FAMILY of

Jesus	Mt 1:1-17

    FULFILLMENT through

Jesus	Mt 17:1-8; Mk 9:2-8; Lk 9:28-36

    concerning IGNORANCE

People	Jn 7:25-31
Pharisees	Jn 8:12-20

    concerning MARRIAGE

Jesus	Jn 4:1-26

    WITNESS to

Demons	Mk 3:7-12
Peter	Mk 8:27-30; Lk 9:18-22
Shepherds	Lk 2:1-20

of MISSION
    of LOVE

Jesus	Jn 13:1-20

    OBEDIENCE in

Jonah	Jon 3:1-10

    WITNESS to

Jeremiah	Jer 6:27-30
Paul	Acts 20:1-4; 5-16; 21:1-14; 15-26; Rom 15:25-33; Tit 1:1-4
Peter	2 Pet 1:12-15
Tychicus	Eph 6:21-22

of OBEDIENCE
    to DEITY

Jesus	Jn 8:21-59; 14:27-31
Psalmist	Ps 119:33-40

through **OBEDIENCE**
  of **FOLLOWER**
    Jesus   1 Jn 2:1-6

OBEDIENCE to
  INSTRUCTION on
    Darius   *1 Esd 6:7-26
    God   Ex 6:28-30
    Israelites   Is 50:1-11
    Jesus   Jn 13:1-20
    Paul   2 Tim 3:14-17
    Solomon   Prov 22:17-21
  MEDITATION on
    Psalmist   Ps 119:25-32;
                97-104
  in **MISSION**
    Jonah   Jon 3:1-10
  REVELATION on
    Ananias   Acts 9:1-19
    Cornelius   Acts 10:1-11:18
    Philadelphians Rev 3:7-13
    Wise Men   Mt 2:1-12
  SELF-REALIZATION of
    Jesus   Lk 2:41-52

of **OLD AGE**
  INSTRUCTION on
    Sirach   *Sir 8:1-19;
                42:8

ONENESS in
  Maiden   Song 6:2-3

of **OPPRESSION**
  by **DEITY**
    Israelites   Ex 2:23b-25;
                Acts 6:8-8:3
  INSTRUCTION on
    Solomon   Prov 29:1-27
  by **MESSIANIC FIGURE**
    Demons   Mk 1:32-34;
                Lk 4:40-41

of **ORDER**
  by **DEITY**
    God   Ps 87:4-6
  in **ENVIRONMENT**
    Israelites   Num 3:40-51
  INSTRUCTION on
    Joshua   Josh 18:1-10
  REVELATION on
    Ezekiel   Ezek 40:6-16;
                17-19;
                20-27;
                28-37;
                38-43;
                44-47;
                48-49;
                41:1-4;
                5-11;
                12;
                13-15a;
                15b-26;
                42:1-10a;
                10b-12;
                13-14;
                15-20;
                47:1-12
  TRADITION of
    Samuel   1 Sam 7:2-17

in **WORSHIP**
  Women   1 Cor 14:34-40

of **PARADOX**
  in **ENVIRONMENT**
    Samsom   Judg 14:10-20

of **PATIENCE**
  INSTRUCTION on
    Paul   1 Cor 13:4-7;
                Phil 4:1-9
    Sirach   *Sir 1:22-30
  REVELATION on
    Ephesus   Rev 2:1-7
    Habakkuk   Hab 2:1-4
    Israelites   Is 49:1-26
    Thyatira   Rev 2:18-29

of **POLITICS**
    David   1 Chr 27:1-31
  in **ENVIRONMENT**
    Romans   *1 Mc 8:1-32
  INSTRUCTION on
    Jephthah   Judg 11:12-28
    Moses   Num 13:17b-20
  REVELATION on
    Daniel   Dan 2:24-45

of **POVERTY**
  INSTRUCTION on
    Solomon   Prov 29:1-27
  REVELATION on
    Smyrna   Rev 2:8-11

PRAISE of
    Solomon   1 Kgs 4:29-34
  of **DEITY**
    Isaiah   Is 28:23-29
    Mankind   Ps 48:9-14
    Shepherds   Lk 2:1-20
  INSTRUCTION on
    Baruch   *Bar 3:24-37
    Jesus   Lk 4:14-15
    Preacher   Eccl 9:1-16;
                17-10:20
    Sirach   *Sir 1:11-20;
                4:11-19;
                6:18-37;
                10:26-11:1;
                14:20-27;
                15:1-10;
                20:24-31;
                24:1-34;
                37:7-26;
                39:1-11
    Solomon   *Wis 6:12-25;
                7:7-14;
                15-8:1;
                2-21
  of **MESSIANIC FIGURE**
    Disciples   Mt 14:28-33
  in **WORSHIP**
    Crowd   Mt 15:29-31

of **PRIDE**
    Elihu   Job 32:11-14
  INSTRUCTION on
    Paul   1 Cor 8:1-3

PROPHECY of
  of **ACCEPTANCE**
    Isaiah   Is 29:17-24
    Zedekiah   Jer 32:1-8
  of **BLASPHEMY**
    Gentiles   Mk 10:32-34
  of **CAPTIVITY**
    Jesus   Mk 10:32-34;
                         Lk 18:31-34
  of **DEATH**
    Jesus   Mt 16:21-28;
                         Mk 8:31-33;
                         10:32-34;
                         Lk 5:33-35;
                         9:18-22;
                         13:31-33
  of **DESTRUCTION**
    Edomites   Obad 1:5-9
  of **EVIL**
    Judahites   Jer 17:1-4
  is **FULFILLed**
    Agabus   Acts 11:27-30
    Isaiah   Mt 13:10-17
    Jeremiah   Jer 44:29-30
    Jesus   Mk 11:1-10;
                         Lk 19:28-38

  of **IGNORANCE**
    Disciples   Lk 18:31-34
    Egyptians   Is 19:1-15
    Isaiah   Is 29:9-12
    Jeremiah   Jer 14:17-18
  of **KILLING**
    Jesus   Jn 16:1-4
  of **LIFE**
    Ezekiel   Ezek 11:22-25
  of **PRUDENCE**
    Isaiah   Is 28:1-13
  of **REJECTION**
    Isaiah   Is 31:1-3
    Israelites   Jer 6:16-21
    Jesus   Mk 8:31-33;
                         Lk 9:18-22;
                         Jn 16:1-4
    Scribes   Mt 17:9-13;
                         Mk 9:9-13
  of **SACRIFICE**
    Jesus   Mt 20:17-19;
                         Lk 18:31-34

  of **SUFFERING**
    Agabus   Acts 11:27-30
    Jesus   Mt 16:21-28;
                         17:9-13;
                         Mk 8:31-33;
                         9:9-13;
                         10:32-34;
                         Lk 9:18-22;
                         18:31-34
  concerning **WISDOM**
    Isaiah   Is 28:1-13;
                         52:13-53:12
  of **WITNESS**
    Holy Spirit   Mk 13:9-13
    Jesus   Lk 21:7-19
    Unbelievers 1 Cor 14:13-25

of **PRUDENCE**
  INSTRUCTION on
    John   1 Jn 2:12-17

INSTRUCTION on (cont'd)
    Preacher   Eccl 7:1-22
    Sirach   *Sir 37:7-26
    Solomon   Prov 13:1-25;
                         14:1-35;
                         25:1-28
    Wisdom   Prov 8:1-21
  PROPHECY of
    Isaiah   Is 28:1-13

REJECTION of
    Gedaliah   Jer 40:13-16
    Rehoboam   1 Kgs 12:1-20;
                         2 Chr 10:1-12:16
  of **FALSE BELIEF**
    Paul   Col 2:1-5;
                         1 Tim 6:20-21
    Sirach   *Sir 34:1-8
  INSTRUCTION on
    Baruch   *Bar 3:9-14
    Job   Job 16:1-6;
                         21:28-34
    Wisdom   Prov 1:20-33;
                         8:32-36
  of **MESSIANIC FIGURE**
    Jesus   Jn 18:1-11

of **REJECTION**
  of **DEITY**
    Galatian   Gal 4:8-11
    Israelites   Ex 16:1-21;
                         Num 14:26-38
  PROPHECY of
    Isaiah   Is 31:1-3
    Israelites   Jer 6:16-21
    Jesus   Mk 8:31-33;
                         Lk 9:18-22;
                         Jn 16:1-4
    Scribes   Mt 17:9-13;
                         Mk 9:9-13
  REVELATION on
    Judahites   Jer 3:6-11
    Mankind   Rev 9:13-21

of **REPENTANCE**
  of **DEITY**
    Manasseh   2 Chr 33:1-25
    Pharaoh   Gen 12:9-13:1
  REVELATION on
    Abimelech   Gen 20:1-18
    Israelites   Ezek 43:6-12

REVELATION on
  of **ANXIETY**
    Daniel   Dan 7:28
    Ethiopians   Ezek 30:6-9
  of **CAPTIVITY**
    Daniel   Dan 11:21-45
  of **DEATH**
    Joseph   Mt 2:13-15;
                         19-23
    Moses   Deut 31:14-23
  of **DESTRUCTION**
    Daniel   Dan 9:1-3
  of **DIGNITY**
    King   Ezek 28:11-19
  of **DISCIPLESHIP**
    Holy Spirit   1 Cor 2:10-16
  of **DISOBEDIENCE**
    Jeremiah   Jer 18:1-12

of ENEMY
Moses	Num 13:1-17a

of EVIL
God	*2 Esd 16:51-78
Sardis	Rev 3:1-6

of FAITH
Pergamum	Rev 2:12-17
Thyatira	Rev 2:18-19

of HERESY
Smyrna	Rev 2:8-11

of IGNORANCE
Daniel	Dan 12:5-13
Isaiah	Is 6:1-13
Job	Job 38:1-3
John	Rev 10:1-11; 19:11-16

of INDIFFERENCE
Laodicea	Rev 3:14-22

of JOY
Israelites	Is 51:17-52:12

of KILLING
Daniel	Dan 11:21-45

of LEADERSHIP
Ezekiel	Ezek 33:30-33
Israelites	Deut 4:15-31; Is 51:17-52:12; Ezek 39:17-24; 25-29
Mankind	Ezek 38:14-16; 17-23; 39:1-16
Philistines	Ezek 25:15-17

of LIFE
Jesus	Jn 1:1-18
Job	Job 39:1-4

of LOVE
Israelites	Is 49:1-26

of OBEDIENCE
Ananias	Acts 9:1-19
Cornelius	Acts 10:1-11:18
Philadelphians	Rev 3:7-13
Wise Men	Mt 2:1-12

of ORDER
Ezekiel	Ezek 40:6-16; 17-19; 20-27; 28-37; 38-43; 44-47; 48-49; 41:1-4; 5-11; 12; 13-15a; 15b-26; 42:1-10a; 10b-12; 13-14; 15-20; 47:1-12

of PATIENCE
Ephesus	Rev 2:1-7
Habakkuk	Hab 2:1-4
Israelites	Is 49:1-26
Thyatira	Rev 2:18-29

of POLITICS
Daniel	Dan 2:24-45

of POVERTY
Smyrna	Rev 2:8-11

of REJECTION
Judahites	Jer 3:6-11
Mankind	Rev 9:13-21

of REPENTANCE
Abimelech	Gen 20:1-18
Israelites	Ezek 43:6-12

of SACREDNESS
Israelites	Ezek 43:6-12

of SERVICE
Thyatira	Rev 2:18-29

of SUFFERING
Ephesus	Rev 2:1-7
Smyrna	Rev 2:8-11
Thyatira	Rev 2:18-29

of VICTORY
Abraham	Gen 15:1-21

of WILL
God	Mt 11:25-26
Jesus	Mt 11:27

concerning WISDOM
Believers	Dan 12:5-13
Daniel	Dan 11:21-45; 12:1-4
Gabriel	Dan 8:15-25; 9:20-23
Jeremiah	Jer 16:19-21
John	Rev 13:11-18

of WITNESS
Amos	Amos 1:1-2
God	Is 41:1-42:4
Habakkuk	Hab 1:1
Haggai	Hag 1:1-11
Hosea	Hos 1:1
Isaiah	Is 1:1
Jeremiah	Jer 30:1-3; 46:1
Joel	Joel 1:1
Jonah	Jon 1:1-17; 3:1-10
Malachi	Mal 1:1
Micah	Mic 1:1
Nahum	Nah 1:1-9
Obadiah	Obad 1:1a
Prophets	Num 12:4-10
Zechariah	Zech 1:1-6; 4:6b-10a
Zephaniah	Zeph 1:1

REWARDs of
Daniel	Dan 2:46-49

of DEITY
Hannah	1 Sam 2:1-10
Solomon	1 Kgs 8:22-53

in ENVIRONMENT
Hiram	1 Kgs 9:10-14

INSTRUCTION on
Father	Prov 4:1-9
Preacher	Eccl 9:17-10:20
Sirach	*Sir 51:13-30
Solomon	Prov 19:1-29

of SACREDNESS
REVELATION on
Israelites	Ezek 43:6-12

TRADITION of
Nehemiah	*2 Mc 2:9-15
Priests	*1 Esd 5:36-43

of SACRIFICE
PROPHECY of
Jesus	Mt 20:17-19; Lk 18:31-34

in **WORSHIP**		
Bethelites	Zech 7:1-3	
Egyptians	Is 19:18-25	
of **SADNESS**		
INSTRUCTION on		
Preacher	Eccl 1:12-2:26	
SCRIPTURES on		
of **FULFILLMENT**		
Disciples	Jn 2:12-22	
of **WISDOM**		
Jesus	Lk 24:13-35	
of **WITNESS**		
Dositheus	*Esth 11:1	
Isaiah	Mt 13:10-17;	
	Acts 28:17-31	
Paul	Acts 28:17-31	
SELF-REALIZATION of		
of **DEATH**		
Jesus	Mt 26:36-46;	
	Mk 14:32-42;	
	Lk 22:39-46	
Ungodly Men	*Wis 5:1-14	
of **ENEMY**		
Jesus	Mt 26:36-46;	
	Mk 14:32-42	
of **EVIL**		
David	Ps 51:3-12	
of **FULFILLMENT**		
Paul	1 Cor 13:8-13	
of **GUILT**		
Pharisees	Mt 21:45-46	
of **IGNORANCE**		
Agur	Prov 30:1-14	
of **OBEDIENCE**		
Jesus	Lk 2:41-52	
concerning **WISDOM**		
Preacher	Eccl 1:12-2:26	
of **WITNESS**		
John the Baptist	Jn 3:31-36	
Leper	Mk 1:40-45	
of **SERVICE**		
MEDITATION on		
Psalmist	Ps 121:1	
REVELATION on		
Thyatira	Rev 2:18-29	
in **WORSHIP**		
Levites	1 Chr 9:17-34;	
	Neh 12:24-26	
of **SHARING**		
INSTRUCTION on		
Paul	1 Thes 5:25-28	
of **SPIRIT**		
Zophar	Job 20:1-3	
by **DEITY**		
God	Prov 17:1-28	
Jesus	Lk 10:21-22	
Mankind	1 Sam 16:1-13;	
	1 Kgs 8:22-53;	
	1 Chr 28:1-29:30;	
	2 Chr 5:1-7:10	
of **SPIRIT** (of one's heart)		
INSTRUCTION on		
Jesus	Lk 8:16-18;	
	12:1-12;	

INSTRUCTION on (cont'd)		
	Jn 14:25-26	
Paul	Rom 2:1-24;	
	1 Cor 4:1-5	
of **MESSIANIC FIGURE**		
Jesus	Jn 2:23-25	
concerning **STEALING**		
through **FALSE BELIEF**		
Lawyers	Lk 11:45-52	
concerning **SUFFERING**		
David	Ps 13:1-4;	
	38:3-10	
Israelites	Ex 3:7-10;	
	Neh 9:9-11	
of **FOLLOWERs**		
God	*2 Esd 16:51-78	
INSTRUCTION on		
Paul	2 Cor 1:8-11	
PROPHECY of		
Agabus	Acts 11:27-30	
Jesus	Mt 16:21-28;	
	17:9-13;	
	Mk 8:31-33;	
	9:9-13;	
	10:32-34;	
	Lk 9:18-22;	
	18:31-34	
REVELATION on		
Ephesus	Rev 2:1-7	
Smyrna	Rev 2:8-11	
Thyatira	Rev 2:18-29	
of **TEMPERANCE**		
INSTRUCTION on		
Peter	2 Pet 1:5-7	
Preacher	Eccl 12:12-14	
Sirach	*Sir 4:11-19	
Solomon	Prov 29:1-27	
of **TRADITIONs**		
of **FAMILY**		
Abraham	Gen 11:27-32	
Asher	1 Chr 7:20-40	
Baruch	*Bar 1:1-4	
Danites	Judg 18:27-31	
David	Ruth 4:13-22;	
	2 Sam 3:1-16	
Elimelech	Ruth 1:1-18	
Esau	Gen 36:1-19	
Ezra	*2 Esd 1:1-3	
Isaac	Gen 25:19-26	
Israel	Ex 1:1-7	
Jacob	Gen 35:22b-26;	
	46:8-27	
Jesus	Lk 3:23-38	
Judah	Gen 38:1-11	
Mattathias	*1 Mc 2:1-5	
Moses	Num 3:1-4	
Noah	Gen 10:1-32	
Seir	Gen 36:20-30	
Shem	Gen 11:10-26	
Tobit	*Tb 1:1-2	
of **IGNORANCE**		
Rehoboam	*Sir 47:23-25	
of **LEADERSHIP**		
John	*1 Mc 16:18-24	
of **LIFE**		
Kohath	Num 4:1-20	

of **ORDER**
  Samuel   1 Sam 7:2-17
of **SACREDNESS**
  Nehemiah   *2 Mc 2:9-15
  Priests   *1 Esd 5:36-43
of **VICTORY**
  Israelites   Josh 12:1-6;
                   7-24;
                   2 Sam 23:8-39;
                   1 Chr 11:1-12:40
concerning **WISDOM**
  Bildad   Job 8:8-9
  Sirach   *Sir Intro
  Solomon   *Sir 47:12-22
of **WITNESS**
  Maccabeus   *2 Mc 2:19-32;
                   15:37-39

of **VICTORY**
  through **DEITY**
    Egyptians   Ex 14:15-22
  of **FOLLOWERs**
    Disciples   Jn 8:21-59
  MEDITATION on
    Paul   2 Tim 4:6-8
  REVELATION on
    Abraham   Gen 15:1-21
  TRADITIONs of
    Israelites   Josh 12:1-6;
                   7-24;
                   2 Sam 23:8-39;
                   1 Chr 11:1-12:40

VICTORY through
INSTRUCTION on
  Solomon   Prov 23:15-24:22

of **VIOLENCE**
  through **DEITY**
    Israelites   Judg 3:1-6
  in **ENVIRONMENT**
    Mordecai   *Esth 12:1-16
  INSTRUCTION on
    Esther   Esth 2:19-23

of **WEALTH**
  Maiden   Song 8:11-12
  in **ENVIRONMENT**
    Solomon   1 Kgs 7:1-12;
                   10:14-29
  INSTRUCTION on
    Moses   Num 13:17b-20
    Solomon   *Wis 7:7-14

of **WILL**
  of **DEITY**
    Believers   Eph 1:3-14;
                   5:15-20
    God   Lk 16:14-15
    Jesus   Lk 9:46-48
    Paul   Col 1:9-14
  of **MESSIANIC FIGURE**
    People   Jn 7:1-14
  REVELATION on
    God   Mt 11:25-26
    Jesus   Mt 11:27

on **WISDOM**
  Daniel   Dan 4:4-9
  Ezra   Ezra 7:11-12
  Solomon   1 Kgs 4:29-34

of **DEITY**
  Asaph   Ps 73:13-20
  Elihu   Job 34:21-28
  Ezra   *2 Esd 14:19-48
  God   Ps 19:4c-6;
                   33:13-19;
                   94:8-11;
                   139:1-6;
                   13-18;
                   Prov 5:15-23;
                   Is 28:23-29;
                   40:12-31;
                   1 Cor 3:18-23;
                   Heb 4:1-13;
                   1 Jn 3:19-24
  Job   Job 28:23-28
  Sennacherib   2 Kgs 19:9b-37
in **ENVIRONMENT**
  Job   Job 12:7-12
  Solomon   1 Kgs 10:14-29
of **FOLLOWERs**
  Holy Spirit   1 Cor 12:4-11
INSTRUCTION on
  Baruch   *Bar 3:9-14;
                   24-37;
                   4:1-4
  Eliphaz   Job 15:7-11
  God   Hos 6:4-6
  Holy Spirit   Jn 14:25-26
  Hosea   Hos 14:9
  Jesus   Mt 7:24-27;
                   Lk 6:46-49
  Job   Job 28:1-13;
                   14-22
  Nebuchadnezzar Dan 4:18
  Preacher   Eccl 1:2-11;
                   7:1-22;
                   8:1-9;
                   10-17;
                   12:8-11
  Psalmist   Ps 49:1-4
  Sirach   *Sir 1:1-10;
                   11-20;
                   22-30;
                   3:17-31;
                   4:11-19;
                   5:1-6:1;
                   18-37;
                   8:1-19;
                   9:14-18;
                   10:26-11:1;
                   14:20-27;
                   15:1-10;
                   18:27-33;
                   19:20-24;
                   20:1-8;
                   9-17;
                   18-23;
                   24-31;
                   21:8-28;
                   22:16-18;
                   24:1-34;
                   25:3-6;
                   7-11;
                   27:8-15;
                   32:14-24;
                   33:4-6;
                   16-23;
                   34:9-12;
                   37:7-26;
                   38:24-34;

KNOWLEDGE (cont'd)

through **SERVICE**
Levites | 1 Chr 9:17-34; Neh 12:24-26

of **WORSHIP's**
ORDER
Women | 1 Cor 14:34-40

of **YOUTH**
INSTRUCTION on
Paul | Gal 4:1-3

LAW

ACCEPTANCE of
of **DEITY**
Peter | 2 Pet 3:1-2
Psalmist | Ps 93:5
INSTRUCTION on
Moses | Deut 4:1-14
Paul | Acts 24:1-27 26:1-32

PROPHECY of
Isaiah | Is 2:1-5
SCRIPTURES on
John | Rev 22:6-21

ALIENATION through
caused by **FALSE BELIEF**
Jesus | Gal 5:2-6
REVELATION on
Moses | Num 5:1-4

concerning **ANGER**
INSTRUCTION on
Jesus | Mt 5:21-26

BLASPHEMY against
through **FALSE BELIEF**
Israelites | Deut 18:9-22

concerning **BLASPHEMY**
Moses | Ex 22:21-31; Lev 19:1-37
INSTRUCTION on
God | Ex 20:1-17
Moses | Deut 5:1-21
REVELATION on
Moses | Lev 18:1-30; 24:10-23

of **BLESSING**
INSTRUCTION on
God | Ps 94:12-15
Moses | Deut 11:26-32
Solomon | Prov 3:1-35
MEDITATION on
Mankind | Ps 1:1-3

concerning **CAPTIVITY**
Moses | Ex 21:2-11
INSTRUCTION on
Moses | Deut 15:12-18; 23:15-25:19
Paul | Rom 7:1-6
REVELATION on
Moses | Lev 25:39-55

COMPASSION in
INSTRUCTION on
Jesus | Mt 12:9-14
Moses | Deut 23:15-25:1

CONDEMNATION of
Moses | Lev 11:1-47
through **FALSE BELIEF**
Moses | Lev 20:1-27
Paul | Col 2:16-23

CONDEMNATION through
INSTRUCTION on
Moses | Deut 11:26-32; 27:11-26
Paul | Rom 3:31-4:25; Gal 3:10-14

COVENANT of
DISOBEDIENCE to
Ephramites | Ps 78:9-20
Isaiah | Is 24:1-12
Israelites | Deut 29:16-29; Ezek 44:6-9; Hos 8:1-3
EVIL against
God | Ps 50:16-21
GOOD in
Sirach | *Sir 42:1-5
IDOLATRY against
Moses | Ex 34:12-28
LEADERSHIP through
Moses | *Sir 45:1-5
concerning **MARRIAGE**
Israelites | Ezra 10:1-6; Neh 10:28-30
OBEDIENCE to
Josiah | 2 Kgs 23:1-3; 2 Chr 34:1-35:2?
Judahites | 2 Kgs 23:1-3
REJECTION of
God | Heb 8:6-13
Israelites | Ezek 20:9-26
Jesus | Eph 2:11-22
Paul | Gal 4:21-26
SACREDNESS of
Moses | Ex 34:12-28
WISDOM in
Sirach | *Sir 24:1-34
WITNESS to
Israelites | Jer 31:31-34
concerning **COVETOUSNESS**
INSTRUCTION on
God | Ex 20:1-17
Moses | Deut 5:1-21; 7:17-26
Paul | Rom 7:7-13; 13:8-10

concerning **DEATH**
Elders | *Susa 1:60-64
Moses | Num 19:11-13
through **FALSE BELIEF**
Author | Heb 10:19-31
INSTRUCTION on
Moses | Deut 21:22-23
Paul | Rom 7:1-6; 2 Cor 3:7-11; Gal 2:17-19

REVELATION on
  Moses   Lev 7:22-27;
                          Num 19:14-22;
                          27:1-11
  Priests   Lev 21:1-22:33;
                          Ezek 44:15-31
TRADITION of
  Jesus   Jn 18:28-19:16
of **DEITY**
  ACCEPTANCE of
    Peter   2 Pet 3:1-2
    Psalmist   Ps 93:5
  DISCIPLESHIP to
    Moses   Deut 10:1-11
  DISOBEDIENCE to
    Babylonians 2 Kgs 17:24-41
    Israelites   Neh 9:16-18;
                      26-31;
                      Dan 9:4-19
    Jason   *2 Mc 4:7-17
    Judahites   Jer 7:21-28;
                      29-8:3
    Pharisees   Mt 15:3-9;
                      Mk 7:1-23
  FAITH in
    Psalmist   Ps 119:41-48;
                      65-72
  FULFILLMENT of
    Israelites   *2 Esd 2:33-41;
                      *Bar 2:1-10
  GOOD in
    David   Ps 19:7-10
    God   Ps 119:137-144
    Psalmist   Ps 119:169-176
  HOPE in
    Psalmist   Ps 119:73-80;
                      145-152
  JOY in
    Mankind   Ps 1:1-3;
                      112:1
    Psalmist   Ps 119:161-168
  LEADERSHIP through
    Psalmist   Ps 119:105-112
  LOVE of
    Believers   1 Jn 4:19-5:5
    God   1 Jn 3:19-24
    Psalmist   Ps 119:33-40;
                      65-72;
                      73-80;
                      89-96;
                      105-112;
                      113-120;
                      121-128;
                      137-144;
                      153-160;
                      161-168
  OBEDIENCE to
    David   2 Sam 22:1-51;
                      Ps 40:6-10
    God   Eccl 12:12-14
    Israelites   Ps 105:43-45
    Psalmist   Ps 119:41-48;
                      49-56;
                      57-64;
                      65-72;
                      81-88;
                      97-104;
                      105-112;
                      113-120;

OBENIENCE to (cont'd)
  Psalmist   121-128;
                      129-136;
                      137-144;
                      153-160;
                      161-168;
                      169-176
  Sirach   *Sir 1:22-30;
                      17:1-14;
                      32:14-24
PEACE through
  Psalmist   Ps 119:161-168
PRAISE of
  David   Ps 19:7-10;
                      56:10-13
  Ezra   Neh 9:12-15
                      *2 Esd 9:26-37
  Psalmist   Ps 119:9-16;
                      89-96;
                      129-136;
                      161-168;
                      169-176
REJECTION of
  Israelites   Jer 6:16-21;
                      *2 Esd 2:33-41
  Judahites   Jer 8:8-13;
                      Amos 2:4-5
WISDOM in
  Ezra   *1 Esd 8:1-7
  Psalmist   *Ps 119:73-80;
                      97-104
  Sirach   *Sir 6:18-37
WITNESS to
  God   Rom 3:21-30
  Psalmist   Ps 119:9-16;
                      41-48

of **DESTRUCTION**
  INSTRUCTION on
    Moses   Deut 20:10-18

of **DISCIPLESHIP**
  INSTRUCTION on
    God   1 Cor 14:34-40

DISCIPLESHIP to
  of **DEITY**
    Moses   Deut 10:1-11

DISOBEDIENCE to
  Daniel   Dan 6:10-15
  Disciples   Mt 12:1-8;
                      15:1-2;
                      Mk 2:23-28;
                      7:1-23;
                      Lk 6:1-5
  Israelites   Num 15:32-36;
                      Ezra 9:1-2;
                      Mal 3:6-12
  Sinners   1 Tim 1:8-11
of **COVENANT**
  Ephraimites Ps 78:9-20
  Isaiah   Is 24:1-12
  Israelites   Deut 29:16-29;
                      Ezek 44:6-9;
                      Hos 8:1-3
of **DEITY**
  Babylonians 2 Kgs 17:24-41
  Israelites   Neh 9:16-18;
                      26-31;

REVELATION on (cont'd)
    Israelites   Ezek 45:10-12;
                      47:13-20;
                      48:1-7;
                      8-22;
                      23-29;
                      30-35
    Priests   Ezek 46:19-24

PEACE through
  of DEITY
    Psalmist   Ps 119:161-168

concerning PIETY
  REVELATION on
    Israelites   Ezek 46:9-10
    Moses   Lev 24:1-4;
                      Num 9:1-14

concerning POVERTY
  Moses   Lev 5:5-13
  in ENVIRONMENT
    Levites   Lev 25:29-34
  INSTRUCTION on
    Moses   Deut 23:15-25:19
  REVELATION on
    Moses   Lev 25:25-28;
                      29-34;
                      35-38;
                      39-55;
                      27:1-34

PRAISE of
  of DEITY
    David   Ps 19:7-10;
                      56:10-13
    Ezra   Neh 9:12-15;
                      *2 Esd 9:26-37
    Psalmist   Ps 119:9-16;
                      89-96;
                      129-136;
                      161-168;
                      169-176
  INSTRUCTION on
    Asaph   Ps 81:1-5b
  in WORSHIP
    Psalmist   Ps 119:1-8;
                      57-64

concerning PURIFICATION
  INSTRUCTION on
    Jesus   Mt 8:2-4;
                      Mk 1:40-45;
                      Lk 5:12-16
    Moses   Deut 23:9-14
    Paul   Rom 2:25-3:20
  REVELATION on
    Moses   Lev 12:1-8;
                      13:1-59;
                      14:1-32;
                      33-54;
                      15:1-33;
                      16:29-34;
                      21:1-22:33;
                      Num 5:1-4
  TRADITION of
    Jesus   Lk 2:21-40
    Paul   Acts 21:15-26

REJECTION of
  of DEITY
    Israelites   Jer 6:16-21;
                      *2 Esd 2:33-41
    Judahites   Jer 8:8-13;
                      Amos 2:4-5
  through FALSE BELIEF
    Paul   Gal 6:11-18;
                      Col 2:16-23
  INSTRUCTION on
    Author   Heb 7:1-28;
                      10:1-18
    Jesus   Mt 9:16-17;
                      Mk 2:18-22;
                      Lk 5:36-39
    Moses   Deut 23:1-8
    Paul   Gal 2:15-16;
                      3:15-18
  by MESSIANIC FIGURE
    Jesus   Lk 13:10-17
  PROPHECY of
    Israelites   Hos 4:4-15
  as TRADITION
    Disciples   Mt 15:1-2

causing REPENTANCE
  SELF-REALIZATION of
    Josiah   2 Kgs 22:3-20;
                      2 Chr 34:1-35:27

REVELATION on
  Moses   Lev 19:1-37
  concerning CAPTIVITY
    Moses   Lev 25:39-55
  concerning DEATH
    Moses   Lev 7:22-27;
                      Num 19:14-22;
                      27:1-11
    Priests   Lev 21:1-22:33;
                      Ezek 44:15-31
  concerning FAMILY
    Moses   Ex 21:1;
                      Lev 18:1-30;
                      Num 27:1-11;
                      30:1-16
  concerning GUILT
    Moses   Lev 7:1-10
  concerning KILLING
    Moses   Num 35:16-25;
                      26-34
  concerning LIFE
    Moses   Lev 7:22-27;
                      17:10-14;
                      15-16;
                      18:1-30
    Solomon   1 Kgs 3:1-15
  concerningMARRIAGE
    Priests   Ezek 44:15-31
  concerning ORDER
    Ezekiel   Ezek 43:13-17
    Israelites   Ezek 45:10-12;
                      47:13-20;
                      48:1-7;
                      8-22;
                      23-29;
                      30-35
    Priests   Ezek 46:19-24

concerning **PIETY**
Israelites	Ezek 46:9-10
Moses	Lev 24:1-4;
	Num 9:1-14

concerning **POVERTY**
Moses	Lev 25:25-28;
	29-34;
	35-38;
	39-55;
	27:1-34

concerning **PURIFICATION**
Moses	Lev 12:1-8;
	13:1-59;
	14:1-32;
	33-54;
	15:1-33;
	16:29-34;
	21:1-22:33;
	Num 5:1-4

concerning **SACREDNESS**
Ezekiel	Ezek 44:4-5
Israelites	Ezek 48:8-22
Moses	Lev 20:1-27;
	21:1-22:33;
	23:1-4;
	5-8;
	15-22;
	23-25;
	26-32;
	33-44;
	24:5-9;
	25:1-7;
	20-22;
	26:1-46;
	27:1-34;
	Num 6:1-21
Prince	Ezek 44:1-3;
	46:1-8

concerning **SACRIFICE**
Moses	Ex 20:24-26;
	Lev 1:1-17;
	2:1-16;
	3:1-17;
	4:1-35;
	6:8-13;
	14-23;
	24-30;
	7:11-21;
	28-36;
	37-38;
	21:1-22:33;
	Num 15:22-31;
	19:1-10;
	29:7-11;
	12-40
Priests	Ezek 46:19-24
Prince	Ezek 46:11-15

concerning **SEX**
Moses	Lev 18:1-30;
	20:1-27

concerning **SHARING**
Israelites	Ezek 47:21-23
Prince	Ezek 46:16-18

concerning **TEMPERANCE**
Moses	Lev 11:1-47

concerning **VIOLENCE**
Moses	Lev 24:10-23

concerning **WEALTH**
Israelites	Ezek 45:10-12;
	47:21-23

concerning **WEALTH** (cont'd)
Moses	Lev 25:23-24
Prince	Ezek 46:16-18

concerning **REVENGE**
Jesus	Mt 5:38-42
Moses	Lev 19:1-37

SACREDNESS of
Moses	Ex 22:21-31;
	23:10-13

in **ENVIRONMENT**
Levites	Deut 18:1-8

INSTRUCTION on
Artaxerxes	Ezra 7:20-24
Ezra	Ezra 7:6-10;
	Neh 7:33b-8:2;
	3-8;
	13-18;
	*1 Esd 8:1-7;
	8-24;
	9:37-48
Jesus	Lk 13:10-17;
	16:16-18
Joshua	Josh 8:30-35
Moses	Ex 16:22-30;
	34:29-35;
	35:1-3;
	Deut 16:13-15;
	31:24-29
Paul	Rom 7:7-13

MESSIANIC FIGURE on
Jesus	Lk 14:1-6

REVELATION on
Ezekiel	Ezek 44:4-5
Israelites	Ezek 48:8-22
Moses	Lev 20:1-27;
	21:1-22:33;
	23:1-4;
	5-8;
	15-22;
	23-25;
	26-32;
	33-44;
	24:5-9;
	25:1-7;
	20-22;
	26:1-46;
	27:1-34;
	Num 6:1-21
Prince	Ezek 44:1-3;
	46:1-8

TRADITION of
Priest	Lev 21:1-22:33

concerning **SACRIFICE**
Moses	Ex 22:21-31;
	29:36b-42a;
	Lev 7:1-10;
	19:1-37;
	Num 28:3-8;
	9-10;
	11-15;
	16-25;
	26-31;
	29:1-6

INSTRUCTION on
Moses	Deut 16:1-8;
	26:1-11;
	12-15

REVELATION on
Moses   Ex 20:24-26;
    Lev 1:1-17;
    2:1-16;
    3:1-17;
    4:1-35;
    6:8-13;
    14-23;
    24-30;
    7:11-21;
    28-36;
    37-38;
    21:1-22:33;
    Num 15:22-31;
    19:1-10;
    29:7-11;
    12-40
Priests   Ezek 46:19-24
Prince   Ezek 46:11-15
in WORSHIP
High Priest   Heb 9:1-14

SELF-REALIZATION of
as GOOD
Paul   Rom 7:14-25
causing REPENTANCE
Josiah   2 Kgs 22:3-20;
    2 Chr 34:1-35:27

concerning SERVICE
Moses   Ex 21:2-11;
    23:1-9
Slaves   Lev 25:39-55
INSTRUCTION on
Ezra   Ezra 7:13-14
Moses   Deut 22:1-12;
    23:15-25:19
Slaves   Deut 15:12-18

concerning SEX
Moses   Ex 22:18-20;
    Lev 19:1-37
INSTRUCTION on
God   Ex 20:1-17
Jesus   Mt 5:27-30;
    19:16-22;
    Mk 10:17-22
Moses   Deut 5:1-21;
    22:13-30;
    23:15-25:19
Paul   Rom 13:8-10
REVELATION on
Moses   Lev 18:1-30;
    20:1-27

concerning SHARING
Moses   Ex 22:21-31
REVELATION on
Israelites   Ezek 47:21-23
Prince   Ezek 46:16-18
TRADITION of
David   1 Sam 30:1-31

concerning SPIRIT
INSTRUCTION on
Paul   Rom 2:25-3:20

concerning STEALING
Moses   Ex 21:33-22:17

INSTRUCTION on
God   Ex 20:1-17
Jesus   Mt 19:16-22;
    Mk 10:17-22
Moses   Deut 5:1-21;
    23:15-25:19
Nathan   2 Sam 12:1-31
Paul   Rom 13:8-10

concerning TEMPERANCE
INSTRUCTION on
God   Lev 10:1-20
REVELATION on
Moses   Lev 11:1-47

concerning TEMPTATION
Moses   Lev 19:1-37
INSTRUCTION on
Moses   Deut 27:11-26

TRADITION of
concerning DEATH
Jesus   Jn 18:28-19:16
concerning FAMILY
Boaz   Ruth 3:1-18;
    4:1-12
Judah   Gen 38:1-11
Ruth   Ruth 3:1-18
concerning IDOLATRY
Galatian   Gal 4:8-11
concerning MARRIAGE
Boaz   Ruth 4:1-12
Priest   Lev 21:1-22:33
concerning OBEDIENCE
Amaziah   2 Kgs 14:5-6
Corinthians   1 Cor 11:2-16
Judeans   Acts 15:1-5
Pharisees   Acts 15:1-5
Priests   Mt 27:3-10
concerning PURIFICATION
Jesus   Lk 2:21-40
Paul   Acts 21:15-26
concerning SACREDNESS
Priest   Lev 21:1-22:33
concerning SHARING
David   1 Sam 30:1-31

VICTORY in
INSTRUCTION on
Jesus   Jn 12:44-50

concerning VIOLENCE
Moses   Ex 21:12-17;
    18-32
INSTRUCTION on
Moses   Deut 20:19-20
REVELATION on
Moses   Lev 24:10-23

concerning WEALTH
INSTRUCTION on
Moses   Deut 15:1-11;
    23:15-25:19
REVELATION on
Israelites   Ezek 45:10-12;
    47:21-23
Moses   Lev 25:23-24
Prince   Ezek 46:16-18

in AUTHORITY (cont'd)

Jephthah	Judg 11:4-11
Jeroboam	1 Kgs 12:1-20; 2 Kgs 14:15-16; 23-29; 2 Chr 10:1-12:16; 13:1-22
Jesus	Col 2:6-15
Joash	2 Kgs 11:4-20; 21-12:3; 2 Chr 21:1-23:21; 24:1-27
John	*1 Mc 16:1-3
Jonathan	*1 Mc 9:28-31; 10:1-14
Joseph	Gen 41:1-57
Josiah	2 Kgs 21:19-26; 22:1-2; 2 Chr 33:1-25; 34:1-35:27
Jotham	2 Kgs 15:1-7; 32-38; 2 Chr 26:1-28:27
Manasseh	2 Kgs 20:12-21; 21:1-18; 2 Chr 32:1-33; 33:1-25
Menahem	2 Kgs 15:13-15; 16-22
Moses	Num 1:1-19
Nadab	1 Kgs 14:19-20; 15:25-32
Nehemiah	Neh 5:14-19
Omri	1 Kgs 16:15-22; 23-28
Pekah	2 Kgs 15:23-26; 27-31
Pekahiah	2 Kgs 15:16-22; 23-26
Rehoboam	1 Kgs 11:41-43; 14:21-24; 2 Chr 9:1-31
Samuel	1 Sam 8:1-22
Saul	1 Sam 11:1-5
Shallum	2 Kgs 15:8-12; 13-15
Simon	*1 Mc 13:1-11
Solomon	1 Kgs 2:5-12; 3:1-15; 4:1-6; 1 Chr 23:1-26:32; 2 Chr 1:1-17; 9:1-31
Tibni	1 Kgs 16:15-22
Tola	Judg 10:1-2
Uzziah	2 Chr 26:1-28:27
Zechariah	2 Kgs 14:23-29; 15:8-12
Zedekiah	2 Kgs 24:8-17; 18-25:7; 2 Chr 36:1-23; Jer 52:1-3
Zerubbabel	Hag 2:20-23
Zimri	1 Kgs 16:8-14; 15-22

over FOLLOWERs

Jesus	Mt 4:23-25; 1 Cor 11:2-16
Paul	Eph 1:1-2; Col 1:1-2

INSTRUCTION on

David	1 Kgs 2:1-4
Elisha	2 Kgs 9:1-13
Ezra	Ezra 7:25-26
Jesus	Mt 7:28-29
Joshua	Josh 1:12-18
Jotham	Judg 9:7-15
Moses	Deut 1:9-18; 16:18-20; 17:14-20
Nehemiah	Neh 7:1-3
Paul	1 Cor 11:2-16
Samuel	1 Sam 12:1-25
Solomon	1 Kgs 1:28-40

PROPHECY of

Balaam	Num 23:27-24:13
Believers	Rev 2:18-29
Deborah	Judg 4:4-5
Eliakim	Is 22:15-25
God	Jer 30:18-22
Isaiah	Is 15:1-16:14
Israelites	Hos 8:8-10
Jesus	Lk 1:26-38
Obadiah	Obad 1:17-21
Samuel	1 Sam 13:1-23

REVELATION on

Daniel	Dan 7:17-27; 8:15-25; 11:1-4; 5-20; 21-45
God	Jer 30:23-31:1
Isaiah	Is 6:1-13
Jeremiah	Jer 1:4-10; 16:19-21; 33:14-26
John	Rev 4:1-11; 12:1-6; 17:6b-18; 19:11-16
Moses	Num 27:12-23
Samuel	1 Sam 8:1-22

SELF-REALIZATION of

David	2 Sam 5:6-16; 1 Chr 14:1-17
Wisdom	Prov 8:1-21

AUTHORITY of
of MESSIANIC FIGURE

David	2 Sam 2:1-7; 5:1-5; 1 Chr 11:1-12:40
Jesus	Heb 1:2b-4; 5-14
Joshua	Num 27:12-23
Solomon	1 Chr 28:1-29:30
Zechariah	Zech 9:1-12

in MISSION

Paul	1 Tim 1:1-2

BEHAVIOR revealing
in ENVIRONMENT

Paul	Acts 13:13

INSTRUCTION on

Artaxerxes	Ezra 7:11-12
Lemuel	Prov 31:1-9

REVELATION on

Moses	Ex 12:1-14

COMMITMENT to
　of MESSIANIC FIGURE
　　Mankind　　　　　　Phil 2:5-11
　REVELATION on
　　Israelites　　　　　Ezek 20:5-8

in COMMUNITY
　　Deborah　　　　　　Judg 5:6-9
　　Esau　　　　　　　Gen 36:31-43
　　Kings　　　　　　　Gen 36:31-43
　　Moses　　　　　　　Ex 15:22-27
　PROPHECY of
　　Isaiah　　　　　　Is 3:1-7
　REVELATION on
　　Israelites　　　　　Jer 30:18-22;
　　　　　　　　　　　Ezek 37:15-28
　　Priests　　　　　　Ezek 44:15-31

CONFRONTATION with
　　Bathsheba　　　　　1 Kgs 1:15-21
　　David　　　　　　　1 Chr 11:1-12:40
　　Israelites　　　　　Num 16:1-2
　　Nathan　　　　　　1 Kgs 1:22-27

by COVENANT
　AUTHORITY of
　　David　　　　　　　2 Sam 5:1-5;
　　　　　　　　　　　1 Chr 11:1-12:40

through COVENANT
　ETERNAL
　　David　　　　　　　2 Sam 7:1-29;
　　　　　　　　　　　Ps 89:19-37
　of FIDELITY
　　Jehoiada　　　　　2 Kgs 11:4-20
　of LAW
　　Moses　　　　　　　*Sir 45:1-5
　PROMISE in
　　Jehoiada　　　　　2 Kgs 11:4-20;
　　　　　　　　　　　2 Chr 21:1-23:21

in the CREATION
　REVELATION on
　　John　　　　　　　Rev 12:1-6
　　Moses　　　　　　　Num 11:14-24a

by DEITY
　AUTHORITY of
　　God　　　　　　　Ps 47:5-9;
　　　　　　　　　　　66:5-7;
　　　　　　　　　　　93:1-2;
　　　　　　　　　　　103:19-22;
　　　　　　　　　　　Is 40:1-11;
　　　　　　　　　　　51:1-16;
　　　　　　　　　　　11:15-19;
　　　　　　　　　　　Rev 19:6-10
　　Israelites　　　　　Ex 15:1-18;
　　　　　　　　　　　Ps 77:11-20;
　　　　　　　　　　　Jer 31:31-34

from DEITY
　AUTHORITY for
　　Jesus　　　　　　　Mt 28:16-20;
　　　　　　　　　　　Acts 2:14-36;
　　　　　　　　　　　Eph 1:15-2:10;
　　　　　　　　　　　Phil 2:5-11
　　Judah　　　　　　Judg 1:1-21
　　King　　　　　　　Prov 21:1-31
　　Maccabeus　　　　*2 Mc 15:6-10
　　Mankind　　　　　Jer 32:26-44;
　　　　　　　　　　　Zech 14:1-21

AUTHORITY for (cont'd)
　　Moses　　　　　　　Ex 32:30-35
　　Paul　　　　　　　Gal 1:1-5
　　Solomon　　　　　Ps 72:8-14

of DEITY
　ETERNAL
　　David　　　　　　　Ps 110:1-4
　　God　　　　　　　Ex 15:1-18;
　　　　　　　　　　　Deut 33:1-29;
　　　　　　　　　　　Ps 9:5-8;
　　　　　　　　　　　10:12-18;
　　　　　　　　　　　29:10-11;
　　　　　　　　　　　145:10-13a;
　　　　　　　　　　　146:10;
　　　　　　　　　　　Jer 10:1-16;
　　　　　　　　　　　Lam 5:1-22;
　　　　　　　　　　　Rev 11:15-19
　　King　　　　　　　Ps 61:6-7
　FIDELITY of
　　Believers　　　　　Heb 13:1-25
　　Israelites　　　　　Deut 31:1-8;
　　　　　　　　　　　Hos 2:16-20;
　　　　　　　　　　　21-23

　JUDGMENT on
　　David　　　　　　　Ps 139:23-24
　　God　　　　　　　Is 33:17-24
　KNOWLEDGE of
　　Ahab　　　　　　　1 Kgs 20:1-43
　　Ammonites　　　　Ezek 25:1-7
　　Edomites　　　　　Ezek 35:1-15
　　Egyptians　　　　Ex 7:1-7;
　　　　　　　　　　　14:1-14;
　　　　　　　　　　　Ezek 29:6-9a;
　　　　　　　　　　　9b-16;
　　　　　　　　　　　17-21;
　　　　　　　　　　　30:6-9;
　　　　　　　　　　　13-19;
　　　　　　　　　　　20-26;
　　　　　　　　　　　32:1-16
　　Ezekiel　　　　　Ezek 11:1-13;
　　　　　　　　　　　15:1-8;
　　　　　　　　　　　24:15-24;
　　　　　　　　　　　25-27;
　　　　　　　　　　　33:23-29
　　God　　　　　　　Heb 8:6-13
　　Israelites　　　　　Ex 5:6-14;
　　　　　　　　　　　Ezek 6:1-7;
　　　　　　　　　　　8-10;
　　　　　　　　　　　11-14;
　　　　　　　　　　　7:1-27;
　　　　　　　　　　　12:1-16;
　　　　　　　　　　　17-20;
　　　　　　　　　　　13:17-23;
　　　　　　　　　　　16:53-63;
　　　　　　　　　　　17:11-21;
　　　　　　　　　　　20:9-26;
　　　　　　　　　　　40-44;
　　　　　　　　　　　22:1-16;
　　　　　　　　　　　28:24-26;
　　　　　　　　　　　34:17-22;
　　　　　　　　　　　25-31;
　　　　　　　　　　　36:8-15;
　　　　　　　　　　　37:1-14;
　　　　　　　　　　　15-28;
　　　　　　　　　　　Hos 2:16-20;
　　　　　　　　　　　Joel 3:16b-21
　　Joel　　　　　　　Joel 2:18-27
　　Mankind　　　　　1 Kgs 8:54-61;

in **AUTHORITY** (cont'd)

Pekah	2 Kgs 15:23-26
Rehoboam	1 Kgs 11:41-43
Samuel	1 Sam 8:1-22
Saul	1 Sam 11:1-15
Simon	*1 Mc 13:1-11
Tola	Judg 10:1-2

BEHAVIOR of

Paul	Acts 13:13

over **COMMUNITY**

Moses	Ex 15:22-27

JUDGMENT of

Israelites	Ps 122:3-5

KNOWLEDGE of

Israelites	Num 33:5-15; 16-36; 37-49

PROMISE of

David	1 Kgs 1:11-14

RESPECT for

David	2 Sam 8:1-18
Tobit	*Tb 1:10-22

SECURITY in

Raphael	*Tb 5:1-21

SIN against

Israelites	Ezek 34:1-10

EQUALITY of
of **DEITY**

God	Is 46:1-13

of **FOLLOWERs**

Jesus	Jn 13:1-20; 15:18-25
Paul	2 Cor 12:11-13

ETERNAL
COVENANT of

David	2 Sam 7:1-29; Ps 89:19-37

of **DEITY**

David	Ps 110:1-4
God	Ex 15:1-18; Deut 33:1-29; Ps 9:5-8; 10:12-18; 29:10-11; 145:10-13a; 146:10; Jer 10:1-16; Lam 5:1-22; Rev 11:15-19
King	Ps 61:6-7

of **MESSIANIC FIGURE**

Jesus	Heb 1:5-14
King	Ps 45:2-9

PROPHECY of

Jesus	Lk 1:26-38

REVELATION on

Daniel	Dan 7:2-14
Isaiah	Is 60:1-22

FALSE BELIEF in
revealing **disHONESTY**

Satan	Rev 12:7-9

revealing **SIN**

Satan	1 Jn 3:4-10

FIDELITY of
to **COVENANT**

Jehoiada	2 Kgs 11:4-20

to **DEITY**

Believers	Heb 13:1-25
Israelites	Deut 31:1-8; Hos 2:16-20; 21-23

of **FOLLOWERs**

Holy Spirit	Gal 5:25-6:6

INSTRUCTION on

Bishop	Tit 1:9-16
Jotham	Judg 9:7-15

REVELATION on

John	Rev 19:11-16

of **FOLLOWERs**
ELECTION to

Joshua	Deut 31:1-8

EQUALITY of

Jesus	Jn 13:1-20; 15:18-25
Paul	2 Cor 12:11-13

FIDELITY of

Holy Spirit	Gal 5:25-6:6

KNOWLEDGE of

Jesus	Jn 10:1-18

concerning **LAW**

Holy Spirit	Gal 5:16-21

MOTIVATION for

Paul	1 Cor 10:23-11:1

PROMISE of

Jesus	Mt 16:13-20

PROVIDENCE through

Israelites	Num 10:11-28; 33-36

RITE by

Paul	Acts 14:19-28

SIGNS of

Ezekiel	Ezek 1:4-28

revealing **TRUTH**

Paul	1 Cor 4:14-21

FREEDOM through
REVELATION on

Cyrus	Is 44:24-45:13

HONESTY of
in **MISSION**

Paul	2 Cor 1:15-22

REVELATION on

Daniel	Dan 11:21-45

disHONESTY of
revealing **FALSE BELIEF**

Satan	Rev 12:7-9

INSTRUCTION on

Artaxerxes	Ezra 7:11-12
Lemuel	Prov 31:1-9

in **AUTHORITY**

David	1 Kgs 2:1-4
Elisha	2 Kgs 9:1-13
Ezra	Ezra 7:25-26
Jesus	Mt 7:28-29
Joshua	Josh 1:12-18
Jotham	Judg 9:7-15
Moses	Deut 1:9-18; 16:18-20; 17:14-20
Nehemiah	Neh 7:1-3
Paul	1 Cor 11:2-16
Samuel	1 Sam 12:1-25
Solomon	1 Kgs 1:28-40

for **JUDGMENT**
James	Jas 3:1-12
Moses	Deut 1:9-18; 16:18-20

concerning **LAW**
Moses	Deut 17:14-20
Samuel	1 Sam 10:17-27

concerning **MEDIATION**
Jethro	Ex 18:13-26

concerning **PROVIDENCE**
Joshua	Josh 24:1-13
Moses	Deut 29:1-15

as **QUALITY OF LIFE**
Elders	1 Pet 5:1-5

in **RITE**
David	1 Kgs 1:28-40

as **VIRTUE**
Solomon	Prov 11:1-31

JUDGMENT of
in **ENVIRONMENT**
Israelites	Ps 122:3-5

INSTRUCTION on
James	Jas 3:1-12
Moses	Deut 1:9-18; 16:18-20

JUDGMENT on
of **DEITY**
David	Ps 139:23-24
God	Is 33:17-24

PROPHECY of
Deborah	Judg 4:4-5
Isaiah	Is 24:18c-23; 51:17-52:12

REVELATION on
Egyptians	Ezek 32:1-16
God	Is 41:1-42:4

KNOWLEDGE of
Daughters	Song 3:6-11
David	1 Chr 27:1-31
Israelites	Num 33:1-4

of **DEITY**
Ahab	1 Kgs 20:1-43
Ammonites	Ezek 25:1-7
Edomites	Ezek 35:1-15
Egyptians	Ex 7:1-7; 14:1-14; Ezek 29:6-9a; 9b-16; 17-21; 30:6-9; 13-19; 20-26; 32:1-16
Ezekiel	Ezek 11:1-13; 15:1-8; 24:15-24; 25-27; 33:23-29
God	Heb 8:6-13
Israelites	Ex 5:6-14; Ezek 6:1-7; 8-10; 11-14; 7:1-27; 12:1-16; 17-20; 13:17-23;

of **DEITY** (cont'd)
Israelites	16:53-63; 17:11-21; 20:9-26; 40-44; 22:1-16; 28:24-26; 34:17-22; 25-31; 36:8-15; 37:1-14; 15-28; Hos 2:16-20; Joel 3:16b-21
Joel	Joel 2:18-27
Mankind	1 Kgs 8:54-61; Ps 59:13c-15; Ezek 36:22-32; 37-38
Moabites	Ezek 25:8-11
Moses	Ex 7:14-25
Prophetesses	Ezek 13:17-23
Sidon	Ezek 28:20-23
Tyre	Ezek 26:1-6

in **ENVIRONMENT**
Israelites	Num 33:5-15; 16-36; 37-49

of **FOLLOWER**
Jesus	Jn 10:1-18

REVELATION on
Ezekiel	Ezek 33:30-33
Israelites	Deut 4:15-31; Is 51:17-52:12; Ezek 39:17-24; 25-29
Mankind	Ezek 38:14-16; 17-23; 39:1-16
Philistines	Ezek 25:15-17

TRADITION of
John	*1 Mc 16:18-24

LAW concerning
of **FOLLOWER**s
Holy Spirit	Gal 5:16-21

INSTRUCTION on
Moses	Deut 17:14-20
Samuel	1 Sam 10:17-27

in **LAW**
COVENANT of
Moses	*Sir 45:1-5

by **DEITY**
Psalmist	Ps 119:105-112

MEDIATION of
INSTRUCTION on
Jethro	Ex 18:13-26

REVELATION on
Moses	Num 3:5-10

SCRIPTURES on
Isaiah	Mk 1:2-8

MEDITATION on
through **PRAYER**
Moses	Num 11:11-13

of **MESSIANIC FIGURE**
  AUTHORITY in
    David   2 Sam 2:1-7;
                    5:1-5;
                    1 Chr 11:1-12:40
    Jesus   Heb 1:2b-4;
                    5-14
    Joshua   Num 27:12-23
    Solomon   1 Chr 28:1-29:30
    Zechariah   Zech 9:1-12
  COMMITMENT to
    Mankind   Phil 2:5-11
  ELECTION of
    David   1 Sam 16:1-13;
                    Ps 78:67-72;
                    89:19-37
    Jehu   2 Kgs 9:1-13
    Moses   Ex 3:7-10
    Saul   1 Sam 9:1-10:16;
                    11:1-15
    Solomon   1 Chr 28:1-29:30
  through **PROVIDENCE**
    Jesus   Lk 1:26-38
  in **RITE**
    Saul   1 Sam 10:17-27
  in **SALVATION**
    God   2 Kgs 13:1-9
  SIGNS of
    Zechariah   Zech 4:1-6a;
                    10b-14

in **MISSION**
  AUTHORITY of
    Paul   1 Tim 1:1-2
  ELECTION to
    Paul   2 Tim 1:1-2
  HONESTY of
    Paul   2 Cor 1:15-22
  PROMISE of
    Jesus   Mt 4:18-22;
                    Mk 1:16-20
  RESPECT for
    Servants   1 Tim 6:1-2b
  reveals **TRUTH**
    Paul   1 Thes 2:1-12

MOTIVATION for
  of **FOLLOWERs**
    Paul   1 Cor 10:23-11:1

in **NEW AGE**
  REVELATION on
    Daniel   Dan 8:15-25

PRAYER for
  by **DEITY**
    Agur   Prov 30:1-14
    David   Ps 5:8-10
  INSTRUCTION on
    Paul   2 Thes 3:1-2;
                    1 Tim 2:1-7
  MEDITATION on
    Moses   Num 11:11-13

through **PRESENCE**
  of **DEITY**
    David   2 Sam 5:6-16
    Ezra   Ezra 7:27-28
    Gideon   Judg 6:33-35
    Israelites   Lev 25:39-55;
                    Num 23:13-26

of **DEITY** (cont'd)
    Jesus   Lk 4:1-13;
                    Col 1:18-20
    Joshua   Josh 6:22-27
    Othniel   Judg 3:7-11
  PROPHECY of
    David   2 Sam 23:1-7
  TRADITION of
    Solomon   *Wis 18:1-4

PROMISE of
  through **COVENANT**
    Jehoiada   2 Kgs 11:4-20;
                    2 Chr 21:1-23:21
  of **DEITY**
    David   1 Kgs 2:1-4
  in **ENVIRONMENT**
    David   1 Kgs 1:11-14
  of **FOLLOWER**
    Jesus   Mt 16:13-20
  in **MISSION**
    Jesus   Mt 4:18-22;
                    Mk 1:16-20
  REVELATION on
    Solomon   1 Kgs 9:1-9;
                    2 Chr 7:11-22
  SCRIPTURES on
    Prophet   Mt 2:1-12

PROPHECY of
  in **AUTHORITY**
    Balaam   Num 23:27-24:1
    Believers   Rev 2:18-29
    Deborah   Judg 4:4-5
    Eliakim   Is 22:15-25
    God   Jer 30:18-22
    Isaiah   Is 15:1-16:14
    Israelites   Hos 8:8-10
    Jesus   Lk 1:26-38
    Obadiah   Obad 1:17-21
    Samuel   1 Sam 13:1-23
  in **COMMUNITY**
    Isaiah   Is 3:1-7
  for **ETERNITY**
    Jesus   Lk 1:26-38

PROVIDENCE in
    Moses   Ex 23:20-33
  of **DEITY**
    Adversaries Ps 83:9-18
    David   2 Sam 22:1-51;
                    Ps 18:43-45;
                    23:1-4;
                    139:7-12
    Ephraimites Ps 78:9-20
    God   Ps 136:10-22;
                    Prov 10:1-32
    Isaiah   Is 63:7-64:12
    Israelites   Ex 13:17-22;
                    32:30-35;
                    Deut 8:11-20;
                    Josh 5:13-15;
                    Neh 9:12-15;
                    Ps 105:43-45;
                    107:4-9
    Paul   2 Cor 3:4-6

through **PROVIDENCE**
  for **FOLLOWERs**
    Israelites   Num 10:11-28;
                    33-36

INSTRUCTION on
| Joshua | Josh 24:1-13 |
| Moses | Deut 29:1-15 |

of MESSIANIC FIGURE
| Jesus | Lk 1:26-38 |

PROPHECY of
| Isaiah | Is 9:2-7 |
| Jeremiah | Jer 23:1-8 |

REVELATION on
David	Ezek 34:23-24
Isaiah	Is 55:1-13;
	58:1-14
Israelites	Is 48:1-22;
	Jer 3:14b-18;
	Ezek 20:9-26;
	32-39
John	Rev 7:9-17

PUNISHMENT of
PROPHECY of
| Coniah | Jer 22:24-30 |
| Isaiah | Is 9:8-10:4 |

REVELATION on
Ezekiel	Ezek 21:25-27
Solomon	1 Kgs 11:1-13
Zechariah	Zech 10:3-12
Zephaniah	Zeph 1:8-9

as QUALITY OF LIFE
| Joseph | Gen 39:1-23 |

of DEITY
| God | Is 40:12-31 |

INSTRUCTION on
| Elders | 1 Pet 5:1-5 |

RECONCILIATION through
| David | 2 Sam 19:8b-43 |

PROPHECY of
| Micah | Mic 2:12-13 |
| Obadiah | Obad 1:17-21 |

REVELATION on
| Israelites | Hos 1:10-2:1 |
| Judahites | Zech 7:4-8:23 |

in WORSHIP
| Nehemiah | Neh 13:10-14 |

RESPECT for
David	2 Sam 8:1-18;
	1 Chr 18:1-20:8
Israelites	Josh 4:9-19
Job	Job 29:21-25
Moses	Ex 22:21-31
Tobit	*Tb 1:10-22

of DEITY
| Moses | Deut 31:30-32:47 |

INSTRUCTION on
Author	Heb 13:1-25
Paul	2 Cor 8:16-24;
	1 Thes 5:12-22;
	1 Tim 5:17-25;
	6:1-2b
Peter	1 Pet 2:13-17;
	5:1-5
Servants	1 Pet 2:18-20

in MISSION
| Servants | 1 Tim 6:1-2b |

SCRIPTURES on
| Paul | Acts 22:30-23:11 |

through RESURRECTION
by DEITY
| Jesus | Acts 5:17-42 |

REVELATION on
in AUTHROITY
Daniel	Dan 7:17-27;
	8:15-25;
	11:1-4;
	5-20;
	21-45
God	Jer 30:23-31:1
Isaiah	Is 6:1-13
Jeremiah	Jer 1:4-10;
	16:19-21;
	33:14-26
John	Rev 4:1-11;
	12:1-6;
	17:6b-18;
	19:11-16
Moses	Num 27:12-23
Samuel	1 Sam 8:1-22

in COMMUNITY
Israelites	Jer 30:18-22;
	Ezek 37:15-28
Priests	Ezek 44:15-31

in the CREATION
| John | Rev 12:1-6 |
| Moses | Num 11:14-24a |

for ETERNITY
| Daniel | Dan 7:2-14 |
| Isaiah | Is 60:1-22 |

in NEW AGE
| Daniel | Dan 8:15-25 |

RITE of
of FOLLOWERs
| Paul | Acts 14:19-28 |

INSTRUCTION on
| David | 1 Kgs 1:28-40 |

of MESSIANIC FIGURE
| Saul | 1 Sam 10:17-27 |

SALVATION through
of DEITY
God	Is 33:17-24
Israelites	Judg 2:11-19
Psalmist	Ps 80:1-3

of MESSIANIC FIGURE
| God | 2 Kgs 13:1-9 |

SECURITY in
of DEITY
| Asaph | Ps 73:21-28 |

in ENVIRONMENT
| Raphael | *Tb 5:1-21 |

REVELATION on
God	Is 42:5-17
John	Rev 6:12-17
Moses	Num 14:25

SIGNS of
of FOLLOWERs
| Ezekiel | Ezek 1:4-28 |

of MESSIANIC FIGURE
| Zechariah | Zech 4:1-6a; |
| | 10b-14 |

PROPHECY of
| Israelites | Hos 3:1-5 |

REVELATION on	
Daniel	Dan 9:24-27
Israelites	Ex 40:34-38;
	Ezek 19:1-4;
	5-9
John	Rev 9:1-12;
	21:22-27
John the Baptist	Mt 11:7-15
Zechariah	Zech 6:1-8
SELF-REALIZATION of	
Joseph	Gen 37:1-11

SIN of	
Israelites	Mic 3:1-12
in **ENVIRONMENT**	
Israelites	Ezek 34:1-10
through **FALSE BELIEF**	
Satan	1 Jn 3:4-10
INSTRUCTION on	
Solomon	Prov 28:1-28
PROPHECY of	
Isaiah	Is 9:8-10:4
Jerusalemites	Zeph 3:1-5

TRUTH revealed by	
of **FOLLOWER**s	
Paul	1 Cor 4:14-21
in **MISSION**	
Paul	1 Thes 2:1-12

VIRTUE in	
INSTRUCTION on	
Solomon	Prov 11:1-31
PROPHECY of	
Isaiah	Is 9:2-7;
	32:1-8

LIFE

AUTHORITY over	
by **DEITY**	
Bildad	Job 25:1-6
David	Ps 29:3-9
Elihu	Job 33:8-12;
	34:10-15
Eliphaz	Job 5:8-17
Ezra	*2 Esd 6:35-59
God	Job 26:5-14;
	Ps 24:1-2;
	50:7-15;
	66:1-4;
	90:1-12;
	Is 13:1-22;
	Amos 4:13;
	9:5-6;
	Hab 3:3-15;
	Mt 22:23-33;
	Mk 12:18-27;
	Lk 20:27-40
Hannah	1 Sam 2:1-10
Job	Job 9:1-7;
	8-13;
	12:7-12;
	13-25
Judith	*Jdt 16:1-17
Mankind	Ps 8:3-8
Sirach	*Sir 17:1-14;
	33:7-15
Solomon	*Wis 16:1-14

in **ENVIRONMENT**	
God	Gen 1:9-13;
	24-31;
	2:18-20;
	Job 37:1-13
Man	Gen 1:24-31;
	2:18-20;
	9:1-7
INSTRUCTION on	
God	Gen 1:20-23;
	Ex 9:13-35;
	Ps 75:2-5
Solomon	Prov 18:1-24
of **MESSIANIC FIGURE**	
Jesus	Col 1:15-17
REVELATION on	
Ezekiel	Ezek 18:1-4
Isaiah	Is 54:1-17
Job	Job 39:5-8;
	9-12;
	13-18;
	19-25;
	40:15-24;
	41:1-12;
	13-34
John	Rev 13:11-18
SCRIPTURES on	
Hosea	Rom 9:14-29
SELF-REALIZATION of	
Jesus	Jn 17:1-5

BEHAVIOR revealing	
INSTRUCTION on	
Jeremiah	Jer 29:1-23
Maiden	Song 8:14
Preacher	Eccl 3:1-8

BELIEF concerning	
INSTRUCTION on	
Jesus	Jn 8:21-59
Paul	Rom 6:1-14
SCRIPTURES on	
Jesus	Jn 7:37-52

COMMITMENT to	
INSTRUCTION on	
Paul	Rom 8:5-13

CONVERSION to	
REVELATION on	
Ezekiel	Ezek 18:21-24;
	25-29
Israelites	Ezek 18:30-32

COVENANT of	
ELECTION to	
Ezekiel	Ezek 16:8-14
MEDIATION through	
Jesus	Heb 12:12-29
PROVIDENCE through	
God	Gen 1:24-31
RECONCILIATION through	
Author	Heb 9:15-22;
	10:19-31
Jesus	Mt 26:17-30;
	Mk 14:22-26
Moses	Ex 24:1-18
RITE of	
Jesus	Mk 14:22-26
SIGNS of	
Jesus	1 Cor 11:23-26

through PROVIDENCE (cont'd)

David	Ps 17:13-14; Ps 22:12-21; 30:1-5; 40:13-17; 138:7-8
Elihu	Job 33:23-25; 29-30
Elijah	1 Kgs 17:1-24; 19:1-21
Ephraimites	Ps 78:9-20
God	Ps 33:13-19; 37:23-40; 46:8-11; 104:10-13; 14-18; 19-23; 104:27-30; 111:5-9; 136:23-25; 147:7-11; Prov 20:1-30; Eccl 3:9-15; Is 27:2-6; Jn 1:1-18; 2 Cor 5:1-5
Hezekiah	Is 38:1-22
Isaac	Gen 26:1-11; 12-31
Israelites	Ex 9:1-7; 13-35; 10:21-23; 11:1-10; 12:1-14; 13:17-22; 16:1-21; 17:1-7; Deut 8:1-10; Neh 9:12-15; Ps 78:21-31; 105:37-42; Is 1:4-9; 10:17-19; 43:14-44:5
Jesus	Jn 1:1-18
Job	Job 12:7-12
King	Ps 21:1-7; 61:6-7
Mankind	Prov 16:1-33; Eccl 9:1-16
Peter	2 Pet 1:3-4
Psalmist	Ps 49:13-15

through RECONCILIATION

Believers	Rom 8:28-39

RESPECT for

God	Prov 10:1-32; 14:1-35; 19:1-29

RESURRECTION through

Jesus	Jn 6:25-59

through SALVATION

Asaph	Ps 73:21-28
Believers	Ps 91:1-13; 97:10-12
Daniel	Dan 6:16-23
David	Ps 56:10-13; 70:1-5; 86:11-13; 138:7-8; 143:7-12

through SALVATION (cont'd)

Elihu	Job 33:29-30
God	Ps 68:19-23
Peter	Acts 12:1-25
Psalmist	Ps 66:8-12; 116:1-11; 118:15-21; 119:81-88; 89-96

through SECURITY

Baruch	Jer 36:20-26
Believers	Ps 46:1-3; 91:14-16
David	Ps 25:16-21; 36:5-9; 41:1-3
Israelites	Neh 9:12-15; 19-21
Jeremiah	Jer 11:18-12:6; 36:20-26
Job	Job 2:4-6
Levites	Num 18:8-20; Deut 10:1-11; 18:1-8; Josh 13:29-33; Ezek 44:15-31
Solomon	Ps 72:8-14

VIRTUE in

Eliphaz	Job 4:17-21

DEITY over

AUTHORITY of

Bildad	Job 25:1-6
David	Ps 29:3-9
Elihu	Job 33:8-12; 34:10-15
Eliphaz	Job 5:8-17
Ezra	*2 Esd 6:35-59
God	Job 26:5-14; Ps 24:1-2; 50:7-15; 66:1-4; 90:1-12; Is 13:1-22; Amos 4:13; 9:5-6; Hab 3:3-15; Mt 22:23-33; Mk 12:18-27; Lk 20:27-40
Hannah	1 Sam 2:1-10
Job	Job 9:1-7; 9:8-13; 12:7-12; 13-25
Judith	*Jdt 16:1-17
Mankind	Ps 8:3-8
Sirach	*Sir 17:1-14; 33:7-15

DESIRE for

MEDITATION on

Paul	Phil 3:4-16

SELF-REALIZATION of

Jesus	Mt 26:36-46; Mk 14:32-42

through ELECTION
in COVENANT

Ezekiel	Ezek 16:8-14

PROPHECY of
Israelites   Amos 5:4-6
REVELATION on
Ezekiel   Ezek 18:5-9;
                                 14-20
Isaiah   Is 55:1-13
John   Rev 20:4-6
of **FOLLOWERs**
KNOWLEDGE of
Jesus   2 Cor 4:7-12
in **NEW AGE**
Jesus   Jn 13:36-38
PROMISE of
God   Eph 6:1-4
through **RECONCILIATION**
Jesus   Rom 5:6-11;
                                 7:1-6;
                                 Eph 1:3-14
Peter   1 Pet 1:13-2:3
through **SALVATION**
Jesus   2 Tim 2:8-13
SECURITY in
Holy Spirit   2 Cor 5:1-5
of **FREEDOM**
Jehoiachin   Jer 52:31-34
INSTRUCTION on
Paul   1 Cor 7:17-24

INSTRUCTION on
through **FIDELITY**
David   Ps 34:11-14
Israelites   Ezek 20:9-26
of **FREEDOM**
Paul   1 Cor 7:17-24;
                                 Gal 4:27-31
in **NEW AGE**
Holy Spirit   Jn 3:1-21
Jesus   Mt 7:13-14
Paul   Rom 5:12-21;
                                 1 Cor 7:25-35
through **PROVIDENCE**
God   Gen 9:1-7
through **RECONCILIATION**
Author   Heb 9:1-7
Jesus   Heb 13:1-25
through **RESURRECTION**
Jesus   Jn 5:19-47
Paul   Rom 8:5-13;
                                 1 Cor 15:35-41;
                                 42-50
through **RITE**
Moses   Ex 13:3-10
through **SALVATION**
Jesus   Mt 16:21-28;
                                 Mk 8:34-9:1;
                                 Lk 9:23-27;
                                 Jn 5:19-47
Paul   Rom 1:16-17;
                                 6:1-14;
                                 8:5-13
through **SECURITY**
Joshua   Josh 20:1-9
Moses   Deut 19:1-13
over **SIN**
Paul   Rom 6:1-14
Preacher   Eccl 7:1-22

through **STEWARDSHIP**
John   1 Jn 3:11-18
through **TRUTH**
Jesus   Jn 8:12-20;
                                 9:1-41;
                                 14:1-14
Paul   2 Cor 4:7-12
of **VIRTUE**
Solomon   Prov 10:1-32;
                                 12:1-28;
                                 15:1-33;
                                 21:1-31

JUDGMENT on
from **DEITY**
God   Eccl 11:9-12:7
Jesus   2 Tim 4:1-5
Mankind   1 Chr 15:1-16:43
                                 Ps 105:7-15
INSTRUCTION on
Peter   1 Pet 4:1-6
MEDITATION on
Jesus   1 Cor 15:20-28
PROPHECY of
Isaiah   Is 51:17-52:12;
                                 66:1-16
REVELATION on
Israelites   Ezek 34:17-22
Joel   Joel 3:12-16a
John   Rev 14:17-20;
                                 20:11-15

KNOWLEDGE of
Moses   Deut 1:1-5
from **DEITY**
David   Ps 16:9-11;
                                 39:4-6
Israelites   Hos 13:4-6
Jeremiah   Jer 1:4-10
in the **ENVIRONMENT**
Danites   Judg 18:1-6
Israelites   Num 21:10-20;
                                 22:1
Moses   Deut 1:19-46
of **FOLLOWERs**
Jesus   2 Cor 4:7-12
INSTRUCTION on
John   1 Jn 5:13-21
Preacher   Eccl 7:1-22
Solomon   Prov 9:7-12;
                                 13:1-25
Wisdom   Prov 8:32-36
MEDITATION on
Jesus   Mk 11:11
PROPHECY of
Ezekiel   Ezek 11:22-25
REVELATION on
Jesus   Jn 1:1-18
Job   Job 39:1-4
TRADITION of
Kohath   Num 4:1-20

LAW concerning
INSTRUCTION on
Baruch   *Bar 3:9-14
Jesus   Lk 10:25-28
Moses   Deut 4:1-14;
                                 14:3-21;
                                 15:19-23;

INSTRUCTION on (cont'd)
    Moses   22:1-12;
        30:15-20;
        31:30-32:47
    Paul   Rom 9:30-10:21;
        Gal 3:10-14
    Solomon   Prov 19:1-29
REVELATION on
    Moses   Lev 7:22-27;
        17:10-14;
        15-16;
        18:1-30
    Solomon   1 Kgs 3:1-15

through MEDIATION
  of COVENANT
    Jesus   Heb 12:12-29
  from DEITY
    Aaron   Num 16:36-50
    Jesus   1 Tim 2:1-7
  in WORSHIP
    Jesus   Heb 10:19-31

MEDITATION on
  through PROVIDENCE
    Jeremiah   Lam 3:1-66

MESSIANIC FIGURE over
  AUTHORITY of
    Jesus   Col 1:15-17

in MISSION
  revealing TRUTH
    Holy Spirit   2 Cor 3:4-6
    Jesus   Eph 5:3-14

MOTIVATION for
  INSTRUCTION on
    Father   Prov 4:20-27

in NEW AGE
  from DEITY
    Mankind   Rev 21:1-8
  of FOLLOWERs
    Jesus   Jn 13:36-38
  INSTRUCTION on
    Holy Spirit   Jn 3:1-21
    Jesus   Mt 7:13-14
    Paul   Rom 5:12-21;
        1 Cor 7:25-35

  PROPHECY of
    Jesus   Mt 26:57-68;
        Mk 14:53-65;
        Jn 7:32-36

  REVELATION on
    Jesus   Rev 1:1-3
    John   Rev 22:1-5

PRAYER for
    David   Ps 13:1-4;
        18:4-6;
        30:6-10;
        31:13-18;
        59:11;
        64:1-2;
        86:1-7
    Elijah   1 Kgs 17:1-24
    Hezekiah   2 Kgs 20:1-11;
        Is 38:1-22

PRAYER for (cont'd)
    Psalmist   Ps 88:3-9;
        119:25-32;
        33-40;
        105-112;
        145-152;
        153-160;
        169-176
    Rebekah   Gen 25:19-26
    Solomon   Ps 72:5-7;
        15-17
  through MEDITATION
    Jeremiah   Jer 18:18-23

through PRESENCE
  of DEITY
    God   Is 66:1-16
    Hagar   Gen 16:11-16
    Israelites   Jer 30:10-11
    Manoah   Judg 13:15-23
    Simeon   Lk 2:21-40
    Zechariah   Zech 4:1-6a;
        10b-14

PROMISE of
  from DEITY
    Psalmist   Ps 119:49-56;
        113-120;
        153-160
  of FOLLOWERs
    God   Eph 6:1-4
  INSTRUCTION on
    God   Gen 6:1-4
    Jesus   Mt 10:26-39

PROPHECY of
  for ETERNITY
    Israelites   Jer 31:35-37
    Judahites   Joel 3:16b-21
  through FIDELITY
    Israelites   Amos 5:4-6
  in NEW AGE
    Jesus   Mt 26:57-68;
        Mk 14:53-65;
        Jn 7:32-36
  through PROVIDENCE
    Isaiah   Is 4:2-6;
        37:30-32
    Israelites   Is 30:18-26;
        Jer 31:27-28
    Joseph   Gen 41:1-57
    Tyre   Is 23:15-18
  through RECONCILIATION
    Isaiah   Is 11:1-9
  through SALVATION
    Jesus   Mt 16:21-28;
        Mk 8:34-9:1;
        Lk 9:23-27
  through SECURITY
    Baruch   Jer 45:1-5
    Ebedmelech   Jer 39:15-18
    Isaiah   Is 4:2-6;
        25:6-9;
        27:2-6;
        32:15-20;
        37:30-32;
        51:17-52:12
    Jeremiah   Jer 21:1-10;
        32:26-44

through SECURITY (cont'd)

Jerusalemites	Zech 14:1-21
Judahites	Jer 27:16-22;
	38:14-28
Paul	Acts 27:1-28:16
Zedekiah	Jer 34:1-7

through STEWARDSHIP

Isaiah	2 Kgs 20:1-11

through PROVIDENCE
  in COVENANT

God	Gen 1:24-31

of DEITY

Believers	Ps 145:13b-20
David	Ps 17:13-14;
	22:12-21;
	30:1-5;
	40:13-17;
	138:7-8
Elihu	Job 33:23-25;
	29-30
Elijah	1 Kgs 17:1-24;
	19:1-21
Ephraimites	Ps 78:9-20
God	Ps 33:13-19;
	37:23-40;
	46:8-11;
	104:10-13;
	14-18;
	19-23;
	27-30;
	111:5-9;
	136:23-25;
	147:7-11;
	Prov 20:1-30;
	Eccl 3:9-15;
	Is 27:2-6;
	Jn 1:1-18;
	2 Cor 5:1-5
Hezekiah	Is 38:1-22
Isaac	Gen 26:1-11;
	12-31
Israelites	Ex 9:1-7;
	13-35;
	10:21-23;
	11:1-10;
	12:1-14;
	13:17-22;
	16:1-21;
	17:1-7;
	Deut 8:1-10;
	Neh 9:12-15;
	Ps 78:21-31;
	105:37-42;
	Is 1:4-9;
	10:17-19;
	43:14-44:5
Jesus	Jn 1:1-18
Job	Job 12:7-12
King	Ps 21:1-7;
	61:6-7
Mankind	Prov 16:1-33;
	Eccl 9:1-16
Peter	2 Pet 1:3-4
Psalmist	Ps 49:13-15

in the ENVIRONMENT

Ishmael	Gen 21:15-21

INSTRUCTION on

God	Gen 9:1-7

MEDITATION on

Jeremiah	Lam 3:1-66

of MESSIANIC FIGURE

Joseph	Gen 45:1-28

PROPHECY of

Isaiah	Is 4:2-6;
	37:30-32
Israelites	Is 30:18-26;
	Jer 31:27-28
Joseph	Gen 41:1-57
Tyre	Is 23:15-18

REVELATION on

Ezekiel	Ezek 4:9-11;
	11:14-21;
	16:1-7;
	17:22-24;
	33:1-9
God	Is 41:1-42:4
Israelites	Ezek 12:1-16
Jacob	Gen 31:1-16;
	17-43
Job	Job 38:39-41
John	Rev 1:4-20;
	12:1-6

SCRIPTURES on

Moses	Jn 6:25-59

TRADITION of

Moses	Ex 2:1-10

as QUALITY OF LIFE

Maiden	Song 2:1

through RECONCILIATION
  in COVENANT

Author	Heb 9:15-22;
	10:19-31
Jesus	Mt 26:17-30;
	Mk 14:22-26
Moses	Ex 24:1-18

with DEITY

Believers	Rom 8:28-39

in the ENVIRONMENT

Israelites	Jer 40:11-12

of FOLLOWERs

Jesus	Rom 5:6-11;
	7:1-6;
	Eph 1:3-14
Peter	1 Pet 1:13-2:3

INSTRUCTION on

Author	Heb 9:15-22
Jesus	Heb 13:1-25

by MESSIANIC FIGURE

Jesus	1 Pet 2:21-25

PROPHECY of

Isaiah	Is 11:1-9

REVELATION on

Amos	Amos 9:11-12
Jeremiah	Jer 33:12-13
Moses	Lev 17:10-14

RESPECT for
  from DEITY

God	Prov 10:1-32;
	14:1-35;
	19:1-29

through RESURRECTION
  by DEITY

Jesus	Jn 6:25-59

from **DEITY** (cont'd)

David	Ps 25:16-21; 36:5-9; 41:1-3
Israelites	Neh 9:12-15; 19-21
Jeremiah	Jer 11:18-12:6; 36:20-26
Job	Job 2:4-6
Levites	Num 18:8-20; Deut 10:1-11; 18:1-8; Josh 13:29-33; Ezek 44:15-31
Solomon	Ps 72:8-14

in **ENVIRONMENT**

Jacob	Gen 43:1-15
Jeremiah	Jer 26:20-24
Psalmist	Ps 49:5-12

of **FOLLOWERs**

Holy Spirit	2 Cor 5:1-5

INSTRUCTION on

Joshua	Josh 20:1-9
Moses	Deut 19:1-13

in **MESSIANIC FIGURE**

Jesus	Jn 10:1-18

PROPHECY of

Baruch	Jer 45:1-5
Ebedmelech	Jer 39:15-18
Isaiah	Is 4:2-6; 25:6-9; 27:2-6; 32:15-20; 37:30-32; 51:17-52:12
Jeremiah	Jer 21:1-10; 32:26-44
Jerusalemites	Zech 14:1-21
Judahites	Jer 27:16-22; 38:14-28
Paul	Acts 27:1-28:16
Zedekiah	Jer 34:1-7

REVELATION on

Ezekiel	Ezek 3:16-21
God	Is 42:5-17
Israelites	Ezek 6:8-10; 28:24-26; 34:17-22; Amos 9:14-15
Jeremiah	Jer 31:7-14
Jerusalemites	Zech 2:1-5
Joel	Joel 2:18-27
John	Rev 12:13-17

SIGNS of

in **COVENANT**

Jesus	1 Cor 11:23-26

in **ENVIRONMENT**

Rahab	Josh 2:15-24

REVELATION on

Angels	Lk 2:1-20
Ezekiel	Ezek 9:1-11; 47:1-12
John	Rev 4:1-11; 12:1-6; 22:1-5

over **SIN**

INSTRUCTION on

Paul	Rom 6:1-14
Preacher	Eccl 7:1-22

through **STEWARDSHIP**

in **ENVIRONMENT**

Israelites	Lev 25:1-7; 20-22
Noah	Gen 9:20

INSTRUCTION on

John	1 Jn 3:11-18

PROPHECY of

Isaiah	2 Kgs 20:1-11

REVELATION on

Moses	Lev 25:1-7; 20-22

through **TRUTH**

INSTRUCTION on

Jesus	Jn 8:12-20; 9:1-41; 14:1-14
Paul	2 Cor 4:7-12

of **MESSIANIC FIGURE**

Jesus	Jn 4:1-26

in **MISSION**

Holy Spirit	2 Cor 3:4-6
Jesus	Eph 5:3-14

of **VIRTUE**

from **DEITY**

Eliphaz	Job 4:17-21

INSTRUCTION on

Solomon	Prov 10:1-32; 12:1-28; 15:1-33; 21:1-31

REVELATION on

Ezekiel	Ezek 18:5-9; 14-20; 21-24; 25-29; 33:10-20

LOVE

AUTHORITY through

of **DEITY**

Jesus	Jn 5:19-47

BEHAVIOR revealing

Maiden	Song 1:12-14; 16-17; 2:3-7; 4:16; 5:2-8
Saul	1 Sam 16:14-23
Young Man	Song 1:9-11; 15; 2:2; 4:1-15; 5:1

in **ENVIRONMENT**

Samson	Judg 16:4-9
Shechem	Gen 34:1-31

of **FOLLOWERs**

Thessalonians	1 Thes 3:1-10

INSTRUCTION on

Paul	1 Cor 16:13-24; 2 Cor 12:14-18; Eph 4:25-5:2; Phil 2:1-4; 12-18
Preacher	Eccl 3:1-8

of DEITY's
    LAW
        Believers   1 Jn 4:19-5:5
        God   1 Jn 3:19-24
        Psalmist   Ps 119:33-40;
                        65-72;
                        73-80;
                        89-96;
                        105-112;
                        113-120;
                        121-128;
                        137-144;
                        153-160;
                        161-168

DESIRE for
    Maiden   Song 1:2-4;
                        3:1-5;
                        8:1-4;
                        5b-7;
                        14
    Young Man   Song 8:13
    of DEITY
        God   Hos 6:4-6
    INSTRUCTION on
        Paul   1 Cor 14:1-12

ELECTION through
    of DEITY
        Israelites   Mal 1:2-5
        Judahites   Ps 78:67-72
    SELF-REALIZATION of
        Paul   1 Tim 1:12-17

ETERNAL
    COVENANT of
        Isaiah   Is 55:1-13

ETERNITY of
    by DEITY
        David   1 Chr 17:1-27
        God   1 Chr 15:1-16:43;
                        2 Chr 5:1-7:10;
                        Ps 103:14-18;
                        106:1-5;
                        107:1-3;
                        117:1-2;
                        118:1-4;
                        28-29;
                        136:1-3;
                        4-9;
                        10-22;
                        23-25;
                        26;
                        138:7-8;
                        Jer 31:2-6
    INSTRUCTION on
        Paul   1 Cor 13:8-13
    PROPHECY of
        Isaiah   Is 54:1-17

FALSE BELIEF concerning
    causing disHONESTY
        John   1 Jn 4:19-5:5

FIDELITY of
    Maiden   Song 2:3-7;
                        8-17;
                        3:1-5;
                        5:2-8;

FIDELITY of (cont'd)
    Maiden   10-16;
                        6:2-3;
                        7:10-13;
                        8:1-4;
                        5b-7
    Young Man   Song 4:1-15;
                        6:4-10
    through COVENANT
        God   Neh 9:32-37
        Israelites   1 Kgs 8:22-53;
                        2 Chr 5:1-7:10;
                        Hos 2:16-20
    by DEITY
        Asaph   Ps 77:1-10
        David   Ps 5:8-10;
                        13:5-6;
                        18:46-50;
                        36:5-9
        God   Ex 34:5b-9;
                        Deut 7:6-16;
                        1 Chr 15:1-16:43;
                        2 Chr 17:1-20:37;
                        Ps 25:1-7;
                        8-15;
                        26:1-3;
                        31:1-8;
                        13-18;
                        19-24;
                        32:8-11;
                        33:4-9;
                        13-19;
                        20-22;
                        36:10-12;
                        40:11;
                        42:6-11;
                        44:23-26;
                        48:9-14;
                        51:1-2;
                        52:8-9;
                        57:1-3;
                        7-11;
                        59:9-10;
                        16-17;
                        62:8-12;
                        63:1-8;
                        66:13-20;
                        69:13-21;
                        85:4-7;
                        8-13;
                        86:1-7;
                        11-13;
                        14-17;
                        89:1-4;
                        5-18;
                        19-37;
                        90:13-17;
                        92:1-4;
                        94:16-19;
                        100:4-5;
                        103:1-5;
                        6-13;
                        14-18;
                        106:1-5;
                        107:1-3;
                        4-9;
                        10-16;
                        17-22;
                        23-32;
                        39-43;

of FOLLOWERs
   Jesus   Eph 5:21-33
   Woman   Lk 7:36-50
INSTRUCTION on
   Jesus   Lk 7:36-50
   Paul   2 Cor 5:14-19

RESPECT for
   Woman   Mt 26:6-13;
                   Mk 14:3-9
   of DEITY
      God   Ps 147:7-11
      Israelites   Ps 103:6-13;
                   14-18
   in ENVIRONMENT
      David   2 Sam 9:1-13
   INSTRUCTION on
      Jesus   Mt 5:43-47;
                   Lk 6:27-35;
                   Jn 14:15-17
      Paul   1 Cor 13:4-7;
                   Eph 5:21-33;
                   6:1-4

disRESPECT for
   in ENVIRONMENT
      Jacob   Gen 37:1-11

REVELATION on
   as MOTIVATION
      Daniel   Dan 9:20-23
   in PROVIDENCE
      Cyrus   Is 48:1-22
      Isaiah   Is 5:1-7

RITE of
      Maiden   Song 1:1
   by FOLLOWER
      Joseph   Jn 19:17-42
      Nicodemus   Jn 19:17-42
   MEDITATION on
      David   2 Sam 1:17-27

SALVATION through
   of DEITY
      Believer   Ps 145:13b-20;
                   1 Jn 4:7-12;
                   Jas 1:12
      David   Ps 6:1-5;
                   31:13-18
      Jesus   Eph 1:15-2:10
      Mankind   Tit 3:1-7
   of FOLLOWER
      Women   1 Tim 2:8-15
   INSTRUCTION on
      Jesus   Lk 15:1-7;
                   8-10;
                   11-32

SECURITY because of
   COVENANT of
      David   1 Sam 20:1-42
   of DEITY
      David   Ps 18:1-3;
                   31:19-24
      King   Ps 21:1-7
   in ENVIRONMENT
      Isaac   Gen 24:61-67
   of FOLLOWER
      Jesus   Rom 8:28-39

REVELATION on
   Israelites   Is 49:1-26

SELF-REALIZATION of
   through ELECTION
      Paul   1 Tim 1:12-17
   through FIDELITY
      Jesus   Mt 26:36-46;
                   Mk 14:32-42;
                   Lk 22:39-46
   as GIFT
      Paul   1 Cor 13:1-3
   through HONESTY
      Paul   1 Cor 13:1-3
   as MOTIVATION
      Paul   1 Cor 13:1-3
   as QUALITY OF LIFE
      Paul   1 Cor 13:1-3

SIGNS of
   in WORSHIP
      Wise Men   Mt 2:1-12

overcomes SIN
   by DEITY
      Jesus   Rom 5:6-11
   by FOLLOWERs
      Paul   2 Cor 2:5-11

in STEWARDSHIP
   by FOLLOWER
      Joseph   Mt 27:57-61;
                   Mk 15:42-47;
                   Lk 23:50-53
   INSTRUCTION on
      Jesus   Mk 12:41-44;
                   Lk 8:16-18;
                   10:29-37;
                   21:1-4;
                   Jn 13:31-35;
                   21:15-23
      Paul   2 Cor 8:7-15;
                   9:1-5;
                   6-11;
                   1 Tim 6:6-10
   of WORSHIP
      Widow   Lk 21:1-4
      Widows   Mk 12:41-44

of TRUTH
   by FOLLOWERs
      Jesus   Eph 4:7-16
   INSTRUCTION on
      John   1 Jn 2:7-11;
                   12-17
   in MISSION
      Believers   1 Jn 3:11-18
through TRUTH
      John   2 Jn 1:1-3
   of DEITY
      Disciples   Lk 24:50-51;
                   Jn 8:21-59

as VIRTUE
      King   Ps 45:2-9
   of DEITY
      God   Ps 11:4-7;
                   33:4-9;
                   146:7c-9;
                   Prov 15:1-33

LOVE (cont'd)

INSTRUCTION on
  Paul   1 Cor 13:8-13

in **WORSHIP**
  PRAYER for
    Jesus   Jn 17:6-19;
                  20-26
    Paul   2 Cor 13:14;
                  Eph 3:14-19;
                  6:23-24
  PROVIDENCE through
    Ezra   Ezra 7:27-28
  SIGNS of
    Wise Men   Mt 2:1-12
  through **STEWARDSHIP**
    Widow   Lk 21:1-4
    Widows   Mk 12:41-44

LUST

BEHAVIOR revealing
  in **ENVIRONMENT**
    Noah   Gen 9:21-25
  INSTRUCTION on
    Jesus   Mt 5:27-30
    Paul   1 Cor 7:36-38;
                  1 Thes 4:1-12
  TRADITION of
    Esau   Gen 25:27-34

DESIRE for
  INSTRUCTION on
    Preacher   Eccl 6:1-12

in **ENVIRONMENT**
  BEHAVIOR revealing
    Noah   Gen 9:21-25
  through **disHONESTY**
    Amnon   2 Sam 13:1-20
  as **MOTIVATION**
    Elders   *Susa 1:5-18
    Shechem   Gen 34:1-31
  causing **SIN**
    Benjaminites Judg 19:22-26

through **FALSE BELIEF**
  causing **inFIDELITY**
    Israelites   Num 25:1-5
  as **MOTIVATION**
    Herod   Mt 14:1-12;
                  Mk 6:17-29
  causing **SIN**
    Israelites   Ezek 23:5-10;
                  36-49
    Judahites   Ezek 23:11-21
    Peter   2 Pet 2:17-22
    Sinners   2 Pet 2:10b-16;
                  3:3-7

causing **inFIDELITY**
  through **FALSE BELIEF**
    Israelites   Num 25:1-5

causing **disHONESTY**
  in **ENVIRONMENT**
    Amnon   2 Sam 13:1-20
INSTRUCTION on

LUST (cont'd)

INSTRUCTION on (cont'd)
  Jesus   Mt 5:27-30
  Paul   1 Cor 7:36-38;
                1 Thes 4:1-12
as **MOTIVATION**
  Preacher   Eccl 5:8-20
as **QUALITY OF LIFE**
  Isaiah   Is 56:9-57:13
as **SIN**
  Author   Heb 13:1-25
  Jude   Jude 1:14-16
in **STEWARDSHIP**
  Paul   1 Tim 6:6-10

JUDGMENT on
  PROPHECY of
    Isaiah   Is 5:8-24a

LAW concerning
  INSTRUCTION on
    God   Ex 20:1-17
    Moses   Deut 5:1-21

as **MOTIVATION**
  David   2 Sam 11:1-27
  Elders   *Susa 1:5-18
  Shechem   Gen 34:1-31
  through **FALSE BELIEF**
    Herod   Mt 14:1-12;
                  Mk 6:17-29
  INSTRUCTION on
    Preacher   Eccl 5:8-20

PUNISHMENT for
  by **DEITY**
    Gentiles   Rom 1:24-32
  INSTRUCTION on
    Solomon   Prov 21:1-31
  REVELATION on
    Chaldeans   Is 47:1-15
    Judahites   Ezek 23:22-35

as **QUALITY OF LIFE**
  INSTRUCTION on
    Isaiah   Is 56:9-57:13

as **SIN**
  INSTRUCTION on
    Author   Heb 13:1-25
    Jude   Jude 1:14-16

causing **SIN**
  through **FALSE BELIEF**
    Israelites   Ezek 23:5-10;
                  36-49
    Judahites   Ezek 23:11-21
    Peter   2 Pet 2:17-22
    Sinners   2 Pet 2:10b-16;
                  3:3-7

SIN of
  Benjaminites Judg 19:22-26
  Nineveh   Nah 3:1-4

in **STEWARDSHIP**
  INSTRUCTION on
    Paul   1 Tim 6:6-10

in **TRADITION**
  BEHAVIOR revealing
    Esau   Gen 25:27-34

AUTHORITY in
  INSTRUCTION on
    Moses   Deut 17:14-20

BEHAVIOR concerning
    Israelites   *1 Esd 9:16-36
    Joseph   Gen 41:1-57
    Judith   *Jdt 16:21-25
    Levite   Judg 19:1-9
    Moses   Num 12:1-2
    Susanna   *Susa 1:1-4
    Tobiah   *Tb 7:1-18
    Tobit   *Tb 1:3-9
  COVENANT of
    Alexander   *1 Mc 10:51-58
  INSTRUCTION on
    David   2 Sam 3:1-16
    Isaac   Gen 27:41-28:5
    Paul   Eph 5:21-33;
                 Col 3:18-4:1
    Raphael   *Tb 6:1-17
    Sirach   *Sir 25:16-26
    Tobit   *Tb 4:1-21
  PROPHECY of
    Isaiah   Is 3:16-4:1
    Jeremiah   Jer 16:1-13
  REVELATION on
    Hosea   Hos 1:2-3
  TRADITION of
    Ahasuerus   Esth 2:8-18
    Esau   Gen 26:34-35;
                 28:6-9
    God   Gen 2:21-25
    Moses   Ex 2:16-23a

BELIEF concerning
  INSTRUCTION on
    Paul   1 Cor 7:8-16

COMMITMENT to
    Israelites   Judg 21:1-7
  INSTRUCTION on
    Nehemiah   Neh 13:23-29
  TRADITION revealing
    Jehoshaphat   2 Chr 17:1-20:37
  in **COMMUNITY**
    INSTRUCTION on
      Joshua   Josh 23:1-16

CONFRONTATION with
  in **ENVIRONMENT**
    Benjaminites   Judg 21:16-25
    Shechem   Gen 34:1-31

COVENANT of
  BEHAVIOR required in
    Alexander   *1 Mc 10:51-58
  FIDELITY to
    Malachi   Mal 2:10-16
  LAW concerning
    Israelites   Ezra 10:1-6;
                 Neh 10:28-30
  PROMISE in
    Abraham   Gen 24:1-10

DESIRE for
    Adonijah   1 Kgs 2:13-25
    Ahasuerus   Esth 2:1-4
    Samson   Judg 14:1-4

INSTRUCTION on
    Naomi   Ruth 3:1-18

in **ENVIRONMENT**
  BEHAVIOR concerning
    Israelites   *1 Esd 9:16-36
    Joseph   Gen 41:1-57
    Judith   *Jdt 16:21-25
    Levite   Judg 19:1-9
    Moses   Num 12:1-2
    Susanna   *Susa 1:1-4
    Tobiah   *Tb 7:1-18
    Tobit   *Tb 1:3-9
  COMMITMENT to
    Israelites   Judg 21:1-7
  CONFRONTATION with
    Benjaminites   Judg 21:16-25
    Shechem   Gen 34:1-31
  DESIRE for
    Samson   Judg 14:1-4
  in**FIDELITY** to
    David   2 Sam 11:1-27
  PROMISE of
    Caleb   Josh 15:13-19;
                 Judg 1:1-21
  RITE of
    Tobiah   *Tb 8:1-21;
                 11:7-19
  SIN against
    Israelites   *1 Esd 8:68-70

FALSE BELIEF in
  causing in**FIDELITY**
    Israelites   Ezek 16:15-34

FIDELITY in
  INSTRUCTION on
    Author   Heb 13:1-25
    Bishops   1 Tim 3:1-7
    Deacons   1 Tim 3:8-13
    God   Ex 20:1-17
    Hosea   Hos 3:1-5
    Jesus   Mt 5:27-30;
                 31-32;
                 19:3-9;
                 16-22;
                 Mk 10:1-12
    Moses   Deut 5:1-21
    Paul   Rom 7:1-6;
                 13:8-10;
                 1 Cor 7:1-7;
                 8-16;
                 25-35;
                 39-40;
                 1 Thes 4:1-12;
                 1 Tim 5:3-16
    Solomon   Prov 5:15-23
  in **MISSION**
    Women   Tit 2:1-10
  REVELATION on
    Israelites   Ezek 22:1-16
    Moses   Lev 18:1-30;
                 Num 5:11-31

FIDELITY to
    Moses   Ex 21:2-11;
                 Lev 20:1-27

RITE of
David — 1 Sam 18:6-30
in **ENVIRONMENT**
Tobiah — *Tb 8:1-21; 11:7-19

TRADITION of
Abraham — Gen 25:1-6
Isaac — Gen 24:61-67
Jacob — Gen 29:15-30
Leah — Gen 29:15-30
Rachel — Gen 29:15-30
Rebekah — Gen 24:61-67

SIGNS of
REVELATION on
John — Rev 21:9-14

SIN in
Ahab — 1 Kgs 16:29-34
Israelites — Ezra 9:1-2; Neh 13:23-29
Solomon — 1 Kgs 11:1-13
against **DEITY**
Israelites — *1 Esd 8:91-96
in **ENVIRONMENT**
Israelites — *1 Esd 8:68-70
INSTRUCTION on
Jesus — Mt 5:31-32; 19:3-9; Mk 10:1-12; Lk 16:16-18
Moses — Deut 7:1-5
Paul — Rom 7:1-6; 1 Cor 7:8-16
Sirach — *Sir 25:16-26

VIRTUE in
INSTRUCTION on
Lemuel — Prov 31:10-31
Sirach — *Sir 7:1-36; 26:1-4; 13-18; 36:21-26; 40:18-27
Solomon — Prov 18:1-24
Women — 1 Pet 3:1-7

MEDIATION

ACCEPTANCE of
MISSION of
John the Baptist — Mt 3:1-12; Mk 1:2-8; Lk 3:1-6
PROPHECY of
Elijah — Mal 4:4-6

with **ANGER**
of **DEITY**
Moses — Ps 106:19-23

with **ANXIETY**
concerning **SECURITY**
Jesus — Mt 6:25-34

of **COVENANT**
through **DEATH**
Jesus — Heb 9:15-22
for **LIFE**
Jesus — Heb 12:12-29

through **SACRIFICE**
Aaron — Lev 24:5-9
through **SERVICE**
Jesus — Heb 8:6-13

with **DEATH**
through **COVENANT**
Jesus — Heb 9:15-22
by **DEITY**
Jesus — Rom 8:28-39
by **MESSIANIC FIGURE**
Jesus — Heb 2:5-18

by **DEITY**
with **DEATH**
Jesus — Rom 8:28-39

with **DEITY**
in **DISCIPLESHIP**
Jesus — Jn 14:1-14; Rom 8:28-39; Eph 2:11-22; Heb 6:13-20; 7:1-28; 9:23-28
concerning **EVIL**
Mankind — 1 Sam 2:11-26
through **GRACE**
Jesus — Rom 5:1-5
Moses — Ex 32:7-14; Deut 9:7-24; 25-29
for **GUILT**
Aaron — Ex 28:36-39
for **INNOCENCE**
Jesus — 1 Thes 3:11-13
for **LIFE**
Aaron — Num 16:36-50
Jesus — 1 Tim 2:1-7
through **MIRACLE**
Aaron — Num 16:36-50
concerning **REVENGE**
God — Ps 37:1-11
Israelites — Jer 51:1-64
SACREDNESS of
Elihu — Job 33:23-25
concerning **SACRIFICE**
Aaron — Ex 30:1-10
High Priest — Heb 5:1-10
through **SERVICE**
Aaron — Ex 28:1-5
Isaiah — Is 40:1-11
Job — Job 42:7-9
WISDOM in
Elihu — Job 36:1-4
WITNESS to
Israelites — Mal 2:17-3:5

in **DISCIPLESHIP**
by **DEITY**
Jesus — Jn 14:1-14; Rom 8:28-39; Eph 2:11-22; 6:13-20; 7:1-28; 9:23-28

in **ENVIRONMENT**
through **GRACE**
Abigail — 1 Sam 25:1-44
Joab — 2 Sam 13:21-14:33

concerning **EVIL**
  through **DEITY**
    Mankind   1 Sam 2:11-26

for **FOLLOWERs**
  reveals **INNOCENCE**
    Jesus   1 Cor 1:4-9
  VICTORY through
    Jesus   Rom 8:28-39
  through **WILL**
    Holy Spirit   Rom 8:26-27
  through **WISDOM**
    Holy Spirit   Rom 8:26-27

concerning **FULFILLMENT**
  PROPHECY of
    Isaiah   Mt 3:1-12;
            Mk 1:2-8;
            Lk 3:1-6;
            Jn 1:19-51
    John the Baptist   Mt 3:1-12;
            11:7-15;
            Mk 1:2-8;
            Lk 3:1-6;
            7:24-30;
            Jn 1:19-51

through **GRACE**
  of **DEITY**
    Jesus   Rom 5:1-5
    Moses   Ex 32:7-14;
            Deut 9:7-24;
            25-29
  in **ENVIRONMENT**
    Abigail   1 Sam 25:1-44
    Joab   2 Sam 13:21-14:33
  of **MESSIANIC FIGURE**
    Moses   Ex 32:30-35
  PROPHECY of
    John the Baptist   Lk 1:57-80
    Zechariah   Lk 1:57-80
  in **WORSHIP**
    Priest   Num 15:22-31

GRATITUDE for
  PRAYER of
    Jesus   Mt 11:25-26

for **GUILT**
  with **DEITY**
    Aaron   Ex 28:36-39
  INSTRUCTION on
    Moses   Lev 11:1-47
  REVELATION on
    Aaron   Num 18:1-7

for **INNOCENCE**
  with **DEITY**
    Jesus   1 Thes 3:11-13
  of **FOLLOWER**
    Jesus   1 Cor 1:4-9

INSTRUCTION on
  for **GUILT**
    Moses   Lev 11:1-47
  for **KILLING**
    Mordecai   Esth 4:1-17
  of **LEADERSHIP**
    Jethro   Ex 18:13-26
  of **SERVICE**
    Eliphaz   Job 5:1-7

for **KILLING**
  INSTRUCTION on
    Mordecai   Esth 4:1-17

of **LEADERSHIP**
  INSTRUCTION on
    Jethro   Ex 18:13-26
  REVELATION on
    Moses   Num 3:5-10
  SCRIPTURES on
    Isaiah   Mk 1:2-8

for **LIFE**
  with **DEITY**
    Aaron   Num 16:36-50
    Jesus   1 Tim 2:1-7
  through **WORSHIP**
    Jesus   Heb 10:19-31

MEDITATION on
  in **SERVICE**
    Jeremiah   Jer 42:1-6

by **MESSIANIC FIGURE**
  through **DEATH**
    Jesus   Heb 2:5-18
  GRACE of
    Moses   Ex 32:30-35
  SACRIFICE of
    Jesus   1 Tim 2:107
  WITNESS of
    Jesus   1 Tim 2:1-7

through **MIRACLE**
  of **DEITY**
    Aaron   Num 16:36-50

MISSION of
  ACCEPTANCE of
    John the Baptist   Mt 3:1-12;
            Mk 1:2-8;
            Lk 3:1-6
  WITNESS to
    John the Baptist   Jn 3:22-30

MOTIVATION for
  is **WILL**
    Centurion   Mt 8:5-13

for **OPPRESSION**
  REVELATION on
    Ezekiel   Ezek 4:4-8

PRAYER of
  for **SACREDNESS**
    Jesus   Jn 17:6-19

PROPHECY of
  concerning **ACCEPTANCE**
    Elijah   Mal 4:4-6
  through **GRACE**
    John the Baptist   Lk 1:57-80
    Zechariah   Lk 1:57-80
  of **SERVICE**
    Israelites   Deut 18:9-22

REJECTION of
  REVELATION on
    Ezekiel   Ezek 14:12-23
    Jeremiah   Jer 7:16-20;
            11:1-14;
            14:10-12

REVELATION on
  for **GUILT**
    Aaron   Num 18:1-7
  of **LEADERSHIP**
    Moses   Num 3:5-10
  for **OPPRESSION**
    Ezekiel   Ezek 4:4-8
  through **SUFFERING**
    Ezekiel   Ezek 4:4-8

through **REVENGE**
  of **DEITY**
    God   Ps 37:1-11
    Israelites   Jer 51:1-64

SACREDNESS of
  of **DEITY**
    Elihu   Job 33:23-25

through **SACRIFICE**
  for **COVENANT**
    Aaron   Lev 24:5-9
  to **DEITY**
    Aaron   Ex 30:1-10
    High Priest   Heb 5:1-10
  of **MESSIANIC FIGURE**
    Jesus   1 Tim 2:1-7
  in **WORSHIP**
    Priest   Lev 1:1-17;
                   2:1-16;
                   3:1-17;
                   4:1-35;
                   5:5-13;
                   14-6:7;
                   15:1-33

SCRIPTURES on
  of **LEADERSHIP**
    Isaiah   Mk 1:2-8

through **SERVICE**
  for **COVENANT**
    Jesus   Heb 8:6-13
  to **DEITY**
    Aaron   Ex 28:1-5
    Isaiah   Is 40:1-11
    Job   Job 42:7-9
  INSTRUCTION on
    Eliphaz   Job 5:1-7
  MEDITATION on
    Jeremiah   Jer 42:1-6
  PROPHECY of
    Israelites   Deut 18:9-22
  in **WORSHIP**
    David   Ps 20:1-5
    Levites   2 Chr 29:1-36

through **SUFFERING**
    Phinehas   Ps 106:28-31
  REVELATION on
    Ezekiel   Ezek 4:4-8

concerning **TEMPERANCE**
  in **TRADITION**
    Israelites   Lev 3:1-17

VICTORY through
  for **FOLLOWER**
    Jesus   Rom 8:28-39

for **WILL**
  of **FOLLOWER**
    Holy Spirit   Rom 8:26-27

WISDOM in
  with **DEITY**
    Elihu   Job 36:1-4
  for **FOLLOWER**
    Holy Spirit   Rom 8:26-27

WITNESS to
    Joshua   Num 14:5-7
  of **DEITY**
    Israelites   Mal 2:17-3:5
  of **MESSIANIC FIGURE**
    Jesus   1 Tim 2:1-7
  in **MISSION**
    John the Baptist Jn 3:22-30

in **WORSHIP**
  through **GRACE**
    Priest   Num 15:22-31
  for **LIFE**
    Jesus   Heb 10:19-31
  through **SACRIFICE**
    Priest   Lev 1:1-17;
                   2:1-16;
                   3:1-17;
                   4:1-35;
                   5:5-13;
                   14-6:7;
                   15:1-33
  for **SERVICE**
    David   Ps 20:1-5
    Levites   2 Chr 29:1-36

MEDITATION

on **ACCEPTANCE**
  of **PUNISHMENT**
    Jeremiah   Jer 10:17-22;
                   Lam 3:1-66

on **ANGER**
    Jeremiah   Jer 10:23-25
  as Divine **PUNISHMENT**
    Jeremiah   Lam 2:1-22

on **ANXIETY**
    David   Ps 39:1-3
    Jesus   Jn 12:27-36a
    Pilate   Jn 18:28-19:16
  in **PUNISHMENT**
    Jeremiah   Jer 10:17-22
  as **QUALITY OF LIFE**
    Jeremiah   Jer 15:10-21
  concerning **SECURITY**
    Jesus   Mt 6:25-34
  caused by **SIN**
    God   Jer 9:2-9

on **BEHAVIOR**
  caused by **ANXIETY**
    David   Ps 39:1-3
    Jesus   Jn 12:27-36a
    Pilate   Jn 18:28-19:16

revealing **COMPASSION**
  Jesus   Lk 13:34-35
revealing **DESPAIR**
  Jeremiah   Jer 12:7-13
  Job   Job 7:7-11;
                        9:30-35;
                        14:18-22
of **ENEMY**
  David   Ps 56:5-6a;
                        62:3-4
revealing **FEAR**
  Pilate   Jn 18:28-19:16
revealing **GRIEF**
  Jeremiah   Jer 12:7-13
revealing **HATE**
  Job   Job 10:1-7
revealing **KILLING**
  Saul   1 Chr 10:1-14
revealing **OPPRESSION**
  Preacher   Eccl 3:16-4:3
revealing **REPENTANCE**
  Nineveh   Jon 3:1-10
revealing **SUFFERING**
  Job   Job 7:7-11;
                        12-16

on **BELIEF**
  in **COMPASSION**
    Jeremiah   Lam 3:1-66
  in **DEATH**
    Job   Job 7:7-11
  in **INNOCENCE**
    Job   Job 16:12-17
  in **OBEDIENCE**
    Paul   2 Thes 3:3-5

on **BLESSING**
  of **LAW**
    Mankind   Ps 1:1-3
  on **SIN**
    Asaph   Ps 73:1-3;
                        4-12
    Jeremiah   Jer 11:18-12:6

on **CAPTIVITY**
  as **PUNISHMENT**
    Jeremiah   Lam 1:1-22

on **COMMITMENT**
  through **FAITH**
    Daniel   Dan 1:8-16
  FEAR of
    Pharisees   Mt 21:45-46

on **COMPASSION**
  Jesus   Lk 13:34-35
  BELIEF in
    Jeremiah   Lam 3:1-66
  PRAYER for
    Israelites   Jer 14:7-9
    Jeremiah   Lam 3:1-66

on **COMPULSION**
  of **GRIEF**
    Jeremiah   Lam 3:1-66
  of **OPPRESSION**
    Jeremiah   Lam 3:1-66
  of **SUFFERING**
    Jeremiah   Lam 3:1-66

on **CONDEMNATION**
  of **CREATION**
    Job   Job 3:1-10
  of dis**HONESTY**
    Jeremiah   Jer 4:9-10
  of **SIN**
    David   Ps 52:1-4

on **CONFRONTATION**
  with **DOUBT**
    Ezekiel   Ezek 20:45-49

on **CONVERSION**
  Jeremiah   Jer 5:1-14

on **CREATION**
  CONDEMNATION of
    Job   Job 3:1-10
  GRIEF in
    Job   Job 3:1-10
  ONENESS of
    Jesus   Eph 1:3-14

on **DEATH**
  David   2 Sam 1:17-27
  Job   Job 7:7-11
  Paul   2 Tim 4:6-8
  as a **DESIRE**
    Job   Job 3:11-19;
                        20-26;
                        7:12-16
  concerning **JUDGMENT**
    Adam   1 Cor 15:20-28
  as **PUNISHMENT**
    Psalmist   Ps 49:13-15
  as **QUALITY OF LIFE**
    Job   Job 14:7-12
    Preacher   Eccl 3:16-4:3
    Psalmist   Ps 49:5-12
  resulting in **RECONCILIATION**
    Jesus   Col 1:21-23

on **DESIRE**
  for **DEATH**
    Job   Job 3:11-19;
                        20-26;
                        7:12-16
  for **LIFE**
    Paul   Phil 3:4-16
  for **PEACE**
    David   Ps 55:3b-8
    Job   Job 3:11-19
  for **REWARD**
    Paul   Phil 3:4-16
  for **WISDOM**
    Preacher   Eccl 7:23-29

on **DESPAIR**
  Jeremiah   Jer 12:7-13
  Job   Job 7:7-11;
                        9:30-35;
                        14:18-22
  over **JUDGMENT**
    Job   Job 19:7-12
  as **QUALITY OF LIFE**
    David   Ps 38:3-10
    Job   Job 7:1-6;
                        14:7-12;
                        17:1-5;
                        11-16

caused by **SIN**
    Jeremiah   Jer 8:18-9:1

on **DESTRUCTION**
  as **PUNISHMENT**
    Jeremiah   Lam 2:1-22
  caused by **SIN**
    David   Ps 101:5-7;
        8

on **DOUBT**
  in **RESURRECTION**
    Job   Job 14:7-12

on **EQUALITY**
  in **LIFE**
    Preacher   Eccl 3:16-4:3

on **ETERNAL**
  REJECTION
    Job   Job 7:12-16

on **FAITH**
  in **COMMITMENT**
    Daniel   Dan 1:8-16
  in **LAW**
    Psalmist   Ps 119:73-80
  in **TRUTH**
    Paul   Eph 1:3-14

on **FEAR**
    Pilate   Jn 18:28-19:16
  in **COMMITMENT**
    Pharisees   Mt 21:45-46
  as **QUALITY OF LIFE**
    Job   Job 7:12-16
  because of **inSECURITY**
    David   Ps 55:3b-8

on **FIDELITY**
  in **FRIENDSHIP**
    Job   Job 6:14-20
  in **LOVE**
    Paul   2 Thes 3:3-5
  through **REPENTANCE**
    Paul   2 Cor 7:5-13a
  REWARDs for
    David   Ps 101:5-7

on **FULFILLMENT**
  of **NEW AGE**
    Paul   Phil 1:3-11
  through **PROVIDENCE**
    David   Ps 143:5-6
    Jeremiah   Lam 2:1-22

on **GIFT**
  of **HOPE**
    Paul   1 Cor 1:4-9

on **GRACE**
  through **PRAYER**
    Israelites   Jer 14:7-9

on **GRATITUDE**
  PRAYER of
    Jesus   Lk 10:21-22
    Paul   Eph 1:15-2:10
  as **VIRTUE**
    Isaiah   Is 61:1-11

on **GRIEF**
    Jeremiah   Jer 12:7-13
  through **COMPULSION**
    Jeremiah   Lam 3:1-66
  in the **CREATION**
    Job   Job 3:1-10
  PRAYER concerning
    Job   Job 16:18-22
  through **PUNISHMENT**
    Jeremiah   Lam 1:1-22;
        2:1-22
  as **QUALITY OF LIFE**
    Asaph   Ps 77:1-10
  RITE of
    David   2 Sam 1:17-27
  caused by **SIN**
    Jeremiah   Jer 8:18-9:1

on **GUILT**
  PRAYER concerning
    Israelites   Jer 14:7-9
  of **SIN**
    Judahites   Lam 5:1-22

on **HATE**
    Job   Job 10:1-7
  as **MOTIVATION**
    Job   Job 9:20-24
  of **SIN**
    David   Ps 26:4-6a

on **disHONESTY**
  causing **OPPRESSION**
    David   Ps 62:3-4

on **HOPE**
  as **GIFT**
    Paul   1 Cor 1:4-9
  in **PRAYER**
    Paul   Eph 1:15-2:10
  in **RESURRECTION**
    Paul   Phil 3:4-16

on **HUMILITY**
  as **PUNISHMENT**
    Jeremiah   Lam 2:1-22

on **IGNORANCE**
  of **KNOWLEDGE**
    Jeremiah   Jer 5:1-14

on **INDIFFERENCE**
  as **MOTIVATION**
    Preacher   Eccl 1:12-2:26

on **JOY**
  in **PRAYER**
    Paul   Phil 1:3-11
  of **RECONCILIATION**
    Paul   2 Cor 7:5-13a
  of **SALVATION**
    Isaiah   Is 61:1-11

on **JUDGMENT**
  of **DEATH**
    Adam   1 Cor 15:20-28
  of **DESPAIR**
    Job   Job 19:7-12
  on **DISCIPLESHIP**
    Paul   1 Cor 11:27-34

on **ENEMY**
　Psalmist　　　　　Ps 120:3-4
of **INNOCENCE**
　Job　　　　　　　Job 34:5-9
　Pilate　　　　　　Jn 18:28-19:16
for **KILLING**
　Pilate　　　　　　Jn 18:28-19:16
for **LIFE**
　Jesus　　　　　　1 Cor 15:20-28

on **JUSTICE**
　PRAYER for
　　Jeremiah　　　　Lam 1:1-22
　　Job　　　　　　Job 16:18-22
　through **RECONCILIATION**
　　Jeremiah　　　　Jer 5:1-14
　for **SIN**
　　Preacher　　　　Eccl 3:16-4:3

on **KILLING**
　Saul　　　　　　　1 Chr 10:1-14

on **KNOWLEDGE**
　of **DEATH**
　　Paul　　　　　　2 Tim 4:6-8
　of **EVIL**
　　Jesus　　　　　　Mt 22:15-22;
　　　　　　　　　　Mk 12:13-17;
　　　　　　　　　　Lk 20:19-26
　of **IGNORANCE**
　　Jeremiah　　　　Jer 5:1-14
　of **LIFE**
　　Jesus　　　　　　Mk 11:11
　of **LOVE**
　　Daughters　　　　Song 5:9
　of **OBEDIENCE**
　　Psalmist　　　　Ps 119:25-32;
　　　　　　　　　　97-104
　of **SERVICE**
　　Psalmist　　　　Ps 121:1
　of **VICTORY**
　　Paul　　　　　　2 Tim 4:6-8

on **LAW**
　concerning **LOVE**
　　Psalmist　　　　Ps 119:9-16;
　　　　　　　　　　17-24;
　　　　　　　　　　41-48;
　　　　　　　　　　97-104

on **LEADERSHIP**
　through **PRAYER**
　　Moses　　　　　Num 11:11-13

on **LIFE**
　through **PROVIDENCE**
　　Jeremiah　　　　Lam 3:1-66

on **MEDIATION**
　of **SERVICE**
　　Jeremiah　　　　Jer 42:1-6

on **MOTIVATION**
　as **HATE**
　　Job　　　　　　Job 9:20-24
　as **INDIFFERENCE**
　　Preacher　　　　Eccl 1:12-2:26
　through **WILL**
　　Centurion　　　　Lk 7:1-10

on **OBEDIENCE**
　to **BELIEF**
　　Paul　　　　　　2 Thes 3:3-5

on **ONENESS**
　in the **CREATION**
　　Jesus　　　　　　Eph 1:3-14

on **OPPRESSION**
　　Preacher　　　　Eccl 3:16-4:3
　through **COMPULSION**
　　Jeremiah　　　　Lam 3:1-66
　caused by **disHONESTY**
　　David　　　　　Ps 62:3-4
　as **PUNISHMENT**
　　Jeremiah　　　　Lam 2:1-22
　　Judahites　　　　Lam 5:1-22
　as **QUALITY OF LIFE**
　　David　　　　　Ps 40:12
　　Psalmist　　　　Ps 42:6-11;
　　　　　　　　　　102:1-11

on **PATIENCE**
　in **SALVATION**
　　Jeremiah　　　　Lam 3:1-66

on **PRAISE**
　through **PRAYER**
　　Jesus　　　　　　Lk 10:21-22
　　Paul　　　　　　2 Cor 1:3-7
　of **PROVIDENCE**
　　Isaiah　　　　　Is 25:1-5

through **PRAYER**
　for **COMPASSION**
　　Israelites　　　　Jer 14:7-9
　　Jeremiah　　　　Lam 3:1-66
　for **GRACE**
　　Israelites　　　　Jer 14:7-9
　of **GRATITUDE**
　　Jesus　　　　　　Lk 10:21-22
　　Paul　　　　　　Eph 1:15-2:10
　concerning **GRIEF**
　　Job　　　　　　Job 16:18-22
　concerning **GUILT**
　　Israelites　　　　Jer 14:7-9
　of **HOPE**
　　Paul　　　　　　Eph 1:15-2:10
　of **JOY**
　　Paul　　　　　　Phil 1:3-11
　for **JUSTICE**
　　Jeremiah　　　　Lam 1:1-22
　　Job　　　　　　Job 16:18-22
　for **LEADERSHIP**
　　Moses　　　　　Num 11:11-13
　for **LIFE**
　　Jeremiah　　　　Jer 18:18-23
　of **PRAISE**
　　Jesus　　　　　　Lk 10:21-22
　　Paul　　　　　　2 Cor 1:3-7
　concerning **REJECTION**
　　Jeremiah　　　　Lam 3:1-66
　for **WISDOM**
　　Jesus　　　　　　Lk 10:21-22
　　Paul　　　　　　Eph 1:15-2:10

on **PRIDE**
　as **QUALITY OF LIFE**
　　Preacher　　　　Eccl 3:16-4:3;
　　　　　　　　　　4-12;
　　　　　　　　　　13-16

on **PROMISE**
　of **LOVE**
　　Psalmist　　　　　Ps 119:145-152

on **PROVIDENCE**
　of **ENEMY**
　　Jeremiah　　　　　Lam 1:1-22
　of **LIFE**
　　Jeremiah　　　　　Lam 3:1-66

on **QUALITY OF LIFE**
　as **ANXIETY**
　　Jeremiah　　　　　Jer 15:10-21
　as **DEATH**
　　Job　　　　　　　Job 14:7-12
　　Preacher　　　　　Eccl 3:16-4:3
　　Psalmist　　　　　Ps 49:5-12
　as **DESPAIR**
　　David　　　　　　Ps 38:3-10
　　Job　　　　　　　Job 7:1-6;
　　　　　　　　　　14:7-12;
　　　　　　　　　　17:1-5;
　　　　　　　　　　11-16
　as **FEAR**
　　Job　　　　　　　Job 7:12-16
　as **GRIEF**
　　Asaph　　　　　　Ps 77:1-10
　as **OPPRESSION**
　　David　　　　　　Ps 40:12
　　Psalmist　　　　　Ps 42:6-11;
　　　　　　　　　　102:1-11
　as **PRIDE**
　　Preacher　　　　　Eccl 3:16-4:3;
　　　　　　　　　　4-12;
　　　　　　　　　　13-16
　as **SPIRIT**
　　Asaph　　　　　　Ps 77:1-10
　as **SUFFERING**
　　Job　　　　　　　Job 7:1-6;
　　　　　　　　　　14:18-22
　　Psalmist　　　　　Ps 102:1-11

on **RECONCILIATION**
　through **DEATH**
　　Jesus　　　　　　Col 1:21-23
　through **JUSTICE**
　　Jeremiah　　　　　Jer 5:1-14
　through **REPENTANCE**
　　Paul　　　　　　 2 Cor 7:5-13a

on **REJECTION**
　of **CONVERSION**
　　Jeremiah　　　　　Jer 5:1-14
　for **ETERNITY**
　　Job　　　　　　　Job 7:12-16
　of **PRAYER**
　　Jeremiah　　　　　Lam 3:1-66
　as **PUNISHMENT**
　　Jeremiah　　　　　Jer 5:1-14
　of **SIN**
　　David　　　　　　Ps 26:4-6a;
　　　　　　　　　　39:1-3;
　　　　　　　　　　101:2c-4
　　Jeremiah　　　　　Jer 5:1-14

on **REPENTANCE**
　　Nineveh　　　　　Jon 3:1-10
　through **FIDELITY**
　　Paul　　　　　　 2 Cor 7:5-13a
　through **RECONCILIATION**
　　Paul　　　　　　 2 Cor 7:5-13a

　from **SIN**
　　David　　　　　　Ps 38:17-22;
　　　　　　　　　　41:4-10

on **RESPECT**
　for **EVIL**
　　Asaph　　　　　　Ps 73:4-12
　for **FRIENDSHIP**
　　David　　　　　　Ps 38:11-16

on **REVENGE**
　as **PUNISHMENT**
　　Jeremiah　　　　　Jer 10:23-25

on **REWARD**
　for **FIDELITY**
　　David　　　　　　Ps 101:5-7

on **RITE**
　related to **DEATH**
　　David　　　　　　2 Sam 1:17-27
　of **GRIEF**
　　David　　　　　　2 Sam 1:17-27
　of **LOVE**
　　David　　　　　　2 Sam 1:17-27

on **SADNESS**
　as **PUNISHMENT**
　　Jeremiah　　　　　Lam 1:1-22;
　　　　　　　　　　3:1-66

on in**SECURITY**
　because of **FEAR**
　　David　　　　　　Ps 55:3b-8

on **SIN**
　　David　　　　　　Ps 52:1-4
　causing **DESPAIR**
　　Jeremiah　　　　　Jer 8:18-9:1
　causing **DESTRUCTION**
　　David　　　　　　Ps 101:5-7;
　　　　　　　　　　8
　against **FRIENDSHIP**
　　David　　　　　　Ps 55:12-14
　causing **GRIEF**
　　Jeremiah　　　　　Jer 8:18-9:1
　causing **GUILT**
　　Judahites　　　　　Lam 5:1-22
　causing **SUFFERING**
　　David　　　　　　Ps 38:3-10
　　Jeremiah　　　　　Lam 1:1-22
　in **WEALTH**
　　Asaph　　　　　　Ps 73:4-12

on **SPIRIT**
　as **QUALITY OF LIFE**
　　Asaph　　　　　　Ps 77:1-10

on **SUFFERING**
　　Job　　　　　　　Job 7:7-11;
　　　　　　　　　　12-16
　through **COMPULSION**
　　Jeremiah　　　　　Lam 3:1-66
　as **PUNISHMENT**
　　Jeremiah　　　　　Lam 2:1-22
　as **QUALITY OF LIFE**
　　Job　　　　　　　Job 7:1-6;
　　　　　　　　　　14:18-22
　　Psalmist　　　　　Ps 102:1-11

in **LEADERSHIP** (cont'd)

Jesus	Heb 1:2b-4; 5-14
Joshua	Num 27:12-23
Solomon	1 Chr 28:1-29:30
Zechariah	Zech 9:1-12

over **LIFE**

Jesus	Col 1:15-17

MIRACLE through

Demon	Mk 1:21-28; Lk 4:31-37

over **POLITICS**

Psalmist	Ps 2:7-9

over **PURIFICATION**

Holy Spirit	Jn 1:19-51

SACREDNESS in

Jesus	Mt 12:1-8; Mk 2:23-28; Lk 6:1-5

concerning **SERVICE**

Jesus	Heb 7:1-28

VICTORY in

Jesus	Mt 8:28-34; Mk 5:1-20; Lk 8:26-39

WISDOM in

Jesus	Mt 22:41-46; Mk 12:35-37a; Lk 20:41-44

WITNESS to

Peter	2 Pet 1:16-19a

BEHAVIOR concerning

DOUBT as

Caiaphas	Mt 26:57-68; Mk 14:53-65

FAITH as

Blind	Mk 8:22-26
Crowd	Mk 6:53-56

FEAR as

Disciples	Mt 14:22-27; Mk 6:45-52; Jn 6:16-24

OBEDIENCE as

Disciples	Mk 9:9-13

OPPRESSION as

Jew	Jn 5:1-18
People	Lk 22:63-65
Soldiers	Mt 27:27-31; Mk 15:16-20

REJECTION as

Crowd	Mt 27:11-26
People	Lk 9:51-56; 22:63-65
Soldiers	Mt 27:27-31; Mk 15:16-20

BEHAVIOR of

resulting in **ALIENATION**

Jesus	Mt 21:12-17; Mk 11:15-19; Lk 19:45-46

ANGER as

Jesus	Mt 21:12-17; Mk 10:13-16; 11:15-19; Lk 9:51-56

BLESSING as

Peter	Mt 16:13-20

COMPASSION as

COMPASSION as (cont'd)

Crowd	Mk 8:1-10
Jesus	Mk 1:40-45; 5:21-24; Lk 7:11-17; 8:40-56; Jn 11:1-57

CONDEMNATION as

Crowd	Lk 11:14-23
Jesus	Mk 11:12-14
Scribes	Mk 3:20-30

HEALING as

Blind	Mk 8:22-26; Lk 18:35-43; Jn 9:1-41
Crowd	Mt 19:1-2; Mk 6:53-56
Deaf	Mk 7:31-37
Demon	Lk 13:10-17
Jesus	Mt 8:2-4; 5-13; 14-17; 28-34; 12:9-14; 22-32; 14:13-21; 15:29-31; 17:14-20; 20:29-34; Mk 1:29-31; 32-34; 40-45; 2:1-12; 3:1-6; 7-12; 5:1-20; 35-43; 9:14-29; 10:46-52; Lk 4:40-41; 5:12-16; 17-26; 6:6-11; 17-19; 7:1-10; 11-17; 8:36-39; 40-56; 9:10-11; 37-43a; 11:14-23; 14:1-6; 22:47-54a; Jn 5:1-18
Lazarus	Jn 11:1-57
Lepers	Lk 17:11-19
Woman	Mk 7:24-30

HUMILITY as

Jesus	Mt 21:1-11; Mk 11:1-10; Lk 19:28-38; Jn 13:1-20

IGNORANCE of

Crowd	Lk 11:14-23

INNOCENCE as

Jesus	Mt 12:1-8

LOVE as

Jesus	Mk 10:17-22
Lazarus	Jn 11:1-57

MIRACLE as

Blind	Mk 8:22-26;
	Lk 18:35-43;
	Jn 9:1-41
Crowd	Mk 6:53-56
Deaf	Mk 7:31-37
Demon	Lk 13:10-17
Jesus	Mt 8:2-4;
	14-17;
	23-27;
	28-34;
	12:9-14;
	22-32;
	17:14-20;
	Mk 1:29-31;
	32-34;
	35-39;
	40-45;
	2:1-12;
	3:1-6;
	7-12;
	4:35-41;
	5:1-20;
	6:30-44;
	9:14-29;
	10:46-52;
	Lk 4:40-41;
	5:1-11;
	12-16;
	17-26;
	6:6-11;
	17-19;
	7:11-17;
	8:22-25;
	26-39;
	9:10-11;
	12-17;
	37-43a;
	11:14-23;
	14:1-6;
	22:47-54a;
	Jn 5:1-18;
	6:1-15;
	21:1-14
Lazarus	Jn 11:1-57
Lepers	Lk 17:11-19
Woman	Mk 7:24-30

PURIFICATION as

Jesus	Jn 3:22-30

SACREDNESS as

Jesus	Jn 5:1-18

SADNESS as

Jesus	Jn 11:1-57

SERVICE as

Crowd	Mk 6:53-56
Jesus	Jn 13:1-20

SUFFERING as

Soldiers	Mt 27:27-31;
	Mk 15:16-20

TEMPERANCE as

Peter	Mt 16:21-28;
	Mk 8:31-33

revealing **WILL of God**

Jesus	Lk 2:41-52

BELIEF in

ACCEPTANCE of

Blind	Jn 9:1-41
Crowd	Mt 21:1-11;

ACCEPTANCE of (cont'd)

Crowd	Mk 11:1-10;
	Lk 19:28-38
Jews	Jn 11:1-57
People	Jn 7:25-31;
	37-52
Samaritans	Jn 4:27-42

CONDEMNATION of

Jews	Jn 8:21-59

through **FAITH**

Blind	Lk 18:35-43;
	Jn 9:1-41
Jews	Jn 12:9-11
Martha	Jn 11:1-57
Mary	Jn 2:1-11
Official	Jn 4:43-54

HEALING through

Blind	Mk 10:46-52;
	Lk 18:35-43;
	Jn 9:1-41
Jesus	Mt 9:18-26;
	9:27-31;
	14:34-36
Martha	Jn 11:1-57
Mary	Jn 11:1-57
Official	Jn 4:43-54
Woman	Mk 5:25-34;
	Lk 8:40-56

IGNORANCE of

People	Jn 7:1-14

MIRACLE because of

Disciples	Jn 2:1-11
Jesus	Mt 9:27-31
Woman	Mk 5:25-34;
	Lk 8:40-56

REJECTION of

People	Jn 7:37-52;
	12:36b-43

WITNESS to

Blind	Jn 9:1-41
Crowd	Mt 21:1-11;
	Mk 11:1-10;
	Lk 19:28-38
Disciples	Jn 2:1-11
Peter	Mt 16:13-20

un**BELIEF** in

causing **DOUBT**

People	Jn 7:25-31;
	12:36b-43

BLASPHEMY against

Pharisees	Mt 9:32-34

BEHAVIOR of

Jews	Jn 8:21-59
People	Lk 22:63-65
Scribes	Mk 3:20-30
Soldiers	Mt 27:27-31;
	Mk 15:16-20

CONFRONTATION with

Crowd	Lk 11:14-23
Herod	Lk 23:6-16
Pharisees	Mt 12:22-32
Priests	Lk 23:33-38
Scribes	Mt 9:1-8;
	Mk 2:1-12;
	Lk 5:17-26
Soldiers	Lk 23:33-38

dis**HONESTY** in

disHONESTY in (cont'd)
Jews   Jn 7:15-24
JUDGMENT of
Jesus   Mt 21:12-17;
    Mk 11:15-19;
    Lk 19:45-46
People   Lk 23:1-5
Priests   Lk 22:66-71
RECONCILIATION overcomes
Paul   1 Tim 1:12-17
SIN of
Crowd   Mt 27:33-44;
    Mk 15:21-32

BLESSING of
BEHAVIOR reveals
Peter   Mt 16:13-20
RESPECT through
David   2 Sam 2:1-7
through STEWARDSHIP
Jesus   Mt 14:13-21;
    Mk 6:30-44;
    8:1-10;
    Lk 9:12-17;
    Jn 6:1-15

CAPTIVITY of
by AUTHORITY
Jesus   Mt 27:27-31
Annas   Jn 18:12-27
Caiaphas   Mt 26:57-68;
    Mk 14:53-65;
    Jn 18:12-27
Jesus   Mt 26:47-56;
    Mk 14:43-50;
    Lk 22:47-54a
Pilate   Mt 27:1-2;
    Mk 15:1-5

DESIRE for
People   Jn 7:25-31

COMMITMENT to
LEADERSHIP of
Mankind   Phil 2:5-11

COMPASSION of
BEHAVIOR revealing
Crowd   Mk 8:1-10
Jesus   Mk 1:40-45;
    5:21-24;
    Lk 7:11-17;
    8:40-56;
    Jn 11:1-57
CONFRONTATION with
Crowd   Mk 6:30-44
Jesus   Mt 14:13-21;
    15:32-39

as MOTIVATION
Jesus   Mt 20:29-34
RESPECT for
David   1Sam 23:14-24;
    22:26:1-25

CONDEMNATION by
Jesus   Mk 11:12-14
through AUTHORITY
Jesus   Mt 21:18-22;
    Mk 11:20-26
Pharisees   Mt 12:22-32

CONDEMNATION of
Crowd   Lk 11:14-23
Scribes   Mk 3:20-30
CONFRONTATION with
Jesus   Lk 13:10-17;
    Jn 2:12-22
Jews   Jn 5:1-18
Pharisees   Mt 12:1-8;
    Mk 2:23-28;
    Lk 6:1-5
Priests   Lk 23:33-38
Soldiers   Lk 23:33-38
DESIRE for
Pharisees   Mt 12:9-14;
    22:15-22;
    Mk 3:1-6;
    12:13-17;
    Lk 6:6-11
Priests   Mt 27:1-2;
    Lk 20:19-26
Scribes   Lk 20:19-26
JUDGMENT on
Caiaphas   Mt 26:57-68;
    Mk 14:53-65
People   Lk 23:1-5
Priests   Lk 22:66-71
Satan   Jn 16:5-11
PROVIDENCE through
Peter   Mt 16:21-28;
    Mk 8:31-33
as PUNISHMENT
Crowd   Mk 15:6-15;
    Lk 23:18-25
SIN of
Crowd   Mt 27:33-44;
    Mk 15:21-32
Jesus   Mk 11:15-19

CONFRONTATION of
resulting in CAPTIVITY
Annas   Jn 18:12-27
Caiaphas   Mt 26:57-68;
    Mk 14:53-65;
    Jn 18:12-27
Jesus   Mt 26:47-56;
    Mk 14:43-50;
    Lk 22:47-54a
Pilate   Mt 27:1-2;
    Mk 15:1-5
COMPASSION in
Crowd   Mk 6:30-44
Jesus   Mt 14:13-21;
    15:32-39
with CONDEMNATION
Jesus   Lk 13:10-17;
    Jn 2:12-22
Jews   Jn 5:1-18
Pharisees   Mt 12:1-8;
    Mk 2:23-28;
    Lk 6:1-5
Priests   Lk 23:33-38
Soldiers   Lk 23:33-38
with DISCIPLESHIP
Andrew   Jn 1:19-51
Peter   Jn 1:19-51
with DOUBT
Jews   Jn 5:1-18
with EVIL
Priests   Mk 11:15-19

with **FAITH**
Criminal | Lk 23:39-43
Crowd | Lk 6:17-19
Jesus | Mt 9:18-26
Lepers | Lk 17:11-19
Woman | Mk 5:25-34;
 | Lk 8:40-56
with **TEMPTATION**
Satan | Mt 4:1-11;
 | Mk 1:12-13;
 | Lk 4:1-13
in **VICTORY**
Psalmist | Ps 2:7-9
with **VIOLENCE**
Demons | Mt 8:28-34;
 | Mk 5:1-20;
 | Lk 8:26-39
with **WEALTH**
Queen of Sheba | 2 Chr 9:1-31;
 | 1 Kgs 10:1-13
with **WISDOM**
Queen of Sheba | 1 Kgs 10:1-13

CONFRONTATION with
ACCEPTANCE of
Nathanael | Jn 1:19-51
causing **ALIENATION**
Jesus | Jn 2:12-22
ANGER in
Jesus | Mk 3:1-6
BLASPHEMY in
Crowd | Lk 11:14-23
Herod | Lk 23:6-16
Pharisees | Mt 12:22-32
Priests | Lk 23:33-38
Scribes | Mt 9:1-8;
 | Mk 2:1-12;
 | Lk 5:17-26
Soldiers | Lk 23:33-38
FEAR of
Demon | Mk 1:21-28;
 | Lk 4:31-37
through **GRACE**
David | 1 Sam 23:14-24;
 | 22:26:1-25
INDIFFERENCE in
Pharisees | Mk 3:1-6
MIRACLE by
Samuel | 1 Sam 28:3-25
PRUDENCE in
Pilate | Mk 15:1-5
REJECTION in
Jesus | Mt 11:16-19;
 | Lk 7:31-35
Jews | Jn 5:1-18
SACRIFICE in
Disciples | Mt 9:14-15;
 | Mk 2:18-22;
 | Lk 5:33-35
Pharisees | Mk 2:18-22;
 | Lk 5:33-35

COURAGE of
RESPECT for
Paul | Phil 1:12-30

CREATION by
of **LIFE**
Jesus | Lk 7:11-17;
 | Heb 1:2b-4;
 | 5-14
Lazarus | Jn 11:1-57

of **ORDER**
Jesus | Col 1:15-17

DEATH of
DESIRE for
Pharisees | Mt 12:9-14
Priests | Mt 27:1-2
JUDGMENT on
Caiaphas | Mt 26:57-68;
 | Mk 14:53-65
provides **MEDIATION**
Jesus | Heb 2:5-18
provides **PROVIDENCE**
Jesus | Mt 27:45-56
as **PUNISHMENT**
Crowd | Mt 27:33-44;
 | Mk 15:21-32
Jesus | Lk 23:33-38;
 | Jn 19:17-42
RESURRECTION through
Ezra | *2 Esd 2:42-48
Jesus | Mt 12:38-42;
 | Lk 11:29-32
for **SINs**
Believers | Gal 5:22-24

DEATH overcome by
through **AUTHORITY**
Lazarus | Jn 11:1-57
Satan | Heb 2:5-18

DESIRE by
for **FULFILLMENT**
Jesus | Mt 14:13-21;
 | 15:32-39;
 | Mk 6:30-44;
 | 8:1-10;
 | Lk 9:12-17;
 | Jn 6:1-15
John the Baptist | Mt 11:2-6;
 | Lk 7:18-23
Queen of Sheba | 1 Kgs 10:1-13;
 | 2 Chr 9:1-31
for **GRACE**
Demons | Lk 8:26-39
Jesus | Mt 9:10-13
for **WISDOM**
Jesus | Mt 16:13-20
to **WITNESS**
Jesus | Lk 2:41-52

DESPAIR of
PRAYER revealing
Jesus | Mt 27:45-56

DESTRUCTION by
of **AUTHORITY**
Satan | Heb 2:5-18
of **SIN**
Isaiah | Is 11:1-9

DESTRUCTION of
DESIRE for
Pharisees | Mk 3:1-6;
 | Lk 6:6-11
Priests | Mk 11:15-19;
 | Lk 19:47-48
through **disRESPECT**
Disciples | Mt 26:47-56;
 | Mk 14:43-50;
 | Lk 22:47-54a

DIGNITY of
   AUTHORITY of
      Jesus   Mt 12:1-8;
                              Mk 2:23-28;
                              Lk 6:1-5
   RESPECT for
      Jesus   Heb 2:5-18

DISCIPLESHIP to
   CONFRONTATION with
      Andrew   Jn 1:19-51
      Peter   Jn 1:19-51
   ELECTION to
      Believers   Lk 10:1-16
      Jesus   Mk 10:17-22;
                              Lk 18:18-27
      Man   Mt 19:16-22
      Jesus   Jn 14:1-14
      Paul   2 Cor 13:5-10

DISOBEDIENCE by
   to LAW
      Jesus   Jn 5:1-18

DOUBT in
   of AUTHORITY
      Crowd   Mt 9:18-26;
                              Mk 5:35-43;
                              Lk 8:40-56
      Elders   Mk 11:27-33;
                              Lk 20:1-8
      Pharisees   Lk 5:17-26
      Priests   Mt 21:23-27;
                              Mk 11:27-33;
                              Lk 20:1-8
   BEHAVIOR revealing
      Caiaphas   Mt 26:57-68;
                              Mk 14:53-65
   because of unBELIEF
      People   Jn 7:25-31;
                              12:36b-43
   CONFRONTATION with
      Jews   Jn 5:1-18
   concerning RESURRECTION
      Disciples   Mk 9:9-13
   concerning SIGNS
      Pharisees   Mt 12:38-42;
                              16:1-4;
                              Mk 8:11-13
   concerning TRUTH
      Jews   Jn 8:21-59
      Nicodemus   Jn 3:1-21
      People   Jn 7:1-14
   concerning VIRTUE
      Pharisees   Mt 9:10-13;
                              Mk 2:15-17;
                              Lk 5:29-32

ELECTION by
   ACCEPTANCE of
      Noah   Gen 6:5-22
   to DISCIPLESHIP
      Believers   Lk 10:1-16
      Jesus   Mk 10:17-22;
                              Lk 18:18-27
      Man   Mt 19:16-22
   FULFILLMENT through
      Jesus   1 Pet 1:13-2:3

ELECTION of
   for KILLING

---

for KILLING (cont'd)
      Jesus   Acts 2:14-36
   to LEADERSHIP
      David   1 Sam 16:1-13;
                            Ps 78:67-72;
                            89:19-37
      Jehu   2 Kgs 9:1-13
      Moses   Ex 3:7-10
      Saul   1 Sam 9:1-10:16;
                            11:1-15
      Solomon   1 Chr 28:1-29:30
   SACREDNESS in
      Jesus   Jn 7:25-31

EQUALITY of
   in LIFE
      Jesus   Heb 2:5-18

FAITH in
      Blind   Mk 8:22-26;
                            Lk 18:35-43;
                            Jn 9:1-41
      Crowd   Mk 6:53-56
      Jews   Jn 12:9-11
      Martha   Jn 11:1-57
      Mary   Jn 2:1-11
      Official   Jn 4:43-54
   concerning AUTHORITY
      Jesus   Mt 8:23-27;
                            9:27-31;
                            Mk 4:35-41;
                            Lk 8:22-25
   CONFRONTATION with
      Criminal   Lk 23:39-43
      Crowd   Lk 6:17-19
      Jesus   Mt 9:18-26
      Lepers   Lk 17:11-19
      Woman   Mk 5:25-34;
                            Lk 8:40-56
   KNOWLEDGE of
      Disciples   Jn 16:29-33
      Peter   Mk 8:27-30;
                            Lk 9:18-22
   as MOTIVATION
      Jesus   Mt 9:27-31
      People   Mk 14:34-36
      Woman   Mk 7:24-30
   in NEW AGE
      Colossians   Col 1:3-8
   through RESURRECTION
      Disciples   Jn 21:1-14
   SALVATION through
      Jesus   Jn 1:1-18
   SIGNS of
      Centurion   Mt 27:45-56
      Jesus   Jn 2:23-25;
                          6:1-15
   in overcoming SIN
      Paralytic   Mt 9:1-8;
                          Mk 2:1-12;
                          Lk 5:17-26
   as TRUTH
      Disciples   Lk 24:50-51
      Jesus   Jn 4:1-26

FAMILY of
   FIDELITY of
      Psalmist   Ps 132:6-10
   KNOWLEDGE of
      Jesus   Mt 1:1-17
   SALVATION through
      Jesus   Mt 1:18-25

REJECTION as (cont'd)
    People   Lk 23:1-5
    Priests   Lk 22:66-71
    through **WITNESS**
        Jesus   Mt 27:11-26;
                          Mk 15:1-5

JUDGMENT by
    against **BLASPHEMY**
        Jesus   Mt 21:12-17;
                          Mk 11:15-19;
                          Lk 19:45-46
        People   Lk 23:1-5
        Priests   Lk 22:66-71
    on **EVIL**
        Satan   Mt 16:21-28;
                          Mk 8:31-33
    on **STEALING**
        Jesus   Mt 21:12-17;
                          Mk 11:15-19;
                          Lk 19:45-46

JUSTICE for
    by **AUTHORITY**
        Pilate   Mt 27:11-26;
                          Mk 15:6-15
    in **JUDGMENT**
        Isaiah   Is 11:1-9
    in **NEW AGE**
        Angel   *2 Esd 11:1-12:39;
                          13:1-50

KILLING of
    DESIRE for
        Jews   Jn 5:1-18
        Priests   Lk 22:1-2
    ELECTION for
        Jesus   Acts 2:14-36
    is **JUDGMENT**
        Crowd   Mt 27:11-26;
                          Mk 15:6-15;
                          Lk 23:18-25

KNOWLEDGE of
    ACCEPTANCE of
        Jesus   Jn 2:23-25;
                          6:60-71
        Peter   Mt 16:13-20
    concerning **EVIL**
        Pharisees   Lk 5:17-26
        Scribes   Mt 9:1-8;
                          Mk 2:1-12
    concerning **FAITH**
        Disciples   Jn 16:29-33
        Peter   Mk 8:27-30;
                          Lk 9:18-22
    concerning **FAMILY**
        Jesus   Mt 1:1-17
    FULFILLMENT through
        Jesus   Mt 17:1-8;
                          Mk 9:2-8;
                          Lk 9:28-36
    concerning **HATE**
        People   Jn 7:1-14
    concerning **HEALING**
        Jesus   Mk 5:25-34
    concerning **IGNORANCE**
        People   Jn 7:25-31
        Pharisees   Jn 8:12-20

concerning **MARRIAGE**
    Jesus   Jn 4:1-26
concerning **OPPRESSION**
    Demons   Mk 1:32-34;
                        Lk 4:40-41
PRAISE of
    Disciples   Mt 14:28-33
REJECTION of
    Jesus   Jn 18:1-11
concerning **SPIRIT**
    Jesus   Jn 2:23-25
concerning **WILL**
    People   Jn 7:1-14
concerning **WISDOM**
    Jesus   Mt 11:27;
                    Jn 7:1-14

WITNESS to
    Demons   Mk 3:7-12
    Peter   Mk 8:27-30;
                    Lk 9:18-22
    Shepherds   Lk 2:1-20

LEADERSHIP of
    AUTHORITY in
        David   2 Sam 2:1-7;
                       5:1-5;
                       1 Chr 11:1-12:40
        Jesus   Heb 1:2b-4;
                       5-14
        Joshua   Num 27:12-23
        Solomon   1 Chr 28:1-29:30
        Zechariah   Zech 9:1-12
    COMMITMENT to
        Mankind   Phil 2:5-11
    ELECTION to
        David   1 Sam 16:1-13;
                       Ps 78:67-72;
                       89:19-37
        Jehu   2 Kgs 9:1-13
        Moses   Ex 3:7-10
        Saul   1 Sam 9:1-10:16;
                       11:1-15
        Solomon   1 Chr 28:1-29:30
    ETERNAL
        Jesus   Heb 1:5-14
        King   Ps 45:2-9
    PROVIDENCE through
        Jesus   Lk 1:26-38
    RITE of
        Saul   1 Sam 10:17-27
    SALVATION through
        God   2 Kgs 13:1-9
    SIGNS of
        Zechariah   Zech 4:1-6a;
                       10b-14

LIFE through
    as **CREATION**
        Jesus   Lk 7:11-17;
                       Heb 1:2b-4;
                       5-14
        Lazarus   Jn 11:1-57
    as **EQUALITY**
        Jesus   Heb 2:5-18
    as **ETERNAL**
        Jesus   Jn 3:31-36;
                       Col 1:15-17;
                       2 Tim 1:8-14;
                       Heb 1:5-14;
                       7:1-28

IGNORANCE of
Jesus   Lk 12:39-40
JUSTICE in
Angel   *2 Esd 11:1-12:39;
                         13:1-50
OBEDIENCE to
Jesus   Lk 12:39-40
REJECTION of
Jesus   Acts 4:1-22
SACRIFICE in
Jesus   Heb 8:1-5
SERVICE to
Jesus   Heb 8:1-5
VICTORY in
Jesus   Jn 16:29-33
WEALTH in
Man   Mt 19:16-22

OBEDIENCE to
BEHAVIOR revealing
Disciples   Mk 9:9-13
in NEW AGE
Jesus   Lk 12:39-40
PROVIDENCE in
Jesus   Jn 18:1-11
SALVATION through
Jesus   Heb 5:1-10

OPPRESSION of
BEHAVIOR revealing
Jews   Jn 5:1-18
People   Lk 22:63-65
Soldiers   Mt 27:27-31;
                         Mk 15:16-20
KNOWLEDGE of
Demons   Mk 1:32-34;
                         Lk 4:40-41
SIN of
Crowd   Mt 27:33-44;
                         Mk 15:21-32

ORDER of
in CREATION
Jesus   Col 1:15-17

PATIENCE in
FIDELITY of
Jesus   Lk 12:39-40
SALVATION through
Jesus   Heb 9:23-28

PEACE from
through RECONCILIATION
Isaiah   Is 11:1-9

PEACE through
PRAYER for
Jesus   Mt 14:22-27
SECURITY in
Disciples   Jn 16:29-33
Zechariah   Zech 9:1-12

POLITICS of
AUTHORITY in
Psalmist   Ps 2:7-9

POVERTY of
SALVATION through
Jesus   2 Cor 8:7-15

PRAISE of
COMPULSION in
Holy Spirit   1 Cor 12:1-3
KNOWLEDGE of
Disciples   Mt 14:28-33
PRAYER for
God   *2 Esd 2:33-41
RESPECT for
Crowd   Mt 21:1-11;
                         Mk 11:1-10;
                         Lk 19:28-38
RITE of
David   2 Sam 23:1-7
Woman   Mt 26:6-13;
                         Mk 14:3-9
SALVATION through
Anna   Lk 2:21-40
TRUTH in
Holy Spirit   Jn 16:12-15

PRAYER of
for COMPASSION
Jesus   Heb 5:1-10
in DESPAIR
Jesus   Mt 27:45-56
for FULFILLMENT
Holy Spirit   Jn 14:15-17
for GRACE
People   Lk 23:33-38
for GRATITUDE
Jesus   Mt 15:32-39;
                         Jn 11:1-57
for HEALING
Jesus   Mt 21:12-17
of JOY
God   *2 Esd 2:33-41
for PEACE
Jesus   Mt 14:22-27
for PRAISE
God   *2 Esd 2:33-41

PRESENCE of
in DISCIPLESHIP
Jesus   Jn 14:1-14
Paul   2 Cor 13:5-10
FULFILLMENT through
Holy Spirit   Jn 14:15-17
Jesus   Mt 11:2-6;
                         Lk 7:18-23
in HEALING
Holy Spirit   Acts 10:1-11:18
JOY of
Holy Spirit   Lk 10:21-22

PROMISE by
for FULFILLMENT
Jesus   Acts 1:1-5
for VICTORY
Jesus   Jn 14:27-31
Zechariah   Zech 9:1-12

PRUDENCE of
in CONFRONTATION
Pilate   Mk 15:1-5

PUNISHMENT of the
CONDEMNATION as
Crowd   Mk 15:6-15;
                         Lk 23:18-25

DEATH as
Crowd — Mt 27:33-44; Mk 15:21-32
Jesus — Lk 23:33-38; Jn 19:17-42
REJECTION as
Jesus — Lk 23:33-38

PUNISHMENT by
REVENGE as
Jehu — 2 Kgs 9:1-13

PURIFICATION by
for **SIN**
Jesus — Heb 1:2b-4

PURIFICATION of
BEHAVIOR revealing
Jesus — Jn 3:22-30
for **RECONCILIATION**
Jesus — Heb 9:1-14
as **STEWARDSHIP**
Jesus — Jn 13:1-20

QUALITY OF LIFE of
HEALING as
Jesus — 1 Pet 2:21-25
HUMILITY as
Zechariah — Zech 9:1-12
WISDOM as
Jesus — Lk 2:21-40; 41-52

RECONCILIATION through
by **GRACE**
Jesus — Rom 5:6-11; Heb 1:2b-4; 2:5-18
HOPE in
Isaiah — Is 11:1-9; 10-16
LIFE in
Jesus — 1 Pet 2:21-25
PEACE in
Isaiah — Is 11:1-9
by **PURIFICATION**
Jesus — Heb 9:1-14
SACRIFICE in
Israelites — Mal 2:17-3:5
Jesus — Heb 9:23-28
SUFFERING in
Jesus — Heb 2:5-18
TEMPTATION in
Jesus — Heb 2:5-18

REJECTION by
of **LAW**
Jesus — Lk 13:10-17

REJECTION of
BEHAVIOR revealing
Crowd — Mt 27:11-26
People — Lk 9:51-56; 22:63-65
Soldiers — Mt 27:27-31; Mk 15:16-20
CONFRONTATION with
Jesus — Mt 11:16-19; Lk 7:31-35
Jews — Jn 5:1-18

JUDGMENT on
Caiaphas — Mt 26:57-68; Mk 14:53-65
People — Lk 23:1-5
Priests — Lk 22:66-71
KNOWLEDGE of
Jesus — Jn 18:1-11
in **NEW AGE**
Jesus — Acts 4:1-22
as **PUNISHMENT**
Jesus — Lk 23:33-38
revealing dis**RESPECT**
Crowd — Mk 6:1-6
People — Mt 13:53-58; Lk 4:16-30
SIN in
Crowd — Mt 27:33-44; Mk 15:21-32
Jesus — Jn 1:1-18
concerning **TRUTH**
Jews — Jn 8:21-59
People — Jn 1:1-18
Pharisees — Jn 8:12-20

RESPECT for
ACCEPTANCE of
Jesus — Heb 1:5-14
Jews — Mt 21:12-17
through **BLESSING**
David — 2 Sam 2:1-7
through **COMPASSION**
David — 1 Sam 23:14-24:22; 26:1-25
revealed by **COURAGE**
Paul — Phil 1:12-30
DIGNITY of
Jesus — Heb 2:5-18
revealed in **FEAR**
Crowd — Mt 9:32-34; 1-8
Disciples — Mt 17:1-8; Lk 9:28-36
God — Is 11:1-9
FULFILLMENT of
Jesus — Heb 1:5-14
through **PRAISE**
Crowd — Mt 21:1-11; Mk 11:1-10; Lk 19:28-38
through **WITNESS**
Centurion — Mt 27:45-56

dis**RESPECT** against
DESTRUCTION through
Disciples — Mt 26:47-56; Mk 14:43-50; Lk 22:47-54a

dis**RESPECT** for
results in **REJECTION**
Crowd — Mk 6:1-6
People — Mt 13:53-58; Lk 4:16-30
brings **REVENGE**
David — 2 Sam 1:1-16

RESURRECTION of
from **DEATH**
Ezra — *2 Esd 2:42-48
Jesus — Mt 12:38-42; Lk 11:29-32

DOUBT in
    Disciples   Mk 9:9-13
FAITH in
    Disciples   Jn 21:1-14
FULFILLMENT through
    Jesus   Jn 20:1-29
WITNESS to
    Jesus   Acts 1:1-5

REVENGE by
  as PUNISHMENT
    Jehu   2 Kgs 9:1-13
  for disRESPECT
    David   2 Sam 1:1-16

RITE of
  revealing LEADERSHIP
    Saul   1 Sam 10:17-27
  revealing PRAISE
    David   2 Sam 23:1-7
    Woman   Mt 26:6-13;
                Mk 14:3-9

SACREDNESS in
    Joshua   Num 27:12-23
    Mary   Jn 12:1-8

SACRIFICE of
  CONFRONTATION with
    Disciples   Mt 9:14-15;
                Mk 2:18-22;
                Lk 5:33-35
    Pharisees   Mk 2:18-22;
                Lk 5:33-35
  MEDIATION through
    Jesus   1 Tim 2:1-7
  for NEW AGE
    Jesus   Heb 8:1-5
  PROVIDENCE through
    Jesus   Mt 27:45-56
  RECONCILIATION through
    Israelites   Mal 2:17-3:5
    Jesus   Heb 9:23-28
  SALVATION through
    Jesus   Heb 9:1-14
  for SIN
    Jesus   Gal 1:1-5
  VIRTUE in
    Jesus   Heb 9:1-14

SADNESS of
  BEHAVIOR revealing
    Jesus   Jn 11:1-57

SALVATION by
  ACCEPTANCE of
    Jesus   Jn 10:1-18
  FAITH in
    Jesus   Jn 1:1-18
  FAMILY of
    Jesus   Mt 1:18-25
  through GRACE
    Believers   1 Pet 1:13-2:3
    Jesus   2 Cor 8:7-15
  HOPE in
    Believers   1 Pet 1:13-2:3
  through LEADERSHIP
    God   2 Kgs 13:1-9
  LIFE through
    Jesus   Mt 9:18-26;
                Mk 5:35-43;
                Lk 2:1-20;
                8:40-56

MIRACLE of
    Jesus   Mt 9:18-26;
                Mk 5:35-43;
                Lk 8:40-56
  through OBEDIENCE
    Jesus   Heb 5:1-10
  through PATIENCE
    Jesus   Heb 9:23-28
  concerning POVERTY
    Jesus   2 Cor 8:7-15
  PRAISE of
    Anna   Lk 2:21-40
  through SACRIFICE
    Jesus   Heb 9:1-14
  through SUFFERING
    Jesus   Heb 2:5-18
  VICTORY of
    Jesus   Heb 2:5-18

SECURITY in
  for LIFE
    Jesus   Jn 10:1-18
  for PEACE
    Disciples   Jn 16:29-33
    Zechariah   Zech 9:1-12

SERVICE of
  BEHAVIOR revealing
    Crowd   Mk 6:53-56
    Jesus   Jn 13:1-20
  for ETERNITY
    Jesus   Heb 7:1-28
  in NEW AGE
    Jesus   Heb 8:1-5
  PROVIDENCE through
    Cyrus   Is 44:24-45:13
  SIGNS of
    Jesus   Mt 11:2-6;
                Lk 7:18-23
  VIRTUE in
    Jesus   Heb 7:1-28

SERVICE to
  COMPULSION in
    Simon   Mt 27:32;
                Mk 15:21-32

SHARING by
  SIGNS of
    Jesus   Mt 14:13-21;
                15:32-39;
                Mk 6:30-44;
                8:1-10;
                Lk 9:12-17;
                Jn 6:1-15

SIGNS by
  of HEALING
    Jesus   Mt 9:10-13;
                11:2-6;
                Mk 2:15-17;
                Lk 5:29-32;
                7:18-23;
                Jn 4:43-54
  of LEADERSHIP
    Zechariah   Zech 4:1-6a;
                10b-14
  of MIRACLEs
    Jesus   Mt 8:28-34;
                9:32-34;
                11:2-6;

PROMISE of
Jesus	Jn 14:27-31
Zechariah	Zech 9:1-12

VIRTUE of
DOUBT of
Pharisees	Mt 9:10-13;
	Mk 2:15-17;
	Lk 5:29-32

in **SACRIFICE**
Jesus	Heb 9:1-14

in **SERVICE**
Jesus	Heb 7:1-28

WEALTH of
CONFRONTATION with
Queen of Sheba	1 Kgs 10:1-13;
	2 Chr 9:1-31

in **NEW AGE**
Man	Mt 19:16-22

WILL of
BEHAVIOR revealing
Jesus	Lk 2:41-52

KNOWLEDGE of
People	Jn 7:1-14

PROVIDENCE through
Jesus	Lk 22:14-23

WISDOM of
concerning **AUTHORITY**
Jesus	Mt 22:41-46;
	Mk 12:35-37a;
	Lk 20:41-44

CONFRONTATION with
Queen of Sheba	1 Kgs 10:1-13

DESIRE for
Jesus	Mt 16:13-20

KNOWLEDGE of
Jesus	Mt 11:27;
	Jn 7:1-14

as **QUALITY OF LIFE**
Jesus	Lk 2:21-40;
	41-52

WITNESS by
DESIRE for
Jesus	Lk 2:41-52

to **FREEDOM**
Isaiah	Is 61:1-11

JUDGMENT on
Jesus	Mt 27:11-26;
	Mk 15:1-5

WITNESS to
Peter	2 Pet 1:16-19a

through **BELIEF**
Blind	Jn 9:1-41
Crowd	Mt 21:1-11;
	Mk 11:1-10;
	Lk 19:28-38
Disciples	Jn 2:1-11
Peter	Mt 16:13-20

CONVERSION through
Centurion	Mk 15:33-41

FIDELITY of
Ezra	*2 Esd 2:42-48

through **KNOWLEDGE**
Demons	Mk 3:7-12
Peter	Mk 8:27-30;
	Lk 9:18-22
Shepherds	Lk 2:1-20

concerning **MEDIATION**
Jesus	1 Tim 2:1-7

RESPECT for
Centurion	Mt 27:45-56

RESURRECTION of
Jesus	Acts 1:1-5

SIGNS of
Jesus	Mt 11:2-6;
	Lk 7:18-23
John the Baptist	Jn 1:19-51

concerning **TRUTH** of
Holy Spirit	1 Cor 12:1-3
Jesus	Mk 1:1
John	Jn 19:17-42
Peter	2 Pet 1:16-19a

MIRACLE

by **AUTHORITY**
God	Ps 114:7-8
Israelites	Ex 15:1-18
Jesus	Mt 8:5-13;
	Lk 7:1-10
Psalmist	Ps 114:3-6

of **DEITY**
God	Mic 1:2-4;
	Nah 1:1-9;
	2 Cor 4:7-12
Jesus	Lk 11:14-23

of **FOLLOWERs**
Demons	Mk 6:7-13;
	Lk 9:1-6
Jesus	Mt 10:1

of **MESSIANIC FIGURE**
Demon	Mk 1:21-28;
	Lk 4:31-37

in **MISSION**
Holy Spirit	Rom 15:14-24

PROPHECY of
Moses	Deut 34:1-12

REVELATION on
Israelites	Deut 11:1-25

BEHAVIOR revealing
Elijah	2 Kgs 2:1-18
Elisha	2 Kgs 2:1-18
Israelites	Josh 3:14-17
Jesus	Mt 14:22-27;
	Mk 6:45-52;
	Lk 4:38-39;
	Jn 6:16-24
Moses	Ex 14:23-31;
	17:8-16
Paul	Acts 16:16-24
Peter	Acts 3:1-26;
	5:11-16;
	9:32-43
Philip	Acts 8:4-13

by **DEITY**
Elijah	*Sir 48:1-11

by **MESSIANIC FIGURE**
Blind	Mk 8:22-26;
	Lk 18:35-43;
	Jn 9:1-41
Crowd	Mk 6:53-56
Deaf	Mk 7:31-37
Demon	Lk 13:10-17

for **HEALING**
  Apostles   Mt 10:7-8
HUMILITY of
  Titus   Tit 3:1-7
JUSTICE in
  Paul   2 Cor 13:5-10
LEADERSHIP of
  Paul   1 Tim 1:1-2
MIRACLE by
  Holy Spirit   Rom 15:14-24
OBEDIENCE to
  Titus   Tit 3:1-7
SERVICE to
  Apostles   Mt 10:7-8
  Elders   1 Pet 5:1-5
  Paul   Tit 1:1-4
WILL of
  Paul   1 Cor 1:1-3
WITNESS to
  Israelites   Ps 106:6-12
  Paul   2 Cor 2:14-17
  Pharaoh   Ex 9:13-35;
                   Rom 9:14-29
  Titus   Tit 2:11-15

BEHAVIOR in
  revealing **ALIENATION**
    Barnabas   Acts 15:30-41
    Paul   Acts 15:30-41
  revealing **COURAGE**
    Paul   1 Thes 2:1-12
  revealing **DISOBEDIENCE**
    Jonah   Jon 1:1-17
  revealing **FULFILLMENT**
    Jesus   Eph 4:7-16
  revealing **HEALING**
    Jesus   Mt 9:35
  revealing **IGNORANCE**
    Joseph   Lk 2:41-52
    Mary   Lk 2:41-52
  revealing **MIRACLE**
    Jesus   Mt 9:35
  revealing **PRUDENCE**
    Paul   1 Thes 2:1-12
  revealing **PURIFICATION**
    John the Baptist Jn 3:22-30
  revealing **SACRIFICE**
    Paul   2 Cor 11:7-15
  revealing **SERVICE**
    Paul   1 Thes 2:1-12
  revealing **SHARING**
    Paul   2 Cor 11:7-15;
                  1 Thes 2:1-12

BELIEF in
  results in **HEALING**
    Jesus   Mt 15:21-28
  of **LOVE**
    Men   Tit 2:1-10
  results in **MIRACLE**
    Jesus   Mt 15:21-28
  WITNESS to
    Paul   2 Cor 4:13-15

of **BELIEF**
  resulting in **ONENESS**
    Believers   Eph 4:7-16

to cause **BELIEF**

to cause **BELIEF** (cont'd)
  resulting in **PURIFICATION**
    John the Baptist Mt 3:1-12;
                  Lk 3:1-6

BLESSING of
  as **GIFT**
    Believers   1 Cor 14:1-12
  as **JUDGMENT**
    Apostles   Mt 10:9-15
to **BROTHERHOOD**
  LOVE in
    Paul   Col 2:1-5;
                  1 Thes 2:1-12
  SERVICE in
    Paul   2 Cor 5:11-13
  WITNESS to
    Holy Spirit   2 Cor 3:1-3

CAPTIVITY in
  FREEDOM from
    Jesus   Lk 4:16-30
  as **STEWARDSHIP**
    Paul   Philm 1:1-3

CHAOS in
  through **FIDELITY**
    Jesus   Mt 10:26-39;
                 Lk 12:51-53

COMMITMENT to
  through **LOVE**
    Timothy   1 Tim 1:3-7
  through **OBEDIENCE**
    Paul   2 Cor 13:5-10
  through **SACRIFICE**
    Paul   1 Cor 9:15-23
  through **SERVICE**
    Paul   1 Cor 9:15-23;
                  Gal 6:11-18;
                  Col 2:1-5
  through **WITNESS**
    Paul   Acts 19:21-22
to **COMMUNITY**
  DOUBT in
    Jesus   Mt 13:53-58;
                 Mk 6:1-6;
                 Lk 4:16-30
  REJECTION of
    Jesus   Lk 13:34-35

COMPASSION in
  of **STEWARDSHIP**
    Isaiah   Is 61:1-11

COMPULSION in
  to **ANGER**
    Ezekiel   Ezek 3:12-15
  for **FULFILLMENT**
    Ezekiel   Ezek 3:12-15

for **CONDEMNATION**
  of **SIN**
    Jonah   Jon 1:1-17

of **CONDEMNATION**
  as **JUDGMENT**
    Holy Spirit   Jn 16:5-11

against **EVIL**
    RECONCILIATION in
      Jesus   1 Cor 15:20-28
    SALVATION through
      Jesus   1 Tim 1:12-17

FAITH in
    results in **AUTHORITY**
      Disciples   Mk 6:7-13;
                      Lk 9:1-6
      Paul   Eph 3:1-13
    FIDELITY of
      Timothy   1 Tim 1:18-20
    PROMISE of
      Apostles   Mt 10:16-22
    as **QUALITY OF LIFE**
      Timothy   1 Tim 1:3-7
    STEWARDSHIP of
      Believers   Acts 11:19-21
    of **TRUTH**
      John the Baptist   Jn 1:1-18
      Paul   1 Cor 15:1-11;
                      2 Cor 10:12-18;
                      1 Tim 2:1-7
      Thessalonians   1 Thes 2:13-16

to **FAMILY**
    urging **FIDELITY**
      Women   Tit 2:1-10
    causes **inFIDELITY**
      Jesus   Lk 12:51-53
    as **QUALITY OF LIFE**
      Bishop   Tit 1:5-8

FIDELITY in
    results in **DEATH**
      Paul   Acts 21:1-14
    DIGNITY through
      Paul   2 Cor 1:15-22
    of **DISCIPLESHIP**
      Paul   2 Cor 1:15-22
    of **FAITH**
      Timothy   1 Tim 1:18-20
    to **FAMILY**
      Jesus   Lk 12:51-53
      Women   Tit 2:1-10
    FULFILLMENT through
      Jesus   Jn 10:1-18
    through **GRACE**
      Paul   2 Cor 4:1-6
    of **LOVE**
      Women   Tit 2:1-10
    of **MARRIAGE**
      Women   Tit 2:1-10
    causes **OPPRESSION**
      Paul   2 Cor 4:7-12
    SACRIFICE through
      Jesus   Jn 10:1-18
      Paul   Acts 21:1-14;
                      2 Cor 6:3-10;
                      Gal 6:11-18
    of **SERVICE**
      Paul   2 Cor 6:3-10
      Servants   1 Tim 6:1-2b
      Slaves   Tit 2:1-10
    SUFFERING through
      Paul   2 Cor 4:7-12;
                      6:3-10
    TEMPERANCE in
      Men   Tit 2:1-10

WITNESS to
    Epaphras   Col 1:3-8

inFIDELITY to
    resulting in **ALIENATION**
      Jesus   Lk 12:51-53
    causes **CHAOS**
      Jesus   Mt 10:26-39;
                      Lk 12:51-53

FREEDOM in
    from **CAPTIVITY**
      Jesus   Lk 4:16-30
    REWARDs of
      Paul   1 Cor 9:15-23

FRIENDSHIP in
    DESIRE for
      Paul   1 Thes 2:17-20

FULFILLMENT of
    BEHAVIOR revealing
      Jesus   Eph 4:7-16
    COMPULSION in
      Ezekiel   Ezek 3:12-15
    FIDELITY in
      Jesus   Jn 10:1-18
    of **LAW**
      Jesus   2 Cor 3:12-18
    of **NEW AGE**
      Jesus   Lk 13:31-33
    PRAYER for
      Jesus   Jn 17:1-5
    PRESENCE in
      Jesus   Lk 4:16-30
    SIGNS of
      Israelites   *1 Esd 7:1-9
    of **TRUTH**
      Paul   2 Tim 4:1-5
    VIRTUE in
      Holy Spirit   Jn 16:5-11

GIFT in
    BLESSING as
      Believers   1 Cor 14:1-12

GOOD in
    VIRTUE as
      Bishop   Tit 1:5-8

GRACE in
    FIDELITY through
      Paul   2 Cor 4:1-6
    PRAYER for
      Jude   Jude 1:1-2
      Peter   2 Pet 1:1-2
    RECONCILIATION through
      Jesus   Rom 3:31-4:25
    SALVATION through
      Jesus   Lk 19:1-10
    STEWARDSHIP by
      Paul   Eph 3:1-13
    through **TRUTH**
      Paul   Rom 15:14-24;
                      1 Cor 15:1-11

HEALING in
    Jesus   Mk 1:35-39
    AUTHORITY for
      Apostles   Mt 10:7-8

provides WISDOM
　Apostles　　　　　Mt 10:16-22

PRUDENCE in
　BEHAVIOR revealing
　　Paul　　　　　　1 Thes 2:1-12
　concerning TRUTH
　　Paul　　　　　　1 Cor 1:13-17

PUNISHMENT in
　for REPENTANCE
　　Jeremiah　　　　Jer 6:27-30

PURIFICATION in
　BEHAVIOR revealing
　　John the Baptist　Jn 3:22-30
　BELIEF in
　　John the Baptist　Mt 3:1-12;
　　　　　　　　　　Lk 3:1-6

of PURIFICATION
　CONVERSION through
　　Disciples　　　　Mt 28:16-20

as QUALITY OF LIFE
　FAITH in
　　Timothy　　　　1 Tim 1:3-7

QUALITY OF LIFE in
　of FAMILY
　　Bishop　　　　　Tit 1:5-8
　HUMILITY as
　　Bishop　　　　　Tit 1:5-8
　　Women　　　　　Tit 2:1-10
　MARRIAGE as
　　Bishop　　　　　Tit 1:5-8
　OBEDIENCE as
　　Jesus　　　　　　Phil 2:5-11
　PRIDE as
　　Paul　　　　　　2 Cor 11:16-20
　SERVICE as
　　Bishop　　　　　Tit 1:5-8
　　James　　　　　　Jas 1:1
　　Jude　　　　　　Jude 1:1-2
　　Paul　　　　　　Phil 1:1-2
　　Peter　　　　　　1 Pet 1:1-2;
　　　　　　　　　　2 Pet 1:1-2
　　Timothy　　　　Phil 1:1-2
　SHARING as
　　Bishop　　　　　Tit 1:5-8
　SPIRIT as
　　Jesus　　　　　　Mt 11:28-30
　TEMPERANCE as
　　Bishop　　　　　Tit 1:5-8
　　Paul　　　　　　1 Cor 9:24-27

RECONCILIATION in
　against EVIL
　　Jesus　　　　　　1 Cor 15:20-28
　by GRACE
　　Jesus　　　　　　Rom 3:31-4:25

of RECONCILIATION
　through HEALING
　　Jesus　　　　　　Mt 9:10-13
　through REPENTANCE
　　Jesus　　　　　　Mt 9:10-13;
　　　　　　　　　　Lk 5:29-32
　through SACRIFICE
　　Jesus　　　　　　Mt 20:20-28;
　　　　　　　　　　Mk 10:35-45

　through SERVICE
　　Jesus　　　　　　Mt 20:20-28;
　　　　　　　　　　Mk 10:35-45
　WITNESS to
　　Paul　　　　　　Acts 26:1-32;
　　　　　　　　　　2 Cor 5:14-19;
　　　　　　　　　　20-6:2

REJECTION of
　by COMMUNITY
　　Jesus　　　　　　Lk 13:34-35
　in CONFRONTATION
　　John the Baptist　Mt 11:16-19;
　　　　　　　　　　Lk 7:31-35

of REPENTANCE
　CONVERSION through
　　Jesus　　　　　　Mt 4:17;
　　　　　　　　　　9:10-13

　PUNISHMENT in
　　Jeremiah　　　　Jer 6:27-30
　of SIN
　　John the Baptist　Lk 3:1-6

REPENTANCE through
　of RECONCILIATION
　　Jesus　　　　　　Mt 9:10-13;
　　　　　　　　　　Lk 5:29-32

RESPECT in
　revealed through HUMILITY
　　Slaves　　　　　Tit 2:1-10
　for LEADERSHIP
　　Servants　　　　1 Tim 6:1-2b
　through OBEDIENCE
　　Servants　　　　1 Tim 6:1-2b
　through PATIENCE
　　Paul　　　　　　2 Cor 6:3-10

of RESURRECTION
　ACCEPTANCE of
　　Paul　　　　　　1 Cor 15:1-11
　DEATH in
　　Jesus　　　　　　2 Cor 5:14-19

REWARD of
　FREEDOM as
　　Paul　　　　　　1 Cor 9:15-23
　as MOTIVATION
　　Paul　　　　　　1 Cor 9:24-27
　of NEW AGE
　　Jesus　　　　　　Mt 5:17-20
　SALVATION as
　　Apostles　　　　Mt 10:16-22

SACREDNESS in
　of NEW AGE
　　Holy Spirit　　　2 Cor 3:7-11
　SIGNS of
　　Israelites　　　　*1 Esd 7:1-9

SACRIFICE in
　BEHAVIOR revealing
　　Paul　　　　　　2 Cor 11:7-15
　COMMITMENT to
　　Paul　　　　　　1 Cor 9:15-23
　FIDELITY in
　　Jesus　　　　　　Jn 10:1-18
　　Paul　　　　　　Acts 21:1-14;
　　　　　　　　　　2 Cor 6:3-10;
　　　　　　　　　　Gal 6:11-18

WITNESS to (cont'd)

Men	Tit 2:1-10
Paul	Acts 14:1-7;
	19-28;
	16:1-5;
	17:10-15;
	18:1-17;
	18-23;
	Rom 1:1-7;
	15:14-24;
	1 Cor 1:13-17;
	2:1-5;
	15:1-11;
	16:5-12;
	2 Cor 2:12-13;
	10:12-18;
	11:7-15;
	Eph 6:19-20;
	Col 1:25-27;
	1 Thes 2:1-12
Peter	2 Pet 1:12-15
Timothy	Acts 16:1-5;
	1 Tim 1:3-7

VICTORY in
　SIGNS of

Jesus	Mt 11:28-30

VIRTUE in
　reveals DIGNITY

Men	Tit 2:1-10

　FULFILLMENT through

Holy Spirit	Jn 16:5-11

　as GOOD

Bishop	Tit 1:5-8

WILL in
　of TRUTH

Jesus	Mk 1:35-39;
	Lk 4:42-44

WISDOM in
　CONFRONTATION with

Apostles	Mt 10:16-22

　DESIRE for

Paul	Col 2:1-5

　of NEW AGE

Jesus	Lk 4:16-30

　PROVIDENCE through

Apostles	Mt 10:16-22

　of TRUTH

Jesus	Lk 4:42-44
Paul	Col 1:28-29

of WITNESS
　AUTHORITY in

Israelites	Ps 106:6-12
Paul	2 Cor 2:14-17
Pharaoh	Ex 9:13-35;
	Rom 9:14-29
Titus	Tit 2:11-15

　BELIEF in

Paul	2 Cor 4:13-15

　to BROTHERHOOD

Holy Spirit	2 Cor 3:1-3

　COMMITMENT to

Paul	Acts 19:21-22

　ELECTION to

Barnabas	Acts 13:1-3
Ezekiel	Ezek 3:4-9

ELECTION to (cont'd)

Gentiles	Gal 1:18-2:10
Jesus	Jn 8:21-59
John the Baptist	Jn 1:1-18
Paul	2 Cor 1:1-2
Saul	Acts 13:1-3

FIDELITY in

Epaphras	Col 1:3-8

HONESTY in

Paul	2 Cor 2:14-17

JUDGMENT on

Ezekiel	Ezek 33:1-9

KNOWLEDGE of

Jeremiah	Jer 6:27-30
Paul	Acts 20:1-4;
	5-16;
	21:1-14;
	15-26;
	Rom 15:25-33;
	Tit 1:1-4
Peter	2 Pet 1:12-15
Tychicus	Eph 6:21-22

MEDIATION through

John the Baptist	Jn 3:22-30

to NEW AGE

Jesus	Mt 9:35

RECONCILIATION through

Paul	Acts 26:1-32;
	2 Cor 5:14-19;
	20-6:2

SALVATION through

Isaiah	Is 49:1-26
Jesus	Mt 9:35

concerning SIN

Ezekiel	Ezek 3:16-21;
	11:1-13;
	33:1-9
Micah	Mic 3:1-12

STEWARDSHIP of

Apostles	Mt 10:5-6
Believers	Lk 10:1-16
Jesus	Mt 11:1

to TRUTH

Apostles	Acts 6:1-7;
	16:11-15
Barnabas	Acts 14:1-7
Believers	Acts 11:19-21
Bishop	Tit 1:9-16
Church	Eph 3:1-13;
	1 Tim 3:14-16
Disciples	Mk 6:7-13;
	Lk 9:1-6;
	Jn 17:6-19
Ezekiel	Ezek 3:16-21;
	22-27;
	38:1-2
Isaiah	Is 61:1-11
Jesus	Mt 9:35;
	Lk 4:42-44;
	Jn 4:27-42;
	18:28-19:16
Men	Tit 2:1-10
Paul	Acts 14:1-7;
	19-28;
	16:1-5;
	17:10-15;
	18:1-17;
	18-23;
	Rom 1:1-7;
	15:14-24;

of **MESSIANIC FIGURE**
   Jesus   Mt 9:27-31
   People   Mt 14:34-36
   Woman   Mk 7:24-30
SELF-REALIZATION of
   Jesus   Mt 26:36-46;
                      Mk 14:32-42;
                      Lk 22:39-46

FALSE BELIEF as
  for **ANGER**
     Herod   Mt 2:16-18
  for **ANXIETY**
     Priests   Mt 27:62-66
  for **DOUBT**
     Priests   Mt 27:62-66
  for **LUST**
     Herod   Mt 14:1-12;
                  Mk 6:17-2
  for **REJECTION**
     Priests   Mt 28:11-15
  for **SACRIFICE**
     Paul   Col 2:16-23
  for **SELFISHNESS**
     Herod   Mt 14:1-12;
                  Mk 6:17-29
  for **SUFFERING**
     Zechariah   Zech 10:1-2
  for **VIOLENCE**
     Satan   Rev 20:7-10

FEAR as
     Abraham   Gen 12:9-13:1;
                  20:1-18;
                  22:1-19
     Israelites   Num 14:1-2;
                  3-4
     Jacob   Gen 33:1-16;
                  42:26-38;
                  43:1-15
     Micah   Judg 18:21-26
     Nations   Ps 2:4-6
     Pharaoh   Ex 1:8-14;
                  15-22
     Rebekah   Gen 27:41-28:5
  of **FOLLOWERs**
     Disciples   Mt 26:47-56
  INSTRUCTION on
     Moses   Ex 4:10-16
  concerning **MESSIANIC FIGURE**
     Pharisees   Mt 22:41-46
  PROPHECY of
     Disciples   Mk 14:43-50
     Tyre   Ezek 26:15-18
  REVELATION on
     Elihu   Job 33:15-18

of **FOLLOWERs**
  DISCIPLESHIP as
     Jesus   Mt 9:36-38
  FEAR as
     Disciples   Mt 26:47-56
  JOY as
     Holy Spirit   1 Thes 1:2-10
     Paul   Philm 1:4-7
  in **LEADERSHIP**
     Paul   1 Cor 10:23-11:1

FULFILLMENT as
  INSTRUCTION on
     Jesus   Mt 11:28-30;
                  13:44-46

PROPHECY of
     Jesus   Mt 4:12-16

GREED as
  in **ENVIRONMENT**
     Ptolemy   *1 Mc 11:1-19

GRIEF as
  PROPHECY of
     Tyre   Ezek 26:15-18
  REVELATION on
     Ezekiel   Ezek 21:1-7;
                  8-17
  in **WORSHIP**
     Job   Job 1:20-21

HATE as
  in **ENVIORNMENT**
     Esau   Gen 27:41-28:5
  MEDITATION on
     Job   Job 9:20-24

HOPE as
  INSTRUCTION on
     Jesus   Mt 13:44-46;
                  Lk 13:6-9
  in **MISSION**
     Paul   1 Thes 2:17-20

IDOLATRY as
  INSTRUCTION on
     Paul   1 Cor 10:23-11:

IGNORANCE as
     Abimelech   Gen 20:1-18

INDIFFERENCE as
  MEDITATION on
     Preacher   Eccl 1:12-2:26

INSTRUCTION on
  through **ANGER**
     Sirach   *Sir 20:1-8
  through **DESTRUCTION**
     Psalmist   Ps 146:3-4
  through **DOUBT**
     Uzziah   *Jdt 8:28-36
  through **EVIL**
     David   1 Sam 23:14-24
  through **FAITH**
     Jesus   Lk 13:6-9
     Paul   Rom 9:30-10:2
  through **FEAR**
     Moses   Ex 4:10-16
  through **FULFILLMENT**
     Jesus   Mt 11:28-30;
                  13:44-46
  through **HOPE**
     Jesus   Mt 13:44-46;
                  Lk 13:6-9
  of **IDOLATRY**
     Paul   1 Cor 10:23-11:
  through **JOY**
     Paul   2 Cor 1:23-2:4
  for **LIFE**
     Father   Prov 4:20-27
  through **LOVE**
     Author   Heb 10:19-31
     James   Jas 4:1-10
     Jesus   Mt 5:43-47;
                  Lk 6:27-35;

through **LOVE** (cont'd)

Jesus	13:6-9
Paul	2 Cor 1:23-2:4

through **LUST**

Preacher	Eccl 5:8-20

for **MARRIAGE**

Paul	1 Cor 7:36-38

through **OPPRESSION**

Jeremiah	Jer 13:15-17

for **PURIFICATION**

Paul	1 Cor 15:29-34

through **REWARDs**

Jesus	Mt 6:1; 2-4; 16-18

for **SACRIFICE**

God	Is 1:10-17
Zechariah	Zech 7:4-8:23

through **SELFISHNESS**

Zechariah	Zech 7:4-8:23

for **SERVICE**

Author	Heb 10:19-31

for **SHARING**

Jesus	Mt 11:28-30

for **SUFFERING**

Paul	2 Cor 1:23-2:4

for **TEMPTATION**

James	Jas 1:13-15

for **VIOLENCE**

James	Jas 4:1-10

JEALOUSY as

of **DEITY**

God	Zeph 1:17-18; Zech 7:4-8:23
Israelites	Zech 1:7-17

in **ENVIRONMENT**

Sarah	Gen 21:8-10

REVELATION on

God	Zeph 3:8

JOY as

from **DEITY**

David	Ps 4:6-8

of **FOLLOWERs**

Holy Spirit	1 Thes 1:2-10
Paul	Philm 1:4-7

INSTRUCTION on

Paul	2 Cor 1:23-2:4

in **MISSION**

Paul	1 Thes 2:17-20

REVELATION on

Jeremiah	Jer 33:1-9

LEADERSHIP as

of **FOLLOWER**

Paul	1 Cor 10:23-11:1

for **LIFE**

INSTRUCTION on

Father	Prov 4:20-27

LOVE as

Daughters	Song 6:1
Maiden	Song 5:10-16; 6:11-12; 7:10-13; 8:5b-7
Young Man	Song 6:4-10; 7:1-9

of **DEITY**

Believers	1 Jn 4:19-5:5
Jesus	Jn 3:1-21; Rom 5:6-11; Eph 1:15-2:10

INSTRUCTION on

Author	Heb 10:19-31
James	Jas 4:1-10
Jesus	Mt 5:43-47; Lk 6:27-35; 13:6-9
Paul	2 Cor 1:23-2:4

in **MISSION**

Jesus	Lk 15:1-7; Gal 2:20-21
Paul	1 Thes 2:17-20

REVELATION on

Daniel	Dan 9:20-23

SELF-REALIZATION of

Paul	1 Cor 13:1-3

LUST as

David	2 Sam 11:1-27

in **ENVIRONMENT**

Elders	*Susa 1:5-18
Shechem	Gen 34:1-31

through **FALSE BELIEF**

Herod	Mt 14:1-12; Mk 6:17-29

INSTRUCTION on

Preacher	Eccl 5:8-20

for **MARRIAGE**

INSTRUCTION on

Paul	1 Cor 7:36-38

MEDIATION as

of **WILL**

Centurion	Mt 8:5-13

MEDITATION on

as **HATE**

Job	Job 9:20-24

as **INDIFFERENCE**

Preacher	Eccl 1:12-2:26

as **WILL**

Centurion	Lk 7:1-10

concerning **MESSIANIC FIGURE**

FEAR as

Pharisees	Mt 22:41-46

of **MESSIANIC FIGURE**

COMPASSION as

Jesus	Mt 20:29-34

FAITH as

Jesus	Mt 9:27-31
People	Mt 14:34-36
Woman	Mk 7:24-30

in **MISSION**

HOPE as

Paul	1 Thes 2:17-20

JOY as

Paul	1 Thes 2:17-20

LOVE as

Jesus	Lk 15:1-7; Gal 2:20-21
Paul	1 Thes 2:17-20

REWARDs as

Paul	1 Cor 9:24-27

SERVICE as
  Apostles   Mt 10:5-6
  Paul   2 Cor 11:7-15

OBEDIENCE as
  in ENVIRONMENT
    Caleb   Josh 14:6-15

OLD AGE as
  in ENVIRONMENT
    Naomi   Ruth 1:1-18

through OPPRESSION
  INSTRUCTION on
    Jeremiah Jer 13:15-17

through POLITICS
  Israelites   Neh 11:1-2
  in ENVIRONMENT
    Jonathan *1 Mc 10:45-50

through POVERTY
  in ENVIRONMENT
    Jacob   Gen 42:1-6;
             43:1-15

through PRAISE
  Daughters Song 6:13
  of DEITY
    David   Ps 40:1-3

PROPHECY of
  for FULFILLMENT
    Jesus   Mt 4:12-16
  as GRIEF
    Tyre   Ezek 26:15-18
  for REPENTANCE
    Israelites 2 Kgs 17:7-23
  to WITNESS
    Holy Spirit 2 Pet 1:19b-21

for PURIFICATION
  INSTRUCTION on
    Paul   1 Cor 15:29-34

for REJECTION
  FALSE BELIEF as
    Priests   Mt 28:11-15

REPENTANCE as
  of DEITY
    Israelites Neh 9:26-31
    People   Rom 2:1-24
  PROPHECY of
    Israelites 2 Kgs 17:7-23

for REPENTANCE
  REVELATION on
    Israelites Hos 2:2-8
    Judahites Jer 18:1-12

REVELATION on
  God   Judg 9:22-25
  through ANGER
    Daniel   Dan 11:5-20
    God   Zeph 3:8
  through ANXIETY
    Daniel   Dan 7:15-16;
             8:26-27

through DISCIPLESHIP
  Satan   Rev 12:13-17
through ENVIRONMENT
  Pharaoh   Ex 5:6-14;
           15-21
through FEAR
  Elihu   Job 33:15-18
through GRIEF
  Ezekiel   Ezek 21:1-7;
           8-17
through JEALOUSY
  God   Zeph 3:8
through JOY
  Jeremiah Jer 33:1-9
through LOVE
  Daniel   Dan 9:20-23
for REPENTANCE
  Israelites Hos 2:2-8
  Judahites Jer 18:1-12
for VIOLENCE
  Joel   Joel 3:9-11

for REVENGE
  Absalom   2 Sam 13:21-14:
  in ENVIRONMENT
    Haman   Esth 3:1-6

through REWARDs
  INSTRUCTION on
    Jesus   Mt 6:1;
           2-4;
           16-18
  in MISSION
    Paul   1 Cor 9:24-27

SACRIFICE as
  through FALSE BELIEF
    Paul   Col 2:16-23
  INSTRUCTION on
    God   Is 1:10-17
    Zechariah Zech 7:4-8:23

SELFISHNESS as
  Abimelech Judg 9:1-6
  through FALSE BELIEF
    Herod   Mt 14:1-12;
           Mk 6:17-29
  INSTRUCTION on
    Zechariah Zech 7:4-8:23

SELF-REALIZATION as
  for FAITH
    Jesus   Mt 26:36-46;
           Mk 14:32-42;
           Lk 22:39-46
  for LOVE
    Paul   1 Cor 13:1-3

SERVICE as
  INSTRUCTION on
    Author   Heb 10:19-31
  for MISSION
    Apostles Mt 10:5-6
    Paul   2 Cor 11:7-15

SEX as
  Abimelech Gen 20:1-18
  in ENVIRONMENT
    Holofernes *Jdt 12:1-20
    Pharaoh   Gen 12:9-13:1

SHARING as
  INSTRUCTION on
    Jesus   Mt 11:28-30

through SPIRIT
  of DEITY
    Cyrus   *1 Esd 2:1-7
    Daniel   *Susa 1:42-51
    Israelites   Ex 35:30-36:7
    Mankind   1 Sam 16:1-13
    Zerubbabel   Zech 4:6b-10a

SUFFERING as
  in ENVIRONMENT
    Haman   *Esth 12:1-16
    Moses   Ex 2:11-15
  through FALSE BELIEF
    Zechariah   Zech 10:1-2
  INSTRUCTION on
    Paul   2 Cor 1:23-2:4

for TEMPTATION
  INSTRUCTION on
    James   Jas 1:13-15

VICTORY as
  in ENVIRONMENT
    Danites   Judg 18:11-13

for VIOLENCE
  FALSE BELIEF as
    Satan   Rev 20:7-10
  INSTRUCTION on
    James   Jas 4:1-10
  REVELATION on
    Joel   Joel 3:9-11

WEALTH as
  in ENVIRONMENT
    Ahaz   2 Kgs 16:5-9
    Danites   Judg 18:11-13
    Jacob   Gen 30:25-43

for WILL
  MEDITATION on
    Centurion   Mt 8:5-13
                            Lk 7:1-10

for WITNESS
  PROPHECY of
    Holy Spirit   2 Pet 1:19b-21

for WORSHIP
  ACCEPTANCE as
    Shepherds   Lk 2:1-20
  GRIEF as
    Job   Job 1:20-21

NEW AGE

ACCEPTANCE of
  INSTRUCTION on
    Apollos   Acts 18:24-28
    Jesus   Mt 9:16-17;
                            18:1-4;
                            22:1-14;
                            Mk 2:18-22;
                            Lk 5:36-39;

INSTRUCTION on (cont'd)
    Jesus   14:15-24
    Paul   1 Cor 15:1-11;
                            Gal 2:17-19;
                            Eph 4:17-24;
                            Col 2:6-15;
                            3:1-4;
                            5-17;
                            1 Tim 6:11-16
  with MESSIANIC FIGURE
    Ezra   *2 Esd 2:33-41
  PROPHECY of
    Believers   Lk 10:17-20
  REVELATION of
    Isaiah   Is 57:14-21
    Israelites   Mal 2:17-3:5
  through SELF-REALIZATION
    Criminal   Lk 23:39-43
    John the Baptist   Jn 3:22-30

ALIENATION in
  PROPHECY of
    Jesus   Jn 7:32-36

BLESSING in
  PROPHECY of
    Israelites   Is 27:2-6
    Joel   Joel 3:16b-21
  REVELATION on
    Amos   Amos 9:13
    Isaiah   Is 60:1-22

CHAOS in
  PROPHECY of
    Jesus   Mt 24:29-31;
                            Mk 13:24-27

CONDEMNATION in
  of FOLLOWERs
    Pharisees   Mt 23:13
  INSTRUCTION on
    Paul   Gal 5:16-21
  PROPHECY of
    Jesus   Lk 17:22-37
  REVELATION on
    Jesus   Lk 17:22-37

COURAGE in
  PROPHECY of
    Isaiah   Is 35:1-10

COVENANT in
  FULFILLMENT of
    Jesus   2 Cor 3:12-18;
                            Heb 8:6-13
  through GRACE
    Paul   Gal 4:21-26
  WITNESS to
    Paul   1 Cor 11:23-26

COVETOUSNESS in
  INSTRUCTION on
    Jesus   Lk 12:22-31

of DEITY
  FULFILLMENT of
    God   Mt 24:34-36
  HOPE in
    Believers   1 Jn 2:28-3:3
    Isaiah   Is 28:1-13
    Paul   1 Cor 1:4-9

PROPHECY of (cont'd)
Zechariah	Zech 14:1-21
Zephaniah	Zeph 1:7

REVELATION on
Angels	Lk 2:1-20
Daniel	Dan 9:24-27; 11:21-45; 12:1-4; 5-13
Isaiah	Is 66:17-24
Joel	Joel 2:30-32
John	Rev 11:15-19; 14:14-16; 17-20; 21:1-8; 9-14; 22:6-21

SCRIPTURES on
Jesus	Lk 21:20-24

GOOD in
REVELATION on
God	*2 Esd 2:10-14; 15-32

GRACE in
COVENANT of
Paul	Gal 4:21-26

INSTRUCTION on
Jesus	Mt 20:1-16; Mk 4:26-29; Lk 13:18-19
Paul	Acts 28:17-31; Rom 5:1-5; 11:1-6; 2 Cor 5:1-5

GRIEF in
REVELATION on
Ezekiel	Ezek 30:1-5

HOPE in
of DEITY
Believers	1 Jn 2:28-3:3
Isaiah	Is 28:1-13
Paul	1 Cor 1:4-9

by FOLLOWERs
Paul	Tit 3:1-7

INSTRUCTION on
Jesus	Mt 4:23-25; 10:7-8; Lk 8:1-3; 9:10-11; 12:35-38; 13:18-19
Paul	2 Cor 3:7-11; 4:16-18; 1 Thes 4:13-18; Tit 2:11-15
Peter	1 Pet 1:13-2:3; 2 Pet 3:11-13

through MESSIANIC FIGURE
Jesus	Lk 12:39-40; Heb 9:23-28

PROPHECY of
Isaiah	Is 33:17-24; 35:1-10
Malachi	Mal 4:4-6

HUMILITY in
INSTRUCTION on

INSTRUCTION on (cont'd)
Jesus	Mt 18:1-4

IGNORANCE of
through FALSE BELIEF
Pharisees	Jn 7:32-36

by FOLLOWERs
Apostles	Acts 1:6-11

INSTRUCTION on
Jesus	Mt 24:42-44; 25:1-13; Mk 13:28-37; Lk 12:54-56; 21:34-36
Paul	1 Thes 5:1-11
Preacher	Eccl 6:1-12

of MESSIANIC FIGURE
Jesus	Lk 12:39-40

PROPHECY of
Jesus	Mt 24:37-41; Jn 8:21-59

REVELATION on
Mankind	2 Pet 3:8-10

INNOCENCE in
INSTRUCTION on
Jesus	Lk 18:15-17

INSTRUCTION on
concerning ACCEPTANCE
Apollos	Acts 18:24-28
Jesus	Mt 9:16-17; 18:1-4; 22:1-14; Mk 2:18-22; Lk 5:36-39; 14:15-24
Paul	1 Cor 15:1-11; Gal 2:17-19; Eph 4:17-24; Col 2:6-15; 3:1-4; 5-17; 1 Tim 6:11-16

concerning COVETOUSNESS
Jesus	Lk 12:22-31

concerning DISCIPLESHIP
Jesus	Lk 9:57-62; 22:28-30
Paul	Gal 6:11-18

concerning EVIL
God	*2 Esd 14:1-18

concerning FAITH
Author	Heb 11:1-40
Jesus	Mk 4:26-29; Lk 13:18-19; 18:1-8; 15-17
Paul	Rom 9:30-10:21

concerning FULFILLMENT
Author	Heb 12:12-29
Jesus	Mt 10:23; 13:31-33; 47-50; 22:1-14; 25:31-46; 26:17-30; Mk 4:26-29; 30-32; 10:23-27; Lk 12:49-50;

concerning **FULFILLMENT**
Jesus	13:18-19;
	20-21;
	16:16-18;
	17:20-21;
	Jn 12:20-26
Paul	Acts 17:1-9;
	Rom 13:11-14;
	1 Cor 15:20-28;
	42-50;
	51-58;
	2 Cor 5:20-6:2;
	Eph 1:15-2:10;
	1 Thes 5:1-11

concerning **GRACE**
Jesus	Mt 20:1-16;
	Mk 4:26-29;
	Lk 13:18-19
Paul	Acts 28:17-31;
	Rom 5:1-5;
	11:1-6;
	2 Cor 5:1-5

concerning **HOPE**
Jesus	Mt 4:23-25;
	10:7-8;
	Lk 8:1-3;
	9:10-11;
	12:35-38;
	13:18-19
Paul	2 Cor 3:7-11;
	4:16-18;
	1 Thes 4:13-18;
	Tit 2:11-15
Peter	1 Pet 1:13-2:3;
	2 Pet 3:11-13

concerning **HUMILITY**
Jesus	Mt 18:1-4

concerning **IGNORANCE**
Jesus	Mt 24:42-44;
	25:1-13;
	Mk 13:28-37;
	Lk 12:54-56;
	21:34-36
Paul	1 Thes 5:1-11
Preacher	Eccl 6:1-12

concerning **INNOCENCE**
Jesus	Lk 18:15-17

revealing **JOY**
God	Is 65:1-25
John	Rev 12:10-12
John the Baptist	Jn 3:22-30
Paul	Rom 14:1-23

concerning **JUSTICE**
Angel	*2 Esd 5:43-6:6
Jesus	Mt 20:1-16;
	25:31-46

concerning **LIFE**
Holy Spirit	Jn 3:1-21
Jesus	Mt 7:13-14
Paul	Rom 5:12-21;
	1 Cor 7:25-35

concerning **LOVE**
James	Jas 2:1-13

concerning **OBEDIENCE**
Jesus	Mt 7:21-23;
	21:33-43;
	Lk 12:35-38;
	41-46;
	13:22-30

concerning **PATIENCE**
James	Jas 5:7-11

concerning **PATIENCE** (cont'd)
Jesus	Lk 12:35-38
Paul	Rom 8:14-25

concerning **PEACE**
Author	Heb 4:1-13
Paul	Rom 14:1-23

concerning **POVERTY**
James	Jas 2:1-13
Jesus	Lk 6:20-23

concerning **PRAISE**
Paul	Rom 14:1-23

concerning **PRUDENCE**
Paul	2 Thes 2:1-3a

concerning **PURIFICATION**
Holy Spirit	Jn 3:1-21
Paul	Rom 6:1-14;
	1 Cor 6:9-11

concerning **REPENTANCE**
Jesus	Mt 4:17;
	Mk 1:14-15
Paul	1 Cor 6:9-11

concerning **REWARDs**
Jesus	Mt 5:3-12;
	19:27-30;
	20:1-16;
	24:45-51;
	25:1-13;
	Mk 10:28-31;
	Lk 6:20-23;
	14:12-14;
	16:1-9;
	18:28-30;
	Jn 4:27-42;
	14:1-14
Paul	2 Cor 4:16-18
Peter	2 Pet 1:8-11

concerning **SACRIFICE**
Jesus	Mt 9:14-15;
	13:44-46;
	Mk 2:18-22;
	Lk 5:33-35;
	Heb 10:1-18

concerning **SPIRIT**
Paul	Rom 7:1-6;
	8:5-13;
	Eph 4:17-24

concerning **SUFFERING**
Paul	Acts 14:19-28;
	Rom 8:14-25;
	2 Cor 4:16-18;
	2 Thes 1:5-7a

concerning **VICTORY**
Ephesus	Rev 2:1-7
Jesus	Mt 13:36-43;
	19:27-30;
	Mk 10:28-31;
	Lk 13:18-19;
	18:28-30
Laodicea	Rev 3:14-22
Paul	1 Cor 15:20-28;
	Col 3:1-4
Pergamum	Rev 2:12-17
Philadelphians	Rev 3:7-13
Sardis	Rev 3:1-6
Smyrna	Rev 2:8-11

concerning **WEALTH**
Jesus	Mk 10:17-22;
	23-27;
	Lk 12:32-34;
	18:18-27

concerning **WILL**

concerning **WISDOM** (cont'd)
    Hezekiah   *Sir 48:17-25
    Isaiah   Is 35:1-10
    Zechariah   Lk 1:57-80
concerning **WITNESS**
    John the Baptist   Mt 3:1-12;
            Lk 3:15-17

PRUDENCE in
  of **FOLLOWER**s
    Scribe   Mt 13:51-52
  INSTRUCTION on
    Paul   2 Thes 2:1-3a

PURIFICATION in
  of **FOLLOWER**s
    Jesus   Gal 3:26-29
  INSTRUCTION on
    Holy Spirit   Jn 3:1-21
    Paul   Rom 6:1-14;
            1 Cor 6:9-11
  PROPHECY of
    John the Baptist   Mt 3:1-12;
            Lk 3:15-17

REJECTION in
  of **FOLLOWER**s
    Jesus   Mk 10:17-22
    Man   Mt 19:16-22
  of **MESSIANIC FIGURE**
    Jesus   Acts 4:1-22
  PROPHECY of
    Jesus   Mk 8:34-9:1;
            Lk 9:23-27

REPENTANCE in
  of **DEITY**
    John the Baptist   Mt 3:1-12
  INSTRUCTION on
    Jesus   Mt 4:17;
            Mk 1:14-15
    Paul   1 Cor 6:9-11

REVELATION on
  concerning **FULFILLMENT**
    Angels   Lk 2:1-20
    Daniel   Dan 9:24-27;
            11:21-45;
            12:1-4;
            5-13
    Isaiah   Is 66:17-24
    Joel   Joel 2:30-32
    John   Rev 11:15-19;
            14:14-16;
            17-20;
            21:1-8;
            9-14;
            22:6-21
  concerning **GOOD**
    God   *2 Esd 2:10-14;
            15-32
  concerning **GRIEF**
    Ezekiel   Ezek 30:1-5
  concerning **IGNORANCE**
    Mankind   2 Pet 3:8-10
  concerning **JUSTICE**
    Angel   *2 Esd 6:7-28
  concerning **LEADERSHIP**
    Daniel   Dan 8:15-25
  concerning **LIFE**
    Jesus   Rev 1:1-3

concerning **LIFE** (cont'd)
    John   Rev 22:1-5
concerning **ORDER**
    Daniel   Dan 2:24-45
    John   Rev 21:9-14;
            15-17;
            18-21;
            22-27
concerning **PEACE**
    Isaiah   Is 65:1-25
concerning **REWARD**
    Daniel   Dan 12:5-13
concerning **SACREDNESS**
    John   Rev 21:22-27
concerning **VICTORY**
    Daniel   Dan 7:2-14;
            17-27
    Isaiah   Is 60:1-22
    John   Rev 7:9-17;
            12:10-12;
            20:11-15
concerning **WEALTH**
    John   Rev 21:18-21
concerning **WISDOM**
    Daniel   Dan 10:10-21
    God   Is 42:5-17
concerning **WITNESS**
    Daniel   Dan 10:10-21
    God   Is 42:5-17
    Jesus   Rev 22:6-21
    John   Rev 1:1-3;
            10:1-11;
            19:11-16;
            22:6-21

REWARDs concerning
  INSTRUCTION on
    Jesus   Mt 5:3-12;
            19:27-30;
            20:1-16;
            24:45-51;
            25:1-13;
            Mk 10:28-31;
            Lk 6:20-23;
            14:12-14;
            16:1-9;
            18:28-30;
            Jn 4:27-42;
            14:1-14
    Paul   2 Cor 4:16-18
    Peter   2 Pet 1:8-11
is **REWARD**
  for **MISSION**
    Jesus   Mt 5:17-20
  REVELATION on
    Daniel   Dan 12:5-13

SACREDNESS of
  MISSION of
    Holy Spirit   2 Cor 3:7-11
  REVELATION on
    John   Rev 21:22-27
  in **WORSHIP**
    God   Gen 4:25-26

SACRIFICE in
  INSTRUCTION on
    Jesus   Mt 9:14-15;
            13:44-46;
            Mk 2:18-22;

INSTRUCTION on (cont'd)
Jesus   Lk 5:33-35;
    Heb 10:1-18
by MESSIANIC FIGURE
Jesus   Heb 8:1-5

SCRIPTURES on
concerning FULFILLMENT
Jesus   Lk 21:20-24

SERVICE in
of DEITY
Israelites   Is 43:14-44:5
by MESSIANIC FIGURE
Jesus   Heb 8:1-5

SPIRIT in
of DEITY
Believers   1 Cor 2:6-9
INSTRUCTION on
Paul   Rom 7:1-6;
    8:5-13;
    Eph 4:17-24

SUFFERING in
INSTRUCTION on
Paul   Acts 14:19-28;
    Rom 8:14-25;
    2 Cor 4:16-18;
    2 Thes 1:5-7a

VICTORY in
of DEITY
Mankind   Rev 21:1-8
INSTRUCTION on
Ephesus   Rev 2:1-7
Jesus   Mt 13:36-43;
    19:27-30;
    Mk 10:28-31;
    Lk 13:18-19;
    18:28-30
Laodicea   Rev 3:14-22
Paul   1 Cor 15:20-28;
    Col 3:1-4
Pergamum   Rev 2:12-17
Philadelphians   Rev 3:7-13
Sardis   Rev 3:1-6
Smyrna   Rev 2:8-11
through MESSIANIC FIGURE
Jesus   Jn 16:29-33
PROPHECY of
Balaam   Num 23:27-24:13
Isaiah   Is 9:1;
    25:6-9;
    51:17-52:12;
    13-53:12
Jesus   Mt 26:57-68;
    Mk 14:53-65;
    Lk 21:25-28
Obadiah   Obad 1:17-21
REVELATION on
Daniel   Dan 7:2-14;
    17-27
Isaiah   Is 60:1-22
John   Rev 7:9-17;
    12:10-12;
    20:11-15

VIOLENCE in
PROPHECY of
Angel   *2 Esd 5:1-15

WEALTH concerning
INSTRUCTION on
Jesus   Mk 10:17-22;
    23-27;
    Lk 12:32-34;
    18:18-27
MESSIANIC FIGURE on
Man   Mt 19:16-22
REVELATION on
John   Rev 21:18-21

WILL in
of DEITY
Believers   Lk 12:32-34
INSTRUCTION on
Jesus   Lk 14:15-24

WISDOM in
INSTRUCTION on
Paul   1 Cor 2:6-9;
    2 Cor 3:7-11;
    2 Thes 2:3b-10
MISSION of
Jesus   Lk 4:16-30
PROPHECY of
Hezekiah   *Sir 48:17-25
Isaiah   Is 35:1-10
Zechariah   Lk 1:57-80
REVELATION on
Daniel   Dan 10:10-21
God   Is 42:5-17

WITNESS to
COVENANT of
Paul   1 Cor 11:23-26
by FOLLOWERs
Stephen   Acts 6:8-8:3
INSTRUCTION on
Angel   *2 Esd 2:42-48
Jesus   Lk 17:20-21
Paul   Gal 4:27-31
Philip   Acts 8:4-13
MISSION of
Jesus   Mt 9:35
PROPHECY of
John the Baptist   Mt 3:1-12;
    Lk 3:15-17
REVELATION on
Daniel   Dan 10:10-21
God   Is 42:5-17
Jesus   Rev 22:6-21
John   Rev 1:1-3;
    10:1-11;
    19:11-16;
    22:6-21

WORSHIP in
SACREDNESS of
God   Gen 4:25-26

YOUTH in
INSTRUCTION on
Jesus   Mt 19:13-15;
    Mk 10:13-16;
    Lk 18:15-17

OBEDIENCE

to AUTHORITY

to AUTHORITY (cont'd)
　by FOLLOWERs
　　God　　　　　　　2 Chr 14:1-16:14
　INSTRUCTION on
　　Demon　　　　　Mk 1:21-28;
　　　　　　　　　　Lk 4:31-37
　　Jesus　　　　　Mt 7:24-27;
　　　　　　　　　　Lk 6:46-49;
　　　　　　　　　　24:44-49
　　Paul　　　　　Rom 13:1-7;
　　　　　　　　　　2 Cor 10:1-6;
　　　　　　　　　　Tit 3:8-11
　　Peter　　　　　Lk 5:1-11;
　　　　　　　　　　1 Pet 2:13-17;
　　　　　　　　　　5:1-5
　　Preacher　　　Eccl 8:1-9
　　Servants　　　1 Pet 2:18-20
　　Solomon　　　Prov 23:15-24:22
　　Women　　　　1 Cor 14:34-40;
　　　　　　　　　　Eph 5:21-33;
　　　　　　　　　　1 Tim 2:8-15;
　　　　　　　　　　Tit 2:1-10;
　　　　　　　　　　1 Pet 3:1-7
　in MISSION
　　Titus　　　　　Tit 3:1-7
　PROPHECY of
　　Israelites　　　*Bar 2:11-23

BEHAVIOR revealing
　to COVENANT
　　Noah　　　　　Gen 6:5-22
　to DEITY
　　Balaam　　　　Num 22:5-14;
　　　　　　　　　　15-21
　　Ezra　　　　　*2 Esd 14:19-48
　　Joseph　　　　Mt 1:18-25
　in ENVIRONMENT
　　Jacob　　　　　Gen 46:1-7
　of FOLLOWERs
　　Abraham　　　Gen 12:1-8;
　　　　　　　　　　13:14-18
　　Disciples　　　Mt 21:1-11;
　　　　　　　　　　Mk 11:1-10;
　　　　　　　　　　Lk 19:28-38
　INSTRUCTION on
　　Abraham　　　Gen 21:11-14
　　Angel　　　　　Gen 16:7-10
　　Author　　　　Heb 12:12-29
　　Esau　　　　　Gen 27:1-40
　　God　　　　　Gen 2:16-17
　　Isaiah　　　　Is 18:1-7
　　Israelites　　　Ex 12:50-51;
　　　　　　　　　　Josh 4:1-8
　　Joshua　　　　Num 14:8-9;
　　　　　　　　　　Josh 11:1-15
　　Moses　　　　Ex 34:1-5a
　　Paul　　　　　1 Cor 4:14-21;
　　　　　　　　　　2 Cor 13:11-13;
　　　　　　　　　　Eph 5:21-33;
　　　　　　　　　　Col 3:18-4:1;
　　　　　　　　　　1 Thes 4:1-12
　　Zedekiah　　　Jer 32:9-15
　to MESSIANIC FIGURE
　　Disciples　　　Mk 9:9-13
　REVELATION on
　　Aaron　　　　Ex 4:27-31
　　Elijah　　　　1 Kgs 19:1-21
　　Ezekiel　　　Ezek 8:5-6;
　　　　　　　　　　7-13
　　Isaac　　　　Gen 26:1-11
　　Isaiah　　　　Is 8:11-15

REVELATION on (cont'd)
　　Jacob　　　　Gen 31:1-6
　　Jeremiah　　　Jer 18:1-12;
　　　　　　　　　　35:1-5
　　Paul　　　　　Acts 16:6-10
　in WORSHIP
　　Ezra　　　　　*2 Esd 9:26-37

BELIEF in
　Believers　　　Heb 11:1-40
　of FOLLOWERs
　　Paul　　　　　Philm 1:21-25
　MEDITATION on
　　Paul　　　　　2 Thes 3:3-5

in BROTHERHOOD
　INSTRUCTION on
　　Believers　　　Acts 15:6-29

COMMITMENT through
　to DEITY
　　Psalmist　　　Ps 119:9-16;
　　　　　　　　　　105-112

to COMMITMENT
　INSTRUCTION on
　　Asaph　　　　Ps 76:10-12
　　Darius　　　　Ezra 6:1-12
　　Esther　　　　Esth 4:1-17
　　Paul　　　　　Rom 8:5-13;
　　　　　　　　　　2 Cor 2:5-11
　　Peter　　　　Acts 2:37-41
　to MISSION
　　Paul　　　　　2 Cor 13:5-10
　REVELATION on
　　Moses　　　　Num 30:1-16

of COMMUNITY
　INSTRUCTION on
　　Ezra　　　　　*1 Esd 9:1-15
　　Joshua　　　　Josh 1:12-18
　　Moses　　　　Lev 24:10-23
　COMPULSION to
　　Darius　　　　Dan 6:10-15;
　　　　　　　　　　16-23

in CONFRONTATION
　to DEITY
　　Joshua　　　　Josh 10:28-43
　in ENVIRONMENT
　　Israelites　　　Josh 6:8-14
　PROPHECY of
　　Amaziah　　　2 Chr 25:1-28
　　Rehoboam　　1 Kgs 12:21-24;
　　　　　　　　　　2 Chr 10:1-12:16

CONVERSION through
　REVELATION on
　　Paul　　　　　Acts 26:1-32

to COVENANT
　BEHAVIOR required
　　Noah　　　　　Gen 6:5-22
　ELECTION through
　　Moses　　　　Ex 19:1-8;
　　　　　　　　　　Deut 29:1-15
　FIDELITY through
　　God　　　　　Judg 2:1-5;
　　　　　　　　　　Ps 25:8-15;
　　　　　　　　　　103:14-18;
　　　　　　　　　　132:11-18

in RITE	
Disciples	Mt 26:17-30
SALVATION through	
Holy Spirit	Gal 5:16-21
to TRUTH	
Believers	1 Pet 1:13-2:3
Corinthians	2 Cor 9:12-15
Disciples	Jn 8:21-59
John	1 Jn 3:19-24
VIRTUE in	
Noah	Gen 7: 1-24

FREEDOM through	
to DEITY	
Psalmist	Ps 119:41-48
INSTRUCTION on	
God	Ex 6:10-13
Paul	Rom 6:15-23
PROPHECY of	
Israelites	2 Chr 26:1-28:27
Judahites	Jer 7:1-15

HONESTY of	
Joseph	Gen 42:18-25
to DEITY	
Sirach	*Sir 1:22-30

INSTRUCTION on	
Abraham	Gen 21:11-14
Angel	Gen 16:7-10
Author	Heb 12:12-29;
	13:1-25
Esau	Gen 27:1-40
God	Gen 2:16-17
Isaiah	Is 18:1-7
Israelites	Ex 12:50-51;
	Josh 4:1-8
Joshua	Num 14:8-9;
	Josh 11:1-15
Moses	Ex 34:1-5a
Paul	1 Cor 4:14-21;
	2 Cor 13:11-13;
	Eph 5:21-33;
	Col 3:18-4:1;
	1 Thes 4:1-12
Zedekiah	Jer 32:9-15
to AUTHORITY	
Demon	Mk 1:21-28;
	Lk 4:31-37
Jesus	Mt 7:24-27;
	Lk 6:46-49;
	24:44-49
Paul	Rom 13:1-7;
	2 Cor 10:1-6;
	Tit 3:8-11
Peter	Lk 5:1-11;
	1 Pet 2:13-17;
	5:1-5
Preacher	Eccl 8:1-9
Servants	1 Pet 2:18-20
Solomon	Prov 23:15-24:22
Women	1 Cor 14:34-40;
	Eph 5:21-33;
	1 Tim 2:8-15;
	Tit 2:1-10;
	1 Pet 3:1-7
to BROTHERHOOD	
Believers	Acts 15:6-29
to COMMITMENT	
Asaph	Ps 76:10-12
Darius	Ezra 6:1-12

to COMMITMENT (cont'd)	
Esther	Esth 4:1-17
Paul	Rom 8:5-13;
	2 Cor 2:5-11
Peter	Acts 2:37-41
to COMMUNITY	
Ezra	*1 Esd 9:1-15
Joshua	Josh 1:12-18
Moses	Lev 24:10-23
in CREATION	
Zerubbabel	Ezra 4:3
through FIDELITY	
Aaron	Ex 7:14-25
Abraham	Gen 22:1-19
Author	Heb 2:1-4;
	3:6b-11;
	12-19;
	4:1-13
Barnabas	Acts 11:22-24
Believers	Rev 14:9-12
David	Ps 15:5c
Father	Prov 4:20-27
God	Ps 95:7d-11
James	Jas 1:22-25
Jesus	Mt 21:28-32;
	23:5-12;
	24:45-51;
	Lk 14:25-27;
	28-33;
	19:11-27;
	Jn 7:53-8:11;
	10:1-18;
	16:1-4
Joshua	Josh 24:14-15
Malachi	Mal 2:10-16
Mattathias	*1 Mc 2:49-70
Moses	Ex 8:1-15;
	9:8-12
Moses	Ex 9:13-35;
	10:1-20;
	21-23;
	11:1-10;
	14:15-22;
	23-31
Paul	Eph 5:3-14;
	6:5-9;
	Phil 2:12-18;
	4:1-9;
	Col 1:21-23
Peter	1 Pet 5:12-14
Samuel	1 Sam 12:1-25
Solomon	Prov 6:20-7:27
Wisdom	Prov 8:32-36
to KNOWLEDGE	
Darius	*1 Esd 6:7-26
God	Ex 6:28-30
Israelites	Is 50:1-11
Jesus	Jn 13:1-20
Paul	2 Tim 3:14-17
Solomon	Prov 22:17-21
to LAW	
Artaxerxes	Ezra 7:25-26
Asaph	Ps 78:1-8
David	1 Kgs 2:1-4;
	1 Chr 15:1-16:43;
	28:1-29:30
Ezra	Ezra 10:7-15
Father	Prov 4:1-9
God	Ex 16:22-30;
	Ps 119:1-8
Isaiah	Is 1:10-17

INSTRUCTION on (cont'd)
Darius	*1 Esd 6:7-26
God	Ex 6:28-30
Israelites	Is 50:1-11
Jesus	Jn 13:1-20
Paul	2 Tim 3:14-17
Solomon	Prov 22:17-21

MEDITATION on
Psalmist	Ps 119:25-32; 97-104

in MISSION
Jonah	Jon 3:1-10

REVELATION on
Ananias	Acts 9:1-19
Cornelius	Acts 10:1-11:18
Philadelphians	Rev 3:7-13
Wise Men	Mt 2:1-12

SELF-REALIZATION of
Jesus	Lk 2:41-52

to LAW
Amaziah	2 Chr 25:1-28
Darius	Dan 6:1(23
Hezekiah	2 Kgs 18:4-8
Israelites	Num 5:1-4; Neh 12:44-13:3
Josiah	2 Kgs 23:24-25a
Moses	Ex 23:10-13; Lev 19:1-37; Num 15:37-41; Deut 15:1-11

COVENANT of
Josiah	2 Kgs 23:1-3; 2 Chr 34:1-35:27
Judahites	2 Kgs 23:1-3

of DEITY
David	2 Sam 22:1-51; Ps 40:6-10
God	Eccl 12:12-14
Israelites	Ps 105:43-45
Psalmist	Ps 119:41-48; 49-56; 57-64; 65-72; 81-88; 97-104; 105-112; 113-120; 121-128; 129-136; 137-144; 153-160; 161-168; 169-176
Sirach	*Sir 1:22-30; 17:1-14; 32:14-24

FALSE BELIEF concerning
Jews	Jn 18:28-19:16
Paul	Gal 5:2-6
Priests	Mal 1:6-2:9

INSTRUCTION on
Artaxerxes	Ezra 7:25-26
Asaph	Ps 78:1-8
David	1 Kgs 2:1-4; 1 Chr 15:1-16:43; 28:1-29:30
Ezra	Ezra 10:7-15
Father	Prov 4:1-9
God	Ex 16:22-30; Ps 119:1-8

INSTRUCTION on (cont'd)
Isaiah	Is 1:10-17
Israelites	Ezek 20:9-26; Mal 4:4-6
James	Jas 2:1-13
Jesus	Mt 17:24-27; 19:16-22; 22:15-22; 34-40; 23:1-3; 12:13-17; 28-34; Lk 10:25-28; 18:18-27; 20:19-26; Jn 14:15-17; 18-24; 15:1-11; 12-17
John	1 Jn 2:7-11; 4:19-5:5; 2 Jn 1:4-6
Joshua	Josh 23:1-16
Moses	Ex 24:1-18; 35:1-3; Deut 4:1-14; 32-40; 5:1-21; 6:1-3; 4-19; 20-25; 8:1-10; 11-20; 11:1-25; 12:1-31; 32-13:18; 16:9-12; 26:16-19; 27:1-10; 11-26; 28:1-14; 30:1-10; 11-14; 15-20; 31:9-13; 30-32:47
Paul	Rom 2:1-24; 25-3:20; 1 Cor 7:17-24; 1 Tim 6:11-16
Peter	1 Pet 2:13-17
Psalmist	Ps 119:33-40
Sirach	*Sir 15:11-20
Solomon	1 Kgs 8:54-61; Prov 3:1-35; 6:20-7:27; 19:1-29; 28:1-28; 29:1-27
Tobit	*Tb 4:1-21

in MISSION
Disciples	Mt 28:16-20

PROPHECY of
Jeremiah	Jer 17:19-27

REVELATION on
Israelites	Ezek 37:15-28; 43:6-12
Joshua	Josh 1:1-9
Moses	Ex 20:1-17; 34:12-28; Deut 5:22-33

REVELATION on (cont'd)
Priests	Ezek 44:15-31
Solomon	1 Kgs 6:1-38; 9:1-9; 2 Chr 7:11-22

SCRIPTURES on
Paul	Gal 3:10-14

SELF-REALIZATION of
Paul	Rom 7:14-25

TRADITION of
Amaziah	2 Kgs 14:5-6
Corinthians	1 Cor 11:2-16
Judeans	Acts 15:1-5
Pharisees	Acts 15:1-5
Priests	Mt 27:3-10

of WORSHIP
Israelites	Neh 8:13-18; 10:34; *1 Esd 7:1-9
Josiah	*1 Esd 1:1-22
Levites	Ezra 6:13-18; Neh 12:24-26

MEDITATION on
to BELIEF
Paul	2 Thes 3:3-5

to KNOWLEDGE
Psalmist	Ps 119:25-32; 97-104

to MESSIANIC FIGURE
BEHAVIOR revealing
Disciples	Mk 9:9-13

in NEW AGE
Jesus	Lk 12:39-40

PROVIDENCE through
Jesus	Jn 18:1-11

SALVATION through
Jesus	Heb 5:1-10

in MISSION
to AUTHORITY
Titus	Tit 3:1-7

COMMITMENT to
Paul	2 Cor 13:5-10

to KNOWLEDGE
Jonah	Jon 3:1-10

to LAW
Disciples	Mt 28:16-20

as QUALITY OF LIFE
Jesus	Phil 2:5-11

RESPECT for
Servants	1 Tim 6:1-2b

SALVATION through
Paul	1 Cor 15:1-11

to TRUTH
Disciples	Mk 6:7-13; Lk 9:1-6
Paul	2 Cor 13:5-10

as MOTIVATION
Caleb	Josh 14:6-15

in NEW AGE
INSTRUCTION on
Jesus	Mt 7:21-23; 21:33-43; Lk 12:35-38; 41-46; 13:22-30

to MESSIANIC FIGURE

---

to MESSIANIC FIGURE (cont'd)
Jesus	Lk 12:39-40

PRAYER for
to DEITY
Author	Heb 13:1-25
Psalmist	Ps 119:1-8

INSTRUCTION on
Jesus	Jn 9:1-41
Paul	2 Cor 13:5-10

in PRESENCE
by FOLLOWER
God	1 Jn 3:19-24

PROPHECY of
Jeroboam	1 Kgs 11:26-40

REVELATION on
Solomon	1 Kgs 6:1-38

PRESENCE through
to DEITY
Amos	Amos 5:14-15
Israelites	Ezek 36:22-32
Jehoshaphat	2 Chr 17:1-20:37
Jesus	Jn 8:21-59

PROMISE of
to DEITY
David	Ps 56:10-13
Israelites	Ex 19:1-8
Psalmist	Ps 119:145-152

INSTRUCTION on
Author	Heb 10:32-39
Israelites	Ex 24:1-18; *1 Esd 9:16-36
People	Jer 42:1-6

PROPHECY of
to AUTHORITY
Israelites	*Bar 2:11-23

in CONFRONTATION
Amaziah	2 Chr 25:1-28
Rehoboam	1 Kgs 12:21-24; 2 Chr 10:1-12:16

in CREATION
Israelites	Hag 1:12-14

through FIDELITY
Micah	Mic 4:1-8
People	Rev 22:6-21

results in FREEDOM
Israelites	2 Chr 26:1-28:27
Judahites	Jer 7:1-15

to LAW
Jeremiah	Jer 17:19-27

in PRESENCE
Jeroboam	1 Kgs 11:26-40

to TRUTH
Israelites	Deut 18:9-22
Jeremiah	Jer 26:7-19

PROVIDENCE through
to COVENANT
Believers	Is 56:1-8
Israelites	Ex 15:22-27

to DEITY
Mankind	Ps 1:1-3

INSTRUCTION on
Achior	*Jdt 5:1-21

to MESSIANIC FIGURE
Jesus	Jn 18:1-11

REVELATION on

REVELATION on (cont'd)
Elijah	1 Kgs 17:1-24; 18:1-46
Ezekiel	Ezek 11:14-21
Israelites	Num 9:15-23
Joseph	Mt 2:19-23

to PUNISHMENT
REVELATION on
Isaiah	Is 65:1-25

as QUALITY OF LIFE
of FOLLOWERs
Disciples	Mk 14:12-16; Lk 22:7-13
Paul	Phil 3:17-21

INSTRUCTION on
Jesus	Lk 16:19-31
Paul	2 Thes 3:6-15

in MISSION
Jesus	Phil 2:5-11

REVELATION on
Ezekiel	Ezek 24:15-24

RECONCILIATION through
of FOLLOWERs
Jesus	Rom 5:12-21

INSTRUCTION on
James	Jas 2:14-26
Paul	Rom 2:1-24

RESPECT through
to DEITY
God	Prov 23:15-24:22; Eccl 12:12-14

INSTRUCTION on
Paul	Eph 6:1-4; 1 Tim 6:1-2b

in MISSION
Servants	1 Tim 6:1-2b

REVELATION on
Aaron	Ex 4:27-31
Elijah	1 Kgs 19:1-21
Ezekiel	Ezek 8:5-6; 7-13
Isaac	Gen 26:1-11
Isaiah	Is 8:11-15
Jacob	Gen 31:1-16
Jeremiah	Jer 18:1-12; 35:1-5
Paul	Acts 16:6-10

to COMMITMENT
Moses	Num 30:1-16

through CONVERSION
Paul	Acts 26:1-32

to ELECTION
Amos	Amos 7:10-17
Jeremiah	Jer 1:4-10
Joshua	Zech 3:1-10

through FIDELITY
Isaiah	Is 58:1-14
Israelites	Jer 3:14b-18; Ezek 37:15-28
Judahites	Zech 7:4-8:23

to KNOWLEDGE
Ananias	Acts 9:1-19
Cornelius	Acts 10:1-11:18
Philadelphians	Rev 3:7-13
Wise Men	Mt 2:1-12

to LAW

to LAW (cont'd)
Israelites	Ezek 37:15-28; 43:6-12
Joshua	Josh 1:1-9
Moses	Ex 20:1-17; 34:12-28; Deut 5:22-33
Priests	Ezek 44:15-31
Solomon	1 Kgs 6:1-38; 9:1-9; 2 Chr 7:11-22

in PRESENCE
Solomon	1 Kgs 6:1-38

to PUNISHMENT
Isaiah	Is 65:1-25

as QUALITY OF LIFE
Ezekiel	Ezek 24:15-24

in RITE
Jacob	Gen 35:1-15
Moses	Ex 40:1-33

in STEWARDSHIP
Jeremiah	Jer 25:15-29

to TRUTH
God	Rom 16:25-27
Jeremiah	Jer 23:23-32; 26:1-6
Paul	Gal 1:18-2:10

as VIRTUE
Believers	Rev 19:6-10

to RITE
by FOLLOWERs
Disciples	Mt 26:17-30

INSTRUCTION on
Aaron	Lev 9:1-24
Abraham	Gen 17:23-27; 21:1-7
God	Gen 17:9-14
Israelites	*1 Esd 9:1-15

REVELATION on
Jacob	Gen 35:1-15
Moses	Ex 40:1-33

TRADITION of
Israelites	*1 Esd 7:10-15

in WORSHIP
Levites	2 Chr 8:1-18

SALVATION through
to DEITY
Mankind	Ps 15:1-5b
Psalmist	Ps 119:145-152

in ENVIRONMENT
God	Gen 8:1-12

of FOLLOWERs
Holy Spirit	Gal 5:16-21

INSTRUCTION on
Angels	Gen 19:12-29
David	Ps 37:23-40
God	Gen 7:1-24; Ps 50:22-23; 81:5c-16; Is 1:18-20
Jesus	Mt 7:21-23; 24-27; 19:16-22; 21:33-43; Mk 10:17-22; 12:1-12; Lk 6:46-49; 13:22-30; 18:18-27;

REVELATION on (cont'd)
   Jeremiah   Jer 23:23-32;
                         26:1-6
   Paul   Gal 1:18-2:10

VIRTUE in
  of FOLLOWER
   Noah   Gen 7:1-24
  INSTRUCTION on
   Isaiah   Is 51:1-16
   Peter   1 Pet 1:13-2:3
  REVELATION on
   Believers   Rev 19:6-10

in WORSHIP
  BEHAVIOR revealing
   Ezra   *2 Esd 9:26-37
  FIDELITY through
   Asa   1 Kgs 15:9-15
   Israelites   Josh 24:16-24
  RITE of
   Levites   2 Chr 8:1-18
  STEWARDSHIP of
   Israelites   Ex 35:4-29

OLD AGE

CONFRONTATION with
  Joshua   Josh 13:1-7

DESIRE for
  INSTRUCTION on
   Peter   1 Pet 1:13-2:3

FIDELITY to
  by DEITY
   Psalmist   Ps 71:1-21

of FOLLOWERs
  concerning TRUTH
   Jesus   Eph 4:7-16

INSTRUCTION on
  concerning KNOWLEDGE
   Sirach   *Sir 8:1-19;
                    42:8
  as QUALITY OF LIFE
   Solomon   Prov 20:1-30
  concerning TRUTH
   Author   Heb 5:11-14;
                    6:1-8
   Peter   2 Pet 3:14-18a

concerning KNOWLEDGE
  INSTRUCTION on
   Sirach   *Sir 8:1-19;
                    42:8

as MOTIVATION
  Naomi   Ruth 1:1-18

as QUALITY OF LIFE
  David   1 Kgs 1:1-4
  Isaac   Gen 27:1-40
  INSTRUCTION on
   Solomon   Prov 20:1-30

RATIONALIZATION concerning
  INSTRUCTION on

INSTRUCTION on (cont'd)
  Paul   1 Cor 14:13-25

RESPECT for
  Elihu   Job 32:2b-5;
                  6-10
  INSTRUCTION on
   Paul   1 Tim 5:1-2;
                  3-16
   Sirach   *Sir 25:3-6;
                  32:1-13
   Solomon   Prov 23:15-24:22
                  *Wis 3:10-19;
                  4:1-9

SECURITY in
  by DEITY
   Believers   Ps 92:12-15

concerning TRUTH
  of FOLLOWERs
   Jesus   Eph 4:7-16
  INSTRUCTION on
   Author   Heb 5:11-14;
                  6:1-8
   Peter   2 Pet 3:14-18a

ONENESS

with the AUTHORITY
  of DEITY
   God   Deut 6:4-19;
                  Is 44:6-8;
                  21-23;
                  46:1-13;
                  Jn 1:1-18
   Jesus   Jn 1:1-18;
                  5:19-47;
                  14:1-14;
                  Col 1:18-20
  REVELATION on
   God   Is 43:8-13

BEHAVIOR revealing
  INSTRUCTION on
   Jesus   Mt 7:12
  SCRIPTURES on
   Paul   Eph 5:21-33

in BELIEF
  of FOLLOWERs
   Believers   Acts 2:42-47
  in MISSION
   Believers   Eph 4:7-16

in BROTHERHOOD
  with DEITY
   Jesus   Jn 8:21-59;
                  17:20-26
  of FOLLOWERs
   Believers   Acts 4:32-5:10;
                  1 Cor 12:12-26;
                  2 Cor 12:11-13;
                  Eph 2:11-22
   Holy Spirit   Eph 4:1-6
  INSTRUCTION on
   Jesus   Mt 12:46-50;
                  Mk 3:31-35;
                  Lk 8:19-21

INSTRUCTION on (cont'd)
  Paul   Rom 12:3-8;
                        14-21;
                        14:1-23;
                        15:1-13;
                        1 Cor 1:10-12;
                        2 Cor 2:5-11;
                        Eph 4:25-5:2
  Peter   1 Pet 3:8-12
in **COMMITMENT**
  to **DEITY**
    Believers   1 Jn 4:13-18
  INSTRUCTION on
    Paul   1 Cor 1:10-12

in **COMMUNITY**
  Canaanites   Judg 1:22-36
  Israelites   Ezra 3:1-3a;
                        Neh 7:33b-8:2
  Jebusites   Josh 15:20-63;
                        Judg 1:1-21
  Psalmist   Ps 133:1-3
  of **FOLLOWERs**
    Believers   Acts 4:32-5:10
  INSTRUCTION on
    Paul   Rom 15:1-13
  REVELATION on
    Israelites   Ezek 37:15-28

in **COVENANT**
  RECONCILIATION through
    Gentiles   Eph 2:11-22

in **CREATION**
  God   Gen 1:24-31;
                        1 Cor 11:2-16;
                        Jas 3:1-12
  Man   Gen 5:1-28
  INSTRUCTION on
    Malachi   Mal 2:10-16
  MEDITATION on
    Jesus   Eph 1:3-14

with **DEITY**
  in **BROTHERHOOD**
    Jesus   Jn 8:21-59;
                        17:20-26
  through **COMMITMENT**
    Believers   1 Jn 4:13-18
  as **GIFT**
    Holy Spirit   1 Cor 12:4-11
  through **PRESENCE**
    Jesus   Jn 14:1-14;
                        18-24;
                        16:29-33
  as **QUALITY OF LIFE**
    God   Is 44:24-45:13;
                        14-25;
                        Zech 14:1-21;
                        Rom 3:21-30;
                        1 Cor 8:4-6;
                        Gal 3:19-25;
                        1 Tim 2:1-7
    Jesus   Jn 10:19-40
  SALVATION through
    God   1 Tim 2:1-7
  TRUTH in
    God   Eph 4:1-6

with **DEITY's**

---

with **DEITY 'S** (cont'd)
  AUTHORITY
    God   Deut 6:4-19;
                        Is 44:6-8;
                        21-23;
                        46:1-13;
                        Jn 1:1-18
    Jesus   Jn 1:1-18;
                        5:19-47;
                        14:1-14;
                        Col 1:18-20

in **ELECTION**
  INSTRUCTION on
    Paul   Rom 9:6-13

in **EQUALITY**
  of **FOLLOWERs**
    Jesus   Gal 3:26-29

in **FIDELITY**
  INSTRUCTION on
    Jesus   Lk 16:13;
                        Jn 15:1-11
    Paul   1 Cor 10:14-22
  REVELATION on
    Ezekiel   Ezek 11:14-21

of **FOLLOWERs**
  in **BELIEF**
    Believers   Acts 2:42-47
  in **BROTHERHOOD**
    Believers   Acts 4:32-5:10;
                        1 Cor 12:12-26;
                        2 Cor 12:11-13;
                        Eph 2:11-22
    Holy Spirit   Eph 4:1-6
  in **COMMUNITY**
    Believers   Acts 4:32-5:10
  in **EQUALITY**
    Jesus   Gal 3:26-29
  in **NEW AGE**
    Gentiles   Eph 3:1-13
  as **QUALITY OF LIFE**
    Jesus   1 Cor 6:12-20
  through **RECONCILIATION**
    Jesus   Eph 2:11-22

GIFT of
  with **DEITY**
    Holy Spirit   1 Cor 12:4-11

INSTRUCTION on
  Jesus   Mt 7:12
  in **BROTHERHOOD**
    Jesus   Mt 12:46-50;
                        Mk 3:31-35;
                        Lk 8:19-21
    Paul   Rom 12:3-8;
                        14-21;
                        14:1-23;
                        15:1-13;
                        1 Cor 1:10-12;
                        2 Cor 2:5-11;
                        Eph 4:25-5:2
    Peter   1 Pet 3:8-12
  in **COMMITMENT**
    Paul   1 Cor 1:10-12
  in **COMMUNITY**
    Paul   Rom 15:1-13
  in **CREATION**

in the **ENVIRONMENT** (cont'd)
Pharaoh	Ex 5:6-14

PROPHECY of
Israelites	Is 14:1-23
Samuel	1 Sam 8:1-22

REVELATION on
John	Rev 7:1-8

BEHAVIOR revealing
Nineveh	Nah 3:1-4

by **DEITY**
Isaiah	Is 52:13-53:12

in **ENVIRONMENT**
Antiochus	*1 Mc 1:54-61
Bacchides	*1 Mc 9:23-27
Jews	*2 Mc 6:1-11

of **FOLLOWERs**
Jews	Acts 17:1-9
Saul	Acts 9:1-19

INSTRUCTION on
Artaxerxes	*Esth 13:1-7
Pharisees	Mt 23:4

MEDITATION on
Preacher	Eccl 3:16-4:3

of **MESSIANIC FIGURE**
Jews	Jn 5:1-18
People	Lk 22:63-65
Soldiers	Mt 27:27-31; Mk 15:16-20

of **COMMUNITY**
Israelites	Neh 1:1-4; 5:1-5
Rehoboam	1 Kgs 12:1-20; 2 Chr 10:1-12:16

through **COMPULSION**
Israel	Ex 2:23b-25; 5:6-14
Israelites	Ex 1:8-14
Simon	Mt 27:32; Mk 15:21-32

MEDITATION on
Jeremiah	Lam 3:1-66

REVELATION on
Ezekiel	Ezek 4:4-8
John	Rev 13:11-18

CONFRONTATION with
David	2 Sam 12:1-31; Ps 54:3
Israelites	Judg 6:1-6; 2 Kgs 13:22-25; Ezra 4:4-5
Jehoiakim	2 Kgs 23:36-24:7
Jeremiah	Jer 37:11-15
Jonathan	*1 Mc 11:38-53
Judahites	2 Kgs 16:5-9; Jer 39:1-14; 52:4-27
Nineveh	Nah 2:6-10
Paul	Acts 16:16-24
Silas	Acts 16:16-24
Zedekiah	Jer 52:4-27

of **FOLLOWERs**
Herod	Acts 12:1-25

INSTRUCTION on
Jesus	Mt 10:23; 24-25

in **MISSION**
Apostles	Mt 10:16-22

PROPHECY of
Gog	Ezek 38:10-13
Isaiah	Is 24:16b-18b

REVELATION on
Daniel	Dan 11:5-20
Ezekiel	Ezek 10:1-22
Gog	Ezek 38:3-9

SCRIPTURES on
Believers	Rom 8:28-39

revealed in **COVENANT SIGNS** of
Paul	Gal 4:21-26

in the **CREATION**
God	Is 24:1-12

by **DEITY**

BEHAVIOR revealing
Isaiah	Is 52:13-53:12

KNOWLEDGE of
Israelites	Ex 2:23b-25; Acts 6:8-8:3

PROVIDENCE through
David	Ps 89:38-51
God	Ps 107:39-43
Israelites	Ps 107:4-9

as **PUNISHMENT**
God	Jer 32:16-25
Israelites	Judg 4:1-3; 10:6-18; 13:1; 2 Kgs 13:1-9
Job	Job 10:13-17; 19:7-12

as **QUALITY OF LIFE**
David	Ps 57:4-6

for **SIN**
Mankind	Ps 10:3-11
Psalmist	Ps 10:1-2

DESIRE for
of **FOLLOWERs**
Gentiles	Acts 14:1-7
Jews	Acts 14:1-7

in the **ENVIRONMENT**
by **AUTHORITY**
Pharaoh	Ex 5:6-14

BEHAVIOR revealing
Antiochus	*1 Mc 1:54-61
Bacchides	*1 Mc 9:23-27
Jews	*2 Mc 6:1-11

CONFRONTATION with
Israelites	Judg 6:1-6; Ezra 4:4-5
Jonathan	*1 Mc 11:38-53
Paul	Acts 16:16-24
Silas	Acts 16:16-24

of **CREATION**
God	Is 24:1-12

through **FIDELITY**
Ungodly Men	*Wis 2:12-20

FREEDOM from
Paul	Gal 4:1-3

EQUALITY in
PROPHECY of
Isaiah	Is 3:8-12

ETERNAL
    REVELATION on
        Sinners   Jer 23:33-40

caused by **FALSE BELIEF**
    PUNISHMENT as
        Peter   2 Pet 2:17-22
        Prophets   Mic 3:1-12

because of **FIDELITY**
    to **DEITY**
        Psalmist   Ps 119:57-64;
                             129-136;
                             153-160
    in **ENVIRONMENT**
        Ungodly Men   *Wis 2:12-20
    of **FOLLOWERs**
        Thessalonians   2 Thes 1:3-4
    INSTRUCTION on
        Jesus   Mt 5:38-42
        Paul   2 Tim 3:10-13
    in **MISSION**
        Paul   2 Cor 4:7-12
    PROPHECY of
        Jesus   Mt 24:9-14;
                             Mk 13:9-13

of **FOLLOWERs**
    BEHAVIOR revealing
        Jews   Acts 17:1-9
        Saul   Acts 9:1-19
    CONFRONTATION with
        Herod   Acts 12:1-25
    DESIRE for
        Gentiles   Acts 14:1-7
        Jews   Acts 14:1-7
    through **FIDELITY**
        Thessalonians   2 Thes 1:3-4
    as **PUNISHMENT**
        Jews   Acts 13:14-52
        Paul   Acts 14:19-28
        Saul   Acts 6:8-8:3

FREEDOM from
    in **ENVIRONMENT**
        Paul   Gal 4:1-3
    INSTRUCTION on
        Manoah   Judg 13:2-7
        Solomon   Prov 6:1-5
    REVELATION on
        Israelites   Ezek 45:1-9
        Manoah   Judg 13:2-7
        Zechariah   Zech 1:18-21

disHONESTY causing
    MEDITATION on
        David   Ps 62:3-4

INSTRUCTION on
    through **FIDELITY**
        Jesus   Mt 5:38-42
        Paul   2 Tim 3:10-13
    as **MOTIVATION**
        Jeremiah   Jer 13:15-17
    as **PUNISHMENT**
        Solomon   Prov 22:1-16
    as **QUALITY OF LIFE**
        Jesus   Mt 10:26-39
    concerning **SECURITY**
        Artaxerxes   *Esth 16:1-24

concerning **SECURITY** (cont'd)
        Isaiah   Is 15:1-16:14
    caused by **SIN**
        Bildad   Job 18:12-15
        James   Jas 5:1-6
    of **TRUTH**
        Jesus   Mt 23:34-39

JUDGMENT on
    PROPHECY of
        Isaiah   Is 3:13-15
    REVELATION on
        Israelites   Mal 2:17-3:5

KNOWLEDGE of
    by **DEITY**
        Israelites   Ex 2:23b-25;
                             Acts 6:8-8:3
    INSTRUCTION on
        Solomon   Prov 29:1-27
    by **MESSIANIC FIGURE**
        Demons   Mk 1:32-34;
                             Lk 4:40-41

LAW concerning
        Moses   Ex 22:21-31;
                             23:1-9;
                             Lev 19:1-37

MEDIATION for
    REVELATION on
        Ezekiel   Ezek 4:4-8

MEDITATION on
        Preacher   Eccl 3:16-4:3
    through **COMPULSION**
        Jeremiah   Lam 3:1-66
    caused by **disHONESTY**
        David   Ps 62:3-4
    as **PUNISHMENT**
        Jeremiah   Lam 2:1-22
        Judahites   Lam 5:1-22
    as **QUALITY OF LIFE**
        David   Ps 40:12
        Psalmist   Ps 42:6-11;
                             102:1-11

against **MESSIANIC FIGURE**
    SIN of
        Crowd   Mt 27:33-44;
                             Mk 15:21-32

by **MESSIANIC FIGURE**
    through **KNOWLEDGE**
        Demons   Mk 1:32-34;
                             Lk 4:40-41

of **MESSIANIC FIGURE**
    BEHAVIOR revealing
        Jews   Jn 5:1-18
        People   Lk 22:63-65
        Soldiers   Mt 27:27-31;
                             Mk 15:16-20

in **MISSION**
    CONFRONTATION with
        Apostles   Mt 10:16-22
    through **FIDELITY**
        Paul   2 Cor 4:7-12

as **MOTIVATION**

as **QUALITY OF LIFE** (cont'd)
David | 4-12;
 | | 109:1-5;
 | | 21-31;
 | | 142:3c-4;
 | | 143:3-4
Paul | 2 Cor 11:21-29
Psalmist | Ps 88:3-9;
 | | 119:145-152;
 | | 129:1-4
Saul | 1 Sam 16:14-23
INSTRUCTION on
Jesus | Mt 10:26-39
MEDITATION on
David | Ps 40:12
Psalmist | Ps 42:6-11;
 | | 102:1-11
PROPHECY of
Ephraimites | Hos 9:1-6
Joel | Joel 1:2-20
REVELATION on
Daniel | Dan 12:1-4
Ezekiel | Ezek 4:9-11

RECONCILIATION through
PROPHECY of
Isaiah | Is 27:12-13
Micah | Mic 4:1-8
REVELATION on
Israelites | Is 51:17-52:12

RESPECT for
Psalmist | Ps 123:3-4

REVELATION on
by **AUTHORITY**
John | Rev 7:1-8
through **COMPULSION**
Ezekiel | Ezek 4:4-8
John | Rev 13:11-18
in **CONFRONTATION**
Daniel | Dan 11:5-20
Ezekiel | Ezek 10:1-22
Gog | Ezek 38:3-9
for **ETERNITY**
Sinners | Jer 23:33-40
as **PUNISHMENT**
Ammonites | Ezek 25:1-7
Chaldeans | Is 47:1-15
Daniel | Dan 4:19-27
Egyptians | Ezek 32:17-32
Eli | 1 Sam 2:27-36
Ezekiel | Ezek 24:15-24
Israelites | Is 43:14-44:5;
 | | Jer 30:18-22;
 | | Ezek 4:16-17;
 | | 5:5-17;
 | | 7:1-27;
 | | 22:17-22;
 | | 23-31
Jeremiah | Jer 25:15-29
John | Rev 14:17-20
Judahites | Ezek 24:1-14
Nebuchadnezzar | Dan 4:28-33
Sidon | Ezek 28:20-23
Zedekiah | Jer 24:1-10
as **QUALITY OF LIFE**
Daniel | Dan 12:1-4
Ezekiel | Ezek 4:9-11
caused by **SIN**
Egyptians | Ezek 29:6-9a

caused by **SIN** (cont'd)
Isaiah | Is 58:1-14

SALVATION from
by **DEITY**
God | Ps 76:7-9;
 | | Rev 7:9-17
Psalmist | Ps 118:10-14;
 | | 119:121-128;
 | | 129-136;
 | | 153-160;
 | | 120:1-2
INSTRUCTION on
Jesus | Mt 5:3-12
REVELATION on
Israelites | Zeph 3:14-20

SCRIPTURES on
in **CONFRONTATION**
Believers | Rom 8:28-39

SECURITY from
by **DEITY**
Hezekiah | Is 38:1-22
Isaiah | Is 19:18-25
Israelites | 1 Chr 15:1-16:4
 | | Ps 105:7-15
INSTRUCTION on
Artaxerxes | *Esth 16:1-24
Isaiah | Is 15:1-16:14
PROPHECY of
Israelites | Zech 9:1-12
REVELATION on
Satan | Rev 20:1-3

as **SIGNS**
PROPHECY of
Jesus | Mt 24:15-22;
 | | Mk 13:14-23;
 | | Lk 21:7-19;
 | | 20-24
Nineveh | Nah 2:11-13
REVELATION on
Ezekiel | Ezek 4:1-3;
 | | 24:25-27
Israelites | Ezek 19:10-14
John | Rev 16:12-16
Zechariah | Zech 1:18-21

SIGNS of
in **COVENANT**
Paul | Gal 4:21-26

caused by **SIN**
Israelites | Amos 2:6-8;
 | | 5:7-13;
 | | 8:4-7
Mankind | Ps 10:3-11
Psalmist | Ps 10:1-2
Samaritans | Amos 3:9-10
Women | Amos 4:1-3
INSTRUCTION on
Bildad | Job 18:12-15
James | Jas 5:1-6
PROPHECY of
Isaiah | Is 52:13-53:12
Micah | Mic 2:1-10
REVELATION on
Egyptians | Ezek 29:6-9a
Isaiah | Is 58:1-14

by SINners		
MESSIANIC FIGURE receives		
Crowd	Mt 27:33-44;	
	Mk 15:21-32	
of TRUTH		
INSTRUCTION on		
Jesus	Mt 23:34-39	
VIRTUE in		
Habakkuk	Hab 1:12-17	

ORDER

by AUTHORITY	
Levites	2 Chr 30:1-31:21
in ENVIRONMENT	
God	Gen 1:1-2;
	3-5;
	6-8;
	9-13;
	14-19;
	24-31;
	2 Sam 22:1-51;
	Ps 18:7-15
INSTRUCTION on	
God	Gen 1:20-23
REVELATION on	
God	*2 Esd 16:51-78
Job	Job 38:12-15
created by AUTHORITY	
of DEITY	
David	Ps 19:1-4b
Ezra	*2 Esd 8:4-36
God	Ps 19:4c-6;
	33:4-9;
	50:1-6;
	65:5-8;
	74:12-17;
	77:11-20;
	89:5-18;
	93:3-4;
	95:1-7c;
	97:1-5;
	104:1-4;
	5-9;
	135:5-7;
	147:12-20
Jeremiah	*Jer 6:60-73
Manasseh	*Mana 1:1-5
Mankind	Ps 8:3-8
Sirach	*Sir 16:24-30;
	17:15-32;
	18:1-14;
	33:7-15;
	39:17-27;
	42:15-43:33
Solomon	*Wis 7:15-8:1;
	9:1-18;
	11:21-12:2;
	13:1-9
BEHAVIOR revealing	
of FOLLOWERs	
Israelites	Num 10:11-28
INSTRUCTION on	
Jesus	Mt 7:13-14
Joshua	Josh 1:10-11

in COMMUNITY	
Gatekeepers	Ezra 2:42
Isaac	Gen 26:32-33
Israelites	Num 1:20-46;
	32:34-38;
	39-42;
	33:1-4;
	Deut 3:12-22;
	Ezra 2:2b-20;
	21-35;
	64;
	65-67;
	Neh 7:4-33a;
	33b-8:2;
	11:3-6
Levites	Ezra 2:40;
	Neh 12:1-7
Moses	Num 3:14-39;
	4:34-49;
	34:1-15;
	16-29;
	35:1-8
Priests	Ezra 2:36-39;
	59-63
Servants	Ezra 2:43-54;
	55-58
Singers	Ezra 2:41
INSTRUCTION on	
Jesus	Mt 10:24-25
REVELATION on	
Moses	Num 1:1-19;
	2:1-34;
	3:40-51;
	26:1-4;
	52-56;
	27:1-11;
	36:1-13
TRADITION of	
Israelites	Num 26:5-51
CONFRONTATION with	
David	1 Chr 11:1-12:40
INSTRUCTION on	
John	Rev 11:1-14
in COVENANT	
PROMISE of	
God	Gen 9;8-19
SECURITY through	
Noah	Gen 9:8-19
SIGNS of	
God	Gen 9:8-19
in the CREATION	
by DEITY	
God	Job 39:9-12;
	Ps 24:1-2;
	3-6;
	33:4-9;
	89:5-18;
	90:1-12;
	102:23-28;
	104:5-9;
	19-23;
	121:2-8;
	135:5-7;
	136:4-9;
	Is 42:5-17;
	44:24-45:13;
	Jer 5:20-25;
	Zech 10:1-2;

by **DEITY** (cont'd)

God	Jn 1:1-18;
	Acts 17:16-34;
	2 Pet 3:3-7
Israelites	Is 45:14-25

CREATION of

in the **ENVIRONMENT**

God	Gen 1:1-2;
	3-5;
	6-8;
	9-13;
	14-19;
	20-23;
	24-31;
	2:4b-7
Israelites	Neh 3:1-5;
	6-12;
	13-14;
	15-31;
	32;
	4:6;
	13-23
Man	Gen 2:8-15

INSTRUCTION on

Nehemiah	Neh 2:16-18

through **MESSIANIC FIGURE**

Jesus	Col 1:15-17

REVELATION on

God	Is 48:1-22
Job	Job 38:4-7;
	8-11

SCRIPTURES on

God	2 Cor 4:1-6

in **WORSHIP**

Ezra	*2 Esd 6:35-59

by **DEITY**

AUTHORITY over

David	Ps 19:1-4b
Ezra	*2 Esd 8:4-36
God	Ps 19:4c-6;
	33:4-9;
	50:1-6;
	65:5-8;
	74:12-17;
	77:11-20;
	89:5-18;
	93:3-4;
	95:1-7c;
	97:1-5;
	104:1-4;
	5-9;
	135:5-7;
	147:12-20
Jeremiah	*Jer 6:60-73
Manasseh	*Mana 1:1-5
Mankind	Ps 8:3-8
Sirach	*Sir 16:24-30;
	17:15-32;
	18:1-14;
	33:7-15;
	39:17-27;
	42:15-43:33
Solomon	*Wis 7:15-8:1;
	9:1-18;
	11:21-12:2;
	13:1-9

CREATION of

God	Job 39:9-12;
	Ps 24:1-2;

CREATION of (cont'd)

God	3-6;
	33:4-9;
	89:5-18;
	90:1-12;
	102:23-28;
	104:5-9;
	19-23;
	121:2-8;
	135:5-7;
	136:4-9;
	Is 42:5-17;
	44:24-45:13;
	Jer 5:20-25;
	Zech 10:1-2;
	Jn 1:1-18;
	Acts 17:16-34;
	2 Pet 3:3-7
Israelites	Is 45:14-25

as **ETERNAL**

God	Eccl 3:9-15

through **PRESENCE**

God	Ps 68:4-14

PROMISE of

God	Gen 8:13-22

PROVIDENCE through

Amos	Amos 3:3-8
God	Ps 65:9-13;
	104:10-13;
	107:23-32;
	147:7-11;
	Jer 31:35-37

DESIRE for

PROPHECY of

Believers	1 Cor 14:34-40

in the **ENVIRONMENT**

by **AUTHORITY**

God	Gen 1:1-2;
	3-5;
	6-8;
	9-13;
	14-19;
	24-31;
	2 Sam 22:1-51;
	Ps 18:7-15

CREATION of

God	Gen 1:1-2;
	3-5;
	6-8;
	9-13;
	14-19;
	20-23;
	24-31;
	2:4b-7
Israelites	Neh 3:1-5;
	6-12;
	13-14;
	15-31;
	32;
	4:6;
	13-23
Man	Gen 2:8-15

KNOWLEDGE of

Israelites	Num 3:40-51

SIGNS of

God	Gen 1:14-19

SIN against

David	2 Sam 24:1-25;
	1 Chr 21:1-22:1

ETERNAL
    by **DEITY**
        God   Eccl 3:9-15
    INSTRUCTION on
        God   Ps 119:89-96

through **FIDELITY**
    INSTRUCTION on
        Jesus   Mt 24:42-44;
                  Mk 13:28-37

of **FOLLOWER**s
    BEHAVIOR revealing
        Israelites   Num 10:11-28

of **GIFT**
    in **WORSHIP**
        Believers   1 Cor 14:26-33

in **HONESTY**
    INSTRUCTION on
        Moses   Deut 19:14

INSTRUCTION on
    Joshua   Josh 18:1-10
    by **AUTHORITY**
        God   Gen 1:20-23
    in **COMMUNITY**
        Jesus   Mt 10:24-25
    through **FIDELITY**
        Jesus   Mt 24:42-44;
                  Mk 13:28-37
    in **HONESTY**
        Moses   Deut 19:14
    in **JUDGMENT**
        Paul   1 Cor 6:1-8
    as **QUALITY OF LIFE**
        Paul   2 Thes 3:6-15
        Preacher   Eccl 3:1-8
        Solomon   Prov 20:1-30

in **JUDGMENT**
    INSTRUCTION on
        Paul   1 Cor 6:1-8
    REVELATION on
        Priests   Ezek 44:15-31
    TRADITION of
        Moses   Ex 18:13-26

KNOWLEDGE of
    by **DEITY**
        God   Ps 87:4-6
    in the **ENVIRONMENT**
        Israelites   Num 3:40-51
    INSTRUCTION on
        Joshua   Josh 18:1-10
    REVELATION on
        Ezekiel   Ezek 40:6-16;
                  17-19;
                  20-27;
                  28-37;
                  38-43;
                  44-47;
                  48-49;
                  41:1-4;
                  5-11;
                  12;
                  13-15a;
                  15b-26;
                  42:1-10a;
                  10b-12;

REVELATION (cont'd)
    Ezekiel   13-14
                  15-20;
                  47:1-12

TRADITION of
    Samuel   1 Sam 7:2-17
    in **WORSHIP**
        Women   1 Cor 14:34-40

LAW concerning
    REVELATION on
        Ezekiel   Ezek 43:13-17
        Israelites   Ezek 45:10-12;
                  47:13-20;
                  48:1-7;
                  8-22;
                  23-29;
                  30-35
        Priests   Ezek 46:19-24

by **MESSIANIC FIGURE**
    CREATION of
        Jesus   Col 1:15-17

in **NEW AGE**
    REVELATION on
        Daniel   Dan 2:24-45
        John   Rev 21:9-14;
                  15-17;
                  18-21;
                  22-27

through **PRESENCE**
    of **DEITY**
        God   Ps 68:4-14

PROMISE of
    in **COVENANT**
        God   Gen 9:8-19
    by **DEITY**
        God   Gen 8:13-22

PROPHECY of
    through **PROVIDENCE**
        Isaiah   Is 17:12-14;
                  18:1-7
    in **STEWARDSHIP**
        Isaiah   Is 18:1-7

through **PROVIDENCE**
    of **DEITY**
        Amos   Amos 3:3-8
        God   Ps 65:9-13;
                  104:10-13;
                  107:23-32;
                  147:7-11;
                  Jer 31:35-37

PROPHECY of
    Isaiah   Is 17:12-14;
                  18:1-7

as **QUALITY OF LIFE**
    INSTRUCTION on
        Paul   2 Thes 3:6-15
        Preacher   Eccl 3:1-8
        Solomon   Prov 20:1-30

REVELATION on
    by **AUTHORITY**
        God   *2 Esd 16:51-78
        Job   Job 38:12-15

ORDER (cont'd)

in **RITE** (cont'd)
    TRADITION of
        Pharisees   Mk 7:1-23

SALVATION through
  by **DEITY**
    God   Ps 118:22-27
  of **FOLLOWERs**
    Jesus   2 Tim 2:8-13
  INSTRUCTION on
    Jesus   Mt 22:1-14;
                   Lk 17:22-37;
                   Jn 12:20-26
  REVELATION on
    Isaiah   Is 66:1-16

SELF-REALIZATION of
  in **BEHAVIOR**
    Paul   Rom 7:14-25
  as **QUALITY OF LIFE**
    Paul   2 Cor 12:1-10

in **SIN**
  INSTRUCTION on
    Paul   Gal 2:17-19
  in **WORSHIP**
    Babylonians   2 Kgs 17:24-41

concerning **STEWARDSHIP**
  INSTRUCTION on
    Jesus   Mt 25:31-46;
                   Lk 22:24-27
  in **MISSION**
    Jesus   Mk 2:15-17

in **TRUTH**
  INSTRUCTION on
    Jesus   Mk 9:33-37;
                   Jn 6:25-59

in **WORSHIP**
  caused by **SIN**
    Babylonians   2 Kgs 17:24-41

PATIENCE

in **AUTHORITY**
  of **DEITY**
    Isaiah   Is 40:12-31

BEHAVIOR revealing
  INSTRUCTION on
    Paul   1 Thes 5:12-22

in **BELIEF**
  of **FOLLOWERs**
    Jesus   1 Tim 1:12-17
  INSTRUCTION on
    Eliphaz   Job 4:1-6

in **COMMITMENT**
  INSTRUCTION on
    Paul   2 Tim 2:20-26

of **DEITY**
  AUTHORITY of
    Isaiah   Is 40:12-31
  in **JUDGMENT**
    Isaiah   Is 26:7-19

with **DEITY**
  PROVIDENCE through
    Jeremiah   Lam 3:1-66
  SALVATION through
    David   Ps 62:1-2;
                   5-7
  as **VIRTUE**
    God   Ex 34:5b-9

FIDELITY through
    Philadelphians   Rev 3:7-13
  to **DEITY**
    David   Ps 38:11-16
    Habakkuk   Hab 3:16-19
  INSTRUCTION on
    David   Ps 37:23-40
    Hosea   Hos 12:2-6
    Jesus   Lk 21:34-36
    Paul   Eph 4:1-6
    Peter   2 Pet 3:14-18a
  to **MESSIANIC FIGURE**
    Jesus   Lk 12:39-40

of **FOLLOWERs**
  PRAYER for
    Paul   Col 1:9-14
  as **QUALITY OF LIFE**
    Holy Spirit   Gal 5:22-24

with **FOLLOWERs**
    Apostles   1 Cor 4:6-13
  BELIEF in
    Jesus   1 Tim 1:12-17

INSTRUCTION on
  to **COMMITMENT**
    Paul   2 Tim 2:20-26
  for **JUDGMENT**
    God   Zeph 3:8
  concerning **NEW AGE**
    James   Jas 5:7-11
    Jesus   Lk 12:35-38
    Paul   Rom 8:14-25
  in **PRESENCE**
    David   Ps 27:13-14
  with **PROMISE**
    Author   Heb 10:32-39
  in **PROVIDENCE**
    Sirach   *Sir 11:10-13
  as **QUALITY OF LIFE**
    Paul   Rom 12:9-13;
                   1 Cor 7:17-24;
                   Col 3:5-17
  in **TRUTH**
    Paul   2 Tim 4:1-5
  as **VIRTUE**
    Peter   2 Pet 3:11-13
    Preacher   Eccl 7:1-22
    Sirach   *Sir 11:10-13
    Solomon   Prov 16:1-33

for **JUDGMENT**
  INSTRUCTION on
    God   Zeph 3:8

in **JUDGMENT**
  by **DEITY**
    Isaiah   Is 26:7-19

KNOWLEDGE of
  INSTRUCTION on

through **BROTHERHOOD**
  in **ENVIRONMENT**
    Israelites   Judg 5:31
  INSTRUCTION on
    Paul   1 Thes 5:12-22

COMMITMENT to
  INSTRUCTION on
    Israelites   Zech 7:4-8:23
    Paul   Rom 8:5-13;
      14:1-23;
      2 Tim 2:20-26;
      Heb 12:12-29

in **COMMUNITY**
    Israelites   Josh 11:16-23
    Psalmist   Ps 133:1-3
  through **COVENANT**
    Solomon   1 Kgs 5:1-18
  INSTRUCTION on
    Paul   Rom 12:14-21;
      15:1-13
  PROPHECY of
    Isaiah   Is 11:10-16

through **CONFRONTATION**
    David   2 Sam 19:8b-43
  COVENANT of
    Maccabeus   *2 Mc 12:10-12
  in **ENVIRONMENT**
    Elisha   2 Kgs 6:8-23
    Israelites   Judg 21:13-15;
      1 Sam 7:2-17
    Joab   2 Sam 2:8-32
    Jonathan   *1 Mc 9:58-73
    Judahites   *1 Mc 9:54-57
    Lysias   *1 Mc 6:55-63
    Maccabeus   *2 Mc 11:13-37;
      13:9-26
    Simon   *1 Mc 13:31-41
  INSTRUCTION on
    Moses   Deut 20:10-18

COVENANT of
  with **AUTHORITY**
    David   2 Sam 3:17-39
  in **COMMUNITY**
    Solomon   1 Kgs 5:1-18
  through **CONFRONTATION**
    Maccabeus   *2 Mc 12:10-12
  for **ETERNITY**
    Israelites   Ezek 37:15-28
  FIDELITY through
    Levi   Mal 1:6-2:9
    Phinehas   *Sir 45:23-24
  dis**HONESTY** in
    Gibeon   Josh 9:3-15
  PROMISE in
    Isaiah   Is 54:1-17
  RECONCILIATION through
    Gentiles   Eph 2:11-22
    Phinehas   Num 25:6-18
  SECURITY in
    Isaac   Gen 26:12-31

SECURITY in (cont'd)
    Israelites   Ezek 34:25-31;
      Hos 2:16-20

from **DEITY**
  through **FIDELITY**
    God   Is 26:1-6
  through **JUDGMENT**
    God   Is 2:1-5
  through **LAW**
    Psalmist   Ps 119:161-168
  PRAYER for
    David   Ps 29:10-11;
      122:6-9
    John   2 Jn 1:1-3;
      3 Jn 1:13-15;
      Rev 1:4-20
    Paul   Col 1:1-2;
      Tit 1:1-4;
      Philm 1:1-3
    Peter   1 Pet 1:1-2;
      5:12-14
    Psalmist   Ps 125:4-5;
      128:5-6;
      131:1-3
  PROMISE of
    Solomon   1 Chr 22:2-19
  through **PROVIDENCE**
    Asa   2 Chr 14:1-16:14
    Believers   Prov 16:1-33
    God   Is 2:1-5
    Isaiah   Is 63:7-64:12
  as **QUALITY OF LIFE**
    God   1 Cor 14:26-33
  through **RECONCILIATION**
    Israelites   Nah 1:10, 12, 13,
      15-2:2;
    Jesus   Col 1:18-20
  SECURITY in
    David   Ps 4:6-8
    God   Ps 147:12-20
  VIRTUE in
    James   Jas 3:13-18
    Solomon   Ps 72:5-7

DESIRE for
    Nebuchadnezzar   Dan 4:1-3
    Psalmist   Ps 120:5-7
  from **DEITY**
    God   Is 27:2-6
    Job   Job 10:18-22
  INSTRUCTION on
    David   Ps 34:11-14
  MEDITATION on
    David   Ps 55:3b-8
    Job   Job 3:11-19
  PROPHECY of
    Isaiah   Is 28:1-13

in **ENVIRONMENT**
  through **BROTHERHOOD**
    Israelites   Judg 5:31
  through **CONFRONTATION**
    Elisha   2 Kgs 6:8-23
    Israelites   Judg 21:13-15;
      1 Sam 7:2-17
    Joab   2 Sam 2:8-32
    Jonathan   *1 Mc 9:58-73

through **CONFRONTATION** (cont'd)
   Judahites   *1 Mc 9:54-57
   Lysias   *1 Mc 6:55-63
   Maccabeus   *2 Mc 11:13-37;
                  13:9-26
   Simon   *1 Mc 13:31-41
 DESIRE for
   Psalmist   Ps 120:5-7
through **FIDELITY**
   David   2 Sam 10:1-19;
                 1 Chr 18:1-20:8
 SECURITY through
   Israelites   Judg 8:24-28

ETERNAL
 through **COVENANT**
   Israelites   Ezek 37:15-28
 from **DEITY**
   Jesus   2 Thes 2:16-17

FALSE BELIEF concerning
 revealing dis**HONESTY**
   Prophets   Jer 14:13-16
 revealing in**SECURITY**
   Moses   Deut 12:1-31

through **FIDELITY**
 to **COVENANT**
   Levi   Mal 1:6-2:9
   Phinehas   *Sir 45:23-24
 to **DEITY**
   God   Is 26:1-6
 in **ENVIRONMENT**
   David   2 Sam 10:1-19;
                 1 Chr 18:1-20:8
 INSTRUCTION on
   Paul   Eph 4:1-6

for **FOLLOWERs**
 PRAYER for
   Paul   1 Cor 1:1-3;
                 Gal 1:1-5;
                 Eph 1:1-2;
                 1 Thes 1:1;
                 2 Thes 1:1-2;
                 3:16;
                 1 Tim 1:1-2;
                 2 Tim 1:1-2
 as **QUALITY OF LIFE**
   Holy Spirit   Gal 5:22-24
 through **RECONCILIATION**
   Jesus   Eph 2:11-22
 through **SALVATION**
   Women   1 Tim 2:8-15
 in **TRUTH**
   John   1 Jn 3:19-24

FREEDOM through
 PROPHECY of
   Judahites   Jer 42:7-22

through **HONESTY**
 PROPHECY of
   Isaiah   Is 52:13-53:12

through dis**HONESTY**
 COVENANT of
   Gibeon   Josh 9:3-15
 FALSE BELIEF in
   Prophets   Jer 14:13-16

INSTRUCTION on
 through **BELIEF**
   Jesus   Jn 14:1-14
 through **BROTHERHOOD**
   Paul   1 Thes 5:12-22
 through **COMMITMENT**
   Israelites   Zech 7:4-8:23
   Paul   Rom 8:5-13; -
                 14:1-23;
                 2 Tim 2:20-26;
                 Heb 12:12-29
 in **COMMUNITY**
   Paul   Rom 12:14-21;
                 15:1-13
 through **CONFRONTATION**
   Moses   Deut 20:10-18
 through **FIDELITY**
   Paul   Eph 4:1-6
 in **NEW AGE**
   Author   Heb 4:1-13
   Paul   Rom 14:1-23
 through **PROMISE**
   Jesus   Mt 11:28-30;
                 Jn 14:27-31
   Paul   Phil 4:1-9
 as **QUALITY OF LIFE**
   Jesus   Mt 5:3-12;
                 21-26
   Paul   2 Cor 13:11-13;
                 Col 3:5-17
   Peter   2 Pet 3:14-18a
 through **RECONCILIATION**
   Paul   Rom 5:1-5
 through **RESURRECTION**
   Solomon   *Wis 3:1-9
 in **RITE**
   Paul   1 Cor 14:34-40
 through **SALVATION**
   Moses   Ex 14:1-14
 in **TRUTH**
   Jesus   Mk 9:49-50
   Paul   Eph 6:10-18
 as **VIRTUE**
   Isaiah   Is 56:9-57:13
   Sirach   *Sir 6:2-17

through **JUDGMENT**
 of **DEITY**
   God   Is 2:1-5

through **LAW**
 of **DEITY**
   Psalmist   Ps 119:161-168

by **MESSIANIC FIGURE**
 PRAYER for
   Jesus   Mt 14:22-27

through **MESSIANIC FIGURE**
 in **RECONCILIATION**
   Isaiah   Is 11:1-9
 SECURITY in
   Disciples   Jn 16:29-33
   Zechariah   Zech 9:1-12

in **MISSION**
 PRAYER for
   Jude   Jude 1:1-2
   Peter   2 Pet 1:1-2

in **NEW AGE**

INSTRUCTION on
Author　Heb 4:1-13
Paul　Rom 14:1-23
PROPHECY of
Isaiah　Is 2:1-5;
　　32:15-20;
　　35:1-10
Micah　Mic 4:1-8
REVELATION on
Isaiah　Is 65:1-25

PRAYER for
David　Ps 29:10-11;
　　122:6-9
John　2 Jn 1:1-3;
　　3 Jn 1:13-15;
　　Rev 1:4-20
Paul　Col 1:1-2;
　　Tit 1:1-4;
　　Philm 1:1-3
Peter　1 Pet 1:1-2;
　　5:12-14
Psalmist　Ps 125:4-5;
　　128:5-6;
　　131:1-3
for FOLLOWERs
Paul　1 Cor 1:1-3;
　　Gal 1:1-5;
　　Eph 1:1-2;
　　1 Thes 1:1;
　　2 Thes 1:1-2;
　　3:16;
　　1 Tim 1:1-2;
　　2 Tim 1:1-2
INSTRUCTION on
Paul　1 Thes 5:23-24;
　　1 Tim 2:1-7
by MESSIANIC FIGURE
Jesus　Mt 14:22-27
in MISSION
Jude　Jude 1:1-2
Peter　2 Pet 1:1-2
in WORSHIP
Paul　Eph 6:23-24;
　　Phil 1:1-2

PROMISE of
through COVENANT
Isaiah　Is 54:1-17
from DEITY
Solomon　1 Chr 22:2-19
INSTRUCTION on
Jesus　Mt 11:28-30;
　　Jn 14:27-31
Paul　Phil 4:1-9
REVELATION on
Isaiah　Is 57:14-21

PROPHECY of
in COMMUNITY
Isaiah　Is 11:10-16
in FREEDOM
Judahites　Jer 42:7-22
through HONESTY
Isaiah　Is 52:13-53:12
in NEW AGE
Isaiah　Is 2:1-5;
　　32:15-20;
　　35:1-10
Micah　Mic 4:1-8
through PROVIDENCE

through PROVIDENCE (cont'd)
Isaiah　Is 9:2-7
Israelites　Jer 46:27-28
through RECONCILIATION
Elijah　Mal 4:4-6
Isaiah　Is 19:18-25;
　　51:17-52:12

through PROVIDENCE
from DEITY
Asa　2 Chr 14:1-16:14
Believers　Prov 16:1-33
God　Is 2:1-5
Isaiah　Is 63:7-64:12
PROPHECY of
Isaiah　Is 9:2-7
Israelites　Jer 46:27-28
REVELATION on
Isaiah　Is 55:1-13;
　　62:1-12
Jeremiah　Jer 31:2-6
Nathan　2 Sam 7:1-29

as QUALITY OF LIFE
of DEITY
God　1 Cor 14:26-33
of FOLLOWERs
Holy Spirit　Gal 5:22-24

INSTRUCTION on
Jesus　Mt 5:3-12;
　　21-26
Paul　2 Cor 13:11-13;
　　Col 3:5-17
Peter　2 Pet 3:14-18a

through RECONCILIATION
in COVENANT
Gentiles　Eph 2:11-22
Phinehas　Num 25:6-18
to DEITY
Israelites　Nah 1:10, 12, 13;
Jesus　Col 1:18-20
of FOLLOWERs
Jesus　Eph 2:11-22
INSTRUCTION on
Paul　Rom 5:1-5
of MESSIANIC FIGURE
Isaiah　Is 11:1-9
PROPHECY of
Elijah　Mal 4:4-6
Isaiah　Is 19:18-25;
　　51:17-52:12
REVELATION on
Israelites　Ezek 45:13-17
Judahites　Zech 7:4-8:23

RESPECT for
Mordecai　Esth 10:1-3
REVELATION on
Israelites　Ezek 36:8-15

through RESURRECTION
INSTRUCTION on
Solomon　*Wis 3:1-9

REVELATION on
through AUTHORITY
John　Rev 6:3-4
in NEW AGE
Isaiah　Is 65:1-25

through **PROMISE**
  Isaiah   Is 57:14-21
through **PROVIDENCE**
  Isaiah   Is 55:1-13;
                    62:1-12
  Jeremiah   Jer 31:2-6
  Nathan   2 Sam 7:1-29
through **RECONCILIATION**
  Israelites   Ezek 45:13-17
  Judahites   Zech 7:4-8:23
through **RESPECT**
  Israelites   Ezek 36:8-15
through **RITE**
  Ezekiel   Ezek 43:18-27
  Moses   Lev 7:28-36
  Priest   Ezek 46:1-8
in **TRUTH**
  Disciples   Lk 9:28-36
as **VIRTUE**
  Isaiah   Is 60:1-22

in **RITE**
  INSTRUCTION on
    Paul   1 Cor 14:34-40
  REVELATION on
    Ezekiel   Ezek 43:18-27
    Moses   Lev 7:28-36
    Priests   Ezek 46:1-8
  in **WORSHIP**
    Aaron   Lev 9:1-24
    Israelites   Josh 8:30-35
    Solomon   1 Kgs 9:25

through **SALVATION**
  of **FOLLOWER**
    Women   1 Tim 2:8-15
  INSTRUCTION on
    Moses   Ex 14:1-14

SECURITY in
  Solomon   1 Kgs 4:20-28
  COVENANT of
    Isaac   Gen 26:12-31
    Israelites   Ezek 34:25-31;
                    Hos 2:16-20
  from **DEITY**
    David   Ps 4:6-8
    God   Ps 147:12-20
  in **ENVIRONMENT**
    Israelites   Judg 8:24-28
  of **MESSIANIC FIGURE**
    Disciples   Jn 16:29-33
    Zechariah   Zech 9:1-12
  REVELATION on
    Isaiah   Is 51:1-16

SIGNS of
  REVELATION on
    Zechariah   Zech 1:7-17

TRADITION of
  BEHAVIOR revealing
    Simon   *1 Mc 14:4-15

in **TRUTH**
  of **FOLLOWERs**
    John   1 Jn 3:19-24
  INSTRUCTION on
    Jesus   Mk 9:49-50
    Paul   Eph 6:10-18
  REVELATION on

REVELATION (cont'd)
  Disciples   Lk 9:28-36
as **VIRTUE**
  of **DEITY**
    James   Jas 3:13-18
    Solomon   Ps 72:5-7
  INSTRUCTION on
    Isaiah   Is 56:9-57:13
    Sirach   *Sir 6:2-17
  REVELATION on
    Isaiah   Is 60:1-22

in **WORSHIP**
  BEHAVIOR revealing
    Women   1 Cor 14:34-40
  PRAYER for
    Paul   Eph 6:23-24;
                    Phil 1:1-2
  RITE of
    Aaron   Lev 9:1-24
    Israelites   Josh 8:30-35
    Solomon   1 Kgs 9:25

PIETY

BEHAVIOR revealing
  INSTRUCTION on
    Jesus   Mt 6:1

in **COVENANT**
  of **STEWARDSHIP**
    Paul   Acts 18:18-23

before **DEITY**
  PRAYER for
    Daniel   Dan 6:10-15;
                    9:1-3
  RESPECT through
    God   Is 29:13-14
  RITE of
    Daniel   Dan 9:1-3

FIDELITY in
  INSTRUCTION on
    Believers   Acts 2:42-47
    Paul   Col 4:2-4;
                    1 Tim 4:11-16

GIFT of
  PROPHECY of
    Paul   1 Tim 4:11-16

INSTRUCTION on
  in **PRAYER**
    Jesus   Mt 6:5-8
    Paul   Rom 12:9-13;
                    1 Tim 2:8-15
  in **RITE**
    Jesus   Mt 6:16-18
  as **SIN**
    Jesus   Mt 23:27-28;
                    Mk 12:37b-40;
                    Lk 20:45-47
  in **STEWARDSHIP**
    Jesus   Mt 6:2-4
    Paul   1 Cor 16:1-4
  of **TRUTH**
    Paul   1 Cor 5:6-8

LAW concerning
    REVELATION on
       Israelites   Ezek 46:9-10
       Moses   Lev 24:1-4;
                           Num 9:1-14

PRAYER revealing
    before **DEITY**
       Daniel   Dan 6:10-15;
                           9:1-3
    INSTRUCTION on
       Jesus   Mt 6:5-8
       Paul   Rom 12:9-13;
                           1 Tim 2:8-15
    REVELATION on
       John   Rev 8:1-6
    in **WORSHIP**
       Abraham   Gen 12:1-8
       Jesus   Mk 6:45-52

as **QUALITY OF LIFE**
    TRADITION of
       Pharisees   Mk 7:1-23

RESPECT through
    before **DEITY**
       God   Is 29:13-14
    TRADITION of
       Women   1 Cor 11:2-16
    in **WORSHIP**
       John   Rev 19:6-10

REVELATION on
    in **PRAYER**
       John   Rev 8:1-6
    in **RITE**
       Moses   Lev 23:5-8
    as **SIN**
       Isaiah   Is 58:1-14

RITE of
    before **DEITY**
       Daniel   Dan 9:1-3
    INSTRUCTION on
       Jesus   Mt 6:16-18
    REVELATION on
       Moses   Lev 23:5-8
    TRADITION of
       Paul   Acts 21:15-26
       Pharisees   Lk 11:37-44
    in **WORSHIP**
       High Priest   Heb 9:1-14
       Israelites   Josh 5:10-12;
                           Ezek 46:1-8
       Job   Job 1:4-5
       Mankind   Zech 14:1-21
       People   Jer 36:8-10

in **SALVATION**
    in **WORSHIP**
       Samaritan   Jn 4:1-26

as **SIN**
       Israelites   Amos 4:4-5
    INSTRUCTION on
       Jesus   Mt 23:27-28;
                           Mk 12:37b-40;
                           Lk 20:45-47
    REVELATION on
       Isaiah   Is 58:1-14

in **STEWARDSHIP**
    COVENANT of
       Paul   Acts 18:18-23
    INSTRUCTION on
       Jesus   Mt 6:2-4
       Paul   1 Cor 16:1-4

TRADITION of
    as **QUALITY OF LIFE**
       Pharisees   Mk 7:1-23
    RESPECT through
       Women   1 Cor 11:2-16
    RITE of
       Paul   Acts 21:15-26
       Pharisees   Lk 11:37-44

of **TRUTH**
    INSTRUCTION on
       Paul   1 Cor 5:6-8

in **WORSHIP**
    PRAYER revealing
       Abraham   Gen 12:1-8
       Jesus   Mk 6:45-52
    RESPECT through
       John   Rev 19:6-10
    RITE of
       High Priest   Heb 9:1-14
       Israelites   Josh 5:10-12;
                           Ezek 46:1-8
       Job   Job 1:4-5
       Mankind   Zech 14:1-21
       People   Jer 36:8-10
    SALVATION through
       Samaritan   Jn 4:1-26

POLITICS

AUTHORITY in
       Absalom   2 Sam 15:1-12
       Adonijah   1 Kgs 1:5-10
       David   1 Chr 18:1-20:8
       Haman   Esth 3:1-6
       Rehoboam   1 Kgs 12:1-20;
                           2 Chr 10:1-12:16
       Saul   1 Sam 13:1-23
       Solomon   1 Kgs 1:41-53;
                           9:15-23
    through **COVENANT**
       David   1 Chr 11:1-12:40
       Jonathan   *1 Mc 10:15-44
       Maccabeus   *2 Mc 14:18-25
       Simon   *1 Mc 14:16-24;
                           15:15-24
    supported by **DEITY**
       David   Ps 108:6-13;
                           110:1-4
       God   Ps 2:4-6;
                           33:10-12;
                           60:6-8;
                           76:10-12;
                           113:2-4
       Israelites   Ps 68:28-35
       Solomon   *Wis 6:1-11;
                           12:12-18
    in **ENVIRONMENT**
       Abner   2 Sam 2:8-32
       David   2 Sam 8:1-18;
                           20:1-26

in **ENVIRONMENT** (cont'd)
Demetrius	*1 Mc 11:1-19; 38-53
Ehud	Judg 3:15-23
Simon	*1 Mc 14:25-49

INSTRUCTION on
Jesus	Mt 22:15-22; Mk 12:13-17; Lk 20:19-26
Mordecai	Esth 8:9-14
Paul	Rom 13:1-7

concerning **MESSIANIC FIGURE**
Psalmist	Ps 2:7-9

PROPHECY of
Deborah	Judg 4:4-5
Jesus	Mt 2:1-12

REVELATION on
God	Is 41:1-42:4
Moses	Ex 3:11-22

TRADITION of
Israelites	2 Sam 23:8-39; 1 Chr 11:1-12:40
Jeconiah	*1 Esd 1:34-36
Jehoiachin	*1 Esd 1:43-45
Jehoiakim	*1 Esd 1:37-42
John	*1 Mc 16:18-24
Josiah	*1 Esd 1:33
Zedekiah	*1 Esd 1:46-58

BEHAVIOR revealing
Ahasuerus	Esth 2:1-4
Alexander	*1 Mc 10:51-58
Esther	Esth 5:1-8
Gideon	Judg 6:33-35
Jonathan	*1 Mc 11:20-37
Menelaus	*2 Mc 4:23-29

through **COVENANT**
Jonathan	*1 Mc 12:1-23

INSTRUCTION on
Demetrius	*1 Mc 11:20-37

COMMITMENT in
Asa	2 Chr 14:1-16:14

in **COMMUNITY**
Levites	Neh 11:19-24

INSTRUCTION on
Moses	Deut 16:18-20

CONFRONTATION with
Asa	1 Kgs 15:16-22
Assyrians	2 Kgs 18:17-19:9a
Bathsheba	1 Kgs 1:15-21
Gaal	Judg 9:26-29
Israelites	Judg 5:12-18
Jehoshaphat	1 Kgs 22:1-40; 2 Chr 17:1-20:37
Nathan	1 Kgs 1:11-14; 22-27

PROPHECY of
Shemaiah	1 Kgs 12:21-24; 2 Chr 10:1-12:16

in **COVENANT**
with **AUTHORITY**
David	1 Chr 11:1-12:40
Jonathan	*1 Mc 10:15-44
Maccabeus	*2 Mc 14:18-25
Simon	*1 Mc 14:16-24; 15:15-24

BEHAVIOR revealing
Jonathan	*1 Mc 12:1-23

DESIRE
Abner	2 Sam 3:1-16

SECURITY in
Maccabeus	*1 Mc 8:1-32

DESIRE for
Tobiah	Neh 6:17-19

in **COVENANT**
Abner	2 Sam 3:1-16

in the **ENVIRONMENT**
AUTHORITY in
Abner	2 Sam 2:8-32
David	2 Sam 8:1-18; 20:1-26
Demetrius	*1 Mc 11:1-19; 38-53
Ehud	Judg 3:15-23
Simon	*1 Mc 14:25-49

BEHAVIOR revealing
Alexander	*1 Mc 10:51-58
Jonathan	*1 Mc 11:20-37
Menelaus	*2 Mc 4:23-29

COMMITMENT to
Asa	2 Chr 14:1-16:14

CONFRONTATION with
Israelites	Judg 5:12-18
Jehoshaphat	1 Kgs 22:1-40; 2 Chr 17:1-20:37

FREEDOM from
Benjaminites	Judg 21:16-25
Israelites	Judg 17:1-6

dis**HONESTY** in
Alcimus	*2 Mc 14:3-17
Gibeon	Josh 9:3-15
Herod	Acts 12:1-25

KNOWLEDGE of
Romans	*1 Mc 8:1-32

as **MOTIVATION**
Jonathan	*1 Mc 10:45-50

PROMISE of
Jonathan	*1 Mc 10:1-14; 15-44

RATIONALIZATION of
Pilate	Mt 27:11-26

FALSE BELIEF involving
JUDGMENT on
Pilate	Mk 15:6-15; Lk 23:18-25

FREEDOM from
Edomites	2 Kgs 8:16-24

in **ENVIRONMENT**
Benjaminites	Judg 21:16-25
Israelites	Judg 17:1-6

dis**HONESTY** in
in **ENVIRONMENT**
Alcimus	*2 Mc 14:3-17
Gibeon	Josh 9:3-15
Herod	Acts 12:1-25

INSTRUCTION on
in **COMMUNITY**
Moses	Deut 16:18-20

in **JUDGMENT**
Paul	Rom 13:1-7

concerning **PUNISHMENT**
Ahasuerus	Esth 1:10-22

in **ENVIRONMENT**
  Levites   Lev 25:29-34
  INSTRUCTION on
    Moses   Deut 23:15-25:19
  REVELATION on
    Moses   Lev 25:25-28;
                         29-34;
                         35-38;
                         39-55;
                         Lev 27:1-34

of **MESSIANIC FIGURE**
  SALVATION through
    Jesus   2 Cor 8:7-15

in **MISSION**
  through **STEWARDSHIP**
    Believers   Rom 15:25-33

MISSION to
  TRUTH as
    Jesus   Lk 4:16-30

as **MOTIVATION**
  Jacob   Gen 42:1-6;
                         43:1-15

in **NEW AGE**
  INSTRUCTION on
    James   Jas 2:1-13
    Jesus   Lk 6:20-23

PROPHECY of
  as **PUNISHMENT**
    Isaiah   Is 3:16-4:1
    Judahites   Jer 17:1-4

PROVIDENCE over
  Moses   Ex 23:10-13;
                       Lev 19:1-37
  by **DEITY**
    David   Ps 9:17-20;
                       35:9-10
    Eliphaz   Job 5:8-17
    God   Ps 68:4-14;
                       113:5-9;
                       146:5-7b
    Hannah   1 Sam 2:1-10
  INSTRUCTION on
    Moses   Lev 23:15-22;
                     Deut 14:22-29
  PROPHECY of
    Isaiah   Is 29:17-24

as **PUNISHMENT**
  INSTRUCTION on
    Solomon   Prov 6:6-11
  PROPHECY of
    Isaiah   Is 3:16-4:1
    Judahites   Jer 17:1-4
  REVELATION on
    Israelites   Hos 2:9-13

as **QUALITY OF LIFE**
  INSTRUCTION on
    James   Jas 1:9-11
    Preacher   Eccl 4:13-16
    Solomon   Prov 24:23-34;
                     28:1-28

RESPECT for
  INSTRUCTION on
    James   Jas 2:1-13
    Solomon   Prov 17:1-28

REVELATION on
  as **PUNISHMENT**
    Israelites   Hos 2:9-13
RITE of
    Moses   Lev 14:1-32

SALVATION through
  of **MESSIANIC FIGURE**
    Jesus   2 Cor 8:7-15

SECURITY in
  by **DEITY**
    God   Ps 12:5-6;
                     14:4-6;
                     132:11-18
    Isaiah   Is 25:1-5
  PROPHECY of
    Isaiah   Is 14:28-32

SIGNS of
  PROPHECY of
    Joseph   Gen 41:1-57

STEWARDSHIP concerning
    David   Ps 41:1-3
    Paul   Gal 1:18-2:10
  INSTRUCTION on
    Jesus   Lk 14:12-14
    Moses   Deut 15:1-11
  in **MISSION**
    Believers   Rom 15:25-33

TRUTH concerning
  in **MISSION**
    Jesus   Lk 4:16-30

VIRTUE in
  INSTRUCTION on
    Solomon   Prov 19:1-29

PRAISE

of **AUTHORITY**
    Bodyguard   *1 Esd 4:1-12
    Israelites   Ex 15:1-18
of **DEITY**
    Crowds   Mt 9:1-8;
                     Mk 2:1-12;
                     Lk 5:17-26
    Darius   Dan 6:25-27
    David   Ps 8:1-2;
                     9;
                     68:28-35
    Elihu   Job 36:26-33
    Israelites   Mal 1:2-5
    Mankind   Ps 22:27-31
    Psalmist   Ps 46:8-11;
                     48:1-3;
                     92:5-11;
                     99:1-3;
                     106:1-5

of **DEITY** (cont'd)

Queen of Sheba	2 Chr 9:1-31
Sirach	*Sir 42:15-43:33
Zedekiah	Jer 32:16-25

INSTRUCTION on

David	Ps 29:1-2
Psalmist	Ps 99:4-5; 150:2

REVELATION of

Isaiah	Is 6:1-13
Jeremiah	Jer 9:23-24

in **WORSHIP**

David	Ps 24:7-10; 138:4-6
Psalmist	Ps 150:2

BEHAVIOR revealing

Maiden	Song 1:12-14; 16-17; 2:3-7; 8-17; 5:10-16
Young Man	Song 1:9-11; 15; 2:2; 4:1-15; 6:4-10; 7:1-9

in **ENVIRONMENT**

Achior	*Jdt 6:14-20
Bodyguard	*1 Esd 3:18-24
Holofernes	*Jdt 11:1-23
Zerubbabel	*1 Esd 4:13-34

of **FOLLOWER**s

Blind	Lk 18:35-43
Crowd	Jn 12:12-19
Jesus	1 Pet 4:12-19

PROPHECY of

Crowd	Lk 7:11-17
Isaiah	Is 24:13-16a

SCRIPTURES on

Jesus	Mt 21:12-17

in **WORSHIP**

Angels	Lk 2:1-20
Lepers	Lk 17:11-19

through **BELIEF**
  in **DEITY**

Followers	Ps 106:6-12

INSTRUCTION on

Peter	1 Pet 1:3-9

in **MISSION**

Believers	Eph 1:3-14

of **BROTHERHOOD**
  INSTRUCTION on

Paul	Eph 5:15-20

by **COMMUNITY**

Psalmist	Ps 87:1-3

INSTRUCTION on

David	Ps 34:1-3

PROPHECY of

Isaiah	Is 60:1-22

COMPULSION of
  INSTRUCTION on

Jesus	Lk 19:39-40

of **MESSIANIC FIGURE**

Holy Spirit	1 Cor 12:1-3

during **CONFRONTATION**

Solomon	Song 3:6-11

CONVERSION revealed in
  of **DEITY**

Mankind	Rev 11:1-14

COVENANT of
  ELECTION to

Ezra	Neh 9:7-8

of the **CREATION**

Azariah	*Azar 1:28-68
David	Ps 8:1-2; 19:1-4b; 65:9-13; 124:6-8
Ethan	Ps 89:5-18
Ezra	Neh 9:6
Psalmist	Ps 98:7-9; 104:24-26
Sirach	*Sir 42:15-43:33

INSTRUCTION on

Psalmist	Ps 148:1-6; 7-14; 150:6

REVELATION on

Isaiah	Is 55:1-13

in **WORSHIP**

John	Rev 5:1-14
Psalmist	Ps 136:4-9; 150:6

of **DEITY**

Paul	Gal 1:1-5

through **BELIEF**

Followers	Ps 106:6-12

for **COMMUNITY**

Psalmist	Ps 87:1-3

CONVERSION revealed in

Mankind	Rev 11:1-14

ETERNAL

David	Ps 86:11-13; 145:21
God	Ps 111:10
Levites	Neh 9:5b
Psalmist	Ps 102:12-22; 106:47-48; 115:12-18

FIDELITY of

David	Ps 57:7-11; 145:1-3
Ethan	Ps 89:1-4
Psalmist	Ps 71:22-24

HONESTY of

Jesus	Jn 7:15-24

MOTIVATION for

David	Ps 40:1-3

PRAYER of

Azariah	*Azar 1:1-10
Daniel	Dan 2:20-23
David	Ps 18:25-30; 30:11-12; 34:1-3; 36:5-9; 57:4-6; 70:1-5; 86:8-10
Ethan	Ps 89:5-18
Ezra	*2 Esd 8:4-36
God	Ps 76:10-12

PRAYER of (cont'd)

Habakkuk	Hab 3:3-15
Hezekiah	Is 37:8-20
Isaiah	Is 51:1-16
Israelites	*Bar 3:1-8
Jews	*2 Mc 1:10-17
John	Rev 1:4-20
Jude	Jude 1:24-25
Maccabeus	*2 Mc 10:24-38
Mary	Lk 1:39-56
Paul	1 Tim 1:12-17
Peter	2 Pet 3:18b
Psalmist	Ps 112:1; 113:5-9; 115:1-2
Sirach	*Sir 39:12-16; 28-35; 51:1-12
Zedekiah	Jer 32:16-25

in **PRESENCE**

Asaph	Ps 76:1-3
Psalmist	Ps 84:3-4

PROMISE of

Asaph	Ps 79:5-13
David	Ps 69:29-36; 109:21-31
Manasseh	*Mana 1:11-15

for **PROVIDENCE**

Asaph	Ps 76:4-6
Daniel	Dan 2:20-23
David	2 Sam 22:1-51; Ps 18:46-50; 29:3-9; 30:1-5; 35:9-10; 40:4-5; 139:13-18
Isaiah	Is 26:7-19
Jesus	Jn 9:1-41; 1 Pet 4:7-11
Psalmist	Ps 66:5-7; 13-20; 84:10-12; 98:1-3; 148:7-14

for **RECONCILIATION**

Jesus	Heb 13:1-25

revealing **RESPECT**

Amos	Amos 4:13; 9:5-6
David	2 Sam 22:1-51; Ps 18:1-3
Eleazar	*2 Mc 6:18-31
Jesus	Phil 2:5-11
Nebuchadnezzar	Dan 4:1-3; 34-35; 36-37
Psalmist	Ps 113:2-4

through **RITE**

Asaph	Ps 75:9-10
David	Ps 9:1-4; 13:5-6; 18:46-50; 26:6b-7; 27:4-6; 30:1-5; 59:9-10; 63:1-8; 65:1-4; 144:9-11; *Sir 47:1-11

through **RITE** (cont'd)

God	Rev 4:1-11
Jeremiah	Jer 20:7-18
Psalmist	Ps 66:8-12; 87:7; 147:1-6

for **SALVATION**

David	Ps 9:13-14; 40:13-17
God	Rev 19:1-5
Psalmist	Ps 67:1-7

for **SECURITY**

David	Ps 59:16-17
Eliphaz	Job 5:8-17

through **STEWARDSHIP**

Psalmist	Ps 116:12-19

through **TRUTH**

Disciples	Lk 24:50-51

through **VIRTUE** in

Psalmist	Ps 71:1-21; 111:2-4

in **WORSHIP**

Hilkaiah	*Susa 1:60-64

of **DEITY'S**

AUTHORITY

Crowds	Mt 9:1-8; Mk 2:1-12; Lk 5:17-26
Darius	Dan 6:25-27
David	Ps 8:1-2; 9; 68:28-35
Elihu	Job 36:26-33
Israelites	Mal 1:2-5
Mankind	Ps 22:27-31
Psalmist	Ps 46:8-11; 48:1-3; 92:5-11; 99:1-3; 106:1-5
Queen of Sheba	2 Chr 9:1-31
Sirach	*Sir 42:15-43:33
Zedekiah	Jer 32:16-25

CREATION

Azariah	*Azar 1:28-68
David	Ps 8:1-2; 19:1-4b; 65:9-13; 124:6-8
Ethan	Ps 89:5-18
Ezra	Neh 9:6
Psalmist	Ps 98:7-9; 104:24-26
Sirach	*Sir 42:15-43:33

for **ELECTION**

Israelites	Is 42:18-43:7

JUDGMENT

Psalmist	Ps 97:6-9
Solomon	*Wis 17:1-21

KNOWLEDGE

Isaiah	Is 28:23-29
Mankind	Ps 48:9-14
Shepherds	Lk 2:1-20

LAW

David	Ps 19:7-10; 56:10-13
Ezra	Neh 9:12-15; *2 Esd 9:26-37
Psalmist	Ps 119:9-16; 89-96;

LAW (cont'd)
Psalmist — 129-136; 161-168; 169-176

of ELECTION
in COVENANT
Ezra — Neh 9:7-8
by DEITY
Israelites — Is 42:18-43:7
to MISSION
Believers — Eph 1:3-14
PROPHECY of
Jesus — Jn 13:31-35

in ENVIRONMENT
of AUTHORITY
Bodyguard — *1 Esd 4:1-12
BEHAVIOR revealing
Achior — *Jdt 6:14-20
Bodyguard — *1 Esd 3:18-24
Holofernes — *Jdt 11:1-23
Zerubbabel — *1 Esd 4:13-34
revealing RESPECT
Jonathan — *1 Mc 10:59-66; 67-89; 11:38-53
Judith — *Jdt 13:11-20; 15:8-13
Maccabeus — *1 Mc 3:1-9; 5:63-64
Romans — *1 Mc 8:1-32
Simon — *1 Mc 14:25-49
Zerubbabel — *1 Esd 4:42-57
for TRUTH
Zerubbabel — *1 Esd 4:35-41

ETERNAL
Psalmist — Ps 45:16-17
of DEITY
David — Ps 86:11-13; 145:21
God — Ps 111:10
Levites — Neh 9:5b
Psalmist — Ps 102:12-22; 106:47-48; 115:12-18
by FOLLOWERs
Jesus — Heb 13:1-25
in WORSHIP
God — Rev 4:1-11

of FIDELITY
Caleb — *Sir 46:1-10
of DEITY
David — Ps 57:7-11; 145:1-3
Ethan — Ps 89:1-4
Psalmist — Ps 71:22-24
of FOLLOWERs
Timothy — 1 Thes 3:1-10
in WORSHIP
David — Ps 22:22-26
Psalmist — Ps 146:1-2

by FOLLOWERs
BEHAVIOR revealing
Blind — Lk 18:35-43
Crowd — Jn 12:12-19
Jesus — 1 Pet 4:12-19

of FIDELITY
Timothy — 1 Thes 3:1-10
through PRAYER
Paul — 2 Thes 1:11-12
as QUALITY OF LIFE
Demetrius — 3 Jn 1:12
John — 3 Jn 1:3-8
RECONCILIATION through
Titus — 2 Cor 7:13b-16
in RITE
King — Ps 45:1
for STEWARDSHIP
Paul — 2 Cor 8:1-6

GIFT of
TRADITION of
Sirach — *Sir 44:1-15

HONESTY of
of DEITY
Jesus — Jn 7:15-24

INSTRUCTION on
Psalmist — Ps 113:1
of AUTHORITY
David — Ps 29:1-2
Psalmist — Ps 99:4-5; 150:2
through BELIEF
Peter — 1 Pet 1:3-9
of BROTHERHOOD
Paul — Eph 5:15-20
by COMMUNITY
David — Ps 34:1-3
through COMPULSION
Jesus — Lk 19:39-40
of CREATION
Psalmist — Ps 148:1-6; 7-14; 150:6
of JUDGMENT
Solomon — Prov 27:1-27
of KNOWLEDGE
Baruch — *Bar 3:24-37
Jesus — Lk 4:14-15
Preacher — Eccl 9:1-16; 17-10:20
Sirach — *Sir 1:11-20; 4:11-19; 6:18-37; 10:26-11:1; 14:20-27; 15:1-10; 20:24-31; 24:1-34; 37:7-26; 39:1-11
Solomon — *Wis 6:12-25; 7:7-14; 15-8:1; 2-21
of NEW AGE
Paul — Rom 14:1-23
on PRAYER
Jeremiah — Jer 13:15-17
Jesus — Lk 11:1-4
Paul — 1 Cor 14:13-25; Phil 4:1-9
Psalmist — Ps 117:1-2; 150:1;

of **PROVIDENCE** (cont'd)
   INSTRUCTION on
      Psalmist   Ps 107:23-32;
                    147:12-20
   MEDITATION on
      Isaiah   Is 25:1-5
   in **WORSHIP**
      David   1 Chr 15:1-16:43

for **QUALITY OF LIFE**
   of **FOLLOWER**
      Demetrius   3 Jn 1:12
      John   3 Jn 1:3-8

of **RECONCILIATION**
   INSTRUCTION on
      Moses   Deut 31:30-32:47

RECONCILIATION through
   of **DEITY**
      Jesus   Heb 13:1-25
   of **FOLLOWER**
      Titus   2 Cor 7:13b-16

revealing **RESPECT**
      Psalmist   Ps 45:16-17
   of **DEITY**
      Amos   Amos 4:13;
                   9:5-6
      David   2 Sam 22:1-51;
                   Ps 18:1-3
      Eleazar   *2 Mc 6:18-31
      Jesus   Phil 2:5-11
      Nebuchadnezzar Dan 4:1-3;
                   34-35;
                   36-37
      Psalmist   Ps 113:2-4
   in **ENVIRONMENT**
      Jonathan   *1 Mc 10:59-66;
                   67-89;
                   11:38-53
      Judith   *Jdt 13:11-20;
                   15:8-13
      Maccabeus   *1 Mc 3:1-9;
                   5:63-64
      Romans   *1 Mc 8:1-32
      Simon   *1 Mc 14:25-49
      Zerubbabel   *1 Esd 4:42-57
   INSTRUCTION on
      Believers   Rev 19:1-5
      David   Ps 22:22-26
      God   Rev 14:6-7
   of **MESSIANIC FIGURE**
      Crowd   Mt 21:1-11;
                   Mk 11:1-10;
                   Lk 19:28-38

   REVELATION on
      Israelites   Zeph 3:14-20
   TRADITION of
      Aaron   *Sir 45:6-22
      Abraham   *Sir 44:19-21
      Adam   *Sir 49:11-16
      David   *Sir 45:25-26;
                   47:1-11
      Elijah   *Sir 48:1-11
      Elisha   *Sir 48:12-14
      Enoch   *Sir 44:16-18;
                   49:11-16
      Ezekiel   *Sir 49:8-10
      Hezekiah   *Sir 48:17-25

TRADITION of (cont'd)
      Jacob   *Sir 44:23
      Jeshua   *Sir 49:11-16
      Joseph   *Sir 49:11-16
      Joshua   *Sir 46:1-10
      Josiah   *Sir 49:1-3
      Judges   *Sir 46:11-12
      Maccabeus   *1 Mc 9:1-22
      Moses   *Sir 45:1-5
      Nehemiah   *Sir 49:11-16
      Noah   *Sir 44:16-18
      Phinehas   *Sir 45:23-24
      Prophets   *Sir 49:8-10
      Samuel   *Sir 46:13-20
      Seth   *Sir 49:11-16
      Shem   *Sir 49:11-16
      Simon   *Sir 50:1-21;
                   *1 Mc 14:4-15
      Sirach   *Sir 44:1-15
      Solomon   *Sir 47:12-22
      Zerubbabel   *Sir 49:11-16
   in **WORSHIP**
      God   Rev 4:1-11;
                   7:9-17;
                   11:15-19;
                   15:1-16:1;
                   19:1-5
      John   Rev 5:1-14
      Nebuchadnezzar Dan 2:46-49
      Paul   Rom 11:33-36
      Psalmist   Ps 96:7-9

REVELATION of
   of **AUTHORITY**
      Isaiah   Is 6:1-13
      Jeremiah   Jer 9:23-24
   of **CREATION**
      Isaiah   Is 55:1-13
   of **PRESENCE**
      Jesus   Jn 12:27-36a
   revealing **RESPECT**
      Israelites   Zeph 3:14-20
   of **SALVATION**
      Isaiah   Is 60:1-22

RITE of
   of **DEITY**
      Asaph   Ps 75:9-10
      David   Ps 9:1-4;
                   13:5-6;
                   18:46-50;
                   26:6b-7;
                   27:4-6;
                   30:1-5;
                   59:9-10;
                   63:1-8;
                   65:1-4;
                   144:9-11;
                   *Sir 47:1-11
      God   Rev 4:1-11
      Jeremiah   Jer 20:7-18
      Psalmist   Ps 66:8-12;
                   87:7;
                   147:1-6
   by **FOLLOWER**
      King   Ps 45:1
   INSTRUCTION on
      David   1 Chr 15:1-16:43;
                   Ps 9:9-12;
                   24:7-10;

INSTRUCTION on (cont'd)

David	68:4-14
Deborah	Judg 5:10-11
God	Is 44:6-8; 21-23
Isaiah	Is 42:5-17
James	Jas 5:13
Jeremiah	Jer 31:7-14
Psalmist	Ps 33:1-3; 47:1-4; 5-9; 66:1-4; 95:1-7c; 96:1-6; 98:4-6; 100:1-3; 105:1-6; 135:1-4; 149:1-4; 150:3-5

of MESSIANIC FIGURE

David	2 Sam 23:1-7
Woman	Mt 26:6-13; Mk 14:3-9

PROPHECY of

Isaiah	Is 12:1-6

TRADITION of

Mordecai	*Esth 10:4-13

in WORSHIP

Believers	Acts 2:42-47
David	2 Sam 6:1-23; 22:1-51; Ps 7:17; 21:8-13; 51:13-17; 61:8; 108:1-5; 138:4-6
Deborah	Judg 5:2-5
Hannah	1 Sam 1:1-28
Hezekiah	2 Chr 30:1-31:21
Israelites	Ezra 3:10-11; *1 Esd 5:59-65
Jehoshaphat	2 Chr 17:1-20:37
Judith	*Jdt 15:8-13; 16:1-17
Lame	Acts 3:1-26
Levites	2 Chr 29:1-36; Neh 12:24-26; 44-13:3
Paul	Acts 16:25-40
Psalmist	Ps 92:1-4; 104:31-35; 111:1; 118:22-27; 146:1-2; 150:3-5
Simon	*Sir 50:1-21
Solomon	2 Chr 5:1-7:10

for SALVATION
by DEITY

David	Ps 9:13-14; 40:13-17
God	Rev 19:1-5
Psalmist	Ps 67:1-7

INSTRUCTION on

David	Ps 69:29-36

by MESSIANIC FIGURE

Anna	Lk 2:21-40

PROPHECY of

Isaiah	Is 26:1-6; 62:1-12

REVELATION on

Isaiah	Is 60:1-22

SCRIPTURES on

Jesus	Mt 21:12-17

for SECURITY
DEITY receives

David	Ps 59:16-17
Eliphaz	Job 5:8-17

SELF-REALIZATION of
in PRAYER

Jesus	Jn 17:1-5

SIGNS of
INSTRUCTION on

God	Rev 19:6-10

of STEWARDSHIP

Psalmist	Ps 116:12-19

of FOLLOWERs

Paul	2 Cor 8:1-6

INSTRUCTION on

Paul	2 Cor 9:12-15

in MISSION

Isaiah	Is 61:1-11

TRADITION of
of FIDELITY

Caleb	*Sir 46:1-10

of GIFT

Sirach	*Sir 44:1-15

revealing RESPECT

Aaron	*Sir 45:6-22
Abraham	*Sir 44:19-21
Adam	*Sir 49:11-16
David	*Sir 45:25-26; 47:1-11
Elijah	*Sir 48:1-11
Elisha	*Sir 48:12-14
Enoch	*Sir 44:16-18; 49:11-16
Ezekiel	*Sir 49:8-10
Hezekiah	*Sir 48:17-25
Jacob	*Sir 44:23
Jeshua	*Sir 49:11-16
Joseph	*Sir 49:11-16
Joshua	*Sir 46:1-10
Josiah	*Sir 49:1-3
Judges	*Sir 46:11-12
Maccabeus	*1 Mc 9:1-22
Moses	*Sir 45:1-5
Nehemiah	*Sir 49:11-16
Noah	*Sir 44:16-18
Phinehas	*Sir 45:23-24
Prophets	*Sir 49:8-10
Samuel	*Sir 46:13-20
Seth	*Sir 49:11-16
Shem	*Sir 49:11-16
Simon	*Sir 50:1-21; *1 Mc 14:4-15
Sirach	*Sir 44:1-15
Solomon	*Sir 47:12-22
Zerubbabel	*Sir 49:11-16

in **RITE**
  Mordecai   *Esth 10:4-13

of **TRUTH**
  Disciples   Lk 24:50-51
  Zerubbabel   *1 Esd 4:35-41
  through **WORSHIP**
  Nebuchadnezzar   Dan 3:28-30

VIRTUE in
  of **DEITY**
    Psalmist   Ps 71:1-21;
                  111:2-4

  INSTRUCTION on
    Psalmist   Ps 99:6-9

of **VIRTUE**
  Sirach   *Sir 26:13-18
  Solomon   Prov 27:1-27
  Wife   Prov 31:10-31
  PROPHECY of
  Isaiah   Is 61:1-11
  in **WORSHIP**
  David   Ps 145:4-7

in **WORSHIP**
  through **PRAYER**
    Azariah   *Azar 1:28-68
    Believers   Acts 4:23-31
    David   2 Sam 7:1-29;
                 1 Chr 17:1-27;
                 28:1-29:30;
                 Ps 29:1-2;
                 31:19-24;
                 35:17-18;
                 22-28;
                 138:1-3
    Ezra   Neh 9:6;
                 *1 Esd 8:25-27;
                 *2 Esd 13:51-58
    Hannah   1 Sam 2:1-10
    Israelites   *Jdt 13:11-20
    Levites   Neh 9:5b
    Manasseh   *Mana 1:1-5
    Paul   Rom 16:25-27;
                 2 Cor 2:14-17;
                 Eph 3:20-21;
                 Phil 4:10-20;
                 1 Tim 6:11-16
    Psalmist   Ps 42:1-5;
                 6-11;
                 43:1-5;
                 119:105-112;
                 135:19-21;
                 146:10;
                 150:1
    Servant   Gen 24:11-27
    Sirach   *Sir 50:22-24
    Solomon   1 Kgs 8:22-53;
                 *Wis 12:12-18;
                 15:1-6
    Tobiah   *Tb 8:1-21
    Tobit   *Tb 13:1-18
    Zerubbabel   *1 Esd 4:58-63
  RITE of
    Believers   Acts 2:42-47
    David   2 Sam 6:1-23;
                 22:1-51;
                 Ps 7:17;
                 21:8-13;

RITE of (cont'd)
  David   51:13-17;
               61:8;
               108:1-5;
               138:4-6
  Deborah   Judg 5:2-5
  Hannah   1 Sam 1:1-28
  Hezekiah   2 Chr 30:1-31:21
  Israelites   Ezra 3:10-11;
               *1 Esd 5:59-65
  Jehoshaphat   2 Chr 17:1-20:37
  Judith   *Jdt 15:8-13;
               16:1-17
  Lame   Acts 3:1-26
  Levites   2 Chr 29:1-36;
               Neh 12:24-26;
               44:13-3
  Paul   Acts 16:25-40
  Psalmist   Ps 92:1-4;
               104:31-35;
               111:1;
               118:22-27;
               146:1-2;
               150:3-5
  Simon   *Sir 50:1-21
  Solomon   2 Chr 5:1-7:10

through **WORSHIP**
  of **AUTHORITY**
    David   Ps 24:7-10;
               138:4-6
    Psalmist   Ps 150:2
  BEHAVIOR revealing
    Angels   Lk 2:1-20
    Lepers   Lk 17:11-19
  CREATION receives
    John   Rev 5:1-14
    Psalmist   Ps 136:4-9;
               150:6
  of **DEITY**
    Hilkaiah   *Susa 1:60-64
  FIDELITY receives
    David   Ps 22:22-26
    Psalmist   Ps 146:1-2
  because of **KNOWLEDGE**
    Crowd   Mt 15:29-31
  LAW receives
    Psalmist   Ps 119:1-8;
               57-64
  for **PROVIDENCE**
    David   1 Chr 15:1-16:43
  revealing **RESPECT**
    God   Rev 4:1-11;
               7:9-17;
               11:15-19;
               15:1-16:1;
               19:1-5
    John   Rev 5:1-14
    Nebuchadnezzar   Dan 2:46-49
    Paul   Rom 11:33-36
    Psalmist   Ps 96:7-9
  of **TRUTH**
    Nebuchadnezzar   Dan 3:28-30
  VIRTUE in
    David   Ps 145:4-7

PRAYER

for **ACCEPTANCE**
    Jesus   Jn 17:6-19;
                           20-26
    Moses   Ex 33:12-23
    Nehemiah   Neh 1:5-11a

ACCEPTANCE of
  by **DEITY**
    Agur   Prov 30:1-14
    Asaph   Ps 74:1-2
    Azariah   *Azar 1:11-22
    Believers   1 Pet 3:8-12
    David   Ps 6:8-10;
                           19:11-14;
                           141:1-2
    Israelites   Hos 5:15-6:3;
                           *Bar 2:11-23
    Judahites   Lam 5:1-22
    Psalmist   Ps 44:23-26;
                           84:8-9

  INSTRUCTION on
    Jesus   Mt 6:9-13;
                           Lk 18:9-14
    Men   1 Pet 3:1-7
    Paul   Rom 15:25-33

concerning **ANGER**
    Asaph   Ps 79:5-13
    Followers   Ps 80:4-7
  MEDITATION on
    Jeremiah   Jer 10:23-25

ANXIETY revealed in
    David   Ps 6:1-5;
                           6-7;
                           22:6-11;
                           25:16-21;
                           31:9-12
    Habakkuk   Hab 1:12-17
    Moses   Ex 17:1-7

BLASPHEMY in
    Priest   *1 Mc 7:36-38

for **BLESSING**
  of **DEITY**
    David   1 Chr 17:1-27;
                           Ps 4:1;
                           29:10-11;
                           72:18-20;
                           103:1-5;
                           122:6-9;
                           144:12-15
    Ezra   Ezra 7:27-28
    Isaac   Gen 27:41-28:5
    Israelites   *Bar 1:5-14
    Jews   *2 Mc 1:1-9
    Job   Job 42:10-17
    John   3 Jn 1:1-2
    Moses   Ps 90:13-17
    Peter   1 Pet 1:3-9
    Psalmist   Ps 44:23-26;
                           67:1-7;
                           115:12-18;
                           126:4-6;
                           128:5-6;
                           132:6-10
    Sirach   *Sir 50:22-24
    Solomon   2 Chr 5:1-7:10;
                           Ps 72:5-7;
                           15-17

  in **ENVIRONMENT**
    Judith   *Jdt 13:11-20
  of **FOLLOWER**s
    Paul   2 Cor 1:1-2;
                           2 Thes 2:16-17

BLESSING in
  INSTRUCTION on
    Jesus   Mt 7:7-11
    Moses   Deut 26:12-15
    Paul   1 Cor 14:13-25
    Psalmist   Ps 134:1-3
  TRADITION of
    Noah   Gen 9:26-27
  in **WORSHIP**
    David   2 Sam 7:1-29;
                           21:1-14;
                         1 Chr 28:1-29:30
                         Ps 20:1-5;
                         103:19-22
    Moses   Num 10:33-36

for **COMPASSION**
  of **DEITY**
    Asaph   Ps 83:1
    Daniel   Dan 2:14-19
    David   Ps 4:1;
                         6:1-5;
                         28:1-5;
                         30:6-10;
                         38:1-2
    Ethan   Ps 89:38-51
    Ezekiel   Ezek 4:12-15
    Isaiah   Is 63:7-64:12
    Israelites   Jer 14:19-22
    Jeremiah   Jer 11:18-12:6;
                           15:10-21
    Job   Job 10:8-12
    Joel   Joel 1:2-20
    Judahites   Lam 5:1-22
    Maccabeus   *2 Mc 8:1-7;
                           10:1-9
    Moses   Ps 90:13-17
    Psalmist   Ps 102:12-22;
                           106:1-5;
                           123:3-4
    Sirach   *Sir 36:1-10;
                         11-17

  MEDITATION on
    Israelites   Jer 14:7-9
    Jeremiah   Lam 3:1-66
  of **MESSIANIC FIGURE**
    Jesus   Heb 5:1-10
  SELF-REALIZATION of
    Israelites   Jer 14:7-9
    Jesus   Mt 26:36-46;
                           Mk 14:32-42

  in **WORSHIP**
    Israelites   *Jdt 6:14-20
    Manasseh   *Mana 1:6-7
    Moses   Deut 3:23-29;
                         9:25-29

for **CONDEMNATION**
    David   Ps 109:6-20;
                           21-31
    Nehemiah   Neh 4:4-5

for **COURAGE**
  in **WORSHIP**
    Believers   Acts 4:23-31

for **COVENANT**	
FULLFILLMENT of	
Asaph	Ps 74:18-23
for **DEATH**	
Jeremiah	Jer 18:18-23
INSTRUCTION on	
Angel	*2 Esd 7:100-115
concerning **DEFEAT**	
Job	Job 7:17-21
concerning **DESPAIR**	
Psalmist	Ps 43:1-5
of **MESSIANIC FIGURE**	
Jesus	Mt 27:45-56
for **DESTRUCTION**	
David	Ps 68:28-35; 69:22-28
Isaiah	Is 26:7-19
Jeremiah	Jer 17:14-18; 18:18-23
with **DIGNITY**	
Believer	1 Cor 11:2-16
for **DISCIPLESHIP**	
David	Ps 25:1-7
Ezra	*2 Esd 8:4-36
INSTRUCTION on	
Author	Heb 13:1-25
Jesus	Mt 9:36-38; Lk 11:1-4
in **MISSION**	
Believers	Lk 10:1-16
through **WORSHIP**	
Abraham	Gen 21:22-34
Isaac	Gen 26:12-31
concerning **ENEMY**	
Asaph	Ps 74:10-11
David	Ps 13:1-4; 25:16-21; 35:4-8; 22-28; 56:1-4; 143:3-4
Esther	*Esth 14:1-19
Judith	*Jdt 9:1-14
Maccabeus	*1 Mc 3:46-60; *2 Mc 11:1-12; 13:9-26; 14:3-17; 15:20-27
Mordecai	*Esth 13:8-18
Priest	*1 Mc 7:36-38
Sirach	*Sir 36:1-10
concerning **EVIL**	
David	Ps 40:12
Sirach	*Sir 22:27-23:6
of **FAITH**	
Isaiah	Is 26:7-19; 33:1-6
Israelites	Hos 5:15-6:3
of **FOLLOWERs**	
Believers	Acts 2:42-47
Paul	1 Thes 3:11-13

INSTRUCTION on	
Holy Spirit	Jude 1:20
James	Jas 1:5-8
Jesus	Mt 21:18-22; Mk 9:14-29; 11:20-26; Lk 18:1-8; Jn 16:25-28
in **WORSHIP**	
Jesus	Lk 22:31-32; Jn 17:6-19; 20-26
Paul	Eph 3:14-19; 6:23-24
for **FAMILY**	
Elijah	1 Kgs 19:1-21
Hannah	1 Sam 1:1-28
Isaac	Gen 25:19-26
Psalmist	Ps 128:5-6
Sirach	*Sir 36:11-17
SCRIPTURES on	
Elijah	Rom 11:1-6
concerning **FEAR**	
David	1 Sam 23:1-13
Jacob	Gen 32:1-23
by **FOLLOWERs**	
for **BLESSING**	
Paul	2 Cor 1:1-2; 2 Thes 2:16-17
for **FAITH**	
Believers	Acts 2:42-47
Paul	1 Thes 3:11-13
for **FRIENDSHIP**	
Paul	1 Thes 3:1-10
FULFILLMENT of	
John	1 Jn 3:19-24
Paul	2 Thes 1:11-12
Servant	Gen 24:11-27
for **GRACE**	
Paul	1 Cor 16:13-24; Gal 1:1-5; Eph 1:1-2; Col 4:15-18; 1 Thes 1:1; 3:11-13; 5:25-28; 2 Thes 1:1-2; 11-12; 3:17-18; 1 Tim 1:1-2; 6:20-21; 2 Tim 1:1-2; 15-18; 4:19-22
of **GRATITUDE**	
Paul	Col 1:3-8; 1 Thes 1:2-10; 2:13-16; 2 Thes 2:13-15; 2 Tim 1:3-7; Philm 1:4-7
for **LOVE**	
Paul	Phil 1:3-11; 1 Thes 3:11-13
for **PATIENCE**	
Paul	Col 1:9-14

for PEACE
  Paul   1 Cor 1:1-3;
                                Gal 1:1-5;
                                Eph 1:1-2;
                                1 Thes 1:1;
                                2 Thes 1:1-2;
                                3:16;
                                1 Tim 1:1-2;
                                2 Tim 1:1-2
  of PRAISE
  Paul   2 Thes 1:11-12
  for SERVICE
  Paul   Col 4:2-4
  for WISDOM
  Paul   Phil 1:3-11;
                                Col 1:9-14
  for WITNESS
  Paul   Philm 1:4-7

for FRIENDSHIP
  of FOLLOWERs
  Paul   1 Thes 3:1-10

concerning FULFILLMENT
  through DEITY
  Believers   Ps 34:15-22;
                                145:13b-20
  Daniel   Dan 2:20-23
  David   2 Sam 22:1-51;
                                Ps 3:3-6;
                                5:1-3;
                                13:1-4;
                                17:1-2;
                                6-7;
                                18:1-3;
                                4-6;
                                20:6-9;
                                22:1-5;
                                25:16-21;
                                28:1-5;
                                6-7;
                                30:1-5;
                                31:1-8;
                                19-24;
                                34:4-10;
                                40:1-3;
                                61:4-5;
                                138:1-3
  Elijah   1 Kgs 17:1-24
  Elisha   2 Kgs 6:8-23
  Ezekiel   Ezek 4:12-15
  God   Ps 99:6-9;
                                Prov 2:1-22
  Hannah   1 Sam 1:1-28
  Hezekiah   2 Chr 30:1-31:21;
                                32:1-33;
                                Is 38:1-22
  Isaac   Gen 25:19-26
  Israelites   Neh 9:26-31;
                                Ps 78:21-31;
                                107:4-9;
                                10-16
  Jabez   1 Chr 4:1-23
  Jehoahaz   2 Kgs 13:1-9
  Job   Job 42:7-9
  Jonah   Jon 2:1-10
  Manasseh   2 Chr 33:1-25
  Manoah   Judg 13:9-14
  Moses   Num 14:11-24
  People   Ps 107:17-22;
                                23-32

through DEITY (cont'd)
  Prophet   1 Kgs 13:1-34
  Psalmist   Ps 10:12-18;
                                66:13-20;
                                102:12-22;
                                116:1-11;
                                118:5-9;
                                15-21
  Sarah   *Tb 3:16-17
  Sirach   *Sir 51:1-12
  Solomon   1 Kgs 8:22-53;
                                *Wis 7:7-14
  Susanna   *Susa 1:42-51
  Tobiah   *Tb 3:16-17

for FULFILLMENT
  of COVENANT
  Asaph   Ps 74:18-23
  by MESSIANIC FIGURE
  Holy Spirit   Jn 14:15-17
  of MISSION
  Jesus   Jn 17:1-5

FULFILLMENT of
  Eli   1 Sam 1:1-28
  Ezra   Ezra 8:21-23;
                                Neh 9:9-11
  John   1 Jn 3:19-24
  Paul   2 Thes 1:11-12
  Samuel   1 Sam 7:2-17
  Servant   Gen 24:11-27
  INSTRUCTION on
  Eliphaz   Job 22:21-30
  James   Jas 1:5-8;
                                5:14-18
  Jesus   Mt 6:9-13;
                                7:7-11;
                                18:18-20;
                                21:18-22;
                                Mk 11:20-26;
                                Lk 11:9-13;
                                18:1-8;
                                Jn 14:1-14;
                                15:1-11;
                                12-17;
                                16:16-24
  John   1 Jn 5:13-21
  PROPHECY of
  Israelites   Is 30:18-26
  Jeremiah   Jer 29:1-23
  REVELATION on
  Daniel   Dan 10:10-21
  David   2 Sam 5:17-25;
                                1 Chr 14:1-17
  Gabriel   Lk 1:5-25
  God   Is 41:1-42:4
  Isaiah   2 Kgs 20:1-11;
                                Is 58:1-14;
                                65:1-25
  Israelites   Zech 10:3-12;
                                13:7-9
  Jeremiah   Jer 11:18-12:6;
                                15:10-21;
                                31:15-22;
                                33:1-9
  Psalmist   Ps 2:7-9
  Solomon   2 Chr 7:11-22

for GOOD
  Psalmist   Ps 125:4-5

in **WORSHIP**	
Ezra	Neh 9:7-8
for **GRACE**	
Jehoahaz	2 Kgs 13:1-9
Moses	Num 11:1-3
Paul	1 Cor 16:13-24;
	Gal 1:1-5;
	Eph 1:1-2;
	Col 4:15-18;
	1 Thes 1:1;
	3:11-13;
	5:25-28;
	2 Thes 1:1-2;
	11-12;
	3:17-18;
	1 Tim 1:1-2;
	6:20-21;
	2 Tim 1:1-2;
	15-18;
	4:19-22;
	Tit 3:12-15
of **DEITY**	
Amos	Amos 7:1-3;
	4-6
Author	Heb 13:1-25
Daniel	Dan 9:4-19
David	Ps 9:13-14;
	25:8-15;
	27:7-12;
	39:7-13;
	40:11;
	41:4-10;
	51:1-2;
	3-12;
	13-17;
	57:1-3
Ezekiel	Ezek 9:1-11
Habakkuk	Hab 3:1;
	2
Isaiah	Is 33:1-6;
	63:7-64:12
Israelites	Neh 9:26-31;
	Jer 14:19-22;
	Hos 5:15-6:3;
	*Bar 2:11-23;
	3:1-8
Jeremiah	Jer 17:14-18
Joel	Joel 1:2-20
John	2 Jn 1:1-3;
	Rev 1:4-20;
	22:6-21
Jonah	Jon 1:1-17;
	2:1-10
Judahites	Lam 5:1-22
Moses	Num 12:11-16
Nineveh	Jon 3:1-10
Paul	1 Cor 1:4-9;
	Gal 6:11-18;
	Col 1:1-2;
	Tit 1:1-4;
	Philm 1:1-3;
	21-25
Peter	1 Pet 1:1-2
Psalmist	Ps 119:57-64;
	73-80;
	129-136;
	123:1-2;
	3-4
concerning **FALSE BELIEF**	
Moses	Ex 32:30-35

INSTRUCTION on	
Bildad	Job 8:1-7
Jeremiah	Jer 10:23-25;
	Lam 2:1-22
Jesus	Mt 6:9-13;
	Mk 11:20-26;
	Lk 11:1-4;
	18:9-14
Joel	Joel 2:12-17
John	1 Jn 5:13-21
Malachi	Mal 1:6-2:9
Paul	1 Thes 5:25-28
Peter	Acts 8:14-25
MEDITATION on	
Israelites	Jer 14:7-9
of **MESSIANIC FIGURE**	
People	Lk 23:33-38
in **MISSION**	
Jude	Jude 1:1-2
Peter	2 Pet 1:1-2
PROPHECY of	
Israelites	Is 30:18-26
REVELATION on	
Israelites	Jer 3:1-5
SELF-REALIZATION of	
Israelites	Jer 14:7-9
in **WORSHIP**	
Believers	Acts 4:23-31
David	2 Sam 12:1-31;
	24:1-25;
	1 Chr 21:1-22:1
Ezra	*1 Esd 8:71-90;
	*2 Esd 8:4-36
Hezekiah	2 Kgs 19:9b-37
Israelites	Num 21:4-9;
	Judg 4:1-3;
	6:1-6;
	7-10
Jehoshaphat	2 Chr 17:1-20:37
Manasseh	2 Chr 33:1-25;
	*Mana 1:11-15
Moses	Ex 34:5b-9;
	Num 14:11-24;
	16:16-24;
	Deut 10:1-11
Paul	2 Cor 13:14;
	Eph 6:23-24;
	Phil 1:1-2;
	4:21-23
of **GRATITUDE**	
Asaph	Ps 75:1
Daniel	Dan 6:10-15
David	1 Chr 17:1-27;
	Ps 7:17;
	9:1-4;
	138:1-3
Ezra	Ezra 7:27-28
Hannah	1 Sam 2:1-10
Isaiah	Is 25:1-5
Jonah	Jon 2:1-10
Paul	Eph 5:15-20;
	Phil 1:3-11;
	Col 1:9-14;
	2 Thes 1:3-4
by **FOLLOWER**	
Paul	Col 1:3-8;
	1 Thes 1:2-10;
	2:13-16;
	2 Thes 2:13-15;
	2 Tim 1:3-7;

by **FOLLOWER** (cont'd)
Paul	Philm 1:4-7

INSTRUCTION on
Jesus	Lk 11:1-4
Paul	2 Cor 1:8-11;
	Phil 4:1-9;
	Col 4:2-4;
	1 Thes 5:12-22;
	1 Tim 2:1-7
Psalmist	Ps 136:1-3

concerning **MEDIATION**
Jesus	Mt 11:25-26

MEDITATION on
Jesus	Lk 10:21-22
Paul	Eph 1:15-2:10

by **MESSIANIC FIGURE**
Jesus	Mt 15:32-39;
	Jn 11:1-57

PROPHECY of
Isaiah	Is 12:1-6

SELF-REALIZATION of
Paul	1 Tim 1:12-17

concerning **GRIEF**
David	Ps 6:6-7
Ezra	*2 Esd 6:35-59
Israelites	Judg 20:19-23;
	24-28;
	*Jdt 4:1-15
Tobit	*Tb 3:1-6

INSTRUCTION on
Angel	*2 Esd 6:29-34

MEDITATION on
Job	Job 16:18-22

in **WORSHIP**
Ezra	Ezra 10:1-6
Israelites	Judg 21:1-7
Moses	Ex 5:22-6:1
Nehemiah	Neh 1:1-4

concerning **GUILT**
Israelites	Jer 14:19-22

MEDITATION on
Israelites	Jer 14:7-9

in **WORSHIP**
Ezra	Ezra 9:6-15

concerning **HATE**
INSTRUCTION on
Solomon	Prov 28:1-28

for **HEALING**
Abraham	Gen 20:1-18
David	Ps 6:1-5;
	41:4-10
Egyptians	Is 19:18-25
Hezekiah	2 Chr 32:1-33;
	Is 38:1-22
Israelites	Hos 5:15-6:3
Jeremiah	Jer 17:14-18
Moses	Num 12:11-16
Tobiah	*Tb 3:16-17

INSTRUCTION on
James	Jas 5:14-18
Sirach	*Sir 38:1-15

by **MESSIANIC FIGURE**
Jesus	Mt 21:12-17

for **HOPE**
Hezekiah	Is 36:1-37:4c

for **HOPE** (cont'd)
Israelites	Jer 14:19-22
Jonah	Jon 2:1-10

MEDITATION on
Paul	Eph 1:15-2:10

HUMILITY in
Azariah	*Azar 1:11-22
Israelites	Jer 3:21-4:4
Psalmist	Ps 131:1-3
Sirach	*Sir 22:27-23:6

INSTRUCTION on
Jesus	Mt 6:5-8

SELF-REALIZATION of
Jesus	Mt 26:36-46;
	Mk 14:32-42;
	Lk 22:39-46

IGNORANCE concerning
Job	Job 33:13-14

by **FOLLOWER**s
Believers	Rom 8:26-27

INDIFFERENCE to
by **DEITY**
Job	Job 24:1-12;
	30:16-23
Psalmist	Ps 88:13-14

of **INNOCENCE**
Jeremiah	Jer 15:10-21

INSTRUCTION on
for **DEATH**
Angel	*2 Esd 7:100-11

for **DISCIPLESHIP**
Author	Heb 13:1-25
Jesus	Mt 9:36-38;
	Lk 11:1-4

for **FAITH**
Holy Spirit	Jude 1:20
James	Jas 1:5-8
Jesus	Mt 21:18-22;
	Mk 9:14-29;
	11:20-26;
	Lk 18:1-8;
	Jn 16:25-28

concerning **FULFILLMENT**
Eliphaz	Job 22:21-30
James	Jas 1:5-8;
	5:14-18
Jesus	Mt 6:9-13;
	7:7-11;
	18:18-20;
	21:18-22;
	Mk 11:20-26;
	Lk 11:9-13;
	18:1-8;
	Jn 14:1-14;
	15:1-11;
	12-17;
	16:16-24
John	1 Jn 5:13-21

for **GRACE**
Bildad	Job 8:1-7
Jeremiah	Jer 10:23-25;
	Lam 2:1-22
Jesus	Mt 6:9-13;
	Mk 11:20-26;
	Lk 11:1-4;

in **WORSHIP**
Jesus   Mk 1:35-39;
    Lk 6:12-16

for **SACRIFICE**
Jesus   Jn 12:27-36a

of **SADNESS**
Paul   Acts 20:17-38

SCRIPTURES on
for **FAMILY**
Elijah   Rom 11:1-6
for **SACREDNESS**
Jesus   Mt 21:12-17;
    Mk 11:15-19;
    Lk 19:45-46

through **SELF-REALIZATION**
for **COMPASSION**
Israelites   Jer 14:7-9
Jesus   Mt 26:36-46;
    Mk 14:32-42

for **GRACE**
Israelites   Jer 14:7-9
of **GRATITUDE**
Paul   1 Tim 1:12-17
with **HUMILITY**
Jesus   Mt 26:36-46;
    Mk 14:32-42;
    Lk 22:39-46

for **ONENESS**
Jesus   Jn 17:1-5
of **PRAISE**
Jesus   Jn 17:1-5

for **SERVICE**
by **FOLLOWER**
Paul   Col 4:2-4
INSTRUCTION on
Paul   Col 4:2-4
in **MISSION**
Apostles   Acts 6:1-7

for **SPIRIT**
Paul   2 Tim 4:19-22
INSTRUCTION on
Paul   1 Cor 14:13-25

concerning **SUFFERING**
David   Ps 6:1-5;
    6-7;
    22:6-11;
    25:16-21;
    31:9-12;
    38:11-16;
    142:1-3b
Jeremiah   Jer 18:18-23
Job   Job 10:1-7
INSTRUCTION on
James   Jas 5:13
REVELATION on
Israelites   Jer 2:20-29

for **TEMPERANCE**
INSTRUCTION on
Jesus   Lk 11:1-4

concerning **TEMPTATION**
INSTRUCTION on
Jesus   Mt 26:36-46;

INSTRUCTION on (cont'd)
Jesus   Mk 14:32-42;
    Lk 22:39-46

revealing **TRADITION**
of **BLESSING**
Noah   Gen 9:26-27

for **VICTORY**
David   Ps 20:1-5
Hezekiah   2 Chr 32:1-33
Jacob   Gen 32:1-23
Jesus   Jn 17:6-19
by **DEITY**
David   Ps 3:7-8;
    7:1-2;
    6-8;
    9:17-20;
    12:7-8;
    22:12-21;
    35:1-3;
    17-18;
    22-28;
    38:17-22;
    40:13-17;
    55:1-3a;
    59:1-5;
    60:1-5;
    9-12;
    68:1-3;
    69:1-3;
    4-12;
    108:6-13;
    140:6-8;
    143:7-12
Hezekiah   Is 37:8-20
Isaiah   Is 63:7-64:12
Israelites   Ps 25:22
Job   Job 17:1-5
Psalmist   Ps 43:1-5;
    71:1-21;
    80:1-3;
    14-19;
    118:22-27;
    120:1-2
over **ENVIRONMENT**
Nehemiah   Neh 6:5-9
INSTRUCTION on
Jesus   Mt 6:9-13;
    Lk 21:34-36
Paul   2 Thes 3:1-2

for **WILL**
of **DEITY**
Jesus   Mt 26:36-46;
    Mk 14:32-42;
    Lk 22:39-46

INSTRUCTION on
Jesus   Lk 11:5-8
Paul   Col 4:2-4

for **WISDOM**
David   2 Sam 5:17-25;
    1 Chr 14:1-17;
    Ps 39:4-6
Ezra   *2 Esd 3:1-36
Manoah   Judg 13:8
Moses   Ps 90:1-12
Paul   Eph 3:14-19
Psalmist   Ps 119:17-24;
    169-176

for **WISDOM** (cont'd)
Solomon   1 Kgs 3:1-15;
                       2 Chr 1:1-17;
                       *Wis 7:7-14;
                       9:1-18
Zerubbabel   *1 Esd 4:58-63
by **FOLLOWER**
Paul   Phil 1:3-11;
                       Col 1:9-14
INSTRUCTION on
Isaiah   Is 8:19-22
James   Jas 1:5-8
Paul   1 Cor 14:13-25
Solomon   Prov 2:1-22
MEDITATION through
Jesus   Lk 10:21-22
Paul   Eph 1:5-2:10

for **WITNESS**
Paul   Rom 1:8-15
by **FOLLOWER**
Paul   Philm 1:4-7
INSTRUCTION on
Paul   Rom 15:25-33;
                       Eph 6:19-20;
                       2 Thes 3:1-2
PROPHECY of
Isaiah   Is 37:21

in **WORSHIP**
for **BLESSING**
David   2 Sam 7:1-29;
                       21:1-14;
                       1 Chr 28:1-29:30;
                       Ps 20:1-5;
                       103:19-22
Moses   Num 10:33-36
for **COMPASSION**
Israelites   *Jdt 6:14-20
Manasseh   *Mana 1:6-7
Moses   Deut 3:23-29;
                       9:25-29
for **COURAGE**
Believers   Acts 4:23-31
for **DISCIPLESHIP**
Abraham   Gen 21:22-34
Isaac   Gen 26:12-31
concerning **ENEMY**
Esther   *Esth 14:1-19
Judith   *Jdt 9:1-14
Mordecai   *Esth 13:8-18
for **FAITH**
Jesus   Lk 22:31-32;
                       Jn 17:6-19;
                       20-26
Paul   Eph 3:14-19;
                       6:23-24
for **GOOD**
Ezra   Neh 9:7-8
for **GRACE**
Believers   Acts 4:23-31
David   2 Sam 12:1-31;
                       24:1-25;
                       1 Chr 21:1-22:1
Ezra   *1 Esd 8:71-90;
                       *2 Esd 8:4-36
Hezekiah   2 Kgs 19:9b-37
Israelites   Num 21:4-9;
                       Judg 4:1-3;

for **GRACE** (cont'd)
                       6:1-6;
                       7-10
Jehoshaphat   2 Chr 17:1-20:3
Manasseh   2 Chr 33:1-25;
                       *Mana 1:11-15
Moses   Ex 34:5b-9;
                       Num 14:11-24;
                       16:16-24;
                       Deut 10:1-11
Paul   2 Cor 13:14;
                       Eph 6:23-24;
                       Phil 1:1-2;
                       4:21-23
concerning **GRIEF**
Ezra   Ezra 10:1-6
Israelites   Judg 21:1-7
Moses   Ex 5:22-6:1
Nehemiah   Neh 1:1-4
concerning **GUILT**
Ezra   Ezra 9:6-15
for **JOY**
Jesus   Jn 17:6-19
Psalmist   Ps 84:1-2
Tobit   *Tb 11:7-19
PRAISE as
Azariah   *Azar 1:28-68
Believers   Acts 4:23-31
David   2 Sam 7:1-29;
                       1 Chr 17:1-27;
                       28:1-29:30;
                       Ps 29:1-2;
                       31:19-24;
                       35:17-18;
                       22-28;
                       138:1-3
Ezra   Neh 9:6;
                       *1 Esd 8:25-27;
                       *2 Esd 13:51-58
Hannah   1 Sam 2:1-10
Israelites   *Jdt 13:11-20
Levites   Neh 9:5b
Manasseh   *Mana 1:1-5
Paul   Rom 16:25-27;
                       2 Cor 2:14-17;
                       Eph 3:20-21;
                       Phil 4:10-20;
                       1 Tim 6:11-16
Psalmist   Ps 42:1-5;
                       6-11;
                       43:1-5;
                       119:105-112;
                       135:19-21;
                       146:10;
                       150:1
Servant   Gen 24:11-27
Sirach   *Sir 50:22-24
Solomon   1 Kgs 8:22-53
                       *Wis 12:12-18;
                       15:1-6
Tobiah   *Tb 8:1-21
Tobit   *Tb 13:1-18
Zerubbabel   *1 Esd 4:58-63
for **PURIFICATION**
Hezekiah   2 Chr 30:1-31:21
for **REPENTANCE**
Ezra   Ezra 9:6-15
Nehemiah   Neh 1:5-11a

SACREDNESS of
    Jesus   Mk 1:35-39;
        Lk 6:12-16

through **WORSHIP**
    for **VICTORY**
      David   Ps 20:1-5
      Hezekiah   2 Chr 32:1-33
      Jacob   Gen 32:1-23
      Jesus   Jn 17:6-19

PRESENCE

ACCEPTANCE of the
    of **DEITY**
      Abraham   Gen 18:1-8
      Holy Spirit   Lk 3:21-22
      Isaiah   Is 8:8b-10
      Israelites   Lev 9:1-24
      Lot   Gen 19:1-3
    REVELATION of
      Moses   Ex 33:12-23

ALIENATION from
    of **DEITY**
      Israelites   Amos 7:7-9;
        8:1-3;
        11-14
      Samson   Judg 16:16-22
      Saul   1 Sam 16:14-23

ANGER in
    of **DEITY**
      God   Is 30:27-33
      Saul   1 Sam 11:1-15

BLESSING through
    of **DEITY**
      God   Is 43:14-44:5
      Israelites   Ezek 34:25-31;
        36:8-15
      Zechariah   Lk 1:57-80

COURAGE in
    of **DEITY**
      Believers   Acts 4:23-31
      Ezra   Ezra 7:27-28
      Israelites   Hag 1:15b-2:9
      Joshua   Josh 1:1-9
    for **FOLLOWERs**
      Holy Spirit   Acts 4:23-31
    REVELATION on
      Paul   Acts 18:1-17

of **DEITY**
    Ezekiel   Ezek 40:1-5
    Jesus   1 Pet 3:18-22
    ACCEPTANCE of
      Abraham   Gen 18:1-8
      Holy Spirit   Lk 3:21-22
      Isaiah   Is 8:8b-10
      Israelites   Lev 9:1-24
      Lot   Gen 19:1-3
    ALIENATION from
      Israelites   Amos 7:7-9;
        8:1-3;
        11-14
      Samson   Judg 16:16-22
      Saul   1 Sam 16:14-23

ANGER in
    God   Is 30:27-33
    Saul   1 Sam 11:1-15
BLESSING through
    God   Is 43:14-44:5
    Israelites   Ezek 34:25-31;
        36:8-15
    Zechariah   Lk 1:57-80
COURAGE in
    Believers   Acts 4:23-31
    Ezra   Ezra 7:27-28
    Israelites   Hag 1:15b-2:9
    Joshua   Josh 1:1-9
DESTRUCTION in
    David   Ps 21:8-13
DIGNITY in
    David   1 Chr 11:1-12:40
    Solomon   2 Chr 1:1-17
DISCIPLESHIP in
    Believers   Ps 46:4-7;
        2 Cor 6:14-7:1;
        1 Thes 4:13-18
    David   1 Chr 15:1-16:43;
        Ps 23:1-4
    Holy Spirit   Acts 2:1-13;
        10:1-11:18;
        2 Tim 1:8-14
    Jesus   Jn 14:18-24
    Psalmist   Ps 105:1-6
FAITH in
    Believers   Ps 145:13b-20;
        Eph 3:14-19
    David   Ps 27:13-14;
        139:13-18
    Israelites   Is 42:18-43:7;
        Zeph 3:14-20
    Jeremiah   Jer 42:7-22
in **FAMILY**
    Mankind   Rev 21:1-8
FEAR of
    Egyptians   Is 19:1-15
    Elihu   Job 37:1-13;
        14-22
    Isaiah   Is 63:7-64:12
    Israelites   Deut 5:22-33;
        6:1-3
    Jacob   Gen 28:10-22
    Job   Job 23:15-17
    Saul   1 Sam 18:6-30
    Tobit   *Tb 12:1-22
FULFILLMENT through
    David   Ps 17:15;
        51:3-12
    God   Num 14:11-24;
        Is 6:1-13
    Jesus   Col 2:6-15
    Nehemiah   Neh 1:11b-2:8
GOOD in
    Mankind   Ps 15:1-5b
GRIEF in
    David   Ps 30:6-10
HOPE in
    Believers   Tit 2:11-15
HUMILITY in
    God   Is 57:14-21
IGNORANCE of
    Elihu   Job 37:23-24
    Job   Job 23:8-14;
        35:13-16
    Psalmist   Ps 10:1-2

WISDOM in (cont'd)	
Isaiah	Is 11:1-9
Moses	Ex 4:10-16
Stephen	Acts 6:8-8:3
WITNESS to	
Azariah	2 Chr 14:1-16:14
Balaam	Num 23:27-24:13
Barnabas	Acts 11:22-24
David	2 Sam 23:1-7
Holy Spirit	1 Jn 4:13-18
Isaiah	Is 61:1-11
Israelites	Num 14:10;
	16:16-24
Moses	Num 20:2-13
Peter	Acts 4:1-22
Prophets	Num 11:24b-30
Zechariah	2 Chr 24:1-27
DESTRUCTION in	
of **DEITY**	
David	Ps 21:8-13
REVELATION on	
God	Ezek 38:17-23
DIGNITY in	
of **DEITY**	
David	1 Chr 11:1-12:40
Solomon	2 Chr 1:1-17
DISCIPLESHIP in	
of **DEITY**	
Believers	Ps 46:4-7;
	2 Cor 6:14-7:1;
	1 Thes 4:13-18
David	1 Chr 15:1-16:43;
	Ps 23:1-4
Holy Spirit	Acts 2:1-13;
	10:1-11:18;
	2 Tim 1:8-14
Jesus	Jn 14:18-24
Psalmist	Ps 105:1-6
INSTRUCTION on	
Holy Spirit	Eph 5:15-20
Jesus	Mt 18:18-20
of **MESSIANIC FIGURE**	
Jesus	Jn 14:1-14
Paul	2 Cor 13:5-10
of **ENEMY**	
PROPHECY of	
Isaiah	Is 29:1-8
in **ENVIRONMENT**	
of **MIRACLE**	
God	Ps 77:11-20
of **SACREDNESS**	
God	Ps 68:15-18
Raphael	*Tb 5:1-21
of **WILL**	
God	Job 36:26-33
FAITH in	
of **DEITY**	
Believers	Ps 145:13b-20;
	Eph 3:14-19
David	Ps 27:13-14;
	139:13-18
Israelites	Is 42:18-43:7;
	Zeph 3:14-20
Jeremiah	Jer 42:7-22

INSTRUCTION on	
Jesus	Mt 28:16-20
REVELATION on	
Jesus	Mt 28:16-20
in **WORSHIP**	
Israel	Ex 4:27-31
FALSE BELIEF in	
REJECTION through	
Sennacherib	Is 36:1-37:4c
in **FAMILY**	
by **DEITY**	
Mankind	Rev 21:1-8
REVELATION on	
Moses	Ex 6:2-9
FEAR of	
of **DEITY**	
Egyptians	Is 19:1-15
Elihu	Job 37:1-13;
	14-22
Isaiah	Is 63:7-64:12
Israelites	Deut 5:22-33;
	6:1-3
Jacob	Gen 28:10-22
Job	Job 23:15-17
Saul	1 Sam 18:6-30
Tobit	*Tb 12:1-22
FEAR of Divine	
INSTRUCTION on	
Psalmist	Ps 114:7-8
PROPHECY of	
Isaiah	Is 2:18-22
REVELATION on	
Israelites	Ex 20:18-20;
	Deut 4:1-14
Moses	Ex 3:1-6
Zechariah	Lk 1:5-25
FULFILLMENT through	
of **DEITY**	
David	Ps 17:15;
	51:3-12
God	Num 14:11-24;
	Is 6:1-13
Jesus	Col 2:6-15
Nehemiah	Neh 1:11b-2:8
of **MESSIANIC FIGURE**	
Holy Spirit	Jn 14:15-17
Jesus	Mt 11:2-6;
	Lk 7:18-23
in **MISSION**	
Jesus	Lk 4:16-30
PROPHECY of	
Saul	1 Sam 9:1-10:16
REVELATION on	
Jesus	Lk 24:13-35
in **WORSHIP**	
David	Ps 132:1-5
GOOD in	
of **DEITY**	
Mankind	Ps 15:1-5b
GRATITUDE for	
INSTRUCTION on	
Psalmist	Ps 95:1-7c
GRIEF in	

GRIEF in (cont'd)
  of **DEITY**
    David   Ps 30:6-10

in **HEALING**
  by **MESSIANIC FIGURE**
    Holy Spirit   Acts 10:1-11:18

HOPE in
  of **DEITY**
    Believers   Tit 2:11-15
  REVELATION on
    God   Is 41:1-42:4

HUMILITY in
  of **DEITY**
    God   Is 57:14-21

IGNORANCE of
  of **DEITY**
    Elihu   Job 37:23-24
    Job   Job 23:8-14; 35:13-16
    Psalmist   Ps 10:1-2

INSTRUCTION on
  in **DISCIPLESHIP**
    Holy Spirit   Eph 5:15-20
    Jesus   Mt 18:18-20
  concerning **PATIENCE**
    David   Ps 27:13-14
  of **SPIRIT**
    Paul   Rom 8:5-13; 1 Cor 3:10-17; 6:12-20

JOY in
  of **DEITY**
    Believers   Acts 13:14-52
    David   Ps 16:9-11
    Elihu   Job 33:26-28
    God   Ps 48:1-3
    Israelites   Zech 2:6-13
    King   Ps 21:1-7

JOY through
  by **MESSIANIC FIGURE**
    Holy Spirit   Lk 10:21-22

JUSTICE in
  of **DEITY**
    David   2 Sam 23:1-7
    God   Is 41:1-42:4
    Micah   Mic 3:1-12

LEADERSHIP through
  of **DEITY**
    David   2 Sam 5:6-16
    Ezra   Ezra 7:27-28
    Gideon   Judg 6:33-35
    Israelites   Lev 25:39-55; Num 23:13-26
    Jesus   Lk 4:1-13; Col 1:18-20
    Joshua   Josh 6:22-27
    Othniel   Judg 3:7-11
  PROPHECY of
    David   2 Sam 23:1-7
  TRADITION of
    Solomon   *Wis 18:1-4

LIFE in
  of **DEITY**
    God   Is 66:1-16
    Hagar   Gen 16:11-16
    Israelites   Jer 30:10-11
    Manoah   Judg 13:15-23
    Simeon   Lk 2:21-40
    Zechariah   Zech 4:1-6a; 10b-14

LOVE in
  of **DEITY**
    Believers   1 Jn 4:7-12
    Corinthians   2 Cor 13:11-13
    David   Ps 26:8-12
  of **MESSIANIC FIGURE**
  in **DISCIPLESHIP**
    Jesus   Jn 14:1-14
    Paul   2 Cor 13:5-10
  FULFILLMENT through
    Holy Spirit   Jn 14:15-17
    Jesus   Mt 11:2-6; Lk 7:18-23
  in **HEALING**
    Holy Spirit   Acts 10:1-11; 18
  JOY in
    Holy Spirit   Lk 10:21-22

MIRACLE through
  of **DEITY**
    David   Ps 29:3-9; 144:5-8
    God   2 Sam 22:1-51; Ps 18:7-15; Nah 1:1-9
    Jesus   Jn 14:18-24
  in **ENVIRONMENT**
    God   Ps 77:11-20
  REVELATION on
    God   Ezek 38:17-23
    Joshua   Josh 3:1-13

in **MISSION**
  FULFILLMENT through
    Jesus   Lk 4:16-30

OBEDIENCE in
  by **FOLLOWERs**
    God   1 Jn 3:19-24
  PROPHECY of
    Jeroboam   1 Kgs 11:26-40
  REVELATION on
    Solomon   1 Kgs 6:1-38

OBEDIENCE through
  of **DEITY**
    Amos   Amos 5:14-15
    Israelites   Ezek 36:22-32
    Jehoshaphat   2 Chr 17:1-20:37
    Jesus   Jn 8:21-59

ONENESS in
  of **DEITY**
    Jesus   Jn 14:1-14; 18-24; 16:29-33

ORDER in
  of **DEITY**
    God   Ps 68:4-14

PATIENCE in
  of **DEITY**
    Jesus   Heb 10:1-18
  INSTRUCTION on
    David   Ps 27:13-14

PRAISE in
  of **DEITY**
    Asaph   Ps 76:1-3
    God   Ps 140:12-13
    Psalmist   Ps 84:3-4
  REVELATION on
    Jesus   Jn 12:27-36a

PROPHECY of
    David   2 Sam 23:1-7
    Isaiah   Is 2:18-22
    Jeroboam   1 Kgs 11:26-40
    Saul   1 Sam 9:1-10:16
  of **ENEMY**
    Isaiah   Is 29:1-8
  of **SACREDNESS**
    Jeremiah   *2 Mc 2:1-8
  of **SADNESS**
    Israelites   Amos 5:16-17
  of **SUFFERING**
    Israelites   Amos 5:16-17
  of **WITNESS**
    Isaiah   Is 60:1-22
    Micah   Mic 1:2-4

PURIFICATION in
  of **DEITY**
    Jesus   Jn 1:19-51

REVELATION on
  in **FAMILY**
    Moses   Ex 6:2-9
  concerning **FULFILLMENT**
    Jesus   Lk 24:13-35
  concerning **MIRACLE**
    God   Ezek 38:17-23
    Joshua   Josh 3:1-13
  concerning **PRAISE**
    Jesus   Jn 12:27-36a
  as **SACREDNESS**
    Gideon   Judg 6:11-32
    Israelites   1 Kgs 8:1-13;
                     Ezek 48:30-35
    Jacob   Gen 28:10-22;
                     32:1-23
    Moses   Ex 3:1-6;
                     19:9-15;
                     16:25;
                     34:1-5a;
                     5b-9;
                     Acts 6:8-8:3
    Raphael   *Tb 12:1-22
    Solomon   1 Kgs 9:1-9;
                     2 Chr 7:11-22
  concerning **SERVICE**
    Priests   Ezek 44:15-31
  of **SPIRIT**
    Holy Spirit   Joel 2:28-29
  of **WILL**
    Moses   Ex 3:11-22
  provides **WISDOM**
    Disciples   Jn 14:18-24
  WITNESS to
    Ezekiel   Ezek 1:1-3
    Heliodorus   *2 Mc 3:1-40

REWARDs of
  of **DEITY**
    David   Ps 23:5-6;
                     41:11-12
    God   Ps 24:3-6
  SACREDNESS in
    Moses   Ex 29:42b-46;
                     Lev 16:1-5
  of **DEITY**
    David   1 Sam 16:1-13;
                     Ps 27:4-6;
                     63:1-8
    God   Num 5:1-4;
                     16:36-50

SACREDNESS of
  of **DEITY**
    God   Ps 11:4-7;
                     Ezek 44:4-5;
                     Hab 2:18-20;
                     Hag 1:1-11
    Israelites   Ex 40:34-38;
                     Deut 5:22-33;
                     Ezek 43:6-12
    Joshua   Josh 5:13-15
    Moses   Ex 24:1-18;
                     34:29-35;
                     2 Cor 3:7-11
    Psalmist   Ps 84:1-2
    Solomon   2 Chr 5:1-7:10
  in **ENVIRONMENT**
    God   Ps 68:15-18
    Raphael   *Tb 5:1-21
  PROPHECY of
    Jeremiah   *2 Mc 2:1-8
  REVELATION concerning
    Gideon   Judg 6:11-32
    Israelites   1 Kgs 8:1-13;
                     Ezek 48:30-35
    Jacob   Gen 28:10-22;
                     32:1-23
    Moses   Ex 3:1-6;
                     19:9-15;
                     16-25;
                     34:1-5a;
                     5b-9;
                     Acts 6:8-8:3
    Raphael   *Tb 12:1-22
    Solomon   1 Kgs 9:1-9;
                     2 Chr 7:11-22
  in **WORSHIP**
    Moses   Ex 33:7-11
    Psalmist   Ps 132:6-10

SADNESS in
  PROPHECY of
    Israelites   Amos 5:16-17

SERVICE in
  of **DEITY**
    Israelites   Ex 31:1-11
    Jesus   Heb 8:1-5;
                     9:23-28
    Nehemiah   Neh 2:16-18
    Saul   1 Sam 19:18-24
  REVELATION on
    Priests   Ezek 44:15-31

of **SPIRIT**
  of **DEITY**
    Daniel   Dan 4:18

CONFRONTATION with (cont'd)
  INSTRUCTION on
    Preacher　　　　　　Eccl 11:1-8
  REVELATION on
    Gideon　　　　　　　Judg 7:1-8

CONVERSION revealed in
  before DEITY
    Mankind　　　　　　Ps 22:27-31

in the CREATION
  through FALSE BELIEF
    Egyptians　　　　　Ezek 29:9b-16

DESIRE for
  by DEITY
    Mankind　　　　　　Ps 10:3-11
  INSTRUCTION on
    Preacher　　　　　　Eccl 6:1-12

through FALSE BELIEF
  in CREATION
    Egyptians　　　　　Ezek 29:9b-16
  revealing inFIDELITY
    Pharisees　　　　　Lk 11:37-44
  revealing disRESPECT
    Egyptians　　　　　Ezek 32:1-16
  revealing SIN
    Israelites　　　　　Ezek 16:15-34
  revealing unTRUTH
    Paul　　　　　　　1 Tim 6:2c-5

revealing inFIDELITY
  through FALSE BELIEF
    Pharisees　　　　　Lk 11:37-44
  INSTRUCTION on
    Jesus　　　　　　　Mk 9:38-41;
　　　　　　　　　　　Lk 9:49-50

of FOLLOWERs
  BEHAVIOR revealing
    Thessalonians　　　1 Thes 2:17-20

INSTRUCTION on
  in BROTHERHOOD
    Paul　　　　　　　2 Cor 1:12-14;
　　　　　　　　　　　5:11-13;
　　　　　　　　　　　7:2-4
  in COMMITMENT
    Paul　　　　　　　2 Cor 5:11-13
  caused by inFIDELITY
    Jesus　　　　　　　Mk 9:38-41;
　　　　　　　　　　　Lk 9:49-50
  of KNOWLEDGE
    Paul　　　　　　　1 Cor 8:1-3
  as QUALITY OF LIFE
    Preacher　　　　　Eccl 1:2-11;
　　　　　　　　　　　12-2:26;
　　　　　　　　　　　5:8-20;
　　　　　　　　　　　9:1-16;
　　　　　　　　　　　11:9-12:7;
　　　　　　　　　　　8-11
  as SIN
    Elihu　　　　　　　Job 35:9-12
    James　　　　　　　Jas 4:1-10;
　　　　　　　　　　　13-16
    Jesus　　　　　　　Lk 18:9-14
    Moses　　　　　　　Deut 8:11-20
    Sirach　　　　　　*Sir 3:17-31;
　　　　　　　　　　　10:12-25

as SIN (cont'd)
    Solomon　　　　　Prov 11:1-31;
　　　　　　　　　　　21:1-31
  in STEWARDSHIP
    Jesus　　　　　　　Mt 6:2-4
  concerning TRUTH
    David　　　　　　　Ps 4:2-5

JUDGMENT on
  by DEITY
    God　　　　　　　　Is 2:12-17
  INSTRUCTION on
    Preacher　　　　　Eccl 8:10-17
  PROPHECY of
    Isaiah　　　　　　　Is 5:8-24a
    Moabites　　　　　Jer 48:1-47
  of KNOWLEDGE
    Elihu　　　　　　　Job 32:11-14
  INSTRUCTION on
    Paul　　　　　　　1 Cor 8:1-3

MEDITATION on
  as QUALITY OF LIFE
    Preacher　　　　　Eccl 3:16-4:3;
　　　　　　　　　　　4-12;
　　　　　　　　　　　13-16

in MISSION
  as QUALITY OF LIFE
    Paul　　　　　　　2 Cor 11:16-20

PROPHECY of
  as SIN
    Edomites　　　　　Obad 1:1b-4
    Ezekiel　　　　　　Ezek 16:44-52
    Nineveh　　　　　　Zeph 2:15

PUNISHMENT for
  by DEITY
    Assyrians　　　　　Is 10:5-16
    Eliphaz　　　　　　Job 22:21-30
    God　　　　　　　　Is 2:12-17
    Hezekiah　　　　　2 Chr 32:1-33
  in ENVIRONMENT
    Azariah　　　　　　*1 Mc 5:55-62
  INSTRUCTION on
    Jesus　　　　　　　Mk 12:37b-40;
　　　　　　　　　　　Lk 20:45-47
    Sirach　　　　　　*Sir 10:12-25
    Solomon　　　　　Prov 18:1-24
  PROPHECY of
    Ephraimites　　　　Hos 5:8-14
    Isaiah　　　　　　　Is 13:1-22;
　　　　　　　　　　　28:1-13
    Moab　　　　　　　Is 15:1-16:14
    Moabites　　　　　Is 25:10-12
    Tyre　　　　　　　Is 23:1-14
  REVELATION on
    Egyptians　　　　　Ezek 31:10-18
    Habakkuk　　　　　Hab 2:5-6a
    Israelites　　　　　Ezek 7:1-27
    Judahites　　　　　Jer 13:1-11
    Malachi　　　　　　Mal 3:13-4:3
  as QUALITY OF LIFE
    Judah　　　　　　　Gen 38:12-23
    Mankind　　　　　　Gen 11:1-9
    Paul　　　　　　　2 Cor 11:21-29
    Tyre　　　　　　　Ezek 27:1-9a
  INSTRUCTION on
    Preacher　　　　　Eccl 1:2-11;

INSTRUCTION on (cont'd)
Preacher   12-2:26;
5:8-20;
9:1-16;
11:9-12:7;
8-11
MEDITATION on
Preacher   Eccl 3:16-4:3;
4-12;
13-16
in **MISSION**
Paul   2 Cor 11:16-20

revealing disRESPECT
Belshazzar   Dan 5:18-25
through **FALSE BELIEF**
Egyptians   Ezek 32:1-16

REVELATION on
in **CONFRONTATION**
Gideon   Judg 7:1-8
as **SIN**
Ammonites   Zeph 2:8-12
Egyptians   Ezek 31:10-18
Israelites   Jer 3:1-5
King   Ezek 28:11-19
Moabites   Zeph 2:8-12
Tyre   Ezek 28:1-10

in **RITE**
of **WORSHIP**
Hypocrites   Mt 6:16-18

SIGNS of
INSTRUCTION on
Paul   2 Tim 3:1-9

as **SIN**
Edomites   Obad 1:10-14
Ephraimites   Hos 12:7-9
Israelites   Amos 6:12-14
INSTRUCTION on
Elihu   Job 35:9-12
James   Jas 4:1-10;
13-16
Jesus   Lk 18:9-14
Moses   Deut 8:11-20
Sirach   *Sir 3:17-31;
10:12-25
Solomon   Prov 11:1-31;
21:1-31
PROPHECY of
Edomites   Obad 1:1b-4
Ezekiel   Ezek 16:44-52
Nineveh   Zeph 2:15
REVELATION on
Ammonites   Zeph 2:8-12
Egyptians   Ezek 31:10-18
Israelites   Jer 3:1-5
King   Ezek 28:11-19
Moabites   Zeph 2:8-12
Tyre   Ezek 28:1-10
in **WORSHIP**
Uzziah   2 Chr 26:1-28:27

revealing **SIN**
through **FALSE BELIEF**
Israelites   Ezek 16:15-34

in **STEWARDSHIP**

INSTRUCTION on
Jesus   Mt 6:2-4

concerning **TRUTH**
INSTRUCTION on
David   Ps 4:2-5
in **WORSHIP**
Pharisees   Mt 23:5-12

revealing unTRUTH
through **FALSE BELIEF**
Paul   1 Tim 6:2c-5

in **WORSHIP**
RITE of
Hypocrites   Mt 6:16-18
as **SIN**
Uzziah   2 Chr 26:1-28:27
concerning **TRUTH**
Pharisees   Mt 23:5-12

PROMISE

ACCEPTANCE of
of **DEITY**
Israelites   Jer 31:35-37
REVELATION of
Ezekiel   Ezek 43:18-27
Jesus   Mt 11:7-15
Mary   Lk 1:26-38

of **ALIENATION**
Israelites   *1 Esd 8:91-96;
9:1-15

INSTRUCTION on
Ezra   *1 Esd 9:1-15
PROPHECY of
Micah   Mic 4:9-5:6

of **BLESSING**
Moses   Ex 23:20-33
in **COVENANT**
Abraham   Gen 13:14-18;
17:1-8;
*Sir 44:19-21;
Gal 3:15-18
God   Gen 12:1-8;
Acts 3:1-26
Israelites   Deut 7:6-16
Moses   Deut 29:1-15
of **DEITY**
Abraham   Gen 22:1-19
Caleb   Num 14:11-24;
Deut 1:19-46
Isaac   Gen 26:1-11
Jacob   Gen 28:10-22
INSTRUCTION on
Darius   Ezra 6:1-12
Jesus   Mt 5:3-12;
11:28-30;
Lk 6:20-23;
Jn 14:18-24
Moses   Deut 15:1-11
PROPHECY of
Isaiah   Is 60:1-22
Israelites   Hag 1:15a;
2:15-19
REVELATION on

REVELATION on (cont'd)
Gabriel | Lk 1:26-38
Isaiah | Is 65:1-25
Israelites | Is 49:1-26
Jacob | Gen 35:1-15
Joshua | Zech 3:1-10
Moses | Ex 20:24-26

concerning **CAPTIVITY**
INSTRUCTION on
Baruch | *Bar 4:17-20
PROPHECY of
Abraham | Gen 15:1-21

of **CHAOS**
PROPHECY of
Jesus | Mk 13:1-2

in **COVENANT**
of **BLESSING**
Abraham | Gen 13:14-18;
 | 17:1-8;
 | *Sir 44:19-21;
 | Gal 3:15-18
God | Gen 12:1-8;
 | Acts 3:1-26
Israelites | Deut 7:6-16
Moses | Deut 29:1-15
with **FAMILY**
Abraham | Gen 13:14-18;
 | 15:1-21;
 | 17:1-8
Azariah | *Azar 1:11-22
David | 1 Sam 23:14-24:22
God | Gen 17:15-22
Jacob | *Sir 44:23
of **FRIENDSHIP**
Jonathan | 1 Sam 17:1-18:5;
 | 23:14-24:22
FULFILLMENT of
Abraham | Gal 3:15-18;
 | Heb 6:13-20
God | Ex 6:2-9;
 | Lev 26:1-46;
 | Deut 4:15-31;
 | Ps 89:19-37
Israelites | Deut 7:6-16
Jeremiah | Jer 33:14-26
Jesus | Gal 3:26-29
Solomon | 1 Kgs 8:22-53
of **GRACE**
Zechariah | Lk 1:57-80
HOPE through
Paul | Gal 4:21-26;
 | 27-31
of **JUSTICE**
Israelites | Hos 2:16-20
for **LEADERSHIP**
Jehoiada | 2 Kgs 11:4-20;
 | 2 Chr 21:1-23:21
of **MARRIAGE**
Abraham | Gen 24:1-10
of **MIRACLE**
Moses | Ex 34:10-11
for **ORDER**
God | Gen 9:8-19
for **PATIENCE**
Abraham | Heb 6:13-20
of **PEACE**
Isaiah | Is 54:1-17

REJECTION of
God | Ps 89:38-51
for **VICTORY**
Moses | Ex 34:10-11

of **COVETOUSNESS**
by **DEITY**
Abraham | Gen 26:1-11

of **DEATH**
Pharaoh | Ex 10:28-29
PROPHECY of
Moses | Ex 11:1-10

of **DEFEAT**
PROPHECY of
Arabia | Is 21:13-17
Kedar | Is 21:13-17
REVELATION of
Daniel | Dan 11:1-4

by **DEITY**
of **MIRACLE**
God | Is 29:13-14

of **DEITY**
ACCEPTANCE of
Israelites | Jer 31:35-37
of **BLESSING**
Abraham | Gen 22:1-19
Caleb | Num 14:11-24;
 | Deut 1:19-46
Isaac | Gen 26:1-11
Jacob | Gen 28:10-22
concerning **COVETOUSNESS**
Abraham | Gen 26:1-11
for **DESTRUCTION**
God | Is 5:8-24a;
 | Jer 4:27-29
concerning **DISOBEDIENCE**
Zedekiah | *1 Esd 1:46-58
DOUBT in
Israelites | Ps 106:24-27
Sarah | Gen 16:1-6;
 | 18:9-15
concerning the **ENEMY**
Uzziah | *Jdt 7:23-32
to **FAMILY**
Abraham | Gen 17:15-22;
 | 22:1-19
Believers | Rom 9:6-13
David | 2 Sam 7:1-29;
 | 1 Chr 17:1-27;
 | Ps 132:11-18
Isaac | Gen 26:12-31
Ishmael | Gen 21:15-21
Sarah | Gen 17:15-22
through **FEAR**
Psalmist | Ps 119:33-40
FULFILLMENT of
Abraham | Gen 21:1-7
Believers | Eccl 5:1-7;
 | Heb 11:1-40
Egyptians | Ezek 30:10-12
Ezekiel | Ezek 28:1-10
Ezra | Neh 9:7-8
God | Ps 12:5-6;
 | Ps 18:25-30;
 | Is 14:24-27;
 | 45:14-25;
 | 46:1-13;

FULFILLMENT of (cont'd)

God	Jer 4:27-29;
	2 Pet 3:8-10
Hagar	Gen 16:11-16
Israelites	Josh 21:8-45;
	Neh 9:22-25;
	Ps 105:37-42;
	Ezek 37:1-14
Jesus	Rom 15:1-13
Joshua	Josh 23:1-16
Moses	Ex 4:27-31;
	23:20-33;
	Deut 23:15-25:19
Solomon	1 Kgs 8:54-61

for GOOD

Solomon	*Wis 15:1-6

through GRACE

Antiochus	*2 Mc 9:5-29
Manasseh	*Mana 1:6-7
Peter	2 Pet 1:3-4

GRATITUDE for

David	Ps 142:5-7

HUMILITY in

God	Ps 37:1-11

LEADERSHIP through

David	1 Kgs 2:1-4

for LIFE

Psalmist	Ps 119:49-56;
	113-120;
	153-160

LOVE of

Psalmist	Ps 119:137-144

concerning MARRIAGE

Sarah	*Tb 3:16-17

concerning ORDER

God	Gen 8:13-22

for PEACE

Solomon	1 Chr 22:2-19

PRAISE of

Asaph	Ps 79:5-13
David	Ps 69:29-36;
	109:21-31
Manasseh	*Mana 1:11-15

of REWARDs

Abraham	Gen 18:16-22
Israelites	Deut 26:16-19

SACREDNESS in

David	Ps 132:1-5

of VICTORY

David	Ps 110:1-4
God	Ps 50:7-15
Peter	2 Pet 1:3-4

of WILL

Solomon	1 Kgs 3:1-15

WITNESS to

Holy Spirit	Jn 15:26-27

to DEITY

concerning ALIENATION

Israelites	*1 Esd 8:91-96;

concerning OBEDIENCE

David	Ps 56:10-13
Israelites	Ex 19:1-8
Psalmist	Ps 119:145-152

of REJECTION

Abraham	Gen 14:21-24

of SACRIFICE

Jonah	Jon 2:1-10

of DESTRUCTION

Angels	Gen 19:12-29
Gideon	Judg 8:4-9

by DEITY

God	Is 5:8-24a;
	Jer 4:27-29

PROPHECY of

Israelites	Hos 4:4-15
Jesus	Lk 21:5-6

REVELATION on

Daniel	Dan 11:5-20
Ezekiel	Ezek 12:17-20

of WORSHIP

Nicanor	*2 Mc 14:31-33

of DISCIPLESHIP

INSTRUCTION on

Holy Spirit	Acts 2:37-41

concerning DISOBEDIENCE

to DEITY

Zedekiah	*1 Esd 1:46-58

DOUBT in

of DEITY

Israelites	Ps 106:24-27
Sarah	Gen 16:1-6;
	18:9-15

REVELATION on

Abraham	Gen 15:1-21;
	17:15-22
Zechariah	Lk 1:5-25

concerning ENEMY

by DEITY

Uzziah	*Jdt 7:23-32

of FAITH

by FOLLOWERs

Holy Spirit	Gal 3:10-14
Peter	Mt 26:31-35;
	Mk 14:27-31;
	Lk 22:33-34

INSTRUCTION on

Author	Heb 6:9-12

in MISSION

Apostles	Mt 10:16-22

to FAMILY

Psalmist	Ps 45:16-17

through COVENANT

Abraham	Gen 13:14-18;
	15:1-21;
	17:1-8
Azariah	*Azar 1:11-22
David	1 Sam 23:14-24:2
God	Gen 17:15-22
Jacob	*Sir 44:23

by DEITY

Abraham	Gen 17:15-22;
	22:1-19
Believers	Rom 9:6-13
David	2 Sam 7:1-29;
	1 Chr 17:1-27;
	Ps 132:11-18
Isaac	Gen 26:12-31
Ishmael	Gen 21:15-21
Sarah	Gen 17:15-22

of FOLLOWERs

Jesus	Gal 3:26-29

of **GOOD**
  to **DEITY**
    Solomon　　　*Wis 15:1-6

of **GRACE**
  in **COVENANT**
    Zechariah　　　Lk 1:57-80

through **GRACE**
  of **DEITY**
    Antiochus　　　*2 Mc 9:5-29
    Manasseh　　　*Mana 1:6-7
    Peter　　　2 Pet 1:3-4
  INSTRUCTION on
    Jesus　　　Mt 5:3-12;
    　　　Lk 6:20-23
  REVELATION on
    Isaiah　　　Is 57:14-21;
    　　　65:1-25

GRATITUDE for
  of **DEITY**
    David　　　Ps 142:5-7

of **HEALING**
  PROPHECY of
    Isaiah　　　Mt 8:14-17

HOPE in
  INSTRUCTION on
    John the Baptist　　　Mt 3:1-12;
    　　　Mk 1:2-8
  PROPHECY of
    Isaiah　　　Is 10:24-27c

HOPE through
  in **COVENANT**
    Paul　　　Gal 4:21-26;
    　　　27-31

is for **HUMILITY**
  DEITY gives
    God　　　Ps 37:1-11

causing **IDOLATRY**
  INSTRUCTION on
    Jesus　　　Mt 5:33-37

of **INDIFFERENCE**
  INSTRUCTION on
    God　　　Ex 4:18-23
  REVELATION on
    Pharaoh　　　Ex 7:1-7

INSTRUCTION on
  of **ALIENATION**
    Ezra　　　*1 Esd 9:1-15
  of **BLESSING**
    Darius　　　Ezra 6:1-12
    Jesus　　　Mt 5:3-12;
    　　　11:28-30;
    　　　Lk 6:20-23;
    　　　Jn 14:18-24
    Moses　　　Deut 15:1-11
  concerning **CAPTIVITY**
    Baruch　　　*Bar 4:17-20
  of **DISCIPLESHIP**
    Holy Spirit　　　Acts 2:37-41
  of **FAITH**
    Author　　　Heb 6:9-12

to **FAMILY**
  God　　　*2 Esd 2:10-14
  Paul　　　Gal 4:27-31
concerning **FULFILLMENT**
  God　　　Num 30:1-16
  Jesus　　　Mt 5:3-12;
  　　　33-37;
  　　　10:23;
  　　　16:13-20;
  　　　18:18-20;
  　　　Lk 6:20-23
  Paul　　　Acts 13:14-52
  Sirach　　　*Sir 18:19-26
of **GRACE**
  Jesus　　　Mt 5:3-12;
  　　　Lk 6:20-23
of **HOPE**
  John the Baptist　　　Mt 3:1-12;
  　　　Mk 1:2-8
causing **IDOLATRY**
  Jesus　　　Mt 5:33-37
of **INDIFFERENCE**
  God　　　Ex 4:18-23
of **JOY**
  Bildad　　　Job 8:20-22
  God　　　*2 Esd 2:15-32
of **KILLING**
  God　　　Ex 4:18-23
of **LIFE**
  God　　　Gen 6:1-4
  Jesus　　　Mt 10:26-39
of **LOVE**
  Angel　　　*2 Esd 5:31-42
of **OBEDIENCE**
  Author　　　Heb 10:32-39
  Israelites　　　Ex 24:1-18;
  　　　*1 Esd 9:16-36
  People　　　Jer 42:1-6
revealing **PARADOX**
  Jesus　　　Mt 10:26-39
of **PATIENCE**
  Author　　　Heb 10:32-39
of **PEACE**
  Jesus　　　Mt 11:28-30;
  　　　Jn 14:27-31
  Paul　　　Phil 4:1-9
of **SERVICE**
  Moses　　　Num 32:20-33
of **VICTORY**
  Bildad　　　Job 8:20-22
  Moses　　　Deut 7:17-26;
  　　　11:1-25
of **WEALTH**
  Artaxerxes　　　Ezra 7:20-24
  Moses　　　Deut 28:1-14;
  　　　30:1-10
  Nehemiah　　　Neh 5:6-13
of **WISDOM**
  Angel　　　*2 Esd 6:29-34
  Jesus　　　Jn 14:25-26

of **JOY**
  INSTRUCTION on
    Bildad　　　Job 8:20-22
    God　　　*2 Esd 2:15-32
  REVELATION on
    God　　　Is 41:1-42:4
    Isaiah　　　Is 60:1-22
    Jeremiah　　　Jer 31:2-6

of **JUSTICE**
    in **COVENANT**
        Israelites   Hos 2:16-20

of **KILLING**
    INSTRUCTION on
        God   Ex 4:18-23

for **LEADERSHIP**
    of **FOLLOWER**
        Jesus   Mt 16:13-20

of **LEADERSHIP**
    through **COVENANT**
        Jehoiada   2 Kgs 11:4-20;
                           2 Chr 21:1-23:21

    in **ENVIRONMENT**
        David   1 Kgs 1:11-14
    in **MISSION**
        Jesus   Mt 4:18-22;
                           Mk 1:16-20

    REVELATION on
        Solomon   1 Kgs 9:1-9;
                           2 Chr 7:11-22

    SCRIPTURES on
        Prophet   Mt 2:1-12

LEADERSHIP through
    of **DEITY**
        David   1 Kgs 2:1-4

for **LIFE**
    of **FOLLOWER**
        God   Eph 6:1-4

of **LIFE**
    INSTRUCTION on
        God   Gen 6:1-4
        Jesus   Mt 10:26-39

LIFE through
    of **DEITY**
        Psalmist   Ps 119:49-56;
                           113-120;
                           153-160

of **LOVE**
        Maiden   Song 7:10-13
    by **DEITY**
        Psalmist   Ps 119:137-144
    INSTRUCTION on
        Angel   *2 Esd 5:31-42
    MEDITATION on
        Psalmist   Ps 119:145-152

of **MARRIAGE**
    in **COVENANT**
        Abraham   Gen 24:1-10
    by **DEITY**
        Sarah   *Tb 3:16-17
    in **ENVIRONMENT**
        Caleb   Josh 15:13-19;
                           Judg 1:1-21

    TRADITION for
        Jacob   Gen 29:15-30
        Rebekah   Gen 24:28-60

MEDITATION on
    of **LOVE**
        Psalmist   Ps 119:145-152

through **MESSIANIC FIGURE**
    of **FULFILLMENT**
        Jesus   Acts 1:1-5
    for **VICTORY**
        Jesus   Jn 14:27-31
        Zechariah   Zech 9:1-12

of **MIRACLE**
    in **COVENANT**
        Moses   Ex 34:10-11
    by **DEITY**
        God   Is 29:13-14
    REVELATION on
        Gabriel   Lk 1:5-25
        Joshua   Josh 6:1-7

in **MISSION**
    of **FAITH**
        Apostles   Mt 10:16-22
    of **LEADERSHIP**
        Jesus   Mt 4:18-22;
                           Mk 1:16-20

of **OBEDIENCE**
    to **DEITY**
        David   Ps 56:10-13
        Israelites   Ex 19:1-8
        Psalmist   Ps 119:145-152
    INSTRUCTION on
        Author   Heb 10:32-39
        Israelites   Ex 24:1-18;
                           *1 Esd 9:16-36
        People   Jer 42:1-6

of **ORDER**
    in **COVENANT**
        God   Gen 9:8-19
    by **DEITY**
        God   Gen 8:13-22

PARADOX in
    INSTRUCTION on
        Jesus   Mt 10:26-39
    PROPHECY of
        Jesus   Mt 16:21-28;
                           Mk 8:34-9:1;
                           Lk 9:23-27

PATIENCE with
    in **COVENANT**
        Abraham   Heb 6:13-20
    INSTRUCTION on
        Author   Heb 10:32-39

of **PEACE**
    in **COVENANT**
        Isaiah   Is 54:1-17
    by **DEITY**
        Solomon   1 Chr 22:2-19
    INSTRUCTION on
        Jesus   Mt 11:28-30;
                           Jn 14:27-31
        Paul   Phil 4:1-9
    REVELATION on
        Isaiah   Is 57:14-21

concerning **POLITICS**
    in **ENVIRONMENT**
        Jonathan   *1 Mc 10:1-14;
                           15-44

PRAISE of
  of DEITY

Asaph	Ps 79:5-13
David	Ps 69:29-36; 109:21-31
Manasseh	*Mana 1:11-15

PROPHECY of
  of ALIENATION

Micah	Mic 4:9-5:6

  of BLESSING

Isaiah	Is 60:1-22
Israelites	Hag 1:15a; 2:15-19

  of CAPTIVITY

Abraham	Gen 15:1-21

  of CHAOS

Jesus	Mk 13:1-2

  of DEATH

Moses	Ex 11:1-10

  of DEFEAT

Arabia	Is 21:13-17
Kedar	Is 21:13-17

  of DESTRUCTION

Israelites	Hos 4:4-15
Jesus	Lk 21:5-6

  to FAMILY

Angel	Gen 16:7-10
God	Gen 18:9-15

  of FULFILLMENT

Belshazzar	Dan 5:30-31
Holy Spirit	Acts 2:1-13
Isaiah	Is 21:1-10
Tyre	Ezek 26:7-14

  of HEALING

Isaiah	Mt 8:14-17

  concerning SUFFERING

Elijah	1 Kgs 17:1-24
Lamech	Gen 5:29-32

  of VICTORY

Isaiah	Is 10:24-27c

  of WEALTH

Abraham	Gen 15:1-21
Isaiah	Is 60:1-22

REJECTION of
  in COVENANT

God	Ps 89:38-51

  of DEITY

Abraham	Gen 14:21-24

  in ENVIRONMENT

Eupator	*1 Mc 6:55-63
Jonathan	*1 Mc 10:45-50

  INSTRUCTION on

Israel	Ex 6:2-9
Sirach	*Sir 23:7-11

REVELATION on
  of BLESSING

Gabriel	Lk 1:26-38
Isaiah	Is 65:1-25
Israelites	Is 49:1-26
Jacob	Gen 35:1-15
Joshua	Zech 3:1-10
Moses	Ex 20:24-26

  of DEFEAT

Daniel	Dan 11:1-4

  of DESTRUCTION

Daniel	Dan 11:5-20
Ezekiel	Ezek 12:17-20

  to FAMILY

Abraham	Gen 12:1-8; 15:1-21
Hagar	Gen 21:11-14
Jacob	Gen 35:1-15

  of FULFILLMENT

Ammonites	Ezek 21:28-32
Daniel	Dan 11:21-45
Ezekiel	Ezek 12:21-28; 17:22-24; 21:8-17; 34:23-24
God	Jer 32:16-25; 2 Pet 3:11-13
Israelites	Ezek 22:1-16; 36:33-36; 47:13-20
Jeremiah	Jer 33:14-26
Judahites	Ezek 23:22-35; 24:1-14
Samuel	1 Sam 3:1-4:1a
Simeon	Lk 2:21-40

  through GRACE

Isaiah	Is 57:14-21; 65:1-25

  of INDIFFERENCE

Pharaoh	Ex 7:1-7

  of JOY

God	Is 41:1-42:4
Isaiah	Is 60:1-22
Jeremiah	Jer 31:2-6

  of LEADERSHIP

Solomon	1 Kgs 9:1-9; 2 Chr 7:11-22

  of MIRACLE

Gabriel	Lk 1:5-25
Joshua	Josh 6:1-7

  of PEACE

Isaiah	Is 57:14-21

  of REVENGE

Jeremiah	Jer 15:1-4

  of REWARDs

Nebuchadnezzar	Ezek 29:17-21

  of SACREDNESS

Moses	Ex 33:12-23

  of VICTORY

Joshua	Josh 3:1-13; 6:1-7
Moses	Ex 5:22-6:1

  of VIOLENCE

Ezekiel	Ezek 12:17-20

  of WEALTH

Isaiah	Is 54:1-17
Jeremiah	Jer 31:23-26
Moses	Num 11:14-24a; Deut 1:6-8
Nebuchadnezzar	Ezek 29:17-21

  of WILL

Solomon	2 Chr 1:1-17

  of WISDOM

Daniel	Dan 5:10-17
Solomon	1 Kgs 3:1-15

of REVENGE
  REVELATION on

Jeremiah	Jer 15:1-4

of REWARDs

Belshazzar	Dan 5:7-9; 10-17
Moses	Num 32:20-33

by **DEITY**	
Abraham	Gen 18:16-22
Israelites	Deut 26:16-19
in **ENVIRONMENT**	
Israelites	Josh 2:8-14
of **FOLLOWERs**	
Jesus	Mt 19:27-30; Mk 10:28-31; Lk 18:28-30
REVELATION on	
Nebuchadnezzar	Ezek 29:17-21
of **SACREDNESS**	
to **DEITY**	
David	Ps 132:1-5
REVELATION on	
Moses	Ex 33:12-23
in **WORSHIP**	
Israelites	Neh 10:31
of **SACRIFICE**	
to **DEITY**	
Jonah	Jon 2:1-10
in **WORSHIP**	
Psalmist	Ps 66:13-20

SADNESS in
because of **SELF-REALIZATION**	
Herod	Mt 14:1-12; Mk 6:17-29

SCRIPTURES on
to **FAMILY**	
Abraham	Acts 6:8-8:3; Gal 3:15-18
of **FULFILLMENT**	
Jesus	Lk 22:35-38
Paul	Acts 26:1-32; 1 Cor 2:6-9; Gal 4:27-31
of **LEADERSHIP**	
Prophet	Mt 2:1-12
of **SERVICE**	
Israelites	Num 32:16-19
INSTRUCTION on	
Moses	Num 32:20-33
of **SUFFERING**	
PROPHECY of	
Elijah	1 Kgs 17:1-24
Lamech	Gen 5:29-32

in **TRADITION**
of **MARRIAGE**	
Jacob	Gen 29:15-30
Rebekah	Gen 24:28-60

of **VICTORY**
Moses	Lev 26:1-46
in **COVENANT**	
Moses	Ex 34:10-11
by **DEITY**	
David	Ps 110:1-4
God	Ps 50:7-15
Peter	2 Pet 1:3-4
INSTRUCTION on	
Bildad	Job 8:20-22
Moses	Deut 7:17-26; 11:1-25

by **MESSIANIC FIGURE**	
Jesus	Jn 14:27-31
Zechariah	Zech 9:1-12
PROPHECY of	
Isaiah	Is 10:24-27c
REVELATION on	
Joshua	Josh 3:1-13; 6:1-7
Moses	Ex 5:22-6:1

of **VIOLENCE**
in **ENVIRONMENT**	
Danites	Judg 18:21-26
REVELATION on	
Ezekiel	Ezek 12:17-20

of **WEALTH**
Young Man	Song 1:9-11
INSTRUCTION on	
Artaxerxes	Ezra 7:20-24
Moses	Deut 28:1-14; 30:1-10
Nehemiah	Neh 5:6-13
PROPHECY of	
Abraham	Gen 15:1-21
Isaiah	Is 60:1-22
REVELATION on	
Isaiah	Is 54:1-17
Jeremiah	Jer 31:23-26
Moses	Num 11:14-24a; Deut 1:6-8
Nebuchadnezzar	Ezek 29:17-21
in **WORSHIP**	
Israelites	*1 Esd 5:44-46

of **WILL**
of **DEITY**	
Solomon	1 Kgs 3:1-15
REVELATION on	
Solomon	2 Chr 1:1-17

of **WISDOM**
INSTRUCTION on	
Angel	*2 Esd 6:29-34
Jesus	Jn 14:25-26
REVELATION on	
Daniel	Dan 5:10-17
Solomon	1 Kgs 3:1-15

WITNESS to
of **DEITY**	
Holy Spirit	Jn 15:26-27

in **WORSHIP**
SACREDNESS as	
Israelites	Neh 10:31
SACRIFICE as	
Psalmist	Ps 66:13-20
WEALTH as	
Israelites	*1 Esd 5:44-46

PROPHECY

ACCEPTANCE of
concerning **CONFRONTATION**	
Hezekiah	Is 39:1-8

of **ACCEPTANCE**
of **JUDGMENT**

revealing **DEATH**
   Jesus   Jn 21:15-23
   Shallum   Jer 22:10-12
   Zedekiah   Jer 34:1-7
revealing **DISOBEDIENCE**
   Jeremiah   Jer 22:20-23
   Zedekiah   *1 Esd 1:46-58
revealing **FULFILLMENT**
   Isaiah   Is 37:36-38;
                Mt 4:12-16;
                12:15-21
   Jeremiah   Mt 2:16-18;
                27:3-10
   Jesus   Mt 8:14-17;
                Lk 18:31-34;
                Jn 12:12-19;
                Acts 3:1-26
   Jonah   2 Kgs 14:23-29
revealing **GRIEF**
   Amos   Amos 5:1-3
   Jeremiah   Jer 14:17-18
revealing **JOY**
   Isaiah   Is 24:13-16a
revealing **JUSTICE**
   Jeremiah   Jer 21:11-12
revealing **MARRIAGE**
   Isaiah   Is 3:16-4:1
   Jeremiah   Jer 16:1-13
revealing **PARADOX**
   Isaiah   Is 11:1-9
revealing **PRAISE**
   Crowd   Lk 7:11-17
   Isaiah   Is 24:13-16a
revealing **PRIDE**
   Jeremiah   Jer 4:30-31
revealing **SADNESS**
   Judahites   Jer 9:10-22
revealing **SPIRIT**
   Saul   1 Sam 19:18-24

of **BELIEF**
 in **BLESSING**
   Elizabeth   Lk 1:39-56
   Jeremiah   Jer 17:5-8
 through **DESTRUCTION**
   Jonah   Jon 3:1-10
   Tobit   *Tb 14:1-15
 through **HOPE**
   Holy Spirit   Jn 7:37-52

of **BLASPHEMY**
 through **inFIDELITY**
   Paul   1 Tim 4:1-5
 as **disRESPECT**
   Ezekiel   Ezek 24:15-24
 as **SIN**
   Isaiah   Is 3:8-12
   Jerusalemites Zeph 3:1-5
   Sennacherib Is 37:22-29

of **BLESSING**
   Jesus   Lk 13:34-35
 in **BELIEF**
   Elizabeth   Lk 1:39-56
   Jeremiah   Jer 17:5-8
 through **ELECTION**
   Gabriel   Lk 1:5-25
   Prophet   Judg 6:7-10
 through **FIDELITY**
   Jeremiah   Jer 7:21-28;
                12:14-17

in **NEW AGE**
   Israelites   Is 27:2-6
   Joel   Joel 3:16b-21
through **PROMISE**
   Isaiah   Is 60:1-22
   Israelites   Hag 1:15a;
                2:15-19
through **PROVIDENCE**
   Balaam   Num 22:41-23:12;
                13-26;
                27-24:13
   Isaiah   Is 52:13-53:12
   Israelites   Deut 30:11-14;
                Is 30:18-26;
                Jer 31:27-28;
                Hos 12:10-14;
                14:4-8
as **QUALITY OF LIFE**
   Jacob   Gen 49:1-28
in **RECONCILIATION**
   Hananiah   Jer 28:1-17
   Israelites   Zeph 3:14-20
   Judahites   Zeph 2:4-7
   Zechariah   Zech 9:1-12
in **SECURITY**
   Isaiah   Is 54:1-17
   Israelites   Zech 9:13-17
of **VIRTUE**
   Isaiah   Is 3:8-12

of **CAPTIVITY**
   Jesus   Mt 20:17-19
 caused by **inFIDELITY**
   Jesus   Mt 26:36-46;
                Mk 14:32-42
   Judahites   Jer 38:14-28
 because of **KNOWLEDGE**
   Jesus   Mk 10:32-34;
                Lk 18:31-34
 PROMISE concerning
   Abraham   Gen 15:1-21
 as **PUNISHMENT**
   Assyrians   Is 31:4-9
   Babylonian   Jer 25:8-14
   Coniah   Jer 22:24-30
   Egyptians   Jer 46:13-26
   Ephraimites Hos 9:1-6
   Isaiah   Is 24:18c-23
   Israelites   Hos 11:5-7
   Jeremiah   Jer 5:18-19;
                20:1-6;
                21:1-10;
                22:20-23;
                34:13-22;
                43:8-13
   Judahites   Jer 13:18-19;
                17:1-4;
                25:8-14
   Moabites   Jer 48:1-47
 as **QUALITY OF LIFE**
   Shallum   Jer 22:10-12

of **CHAOS**
 in **COMMUNITY**
   Isaiah   Is 3:1-7
 in the **NEW AGE**
   Jesus   Mt 24:29-31;
                Mk 13:24-27
 as **PUNISHMENT**
   Isaiah   Is 13:1-22;
                22:1-14;

as **PUNISHMENT** (cont'd)

Isaiah	24:1-12; 34:1-17
Jeremiah	Jer 13:12-14; 23:1-8
Jesus	Lk 19:41-44; 23:27-32

of **COMMITMENT**
  to **SACRIFICE**

Jesus	Mt 16:21-28; Mk 8:34-9:1; Lk 9:23-27

  to **SERVICE**

Zedekiah	Jer 27:12-15

of **COMPASSION**
  for **ETERNITY**

Isaiah	Is 54:1-17

  through **PROVIDENCE**

Isaiah	Is 14:1-23
Jerusalemites	Zech 12:1-13:6

  in **RECONCILIATION**

Israelites	Hos 11:8-9
Judahites	Jer 12:14-17

  in **SALVATION**

Isaiah	Is 40:1-11

of **COMPULSION**
  of **EVIL**

Habakkuk	Hab 2:15-16

  of **SACRIFICE**

Caiaphas	Jn 11:1-57

  to **WITNESS**

God	Amos 3:3-8

of **CONDEMNATION**
  of **COMMUNITY**

Joshua	Josh 6:22-27; 7:6-26

  in **CONFRONTATION**

Priests	Mk 10:32-34
Scribes	Mk 10:32-34
Shemaiah	1 Kgs 12:21-24; 2 Chr 10:1-12:16

  through **inFIDELITY**

Isaiah	Is 8:19-22
Jeremiah	Jer 17:5-8

  as **JUDGMENT**

Amos	Amos 3:13-15
Ephraimites	Hos 7:8-12
Ezekiel	Ezek 16:44-52
Habakkuk	Hab 2:9-11; 12-14; 15-16; 17; 18-20
Isaiah	Is 30:1-7; 27-33; 31:1-3; 33:1-6; 34:1-17
Israelites	Ezek 16:53-63; Hos 5:1-2; 10:1-8; 12:10-14; Amos 4:4-5; 5:7-13; 6:1-7

as **JUDGMENT** (cont'd)

Jeremiah	Jer 4:13-18; 21:13-14
Jerusalemites	Zeph 3:1-5
Jesus	Mt 11:20-24
Micah	Mic 3:1-12
Moabites	Jer 48:1-47
Nineveh	Nah 3:1-4; 5-19
Priests	Mal 1:6-2:9
Prophets	Jer 23:13-15
Shemaiah	Jer 29:24-32
Zephaniah	Zeph 2:4-7

  in **NEW AGE**

Jesus	Lk 17:22-37

  as **PUNISHMENT**

Shebna	Is 22:15-25

  of **RITE**

Haggai	Hag 2:10-14

  of **SIN**

Enoch	Jude 1:14-16
Isaiah	Is 2:6-11; 5:8-24a
Jeremiah	Jer 22:13-19; 23:1-8
Judahites	Jer 25:8-14
Micah	Mic 2:1-10
Nathan	2 Sam 12:1-31
Sennacherib	Is 37:22-29

concerning **CONFRONTATION**
  ACCEPTANCE of

Hezekiah	Is 39:1-8

of **CONFRONTATION**
  resulting in **ALIENATION**

Jerusalemites	Zech 14:1-21

  with **ANGER**

Zephaniah	Zeph 2:1-2

  with **ANXIETY**

Babylonians	Jer 50:1-46
Zechariah	Zech 9:1-12

  with **CAPTIVITY**

Babylonians	Jer 50:1-46
Isaiah	2 Kgs 20:12-21; Is 39:1-8
Jeremiah	Jer 32:26-44
Jerusalemites	Zech 14:1-21
Jesus	Lk 9:43b-45
Judahites	Jer 37:16-21
Smyrna	Rev 2:8-11
Zedekiah	Jer 34:1-7

  with **CONDEMNATION**

Priests	Mk 10:32-34
Scribes	Mk 10:32-34
Shemaiah	1 Kgs 12:21-24; 2 Chr 10:1-12:16

  with **DEATH**

Ethiopians	Zeph 2:8-12
Isaiah	Is 52:13-53:12
Jeroboam	Amos 7:10-17
Tyre	Ezek 26:7-14

  with **DEFEAT**

Ammonites	Jer 49:1-6
Assyrians	Is 31:4-9
Babylonians	Jer 50:1-46; 51:1-64
Edomites	Jer 49:7-22
Egyptian	Is 20:1-6

with **DEFEAT** (cont'd)

Egyptians	Jer 46:2-12; 13-26
Isaiah	Is 9:8-10:4
Israelites	Jer 5:15-17; 6:9-15
Jeremiah	Jer 6:1-8; 8:14-17; 20:1-6; 21:1-10; 32:1-8; 26-44; 43:8-13
Jerusalemites	Zech 14:1-21
Judahites	Jer 37:3-10
Micaiah	1 Kgs 22:1-40; 2 Chr 17:1-20:37
Moabites	Jer 48:1-47
Nineveh	Nah 3:5-19
Philistines	Jer 47:1-7
Samaritans	Amos 3:11-12
Tyre	Ezek 26:7-14
Zedekiah	Jer 34:1-7

with **DESTRUCTION**

Adversaries	Zech 12:1-13:6
Ammonites	Jer 49:1-6
Babylonians	Is 13:1-22; 21:1-10; Jer 50:1-46; 51:1-64
Canaanites	Is 23:1-14
Edomites	Jer 49:7-22
Egyptians	Jer 46:2-12; 13-26
Elamites	Jer 49:34-39
Hazorites	Jer 49:28-33
Isaiah	Is 8:5-8a; 30:8-17
Israelites	Hos 10:9-15; 11:5-7
Jeremiah	Jer 6:22-26; 10:17-22; 21:1-10
Judahites	Jer 25:8-14; 37:3-10
Moabites	Jer 48:1-47
Philistines	Jer 47:1-7
Tyre	Ezek 26:7-14
Zedekiah	Jer 34:1-7

with **DISOBEDIENCE**

Ahab	1 Kgs 22:1-40; 2 Chr 17:1-20:37
Josiah	*1 Esd 1:25-32

with **DOUBT**

Zedekiah	Jer 32:1-8

with **ENEMY**

Isaiah	Is 8:8b-10
Israelites	Nah 2:1-5
Jeremiah	Jer 6:22-26

with **EVIL**

Judahites	Jer 4:5-8

with **FEAR**

Damascenes	Jer 49:23-27
Saul	1 Sam 28:3-25
Zechariah	Zech 9:1-12

FULFILLMENT of

Elisha	2 Kgs 3:1-27
Israelites	Judg 20:29-36
Jeremiah	Jer 39:1-14

FULFILLMENT of (cont'd)

Jesus	Mt 26:47-56; Mk 14:12-16; 43-50; Lk 22:7-13
Joash	2 Kgs 13:22-25
Micaiah	1 Kgs 22:1-40; 2 Chr 17:1-20:37

with **GRIEF**

Jerusalemites	Zech 12:1-13:6

with **HATE**

Jeremiah	Jer 4:30-31

with **KILLING**

Gentiles	Mk 10:32-34
Jesus	Mt 16:21-28; 17:22-23; 20:17-19; 26:1-2; Mk 8:31-33; 9:30-32; Lk 9:18-22; 43b-45; 18:31-34

with **MIRACLE**

Assyrians	Is 31:4-9

with **OPPRESSION**

Gog	Ezek 38:10-13
Isaiah	Is 24:16b-18b

with **POLITICS**

Shemaiah	1 Kgs 12:21-24; 2 Chr 10:1-12:16

with **REVENGE**

Micah	Mic 4:9-5:6

with **SACREDNESS**

Saul	1 Sam 19:18-24

with **VICORY**

Ahithophel	2 Sam 16:15-17:29
Babylonians	Jer 46:13-26
Balaam	Num 24:14-25
Deborah	Judg 4:6-9
Elisha	2 Kgs 3:1-27; 13:14-19
Hezekiah	Is 38:1-22
Isaiah	Is 29:1-8
Israelites	Zech 9:13-17
Jerusalemites	Zech 14:1-21
Joshua	Josh 17:14-18
Samuel	1 Sam 15:1-35

with **VIOLENCE**

Ammonites	Jer 49:1-6
Babylonians	Jer 43:8-13; 50:1-46; 51:1-64
Damascenes	Jer 49:23-27
Edomites	Jer 49:7-22
Egyptians	Jer 46:2-12; 13-26
Ephraimites	Hos 7:13-16
Gog	Ezek 38:10-13
Hazorites	Jer 49:28-33
Israelites	Deut 28:15-68; Hos 10:9-15; 11:5-7; Amos 6:12-14; Nah 2:1-5
Jeremiah	Jer 6:1-8; 21:1-10
Jerusalemites	Zech 12:1-13:6; 14:1-21

with **VIOLENCE** (cont'd)

Joel	Joel 1:2-20
Judahites	Jer 25:8-14;
	37:3-10
Micah	Mic 4:9-5:6
Moabites	Jer 48:1-47
Nineveh	Nah 3:5-19
Philistines	Jer 47:1-7
Samaria	Hos 13:15-16
Samaritans	Amos 3:11-12
Tyre	Ezek 26:7-14

with **WEALTH**

Isaiah	2 Kgs 20:12-21
Jeremiah	Jer 20:1-6

of **CONVERSION**

through **FAITH**

Isaiah	Is 2:1-5;
	17:7-8

from **IDOLATRY**

Israelites	Is 31:4-9

through **REPENTANCE**

Isaiah	Is 10:20-23
Israelites	Ezek 16:53-63;
	Hos 14:4-8
Jeremiah	Jer 12:14-17

of **COURAGE**

in **NEW AGE**

Isaiah	Is 35:1-10

in **SECURITY**

Isaiah	Is 37:4d-7;
	54:1-17
Israelites	Jer 46:27-28
Micah	Mic 4:1-8

concerning **CREATION**

of **LIFE**

Ezekiel	Ezek 37:1-14
Isaiah	Is 7:10-17;
	9:2-7

of **MIRACLE**

Zechariah	Zech 14:1-21

of **SACREDNESS** (sanctuary)

Haggai	Ezra 5:1-2;
	Hag 1:1-11
Jeremiah	Jer 31:38-40
Zechariah	Ezra 5:1-2

of **DEATH**

Ezekiel	Ezek 24:15-24
Hezekiah	Is 38:1-22
Huldah	2 Kgs 22:3-20
Jesus	Jn 12:27-36a
Joseph	Gen 40:1-23

as **PUNISHMENT**

Ahab	1 Kgs 21:17-29
Ahijah	1 Kgs 14:1-18
Amaziah	Amos 7:10-17
Coniah	Jer 22:24-30
Edomites	Obad 1:5-9
Elijah	2 Kgs 1:1-18
Ephraimites	Hos 7:13-16;
	9:10-17
Isaiah	Is 3:16-4:1
Israelites	Ezek 16:35-43;
	Amos 2:13-16;
	5:1-3;
	6:8-11
Jehoiakim	Jer 22:13-19

as **PUNISHMENT** (cont'd)

Jeremiah	Jer 16:1-13;
	20:1-6;
	21:1-10;
	29:1-23;
	42:7-22;
	43:8-13;
	44:20-28
Jezebel	Rev 2:18-29
Judahites	Jer 9:10-22;
	42:7-22;
	44:1-14
Obadiah	Obad 1:17-21
Samaria	Hos 13:15-16
Samuel	1 Sam 28:3-25
Shebna	Is 22:15-25

as **QUALITY OF LIFE**

Isaiah	Is 40:1-11

before **RESURRECTION**

Jesus	Mt 17:22-23;
	20:17-19;
	Mk 9:30-32;
	Lk 18:31-34;
	Jn 2:12-22;
	16:25-28

resulting from **SIN**

Jeremiah	Jer 31:29-30
Isaiah	2 Kgs 20:1-11

of **DEFEAT**

Eliakim	Is 22:15-25

in **CONFRONTATION**

Ammonites	Jer 49:1-6
Assyrians	Is 31:4-9
Babylonians	Jer 50:1-46;
	51:1-64
Edomites	Jer 49:7-22
Egyptian	Is 20:1-6;
	Jer 46:2-12;
	46:13-26
Isaiah	Is 9:8-10:4
Israelites	Jer 5:15-17;
	6:9-15
Jeremiah	Jer 6:1-8;
	8:14-17;
	20:1-6;
	21:1-10;
	32:1-8;
	26-44;
	43:8-13
Jerusalemites	Zech 14:1-21
Judahites	Jer 37:3-10
Micaiah	1 Kgs 22:1-40;
	2 Chr 17:1-20:37
Moabites	Jer 48:1-47
Nineveh	Nah 3:5-19
Philistines	Jer 47:1-7
Samaritans	Amos 3:11-12
Tyre	Ezek 26:7-14
Zedekiah	Jer 34:1-7

as **PUNISHMENT**

Edomites	Obad 1:1b-4
Isaiah	Is 5:24b-30;
	30:8-17
Israelites	Amos 2:13-16
Micah	Mic 1:10-16
Samuel	1 Sam 28:3-25
Sennacherib	Is 37:22-29
Zechariah	Zech 11:1-3

concerning **DESIRE**
　for **DEATH**
　　Jeremiah　　　　Jer 7:29-8:3
　for **DESTRUCTION**
　　Israelites　　　　Hos 10:1-8
　for **KILLING**
　　Israelites　　　　Jer 18:18-23
　for **OBEDIENCE**
　　Isaiah　　　　　Is 2:1-5
　for **ORDER**
　　Believers　　　　1 Cor 14:34-40
　for **PEACE**
　　Isaiah　　　　　Is 28:1-13
　for **VICTORY**
　　Zedekiah　　　　Jer 21:1-10
　for **WEALTH**
　　Gog　　　　　　Ezek 38:10-13
　for **WISDOM**
　　Isaiah　　　　　Is 21:11-12

of **DESPAIR**
　in **NEW AGE**
　　Amos　　　　　Amos 5:18-20
　as **PUNISHMENT**
　　Egyptians　　　　Is 19:1-15
　　Isaiah　　　　　Is 8:19-22;
　　　　　　　　　　21:1-10
　as **QUALITY OF LIFE**
　　Isaiah　　　　　Is 51:17-52:12

of **DESTRUCTION**
　　Israelites　　　　Hos 10:1-8
　of **AUTHORITY**
　　Elisha　　　　　2 Kgs 8:7-15
　through **BELIEF**
　　Jonah　　　　　Jon 3:1-10
　　Tobit　　　　　*Tb 14:1-15
　in **CONFRONTATION**
　　Adversaries　　　Zech 12:1-13:6
　　Ammonites　　　Jer 49:1-6
　　Babylonians　　　Is 13:1-22;
　　　　　　　　　　21:1-10;
　　　　　　　　　　Jer 50:1-46;
　　　　　　　　　　51:1-64
　　Canaanites　　　Is 23:1-14
　　Edomites　　　　Jer 49:7-22
　　Egyptians　　　　Jer 46:2-12;
　　　　　　　　　　13-26
　　Elamites　　　　Jer 49:34-39
　　Hazorites　　　　Jer 49:28-33
　　Isaiah　　　　　Is 8:5-8a;
　　　　　　　　　　30:8-17
　　Israelites　　　　Hos 10:9-15;
　　　　　　　　　　11:5-7
　　Jeremiah　　　　Jer 6:22-26;
　　　　　　　　　　10:17-22;
　　　　　　　　　　21:1-10
　　Judahites　　　　Jer 25:8-14;
　　　　　　　　　　37:3-10
　　Moabites　　　　Jer 48:1-47
　　Philistines　　　Jer 47:1-7
　　Tyre　　　　　　Ezek 26:7-14
　　Zedekiah　　　　Jer 34:1-7
　of **CREATION**
　　Jeremiah　　　　Jer 4:23-26
　for **ETERNITY**
　　Damascenes　　　Is 17:1-6
　　Isaiah　　　　　Is 34:1-17
　through **inFIDELITY**
　　Jeremiah　　　　Jer 12:14-17

through **inFIDELITY** (cont'd)
　　Judahites　　　　Jer 9:10-22;
　　　　　　　　　　38:14-28
　as **JUDGMENT**
　　Israelites　　　　Amos 9:1-4
　　Joel　　　　　　Joel 2:1-11
　in **NEW AGE**
　　Jesus　　　　　Lk 17:22-37
　as **PUNISHMENT**
　　Ammonites　　　Amos 1:13-15
　　Amos　　　　　Amos 1:3-5
　　Assyrians　　　　Zeph 2:13-14
　　Baasha　　　　　1 Kgs 15:33-16:7
　　Edomites　　　　Jer 49:7-22;
　　　　　　　　　　Amos 1:11-12
　　Ephraimites　　　Is 28:1-13;
　　　　　　　　　　Hos 5:3-7;
　　　　　　　　　　8-14;
　　　　　　　　　　13:15-16
　　Habakkuk　　　　Hab 2:12-14:17
　　Isaiah　　　　　Is 10:20-23;
　　　　　　　　　　33-34;
　　　　　　　　　　17:12-14;
　　　　　　　　　　19:1-15;
　　　　　　　　　　21:1-10;
　　　　　　　　　　22:1-14;
　　　　　　　　　　24:1-12;
　　　　　　　　　　26:20-27:1;
　　　　　　　　　　28:14-22;
　　　　　　　　　　30:27-33;
　　　　　　　　　　31:1-3;
　　　　　　　　　　32:9-14;
　　　　　　　　　　33:1-6;
　　　　　　　　　　7-16;
　　　　　　　　　　34:1-17;
　　　　　　　　　　66:1-16
　　Israelites　　　　Jer 5:15-17;
　　　　　　　　　　6:16-21;
　　　　　　　　　　11:15-17;
　　　　　　　　　　Ezek 16:35-43;
　　　　　　　　　　Hos 8:4-7;
　　　　　　　　　　11-14;
　　　　　　　　　　10:1-8;
　　　　　　　　　　13:7-8;
　　　　　　　　　　9-11;
　　　　　　　　　　Amos 3:13-15;
　　　　　　　　　　5:4-6;
　　　　　　　　　　6:8-11;
　　　　　　　　　　7:10-17
　　Jeremiah　　　　Jer 4:13-18;
　　　　　　　　　　19-22;
　　　　　　　　　　23-26;
　　　　　　　　　　5:1-14;
　　　　　　　　　　6:1-8;
　　　　　　　　　　7:29-8:3;
　　　　　　　　　　14-17;
　　　　　　　　　　13:12-14;
　　　　　　　　　　14:10-12;
　　　　　　　　　　17-18;
　　　　　　　　　　16:1-13;
　　　　　　　　　　17:19-27;
　　　　　　　　　　21:13-14;
　　　　　　　　　　22:1-9;
　　　　　　　　　　20-23;
　　　　　　　　　　29:1-23;
　　　　　　　　　　32:26-44;
　　　　　　　　　　34:13-22;
　　　　　　　　　　43:8-13;
　　　　　　　　　　44:20-28;
　　　　　　　　　　45:1-5

as PUNISHMENT (cont'd)

Jeroboam	1 Kgs 13:1-34
Jesus	Lk 19:41-44
Joel	Joel 3:16b-21
John the Baptist	Mt 3:1-12; Lk 3:7-9; 15-17
Judahites	Jer 4:5-8
Micah	Mic 1:5-9; 2:1-10; 3:1-12; 5:7-15
Moabites	Is 25:10-12; Amos 2:1-3
Nineveh	Nah 1:11; 14; 2:11-13; 3:5-19; Zeph 2:13-14; 15
Philistines	Amos 1:6-8
Shebna	Is 22:15-25
Tyre	Is 23:1-14; Ezek 26:7-14; 19-21; Amos 1:9-10; Zech 9:1-12
Women	Amos 4:1-3
Zechariah	Zech 9:13-17; 11:1-3
Zedekiah	Jer 27:12-15
Zephaniah	Zeph 1:14-16; 17-18; 2:4-7

as QUALITY OF LIFE

Jeremiah	Jer 4:30-31
Joel	Joel 1:2-20

caused by SIN

Eliezer	2 Chr 17:1-20:37
Isaiah	Is 1:27-31
Moses	Num 32:6-15

overcome by STEWARDSHIP

Isaiah	Is 60:1-22
Israelites	Jer 51:1-64

of DIGNITY
  of AUTHORITY

Jesus	Mt 24:29-31; Mk 13:24-27

  in PRAYER

Believer	1 Cor 11:2-16

of DISCIPLESHIP
  in NEW AGE

Jesus	Mk 8:34-9:1; Lk 9:23-27

of DISOBEDIENCE

Ahab	1 Kgs 22:1-40; 2 Chr 17:1-20:37
Jeremiah	Jer 22:20-23
Josiah	*1 Esd 1:25-32
Zedekiah	*1 Esd 1:46-58

  through inFIDELITY

Ahijah	1 Kgs 14:1-18
Jeremiah	Jer 42:7-22
Moses	Deut 31:24-29

  to LAW

Jerusalemites	Zeph 3:1-5

as SIN

Isaiah	Is 3:8-12

  to TRUTH

Johanan	Jer 43:4-7
Judahites	Jer 25:1-7; 42:7-22

concerning DOUBT

Zedekiah	Jer 32:1-8

  as SIN

Jerusalemites	Zeph 3:1-5

  of TRUTH

Jeremiah	Jer 38:1-13

of ELECTION
  as BLESSING

Gabriel	Lk 1:5-25
Prophet	Judg 6:7-10

  for DEATH

Jesus	Jn 13:31-35

  of LEADERSHIP

Gabriel	Lk 1:5-25
God	Jer 50:1-46
Jeroboam	1 Kgs 11:26-40
Micah	Mic 4:9-5:6
Samuel	1 Sam 9:1-10:16

  for SACRIFICE

Jesus	Mt 16:21-28

  for SERVICE

Elisha	1 Kgs 19:1-21
Jeremiah	Jer 1:4-10

  for VICTORY

Israelites	Is 27:12-13
Jesus	Mt 24:29-31; Mk 13:24-27

concerning ENEMY
  in CONFRONTATION

Isaiah	Is 8:8b-10
Israelites	Nah 2:1-5
Jeremiah	Jer 6:22-26

of EQUALITY
  in EVIL

Isaiah	Is 52:13-53:12

  in OPPRESSION

Isaiah	Is 3:8-12

of ETERNAL
  ANGER

Judahites	Jer 17:1-4

  COMPASSION

Isaiah	Is 54:1-17

  DESTRUCTION

Damascenes	Is 17:1-6
Isaiah	Is 34:1-17

  FAITH

Isaiah	Is 32:15-20

  FULFILLMENT

Jeremiah	Jer 31:38-40

  JOY

Isaiah	Is 51:1-16; 61:1-11

  LEADERSHIP

Jesus	Lk 1:26-38

  LIFE

Israelites	Jer 31:35-37
Judahites	Joel 3:16b-21

  LOVE

Isaiah	Is 54:1-17

concerning **EVIL**
  resulting in **PUNISHMENT**

Amos	Amos 1:3-5; 6-8
Angel	*2 Esd 7:33-44; 13:1-50
Babylonians	Jer 50:1-46
Ephraimites	Hos 7:8-12; 9:1-6; 13:1-3
Habakkuk	Hab 2:9-11; 12-14:17; 15-16
Isaiah	Is 1:27-31; 5:8-24a; 24b-30; 13:1-22; 22:1-14; 24:1-12; 16b-18b; 18c-23; 26:20-27:1; 28:1-13; 30:1-7; 31:1-3; 56:9-57:13
Israelites	Jer 6:16-21; 11:15-17; Ezek 16:35-43; Hos 4:4-15; 5:1-2; 12:10-14; Amos 3:1-2; 6:12-14
Jehoiakim	Jer 22:13-19
Jeremiah	Jer 5:1-14; 26-29; 6:1-8; 9-15; 13:20-27; 14:10-12; 19:1-15; 21:11-12; 22:20-23; 23:1-8; 32:26-44; 45:1-5
Judahites	Jer 7:1-15; 8:8-13; 25:8-14 Jer 35:6-17
Micah	Mic 1:5-9; 10-16; 2:1-10
Nathan	2 Sam 12:1-31
Prophets	Jer 23:9-12; 13-15; 16-22
Zephaniah	Zeph 1:17-18

of **EVIL**
  through **COMPULSION**

Habakkuk	Hab 2:15-16

  in **CONFRONTATION**

Judahites	Jer 4:5-8

  through **inFIDELITY**

Jesus	Mt 26:17-30; Mk 14:17-21

  through **disHONESTY**

Prophets	Jer 5:30-31

  as **QUALITY OF LIFE**

Isaiah	Is 32:1-8

  causing **SIN**

Isaiah	Is 24:16b-18b
Jerusalemites	Zeph 3:1-5

of **FAITH**
  in **AUTHORITY**

Isaiah	Is 30:8-17

  in **BROTHERHOOD**

Jesus	Mt 16:13-20

  in **CONVERSION**

Isaiah	Is 2:1-5; 17:7-8

  for **ETERNITY**

Isaiah	Is 32:15-20

  in **NEW AGE**

Micah	Mic 4:1-8

  in **PROVIDENCE**

Holy Spirit	Mk 13:9-13
Israelites	Jer 46:27-28
Jesus	Lk 21:7-19

  in **RECONCILIATION**

Tyre	Is 23:15-18

  in **SALVATION**

Isaiah	Is 12:1-6; 28:14-22; 33:7-16
Jesus	Mt 24:9-14; Mk 13:9-13; Lk 21:7-19

  in **SECURITY**

Edomites	Jer 49:7-22
Isaiah	Is 54:1-17
Jeremiah	Jer 17:5-8

concerning **FEAR**
  in **CONFRONTATION**

Damascenes	Jer 49:23-27
Saul	1 Sam 28:3-25
Zechariah	Zech 9:1-12

  revealing **FIDELITY**

Israelites	Hos 11:10-11

of **FEAR**
  of **JUDGMENT**

Joel	Joel 2:1-11

  as **MOTIVATION**

Disciples	Mk 14:43-50
Tyre	Ezek 26:15-18

  of divine **PRESENCE**

Isaiah	Is 2:18-22

  of **PUNISHMENT**

Isaiah	Is 2:18-22; 30:27-33

of **FIDELITY**
  through **ANGER**

God	2 Chr 36:1-23

  through **ANXIETY**

Jesus	Jn 13:21-30

  as **BLESSING**

Jeremiah	Jer 7:21-28; 12:14-17

  through **FEAR**

Israelites	Hos 11:10-11

in **JUSTICE**
     Judahites   Jer 7:1-15
in **LIFE**
     Israelites   Amos 5:4-6
through **OBEDIENCE**
     Micah   Mic 4:1-8
     People   Rev 22:6-21
causing **OPPRESSION**
     Jesus   Mt 24:9-14;
         Mk 13:9-13
resulting in **REJECTION**
     Isaiah   Is 29:15-16
     Jesus   Mt 26:31-35;
         Mk 14:27-31;
         Lk 22:14-23;
         31-32;
         33-34;
         Jn 13:1-20;
         21-30;
         36-38;
         16:29-33
     Judahites   2 Chr 24:1-27
     Peter   Mt 26:69-75;
         Mk 14:66-72;
         Lk 22:54b-62;
         Jn 18:12-27
in **REPENTANCE**
     Prophets   2 Chr 24:1-27
in **SERVICE**
     Ezekiel   Ezek 16:44-52

of in**FIDELITY**
through **BLASPHEMY**
     Paul   1 Tim 4:1-5
causing **CAPTIVITY**
     Jesus   Mt 26:36-46;
         Mk 14:32-42
     Judahites   Jer 38:14-28
resulting in **DESTRUCTION**
     Jeremiah   Jer 12:14-17
     Judahites   Jer 9:10-22;
         38:14-28
through **DISOBEDIENCE**
     Ahijah   1 Kgs 14:1-18
     Jeremiah   Jer 42:7-22
     Moses   Deut 31:24-29
of **ENEMY**
     Jesus   Mt 26:17-30;
         Mk 14:17-21;
         Lk 22:14-23;
         Jn 13:21-30
through **EVIL**
     Jesus   Mt 26:17-30;
         Mk 14:17-21

of **FREEDOM**
from **CAPTIVITY**
     Israelites   Is 14:1-23
     Jacobites   Mic 5:7-15
     Jeremiah   *Jer 6:2-3
     Obadiah   Obad 1:17-21
through **GRACE**
     Obed   2 Chr 26:1-28:27
through **OBEDIENCE**
     Israelites   2 Chr 26:1-28:27
     Judahites   Jer 7:1-15
through **PEACE**
     Judahites   Jer 42:7-22

FULFILLMENT of

FULFILLMENT of (cont'd)
in **CONFRONTATION**
     Elisha   2 Kgs 3:1-27
     Israelites   Judg 20:29-36
     Jeremiah   Jer 39:1-14
     Jesus   Mt 26:47-56;
         Mk 14:12-16;
         43-50;
         Lk 22:7-13
     Joash   2 Kgs 13:22-25
     Micaiah   1 Kgs 22:1-40;
         2 Chr 17:1-20:37
on **CREATION**
     Jesus   Lk 2:1-20
     Prophet   Mt 1:18-25
     Samson   Judg 13:24-25
in **ELECTION**
     Jesus   Lk 4:16-30
     John the Baptist   Lk 1:57-80
concerning in**FIDELITY**
     Peter   Mt 26:69-75;
         Mk 14:66-72;
         Lk 22:54b-62;
         Jn 18:12-27
of **GIFT**
     Joel   Acts 2:14-36
of **JUDGMENT**
     God   1 Sam 4:1b-22
of **KNOWLEDGE**
     Agabus   Acts 11:27-30
     Isaiah   Mt 13:10-17
     Jeremiah   Jer 44:29-30;
         Mk 11:1-10;
         Lk 19:28-38
of **LAW**
     Jesus   Lk 24:44-49;
         Jn 18:28-19:16
MOTIVATION for
     Jesus   Mt 4:12-16
through **PRESENCE**
     Saul   1 Sam 9:1-10:16
of **PROMISE**
     Belshazzar   Dan 5:30-31
     Holy Spirit   Acts 2:1-13
     Isaiah   Is 21:1-10
     Tyre   Ezek 26:7-14
through **PROVIDENCE**
     Babylonians   Jer 51:1-64
     Elijah   1 Kgs 18:1-46
     Elisha   2 Kgs 7:3-20
     Isaiah   Is 9:2-7
     Israelites   Ezra 6:13-18
     Jahaziel   2 Chr 17:1-20:37
     Jeremiah   Ezra 1:1
     Prophet   Mt 2:13-15
of **PUNISHMENT**
     Ahijah   1 Kgs 14:1-18;
         15:25-32
     Elijah   2 Kgs 1:1-18;
         9:30-37;
         10:1-14
     God   1 Kgs 2:26-27
     Israelites   Num 26:63-65
     Jehoram   2 Chr 21:1-23:21
     Jehu   1 Kgs 16:8-14;
         2 Kgs 9:14-29
     Jeremiah   2 Chr 36:1-23;
         Jer 28:1-17;
         *Sir 49:4-7
     Joshua   1 Kgs 16:29-34
     Josiah   2 Kgs 23:16-20

in SALVATION
    Isaiah   Is 52:13-53:12
    Jesus   Lk 23:39-43
    Judahites   Jer 23:1-8
    Simeon   Lk 2:21-40
in SECURITY
    Israelites   Hos 12:10-14
    Judahites   Jer 23:1-8
over SIN
    Isaiah   Is 33:17-24;
                       40:1-11
    Israelites   Ezek 16:53-63

of GRATITUDE
through PRAYER
    Isaiah   Is 12:1-6
in RITE
    Isaiah   Is 26:1-6

of GRIEF
    Amos   Amos 5:1-3
    Jeremiah   Jer 14:17-18
in CONFRONTATION
    Jerusalemites   Zech 12:1-13:6
as MOTIVATION
    Tyre   Ezek 26:15-18
in PROVIDENCE
    Egyptians   Is 19:1-15
through PUNISHMENT
    Moabites   Jer 48:1-47
through RESPECT
    Isaiah   Is 52:13-53:12

of HATE
in CONFRONTATION
    Jeremiah   Jer 4:30-31
as SIN
    Prophet   Hos 9:7-9

of HEALING
as QUALITY OF LIFE
    Isaiah   Is 52:13-53:12
through RECONCILIATION
    Israelites   Hos 6:10-7:2;
                     14:4-8

of HERESY
through disHONESTY
    Apostles   Jude 1:17-19
    Jesus   Mt 24:4-8;
                     Mk 13:3-8
concerning TRUTH
    Paul   1 Tim 4:1-5

of disHONESTY
of ENEMY
    Hushai   2 Sam 16:15-17:29
through EVIL
    Prophets   Jer 5:30-31
causing HERESY
    Apostles   Jude 1:17-19
    Jesus   Mt 24:4-8;
                     Mk 13:3-8
in SELFISHNESS
    Jeremiah   Jer 22:13-19
in SEX
    Prophets   Jer 23:13-15
with WEALTH
    Jeremiah   Jer 17:11

of HOPE
in BELIEF
    Holy Spirit   Jn 7:37-52
in HONESTY
    Hananiah   Jer 28:1-17
in NEW AGE
    Isaiah   Is 33:17-24;
                     35:1-10
    Malachi   Mal 4:4-6
in PROMISE
    Isaiah   Is 10:24-27c
in PROVIDENCE
    Elisha   2 Kgs 6:32-7:2
    Isaiah   Is 29:1-8;
                     30:18-26
in RECONCILIATION
    Jeremiah   Jer 29:1-23
    Micah   Mic 2:12-13
in SALVATION
    Isaiah   Is 25:6-9
in SECURITY
    Isaiah   Is 37:33-35;
                     62:1-12
in SIGNS
    Isaiah   Is 7:10-17;
                     37:30-32

of HUMILITY
through PROVIDENCE
    Isaiah   Is 2:6-11;
                     17:1-6
as PUNISHMENT
    Babylonians   Jer 50:1-46
    Ezekiel   Ezek 16:44-52
    Habakkuk   Hab 2:15-16
    Isaiah   Is 3:16-4:1;
                     5:8-24a
    Israelites   Ezek 16:53-63;
                     Hos 4:4-15;
                     10:1-8
    Jeremiah   Jer 13:20-27;
                     22:20-23
    Judahites   Jer 13:18-19
    Moabites   Jer 48:1-47
    Nineveh   Nah 3:5-19
revealing RESPECT
    Edomites   Obad 1:1b-4
    God   Zeph 2:8-12
    Isaiah   Is 30:1-7;
                     60:1-22

of IDOLATRY
as SIN
    Ahijah   1 Kgs 14:1-18
    Jeremiah   Jer 5:1-14

of IGNORANCE
of JUDGMENT
    Isaiah   Is 5:8-24a
of KNOWLEDGE
    Disciples   Lk 18:31-34
    Egyptians   Is 19:1-15
    Isaiah   Is 29:9-12
    Jeremiah   Jer 14:17-18
of NEW AGE
    Jesus   Mt 24:37-41;
                     Jn 8:21-59
of SALVATION
    Caiaphas   Jn 11:1-57

of **TRUTH**
Disciples   Lk 9:43b-45

of **INDIFFERENCE**
as **PUNISHMENT**
Isaiah   Is 32:9-14

of **INNOCENCE**
as **QUALITY OF LIFE**
Isaiah   Is 52:13-53:12

of **JOY**
Isaiah   Is 24:13-16a
in **BROTHERHOOD**
Isaiah   Is 62:1-12
for **ETERNITY**
Isaiah   Is 51:1-16;
                         61:1-11
in **NEW AGE**
Isaiah   Is 35:1-10
Jesus   Jn 16:16-24
in **PROVIDENCE**
Isaiah   Is 9:2-7;
                         60:1-22
Jeremiah   Jer 32:26-44
in **SALVATION**
Isaiah   Is 12:1-6;
                         25:6-9;
                         35:1-10
in **SECURITY**
Jesus   Jn 16:16-24

of **JUDGMENT**
on **ALIENATION**
Jesus   Jn 12:27-36a
on **ANGER**
Isaiah   Is 34:1-17;
                         59:1-21;
                         66:1-16
on **BLASPHEMY**
Isaiah   Is 5:8-24a
as **CONDEMNATION**
Amos   Amos 3:13-15
Ephraimites   Hos 7:8-12
Ezekiel   Ezek 16:44-52
Habakkuk   Hab 2:9-11;
                         12-14;
                         15-16;
                         17;
                         18-20
Isaiah   Is 30:1-7;
                         27-33;
                         31:1-3;
                         33:1-6;
                         34:1-17
Israelites   Ezek 16:53-63;
                         Hos 5:1-2;
                         10:1-8;
                         12:10-14;
                         Amos 4:4-5;
                         5:7-13;
                         6:1-7
Jeremiah   Jer 4:13-18;
                         21:13-14
Jerusalemites   Zeph 3:1-5
Jesus   Mt 11:20-24
Micah   Mic 3:1-12
Moabites   Jer 48:1-47
Nineveh   Nah 3:1-4;
                         5-19

as **CONDEMNATION** (cont'd)
Priests   Mal 1:6-2:9
Prophets   Jer 23:13-15
Shemaiah   Jer 29:24-32
Zephaniah   Zeph 2:4-7
on **DEATH**
Ezra   *2 Esd 14:19-48
on **DESTRUCTION**
Israelites   Amos 9:1-4
Joel   Joel 2:1-11
on **DISOBEDIENCE**
Jesus   Mt 11:20-24
on **EVIL**
Isaiah   Is 3:16-4:1
Jesus   Mt 11:20-24
with **GRACE**
Israelites   Hos 11:8-9
of **GUILT**
Babylonians   Jer 51:1-64
Ephraimites   Hos 5:3-7;
                         12:7-9
Isaiah   Is 13:1-22;
                         24:1-12
Israelites   Ezek 16:44-52
Samaria   Hos 13:15-16
on **IDOLATRY**
Asa   2 Chr 14:1-16:14
Babylonians   Jer 51:1-64
Israelites   Jer 11:15-17
on **IGNORANCE**
Isaiah   Is 5:8-24a
on **JUSTICE**
Angel   *2 Esd 7:33-44;
                         8:63-9:25
Isaiah   Is 15:1-16:14
Israelites   Ezek 16:35-43
Jeremiah   Jer 31:31-34
Obadiah   Obad 1:15-16
by **LEADERSHIP**
Deborah   Judg 4:4-5
on **LEADERSHIP**
Isaiah   Is 24:18c-23;
                         51:17-52:12
on **LIFE**
Isaiah   Is 51:17-52:12;
                         66:1-16
on **LUST**
Isaiah   Is 5:8-24a
on **OPPRESSION**
Isaiah   Is 3:13-15
on **PRIDE**
Isaiah   Is 5:8-24a
Moabites   Jer 48:1-47
on **REJECTION**
Jesus   Lk 22:14-23
on **REPENTANCE**
Holy Spirit   Neh 9:26-31
Jesus   Mt 11:20-24
on **REVENGE**
Babylonian   Jer 25:8-14
Isaiah   Is 34:1-17
Jeremiah   Jer 4:11-12
Jesus   Lk 21:20-24
on **VIOLENCE**
Joel   Joel 2:1-11
on **WISDOM**
Isaiah   Is 32:1-8

on **JUSTICE**
Jeremiah   Jer 21:11-12

in AUTHORITY
  Isaiah   Is 9:2-7;
                        32:1-8
in JUDGMENT
  Angel   *2 Esd 7:33-44;
                        8:63-9:25
  Isaiah   Is 15:1-16:14
  Israelites   Ezek 16:35-43
  Jeremiah   Jer 31:31-34
  Obadiah   Obad 1:15-16
in NEW AGE
  Angel   *2 Esd 8:63-9:25;
                        11:1-12:39
  Isaiah   Is 32:15-20
in PUNISHMENT
  Babylonians   Jer 50:1-46
  Edomites   Obad 1:15-16
  Isaiah   Is 3:8-12;
                        27:7-11
  Israelites   Jer 46:27-28;
                        Ezek 16:35-43;
                        Hos 4:4-15;
                        12:2-6
  Jeremiah   Jer 21:13-14;
                        31:29-30
in RECONCILIATION
  Isaiah   Is 1:27-31
in SALVATION
  Isaiah   Is 1:27-31
as VIRTUE
  Isaiah   Is 28:14-22
  Jeremiah   Jer 22:1-9;
                        23:1-8

of KILLING
  in CONFRONTATION
    Gentiles   Mk 10:32-34
    Jesus   Mt 16:21-28;
                        17:22-23;
                        20:17-19;
                        26:1-2;
                        Mk 8:31-33;
                        9:30-32;
                        Lk 9:18-22;
                        43b-45;
                        18:31-34

  as PUNISHMENT
    Habakkuk   Hab 2:12-14;
                        17
    Jehu   2 Chr 21:1-23:21
    Prophet   2 Kgs 9:1-13

of KNOWLEDGE
  of BLASPHEMY
    Gentiles   Mk 10:32-34
  of CAPTIVITY
    Jesus   Mk 10:32-34;
                        Lk 18:31-34
  of DEATH
    Jesus   Mt 16:21-28;
                        Mk 8:31-33;
                        10:32-34;
                        Lk 5:33-35;
                        9:18-22;
                        13:31-33
  of DESTRUCTION
    Edomites   Obad 1:5-9
  of EVIL
    Judahites   Jer 17:1-4

of FULFILLMENT
  Agabus   Acts 11:27-30
  Isaiah   Mt 13:10-17
  Jeremiah   Jer 44:29-30
  Jesus   Mk 11:1-10;
                        Lk 19:28-38
of IGNORANCE
  Disciples   Lk 18:31-34
  Egyptians   Is 19:1-15
  Isaiah   Is 29:9-12
  Jeremiah   Jer 14:17-18
of KILLING
  Jesus   Jn 16:1-4
of LIFE
  Ezekiel   Ezek 11:22-25
of PRUDENCE
  Isaiah   Is 28:1-13
of REJECTION
  Isaiah   Is 31:1-3
  Israelites   Jer 6:16-21
  Jesus   Mk 8:31-33;
                        Lk 9:18-22;
                        Jn 16:1-4
  Scribes   Mt 17:9-13;
                        Mk 9:9-13
of SACRIFICE
  Jesus   Mt 20:17-19;
                        Lk 18:31-34
of SUFFERING
  Agabus   Acts 11:27-30
  Jesus   Mt 16:21-28;
                        17:9-13;
                        Mk 8:31-33;
                        9:9-13;
                        10:32-34;
                        Lk 9:18-22;
                        18:31-34
concerning WISDOM
  Isaiah   Is 28:1-13;
                        52:13-53:12
of WITNESS
  Holy Spirit   Mk 13:9-13
  Jesus   Lk 21:7-19
  Unbelievers   1 Cor 14:13-25

of LAW
  concerning OBEDIENCE
    Jeremiah   Jer 17:19-27
  concerning REJECTION
    Israelites   Hos 4:4-15

of LEADERSHIP
  in AUTHORITY
    Balaam   Num 23:27:24-13
    Believers   Rev 2:18-29
    Deborah   Judg 4:4-5
    Eliakim   Is 22:15-25
    God   Jer 30:18-22
    Isaiah   Is 15:1-16:14
    Israelites   Hos 8:8-10
    Jesus   Lk 1:26-38
    Obadiah   Obad 1:17-21
    Samuel   1 Sam 13:1-23
  in COMMUNITY
    Isaiah   Is 3:1-7
  through ELECTION
    Gabriel   Lk 1:5-25
    God   Jer 50:1-46
    Jeroboam   1 Kgs 11:26-40

through **ELECTION** (cont'd)
Micah	Mic 4:9-5:6
Samuel	1 Sam 9:1-10:16

ETERNAL
Jesus	Lk 1:26-38

concerning **JUDGMENT**
Deborah	Judg 4:4-5

JUDGMENT on
Isaiah	Is 24:18c-23; 51:17-52:12

through **PROVIDENCE**
Isaiah	Is 9:2-7
Jeremiah	Jer 23:1-8

of **LIFE**
Ezekiel	Ezek 37:1-14
Isaiah	Is 7:10-17; 9:2-7

for **ETERNITY**
Israelites	Jer 31:35-37
Judahites	Joel 3:16b-21

through **FIDELITY**
Israelites	Amos 5:4-6

in **NEW AGE**
Jesus	Mt 26:57-68; Mk 14:53-65; Jn 7:32-36

through **PROVIDENCE**
Isaiah	Is 4:2-6; 37:30-32
Israelites	Is 30:18-26; Jer 31:27-28
Joseph	Gen 41:1-57
Tyre	Is 23:15-18

through **RECONCILIATION**
Isaiah	Is 11:1-9

through **SALVATION**
Jesus	Mt 16:21-28; Mk 8:34-9:1; Lk 9:23-27

through **SECURITY**
Baruch	Jer 45:1-5
Ebedmelech	Jer 39:15-18
Isaiah	Is 4:2-6; 25:6-9; 27:2-6; 32:15-20; 37:30-32; 51:17-52:12
Jeremiah	Jer 21:1-10; 32:26-44
Jerusalemites	Zech 14:1-21
Judahites	Jer 27:16-22; 38:14-28
Paul	Acts 27:1-28:16
Zedekiah	Jer 34:1-7

through **STEWARDSHIP**
Isaiah	2 Kgs 20:1-11

of **LOVE**
for **ETERNITY**
Isaiah	Is 54:1-17

of **MARRIAGE**
Isaiah	Is 3:16-4:1
Jeremiah	Jer 16:1-13

of **MEDIATION**
for **ACCEPTANCE**
Elijah	Mal 4:4-6

FULFILLMENT of
Isaiah	Mt 3:1-12; Mk 1:2-8; Lk 3:1-6; Jn 1:19-51
John the Baptist	Mt 3:1-12; 11:7-15; Mk 1:2-8; Lk 3:1-6; 7:24-30; Jn 1:19-51

through **GRACE**
John the Baptist	Lk 1:57-80
Zechariah	Lk 1:57-80

of **SERVICE**
Israelites	Deut 18:9-22

of **MIRACLE**
by **AUTHORITY**
Moses	Deut 34:1-12

in **CONFRONTATION**
Assyrians	Is 31:4-9

in the **CREATION**
Zechariah	Zech 14:1-21

through **PROVIDENCE**
Israelites	Ezek 37:1-14

as **PUNISHMENT**
Jeremiah	Jer 7:29-8:3

of **MOTIVATION**
as **ANGER**
Israelites	Ezek 16:35-43

as **FEAR**
Disciples	Mk 14:43-50
Tyre	Ezek 26:15-18

as **FULFILLMENT**
Jesus	Mt 4:12-16

as **GRIEF**
Tyre	Ezek 26:15-18

as **REPENTANCE**
Israelites	2 Kgs 17:7-23

as **WITNESS**
Holy Spirit	2 Pet 1:19b-21

of **NEW AGE**
concerning **ACCEPTANCE**
Believers	Lk 10:17-20

concerning **ALIENATION**
Jesus	Jn 7:32-36

concerning **BLESSING**
Israelites	Is 27:2-6
Joel	Joel 3:16b-21

concerning **CHAOS**
Jesus	Mt 24:29-31; Mk 13:24-27

concerning **CONDEMNATION**
Jesus	Lk 17:22-37

concerning **COURAGE**
Isaiah	Is 35:1-10

concerning **DESPAIR**
Amos	Amos 5:18-20

concerning **DESTRUCTION**
Jesus	Lk 17:22-37

concerning **DISCIPLESHIP**
Jesus	Mk 8:34-9:1; Lk 9:23-27

concerning **FULFILLMENT**
Angel	*2 Esd 7:19-32
Angels	Lk 2:1-20
Isaiah	Is 11:1-9;

concerning **FUFILLMENT** (cont'd)
Isaiah	24:18c-23;
	32:15-20;
	33:17-24;
	51:17-52:12;
	60:1-22
Jesus	Mt 16:21-28;
	24:1-3;
	4-8;
	9-14;
	15-22;
	23-28;
	29-31;
	32-33;
	34-36;
	37-41;
	42-44;
	Mk 1:14-15;
	8:34-9:1;
	13:3-8;
	9-13;
	14-23;
	24-27;
	28-37;
	14:22-26;
	Lk 9:23-27;
	21:7-19;
	20-24;
	25-28;
	29-31;
	32-33;
	22:14-23;
	Jn 16:16-24
Joel	Joel 1:2-20
Zechariah	Zech 14:1-21
Zephaniah	Zeph 1:7

concerning **HOPE**
Isaiah	Is 33:17-24;
	35:1-10
Malachi	Mal 4:4-6

concerning **IGNORANCE**
Jesus	Mt 24:37-41;
	Jn 8:21-59

concerning **JOY**
Isaiah	Is 35:1-10
Jesus	Jn 16:16-24

concerning **JUSTICE**
Angel	*2 Esd 8:63-9:25;
	11:1-12:39
Isaiah	Is 32:15-20

concerning **LIFE**
Jesus	Mt 26:57-68;
	Mk 14:53-65;
	Jn 7:32-36

concerning **OPPRESSION**
Amos	Amos 5:18-20

concerning **PEACE**
Isaiah	Is 2:1-5;
	32:15-20;
	35:1-10
Micah	Mic 4:1-8

concerning **PRAISE**
Zechariah	Lk 1:57-80

concerning **PURIFICATION**
John the Baptist	Mt 3:1-12;
	Lk 3:15-17

concerning **REJECTION**
Jesus	Mk 8:34-9:1;
	Lk 9:23-27

concerning **VICTORY**
Balaam	Num 23:27-24:13
Isaiah	Is 9:1;
	25:6-9;
	51:17-52:12;
	13-53:12
Jesus	Mt 26:57-68;
	Mk 14:53-65;
	Lk 21:25-28
Obadiah	Obad 1:17-21

concerning **VIOLENCE**
Angel	*2 Esd 5:1-15

concerning **WISDOM**
Hezekiah	*Sir 48:17-25
Isaiah	Is 35:1-10
Zechariah	Lk 1:57-80

concerning **WITNESS**
John the Baptist	Mt 3:1-12;
	Lk 3:15-17

of **OBEDIENCE**
  to **AUTHORITY**
Israelites	*Bar 2:11-23

  in **CONFRONTATION**
Amaziah	2 Chr 25:1-28
Rehoboam	1 Kgs 12:21-24;
	2 Chr 10:1-12:16

  in **CREATION**
Israelites	Hag 1:12-14

  through **FIDELITY**
Micah	Mic 4:1-8
People	Rev 22:6-21

  resulting in **FREEDOM**
Israelites	2 Chr 26:1-28:27
Judahites	Jer 7:1-15

  to **LAW**
Jeremiah	Jer 17:19-27

  in **PRESENCE**
Jeroboam	1 Kgs 11:26-40

  to **TRUTH**
Israelites	Deut 18:9-22
Jeremiah	Jer 26:7-19

of **ONENESS**
  through **RECONCILIATION**
Jeremiah	Jer 32:26-44

of **OPPRESSION**
  by **AUTHORITY**
Israelites	Is 14:1-23
Samuel	1 Sam 8:1-22

  in **CONFRONTATION**
Gog	Ezek 38:10-13
Isaiah	Is 24:16b-18b

  through **FIDELITY**
Jesus	Mt 24:9-14;
	Mk 13:9-13

  in **NEW AGE**
Amos	Amos 5:18-20

  as **PUNISHMENT**
Babylonians	Jer 50:1-46
Egyptians	Is 19:1-15
Ephraimites	Hos 5:8-14;
	7:8-12;
	12:7-9
Habakkuk	Hab 2:6b-8
Isaiah	Is 3:1-7;
	5:24b-30;
	28:1-13

as **PUNISHMENT** (cont'd)

Israelites	Ezek 16:35-43; Hos 8:1-3; 8-10; 11:5-7; Amos 2:13-16; 6:12-14; 8:11-14
Jeremiah	Jer 13:20-27; 29:1-23; 32:26-44; 34:13-22
Micah	Mic 7:1-6
Moabites	Jer 48:1-47
Nineveh	Nah 3:5-19

as **QUALITY OF LIFE**

Ephraimites	Hos 9:1-6
Joel	Joel 1:2-20

in **RECONCILIATION**

Isaiah	Is 27:12-13
Micah	Mic 4:1-8

in **SECURITY**

Israelites	Zech 9:1-12

caused by **SIN**

Isaiah	Is 52:13-53:12
Micah	Mic 2:1-10

of **ORDER**

Believers	1 Cor 14:34-40
Jesus	Mt 24:32-33; Mk 13:28-37; Lk 21:29-31

through **PROVIDENCE**

Isaiah	Is 17:12-14; 18:1-7

in **STEWARDSHIP**

Isaiah	Is 18:1-7

of **PARADOX**

in **BEHAVIOR**

Isaiah	Is 11:1-9

in **PROMISE**

Jesus	Mt 16:21-28; Mk 8:34-9:1; Lk 9:23-27

of **PATIENCE**

in **SALVATION**

Jesus	Mk 13:9-13; Lk 21:7-19

concerning **PEACE**

Isaiah	Is 28:1-13

in **COMMUNITY**

Isaiah	Is 11:10-16

resulting in **FREEDOM**

Judahites	Jer 42:7-22

through **HONESTY**

Isaiah	Is 52:13-53:12

in **NEW AGE**

Isaiah	Is 2:1-5; 32:15-20; 35:1-10
Micah	Mic 4:1-8

through **PROVIDENCE**

Isaiah	Is 9:2-7
Israelites	Jer 46:27-28

through **RECONCILIATION**

Elijah	Mal 4:4-6

through **RECONCILIATION** (cont'd)

Isaiah	Is 19:18-25; 51:17-52:12

of **PIETY**

as **GIFT**

Paul	1 Tim 4:11-16

of **POLITICS**

of **AUTHORITY**

Deborah	Judg 4:4-5
Jesus	Mt 2:1-12

in **CONFRONTATION**

Shemaiah	1 Kgs 12:21-24; 2 Chr 10:1-12:16

of **POVERTY**

in **PROVIDENCE**

Isaiah	Is 29:17-24

as **PUNISHMENT**

Isaiah	Is 3:16-4:1
Judahites	Jer 17:1-4

of **PRAISE**

Crowd	Lk 7:11-17
Isaiah	Is 24:13-16a

by **COMMUNITY**

Isaiah	Is 60:1-22

of **ELECTION**

Jesus	Jn 13:31-35

of **NEW AGE**

Zechariah	Lk 1:57-80

in **RITE**

Isaiah	Is 12:1-6

of **SALVATION**

Isaiah	Is 26:1-6; 62:1-12

as **VIRTUE**

Isaiah	Is 61:1-11

of **PRAYER**

Believer	1 Cor 11:2-16
Israelites	Is 30:18-26
Jeremiah	Jer 29:1-23

for **GRACE**

Israelites	Is 30:18-26

of **GRATITUDE**

Isaiah	Is 12:1-6

concerning **REJECTION**

Israelites	Mic 3:1-12
Jeremiah	Jer 14:10-12
Moab	Is 15:1-16:14
Samuel	1 Sam 8:1-22

for **WITNESS**

Isaiah	Is 37:21

of **PRESENCE**

of **ENEMY**

Isaiah	Is 29:1-8

of **FEAR**

Isaiah	Is 2:18-22

concerning **FULFILLMENT**

Saul	1 Sam 9:1-10:16

in **LEADERSHIP**

David	2 Sam 23:1-7

of **PRIDE**

Jeremiah	Jer 4:30-31

as **SIN**

Edomites	Obad 1:1b-4

as **ALIENATION** (cont'd)

Nineveh	Nah 1:11; 14
Women	Amos 4:1-3
Zephaniah	Zeph 2:4-7

through **ANGER**

God	Mic 5:7-15
Isaiah	Is 13:1-22
Israelites	Hos 13:9-11
Jeremiah	Jer 6:9-15
Judahites	Jer 4:5-8; 42:7-22
Prophets	Jer 23:16-22

for **BLASPHEMY**

Jeremiah	Jer 32:26-44
Moabites	Jer 48:1-47

as **CAPTIVITY**

Assyrians	Is 31:4-9
Babylonian	Jer 25:8-14
Coniah	Jer 22:24-30
Egyptians	Jer 46:13-26
Ephraimites	Hos 9:1-6
Isaiah	Is 24:18c-23
Israelites	Hos 11:5-7
Jeremiah	Jer 5:18-19; 20:1-6; 21:1-10; 22:20-23; 34:13-22; 43:8-13
Judahites	Jer 13:18-19; 17:1-4; 25:8-14
Moabites	Jer 48:1-47

as **CHAOS**

Isaiah	Is 13:1-22; 22:1-14; 24:1-12; 34:1-17
Jeremiah	Jer 13:12-14; 23:1-8
Jesus	Lk 19:41-44; 23:27-32

as **CONDEMNATION**

Shebna	Is 22:15-25

for **COVETOUSNESS**

Habakkuk	Hab 2:6b-8

as **DEATH**

Ahab	1 Kgs 21:17-29
Ahijah	1 Kgs 14:1-18
Amaziah	Amos 7:10-17
Coniah	Jer 22:24-30
Edomites	Obad 1:5-9
Elijah	2 Kgs 1:1-18
Ephraimites	Hos 7:13-16; 9:10-17
Isaiah	Is 3:16-4:1
Israelites	Ezek 16:35-43; Amos 2:13-16; 5:1-3; 6:8-11
Jehoiakim	Jer 22:13-19
Jeremiah	Jer 16:1-13; 20:1-6; 21:1-10; 29:1-23; 42:7-22; 43:8-13; 44:20-28
Jezebel	Rev 2:18-29

as **DEATH** (cont'd)

Judahites	Jer 9:10-22; 42:7-22; 44:1-14
Obadiah	Obad 1:17-21
Samaria	Hos 13:15-16
Samuel	1 Sam 28:3-25
Shebna	Is 22:15-25

as **DEFEAT**

Edomites	Obad 1:1b-4
Isaiah	Is 5:24b-30; 30:8-17
Israelites	Amos 2:13-16
Micah	Mic 1:10-16
Samuel	1 Sam 28:3-25
Sennacherib	Is 37:22-29
Zechariah	Zech 11:1-3

as **DESPAIR**

Egyptians	Is 19:1-15
Isaiah	Is 8:19-22; 21:1-10

as **DESTRUCTION**

Ammonites	Amos 1:13-15
Amos	Amos 1:3-5
Assyrians	Zeph 2:13-14
Baasha	1 Kgs 15:33-16:7
Edomites	Jer 49:7-22; Amos 1:11-12
Ephraimites	Is 28:1-13; Hos 5:3-7; 8-14; 13:15-16
Habakkuk	Hab 2:12-14; 17
Isaiah	Is 10:20-23; 33-34; 17:12-14; 19:1-15; 21:1-10; 22:1-14; 24:1-12; 26:20-27:1; 28:14-22; 30:27-33; 31:1-3; 32:9-14; 33:1-6; 7-16; 34:1-17; 66:1-16
Israelites	Jer 5:15-17; 6:16-21; 11:15-17; Ezek 16:35-43; Hos 8:4-7; 11-14; 10:1-8; 13:7-8; 9-11; Amos 3:13-15; 5:4-6; 6:8-11; 7:10-17
Jeremiah	Jer 4:13-18; 19-22; 23-26; 5:1-14; 6:1-8; 7:29-8:3; 14-17;

as **DESTRUCTION** (cont'd)

Jeremiah	13:12-14;
	14:10-12;
	17-18;
	16:1-13;
	17:19-27;
	21:13-14;
	22:1-9;
	20-23;
	29:1-23;
	32:26-44;
	34:13-22;
	43:8-13;
	44:20-28;
	45:1-5
Jeroboam	1 Kgs 13:1-34
Jesus	Lk 19:41-44
Joel	Joel 3:16b-21
John the Baptist	Mt 3:1-12;
	Lk 3:7-9;
	15-17
Judahites	Jer 4:5-8;
	8:8-13;
	9:10-22;
	44:1-14;
	Hos 5:3-7;
	Amos 2:4-5
Micah	Mic 1:5-9;
	2:1-10;
	3:1-12;
	5:7-15
Moabites	Is 25:10-12;
	Amos 2:1-3
Nineveh	Nah 1:11;
	14;
	2:11-13;
	3:5-19;
	Zeph 2:13-14;
	15
Philistines	Amos 1:6-8
Shebna	Is 22:15-25
Tyre	Is 23:1-14;
	Ezek 26:7-14;
	19-21;
	Amos 1:9-10;
	Zech 9:1-12
Women	Amos 4:1-3
Zechariah	Zech 9:13-17;
	11:1-3
Zedekiah	Jer 27:12-15
Zephaniah	Zeph 1:14-16;
	17-18;
	2:4-7

for **DISOBEDIENCE**

Ahijah	1 Kgs 11:26-40
Amaziah	2 Chr 25:1-28
Asa	2 Chr 14:1-16:14
God	Mic 5:7-15
Huldah	2 Kgs 22:3-20;
	14:1-18
Jeremiah	Jer 17:19-27;
	29:1-23;
	34:13-22
Jeroboam	1 Kgs 13:1-34;
	14:1-18
Judahites	Jer 44:1-14
Samuel	1 Sam 13:1-23;
	28:3-25
Zedekiah	Jer 22:1-9

for **DOUBT**

Israelites	Jer 18:18-23

for **ENEMY**

Baruch	*Bar 4:21-37
Isaiah	Is 17:12-14
Joel	Joel 3:16b-21
Judahites	Zeph 2:4-7
Micah	Mic 1:10-16
Zechariah	Zech 2:6-13

for **EVIL**

Amos	Amos 1:3-5;
	6-8
Angel	*2 Esd 7:33-44;
	13:1-50
Babylonians	Jer 50:1-46
Ephraimites	Hos 7:8-12;
	9:1-6;
	13:1-3
Habakkuk	Hab 2:9-11;
	12-14;
	15-16;
	17
Isaiah	Is 1:27-31;
	5:8-24a;
	24b-30;
	13:1-22;
	22:1-14;
	24:1-12;
	16b-18b;
	18c-23;
	26:20-27:1;
	28:1-13;
	30:1-7;
	31:1-3;
	56:9-57:13
Israelites	Jer 6:16-21;
	11:15-17;
	Ezek 16:35-43;
	Hos 4:4-15;
	5:1-2;
	12:10-14;
	Amos 3:1-2;
	6:12-14
Jehoiakim	Jer 22:13-19
Jeremiah	Jer 5:1-14;
	26-29;
	6:1-8;
	9-15;
	13:20-27;
	14:10-12;
	19:1-15;
	21:11-12;
	22:20-23;
	23:1-8;
	32:26-44;
	45:1-5
Judahites	Jer 7:1-15;
	8:8-13;
	25:8-14;
	35:6-17
Micah	Mic 1:5-9;
	10-16;
	2:1-10
Nathan	2 Sam 12:1-31
Prophets	Jer 23:9-12;
	13-15;
	16-22
Zephaniah	Zeph 1:17-18

resulting in **GRIEF**

Moabites	Jer 48:1-47

for **HERESY**
John	Rev 22:6-21

as **HUMILITY**
Babylonians	Jer 50:1-46
Ezekiel	Ezek 16:44-52
Habakkuk	Hab 2:15-16
Isaiah	Is 3:16-4:1;
	5:8-24a
Israelites	Ezek 16:53-63;
	Hos 4:4-15;
	10:1-8
Jeremiah	Jer 13:20-27;
	22:20-23
Judahites	Jer 13:18-19
Moabites	Jer 48:1-47
Nineveh	Nah 3:5-19

for **IDOLATRY**
Babylonians	Jer 50:1-46;
	51:1-64
Egyptians	Jer 46:13-26
Elijah	1 Kgs 21:17-29
Habakkuk	Hab 2:18-20
Isaiah	Is 2:6-11
Israelites	Ezek 16:35-43;
	Amos 3:13-15;
	5:26-27
Jeremiah	Jer 32:26-44
Judahites	Jer 44:1-14
Micah	Mic 1:5-9
Moabites	Jer 48:1-47
Zechariah	Zech 12:1-13:6

for **IGNORANCE**
Israelites	Hos 4:4-15
Jesus	Lk 19:41-44

for **INDIFFERENCE**
Isaiah	Is 32:9-14

through **JUSTICE**
Babylonians	Jer 50:1-46
Edomites	Obad 1:15-16
Isaiah	Is 3:8-12;
	27:7-11
Israelites	Jer 46:27-28;
	Ezek 16:35-43;
	Hos 4:4-15;
	12:2-6
Jeremiah	Jer 21:13-14;
	31:29-30

for **KILLING**
Habakkuk	Hab 2:12-14;
	17
Jehu	2 Chr 21:1-23:21
Prophet	2 Kgs 9:1-13

of **LEADERSHIP**
Coniah	Jer 22:24-30
Isaiah	Is 9:8-10:4

through **MIRACLE**
Jeremiah	Jer 7:29-8:3

as **OPPRESSION**
Babylonians	Jer 50:1-46
Egyptians	Is 19:1-15
Ephraimites	Hos 5:8-14;
	7:8-12;
	12:7-9
Habakkuk	Hab 2:6b-8
Isaiah	Is 3:1-7;
	5:24b-30;
	28:1-13
Israelites	Ezek 16:35-43;
	Hos 8:1-3;
	8-10;

as **OPPRESSION** (cont'd)
Israelites	11:5-7;
	Amos 2:13-16;
	6:12-14;
	8:11-14
Jeremiah	Jer 13:20-27;
	29:1-23;
	32:26-44;
	34:13-22
Micah	Mic 7:1-6
Moabites	Jer 48:1-47
Nineveh	Nah 3:5-19

as **POVERTY**
Isaiah	Is 3:16-4:1
Judahites	Jer 17:1-4

for **PRIDE**
Ephraimites	Hos 5:8-14
Isaiah	Is 13:1-22;
	28:1-13
Moab	Is 15:1-16:14
Moabites	Is 25:10-12
Tyre	Is 23:1-14

concerning **REJECTION**
Ephraimites	Hos 9:10-17
Isaiah	Is 8:5-8a;
	10:5-16;
	17:9-11;
	28:1-13;
	30:1-7
Israelites	Ezek 16:35-43;
	Hos 4:4-15;
	11:5-7;
	Amos 4:6-12;
	5:4-6;
	Mic 3:1-12;
	Hag 1:15a;
	2:15-19
Jeremiah	Jer 13:20-27;
	19:1-15;
	29:1-23;
	32:26-44;
	34:13-22;
	*Sir 49:4-7
Jesus	Lk 19:41-44
Judahites	Jer 9:10-22
People	Acts 3:1-26
Priests	Mal 1:6-2:9
Sennacherib	Is 37:22-29
Shemaiah	Jer 29:24-32
Zedekiah	Jer 27:12-15

as **REVENGE**
Babylonians	Jer 50:1-46;
	51:1-64
Edomites	Obad 1:15-16
Egyptians	Jer 46:2-12;
	13-26
Habakkuk	Hab 2:6b-8;
	15-16
Israelites	Jer 6:16-21
Jeremiah	Jer 5:1-14;
	26-29
Joel	Joel 3:16b-21
Micah	Mic 5:7-15

as **SACRIFICE**
Isaiah	Is 34:1-17
Israelites	Ezek 16:35-43

as **SADNESS**
Isaiah	Is 3:16-4:1
Judahites	Jer 25:8-14

as **SADNESS** (cont'd)
Zechariah	Zech 11:1-3

as **SUFFERING**
Elijah	2 Chr 21:1-23:21
Ephraimites	Hos 9:10-17; 13:12-14
Habakkuk	Hab 2:6b-8
Haggai	Hag 1:1-11
Huldah	2 Chr 34:1-35:27
Isaiah	Is 8:19-22; 17:9-11; 24:1-12; 29:1-8
Jeremiah	Jer 4:19-22; 10:17-22; 14:1-6; 10-12; 21:1-10
Jesus	Lk 23:27-32
Moab	Is 15:1-16:14
Moabites	Jer 48:1-47
People	Zech 14:1-21
Prophets	Jer 23:9-12; 13-15
Zephaniah	Zeph 1:17-18

for **VIOLENCE**
Habakkuk	Hab 2:12-14; 17
Isaiah	Is 3:16-4:1
Jeremiah	Jer 22:13-19

through **WITNESS**
Amos	Amos 3:13-15

of **PURIFICATION**
in **NEW AGE**
John the Baptist	Mt 3:1-12; Lk 3:15-17

through **RECONCILIATION**
Isaiah	Is 4:2-6
Jerusalemites	Zech 12:1-13:6

of **QUALITY OF LIFE**
as **BLESSING**
Jacob	Gen 49:1-28

as **CAPTIVITY**
Shallum	Jer 22:10-12

as **DEATH**
Isaiah	Is 40:1-11

as **DESPAIR**
Isaiah	Is 51:17-52:12

as **DESTRUCTION**
Jeremiah	Jer 4:30-31
Joel	Joel 1:2-20

as **EVIL**
Isaiah	Is 32:1-8

as **GOOD**
Isaiah	Is 32:1-8

as **HEALING**
Isaiah	Is 52:13-53:12

as **INNOCENCE**
Isaiah	Is 52:13-53:12

as **OPPRESSION**
Ephraimites	Hos 9:1-6
Joel	Joel 1:2-20

condition for **REWARDs**
Jeremiah	Jer 17:11

as **SADNESS**
Isaiah	Is 15:1-16:14
Joel	Joel 1:2-20

as **SPIRIT**

as **SPIRIT** (cont'd)
Believers	1 Cor 14:26-33

as **SUFFERING**
Ephraimites	Hos 9:1-6
Isaiah	Is 33:7-16; 51:17-52:12
Jeremiah	Jer 4:30-31

of **RECONCILIATION**
Judahites	Jer 27:16-22

from **CAPTIVITY**
Jeremiah	Jer 23:1-8

through **COMPASSION**
Israelites	Hos 11:8-9
Judahites	Jer 12:14-17

through **DEATH**
Jesus	Jn 12:27-36a

through **DESTRUCTION**
Isaiah	Is 25:6-9

from **EVIL**
Isaiah	Is 25:6-9; 52:13-53:12

through **FAITH**
Tyre	Is 23:15-18

of **FAMILY**
Baruch	*Bar 5:5-9

through **FEAR**
Israelites	Hos 11:10-11

through **FULFILLMENT**
Israelites	Mic 4:9-5:6
Jeremiah	Jer 31:38-40

through **GRACE**
Ammonites	Jer 49:1-6
Elamites	Jer 49:34-39
Isaiah	Is 4:2-6; 27:7-11; 52:13-53:12; 54:1-17
Israelites	Jer 31:31-34; 50:1-46; Hos 14:4-8; Zeph 3:14-20
Judahites	Jer 12:14-17
Moabites	Jer 48:1-47

from **GUILT**
Isaiah	Is 27:7-11

through **HEALING**
Israelites	Hos 6:10-7:2; 14:4-8

through **HOPE**
Jeremiah	Jer 29:1-23
Micah	Mic 2:12-13

through **JUSTICE**
Isaiah	Is 1:27-31

through **LEADERSHIP**
Micah	Mic 2:12-13
Obadiah	Obad 1:17-21

to **LIFE**
Isaiah	Is 11:1-9

to **ONENESS**
Jeremiah	Jer 32:26-44

through **OPPRESSION**
Isaiah	Is 27:12-13
Micah	Mic 4:1-8

through **PEACE**
Elijah	Mal 4:4-6
Isaiah	Is 19:18-25; 51:17-52:12

through **PURIFICATION**
Isaiah	Is 4:2-6
Jerusalemites	Zech 12:1-13:6

through **REPENTANCE**
Isaiah   Is 59:1-21
Jeremiah   Jer 26:7-19;
                       29:1-23
Judahites   Jer 7:1-15;
                       35:6-17
Tyre   Is 23:15-18
through **SERVICE**
Tyre   Is 23:15-18
through **VICTORY**
Israelites   Nah 2:1-5
through **WEALTH**
Jeremiah   Jer 32:26-44
Judahites   Zeph 2:4-7
of **REJECTION**
caused by in**FIDELITY**
Isaiah   Is 29:15-16
Jesus   Mt 26:31-35;
                       Mk 14:27-31;
                       Lk 22:14-23;
                       31-32;
                       33-34;
                       Jn 13:1-20;
                       21-30;
                       36-38;
                       16:29-33
Judahites   2 Chr 24:1-27
Peter   Mt 26:69-75;
                       Mk 14:66-72;
                       Lk 22:54b-62;
                       Jn 18:12-27
caused by dis**HONESTY**
Prophets   Jer 27:12-15;
                       16-22
of **LAW**
Israelites   Hos 4:4-15
of **NEW AGE**
Jesus   Mk 8:34-9:1;
                       Lk 9:23-27
of **PRAYER**
Israelites   Mic 3:1-12
Jeremiah   Jer 14:10-12
Moab   Is 15:1-16:14
Samuel   1 Sam 8:1-22
of **PROVIDENCE**
Isaiah   Is 5:8-24a
as **PUNISHMENT**
Ephraimites   Hos 9:10-17
Isaiah   Is 8:5-8a;
                       10:5-16;
                       17:9-11;
                       28:1-13;
                       30:1-7
Israelites   Ezek 16:35-43;
                       Hos 4:4-15;
                       11:5-7
                       Amos 4:6-12;
                       5:4-6;
                       Mic 3:1-12;
                       Hag 1:15a;
                       2:15-19
Jeremiah   Jer 13:20-27;
                       19:1-15;
                       29:1-23;
                       32:26-44;
                       34:13-22;
                       *Sir 49:4-7
Jesus   Lk 19:41-44
Judahites   Jer 9:10-22
People   Acts 3:1-26

as **PUNISHMENT** (cont'd)
Priests   Mal 1:6-2:9
Sennacherib   Is 37:22-29
Shemaiah   Jer 29:24-32
Zedekiah   Jer 27:12-15
revealing dis**RESPECT**
Isaiah   Is 22:1-14;
                       52:13-53:12
of **SIN**
Isaiah   Is 2:6-11;
                       3:8-12
Jerusalemites   Zeph 3:1-5
Jesus   Jn 6:60-71
of **TRUTH**
Amaziah   Amos 7:10-17
Apostles   Jude 1:17-19
Israelites   Jer 44:15-19
Judahites   Jer 25:1-7;
                       35:6-7
Paul   1 Tim 4:1-5
People   Jer 43:1-3
Zedekiah   Jer 37:1-2
of **REPENTANCE**
through **FIDELITY**
Prophets   2 Chr 24:1-27
as **MOTIVATION**
Israelites   2 Kgs 17:7-23
of **SIN**
Isaiah   Is 17:7-8
as **VIRTUE**
Isaiah   Is 1:27-31
of **RESPECT**
revealing **GRIEF**
Isaiah   Is 52:13-53:12
revealing **HUMILITY**
Edomites   Obad 1:1b-4
God   Zeph 2:8-12
Isaiah   Is 30:1-7;
                       60:1-22
in **SADNESS**
Isaiah   Is 52:13-53:12
in **WEALTH**
Isaiah   Is 61:1-11
in **WISDOM**
Judahites   Jer 8:8-13
of dis**RESPECT**
results in **ALIENATION**
Israelites   Deut 28:15-68
revealing **BLASPHEMY**
Ezekiel   Ezek 24:15-24
through **IDOLATRY**
Isaiah   Is 17:7-8
in **REJECTION**
Isaiah   Is 22:1-14;
                       52:13-53:12
of **RESURRECTION**
from **DEATH**
Jesus   Mt 17:22-23;
                       20:17-19;
                       Mk 9:30-32;
                       Lk 18:31-34;
                       Jn 2:12-22;
                       16:25-28
of **REVENGE**
in **CONFRONTATION**
Micah   Mic 4:9-5:6

as **HERESY** (cont'd)
Jesus	Mt 24:9-14; 23-28; Mk 13:14-23

as **OPPRESSION**
Jesus	Mt 24:15-22; Mk 13:14-23; Lk 21:7-19; 20-24
Nineveh	Nah 2:11-13

of **ORDER**
Jesus	Mt 24:32-33; Mk 13:28-37; Lk 21:29-31

as **SUFFERING**
Amos	Amos 1:1-2
Jesus	Mt 24:4-8; 15-22; Mk 13:3-8; 14-23; Lk 17:22-37; 21:7-19

of **TEMPTATION**
Jesus	Mt 24:23-28; Mk 13:14-23

as **VIOLENCE**
Jesus	Mt 24:1-3; 4-8; Mk 13:3-8; Lk 21:7-19

SIGNS of
HOPE in
Isaiah	Is 7:10-17; 37:30-32

of **SIGNS**
of **ACCEPTANCE**
Joseph	Gen 40:1-23

of **BLASPHEMY**
Jesus	Mt 24:9-14; 15-22; 23-28; Mk 13:14-23; Lk 21:7-19

of **CAPTIVITY**
Egyptian	Is 20:1-6

of **CONDEMNATION**
Haggai	Hag 2:10-14

of **DEATH**
Ezekiel	Ezek 24:15-24
Joseph	Gen 40:1-23

of **DESPAIR**
Isaiah	Is 7:18-25

of **ENEMY**
Isaiah	2 Kgs 19:9b-37

of **FAMILY**
Angel	*2 Esd 9:38-10:59

of **FEAR**
Jesus	Lk 21:25-28

of **FULFILLMENT**
Elijah	Mk 9:9-13
Isaiah	Is 27:7-11; 38:1-22; 48:1-22; Mt 13:34-35
Jesus	Mt 21:1-11; 24:1-3; 29-31; 32-33;

of **FULFILLMENT** (cont'd)
Jesus	37-41; Mk 13:24-27; 28-37; Lk 21:29-31
Joel	Acts 2:14-36
John the Baptist	Mt 17:9-13
Joseph	Gen 40:1-23; 41:1-57
Prophet	1 Kgs 13:1-34
Samuel	1 Sam 9:1-10:16

of **GRIEF**
Jeremiah	Mt 2:16-18

of **HATE**
Jesus	Mt 24:9-14; Mk 13:9-13; Lk 21:7-19

of **INDIFFERENCE**
Jesus	Lk 17:22-37

of **JUSTICE**
Angel	*2 Esd 4:33-52

of **KILLING**
Jesus	Mt 24:9-14

of **LEADERSHIP**
Israelites	Hos 3:1-5

of **MIRACLE**
Isaiah	2 Kgs 20:1-11
Jeroboam	1 Kgs 13:1-34
Jesus	Jn 1:19-51
Micah	Mic 1:2-4; 7:7-20

of **POVERTY**
Joseph	Gen 41:1-57

of **REJECTION**
Jesus	Lk 17:22-37

of **SACREDNESS**
Haggai	Hag 2:10-14; *1 Esd 6:1-2
Zechariah	*1 Esd 6:1-2

of **VICTORY**
Isaiah	Is 7:10-17

of **WITNESS**
Believers	1 Cor 14:13-25
Ezekiel	Ezek 11:22-25
Isaiah	Is 8:16-18

of **SIN**
causing **ALIENATION**
Isaiah	Is 29:17-24; 52:13-53:12
Jesus	Mt 24:9-14

of **BLASPHEMY**
Isaiah	Is 3:8-12
Jerusalemites	Zeph 3:1-5
Sennacherib	Is 37:22-29

of **COVETOUSNESS**
Micah	Mic 2:1-10

resulting in **DEATH**
Jeremiah	Jer 31:29-30

resulting in **DESTRUCTION**
Eliezer	2 Chr 17:1-20:37
Isaiah	Is 1:27-31
Moses	Num 32:6-15

of **DISOBEDIENCE**
Isaiah	Is 3:8-12

of **DOUBT**
Jerusalemites	Zeph 3:1-5

through **EVIL**
Isaiah	Is 24:16b-18b
Jerusalemites	Zeph 3:1-5

forgiven by **GRACE**
Isaiah   Is 33:17-24;
    40:1-11
Israelites   Ezek 16:53-63
of **HATE**
Prophet   Hos 9:7-9
of **IDOLATRY**
Ahijah   1 Kgs 14:1-18
Jeremiah   Jer 5:1-14
in **LEADERSHIP**
Isaiah   Is 9:8-10:4
Jerusalemites   Zeph 3:1-5
causing **OPPRESSION**
Isaiah   Is 52:13-53:12
Micah   Mic 2:1-10
of **PRIDE**
Edomites   Obad 1:1b-4
Ezekiel   Ezek 16:44-52
Nineveh   Zeph 2:15
in **REVENGE**
Judahites   Jer 25:8-14
causing **SACRIFICE**
Isaiah   Is 52:13-53:12
in **SEX**
Jeremiah   Jer 5:1-14;
    13:20-27
causing **SUFFERING**
Isaiah   Is 52:13-53:12

of **SPIRIT**
as **GIFT**
Elders   Num 11:24b-30
Holy Spirit   Joel 2:28-29
as **QUALITY OF LIFE**
Believers   1 Cor 14:26-33

of **STEWARDSHIP**
concerning **DEATH**
Isaiah   2 Kgs 20:1-11
concerning **DESTRUCTION**
Isaiah   Is 60:1-22
Israelites   Jer 51:1-64
concerning **FAMILY**
Isaiah   Is 54:1-17
in **FULFILLMENT**
Isaiah   Is 52:13-53:12
in **LIFE**
Isaiah   2 Kgs 20:1-11
in **ORDER**
Isaiah   Is 18:1-7
as **WITNESS**
Jesus   Mk 8:34-9:1;
    Lk 9:23-27

of **SUFFERING**
in **PRESENCE**
Israelites   Amos 5:16-17
in **PROVIDENCE**
Isaiah   Is 17:1-6
Israelites   Is 14:1-23
as **PUNISHMENT**
Elijah   2 Chr 21:1-23:21
Ephraimites   Hos 9:10-17;
    13:12-14
Habakkuk   Hab 2:6b-8
Haggai   Hag 1:1-11
Huldah   2 Chr 34:1-35:27
Isaiah   Is 8:19-22;
    17:9-11;
    24:1-12;
    29:1-8

as **PUNISHMENT** (cont'd)
Jeremiah   Jer 4:19-22;
    10:17-22;
    14:1-6;
    10-12;
    21:1-10
Jesus   Lk 23:27-32
Moab   Is 15:1-16:14
Moabites   Jer 48:1-47
People   Zech 14:1-21
Prophets   Jer 23:9-12;
    13-15
Zephaniah   Zeph 1:17-18
as **QUALITY OF LIFE**
Ephraimites   Hos 9:1-6
Isaiah   Is 33:7-16;
    51:17-52:12
Jeremiah   Jer 4:30-31
in **SALVATION**
Jesus   Mt 24:9-14;
    Mk 13:9-13;
    Lk 21:7-19
caused by **SIN**
Isaiah   Is 52:13-53:12

of **TEMPERANCE**
in **RITE**
Nazirites   Amos 2:9-12

of **VICTORY**
in **BROTHERHOOD**
Jesus   Mt 16:13-20
in **CONFRONTATION**
Ahithophel   2 Sam 16:15-17:29
Babylonians   Jer 46:13-26
Balaam   Num 24:14-25
Deborah   Judg 4:6-9
Elisha   2 Kgs 3:1-27;
    13:14-19
Hezekiah   Is 38:1-22
Isaiah   Is 29:1-8
Israelites   Zech 9:13-17
Jerusalemites   Zech 14:1-21
Joshua   Josh 17:14-18
Samuel   1 Sam 15:1-35
in **NEW AGE**
Balaam   Num 23:27-24:13
Isaiah   Is 9:1;
    25:6-9;
    51:17-52:12;
    13-53:12
Jesus   Mt 26:57-68;
    Mk 14:53-65;
    Lk 21:25-28
Obadiah   Obad 1:17-21
through **PROVIDENCE**
Ahab   1 Kgs 20:1-43
Amaziah   2 Chr 25:1-28
Ehud   Judg 3:26-30
Isaiah   2 Kgs 19:9b-37;
    Is 9:2-7;
    11:10-16;
    14:1-23;
    26:1-6;
    37:33-35;
    40:12-31;
    51:17-52:12
Jacobites   Mic 5:7-15
Jahaziel   2 Chr 17:1-20:37

through **PROVIDENCE** (cont'd)
Jerusalemites	Zech 12:1-13:6
Joshua	Josh 10:16-27
Judahites	Zech 12:1-13:6
Micah	Mic 4:9-5:6

in **RECONCILIATION**
Israelites	Nah 2:1-5

in **RESURRECTION**
Jesus	Mt 16:21-28;
	20:17-19;
	Lk 9:18-22;
	18:31-34;
	Jn 2:12-22

in **SALVATION**
Isaiah	Is 11:10-16;
	51:17-52:12
Jesus	Mt 16:21-28;
	24:9-14;
	Mk 8:34-9:1;
	30-32;
	13:9-13;
	Lk 9:23-27;
	21:7-19

in **VIRTUE**
Isaiah	Is 52:13-53:12

of **VIOLENCE**
in **CONFRONTATION**
Ammonites	Jer 49:1-6
Babylonians	Jer 43:8-13;
	50:1-46;
	51:1-64
Damascenes	Jer 49:23-27
Edomites	Jer 49:7-22
Egyptians	Jer 46:2-12;
	13-26
Ephraimites	Hos 7:13-16
Gog	Ezek 38:10-13
Hazorites	Jer 49:28-33
Israelites	Deut 28:15-68;
	Hos 10:9-15;
	11:5-7;
	Amos 6:12-14;
	Nah 2:1-5
Jeremiah	Jer 6:1-8;
	21:1-10
Jerusalemites	Zech 12:1-13:6;
	14:1-21
Joel	Joel 1:2-20
Judahites	Jer 25:8-14;
	37:3-10
Micah	Mic 4:9-5:6
Moabites	Jer 48:1-47
Nineveh	Nah 3:5-19
Philistines	Jer 47:1-7
Samaria	Hos 13:15-16
Samaritans	Amos 3:11-12
Tyre	Ezek 26:7-14

in **NEW AGE**
Angel	*2 Esd 5:1-15

through **PROVIDENCE**
Egyptians	Is 19:1-15

as **PUNISHMENT**
Habakkuk	Hab 2:12-14;
	17
Isaiah	Is 3:16-4:1
Jeremiah	Jer 22:13-19

of **VIRTUE**
in **ACCEPTANCE**
Isaiah	Is 52:13-53:12

as **BLESSING**
Isaiah	Is 3:8-12

in **JUSTICE**
Isaiah	Is 28:14-22
Jeremiah	Jer 22:1-9;
	23:1-8

in **LEADERSHIP**
Isaiah	Is 9:2-7;
	32:1-8

in **REPENTANCE**
Isaiah	Is 1:27-31

in **VICTORY**
Isaiah	Is 52:13-53:12

concerning **WEALTH**
Isaiah	2 Kgs 20:12-21
Jeremiah	Jer 20:1-6

through dis**HONESTY**
Jeremiah	Jer 17:11

through **PROVIDENCE**
Isaiah	Is 52:13-53:12

through **RECONCILIATION**
Jeremiah	Jer 32:26-44
Judahites	Zeph 2:4-7

of **WILL**
in **SALVATION**
Jesus	Mt 24:15-22;
	Mk 13:14-23

on **WISDOM**
of **AUTHORITY**
Holy Spirit	Jn 16:12-15

in **NEW AGE**
Hezekiah	*Sir 48:17-25
Isaiah	Is 35:1-10
Zechariah	Lk 1:57-80

through **PROVIDENCE**
Isaiah	Is 29:9-12
Jesus	Mk 13:9-13;
	Lk 21:7-19
Solomon	*Wis 11:1-20

of **WITNESS**
to **AUTHORITY**
John	Rev 11:1-14

through **COMPULSION**
God	Amos 3:3-8

as **GIFT**
Believers	1 Cor 14:1-12

as **MOTIVATION**
Holy Spirit	2 Pet 1:19b-21

in **NEW AGE**
John the Baptist	Mt 3:1-12;
	Lk 3:15-17

to **PRESENCE**
Isaiah	Is 60:1-22
Micah	Mic 1:2-4

to **PROVIDENCE**
Isaiah	Is 12:1-6

to **PUNISHMENT**
Amos	Amos 3:13-15

to **SALVATION**
Believers	1 Pet 1:10-12
Isaiah	Is 62:1-12
Mankind	Is 51:17-52:12

through **STEWARDSHIP**
Jesus	Mk 8:34-9:1;
	Lk 9:23-27

to **TRUTH**

to **TRUTH** (cont'd)

Holy Spirit	1 Pet 1:10-12
Isaiah	Is 40:1-11
Jeremiah	Jer 51:1-64
Jesus	Mt 24:9-14;
	Mk 13:9-13;
	Lk 21:7-19

PROVIDENCE

ACCEPTANCE of
  of **DEITY**

Cyrus	Is 45:14-25
Jacob	Gen 28:10-22
Job	Job 1:20-21;
	2:9-10

  INSTRUCTION on

God	Is 46:1-13
James	Jas 4:13-16
Preacher	Eccl 5:8-20

  through **MESSIANIC FIGURE**

Jesus	Jn 18:1-11

  PROPHECY of

Zedekiah	Jer 27:12-15

  REVELATION of

People	Jer 27:1-11

  through **SELF-REALIZATION**

Magicians	Ex 8:16-19

ALIENATION from
  of **DEITY**

Israelites	2 Kgs 10:32-33

ANGER in
  PROPHECY of

Elamites	Jer 49:34-39

  REVELATION of

Israelites	Ezek 20:32-39

ANXIETY concerning the
  of **DEITY**

Habakkuk	Hab 1:12-17

BLESSING through

Moses	Lev 26:1-46;
	Deut 2:1-25

  of **DEITY**

Assyrians	Is 19:18-25
Baruch	*Bar 5:1-4
Believers	Ps 97:10-12
David	Ps 13:5-6;
	16:5-8;
	18:31-42;
	22:6-11;
	23:1-4;
	5-6;
	89:19-37
Egyptians	Is 19:18-25
God	Ps 67:1-7;
	68:4-14;
	107:33-38;
	113:5-9;
	127:1-2;
	147:12-20
Isaac	Gen 25:7-11
Israelites	Deut 4:32-40;
	2 Chr 30:1-31:21;
	Ps 78:40-55;

  of **DEITY** (cont'd)

Israelites	105:23-25;
	Is 19:18-25;
	Hos 2:16-20;
	13:4-6;
	Amos 2:9-12
Joseph	Gen 39:1-23
Judahites	2 Chr 17:1-20:37
Mankind	Ps 8:3-8;
	Zech 10:1-2
Melchizedek	Gen 14:17-20
Nebuchadnezzar	*Bar 1:5-14
Psalmist	Ps 66:8-12;
	85:1-3;
	92:5-11
Solomon	1 Chr 28:1-29:30

  INSTRUCTION on

God	Ps 81:5c-16
Moses	Deut 6:20-25;
	16:13-15;
	28:1-14
Nehemiah	Neh 2:19-20
Paul	2 Cor 9:6-11

  PROPHECY on

Balaam	Num 22:41-23:12;
	13-26;
	27-24:13
Isaiah	Is 52:13-53:12
Israelites	Deut 30:11-14;
	Is 30:18-26;
	Jer 31:27-28;
	Hos 12:10-14;
	14:4-8

  REVELATION on

Balaam	Num 22:5-14
Ezekiel	Ezek 16:1-7;
	17:22-24
God	Is 42:5-17
Isaiah	Is 55:1-13
Israelites	Ezek 36:8-15;
	37-38;
	Hos 2:14-15;
	Mic 6:1-5
Jeremiah	Jer 31:7-14
Joel	Joel 2:18-27
Nathan	2 Sam 7:1-29;
	1 Chr 17:1-27

in **CAPTIVITY**

Manasseh	2 Chr 33:1-25

  by **DEITY**

God	Ps 107:10-16
Joseph	Ps 105:16-22

  PROPHECY of

Jeremiah	Jer 28:1-17
Judahites	Jer 27:16-22
Zedekiah	Jer 27:12-15

over **CHAOS**
  by **DEITY**

Philistines	1 Sam 7:2-17

through **COMPASSION**
  of **DEITY**

God	Gen 3:20-24;
	Ps 103:6-13
Jonah	Jon 4:1-11
Solomon	*Wis 18:20-25

  for **FOLLOWER**

God	Ps 135:13-14

JOY in (cont'd)

David	Ps 20:1-5; 30:11-12; 31:1-8; 63:1-8
Ezra	*1 Esd 8:25-27
God	Ps 127:3-5; Eccl 1:12-2:26; 6:1-12
Habakkuk	Hab 3:16-19
Israelites	1 Kgs 8:62-66; Ezra 6:19-22
Preacher	Eccl 5:8-20
Psalmist	Ps 92:1-4; 126:1-3

JUSTICE in

God	Ezra 9:6-15; Ps 140:12-13
Hannah	1 Sam 2:1-10

in LEADERSHIP

Adversaries	Ps 83:9-18
David	2 Sam 22:1-51; Ps 18:43-45; 23:1-4; 139:7-12
Ephraimites	Ps 78:9-20
God	Ps 136:10-22; Prov 10:1-32
Isaiah	Is 63:7-64:12
Israelites	Ex 13:17-22; 32:30-35; Deut 8:11-20; Josh 5:13-15; Neh 9:12-15; Ps 105:43-45; 107:4-9
Paul	2 Cor 3:4-6

LIFE through

Believers	Ps 145:13b-20
David	Ps 17:13-14; 22:12-21; 30:1-5; 40:13-17; 138:7-8
Elihu	Job 33:23-25; 29-30
Elijah	1 Kgs 17:1-24; 19:1-21
Ephraimites	Ps 78:9-20
God	Ps 33:13-19; 37:23-40; 46:8-11; 104:10-13; 14-18; 19-23; 27-30; 111:5-9; 136:23-25; 147:7-11; Prov 20:1-30; Eccl 3:9-15; Is 27:2-6; Jn 1:1-18; 2 Cor 5:1-5
Hezekiah	Is 38:1-22
Isaac	Gen 26:1-11; 12-31
Israelites	Ex 9:1-7; 13-35; 10:21-23;

LIFE through (cont'd)

Israelites	11:1-10; 12:1-14; 13:17-22; 16:1-21; 17:1-7; Deut 8:1-10; Neh 9:12-15; Ps 78:21-31; 105:37-42; Is 1:4-9; 10:17-19; 43:14-44:5
Jesus	Jn 1:1-18
Job	Job 12:7-12
King	Ps 21:1-7; 61:6-7
Mankind	Prov 16:1-33; Eccl 9:1-16
Peter	2 Pet 1:3-4
Psalmist	Ps 49:13-15

LOVE in

Believers	1 Cor 2:6-9
Ezra	*2 Esd 3:1-36
Israelites	Hos 11:1-4
Jesus	2 Thes 2:16-17
Job	Job 10:8-12
Psalmist	Ps 116:1-11

in MARRIAGE

God	Prov 19:1-29
Samson	Judg 14:1-4

MIRACLE through

Assyrians	2 Kgs 19:9b-37
Elijah	1 Kgs 17:1-24
Elisha	2 Kgs 2:19-22; 4:42-44
Ephraimites	Ps 78:9-20
Ezekiel	Ezek 33:21-22
God	Ps 66:5-7; 135:8-12; 136:10-22; Hab 3:3-15
Isaiah	Is 63:7-64:12
Israelites	Ex 13:17-22; 14:15-22; Num 11:31-35; Josh 6:15-21; Neh 9:9-11; 12-15; Ps 78:21-31; 106:6-12; Is 42:18-43:7
Jonah	Jon 4:1-11
Samson	Judg 15:9-20

through OBEDIENCE

Mankind	Ps 1:1-3

through OPPRESSION

David	Ps 89:38-51
God	Ps 107:39-43
Israelites	Ps 107:4-9

through ORDER

Amos	Amos 3:3-8
God	Ps 65:9-13; 104:10-13; 107:23-32; 147:7-11; Jer 31:35-37

through PATIENCE

Jeremiah	Lam 3:1-66

PEACE through

Asa	2 Chr 14:1-16:14
Believers	Prov 16:1-33
God	Is 2:1-5
Isaiah	Is 63:7-64:12

over **POVERTY**

David	Ps 9:17-20; 35:9-10
Eliphaz	Job 5:8-17
God	Ps 68:4-14; 113:5-9; 146:5-7b
Hannah	1 Sam 2:1-10

PRAISE for

Asaph	Ps 76:4-6
Daniel	Dan 2:20-23
David	2 Sam 22:1-51; 18:46-50; 29:3-9; 30:1-5; 35:9-10; 40:4-5; 139:13-18
Isaiah	Is 26:7-19
Jesus	Jn 9:1-41; 1 Pet 4:7-11
Psalmist	Ps 66:5-7; 66:13-20; 84:10-12; 98:1-3; 148:7-14

PURIFICATION through

God	Is 1:24-26

REJECTION of

David	Ps 60:1-5
Ephraimites	Hos 7:13-16
Followers	Ps 80:8-13
Israelites	Neh 9:16-18; Ps 78:9-20; Jer 2:1-13; Amos 4:6-12
Psalmist	Ps 88:15-18
Sinners	2 Pet 3:3-7

through **REPENTANCE**

God	2 Tim 2:20-26
Israelites	*Bar 2:27-35

REVENGE in

David	Ps 18:46-50
God	1 Sam 25:1-44

REWARDs in

God	Ps 127:3-5
Israelites	Ps 105:43-45

in **SACRIFICE**

Abraham	Gen 22:1-19

SERVICE through

Jesus	Mk 1:12-13

over **SUFFERING**

Asaph	Ps 77:1-10
David	Ps 20:1-5; 31:1-8; 32:3-7; 34:4-10; 60:1-5
Elihu	Job 36:5-15; 16-25
Followers	Ps 80:4-7
God	Ps 107:33-38; 39-43; 140:12-13; 146:7c-9; 147:1-6

over **SUFFERING** (cont'd)

Israelites	Ps 78:32-39
Psalmist	Ps 88:3-9; 15-18; 119:49-56
Sirach	*Sir 35:12-20
Solomon	*Wis 16:1-14

in **VICTORY**

Abijah	2 Chr 13:1-22
Asa	2 Chr 14:1-16:14
Believers	Ps 47:1-4; Eph 6:10-18
Cyrus	Is 44:24-45:13
David	2 Sam 8:1-18; 22:1-51; 1 Chr 18:1-20:8; Ps 9:1-4; 18:16-19; 46-50; 20:6-9; 21:8-13; 22:1-5; 27:1-3; 4-6; 35:9-10; 59:16-17; 61:4-5; 89:19-37; 110:5-7; 124:1-5; 144:9-11
Gideon	Judg 8:1-3
God	Ps 33:13-19; 48:4-8; 55:15-19; 68:4-14; 19-23; 69:29-36; 89:5-18; 118:15-21; 136:10-22; 149:1-4; Prov 21:1-31
Hezekiah	2 Kgs 20:1-11
Isaiah	Is 59:1-21
Israelites	Ex 3:7-10; Num 21:33-35; Deut 1:19-46; 2:26-3:11; 12-22; 9:1-6; 12:1-31; 31:1-8; Josh 11:16-23; Judg 4:10-16; 7:16-22; 1 Sam 19:1-10; 1 Chr 15:1-16:43; Neh 4:13-23; Ps 44:1-3; 4-8; 105:7-15; 23-25; 106:6-12; Is 43:14-44:5
Jacob	Gen 46:1-7
Jephthah	Judg 11:29-33
Jeroboam	2 Kgs 14:23-29
Jesus	Rom 8:1-4; Col 2:6-15

REVELATION on (cont'd)
Jeremiah   Jer 1:11-12;
                         31:7-14
Jesus   Jn 12:20-26

through **GOOD**
of **DEITY**
Believers   Ps 92:12-15;
                         Rom 8:28-39
God   Ps 85:8-13;
                         118:15-21
James   Jas 1:16-18
Sirach   *Sir 39:28-35
INSTRUCTION on
Eliphaz   Job 5:18-27

through **GRACE**
of **DEITY**
David   Ps 23:5-6
God   Ps 147:1-6
Israelites   2 Kgs 13:22-25;
                         Neh 9:19-21;
                         Is 1:4-9
Jesus   2 Thes 2:16-17
Solomon   *Wis 16:1-14
INSTRUCTION on
Paul   1 Cor 3:5-9
PROPHECY of
Isaiah   Is 60:1-22
REVELATION on
Ezekiel   Ezek 16:8-14;
                         17:22-24
Israelites   Is 51:17-52:12
Jeremiah   Jer 31:2-6
Joel   Joel 2:18-27

GRATITUDE for
of **DEITY**
David   Ps 30:11-12;
                         40:6-10;
                         52:8-9;
                         54:6-7;
                         86:11-13;
                         144:1-2
Isaiah   Is 26:7-19
INSTRUCTION on
Psalmist   Ps 107:4-9;
                         10-16;
                         17-22;
                         23-32;
                         136:4-9;
                         10-22;
                         23-25;
                         26
REVELATION on
Isaiah   Is 51:1-16
in **WORSHIP**
David   2 Sam 22:1-51

GRIEF in
of **DEITY**
Psalmist   Ps 119:25-32
PROPHECY of
Egyptians   Is 19:1-15

HEALING through
of **DEITY**
Abimelech   Gen 20:1-18
David   Ps 41:1-3

of **DEITY** (cont'd)
God   Ps 103:1-5;
                         146:7c-9
People   Ps 107:17-22
REVELATION on
Israelites   Ezek 34:11-16
Jeremiah   Jer 30:12-17

HOPE in
of **DEITY**
David   Ps 9:17-20
Eliphaz   Job 5:8-17
Jesus   2 Thes 2:16-17
Psalmist   Ps 130:5-6
INSTRUCTION on
Psalmist   Ps 130:7-8
through **MESSIANIC FIGURE**
Gentiles   Mt 12:15-21;
                         Rom 15:1-13
PROPHECY of
Elisha   2 Kgs 6:32-7:2
Isaiah   Is 29:1-8;
                         30:18-26
REVELATION on
Ezekiel   Ezek 17:22-24

HUMILITY concerning
of **DEITY**
David   Ps 144:3-4
God   Ps 149:1-4
Israelites   Deut 8:1-10
Mankind   Ps 18:25-30
PROPHECY of
Isaiah   Is 2:6-11;
                         17:1-6
REVELATION on
Israelites   Zeph 3:11-13
Paul   2 Cor 12:1-10

IDOLATRY revealed in
of **DEITY**
Solomon   *Wis 14:1-11

IGNORANCE of
of **DEITY**
Elihu   Job 34:34-37
Ephraimites   Hos 11:1-4
Israelites   Judg 2:6-10;
                         Hos 2:2-8
Mankind   Prov 20:1-30
through **FALSE BELIEF**
Isaiah   Is 44:9-20
INSTRUCTION on
Preacher   Eccl 9:1-16

INDIFFERENCE to
of **DEITY**
Isaiah   Is 63:7-64:12
Pharaoh   Ex 9:8-12;
                         10:1-20;
                         27;
                         11:1-10;
                         14:1-14;
                         15-22

INSTRUCTION on
over **ENEMY**
God   *2 Esd 1:4-23

for **FAMILY**
  Moses   Deut 31:30-32:47
through **GOOD**
  Eliphaz   Job 5:18-27
through **GRACE**
  Paul   1 Cor 3:5-9
concerning **IGNORANCE**
  Preacher   Eccl 9:1-16
of **LEADERSHIP**
  Joshua   Josh 24:1-13
  Moses   Deut 29:1-15
in **LIFE**
  God   Gen 9:1-7
through **LOVE**
  Moses   Deut 30:1-10
through **OBEDIENCE**
  Achior   *Jdt 5:1-21
through **PATIENCE**
  Sirach   *Sir 11:10-13
concerning **POVERTY**
  Moses   Lev 23:15-22;
                   Deut 14:22-29
through **PRUDENCE**
  Isaiah   Is 28:23-29
through **TEMPTATION**
  Paul   1 Cor 10:1-13
in **VICTORY**
  Joshua   Josh 24:1-13
concerning **WEALTH**
  Jesus   Lk 12:22-31
concerning **WISDOM**
  Jesus   Mk 4:10-20
  Paul   2 Tim 2:1-7
  Solomon   Prov 2:1-22
for **YOUTH**
  Jesus   Mt 18:5-6;
                   Lk 9:46-48;
                   17:1-6

in **JEALOUSY**
  of **DEITY**
    Israelites   Rom 11:7-24

JOY in
  of **DEITY**
    Asaph   Ps 75:9-10
    Baruch   *Bar 5:5-9
    David   Ps 20:1-5;
                  30:11-12;
                  31:1-8;
                  63:1-8
    Ezra   *1 Esd 8:25-27
    God   Ps 127:3-5;
                  Eccl 1:12-2:26;
                  6:1-12
    Habakkuk   Hab 3:16-19
    Israelites   1 Kgs 8:62-66;
                  Ezra 6:19-22
    Preacher   Eccl 5:8-20
    Psalmist   Ps 92:1-4;
                  126:1-3
  INSTRUCTION on
    Moses   Deut 26:1-11
  PROPHECY of
    Isaiah   Is 9:2-7;
                  60:1-22
    Jeremiah   Jer 32:26-44
  REVELATION on
    Isaiah   Is 51:5-16
    Jeremiah   Jer 33:10-11
    Joel   Joel 2:18-27

JUSTICE in
  of **DEITY**
    God   Ezra 9:6-15;
                  Ps 140:12-13
    Hannah   1 Sam 2:1-10
  INSTRUCTION on
    Angel   *2 Esd 5:43-6:6
  REVELATION on
    Israelites   Ezek 34:11-16

in **LEADERSHIP**
  Moses   Ex 23:20-33
  by **DEITY**
    Adversaries   Ps 83:9-18
    David   2 Sam 22:1-51;
                  Ps 18:43-45;
                  23:1-4;
                  139:7-12
    Ephraimites   Ps 78:9-20
    God   Ps 136:10-22;
                  Prov 10:1-32
    Isaiah   Is 63:7-64:12
    Israelites   Ex 13:17-22;
                  32:30-35;
                  Deut 8:11-20;
                  Josh 5:13-15;
                  Neh 9:12-15;
                  Ps 105:43-45;
                  107:4-9
    Paul   2 Cor 3:4-6

LEADERSHIP through
  of **FOLLOWERs**
    Israelites   Num 10:11-28;
                  33-36
  INSTRUCTION on
    Joshua   Josh 24:1-13
    Moses   Deut 29:1-15
  of **MESSIANIC FIGURE**
    Jesus   Lk 1:26-38
  PROPHECY of
    Isaiah   Is 9:2-7
    Jeremiah   Jer 23:1-8
  REVELATION on
    David   Ezek 34:23-24
    Isaiah   Is 55:1-13;
                  58:1-14
    Israelites   Is 48:1-22;
                  Jer 3:14b-18;
                  Ezek 20:9-26;
                  32-39
    John   Rev 7:9-17

LIFE through
  in **COVENANT**
    God   Gen 1:24-31
  of **DEITY**
    Believers   Ps 145:13b-20
    David   Ps 17:13-14;
                  22:12-21;
                  30:1-5;
                  40:13-17;
                  138:7-8
    Elihu   Job 33:23-25;
                  29-30
    Elijah   1 Kgs 17:1-24;
                  19:1-21
    Ephraimites   Ps 78:9-20
    God   Ps 33:13-19;
                  37:23-40;

of **DEITY** (cont'd)

Isaiah	Is 63:7-64:12
Israelites	Ex 13:17-22;
	14:15-22;
	Num 11:31-35;
	Josh 6:15-21;
	Neh 9:9-11;
	12-15;
	Ps 78:21-31;
	106:6-12;
	Is 42:18-43:7
Jonah	Jon 4:1-11
Samson	Judg 15:9-20

for **FOLLOWERs**

Jesus	Lk 24:50-51

PROPHECY of

Israelites	Ezek 37:1-14

REVELATION on

Elijah	1 Kgs 19:1-21

TRADITION of

Solomon	*Wis 19:1-12;
	18-22

n **MISSION**

through **DISCIPLESHIP**

Holy Spirit	Acts 16:6-10

through **WISDOM**

Apostles	Mt 10:16-22

through **OBEDIENCE**

to **COVENANT**

Believers	Is 56:1-8
Israelites	Ex 15:22-27

to **DEITY**

Mankind	Ps 1:1-3

INSTRUCTION on

Achior	*Jdt 5:1-21

to **MESSIANIC FIGURE**

Jesus	Jn 18:1-11

REVELATION on

Elijah	1 Kgs 17:1-24;
	18:1-46;
Ezekiel	Ezek 11:14-21
Israelites	Num 9:15-23
Joseph	Mt 2:19-23

through **ONENESS**

REVELATION on

John	Rev 17:6b-18

n **OPPRESSION**

by **DEITY**

David	Ps 89:38-51
God	Ps 107:39-43
Israelites	Ps 107:4-9

n **ORDER**

by **DEITY**

Amos	Amos 3:3-8
God	Ps 65:9-13;
	104:10-13;
	107:23-32;
	147:7-11;
	Jer 31:35-37

PROPHECY of

Isaiah	Is 17:12-14;
	18:1-7

through **PATIENCE**

Jeremiah	Lam 3:1-66

INSTRUCTION on

Sirach	*Sir 11:10-13

PEACE through

of **DEITY**

Asa	2 Chr 14:1-16:14
Believers	Prov 16:1-33
God	Is 2:1-5
Isaiah	Is 63:7-64:12

PROPHECY of

Isaiah	Is 9:2-7
Israelites	Jer 46:27-28

REVELATION on

Isaiah	Is 55:1-13;
	62:1-12
Jeremiah	Jer 31:2-6
Nathan	2 Sam 7:1-29

over **POVERTY**

Moses	Ex 23:10-13;
	Lev 19:1-37

by **DEITY**

David	Ps 9:17-20;
	35:9-10
Eliphaz	Job 5:8-17
God	Ps 68:4-14;
	113:5-9;
	146:5-7b
Hannah	1 Sam 2:1-10

INSTRUCTION on

Moses	Lev 23:15-22;
	Deut 14:22-29

PROPHECY of

Isaiah	Is 29:17-24

PRAISE of

of **DEITY**

Asaph	Ps 76:4-6
Daniel	Dan 2:20-23
David	2 Sam 22:1-51;
	Ps 18:46-50;
	29:3-9;
	30:1-5;
	35:9-10;
	40:4-5;
	139:13-18
Isaiah	Is 26:7-19
Jesus	Jn 9:1-41;
	1 Pet 4:7-11
Psalmist	Ps 66:5-7;
	13-20;
	84:10-12;
	98:1-3;
	148:7-14

INSTRUCTION on

Psalmist	Ps 107:23-32;
	147:12-20

MEDITATION on

Isaiah	Is 25:1-5

in **WORSHIP**

David	1 Chr 15:1-16:43

PROPHECY of

through **ANGER**

Elamites	Jer 49:34-39

as **BLESSING**

Balaam	Num 22:41-23:12;
	13-26;
	27-24:13
Isaiah	Is 52:13-53:12

as BLESSING (cont'd)
| Israelites | Deut 30:11-14;
Is 30:18-26;
Jer 31:27-28;
Hos 12:10-14;
14:4-8 |

in CAPTIVITY
Jeremiah	Jer 28:1-17
Judahites	Jer 27:16-22
Zedekiah	Jer 27:12-15

through COMPASSION
| Isaiah | Is 14:1-23 |
| Jerusalemites | Zech 12:1-13:6 |

in DEATH
| Jesus | Jn 12:1-8 |

in DESTRUCTION
Babylonians	Jer 51:1-64
Damascenes	Jer 49:23-27
Isaiah	Is 11:10-16

over ENEMY
| Isaiah | 2 Kgs 18:17-19:9a |

over EVIL
| Elamites | Jer 49:34-39 |

for FAMILY
| Joseph | Gen 50:22-26 |

because of FEAR
Elamites	Jer 49:34-39
Isaiah	Is 19:16-17
Jeremiah	Jer 32:26-44

through GRACE
| Isaiah | Is 60:1-22 |

through LEADERSHIP
| Isaiah | Is 9:2-7 |
| Jeremiah | Jer 23:1-8 |

in LIFE
Isaiah	Is 4:2-6; 37:30-32
Israelites	Is 30:18-26; Jer 31:27-28
Joseph	Gen 41:1-57
Tyre	Is 23:15-18

through ORDER
| Isaiah | Is 17:12-14;
18:1-7 |

over POVERTY
| Isaiah | Is 29:17-24 |

concerning REJECTION
| Isaiah | Is 5:8-24a |

concerning SACREDNESS
| Cyrus | 2 Chr 36:1-23 |

concerning SERVICE
Holy Spirit	1 Pet 1:10-12
Isaiah	Is 40:1-11
Judahites	Jer 27:16-22

concerning SUFFERING
| Isaiah | Is 17:1-6 |
| Israelites | Is 14:1-23 |

concerning TEMPTATION
| Israelites | Jer 6:16-21 |

concerning VICTORY
Ahab	1 Kgs 20:1-43
Amaziah	2 Chr 25:1-28
Ehud	Judg 3:26-30
Isaiah	2 Kgs 19:9b-37; Is 9:2-7; 11:10-16; 14:1-23; 26:1-6; 37:33-35; 40:12-31; 51:17-52:12

concerning VICTORY (cont'd)
Jacobites	Mic 5:7-15
Jahaziel	2 Chr 17:1-20:3
Jerusalemites	Zech 12:1-13:6
Joshua	Josh 10:16-27
Judahites	Zech 12:1-13:6
Micah	Mic 4:9-5:6

in VIOLENCE
| Egyptians | Is 19:1-15 |

concerning WEALTH
| Isaiah | Is 52:13-53:12 |

concerning WISDOM
Isaiah	Is 29:9-12
Jesus	Mk 13:9-13; Lk 21:7-19
Solomon	*Wis 11:1-20

concerning WITNESS
| Isaiah | Is 12:1-6 |

through PRUDENCE
INSTRUCTION on
| Isaiah | Is 28:23-29 |

PURIFICATION through
of DEITY
| God | Is 1:24-26 |

REJECTION of
of DEITY
David	Ps 60:1-5
Ephraimites	Hos 7:13-16
Followers	Ps 80:8-13
Israelites	Neh 9:16-18; Ps 78:9-20; Jer 2:1-13; Amos 4:6-12
Psalmist	Ps 88:15-18
Sinners	2 Pet 3:3-7

through FALSE BELIEF
| Ephraimites | Hos 11:1-4 |

PROPHECY of
| Isaiah | Is 5:8-24a |

REVELATION on
| Israelites | Jer 2:20-29 |

REPENTANCE through
of DEITY
| God | 2 Tim 2:20-26 |
| Israelites | *Bar 2:27-35 |

REVELATION on
| Israelites | Ezek 12:1-16 |

REVELATION on
through ANGER
| Israelites | Ezek 20:32-39 |

as BLESSING
Balaam	Num 22:5-14
Ezekiel	Ezek 16:1-7; 17:22-24
God	Is 42:5-17
Isaiah	Is 55:1-13
Israelites	Ezek 36:8-15; 37-38; Hos 2:14-15; Mic 6:1-5
Jeremiah	Jer 31:7-14
Joel	Joel 2:18-27
Nathan	2 Sam 7:1-29; 1 Chr 17:1-27

of DEITY
| God | 1 Sam 25:1-44 |

for **FAMILY**
Isaiah   Is 51:1-16;
                        66:17-24
concerning **FEAR**
God   Is 41:1-42:4
Jeremiah   Jer 4:9-10
through **GRACE**
Ezekiel   Ezek 16:8-14;
                        17:22-24
Israelites   Is 51:17-52:12
Jeremiah   Jer 31:2-6
Joel   Joel 2:18-27
through **HEALING**
Israelites   Ezek 34:11-16
Jeremiah   Jer 30:12-17
through **LEADERSHIP**
David   Ezek 34:23-24
Isaiah   Is 55:1-13;
                        58:1-14
Israelites   Is 48:1-22;
                        Jer 3:14b-18;
                        Ezek 20:9-26;
                        32-29
John   Rev 7:9-17
resulting in **LIFE**
Ezekiel   Ezek 4:9-11;
                        11:14-21;
                        16:1-7;
                        17:22-24;
                        33:1-9
God   Is 41:1-42:4
Israelites   Ezek 12:1-16
Jacob   Gen 31:1-16;
                        17-43
Job   Job 38:39-41
John   Rev 1:4-20;
                        12:1-6
through **LOVE**
Cyrus   Is 48:1-22
Isaiah   Is 5:1-7
concerning **OBEDIENCE**
Elijah   1 Kgs 17:1-24;
                        18:1-46
Ezekiel   Ezek 11:14-21
Israelites   Num 9:15-23
Joseph   Mt 2:19-23
concerning **ONENESS**
John   Rev 17:6b-18
concerning **REPENTANCE**
Israelites   Ezek 12:1-16
concerning **SERVICE**
Babylonians   Jer 27:1-11
Ezekiel   Ezek 16:8-14
God   Is 41:1-42:4
Israelites   Is 49:1-26;
                        Ezek 20:40-44;
                        34:11-16
Nations   Zeph 3:9-10
Philip   Acts 8:26-40
concerning **SPIRIT**
Israelites   Ezek 36:22-32
concerning **SUFFERING**
Gog   Ezek 38:17-23
concerning **VICTORY**
Babylonians   Ezek 30:6-9;
                        20-26
Cyrus   Is 44:24-45:13
David   1 Sam 23:1-13;
                        2 Sam 5:17-25;
                        1 Chr 14:1-17

concerning **VICTORY** (cont'd)
Gideon   Judg 7:1-8
God   Is 41:1-42:4
Israelites   Is 45:14-25;
                        49:1-26;
                        Zeph 3:14-20
Joshua   Josh 11:1-15;
                        13:1-7
Moses   Ex 14:15-22
concerning **VIOLENCE**
God   Ezek 38:17-23;
                        39:1-16
concerning **WEALTH**
Cyrus   Is 45:14-25
Israelites   Ezek 34:25-31;
                        Hag 1:15b-2:9
Moses   Ex 33:1-6;
                        Lev 25:1-7;
                        20-22;
                        Num 34:1-15
concerning **WILL**
Jeremiah   Jer 18:1-12
concerning **WISDOM**
Daniel   Dan 1:17-21;
                        2:14-19
Israelites   Jer 3:14b-18
Judahites   Jer 24:1-10
concerning **WITNESS**
Ezekiel   Ezek 3:22-27
God   Heb 1:1-2a
Isaiah   Is 66:1-16
Paul   Acts 22:30-23:11

REVENGE in
of **DEITY**
David   Ps 18:46-50
God   1 Sam 25:1-44

REWARDs in
of **DEITY**
God   Ps 127:3-5
Israelites   Ps 105:43-45

SACREDNESS in
through **COVENANT**
Aaron   Num 18:8-20
of **DEITY**
Israelites   Ezra 5:3-5
PROPHECY of
Cyrus   2 Chr 36:1-23
TRADITION of
Aaron   Ex 16:31-36

through **SACRIFICE**
to **DEITY**
Abraham   Gen 22:1-19
by **MESSIANIC FIGURE**
Jesus   Mt 27:45-56

SCRIPTURES on
in **LIFE**
Moses   Jn 6:25-59
through **WILL**
God   Rom 9:14-29

SELF-REALIZATION of
Magicians   Ex 8:16-19

SERVICE through
Aaron   Num 18:21-24

of **DEITY**
Jesus — Mk 1:12-13
of **MESSIANIC FIGURE**
Cyrus — Is 44:24-45:13
PROPHECY of
Holy Spirit — 1 Pet 1:10-12
Isaiah — Is 40:1-11
Judahites — Jer 27:16-22
REVELATION on
Babylonians — Jer 27:1-11
Ezekiel — Ezek 16:8-14
God — Is 41:1-42:4
Israelites — Is 49:1-26;
Ezek 20:40-44;
34:11-16
Nations — Zeph 3:9-10
Philip — Acts 8:26-40

through **SPIRIT**
REVELATION on
Israelites — Ezek 36:22-32

concerning **SUFFERING**
Asaph — Ps 77:1-10
David — Ps 20:1-5;
31:1-8;
32:3-7;
34:4-10;
60:1-5
Elihu — Job 36:5-15;
16-25
Followers — Ps 80:4-7
God — Ps 107:33-38;
39-43;
140:12-13;
146:7c-9;
147:1-6
Israelites — Ps 78:32-39
Psalmist — Ps 88:3-9;
15-18;
119:49-56
Sirach — *Sir 35:12-20
Solomon — *Wis 16:1-14

through **SUFFERING**
of **FOLLOWER**s
God — *Wis 16:15-29
PROPHECY of
Isaiah — Is 17:1-6
Israelites — Is 14:1-23
REVELATION on
Gog — Ezek 38:17-23

through **TEMPTATION**
INSTRUCTION on
Paul — 1 Cor 10:1-13
PROPHECY of
Israelites — Jer 6:16-21

in **VICTORY**
Israelites — Ex 17:8-16
Moses — Ex 23:20-33
by **DEITY**
Abijah — 2 Chr 13:1-22
Asa — 2 Chr 14:1-16:14
Believers — Ps 47:1-4;
Eph 6:10-18
Cyrus — Is 44:24-45:13
David — 2 Sam 8:1-18;
22:1-51;

by **DEITY** (cont'd)
David — 1 Chr 18:1-20:8
Ps 9:1-4;
18:16-19;
46-50;
20:6-9;
21:8-13;
22:1-5;
27:1-3;
4-6;
35:9-10;
59:16-17;
61:4-5;
89:19-37;
110:5-7;
124:1-5;
144:9-11
Gideon — Judg 8:1-3
God — Ps 33:13-19;
48:4-8;
55:15-19;
68:4-14;
19-23;
69:29-36;
89:5-18;
118:15-21;
136:10-22;
149:1-4;
Prov 21:1-31
Hezekiah — 2 Kgs 20:1-11
Isaiah — Is 59:1-21
Israelites — Ex 3:7-10;
Num 21:33-35;
Deut 1:19-46;
2:26-3:11;
12-22;
9:1-6;
12:1-31;
31:1-8;
Josh 11:16-23;
Judg 4:10-16;
7:16-22;
1 Sam 19:1-10;
1 Chr 15:1-16:
Neh 4:13-23;
Ps 44:1-3;
4-8;
105:7-15;
23-25;
106:6-12;
Is 43:14-44:5
Jacob — Gen 46:1-7
Jephthah — Judg 11:29-33
Jeroboam — 2 Kgs 14:23-29
Jesus — Rom 8:1-4;
Col 2:6-15
Joshua — Num 14:8-9;
Josh 23:1-16
Judah — Judg 1:1-21
Maccabeus — *1 Mc 4:1-35
Mankind — Ps 18:25-30
Paul — 2 Tim 3:10-13
Psalmist — Ps 92:5-11;
94:16-19
Uzziah — 2 Chr 26:1-28:
in **ENVIRONMENT**
God — Ps 68:15-18
Joshua — Josh 10:28-43
INSTRUCTION on
Joshua — Josh 24:1-13

PROPHECY of
Ahab	1 Kgs 20:1-43
Amaziah	2 Chr 25:1-28
Ehud	Judg 3:26-30
Isaiah	2 Kgs 19:9b-37;
	Is 9:2-7;
	11:10-16;
	14:1-23;
	26:1-6;
	37:33-35;
	40:12-31;
	51:17-52:12
Jacobites	Mic 5:7-15
Jahaziel	2 Chr 17:1-20:37
Jerusalemites	Zech 12:1-13:6
Joshua	Josh 10:16-27
Judahites	Zech 12:1-13:6
Micah	Mic 4:9-5:6

REVELATION on
Babylonians	Ezek 30:6-9;
	20-26
Cyrus	Is 44:24-45:13
David	1 Sam 23:1-13;
	2 Sam 5:17-25;
	1 Chr 14:1-17
Gideon	Judg 7:1-8
God	Is 41:1-42:4
Israelites	Is 45:14-25;
	49:1-26;
	Zeph 3:14-20
Joshua	Josh 11:1-15;
	13:1-7
Moses	Ex 14:15-22

concerning VIOLENCE
by DEITY
David	2 Sam 22:1-51;
	Ps 18:31-42
God	2 Chr 17:1-20:37
Hezekiah	2 Chr 32:1-33
Israelites	Ex 14:1-14;
	Deut 1:19-46
Jonah	Jon 1:1-17
Judahites	2 Kgs 15:32-38

VIOLENCE through
PROPHECY of
Egyptians	Is 19:1-15

REVELATION on
Gog	Ezek 38:17-23;
	39:1-16

WEALTH through
Isaac	Gen 25:1-6

in COVENANT
Moses	Ex 34:12-28

of DEITY
Cyrus	Is 44:24-45:13
David	Ps 30:6-10
God	Ps 112:2-4;
	Eccl 6:1-12;
	1 Tim 6:17-19
Israelites	Ex 11:1-10;
	12:33-36;
	Deut 8:11-20;
	17:14-20;
	Josh 5:10-12;
	2 Chr 17:1-20:37;
	Neh 9:22-25;
	Ps 105:37-42;
	Hos 2:2-8

of DEITY (cont'd)
Job	Job 42:10-17
King	Ps 45:2-9
Psalmist	Ps 72:1-4
Solomon	1 Kgs 3:1-15;
	2 Chr 1:1-17

in ENVIRONMENT
Danites	Judg 18:7-10

INSTRUCTION on
Jesus	Lk 12:22-31

PROPHECY of
Isaiah	Is 52:13-53:12

REVELATION on
Cyrus	Is 45:14-25
Israelites	Ezek 34:25-31;
	Hag 1:15b-2:9
Moses	Ex 33:1-6;
	Lev 25:1-7;
	20-22;
	Num 34:1-15

in WORSHIP
Israelites	Deut 26:1-11

through WILL
of DEITY
God	Ps 135:5-7;
	Mt 10:26-39
James	Jas 1:16-18
Job	Job 12:13-25

in ENVIRONMENT
God	Job 37:1-13

of MESSIANIC FIGURE
Jesus	Lk 22:14-23

REVELATION on
Jeremiah	Jer 18:1-12

SCRIPTURES on
God	Rom 9:14-29

WISDOM through
for FOLLOWERs
Holy Spirit	Mt 10:16-22;
	Lk 12:1-12;
	Jn 14:25-26;
	1 Cor 2:1-5

INSTRUCTION on
Jesus	Mk 4:10-20
Paul	2 Tim 2:1-7
Solomon	Prov 2:1-22

PROPHECY of
Isaiah	Is 29:9-12
Jesus	Mk 13:9-13;
	Lk 21:7-19
Solomon	*Wis 11:1-20

REVELATION on
Daniel	Dan 1:17-21;
	2:14-19
Israelites	Jer 3:14b-18
Judahites	Jer 24:1-10

through WISDOM
of DEITY
Believers	1 Jn 2:24-27
Cyrus	Is 44:24-45:13
God	Eccl 1:12-2:26;
	Is 44:24-45:13
Isaiah	Is 50:1-11
James	Jas 1:5-8
Solomon	2 Chr 1:1-17

in MISSION
Apostles	Mt 10:16-22

in **BEHAVIOR** (cont'd)

God	Gen 6:5-22
Isaiah	Is 8:8b-10
James	Jas 3:1-12
Jesus	Mt 5:21-26;
	33-37;
	7:15-20;
	Lk 10:38-42;
	21:34-36
Maiden	Song 3:1-5
Paul	1 Cor 10:23-11:1;
	Eph 5:15-20;
	Col 4:5-6;
	1 Thes 5:1-11;
	1 Tim 5:3-16;
	17-25
Preacher	Eccl 5:1-7
Sirach	*Sir 8:1-19;
	13:1-13;
	18:19-26;
	27-33;
	31:12-24
Solomon	Prov 1:2-6;
	5:1-14;
	10:1-32;
	22:1-16;
	22-23:14

in **BROTHERHOOD**

Paul	2 Thes 3:6-15

in **CONFRONTATION**

Jesus	Mt 7:6

in the **CREATION**

Paul	1 Cor 3:10-17

in **FREEDOM**

Gamaliel	Acts 5:17-42
Peter	1 Pet 2:13-17

as **GIFT**

Jesus	Mt 25:14-30

in **HONESTY**

Jesus	Lk 16:10-12

in **JUDGMENT**

Jesus	Jn 7:15-24

with **KNOWLEDGE**

John	1 Jn 2:12-17
Preacher	Eccl 7:1-22
Sirach	*Sir 37:7-26
Solomon	Prov 13:1-25;
	14:1-35;
	25:1-28
Wisdom	Prov 8:1-21

in **NEW AGE**

Paul	2 Thes 2:1-3a

in **PROVIDENCE**

Isaiah	Is 28:23-29

as **QUALITY OF LIFE**

Bishops	1 Tim 3:1-7
James	Jas 1:19-21

in **RECONCILIATION**

Jesus	Lk 12:57-59

in **STEWARDSHIP**

Jesus	Mt 18:12-14;
	22:15-22;
	Lk 16:1-9;
	19:11-27
Paul	Rom 13:1-7;
	14:1-23
Sirach	*Sir 29:14-20
Women	1 Pet 3:1-7

with **TRUTH**

James	Jas 1:26

with **TRUTH** (cont'd)

Jesus	Mt 13:1-3a;
	Mk 4:1-9;
	Lk 11:33-36
Paul	2 Tim 2:14-19
Peter	1 Pet 3:13-17

as **VIRTUE**

Jesus	Mt 25:1-13
Paul	1 Cor 15:29-34
Sirach	*Sir 11:2-9
Solomon	Prov 12:1-28;
	24:23-34

in **JUDGMENT**
INSTRUCTION on

Jesus	Jn 7:15-24

with **KNOWLEDGE**
INSTRUCTION on

John	1 Jn 2:12-17
Preacher	Eccl 7:1-22
Sirach	*Sir 37:7-26
Solomon	Prov 13:1-25;
	14:1-35;
	25:1-28
Wisdom	Prov 8:1-21

PROPHECY of

Isaiah	Is 28:1-13

by **MESSIANIC FIGURE**
in **CONFRONTATION**

Pilate	Mk 15:1-5

in **MISSION**
BEHAVIOR revealing

Paul	1 Thes 2:1-12

with **TRUTH**

Paul	1 Cor 1:13-17

in **NEW AGE**
of **FOLLOWER**

Scribe	Mt 13:51-52

INSTRUCTION on

Paul	2 Thes 2:1-3a

PROPHECY of
with **KNOWLEDGE**

Isaiah	Is 28:1-13

in **PROVIDENCE**
INSTRUCTION on

Isaiah	Is 28:23-29

as **QUALITY OF LIFE**
INSTRUCTION on

Bishops	1 Tim 3:1-7
James	Jas 1:19-21

in **RATIONALIZATION**

Jesus	Mk 11:27-33;
	Lk 20:1-8

in **RECONCILIATION**
INSTRUCTION on

Jesus	Lk 12:57-59

SECURITY in
INSTRUCTION on

Solomon	Prov 27:1-27

PRUDENCE (cont'd)

SIGNS of
  INSTRUCTION on
    Jesus   Mt 9:16-17;
                    16:1-4;
                    Mk 2:18-22;
                    Lk 5:36-39;
                    12:54-56

concerning SIN
  Ungodly Men   *Wis 2:6-11

in STEWARDSHIP
  of FOLLOWER
    Mary   Lk 10:38-42
  INSTRUCTION on
    Jesus   Mt 18:12-14;
                    22:15-22;
                    Lk 16:1-9;
                    19:11-27
    Paul   Rom 13:1-7;
                    14:1-23
    Sirach   *Sir 29:14-20
    Women   1 Pet 3:1-7

with TRUTH
  INSTRUCTION on
    James   Jas 1:26
    Jesus   Mt 13:1-3a;
                    Mk 4:1-9;
                    Lk 11:33-36
    Paul   2 Tim 2:14-19
    Peter   1 Pet 3:13-17
  in MISSION
    Paul   1 Cor 1:13-17

VIRTUE in
  INSTRUCTION on
    Jesus   Mt 25:1-13
    Paul   1 Cor 15:29-34
    Sirach   *Sir 11:2-9
    Solomon   Prov 12:1-28;
                    24:23-34

in WORSHIP
  DESIRE for
    Herod   Mt 2:1-12

PUNISHMENT

ACCEPTANCE of
  by DEITY
    Daniel   Dan 9:4-19
    Elihu   Job 36:16-25
    Micah   Mic 7:7-20
  INSTRUCTION on
    Author   Heb 12:3-11
    Eliphaz   Job 5:8-17
    God   Ezek 6:11-14
    Solomon   Prov 3:1-35
  MEDITATION on
    Jeremiah   Jer 10:17-22;
                    Lam 3:1-66

ALIENATION as
  Israelites   Lev 26:1-46;
                    Zech 11:4-14
  Moses   Lev 17:1-9;
                    10-14;

PUNISHMENT (cont'd)

ALIENATION as (cont'd)
  Moses   18:1-30;
                19:1-37;
                Num 15:22-31
  by DEITY
    Babylonians Is 14:1-23
    Bethelites   Zech 7:4-8:23
    Edomites   Ezek 35:1-15
    God   Gen 11:1-9;
                Ps 37:12-22;
                53:4-5;
                2 Thes 1:7b-10
    Israelites   Num 14:39-45;
                2 Chr 10:1-12:1
                Is 9:8-10:4;
                Ezek 20:9-26
    Jonah   Jon 1:1-17
    Judahites   2 Kgs 23:25b-3
                24:18-25:7
    Priests   Mal 1:6-2:9
  in ENVIRONMENT
    Cain   Gen 4:1-16
    God   Gen 3:20-24
  for FALSE BELIEF
    Author   Heb 6:1-8
    Israelites   Jer 18:13-17
  INSTRUCTION on
    Bildad   Job 18:16-18;
                19-21
    Eliphaz   Job 22:12-20
    Ephesus   Rev 2:1-7
    Jesus   Mt 25:14-30
    Nehemiah   Neh 13:4-9
    Paul   1 Cor 5:1-5
  PROPHECY of
    Ammonites   Amos 1:13-15
    Amos   Amos 1:3-5;
                6-8
    Coniah   Jer 22:24-30
    Edomites   Obad 1:10-14
    Ephraimites Hos 5:3-7;
                9:10-17
    God   Hos 5:8-14
    Habakkuk   Hab 2:9-11
    Isaiah   Is 34:1-17
    Israelites   Ezek 16:44-52;
                Amos 5:26-27;
                6:1-7;
                7:10-17
    Judahites   Jer 7:1-15
    Micah   Mic 1:10-16;
                5:7-15
    Nineveh   Nah 1:11;
                14
    Women   Amos 4:1-3
    Zephaniah   Zeph 2:4-7
  REVELATION of
    Ammonites   Ezek 25:1-7
    Egyptians   Ezek 29:1-5;
                6-9a
    Ezekiel   Ezek 14:1-11;
                12-23
    Hosea   Hos 1:8-9
    Israelites   Ezek 39:17-24;
                Amos 8:1-3;
                Zech 13:7-9
    Jeremiah   Jer 23:33-40
    Joel   Joel 3:4-8
    Judahites   Jer 3:6-11;
                Ezek 23:11-21

CAPTIVITY as
Israelites   2 Kgs 17:7-23;
     Neh 9:32-37;
     Ps 106:40-46;
     *Bar 2:1-10
CONDEMNATION as
Israelites   Is 9:8-10:4
DEATH as
Ahaziah   2 Chr 21:1-23:21
David   1 Chr 21:1-22:1;
     Ps 55:15-19
Elihu   Job 36:5-15
God   1 Sam 25:1-44;
     Ps 55:23
Israelites   Num 11:31-35;
     16:36-50;
     21:4-9;
     2 Sam 24:1-25;
     Ps 78:21-31;
     *1 Esd 1:46-58
Judahites   2 Chr 26:1-28:27
Onan   Gen 38:1-11
Solomon   1 Kgs 1:41-53
DEFEAT as
Israelites   Num 14:39-45
DESTRUCTION as
Asaph   Ps 83:9-18
Assyrians   Is 10:24-27c;
     14:24-27
Babylonians   Is 14:1-23
David   Ps 21:8-13;
     63:9-10;
     68:1-3
God   2 Chr 36:1-23;
     Nah 1:10,12,13;
     15-2:2;
     1 Cor 3:10-17;
     Rev 11:15-19
Isaiah   Is 63:1-6
Israelites   Num 16:25-35;
     Deut 2:1-25;
     Is 9:8-10:4;
     17-19;
     Jer 12:7-13;
     Jude 1:5-7
Judahites   2 Kgs 23:25b-30
Mankind   Ps 64:7-10
Sinners   2 Pet 3:3-7
Zophar   Job 20:4-29
DISCIPLESHIP through
Psalmist   Ps 118:15-21
for DISOBEDIENCE
Azariah   *Azar 1:1-10
David   Ps 55:15-19;
     89:19-37
God   Judg 9:56-57;
     Ps 95:7d-11;
     119:17-24
Israelites   Num 16:25-35;
     Josh 7:6-26;
     Judg 10:6-18;
     2 Kgs 18:9-12;
     Neh 9:32-37;
     Ps 106:24-27;
     Jer 32:16-25;
     *Bar 2:1-10;
     24-26;
     Heb 4:1-13
Jehoshaphat   2 Chr 17:1-20:37
Judahites   2 Kgs 23:36-24:7

for DISOBEDIENCE (cont'd)
Moses   Deut 31:30-32:≀
Psalmist   Ps 137:4-6
Saul   1 Chr 10:1-14
Uzzah   2 Sam 6:1-23;
     1 Chr 13:1-14
for DOUBT
Princes   Ezek 11:1-13
of ENEMY
Asaph   Ps 79:5-13
Azariah   *Azar 1:1-10
David   Ps 5:8-10;
     6:8-10;
     31:13-18;
     35:19-21;
     40:13-17;
     41:4-10;
     54:4-5;
     59:11;
     63:9-10;
     69:22-28;
     109:6-20;
     21-31;
     143:7-12
God   Ps 97:1-5;
     Nah 1:1-9,10,
     13,15-2:2
Isaiah   Is 25:1-5;
     63:7-64:12
Psalmist   Ps 71:1-21;
     80:14-19;
     129:5-8
for EVIL
Angels   2 Pet 2:4-10a
Asaph   Ps 83:2-8
Babylonians   Is 14:1-23
Bildad   Job 8:10-19
Chaldeans   Hab 1:12-17
David   Ps 3:7-8;
     7:3-5;
     9-11;
     12-16;
     12:1-4;
     28:1-5;
     31:13-18;
     35:4-8;
     39:7-13;
     59:1-5;
     12-13b;
     139:19-22;
     140:9-11;
     141:5-7;
     8-10
Ephraimites   Hos 9:10-17
Gentiles   Rom 1:24-32
God   Ps 11:4-7;
     31:19-24;
     34:15-22;
     37:1-11;
     23-40;
     50:16-21;
     52:5-7;
     53:4-5;
     68:19-23;
     73:13-20;
     125:4-5;
     146:7c-9;
     147:1-6;
     Prov 10:1-32;
     16:1-33;
     22:22-23:14;

WISDOM in
  Sirach   *Sir 32:14-24

causing **DESPAIR**
  INSTRUCTION on
    Isaiah   Is 59:1-21
    Jeremiah   Jer 6:22-26
  PROPHECY of
    Egyptians   Is 19:1-15
    Isaiah   Is 8:19-22;
                    21:1-10

DESTRUCTION as
  Israelites   Judg 6:1-6;
                    21:8-12
  Moses   Ex 21:33-22:17;
                    Lev 26:1-46
  by **DEITY**
    Asaph   Ps 83:9-18
    Assyrians   Is 10:24-27c;
                    14:24-27
    Babylonians   Is 14:1-23
    David   Ps 21:8-13;
                    63:9-10;
                    68:1-3
    God   2 Chr 36:1-23;
                    Nah 1:10,12,13,
                    15-2:2;
                    1 Cor 3:10-17;
                    Rev 11:15-19
    Isaiah   Is 63:1-6
    Israelites   Num 16:25-35;
                    Deut 2:1-25;
                    Is 9:8-10:4;
                    17-19;
                    Jer 12:7-13;
                    Jude 1:5-7
    Judahites   2 Kgs 23:25b-30
    Mankind   Ps 64:7-10
    Sinners   2 Pet 3:3-7
    Zophar   Job 20:4-29
  for **FALSE BELIEF**
    Author   Heb 6:1-8
    Moses   Num 33:50-56
    Peter   2 Pet 3:14-18a
    Prophets   2 Pet 2:1-3;
                    Rev 19:17-21
    Sinners   2 Pet 2:10b-16
  INSTRUCTION on
    Eliphaz   Job 15:17-35
    God   Is 1:18-20;
                    *2 Esd 2:8-9
    Joshua   Josh 23:1-16
    Moses   Deut 6:4-19;
                    8:11-20;
                    28:15-68

  MEDITATION on
    Jeremiah   Lam 2:1-22
  PROPHECY of
    Ammonites   Amos 1:13-15
    Amos   Amos 1:3-5
    Assyrians   Zeph 2:13-14
    Baasha   1 Kgs 15:33-16:7
    Edomites   Jer 49:7-22;
                    Amos 1:11-12
    Ephraimites   Is 28:1-13;
                    Hos 5:3-7;
                    8-14;
                    13:15-16
    Habakkuk   Hab 2:12-14:17

PROPHECY of (cont'd)
  Isaiah   Is 10:20-23;
                    33-34;
                    17:12-14;
                    19:1-15;
                    21:1-10;
                    22:1-14;
                    24:1-12;
                    26:20-27:1;
                    28:14-22;
                    30:27-33;
                    31:1-3;
                    32:9-14;
                    33:1-6;
                    7-16;
                    34:1-17;
                    66:1-16
  Israelites   Jer 5:15-17;
                    6:16-21;
                    11:15-17;
                    Ezek 16:35-43;
                    Hos 8:4-7;
                    11-14;
                    10:1-8;
                    13:7-8;
                    9-11;
                    Amos 3:13-15;
                    5:4-6;
                    6:8-11;
                    7:10-17
  Jeremiah   Jer 4:13-18;
                    19-22;
                    23-26;
                    5:1-14;
                    6:1-8;
                    7:29-8:3;
                    14-17;
                    13:12-14;
                    14:10-12;
                    17-18;
                    16:1-13;
                    17:19-27;
                    21:13-14;
                    22:1-9;
                    20-23;
                    29:1-23;
                    32:26-44;
                    34:13-22;
                    43:8-13;
                    44:20-28;
                    45:1-5
  Jeroboam   1 Kgs 13:1-34
  Jesus   Lk 19:41-44
  Joel   Joel 3:16b-21
  John the Baptist Mt 3:1-12;
                    Lk 3:7-9;
                    15-17
  Judahites   Jer 4:5-8;
                    8:8-13;
                    9:10-22;
                    44:1-14;
                    Hos 5:3-7;
                    Amos 2:4-5
  Micah   Mic 1:5-9;
                    2:1-10;
                    3:1-12;
                    5:7-15
  Moabites   Is 25:10-12;
                    Amos 2:1-3

PROPHECY of (cont'd)

Nineveh	Nah 1:11; 14; 2:11-13; 3:5-19; Zeph 2:13-14; 15
Philistines	Amos 1:6-8
Shebna	Is 22:15-25
Tyre	Is 23:1-14; Ezek 26:7-14; 19-21; Amos 1:9-10; Zech 9:1-12
Women	Amos 4:1-3
Zechariah	Zech 9:13-17; 11:1-3
Zedekiah	Jer 27:12-15
Zephaniah	Zeph 1:14-16; 17-18; 2:4-7

REVELATION on

Ammonites	Ezek 21:28-32; 25:1-7; Zeph 2:8-12
Belshazzar	Dan 5:26-28
Chaldeans	Is 47:1-15
Edomites	Ezek 25:12-14; 35:1-15
Egyptians	Ezek 29:1-5; 6-9a; 9b-16; 30:13-19; 31:10-18; 32:1-16
Ezekiel	Ezek 6:1-7; 13:1-16; 14:1-11; 20:45-49; 21:25-27
God	Is 41:1-42:4
Gog	Ezek 39:1-16
Isaiah	Is 5:1-7; 6:1-13; 56:9-57:13; 65:1-25
Israelites	Jer 2:14-19; 5:1-14; Ezek 5:5-17; 6:11-14; 7:1-27; 21:1-7; 8-17; 22:1-16; 23:5-10; 36-49; Hos 1:4-5; 2:9-13; Amos 7:7-9; 8:8-10; 9:1-4; Zech 13:7-9
Jacobites	Amos 9:8-10
Jehu	1 Kgs 15:33-16:7
Jeremiah	Jer 15:1-4; 5-9; 19:1-15; 25:15-29; 30-38
Jesus	2 Thes 1:7b-10

REVELATION on (cont'd)

John	Rev 11:1-14; 18:4-20
Judahites	Jer 13:1-11; Ezek 23:22-35; 24:1-14
Malachi	Mal 3:13-4:3
Micah	Mic 6:9-16
Moabites	Ezek 25:8-11; Zeph 2:8-12
Nations	Zeph 3:6-7
People	Jer 27:1-11
Philistines	Ezek 25:15-17
Prophets	2 Kgs 21:1-18; Jer 14:13-16
Solomon	2 Chr 7:11-22
Tyre	Ezek 26:1-6; 27:25b-36; 28:1-10
Zechariah	Zech 5:1-4
Zedekiah	Jer 24:1-10; Zeph 1:2-6; 10-11; 12-13

DISCIPLESHIP through

by **DEITY**

Psalmist	Ps 118:15-21

for **DISOBEDIENCE**

Moses	Lev 26:1-46
Nebuchadnezzar	*Jdt 1:1-2:20
Shadrach	Dan 3:19-23
Solomon	*Wis 11:1-20

to **COVENANT**

Israelites	Judg 2:1-5

to **DEITY**

Azariah	*Azar 1:1-10
David	Ps 55:15-19; 89:19-37
God	Judg 9:56-57; Ps 95:7d-11; 119:17-24
Israelites	Num 16:25-35; Josh 7:6-26; Judg 10:6-18; 2 Kgs 18:9-12; Neh 9:32-37; Ps 106:24-27; Jer 32:16-25; *Bar 2:1-10; 24-26; Heb 4:1-13
Jehoshaphat	2 Chr 17:1-20:37
Judahites	2 Kgs 23:36-24:7
Moses	Deut 31:30-32:47
Psalmist	Ps 137:4-6
Saul	1 Chr 10:1-14
Uzzah	2 Sam 6:1-23; 1 Chr 13:1-14

caused by **FALSE BELIEF**

Author	Heb 6:1-8

INSTRUCTION on

Achior	*Jdt 5:1-21
Agur	Prov 30:15-33
Artaxerxes	Ezra 7:25-26; *1 Esd 8:8-24
Ezra	*1 Esd 9:1-15
God	Gen 2:16-17; 3:14-19

INSTRUCTION on (cont'd)		by **DEITY** (cont'd)	
Jeremiah	Jer 44:20-28	David	31:13-18;
Jesus	Lk 12:41-46;		35:19-21;
	47-48		40:13-17;
Joshua	Josh 23:1-16;		41:4-10;
	24:16-24		54:4-5;
Lot	Gen 19:12-29		59:11;
Moses	Deut 28:15-68;		63:9-10;
	29:16-29		69:22-28;
Nebuchadnezzar	Dan 3:1-6;		109:6-20;
	13-15		21-31;
Paul	Rom 2:1-24;		143:7-12;
	2 Cor 10:1-6;		97:1-5;
	13:1-4;		Nah 1:1-9,10,12
	2 Thes 3:6-15		13,15-2:2
Solomon	Prov 5:1-14;	Isaiah	Is 25:1-5;
	*Wis 6:1-11		63:7-64:12
PROPHECY of		Psalmist	Ps 71:1-21;
Ahijah	1 Kgs 11:26-40		80:14-19;
Amaziah	2 Chr 25:1-28		129:5-8
Asa	2 Chr 14:1-16:14		
God	Mic 5:7-15	**INSTRUCTION** on	
Huldah	2 Kgs 22:30-20	God	Is 1:24-26
Jeremiah	Jer 17:19-27;	**PROPHECY** of	
	29:1-23;	Baruch	*Bar 4:21-37
	34:13-22	Isaiah	Is 17:12-14
Jeroboam	1 Kgs 13:1-34;	Joel	Joel 3:16b-21
	14:1-18	Judahites	Zeph 2:4-7
Judahites	Jer 44:1-14	Micah	Mic 1:10-16
Samuel	1 Sam 13:1-23;	Zechariah	Zech 2:6-13
	28:3-25	**REVELATION** on	
Zedekiah	Jer 22:1-9	Ezekiel	Ezek 36:1-7
REVELATION on		God	Is 1:24-26;
Ezekiel	Ezek 3:16-21;		*2 Esd 15:1-16:5
	11:1-13	Israelites	Is 51:17-52:12;
Holy Spirit	Heb 3:6b-11		Zeph 2:8-12
Isaiah	Is 31:4-9	Jeremiah	Jer 30:12-17
Israelites	Num 14:26-38;	Zechariah	Zech 1:18-21
	Is 48:1-22;		
	Jer 9:25-26	for **EVIL**	
Jeremiah	Jer 16:1-13;	against **DEITY**	
	23:33-40	Angels	2 Pet 2:4-10a
Judahites	Jer 13:1-11	Asaph	Ps 83:2-8
Moses	Num 16:36-50	Babylonians	Is 14:1-23
Nathan	2 Sam 7:1-29;	Bildad	Job 8:10-19
	1 Chr 17:1-27	Chaldeans	Hab 1:12-17
Solomon	1 Kgs 9:1-9;	David	Ps 3:7-8;
	11:1-13		7:3-5;
			9-11;
for **DOUBT**			12-16;
Moses	Num 12:4-10;		12:1-4;
	20:2-13		28:1-5;
of **DEITY**			31:13-18;
Princes	Ezek 11:1-13		35:4-8;
through **FALSE BELIEF**			39:7-13;
Israelites	Jer 5:1-14		59:1-5;
INSTRUCTION on			12-13b;
Author	Heb 3:12-19		139:19-22;
PROPHECY of			140:9-11;
Israelites	Jer 18:18-23		141:5-7;
REVELATION on			8-10
Gabriel	Lk 1:5-25	Ephraimites	Hos 9:10-17
God	Num 12:11-16	Gentiles	Rom 1:24-32
		God	Ps 11:4-7;
of **ENEMY**			31:19-24;
by **DEITY**			34:15-22;
Asaph	Ps 79:5-13		37:1-11;
Azariah	*Azar 1:1-10		23-40;
David	Ps 5:8-10;		50:16-21;
	6:8-10;		52:5-7;

PROPHECY of (cont'd)

Jeremiah	6:1-8;
	9-15;
	13:20-27;
	14:10-12;
	19:1-15;
	21:11-12;
	22:20-23;
	23:1-8;
	32:26-44;
	45:1-5
Judahites	Jer 7:1-15;
	8:8-13;
	25:8-14;
	35:6-17
Micah	Mic 1:5-9;
	10-16;
	2:1-10
Nathan	2 Sam 12:1-31
Prophets	Jer 23:9-12;
	13-15;
	16-22
Zephaniah	Zeph 1:17-18

REVELATION on

Chaldeans	Is 47:1-15
Egyptians	Ezek 32:17-32
Ezekiel	Ezek 8:16-18;
	9:1-11;
	11:14-21;
	20:45-49
God	Gen 20:1-18;
	Ps 9:15-16;
	*2 Esd 15:1-16:50
Habakkuk	Hab 2:1-4
Isaiah	Is 51:1-16;
	57:14-21;
	65:1-25;
	66:1-16
Israelites	Is 50:1-11;
	Jer 2:14-19;
	3:1-5;
	30:10-11;
	Ezek 5:5-17;
	7:1-27;
	15:1-8;
	17:11-21;
	20:32-39;
	21:18-24;
	22:1-16;
	23:5-10;
	36-49;
	36:16-21;
	39:17-24;
	Hos 2:2-8;
	Amos 9:8-10
Jehoiakim	Jer 36:27-32
Jeremiah	Jer 1:13-16;
	3:21-4:4;
	11:1-14;
	18-12:6;
	14:13-16;
	16:16-18;
	18:1-12;
	19:1-15;
	25:15-29;
	30:12-17;
	23-31:1
John	Rev 18:1-3
Judahites	Jer 9:2-9;
	Ezek 23:11-21

REVELATION of (cont'd)

Micah	Mic 6:9-16
Prophetesses	Ezek 13:17-23
Prophets	Ezek 13:1-16
Sinners	Rev 21:1-8
Solomon	2 Chr 7:11-22
Zechariah	Zech 5:1-4
Zephaniah	Zeph 1:8-9

SELF-REALIZATION of

Israelites	*Bar 1:15-21
Ungodly Men	*Wis 5:1-14

TRADITION on

Solomon	*Wis 10:1-21;
	19:13-17;
	*Sir 47:12-22

for **FALSE BELIEF**

ALIENATION as

Author	Heb 6:1-8
Israelites	Jer 18:13-17

ANGER as

God	Rev 14:9-12

causing **BLASPHEMY**

Author	Heb 6:1-8

causing **CHAOS**

Israelites	Jer 18:13-17

CONDEMNATION as

Israelites	Deut 29:16-29

DEATH as

Ahaziah	2 Kgs 1:1-18
Ananias	Acts 4:32-5:10
Cyrus	*Bel 1:8-9;
	21-22
Darius	Dan 6:4-9
Elijah	1 Kgs 18:1-46
False Prophet	Rev 19:17-21
God	Num 3:1-4;
	25:1-5
Hananiah	Jer 28:1-17
Jews	*2 Mc 12:38-45
John	1 Jn 3:11-18
Moses	Ex 21:33-22:17;
	Lev 20:1-27;
	Deut 12:32-13:18
Sapphira	Acts 4:32-5:10
Sinners	2 Pet 2:10b-16

DESTRUCTION as

Author	Heb 6:1-8
Moses	Num 33:50-56
Peter	2 Pet 3:14-18a
Prophets	2 Pet 2:1-3;
	Rev 19:17-21
Sinners	2 Pet 2:10b-16

causing **DISOBEDIENCE**

Author	Heb 6:1-8

causing **DOUBT**

Israelites	Jer 5:1-14

is **HUMILITY**

Ephraimites	Hos 4:17-19
Prophets	Mic 3:1-12

causing **IDOLATRY**

Baruch	*Bar 4:5-16
God	Rev 14:9-12
Israelites	Deut 29:16-29

JUSTICE in

God	*Wis 12:23-27
Sinners	2 Pet 2:10b-16

OPPRESSION as

Peter	2 Pet 2:17-22
Prophets	Mic 3:1-12

REJECTION as
  Author   Heb 6:1-8

in **FAMILY**
  by **DEITY**
    Believers   Heb 12:3-11
    Israelites   Deut 8:1-10
  INSTRUCTION on
    Sirach   *Sir 30:1-13;
        42:1-5
    Solomon   Prov 19:1-29

FEAR of
  Israelites   Lev 26:1-46
  by **DEITY**
    God   Ps 14:4-6
    Israelites   Num 16:25-35
  of **FOLLOWER**s
    Magistrates   Acts 16:25-40
  INSTRUCTION on
    Moses   Deut 19:15-21
  PROPHECY of
    Isaiah   Is 2:18-22;
        30:27-33
  REVELATION on
    Egyptians   Ezek 30:13-19
    Israelites   Ezek 4:16-17

of **FOLLOWER**s
  CAPTIVITY as
    Peter   Acts 12:1-25
  DEATH as
    Rulers   Acts 6:8-8:3
  FEAR of
    Magistrates   Acts 16:25-40
  OPPRESSION as
    Jews   Acts 13:14-52
    Paul   Acts 14:19-28
    Saul   Acts 6:8-8:3
  REJECTION as
    Jesus   Heb 10:19-31
  SADNESS in
    Jesus   Lk 23:27-32
  SUFFERING as
    Paul   Acts 14:19-28
  WITNESS to
    Women   Lk 23:46-49

FULFILLMENT of
  PROPHECY of
    Ahijah   1 Kgs 14:1-18;
        15:25-32
    Elijah   2 Kgs 1:1-18;
        9:30-37;
        10-14
    God   1 Kgs 2:26-27
    Israelites   Num 26:63-65
    Jehoram   2 Chr 21:1-23:21
    Jehu   1 Kgs 16:8-14;
        2 Kgs 9:14-29
    Jeremiah   2 Chr 36:1-23;
        Jer 28:1-17;
        *Sir 49:4-7
    Joshua   1 Kgs 16:29-34
    Josiah   2 Kgs 23:16-20
    Judahites   2 Kgs 23:36-24:7
    Paul   Acts 13:4-12
    Tobiah   *Tb 14:1-15
  REVELATION on
    Ezekiel   Ezek 12:21-28;
        33:21-22

REVELATION on (cont'd)
  Israelites   Ezek 6:8-10
  Nebuchadnezzar   Dan 4:28-33

FULFILLMENT through
  Gideon   Judg 8:13-17
  by **DEITY**
    God   Rev 15:1-16:1

through **GOOD**
  of **DEITY**
    Psalmist   Ps 119:65-72

through **GRACE**
  Solomon   1 Kgs 1:41-53
  of **DEITY**
    Job   Job 35:13-16

for **GREED**
  INSTRUCTION on
    Sirach   *Sir 14:3-19
  REVELATION on
    Eli   1 Sam 2:27-36

GRIEF through
  Micah   Mic 1:5-9
  INSTRUCTION on
    Baruch   *Bar 4:5-16;
        17-20
  MEDITATION on
    Jeremiah   Lam 1:1-22;
        2:1-22
  PROPHECY of
    Moabites   Jer 48:1-47
  REVELATION on
    Judahites   Ezek 24:1-14

for **GUILT**
  Moses   Ex 23:1-9
  by **DEITY**
    God   Nah 1:1-9
  INSTRUCTION on
    Moses   Deut 27:11-26
    Zophar   Job 11:1-6'
  SELF-REALIZATION of
    Joseph   Gen 42:18-25

for **HATE**
  REVELATION on
    Edomites   Ezek 35:1-15

for **HERESY**
  PROPHECY of
    John   Rev 22:6-21

for dis**HONESTY**
  INSTRUCTION on
    Sirach   *Sir 27:22-29

HUMILITY as
  Israelites   Lev 26:1-46
  before **DEITY**
    Jeremiah   Jer 17:13
  for **FALSE BELIEF**
    Ephraimites   Hos 4:17-19
    Prophets   Mic 3:1-12
  MEDITATION on
    Jeremiah   Lam 2:1-22
  PROPHECY of
    Babylonians   Jer 50:1-46
    Ezekiel   Ezek 16:44-52

PROPHECY of (cont'd)
Habakkuk	Hab 2:15-16
Isaiah	Is 3:16-4:1; 5:8-24a
Israelites	Ezek 16:53-63; Hos 4:4-15; 10:1-8
Jeremiah	Jer 13:20-27; 22:20-23
Judahites	Jer 13:18-19
Moabites	Jer 48:1-47
Nineveh	Nah 3:5-19

REVELATION on
Israelites	Jer 2:20-29; 30-37; Hos 2:9-13
Jeremiah	Jer 15:1-4; 5-9
Levites	Ezek 44:10-14

for **IDOLATRY**
before **DEITY**
Israelites	Ps 78:56-66; Ezek 43:6-12
Moses	Deut 31:30-32:47

through **FALSE BELIEF**
Baruch	*Bar 4:5-16
God	Rev 14:9-12
Israelites	Deut 29:16-29

INSTRUCTION on
Moses	Deut 4:15-31; 16:21-17:7
Solomon	*Wis 14:12-31; 16:1-14

PROPHECY of
Babylonians	Jer 50:1-46; 51:1-64
Egyptians	Jer 46:13-26
Elijah	1 Kgs 21:17-29
Habakkuk	Hab 2:18-20
Isaiah	Is 2:6-11
Israelites	Ezek 16:35-43; Amos 3:13-15; 5:26-27
Jeremiah	Jer 32:26-44
Judahites	Jer 44:1-14
Micah	Mic 1:5-9
Moabites	Jer 48:1-47
Zechariah	Zech 12:1-13:6

REVELATION on
Egyptians	Ezek 30:13-19
Ezekiel	Ezek 14:1-11
God	Is 42:5-17
Isaiah	Is 56:9-57:13
Israelites	Ezek 6:8-10; Hos 2:9-13
Jeremiah	Jer 7:16-20; 11:1-14; 16:1-13; 16-18; 19:1-15
John	Rev 16:2
Judahites	Ezek 23:22-35
Levites	Ezek 44:10-14

for **IGNORANCE**
INSTRUCTION on
Jesus	Lk 12:47-48
Solomon	Prov 10:1-32; 26:1-28

PROPHECY of
Israelites	Hos 4:4-15
Jesus	Lk 19:41-44

REVELATION on
God	Gen 12:9-13:1

for **INDIFFERENCE**
by **DEITY**
God	Is 29:13-14
Israelites	Is 42:18-43:7; Amos 4:6-12

PROPHECY of
Isaiah	Is 32:9-14

REVELATION on
Zephaniah	Zeph 1:12-13

INNOCENCE of
by **DEITY**
Job	Job 9:14-19; 20-24

in **ENVIRONMENT**
Benjamin	Gen 44:1-34
Joseph	Gen 39:1-23

INSTRUCTION on
Author	Heb 12:3-11
Eliphaz	Job 5:8-17
God	Ezek 6:11-14
Solomon	Prov 3:1-35

as **ALIENATION**
Bildad	Job 18:16-18; 19-21
Eliphaz	Job 22:12-20
Ephesus	Rev 2:1-7
Jesus	Mt 25:14-30
Nehemiah	Neh 13:4-9
Paul	1 Cor 5:1-5

through **ANGER**
Job	Job 19:25-29
Solomon	Prov 19:1-29

for **BLASPHEMY**
Paul	1 Tim 1:18-20

as **CAPTIVITY**
Baruch	*Bar 4:5-16
Jeremiah	*Jer 6:2-3
Moses	Deut 28:15-68

as **CONDEMNATION**
David	1 Kgs 2:5-12

as **DEATH**
Angel	*2 Esd 7:75-87
Antiochus	*1 Mc 1:41-53
Darius	Dan 6:24; *1 Esd 6:27-34
God	Ps 82:2-7
Israelites	Judg 20:12-17
Jesus	Mt 15:3-9; Mk 7:1-23
Moses	Ex 32:25-29; 35:1-3; Lev 20:1-27; Deut 16:21-17:7; 8-13; 21:18-21; 22-23; 23:15-25:19; 28:15-68
Nebuchadnezzar	Dan 3:1-6; 13-15
Prophet	1 Kgs 20:1-43
Solomon	Prov 5:15-23; 9:13-18

causing **DESPAIR**
　Isaiah　　　　　Is 59:1-21
　Jeremiah　　　　Jer 6:22-26
as **DESTRUCTION**
　Eliphaz　　　　　Job 15:17-35
　God　　　　　　Is 1:18-20;
　　　　　　　　　*2 Esd 2:8-9
　Joshua　　　　　Josh 23:1-16
　Moses　　　　　Deut 6:4-19;
　　　　　　　　　8:11-20;
　　　　　　　　　28:15-68

for **DISOBEDIENCE**
　Achior　　　　　*Jdt 5:1-21
　Agur　　　　　　Prov 30:15-33
　Artaxerxes　　　Ezra 7:25-26;
　　　　　　　　　*1 Esd 8:8-24
　Ezra　　　　　　*1 Esd 9:1-15
　God　　　　　　Gen 2:16-17;
　　　　　　　　　3:14-19
　Jeremiah　　　　Jer 44:20-28
　Jesus　　　　　　Lk 12:41-46;
　　　　　　　　　47-48
　Joshua　　　　　Josh 23:1-16;
　　　　　　　　　24:16-24
　Lot　　　　　　Gen 19:12-29
　Moses　　　　　Deut 28:15-68;
　　　　　　　　　29:16-29
　Nebuchadnezzar　Dan 3:1-6;
　　　　　　　　　13-15
　Paul　　　　　　Rom 2:1-24;
　　　　　　　　　2 Cor 10:1-6;
　　　　　　　　　13:1-4;
　　　　　　　　　2 Thes 3:6-15
　Solomon　　　　Prov 5:1-14;
　　　　　　　　　*Wis 6:1-11

for **DOUBT**
　Author　　　　　Heb 3:12-19
of **ENEMY**
　God　　　　　　Is 1:24-26
for **EVIL**
　Angel　　　　　*2 Esd 7:62-74;
　　　　　　　　　75-87;
　　　　　　　　　8:37-62
　Baruch　　　　　*Bar 4:5-16
　Bildad　　　　　Job 18:5-7;
　　　　　　　　　8-11;
　　　　　　　　　12-15;
　　　　　　　　　16-18;
　　　　　　　　　19-21
　David　　　　　Ps 32:8-11
　Eliphaz　　　　　Job 15:17-35;
　　　　　　　　　22:1-5;
　　　　　　　　　6-11
　God　　　　　　Ps 81:5c-16;
　　　　　　　　　*Wis 12:19-22
　Isaiah　　　　　Is 59:1-21
　Jeremiah　　　　Jer 44:20-28;
　　　　　　　　　*Jer 6:2-3
　Jesus　　　　　　Mt 13:24-30;
　　　　　　　　　47-50;
　　　　　　　　　24:45-51
　Job　　　　　　Job 21:19-27;
　　　　　　　　　31:1-4;
　　　　　　　　　38-40
　Moses　　　　　Deut 17:8-13;
　　　　　　　　　30:15-20
　Pergamum　　　Rev 2:12-17
　Preacher　　　　Eccl 8:10-17
　Sardis　　　　　Rev 3:1-6
　Sirach　　　　　*Sir 16:6-23;
　　　　　　　　　21:1-7;

for **EVIL** (cont'd)
　Sirach　　　　　8-28;
　　　　　　　　　26:28;
　　　　　　　　　27:3-7;
　　　　　　　　　40:12-17;
　　　　　　　　　41:5-13
　Solomon　　　　Prov 6:12-15;
　　　　　　　　　11:1-31;
　　　　　　　　　13:1-25;
　　　　　　　　　15:1-33;
　　　　　　　　　17:1-28;
　　　　　　　　　19:1-29;
　　　　　　　　　20:1-30;
　　　　　　　　　21:1-31;
　　　　　　　　　22:1-16;
　　　　　　　　　23:15-24:22;
　　　　　　　　　23-34;
　　　　　　　　　*Wis 1:6-11;
　　　　　　　　　3:10-19;
　　　　　　　　　4:1-9;
　　　　　　　　　10-20;
　　　　　　　　　16:15-29;
　　　　　　　　　17:1-21

for **GREED**
　Sirach　　　　　*Sir 14:3-19
resulting in **GRIEF**
　Baruch　　　　　*Bar 4:5-16;
　　　　　　　　　17-20
for **GUILT**
　Moses　　　　　Deut 27:11-26
　Zophar　　　　　Job 11:1-6
for **disHONESTY**
　Sirach　　　　　*Sir 27:22-29
for **IDOLATRY**
　Moses　　　　　Deut 4:15-31;
　　　　　　　　　16:21-17:7
　Solomon　　　　*Wis 14:12-31;
　　　　　　　　　16:1-14
for **IGNORANCE**
　Jesus　　　　　　Lk 12:47-48
　Solomon　　　　Prov 10:1-32;
　　　　　　　　　26:1-28
for **KILLING**
　Jehoiada　　　　2 Kgs 11:4-20
　Jehu　　　　　　2 Kgs 10:1-14
　Moses　　　　　Deut 19:1-13
　Solomon　　　　1 Kgs 2:13-25;
　　　　　　　　　28-35;
　　　　　　　　　36-46;
　　　　　　　　　Prov 28:1-28
with **LOVE**
　Laodicea　　　　Rev 3:14-22
　Solomon　　　　Prov 13:1-25
for **LUST**
　Solomon　　　　Prov 21:1-31
as **OPPRESSION**
　Solomon　　　　Prov 22:1-16
through **POLITICS**
　Ahasuerus　　　Esth 1:10-22
of **POVERTY**
　Solomon　　　　Prov 6:6-11
for **PRIDE**
　Jesus　　　　　　Mk 12:37b-40;
　　　　　　　　　Lk 20:45-47
　Sirach　　　　　*Sir 10:12-25
　Solomon　　　　Prov 18:1-24
of **REJECTION**
　John the Baptist　Mt 3:1-12
　Paul　　　　　　2 Thes 3:6-15
　Solomon　　　　Prov 13:1-25
　Wisdom　　　　Prov 1:20-33

through **POLITICS**
  INSTRUCTION on
    Ahasuerus   Esth 1:10-22

POVERTY as
  INSTRUCTION on
    Solomon   Prov 6:6-11
  PROPHECY of
    Isaiah   Is 3:16-4:1
    Judahites   Jer 17:1-4
  REVELATION on
    Israelites   Hos 2:9-13

for **PRIDE**
  by **DEITY**
    Assyrians   Is 10:5-16
    Eliphaz   Job 22:21-30
    God   Is 2:12-17
    Hezekiah   2 Chr 32:1-33
  in **ENVIRONMENT**
    Azariah   *1 Mc 5:55-62
  INSTRUCTION on
    Jesus   Mk 12:37b-40;
              Lk 20:45-47
    Sirach   *Sir 10:12-25
    Solomon   Prov 18:1-24
  PROPHECY of
    Ephraimites   Hos 5:8-14
    Isaiah   Is 13:1-22;
              28:1-13
    Moab   Is 15:1-16:14
    Moabites   Is 25:10-12
    Tyre   Is 23:1-14
  REVELATION on
    Egyptians   Ezek 31:10-18
    Habakkuk   Hab 2:5-6a
    Israelites   Ezek 7:1-27
    Judahites   Jer 13:1-11
    Malachi   Mal 3:13-4:3

PROPHECY of
  as **ALIENATION**
    Ammonites   Amos 1:13-15
    Amos   Amos 1:3-5;
              6-8
    Coniah   Jer 22:24-30
    Edomites   Obad 1:10-14
    Ephraimites   Hos 5:3-7;
              9:10-17
    God   Hos 5:8-14
    Habakkuk   Hab 2:9-11
    Isaiah   Is 34:1-17
    Israelites   Ezek 16:44-52;
              Amos 5:26-27;
              6:1-7;
              7:10-17
    Judahites   Jer 7:1-15
    Micah   Mic 1:10-16
              5:7-15
    Nineveh   Nah 1:11;
              14
    Women   Amos 4:1-3
    Zephaniah   Zeph 2:4-7
  through **ANGER**
    God   Mic 5:7-15
    Isaiah   Is 13:1-22
    Israelites   Hos 13:9-11
    Jeremiah   Jer 6:9-15
    Judahites   Jer 4:5-8;
              42:7-22
    Prophets   Jer 23:16-22

for **BLASPHEMY**
  Jeremiah   Jer 32:26-44
  Moabites   Jer 48:1-47
as **CAPTIVITY**
  Assyrians   Is 31:4-9
  Babylonians   Jer 25:8-14
  Coniah   Jer 22:24-30
  Egyptians   Jer 46:13-26
  Ephraimites   Hos 9:1-6
  Isaiah   Is 24:18c-23
  Israelites   Hos 11:5-7
  Jeremiah   Jer 5:18-19;
              20:1-6;
              21:1-10;
              22:20-23;
              34:13-22;
              43:8-13
  Judahites   Jer 13:18-19;
              17:1-4;
              25:8-14
  Moabites   Jer 48:1-47
for **CHAOS**
  Isaiah   Is 13:1-22;
              22:1-14;
              24:1-12;
              34:1-17
  Jeremiah   Jer 13:12-14;
              23:1-8
  Jesus   Lk 19:41-44;
              23:27-32
as **CONDEMNATION**
  Shebna   Is 22:15-25
for **COVETOUSNESS**
  Habakkuk   Hab 2:6b-8
as **DEATH**
  Ahab   1 Kgs 21:17-29
  Ahijah   1 Kgs 14:1-18
  Amaziah   Amos 7:10-17
  Coniah   Jer 22:24-30
  Edomites   Obad 1:5-9
  Elijah   2 Kgs 1:1-18
  Ephraimites   Hos 7:13-16;
              9:10-17
  Isaiah   Is 3:16-4:1
  Israelites   Ezek 16:35-43;
              Amos 2:13-16;
              5:1-3;
              6:8-11
  Jehoiakim   Jer 22:13-19
  Jeremiah   Jer 16:1-13;
              20:1-6;
              21:1-10;
              29:1-23;
              42:7-22;
              43:8-13;
              44:20-28
  Jezebel   Rev 2:18-29
  Judahites   Jer 9:10-22;
              42:7-22;
              44:1-14
  Obadiah   Obad 1:17-21
  Samaria   Hos 13:15-16
  Samuel   1 Sam 28:3-25
  Shebna   Is 22:15-25
as **DEFEAT**
  Edomites   Obad 1:1b-4
  Isaiah   Is 5:24b-30;
              30:8-17
  Israelites   Amos 2:13-16
  Micah   Mic 1:10-16
  Samuel   1 Sam 28:3-25

as DEFEAT (cont'd)	
Sennacherib	Is 37:22-29
Zechariah	Zech 11:1-3
causing **DESPAIR**	
Egyptians	Is 19:1-15
Isaiah	Is 8:19-22;
	21:1-10
as **DESTRUCTION**	
Ammonites	Amos 1:13-15
Amos	Amos 1:3-5
Assyrians	Zeph 2:13-14
Baasha	1 Kgs 15:33-16:7
Edomites	Jer 49:7-22;
	Amos 1:11-12
Ephraimites	Is 28:1-13;
	Hos 5:3-7;
	8-14;
	13:15-16
Habakkuk	Hab 2:12-14;
	17
Isaiah	Is 10:20-23;
	33-34;
	17:12-14;
	19:1-15;
	21:1-10;
	22:1-14;
	24:1-12;
	26:20-27:1;
	28:14-22;
	30:27-33;
	31:1-3;
	32:9-14;
	33:1-6;
	7-16;
	34:1-17;
	66:1-16
Israelites	Jer 5:15-17;
	6:16-21;
	11:15-17;
	Ezek 16:35-43;
	Hos 8:4-7;
	11-14;
	10:1-8;
	13:7-8;
	9-11;
	Amos 3:13-15;
	5:4-6;
	6:8-11;
	7:10-17
Jeremiah	Jer 4:13-18;
	19-22;
	23-26;
	5:1-14;
	6:1-8;
	7:29-8:3;
	14-17;
	13:12-14;
	14:10-12;
	17-18;
	16:1-13;
	17:19-27;
	21:13-14;
	22:1-9;
	20-23;
	29:1-23;
	32:26-44;
	34:13-22;
	43:8-13;
	44:20-28;
	45:1-5

as **DESTRUCTION** (cont'd)	
Jeroboam	1 Kgs 13:1-34
Jesus	Lk 19:41-44
Joel	Joel 3:16b-21
John the Baptist	Mt 3:1-12;
	Lk 3:7-9;
	15-17
Judahites	Jer 4:5-8;
	8:8-13;
	9:10-22;
	44:1-14;
	Hos 5:3-7;
	Amos 2:4-5
Micah	Mic 1:5-9;
	2:1-10;
	3:1-12;
	5:7-15
Moabites	Is 25:10-12;
	Amos 2:1-3
Nineveh	Nah 1:11;
	14;
	2:11-13;
	3:5-19;
	Zeph 2:13-14;
	15
Philistines	Amos 1:6-8
Shebna	Is 22:15-25
Tyre	Is 23:1-14;
	Ezek 26:7-14;
	19-21;
	Amos 1:9-10;
	Zech 9:1-12
Women	Amos 4:1-3
Zechariah	Zech 9:13-17;
	11:1-3;
	Jer 27:12-15
Zephaniah	Zeph 1:14-16;
	17-18;
	2:4-7
for **DISOBEDIENCE**	
Ahijah	1 Kgs 11:26-40
Amaziah	2 Chr 25:1-28
Asa	2 Chr 14:1-16:14
God	Mic 5:7-15
Huldah	2 Kgs 22:3-20
Jeremiah	Jer 17:19-27;
	29:1-23;
	34:13-22
Jeroboam	1 Kgs 13:1-34;
	14:1-18
Judahites	Jer 44:1-14
Samuel	1 Sam 13:1-23;
	28:3-25
Zedekiah	Jer 22:1-9
for **DOUBT**	
Israelites	Jer 18:18-23
of **ENEMY**	
Baruch	*Bar 4:21-37
Isaiah	Is 17:12-14
Joel	Joel 3:16b-21
Judahites	Zeph 2:4-7
Micah	Mic 1:10-16
Zechariah	Zech 2:6-13
for **EVIL**	
Amos	Amos 1:3-5;
	6-8
Angel	*2 Esd 7:33-44;
	13:1-50
Babylonians	Jer 50:1-46
Ephraimites	Hos 7:8-12;

for **EVIL** (cont'd)

Ephraimites	9:1-6; 13:1-3
Habakkuk	Hab 2:9-11; 12-14; 15-16; 17
Isaiah	Is 1:27-31; 5:8-24a; 24b-30; 13:1-22; 22:1-14; 24:1-12; 16b-18b; 18c-23; 26:20-27:1; 28:1-13; 30:1-7; 31:1-3; 56:9-57:13
Israelites	Jer 6:16-21; 11:15-17; Ezek 16:35-43; Hos 4:4-15; 5:1-2; 12:10-14; Amos 3:1-2; 6:12-14
Jehoiakim	Jer 22:13-19
Jeremiah	Jer 5:1-14; 26-29; 6:1-8; 9-15; 13:20-27; 14:10-12; 19:1-15; 21:11-12; 22:20-23; 23:1-8; 32:26-44; 45:1-5
Judahites	Jer 7:1-15; 8:8-13; 25:8-14; 35:6-17
Micah	Mic 1:5-9; 10-16; 2:1-10
Nathan	2 Sam 12:1-31
Prophets	Jer 23:9-12; 13-15; 16-22
Zephaniah	Zeph 1:17-18

resulting in **GRIEF**

Moabites	Jer 48:1-47

for **HERESY**

John	Rev 22:6-21

as **HUMILITY**

Babylonians	Jer 50:1-46
Ezekiel	Ezek 16:44-52
Habakkuk	Hab 2:15-16
Isaiah	Is 3:16-4:1; 5:8-24a
Israelites	Ezek 16:53-63; Hos 4:4-15; 10:1-8
Jeremiah	Jer 13:20-27; 22:20-23
Judahites	Jer 13:18-19
Moabites	Jer 48:1-47
Nineveh	Nah 3:5-19

for **IDOLATRY**

Babylonians	Jer 50:1-46; 51:1-64
Egyptians	Jer 46:13-26
Elijah	1 Kgs 21:17-29
Habakkuk	Hab 2:18-20
Isaiah	Is 2:6-11
Israelites	Ezek 16:35-43; Amos 3:13-15; 5:26-27
Jeremiah	Jer 32:26-44
Judahites	Jer 44:1-14
Micah	Mic 1:5-9
Moabites	Jer 48:1-47
Zechariah	Zech 12:1-13:6

for **IGNORANCE**

Israelites	Hos 4:4-15
Jesus	Lk 19:41-44

for **INDIFFERNCE**

Isaiah	Is 32:9-14

with **JUSTICE**

Babylonians	Jer 50:1-46
Edomites	Obad 1:15-16
Isaiah	Is 3:8-12; 27:7-11
Israelites	Jer 46:27-28; Ezek 16:35-43; Hos 4:4-15; 12:2-6
Jeremiah	Jer 21:13-14; 31:29-30

as **KILLING**

Habakkuk	Hab 2:12-14; 17
Jehu	2 Chr 21:1-23:21
Prophet	2 Kgs 9:1-13

of **LEADERSHIP**

Coniah	Jer 22:24-30
Isaiah	Is 9:8-10:4

through **MIRACLE**

Jeremiah	Jer 7:29-8:3

as **OPPRESSION**

Babylonians	Jer 50:1-46
Egyptians	Is 19:1-15
Ephraimites	Hos 5:8-14; 7:8-12; 12:7-9
Habakkuk	Hab 2:6b-8
Isaiah	Is 3:1-7; 5:24b-30; Is 28:1-13
Israelites	Ezek 16:35-43; Hos 8:1-3; 8-10; 11:5-7; Amos 2:13-16; 6:12-14; 8:11-14
Jeremiah	Jer 13:20-27; 29:1-23; 32:26-44; 34:13-22
Micah	Mic 7:1-6
Moabites	Jer 48:1-47
Nineveh	Nah 3:5-19

as **POVERTY**

Isaiah	Is 3:16-4:1
Judahites	Jer 17:1-4

for **PRIDE**

Ephraimites	Hos 5:8-14
Isaiah	Is 13:1-22;

REVELATION on (cont'd)
Jeremiah	Jer 16:1-13;
	19:1-15
Judahites	Ezek 23:22-35
Moses	Num 14:11-24;
	20:2-13
Nations	Zeph 3:6-7
People	Jer 27:1-11
Zedekiah	Jer 24:1-10
Zephaniah	Zeph 1:2-6
in WORSHIP	
God	Zech 14:1-21

REPENTANCE of
by DEITY
David	1 Chr 21:1-22:1
God	Ex 32:7-14;
	Jer 42:7-22;
	Amos 7:1-3;
	4-6;
	Jon 3:1-10
Israelites	2 Sam 24:1-25;
	1 Chr 21:1-22:1
Rehoboam	2 Chr 10:1-12:16
in MISSION	
Jeremiah	Jer 6:27-30

REVELATION on
as ALIENATION
Ammonites	Ezek 25:1-7
Egyptians	Ezek 29:1-5;
	6-9a
Ezekiel	Ezek 14:1-11;
	12-23
Hosea	Hos 1:8-9
Israelites	Ezek 39:17-24;
	Amos 8:1-3;
	Zech 13:7-9
Jeremiah	Jer 23:33-40
Joel	Joel 3:4-8
Judahites	Jer 3:6-11;
	Ezek 23:11-21
King	Ezek 28:11-19
Levites	Ezek 44:10-14
Moses	Lev 21:1-22:33;
	23:26-32
Nations	Zeph 3:6-7
?.b.chadnezzar	Dan 4:28-33
Prophetesses	Ezek 13:17-23
Samuel	1 Sam 3:1-4:1a
Satan	Rev 12:7-9
Solomon	1 Kgs 11:1-13
Zechariah	Zech 5:1-4
Zephaniah	Zeph 1:2-6;
	10-11

through ANGER
Edomites	Ezek 25:12-14;
	35:1-15
Egyptians	Ezek 30:13-19
Ezekiel	Ezek 8:16-18;
	13:1-16;
	36:1-7
Israelites	Num 11:1-3;
	Ezek 5:5-17;
	6:11-14;
	7:1-27;
	19:10-14;
	22:17-22;
	23-31;
	36:16-21

through ANGER (cont'd)
Jeremiah	Jer 7:16-20;
	25:30-38;
	30:23-31:1;
	33:1-9
John	Rev 14:17-20
Judahites	Ezek 23:22-35;
	24:1-14
Philistines	Ezek 25:15-17
Rulers	Zech 10:3-12

for BLASPHEMY
Israelites	Ezek 5:5-17
Jeremiah	Jer 19:1-15
Samuel	1 Sam 3:1-4:1a
Zechariah	Zech 5:1-4

as CAPTIVITY
Ammonites	Ezek 25:1-7;
	Zeph 2:8-12
Egyptians	Ezek 30:13-19;
	32:1-16
Israelites	Ezek 21:18-24
Jeremiah	Jer 15:10-21
Joel	Joel 3:4-8
Moabites	Ezek 25:8-11;
	Zeph 2:8-12

as CONDEMNATION
Zedekiah	Jer 24:1-10

as DEATH
Ammonites	Ezek 21:28-32
Egyptians	Ezek 29:1-5;
	30:13-19;
	32:1-16;
	17-32
Eli	1 Sam 2:27-36
Elijah	1 Kgs 21:17-29
Ezekiel	Ezek 6:1-7;
	9:1-11;
	11:1-13
God	Gen 2:16-17;
	Lev 10:1-20
Israelites	Num 14:26-38;
	Ezek 6:11-14;
	7:1-27;
	12:1-16;
	17:11-21;
	21:8-17;
	23:5-10;
	Amos 8:1-3;
	9:1-4
Jehoiakim	Jer 36:27-32
Jeremiah	Jer 11:18-12:6;
	15:1-4;
	5-9;
	19:1-15;
	25:30-38;
	33:1-9
John	Rev 11:1-14;
	16:3
King	Ezek 28:11-19
Moses	Lev 21:1-22:33;
	Num 15:32-36;
	27:12-23;
	Deut 32:48-52
Sidon	Ezek 28:20-23
Tyre	Ezek 28:1-10

as DEFEAT
Ammonites	Ezek 25:1-7
Israelites	Hos 1:4-5
John	Rev 14:8

as DESTRUCTION

as **DESTRUCTION** (cont'd)

Ammonites	Ezek 21:28-32; 25:1-7; Zeph 2:8-12
Belshazzar	Dan 5:26-28
Chaldeans	Is 47:1-15
Edomites	Ezek 25:12-14; 35:1-15
Egyptians	Ezek 29:1-5; 6-9a; 9b-16; 30:13-19; 31:10-18; 32:1-16
Ezekiel	Ezek 6:1-7; 13:1-16; 14:1-11; 20:45-49; 21:25-27
God	Is 41:1-42:4
Gog	Ezek 39:1-16
Isaiah	Is 5:1-7; 6:1-13; 56:9-57:13; 65:1-25
Israelites	Jer 2:14-19; 5:1-14; Ezek 5:5-17; 6:11-14; 7:1-27; 21:1-7; 8-17; 22:1-16; 23:5-10; 36-49; Hos 1:4-5; 2:9-13; Amos 7:7-9; 8:8-10; 9:1-4; Zech 13:7-9
Jacobites	Amos 9:8-10
Jehu	1 Kgs 15:33-16:7
Jeremiah	Jer 15:1-4; 5-9; 19:1-15; 25:15-29; 30-38
Jesus	2 Thes 1:7b-10
John	Rev 11:1-14; 18:4-20
Judahites	Jer 13:1-11; Ezek 23:22-35; 24:1-14
Malachi	Mal 3:13-4:3
Micah	Mic 6:9-16
Moabites	Ezek 25:8-11; Zeph 2:8-12
Nations	Zeph 3:6-7; 8
People	Jer 27:1-11
Philistines	Ezek 25:15-17
Prophets	2 Kgs 21:1-18; Jer 14:13-16
Solomon	2 Chr 7:11-22
Tyre	Ezek 26:1-6; 27:25b-36; 28:1-10
Zechariah	Zech 5:1-4
Zedekiah	Jer 24:1-10

as **DESTRUCTION** (cont'd)

Zephaniah	Zeph 1:2-6; 10-11; 12-13

for **DISOBEDIENCE**

Ezekiel	Ezek 3:16-21; 11:1-13
Holy Spirit	Heb 3:6b-11
Isaiah	Is 31:4-9
Israelites	Num 14:26-38; Is 48:1-22; Jer 9:25-26
Jeremiah	Jer 16:1-13; 23:33-40
Judahites	Jer 13:1-11
Moses	Num 16:36-50
Nathan	2 Sam 7:1-29; 1 Chr 17:1-27
Solomon	1 Kgs 9:1-9; 11:1-13

for **DOUBT**

Gabriel	Lk 1:5-25
God	Num 12:11-16

of **ENEMY**

Ezekiel	Ezek 36:1-7
God	Is 1:24-26; *2 Esd 15:1-16:50
Israelites	Is 51:17-52:12; Zeph 2:8-12
Jeremiah	Jer 30:12-17
Zechariah	Zech 1:18-21

for **EVIL**

Chaldeans	Is 47:1-15
Egyptians	Ezek 32:17-32
Ezekiel	Ezek 8:16-18; 9:1-11; 11:14-21; 20:45-49
God	Gen 20:1-18; Ps 9:15-16; *2 Esd 15:1-16:50
Habakkuk	Hab 2:1-4
Isaiah	Is 51:1-16; 57:14-21; 65:1-25; 66:1-16
Israelites	Is 50:1-11; Jer 2:14-19; 3:1-5; 30:10-11; Ezek 5:5-17; 7:1-27; 15:1-8; 17:11-21; 20:32-39; 21:18-24; 22:1-16; 23:5-10; 36-49; 36:16-21; 39:17-24; Hos 2:2-8; Amos 9:8-10
Jehoiakim	Jer 36:27-32
Jeremiah	Jer 1:13-16; 3:21-4:4; 11:1-14; 18-12:6; 14:13-16; 16:16-18;

by **DEITY** (cont'd)
God	Rev 16:4-7
Israelites	Ex 32:30-35;
	Neh 9:26-31;
	Is 1:4-9
Job	Job 10:13-17;
	19:7-12
Uzziah	2 Chr 26:1-28:27

of **FOLLOWER**
Paul	Acts 14:19-28

INSTRUCTION on
Israelites	Is 50:1-11
Jesus	Mt 13:47-50;
	18:7-9;
	Mk 9:42-48
Moses	Deut 28:15-68

MEDITATION on
Jeremiah	Lam 2:1-22

PROPHECY of
Elijah	2 Chr 21:1-23:21
Ephraimites	Hos 9:10-17;
	13:12-14
Habakkuk	Hab 2:6b-8
Haggai	Hag 1:1-11
Huldah	2 Chr 34:1-35:27
Isaiah	Is 8:19-22;
	17:9-11;
	24:1-12;
	29:1-8
Jeremiah	Jer 4:19-22;
	10:17-22;
	14:1-6;
	10-12;
	21:1-10
Jesus	Lk 23:27-32
Moab	Is 15:1-16:14
Moabites	Jer 48:1-47
People	Zech 14:1-21
Prophets	Jer 23:9-12;
	13-15
Zephaniah	Zeph 1:17-18

REVELATION on
Egyptians	Ezek 30:13-19
Ezekiel	Ezek 14:12-23
Isaiah	Is 65:1-25;
	66:1-16
Israelites	Jer 2:14-19;
	3:1-5;
	Ezek 4:16-17;
	7:1-27;
	Amos 8:8-10;
	11-14
Jeremiah	Jer 14:13-16;
	15:1-4;
	5-9;
	25:15-29;
	30:12-17
John	Rev 15:1-16:1;
	2;
	8-9;
	10-11;
	18:4-20;
	20:11-15
Micah	Mic 6:9-16
Rulers	Zech 11:15-17
Sinners	Rev 21:1-8

for **TEMPTATION**
INSTRUCTION on
Jesus	Mt 18:5-6;

INSTRUCTION on (cont'd)
Jesus	Mk 9:42-48;
	Lk 17:1-6

TRADITION concerning
by **DEATH**
Pharisees	Jn 7:53-8:11

for **DISOBEDIENCE**
Solomon	*Wis 11:1-20

for **EVIL**
Solomon	*Wis 10:1-21;
	19:13-17;
	*Sir 47:12-22

TRADITION reveals
as **CAPTIVITY**
Israelites	*Sir 48:15-16;
	49:4-7

concerning **VIOLENCE**
REVELATION on
Amos	Amos 7:7-9
Ezekiel	Ezek 6:1-7;
	11:1-13;
	14:12-23
God	*2 Esd 15:1-16:5
Isaiah	Is 54:1-17
Israelites	Ezek 5:5-17;
	7:1-27;
	21:8-17
Jeremiah	Jer 25:30-38
Zephaniah	Zeph 1:8-9

for **VIOLENCE**
INSTRUCTION on
Solomon	Prov 21:1-31

PROPHECY of
Habakkuk	Hab 2:12-14;
	17
Isaiah	Is 3:16-4:1
Jeremiah	Jer 22:13-19

for **WEALTH**
INSTRUCTION on
James	Jas 5:1-6

WILL in
by **DEITY**
Tyre	Is 23:1-14

WISDOM in
by **DEITY**
Sirach	*Sir 32:14-24

WITNESS to
of **FOLLOWER**
Women	Lk 23:46-49

PROPHECY of
Amos	Amos 3:13-15

for false **WORSHIP**
ALIENATION as
Israelites	Ex 30:22-33;
	34-38

DEATH as
Alcimus	*1 Mc 9:54-57
Israelites	Ex 30:17-21;
	31:12-17

in **BROTHERHOOD**
  Peter — Acts 10:1-11:18
of **CREATION**
  Holy Spirit — Jn 3:1-21
resulting in **FIDELITY**
  Elisha — 2 Kgs 5:1-19
as **MOTIVATION**
  Paul — 1 Cor 15:29-34
in **NEW AGE**
  Holy Spirit — Jn 3:1-21
  Paul — Rom 6:1-14;
    1 Cor 6:9-11
as **QUALITY OF LIFE**
  Jesus — Lk 11:37-44
as **RITE**
  David — 1 Chr 15:1-16:43
  Isaiah — Is 51:17-52:12
  Jesus — Mt 23:25-26
  Moses — Ex 19:9-15;
    Deut 21:1-9
  Nehemiah — Neh 13:4-9
for **SALVATION**
  Holy Spirit — Jn 3:1-21
  Paul — 1 Cor 3:10-17;
    6:9-11;
    Col 2:6-15
  Peter — 1 Pet 3:18-22
of **SIN**
  Peter — Acts 2:37-41
through **TRUTH**
  Believers — 1 Pet 1:13-2:3
  Jesus — Jn 15:1-11
as **VIRTUE**
  Paul — 2 Cor 6:14-7:1

JUDGMENT on
  INSTRUCTION on
    Paul — Rom 14:1-23
  REVELATION on
    Israelites — Is 48:1-22;
      Ezek 20:32-39

LAW concerning
  INSTRUCTION on
    Jesus — Mt 8:2-4;
      Mk 1:40-45;
      Lk 5:12-16
    Moses — Deut 23:9-14
    Paul — Rom 2:25-3:20
  REVELATION on
    Moses — Lev 12:1-8;
      13:1-59;
      14:1-32;
      33-54;
      15:1-33;
      16:29-34;
      21:1-22:33;
      Num 5:1-4
  TRADITION of
    Jesus — Lk 2:21-40
    Paul — Acts 21:15-26

by **MESSIANIC FIGURE**
  for **SIN**
    Jesus — Heb 1:2b-4
  as **STEWARDSHIP**
    Jesus — Jn 13:1-20

by **MESSIANIC FIGURE's**
  AUTHORITY
    Holy Spirit — Jn 1:19-51

of **MESSIANIC FIGURE**
  BEHAVIOR revealing
    Jesus — Jn 3:22-30
  for **RECONCILIATION**
    Jesus — Heb 9:1-14

MISSION of
  BEHAVIOR revealing
    John the Baptist — Jn 3:22-30
  BELIEF in
    John the Baptist — Mt 3:1-12;
      Lk 3:1-6
  CONVERSION through
    Disciples — Mt 28:16-20

MOTIVATION for
  INSTRUCTION on
    Paul — 1 Cor 15:29-34

in **NEW AGE**
  of **FOLLOWERs**
    Jesus — Gal 3:26-29
  INSTRUCTION on
    Holy Spirit — Jn 3:1-21
    Paul — Rom 6:1-14;
      1 Cor 6:9-11
  PROPHECY of
    John the Baptist — Mt 3:1-12;
      Lk 3:15-17

PRAYER for
  by **DEITY**
    David — Ps 51:3-12
  in **WORSHIP**
    Hezekiah — 2 Chr 30:1-31:21

in **PRESENCE**
  of **DEITY**
    Jesus — Jn 1:19-51

PROPHECY of
  in **NEW AGE**
    John the Baptist — Mt 3:1-12;
      Lk 3:15-17
  through **PROVIDENCE**
    of **DEITY**
      God — Is 1:24-26

as **QUALITY OF LIFE**
  INSTRUCTION on
    Jesus — Lk 11:37-44

RECONCILIATION through
  Priest — Lev 14:33-54
  COVENANT of
    Jesus — Heb 9:15-22
  of **FOLLOWER**
    Jesus — Eph 5:21-33;
      Tit 2:11-15
  INSTRUCTION on
    Author — Heb 10:19-31
    John the Baptist — Lk 3:1-6
  by **MESSIANIC FIGURE**
    Jesus — Heb 9:1-14
  PROPHECY of
    Isaiah — Is 4:2-6
    Jerusalemites — Zech 12:1-13:6
  REVELATION on
    Ezekiel — Ezek 43:15-27
    Israelites — Ezek 36:22-32;
      33-36

REVELATION on
　　through COMMITMENT
　　　　Judahites　　　　Jer 3:21-4:4

RITE of
　　　　Israelites　　　　Josh 5:2-9
　　　　Levites　　　　Num 8:5-22
　　　　Moses　　　　Lev 16:1-5;
　　　　　　　　　　11-28;
　　　　　　　　　　Num 19:1-10;
　　　　　　　　　　11-13;
　　　　　　　　　　14-22
　　of FOLLOWERs
　　　　Believers　　　　Acts 8:4-13
　　　　Corinthians　　　Acts 18:1-17
　　　　Ephesians　　　Acts 19:1-12
　　　　Jailer　　　　Acts 16:25-40
　　　　Lydia　　　　Acts 16:11-15
　　　　Saul　　　　Acts 9:1-19
　　　　Timothy　　　Acts 16:1-5
　　INSTRUCTION on
　　　　David　　　　1 Chr 15:1-16:43
　　　　Isaiah　　　　Is 51:17-52:12
　　　　Jesus　　　　Mt 23:25-26
　　　　Moses　　　　Ex 19:9-15;
　　　　　　　　　　Deut 21:1-9
　　　　Nehemiah　　　Neh 13:4-9
　　REVELATION on
　　　　Ezekiel　　　Ezek 16:8-14
　　　　Israelites　　　Ezek 45:18-25
　　　　Joshua　　　Josh 5:2-9
　　　　Moses　　　　Lev 17:15-16;
　　　　　　　　　　Num 6:1-21
　　　　Priests　　　Ezek 44:15-31
　　TRADITION of
　　　　Jesus　　　　Lk 2:21-40
　　　　Jews　　　　*2 Mc 2:16-18
　　　　Leper　　　　Mt 8:2-4;
　　　　　　　　　　Mk 1:40-45;
　　　　　　　　　　Lk 5:12-16
　　　　Pharisees　　Lk 11:37-44
　　in WORSHIP
　　　　Ethiopian　　Acts 8:26-40
　　　　Israelites　　*1 Esd 7:10-15
　　　　Jews　　　　*2 Mc 1:18-36
　　　　Levites　　　Ezra 6:19-22;
　　　　　　　　　　Neh 12:30;
　　　　　　　　　　44-13:3
　　　　Maccabeus　　*1 Mc 4:36-61

SALVATION through
　　by DEITY
　　　　Believers　　Tit 3:1-7
　　FALSE BELIEF concerning
　　　　Judeans　　Acts 15:1-5
　　INSTRUCTION on
　　　　Holy Spirit　　Jn 3:1-21
　　　　Paul　　　　1 Cor 3:10-17;
　　　　　　　　　　6:9-11;
　　　　　　　　　　Col 2:6-15
　　　　Peter　　　1 Pet 3:18-22

SIGNS of
　　REVELATION on
　　　　Israelites　　Mal 2:17-3:5
　　TRADITION of
　　　　Israelites　　Ex 30:17-21
　　of SIN
　　　　Moses　　　Lev 16:29-34

INSTRUCTION on
　　　　Peter　　　Acts 2:37-41
　　by MESSIANIC FIGURE
　　　　Jesus　　　Heb 1:2b-4

in STEWARDSHIP
　　by MESSIANIC FIGURE
　　　　Jesus　　　Jn 13:1-20

through TRUTH
　　INSTRUCTION on
　　　　Believers　　1 Pet 1:13-2:3
　　　　Jesus　　　Jn 15:1-11

VIRTUE in
　　INSTRUCTION in
　　　　Paul　　　　2 Cor 6:14-7:1

in WORSHIP
　　COMMITMENT through
　　　　Converts　　Mt 3:1-12;
　　　　　　　　　　Mk 1:2-8
　　of disHONESTY
　　　　Author　　Heb 10:19-31
　　PRAYER for
　　　　Hezekiah　　2 Chr 30:1-31:21
　　RITE of
　　　　Ethiopian　　Acts 8:26-40
　　　　Israelites　　*1 Esd 7:10-15
　　　　Jews　　　　*2 Mc 1:18-36
　　　　Levites　　　Ezra 6:19-22;
　　　　　　　　　　Neh 12:30;
　　　　　　　　　　44-13:3;
　　　　　　　　　　*1 Mc 4:36-61

QUALITY OF LIFE

as ACCEPTANCE
　　by DEITY
　　　　God　　　　Mic 6:6-8
　　　　Sirach　　　*Sir 41:1-4
　　INSTRUCTION on
　　　　Jesus　　　Mk 9:33-37
　　　　Maiden　　Song 1:5-6
　　　　Paul　　　　1 Cor 7:17-24;
　　　　　　　　　　25-35

ALIENATION as
　　　　Moses　　　Lev 13:1-59

INSTRUCTION on
　　　　Job　　　　Job 30:1-18
　　REVELATION on
　　　　Jeremiah　　Jer 16:1-13

ANGER as
　　INSTRUCTION on
　　　　Solomon　　Prov 19:1-29

ANXIETY as
　　　　Daughters　　Song 8:8-9
　　　　David　　　Ps 69:13-21
　　　　Jeremiah　　Jer 20:7-18
　　MEDITATION on
　　　　Jeremiah　　Jer 15:10-21

SELF-REALIZATION of
David   Ps 55:1-3a;
                    3b-8

BLASPHEMY as
    Pharisees   Mk 7:1-23

BLESSING as
    of **DEITY**
       Isaac   Gen 26:12-31
    INSTRUCTION on
       Wisdom   Prov 8:1-21
    PROPHECY of
       Jacob   Gen 49:1-28
    REVELATION on
       Isaiah   Is 66:1-16

CAPTIVITY as
    Israelites   Is 42:18-43:7
    Jeremiah   Jer 32:1-8;
                    33:1-9
    Jonah   Jon 1:1-17
    Samson   Judg 16:16-22
    INSTRUCTION on
       Paul   2 Cor 6:11-13
    PROPHECY of
       Shallum   Jer 22:1-112

COMPASSION as
    of **DEITY**
       God   Ex 22:21-31
    INSTRUCTION on
       Jesus   Mt 18:23-35
       Paul   Col 3:5-17

CONDEMNATION as
    of **DEITY**
       Judahites   Jer 9:2-9
    INSTRUCTION on
       Bildad   Job 18:5-7;
                    8-11
       Jesus   Lk 6:24-26
       Laodicea   Rev 3:14-22

DEATH as
    Mankind   Ps 103:14-18;
                    144:3-4;
                    Jas 1:9-11;
                    1 Pet 1:13-2:3
    INSTRUCTION on
       James   Jas 4:13-16
       Preacher   Eccl 11:9-12:7
       Psalmist   Ps 49:16-20
       Sirach   *Sir 10:6-11;
                    11:14-20;
                    14:3-19;
                    17:15-32;
                    18:1-14;
                    41:1-4
    MEDITATION on
       Job   Job 14:7-12
       Preacher   Eccl 3:16-4:3
       Psalmist   Ps 49:5-12
    PROPHECY of
       Isaiah   Is 40:1-11
    SELF-REALIZATION of
       David   1 Chr 28:1-29:30
       Job   Job 13:28-14:6
       Moses   Ps 90:1-12
       Ungodly Men   *Wis 1:16-2:5

DEFEAT as a
    SELF-REALIZATION of
       Job   Job 13:28-14:6

of **DEITY**
    BLESSING as
       Isaac   Gen 26:12-31
    COMPASSION as
       God   Ex 22:21-31
    CONDEMNATION as
       Judahites   Jer 9:2-9
    GOOD as
       God   Nah 1:1-9
    GRACE as
       Believers   Jas 4:1-10
       God   Deut 4:15-31;
                    Ps 86:14-17;
                    111:2-4;
                    119:153-160;
                    Is 30:18-26;
                    Joel 2:12-17;
                    Jas 5:7-11
       Jonah   Jon 4:1-11
    HATE as
       God   Is 1:10-17
       Isaiah   Is 61:1-11
    JEALOUSY as
       God   Ex 34:12-28;
                    Deut 4:15-31;
                    5:1-21
    JUSTICE as
       God   Is 30:18-26
    LEADERSHIP as
       God   Is 40:12-31
    LOVE as
       God   1 Jn 4:7-12;
                    13-18
       Isaiah   Is 61:1-11
    ONENESS as
       God   Is 44:24-45:13;
                    14-25;
                    Zech 14:1-21;
                    Rom 3:21-30;
                    1 Cor 8:4-6;
                    Gal 3:19-25;
                    1 Tim 2:1-7
       Jesus   Jn 10:19-40
    PEACE as
       God   1 Cor 14:26-33
    SPIRIT as
       God   2 Kgs 19:9b-37
    WILL as
       Isaiah   Is 52:13-53:12

DESPAIR as
       David   Ps 22:12-21;
                    143:3-4
       Job   Job 6:1-7;
                    21:1-6
       Psalmist   Ps 88:15-18
    MEDITATION on
       David   Ps 38:3-10
       Job   Job 7:1-6;
                    14:7-12;
                    17:1-5;
                    11-16
    PROPHECY of
       Isaiah   Is 51:17-52:12
    SELF-REALIZATION of
       Job   Job 19:13-19

INSTRUCTION on (cont'd)
　Jesus　　　　　Mt 7:15-20;
　　　　　　　　12:33-37;
　　　　　　　　Lk 6:36-45
　John　　　　　3 Jn 1:12
PROPHECY of
　Isaiah　　　　Is 32:1-8

GRACE as
　of DEITY
　　Believers　　Jas 4:1-10
　　God　　　　Deut 4:15-31;
　　　　　　　　Ps 86:14-17;
　　　　　　　　111:2-4;
　　　　　　　　119:153-160;
　　　　　　　　Is 30:18-26;
　　　　　　　　Joel 2:12-17;
　　　　　　　　Jas 5:7-11
　　Jonah　　　Jon 4:1-11
　INSTRUCTION on
　　Jesus　　　Mt 18:23-35
　　Paul　　　Rom 12:14-21;
　　　　　　　Col 3:5-17

GREED as
　through FALSE BELIEF
　　Pharisees　　Lk 16:14-15
　INSTRUCTION on
　　Solomon　　Prov 28:1-28

GRIEF as
　Naomi　　　　Ruth 1:1-18
　INSTRUCTION on
　　Jesus　　　Mt 5:3-12;
　　　　　　　Lk 6:20-23
　　Preacher　　Eccl 1:12-2:26
　MEDITATION on
　　Asaph　　　Ps 77:1-10
　REVELATION on
　　Zephaniah　Zeph 1:10-11
　SELF-REALIZATION of
　　Naomi　　　Ruth 1:19-22

HATE as
　of DEITY
　　God　　　　Is 1:10-17
　　Isaiah　　　Is 61:1-11
　through FALSE BELIEF
　　Believers　　Jude 1:21-23

HEALING as
　Naaman　　　Lk 4:16-30
　by MESSIANIC FIGURE
　　Jesus　　　1 Pet 2:21-25
　PROPHECY of
　　Isaiah　　　Is 52:13-53:12

HOPE as
　INSTRUCTION on
　　Paul　　　　Rom 5:1-5;
　　　　　　　12:9-13
　　Preacher　　Eccl 9:1-16

HUMILITY as
　James　　　　Jas 4:1-10
　INSTRUCTION on
　　Bishops　　1 Tim 3:1-7
　　James　　　Jas 1:9-11
　　Jeremiah　Jer 13:15-17

INSTRUCTION on (cont'd)
　Jesus　　　　Mt 5:3-12;
　　　　　　　18:1-4;
　　　　　　　20:20-28;
　　　　　　　Mk 10:35-45;
　　　　　　　Lk 6:20-23;
　　　　　　　18:9-14
　Paul　　　　Rom 12:3-8;
　　　　　　　1 Cor 3:18-23;
　　　　　　　Gal 5:25-6:6;
　　　　　　　Col 3:5-17
　of MESSIANIC FIGURE
　　Zechariah　Zech 9:1-12
　in MISSION
　　Bishop　　Tit 1:5-8
　　Women　　Tit 2:1-10

IDOLATRY as
　through FALSE BELIEF
　　Psalmist　　Ps 115:3-8;
　　　　　　　135:15-18

IGNORANCE as
　INSTRUCTION on
　　Isaiah　　　Is 56:9-57:13
　　Solomon　　Prov 9:13-18;
　　　　　　　18:1-24

INDIFFERENCE as
　Israelites　　Hos 4:16
　REVELATION on
　　Jeremiah　Jer 7:21-28

INNOCENCE as
　before DEITY
　　David　　　Ps 18:20-24
　PROPHECY of
　　Isaiah　　　Is 52:13-53:12

INSTRUCTION on
　as ACCEPTANCE
　　Jesus　　　Mk 9:33-37
　　Maiden　　Song 1:5-6
　　Paul　　　1 Cor 7:17-24;
　　　　　　　25-35
　as ALIENATION
　　Job　　　　Job 30:1-8
　as ANGER
　　Solomon　　Prov 19:1-29
　as BLESSING
　　Wisdom　　Prov 8:1-21
　as CAPTIVITY
　　Paul　　　2 Cor 6:11-13
　as COMPASSION
　　Jesus　　　Mt 18:23-35
　　Paul　　　Col 3:5-17
　as CONDEMNATION
　　Bildad　　Job 18:5-7;
　　　　　　　8-11
　　Jesus　　　Lk 6:24-26
　　Laodicea　Rev 3:14-22
　as DEATH
　　James　　Jas 4:13-16
　　Preacher　Eccl 11:9-12:7
　　Psalmist　Ps 49:16-20
　　Sirach　　*Sir 10:6-11;
　　　　　　　11:14-20;
　　　　　　　14:3-19;
　　　　　　　17:15-32;

LOVE as
    Naomi   Ruth 4:13-22
    of **DEITY**
        God   1 Jn 4:7-12;
                            13-18
        Isaiah   Is 61:1-11
    of **FOLLOWERs**
        Holy Spirit   Gal 5:22-24
    INSTRUCTION on
        Jesus   Mk 9:49-50
        Paul   1 Cor 8:7-13;
                            13:8-13;
                            Eph 6:5-9;
                            Col 3:5-17;
                            1 Thes 5:1-11
        Wisdom   Prov 8:1-21
    SELF-REALIZATION of
        Paul   1 Cor 13:1-13

LUST as
    INSTRUCTION on
        Isaiah   Is 56:9-57:13

concerning **MARRIAGE**
    INSTRUCTION on
        Solomon   Prov 12:1-28
    in **MISSION**
        Bishop   Tit 1:5-8

MEDITATION on
    as **ANXIETY**
        Jeremiah   Jer 15:10-21
    as **DEATH**
        Job   Job 14:7-12
        Preacher   Eccl 3:16-4:3
        Psalmist   Ps 49:5-12
    as **DESPAIR**
        David   Ps 38:3-10
        Job   Job 7:1-6;
                            14:7-12;
                            17:1-5;
                            11-16
    as **FEAR**
        Job   Job 7:12-16
    as **GRIEF**
        Asaph   Ps 77:1-10
    as **OPPRESSION**
        David   Ps 40:12
        Psalmist   Ps 42:6-11;
                            102:1-11
    as **PRIDE**
        Preacher   Eccl 3:16-4:3;
                            4-12;
                            13-16
    as **SPIRIT**
        Asaph   Ps 77:1-10
    as **SUFFERING**
        Job   Job 7:1-6;
                            14:18-22
        Psalmist   Ps 102:1-11
    of **MESSIANIC FIGURE**
        as **HEALING**
            Jesus   1 Pet 2:21-25
        as **HUMILITY**
            Zechariah   Zech 9:1-12
        as **WISDOM**
            Jesus   Lk 2:21-40;
                          41-52

in **MISSION**
    FAITH as
        Timothy   1 Tim 1:3-7
    of **FAMILY**
        Bishop   Tit 1:5-8
    HUMILITY as
        Bishop   Tit 1:5-8
        Women   Tit 2:1-10
    concerning **MARRIAGE**
        Bishop   Tit 1:5-8
    OBEDIENCE as
        Jesus   Phil 2:5-11
    PRIDE as
        Paul   2 Cor 11:16-20
    SERVICE as
        Bishop   Tit 1:5-8
        James   Jas 1:1
        Jude   Jude 1:1-2
        Paul   Phil 1:1-2
        Peter   1 Pet 1:1-2;
                        2 Pet 1:1-2
        Timothy   Phil 1:1-2
    SHARING as
        Bishop   Tit 1:5-8
    SPIRIT as
        Jesus   Mt 11:28-30
    TEMPERANCE as
        Bishop   Tit 1:5-8
        Paul   1 Cor 9:24-27

OBEDIENCE as
    of **FOLLOWERs**
        Disciples   Mk 14:12-16;
                        Lk 22:7-13
        Paul   Phil 3:17-21
    INSTRUCTION on
        Jesus   Lk 16:19-31
        Paul   2 Thes 3:6-15
    in **MISSION**
        Jesus   Phil 2:5-11
    REVELATION on
        Ezekiel   Ezek 24:15-24

OLD AGE as
        David   1 Kgs 1:1-4
        Isaac   Gen 27:1-40
    INSTRUCTION on
        Solomon   Prov 20:1-30

ONENESS as
        Jesus   1 Cor 8:4-6
    with **DEITY**
        God   Is 44:24-45:13;
                        14-25;
                        Zech 14:1-21;
                        Rom 3:21-30;
                        1 Cor 8:4-6;
                        Gal 3:19-25;
                        1 Tim 2:1-7
        Jesus   Jn 10:19-40
    of **FOLLOWERs**
        Jesus   1 Cor 6:12-20
    INSTRUCTION on
        Man   Gen 2:21-25
        Paul   Phil 2:1-4

OPPRESSION as
        David   Ps 56:1-4;
                        57:4-6;
                        69:1-3;

OPPRESSION as (cont'd)
David	4-12; 109:1-5; 21-31; 142:3c-4; 143:3-4
Paul	2 Cor 11:21-29
Psalmist	Ps 88:3-9; 119:145-152; 129:1-4
Saul	1 Sam 16:14-23

INSTRUCTION on
Jesus	Mt 10:26-39

MEDITATION on
David	Ps 40:12
Psalmist	Ps 42:6-11; 102:1-11

PROPHECY of
Ephraimites	Hos 9:1-6
Joel	Joel 1:2-20

REVELATION on
Daniel	Dan 12:1-4
Ezekiel	Ezek 4:9-11

ORDER as
INSTRUCTION on
Paul	2 Thes 3:6-15
Preacher	Eccl 3:1-8
Solomon	Prov 20:1-30

PARADOX as
Israelites	Hos 1:10-2:1

INSTRUCTION on
James	Jas 3:1-12
Jesus	Mt 19:27-30; 20:1-16; Mk 10:28-31; Lk 9:46-48; 18:9-14
Paul	1 Cor 4:6-13; 7:17-24
Sirach	*Sir 20:9-17

SELF-REALIZATION of
Paul	2 Cor 12:1-10

PATIENCE as
of FOLLOWERs
Holy Spirit	Gal 5:22-24

INSTRUCTION on
Paul	Rom 12:9-13; 1 Cor 7:17-24; Col 3:5-17

SELF-REALIZATION of
Paul	Phil 4:10-20

PEACE as
of DEITY
God	1 Cor 14:26-33

of FOLLOWERs
Holy Spirit	Gal 5:22-24

INSTRUCTION on
Jesus	Mt 5:3-12; 21-26
Paul	2 Cor 13:11-13; Col 3:5-17;
Peter	2 Pet 3:14-18a

PIETY as
Pharisees	Mk 7:1-23

POVERTY as
INSTRUCTION on
James	Jas 1:9-11
Preacher	Eccl 4:13-16
Solomon	Prov 24:23-34; 28:1-28

PRAISE for
of FOLLOWERs
Demetrius	3 Jn 1:12
John	3 Jn 1:3-8

PRIDE as
Judah	Gen 38:12-23
Mankind	Gen 11:1-9
Paul	2 Cor 11:21-29
Tyre	Ezek 27:1-9a

INSTRUCTION on
Preacher	Eccl 1:2-11; 12-2:26; 5:8-20; 9:1-16; 11:9-12:7; 8-11

MEDITATION on
Preacher	Eccl 3:16-4:3; 4-12; 13-16

in MISSION
Paul	2 Cor 11:16-20

PROPHECY of
as BLESSING
Jacob	Gen 49:1-28

as CAPTIVITY
Shallum	Jer 22:10-12

as DEATH
Isaiah	Is 40:1-11

as DESPAIR
Isaiah	Is 51:17-52:12

as DESTRUCTION
Jeremiah	Jer 4:30-31
Joel	Joel 1:2-20

as EVIL
Isaiah	Is 32:1-8

as GOOD
Isaiah	Is 32:1-8

as HEALING
Isaiah	Is 52:13-53:12

as INNOCENCE
Isaiah	Is 52:13-53:12

as OPPRESSION
Ephraimites	Hos 9:1-6
Joel	Joel 1:2-20

as SADNESS
Isaiah	Is 15:1-16:14
Joel	Joel 1:2-20

as SPIRIT
Believers	1 Cor 14:26-33

as SUFFERING
Ephraimites	Hos 9:1-6
Isaiah	Is 33:7-16; 51:17-52:12
Jeremiah	Jer 4:30-31

PRUDENCE as
INSTRUCTION on
Bishops	1 Tim 3:1-7
James	Jas 1:19-21

WISDOM as (cont'd)
  of MESSIANIC FIGURE
    Jesus   Lk 2:21-40;
                41-52

WISDOM concerning
  INSTRUCTION on
    Jesus   Mt 6:5-8
    Paul   Rom 8:5-13;
               1 Cor 3:18-23
    Preacher   Eccl 4:13-16
    Solomon   Prov 13:1-25
    Wisdom   Prov 8:32-36

WITNESS to
  of FOLLOWERs
    Demetrius   3 Jn 1:12
  INSTRUCTION on
    Paul   Rom 2:1-24;
               Phil 1:12-30
    Women   1 Pet 3:1-7

YOUTH as
  God   Is 40:12-31
  INSTRUCTION on
    Solomon   Prov 20:1-30

RATIONALIZATION

ACCEPTANCE of
  from DEITY
    James   Jas 3:13-18

caused by ANXIETY
  SELF-REALIZATION of
    Paul   2 Cor 12:19-21

before DEITY
  concerning ACCEPTANCE
    James   Jas 3:13-18
  concerning SUFFERING
    Job   Job 6:1-7
  concerning TEMPTATION
    Satan   Mt 4:1-11;
               Lk 4:1-13
    Serpent   Gen 3:1-8

through FALSE BELIEF
  causing IDOLATRY
    Israelites   Ex 32:15-24
  WITNESS to
    Micah   Mic 2:1-10

of HATE
    Moses   Lev 19:1-37

causing IDOLATRY
  through FALSE BELIEF
    Israelites   Ex 32:15-24

INSTRUCTION on
  in OLD AGE
    Paul   1 Cor 14:13-25
  of ONENESS
    Jesus   Mt 12:22-32;
               Mk 3:20-30
  revealing PARADOX
    Jesus   Mt 5:38-42

revealing PARADOX (cont'd)
    Paul   1 Cor 6:1-18
    Peter   1 Pet 2:18-20
  of POLITICS
    Gamaliel   Acts 5:17-42
  of SERVICE
    Jesus   Lk 13:10-17
  of WISDOM
    Jesus   Mk 12:13-17;
               Lk 20:19-26

in OLD AGE
  INSTRUCTION on
    Paul   1 Cor 14:13-25

of ONENESS
  INSTRUCTION on
    Jesus   Mt 12:22-32;
               Mk 3:20-30

revealing PARADOX
  INSTRUCTION on
    Jesus   Mt 5:38-42
    Paul   1 Cor 6:1-8
    Peter   1 Pet 2:18-20
  TRADITION of
    Pharisees   Mt 15:3-9

of PATIENCE
    Job   Job 21:1-6

of POLITICS
  in ENVIRONMENT
    Pilate   Mt 27:11-26
  INSTRUCTION on
    Gamaliel   Acts 5:17-42

of PRUDENCE
  in ENVIRONMENT
    Jesus   Mk 11:27-33;
               Lk 20:1-8

SCRIPTURES on
  in TEMPTATION
    Jesus   Mt 4:1-11;
               Lk 4:1-13

of SELFISHNESS
  in ENVIRONMENT
    Pilate   Mt 27:11-26

SELF-REALIZATION of
  caused by ANXIETY
    Paul   2 Cor 12:19-21

of SERVICE
  INSTRUCTION on
    Jesus   Lk 13:10-17

of SUFFERING
  before DEITY
    Job   Job 6:1-7

of TEMPTATION
  before DEITY
    Satan   Mt 4:1-11;
               Lk 4:1-13
    Serpent   Gen 3:1-8
  SCRIPTURES on
    Jesus   Mt 4:1-11;
               Lk 4:1-13

RATIONALIZATION (cont'd)

of TRADITION
  PARADOX in
    Pharisees   Mt 15:3-9

through WISDOM
  INSTRUCTION as
    Jesus   Mk 12:13-17;
                  Lk 20:19-26

WITNESS to
  through FALSE BELIEF
    Micah   Mic 2:1-10

RECONCILIATION

ACCEPTANCE of
  COVENANT of
    Gentiles   Eph 2:11-22
  with DEITY
    God   2 Cor 5:14-19
    Jesus   Gal 4:4-7
  INSTRUCTION on
    Jesus   Mt 18:15-17
    Paul   2 Cor 5:20-6:2

through ACCEPTANCE
  REVELATION on
    Israelites   Ezek 20:40-44;
                  Hos 2:14-15
    Moses   Lev 1:1-17

ALIENATION from
  through FALSE BELIEF
    Author   Heb 6:1-8;
                  10:19-31
  with MESSIANIC FIGURE
    Pharisees   Mt 23:34-39

from ALIENATION
  INSTRUCTION on
    Jesus   Mt 5:21-26
  PROPHECY of
    Isaiah   Is 54:1-17

overcomes BLASPHEMY
  ENVIRONMENT
    Nebuchadnezzar   Dan 4:36-37
  against MESSIANIC FIGURE
    Paul   1 Tim 1:12-17
  REVELATION of
    Israelites   Ezek 36:16-21;
                  22-32

BLESSING in
  with DEITY
    David   Ps 32:1-2
  PROPHECY of
    Hananiah   Jer 28:1-17
    Israelites   Zeph 3:14-20
    Judahites   Zeph 2:4-7
    Zechariah   Zech 9:1-12
  REVELATION on
    Amos   Amos 9:11-12
    Israelites   Ezek 28:24-26;
                  36:33-36;
                  37:15-28;
                  Hos 2:21-23;
                  Amos 9:14-15;

RECONCILIATION (cont'd)

REVELATION on (cont'd)
  Israelites   Zech 1:7-17;
                  7:4-8:23;
                  10:3-12
  SCRIPTURES on
    Jesus   Gal 3:10-14

from CAPTIVITY
  PROPHECY of
    Jeremiah   Jer 23:1-8
  REVELATION on
    Israelites   Ezek 28:24-26

through COMPASSION
  of DEITY
    Followers   Ps 80:4-7
    God   Mic 7:7-20
    Israelites   Deut 30:1-10
  PROPHECY of
    Israelites   Hos 11:8-9
    Judahites   Jer 12:14-17
  REVELATION on
    Israelites   Jer 30:18-22;
                  Zech 1:7-17

COURAGE through
  with DEITY
    Israelites   Is 42:18-43:7

COVENANT of
  ACCEPTANCE of
    Gentiles   Eph 2:11-22
  through DEATH
    Jesus   Heb 9:15-22
  FAITH in
    Jesus   Gal 3:19-25
  FULFILLMENT of
    Jesus   Heb 9:15-22
  JUSTICE in
    Abimelech   Gen 21:22-34
    Abraham   Gen 21:22-34
  LIFE through
    Author   Heb 9:15-22;
                  10:19-31
    Jesus   Mt 26:17-30;
                  Mk 14:22-26
    Moses   Ex 24:1-18
  ONENESS in
    Gentiles   Eph 2:11-22
  PEACE through
    Gentiles   Eph 2:11-22
    Phinehas   Num 25:6-18
  through PURIFICATION
    Jesus   Heb 9:15-22
  through REPENTANCE
    Israelites   Lev 26:1-46
  through SACRIFICE
    Jesus   Mt 26:17-30;
                  Mk 14:22-26
  WITNESS to
    Holy Spirit   Heb 10:1-18
    Jacob   Gen 31:44-55

through DEATH
  Jesus   Heb 9:15-22;
               1 Pet 3:18-22
  Mankind   Rev 5:1-14
for FOLLOWERs
  Jesus   Eph 2:11-22

INSTRUCTION on	
Jesus	Rom 5:12-21
MEDITATION on	
Jesus	Col 1:21-23
PROPHECY of	
Jesus	Jn 12:27-36a
with DEITY	
ACCEPTANCE of	
God	2 Cor 5:14-19
Jesus	Gal 4:4-7
BLESSING in	
David	Ps 32:1-2
through COMPASSION	
Followers	Ps 80:4-7
God	Mic 7:7-20
Israelites	Deut 30:1-10
COURAGE in	
Israelites	Is 42:18-43:7
through DEATH	
Mankind	Rev 5:1-14
through DESTRUCTION	
Isaiah	Is 9:8-10:4
through DISCIPLESHIP	
God	Ps 111:5-9
through EVIL	
Jesus	1 Jn 2:1-6
through FAITH	
Israelites	Is 10:20-23
through GRACE	
Believers	1 Pet 1:3-9
God	Is 1:24-26;
	44:6-8;
	21-23;
	Mic 7:7-20;
	Mt 6:14-15
Isaiah	Is 63:7-64:12
Psalmist	Ps 85:4-7
JOY through	
Jesus	Rom 5:6-11
LIFE through	
Believers	Rom 8:28-39
through LOVE	
Israelites	Is 42:18-43:7;
	Zech 10:3-12
Jesus	1 Jn 4:7-12
PEACE through	
Israelites	Nah 1:10,12,13;
	15-2:2
Jesus	Col 1:18-20
through PRAISE	
Jesus	Heb 13:1-25
through REJECTION	
Israelites	Rom 11:7-24
through REPENTANCE	
Egyptians	Is 19:18-25
God	Ex 32:7-14
Israelites	Judg 3:7-11;
	Rom 11:7-24
Solomon	2 Chr 5:1-7:10
through REVENGE	
David	2 Sam 21:1-14
REWARDs of	
Isaiah	Is 40:1-11
through SACRIFICE	
High Priest	Heb 5:1-10
through SUFFERING	
Aaron	Num 16:36-50
through VICTORY	

through VICTORY (cont'd)	
Isaiah	Is 63:1-6
Israelites	Nah 1:10,12,13;
	15-2:2
WEALTH of	
Israelites	Zeph 3:14-20
through DESTRUCTION	
by DEITY	
Isaiah	Is 9:8-10:4
PROPHECY of	
Isaiah	Is 25:6-9
through DISCIPLESHIP	
to DEITY	
God	Ps 111:5-9
for EVIL	
against DEITY	
Jesus	1 Jn 2:1-6
of FOLLOWERs	
Believers	Gal 5:25-6:6
INSTRUCTION on	
Paul	Rom 8:1-4
in MISSION	
Jesus	1 Cor 15:20-28
PROPHECY of	
Isaiah	Is 25:6-9;
	52:13-53:12
through FAITH	
in COVENANT	
Jesus	Gal 3:19-25
in DEITY	
Israelites	Is 10:20-23
of FOLLOWERs	
Jesus	Gal 3:26-29
INSTRUCTION on	
Paul	Rom 3:21-30;
	31-4:25;
	5:1-5;
	9:30-10:21;
	Gal 2:15-16;
	3:6-9;
	10-14;
	5:2-6
PROPHECY of	
Tyre	Is 23:15-18
REVELATION on	
Israelites	Is 50:1-11
in FAMILY	
Benjaminites	Judg 21:13-15
David	1 Sam 30:1-31;
	2 Sam 13:21-14:33
Israelites	Judg 21:13-15
Tobiah	*Tb 10:1-11:6
PROPHECY of	
Baruch	*Bar 5:5-9
through WORSHIP	
Jews	*2 Mc 1:19-36;
	2:16-18
through FEAR	
PROPHECY of	
Israelites	Hos 11:10-11
for FOLLOWERs	
through DEATH	
Jesus	Eph 2:11-22

of **FOLLOWER**s
   from **EVIL**
      Believers   Gal 5:25-6:6
   through **FAITH**
      Jesus   Gal 3:26-29
   as **FULFILLMENT**
      Holy Spirit   Eph 4:25-5:2
   in **LIFE**
      Jesus   Rom 5:6-11;
                 7:1-6;
                 Eph 1:3-14
      Peter   1 Pet 1:13-2:3
   through **LOVE**
      Jesus   Eph 5:21-33
      Woman   Lk 7:36-50
   through **OBEDIENCE**
      Jesus   Rom 5:12-21
   ONENESS in
      Jesus   Eph 2:11-22
   PEACE in
      Jesus   Eph 2:11-22
   PRAISE of
      Titus   2 Cor 7:13b-16
   PURIFICATION through
      Jesus   Eph 5:21-33;
                 Tit 2:11-15
   SACREDNESS in
      Jesus   1 Cor 1:26-31;
                 6:9-11;
                 Eph 5:21-33

through **FRIENDSHIP**
   in **ENVIRONMENT**
      Naomi   Ruth 1:19-22

FULFILLMENT through
   COVENANT of
      Jesus   Heb 9:15-22
   of **FOLLOWER**s
      Holy Spirit   Eph 4:25-5:2
   INSTRUCTION on
      Jesus   Heb 10:1-18
   PROPHECY of
      Israelites   Mic 4:9-5:6
      Jeremiah   Jer 31:38-40
   REVELATION on
      Jeremiah   Jer 31:23-26
   SCRIPTURES on
      Jesus   1 Cor 15:1-11

through **GRACE**
   of **DEITY**
      Believers   1 Pet 1:3-9
      God   Is 1:24-26;
                 44:6-8;
                 21-23;
                 Mic 7:7-20;
                 Mt 6:14-15
      Isaiah   Is 63:7-64:12
      Psalmist   Ps 85:4-7
   INSTRUCTION on
      Jesus   Mt 6:14-15;
                 18:21-22
      Moses   Deut 30:1-10
      Paul   Rom 3:21-30;
                 5:1-5;
                 12-21;
                 Gal 2:15-16;
                 20-21;
                 3:10-14;
                 Col 1:9-14

of **MESSIANIC FIGURE**
   Jesus   Rom 5:6-11;
                 Heb 1:2b-4;
                 2:5-18
   in **MISSION**
      Jesus   Rom 3:31-4:25
   PROPHECY of
      Ammonites   Jer 49:1-6
      Elamites   Jer 49:34-39
      Isaiah   Is 4:2-6;
                 27:7-11;
                 52:13-53:12;
                 54:1-17
      Israelites   Jer 31:31-34;
                 50:1-46;
                 Hos 14:4-8;
                 Zeph 3:14-20
      Judahites   Jer 12:14-17
      Moabites   Jer 48:1-47
   REVELATION on
      Amos   Amos 9:11-12
      Israelites   Jer 30:10-11;
                 18-22;
                 31:15-22;
                 Ezek 20:40-44;
                 34:11-16;
                 36:33-36;
                 37:1-14;
                 39:25-29;
                 Hos 1:10-2:1;
                 21-23
      Jeremiah   Jer 3:12-14a;
                 16:14-15;
                 30:12-17;
                 31:7-14;
                 33:14-26
      Judahites   Jer 24:1-10
      Moses   Lev 5:5-13;
                 14-6:7
   SCRIPTURES on
      Peter   Acts 15:6-29

GRATITUDE for
   REVELATION on
      Israelites   Jer 30:18-22
      Jeremiah   Jer 33:10-11

through **GUILT**
   Moses   Lev 16:11-28
   INSTRUCTION on
      Moses   Deut 21:1-9
      Solomon   1 Kgs 2:28-35
   PROPHECY of
      Isaiah   Is 27:7-11
   REVELATION on
      Israelites   Is 43:14-44:5

through **HEALING**
   Jesus   Mt 9:10-13
   PROPHECY of
      Israelites   Hos 6:10-7:2;
                 14:4-8
   REVELATION on
      Jeremiah   Jer 33:1-9

HOPE in
   through **MESSIANIC FIGURE**
      Isaiah   Is 11:1-9;
                 10-16
   PROPHECY of
      Jeremiah   Jer 29:1-23

PROPHECY of
  Isaiah   Is 11:1-9
REVELATION on
  Amos   Amos 9:11-12
  Jeremiah   Jer 33:12-13
  Moses   Lev 17:10-14

through LOVE
  of DEITY
    Israelites   Is 42:18-43:7;
                   Zech 10:3-12
    Jesus   1 Jn 4:7-12
  of FOLLOWER
    Jesus   Eph 5:21-33
    Woman   Lk 7:36-50
  INSTRUCTION on
    Jesus   Lk 7:36-50
    Paul   2 Cor 5:14-19

MEDITATION on
  through DEATH
    Jesus   Col 1:21-23
  through JUSTICE
    Jeremiah   Jer 5:1-14
  through REPENTANCE
    Paul   2 Cor 7:5-13a

by MESSIANIC FIGURE
  ALIENATION from
    Pharisees   Mt 23:34-39
  for BLASPHEMY
    Paul   1 Tim 1:12-17
  through GRACE
    Jesus   Rom 5:6-11;
                   Heb 1:2b-4;
                   2:5-18
  HOPE in
    Isaiah   Is 11:1-9;
                   10-16
  LIFE through
    Jesus   1 Pet 2:21-25
  PEACE in
    Isaiah   Is 11:1-9
  through PURIFICATION
    Jesus   Heb 9:1-14
  SACRIFICE in
    Israelites   Mal 2:17-3:5
    Jesus   Heb 9:23-28
  SUFFERING in
    Jesus   Heb 2:5-18
  TEMPTATION in
    Jesus   Heb 2:5-18

MISSION of
  over EVIL
    Jesus   1 Cor 15:20-28
  by GRACE
    Jesus   Rom 3:31-4:25
  through HEALING
    Jesus   Mt 9:10-13
  through REPENTANCE
    Jesus   Mt 9:10-13;
                   Lk 5:29-32
  through SACRIFICE
    Jesus   Mt 20:20-28;
                   Mk 10:35-45
  through SERVICE
    Jesus   Mt 20:20-28;
                   Mk 10:35-45
  WITNESS to
    Paul   Acts 26:1-32;

WITNESS to (cont'd)
  Paul   2 Cor 5:14-19;
                   20-6:2

through OBEDIENCE
  of FOLLOWERs
    Jesus   Rom 5:12-21
  INSTRUCTION on
    James   Jas 2:14-26
    Paul   Rom 2:1-24

through ONENESS
  Jesus   2 Cor 5:14-19
  in COVENANT
    Gentiles   Eph 2:11-22
  of FOLLOWERs
    Jesus   Eph 2:11-22
  INSTRUCTION on
    Jesus   Mt 5:21-26
  PROPHECY of
    Jeremiah   Jer 32:26-44
  REVELATION on
    Israelites   Jer 3:14b-18
    Judahites   Jer 3:14b-18

through OPPRESSION
  PROPHECY of
    Isaiah   Is 27:12-13
    Micah   Mic 4:1-8
  REVELATION on
    Israelites   Is 51:17-52:12

PEACE through
  Israelites   Nah 1:10,12,13;
                   15-2:2
  Jesus   Col 1:18-20
  COVENANT of
    Gentiles   Eph 2:11-22
    Phinehas   Num 25:6-18
  of FOLLOWERs
    Jesus   Eph 2:11-22
  INSTRUCTION on
    Paul   Rom 5:1-5
  of MESSIANIC FIGURE
    Isaiah   Is 11:1-9
  PROPHECY of
    Elijah   Mal 4:4-6
    Isaiah   Is 19:18-25;
                   51:17-52:12
  REVELATION on
    Israelites   Ezek 45:13-17
    Judahites   Zech 7:4-8:23

through POLITICS
  David   2 Sam 19:8b-43

through PRAISE
  of DEITY
    Jesus   Heb 13:1-25
  of FOLLOWER
    Titus   2 Cor 7:13b-16
  INSTRUCTION on
    Moses   Deut 31:30-32:47

PROPHECY of
  Judahites   Jer 27:16-22
  from ALIENATION
    Isaiah   Is 54:1-17
  as BLESSING

as **BLESSING** (cont'd)

Hananiah	Jer 28:1-17
Israelites	Zeph 3:14-20
Judahites	Zeph 2:4-7
Zechariah	Zech 9:1-12

from **CAPTIVITY**

Jeremiah	Jer 23:1-8

through **COMPASSION**

Israelites	Hos 11:8-9
Judahites	Jer 12:14-17

through **DEATH**

Jesus	Jn 12:27-36a

through **DESTRUCTION**

Isaiah	Is 25:6-9

for **EVIL**

Isaiah	Is 25:6-9; 52:13-53:12

through **FAITH**

Tyre	Is 23:15-18

in **FAMILY**

Baruch	*Bar 5:5-9

through **FEAR**

Israelites	Hos 11:10-11

through **FULFILLMENT**

Israelites	Mic 4:9-5:6
Jeremiah	Jer 31:38-40

through **GRACE**

Ammonites	Jer 49:1-6
Elamites	Jer 49:34-39
Isaiah	Is 4:2-6; 27:7-11; 52:13-53:12; 54:1-17
Israelites	Jer 31:31-34; 50:1-46; Hos 14:4-8; Zeph 3:14-20
Judahites	Jer 12:14-17
Moabites	Jer 48:1-47

through **GUILT**

Isaiah	Is 27:7-11

through **HEALING**

Israelites	Hos 6:10-7:2; 14:4-8

through **LEADERSHIP**

Micah	Mic 2:12-13
Obadiah	Obad 1:17-21

in **LIFE**

Isaiah	Is 11:1-9

in **ONENESS**

Jeremiah	Jer 32:26-44

through **OPPRESSION**

Isaiah	Is 27:12-13
Micah	Mic 4:1-8

through **PURIFICATION**

Isaiah	Is 4:2-6
Jerusalemites	Zech 12:1-13:6

through **REPENTANCE**

Isaiah	Is 59:1-21
Jeremiah	Jer 26:7-19; 29:1-23
Judahites	Jer 7:1-15; 35:6-17
Tyre	Is 23:15-18

through **SERVICE**

Tyre	Is 23:15-18

through **VICTORY**

Israelites	Nah 2:1-5

through **WEALTH**

Jeremiah	Jer 32:26-44
Judahites	Zeph 2:4-7

through **PRUDENCE**
INSTRUCTION on

Jesus	Lk 12:57-59

through **PURIFICATION**

Priest	Lev 14:33-54

COVENANT of

Jesus	Heb 9:15-22

of **FOLLOWER**

Jesus	Eph 5:21-33; Tit 2:11-15

INSTRUCTION on

Author	Heb 10:19-31
John the Baptist	Lk 3:1-6

by **MESSIANIC FIGURE**

Jesus	Heb 9:1-14

PROPHECY of

Isaiah	Is 4:2-6
Jerusalemites	Zech 12:1-13:6

REVELATION on

Ezekiel	Ezek 43:18-27
Israelites	Ezek 36:22-32; 33-36

through **REJECTION**

Israelites	Rom 11:7-24

of **FALSE BELIEF**

Author	Heb 6:1-8; 10:19-31

through **REPENTANCE**
in **COVENANT**

Israelites	Lev 26:1-46

of **DEITY**

Egyptians	Is 19:18-25
God	Ex 32:7-14
Israelites	Judg 3:7-11; Rom 11:7-24
Solomon	2 Chr 5:1-7:10

INSTRUCTION on

Jesus	Mt 18:15-17; 21:28-32; Lk 12:57-59; 13:1-5; 18:9-14
John the Baptist	Lk 3:1-6
Moses	Deut 30:1-10

MEDITATION on

Paul	2 Cor 7:5-13a

MISSION of

Jesus	Mt 9:10-13; Lk 5:29-32

PROPHECY of

Isaiah	Is 59:1-21
Jeremiah	Jer 26:7-19; 29:1-23
Judahites	Jer 7:1-15; 35:6-17
Tyre	Is 23:15-18

REVELATION on

Israelites	Jer 3:14b-18; 21-4:4; Ezek 39:25-29; Mal 3:6-12
Jeremiah	Jer 15:10-21; 18:1-12
Judahites	Jer 24:1-10
Solomon	2 Chr 7:11-22

SCRIPTURES on

Israelites	Neh 1:5-11a

SELF-REALIZATION of

David	2 Sam 12:1-31a

REVELATION on
  through **ACCEPTANCE**
Israelites	Ezek 20:40-44;
	Hos 2:14-15
Moses	Lev 1:1-17
over **BLASPHEMY**
Israelites	Ezek 36:16-21;
	22-32
as **BLESSING**
Amos	Amos 9:11-12
Israelites	Ezek 28:24-26;
	36:33-36;
	37:15-28;
	Hos 2:21-23;
	Amos 9:14-15;
	Zech 1:7-17;
	7:4-8:23;
	10:3-12
through **CAPTIVITY**
Israelites	Ezek 28:24-26
through **COMPASSION**
Israelites	Jer 30:18-22;
	Zech 1:7-17
through **FAITH**
Israelites	Is 50:1-11
through **FULFILLMENT**
Jeremiah	Jer 31:23-26
through **GRACE**
Amos	Amos 9:11-12
Israelites	Jer 30:10-11;
	18-22;
	31:15-22;
	Ezek 20:40-44;
	34:11-16;
	36:33-36;
	37:1-14;
	39:25-29;
	Hos 1:10-2:1;
	21-23
Jeremiah	Jer 3:12-14a;
	16:14-15;
	30:12-17;
	31:7-14;
	33:14-26
Judahites	Jer 24:1-10
Moses	Lev 5:5-13;
	14-6:7
through **GUILT**
Israelites	Is 43:14-44:5
through **HEALING**
Jeremiah	Jer 33:1-9
through **IGNORANCE**
Israelites	Ezek 45:18-25
through **LEADERSHIP**
Israelites	Hos 1:10-2:1
Judahites	Zech 7:4-8:23
resulting in **LIFE**
Amos	Amos 9:11-12
Jeremiah	Jer 33:12-13
Moses	Lev 17:10-14
through **ONENESS**
Israelites	Jer 3:14b-18
Judahites	Jer 3:14b-18
through **OPPRESSION**
Israelites	Is 51:17-52:12
through **PURIFICATION**
Ezekiel	Ezek 43:18-27
Israelites	Ezek 36:22-32;
	33-36

  through **REPENTANCE**
Israelites	Jer 3:14b-18;
	21-4:4
	Ezek 39:25-29;
	Mal 3:6-12
Jeremiah	Jer 15:10-21;
	18:1-12
Judahites	Jer 24:1-10
Solomon	2 Chr 7:11-22
through **SACRIFICE**
Moses	Ex 34:12-28;
	Lev 23:26-32;
	Num 3:40-51
through **SUFFERING**
Moses	Lev 23:26-32
through **WEALTH**
Egyptians	Ezek 29:9b-16
Israelites	Ezek 39:25-29;
	Joel 3:1-3;
	Amos 9:14-15
Jeremiah	Jer 33:12-13

through **REVENGE**
  of **DEITY**
  | David | 2 Sam 21:1-14 |

REWARDs of
  with **DEITY**
  | Isaiah | Is 40:1-11 |
  INSTRUCTION on
James	Jas 5:19-20
Jesus	Mt 5:3-12;
	Lk 6:20-23
  PROPHECY of
  | Isaiah | Is 52:13-53:12; |
  | | 62:1-12 |
  REVELATION on
  | Ezekiel | Ezek 11:14-21 |
  | Israelites | Zech 10:3-12 |

SACREDNESS in
  of **FOLLOWER**
Jesus	1 Cor 1:26-31;
	6:9-11;
	Eph 5:21-33
  INSTRUCTION on
  | Nehemiah | Neh 13:15-22 |
  | Paul | 1 Cor 7:8-16 |
  REVELATION on
  | Moses | Lev 16:11-28 |

through **SACRIFICE**
High Priest	Heb 5:1-10
Jacob	Gen 32:1-23
Moses	Ex 29:19-36a;
	30:11-16;
	Lev 12:1-8;
	16:6-10;
	Num 28:26-31;
	29:1-6
  COVENANT of
  | Jesus | Mt 26:17-30; |
  | | Mk 14:22-26 |
  INSTRUCTION on
  | Jesus | Heb 10:1-18 |
  | Moses | Lev 9:1-24 |
  of **MESSIANIC FIGURE**
  | Israelites | Mal 2:17-3:5 |
  | Jesus | Heb 9:23-28 |

MISSION of
  Jesus   Mt 20:20-28;
                      Mk 10:35-45
REVELATION on
  Moses   Ex 34:12-28;
                      Lev 23:26-32;
                      Num 3:40-51
TRADITION of
  Aaron   Ex 30:1-10
  Priest   Lev 4:1-35;
                      7:1-10
in WORSHIP
  Aaron   Lev 16:1-5;
                      1 Chr 6:49-53
  Moses   Lev 8:1-36
  Noah   Gen 8:13-22
  Priest   Lev 15:1-33;
                      Num 15:22-31

SCRIPTURES on
  as BLESSING
    Jesus   Gal 3:10-14
  through FULFILLMENT
    Jesus   1 Cor 15:1-11
  through GRACE
    Peter   Acts 15:6-29
  through REPENTANCE
    Israelites   Neh 1:5-11a

SELF-REALIZATION of
  through REPENTANCE
    David   2 Sam 12:1-31

through SERVICE
  INSTRUCTION on
    James   Jas 2:14-26
  MISSION of
    Jesus   Mt 20:20-28;
                    Mk 10:35-45
  PROPHECY of
    Tyre   Is 23:15-18
  TRADITION of
    Priest   Lev 16:29-34

through SUFFERING
    Aaron   Num 16:36-50
  INSTRUCTION on
    Jesus   Heb 13:1-25
  of MESSIANIC FIGURE
    Jesus   Heb 2:5-18
  REVELATION on
    Moses   Lev 23:26-32

through TEMPTATION
  of MESSIANIC FIGURE
    Jesus   Heb 2:5-18

TRADITION of
  through SACRIFICE
    Aaron   Ex 30:1-10
    Priest   Lev 4:1-35;
                    7:1-10
  through SERVICE
    Priest   Lev 16:29-34

VICTORY in
  with DEITY
    Isaiah   Is 63:1-6
    Israelites   Nah 1:10,12,13;
                    15-2:2

PROPHECY of
  Israelites   Nah 2:1-5
REVELATION on
  Daniel   Dan 8:13-14

WEALTH through
  with DEITY
    Israelites   Zeph 3:14-20
  in ENVIRONMENT
    Nebuchadnezzar Dan 4:36-37
  PROPHECY of
    Jeremiah   Jer 32:26-44
    Judahites   Zeph 2:4-7
  REVELATION on
    Egyptians   Ezek 29:9b-16
    Israelites   Ezek 39:25-29;
                    Joel 3:1-3;
                    Amos 9:14-15
    Jeremiah   Jer 33:12-13

WITNESS to
  COVENANT of
    Holy Spirit   Heb 10:1-18
    Jacob   Gen 31:44-55
  MISSION of
    Paul   Acts 26:1-32;
                  2 Cor 5:14-19;
                  20-6:2

through WORSHIP
  for FAMILY
    Jews   *2 Mc 1:18-36;
                  2:16-18
  for LEADERSHIP
    Nehemiah   Neh 13:10-14
  with SACRIFICE
    Aaron   Lev 16:1-5;
                  1 Chr 6:49-53
    Moses   Lev 8:1-36
    Noah   Gen 8:13-22
    Priest   Lev 15:1-33;
                  Num 15:22-31

REJECTION

of AUTHORITY
  Israelites   1 Kgs 12:1-20;
                  2 Chr 10:1-12:16
  Sheba   2 Sam 20:1-26
of COVENANT
  Israelites   Zech 11:4-14
  Ptolemy   *1 Mc 11:1-19
of DEITY
  Ephraimites   Hos 7:3-7
  Saul   1 Sam 15:1-35
  through FALSE BELIEF
    Diotrephes   3 Jn 1:9-11
    Sinners   Jude 1:8-10
  REVELATION of
    Pharaoh   Ex 7:1-7

BEHAVIOR revealing
  of COVENANT
    Isaiah   Is 33:7-16
  of DEITY
    Israelites   Is 1:2-3;
                  4-9
  through FALSE BELIEF

through **FALSE BELIEF** (cont'd)
    Pharisees   Lk 11:53-54;
                        19:39-40
of **FOLLOWERs**
    Gentiles   Acts 14:1-7
    Jews   Acts 14:1-7;
                        17:10-15;
                        18:1-17
    Judas   Mt 26:47-56;
                        Mk 14:43-50;
                        Lk 22:47-54a
    Peter   Mt 26:69-75;
                        Mk 14:66-72;
                        Lk 22:54b-62;
                        Jn 18:12-27
of **MESSIANIC FIGURE**
    Crowd   Mt 27:11-26
    People   Lk 9:51-56;
                        22:63-65
    Soldiers   Mt 27:27-31;
                        Mk 15:16-20
REVELATION on
    Zechariah   Zech 7:4-8:23

of **BELIEF**
    through **FALSE BELIEF**
        Daniel   *Bel 1:3-7
    INSTRUCTION on
        Jesus   Lk 10:1-16
        Jews   Acts 28:17-31
        Paul   2 Cor 6:14-7:1
    in **MESSIANIC FIGURE**
        People   Jn 7:37-52;
                        12:36b-43

of **unBELIEF**
    in **DEITY**
        Israelites   Is 49:1-26;
                        Ezek 9:1-11
    by **FOLLOWERs**
        Jews   Acts 13:14-52
    INSTRUCTION on
        Achior   *Jdt 5:22-6:13
        Elihu   Job 35:1-4
        Jesus   Mt 7:6

of **BROTHERHOOD**
    COVENANT of
        Tyre   Amos 1:9-10
    in **ENVIRONMENT**
        Levite   Judg 19:10-15

by **COMMUNITY**
    Jesus   Mt 13:53-58;
                        Mk 6:1-6;
                        Lk 4:16-30
    Moses   Num 16:3-11
of **DEITY**
    Israelites   2 Kgs 17:7-23
    Mankind   Ps 2:1-3
    Psalmist   Ps 44:9-16
of **MISSION**
    Jesus   Lk 13:34-35
SELF-REALIZATION on
    Job   Job 19:13-19

of **COMMUNITY**
    by **FOLLOWERs**
        Jesus   Mt 19:27-30;
                      Mk 10:28-31;

by **FOLLOWERs** (cont'd)
    Jesus   Lk 18:28-30

through **COMPULSION**
    Eleazar   *2 Mc 6:18-31

CONFRONTATION with
    Jesus   Lk 10:1-16
    in the **ENVIRONMENT**
        Jephthah   Judg 11:1-3
    through **FALSE BELIEF**
        Herod   Lk 23:6-16
        Paul   Tit 2:11-15
        Pharisees   Lk 16:14-15
    of **FOLLOWERs**
        Apostles   1 Cor 4:6-13
    of **MESSIANIC FIGURE**
        Jesus   Mt 11:16-19;
                      Lk 7:31-35
        Jews   Jn 5:1-18
    in **MISSION**
        John the Baptist Mt 11:16-19;
                      Lk 7:31-35
    REVELATION on
        Israelites   Ezek 21:1-7

CONVERSION through
    INSTRUCTION on
        Paul   Gal 2:17-19
    MEDITATION on
        Jeremiah   Jer 5:1-14

of **COVENANT**
    by **AUTHORITY**
        Israelites   Zech 11:4-14
        Ptolemy   *1 Mc 11:1-19
    BEHAVIOR revealing
        Isaiah   Is 33:7-16
    of **BROTHERHOOD**
        Tyre   Amos 1:9-10
    of **ELECTION**
        Israelites   Rom 9:1-5
    through **inFIDELITY**
        Israelites   Ps 106:19-23;
                      Ezek 16:53-63;
                      17:11-21
    of **FREEDOM**
        People   Jer 34:13-22
    of **LAW**
        God   Heb 8:6-13
        Israelites   Ezek 20:9-26
        Jesus   Eph 2:11-22
        Paul   Gal 4:21-26
    of **PROMISE**
        God   Ps 89:38-51
    through **disRESPECT**
        Zechariah   Zech 11:4-14

by **DEITY**
    of **AUTHORITY**
        Ephraimites   Hos 7:3-7
      . Saul   1 Sam 15:1-35
    for **inFIDELITY**
        Ephraimites   Hos 7:8-12
        God   Ps 52:5-7
        Isaiah   Is 63:7-64:12
        Israelites   Ps 106:24-27;
                      Ezek 22:1-16;
                      Hos 8:11-14

for **in**FIDELITY (cont'd)
Job	Job 21:14-18; 34:5-9

for dis**HONESTY**
Isaiah	Is 56:9-57:13
Judahites	Jer 9:2-9

KNOWLEDGE of
Galatian	Gal 4:8-11
Israelites	Ex 16:1-21; Num 14:26-38
Mankind	Ps 10:3-11

of **PRAYER**
Adversaries	Ps 18:31-42
God	Is 1:10-17
Habakkuk	Hab 1:2-4
Jeremiah	Lam 3:1-66
Job	Job 19:7-12
Moses	Deut 3:23-29
Saul	1 Sam 28:3-25

of **PROMISE**
Abraham	Gen 14:21-24

of **PROVIDENCE**
David	Ps 60:1-5
Ephraimites	Hos 7:13-16
Followers	Ps 80:8-13
Israelites	Neh 9:16-18; Ps 78:9-20; Jer 2:1-13; Amos 4:6-12
Psalmist	Ps 88:15-18
Sinners	2 Pet 3:3-7

PUNISHMENT of
God	Ps 68:4-14; Hos 6:4-6
Israelites	Neh 9:26-31; Ps 95:7d-11; Is 9:8-10:4; 30:8-17; Heb 3:12-19
Jeremiah	Jer 17:13
Judahites	Jer 7:29-8:3
Psalmist	Ps 119:113-120

RECONCILIATION through
Israelites	Rom 11:7-24

of **RITE**
Israelites	Amos 5:21-25; Mal 2:10-16
Priests	Mal 1:6-2:9

SIGNS of
Ahaz	Is 7:10-17
Israelites	Ps 78:40-55
Jesus	Jn 15:18-25

of **SIN**
Believers	Heb 6:1-8; 10:19-31
David	Ps 140:6-8
Elihu	Job 34:34-37
Gentiles	Rom 1:24-32
Israelites	Ps 78:56-66; Jer 2:1-13; 6:27-30; Hos 10:1-8; 13:4-6; *2 Esd 1:24-40
Mankind	Ps 14:1-3
Sinners	Jn 9:1-41
Sirach	*Sir 15:11-20

of **STEWARDSHIP**
Cain	Gen 4:1-16

of **TRUTH**
God	Rom 1:18
Judahites	Jer 7:21-28; 8:4-7
Mankind	Rev 16:8-9; 10-11

of **DEITY**
BEHAVIOR revealing
Israelites	Is 1:2-3; 4-9

BELIEF in
Israelites	Is 49:1-26; Ezek 9:1-11

by **COMMUNITY**
Israelites	2 Kgs 17:7-23
Mankind	Ps 2:1-3
Psalmist	Ps 44:9-16

CONFRONTATION with
Jesus	Lk 10:1-16

revealing dis**RESPECT**
Israelites	Jer 6:9-15

DESIRE for
Ahab	1 Kgs 21:1-4

of **ELECTION**
to **COVENANT**
Israelites	Rom 9:1-5

by **DEITY**
Ephraimites	Ps 78:67-72
Saul	1 Sam 13:1-23

of **FOLLOWER**
Judas	Jn 6:60-71

REVELATION on
Eli	1 Sam 2:27-36

TRADITION of
Esau	Gen 27:1-40

of **EQUALITY**
with **DEITY**
Bildad	Job 25:1-6
Ezra	*2 Esd 4:1-12; 5:31-42
Job	Job 9:1-7; 8-13; 14-19; 30-35
Zophar	Job 11:7-12

ETERNAL
MEDITATION on
Job	Job 7:12-16

FALSE BELIEF causing
of **JUDGMENT**
Jews	Jn 18:28-19:16
Priests	Jn 12:9-11

of **KNOWLEDGE**
Paul	Col 2:1-5; 1 Tim 6:20-21
Sirach	*Sir 34:1-8

of **LAW**
Paul	Gal 6:11-18; Col 2:16-23

as **MOTIVATION**
Priests	Mt 28:11-15

of **PRESENCE**
Sennacherib	Is 36:1-37:4c

through inFIDELITY
Jesus	2 Tim 2:8-13
Paul	2 Tim 1:15-18

as PUNISHMENT
Jesus	Heb 10:19-31

of TRUTH
Jews	Acts 21:27-22:29
Peter	2 Pet 2:17-22

of FREEDOM
  through COVENANT
People	Jer 34:13-22

FREEDOM through
  by FOLLOWERs
Satan	Jas 4:1-10

of HONESTY
  caused by FALSE BELIEF
Israelites	Jer 5:1-14
James	Jas 1:26
Jesus	1 Jn 2:18-23; 4:1-3
Paul	Tit 1:9-16
Shemaiah	Jer 29:24-32

  PROPHECY of
Prophets	Jer 27:12-15; 16-22

of disHONESTY
  by DEITY
Isaiah	Is 56:9-57:13
Judahites	Jer 9:2-9

  INSTRUCTION on
Jeremiah	Jer 29:1-23
Jesus	Jn 10:1-18
Paul	2 Thes 2:1-3a

INSTRUCTION on
  of BELIEF
Achior	*Jdt 5:22-6:13
Elihu	Job 35:1-4
Jesus	Mt 7:6; Lk 10:1-16
Jews	Acts 28:17-31
Paul	2 Cor 6:14-7:1

  of inFIDELITY
Author	Heb 3:12-19
Jesus	Mt 8:18-22; 23:34-39; Lk 9:57-62; 12:1-12

  of disHONESTY
Jeremiah	Jer 29:1-23
Jesus	Jn 10:1-18
Paul	2 Thes 2:1-3a

  through JUDGMENT
Jesus	Mt 10:26-39; 12:38-42; 22:1-14; Lk 10:1-16; 11:29-32; 14:15-24; Jn 5:19-47; 12:44-50

  of KNOWLEDGE
Baruch	*Bar 3:9-14
Job	Job 16:1-6; 21:28-34
Wisdom	Prov 1:20-33; 8:32-36

of LAW
  Author
Author	Heb 7:1-28; 10:1-18
Jesus	Mt 9:16-17; Mk 2:18-22; Lk 5:36-39
Moses	Deut 23:1-8
Paul	Gal 2:15-16; 3:15-18

of PRAYER
Elihu	Job 35:9-12
James	Jas 4:1-10

of PROMISE
Israel	Ex 6:2-9
Sirach	*Sir 23:7-11

as PUNISHMENT
John the Baptist	Mt 3:1-12
Paul	2 Thes 3:6-15
Solomon	Prov 13:1-25
Wisdom	Prov 1:20-33

through disRESPECT
Israelites	Is 30:8-17

of RESURRECTION
Disciples	Lk 24:1-12

of RITE
Antiochus	*1 Mc 1:41-53
God	Is 1:10-17
Paul	Gal 5:2-6

of SIN
Author	Heb 3:12-19; 12:1-2
David	Ps 37:23-40
Father	Prov 4:10-19; 20-27
God	Is 1:18-20
Isaiah	Is 59:1-21
James	Jas 1:19-21
Jeremiah	Jer 5:20-25
Jesus	Mt 12:22-32; 21:33-43; Mk 12:1-12; Lk 20:9-18
John	1 Jn 2:12-17
Paul	1 Cor 15:29-34; 2 Cor 6:14-7:1; 2 Tim 2:14-19; 20-26; 3:1-9
Peter	1 Pet 4:1-6
Sirach	*Sir 7:1-36; 9:11-12; 12:1-7; 8-18; 18:27-33; 19:4-12; 21:1-7
Solomon	Prov 1:10-19; 5:1-14; 23:15-24:22

of TRUTH
Baruch	Jer 36:20-26
James	Jas 4:17
Jesus	Mt 7:6; 11:20-24; 13:3b-9; 10-17; 18-23; Mk 4:1-9; 10-20; Lk 8:4-8; 11-15;

of TRUTH (cont'd)
Jesus   Jn 3:1-21
John the Baptist   Jn 3:31-36
Paul   Rom 1:19-23;
    1 Tim 4:6-10;
    2 Tim 4:1-5
Pharisees   Mt 15:3-9;
    Mk 7:1-23
of VIRTUE
Sirach   *Sir 26:28

JUDGMENT of
of MESSIANIC FIGURE
Caiaphas   Mt 26:57-68;
    Mk 14:53-65
People   Lk 23:1-5
Priests   Lk 22:66-71
PROPHECY of
Jesus   Lk 22:14-23
REVELATION on
Israelites   Mal 2:17-3:5
TRADITION of
Paul   Col 2:16-23

of JUDGMENT
by DEITY
Job   Job 7:17-21
FALSE BELIEF causing
Jews   Jn 18:28-19:16
Priests   Jn 12:9-11

through JUDGMENT
INSTRUCTION on
Jesus   Mt 10:26-39;
    12:38-42;
    22:1-14;
    Lk 10:1-16;
    11:29-32;
    14:15-24;
    Jn 5:19-47;
    12:44-50

KNOWLEDGE of
of DEITY
Galatian   Gal 4:8-11
Israelites   Ex 16:1-21;
    Num 14:26-38
Mankind   Ps 10:3-11
PROPHECY of
Isaiah   Is 31:1-3
Israelites   Jer 6:16-21
Jesus   Mk 8:31-33;
    Lk 9:18-22;
    Jn 16:1-4
Scribes   Mt 17:9-13;
    Mk 9:9-13
REVELATION on
Judahites   Jer 3:6-11
Mankind   Rev 9:13-21

of KNOWLEDGE
Gedaliah   Jer 40:13-16
Rehoboam   1 Kgs 12:1-20;
    2 Chr 10:1-12:16
caused by FALSE BELIEF
Paul   Col 2:1-5;
    1 Tim 6:20-21
Sirach   *Sir 34:1-8
INSTRUCTION on
Baruch   *Bar 3:9-14

INSTRUCTION on (cont'd)
Job   Job 16:1-6;
    21:28-34
Wisdom   Prov 1:20-33;
    8:32-36
of MESSIANIC FIGURE
Jesus   Jn 18:1-11

of LAW
COVENANT of
God   Heb 8:6-13
Israelites   Ezek 20:9-26
Jesus   Eph 2:11-22
Paul   Gal 4:21-26
of DEITY
Israelites   Jer 6:16-21;
    *2 Esd 2:33-41
Judahites   Jer 8:8-13;
    Amos 2:4-5
FALSE BELIEF causing
Paul   Gal 6:11-18;
    Col 2:16-23
INSTRUCTION on
Author   Heb 7:1-28;
    10:1-18
Jesus   Mt 9:16-17;
    Mk 2:18-22;
    Lk 5:36-39
Moses   Deut 23:1-8
Paul   Gal 2:15-16;
    3:15-18
by MESSIANIC FIGURE
Jesus   Lk 13:10-17
PROPHECY of
Israelites   Hos 4:4-15
TRADITION of
Disciples   Mt 15:1-2

of MEDIATION
REVELATION on
Ezekiel   Ezek 14:12-23
Jeremiah   Jer 7:16-20;
    11:1-14;
    14:10-12

MEDITATION on
of CONVERSION
Jeremiah   Jer 5:1-14
for ETERNITY
Job   Job 7:12-16
of PRAYER
Jeremiah   Lam 3:1-66
as PUNISHMENT
Jeremiah   Jer 5:1-14
of SIN
David   Ps 26:4-6a;
    39:1-3;
    101:2c-4
Jeremiah   Jer 5:1-14

by MESSIANIC FIGURE
of LAW
Jesus   Lk 13:10-17

of MESSIANIC FIGURE
BEHAVIOR revealing
Crowd   Mt 27:11-26
People   Lk 9:51-56;
    22:63-65
Soldiers   Mt 27:27-31;
    Mk 15:16-20

BELIEF in
  People   Jn 7:37-52;
                          12:36b-43
CONFRONTATION with
  Jesus   Mt 11:16-19;
                          Lk 7:31-35
  Jews   Jn 5:1-18
JUDGMENT of
  Caiaphas   Mt 26:57-68;
                          Mk 14:53-65
  People   Lk 23:1-5
  Priests   Lk 22:66-71
KNOWLEDGE of
  Jesus   Jn 18:1-11
in **NEW AGE**
  Jesus   Acts 4:1-22
as **PUNISHMENT**
  Jesus   Lk 23:33-38
revealing dis**RESPECT**
  Crowd   Mk 6:1-6
  People   Mt 13:53-58;
                          Lk 4:16-30
SIN in
  Crowd   Mt 27:33-44;
                          Mk 15:21-32
  Jesus   Jn 1:1-18
TRUTH in
  Jews   Jn 8:21-59
  People   Jn 1:1-18
  Pharisees   Jn 8:12-20

of **MISSION**
  by **COMMUNITY**
    Jesus   Lk 13:34-35
  CONFRONTATION with
    John the Baptist   Mt 11:16-19;
                          Lk 7:31-35

MOTIVATION for
  FALSE BELIEF causing
    Priests   Mt 28:11-15

in **NEW AGE**
  of **MESSIANIC FIGURE**
    Jesus   Acts 4:1-22
  PROPHECY of
    Jesus   Mk 8:34-9:1;
                          Lk 9:23-27

of **NEW AGE**
  by **FOLLOWER**
    Jesus   Mk 10:17-22
    Man   Mt 19:16-22

of **PRAYER**
  Moses   Num 16:12-15
  Paul   2 Cor 12:1-10
  by **DEITY**
    Adversaries   Ps 18:31-42
    God   Is 1:10-17
    Habakkuk   Hab 1:2-4
    Jeremiah   Lam 3:1-66
    Job   Job 19:7-12
    Moses   Deut 3:23-29
    Saul   1 Sam 28:3-25
  INSTRUCTION on
    Elihu   Job 35:9-12
    James   Jas 4:1-10
  MEDITATION on
    Jeremiah   Lam 3:1-66

PROPHECY of
  Israelites   Mic 3:1-12
  Jeremiah   Jer 14:10-12
  Moab   Is 15:1-16:14
  Samuel   1 Sam 8:1-22
REVELATION on
  Israelites   Ezek 20:30-31
  Jeremiah   Jer 11:1-14;
                          15:1-4

of **PRESENCE**
  FALSE BELIEF causes
    Sennacherib   Is 36:1-37:4c
of **PROMISE**
  in **COVENANT**
    God   Ps 89:38-51
  by **DEITY**
    Abraham   Gen 14:21-24
  in **ENVIRONMENT**
    Eupator   *1 Mc 6:55-63
    Jonathan   *1 Mc 10:45-50
  INSTRUCTION on
    Israel   Ex 6:2-9
    Sirach   *Sir 23:7-11

PROPHECY of
  through in**FIDELITY**
    Isaiah   Is 29:15-16
    Jesus   Mt 26:31-35;
                          Mk 14:27-31;
                          Lk 22:14-23;
                          31-32;
                          33-34;
                          Jn 13:1-20;
                          21-30;
                          36-38;
                          Jn 16:29-33
    Judahites   2 Chr 24:1-27
    Peter   Mt 26:69-75;
                          Mk 14:66-72;
                          Lk 22:54b-62;
                          Jn 18:12-27
  of dis**HONESTY**
    Prophets   Jer 27:12-15;
                          16-22
  of **JUDGMENT**
    Jesus   Lk 22:14-23
  of **KNOWLEDGE**
    Isaiah   Is 31:1-3
    Israelites   Jer 6:16-21
    Jesus   Mk 8:31-33;
                          Lk 9:18-22;
                          Jn 16:1-4
    Scribes   Mt 17:9-13;
                          Mk 9:9-13
  of **LAW**
    Israelites   Hos 4:4-15
  in **NEW AGE**
    Jesus   Mk 8:34-9:1;
                          Lk 9:23-27
  concerning **PRAYER**
    Israelites   Mic 3:1-12
    Jeremiah   Jer 14:10-12
    Moab   Is 15:1-16:14
    Samuel   1 Sam 8:1-22
  of **PROVIDENCE**
    Isaiah   Is 5:8-24a
  as **PUNISHMENT**
    Ephraimites   Hos 9:10-17

as **PUNISHMENT** (cont'd)

Isaiah	Is 8:5-8a; 10:5-16; 17:9-11; 28:1-13; 30:1-7
Israelites	Ezek 16:35-43; Hos 4:4-15; 11:5-7; Amos 4:6-12; 5:4-6; Mic 3:1-12; Hag 1:15a; 2:15-19
Jeremiah	Jer 13:20-27; 19:1-15; 29:1-23; 32:26-44; 34:13-22; *Sir 49:4-7
Jesus	Lk 19:41-44
Judahites	Jer 9:10-22
People	Acts 3:1-26
Priests	Mal 1:6-2:9
Sennacherib	Is 37:22-29
Shemaiah	Jer 29:24-32
Zedekiah	Jer 27:12-15

through **disRESPECT**

Isaiah	Is 22:1-14; 52:13-53:12

of **SIN**

Isaiah	Is 2:6-11; 3:8-12
Jerusalemites	Zeph 3:1-5
Jesus	Jn 6:60-71

of **TRUTH**

Amaziah	Amos 7:10-17
Apostles	Jude 1:17-19
Israelites	Jer 44:15-19
Judahites	Jer 25:1-7; 35:6-17
Paul	1 Tim 4:1-5
People	Jer 43:1-3
Zedekiah	Jer 37:1-2

of **PROVIDENCE**
  of **DEITY**

David	Ps 60:1-5
Ephraimites	Hos 7:13-16
Followers	Ps 80:8-13
Israelites	Neh 9:16-18; Ps 78:9-20; Jer 2:1-13; Amos 4:6-12
Psalmist	Ps 88:15-18
Sinners	2 Pet 3:3-7

  caused by **FALSE BELIEF**

Ephraimites	Hos 11:1-4

  PROPHECY of

Isaiah	Is 5:8-24a

  REVELATION on

Israelites	Jer 2:20-29

as **PUNISHMENT**

Israelites	Deut 1:19-46
Michal	2 Sam 6:1-23

  by **DEITY**

God	Ps 68:4-14; Hos 6:4-6
Israelites	Neh 9:26-31;

by **DEITY** (cont'd)

Israelites	Ps 95:7d-11; Is 9:8-10:4; 30:8-17; Heb 3:12-19
Jeremiah	Jer 17:13
Judahites	Jer 7:29-8:3
Psalmist	Ps 119:113-120

caused by **FALSE BELIEF**

Author	Heb 6:1-8

of **FOLLOWER**s

Jesus	Heb 10:19-31

INSTRUCTION on

John the Baptist	Mt 3:1-12
Paul	2 Thes 3:6-15
Solomon	Prov 13:1-25
Wisdom	Prov 1:20-33

MEDITATION on

Jeremiah	Jer 5:1-14

of **MESSIANIC FIGURE**

Jesus	Lk 23:33-38

PROPHECY of

Ephraimites	Hos 9:10-17
Isaiah	Is 8:5-8a; 10:5-16; 17:9-11; 28:1-13; 30:1-7
Israelites	Ezek 16:35-43; Hos 4:4-15; 11:5-7; Amos 4:6-12; 5:4-6; Mic 3:1-12; Hag 1:15a; 2:15-19
Jeremiah	Jer 13:20-27; 19:1-15; 29:1-23; 32:26-44; 34:13-22; *Sir 49:4-7
Jesus	Lk 19:41-44
Judahites	Jer 9:10-22
People	Acts 3:1-26
Priests	Mal 1:6-2:9
Sennacherib	Is 37:22-29
Shemaiah	Jer 29:24-32
Zedekiah	Jer 27:12-15

REVELATION on

Ezekiel	Ezek 14:1-11
Israelites	Num 14:26-38; Jer 2:14-19; 30-37; Ezek 20:32-39; Hos 2:2-8; 9-13
Jehoiakim	Jer 36:27-32
Jeremiah	Jer 16:1-13; 19:1-15
Judahites	Ezek 23:22-35
Moses	Num 14:11-24; 20:2-13
Nations	Zeph 3:6-7
People	Jer 27:1-11
Zedekiah	Jer 24:1-10
Zephaniah	Zeph 1:2-6

as **QUALITY OF LIFE**
  REVELATION on

PROPHECY of
   Jesus   Lk 17:22-37
REVELATION on
   Hosea   Hos 1:2-3;
                   8-9
   John   Rev 13:11-18;
                   14:1-5
SCRIPTURES on
   Isaiah   1 Cor 14:13-25

SIN of
  of **MESSIANIC FIGURE**
    Crowd   Mt 27:33-44;
                 Mk 15:21-32
    Jesus   Jn 1:1-18
  of **SIN**
    Israelites   Hos 4:1-3
    Joseph   Gen 39:1-23
    Judahites   Jer 7:1-15
    Mankind   Ps 112:10
    Susanna   *Susa 1:19-27
  by **DEITY**
    Believers   Heb 6:1-8;
                 10:19-31
    David   Ps 140:6-8
    Elihu   Job 34:34-37
    Gentiles   Rom 1:24-32
    Israelites   Ps 78:56-66;
                 Jer 2:1-13;
                 6:27-30;
                 Hos 10:1-8;
                 13:4-6;
                 *2 Esd 1:24-40
    Mankind   Ps 14:1-3
    Sinners   Jn 9:1-41
    Sirach   *Sir 15:11-20
  INSTRUCTION on
    Author   Heb 3:12-19;
                 12:1-2
    David   Ps 37:23-40
    Father   Prov 4:10-19;
                 20-27
    God   Is 1:18-20
    Isaiah   Is 59:1-21
    James   Jas 1:19-21
    Jeremiah   Jer 5:20-25
    Jesus   Mt 12:22-32;
                 21:33-43;
                 Mk 12:1-12;
                 Lk 20:9-18
    John   1 Jn 2:12-17
    Paul   1 Cor 15:29-34;
                 2 Cor 6:14-7:1;
                 2 Tim 2:14-19;
                 20-26;
                 3:1-9
    Peter   1 Pet 4:1-6
    Sirach   *Sir 7:1-36;
                 9:11-12;
                 12:1-7;
                 8-18;
                 18:27-33;
                 19:4-12;
                 21:1-7
    Solomon   Prov 1:10-19;
                 5:1-14;
                 23:15-24:22

MEDITATION on
    David   Ps 26:4-6a;

MEDITATION on (cont'd)
    David   39:1-3;
                 101:2c-4
    Jeremiah   Jer 5:1-14
  in **MISSION**
    Holy Spirit   Jn 16:5-11
PROPHECY of
    Isaiah   Is 2:6-11;
                 3:8-12
    Jerusalemites   Zeph 3:1-5
    Jesus   Jn 6:60-71
REVELATION on
    Ezekiel   Ezek 12:1-16
    Isaiah   Is 65:1-25
    Israelites   Jer 3:1-5;
                 Ezek 5:5-17;
                 20:5-8
    Jesus   Jn 1:1-18

through **SIN**
  caused by **FALSE BELIEF**
    Israelites   Hos 2:2-8
    Jeremiah   *Jer 6:8-40;
                 45-59;
                 60-73
    Paul   Phil 3:1-3;
                 Tit 3:8-11
    Pharisees   Lk 7:24-30

of **STEWARDSHIP**
  by **DEITY**
    Cain   Gen 4:1-16
  REVELATION on
    Cain   Gen 4:1-16

of **TRADITION**
  of **ELECTION**
    Esau   Gen 27:1-40
  of **JUDGMENT**
    Paul   Col 2:16-23
  of **LAW**
    Disciples   Mt 15:1-2
  of **RITE**
    Pharaoh   Ex 5:1-5
  of **SECURITY**
    Esau   Gen 25:27-34

of **TRUTH**
    Israelites   Num 14:10;
                 Amos 5:7-13
  of **DEITY**
    God   Rom 1:18
    Judahites   Jer 7:21-28;
                 8:4-7
    Mankind   Rev 16:8-9;
                 10-11
  through **FALSE BELIEF**
    Galatians   Gal 4:12-20
    Israelites   Is 48:1-22
    Jezebel   Rev 2:18-29
    John   2 Jn 1:7-11
    Pharisees   Jn 7:32-36;
                 9:1-41
    Priests   Mt 28:11-15
    Sinners   Jude 1:3-4
  of **FOLLOWERs**
    Jews   Acts 21:27-22:29
    Peter   2 Pet 2:17-22
  INSTRUCTION on
    Baruch   Jer 36:20-26

REVELATION on (cont'd)
  Jeremiah   31:2-6
  Prophets   Jer 23:16-22
  Zechariah   Zech 1:1-6
SELF-REALIZATION of
  Criminal   Lk 23:39-43
  Nebuchadnezzar Dan 4:34-35

through COVENANT
 of RECONCILIATION
  Israelites   Lev 26:1-46

before DEITY
 CONVERSION through
  David   Ps 32:3-7;
                51:3-12
  Ephraim   Jer 31:15-22
  God   Num 23:13-26;
                1 Sam 15:1-35;
                1 Chr 21:1-22:1;
                Ezek 24:1-14;
                Joel 2:12-17;
                Jon 3:1-10
  Israelites   Hos 3:1-5;
                5:15-6:3
 DESIRE for
  Israelites   Ezek 33:10-20
  Mankind   2 Pet 3:8-10
 of disHONESTY
  Israelites   Ps 78:32-39
 JUDGMENT on
  God   Jon 4:1-11
 KNOWLEDGE of
  Manasseh   2 Chr 33:1-25
  Pharaoh   Gen 12:9-13:1
 MOTIVATION for
  Israelites   Neh 9:26-31
  People   Rom 2:1-24
 in NEW AGE
  John the Baptist Mt 3:1-12
 through PRAYER
  Daniel   Dan 9:4-19
  Israelites   1 Sam 12:1-25;
                Hos 5:15-6:3
 through PROVIDENCE
  God   2 Tim 2:20-26
  Israelites   *Bar 2:27-35
 revealing RESPECT
  People   Mic 7:7-20
 of SIN
  David   Ps 7:12-16;
                19:11-14;
                51:1-2
  Israelites   Num 14:39-45;
                *Bar 2:27-35
  Sirach   *Sir 17:15-32

by DEITY
  Heliodorus   *2 Mc 3:1-40
  Israelites   Rom 11:7-24
 to COMMITMENT
  Israelites   Jer 3:21-4:4
 CONFRONTATION with
  Job   Job 42:1-6

of DEITY
 concerning PUNISHMENT
  David   1 Chr 21:1-22:1
  God   Ex 32:7-14;

concerning PUNISHMENT (cont'd)
  God   Jer 42:7-22;
                Amos 7:1-3;
                4-6;
                Jon 3:1-10
  Israelites   2 Sam 24:1-25;
                1 Chr 21:1-22:1
  Rehoboam   2 Chr 10:1-12:1
RECONCILIATION through
  Egyptians   Is 19:18-25
  God   Ex 32:7-14
  Israelites   Judg 3:7-11;
                Rom 11:7-24
  Solomon   2 Chr 5:1-7:10
SALVATION through
  Israelites   Judg 3:15-23

DESIRE for
 by DEITY
  Israelites   Ezek 33:10-20
  Mankind   2 Pet 3:8-10
 INSTRUCTION on
  Paul   2 Cor 12:19-21;
                Gal 4:12-20
 REVELATION on
  Ezekiel   Ezek 18:21-24
  Jeremiah   Jer 26:1-6;
                36:1-7

concerning FALSE BELIEF
 BEHAVIOR revealing
  Magicians   Acts 19:13-20

FIDELITY through
 INSTRUCTION on
  Ephesus   Rev 2:1-7
  Jeremiah   Jer 6:16-21
  Jesus   Lk 16:19-31;
                Jn 7:53-8:11
  Samuel   1 Sam 7:2-17
  Zephaniah   Zeph 2:3
 MEDITATION on
  Paul   2 Cor 7:5-13a
 PROPHECY of
  Prophets   2 Chr 24:1-27
 REVELATION on
  Judahites   Jer 3:21-4:4

for inFIDELITY
 through SELF-REALIZATION
  Peter   Mt 26:69-75;
                Mk 14:66-72;
                Lk 22:54b-62

of FOLLOWERs
 results in CONVERSION
  Jailer   Acts 16:25-40
  Thessalonians 1 Thes 1:2-10
  Zacchaeus   Lk 19:1-10

GIFT through
 INSTRUCTION on
  Holy Spirit   Acts 2:37-41

of disHONESTY
 before DEITY
  Israelites   Ps 78:32-39
 INSTRUCTION on
  John the Baptist Lk 3:7-9;
                10-14

resulting in **RECONCILIATION** (cont'd)
Tyre   Is 23:15-18

PROPHECY of
in **JUDGMENT**
Holy Spirit   Neh 9:26-31
Jesus   Mt 11:20-24
as **MOTIVATION**
Israelites   2 Kgs 17:7-23
of **SIN**
Isaiah   Is 17:7-8
as **VIRTUE**
Isaiah   Is 1:27-31

through **PROVIDENCE**
of **DEITY**
God   2 Tim 2:20-26
Israelites   *Bar 2:27-35
REVELATION on
Israelites   Ezek 12:1-16

of **PUNISHMENT**
by **DEITY**
David   1 Chr 21:1-22:1
God   Ex 32:7-14;
                            Jer 42:7-22;
                            Amos 7:1-3;
                            4-6;
                            Jon 3:1-10
Israelites   2 Sam 24:1-25;
                            1 Chr 21:1-22:1
Rehoboam   2 Chr 10:1-12:16

as **QUALITY OF LIFE**
REVELATION on
Israelites   Ezek 36:22-32

RECONCILIATION through
COVENANT of
Israelites   Lev 26:1-46
of **DEITY**
Egyptians   Is 19:18-25
God   Ex 32:7-14
Israelites   Judg 3:7-11;
                            Rom 11:7-24
Solomon   2 Chr 5:1-7:10
INSTRUCTION on
Jesus   Mt 18:15-17;
                            21:28-32;
                            Lk 12:57-59;
                            18:9-14
John the Baptist   Lk 3:1-6
Moses   Deut 30:1-10
MEDITATION on
Paul   2 Cor 7:5-13a
MISSION of
Jesus   Mt 9:10-13;
                            Lk 5:29-32

PROPHECY of
Isaiah   Is 59:1-21
Jeremiah   Jer 26:7-19;
                            29:1-23
Judahites   Jer 7:1-15;
                            35:6-17
Tyre   Is 23:15-18
REVELATION on
Israelites   Jer 3:14b-18;
                            21-4:4;
                            Ezek 39:25-29;
                            Mal 3:6-12

REVELATION on (cont'd)
Jeremiah   Jer 15:10-21;
                            18:1-12
Judahites   Jer 24:1-10
Solomon   2 Chr 7:11-22
SCRIPTURES on
Israelites   Neh 1:5-11a
SELF-REALIZATION of
David   2 Sam 12:1-31

revealing **RESPECT**
before **DEITY**
People   Mic 7:7-20

REVELATION on
concerning **JUDGMENT**
Jesus   Mt 11:20-24
as **MOTIVATION**
Israelites   Hos 2:2-8
Judahites   Jer 18:1-12
as **QUALITY OF LIFE**
Israelites   Ezek 36:22-32
of **SIN**
Manasseh   2 Chr 33:1-25
Moses   Num 5:5-10

SALVATION through
of **DEITY**
Israelites   Judg 3:15-23
INSTRUCTION on
Israelites   Hos 10:9-15
Jesus   Mt 21:28-32;
                            Lk 15:1-7;
                            8-10;
                            11-32;
                            19:1-10
Paul   2 Cor 7:5-13a
PROPHECY of
Isaiah   Is 30:8-17;
                            59:1-21
Jeremiah   Jer 4:13-18

SECURITY in
INSTRUCTION on
Zophar   Job 11:13-20
PROPHECY of
Judahites   Jer 4:13-18

SELF-REALIZATION causes
Israelites   Ex 33:1-6
Criminal   Lk 23:39-43
Nebuchadnezzar   Dan 4:34-35
for in**FIDELITY**
Peter   Mt 26:69-75;
                            Mk 14:66-72;
                            Lk 22:54b-62

SELF-REALIZATION of
caused by **LAW**
Josiah   2 Kgs 22:3-20;
                            2 Chr 34:1-35:27
of **SIN**
Daniel   Dan 9:4-19
Hezekiah   2 Chr 32:1-33
Judas   Mt 27:3-10

SIGNS of
REVELATION on
Moses   Deut 31:14-23

REPENTANCE (cont'd)

of **SIN**
Israelites	Deut 1:19-46; Judg 10:6-18
Saul	1 Sam 15:1-35

against **DEITY**
David	Ps 7:12-16; 19:11-14; 51:1-2
Israelites	Num 14:39-45; *Bar 2:27-35
Sirach	*Sir 17:15-32

INSTRUCTION on
Eli	1 Sam 2:11-26
Eliphaz	Job 22:21-30
Ezra	Ezra 10:7-15
God	Is 1:10-17
Isaiah	Is 28:14-22
Israelites	Is 31:4-9
Jesus	Lk 17:1-6; 24:44-49
John	1 Jn 1:5-10
John the Baptist	Mk 1:2-8
Paul	Rom 6:1-14; 1 Cor 15:29-34
Peter	Acts 3:1-26; 1 Pet 4:1-6
Sirach	*Sir 34:23-26
Solomon	Prov 28:1-28

MEDITATION on
David	Ps 38:17-22; 41:4-10

MISSION of
John the Baptist	Lk 3:1-6

PROPHECY of
Isaiah	Is 17:7-8

REVELATION on
Manasseh	2 Chr 33:1-25
Moses	Num 5:5-10

SELF-REALIZATION of
Daniel	Dan 9:4-19
Hezekiah	2 Chr 32:1-33
Judas	Mt 27:3-10

in **WORSHIP**
Israelites	Neh 9:1-5a

through **TRUTH**
INSTRUCTION on
Jeremiah	Jer 36:1-7
Paul	Acts 17:16-34

VIRTUE in
PROPHECY of
Isaiah	Is 1:27-31

in **WORSHIP**
PRAYER of
Ezra	Ezra 9:6-15
Nehemiah	Neh 1:5-11a

RESPECT

ACCEPTANCE of
for **DEITY**
Jesus	Lk 2:21-40; 41-52

RESPECT (cont'd)

for **FOLLOWER**
Apostles	Gal 1:18-2:10
Paul	Gal 1:18-2:10

INSTRUCTION on
Jesus	Mt 26:6-13; Mk 14:3-9; Jn 5:19-47

for **MESSIANIC FIGURE**
Jesus	Heb 1:5-14
Jews	Mt 21:12-17

REVELATION of
Eli	1 Sam 2:27-36

in **WORSHIP**
Believers	Heb 12:12-29

BLESSING as
INSTRUCTION on
David	1 Chr 15:1-16:43
Psalmist	Ps 96:1-6; 135:19-21

of **MESSIANIC FIGURE**
David	2 Sam 2:1-7

REVELATION on
Israelites	Jer 30:18-22

BLESSING in
Saul	1 Sam 26:1-55

for **DEITY**
Believers	Ps 33:13-19; Ps 128:1-2; 3-4; Eccl 8:10-17
David	Ps 31:19-24
God	Ps 115:12-18; Prov 28:1-28
King	Ps 21:1-7
Mankind	Ps 112:1
Psalmist	Ps 71:1-21

of **FOLLOWER**
Peter	1 Pet 4:12-19

for **COMPASSION**
of **DEITY**
David	Ps 69:13-21

of **MESSIANIC FIGURE**
David	1 Sam 23:14-24:22; 26:1-25

for **COURAGE**
Maccabeus	*2 Mc 8:1-7

for **DEATH**
Israelites	1 Sam 31:1-13
Jonathan	*1 Mc 13:25-30
Tobit	*Tb 1:10-22; 2:1-8

INSTRUCTION on
Sirach	*Sir 38:16-23

for **DEITY**
ACCEPTANCE of
Jesus	Lk 2:21-40; 41-52

BLESSING in
Believers	Ps 33:13-19; 128:1-2; 3-4; Eccl 8:10-17
David	Ps 31:19-24

BLESSING in (cont'd)	
God	Ps 115:12-18; Prov 28:1-28
King	Ps 21:1-7
Mankind	Ps 112:1
Psalmist	Ps 71:1-21
COMPASSION of	
David	Ps 69:13-21
CONDEMNATION of	
Job	Job 17:6-10
DIGNITY of	
David	Ps 18:46-50; 145:1-3
God	Ps 104:1-4
Mankind	Ps 8:3-8
from **ENEMY**	
David	Ps 18:43-45
God	Ps 132:11-18
through **FAITH**	
David	2 Sam 22:1-51; Ps 18:1-3
through **FEAR**	
Babylonians	2 Kgs 17:24-41
Darius	Dan 6:25-27
David	Ps 19:7-10
God	Prov 23:15-24:22; Is 33:1-6
Isaiah	Is 8:11-15; 59:1-21
Israelites	Deut 4:1-14; 6:20-25; Hos 3:1-5; Hag 1:12-14
Job	Job 1:1
Jonah	Jon 1:1-17
Kings	Ps 2:10-11
Mankind	Ps 15:1-5b; 33:4-9
Micah	Mic 7:7-20
Moses	Deut 6:4-19
Nehemiah	Neh 1:11b-2:8
Peter	1 Pet 2:13-17
Psalmist	Ps 67:1-7; 99:1-3
Sirach	*Sir 25:7-11; 32:14-24; 40:18-27
Wisdom	Prov 1:20-33
FRIENDSHIP of	
Mankind	Ps 15:1-5b
FULFILLMENT through	
Believers	Ps 145:13b-20
HUMILITY in	
God	Ps 138:4-6
Job	Job 30:9-15
JOY in	
Believers	Prov 15:1-33
David	Ps 34:4-10
JUSTICE of	
God	Ps 33:4-9
Nebuchadnezzar	Dan 4:36-37
concerning **LEADERSHIP**	
Moses	Deut 31:30-32:47
LIFE from	
God	Prov 10:1-32; 14:1-35; 19:1-29
LOVE of	
God	Ps 147:7-11
Israelites	Ps 103:6-13; 14-18

through **MIRACLE**	
David	Ps 29:3-9
through **OBEDIENCE**	
God	Prov 23:15-24:22 Eccl 12:12-14
through **PIETY**	
God	Is 29:13-14
through **PRAISE**	
Amos	Amos 4:13; 9:5-6
David	2 Sam 22:1-51; Ps 18:1-3
Eleazer	*2 Mc 6:18-31
Jesus	Phil 2:5-11
Nebuchadnezzar	Dan 4:1-3; 34-35; 36-37
Psalmist	Ps 113:2-4
REJECTION of	
Israelites	Jer 6:9-15
through **REPENTANCE**	
People	Mic 7:7-20
REWARDs of	
God	Ps 112:2-4
Israelites	Mal 3:13-4:3
SACREDNESS in	
Israelites	Is 29:17-24
through **SACRIFICE**	
David	Ps 20:1-5
through **SERVICE**	
God	Jn 12:20-26
Kings	Ps 2:10-11
through **WEALTH**	
Believer	Prov 22:1-16
Kings	Ps 68:28-35
Solomon	Ps 72:15-17
is **WISDOM**	
Micah	Mic 6:9-16
results in **WISDOM**	
God	Prov 2:1-22; 9:7-12; 14:1-35
Mankind	Ps 111:10; Prov 1:7
Solomon	Prov 3:1-35
WITNESS to	
Ezekiel	Ezek 44:4-5
for **DEITY's**	
WISDOM	
Job	Job 9:1-7; 26:5-14; 28:23-28
for **DIGNITY**	
Uzziah	2 Chr 26:1-28:27
of **DEITY**	
David	Ps 18:46-50; 145:1-3
God	Ps 104:1-4
Mankind	Ps 8:3-8
in **ENVIRONMENT**	
Tyre	Ezek 27:1-9a; 9b-11
INSTRUCTION on	
Paul	Rom 12:9-13; 13:1-7
Preacher	Eccl 7:1-22
Solomon	Prov 26:1-28
Wife	Prov 31:10-31

through PIETY
  TRADITION of
    Women   1 Cor 11:2-16
  in WORSHIP
    John   Rev 19:6-10

in POLITICS
  INSTRUCTION on
    Peter   1 Pet 2:13-17

for POVERTY
  INSTRUCTION on
    James   Jas 2:1-13
    Solomon   Prov 17:1-28

PRAISE revealing
  Psalmist   Ps 45:16-17
  of DEITY
    Amos   Amos 4:13;
        9:5-6
    David   2 Sam 22:1-51;
        Ps 18:1-3
    Eleazer   *2 Mc 6:18-31
    Jesus   Phil 2:5-11
    Nebuchadnezzar   Dan 4:1-3;
        34-35;
        36-37
    Psalmist   Ps 113:2-4
  in ENVIRONMENT
    Jonathan   *1 Mc 10:59-66;
        67-89;
        11:38-53
    Judith   *Jdt 13:11-20;
        15:8-13
    Maccabeus   *1 Mc 3:1-9;
        5:63-64
    Romans   *1 Mc 8:1-32
    Simon   *1 Mc 14:25-49
    Zerubbabel   *1 Esd 4:42-57
  INSTRUCTION on
    Believers   Rev 19:1-5
    David   Ps 22:22-26
    God   Rev 14:6-7
  for MESSIANIC FIGURE
    Crowd   Mt 21:1-11;
        Mk 11:1-10;
        Lk 19:28-38

REVELATION on
  Israelites   Zeph 3:14-20
TRADITION of
  Aaron   *Sir 45:6-22
  Abraham   *Sir 44:19-21
  Adam   *Sir 49:11-16
  David   *Sir 45:25-26;
      47:1-11
  Elijah   *Sir 48:1-11
  Elisha   *Sir 48:12-14
  Enoch   *Sir 44:16-18;
      49:11-16
  Ezekiel   *Sir 49:8-10
  Hezekiah   *Sir 48:17-25
  Jacob   *Sir 44:23
  Jeshua   *Sir 49:11-16
  Joseph   *Sir 49:11-16
  Joshua   *Sir 46:1-10
  Josiah   *Sir 49:1-3
  Judges   *Sir 46:11-12
  Maccabeus   *1 Mc 9:1-22
  Moses   *Sir 45:1-5
  Nehemiah   *Sir 49:11-16

TRADITION of (cont'd)
  Noah   *Sir 44:16-18
  Phinehas   *Sir 45:23-24
  Prophets   *Sir 49:8-10
  Samuel   *Sir 46:13-20
  Seth   *Sir 49:11-16
  Shem   *Sir 49:11-16
  Simon   *Sir 50:1-21;
      *1 Mc 14:4-15
  Sirach   *Sir 44:1-15
  Solomon   *Sir 47:12-22
  Zerubbabel   *Sir 49:11-16
  in WORSHIP
    God   Rev 4:1-11;
        7:9-17;
        11:15-19;
        15:1-16:1;
        19:1-5
    John   Rev 5:1-14
    Nebuchadnezzar   Dan 2:46-49
    Paul   Rom 11:33-36
    Psalmist   Ps 96:7-9

PROPHECY of
  in SADNESS
    Isaiah   Is 52:13-53:12
  in WEALTH
    Isaiah   Is 61:1-11
  in WISDOM
    Judahites   Jer 8:8-13

REJECTION of
  for DEITY
    Israelites   Jer 6:9-15
  INSTRUCTION on
    Israelites   Is 30:8-17

for REPENTANCE
  of DEITY
    People   Mic 7:7-20
  in ENVIRONMENT
    Saul   1 Sam 23:14-24

REVELATION on
  for FAMILY
    Israelites   Ezek 22:1-16
  through FEAR
    Disciples   Mk 9:2-8
    Isaiah   Is 66:1-16
    Jeremiah   Jer 33:1-9
  through HUMILITY
    Isaiah   Is 66:1-16
  for PATIENCE
    Isaiah   Is 56:9-57:13
  for PEACE
    Israelites   Ezek 36:8-15
  through VICTORY
    Israelites   Is 45:14-25
  through WITNESS
    Ezekiel   Ezek 43:1-5

REWARDs for
  of DEITY
    God   Ps 112:2-4
    Israelites   Mal 3:13-4:3
  INSTRUCTION on
    Elders   1 Tim 5:17-25
    Solomon   Prov 13:1-25

SACREDNESS in

SACREDNESS in (cont'd)	
for DEITY	
Israelites	Is 29:17-24
INSTRUCTION on	
Jesus	Mt 23:16-22
through SACRIFICE	
to DEITY	
David	Ps 20:1-5
in SADNESS	
PROPHECY of	
Isaiah	Is 52:13-53:12
SCRIPTURES on	
for LEADERSHIP	
Paul	Acts 22:30-23:11
for SERVICE	
Job	Job 29:7-13;
	14-20
to DEITY	
God	Jn 12:20-26
Kings	Ps 2:10-11
INSTRUCTION on	
Sirach	*Sir 38:24-34
Solomon	Prov 27:1-27
for SEX	
Zerubbabel	*1 Esd 4:13-34
INSTRUCTION on	
Sirach	*Sir 41:14-23
for SUFFERING	
David	Ps 35:11-16
TRADITION of	
through PIETY	
Women	1 Cor 11:2-16
through PRAISE	
Aaron	*Sir 45:6-22
Abraham	*Sir 44:19-21
Adam	*Sir 49:11-16
David	*Sir 45:25-26;
	47:1-11
Elijah	*Sir 48:1-11
Elisha	*Sir 48:12-14
Enoch	*Sir 44:16-18;
	49:11-16
Ezekiel	*Sir 49:8-10
Hezekiah	*Sir 48:17-25
Jacob	*Sir 44:23
Jeshua	*Sir 49:11-16
Joseph	*Sir 49:11-16
Joshua	*Sir 46:1-10
Josiah	*Sir 49:1-3
Judges	*Sir 46:11-12
Maccabeus	*1 Mc 9:1-22
Moses	*Sir 45:1-5
Nehemiah	*Sir 49:11-16
Noah	*Sir 44:16-18
Phinehas	*Sir 45:23-24
Prophets	*Sir 49:8-10
Samuel	*Sir 46:13-20
Seth	*Sir 49:11-16
Shem	*Sir 49:11-16
Simon	*Sir 50:1-21;
	*1 Mc 14:4-15
Sirach	*Sir 44:1-15
Solomon	*Sir 47:12-22
Zerubbabel	*Sir 49:11-16

through VICTORY	
REVELATION on	
Israelites	Is 45:14-25
through WEALTH	
Believer	Prov 22:1-16
David	1 Chr 28:1-29:30
Hezekiah	2 Chr 32:1-33
Jehoshaphat	2 Chr 17:1-20:37
Kings	Ps 68:28-35
Solomon	Ps 72:15-17
Tyre	Ezek 27:12-25a
INSTRUCTION on	
Psalmist	Ps 45:10-12
Sirach	*Sir 40:28-20
PROPHECY of	
Isaiah	Is 61:1-11
for WISDOM	
of DEITY	
Job	Job 9:1-7;
	26:5-14;
	28:23-28
INSTRUCTION on	
Believers	Prov 15:1-33
Father	Prov 4:1-9
Isaiah	Is 29:15-16
Sirach	*Sir 9:14-18;
	37:7-26;
	39:1-11
Solomon	*Wis 8:2-21
PROPHECY of	
Judahites	Jer 8:8-13
WISDOM in	
Darius	*1 Esd 3:1-17
Elihu	Job 32:11-14
WISDOM results from	
for DEITY	
God	Prov 2:1-22;
	9:7-12;
	14:1-35
Mankind	Ps 111:10;
	Prov 1:7
for WITNESS	
INSTRUCTION on	
Isaiah	Is 51:17-52:12
Peter	1 Pet 2:11-12
WITNESS to	
for DEITY	
Ezekiel	Ezek 44:4-5
of FOLLOWERs	
Mary	Mk 15:33-41
Salome	Mk 15:33-41
for MESSIANIC FIGURE	
Centurion	Mt 27:45-56
REVELATION on	
Ezekiel	Ezek 43:1-5
in WORSHIP	
ACCEPTANCE of	
Believers	Heb 12:12-29
through DIGNITY	
Women	1 Cor 11:2-16
FEAR revealing	
David	1 Chr 15:1-16:43;
	Ps 5:8-10

RESPECT (cont'd)

revealing GRATITUDE
David   1 Chr 15:1-16:43
God   Rev 4:1-11;
                         7:9-17;
                         11:15-19
through HUMILITY
Women   1 Cor 11:2-16
for JUSTICE
God   Rev 15:1-16:1
through PIETY
John   Rev 19:6-10
PRAISE revealing
God   Rev 4:1-11;
                         7:9-17;
                         11:15-19;
                         15:1-16:1;
                         19:1-5
John   Rev 5:1-14
Nebuchadnezzar   Dan 2:46-49
Paul   Rom 11:33-36
Psalmist   Ps 96:7-9

for YOUTH
INSTRUCTION on
Jesus   Mt 18:10
Paul   1 Tim 4:11-16;
                         5:1-2

disRESPECT

results in ALIENATION
PROPHECY of
Israelites   Deut 28:15-68

ANGER resulting from
Sanballat   Neh 4:1-3

through BLASPHEMY
against DEITY
Priests   Mal 1:6-2:9
PROPHECY of
Ezekiel   Ezek 24:15-24
in WORSHIP
Judahites   Jer 7:29-8:3

reveals CONDEMNATION
David   Ps 22:6-11;
                         31:9-12
by DEITY
Job   Job 17:6-10
REVELATION on
God   Is 44:24-45:13

against DEITY
through BLASPHEMY
Priests   Mal 1:6-2:9

to DEITY
as EVIL
David   Ps 36:1-4
Judahites   Jer 7:29-8:3
Wisdom   Prov 8:1-21

DESTRUCTION through
against MESSIANIC FIGURE
Disciples   Mt 26:47-56;
                         Mk 14:43-50;
                         Lk 22:47-54a

disRESPECT (cont'd)

DISOBEDIENCE in
Mordecai   Esth 3:1-6

DOUBT revealed in
caused by FALSE BELIEF
Moabites   Ezek 25:8-11
INSTRUCTION on
Moses   Ex 6:10-13;
                         28-30
of ENEMY
for DEITY
David   Ps 18:43-45
God   Ps 132:11-18
as EVIL
against DEITY
David   Ps 36:1-4
Judahites   Jer 7:29-8:3
Wisdom   Prov 8:1-21
INSTRUCTION on
Sirach   *Sir 4:20-31;
                         41:14-23
Solomon   Prov 18:1-24
MEDITATION on
Asaph   Ps 73:4-12

caused by FALSE BELIEF
through DOUBT
Moabites   Ezek 25:8-11
through PRIDE
Egyptians   Ezek 32:1-16

for FOLLOWER
BLESSING through
Peter   1 Pet 4:12-19

for GRACE
REVELATION on
God   Ezek 36:16-21

HATE of
REVELATION on
Israelites   Ezek 5:5-17
Judahites   Ezek 23:22-35

causing HUMILITY
PROPHECY of
Edomites   Obad 1:1b-4
God   Zeph 2:8-12
Isaiah   Is 30:1-7;
                         60:1-22
REVELATION on
Isaiah   Is 66:1-16

for IDOLATRY
PROPHECY of
Isaiah   Is 17:7-8

INSTRUCTION on
through EVIL
Sirach   *Sir 4:20-31;
                         41:14-23
Solomon   Prov 18:1-24

MEDITATION on
as EVIL
Asaph   Ps 73:4-12

against MESSIANIC FIGURE
DESTRUCTION through

DESTRUCTION through (cont'd)
Disciples   Mt 26:47-56;
           Mk 14:43-50;
           Lk 22:47-54a
through **REJECTION**
Crowd   Mk 6:1-6
People   Mt 13:53-58;
           Lk 4:16-30
through **REVENGE**
David   2 Sam 1:1-16

through **OPPRESSION**
Psalmist   Ps 123:3-4

through **PIETY**
before **DEITY**
God   Is 29:13-14

through **PRIDE**
Belshazzar   Dan 5:18-25
caused by **FALSE BELIEF**
Egyptians   Ezek 32:1-16

PROPHECY of
causing **ALIENATION**
Israelites   Deut 28:15-68
through **BLASPHEMY**
Ezekiel   Ezek 24:15-24
causing **GRIEF**
Isaiah   Is 52:13-53:12
causing **HUMILITY**
Edomites   Obad 1:1b-4
God   Zeph 2:8-12
Isaiah   Is 30:1-7;
           60:1-22
for **IDOLATRY**
Isaiah   Is 17:7-8
in **REJECTION**
Isaiah   Is 22:1-14;
           52:13-53:12

causes **REJECTION**
Job   Job 30:1-8;
           9-15
of **COVENANT**
Zechariah   Zech 11:4-14

results in **REJECTION**
of **MESSIANIC FIGURE**
Crowd   Mk 6:1-6
People   Mt 13:53-58;
           Lk 4:16-30

through **REJECTION**
PROPHECY of
Isaiah   Is 22:1-14;
           52:13-53:12
REVELATION on
Israelites   Jer 2:14-19
in **WORSHIP**
John   Rev 22:6-21

REVELATION on
for **GRACE**
God   Ezek 36:16-21

REVENGE through
for **MESSIANIC FIGURE**
David   2 Sam 1:1-16

in **WORSHIP**

through **BLASPHEMY**
Judahites   Jer 7:29-8:3
through **REJECTION**
John   Rev 22:6-21

RESURRECTION

ACCEPTANCE of the
INSTRUCTION on
Paul   Acts 17:1-9;
           24:1-27;
           1 Cor 15:29-34
Women   Lk 24:1-12
in **MISSION**
Paul   1 Cor 15:1-11
PROPHECY of
Jesus   Mt 26:31-35;
           Mk 14:27-31

ANXIETY concerning the
through **FALSE BELIEF**
Priest   Acts 4:1-22

resulting in **CONDEMNATION**
INSTRUCTION on
Jesus   Jn 5:19-47

from **DEATH**
Isaiah   Is 26:7-19
INSTRUCTION on
God   *2 Esd 2:15-32
Jesus   Mt 22:23-33;
           Mk 12:18-27;
           Lk 20:27-40
Paul   Rom 6:1-14;
           1 Cor 15:12-19;
           51-58
of **MESSIANIC FIGURE**
Ezra   *2 Esd 2:42-48
Jesus   Mt 12:38-42
           Lk 11:29-32
in **MISSION**
Jesus   2 Cor 5:14-19
PROPHECY of
Jesus   Mt 17:22-23;
           20:17-19;
           Mk 9:30-32;
           Lk 18:31-34;
           Jn 2:12-22;
           16:25-28
TRADITION of
Elijah   *Sir 48:1-11
by **DEITY**
through **ACCEPTANCE**
Israelites   Rom 11:7-24
from **DEATH**
Isaiah   Is 26:7-19
FAITH in
Maccabeus   *2 Mc 12:38-45
HOPE in
Believers   1 Pet 1:13-2:3
LEADERSHIP of
Jesus   Acts 5:17-42
LIFE from
Jesus   Jn 6:25-59
VICTORY through
Jesus   Acts 2:14-36

WITNESS to
Apostles   Acts 5:17-42

DOUBT in
caused by FALSE BELIEF
Sadducees   Mk 12:18-27;
Lk 20:27-40
by FOLLOWER
Thomas   Jn 20:1-29
INSTRUCTION on
Disciples   Lk 24:1-12
MEDITATION on
Job   Job 14:7-12
of MESSIANIC FIGURE
Disciples   Mk 9:9-13

in ENVIRONMENT
WITNESS to
Saints   Mt 27:25-56

FAITH in
Believers   Heb 11:1-40
through DEITY
Maccabeus   *2 Mc 12:38-45
by FOLLOWERs
Disciples   Jn 20:1-29
Mary   Jn 20:1-29
Thomas   Jn 20:1-29
INSTRUCTION on
Jesus   Jn 11:1-57
Paul   1 Cor 15:12-19;
29-34;
35-41;
2 Cor 4:13-15;
Col 2:6-15;
2 Tim 2:8-13
of MESSIANIC FIGURE
Disciples   Jn 21:1-14

FALSE BELIEF in
causing ANXIETY
Priest   Acts 4:1-22
causing DOUBT
Sadducees   Mk 12:18-27;
Lk 20:27-40
causing HERESY
Unbelievers   1 Cor 15:12-19

FULFILLMENT through the
INSTRUCTION on
Men   Lk 24:1-12
Paul   1 Cor 15:12-19;
20-28
Peter   Acts 2:14-36
of MESSIANIC FIGURE
Jesus   Jn 20:1-29
PROPHECY of
Jesus   Mt 28:1-8
SCRIPTURES on
David   Acts 2:14-36

of GOOD
INSTRUCTION on
Solomon   *Wis 4:1-9;
5:15-23

through GRACE
INSTRUCTION on
Jesus   Lk 24:44-49
REVELATION on
Daniel   Dan 12:1-4

HOPE through
Believers   1 Pet 1:13-2:3
for FOLLOWERs
Jesus   1 Pet 1:3-9
INSTRUCTION on
Paul   1 Cor 15:12-19;
29-34;
51-58;
1 Thes 4:13-18
Peter   Acts 2:14-36
MEDITATION on
Paul   Phil 3:4-16

IGNORANCE of
INSTRUCTION on
Jesus   Mk 9:9-13
SCRIPTURES on
Sadducees   Mt 22:23-33;
Mk 12:18-27;
Lk 20:27-40

INSTRUCTION on
from DEATH
God   *2 Esd 2:15-32
Jesus   Mt 22:23-33;
Mk 12:18-27;
Lk 20:27-40
Paul   Rom 6:1-14;
1 Cor 15:12-19;
51-58
of GOOD
Solomon   *Wis 4:1-9;
5:15-23
through GRACE
Jesus   Lk 24:44-49
of LIFE
Jesus   Jn 5:19-47
Paul   Rom 8:5-13;
1 Cor 15:35-41;
42-50
concerning MARRIAGE
Jesus   Mt 22:23-33;
Mk 12:18-27;
Lk 20:27-40
as MIRACLE
Paul   1 Cor 15:35-41
of YOUTH
Solomon   *Wis 4:10-20

JOY in
Mary   Mt 28:1-8
REVELATION on
Mary   Mt 28:1-8

LEADERSHIP through
by DEITY
Jesus   Acts 5:17-42

LIFE through
by DEITY
Jesus   Jn 6:25-59
INSTRUCTION on
Jesus   Jn 5:19-47
Paul   Rom 8:5-13;
1 Cor 15:35-41;
42-50
REVELATION on
John   Rev 20:11-15
Prophets   Rev 11:1-14

concerning MARRIAGE

concerning MARRIAGE (cont'd)
    INSTRUCTION on
      Jesus   Mt 22:23-33;
                     Mk 12:18-27;
                     Lk 20:27-40

of MESSIANIC FIGURE
    from DEATH
      Ezra   *2 Esd 2:42-48
      Jesus   Mt 12:38-42;
                     Lk 11:29-32
    DOUBT in
      Disciples   Mk 9:9-13
    FAITH in
      Disciples   Jn 21:1-14
    FULFILLMENT through
      Jesus   Jn 20:1-29
    WITNESS to
      Jesus   Acts 1:1-5

MIRACLE in
    Angel   Mt 28:1-8
    INSTRUCTION on
      Paul   1 Cor 15:35-41
    REVELATION on
      Angel   Mt 28:1-8

MISSION revealing
    ACCEPTANCE of
      Paul   1 Cor 15:1-11
    from DEATH
      Jesus   2 Cor 5:14-19

PARADOX in
    INSTRUCTION on
      Paul   1 Cor 15:35-41;
                     42-50

PEACE through
    INSTRUCTION on
      Solomon   *Wis 3:1-9

PROPHECY of
    from DEATH
      Jesus   Mt 17:22-23;
                     20:17-19;
                     Mk 9:30-32;
                     Lk 18:31-34;
                     Jn 2:12-22;
                     16:25-28
    FULFILLMENT of
      Jesus   Mt 28:1-8

REJECTION of
    INSTRUCTION on
      Disciples   Lk 24:1-12

REVELATION on
    through GRACE
      Daniel   Dan 12:1-4
    as MIRACLE
      Angel   Mt 28:1-8

REWARDs of
    INSTRUCTION on
      Jesus   Lk 14:12-14

SACREDNESS in
    INSTRUCTION on
      Paul   Col 3:1-4

SCRIPTURES on
    FULFILLMENT of
      David   Acts 2:14-36

SERVICE through
    REVELATION on
      John   Rev 20:4-6

SPIRIT of
    INSTRUCTION on
      Paul   1 Cor 15:42-50

SUFFERING in
    SCRIPTURES on
      Jesus   Lk 24:44-49

TRADITION of
    from DEATH
      Elijah   *Sir 48:1-11

VICTORY through
    by DEITY
      Jesus   Acts 2:14-36
    INSTRUCTION on
      Paul   Rom 7:1-6
    PROPHECY of
      Jesus   Mt 16:21-28;
                     20:17-19;
                     Lk 9:18-22;
                     18:31-34;
                     Jn 2:12-22

WISDOM concerning
    INSTRUCTION on
      Jesus   Mt 22:23-33;
                     Mk 12:18-27;
                     Lk 20:27-40
      Solomon   *Wis 8:2-21
    SCRIPTURES on
      Jesus   Mt 22:23-33;
                     Mk 12:18-27;
                     Lk 20:27-40

WITNESS to
    Disciples   Jn 21:1-14
    Mary   Mt 28:1-8
    by DEITY
      Apostles   Acts 5:17-42
    in ENVIRONMENT
      Saints   Mt 27:45-56
    by FOLLOWERs
      Apostles   Acts 1:6-11
      Disciples   Jn 20:1-29
      Mary   Jn 20:1-29
      Matthias   Acts 1:12-26
      Thomas   Jn 20:1-29
    INSTRUCTION on
      Apostles   Acts 4:32-5:10
      Jesus   Mt 28:9-10
      Paul   Acts 22:30-23:11;
                     26:1-32;
                     1 Cor 15:1-11;
                     12-19;
                     20-28
      Peter   Acts 3:1-26
    of MESSIANIC FIGURE
      Jesus   Acts 1:1-5
    REVELATION on
      Angel   Mt 28:1-8
      Disciples   Jn 21:1-14
      Mary   Mt 28:1-8

revealing **GRIEF**
Tyre — Ezek 27:25b-36
revealing **JOY**
Israelites — Zeph 3:14-20
revealing **LEADERSHIP**
Moses — Ex 12:1-14
revealing **MARRIAGE**
Hosea — Hos 1:2-3
revealing **MIRACLE**
Jesus — Acts 1:6-11
Manoah — Judg 13:15-23
Moses — Ex 14:23-31
revealing **OBEDIENCE**
Aaron — Ex 4:27-31
Elijah — 1 Kgs 19:1-21
Ezekiel — Ezek 8:5-6; 7-13
Isaac — Gen 26:1-11
Isaiah — Is 8:11-15
Jacob — Gen 31:1-16
Jeremiah — Jer 18:1-12; 35:1-5
Paul — Acts 16:6-10
revealing **PARADOX**
Isaiah — Is 58:1-14
revealing **REJECTION**
Zechariah — Zech 7:4-8:23
revealing **REWARDs**
Jeremiah — Jer 31:15-22
revealing **SACREDNESS**
Nathan — 1 Chr 17:1-27
revealing **SELFISHNESS**
Ezekiel — Ezek 33:30-33; 34:17-22
Isaiah — Is 58:1-14
revealing **SUFFERING**
John — Rev 12:1-6
revealing **WITNESS**
Believers — 1 Cor 14:26-33

on **BLASPHEMY**
in **BEHAVIOR**
Daniel — Dan 11:21-45
against **LAW**
Moses — Lev 18:1-30; 24:10-23
in **RITE**
Israelites — Ezek 44:6-9
as **SIN**
Ezekiel — Ezek 8:16-18
Isaiah — Is 65:1-25
Israelites — Ezek 8:5-6; 20:27-29; 22:1-16; Mal 3:13-4:3
Prophetesses — Ezek 13:17-23

on **BLESSING**
through **CONVERSION**
Isaiah — Is 58:1-14
Judahites — Jer 24:1-10
being **DESIREd**
People — Zech 7:4-8:23
through **ELECTION**
Abraham — Gen 12:1-8
Israelites — Ezek 20:5-8
through **FIDELITY**
Isaiah — Is 56:1-8
Israelites — Jer 3:21-4:4
Joshua — Josh 1:1-9

through **FIDELITY** (cont'd)
Moses — Deut 5:22-33
Solomon — 1 Kgs 9:1-9
in **FREEDOM**
Moses — Ex 11:1-10
in **NEW AGE**
Amos — Amos 9:13
Isaiah — Is 60:1-22
through **PROMISE**
Gabriel — Lk 1:26-38
Isaiah — Is 65:1-25
Israelites — Is 49:1-26
Jacob — Gen 35:1-15
Joshua — Zech 3:1-10
Moses — Ex 20:24-26
in **PROVIDENCE**
Balaam — Num 22:5-14
Ezekiel — Ezek 16:1-7; 17:22-24
God — Is 42:5-17
Isaiah — Is 55:1-13
Israelites — Ezek 36:8-15; 37-38; Hos 2:14-15; Mic 6:1-5
Jeremiah — Jer 31:7-14
Joel — Joel 2:18-27
Nathan — 2 Sam 7:1-29; 1 Chr 17:1-27
as **QUALITY OF LIFE**
Isaiah — Is 66:1-16
in **RECONCILIATION**
Amos — Amos 9:11-12
Israelites — Ezek 28:24-26; 36:33-36; 37:15-28; Hos 2:21-23; Amos 9:14-15; Zech 1:7-17; 7:4-8:23; 10:3-12
as **RESPECT**
Israelites — Jer 30:18-22
in **STEWARDSHIP**
Israelites — Ezek 44:15-31; Mal 3:6-12

on **CAPTIVITY**
by **COMPULSION**
Ezekiel — Ezek 3:22-27
in **CONFRONTATION**
Babylonians — Jer 27:1-11
Satan — Rev 20:1-3
as **PUNISHMENT**
Ammonites — Ezek 25:1-7; Zeph 2:8-12
Egyptians — Ezek 30:13-19; 32:1-16
Israelites — Ezek 21:18-24
Jeremiah — Jer 15:10-21
Joel — Joel 3:4-8
Moabites — Ezek 25:8-11; Zeph 2:8-12

on **CHAOS**
John — Rev 11:1-14
in **CONFRONTATION**
John — Rev 11:15-19
in **CREATION**
Jeremiah — Jer 4:23-26
John — Rev 8:1-6

caused by SIN
Isaiah	Is 57:14-21

on COMMITMENT
  to FULFILLMENT
Isaiah	Is 55:1-13

  through GUILT
Moses	Lev 4:1-35

  to HEALING
Isaiah	Is 57:14-21

  to LEADERSHIP
Israelites	Ezek 20:5-8

  through LOVE
Ezekiel	Ezek 16:8-14

  through OBEDIENCE
Moses	Num 30:1-16

  through PURIFICATION
Judahites	Jer 3:21-4:4

  through SERVICE
Moses	Num 8:23-26
People	Jer 27:1-11

on COMPASSION
  in BROTHERHOOD
Israelites	Is 49:1-26

  in RECONCILIATION
Israelites	Jer 30:18-22; Zech 1:7-17

  in SALVATION
Israelites	Zech 10:3-12

  in SECURITY
Isaiah	Is 51:1-16

on COMPULSION
  of ACCEPTANCE
Jeremiah	Jer 25:15-29

  of CAPTIVITY
Ezekiel	Ezek 3:22-27

  of OPPRESSION
Ezekiel	Ezek 4:4-8
John	Rev 13:11-18

on CONDEMNATION
Ezekiel	Ezek 34:17-22
Israelites	Is 1:4-9

  of AUTHORITY
Job	Job 38:12-15; 40:6-14

  of CREATION
God	Gen 3:14-19

  for ETERNITY
Mankind	Is 66:17-24

  of inFIDELITY
Israelites	Jer 3:1-5
Jeremiah	Jer 26:1-6

  of disHONESTY
Prophetesses	Ezek 13:17-23
Prophets	Jer 23:23-32; Ezek 13:1-16

  as JUDGMENT
Chaldeans	Is 47:1-15
Edomites	Ezek 35:1-15
Egyptians	Ezek 29:1-5; 30:20-26; 32:17-32
Ezekiel	Ezek 14:12-23; 36:1-7
God	Is 41:1-42:4
Gog	Ezek 38:3-9; 39:1-16
Habakkuk	Hab 2:5-6a

as JUDGMENT (cont'd)
Isaiah	Is 5:1-7; 65:1-25
Israelites	Ezek 5:5-17; 17:11-21; 20:27-29; 22:17-22; 34:1-10; 36:16-21; Hos 2:9-13; Mal 2:17-3:5
Jeremiah	Jer 1:13-16; 25:30-38
Jesus	Mt 11:20-24
Judahites	Ezek 23:22-35; 24:1-14
Moabites	Ezek 25:8-11
Rulers	Zech 11:15-17
Zedekiah	Jer 24:1-10

  in NEW AGE
Jesus	Lk 17:22-37

  as PUNISHMENT
Zedekiah	Jer 24:1-10

  of disRESPECT
God	Is 44:24-45:13

  of SIN
Ezekiel	Ezek 11:1-13
Israelites	Is 43:14-44:5; Hos 1:6-7
Job	Job 40:1-2

on CONFRONTATION
  with ACCEPTANCE
Jesus	Lk 24:13-35

  with ALIENATION
Israelites	Ezek 21:1-7

  with ANGER
Aaron	Num 12:4-10
Gog	Ezek 38:17-23

  with CAPTIVITY
Babylonians	Jer 27:1-11
Satan	Rev 20:1-3

  with CHAOS
John	Rev 11:15-19

  with COURAGE
John	Rev 1:4-20

  with DEATH
Egyptians	Ezek 30:10-12; 31:10-18
Ezekiel	Ezek 30:1-5; 33:23-29
Gog	Ezek 39:1-16
Israelites	Amos 9:8-10

  with DEFEAT
Ammonites	Ezek 21:28-32
Babylonians	Rev 18:21-24
Egyptians	Ezek 29:17-21; 30:10-12; 13-19; 20-26; 32:1-16; 17-32
Ezekiel	Ezek 33:23-29
Gog	Ezek 39:1-16
Israelites	Ezek 21:18-24
Jeremiah	Jer 19:1-15
Judahites	Ezek 23:22-35
Prophets	Rev 11:1-14
Satan	Rev 12:7-9
Tyre	Ezek 26:1-6; 28:1-10

through **OBEDIENCE**
Paul   Acts 26:1-32
through **REPENTANCE**
Daniel   Dan 4:19-27
Ezekiel   Ezek 18:25-29;
                 33:10-20
Isaiah   Is 55:1-13;
                 58:1-14
Israelites   Ezek 18:30-32;
                 20:40-44;
                 44:6-9;
                 Hos 2:14-15
Jeremiah   Jer 3:12-14a;
                 31:2-6
Prophets   Jer 23:16-22
Zechariah   Zech 1:1-6

on **COURAGE**
in **CONFRONTATION**
John   Rev 1:4-20
in **PRESENCE**
Paul   Acts 18:1-17
through **PROVIDENCE**
Paul   Acts 22:30-23:11
in **SECURITY**
Ezekiel   Ezek 2:1-8a;
                 3:4-9
Isaiah   Is 7:1-9
Israelites   Zeph 3:11-13
Joshua   Deut 31:14-23
Paul   Acts 27:1-28:16

on **COVETOUSNESS**
as **SIN**
Habakkuk   Hab 2:5-6a

on **CREATION**
from **CHAOS**
Jeremiah   Jer 4:23-26
John   Rev 8:1-6
of **FAMILY**
Israel   Gen 35:1-15
of **GOOD**
Egyptians   Ezek 31:1-9
of **LEADERSHIP**
John   Rev 12:1-6
Moses   Num 11:14-24a
of **LIFE**
Angels   Lk 2:1-20
Ezekiel   Ezek 37:1-14
Gabriel   Lk 1:5-25;
                 26-38
Isaiah   Is 57:14-21
Israelites   Ezek 36:37-38
Manoah   Judg 13:2-7
Mary   Lk 1:26-38
through **MIRACLE**
Jesus   Mt 1:18-25
Joseph   Mt 1:18-25
of **ORDER**
God   Is 48:1-22
Job   Job 38:4-7;
                 8-11

on **DEATH**
Ezekiel   Ezek 24:15-24
Joshua   Josh 1:1-9
Moses   Lev 16:1-5
in **CONFRONTATION**
Egyptians   Ezek 30:10-12;

in **CONFRONTATION** (cont'd)
Egyptians   31:10-18
Ezekiel   Ezek 30:1-5;
                 33:23-29
Gog   Ezek 39:1-16
Israelites   Amos 9:8-10
as a **DESIRE**
Mankind   Rev 9:1-12
through **FIDELITY**
Ezekiel   Ezek 18:10-13
John   Rev 20:4-6
as **PUNISHMENT**
Ammonites   Ezek 21:28-32
Egyptians   Ezek 29:1-5;
                 30:13-19;
                 32:1-16;
                 17-32
Eli   1 Sam 2:27-36
Elijah   1 Kgs 21:17-29
Ezekiel   Ezek 6:1-7;
                 9:1-11;
                 11:1-13
God   Gen 2:16-17;
                 Lev 10:1-20
Israelites   Num 14:26-38;
                 Ezek 6:11-14;
                 7:1-27;
                 12:1-16;
                 17:11-21;
                 21:8-17;
                 23:5-10;
                 Amos 8:1-3;
                 9:1-4
Jehoiakim   Jer 36:27-32
Jeremiah   Jer 11:18-12:6;
                 15:1-4;
                 5-9;
                 19:1-15;
                 25:30-38;
                 33:1-9
John   Rev 11:1-14;
                 16:3
King   Ezek 28:11-19
Moses   Lev 21:1-22:33;
                 Num 15:32-36;
                 27:12-23;
                 Deut 32:48-52
Sidon   Ezek 28:20-23
Tyre   Ezek 28:1-10
caused by **SIN**
Ezekiel   Ezek 18:1-4;
                 10-13;
                 14-20;
                 21-24;
                 25-29;
                 33:1-9;
                 10-20
Moses   Num 1:47-54

on **DEFEAT**
of **AUTHORITY**
Babylonians   Rev 18:1-3
Daniel   Dan 11:5-20
in **CONFRONTATION**
Ammonites   Ezek 21:28-32
Babylonians   Rev 18:21-24
Egyptians   Ezek 29:17-21;
                 30:10-12;
                 13-19;
                 20-26;

in **CONFRONTATION** (cont'd)
　Egyptians　　　32:1-16;
　　　　　　　　17-32
　Ezekiel　　　　Ezek 33:23-29
　Gog　　　　　　Ezek 39:1-16
　Israelites　　　Ezek 21:18-24
　Jeremiah　　　Jer 19:1-15
　Judahites　　　Ezek 23:22-35
　Prophets　　　Rev 11:1-14
　Satan　　　　　Rev 12:7-9
　Tyre　　　　　Ezek 26:1-6;
　　　　　　　　28:1-10

as **PUNISHMENT**
　Ammonites　　Ezek 25:1-7
　Israelites　　　Hos 1:4-5
　John　　　　　Rev 14:8
caused by **SIN**
　Zephaniah　　Zeph 1:2-6
of **TRUTH**
　Daniel　　　　Dan 8:9-12

on **DESIRE**
　for **BLESSING**
　　People　　　Zech 7:4-8:23
　for **DEATH**
　　Mankind　　Rev 9:1-12
　for **FULFILLMENT**
　　Solomon　　1 Kgs 3:1-15
　for **KILLING**
　　David　　　1 Sam 23:1-13
　for **OBEDIENCE**
　　Balaam　　Num 22:22-35
　for **REPENTANCE**
　　Ezekiel　　Ezek 18:21-24
　　Jeremiah　Jer 26:1-6;
　　　　　　　36:1-7
　for **SACRIFICE**
　　Moses　　　Ex 25:1-9
　for **SERVICE**
　　Isaiah　　　Is 65:1-25
　for **SHARING**
　　Moses　　　Ex 25:1-9
　for **WISDOM**
　　Belshazzar　Dan 5:7-9;
　　　　　　　10-17
　　Daniel　　　Dan 7:15-16;
　　　　　　　8:15-25
　　Nebuchadnezzar　Dan 2:1-13;
　　　　　　　4:4-9
　　Pharaoh　　Gen 41:1-57

on **DESTRUCTION**
　by **AUTHORITY**
　　Daniel　　　Dan 7:2-14;
　　　　　　　17-27;
　　　　　　　8:3-8;
　　　　　　　9-12;
　　　　　　　15-25
　of **COMMUNITY**
　　Psalmist　　Ps 2:7-9
　in **CONFRONTATION**
　　Babylonians　Rev 18:21-24
　　Daniel　　　Dan 9:24-27;
　　　　　　　11:21-45
　　Egyptians　Ezek 30:6-9;
　　　　　　　10-12;
　　　　　　　20-26
　　Ezekiel　　Ezek 30:1-5;
　　　　　　　33:23-29
　　Satan　　　Rev 20:7-10

of **CREATION**
　Isaiah　　　　Is 51:1-16
　John　　　　　Rev 6:12-17
for **ETERNITY**
　Edomites　　Ezek 35:1-15
　Tyre　　　　　Ezek 27:25b-36;
　　　　　　　28:11-19
through in**FIDELITY**
　Isaiah　　　　Is 8:11-15
as **JUDGMENT**
　Amos　　　　Amos 7:1-3;
　　　　　　　4-6
　Daniel　　　Dan 7:2-14
in **NEW AGE**
　Haggai　　　Hag 2:20-23
　Jesus　　　　Lk 17:22-37
as **PUNISHMENT**
　Ammonites　Ezek 21:28-32;
　　　　　　　25:1-7;
　　　　　　　Zeph 2:8-12
　Belshazzar　Dan 5:26-28
　Chaldeans　Is 47:1-15
　Edomites　　Ezek 25:12-14;
　　　　　　　35:1-15
　Egyptians　Ezek 29:1-5;
　　　　　　　6-9a;
　　　　　　　9b-16;
　　　　　　　30:13-19;
　　　　　　　31:10-18;
　　　　　　　32:1-16
　Ezekiel　　Ezek 6:1-7;
　　　　　　　13:1-16;
　　　　　　　14:1-11;
　　　　　　　20:45-49;
　　　　　　　21:25-27
　God　　　　Is 41:1-42:4
　Gog　　　　Ezek 39:1-16
　Isaiah　　　Is 5:1-7;
　　　　　　　6:1-13;
　　　　　　　56:9-57:13;
　　　　　　　65:1-25
　Israelites　Jer 2:14-19;
　　　　　　　5:1-14;
　　　　　　　Ezek 5:5-17;
　　　　　　　6:11-14;
　　　　　　　7:1-27;
　　　　　　　21:1-7;
　　　　　　　8-17;
　　　　　　　22:1-16;
　　　　　　　23:5-10;
　　　　　　　36-49;
　　　　　　　Hos 1:4-5;
　　　　　　　2:9-13;
　　　　　　　Amos 7:7-9;
　　　　　　　8:8-10;
　　　　　　　9:1-4;
　　　　　　　Zech 13:7-9
　Jacobites　Amos 9:8-10
　Jehu　　　1 Kgs 15:33-16:7
　Jeremiah　Jer 15:1-4;
　　　　　　　5-9;
　　　　　　　19:1-15;
　　　　　　　25:15-29;
　　　　　　　30-38
　Jesus　　　2 Thes 1:7b-10
　John　　　Rev 11:1-14;
　　　　　　　18:4-20
　Judahites　Jer 13:1-11;
　　　　　　　Ezek 23:22-35;
　　　　　　　24:1-14

as **PUNISHMENT** (cont'd)

Malachi	Mal 3:13-4:3
Micah	Mic 6:9-16
Moabites	Ezek 25:8-11; Zeph 2:8-12
Nations	Zeph 3:6-7; 8
People	Jer 27:1-11
Philistines	Ezek 25:15-17
Prophets	2 Kgs 21:1-18; Jer 14:13-16
Solomon	2 Chr 7:11-22
Tyre	Ezek 26:1-6; 27:25b-36; 28:1-10
Zechariah	Zech 5:1-4
Zedekiah	Jer 24:1-10
Zephaniah	Zeph 1:2-6; 10-11; 12-13

caused by **SIN**

Believers	Mal 3:13-4:3
Daniel	Dan 8:15-25
Isaiah	Is 66:17-24

on **DIGNITY**

in **AUTHORITY**

Ezekiel	Ezek 1:4-28; 10:1-22
Isaiah	Is 49:1-26
Moses	Ex 7:1-7

in **PROVIDENCE**

Egyptians	Ezek 31:1-9

on **DISOBEDIENCE**

through in**FIDELITY**

Ezekiel	Ezek 3:22-27
Isaiah	Is 65:1-25
Israelites	Jer 2:14-19; 20-29; 5:1-14; Ezek 15:1-8
Moses	Deut 31:14-23
Samuel	1 Sam 8:1-22

to **LAW**

Israelites	Ezek 5:5-17

as **SIN**

Ezekiel	Ezek 12:1-16
Jehu	1 Kgs 15:33-16:7

to **TRUTH**

Ezekiel	Ezek 33:30-33

on **DOUBT**

concerning **COMMUNITY**

Judahites	Jer 9:2-9

in **CONFRONTATION**

Ananias	Acts 9:1-19
Disciples	Lk 24:36-43

of **PROMISE**

Abraham	Gen 15:1-21; 17:15-22
Zechariah	Lk 1:5-25

as **QUALITY OF LIFE**

Zechariah	Lk 1:5-25

as **SIN**

Ezekiel	Ezek 33:23-29

on **ELECTION**

as **BLESSING**

Abraham	Gen 12:1-8
Israelites	Ezek 20:5-8

to **DISCIPLESHIP**

Saul	Acts 9:1-19

through **FAITH**

Believers	Is 56:1-8

of **FAMILY**

Israelites	Zech 13:7-9
Solomon	1 Kgs 11:1-13

of **LEADERSHIP**

Babylonians	Jer 27:1-11
Cyrus	Is 48:1-22
Elijah	1 Kgs 19:1-21
God	1 Sam 2:27-36
Israelites	1 Kgs 11:1-13; Is 49:1-26
Joshua	Deut 31:14-23; Josh 1:1-9; Zech 3:1-10; 6:9-15
Samuel	1 Sam 16:1-13
Zechariah	Zech 11:4-14
Zerubbabel	Hag 2:20-23

through **OBEDIENCE**

Amos	Amos 7:10-17
Jeremiah	Jer 1:4-10
Joshua	Zech 3:1-10

for **SERVICE**

Elisha	1 Kgs 19:1-21
Isaiah	Is 66:17-24
Israelites	Is 43:14-44:5; Jer 30:4-9
Jeremiah	Jer 1:13-16
Levites	Num 18:1-7; Ezek 44:10-14
Moses	Ex 28:40-43
Samuel	1 Sam 3:1-4:1a

by Divine **WILL**

Jesus	Jn 21:15-23
Moses	Num 12:4-10

to **WITNESS**

Ezekiel	Ezek 2:1-8a; 3:10-11; 16-21
Isaiah	Is 6:1-13

on **EQUALITY**

in **DISCIPLESHIP**

Peter	Acts 10:1-11:18

in **JUSTICE**

Moses	Lev 24:10-23

in **LIFE**

Job	Job 41:1-12

in **SHARING**

Israelites	Ezek 47:13-20

on **ETERNAL**

ANGER

Jeremiah	Jer 15:10-21

CONDEMNATION

Mankind	Is 66:17-24

DESTRUCTION

Edomites	Ezek 25:1-15
Tyre	Ezek 27:25b-36; 28:11-19

FULFILLMENT

Isaiah	Is 51:1-16

HUMILITY

Sinners	Jer 23:33-40

LEADERSHIP

Daniel	Dan 7:2-14
Isaiah	Is 60:1-22

on GRATITUDE
  for PROVIDENCE
    Isaiah   Is 51:1-16
  for RECONCILIATION
    Israelites   Jer 30:18-22
    Jeremiah   Jer 33:10-11

on GREED
  as SIN
    Habakkuk   Hab 2:5-6a

on GRIEF
    Tyre   Ezek 27:25b-36
  as MOTIVATION
    Ezekiel   Ezek 21:1-7;
                          8-17
  in NEW AGE
    Ezekiel   Ezek 30:1-5
  through PUNISHMENT
    Judahites   Ezek 24:1-14
  as QUALITY OF LIFE
    Zephaniah   Zeph 1:10-11

on GUILT
  resulting in COMMITMENT
    Moses   Lev 4:1-35
  by the LAW
    Moses   Lev 7:1-10
  of SIN
    Moses   Lev 5:1-4

on HATE
  of disRESPECT
    Israelites   Ezek 5:5-17
    Judahites   Ezek 23:22-35

on HEALING
  by COMMITMENT
    Isaiah   Is 57:14-21
  in CONFRONTATION
    Daniel   Dan 10:10-21
  through PROVIDENCE
    Israelites   Ezek 34:11-16
    Jeremiah   Jer 30:12-17
  in STEWARDSHIP
    Isaiah   Is 58:1-14

on HERESY
  through inFIDELITY
    Israelites   Jer 2:14-19

on HONESTY
  of LEADERSHIP
    Daniel   Dan 11:21-45
  of SACRIFICE
    Isaiah   Is 58:1-14

on disHONESTY
  resulting in ANGER
    Ammonites   Ezek 21:28-32

on HOPE
  in ELECTION
    Israelites   Jer 3:19-20
  in PRESENCE
    God   Is 41:1-42:4
  in PROVIDENCE
    Ezekiel   Ezek 17:22-24
  in RECONCILIATION
    Israelites   Jer 30:4-9

in RECONCILIATION (cont'd)
    Jeremiah   Jer 16:1-15;
                          30:1-3
    Rachel   Jer 31:15-22
    Zedekiah   Jer 32:9-15
  in SALVATION
    Believers   1 Pet 1:13-2:3
  in SECURITY
    Ezekiel   Ezek 11:14-21

on HUMILITY
  before AUTHORITY
    Paul   2 Cor 12:1-10
  for ETERNITY
    Sinners   Jer 23:33-40
  in PROVIDENCE
    Israelites   Zeph 3:11-13
    Paul   2 Cor 12:1-10
  as PUNISHMENT
    Israelites   Jer 2:20-29;
                          30-37;
                          Hos 2:9-13
    Jeremiah   Jer 15:1-4;
                          5-9
    Levites   Ezek 44:10-14
  in RECONCILIATION
    Egyptians   Ezek 29:9b-16
  in RESPECT
    Isaiah   Is 66:1-16

on IDOLATRY
  through inFIDELITY
    Israelites   Ezek 20:5-8
    Judahites   Ezek 23:11-21
  as SIN
    Ezekiel   Ezek 8:7-13;
                          14-15;
                          16-18;
                          22:1-16
    Israelites   Jer 2:1-13;
                          20-29;
                          Ezek 20:27-29;
                          30-31
    Jeremiah   Jer 1:13-16
    Mankind   Rev 9:13-21
    Moses   Ex 20:21-23

on IGNORANCE
  in the CREATION
    Israelites   Is 49:1-26
  of JUDGMENT
    Mankind   2 Pet 3:8-10
  of KNOWLEDGE
    Daniel   Dan 12:5-13
    Isaiah   Is 6:1-13
    Job   Job 38:1-3
    John   Rev 10:1-11;
                          19:11-16
  of NEW AGE
    Mankind   2 Pet 3:8-10
  of PUNISHMENT
    God   Gen 12:9-13:1
  of RECONCILIATION
    Israelites   Ezek 45:18-25
  of TRUTH
    Daniel   Dan 8:26-27

on INDIFFERENCE
  as QUALITY OF LIFE
    Jeremiah   Jer 7:21-28

INSTRUCTION on
    to COMMUNITY
        Mordecai   Esth 8:9-14
    of LAW
        Jesus   Mt 5:38-42
    of PUNISHMENT
        Moses   Deut 28:15-68

on JEALOUSY
    in CONFRONTATION
        Gog   Ezek 38:17-23
    as MOTIVATION
        God   Zeph 3:8
    in PUNISHMENT
        Ezekiel   Ezek 36:1-7
        Israelites   Ezek 5:5-17

on JOY
    in BEHAVIOR
        Israelites   Zeph 3:14-20
    in the CREATION
        Isaiah   Is 55:1-13
    in KNOWLEDGE
        Israelites   Is 51:17-52:12
    as MOTIVATION
        Jeremiah   Jer 33:1-9
    in PRAYER
        Believers   Is 56:1-8
    in PROVIDENCE
        Isaiah   Is 51:1-16
        Jeremiah   Jer 33:10-11
        Joel   Joel 2:18-27
    as QUALITY OF LIFE
        Isaiah   Is 66:1-16
        Jesus   1 Pet 4:12-19
    in RESPECT
        Isaiah   Is 58:1-14
    in RESURRECTION
        Mary   Mt 28:1-8
    in RITE
        Moses   Lev 23:33-44;
                25:8-19

on JUDGMENT
    of ALIENATION
        Hosea   Hos 1:8-9
    against BLASPHEMY
        Ezekiel   Ezek 9:1-11
        Israelites   Mal 2:17-3:5
    as CONDEMNATION
        Chaldeans   Is 47:1-15
        Edomites   Ezek 35:1-15
        Egyptians   Ezek 29:1-5;
                30:20-26;
                32:17-32
        Ezekiel   Ezek 14:12-23;
                36:1-7
        God   Is 41:1-42:4
        Gog   Ezek 38:3-9;
                39:1-16
        Habakkuk   Hab 2:5-6a
        Isaiah   Is 5:1-7;
                65:1-25
        Israelites   Ezek 5:5-17;
                17:11-21;
                20:27-29;
                22:17-22;
                34:1-10;
                36:16-21;
                Hos 2:9-13;
                Mal 2:17-3:5

as CONDEMNATION (cont'd)
    Jeremiah   Jer 1:13-16;
                25:30-38
    Jesus   Mt 11:20-24
    Judahites   Ezek 23:22-35;
                24:1-14
    Moabites   Ezek 25:8-11
    Rulers   Zech 11:15-17
    Zedekiah   Jer 24:1-10
as DESTRUCTION
    Amos   Amos 7:1-3;
                4-6
    Daniel   Dan 7:2-14
concerning DISOBEDIENCE
    Jesus   Mt 11:20-24
against ENEMY
    Isaiah   Is 66:1-16
    Joel   Joel 3:1-3
on EVIL
    God   Ps 9:15-16
    Israelites   Mal 2:17-3:5
    Jesus   Mt 11:20-24
by GRACE
    Israelites   Is 43:14-44:5;
                48:1-22
on GUILT
    Belshazzar   Dan 5:26-28
    Elders   Ezek 20:1-4
    Ezekiel   Ezek 11:1-13;
                22:1-16
    God   Gen 3:14-19
    Israelites   Jer 2:20-29;
                30-37;
                9:1-11;
                21:18-24;
                22:23-31;
                36:22-32
    Jeremiah   Jer 30:12-17
    Sidon   Ezek 28:20-23
on IDOLATRY
    Chaldeans   Is 47:1-15
    John   Rev 17:1-6a
on IGNORANCE
    Mankind   2 Pet 3:8-10
on JUSTICE
    Edomites   Ezek 35:1-15
    Ezekiel   Ezek 18:14-20;
                21-24;
                25-29;
                33:1-9;
                10-20
    Isaiah   Is 5:1-7;
                65:1-25
    Israelites   Ezek 7:1-27;
                9:1-11;
                18:30-32;
                22:23-31
    John   Rev 19:11-16;
                20:11-15;
                22:6-21
    Judahites   Ezek 24:1-14
    Moses   Num 35:16-25
    Zechariah   Zech 7:4-8:23
on LEADERSHIP
    Egyptians   Ezek 32:1-16
    God   Is 41:1-42:4
on LIFE
    Israelites   Ezek 34:17-22
    Joel   Joel 3:12-16a
    John   Rev 14:17-20;

on **LIFE** (cont'd)
John   20:11-15
through **MIRACLE**
Egyptians   Ex 7:1-7
on **OPPRESSION**
Israelites   Mal 2:17-3:5
on **ORDER**
Priests   Ezek 44:15-31
on **PURIFICATION**
Israelites   Is 48:1-22;
     Ezek 20:32-39
on **REJECTION**
Israelites   Mal 2:17-3:5
on **REPENTANCE**
Jesus   Mt 11:20-24
on **REVENGE**
Joel   Joel 3:4-8
concerning **REWARDs**
Daniel   Dan 12:1-4
causing **SADNESS**
John   Rev 18:4-20
on **SEX**
Israelites   Ezek 23:36-49;
     Mal 2:17-3:5
on **VICTORY**
Daniel   Dan 7:17-27
on **WEALTH**
John   Rev 18:4-20
on **WITNESS**
Isaiah   Is 66:17-24
Israelites   Mal 2:17-3:5
John   Rev 20:4-6
Mankind   Ezek 39:17-24

on **JUSTICE**
to **COMMUNITY**
God   Ps 9:15-16
in **CONFRONTATION**
Job   Job 40:6-14
Mordecai   *Esth 11:2-12
concerning **JUDGMENT**
Edomites   Ezek 35:1-15
Ezekiel   Ezek 18:14-20;
     21-24;
     25-29;
     33:1-9;
     10-20
Isaiah   Is 5:1-7;
     65:1-25
Israelites   Ezek 7:1-27;
     9:1-11;
     18:30-32;
     22:23-31
John   Rev 19:11-16;
     20:11-15;
     22:6-21
Judahites   Ezek 24:1-14
Moses   Num 35:16-25
Zechariah   Zech 7:4-8:23
in **LAW**
Israelites   Ezek 45:10-12
Moses   Lev 24:10-23
in **NEW AGE**
Angel   *2 Esd 6:7-28
in **PROVIDENCE**
Israelites   Ezek 34:11-16
in **PUNISHMENT**
Egyptians   Ezek 31:10-18
Ezekiel   Ezek 14:12-23
Israelites   Jer 2:14-19;

in **PUNISHMENT** (cont'd)
Israelites   Ezek 36:16-21;
     39:17-24;
     Amos 8:4-7
Jeremiah   Jer 16:16-18
John   Rev 13:5-10;
     18:4-20
Moses   Lev 24:10-23
as **VIRTUE**
Israelites   Ezek 45:1-9
Jeremiah   Jer 33:14-26

on **KILLING**
in **CONFRONTATION**
Prophets   Rev 11:1-14
DESIREd
David   1 Sam 23:1-13
as **PUNISHMENT**
Elijah   1 Kgs 19:1-21
John   Rev 11:1-14
Mankind   Rev 9:13-21
Moses   Num 35:16-25
as **SIN**
Israelites   Ezek 22:1-16
Mankind   Rev 9:13-21

on **KNOWLEDGE**
of **ANXIETY**
Daniel   Dan 7:28
Ethiopians   Ezek 30:6-9
of **CAPTIVITY**
Daniel   Dan 11:21-45
of **DEATH**
Joseph   Mt 2:13-15;
     19-23
Moses   Deut 31:14-23
of **DESTRUCTION**
Daniel   Dan 9:1-3
of **DIGNITY**
King   Ezek 28:11-19
of **DISCIPLESHIP**
Holy Spirit   1 Cor 2:10-16
of **DISOBEDIENCE**
Jeremiah   Jer 18:1-12
of **DOUBT**
Habakkuk   Hab 1:5-11
of **ENEMY**
Moses   Num 13:1-17a
of **EVIL**
God   *2 Esd 16:51-78
Sardis   Rev 3:1-6
of **FAITH**
Pergamum   Rev 2:12-17
Thyatira   Rev 2:18-29
of **HERESY**
Smyrna   Rev 2:8-11
of **IGNORANCE**
Daniel   Dan 12:5-13
Isaiah   Is 6:1-13
Job   Job 38:1-3
John   Rev 10:1-11;
     19:11-16
of **INDIFFERENCE**
Laodicea   Rev 3:14-22
of **JOY**
Israelites   Is 51:17-52:12
of **KILLING**
Daniel   Dan 11:21-45
of **LEADERSHIP**
Ezekiel   Ezek 33:30-33

of **LEADERSHIP** (cont'd)

Israelites	Deut 4:15-31; Is 51:17-52:12; Ezek 39:17-24; 25-29
Mankind	Ezek 38:14-16; 17-23; 39:1-16
Philistines	Ezek 25:15-17

of **LIFE**

Jesus	Jn 1:1-18
Job	Job 39:1-4

of **LOVE**

Israelites	Is 49:1-26

of **OBEDIENCE**

Ananias	Acts 9:1-19
Cornelius	Acts 10:1-11:18
Philadelphians	Rev 3:7-13
Wise Men	Mt 2:1-12

of **ORDER**

Ezekiel	Ezek 40:6-16; 17-19; 20-27; 28-37; 38-43; 44-47; 48-49; 41:1-4; 5-11; 12; 13-15a; 15b-26; 42:1-10a; 10b-12; 13-14; 15-20; 47:1-12

of **PATIENCE**

Ephesus	Rev 2:1-7
Habakkuk	Hab 2:1-4
Israelites	Is 49:1-26
Thyatira	Rev 2:18-29

of **POLITICS**

Daniel	Dan 2:24-45

of **POVERTY**

Smyrna	Rev 2:8-11

of **REJECTION**

Judahites	Jer 3:6-11
Mankind	Rev 9:13-21

of **REPENTANCE**

Abimelech	Gen 20:1-18
Israelites	Ezek 43:6-12

of **SACREDNESS**

Israelites	Ezek 43:6-12

of **SERVICE**

Thyatira	Rev 2:18-29

of **SUFFERING**

Ephesus	Rev 2:1-7
Smyrna	Rev 2:8-11
Thyatira	Rev 2:18-29

of **VICTORY**

Abraham	Gen 15:1-21

of **WILL**

God	Mt 11:25-26
Jesus	Mt 11:27

concerning **WISDOM**

Believers	Dan 12:5-13
Daniel	Dan 11:21-45; 12:1-4
Gabriel	Dan 8:15-25; 9:20-23

concerning **WISDOM** (cont'd)

Jeremiah	Jer 16:19-21
John	Rev 13:11-18

of **WITNESS**

Amos	Amos 1:1-2
God	Is 41:1-42:4
Habakkuk	Hab 1:1
Haggai	Hag 1:1-11
Hosea	Hos 1:1
Isaiah	Is 1:1
Jeremiah	Jer 30:1-3; 46:1
Joel	Joel 1:1
Jonah	Jon 1:1-17; 3:1-10
Malachi	Mal 1:1
Micah	Mic 1:1
Nahum	Nah 1:1-9
Obadiah	Obad 1:1a
Prophets	Num 12:4-10
Zechariah	Zech 1:1-6; 4:6b-10a
Zephaniah	Zeph 1:1

on **LAW**

Moses	Lev 19:1-37

concerning **ALIENATION**

Moses	Num 5:1-4

concerning **BLASPHEMY**

Moses	Lev 18:1-30; 24:10-23

concerning **CAPTIVITY**

Moses	Lev 25:39-55

concerning **DEATH**

Moses	Lev 7:22-27; Num 19:14-22; 27:1-11
Priests	Lev 21:1-22:33; Ezek 44:15-31

concerning **DISOBEDIENCE**

Israelites	Ezek 5:5-17

concerning **FAMILY**

Moses	Ex 21:1; Lev 18:1-30; Num 27:1-11; 30:1-16

concerning **FULFILLMENT**

Jesus	Gal 4:4-7

concerning **GUILT**

Moses	Lev 7:1-10

concerning **JUSTICE**

Israelites	Ezek 45:10-12
Moses	Lev 24:10-23

concerning **KILLING**

Moses	Num 35:16-25; 26-34

concerning **LIFE**

Moses	Lev 7:22-27; 17:10-14; 15-16; 18:1-30
Solomon	1 Kgs 3:1-15

concerning **MARRIAGE**

Priests	Ezek 44:15-31

concerning **OBEDIENCE**

Israelites	Ezek 37:15-28; 43:6-12
Joshua	Josh 1:1-9

concerning **OBEDIENCE** (cont'd)
Moses	Ex 20:1-17; 34:12-28; Deut 5:22-33
Priests	Ezek 44:15-31
Solomon	1 Kgs 6:1-38; 9:1-9; 2 Chr 7:11-22

concerning **ORDER**
Ezekiel	Ezek 43:13-17
Israelites	Ezek 45:10-12; 47:13-20; 48:1-7; 8-22; 23-29; 30-35
Priests	Ezek 46:19-24

concerning **PIETY**
Israelites	Ezek 46:9-10
Moses	Lev 24:1-4; Num 9:1-14

concerning **POVERTY**
Moses	Lev 25:25-28; 29-34; 35-38; 39-55; 27:1-34

concerning **PURIFICATION**
Moses	Lev 12:1-8; 13:1-59; 14:1-32; 33-54; 15:1-33; 16:29-34; 21:1-22:33; Num 5:1-4

concerning **SACREDNESS**
Ezekiel	Ezek 44:4-5
Israelites	Ezek 48:8-22
Moses	Lev 20:1-27; 21:1-22:33; 23:1-4; 5-8; 15-22; 23-25; 26-32; 33-44; 24:5-9; 25:1-7; 20-22; 26:1-46; 27:1-34; Num 6:1-21
Prince	Ezek 44:1-3; 46:1-8

concerning **SACRIFICE**
Moses	Ex 20:24-26; Lev 1:1-17; 2:1-16; 3:1-17; 4:1-35; 6:8-13; 14-23; 24-30; 7:11-21; 28-36; 37-38; 21:1-22:33; Num 15:22-31; 19:1-10;

concerning **SACRIFICE** (cont'd)
Moses	29:7-11; 12-40
Priests	Ezek 46:19-24
Prince	Ezek 46:11-15

concerning **SEX**
Moses	Lev 18:1-30; 20:1-27

concerning **SHARING**
Israelites	Ezek 47:21-23
Prince	Ezek 46:16-18

concerning **TEMPERANCE**
Moses	Lev 11:1-47

concerning **VIOLENCE**
Moses	Lev 24:10-23

concerning **WEALTH**
Israelites	Ezek 45:10-12; 47:21-23
Moses	Lev 25:23-24
Prince	Ezek 46:16-18

on **LEADERSHIP**
　in **AUTHORITY**
Daniel	Dan 7:17-27; 8:15-25; 11:1-4; 5-20; 21-45
God	Jer 30:23-31:1
Isaiah	Is 6:1-13
Jeremiah	Jer 1:4-10; 16:19-21; 33:14-26
John	Rev 4:1-11; 12:1-6; 17:6b-18; 19:11-16
Moses	Num 27:12-23
Samuel	1 Sam 8:1-22

　in **COMMITMENT**
Israelites	Ezek 20:5-8

　in **COMMUNITY**
Israelites	Jer 30:18-22; Ezek 37:15-28
Priests	Ezek 44:15-31

　in the **CREATION**
John	Rev 12:1-6
Moses	Num 11:14-24a

　for **ETERNITY**
Daniel	Dan 7:2-14
Isaiah	Is 60:1-22

　in **NEW AGE**
Daniel	Dan 8:15-25

　through **PROVIDENCE**
David	Ezek 34:23-24
Isaiah	Is 55:1-13; 58:1-14
Israelites	Is 48:1-22; Jer 3:14b-18; Ezek 20:9-26; 32-39
John	Rev 7:9-17

on **LIFE**
　through **CONVERSION**
Ezekiel	Ezek 18:21-24; 25-29
Israelites	Ezek 18:30-32

　for **ETERNITY**
Daniel	Dan 12:1-4

for **ETERNITY** (cont'd)
John	Rev 22:1-5; 6-21

through **FIDELITY**
Ezekiel	Ezek 18:5-9; 14-20
Isaiah	Is 55:1-13
John	Rev 20:4-6

in **NEW AGE**
Jesus	Rev 1:1-3
John	Rev 22:1-5

through **PROVIDENCE**
Ezekiel	Ezek 4:9-11; 11:14-21; 16:1-7; 17:22-24; 33:1-9
God	Is 41:1-42:4
Israelites	Ezek 12:1-16
Jacob	Gen 31:1-16; 17-43
Job	Job 38:39-41
John	Rev 1:4-20; 12:1-6

through **RECONCILIATION**
Amos	Amos 9:11-12
Jeremiah	Jer 33:12-13
Moses	Lev 17:10-14

through **RESURRECTION**
John	Rev 20:11-15
Prophets	Rev 11:1-14

through **RITE**
Moses	Ex 12:1-14

through **SALVATION**
Prophets	Rev 11:1-14

through **SECURITY**
Ezekiel	Ezek 3:16-21
God	Is 42:5-17
Israelites	Ezek 6:8-10; 28:24-26; 34:17-22; Amos 9:14-15
Jeremiah	Jer 31:7-14
Jerusalemites	Zech 2:1-5
Joel	Joel 2:18-27
John	Rev 12:13-17

through **STEWARDSHIP**
Moses	Lev 25:1-7; 20-22

of **VIRTUE**
Ezekiel	Ezek 18:5-9; 14-20; 21-24; 25-29; 33:10-20

on **LOVE**
as **MOTIVATION**
Daniel	Dan 9:20-23

in **PROVIDENCE**
Cyrus	Is 48:1-22
Isaiah	Is 5:1-7

on **MARRIAGE**
Hosea	Hos 1:2-3

concerning **FIDELITY**
Israelites	Ezek 22:1-16
Moses	Lev 18:1-30; Num 5:11-31

on **MEDIATION**
for **GUILT**
Aaron	Num 18:1-7

of **LEADERSHIP**
Moses	Num 3:5-10

for **OPPRESSION**
Ezekiel	Ezek 4:4-8

for **SUFFERING**
Ezekiel	Ezek 4:4-8

on **MIRACLE**
Jesus	Acts 1:6-11
Manoah	Judg 13:15-23
Moses	Ex 14:23-31

by **AUTHORITY**
Israelites	Deut 11:1-25

in **CONFRONTATION**
Daniel	Dan 10:10-21
Jesus	Lk 24:13-35; 36-43

in the **CREATION**
Jesus	Mt 1:18-25
Joseph	Mt 1:18-25

through **PRESENCE**
God	Ezek 38:17-23
Joshua	Josh 3:1-13

through **PROVIDENCE**
Elijah	1 Kgs 19:1-21

in **RESURRECTION**
Angel	Mt 28:1-8

on **MOTIVATION**
God	Judg 9:22-25

as **ANGER**
Daniel	Dan 11:5-20
God	Zeph 3:8

as **ANXIETY**
Daniel	Dan 7:15-16; 8:26-27

for **DISCIPLESHIP**
Satan	Rev 12:13-17

in **ENVIRONMENT**
Pharaoh	Ex 5:6-14; 15-21

as **FEAR**
Elihu	Job 33:15-18

as **GRIEF**
Ezekiel	Ezek 21:1-7; 8-17

as **JEALOUSY**
God	Zeph 3:8

as **JOY**
Jeremiah	Jer 33:1-9

as **LOVE**
Daniel	Dan 9:20-23

as **REPENTANCE**
Israelites	Hos 2:2-8
Judahites	Jer 18:1-12

as **VIOLENCE**
Joel	Joel 3:9-11

on **NEW AGE**
concerning **CONDEMNATION**
Jesus	Lk 17:22-37

concerning **DESTRUCTION**
Haggai	Hag 2:20-23
Jesus	Lk 17:22-37

concerning **FULFILLMENT**
Angels	Lk 2:1-20

concerning FULFILLMENT (cont'd)

Daniel	Dan 9:24-27; 11:21-45; 12:1-4; 5-13
Isaiah	Is 66:17-24
Joel	Joel 2:30-32
John	Rev 11:15-19; 14:14-16; 17-20; 21:1-8; 9-14; 22:6-21

concerning GOOD

God	*2 Esd 2:10-14; 15-32

concerning GRIEF

Ezekiel	Ezek 30:1-5

concerning IGNORANCE

Mankind	2 Pet 3:8-10

concerning JUSTICE

Angel	*2 Esd 6:7-28

concerning LEADERSHIP

Daniel	Dan 8:15-25

concerning LIFE

Jesus	Rev 1:1-3
John	Rev 22:1-5

concerning ORDER

Daniel	Dan 2:24-45
John	Rev 21:9-14; 15-17; 18-21; 22-27

concerning PEACE

Isaiah	Is 65:1-25

concerning REWARDs

Daniel	Dan 12:5-13

concerning SACREDNESS

John	Rev 21:22-27

concerning VICTORY

Daniel	Dan 7:2-14; 17-27
Isaiah	Is 60:1-22
John	Rev 7:9-17; 12:10-12; 20:11-15

concerning WEALTH

John	Rev 21:18-21

concerning WISDOM

Daniel	Dan 10:10-21
God	Is 42:5-17

concerning WITNESS

Daniel	Dan 10:10-21
God	Is 42:5-17
Jesus	Rev 22:6-21
John	Rev 1:1-3; 10:1-11; 19:11-16; 22:6-21

on OBEDIENCE

Aaron	Ex 4:27-31
Balaam	Num 22:22-35
Elijah	1 Kgs 19:1-21
Ezekiel	Ezek 8:5-6; 7-13
Isaac	Gen 26:1-11
Isaiah	Is 8:11-15
Jacob	Gen 31:1-16
Jeremiah	Jer 18:1-12; 35:1-5

on OBEDIENCE (cont'd)

Paul	Acts 16:6-10

to COMMITMENT

Moses	Num 30:1-16

through CONVERSION

Paul	Acts 26:1-32

to ELECTION

Amos	Amos 7:10-17
Jeremiah	Jer 1:4-10
Joshua	Zech 3:1-10

through FIDELITY

Isaiah	Is 58:1-14
Israelites	Jer 3:14b-18; Ezek 37:15-28
Judahites	Zech 7:4-8:23

to KNOWLEDGE

Ananias	Acts 9:1-19
Cornelius	Acts 10:1-11:18
Philadelphians	Rev 3:7-13
Wise Men	Mt 2:1-12

to LAW

Israelites	Ezek 37:15-28; 43:6-12
Joshua	Josh 1:1-9
Moses	Ex 20:1-17; 34:12-28; Deut 5:22-33
Priests	Ezek 44:15-31
Solomon	1 Kgs 6:1-38; 9:1-9; 2 Chr 7:11-22
Solomon	1 Kgs 6:1-38

in PRESENCE

Solomon	1 Kgs 6:1-38

through PROVIDENCE

Elijah	1 Kgs 17:1-24; 18:1-46
Ezekiel	Ezek 11:14-21
Israelites	Num 9:15-23
Joseph	Mt 2:19-23

to PUNISHMENT

Isaiah	Is 65:1-25

as QUALITY OF LIFE

Ezekiel	Ezek 24:15-24

in RITE

Jacob	Gen 35:1-15
Moses	Ex 40:1-33

in STEWARDSHIP

Jeremiah	Jer 25:15-29

to TRUTH

God	Rom 16:25-27
Jeremiah	Jer 23:23-32; 26:1-6
Paul	Gal 1:18-2:10

as VIRTUE

Believers	Rev 19:6-10

on ONENESS

with AUTHORITY

God	Is 43:8-13

in COMMUNITY

Israelites	Ezek 37:15-28

through FIDELITY

Ezekiel	Ezek 11:14-21

through PROVIDENCE

John	Rev 17:6b-18

through RECONCILIATION

Israelites	Jer 3:14b-18
Judahites	Jer 3:14b-18

on OPPRESSION
  by AUTHORITY
    John   Rev 7:1-8
  through COMPULSION
    Ezekiel   Ezek 4:4-8
    John   Rev 13:11-18
  in CONFRONTATION
    Daniel   Dan 11:5-20
    Ezekiel   Ezek 10:1-22
    Gog   Ezek 38:3-9
  for ETERNITY
    Sinners   Jer 23:33-40
  as PUNISHMENT
    Ammonites   Ezek 25:1-7
    Chaldeans   Is 47:1-15
    Daniel   Dan 4:19-27
    Egyptians   Ezek 32:17-32
    Eli   1 Sam 2:27-36
    Ezekiel   Ezek 24:15-24
    Israelites   Is 43:14-44:5;
                    Jer 30:18-22;
                    Ezek 4:16-17;
                    5:5-17;
                    7:1-27;
                    22:17-22;
                    23-31
    Jeremiah   Jer 25:15-29
    John   Rev 14:17-20
    Judahites   Ezek 24:1-14
    Nebuchadnezzar Dan 4:28-33
    Sidon   Ezek 28:20-23
    Zedekiah   Jer 24:1-10
  as QUALITY OF LIFE
    Daniel   Dan 12:1-4
    Ezekiel   Ezek 4:9-11
  caused by SIN
    Egyptians   Ezek 29:6-9a
    Isaiah   Is 58:1-14

on ORDER
  by AUTHORITY
    God   *2 Esd 16:51-78
    Job   Job 38:12-15
  in COMMUNITY
    Moses   Num 1:1-19;
                    2:1-34;
                    3:40-51;
                    26:1-4;
                    52-56;
                    27:1-11;
                    36:1-13
  in the CREATION
    God   Is 48:1-22
    Job   Job 38:4-7;
                    8-11
  in NEW AGE
    Daniel   Dan 2:24-45
    John   Rev 21:9-14;
                    15-17;
                    18-21;
                    22-27

on PARADOX
  in BEHAVIOR
    Isaiah   Is 58:1-14
  in PUNISHMENT
    Israelites   Jer 9:25-26
  in SALVATION
    Isaiah   Is 66:1-16

on PEACE
  through AUTHORITY
    John   Rev 6:3-4
  in NEW AGE
    Isaiah   Is 65:1-25
  through PROMISE
    Isaiah   Is 57:14-21
  through PROVIDENCE
    Isaiah   Is 55:1-13;
                    62:1-12
    Jeremiah   Jer 31:2-6
    Nathan   2 Sam 7:1-29
  through RECONCILIATION
    Israelites   Ezek 45:13-17
    Judahites   Zech 7:4-8:23
  through RESPECT
    Israelites   Ezek 36:8-15
  through RITE
    Ezekiel   Ezek 43:18-27
    Moses   Lev 7:28-36
    Priest   Ezek 46:1-8
  in TRUTH
    Disciples   Lk 9:28-36
  as VIRTUE
    Isaiah   Is 60:1-22

on PIETY
  in PRAYER
    John   Rev 8:1-6
  in RITE
    Moses   Lev 23:5-8
  as SIN
    Isaiah   Is 58:1-14

on POLITICS
  of AUTHORITY
    God   Is 41:1-42:4
    Moses   Ex 3:11-22

on POVERTY
  as PUNISHMENT
    Israelites   Hos 2:9-13

on PRAISE
  of AUTHORITY
    Isaiah   Is 6:1-13
    Jeremiah   Jer 9:23-24
  of the CREATION
    Isaiah   Is 55:1-13
  of PRESENCE
    Jesus   Jn 12:27-36a
  revealing RESPECT
    Israelites   Zeph 3:14-20
  of SALVATION
    Isaiah   Is 60:1-22

on PRAYER
  concerning FULFILLMENT
    Daniel   Dan 10:10-21
    David   2 Sam 5:17-25;
                    1 Chr 14:1-17
    Gabriel   Lk 1:5-25
    God   Is 41:1-42:4
    Isaiah   2 Kgs 20:1-11;
                    Is 58:1-14;
                    65:1-25
    Israelites   Zech 10:3-12;
                    13:7-9
    Jeremiah   Jer 11:18-12:6;
                    15:10-21;

concerning **FULFILLMENT** (cont'd)
Jeremiah	31:15-22;
	33:1-9
Psalmist	Ps 2:7-9
Solomon	2 Chr 7:11-22

for **GRACE**
Israelites	Jer 3:1-5

for **JOY**
Believers	Is 56:1-8

with **PIETY**
John	Rev 8:1-6

concerning **REJECTION**
Israelites	Ezek 20:30-31
Jeremiah	Jer 11:1-14;
	15:1-4

concerning **SUFFERING**
Israelites	Jer 2:20-29

on **PRESENCE**
to **FAMILY**
Moses	Ex 6:2-9

concerning **FULFILLMENT**
Jesus	Lk 24:13-35

concerning **MIRACLE**
God	Ezek 38:17-23
Joshua	Josh 3:1-13

depends on **OBEDIENCE**
Solomon	1 Kgs 6:1-38

concerning **PRAISE**
Jesus	Jn 12:27-36a

of **SACREDNESS**
Gideon	Judg 6:11-32
Israelites	1 Kgs 8:1-13;
	Ezek 48:30-35
Jacob	Gen 28:10-22;
	32:1-23
Moses	Ex 3:1-6;
	19:9-15;
	16-25;
	34:1-5a;
	5b-9;
	Acts 6:8-8:3
Raphael	*Tb 12:1-22
Solomon	1 Kgs 9:1-9;
	2 Chr 7:11-22

of **SERVICE**
Priests	Ezek 44:15-31

of **SPIRIT**
Holy Spirit	Joel 1:28-29

of **WILL**
Moses	Ex 3:11-22

of **WISDOM**
Disciples	Jn 14:18-24

WITNESS to
Ezekiel	Ezek 1:1-3
Heliodorus	*2 Mc 3:1-40

through **PRESENCE**
results in **FAITH**
Jesus	Mt 28:16-20

on **PRIDE**
in **CONFRONTATION**
Gideon	Judg 7:1-8

as **SIN**
Ammonites	Zeph 2:8-12
Egyptians	Ezek 31:10-18
Israelites	Jer 3:1-5
King	Ezek 28:11-19

as **SIN** (cont'd)
Moabites	Zeph 2:8-12
Tyre	Ezek 28:1-10

on **PROMISE**
of **BLESSING**
Gabriel	Lk 1:26-38
Isaiah	Is 65:1-25
Israelites	Is 49:1-26
Jacob	Gen 35:1-15
Joshua	Zech 3:1-10
Moses	Ex 20:24-26

of **DEFEAT**
Daniel	Dan 11:1-4

of **DESTRUCTION**
Daniel	Dan 11:5-20
Ezekiel	Ezek 12:17-20

to **FAMILY**
Abraham	Gen 12:1-8;
	15:1-21
Hagar	Gen 21:11-14
Jacob	Gen 35:1-15

concerning **FULFILLMENT**
Ammonites	Ezek 21:28-32
Daniel	Dan 11:21-45
Ezekiel	Ezek 12:21-28;
	17:22-24;
	21:8-17;
	34:23-24
God	Jer 32:16-25;
	2 Pet 3:11-13
Israelites	Ezek 22:1-16;
	36:33-36;
	47:13-20
Jeremiah	Jer 33:14-26
Judahites	Ezek 23:22-35;
	24:1-14
Samuel	1 Sam 3:1-4:1a
Simeon	Lk 2:21-40

of **GRACE**
Isaiah	Is 57:14-21;
	65:1-25

of **INDIFFERENCE**
Pharaoh	Ex 7:1-7

of **JOY**
God	Is 41:1-42:4
Isaiah	Is 60:1-22
Jeremiah	Jer 31:2-6

of **LEADERSHIP**
Solomon	1 Kgs 9:1-9;
	2 Chr 7:11-22

of **MIRACLE**
Gabriel	Lk 1:5-25
Joshua	Josh 6:1-7

of **OBEDIENCE**
People	Jer 42:1-6

of **PEACE**
Isaiah	Is 57:14-21

of **REVENGE**
Jeremiah	Jer 15:1-4

of **REWARD**s
Nebuchadnezzar	Ezek 29:17-21

of **SACREDNESS**
Moses	Ex 33:12-23

of **VICTORY**
Joshua	Josh 3:1-13;
	6:1-7
Moses	Ex 5:22-6:1

of **VIOLENCE**
Ezekiel	Ezek 12:17-20

of **WEALTH**
  Isaiah   Is 54:1-17
  Jeremiah   Jer 31:23-26
  Moses   Num 11:14-24a;
                      Deut 1:6-8
  Nebuchadnezzar   Ezek 29:17-21
of **WILL**
  Solomon   2 Chr 1:1-17
of **WISDOM**
  Daniel   Dan 5:10-17
  Solomon   1 Kgs 3:1-15

on **PROVIDENCE**
  through **ANGER**
    Israelites   Ezek 20:32-39
  as **BLESSING**
    Balaam   Num 22:5-14
    Ezekiel   Ezek 16:1-7;
                      17:22-24
    God   Is 42:5-17
    Isaiah   Is 55:1-13
    Israelites   Ezek 36:8-15;
                      37-38;
                      Hos 2:14-15;
                      Mic 6:1-5
    Jeremiah   Jer 31:7-14
    Joel   Joel 2:18-27
    Nathan   2 Sam 7:1-29;
                      1 Chr 17:1-27
  of **DEITY**
    God   1 Sam 25:1-44
  for **FAMILY**
    Isaiah   Is 51:1-16;
                      66:17-24
  concerning **FEAR**
    God   Is 41:1-42:4
    Jeremiah   Jer 4:9-10
  concerning **FULFILLMENT**
    Isaiah   Is 55:1-13
    Israelites   Is 49:1-26
    Jeremiah   Jer 1:11-12;
                      31:7-14
    Jesus   Jn 12:20-26
  through **GRACE**
    Ezekiel   Ezek 16:8-14;
                      17:22-24
    Israelites   Is 51:17-52:12
    Jeremiah   Jer 21:2-6
    Joel   Joel 2:18-27
  concerning **HEALING**
    Israelites   Ezek 34:11-16
    Jeremiah   Jer 30:12-17
  concerning **HUMILITY**
    Israelites   Zeph 3:11-13
    Paul   2 Cor 12:1-10
  through **JUSTICE**
    Israelites   Ezek 34:11-16
  through **LEADERSHIP**
    David   Ezek 34:23-24
    Isaiah   Is 55:1-13;
                      58:1-14
    Israelites   Is 48:1-22;
                      Jer 3:14b-18;
                      Ezek 20:9-26;
                      32-39
    John   Rev 7:9-17
  resulting in **LIFE**
    Ezekiel   Ezek 4:9-11;
                      11:14-21;
                      16:1-7;

resulting in **LIFE** (cont'd)
    Ezekiel   17:22-24;
                      33:1-9
    God   Is 41:1-42:4
    Israelites   Ezek 12:1-16
    Jacob   Gen 31:1-16;
                      17-43
    Job   Job 38:39-41
    John   Rev 1:4-20;
                      12:1-6
  through **LOVE**
    Cyrus   Is 48:1-22
    Isaiah   Is 5:1-7
  through **MIRACLE**
    Elijah   1 Kgs 19:1-21
  concerning **OBEDIENCE**
    Elijah   1 Kgs 7:1-14;
                      18:1-46
    Ezekiel   Ezek 11:14-21
    Israelites   Num 9:15-23
    Joseph   Mt 2:19-23
  through **ONENESS**
    John   Rev 17:6b-18
  concerning **PEACE**
    Isaiah   Is 55:1-13;
                      62:1-12
    Jeremiah   Jer 31:2-6
    Nathan   2 Sam 7:1-29
  concerning **REPENTANCE**
    Israelites   Ezek 12:1-16
  concerning **SERVICE**
    Babylonians   Jer 27:1-11
    Ezekiel   Ezek 16:8-14
    God   Is 41:1-42:4
    Israelites   Is 49:1-26;
                      Ezek 20:40-44;
                      34:11-16
    Nations   Zeph 3:9-10
    Philip   Acts 8:26-40
  concerning **SPIRIT**
    Israelites   Ezek 36:22-32
  concerning **SUFFERING**
    Gog   Ezek 38:17-23
  concerning **VICTORY**
    Babylonians   Ezek 30:6-9;
                      20-26
    Cyrus   Is 44:24-45:13
    David   1 Sam 23:1-13;
                      2 Sam 5:17-25;
                      1 Chr 14:1-17
    Gideon   Judg 7:1-8
    God   Is 41:1-42:4
    Israelites   Is 45:14-25;
                      49:1-26;
                      Zeph 3:14-20
    Joshua   Josh 11:1-15;
                      13:1-7
    Moses   Ex 14:15-22
  concerning **VIOLENCE**
    Gog   Ezek 38:17-23;
                      39:1-16
  concerning **WEALTH**
    Cyrus   Is 45:14-25
    Israelites   Ezek 34:25-31;
                      Hag 1:15b-2:9
    Moses   Ex 33:1-6;
                      Lev 25:1-7;
                      20-22
                      Num 34:1-15

concerning **WILL**
Jeremiah　　　　Jer 18:1-12
concerning **WISDOM**
Daniel　　　　Dan 1:17-21;
　　　　2:14-19
Israelites　　　　Jer 3:14b-18
Judahites　　　　Jer 24:1-10
concerning **WITNESS**
Ezekiel　　　　Ezek 3:22-27
God　　　　Heb 1:1-2a
Isaiah　　　　Is 66:1-16
Paul　　　　Acts 22:30-23:11

on **PUNISHMENT**
as **ALIENATION**
Ammonites　　　　Ezek 25:1-7
Egyptians　　　　Ezek 29:1-5;
　　　　6-9a
Ezekiel　　　　Ezek 14:1-11;
　　　　12-23
Hosea　　　　Hos 1:8-9
Israelites　　　　Ezek 39:17-24;
　　　　Amos 8:1-3;
　　　　Zech 13:7-9
Jeremiah　　　　Jer 23:33-40
Joel　　　　Joel 3:4-8
Judahites　　　　Jer 3:6-11;
　　　　Ezek 23:11-21
King　　　　Ezek 28:11-19
Levites　　　　Ezek 44:10-14
Moses　　　　Lev 21:1-22:33;
　　　　23:26-32
Nations　　　　Zeph 3:6-7
Nebuchadnezzar　　　　Dan 4:28-33
Prophetesses　　　　Ezek 13:17-23
Samuel　　　　1 Sam 3:1-4:1a
Satan　　　　Rev 12:7-9
Solomon　　　　1 Kgs 11:1-13
Zechariah　　　　Zech 5:1-4
Zephaniah　　　　Zeph 1:2-6;
　　　　10-11

through **ANGER**
Edomites　　　　Ezek 25:12-14;
　　　　35:1-15
Egyptians　　　　Ezek 30:13-19
Ezekiel　　　　Ezek 8:16-18;
　　　　13:1-16;
　　　　36:1-7
Israelites　　　　Num 11:1-3;
　　　　5:5-17;
　　　　6:11-14;
　　　　7:1-27;
　　　　19:10-14;
　　　　22:17-22;
　　　　23-31;
　　　　36:16-21
Jeremiah　　　　Jer 7:16-20;
　　　　25:30-38;
　　　　30:23-31:1;
　　　　33:1-9
John　　　　Rev 14:17-20
Judahites　　　　Ezek 23:22-35;
　　　　24:1-14
Philistines　　　　Ezek 25:15-17
Rulers　　　　Zech 10:3-12
for **BLASPHEMY**
Israelites　　　　Ezek 5:5-17
Jeremiah　　　　Jer 19:1-15
Samuel　　　　1 Sam 3:1-4:1a
Zechariah　　　　Zech 5:1-4

as **CAPTIVITY**
Ammonites　　　　Ezek 25:1-7;
　　　　Zeph 2:8-12
Egyptians　　　　Ezek 30:12-19;
　　　　32:1-16
Israelites　　　　Ezek 21:18-24
Jeremiah　　　　Jer 15:10-21
Joel　　　　Joel 3:4-8
Moabites　　　　Ezek 25:8-11;
　　　　Zeph 2:8-12

as **CONDEMNATION**
Zedekiah　　　　Jer 24:1-10
as **DEATH**
Ammonites　　　　Ezek 21:28-32
Egyptians　　　　Ezek 29:1-5;
　　　　30:13-19;
　　　　32:1-16;
　　　　17-32
Eli　　　　1 Sam 2:27-36
Elijah　　　　1 Kgs 21:17-29
Ezekiel　　　　Ezek 6:1-7;
　　　　9:1-11;
　　　　11:1-13
God　　　　Gen 2:16-17;
　　　　Lev 10:1-20
Israelites　　　　Num 14:26-38;
　　　　Ezek 6:11-14;
　　　　7:1-27;
　　　　12:1-6;
　　　　17:11-21;
　　　　21:8-17;
　　　　23:5-10;
　　　　8:1-3;
　　　　9:1-4
Jehoiakim　　　　Jer 36:27-32
Jeremiah　　　　Jer 11:18-12:6;
　　　　15:1-4;
　　　　5-9;
　　　　19:1-15;
　　　　25:30-38;
　　　　33:1-9
John　　　　Rev 11:1-14;
　　　　16:3
King　　　　Ezek 28:11-19
Moses　　　　Lev 21:1-22:33;
　　　　Num 15:32-36;
　　　　27:12-23;
　　　　Deut 32:48-52
Sidon　　　　Ezek 28:20-23
Tyre　　　　Ezek 28:1-10

as **DEFEAT**
Ammonites　　　　Ezek 25:1-7
Israelites　　　　Hos 1:4-5
John　　　　Rev 14:8
as **DESTRUCTION**
Ammonites　　　　Ezek 21:28-32;
　　　　25:1-7;
　　　　Zeph 2:8-12
Belshazzar　　　　Dan 5:26-28
Chaldeans　　　　Is 47:1-15
Edomites　　　　Ezek 25:12-14;
　　　　35:1-15
Egyptians　　　　Ezek 29:1-5;
　　　　6-9a;
　　　　9b-16;
　　　　30:13-19;
　　　　31:10-18;
　　　　32:1-16
Ezekiel　　　　Ezek 6:1-7;
　　　　13:1-16;

as **DESTRUCTION** (cont'd)	
Ezekiel	14:1-11;
	20:45-49;
	21:25-27
God	Is 41:1-42:4
Gog	Ezek 39:1-16
Isaiah	Is 5:1-7;
	6:1-13;
	56:9-57:13
	65:1-25
Israelites	Jer 2:14-19;
	5:1-14;
	Ezek 5:5-17;
	6:11-14;
	7:1-27;
	Ezek 21:1-7;
	8-17;
	22:1-16;
	23:5-10;
	36-49;
	Hos 1:4-5;
	2:9-13;
	Amos 7:7-9;
	8:8-10;
	9:1-4;
	Zech 13:7-9
Jacobites	Amos 9:8-10
Jehu	1 Kgs 15:33-16:7
Jeremiah	Jer 15:1-4;
	5-9;
	19:1-15;
	25:15-29;
	30-38
Jesus	2 Thes 1:7b-10
John	Rev 11:1-14;
	18:4-20
Judahites	Jer 13:1-11;
	Ezek 23:22-35;
	24:1-14
Malachi	Mal 3:13-4:3
Micah	Mic 6:9-16
Moabites	Ezek 25:8-11;
	Zeph 2:8-12
Nations	Zeph 3:6-7;
	8
People	Jer 27:1-11
Philistines	Ezek 25:15-17
Prophets	2 Kgs 21:1-18;
	Jer 14:13-16
Solomon	2 Chr 7:11-22
Tyre	Ezek 26:1-6;
	27:25b-36;
	28:1-10
Zechariah	Zech 5:1-4
Zedekiah	Jer 24:1-10
Zephaniah	Zeph 1:2-6;
	10-11;
	12-13

for **DISOBEDIENCE**	
Ezekiel	Ezek 3:16-21;
	11:1-13
Holy Spirit	Heb 3:6b-11
Isaiah	Is 31:4-9
Israelites	Num 14:26-38;
	Is 48:1-22;
	Jer 9:25-26
Jeremiah	Jer 16:1-13;
	23:33-40
Judahites	Jer 13:1-11
Moses	Num 16:36-50

for **DISOBEDIENCE** (cont'd)	
Nathan	2 Sam 7:1-29;
	1 Chr 17:1-27
Solomon	1 Kgs 9:1-9;
	11:1-13

for **DOUBT**	
Gabriel	Lk 1:5-25
God	Num 12:11-16

of **EMEMY**	
Ezekiel	Ezek 36:1-7
God	Is 1:24-26;
	*2 Esd 15:1-16:50
Israelites	Is 51:17-52:12;
	Zeph 2:8-12
Jeremiah	Jer 30:12-17
Zechariah	Zech 1:18-21

for **EVIL**	
Chaldeans	Is 47:1-15
Egyptians	Ezek 32:17-32
Ezekiel	Ezek 8:16-18;
	9:1-11;
	11:14-21;
	20:45-49
God	Gen 20:1-18;
	Ps 9:15-16;
	*2 Esd 15:1-16:50
Habakkuk	Hab 2:1-4
Isaiah	Is 51:1-16;
	57:14-21;
	65:1-25;
	66:1-16
Israelites	Is 50:1-11;
	Jer 2:14-19;
	3:1-5;
	30:10-11;
	Ezek 5:5-17;
	7:1-27;
	15:1-8;
	17:11-21;
	20:32-39;
	21:18-24;
	22:1-16;
	23:5-10;
	36-49;
	36:16-21;
	39:17-24;
	Hos 2:2-8;
	Amos 9:8-10
Jehoiakim	Jer 36:27-32
Jeremiah	Jer 1:13-16;
	3:21-4:4;
	11:1-14;
	18-12:6;
	14:13-16;
	16:16-18;
	18:1-12;
	19:1-15;
	25:15-29;
	30:12-17;
	23-31:1
John	Rev 18:1-3
Judahites	Jer 9:2-9;
	Ezek 23:11-21
Micah	Mic 6:9-16
Prophetesses	Ezek 13:17-23
Prophets	Ezek 13:1-16
Sinners	Rev 21:1-8
Solomon	2 Chr 7:11-22
Zechariah	Zech 5:1-4
Zephaniah	Zeph 1:8-9

for **GREED**

Eli	1 Sam 2:27-36

resulting in **GRIEF**

Judahites	Ezek 24:1-14

for **HATE**

Edomites	Ezek 35:1-15

as **HUMILITY**

Israelites	Jer 2:20-29; 30-37; Hos 2:9-13
Jeremiah	Jer 15:1-4; 5-9
Levites	Ezek 44:10-14

for **IDOLATRY**

Egyptians	Ezek 30:13-19
Ezekiel	Ezek 14:1-11
God	Is 42:5-17
Isaiah	Is 56:9-57:13
Israelites	Ezek 6:8-10; Hos 2:9-13
Jeremiah	Jer 7:16-20; 11:1-14; 16:1-13; 16-18; 19:1-15
John	Rev 16:2
Judahites	Ezek 23:22-35
Levites	Ezek 44:10-14

for **IGNORANCE**

God	Gen 12:9-13:1

for **INDIFFERENCE**

Zephaniah	Zeph 1:12-13

through **JEALOUSY**

Ezekiel	Ezek 36:1-7
Israelites	Ezek 5:5-17

with **JUSTICE**

Egyptians	Ezek 31:10-18
Ezekiel	Ezek 14:12-23
Israelites	Jer 2:14-19; Ezek 36:16-21; 39:17-24; Amos 8:4-7
Jeremiah	Jer 16:16-18
John	Rev 13:5-10; 18:4-20
Moses	Lev 24:10-23

for **KILLING**

Elijah	1 Kgs 19:1-21
John	Rev 11:1-14
Mankind	Rev 9:13-21
Moses	Num 35:16-25

of **LEADERSHIP**

Ezekiel	Ezek 21:25-27
Solomon	1 Kgs 11:1-13
Zechariah	Zech 10:3-12
Zephaniah	Zeph 1:8-9

for **LUST**

Chaldeans	Is 47:1-15
Judahites	Ezek 23:22-35

as **OPPRESSION**

Ammonites	Ezek 25:1-7
Chaldeans	Is 47:1-15
Daniel	Dan 4:19-27
Egyptians	Ezek 32:17-32
Eli	1 Sam 2:27-36
Ezekiel	Ezek 24:15-24
Israelites	Is 43:14-44:5; Jer 30:18-22; Ezek 4:16-17; 5:5-17;

as **OPPRESSION** (cont'd)

Israelites	7:1-27; 22:17-22; 23-31
Jeremiah	Jer 25:15-29
John	Rev 14:17-20
Judahites	Ezek 24:1-14
Nebuchadnezzar	Dan 4:28-33
Sidon	Ezek 28:20-23
Zedekiah	Jer 24:1-10

through **PARADOX**

Israelites	Jer 9:25-26

as **POVERTY**

Israelites	Hos 2:9-13

for **PRIDE**

Egyptians	Ezek 31:10-18
Habakkuk	Hab 2:5-6a
Israelites	Ezek 7:1-27
Judahites	Jer 13:1-11
Malachi	Mal 3:13-4:3

as **REJECTION**

Ezekiel	Ezek 14:1-11
Israelites	Num 14:26-38; Jer 2:14-19; 30-37; Ezek 20:32-39; Hos 2:2-8; 9-13
Jehoiakim	Jer 36:27-32
Jeremiah	Jer 16:1-13; 19:1-15
Judahites	Ezek 23:22-35
Moses	Num 14:11-24; 20:2-13
Nations	Zeph 3:6-7
People	Jer 27:1-11
Zedekiah	Jer 24:1-10
Zephaniah	Zeph 1:2-6

as **REVENGE**

Chaldeans	Is 47:1-15
Edomites	Ezek 25:12-14
Ezekiel	Ezek 36:1-7
Isaiah	Is 65:1-25; 66:1-16
Israelites	Jer 5:1-14
Jeremiah	Jer 25:15-29
Jesus	2 Thes 1:7b-10
Judahites	Ezek 8:16-18; 24:1-14
Philistines	Ezek 25:15-17

as **SADNESS**

Israelites	Ezek 7:1-27; Amos 8:8-10

for **SELFISHNESS**

Isaiah	Is 66:1-16

for **SEX**

Judahites	Ezek 23:22-35

as **SUFFERING**

Egyptians	Ezek 30:13-19
Ezekiel	Ezek 14:12-23
Isaiah	Is 65:1-25; 66:1-16
Israelites	Jer 2:14-19; 3:1-5; Ezek 4:16-17; 7:1-27; Amos 8:8-10; 11-14
Jeremiah	Jer 14:13-16; 15:1-4;

as **SUFFERING** (cont'd)
Jeremiah	5-9;
	25:15-29;
	30:12-17
John	Rev 15:1-16:1;
	2;
	8-9;
	10-11;
	18:4-20;
	20:11-15
Micah	Mic 6:9-16
Rulers	Zech 11:15-17
Sinners	Rev 21:1-8

for **VIOLENCE**
Amos	Amos 7:7-9
Ezekiel	Ezek 6:1-7;
	11:1-13;
	14:12-23
God	*2 Esd 15:1-16:50
Isaiah	Is 54:1-17
Israelites	Ezek 5:5-17;
	7:1-27;
	21:8-17
Jeremiah	Jer 25:30-38
Zephaniah	Zeph 1:8-9

on **PURIFICATION**
through **COMMITMENT**
Judahites	Jer 3:21-4:4

through **JUDGMENT**
Israelites	Is 48:1-22;
	Ezek 20:32-39

on **QUALITY OF LIFE**
as **ALIENATION**
Jeremiah	Jer 16:1-13

as **BLESSING**
Isaiah	Is 66:1-16

as **DOUBT**
Zechariah	Lk 1:5-25

as **EVIL**
Jeremiah	Jer 2:1-13

as **GRIEF**
Zephaniah	Zeph 1:10-11

as **INDIFFERENCE**
Jeremiah	Jer 7:21-28

as **JOY**
Isaiah	Is 66:1-16
Jesus	1 Pet 4:12-19

as **OBEDIENCE**
Ezekiel	Ezek 24:15-24

as **OPPRESSION**
Daniel	Dan 12:1-4
Ezekiel	Ezek 4:9-11

as **REJECTION**
Isaiah	Is 5:1-7

as **REPENTANCE**
Israelites	Ezek 36:22-32

as condition for **REWARD**s
God	1 Cor 4:1-5
Isaiah	Is 66:1-16
John	Rev 22:6-21

as **SACREDNESS**
Israelites	Lev 19:1-37

as **TEMPERANCE**
Manoah	Judg 13:9-14
Priests	Ezek 44:15-31

as **WEALTH**
Isaiah	Is 66:1-16

on **RECONCILIATION**
through **ACCEPTANCE**
Israelites	Ezek 20:40-44;
	Hos 2:14-15
Moses	Lev 1:1-17

over **BLASPHEMY**
Israelites	Ezek 36:16-21;
	22-32

as **BLESSING**
Amos	Amos 9:11-12
Israelites	Ezek 28:24-26;
	36:33-36;
	37:15-28;
	Hos 2:21-23;
	Amos 9:14-15;
	Zech 1:7-17;
	7:4-8:23;
	10:3-12

from **CAPTIVITY**
Israelites	Ezek 28:24-26

through **COMPASSION**
Israelites	Jer 30:18-22;
	Zech 1:7-17

through **FAITH**
Israelites	Is 50:1-11

through **FULFILLMENT**
Jeremiah	Jer 31:23-26

through **GRACE**
Amos	Amos 9:11-12
Israelites	Jer 30:10-11;
	18-22;
	31:15-22;
	Ezek 20:40-44;
	34:11-16;
	36:33-36;
	37:1-14;
	39:25-29;
	Hos 1:10-2:1;
	21-23
Jeremiah	Jer 3:12-14a;
	16:14-15;
	30:12-17;
	31:7-14;
	33:14-26
Judahites	Jer 24:1-10
Moses	Lev 5:5-13;
	14-6:7

resulting in **GRATITUDE**
Israelites	Jer 30:18-22
Jeremiah	Jer 33:10-11

for **GUILT**
Israelites	Is 43:14-44:5

concerning **HEALING**
Jeremiah	Jer 33:1-9

through **HUMILITY**
Egyptians	Ezek 29:9b-16

for **IGNORANCE**
Israelites	Ezek 45:18-25

concerning **LEADERSHIP**
Israelites	Hos 1:10-2:1
Judahites	Zech 7:4-8:23

resulting in **LIFE**
Amos	Amos 9:11-12
Jeremiah	Jer 33:12-13
Moses	Lev 17:10-14

through **ONENESS**
Israelites	Jer 3:14b-18
Judahites	Jer 3:14b-18

through **OPPRESSION**
Israelites	Is 51:17-52:12

of **SACRIFICE** (cont'd)

Moses	17:1-9;
	23:15-22;
	33-44;
	Num 15:1-16;
	17-21;
	28:1-2;
	3-8;
	9-10;
	29:7-11;
	12-40
Priest	Ezek 46:1-8
Prince	Ezek 45:13-17

of **SERVICE**

Isaiah	Is 58:1-14

of **SHARING**

Isaiah	Is 58:1-14

concerning **STEALING**

Israelites	Mal 3:6-12

concerning **TEMPERANCE**

Nazirites	Judg 13:9-14

on **SACREDNESS**

in **AUTHORITY**

Levites	Num 1:47-54

in **BEHAVIOR**

Nathan	1 Chr 17:1-27

of **BROTHERHOOD**

Peter	Acts 10:1-11:18

of **COMMITMENT**

Moses	Num 6:1-21

in the **CREATION**

Ezekiel	Ezek 45:1-9
Moses	Ex 25:1-9;
	40:1-33
Zechariah	Zech 6:9-15

of **ELECTION**

Jesus	Mk 9:2-8
John	Rev 7:1-8
Manoah	Judg 13:2-7
Moses	Num 3:11-13

in **NEW AGE**

John	Rev 21:22-27

of **PRESENCE**

Gideon	Judg 6:11-32
Israelites	1 Kgs 8:1-13;
	Ezek 48:30-35
Jacob	Gen 28:10-22;
	32:1-23
Moses	Ex 3:1-6;
	19:9-15;
	16-25;
	34:1-5a;
	5b-9;
	Acts 6:8-8:3
Raphael	*Tb 12:1-22
Solomon	1 Kgs 9:1-9;
	2 Chr 7:11-22

as **QUALITY OF LIFE**

Israelites	Lev 19:1-37

in **RECONCILIATION**

Moses	Lev 16:11-28

of **RITE**

Aaron	Ex 12:43-49;
	Num 18:1-7
Ezekiel	Ezek 42:13-14
Joshua	Josh 7:6-26
Moses	Ex 12:1-14;
	43-49;
	Lev 1:1-17;

of **RITE** (cont'd)

Moses	2:1-16;
	5:5-13;
	23:5-8;
	23-25;
	26-32;
	33-44;
	Num 1:47-54;
	9:1-14;
	20:2-13;
	28:16-25;
	26-31;
	29:1-6;
	12-40
Priests	Ezek 44:15-31

concerning **STEWARDSHIP**

Moses	Ex 13:1-2;
	Num 4:1-20;
	21-28;
	29-33

of **TRUTH**

Samaritan	Jn 4:1-26

on **SACRIFICE**

according to **DESIRE**

Moses	Ex 25:1-9

through **FIDELITY**

Nations	Zeph 3:9-10

through **HONESTY**

Isaiah	Is 58:1-14

in **RECONCILIATION**

Moses	Ex 34:12-28;
	Lev 23:26-32;
	Num 3:40-51

in **RITE**

Aaron	Num 18:8-20
Ezekiel	Ezek 40:38-43
Israelites	Ezek 45:18-25;
	Zech 7:4-8:23
Moses	Lev 3:1-17;
	17:1-9;
	23:15-22;
	33-44;
	Num 15:1-16;
	17-21;
	28:1-2;
	3-8;
	9-10;
	29:7-11;
	12-40
Priest	Ezek 46:1-8
Prince	Ezek 45:13-17

for **SIN**

Ezekiel	Ezek 43:18-27
Israelites	Ezek 20:30-31;
	45:18-25
Moses	Lev 5:5-13;
	14-6:7;
	16:6-10;
	11-28;
	Num 28:11-15;
	29:7-11;
	12-40
Priests	Ezek 44:15-31
Prince	Ezek 45:13-17
Samuel	1 Sam 3:1-4:1a

in **STEWARDSHIP**

Israelites	Ezek 46:11-15
Moses	Num 18:25-32

on **SADNESS**
  in **CONFRONTATION**
    John   Rev 1:4-20
  in **JUDGMENT**
    John   Rev 18:4-20
  as **PUNISHMENT**
    Israelites   Ezek 7:1-27;
                 Amos 8:8-10
  for **SIN**
    Ezekiel   Ezek 8:14-15

on **SALVATION**
  from **CAPTIVITY**
    Israelites   Ex 3:7-10;
                 7:1-7;
                 11:1-10;
                 Ezek 20:5-8;
                 Zech 10:3-12
    Moses   Ex 6:2-9
  through **COMPASSION**
    Israelites   Zech 10:3-12
  through **DISCIPLESHIP**
    Heliodorus   *2 Mc 3:1-40
  from **EVIL**
    Elihu   Job 33:15-18
  through **FAITH**
    God   Is 45:14-25
    Israelites   Jer 30:10-11
    Joel   Joel 2:30-32
  for **FAMILY**
    Israelites   Is 49:1-26
    Jesus   Mt 1:18-25
    Noah   Gen 7:1-24
  from **FEAR**
    Believers   Mal 3:13-4:3
  through **FULFILLMENT**
    God   Rev 12:10-12
    Isaiah   Is 51:1-16
    Israelites   Is 49:1-26
    John   Rev 7:1-8
  through **GRACE**
    Believers   1 Pet 1:13-2:3
    Israelites   Is 49:1-26;
                 Ezek 36:22-32;
                 37:15-28;
                 Zech 7:4-8:23;
                 13:7-9
    Jeremiah   Jer 33:14-26
    John   Rev 14:1-5
  for **LIFE**
    Prophets   Rev 11:1-14
  through **MIRACLE**
    God   Heb 2:1-4
    Israelites   Zech 10:3-12
    Moses   Ex 15:22-27;
                 16:1-21;
                 17:1-7
  through **OBEDIENCE**
    Believers   Is 56:1-8
    Moses   Ex 14:15-22
  from **OPPRESSION**
    Israelites   Zeph 3:14-20
  through **PARADOX**
    Isaiah   Is 66:1-16
  through **SUFFERING**
    Israelites   Jer 30:4-9
  through **TEMPERANCE**
    John   Rev 14:1-5
  through **VICTORY**
    Daniel   Dan 12:1-4

through **VICTORY** (cont'd)
    Jeremiah   Jer 15:10-21
    John   Rev 12:1-6
    Judahites   Hos 1:6-7
through **WILL**
    Israelites   Is 45:14-25
through **WISDOM**
    Author   Heb 2:1-4
    Isaiah   Is 56:1-8
through **WITNESS** to
    Author   Heb 2:1-4
    Isaiah   Is 60:1-22
    Israelites   Mic 6:1-5
    Simeon   Lk 2:21-40

on **SECURITY**
  from **ALIENATION**
    Believers   Rev 18:4-20
  from **ANGER**
    Israelites   Is 51:17-52:12
  in **BLESSING**
    Israelites   Ezek 34:11-16;
                 25-31
    Jeremiah   Jer 33:1-9
  in **COMPASSION**
    Isaiah   Is 51:1-16
  in **COURAGE**
    Ezekiel   Ezek 2:1-8a;
                 3:4-9
    Isaiah   Is 7:1-9
    Israelites   Zeph 3:11-13
    Joshua   Deut 31:14-23
    Paul   Acts 27:1-28:16
  in **DEATH**
    Chaldeans   Is 47:1-15
  in **DISCIPLESHIP**
    John   Rev 7:1-8
  from **ENEMY**
    God   Is 41:1-42:4
    Israelites   Ezek 39:25-29
    John   Rev 12:1-6
  through **FAITH**
    Elijah   2 Kgs 1:1-18
    Ezekiel   Ezek 2:1-8a;
                 3:4-9
    God   Is 46:1-13
    Isaiah   Is 7:1-9;
                 51:1-16;
                 56:9-57:13
    Israelites   Zeph 3:11-13;
                 Zech 7:4-8:23
    Jeremiah   Jer 1:4-10
  of **FAMILY**
    Israelites   Ezek 34:1-10
    Jacob   Gen 46:1-7
    Jeremiah   Jer 33:14-26
  in **FULFILLMENT**
    Paul   Acts 27:1-28:16
  through **GRACE**
    Jacobites   Amos 9:8-10
  from **KILLING**
    Joshua   Josh 20:1-9
    Moses   Num 35:9-15
  in **LEADERSHIP**
    God   Is 42:5-17
    John   Rev 6:12-17
    Moses   Num 14:25
  of **LIFE**
    Ezekiel   Ezek 3:16-21
    God   Is 42:5-17

of **LIFE** (cont'd)

Israelites	Ezek 6:8-10; 28:24-26; 34:17-22; Amos 9:14-15
Jeremiah	Jer 31:7-14
Jerusalemites	Zech 2:1-5
Joel	Joel 2:18-27
John	Rev 12:13-17

of **LOVE**

Israelites	Is 49:1-26

through **MIRACLE**

Moses	Num 20:2-13

through **OBEDIENCE**

Isaiah	Is 8:11-15
Israelites	Is 48:1-22
Moses	Ex 4:18-23

from **OPPRESSION**

Satan	Rev 20:1-3

through **PEACE**

Isaiah	Is 51:1-16

through **REVENGE**

Isaiah	Is 54:1-17

through **SERVICE**

Isaiah	Is 58:1-14
Israelites	Is 49:1-26

through **SUFFERING**

God	*2 Esd 16:51-78
John	Rev 9:1-12

in **VICTORY**

Gideon	Judg 7:9-15
Jeremiah	Jer 1:17-19

from **VIOLENCE**

Daniel	Dan 11:21-45

on **SELFISHNESS**
　in **BEHAVIOR**

Ezekiel	Ezek 33:30-33; 34:17-22
Isaiah	Is 58:1-14

on **SERVICE**
　in **COMMITMENT**

Moses	Num 8:23-26
People	Jer 27:1-11

through **ELECTION**

Elisha	1 Kgs 19:1-21
Isaiah	Is 66:17-24
Israelites	Is 43:14-44:5; Jer 30:4-9
Jeremiah	Jer 1:13-16
Levites	Num 18:1-7; Ezek 44:10-14
Moses	Ex 28:40-43
Samuel	1 Sam 3:1-4:1a

through **PROVIDENCE**

Babylonians	Jer 27:1-11
Ezekiel	Ezek 16:8-14
God	Is 41:1-42:4
Israelites	Is 49:1-26; Ezek 20:40-44; 34:11-16
Nations	Zeph 3:9-10
Philip	Acts 8:26-40

through **RESURRECTION**

John	Rev 20:4-6

in **RITE**

Isaiah	Is 58:1-14

in **STEWARDSHIP**

Levites	Num 1:47-54

on **SEX**
　as **SIN**

Israelites	Ezek 22:1-16
Mankind	Rev 9:13-21

on **SHARING**
　to be **DESIRED**

Moses	Ex 25:1-9

with **EQUALITY**

Israelites	Ezek 47:13-20

in **RITE**

Isaiah	Is 58:1-14

in **STEWARDSHIP**

Isaiah	Is 58:1-14

on **SIGNS**
　of **ACCEPTANCE**

Ezekiel	Ezek 17:1-10
Jesus	Mt 17:1-8; Mk 9:2-8; Lk 9:28-36
John	Rev 17:6b-18
Jonah	Mt 12:38-42

in **BLASPHEMY**

Daniel	Dan 8:9-12; 13-14; 9:24-27; 12:5-13
John	Rev 13:1-4; 5-10

of **BLESSING**

God	Mt 3:13-17; Mk 1:9-11
Isaiah	Is 55:1-13
Jesus	Lk 3:21-22

in **CAPTIVITY**

Ezekiel	Ezek 12:1-16; 17:1-10
Israelites	Ezek 17:11-21; 19:1-4; 5-9
Jeremiah	Jer 24:1-10
John	Rev 13:5-10
Zechariah	Zech 5:5-11

in **CHAOS**

John	Rev 6:12-17; 8:12; 16:17-21

in **COMPASSION**

John	Rev 8:13
Jonah	Jon 4:1-11

in **CONDEMNATION**

Israelites	Hos 1:6-7
John	Rev 17:6b-18
Zechariah	Zech 5:1-4

in **DEATH**

Israelites	Ezek 15:1-8
John	Rev 5:1-14; 8:8-9; 10-11; 14:17-20

in **DEFEAT**

Isaiah	Is 8:1-4

in **DESPAIR**

John	Rev 6:12-17

in **DESTRUCTION**

Daniel	Dan 7:2-14
Ezekiel	Ezek 5:1-4; 17:1-10
Israelites	Ezek 15:1-8;

in **DESTRUCTION** (cont'd)
Israelites | 19:10-14
John | Rev 8:7;
| 8-9;
| 12:1-6;
| 16:12-16;
| 17-21;
| 17:6b-18
Zechariah | Zech 5:1-4
concerning **ENEMY**
John | Rev 12:1-6;
| 13:1-4
in **EVIL**
John | Rev 17:1-6a
Zechariah | Zech 5:5-11
Zedekiah | Jer 24:1-10
in **FEAR**
Ezekiel | Ezek 12:17-20
of **FULFILLMENT**
Joel | Joel 3:12-16a
John | Rev 6:9-11;
| 7:1-8;
| 10:1-11;
| 14:14-16;
| 16:17-21
Mordecai | *Esth 10:4-13
in **GRACE**
Zechariah | Zech 3:1-10
in **HEALING**
John | Rev 13:1-4;
| 22:1-5
in **HOPE**
Daniel | Dan 8:13-14
Ezekiel | Ezek 47:1-12
IGNORANCE of
John | Rev 14:1-5
in **JEALOUSY**
Ezekiel | Ezek 8:1-4;
| 5-6
in **JUSTICE**
Ezra | *2 Esd 13:1-50
in **KILLING**
John | Rev 6:3-4;
| 7-8;
| 13:11-18
Mankind | Rev 9:13-21
concerning **LEADERSHIP**
Daniel | Dan 9:24-27
Israelites | Ex 40:34-38;
| Ezek 19:1-4;
| 5-9
John | Rev 9:1-12;
| 21:22-27
John the Baptist | Mt 11:7-15
Zechariah | Zech 6:1-8
in **LIFE**
Angels | Lk 2:1-20
Ezekiel | Ezek 9:1-11;
| 47:1-12
John | Rev 4:1-11;
| 12:1-6;
| 22:1-5
in **MARRIAGE**
John | Rev 21:9-14
in **MIRACLE**
Angel | *2 Esd 6:7-28
Ezekiel | Ezek 2:8b-3:3;
| 8:1-4
Gideon | Judg 6:11-32
Israelites | Num 9:15-23;

in **MIRACLE** (cont'd)
Israelites | 17:1-13
Joel | Joel 2:30-32;
| 3:12-16a
John | Rev 13:11-18
Joshua | Josh 4:1-8
Moses | Ex 3:1-6
Zechariah | Zech 2:1-5
for **OBEDIENCE**
Ezekiel | Ezek 12:1-16;
| 33:1-9
Isaiah | Is 20:1-6
of **ONENESS**
Ezekiel | Ezek 37:15-28
in **OPPRESSION**
Ezekiel | Ezek 4:1-3;
| 24:25-27
Israelites | Ezek 19:10-14
John | Rev 16:12-16
Zechariah | Zech 1:18-21
in **ORDER**
Zechariah | Zech 4:1-6a;
| 10b-14
in **PATIENCE**
John | Rev 6:9-11
in **PEACE**
Zechariah | Zech 1:7-17
in **POLITICS**
Ezra | *2 Esd 11:1-12:39
in **PURIFICATION**
Israelites | Mal 2:17-3:5
in **REJECTION**
Hosea | Hos 1:2-3;
| 8-9
John | Rev 13:11-18;
| 14:1-5
in **REPENTANCE**
Moses | Deut 31:14-23
in **SACREDNESS**
Jews | *2 Mc 5:1-4
Joshua | Josh 3:1-13
Maccabeus | *2 Mc 11:1-12
Moses | Num 8:1-4;
| 15:37-41;
| 16:36-50
Nathan | 2 Sam 7:1-29
in **SACRIFICE**
Daniel | Dan 8:9-12
John | Rev 12:10-12
Moses | Lev 24:5-9
in **SADNESS**
Ezekiel | Ezek 9:1-11
John | Rev 8:13
in **SERVICE**
John | Rev 7:1-8;
| 8:1-6
Moses | Num 10:1-10
in **SEX**
Hosea | Hos 3:1-5
in **SUFFERING**
Ezekiel | Ezek 4:4-8;
| 9-11;
| 12-15
John | Rev 6:5-6;
| 9:1-12;
| 13:1-4;
| 15:1-16:1
in **VICTORY**
Gideon | Judg 7:9-15
John | Rev 6:1-2;

in **VICTORY** (cont'd)
John 7:9-17; 10:1-11
in **VIOLENCE**
Daniel Dan 10:1
Ezekiel Ezek 5:1-4
Israelites Ezek 19:1-4; 5-9
John Rev 16:12-16; 17-21
concerning **WILL**
Mordecai *Esth 11:2-12
concerning **WISDOM**
Daniel Dan 2:24-45
John Rev 17:6b-18
Zechariah Zech 4:1-6a; 10b-14
WITNESS to
Daniel Dan 4:19-27; 5:18-25; 7:1; 8:1-2; 10:2-9
Ezekiel Ezek 1:4-28; 4:1-3; 10:1-22; 24:25-27; 40:1-5; 6-16; 17-19; 20-27; 28-37; 38-43; 44-47; 48-49; 41:1-4; 5-11; 12; 13-15a; 15b-26; 42:1-10a; 10b-12; 13-14; 15-20; 43:13-17; 47:1-12
Isaiah Is 66:17-24
John Rev 1:4-20; 4:1-11; 5:1-14
Nebuchadnezzar Dan 4:10-17

on **SIN**
Joab 2 Sam 3:17-39
resulting in **ALIENATION**
Israelites Zeph 3:11-13
John Rev 22:6-21
Moses Num 19:14-22
causing **ANGER**
Isaiah Is 57:14-21
Solomon 1 Kgs 11:1-13
as **BLASPHEMY**
Ezekiel Ezek 8:16-18
Isaiah Is 65:1-25
Israelites Ezek 8:5-6; 20:27-29; 22:1-16; Mal 3:13-4:3
Prophetesses Ezek 13:17-23
causing **CHAOS**
Isaiah Is 57:14-21

of **COVETOUSNESS**
Habakkuk Hab 2:5-6a
causing **DEATH**
Ezekiel Ezek 18:1-4; 10-13; 14-20; 21-24; 25-29; 33:1-9; 10-20
Moses Num 1:47-54
causing **DEFEAT**
Zephaniah Zeph 1:2-6
causing **DESTRUCTION**
Believers Mal 3:13-4:3
Daniel Dan 8:15-25
Isaiah Is 66:17-24
causing **DISOBEDIENCE**
Ezekiel Ezek 12:1-16
Jehu 1 Kgs 15:33-16:7
as **DOUBT**
Ezekiel Ezek 33:23-29
as **EVIL**
Ezekiel Ezek 8:5-6; 23:1-4
John Rev 14:8
Mankind Rev 9:13-21
of **GREED**
Habakkuk Hab 2:5-6a
causing **GUILT**
Moses Lev 5:1-4
of **IDOLATRY**
Ezekiel Ezek 8:7-13; 14-15; 16-18; 22:1-16
Israelites Jer 2:1-13; 20-29; Ezek 20:27-29; 30-31
Jeremiah Jer 1:13-16
Mankind Rev 9:13-21
Moses Ex 20:21-23
of **KILLING**
Israelites Ezek 22:1-16
Mankind Rev 9:13-21
resulting in **OPPRESSION**
Egyptians Ezek 29:6-9a
Isaiah Is 58:1-14
of **PIETY**
Isaiah Is 58:1-14
of **PRIDE**
Ammonites Zeph 2:8-12
Egyptians Ezek 31:10-18
Israelites Jer 3:1-5
King Ezek 28:11-19
Moabites Zeph 2:8-12
Tyre Ezek 28:1-10
of **REJECTION**
Ezekiel Ezek 12:1-16
Isaiah Is 65:1-25
Israelites Jer 3:1-5; Ezek 5:5-17; 20:5-8
Jesus Jn 1:1-18
causing **SADNESS**
Ezekiel Ezek 8:14-15
of **SEX**
Israelites Ezek 22:1-16
Mankind Rev 9:13-21

of STEALING
   Joel   Joel 3:4-8
   Mankind   Rev 9:13-21
of VIOLENCE
   King   Ezek 28:11-19

on SPIRIT
   in PRESENCE
      Holy Spirit   Joel 2:28-29
   through PROVIDENCE
      Israelites   Ezek 36:22-32

on STEALING
   in RITE
      Israelites   Mal 3:6-12
   as SIN
      Joel   Joel 3:4-8
      Mankind   Rev 9:13-21

on STEWARDSHIP
   in FAMILY
      Moses   Lev 25:25-28
   of HEALING
      Isaiah   Is 58:1-14
   of LIFE
      Moses   Lev 25:1-7;
                 20-22
   of SACRIFICE
      Israelites   Ezek 46:11-15
      Moses   Num 18:25-32
   of SERVICE
      Levites   Num 1:47-54
   of SHARING
      Isaiah   Is 58:1-14
   of WEALTH
      Israelites   Ezek 45:13-17
      Moses   Lev 25:23-24;
                 27:1-34
   of WILL
      Moses   Lev 23:33-44

of SUFFERING
   John   Rev 12:1-6
   by AUTHORITY
      Israelites   Hag 1:1-11
      John   Rev 6:7-8
   in CONFRONTATION
      Holy Spirit   Acts 21:1-14
      John   Rev 9:1-12
   through FIDELITY
      John   Rev 13:5-10;
                 11-18
   through MEDIATION
      Ezekiel   Ezek 4:4-8
   in PROVIDENCE
      God   Ezek 38:17-23
   as PUNISHMENT
      Egyptians   Ezek 30:13-19
      Ezekiel   Ezek 14:12-23
      Isaiah   Is 65:1-25;
                 66:1-16
      Israelites   Jer 2:14-19;
                 3:1-5;
                 Ezek 4:16-17;
                 7:1-27;
                 Amos 8:8-10;
                 11-14
      Jeremiah   Jer 14:13-16;
                 15:1-4;
                 5-9;

as PUNISHMENT (cont'd)
   Jeremiah   25:15-29;
              30:12-17
   John   Rev 15:1-16:1;
              2;
              8-9;
              10-11;
              18:4-20;
              20:11-15
   Micah   Mic 6:9-16
   Rulers   Zech 11:15-17
   Sinners   Rev 21:1-8
in RECONCILIATION
   Moses   Lev 23:26-32
in SALVATION
   Israelites   Jer 30:4-9

on TEMPERANCE
   as QUALITY OF LIFE
      Manoah   Judg 13:9-14
      Priests   Ezek 44:15-31
   in RITE
      Nazirites   Judg 13:9-14
   as VIRTUE
      Mary   Lk 1:26-38

on TRUTH
   concerning DEFEAT
      Daniel   Dan 8:9-12
   FULFILLMENT of
      Ezekiel   Ezek 12:21-28
   through GRACE
      Paul   Gal 1:11-17

on VICTORY
   of AUTHORITY
      Daniel   Dan 8:15-25
      God   Is 41:1-42:4
      John   Rev 13:5-10
   in CONFRONTATION
      Babylonians   Ezek 32:1-16
      Gideon   Judg 6:11-32
      Isaiah   Is 54:1-17
      Israel   Gen 32:24-32
      Israelites   Judg 20:24-28;
                 Ezek 39:1-16;
                 Zeph 2:8-12
      Jeremiah   Jer 1:17-19
      John   Rev 12:10-12;
                 13-17;
                 15:1-16:1;
                 17:6b-18;
                 19:17-21
      Joshua   Josh 8:1-29;
                 10:1-15
      Judahites   Is 7:1-9
      Maccabeus   *2 Mc 15:11-19
      Michael   Rev 12:7-9
      Moses   Num 33:50-56
      Nebuchadnezzar Ezek 29:17-21
   in the CREATION
      Isaiah   Is 54:1-17
   for ETERNITY
      Israelites   Is 45:14-25
   through FIDELITY
      John   Rev 14:13
   in NEW AGE
      Daniel   Dan 7:2-14;
                 17-27
      Isaiah   Is 60:1-22

of **COMMUNITY**
  Ezra   *2 Esd 9:38-10:59
in **CONFRONTATION**
  Balaam   Num 22:15-21
in **ELECTION**
  Jesus   Jn 21:15-23
  Moses   Num 12:4-10
in **PRESENCE**
  Moses   Ex 3:11-22
in **PROVIDENCE**
  Jeremiah   Jer 18:1-12
in **SALVATION**
  Israelites   Is 45:14-25

on **WISDOM**
in **AUTHORITY**
  Holy Spirit   1 Cor 2:10-16
  Isaiah   Is 55:1-13
  Job   Job 38:4-7;
       16-18;
       19-21;
       22-24;
       25-30;
       31-38;
       39-41;
       39:1-4;
       5-8;
       13-18;
       26-30
in the **CREATION**
  Job   Job 38:8-11
in **NEW AGE**
  Daniel   Dan 10:10-21
  God   Is 42:5-17
in **PRESENCE**
  Disciples   Jn 14:18-24
through **PROVIDENCE**
  Daniel   Dan 1:17-21;
       2:14-19
  Israelites   Jer 3:14b-18
  Judahites   Jer 24:1-10
in **TRUTH**
  Daniel   Dan 10:1
  Holy Spirit   Eph 3:1-13
  Paul   Rom 1:19-23;
       Eph 3:1-13;
       Phil 3:4-16
as **VIRTUE**
  Daniel   Dan 12:1-4

on **WITNESS**
  Believers   1 Cor 14:26-33
to **COMMUNITY**
  Ezekiel   Ezek 40:1-5
CONFRONTATION with
  Angel   Judg 6:11-32;
       13:2-7;
       Lk 1:5-25
  Disciples   Lk 24:13-35
  Israelites   Deut 4:32-40;
       Neh 9:12-15
  Jesus   Lk 24:13-35
  Job   Job 40:1-2
  Moses   Ex 20:21-23
to **ELECTION**
  Ezekiel   Ezek 2:1-8a;
       3:10-11;
       16-21
  Isaiah   Is 6:1-13
to **JUDGMENT**

to **JUDGMENT** (cont'd)
  Isaiah   Is 66:17-24
  Israelites   Mal 2:17-3:5
  John   Rev 20:4-6
  Mankind   Ezek 39:17-24
to **NEW AGE**
  Daniel   Dan 10:10-21
  God   Is 42:5-17
  Jesus   Rev 22:6-21
  John   Rev 1:1-3;
       10:1-11;
       19:11-16;
       22:6-21
to **PRESENCE**
  Ezekiel   Ezek 1:1-3
  Heliodorus   *2 Mc 3:1-40
to **PROVIDENCE**
  Ezekiel   Ezek 3:22-27
  God   Heb 1:1-2a
  Isaiah   Is 66:1-16
  Paul   Acts 22:30-23:11
to **RESPECT**
  Ezekiel   Ezek 43:1-5
to **RESURRECTION**
  Angel   Mt 28:1-8
  Disciples   Jn 21:1-14
  Mary   Mt 28:1-8
to **SALVATION**
  Author   Heb 2:1-4
  Isaiah   Is 60:1-22
  Israelites   Mic 6:1-5
  Simeon   Lk 2:21-40
to **SIGNS**
  Daniel   Dan 4:19-27;
       5:18-25;
       7:1;
       8:1-2;
       10:2-9
  Ezekiel   Ezek 1:4-28;
       4:1-3;
       10:1-22;
       24:25-27;
       40:1-5;
       6-16;
       17-19;
       20-27;
       28-37;
       38-43;
       44-47;
       48-49;
       41:1-4;
       5-11;
       12;
       13-15a;
       15b-26;
       42:1-10a;
       10b-12;
       13-14;
       15-20;
       43:13-17;
       47:1-12
  Isaiah   Is 66:17-24
  John   Rev 1:4-20;
       4:1-11;
       5:1-14
  Nebuchadnezzar   Dan 4:10-17
to **SIN**
  Elders   Ezek 20:1-4
  Ezekiel   Ezek 16:1-7;
       22:1-16;

to **SIN** (cont'd)

Ezekiel	23:36-49
Isaiah	Is 58:1-14

to **TRUTH**

Disciples	Mt 17:1-8; Mk 9:2-8; Lk 9:28-36
Ezekiel	Ezek 3:10-11; 4:4-8; 20:45-49; 21:1-7
Isaiah	Is 55:1-13
Jeremiah	Jer 23:23-32; 33-40; 31:7-14; 36:27-32
John	Rev 14:6-7
Paul	Acts 16:6-10

REVENGE

by **AUTHORITY**
of **DEITY**

Asaph	Ps 83:9-18
God	Deut 31:30-32:47
Israelites	Deut 31:30-32:47
Paul	Rom 12:14-21

BEHAVIOR revealing

Amaziah	2 Kgs 14:5-6
Samson	Judg 15:1-18
Tamar	Gen 38:12-23

of **DEITY**

Jeremiah	Lam 3:1-66

for **unBELIEF**

Moses	Num 11:14-24a

by **COMMUNITY**
INSTRUCTION on

Mordecai	Esth 8:9-14

CONFRONTATION with

Levi	Gen 34:1-31
Simeon	Gen 34:1-31

of **DEITY**

Moses	Num 31:1-6

through **FALSE BELIEF**

Edomites	Ezek 25:12-14
Philistines	Ezek 25:15-17

PROPHECY of

Micah	Mic 4:9-5:6

of **DEITY**
BEHAVIOR revealing

Jeremiah	Lam 3:1-66

CONFRONTATION with

Moses	Num 31:1-6

as **JUDGMENT**

David	Ps 109:6-20
God	Rev 16:4-7
Mankind	Ps 58:10-11; Heb 10:19-31

MEDIATION with

God	Ps 37:1-11
Israelites	Jer 51:1-64

PRAYER for

Asaph	Ps 79:5-13

PRAYER for (cont'd)

David	1 Sam 23:14-24:2 Ps 35:22-28; 69:22-28
Jeremiah	Jer 11:18-12:6; 15:10-21; 17:14-18; 18:18-23; 20:7-18
Nehemiah	Neh 4:4-5; 6:10-14
Priest	*1 Mc 7:36-38
Psalmist	Ps 43:1-5; 94:1-3; 119:81-88; 137:7-9

PROVIDENCE in

David	Ps 18:46-50
God	1 Sam 25:1-44

as **PUNISHMENT**

David	Ps 56:6b-9
God	Nah 1:1-9; Rev 19:1-5
Solomon	*Wis 18:5-19
Unbelievers	2 Thes 2:11-12

RECONCILIATION through

David	2 Sam 21:1-14

SALVATION through

David	Ps 54:1-2

for **SIN**

God	Ps 9:9-12; Prov 20:1-30
Isaiah	Is 59:1-21; 63:1-6

VIRTUE in

David	Ps 26:1-3

DESIRE for

David	1 Sam 25:1-44
Haman	Esth 5:9-14

by **FOLLOWERs**

Believers	Rev 6:9-11

in **ENVIRONMENT**
BEHAVIOR revealing

Samson	Judg 15:1-8
Tamar	Gen 38:12-23

CONFRONTATION with

Levi	Gen 34:1-31
Simeon	Gen 34:1-31

MOTIVATION for

Haman	Esth 3:1-6

PUNISHMENT for

David	2 Sam 4:1-12
Gibeonites	2 Sam 21:1-14
Saul	1 Sam 22:1-23

through **FALSE BELIEF**

Herodias	Mk 6:17-29

CONFRONTATION with

Edomites	Ezek 25:12-14
Philistines	Ezek 25:15-17

JUDGMENT on

Priests	Jn 12:9-11

by **FOLLOWERs**
DESIRE for

Believers	Rev 6:9-11

INSTRUCTION on

REVELATION on (cont'd)
Ezekiel	Ezek 36:1-7
Isaiah	Is 65:1-25;
	66:1-16
Israelites	Jer 5:1-14
Jeremiah	Jer 25:15-29
Jesus	2 Thes 1:7b-10
Judahites	Ezek 8:16-18;
	24:1-14
Philistines	Ezek 25:15-17

RECONCILIATION through
of **DEITY**
David	2 Sam 21:1-14

because of dis**RESPECT**
for **MESSIANIC FIGURE**
David	2 Sam 1:1-16

REVELATION on
as **JUDGMENT**
Joel	Joel 3:4-8

as a **PROMISE**
Jeremiah	Jer 15:14

as **PUNISHMENT**
Chaldeans	Is 47:1-15
Edomites	Ezek 25:12-14
Ezekiel	Ezek 36:1-7
Isaiah	Is 65:1-25;
	66:1-16
Israelites	Jer 5:1-14
Jeremiah	Jer 25:15-29
Jesus	2 Thes 1:7b-10
Judahites	Ezek 8:16-18;
	24:1-14
Philistines	Ezek 25:15-17

for **SIN**
John	Rev 18:4-20
Judahites	Jer 9:2-9

SALVATION through
of **DEITY**
David	Ps 54:1-2

PROPHECY of
Isaiah	Is 62:1-12

SECURITY in
REVELATION on
Isaiah	Is 54:1-17

as **SIN**
INSTRUCTION on
Sirach	*Sir 27:30-28:12

for **SIN**
by **DEITY**
God	Ps 9:9-12;
	Prov 20:1-30
Isaiah	Is 59:1-21;
	63:1-6

PROPHECY of
Judahites	Jer 25:8-14

REVELATION on
John	Rev 18:4-20
Judahites	Jer 9:2-9

VIRTUE in
by **DEITY**
David	Ps 26:1-3

by **AUTHORITY**
Daniel	Dan 6:1-3
David	1 Sam 17:1-18:5
Mordecai	Esth 8:1-2

for **FOLLOWER**s
Paul	1 Cor 9:7-14

BEHAVIOR revealing
Daniel	Dan 5:29

by **DEITY**
God	Prov 19:1-29;
	Jer 32:16-25
Jesus	Mt 7:7-11

INSTRUCTION on
Paul	Rom 2:1-24
Sirach	*Sir 4:1-10

REVELATION on
Jeremiah	Jer 31:15-22

for **BELIEF**
in **DEITY**
Believers	Heb 11:1-40

INSTRUCTION on
Author	Heb 10:32-39
Jesus	Jn 11:1-57;
	12:27-36a
Paul	Rom 9:30-10:21;
	11:7-24;
	2 Thes 1:7b-10
Solomon	Prov 28:1-28

PROPHECY of
Jesus	Jn 7:37-52

SCRIPTURES on
People	1 Pet 2:4-10

for **COMMITMENT**
Israelites	Lev 26:1-46

PROPHECY of
Jesus	Mt 16:21-28;
	Mk 8:34-9:1;
	Lk 9:23-27

of **COMMUNITY**
INSTRUCTION on
Darius	*1 Esd 4:42-57

for **CONVERSION**
by **DEITY**
Eliphaz	Job 22:21-30

INSTRUCTION on
Peter	1 Pet 3:8-12
Zophar	Job 11:13-20

REVELATION on
Zechariah	Zech 1:1-6

by **DEITY**
David	Ps 23:5-6;
	41:11-12
God	Ps 24:3-6

BEHAVIOR revealing
God	Prov 19:1-29;
	Jer 32:16-25
Jesus	Mt 7:7-11

for **BELIEF**
Believers	Heb 11:1-40

for **CONVERSION**
Eliphaz	Job 22:21-30

DESIRE for
  Israelites   Amos 5:4-6
  Psalmist   Ps 116:12-19
for **FIDELITY**
  Asa   2 Chr 14:1-16:14
  Believers   Ps 91:1-13;
                     14-16;
                     128:1-2;
                     3-4;
                     Dan 9:4-19;
                     Jn 9:1-41;
                     Col 3:18-4:1;
                     Heb 6:9-12;
                     1 Pet 5:6-11
  Bildad   Job 8:10-19;
                     20-22
  David   Ps 19:11-14
  Elihu   Job 36:5-15
  Ezra   *2 Esd 13:51-58
  God   Ps 25:8-15;
                     Prov 3:1-35;
                     Rev 11:15-19
  Israelites   Ex 19:1-8
  Mankind   Ps 15:1-5b;
                     18:25-30
  Psalmist   Ps 119:25-32
  Sirach   *Sir 2:12-18
KNOWLEDGE of
  Hannah   1 Sam 2:1-10
  Solomon   1 Kgs 8:22-53
PRAYER for
  David   Ps 25:1-7
  Nehemiah   Neh 5:14-19;
                     13:10-14
                     15-22;
                     23-29;
                     30-31
PROMISE of
  Abraham   Gen 18:16-22
  Israelites   Deut 26:16-19
through **PROVIDENCE**
  God   Ps 127:3-5
  Israelites   Ps 105:43-45
through **PUNISHMENT**
  Sirach   *Sir 11:21-28
as **QUALITY OF LIFE**
  God   Job 34:10-15;
                     2 Cor 5:9-10
  Israelites   Ezek 33:10-21
  Jesus   Mt 16:21-28
  Paul   2 Thes 1:5-7a
RECONCILIATION through
  Isaiah   Is 40:1-11
for **RESPECT**
  God   Ps 112:2-4
  Israelites   Mal 3:13-4:3
for **SIN**
  Zophar   Job 20:4-29
for **STEWARDSHIP**
  God   Prov 25:1-28
  Isaiah   Is 49:1-26
  Israelites   2 Chr 30:1-31:21
for **VIRTUE**
  Believers   Ps 58:10-11;
                     92:12-15;
                     Eph 6:5-9;
                     Jas 4:1-10;
                     2 Pet 2:4-10a
  David   2 Sam 22:1-51;
                     Ps 18:20-24;
                     41:11-12

for **VIRTUE** (cont'd)
  Eliphaz   Job 22:1-5
  God   Ps 24:3-6;
                     37:12-22;
                     23-40;
                     75:9-10;
                     Prov 12:1-28
  Psalmist   Ps 125:4-5

DESIRE for
  Ahasuerus   Esth 6:1-5
  Israelites   Num 32:1-5
of **DEITY**
  Israelites   Amos 5:4-6
  Psalmist   Ps 116:12-19
by **FOLLOWERs**
  Paul   Philm 1:15-20
INSTRUCTION on
  Paul   Phil 1:12-30
MEDITATION on
  Paul   Phil 3:4-16

of **ELECTION**
of **FOLLOWERs**
  Jesus   Lk 22:28-30
INSTRUCTION on
  God   *2 Esd 2:15-32
  Paul   Rom 11:7-24
REVELATION on
  Isaiah   Is 65:1-25

is **ETERNITY**
  INSTRUCTION on
    Paul   2 Cor 4:16-18;
                     1 Tim 6:11-16
  REVELATION on
    Isaiah   Is 51:1-16
  TRADITION of
    Levites   Num 18:21-24

for **FIDELITY**
  King   Prov 20:1-30
  Mordecai   Esth 6:6-14
  Moses   Ex 23:20-33
  Nebuchadnezzar Dan 3:28-30
  Ruth   Ruth 2:1-23
to **COVENANT**
  Israelites   1 Kgs 19:1-21
  Moses   Deut 29:1-15
to **DEITY**
  Asa   2 Chr 14:1-16:14
  Believers   Ps 91:1-13;
                     14-16;
                     128:1-2;
                     3-4;
                     Dan 9:4-19;
                     Jn 9:1-41;
                     Col 3:18-4:1;
                     Heb 6:9-12;
                     1 Pet 5:6-11
  Bildad   Job 8:10-19;
                     20-22
  David   Ps 19:11-14
  Elihu   Job 36:5-15
  Ezra   *2 Esd 13:51-58
  God   Ps 25:8-15;
                     Prov 3:1-35;
                     Rev 11:15-19
  Israelites   Ex 19:1-8
  Mankind   Ps 15:1-5b;

for **FIDELITY** (cont'd)

David	1 Kgs 2:5-12;
	Ps 37:1-11
Ephesus	Rev 2:1-7
God	Ps 81:5c-16;
	Is 1:18-20
Israelites	Deut 7:6-16
Jesus	Mt 5:43-47;
	7:21-23;
	10:26-39;
	19:27-30;
	21:28-32;
	24:45-51;
	25:14-30;
	Lk 6:27-35;
	12:35-38;
	13:22-30;
	Jn 14:18-24
John	1 Jn 2:1-6;
	12-17;
	24-27;
	28-3:3;
	19-24;
	2 Jn 1:7-11
Joshua	Josh 22:1-8
Laodicea	Rev 3:14-22
Moses	Deut 4:15-31
Paul	1 Cor 9:24-27;
	15:51-58;
	Gal 6:7-10;
	2 Tim 4:6-8
Pergamum	Rev 2:12-17
Philadelphians	Rev 3:7-13
Sardis	Rev 3:1-6
Servants	1 Pet 2:18-20
Smyrna	Rev 2:8-11
Solomon	*Wis 3:1-9;
	10-19

as **FREEDOM**

Moses	Deut 15:12-18

from **JUDGMENT**

Jesus	Mt 12:33-37
Paul	1 Cor 3:10-17;
	4:1-5;
	2 Cor 5:9-10

of **KNOWLEDGE**

Father	Prov 4:1-9
Preacher	Eccl 9:17-10:20
Sirach	*Sir 51:13-30
Solomon	Prov 19:1-29

as **MOTIVATION**

Jesus	Mt 6:1;
	2-4;
	16-18

concerning **NEW AGE**

Jesus	Mt 5:3-12;
	19:27-30;
	20:1-16;
	24:45-51;
	25:1-13;
	Mk 10:28-31;
	Lk 6:20-23;
	14:12-14;
	16:1-9;
	18:28-30;
	Jn 4:27-42;
	14:1-14
Paul	2 Cor 4:16-18
Peter	2 Pet 1:8-11

of **PRAYER**

Jesus	Lk 11:5-8;
	9-13

for **QUALITY OF LIFE**

Eliphaz	Job 4:7-11
Jesus	Lk 6:24-26
Paul	Gal 6:7-10
Preacher	Eccl 5:8-20

in **RECONCILIATION**

James	Jas 5:19-20
Jesus	Mt 5:3-12;
	Lk 6:20-23

as **RESPECT**

Elders	1 Tim 5:17-25
Solomon	Prov 13:1-25

in **RESURRECTION**

Jesus	Lk 14:12-14

in **SALVATION**

Jesus	Mt 5:3-12;
	10:26-39;
	13:36-43;
	19:27-30;
	25:31-46;
	Mk 10:28-31;
	Lk 6:20-23;
	18:28-30;
	Jn 6:25-59;
	12:44-50
John the Baptist	Jn 3:31-36
Paul	Rom 6:15-23;
	2 Thes 2:13-15;
	2 Tim 4:6-8
Peter	1 Pet 5:1-5;
	2 Pet 1:8-11

in **SECURITY**

Jesus	Mt 10:40-42

for **STEWARDSHIP**

Jesus	Mt 10:40-42;
	25:14-30;
	Mk 4:21-25;
	26-29;
	9:38-41;
	Lk 8:16-18;
	12:41-46;
	16:1-9;
	19:11-27;
	Jn 12:20-26
Paul	1 Cor 3:5-9;
	2 Cor 9:6-11
Preacher	Eccl 11:1-8
Solomon	Prov 3:1-35
Thyatira	Rev 2:18-29

of **TRUTH**

Paul	1 Cor 3:10-17

for **VIRTUE**

Author	Heb 12:3-11
Believers	Prov 15:1-33
James	Jas 1:12;
	5:14-18
Jesus	Mt 5:3-12;
	Lk 6:20-23;
	14:7-11
Paul	1 Cor 6:9-11
Peter	1 Pet 3:8-12;
	13-17
Sirach	*Sir 40:12-17;
	41:5-13
Solomon	Prov 3:1-35;
	10:1-32;
	11:1-31;

for **VIRTUE** (cont'd)
  Solomon   14:1-35;
         16:1-33;
         20:1-30;
         22:1-16;
         *Wis 4:1-9;
         5:15-23

concerning **JUDGMENT**
  INSTRUCTION on
    Jesus   Mt 12:33-37
    Paul   1 Cor 3:10-17;
         4:1-5;
         2 Cor 5:9-10

  REVELATION on
    Daniel   Dan 12:1-4

for **KNOWLEDGE**
  Daniel   Dan 2:46-49
  INSTRUCTION on
    Father   Prov 4:1-9
    Preacher   Eccl 9:17-10:20
    Sirach   *Sir 51:13-30
    Solomon   Prov 19:1-29

KNOWLEDGE of
  of **DEITY**
    Hannah   1 Sam 2:1-10
    Solomon   1 Kgs 8:22-53
  in **ENVIRONMENT**
    Hiram   1 Kgs 9:10-14

MEDITATION on
  for **FIDELITY**
    David   Ps 101:5-7

of **MISSION**
  FREEDOM as
    Paul   1 Cor 9:15-23
  as **MOTIVATION**
    Paul   1 Cor 9:24-27
  in **NEW AGE**
    Jesus   Mt 5:17-20
  SALVATION as
    Apostles   Mt 10:16-22

as **MOTIVATION**
  INSTRUCTION on
    Jesus   Mt 6:1;
         2-4;
         16-18

  in **MISSION**
    Paul   1 Cor 9:24-27

in **NEW AGE**
  INSTRUCTION on
    Jesus   Mt 5:3-12;
         19:27-30;
         20:1-16;
         24:45-51;
         25:1-13;
         Mk 10:28-31;
         Lk 6:20-23;
         14:12-14;
         16:1-9;
         18:28-30;
         Jn 4:27-42;
         14:1-14
    Paul   2 Cor 4:16-18
    Peter   2 Pet 1:8-11

for **MISSION**
  Jesus   Mt 5:17-20
  REVELATION on
    Daniel   Dan 12:5-13

PRAYER for
  of **DEITY**
    David   Ps 25:1-7
    Nehemiah   Neh 5:14-19;
         13:10-14;
         15-22;
         23-29;
         30-31

of **PRAYER**
  INSTRUCTION on
    Jesus   Lk 11:5-8;
         9-13

is **PRESENCE**
  of **DEITY**
    David   Ps 23:5-6;
         41:11-12
    God   Ps 24:3-6

PROMISE of
  Belshazzar   Dan 5:7-9;
         10-17
  Moses   Num 32:20-33
  by **DEITY**
    Abraham   Gen 18:16-22
    Israelites   Deut 26:16-19
  in **ENVIRONMENT**
    Israelites   Josh 2:8-14
  for **FOLLOWERs**
    Jesus   Mt 19:27-30;
         Mk 10:28-31;
         Lk 18:28-30

  REVELATION on
    Nebuchadnezzar   Ezek 29:17-21

PROPHECY of
  for **BELIEF**
    Jesus   Jn 7:37-52
  for **COMMITMENT**
    Jesus   Mt 16:21-28;
         Mk 8:34-9:1;
         Lk 9:23-27

  for **FIDELITY**
    Angel   *2 Esd 7:33-44
    Ebedmelech   Jer 39:15-18
    Isaiah   Is 62:1-12
    Israelites   Is 30:18-26;
         Hag 1:15a;
         2:15-19
    Jeremiah   Jer 17:5-8;
         19-27;
         22:1-9;
         42:7-22
    Joshua   Josh 23:1-16
    People   Rev 22:6-21
    Rechabites   Jer 35:18-19
  for **QUALITY OF LIFE**
    Jeremiah   Jer 17:11
  in **RECONCILIATION**
    Isaiah   Is 52:13-53:12;
         62:1-12
  concerning **SALVATION**
    Isaiah   Is 62:1-12
    Jesus   Mt 24:9-14;
         Lk 23:39-43

for **VIRTUE**
  Isaiah   Is 33:7-16

through **PROVIDENCE**
  of **DEITY**
    God   Ps 127:3-5
    Israelites   Ps 105:43-45

through **PUNISHMENT**
  of **DEITY**
    Sirach   *Sir 11:21-28
  INSTRUCTION on
    Jesus   Mt 25:31-46

for **QUALITY OF LIFE**
  God   Job 34:10-15;
                          2 Cor 5:9-10
  Israelites   Ezek 33:10-20
  Jesus   Mt 16:21-28
  Paul   2 Thes 1:5-7a
  INSTRUCTION on
    Eliphaz   Job 4:7-11
    Jesus   Lk 6:24-26
    Paul   Gal 6:7-10
    Preacher   Eccl 5:8-20
  PROPHECY of
    Jeremiah   Jer 17:11
  REVELATION on
    God   1 Cor 4:1-5
    Isaiah   Is 66:1-16
    John   Rev 22:6-21

RECONCILIATION through
  of **DEITY**
    Isaiah   Is 40:1-11

in **RECONCILIATION**
  INSTRUCTION on
    James   Jas 5:19-20
    Jesus   Mt 5:3-12;
                          Lk 6:20-23
  PROPHECY of
    Isaiah   Is 52:13-53:12;
                          62:1-12
  REVELATION on
    Ezekiel   Ezek 11:14-21
    Israelites   Zech 10:3-12

as **RESPECT**
  in **ENVIRONMENT**
    Mordecai   *Esth 12:1-6
  INSTRUCTION on
    Elders   1 Tim 5:17-25
    Solomon   Prov 13:1-25

for **RESPECT**
  of **DEITY**
    God   Ps 112:2-4
    Israelites   Mal 3:13-4:3

in **RESURRECTION**
  INSTRUCTION on
    Jesus   Lk 14:12-14

REVELATION on
  for **BEHAVIOR**
    Jeremiah   Jer 31:15-22
  of **CONVERSION**
    Zechariah   Zech 1:1-6
  of **ELECTION**
    Isaiah   Is 65:1-25

is **ETERNITY**
  Isaiah   Is 51:1-16
for **FIDELITY**
  Believers   Is 56:1-8
  Caleb   Deut 1:19-46
  God   Is 42:5-17
  Isaiah   Is 56:9-57:13;
                          58:1-14;
                          65:1-25
  Israelites   Ex 15:22-27;
                          Deut 4:32-40
  Jehu   2 Kgs 10:29-31
  John   Rev 14:1-5;
                          13;
                          20:4-6;
                          21:1-8
  Joshua   Zech 3:1-10
  Solomon   2 Chr 7:11-22
for **HONESTY**
  John   Rev 14:1-5
from **JUDGMENT**
  Daniel   Dan 12:1-4
in **NEW AGE**
  Daniel   Dan 12:5-13
as a **PROMISE**
  Nebuchadnezzar   Ezek 29:17-21
for **QUALITY OF LIFE**
  God   1 Cor 4:1-5
  Isaiah   Is 66:1-16
  John   Rev 22:6-21
in **RECONCILIATION**
  Ezekiel   Ezek 11:14-21
  Israelites   Zech 10:3-12
for **STEWARDSHIP**
  Aaron   Num 18:8-20;
                          21-24
for **VIRTUE**
  Ezekiel   Ezek 18:5-9
  Habakkuk   Hab 2:1-4

SALVATION as
  of **MISSION**
    Apostles   Mt 10:16-22
  PROPHECY of
    Isaiah   Is 62:1-12
    Jesus   Mt 24:9-14;
                          Lk 23:29-43

of **SALVATION**
  for **FOLLOWER**
    Jesus   Jn 8:12-20
  INSTRUCTION on
    Jesus   Mt 5:3-12;
                          10:26-39;
                          13:36-43;
                          19:27-30;
                          25:31-46;
                          Mk 10:28-31;
                          Lk 6:20-23;
                          18:28-30;
                          Jn 6:25-59;
                          12:44-50
    John the Baptist   Jn 3:31-36
    Paul   Rom 6:15-23;
                          2 Thes 2:13-15;
                          2 Tim 4:6-8
    Peter   1 Pet 5:1-5;
                          2 Pet 1:8-11

SCRIPTURES on

remembering **CAPTIVITY** (cont'd)
    TRADITION of
      Israelites   Ex 13:11-16

CONDEMNATION of
    by **DEITY**
      Israelites   Amos 5:21-25
    revealing **FALSE BELIEF**
      Israelites   Deut 18:9-22
    INSTRUCTION on
      Moses   Deut 27:11-26
      Paul   1 Cor 11:27-34
    PROPHECY of
      Haggai   Hag 2:10-14

COURAGE through
    INSTRUCTION on
      Isaiah   Is 40:1-11

COVENANT in
    through **GRACE**
      Jesus   Mt 26:17-30;
                      Mk 14:22-26
      LIFE through
        Jesus   Mk 14:22-26
      SACREDNESS in
        Disciples   Mt 26:17-30
        Jesus   Mk 14:22-26
        Moses   Ex 34:12-28
    related to **DEATH**
      Abraham   Gen 23:1-20
      Isaac   Gen 25:7-11
      Joseph   Josh 24:32
    by **FOLLOWER**
      Joseph   Mt 27:57-61;
                    Mk 15:42-47;
                    Lk 23:50-53
    INSTRUCTION on
      Jacob   Gen 49:29-33
    MEDITATION on
      David   2 Sam 1:17-27
    PROPHECY of
      Jesus   Mt 26:6-13;
                    Mk 14:3-9

DIGNITY of
    in **WORSHIP**
      Believers   1 Cor 11:27-34

of **DISCIPLESHIP**
    in **WORSHIP**
      Abraham   Gen 12:1-8;
                    13:2-9;
                    14-18
      Isaac   Gen 26:12-31

DISOBEDIENCE in
    INSTRUCTION on
      Aaron   Lev 10:1-20
    of **WORSHIP**
      Naphtali   *Tb 1:3-9
      Nicanor   *2 Mc 15:1-5

FALSE BELIEF in
    causes **BLASPHEMY**
      Israelites   Ezek 23:36-49
    causes **CONDEMNATION**
      Israelites   Deut 18:9-22

    causes **IDOLATRY**
      Babylonians   Dan 3:7
      Belshazzar   Dan 5:1-4
    causes **JOY**
      Moses   Deut 12:1-31
    concerning **SACREDNESS**
      Moses   Deut 12:1-31
    concerning **SACRIFICE**
      Israelites   Ezek 23:36-49

of **FAMILY**
    REVELATION on
      Israelites   Ex 12:43-49
    in **WORSHIP**
      Job   Job 1:4-5

FEAR in
    INSTRUCTION on
      Moses   Deut 31:9-13

of **FOLLOWER**s
    related to **DEATH**
      Joseph   Mt 27:57-61;
                    Mk 15:42-47;
                    Lk 23:50-53
    for **LEADERSHIP**
      Paul   Acts 14:19-28
    revealing **LOVE**
      Joseph   Jn 19:17-42
      Nicodemus   Jn 19:17-42
    through **OBEDIENCE**
      Disciples   Mt 26:17-30
    PRAISE in
      King   Ps 45:1
    for **PURIFICATION**
      Believers   Acts 8:4-13
      Corinthians   Acts 18:1-17
      Ephesians   Acts 19:1-12
      Jailer   Acts 16:25-40
      Lydia   Acts 16:11-15
      Saul   Acts 9:1-19
      Timothy   Acts 16:1-5
    SACREDNESS of
      Barnabas   Acts 13:1-3
      Disciples   Acts 6:1-7
      Jesus   Mk 2:23-28;
                    Lk 6:1-5
      Paul   2 Cor 13:11-13
      Saul   Acts 13:1-3
    in **SERVICE**
      Joseph   Jn 19:17-42

FULFILLMENT of
    INSTRUCTION on
      Jacob   Gen 50:1-21
      Moses   Lev 8:1-36
    PROPHECY of
      Jesus   Mt 26:17-30

of **GRATITUDE**
    to **DEITY**
      David   Ps 26:6b-7;
                  28:6-7;
                  56:10-13;
                  57:7-11
    INSTRUCTION on
      Moses   Deut 26:1-11
      Psalmist   Ps 97:10-12;
                  100:4-5;
                  147:7-11

PROPHECY of
Isaiah — Is 26:1-6
in **WORSHIP**
Hezekiah — 2 Chr 30:1-31:21
Israelites — Ezra 3:10-11;
Ps 122:3-5
Judahites — Neh 12:31a
Levites — Neh 12:44-13:3
Nehemiah — Neh 12:38-42

of **GRIEF**
Israelites — Deut 34:1-12;
1 Sam 25:1-44;
28:3-25
MEDITATION on
David — 2 Sam 1:17-27
TRADITION of
Israelites — Judg 11:34-40
in **WORSHIP**
Israelites — *Bar 1:5-14

concerning **GUILT**
REVELATION on
Moses — Lev 5:14-6:7;
Num 5:5-10

of **HEALING**
Disciples — Mk 6:7-13
Moses — Lev 13:1-59;
14:1-32
INSTRUCTION on
James — Jas 5:14-18

HUMILITY in
INSTRUCTION on
Jesus — Mt 6:16-18
in **WORSHIP**
Ezra — Ezra 8:21-23

IDOLATRY in
through **FALSE BELIEF**
Babylonians — Dan 3:7
Belshazzar — Dan 5:1-4
INSTRUCTION on
Jeremiah — *Jer 6:41-44
Nebuchadnezzar — Dan 3:13-15
in **WORSHIP**
Ahaziah — 1 Kgs 22:51-53;
2 Chr 17:1-20:37

INSTRUCTION on
related to **DEATH**
Jacob — Gen 49:29-33
of **GRATITUDE**
Moses — Deut 26:1-11
Psalmist — Ps 97:10-12;
100:4-5;
147:7-11
of **HEALING**
James — Jas 5:14-18
revealing **IDOLATRY**
Jeremiah — *Jer 6:41-44
Nebuchadnezzar — Dan 3:13-15
revealing **JOY**
Asaph — Ps 81:1-5b
Isaiah — Is 49:1-26
James — Jas 5:13
Jeremiah — Jer 31:7-14
Mordecai — Esth 9:20-28
Moses — Deut 16:13-15

revealing **JOY** (cont'd)
Psalmist — Ps 33:1-3;
47:1-4;
66:1-4;
97:10-12;
98:4-6;
100:1-3;
149:5-9
Zephaniah — Zeph 3:14-20
of **LEADERSHIP**
David — 1 Kgs 1:28-40
concerning **LIFE**
Moses — Ex 13:3-10
concerning **OBEDIENCE**
Aaron — Lev 9:1-24
Abraham — Gen 17:23-27;
21:1-7
God — Gen 17:9-14
Israelites — *1 Esd 9:1-15
of **PEACE**
Paul — 1 Cor 14:34-40
of **PRAISE**
David — 1 Chr 15:1-16:43
Ps 9:9-12;
24:7-10;
68:4-14
Deborah — Judg 5:10-11
God — Is 44:6-8;
21-23
Isaiah — Is 42:5-17
James — Jas 5:13
Jeremiah — Jer 31:7-14
Psalmist — Ps 33:1-3;
47:1-4;
5-9;
66:1-4;
95:1-7c;
96:1-6;
98:4-6;
100:1-3;
105:1-6;
135:1-4;
149:1-4;
150:3-5
of **PURIFICATION**
David — 1 Chr 15:1-16:43
Isaiah — Is 51:17-52:12
Jesus — Mt 23:25-26
Moses — Ex 19:9-15;
Deut 21:1-9
Nehemiah — Neh 13:4-9
of **SACREDNESS**
Esther — Esth 4:1-17
God — Ex 12:15-20;
20:1-17
Hezekiah — 2 Chr 30:1-31:21
Holy Spirit — Acts 13:1-3
Jesus — Mt 26:17-30;
Lk 22:14-23
Jews — *2 Mc 1:1-9
Joel — Joel 2:12-17
Joshua — Josh 3:1-13
Josiah — 2 Kgs 23:21-23;
2 Chr 34:1-35:27
Moses — Ex 12:21-28;
13:3-10;
11-16;
35:1-3;
Lev 8:1-36;
Deut 5:1-21;

in **WORSHIP**

Jews	*2 Mc 1:18-36
Solomon	2 Chr 5:1-7:10

OBEDIENCE to
by **FOLLOWER**s

Disciples	Mt 26:17-30

INSTRUCTION on

Aaron	Lev 9:1-24
Abraham	Gen 17:23-27; 21:1-7
God	Gen 17:9-14
Israelites	*1 Esd 9:1-15

REVELATION on

Jacob	Gen 35:1-15
Moses	Ex 40:1-33

TRADITION of

Israelites	*1 Esd 7:10-15

in **WORSHIP**

Levites	2 Chr 8:1-18

ORDER in
in **WORSHIP**

Israelites	Neh 12:31b-37; 38-42
Levites	Neh 12:8-9

PARADOX in
TRADITION of

Pharisees	Mk 7:1-23

of **PEACE**
INSTRUCTION on

Paul	1 Cor 14:34-40

REVELATION on

Ezekiel	Ezek 43:18-27
Moses	Lev 7:28-36
Priest	Ezek 46:1-8

in **WORSHIP**

Aaron	Lev 9:1-24
Israelites	Josh 8:30-35
Solomon	1 Kgs 9:25

of **PIETY**
before **DEITY**

Daniel	Dan 9:1-3

INSTRUCTION on

Jesus	Mt 6:16-18

REVELATION on

Moses	Lev 23:5-8

TRADITION of

Paul	Acts 21:15-26
Pharisees	Lk 11:37-44

in **WORSHIP**

High Priest	Heb 9:1-14
Israelites	Josh 5:10-12; Ezek 46:1-8
Job	Job 1:4-5
Mankind	Zech 14:1-21
People	Jer 36:8-10

of **POVERTY**

Moses	Lev 14:1-32

of **PRAISE**
to **DEITY**

Asaph	Ps 75:9-10
David	Ps 9:1-4; 13:5-6; 18:46-50;

to **DEITY** (cont'd)

David	26:6b-7; 27:4-6; 30:1-5; 59:9-10; 63:1-8; 65:1-4; 144:9-11; *Sir 47:1-11
God	Rev 4:1-11
Jeremiah	Jer 20:7-18
Psalmist	Ps 66:8-12; 87:7; 147:1-6

of **FOLLOWER**

King	Ps 45:1

INSTRUCTION on

David	1 Chr 15:1-16:43 Ps 9:9-12; 24:7-10; 68:4-14
Deborah	Judg 5:10-11
God	Is 44:6-8; 21-23
Isaiah	Is 42:5-17
James	Jas 5:13
Jeremiah	Jer 31:7-14
Psalmist	Ps 33:1-3; 47:1-4; 5-9; 66:1-4; 95:1-7c; 96:1-6; 98:4-6; 100:1-3; 105:1-6; 135:1-4; 149:1-4; 150:3-5

of **MESSIANIC FIGURE**

David	2 Sam 23:1-7
Woman	Mt 26:6-13; Mk 14:3-9

PROPHECY of

Isaiah	Is 12:1-6

TRADITION of

Mordecai	*Esth 10:4-13

in **WORSHIP**

Believers	Acts 2:42-47
David	2 Sam 6:1-23; 22:1-51; Ps 7:17; 8-13; Ps 51:13-17; 61:8; 108:1-5; 138:4-6
Deborah	Judg 5:2-5
Hannah	1 Sam 1:1-28
Hezekiah	2 Chr 30:1-31:21
Israelites	Ezra 3:10-11; *1 Esd 5:59-65
Jehoshaphat	2 Chr 17:1-20:37
Judith	*Jdt 15:8-13; 16:1-17
Lame	Acts 3:1-26
Levites	2 Chr 29:1-36; Neh 12:24-26; 44-13:3
Paul	Acts 16:25-40

in **WORSHIP** (cont'd)
  Psalmist   Ps 92:1-4;
                     104:31-35;
                     111:1;
                     118:22-27;
                     146:1-2;
                     150:3-5
  Simon   *Sir 50:1-21
  Solomon   2 Chr 5:1-7:10

PRIDE in
 of **WORSHIP**
  Hypocrites   Mt 6:16-18

PROPHECY of
 concerning **CONDEMNATION**
  Haggai   Hag 2:10-14
 related to **DEATH**
  Jesus   Mt 26:6-13;
              Mk 14:3-9
 of **FULFILLMENT**
  Jesus   Mt 26:17-30
 of **GRATITUDE**
  Isaiah   Is 26:1-6
 of **PRAISE**
  Isaiah   Is 12:1-6
 of **SACREDNESS**
  Zechariah   Zech 14:1-21
  Zephaniah   Zeph 1:7
 of **SACRIFICE**
  Zechariah   Zech 14:1-21
 of **TEMPERANCE**
  Nazirites   Amos 2:9-12

PUNISHMENT for breaking
 INSTRUCTION on
  Nehemiah   Neh 13:15-22
  Israelites   Josh 5:2-9
  Levites   Num 8:5-22
  Moses   Lev 16:1-5;
              11-28;
              Num 19:1-10;
              11-13;
              14-22
 of **FOLLOWERs**
  Believers   Acts 8:4-13
  Corinthians   Acts 18:1-17
  Ephesians   Acts 19:1-12
  Jailer   Acts 16:25-40
  Lydia   Acts 16:11-15
  Saul   Acts 9:1-19
  Timothy   Acts 16:1-5
 INSTRUCTION on
  David   1 Chr 15:1-16:43
  Isaiah   Is 51:17-52:12
  Jesus   Mt 23:25-26
  Moses   Ex 19:9-15;
              Deut 21:1-9
  Nehemiah   Neh 13:4-9
 REVELATION on
  Ezekiel   Ezek 16:8-14
  Israelites   Ezek 45:18-25
  Joshua   Josh 5:2-9
  Moses   Lev 17:15-16;
              Num 6:1-21
  Priests   Ezek 44:15-31
 TRADITION of
  Jesus   Lk 2:21-40
  Jews   *2 Mc 2:16-18
  Leper   Mt 8:2-4;

TRADITION of (cont'd)
  Leper   Mk 1:40-45;
              Lk 5:12-16
  Pharisees   Lk 11:37-44
 in **WORSHIP**
  Ethiopian   Acts 8:26-40
  Israelites   *1 Esd 7:10-15
  Jews   *2 Mc 1:18-36
  Levites   Ezra 6:19-22;
              Neh 12:30;
              44-13:3
  Maccabeus   *1 Mc 4:36-61

REJECTION of
 by **DEITY**
  Israelites   Amos 5:21-25;
              Mal 2:10-16
  Priests   Mal 1:6-2:9
 INSTRUCTION on
  Antiochus   *1 Mc 1:41-52
  God   Is 1:10-17
  Paul   Gal 5:2-6
 REVELATION on
  Israelites   Ezek 44:6-9
 TRADITION of
  Pharaoh   Ex 5:1-5

REVELATION on
 ACCEPTANCE of
  Believers   Is 56:1-8
  Moses   Lev 21:1-22:33
 revealing **BLASPHEMY**
  Israelites   Ezek 44:6-9
 of **FAMILY**
  Israelites   Ex 12:43-49
 concerning **GUILT**
  Moses   Lev 5:14-6:7;
              Num 5:5-10
 of **JOY**
  Moses   Lev 23:33-44;
              25:8-19
 for **LIFE**
  Moses   Ex 12:1-14
 for **PEACE**
  Ezekiel   Ezek 43:18-27
  Moses   Lev 7:28-36
  Priest   Ezek 46:1-8
 of **PIETY**
  Moses   Lev 23:5-8
 of **PURIFICATION**
  Ezekiel   Ezek 16:8-14
  Israelites   Ezek 45:18-25
  Joshua   Josh 5:2-9
  Moses   Lev 17:15-16;
              Num 6:1-21
  Priests   Ezek 44:15-31
 of **SACREDNESS**
  Aaron   Ex 12:43-49;
              Num 18:1-7
  Ezekiel   Ezek 42:13-14
  Joshua   Josh 7:6-26
  Moses   Ex 12:1-14;
              43-49;
              Lev 1:1-17;
              2:1-16;
              5:5-13;
              23:5-8;
              23-25;
              26-32;
              33-44;

in **WORSHIP** (cont'd)
Israelites
9:1-5a
*1 Esd 7:1-9;
*Jdt 16:18-20
Jacob
Gen 28:10-22;
33:17-20;
35:1-15
Levites
1 Chr 23:1-26:32;
Neh 9:1-5a;
12:27-29
Maccabeus
*2 Mc 8:24-33;
12:38-45
Moses
Ex 17:8-16
Paul
1 Cor 11:23-26
Priest
Lev 6:24-30
Saul
1 Sam 14:1-46
Solomon
1 Kgs 8:62-66;
2 Chr 5:1-7:10

of **SACRIFICE**
Adonijah
1 Kgs 1:5-10
Moses
Ex 23:14-19;
29:10-18;
Lev 7:11-21;
14:1-32;
33-54;
23:9-14;
24:5-9;
Num 28:11-15
Nazirite
Num 6:1-21
to **DEITY**
David
Ps 27:4-6;
40:6-10;
51:18-19
God
Ps 51:13-19
Israelites
Amos 5:21-25
Nineveh
Jon 3:1-10
in **ENVIRONMENT**
Jesus
Mk 14:12-16;
Lk 22:7-13

FALSE BELIEF in
Israelites
Ezek 23:36-49
INSTRUCTION on
Abraham
Gen 22:1-19
Ahaz
2 Kgs 16:10-20
Artaxerxes
Ezra 7:15-19
David
Ps 4:2-5
God
Ex 34:12-28;
Job 42:7-9;
Ps 50:7-15
Israelites
*Bar 1:5-14
Moses
Ex 5:1-5;
10:24-26;
12:21-28;
Lev 10:1-20;
Num 16:16-24;
Deut 12:1-31;
15:19-23;
16:1-8;
9-12;
16-17;
21-17:7;
27:1-10
Preacher
Eccl 5:1-7
Psalmist
Ps 107:17-22
PROPHECY of
Zechariah
Zech 14:1-21
REVELATION on
Aaron
Num 18:8-20
Ezekiel
Ezek 40:38-43

REVELATION on (cont'd)
Israelites
Ezek 45:18-25;
Zech 7:4-8:23
Moses
Lev 3:1-17;
17:1-9;
23:15-22;
33-44;
Num 15:1-16;
17-21;
28:1-2;
3-8;
9-10;
29:7-11;
12-40
Priest
Ezek 46:1-8
Prince
Ezek 45:13-17
TRADITION of
Israelites
Ex 12:21-28;
29:36b-42a;
1 Sam 2:11-26;
Neh 10:34
Josiah
*1 Esd 1:1-22
in **WORSHIP**
Abel
Gen 4:1-16
Asa
2 Chr 14:1-16:14
Babylonians
2 Kgs 17:24-41
Balaam
Num 22:41-23:12;
27-24:13
Balak
Num 22:36-40
David
2 Sam 6:1-23;
24:1-25;
1 Chr 15:1-16:43;
21:1-22:1;
Ps 5:1-3
Gideon
Judg 6:11-32
Hannah
1 Sam 1:1-28
Hezekiah
2 Chr 30:1-31:21
Israelites
Num 7:1-89;
Judg 2:1-5;
20:24-28;
21:1-7;
1 Sam 6:1-7:1;
11:1-15;
Ezra 3:1-3a;
3b-6;
Neh 12:43;
*1 Esd 5:47-55;
7:1-9;
10-15;
*Jdt 16:18-20
Jethro
Ex 18:1-12
Jews
*2 Mc 1:18-36
Joash
2 Chr 24:1-27
Joshua
Josh 8:30-35
Josiah
2 Chr 34:1-35:27
Maccabeus
*1 Mc 4:36-61
Manoah
Judg 13:15-23
Moabite
2 Kgs 3:1-27
Moses
Ex 24:1-18;
40:1-33;
Num 28:1-2
Noah
Gen 8:13-22
Psalmist
Ps 96:7-9;
116:12-19
Samuel
1 Sam 7:2-17;
16:1-13
Solomon
1 Kgs 3:1-15;
8:1-13;
62-66;
9:25;

in **WORSHIP** (cont'd)
Solomon — 2 Chr 1:1-17; 2:1-4:22; 5:1-7:10; 8:1-18

of **SERVICE**
  of **FOLLOWER**
    Joseph — Jn 19:17-42
  INSTRUCTION on
    David — 1 Chr 23:1-26:32
  REVELATION on
    Isaiah — Is 58:1-14
  TRADITION of
    Priest — Lev 6:8-13
    Priests — Lev 21:1-22:33; Ezek 44:15-31
  in **WORSHIP**
    Levites — 1 Chr 6:31-48; Neh 12:44-13:3

of **SHARING**
  INSTRUCTION on
    Jesus — Lk 22:14-23
  REVELATION on
    Isaiah — Is 58:1-14

STEALING in
  REVELATION on
    Israelites — Mal 3:6-12

of **TEMPERANCE**
  Nazirites — Num 6:1-21
  PROPHECY of
    Nazirites — Amos 2:9-12
  REVELATION on
    Nazirites — Judg 13:9-14

as **TRADITION**
  ACCEPTANCE of
    Joseph — Gen 43:16-34
  remembering **CAPTIVITY**
    Israelites — Ex 13:11-16
  of **GRIEF**
    Israelites — Judg 11:34-40
  of **JOY**
    Israelites — Esth 9:16-19
    Maccabeus — *1 Mc 4:36-61; 7:39-50; *2 Mc 10:1-9
    Simon — *1 Mc 13:42-53
  of **LIFE**
    Israelites — Ex 13:3-10
  of **MARRIAGE**
    Abraham — Gen 25:1-6
    Isaac — Gen 24:61-67
    Jacob — Gen 29:15-30
    Leah — Gen 29:15-30
    Rachel — Gen 29:15-30
    Rebekah — Gen 24:61-67
  PARADOX in
    Pharisees — Mk 7:1-23
  of **PIETY**
    Paul — Acts 21:15-26
    Pharisees — Lk 11:37-44
  of **PRAISE**
    Mordecai — *Esth 10:4-13
  of **PURIFICATION**
    Jesus — Lk 2:21-40
    Jews — *2 Mc 2:16-18
    Leper — Mt 8:2-4;

of **PURIFICATION** (cont'd)
  Leper — Mk 1:40-45; Lk 5:12-16
  Pharisees — Lk 11:37-44
of **SACREDNESS**
  Aaron — *Sir 45:6-22
  Israel — Gen 32:24-32
  Israelites — Ex 12:15-20; 37-42; 43-49; 13:11-16; Ezra 3:3b-6
  Moses — Ex 4:24-26
  Priest — Lev 6:14-23
  Women — Lk 23:54-56
of **SACRIFICE**
  Israelites — Ex 12:21-28; 29:36b-42a; 1 Sam 2:11-26; Neh 10:34
  Josiah — *1 Esd 1:1-22
of **SERVICE**
  Priest — Lev 6:8-13
  Priests — Lev 21:1-22:33; Ezek 44:15-31
of **VICTORY**
  Maccabeus — *2 Mc 15:28-36

concerning **VICTORY**
  INSTRUCTION on
    Deborah — Judg 5:10-11

of **VICTORY**
  TRADITION as
    Maccabeus — *2 Mc 15:28-36

of **WITNESS**
  to **DEITY**
    David — Ps 26:6b-7
  INSTRUCTION on
    Psalmist — Ps 107:17-22

in **WORSHIP**
  BLESSING through
    David — Ps 26:8-12
  DIGNITY in
    Believers — 1 Cor 11:27-34
  DISCIPLESHIP in
    Abraham — Gen 12:1-8; 13:2-9; 14-18
    Isaac — Gen 26:12-31
  DISOBEDIENCE in
    Naphtali — *Tb 1:3-9
    Nicanor — *2 Mc 15:1-5
  by **FAMILY**
    Job — Job 1:4-5
  for **GRATITUDE**
    Hezekiah — 2 Chr 30:1-31:21
    Israelites — Ezra 3:10-11; Ps 122:3-5
    Judahites — Neh 12:31a
    Levites — Neh 12:44-13:3
    Nehemiah — Neh 12:38-42
  for **GRIEF**
    Israelites — *Bar 1:5-14
  HUMILITY in
    Ezra — Ezra 8:21-23
  IDOLATRY in
    Ahaziah — 1 Kgs 22:51-53; 2 Chr 17:1-20:37

revealing **JOY**
David — 2 Sam 6:1-23; Ps 122:1-2
Deborah — Judg 5:1
Hezekiah — 2 Chr 30:1-31:21
Israelites — Neh 8:13-18; *1 Esd 5:59-65
Maccabeus — *2 Mc 10:1-9
MIRACLE in
Jews — *2 Mc 1:18-36
Solomon — 2 Chr 5:1-7:10
OBEDIENCE to
Levites — 2 Chr 8:1-18
ORDER of
Israelites — Neh 12:31b-37; 38-42
Levites — Neh 12:8-9
for **PEACE**
Aaron — Lev 9:1-24
Israelites — Josh 8:30-35
Solomon — 1 Kgs 9:25
PIETY in
High Priest — Heb 9:1-14
Israelites — Josh 5:10-12; Ezek 46:1-8
Job — Job 1:4-5
Mankind — Zech 14:1-21
People — Jer 36:8-10
PRAISE in
Believers — Acts 2:42-47
David — 2 Sam 6:1-23; 22:1-51; Ps 7:17 21:8-13; 51:13-17; 61:8; 108:1-5; 138:4-6
Deborah — Judg 5:2-5
Hannah — 1 Sam 1:1-28
Hezekiah — 2 Chr 30:1-31:21
Israelites — Ezra 3:10-11; *1 Esd 5:59-65
Jehoshaphat — 2 Chr 17:1-20:37
Judith — *Jdt 15:8-13 *Jdt 16:1-17
Lame — Acts 3:1-26
Levites — 2 Chr 29:1-36; Neh 12:24-26; 44-13:3
Paul — Acts 16:25-40
Psalmist — Ps 92:1-4; 104:31-35; 111:1; 118:22-27; 146:1-2; 150:3-5
Simon — *Sir 50:1-21
Solomon — 2 Chr 5:1-7:10
revealing **PRIDE**
Hypocrites — Mt 6:16-18
for **PURIFICATION**
Ethiopian — Acts 8:26-40
Israelites — *1 Esd 7:10-15
Jews — *2 Mc 1:18-36
Levites — Ezra 6:19-22; Neh 12:30; 44-13:3
Maccabeus — *1 Mc 44:36-61

SACREDNESS of
Aaron — Ex 29:19-36a; 30:22-33; Lev 8:1-36; 10:1-20
Abraham — Gen 15:1-21
David — 2 Sam 8:1-18; 1 Chr 6:31-48; 18:1-20:8; 21:1-22:1; Ps 68:24-27
Eliashib — Neh 3:1-5
Hezekiah — 2 Chr 29:1-36
Israelites — Ex 20:24-26; Lev 23:1-4; Josh 22:9-34; Ezra 6:19-22; Neh 8:3-8; 9:1-5a; *1 Esd 7:1-9; *Jdt 16:18-20
Jacob — Gen 28:10-22; 33:17-20; 35:1-15
Levites — 1 Chr 23:1-26:32; Neh 9:1-5a; 12:27-29
Maccabeus — *2 Mc 8:24-33; 12:38-45
Moses — Ex 17:8-16
Paul — 1 Cor 11:23-26
Priest — Lev 6:24-30
Saul — 1 Sam 14:1-46
Solomon — 1 Kgs 8:62-66; 2 Chr 5:1-7:10
SACRIFICE as
Abel — Gen 4:1-16
Asa — 2 Chr 14:1-16:14
Babylonians — 2 Kgs 17:24-41
Balaam — Num 22:41-23:12; 27-24:13
Balak — Num 22:36-40
David — 2 Sam 6:1-23; 24:1-25; 1 Chr 15:1-16:43; 21:1-22:1; Ps 5:1-3
Gideon — Judg 6:11-32
Hannah — 1 Sam 1:1-28
Hezekiah — 2 Chr 30:1-31:21
Israelites — Num 7:1-89; Judg 2:1-5; 20:24-28; 21:1-7; 1 Sam 6:1-7:1; 11:1-15; Ezra 3:1-3a; 3b-6; Neh 12:43; *1 Esd 5:47-55; 7:1-9; 10-15; *Jdt 16:18-20
Jethro — Ex 18:1-12
Jews — *2 Mc 1:18-36
Joash — 2 Chr 24:1-27
Joshua — Josh 8:30-35
Josiah — 2 Chr 34:1-35:27
Maccabeus — *1 Mc 4:36-61

SACRIFICE as (cont'd)

Manoah	Judg 13:15-23
Moabite	2 Kgs 3:1-27
Moses	Ex 24:1-18; 40:1-33; Num 28:1-2
Noah	Gen 8:13-22
Psalmist	Ps 96:7-9; 116:12-19
Samuel	1 Sam 7:2-17; 16:1-13
Solomon	1 Kgs 3:1-15; 8:1-13; 62-66; 9:25; 2 Chr 1:1-17; 2:1-4:22; 5:1-7:10; 8:1-18

SERVICE as

Levites	1 Chr 6:31-48; Neh 12:44-13:3

SACREDNESS

of AUTHORITY
of DEITY

Jesus	Lk 22:66-71; Jn 10:19-40

in ENVIRONMENT

Menelaus	*2 Mc 4:23-29
Simon	*1 Mc 14:25-49

INSTRUCTION on

Esther	Esth 9:29-32
Jesus	Jn 7:15-24

of MESSIANIC FIGURE

Jesus	Mt 12:1-8; Mk 2:23-28; Lk 6:1-5

REVELATION on

Levites	Num 1:47-54

SCRIPTURES on

Paul	2 Tim 3:14-17

TRADITION of

John	*1 Mc 16:18-24

BEHAVIOR revealing

David	1 Sam 21:1-9
Levites	Ex 32:25-29
Moses	Lev 11:1-47

INSTRUCTION on

Cyrus	*1 Esd 2:1-7
Moses	Deut 22:1-12

of MESSIANIC FIGURE

Jesus	Jn 5:1-18

REVELATION on

Nathan	1 Chr 17:1-27

SCRIPTURES on

David	Mt 12:1-8; Mk 2:23-28

TRADITION of

Jeremiah	*2 Mc 2:1-8

through BELIEF
of FOLLOWERs

Holy Spirit	2 Thes 2:13-15

unBELIEF in
of DEITY

Moses	Num 20:2-13

of BROTHERHOOD
REVELATION on

Peter	Acts 10:1-11:18

of COMMITMENT
INSTRUCTION on

Paul	2 Cor 6:14-7:1

REVELATION on

Moses	Num 6:1-21

to WORSHIP

Israelites	Neh 10:39b

in COMMUNITY

Levites	Josh 13:8-14

INSTRUCTION on

Attharates	*1 Esd 9:49-55

in WORSHIP

Levites	Ezra 8:15-20

CONFRONTATION with
PROPHECY of

Saul	1 Sam 19:18-24

in COVENANT
with AUTHORITY

Jonathan	*1 Mc 10:15-44

ETERNAL

Aaron	*Sir 45:6-22

of LAW

Moses	Ex 34:12-28

of PROVIDENCE

Aaron	Num 18:8-20

in RITE

Disciples	Mt 26:17-30
Jesus	Mk 14:22-26
Moses	Ex 34:12-28

SIGNS of

Israelites	Ex 31:12-17
Ezekiel	Ezek 20:9-26

CREATION of
TRADITION of

Esther	Esth 9:29-32
God	Gen 2:1-4a; Ex 20:1-17
Israelites	Esth 9:16-19
Mordecai	Esth 9:20-28

for WORSHIP

Israelites	Ezra 3:1-3a; 7-9; 10-11; 5:1-2; Hag 1:12-14
Levites	2 Chr 34:1-35:27

CREATION of sanctuary

Israelites	Ex 35:4-29; 36:8-19; 20-34; 35-38; 37:1-9; 10-16; 17-24; 25-28; 29;

CREATION of sanctuary (cont'd)	
Israelites	38:1-7;
	8;
	9-20;
	39:1;
	2-7;
	8-21;
	22-26;
	27-31
Moses	Ex 25:10-22;
	23-30;
	31-40;
	26:1-14;
	15-30;
	31-37;
	27:1-8;
	9-19;
	20-21;
	28:1-5;
	6-12;
	13-30;
	31-35;
	36-39;
	40-43;
	30:1-10;
	17-21;
	Lev 24:1-4
INSTRUCTION on	
Cyrus	2 Chr 36:1-23;
	Ezra 1:2-4
Darius	Ezra 6:1-12
David	1 Chr 22:2-19;
	28:1-29:30
Hezekiah	2 Chr 29:1-36
Jesus	Mt 16:13-20
Joash	2 Kgs 12:4-16
Moses	Ex 35:4-29
Paul	1 Cor 3:10-17;
	1 Tim 4:1-5
Solomon	2 Chr 2:1-4:22
Tattenai	Ezra 5:6-17
PROPHECY of	
Haggai	Ezra 5:1-2;
	Hag 1:1-11
Jeremiah	Jer 31:38-40
Zechariah	Ezra 5:1-2
REVELATION on	
Ezekiel	Ezek 45:1-9
Moses	Ex 25:1-9;
	40:1-33
Zechariah	Zech 6:9-15
of DEITY	
AUTHORITY of	
Jesus	Lk 22:66-71;
	Jn 10:19-40
unBELIEF in	
Moses	Num 20:2-13
PRESENCE of	
David	1 Sam 16:1-13;
	Ps 27:4-6;
	63:1-8
God	Num 5:1-4;
	16:36-50;
	Ps 11:4-7;
	Ezek 44:4-5;
	Hab 2:18-20;
	Hag 1:1-11
Israelites	Ex 40:34-38;
	Deut 5:22-33;

PRESENCE of (cont'd)	
Israelites	Ezek 43:6-12
Joshua	Josh 5:13-15
Moses	Ex 24:1-18;
	34:29-35;
	2 Cor 3:7-11
Psalmist	Ps 84:1-2
Solomon	2 Chr 5:1-7:10
PROMISE concerning	
David	Ps 132:1-5
PROVIDENCE through	
Israelites	Ezra 5:3-5
RESPECT for	
Israelites	Is 29:17-24
in **RITE**	
Nineveh	Jon 3:1-10
SIGNS of	
Moses	Ex 31:18;
	32:15-24
in **STEWARDSHIP**	
Aaron	Ex 29:42b-46
DESIRE for	
INSTRUCTION on	
God	Is 51:1-16
DESIRE for sanctuary	
through **FALSE BELIEF**	
Zerubbabel	Ezra 4:1-2
of **ELECTION**	
Moses	Num 16:3-11
by **DEITY**	
Aaron	Num 17:1-13
Israelites	1 Sam 12:1-25
Jews	Rom 2:25-3:20
Levites	Deut 10:1-11
Solomon	1 Chr 22:2-19
over **FALSE BELIEF**	
Moses	Lev 20:1-27
of **FOLLOWERs**	
Paul	Rom 1:1-7
INSTRUCTION on	
Believers	1 Pet 2:4-10
Moses	Deut 7:6-16;
	14:1-2;
	26:16-19;
	28:1-14
of **MESSIANIC FIGURE**	
Jesus	Jn 7:25-31
PROPHECY of	
Israelites	Zech 2:6-13
REVELATION on	
Jesus	Mk 9:2-8
John	Rev 7:1-8
Manoah	Judg 13:2-7
Moses	Num 3:11-13
TRADITION of	
Levites	Num 3:11-13
for **WORSHIP**	
Aaron	Ex 28:40-43
in **ENVIRONMENT**	
of **AUTHORITY**	
Menelaus	*2 Mc 4:23-29
Simon	*1 Mc 14:25-49
CREATION of sanctuary	
Israelites	Ex 35:4-29
LAW concerning	
Levites	Deut 18:1-8

PRESENCE of	
God	Ps 68:15-18
Raphael	*Tb 5:1-21
SYMBOLS of	
Antiochus	*1 Mc 1:16-24
David	2 Sam 6:1-23
Hiram	1 Kgs 7:15-22;
	23-26;
	27-39;
	40-47
Israelites	1 Sam 4:1b-22
Solomon	1 Kgs 7:48-51
SIN against	
Israelites	Josh 7:1-5
Jason	*2 Mc 4:7-17
in **EQUALITY**	
with **DEITY**	
Jesus	Jn 5:1-18
for **ETERNITY**	
in **COVENANT**	
Aaron	*Sir 45:6-22
of **DEITY**	
God	Ps 93:5
TRADITION of	
Israelites	Ex 27:20-21
Moses	Lev 23:26-32;
	33-44;
	24:1-4
in **WORSHIP**	
Jeremiah	Jer 17:12
FALSE BELIEF concerning	
of **ELECTION**	
Moses	Lev 20:1-27
in **RITE**	
Moses	Deut 12:1-31
through **FALSE BELIEF**	
DESIRE for	
Zerubbabel	Ezra 4:1-2
FIDELITY in	
of **FOLLOWER**s	
Holy Spirit	1 Pet 1:1-2
INSTRUCTION on	
Jesus	Lk 14:34-35
in **WORSHIP**	
Josiah	2 Kgs 23:21-23
Simon	*Sir 50:1-21
of **FOLLOWER**s	
BELIEF of	
Holy Spirit	2 Thes 2:13-15
ELECTION of	
Paul	Rom 1:1-7
FIDELITY in	
Holy Spirit	1 Pet 1:1-2
of **FREEDOM**	
PROPHECY of	
Jeremiah	2 Chr 36:1-23
GIFT for sanctuary	
INSTRUCTION on	
Moses	Ex 35:30-36:7

INSTRUCTION on	
Cyrus	*1 Esd 2:1-7
Moses	Deut 22:1-12
in **AUTHORITY**	
Esther	Esth 9:29-32
Jesus	Jn 7:15-24
of **COMMITMENT**	
Paul	2 Cor 6:14-7:1
of **COMMUNITY**	
Attharates	*1 Esd 9:49-55
of **ELECTION**	
Believers	1 Pet 2:4-10
Moses	Deut 7:6-16;
	14:1-2;
	26:16-19;
	28:1-14
of **FIDELITY**	
Jesus	Lk 14:34-35
of **LAW**	
Artaxerxes	Ezra 7:20-24
Ezra	Ezra 7:6-10;
	Neh 7:33b-8:2;
	3-8;
	13-18;
	*1 Esd 8:1-7;
	8-24;
	Ex 34:12-28
Jesus	Lk 13:10-17;
	16:16-18
Joshua	Josh 8:30-35
Moses	Ex 16:22-30;
	34:29-35;
	35:1-3;
	Deut 16:13-15;
	31:24-29
Paul	Rom 7:7-13
of **PRAYER**	
Paul	1 Thes 5:23-24
as **QUALITY OF LIFE**	
God	Lev 11:1-47
Jesus	Lk 11:37-44
Paul	Rom 2:25-3:20;
	12:1-2;
	Col 3:1-4
in **RECONCILIATION**	
Nehemiah	Neh 13:15-22
Paul	1 Cor 7:8-16
revealing **RESPECT**	
Jesus	Mt 23:16-22
of **RESURRECTION**	
Paul	Col 3:1-4
concerning **RITE**	
Esther	Esth 4:1-17
God	Ex 12:15-20;
	20:1-17
Hezekiah	2 Chr 30:1-31:2]
Holy Spirit	Acts 13:1-3
Jesus	Mt 26:17-30;
	Lk 22:14-23
Jews	*2 Mc 1:1-9
Joel	Joel 2:12-17
Joshua	Josh 3:1-13
Josiah	2 Kgs 23:21-23;
	2 Chr 34:1-35:2]
Moses	Ex 12:21-28;
	13:3-10;
	11-16;

of **DEITY** (cont'd)
  God
    Hab 2:18-20;
    Hag 1:1-11
  Israelites
    Ex 40:34-38;
    Deut 5:22-33;
    Ezek 43:6-12
  Joshua   Josh 5:13-15
  Moses   Ex 24:1-18;
    34:29-35;
    2 Cor 3:7-11
  Psalmist   Ps 84:1-2
  Solomon   2 Chr 5:1-7:10
in **ENVIRONMENT**
  God   Ps 68:15-18
  Raphael   *Tb 5:1-21
PROPHECY of
  Jeremiah   *2 Mc 2:1-8
REVELATION on
  Gideon   Judg 6:11-32
  Israelites   1 Kgs 8:1-13;
    Ezek 48:30-35
  Jacob   Gen 28:10-22;
    32:1-23
  Moses   Ex 3:1-6;
    19:9-15;
    16-25;
    34:1-5a;
    5b-9;
    Acts 6:8-8:3
  Raphael   *Tb 12:1-22
  Solomon   1 Kgs 9:1-9;
    2 Chr 7:11-22
in **WORSHIP**
  Moses   Ex 33:7-11
  Psalmist   Ps 132:6-10

PROMISE of sanctuary
  for **DEITY**
    David   Ps 132:1-5
  REVELATION on
    Moses   Ex 33:12-23
  of **WORSHIP**
    Israelites   Neh 10:31

PROPHECY of
  CONFRONTATION with
    Saul   1 Sam 19:18-24
  of **ELECTION**
    Israelites   Zech 2:6-13
  of **FREEDOM**
    Jeremiah   2 Chr 36:1-23
  in **PRESENCE**
    Jeremiah   *2 Mc 2:1-8
  of **PROVIDENCE**
    Cyrus   2 Chr 26:1-23
  of **RITE**
    Zechariah   Zech 14:1-21
    Zephaniah   Zeph 1:7

in **PROVIDENCE**
  through **COVENANT**
    Aaron   Num 18:8-20
  of **DEITY**
    Israelites   Ezra 5:3-5
  PROPHECY of
    Cyrus   2 Chr 36:1-23
  TRADITION of
    Aaron   Ex 16:31-36

as **QUALITY OF LIFE**

of **FOLLOWERs**
  Holy Spirit   1 Cor 3:10-17;
    6:12-20
INSTRUCTION on
  God   Lev 11:1-47
  Jesus   Lk 11:37-44
  Paul   Rom 2:25-3:20;
    12:1-2;
    Col 3:1-4
REVELATION on
  Israelites   Lev 19:1-37
SCRIPTURES on
  Peter   1 Pet 1:13-2:3

in **RECONCILIATION**
  of **FOLLOWERs**
    Jesus   1 Cor 1:26-31;
    6:9-11;
    Eph 5:21-33
  INSTRUCTION on
    Nehemiah   Neh 13:15-22
    Paul   1 Cor 7:8-16
  REVELATION on
    Moses   Lev 16:11-28

RESPECT for
  of **DEITY**
    Israelites   Is 29:17-24
  INSTRUCTION on
    Jesus   Mt 23:16-22

of **RESURRECTION**
  INSTRUCTION on
    Paul   Col 3:1-4

REVELATION on
  in **AUTHORITY**
    Levites   Num 1:47-54
  of **BEHAVIOR**
    Nathan   1 Chr 17:1-27
  of **BROTHERHOOD**
    Peter   Acts 10:1-11:18
  of **COMMITMENT**
    Moses   Num 6:1-21
  of **ELECTION**
    Jesus   Mk 9:2-8
    John   Rev 7:1-8
    Manoah   Judg 13:2-7
    Moses   Num 3:11-13
  of **LAW**
    Ezekiel   Ezek 44:4-5
    Israelites   Ezek 48:8-22
    Moses   Lev 20:1-27;
    21:1-22:33;
    23:1-4;
    5-8;
    15-22;
    23-25;
    26-32;
    33-44;
    24:5-9;
    25:1-7;
    20-22;
    26:1-46;
    27:1-34;
    Num 6:1-21
    Prince   Ezek 44:1-3;
    46:1-8
  of **NEW AGE**
    John   Rev 21:22-27

SACREDNESS (cont'd)

COMMITMENT to (cont'd)

Israelites	Neh 10:39b

of **COMMUNITY**

Levites	Ezra 8:15-20

SYMBOLS of

Israelites	Ex 25:10-22; 23-30; 31-40; 26:1-14; 15-30; 31-37; 27:1-8; 9-19; 28:1-5; 6-12; 13-30; 31-35; 36-39; 40-43; 30:1-10; 11-16; 33:7-11; 1 Kgs 8:1-13; *1 Esd 6:1-2
Moses	Ex 30:34-38
Solomon	1 Kgs 5:1-18; 6:1-38

SIN against

Jeroboam	1 Kgs 13:1-34

in **STEWARDSHIP**

Israelites	Ex 25:1-9; 27:20-21; 29:10-18; 30:17-21; Neh 10:35-36

WORSHIP through
FIDELITY in

Josiah	2 Kgs 23:21-23
Simon	*Sir 50:1-21

SACRIFICE

BEHAVIOR revealing
of **FOLLOWER**

Paul	1 Cor 9:1-6

in **MISSION**

Paul	2 Cor 11:7-15

in **WORSHIP**

Jacob	Gen 31:44-55

for **BROTHERHOOD**
INSTRUCTION on

Jesus	Jn 15:12-17
John	1 Jn 3:11-18

in **COMMITMENT**
to **DEITY**

Jephthah	Judg 11:29-33
Jonah	Jon 1:1-17

INSTRUCTION on

Jesus	Mt 13:44-46
Paul	Rom 13:11-14; 1 Cor 9:24-27

to **MISSION**

Paul	1 Cor 9:15-23

PROPHECY of

Jesus	Mt 16:21-28; Mk 8:34-9:1;

SACRIFICE (cont'd)

PROPHECY of (cont'd)

Jesus	Lk 9:23-27

through **WORSHIP**

Hannah	1 Sam 1:1-28
Israelites	Neh 10:32-33; 35-36

to **COMMUNITY**
by **FOLLOWERs**

Believers	Acts 4:32-5:10

COMPULSION of
PROPHECY of

Caiaphas	Jn 11:1-57

SELF-REALIZATION of

Jesus	Mt 26:36-46; Mk 14:32-42; Lk 22:39-46

CONFRONTATION with
of **MESSIANIC FIGURE**

Disciples	Mt 9:14-15; Mk 2:18-22; Lk 5:33-35
Pharisees	Mk 2:18-22; Lk 5:33-35

in **COVENANT**
of **MEDIATION**

Aaron	Lev 24:5-9

of **RECONCILIATION**

Jesus	Mt 26:17-30; Mk 14:22-26

SIGNS of

Moses	Ex 12:1-14

to **DEITY**
COMMITMENT to

Jephthah	Judg 11:29-33
Jonah	Jon 1:1-17

MEDIATION in

Aaron	Ex 30:1-10
High Priest	Heb 5:1-10

PRAYER concerning

Jesus	Jn 12:27-36a

PROMISE of

Jonah	Jon 2:1-10

PROVIDENCE through

Abraham	Gen 22:1-19

RECONCILIATION through

High Priest	Heb 5:1-10

RESPECT for

David	Ps 20:1-5

as **RITE**

David	Ps 27:4-6; 40:6-10; 51:18-19
God	Ps 51:13-17
Israelites	Amos 5:21-25
Nineveh	Jon 3:1-10

SECURITY through

Lot	Gen 19:4-11

as **SIN**

God	Prov 15:1-33

through **STEWARDSHIP**

David	Ps 54:6-7

DESIRE for
REVELATION on

Moses	Ex 25:1-9

in WORSHIP (cont'd)
　　Egyptians　　　　Is 19:18-25

LAW concerning
　　Moses　　　　Ex 22:21-31;
　　　　　　　　29:36b-42a;
　　　　　　　　Lev 7:1-10;
　　　　　　　　19:1-37;
　　　　　　　　Num 28:3-8;
　　　　　　　　9-10;
　　　　　　　　11-15;
　　　　　　　　16-25;
　　　　　　　　26-31;
　　　　　　　　29:1-6
　　INSTRUCTION on
　　Moses　　　　Deut 16:1-8;
　　　　　　　　26:1-11;
　　　　　　　　12-15
　　REVELATION on
　　Moses　　　　Ex 20:24-26;
　　　　　　　　Lev 1:1-17;
　　　　　　　　2:1-16;
　　　　　　　　3:1-17;
　　　　　　　　4:1-35;
　　　　　　　　6:8-13;
　　　　　　　　14-23;
　　　　　　　　24-30;
　　　　　　　　7:11-21;
　　　　　　　　28-36;
　　　　　　　　37-38;
　　　　　　　　21:1-22:33;
　　　　　　　　Num 15:22-31;
　　　　　　　　19:1-10;
　　　　　　　　29:7-11;
　　　　　　　　12-40
　　Priests　　　　Ezek 46:19-24
　　Prince　　　　Ezek 46:11-15
　　in WORSHIP
　　High Priest　　Heb 9:1-14

in MEDIATION
　　COVENANT of
　　Aaron　　　　Lev 24:5-9
　　to DEITY
　　Aaron　　　　Ex 30:1-10
　　High Priest　　Heb 5:1-10
　　of MESSIANIC FIGURE
　　Jesus　　　　1 Tim 2:1-7
　　in WORSHIP
　　Priest　　　　Lev 1:1-17;
　　　　　　　　2:1-16;
　　　　　　　　3:1-17;
　　　　　　　　4:1-35;
　　　　　　　　5:5-13;
　　　　　　　　14-6:7;
　　　　　　　　15:1-33

of MESSIANIC FIGURE
　　CONFRONTATION with
　　Disciples　　　Mt 9:14-15;
　　　　　　　　Mk 2:18-22;
　　　　　　　　Lk 5:33-35
　　Pharisees　　　Mk 2:18-22;
　　　　　　　　Lk 5:33-35
　　MEDIATION through
　　Jesus　　　　1 Tim 2:1-7
　　for NEW AGE
　　Jesus　　　　Heb 8:1-5
　　PROVIDENCE through
　　Jesus　　　　Mt 27:45-56

RECONCILIATION through
　　Israelites　　　Mal 2:17-3:5
　　Jesus　　　　Heb 9:23-28
　　SALVATION through
　　Jesus　　　　Heb 9:1-14
　　for SIN
　　Jesus　　　　Gal 1:1-5
　　VIRTUE in
　　Jesus　　　　Heb 9:1-14

in MISSION
　　BEHAVIOR revealing
　　Paul　　　　2 Cor 11:7-15
　　COMMITMENT to
　　Paul　　　　1 Cor 9:15-23
　　FIDELITY in
　　Jesus　　　　Jn 10:1-18
　　Paul　　　　Acts 21:1-14;
　　　　　　　　2 Cor 6:3-10;
　　　　　　　　Gal 6:11-18
　　of RECONCILIATION
　　Jesus　　　　Mt 20:20-28;
　　　　　　　　Mk 10:35-45
　　STEWARDSHIP of
　　Believers　　　Lk 10:1-16

as MOTIVATION
　　through FALSE BELIEF
　　Paul　　　　Col 2:16-23
　　INSTRUCTION on
　　God　　　　Is 1:10-17
　　Zechariah　　Zech 7:4-8:23

in NEW AGE
　　INSTRUCTION on
　　Jesus　　　　Mt 9:14-15;
　　　　　　　　13:44-46;
　　　　　　　　Mk 2:18-22;
　　　　　　　　Lk 5:33-35;
　　　　　　　　Heb 10:1-18
　　by MESSIANIC FIGURE
　　Jesus　　　　Heb 8:1-5

PRAYER concerning
　　to DEITY
　　Jesus　　　　Jn 12:27-36a

PROMISE to
　　to DEITY
　　Jonah　　　　Jon 2:1-10
　　in WORSHIP
　　Psalmist　　　Ps 66:13-20

PROPHECY of
　　in COMMITMENT
　　Jesus　　　　Mt 16:21-28;
　　　　　　　　Mk 8:34-9:1; ·
　　　　　　　　Lk 9:23-27
　　as PUNISHMENT
　　Isaiah　　　　Is 34:1-17
　　Israelites　　　Ezek 16:35-43
　　in RITE
　　Zechariah　　Zech 14:1-21
　　in SALVATION
　　Jesus　　　　Jn 6:25-59
　　for SIN
　　Isaiah　　　　Is 52:13-53:12

PROVIDENCE in
　　to DEITY
　　Abraham　　　Gen 22:1-19

of **MESSIANIC FIGURE**
Jesus   Mt 27:45-56

as **PUNISHMENT**
PROPHECY of
Isaiah   Is 34:1-17
Israelites   Ezek 16:35-43
SELF-REALIZATION of
Jonah   Jon 1:1-17

as **QUALITY OF LIFE**
Paul   1 Cor 15:29-34
INSTRUCTION on
Paul   Rom 12:1-2
Peter   1 Pet 2:4-10

RECONCILIATION through
Moses   Ex 29:19-36a;
30:11-16;
Lev 12:1-8;
16:6-10;
Num 28:26-31;
29:1-6
    COVENANT of
Jesus   Mt 26:17-30;
Mk 14:22-26
    to **DEITY**
High Priest   Heb 5:1-10
    in **ENVIRONMENT**
Jacob   Gen 32:1-23
    INSTRUCTION on
Jesus   Heb 10:1-18
Moses   Lev 9:1-24
    of **MESSIANIC FIGURE**
Israelites   Mal 2:17-3:5
Jesus   Heb 9:23-28
    MISSION of
Jesus   Mt 20:20-28;
Mk 10:35-45
    REVELATION on
Moses   Ex 34:12-28;
Lev 23:26-32;
Num 3:40-51
    TRADITION of
Aaron   Ex 30:1-10
Priest   Lev 4:1-35;
7:1-10
in **WORSHIP**
Aaron   Lev 16:1-5;
1 Chr 6:49-53
Moses   Lev 8:1-36
Noah   Gen 8:13-22
Priest   Lev 15:1-33;
Num 15:22-31

RESPECT through
to **DEITY**
David   Ps 20:1-5

REVELATION on
as **RITE**
Aaron   Num 18:8-20
Ezekiel   Ezek 40:38-43
Israelites   Ezek 45:18-25;
Zech 7:4-8:23
Moses   Lev 3:1-17;
17:1-9;
23:15-22;
33-44;
Num 15:1-16;

as **RITE** (cont'd)
Moses   17-21;
28:1-2;
3-8;
9-10;
29:7-11;
12-40
Priest   Ezek 46:1-8
Prince   Ezek 45:13-17
for **SIN**
Ezekiel   Ezek 43:18-27
Israelites   Ezek 20:30-31;
45:18-25
Moses   Lev 5:5-13;
14-6:7;
16:6-10;
11-28;
Num 28:11-15;
29:7-11;
12-40
Priests   Ezek 44:15-31
Prince   Ezek 45:13-17
Samuel   1 Sam 3:1-4:1a
in **STEWARDSHIP**
Israelites   Ezek 46:11-15
Moses   Num 18:25-32

in **RITE**
Adonijah   1 Kgs 1:5-10
Moses   Ex 23:14-19;
29:10-18;
Lev 7:11-21;
14:1-32;
33-54;
23:9-14;
24:5-9;
Num 28:11-15
Nazirite   Num 6:1-21
to **DEITY**
David   Ps 27:4-6;
40:6-10;
51:18-19
God   Ps 51:13-17
Israelites   Amos 5:21-25
Nineveh   Jon 3:1-10
in **ENVIRONMENT**
Jesus   Mk 14:12-16;
Lk 22:7-13
FALSE BELIEF concerning
Israelites   Ezek 23:36-49
INSTRUCTION on
Abraham   Gen 22:1-19
Ahaz   2 Kgs 16:10-20
Artaxerxes   Ezra 7:15-19
David   Ps 4:2-5
God   Ex 34:12-28;
Job 42:7-9;
Ps 50:7-15
Israelites   *Bar 1:5-14
Moses   Ex 5:1-5;
10:24-26;
12:21-28;
Lev 10:1-20;
Num 16:16-24;
Deut 12:1-31;
15:19-23;
16:1-8;
9-12;
16-17;
21-17:7;

INSTRUCTION on (cont'd)

Moses	27:1-10
Preacher	Eccl 5:1-7
Psalmist	Ps 107:17-22

PROPHECY of

Zechariah	Zech 14:1-21

REVELATION on

Aaron	Num 18:8-20
Ezekiel	Ezek 40:38-43
Israelites	Ezek 45:18-25;
	Zech 7:4-8:23
Moses	Lev 3:1-17;
	17:1-9;
	23:15-22;
	33-44;
	Num 15:1-16;
	17-21;
	28:1-2;
	3-8;
	9-10;
	29:7-11;
	12-40
Priest	Ezek 46:1-8
Prince	Ezek 45:13-17

TRADITION of

Israelites	Ex 12:21-28;
	29:36b-42a;
	1 Sam 2:11-26;
	Neh 10:34
Josiah	*1 Esd 1:1-22

in **WORSHIP**

Abel	Gen 4:1-16
Asa	2 Chr 14:1-16:14
Babylonians	2 Kgs 17:24-41
Balaam	Num 22:41-23:12;
	27-24:13
Balak	Num 22:36-40
David	2 Sam 6:1-23;
	24:1-25;
	1 Chr 15:1-16:43;
	21:1-22:1;
	Ps 5:1-3
Gideon	Judg 6:11-32
Hannah	1 Sam 1:1-28
Hezekiah	2 Chr 30:1-31:21
Israelites	Num 7:1-89;
	Judg 2:1-5;
	20:24-28;
	21:1-7;
	1 Sam 6:1-7:1;
	11:1-15;
	Ezra 3:1-3a;
	3b-6;
	Neh 12:43;
	*1 Esd 5:47-55;
	7:1-9;
	10-15;
	*Jdt 16:18-20
Jethro	Ex 18:1-12
Jews	*2 Mc 1:18-36
Joash	2 Chr 24:1-27
Joshua	Josh 8:30-35
Josiah	2 Chr 34:1-35:27
Maccabeus	*1 Mc 4:36-61
Manoah	Judg 13:15-23
Moabites	2 Kgs 3:1-27
Moses	Ex 24:1-18;
	40:1-33;
	Num 28:1-2
Noah	Gen 8:13-22

in **WORSHIP** (cont'd)

Psalmist	Ps 96:7-9;
	116:12-19
Samuel	1 Sam 7:2-17;
	16:1-13
Solomon	1 Kgs 3:1-15;
	8:1-13;
	62-66;
	9:25;
	2 Chr 1:1-17;
	2:1-4:22;
	5:1-7:10;
	8:1-18

SALVATION through

by **FOLLOWER**

Jesus	1 Pet 1:13-2:3

INSTRUCTION on

God	Ps 50:22-23
Jesus	Jn 12:20-26

of **MESSIANIC FIGURE**

Jesus	Heb 9:1-14

PROPHECY of

Jesus	Jn 6:25-59

SECURITY through

to **DEITY**

Lot	Gen 19:4-11

in **ENVIRONMENT**

Reuben	Gen 42:26-38

as **PUNISHMENT**

Jonah	Jon 1:1-17

SIGNS of

in **COVENANT**

Moses	Ex 12:1-14

INSTRUCTION on

Jesus	Mt 9:14-15;
	Mk 2:18-22;
	Lk 5:33-35

REVELATION on

Daniel	Dan 8:9-12
John	Rev 12:10-12
Moses	Lev 24:5-9

TRADITION of

Israelites	Ex 13:3-10

in **WORSHIP**

Israelites	*1 Esd 5:56-58
Jeroboam	1 Kgs 12:25-33

as **SIN**

against **DEITY**

God	Prov 15:1-33

for **SIN**

Israelites	Ps 106:34-39;
	Amos 4:4-5
Job	Job 1:4-5
Moses	Lev 6:24-30;
	16:1-5;
	Num 28:16-25;
	29:1-6

FALSE BELIEF concerning

Israelites	2 Kgs 17:7-23
Judahites	Jer 7:29-8:3
Priests	Mal 1:6-2:9

INSTRUCTION on

Israelites	*Bar 1:5-14
Jesus	Mt 18:7-9;
	Mk 9:42-48

INSTRUCTION on (cont'd)
Sirach   *Sir 34:18-22
by MESSIANIC FIGURE
Jesus   Gal 1:1-5
PROPHECY of
Isaiah   Is 52:13-53;12
REVELATION on
Ezekiel   Ezek 43:18-27
Israelites   Ezek 20:20-31;
                      45:18-25
Moses   Lev 5:5-13;
                      14-6:7;
                      16:6-10;
                      11-28;
                      Num 28:11-15;
                      29:7-11;
                      12-40
Priests   Ezek 44:15-31
Prince   Ezek 45:13-17
Samuel   1 Sam 3:1-4:1a
TRADITION of
Eli   1 Sam 2:11-26
Israelites   Lev 4:1-35
Ruler   Lev 4:1-35
in WORSHIP
Aaron   Lev 9:1-24
Ahaz   2 Kgs 16:1-4;
                      2 Chr 26:1-28:27
Author   Heb 10:1-18
Heliodorus   *2 Mc 3:1-40
High Priest   Heb 5:1-10
Israelites   Ezra 6:13-18;
                      8:31-36
Levites   2 Chr 29:1-36
Maccabeus   *2 Mc 12:38-45
Manasseh   2 Kgs 21:1-18;
                      2 Chr 33:1-25
Priest   Lev 15:1-33
Priests   Ezra 10:16-19
Saul   1 Sam 13:1-23
in STEWARDSHIP
Moses   Ex 22:21-31;
                      23:14-19;
                      Num 31:25-54
to DEITY
David   Ps 54:6-7
by FOLLOWERs
Believers   Acts 2:42-47
Macedonians   2 Cor 8:1-6
INSTRUCTION on
God   Ex 20:24-26
Jesus   Mt 20:20-28;
                      Mk 10:35-45;
                      12:41-44;
                      Lk 9:57-62;
                      12:32-34;
                      21:1-4
John the Baptist   Lk 3:10-14
Moses   Deut 16:16-17;
                      18:1-8;
                      26:1-11
Paul   Rom 12:1-2;
                      1 Cor 16:1-4;
                      2 Cor 9:6-11
Solomon   Prov 3:1-35
in MISSION
Believers   Lk 10:1-16
REVELATION on
Israelites   Ezek 46:11-15

REVELATION on
Moses   Num 18:25-32
in WORSHIP
Israelites   Ex 30:11-16;
                      1 Chr 23:1-26:32;
                      Neh 10:37a;
                      37b-39a

TRADITION of
in RITE
Israelites   Ex 12:21-28;
                      29:36b-42a;
                      1 Sam 2:11-26;
                      Neh 10:34
Josiah   *1 Esd 1:1-22
for SIN
Eli   1 Sam 2:11-26
Israelites   Lev 4:1-35
Ruler   Lev 4:1-35

VIRTUE in
of MESSIANIC FIGURE
Jesus   Heb 9:1-14
in WORSHIP
Sirach   *Sir 35:1-11

in WORSHIP
BEHAVIOR revealing
Jacob   Gen 31:44-55
COMMITMENT to
Hannah   1 Sam 1:1-28
Israelites   Neh 10:32-33
FIDELITY in
Widow   Lk 21:1-4
Widows   Mk 12:41-44
KNOWLEDGE of
Bethelites   Zech 7:1-3
Egyptians   Is 19:18-25
LAW concerning
High Priest   Heb 9:1-14
MEDIATION through
Priest   Lev 1:1-17;
                      2:1-16;
                      3:1-17;
                      4:1-35;
                      5:5-13;
                      14-6:7;
                      15:1-33
PROMISE of
Psalmist   Ps 6:13-20
RECONCILIATION through
Aaron   Lev 16:1-5;
                      1 Chr 6:49-53
Moses   Lev 8:1-36
Noah   Gen 8:13-22
Priest   Lev 15:1-33;
                      Num 15:22-31
Abel   Gen 4:1-16
Asa   2 Chr 14:1-16:14
Babylonians   2 Kgs 17:24-41
Balaam   Num 22:41-23:12;
                      27-24:13
Balak   Num 22:36-40
David   2 Sam 6:1-23;
                      24:1-25;
                      1 Chr 15:1-16:43;
                      21:1-22:1;
                      Ps 5:1-3
Gideon   Judg 6:11-32
Hannah   1 Sam 1:1-28

RECONCILIATION through (cont'd)

Hezekiah	2 Chr 30:1-31:21
Israelites	Num 7:1-89;
	Judg 2:1-5;
	20:24-28;
	21:1-7;
	1 Sam 6:1-7:1;
	11:1-15;
	Ezra 3:1-3a;
	3b-6;
	Neh 12:43;
	*1 Esd 5:47-55;
	7:1-9;
	10-15;
	*Jdt 16:18-20
Jethro	Ex 18:1-12
Jews	*2 Mc 1:18-36
Joash	2 Chr 24:1-27
Joshua	Josh 8:30-35
Josiah	2 Chr 34:1-35:27
Maccabeus	*1 Mc 4:36-61
Manoah	Judg 13:15-23
Moabite	2 Kgs 3:1-27
Moses	Ex 24:1-18;
	40:1-33;
	Num 28:1-2
Noah	Gen 8:13-22
Psalmist	Ps 96:7-9;
	116:12-19
Samuel	1 Sam 7:2-17;
	16:1-13
Solomon	1 Kgs 3:1-15;
	8:1-13;
	62-66;
	9:25;
	2 Chr 1:1-17;
	2:1-4:22;
	5:1-7:10;
	8:1-18

SIGNS of

Israelites	*1 Esd 5:56-58
Jeroboam	1 Kgs 12:25-33
Aaron	Lev 9:1-24
Ahaz	2 Kgs 16:1-4;
	2 Chr 26:1-28:27
Author	Heb 10:1-18
Heliodorus	*2 Mc 3:1-40
High Priest	Heb 5:1-10
Israelites	Ezra 6:13-18;
	8:31-36
Levites	2 Chr 29:1-36
Maccabeus	*2 Mc 12:38-45
Manasseh	2 Kgs 21:1-18;
	2 Chr 33:1-25
Priest	Lev 15:1-33
Priests	Ezra 10:16-19
Saul	1 Sam 13:1-23

through STEWARDSHIP

Israelites	Ex 30:11-16;
	1 Chr 23:1-26:32;
	Neh 10:37a;
	37b-39a

VIRTUE in

Sirach	*Sir 35:1-11

SADNESS

BEHAVIOR revealing

Nehemiah	Neh 1:11b-2:8

in ENVIRONMENT

Jacob	Gen 42:26-38

of FOLLOWERs

Disciples	Jn 16:5-11

INSTRUCTION on

Preacher	Eccl 7:1-22

of MESSIANIC FIGURE

Jesus	Jn 11:1-57

PROPHECY of

Judahites	Jer 9:10-22

SELF-REALIZATION of

Jesus	Mt 26:36-46;
	Mk 14:32-42

CONFRONTATION with
REVELATION on

John	Rev 1:4-20

in ENVIRONMENT
BEHAVIOR revealing

Jacob	Gen 42:26-38

through inFIDELITY
SELF-REALIZATION of

Peter	Mt 26:69-75;
	Mk 14:66-72;
	Lk 22:54b-62

of FOLLOWER
BEHAVIOR revealing

Disciples	Jn 16:5-11

concerning PUNISHMENT

Jesus	Lk 23:27-32

INSTRUCTION on

Preacher	Eccl 7:1-22

in KNOWLEDGE

Preacher	Eccl 1:12-2:26

as JUDGMENT
REVELATION on

John	Rev 18:4-20

concerning KNOWLEDGE
INSTRUCTION on

Preacher	Eccl 1:12-2:26

MEDITATION on
as PUNISHMENT

Jeremiah	Lam 1:1-22;
	3:1-66

of MESSIANIC FIGURE
BEHAVIOR revealing

Jesus	Jn 11:1-57

of PRAYER
in WORSHIP

Paul	Acts 20:17-38

of PRESENCE
PROPHECY of

Israelites	Amos 5:16-17

in PROMISE
through SELF-REALIZATION

Herod	Mt 14:1-12;
	Mk 6:17-29

PROPHECY of

Judahites	Jer 9:10-22

in PRESENCE	
Israelites	Amos 5:16-17
as PUNISHMENT	
Isaiah	Is 3:16-4:1
Judahites	Jer 25:8-14
Zechariah	Zech 11:1-3
as QUALITY OF LIFE	
Isaiah	Is 15:1-16:14
Joel	Joel 1:2-20
revealing RESPECT	
Isaiah	Is 52:13-53:12

as PUNISHMENT
of FOLLOWERs	
Jesus	Lk 23:27-32
MEDITATION on	
Jeremiah	Lam 1:1-22;
	3:1-66
PROPHECY of	
Isaiah	Is 3:16-4:1
Judahites	Jer 25:8-14
Zechariah	Zech 11:1-3
REVELATION on	
Israelites	Ezek 7:1-27;
	Amos 8:8-10

as QUALITY OF LIFE
Psalmist	Ps 137:1-3
PROPHECY of	
Isaiah	Is 15:1-16:14
Joel	Joel 1:2-20

revealing RESPECT
PROPHECY of	
Isaiah	Is 52:13-53:12

REVELATION on
CONFRONTATION with	
John	Rev 1:4-20
as JUDGMENT	
John	Rev 18:4-20
as PUNISHMENT	
Israelites	Ezek 7:1-27;
	Amos 8:8-10
for SIN	
Ezekiel	Ezek 8:14-15

SELF-REALIZATION of
through inFIDELITY	
Peter	Mt 26:69-75;
	Mk 14:66-72;
	Lk 22:54b-62

through SELF-REALIZATION
of PROMISE	
Herod	Mt 14:1-12;
	Mk 6:17-29

SIGNS of
REVELATION on	
Ezekiel	Ezek 9:1-11
John	Rev 8:13
in WORSHIP	
Israelites	Ezra 3:12-13

for SIN
Israelites	Deut 1:19-46
REVELATION on	
Ezekiel	Ezek 8:14-15

in WORSHIP	
in PRAYER	
Paul	Acts 20:17-38
SIGNS of	
Israelites	Ezra 3:12-13

SALVATION

ACCEPTANCE of
from DEITY	
God	Ps 118:22-27
INSTRUCTION on	
God	Is 46:1-13
Jesus	Jn 6:25-59
Paul	Rom 5:12-21;
	9:30-10:21;
	1 Cor 1:18-25
Peter	2 Pet 3:14-18a
through MESSIANIC FIGURE	
Jesus	Jn 10:1-18
PROPHECY of	
Jesus	Mt 24:37-41;
	Lk 23:39-43
Joel	Acts 2:14-36

from ANGER
INSTRUCTION on	
Zephaniah	Zeph 2:3

through BLESSING
by DEITY	
David	Ps 28:8-9;
	68:19-23
God	Ps 103:1-5
Psalmist	Ps 80:14-19

from CAPTIVITY
Israelites	Ex 15:1-18
by DEITY	
God	Ps 136:10-22
Israelites	Ex 12:37-42;
	50-51;
	Ex 13:3-10;
	11-16;
	16:1-21;
	18:1-12;
	19:1-8;
	Deut 5:1-21;
	6:4-19;
	Ps 105:27-42;
	43-45;
	135:8-12;
	Acts 13:14-52
REVELATION on	
Israelites	Ex 3:7-10;
	7:1-7;
	11:1-10;
	Ezek 20:5-8;
	Zech 10:3-12
Moses	Ex 6:2-9
TRADITION of	
Israelites	Deut 6:20-25

through COMPASSION
Moses	Ex 2:1-10
of DEITY	
Psalmist	Ps 85:4-7
PROPHECY of	
Isaiah	Is 40:1-11

from **DISOBEDIENCE**
  of **FOLLOWERs**
    Gentiles   Rom 11:7-24
  INSTRUCTION on
    Paul   Rom 11:25-32

DOUBT of
  by **DEITY**
    Israelites   Ex 14:1-14;
                  Ps 78:21-31
    Moses   Ex 5:22-6:1
  SELF-REALIZATION of
    Moses   Ex 3:11-22

from **ENEMY**
  by **DEITY**
    Baruch   *Bar 4:21-37
    David   2 Sam 3:17-39;
                  1 Chr 15:1-16:43;
                  3:7-8;
                  55:15-19;
                  69:13-21;
                  86:14-17;
                  109:21-31;
                  124:1-5;
                  144:5-8;
                  9-11
    Hezekiah   *Sir 48:17-25
    Jews   *2 Mc 1:10-17
    Judith   *Jdt 8:28-36
    Mordecai   *Esth 10:4-13
    Psalmist   Ps 44:4-8;
                  106:47-48
    Sirach   *Sir 51:1-12
  INSTRUCTION on
    Baruch   *Bar 4:17-20
    Judith   *Jdt 8:9-27
  PROPHECY of
    Israelites   Zech 2:6-13;
                  9:13-17
    Zechariah   Lk 1:57-80
  TRADITION of
    Solomon   *Wis 18:1-4
  through **WORSHIP**
    David   2 Sam 22:1-51
    Israelites   *Jdt 4:1-15

from **ENVIRONMENT**
  through **COMPASSION**
    Moses   Ex 2:1-10
  of **DEATH**
    Azariah   *Azar 1:23-27
  DOUBT in
    Israelites   Ex 14:1-14
  FULFILLMENT of
    Rahab   Josh 6:22-27

  of **INNOCENCE**
    Daniel   *Susa 1:60-64
  through **JEALOUSY**
    Phinehas   Num 25:6-18
  JOY in
    Cyrus   *Bel 1:40-42
  for **LIFE**
    David   Ps 54:3
  through **MIRACLE**
    Azariah   *Azar 1:23-27

through **OBEDIENCE**
  God   Gen 8:1-12
through **SEX**
  Israelites   Judg 21:8-12
through **VICTORY**
  Othniel   Judg 3:7-11

from **EVIL**
  against **DEITY**
    David   Ps 28:1-5;
                  39:7-13
    Israelites   Ps 130:7-8
    Psalmist   Ps 71:1-21
  INSTRUCTION on
    Solomon   *Wis 4:10-20
  through **MISSION**
    Jesus   1 Tim 1:12-17
  REVELATION on
    Elihu   Job 33:15-18

through **FAITH**
  in **DEITY**
    Believers   1 Pet 1:3-9
    David   1 Sam 17:1-18:
                  Ps 27:1-3;
                  86:1-7
    Habakkuk   Hab 3:1619
    Jesus   Heb 7:1-28
    Job   Job 19:25-29
    Micah   Mic 7:7-20
    Psalmist   Ps 119:121-128
    Shadrach   Dan 3:16-18
    Sirach   *Sir 33:1-3
    Thessalonians   2 Thes 2:13-15
  of **FOLLOWERs**
    Jailer   Acts 16:25-40
    Jesus   1 Jn 5:8-12
    Woman   Lk 7:36-50
  INSTRUCTION on
    Author   Heb 4:1-13;
                  6:9-12
    James   Jas 2:14-26
    Jesus   Mt 21:28-32;
                  22:1-14;
                  Lk 7:36-50;
                  12:32-34;
                  Jn 3:1-21;
                  8:12-20;
                  21-59;
                  12:27-36a
    John the Baptist   Jn 3:31-36
    Paul   Acts 13:14-52;
                  Rom 1:16-17;
                  3:21-30;
                  9:30-10:21;
                  11:1-6;
                  7-24;
                  1 Cor 1:18-25;
                  2 Cor 4:13-15;
                  Gal 3:10-14;
                  5:2-6;
                  Eph 1:15-2:10;
                  Col 1:21-23;
                  1 Thes 4:13-18
  in **MESSIANIC FIGURE**
    Jesus   Jn 1:1-18
  PROPHECY of
    Isaiah   Is 12:1-6;
                  28:14-22;
                  33:7-16

of DEITY (cont'd)
    Paul   2 Cor 5:20-6:2
    Sirach   *Sir 51:1-12
for FOLLOWERs
    Jesus   Eph 1:3-14
INSTRUCTION on
    Jesus   Mt 20:1-16;
                  Jn 3:1-21
    Paul   Rom 9:6-13;
                  11:1-6;
                  25-32;
                  1 Cor 1:26-31;
                  6:12-20;
                  Gal 2:15-16;
                  4:27-31;
                  Eph 1:15-2:10;
                  Col 1:9-14;
                  1 Thes 5:1-11;
                  2 Tim 1:8-14
    Peter   Acts 2:14-36;
                  15:6-29
of MESSIANIC FIGURE
    Believers   1 Pet 1:13-2:3
    Jesus   2 Cor 8:7-15
in MISSION
    Jesus   Lk 19:1-10
PROPHECY of
    Isaiah   Is 52:13-53:12
    Jesus   Lk 23:39-43
    Judahites   Jer 23:1-8
    Simeon   Lk 2:21-40
REVELATION on
    Believers   1 Pet 1:13-2:3
    Israelites   Is 49:1-26;
                  Ezek 36:22-32;
                  37:15-28;
                  Zech 7:4-8:23;
                  13:7-9
    Jeremiah   Jer 33:14-26
    John   Rev 14:1-5
SCRIPTURES on
    Israelites   Rom 11:25-32

GRATITUDE for
  INSTRUCTION on
    Jeremiah   Jer 31:7-14

HOPE in
  by DEITY
    Believers   1 Tim 4:6-10
    David   Ps 38:17-22;
                  39:7-13
    God   Ps 65:5-8
    Psalmist   Ps 119:81-88;
                  161-168;
                  169-176;
                  123:1-2
  of FOLLOWERs
    Thessalonians 1 Thes 1:2-10
  INSTRUCTION on
    Author   Heb 6:9-12
    Baruch   *Bar 4:21-37
    Paul   Rom 8:14-25;
                  Phil 3:17-21;
                  1 Thes 5:1-11
  through MESSIANIC FIGURE
    Believers   1 Pet 1:13-2:3
  PROPHECY of
    Isaiah   Is 25:6-9

REVELATION on
    Believers   1 Pet 1:13-2:3
through HUMILITY
  before DEITY
    Eliphaz   Job 22:21-30
  INSTRUCTION on
    Jesus   Mt 18:1-4
    Paul   1 Cor 1:26-31

IGNORANCE of
  PROPHECY of
    Caiaphas   Jn 11:1-57

from INDIFFERENCE
  in MISSION
    Jesus   Lk 13:34-35

of INNOCENCE
  in ENVIRONMENT
    Daniel   *Susa 1:60-64

INSTRUCTION on
    God   Is 46:1-13
    Jesus   Jn 6:25-59;
                  Acts 4:1-22
    Paul   Rom 5:12-21;
                  9:30-10:21;
                  1 Cor 1:18-25
    Peter   2 Pet 3:14-18a
  from ANGER
    Zephaniah   Zeph 2:3
  from DEATH
    God   *2 Esd 2:15-32
    James   Jas 5:19-20
    Paul   Gal 2:20-21
    Solomon   *Wis 1:12-15
  from DISOBEDIENCE
    Paul   Rom 11:25-32
  from ENEMY
    Baruch   *Bar 4:17-20
    Judith   *Jdt 8:9-27
  from EVIL
    Solomon   *Wis 4:10-20
  through FAITH
    Author   Heb 4:1-13;
                  6:9-12
    James   Jas 2:14-26
    Jesus   Mt 21:28-32;
                  22:1-14;
                  Lk 7:36-50;
                  12:32-34;
                  Jn 3:1-21;
                  8:12-20;
                  21-59;
                  12:27-36a
    John the Baptist Jn 3:31-36
    Paul   Acts 13:14-52;
                  Rom 1:16-17;
                  3:21-30;
                  9:30-10:21;
                  11:1-6;
                  7-24;
                  1 Cor 1:18-25;
                  2 Cor 4:13-15;
                  Gal 3:10-14;
                  5:2-6;
                  Eph 1:15-2:10;
                  Col 1:21-23;
                  1 Thes 4:13-18

INSTRUCTION on
Jesus   Lk 10:17-20;
                     15:1-7;
                     8-10;
                     11-32
Psalmist   Ps 95:1-7c
MEDITATION on
Isaiah   Is 61:1-11
PROPHECY of
Isaiah   Is 12:1-6;
                     25:6-9;
                     35:1-10

through **JUSTICE**
INSTRUCTION on
Angel   *2 Esd 7:116-8:3
Jesus   Mt 20:1-16
PROPHECY of
Isaiah   Is 1:27-31

through **LEADERSHIP**
of **DEITY**
God   Is 33:17-24
Israelites   Judg 2:11-19
Psalmist   Ps 80:1-3
of **MESSIANIC FIGURE**
God   2 Kgs 13:1-9

LIFE through
by **DEITY**
Asaph   Ps 73:21-28
Believers   Ps 91:1-13;
                     97:10-12
Daniel   Dan 6:16-23
David   Ps 56:10-13;
                     70:1-5;
                     86:11-13;
                     138:7-8;
                     143:7-12
Elihu   Job 33:29-30
God   Ps 68:19-23
Peter   Acts 12:1-25
Psalmist   Ps 66:8-12;
                     116:1-11;
                     118:15-21;
                     119:81-88;
                     89-96
in the **ENVIRONMENT**
David   Ps 54:3
of **FOLLOWER**
Jesus   2 Tim 2:8-13
INSTRUCTION on
Jesus   Mt 16:21-28;
                     Mk 8:34-9:1;
                     Lk 9:23-27;
                     Jn 5:19-47
Paul   Rom 1:16-17;
                     6:1-14;
                     8:5-13
by **MESSIANIC FIGURE**
Jesus   Mt 9:18-26;
                     Mk 5:35-43;
                     Lk 2:1-20;
                     8:40-56
PROPHECY of
Jesus   Mt 16:21-28;
                     Mk 8:34-9:1;
                     Lk 9:23-27
REVELATION on
Prophets   Rev 11:1-14

through **LOVE**
of **DEITY**
Believers   Ps 145:13b-20;
                     1 Jn 4:7-12;
                     Jas 1:12
David   Ps 6:1-5;
                     31:13-18
Jesus   Eph 1:15-2:10
Mankind   Tit 3:1-7
of **FOLLOWER**
Women   1 Tim 2:8-15
INSTRUCTION on
Jesus   Lk 15:1-7;
                     8-10;
                     11-32

MEDITATION on
through **PATIENCE**
Jeremiah   Lam 3:1-66

through **MESSIANIC FIGURE**
ACCEPTANCE of
Jesus   Jn 10:1-18
FAITH in
Jesus   Jn 1:1-18
FAMILY of
Jesus   Mt 1:18-25
GRACE of
Believers   1 Pet 1:13-2:3
Jesus   2 Cor 8:7-15
HOPE in
Believers   1 Pet 1:13-2:3
LEADERSHIP for
God   2 Kgs 13:1-9
LIFE through
Jesus   Mt 9:18-26;
                     Mk 5:35-43;
                     Lk 2:1-20;
                     8:40-56
through **MIRACLE**
Jesus   Mt 9:18-26;
                     Mk 5:35-43;
                     Lk 8:40-56
OBEDIENCE to
Jesus   Heb 5:1-10
PATIENCE with
Jesus   Heb 9:23-28
concerning **POVERTY**
Jesus   2 Cor 8:7-15
PRAISE of
Anna   Lk 2:21-40
SACRIFICE of
Jesus   Heb 9:1-14
SUFFERING of
Jesus   Heb 2:5-18
VICTORY of
Jesus   Heb 2:5-18

through **MIRACLE**
by **DEITY**
Daniel   Dan 6:16-23;
                     *Bel 1:31-39
in **ENVIRONMENT**
Azariah   *Azar 1:23-27
by **MESSIANIC FIGURE**
Jesus   Mt 9:18-26;
                     Mk 5:35-43;
                     Lk 8:40-56
REVELATION on
God   Heb 2:1-4

REVELATION on (cont'd)

Israelites	Zech 10:3-12
Moses	Ex 15:22-27; 16:1-21; 17:1-7

MISSION of
　by **GRACE**

Jesus	Lk 19:1-0

　INDIFFERENCE to

Jesus	Lk 13:34-35

　OBEDIENCE to

Paul	1 Cor 15:1-11

　REWARDs of

Apostles	Mt 10:16-22

　SERVICE in

Angels	Heb 1:5-14
Believers	Jude 1:21-23

　SUFFERING in

Apostles	Mt 10:16-22

　WITNESS to

Isaiah	Is 49:1-26
Jesus	Mt 9:35

through **MISSION**
　of **DISCIPLESHIP**

Gentiles	Acts 13:14-52

　against **EVIL**

Jesus	1 Tim 1:12-17

through **OBEDIENCE**
　to **DEITY**

Mankind	Ps 15:1-5b
Psalmist	Ps 119:145-152

　in **ENVIRONMENT**

God	Gen 8:1-12

　of **FOLLOWER**s

Holy Spirit	Gal 5:16-21

　INSTRUCTION on

Angels	Gen 19:12-29
David	Ps 37:23-40
God	Gen 7:1-24; Ps 50:22-23; 81:5c-16; Is 1:18-20
Jesus	Mt 7:21-23; 24-27; 19:16-22; 21:33-43; Mk 10:17-22; 12:1-12; Lk 6:46-49; 13:22-30; 18:18-27; 20:9-18
John	1 Jn 2:12-17
Paul	Rom 2:1-24; 11:7-24; 1 Tim 4:11-16

　to **MESSIANIC FIGURE**

Jesus	Heb 5:1-10

　in **MISSION**

Paul	1 Cor 15:1-11

　REVELATION on

Believers	Is 56:1-8
Moses	Ex 14:15-22

through **ONENESS**
　with **DEITY**

God	1 Tim 2:1-7

INSTRUCTION on

Paul	Rom 9:30-10:21

from **OPPRESSION**
　by **DEITY**

God	Ps 76:7-9; Rev 7:9-17
Psalmist	Ps 118:10-14; 119:121-128; 129-136; 153-160; 120:1-2

　INSTRUCTION on

Jesus	Mt 5:3-12

　REVELATION on

Israelites	Zeph 3:14-20

through **PARADOX**
　by **DEITY**

God	Ps 118:22-27

　of **FOLLOWER**s

Jesus	2 Tim 2:8-13

　INSTRUCTION on

Jesus	Mt 22:1-14; Lk 17:22-37; Jn 12:20-26

　REVELATION on

Isaiah	Is 66:1-16

through **PATIENCE**
　with **DEITY**

David	Ps 62:1-2; 5-7

　INSTRUCTION on

Author	Heb 6:9-12
Jude	Jude 1:21-23
Paul	Rom 2:1-24; 2 Tim 2:8-13

　MEDITATION on

Jeremiah	Lam 3:1-66

　with **MESSIANIC FIGURE**

Jesus	Heb 9:23-28

　PROPHECY of

Jesus	Mk 13:9-13; Lk 21:7-19

PEACE through
　of **FOLLOWER**

Women	1 Tim 2:8-15

　INSTRUCTION on

Moses	Ex 14:1-14

through **PIETY**
　in **WORSHIP**

Samaritan	Jn 4:1-26

through **POVERTY**
　of **MESSIANIC FIGURE**

Jesus	2 Cor 8:7-15

PRAISE of
　by **DEITY**

David	Ps 9:13-14; 40:13-17
God	Rev 19:1-5
Psalmist	Ps 67:1-7

　INSTRUCTION on

David	Ps 69:29-36

　by **MESSIANIC FIGURE**

Anna	Lk 2:21-40

to **LIFE** (cont'd)	
Prophets	Rev 11:1-14
through **MIRACLE**	
God	Heb 2:1-4
Israelites	Zech 10:3-12
Moses	Ex 15:22-27;
	16:1-21;
	17:1-7
through **OBEDIENCE**	
Believers	Is 56:1-8
Moses	Ex 14:15-22
from **OPPRESSION**	
Israelites	Zeph 3:14-20
through **PARADOX**	
Isaiah	Is 66:1-16
through **SUFFERING**	
Israelites	Jer 30:4-9
through **TEMPERANCE**	
John	Rev 14:1-5
through **VICTORY**	
Daniel	Dan 12:1-4
Jeremiah	Jer 15:10-21
John	Rev 12:1-6
Judahites	Hos 1:6-7
through **WILL**	
Israelites	Is 45:14-25
through **WISDOM**	
Author	Heb 2:1-4
Isaiah	Is 56:1-8
through **WITNESS**	
Author	Heb 2:1-4
Isaiah	Is 60:1-22
Israelites	Mic 6:1-5
Simeon	Lk 2:21-40
through **REVENGE**	
of **DEITY**	
David	Ps 54:1-2
PROPHECY of	
Isaiah	Is 62:1-12
REWARDs of	
of **FOLLOWER**	
Jesus	Jn 8:12-20
INSTRUCTION on	
Jesus	Mt 5:3-12;
	10:26-39;
	13:36-43;
	19:27-30;
	25:31-46;
	Mk 10:28-31;
	Lk 6:20-23;
	18:28-30;
	Jn 6:25-59;
	12:44-50
John the Baptist	Jn 3:31-36
Paul	Rom 6:15-23;
	2 Thes 2:13-15;
	2 Tim 4:6-8
Peter	1 Pet 5:1-5;
	2 Pet 1:8-11
in **MISSION**	
Apostles	Mt 10:16-22
PROPHECY of	
Isaiah	Is 62:1-12
Jesus	Mt 24:9-14;
	Lk 23:39-43
through **SACREDNESS**	
in **WORSHIP**	

in **WORSHIP** (cont'd)	
Isaiah	Is 27:12-13
Priests	*2 Mc 14:34-36
through **SACRIFICE**	
of **FOLLOWER**	
Jesus	1 Pet 1:13-2:3
INSTRUCTION on	
God	Ps 50:22-23
Jesus	Jn 12:20-26
of **MESSIANIC FIGURE**	
Jesus	Heb 9:1-14
PROPHECY of	
Jesus	Jn 6:25-59
SCRIPTURES on	
through **DISCIPLESHIP**	
Paul	Eph 6:10-18
through **FAITH**	
Jesus	Jn 20:30-31
Paul	2 Tim 3:14-17
through **GRACE**	
Israelites	Rom 11:25-32
through **WILL**	
God	Mt 21:33-43;
	Mk 12:1-12;
	Lk 20:9-18
Israelites	Rom 9:14-29
SELF-REALIZATION of	
through **FAITH**	
Jesus	Jn 17:1-5
through **SUFFERING**	
Paul	2 Tim 2:8-13
through **SERVICE**	
INSTRUCTION on	
James	Jas 2:14-26
Jesus	Lk 17:7-10;
	19:1-10
in **MISSION**	
Angels	Heb 1:5-14
Believers	Jude 1:21-23
based on **SEX**	
in **ENVIRONMENT**	
Israelites	Judg 21:8-12
through **SHARING**	
Peter	2 Pet 1:3-4
through **SPIRIT**	
of **DEITY**	
David	Ps 31:1-8
INSTRUCTION on	
Paul	1 Cor 5:1-5
through **SUFFERING**	
Believer	Jas 1:12
David	Ps 34:4-10;
	41:1-3;
	69:1-3
Eliphaz	Job 5:18-27
Israelites	*Bar 2:11-23
Paul	2 Cor 1:8-11
People	Ps 107:17-22
Psalmist	Ps 126:4-6
Sirach	*Sir 51:1-12
INSTRUCTION on	
God	Ps 50:7-15

SALVATION (cont'd)

in WORSHIP
 through **PIETY**
  Samaritan   Jn 4:1-26
 through **SACREDNESS**
  Isaiah   Is 27:12-13
  Priests   *2 Mc 14:34-36
 through **VICTORY**
  Miriam   Ex 15:19-21

through **YOUTH**
 INSTRUCTION on
  Jesus   Mt 19:13-15;
      Mk 10:13-16

SCRIPTURES

on **ACCEPTANCE**
 of **BELIEF**
  Jesus   Jn 5:19-47
 through **CONVERSION**
  James   Acts 15:6-29
 of **LAW**
  John   Rev 22:6-21
 of **SIGNS**
  Jonah   Lk 11:29-32

on **AUTHORITY**
 over **LIFE**
  Hosea   Rom 9:14-29
 SACREDNESS in
  Paul   2 Tim 3:14-17
 WISDOM in
  God   1 Cor 1:18-25
 WITNESS to
  David   Mt 22:41-46;
      Mk 12:35-37a;
      Lk 20:41-44
  Paul   2 Tim 3:14-17

on **BEHAVIOR**
 revealing **FULFILLMENT**
  Isaiah   Jn 12:36b-43
  Jesus   Jn 19:17-42
  Judas   Jn 13:1-20
 revealing **JUSTICE**
  Jesus   Mt 12:1-8;
      Mk 2:23-28;
      Lk 6:1-5
 revealing **ONENESS**
  Paul   Eph 5:21-33
 revealing **PRAISE**
  Jesus   Mt 21:12-17
 revealing **SACREDNESS**
  David   Mt 12:1-8;
      Mk 2:23-28

on **BELIEF**
 ACCEPTANCE of
  Jesus   Jn 5:19-47
 concerning **LIFE**
  Jesus   Jn 7:37-52
 REWARDs of
  People   1 Pet 2:4-10
 WITNESS to
  Jesus   Jn 20:30-31

on **BLASPHEMY**
 concerning **JUDGMENT**
  Paul   Rom 2:1-24

on **BLESSING**
 in **RECONCILIATION**
  Jesus   Gal 3:10-14
 of **VIRTUE**
  David   Rom 3:31-4:25

on **COMPASSION**
 in **ELECTION**
  God   Rom 9:14-29

on **COMPULSION**
 for **FULFILLMENT**
  Judas   Acts 1:12-26

on **CONDEMNATION**
 as **JUDGMENT**
  Jesus   Mt 12:38-42;
      Lk 11:29-32
 of **SIN**
  Paul   Gal 3:19-25

on **CONFRONTATION**
 with **FULFILLMENT**
  Jesus   Mt 26:47-56;
      Mk 14:43-50
 with **OPPRESSION**
  Believers   Rom 8:28-39

on **CREATION**
  Adam   1 Cor 15:42-50
  God   2 Cor 4:1-6
  Jeremiah   Jer 30:1-3;
      36:1-7;
      27-32

on **DISCIPLESHIP**
  Paul   Eph 6:10-18

on **DISOBEDIENCE**
  People   1 Pet 2:4-10

on **DOUBT**
 in **PROVIDENCE**
  Habakkuk   Hab 1:5-11
  Paul   Acts 13:14-52

on **ELECTION**
 through **COMPASSION**
  God   Rom 9:14-29
 through **DISOBEDIENCE**
  People   1 Pet 2:4-10
 through **FULFILLMENT**
  Jesus   Lk 4:16-30;
      Jn 13:1-20
 by **GRACE**
  Mankind   Rom 9:14-29
 of **LEADERSHIP**
  Prophet   Acts 3:1-26

on **ENEMY**
 concerning **inFIDELITY**
  Jesus   Mt 26:17-30;
      Mk 14:17-21

on **EQUALITY**
 with **EVIL**
  Paul   Rom 2:25-3:20

on **ETERNAL**
  Isaiah   Is 40:1-11

through **WILL**
    God   Mt 21:33-43;
                            Mk 12:1-12;
                            Lk 20:9-18
    Israelites   Rom 9:14-29

on **SECURITY**
    FULFILLMENT of
    Jesus   Jn 17:6-19;
                         18:1-11

on **SIGNS**
    of **ACCEPTANCE**
    Jonah   Lk 11:29-32
    of **FAITH**
    Jesus   Jn 20:30-31
    of **FULFILLMENT**
    Jesus   Heb 2:5-18
    of **REJECTION**
    Isaiah   1 Cor 14:13-25

on **SIN**
    concerning **CONDEMNATION**
    Paul   Gal 3:19-25

on **SPIRIT**
    of **CREATION**
    Adam   1 Cor 15:42-:9

on **STEWARDSHIP**
    Luke   Lk 2:21-40
    Moses   1 Cor 9:7-14

on **SUFFERING**
    in **RESURRECTION**
    Jesus   Lk 24:44-49

on **TEMPTATION**
    Jesus   Mt 4:1-11;
                         Lk 4:1-13

on **TRUTH**
    Jeremiah   Jer 1:1-3
    FULFILLMENT of
    Believers   Acts 10:1-11:18

on **VIRTUE**
    David   Rom 3:31-4:25
    in **FAITH**
    Abraham   Gal 3:6-9;
                        Jas 2:14-26

on **WILL**
    God   Mt 21:33-43;
                            Mk 12:1-12;
                            Lk 20:9-18;
                            Rom 9:14-29
    Israelites   Rom 9:14-29

on **WISDOM**
    in **AUTHORITY**
    God   1 Cor 1:18-25
    in **KNOWLEDGE**
    Jesus   Lk 24:13-35
    of **RESURRECTION**
    Jesus   Mt 22:23-33;
                         Mk 12:18-27;
                         Lk 20:27-40

on **WITNESS**
    to **AUTHORITY**
    David   Mt 22:41-46;
                         Mk 12:35-37a;
                         Lk 20:41-44
    Paul   2 Tim 3:14-17
    to **BELIEF**
    Jesus   Jn 20:30-31
    to **CREATION**
    Jeremiah   Jer 36:1-7;
                         27-32
    for **ETERNITY**
    Isaiah   Is 40:1-11
    to **GIFT**
    Paul   1 Cor 1:26-31
    to **JUDGMENT**
    Jesus   Jn 8:12-20
    to **KNOWLEDGE**
    Dositheus   *Esth 11:1
    Isaiah   Mt 13:10-17;
                         Acts 28:17-31
    Paul   Acts 28:17-31
    to **TRUTH**
    Jeremiah   Jer 1:1-3

SECURITY

in **ALIENATION**
    from **ENVIRONMENT**
    David   2 Sam 15:13-16:1
    REVELATION on
    Believers   Rev 18:4-20

resulting from **ANGER**
    REVELATION on
    Israelites   Is 51:17-52:12

ANXIETY concerning
    Jacob   Gen 34:1-31
    INSTRUCTION on
    Paul   2 Cor 5:1-5
    MEDITATION on
    Jesus   Mt 6:25-34
    PROPHECY of
    People   Is 20:1-6

BLESSING in
    Mephibosheth 2 Sam 9:1-13
    by **DEITY**
    David   Ps 61:4-5;
                         144:1-2
    Eliphaz   Job 5:18-27
    Israelites   Ps 84:5-7;
                         Joel 3:16b-21
    Mankind   Ps 2:10-11
    PROPHECY of
    Isaiah   Is 54:1-17
    Isarelites   Zech 9:13-17
    REVELATION on
    Israelites   Ezek 34:11-16;
                         25-31
    Jeremiah   Jer 33:1-9

from **CAPTIVITY**
    by **DEITY**
    Isaiah   Is 62:1-12
    TRADITION of
    Egyptians   Gen 47:13-26

through **COMPASSION**

Cain	Gen 4:1-16
David	1 Sam 22:1-23

REVELATION on

Isaiah	Is 51:1-16

COURAGE in
in **DEITY**

David	Ps 56:1-4
God	Ps 91:1-13
Nehemiah	Neh 4:13-23
Psalmist	Ps 118:5-9

INSTRUCTION on

God	Is 41:1-42:4
Solomon	Prov 3:1-35
Zophar	Job 11:13-20

PROPHECY of

Isaiah	Is 37:4d-7; 54:1-17
Israelites	Jer 46:27-28
Micah	Mic 4:1-8

REVELATION on

Ezekiel	Ezek 2:1-8a; 3:4-9
Isaiah	Is 7:1-9
Israelites	Zeph 3:11-13
Joshua	Deut 31:14-23
Paul	Acts 27:1-28:16

through **COVENANT**
with **FAMILY**

David	2 Sam 23:1-7

FULFILLMENT of

God	2 Chr 21:1-23:21

of **LOVE**

David	1 Sam 20:1-42

ORDER in

Noah	Gen 9:8-19

of **PEACE**

Isaac	Gen 26:12-31
Israelites	Ezek 34:25-31; Hos 2:16-20

of **POLITICS**

Maccabeus	*1 Mc 8:1-32

of **SERVICE**

Jesus	Heb 7:1-28

in **DEATH**

David	Ps 16:9-11
Tobiah	*Tb 8:1-21

through **FALSE BELIEF**

Priests	Mt 27:62-66

INSTRUCTION on

Raphael	*Tb 6:1-17
Solomon	Prov 23:15-24:22

PROPHECY of

Huldah	2 Kgs 22:3-20

REVELATION on

Chaldeans	Is 47:1-15

in **DEITY**
BLESSING of

David	Ps 61:4-5; 144:1-2
Eliphaz	Job 5:18-27
Israelites	Ps 84:5-7; Joel 3:16b-21
Mankind	Ps 2:10-11

from **CAPTIVITY**

Isaiah	Is 61:1-12

revealing **COURAGE**

David	Ps 56:1-4
God	Ps 91:1-13
Nehemiah	Neh 4:13-23
Psalmist	Ps 118:5-9

from **DEATH**

David	Ps 16:9-11

from **DESPAIR**

Psalmist	Ps 42:1-5; 6-11

in the face of **DESTRUCTION**

David	Ps 57:1-3

DIGNITY of

David	Ps 25:16-21

in **DISCIPLESHIP**

David	Ps 28:8-9
God	Ps 34:15-22; 91:1-13; 102:23-28

from **ENEMY**

David	2 Sam 22:1-51; Ps 7:1-2; 11:1-3; 17:8-12; 18:16-19; 46-50; 23:5-6; 31:1-8; 13-18; 54:4-5; 57:4-6; 61:1-3; 64:1-2; 70:1-5; 138:7-8; 141:8-10; 142:5-7; 143:7-12
God	Ps 136:23-25
Habakkuk	Hab 3:3-15

from **EVIL**

David	Ps 11:1-3; 12:7-8; 19:11-14; 26:8-12; 36:10-12; 59:1-5; 62:8-12; 64:1-2; 139:19-22; 140:1-5; 141:3-4
God	2 Thes 3:3-5
Jesus	Jn 17:6-19
Job	Job 21:7-13; 14-18; 24:13-25
Psalmist	Ps 43:1-5; 121:2-8

through **FAITH**

Believers	Ps 55:22; Prov 22:17-21
David	Ps 4:2-5; 7:9-11; 11:1-3; 16:1-4; 5-8; 23:1-4; 25:8-15; 27:7-12;

through **FAITH** (cont'd)

David	28:6-7; 56:6b-9; 10-13; 62:1-2; 5-7; 143:7-12
God	Ps 125:1-3; Prov 29:1-27; 30:1-14; Is 26:1-6
Isaiah	Is 25:1-5; 50:1-11
Israelites	Deut 31:1-8
Jehoshaphat	2 Chr 17:1-20:37
Jeremiah	Jer 16:19-21
Mankind	2 Sam 22:1-51; Ps 18:25-30
Moses	Ps 90:1-12
Paul	2 Cor 1:8-11; 2 Tim 4:9-18
Psalmist	Ps 10:12-18; 33:20-22; 46:1-3; 71:1-21; 94:20-23; 118:10-14

in **FAMILY**

Believers	Is 40:1-11

from **FEAR**

Believers	Prov 16:1-33
David	Ps 27:1-3

through **FEAR**

Job	Job 4:1-6

through **FULFILLMENT**

Believers	Heb 6:13-20
David	Ps 38:11-16
Israelites	Is 31:4-9

through **GOOD**

Believers	Prov 18:1-24
God	Ps 37:12-22

GRATITUDE for

David	Ps 124:6-8
Hezekiah	Is 38:1-22

HOPE in

Believers	Ps 146:5-7b
David	Ps 22:12-21; 40:13-17
Habakkuk	Hab 3:16-19
Isaiah	Is 8:16-18
Jeremiah	Lam 3:1-66
Psalmist	Ps 42:1-5; 6-11; 43:1-5; 71:1-21; 94:16-19; 116:1-11; 119:49-56; 113-120

JOY through

Believers	Ps 146:5-7b
David	Ps 16:9-11; 35:9-10
Followers	Ps 64:7-10
Mankind	Ps 5:11-12

JUSTICE of

Believers	Ps 37:23-40

through **LEADERSHIP**

Asaph	Ps 73:21-28

through **LIFE**

Baruch	Jer 36:20-26
Believers	Ps 46:1-3; 91:14-16
David	Ps 25:16-21; 36:5-9; 41:1-3
Israelites	Neh 9:12-15; 19-21
Jeremiah	Jer 11:18-12:6; 36:20-26
Job	Job 2:4-6
Levites	Num 18:8-20; Deut 10:1-11; 18:1-8; Josh 13:29-33; Ezek 44:15-31
Solomon	Ps 72:8-14

through **LOVE**

David	Ps 18:1-3; 31:19-24
King	Ps 21:1-7

through **OBEDIENCE**

Hannah	1 Sam 2:1-10

for **OLD AGE**

Believers	Ps 92:12-15

from **OPPRESSION**

Hezekiah	Is 38:1-22
Isaiah	Is 19:18-25
Israelites	1 Chr 15:1-16:43; Ps 105:7-15

through **PEACE**

David	Ps 4:6-8
God	Ps 147:12-20

in **POLITICS**

Israelites	Judg 2:11-19

for **POVERTY**

God	Ps 12:5-6; 14:4-6; 132:11-18
Isaiah	Is 25:1-5

PRAISE of

David	Ps 59:16-17
Eliphaz	Job 5:8-17

through **SACRIFICE**

Lot	Gen 19:4-11

through **SERVICE**

Believers	Ps 46:4-7
David	Ps 124:6-8
God	Ps 127:1-2; Rev 7:9-17
Psalmist	Ps 121:2-8

for **SUFFERING**

Believers	Ps 33:13-19; 145:13b-20; 2 Pet 2:4-10a
David	Ps 22:22-26; 27:4-6; 32:3-7; 35:17-18; 38:17-22; 40:1-3; 54:6-7
Ezra	*2 Esd 7:1-18
God	Ps 91:1-13
Mankind	Ps 9:9-12; Rev 21:1-8

through **VICTORY**

Believers	Ps 46:8-11

in **PRUDENCE**
Solomon   Prov 27:1-27
in **REJECTION**
Sirach   *Sir 13:1-13
through **REPENTANCE**
Zophar   Job 11:13-20
in **REWARDs**
Jesus   Mt 10:40-42
in **SACREDNESS**
God   Ex 19:16-25
from **SEX**
Solomon   Prov 6:20-7:27
through **SUFFERING**
Servants   1 Pet 2:18-20
Solomon   Prov 6:1-5
from **TEMPTATION**
Paul   1 Tim 5:3-16
from **VIOLENCE**
Artaxerxes   *Esth 16:1-24
Mordecai   Esth 8:9-14
Nehemiah   Neh 7:1-3
in **WEALTH**
Jesus   Lk 12:16-21
Psalmist   Ps 49:16-20
Solomon   Prov 18:1-24
in **WISDOM**
Baruch   *Bar 3:9-14
Father   Prov 4:1-9;
   10-19
Sirach   *Sir 22:16-18
Solomon   Prov 3:1-35;
   28:1-28;
   *Wis 6:12-25
Wisdom   Prov 1:20-33

JOY through
Darius   Dan 6:16-23
in **DEITY**
Believers   Ps 146:5-7b
David   Ps 16:9-11;
   35:9-10
Followers   Ps 64:7-10
Mankind   Ps 5:11-12
INSTRUCTION on
Sirach   *Sir 30:14-25
PROPHECY of
Jesus   Jn 16:16-24

in **JUSTICE**
Joshua   Josh 20:1-9
Moses   Num 35:9-15;
   Deut 4:41-43
of **DEITY**
Believers   Ps 37:23-40
for **FOLLOWER**
Claudius   Acts 23:12-35
INSTRUCTION on
Moses   Deut 19:1-13

from **KILLING**
David   1 Sam 20:1-42
Joash   2 Kgs 11:1-3;
   2 Chr 21:1-23:21
Moses   Num 35:1-8
in **ENVIRONMENT**
David   1 Sam 21:1-9
Jonathan   *1 Mc 9:32-42
Maccabeus   *2 Mc 5:11-7
Moses   Deut 4:41-43

in **LEADERSHIP**
of **DEITY**
Asaph   Ps 73:21-28
in **ENVIRONMENT**
Raphael   *Tb 5:1-21
REVELATION on
God   Is 42:5-17
John   Rev 6:12-17
Moses   Num 14:25

LIFE through
Esther   Esth 7:1-10
Ishmael   Jer 40:13-16
Jeremiah   Jer 38:1-13;
   14-28;
   39:1-14
Moses   Ex 21:1;
   Num 33:16-36;
   35:1-8;
   Deut 4:41-43
in **DEITY**
Baruch   Jer 36:20-26
Believers   Ps 46:1-3;
   91:14-16
David   Ps 25:16-21;
   36:5-9;
   41:1-3
Israelites   Neh 9:12-15;
   19-21
Jeremiah   Jer 11:18-12:6;
   36:20-26
Job   Job 2:4-6
Levites   Num 18:8-20;
   Deut 10:1-11;
   18:1-8;
   Josh 13:29-33;
   Ezek 44:15-31
Solomon   Ps 72:8-14
in **ENVIRONMENT**
Jacob   Gen 43:1-15
Jeremiah   Jer 26:20-24
Psalmist   Ps 49:5-12
of **FOLLOWER**
Holy Spirit   2 Cor 5:1-5
INSTRUCTION on
Joshua   Josh 20:1-9
Moses   Deut 19:1-13
in **MESSIANIC FIGURE**
Jesus   Jn 10:1-18
PROPHECY of
Baruch   Jer 45:1-5
Ebedmelech   Jer 39:15-18
Isaiah   Is 4:2-6;
   25:6-9;
   27:2-6;
   32:15-20;
   37:30-32;
   51:17-52:12
Jeremiah   Jer 21:1-10;
   32:26-44
Jerusalemites   Zech 14:1-21
Judahites   Jer 27:16-22;
   38:14-28
Paul   Acts 27:1-28:16
Zedekiah   Jer 34:1-7
REVELATION on
Ezekiel   Ezek 3:16-21
God   Is 42:5-17
Israelites   Ezek 6:8-10;

REVELATION on (cont'd)
Israelites 28:24-26;
34:17-22;
Amos 9:14-15
Jeremiah Jer 31:7-14
Jerusalemites Zech 2:1-5
Joel Joel 2:18-27
John Rev 12:13-17

through **LOVE**
COVENANT of
David 1 Sam 20:1-42
of **DEITY**
David Ps 18:1-3;
31:19-24
King Ps 21:1-7
in **ENVIRONMENT**
Isaac Gen 24:61-67
of **FOLLOWER**
Jesus Rom 8:28-39
REVELATION on
Israelites Is 49:1-26

through **MEDIATION**
from **ANXIETY**
Jesus Mt 6:25-34

MEDITATION on
from **FEAR**
David Ps 55:3b-8

in **MESSIANIC FIGURE**
LIFE through
Jesus Jn 10:1-18
for **PEACE**
Disciples Jn 16:29-33
Zechariah Zech 9:1-12

in **MIRACLE**
Shadrach Dan 3:26-27
INSTRUCTION on
Elisha 2 Kgs 4:1-7
PROPHECY of
Elisha 2 Kgs 3:1-27
REVELATION on
Moses Num 20:2-13

through **OBEDIENCE**
Moses Lev 26:1-46
to **DEITY**
Hannah 1 Sam 2:1-10
INSTRUCTION on
Jesus Mt 24:42-44;
Mk 13:28-37
Peter 2 Pet 1:8-11
PROPHECY of
Isaiah Is 33:7-16
Jeroboam 1 Kgs 11:26-40
Judahites Jer 38:14-28
REVELATION on
Isaiah Is 8:11-15
Israelites Is 48:1-22
Moses Ex 4:18-23

in **OLD AGE**
by **DEITY**
Believers Ps 92:12-15

from **OPPRESSION**
by **DEITY**

by **DEITY** (cont'd)
Hezekiah Is 38:1-22
Isaiah Is 19:18-25
Israelites 1 Chr 15:1-16:43;
Ps 1-5:7-15
INSTRUCTION on
Artaxerxes *Esth 16:1-24
Isaiah Is 15:1-16:14
PROPHECY of
Israelites Zech 9:1-12
REVELATION on
Satan Rev 20:1-3

in **ORDER**
through **COVENANT**
Noah Gen 9:8-19
INSTRUCTION on
Jesus Lk 22:35-38

through **PEACE**
Solomon 1 Kgs 4:20-28
COVENANT of
Isaac Gen 26:12-31
Israelites Ezek 34:25-31;
Hos 2:16-20
from **DEITY**
David Ps 4:6-8
God Ps 147:12-20
in **ENVIRONMENT**
Israelites Judg 8:24-28
of **MESSIANIC FIGURE**
Disciples Jn 16:29-33
Zechariah Zech 9:1-12
REVELATION on
Isaiah Is 51:1-16

in **POLITICS**
Jehoiada 2 Chr 21:1-23:21
Manahem 2 Kgs 15:16-22
COVENANT of
Maccabeus *1 Mc 8:1-32
by **DEITY**
Israelites Judg 2:11-19
INSTRUCTION on
Nehemiah Neh 7:1-3
PROPHECY of
Isaiah Is 30:1-7

in **POVERTY**
by **DEITY**
God Ps 12:5-6;
14:4-6;
132:11-18
Isaiah Is 25:1-5
PROPHECY of
Isaiah Is 14:28-32

PRAISE for
in **DEITY**
David Ps 59:16-17
Eliphaz Job 5:8-17

PROPHECY of
Israelites Jer 46:27-28
Micah Mic 4:1-8
in **DEATH**
Huldah 2 Kgs 22:3-20
from **DESTRUCTION**
Benjaminites Jer 6:1-8
Israelites Amos 3:11-12

REVELATION on
  Daniel   Dan 11:21-45

through WEALTH
  Hezekiah   2 Kgs 18:13-16
  Jehoiakim   2 Kgs 23:31-35
  Joash   2 Kgs 12:17-18
  Levites   Ezra 8:24-30
  Menahem   2 Kgs 15:16-22
  Moses   Lev 25:8-19
  in ENVIRONMENT
  Jacob   Gen 33:17-20;
                 46:28-47:12
  Levites   Deut 18:1-8
  INSTRUCTION on
  Jesus   Lk 12:16-21
  Psalmist   Ps 49:16-20
  Solomon   Prov 18:1-24
  in WORSHIP
  Micah   Judg 17:7-13

through WILL
  in ENVIRONMENT
  Boaz   Ruth 3:1-18

in WISDOM
  of DEITY
  God   Prov 2:1-22
  INSTRUCTION on
  Baruch   *Bar 3:9-14
  Father   Prov 4:1-9;
                 10-19
  Sirach   *Sir 22:16-18
  Solomon   Prov 3:1-35;
                 28:1-28;
                 *Wis 6:12-25
  Wisdom   Prov 1:20-33

WITNESS to
  in DEITY
  Asaph   Ps 73:21-28
  Paul   1 Cor 1:4-9;
                 2 Cor 3:4-6

in WORSHIP
  through WEALTH
  Micah   Judg 17:7-13

inSECURITY

FALSE BELIEF causing
  in DEATH
  Priests   Mt 27:62-66
  in FAITH
  Israelites   Mic 3:1-12
  in HOPE
  Solomon   *Wis 13:10-19
  in PEACE
  Moses   Deut 12:1-31

through GREED
  Ishmael   Jer 41:4-9

in IDOLATRY
  PROPHECY of
  Jeremiah   Jer 10:1-16

INSTRUCTION on

INSTRUCTION on (cont'd)
  through GREED
  Jesus   Mt 6:19-24
  in KILLING
  Moses   Deut 19:1-13
  Sirach   *Sir 9:13

through KILLING
  INSTRUCTION on
  Moses   Deut 19:1-13
  Sirach   *Sir 9:13
  REVELATION on
  Joshua   Josh 20:1-9
  Moses   Num 35:9-15

in PEACE
  through FALSE BELIEF
  Moses   Deut 12:1-31

PROPHECY of
  in IDOLATRY
  Jeremiah   Jer 10:1-16

REVELATION on
  through KILLING
  Joshua   Josh 20:1-9
  Moses   Num 35:9-15

SELFISHNESS

BEHAVIOR revealing
  in ENVIRONMENT
  Israelites   Ezek 34:1-10
  through FALSE BELIEF
  Demetrius   Acts 19:23-41
  Pharisees   Lk 11:37-44
  of FOLLOWERs
  Disciples   Mt 26:36-46;
                 Mk 14:32-42;
                 Lk 22:39-46
  REVELATION on
  Ezekiel   Ezek 33:30-33;
                 34:17-22
  Isaiah   Is 58:1-14

in ENVIRONMENT
  BEHAVIOR revealing
  Israelites   Ezek 34:1-10
  through disHONESTY
  Absalom   2 Sam 15:1-12
  through RATIONALIZATION
  Pilate   Mt 27:11-26

FALSE BELIEF causing
  Demetrius   Acts 19:23-41
  Pharisees   Lk 11:37-44
  through disHONESTY
  James   Jas 3:13-18
  as MOTIVATION
  Herod   Mt 14:1-12;
                 Mk 6:17-29
  as SIN
  James   Jas 5:1-6
  Lawyers   Lk 11:45-52

of FOLLOWER
  BEHAVIOR revealing
  Disciples   Mt 26:36-46;

BEHAVIOR revealing (cont'd)
 Disciples   Mk 14:32-42;
                      Lk 22:39-46

through disHONESTY
 Absalom   2 Sam 15:1-12
 FALSE BELIEF causing
  James   Jas 3:13-18
 PROPHECY of
  Jeremiah   Jer 22:13-19
 INSTRUCTION on
  Jesus   Lk 11:37-44;
                      12:13-15;
                      16-21;
                      19:11-27
 as MOTIVATION
  Zechariah   Zech 7:4-8:23
 as QUALITY OF LIFE
  Isaiah   Is 56:9-57:13
  Job   Job 21:19-27
 as SIN
  Jesus   Mk 12:37b-40;
                      Lk 20:45-47
  Jude   Jude 1:14-16

JUDGMENT on
 INSTRUCTION on
  Jesus   Lk 11:37-44;
                      12:13-15;
                      16-21;
                      19:11-27

in MISSION
 of TRUTH
  Pharisees   Mt 23:15

as MOTIVATION
 Abimelech   Judg 9:1-6
 FALSE BELIEF causing
  Herod   Mt 14:1-12;
                      Mk 6:17-29
 INSTRUCTION on
  Zechariah   Zech 7:4-8:23

PROPHECY of
 in disHONESTY
  Jeremiah   Jer 22:13-19

PUNISHMENT for
 INSTRUCTION on
  Jesus   Mt 25:31-46
 REVELATION on
  Isaiah   Is 66:1-16

as QUALITY OF LIFE
 INSTRUCTION on
  Isaiah   Is 56:9-57:13
  Job   Job 21:19-27

RATIONALIZATION of
 in ENVIRONMENT
  Pilate   Mt 27:11-26

REVELATION on
 Ezekiel   Ezek 33:30-33;
                      34:17-22
 Isaiah   Is 58:1-14

SIGNS of
 INSTRUCTION on
  Paul   2 Tim 3:1-9

as SIN
 Israelites   Amos 8:4-7;
                      Hag 1:1-11
 through FALSE BELIEF
  James   Jas 5:1-6
  Lawyers   Lk 11:46-52
 INSTRUCTION on
  Jesus   Mk 12:37b-40;
                      Lk 20:45-47
  Jude   Jude 1:14-16

in STEWARDSHIP
 in WORSHIP
  Micah   Judg 17:7-13

in TRUTH
 MISSION of
  Pharisees   Mt 23:15

in WORSHIP
 through STEWARDSHIP
  Micah   Judg 17:7-13

SELF-REALIZATION

of ACCEPTANCE
 by AUTHORITY
  Centurion   Mt 8:5-13;
                      Lk 7:1-10
 through CONVERSION
  Gentiles   Acts 10:1-11:18
 of NEW AGE
  Criminal   Lk 23:39-43
  John the Baptist   Jn 3:22-30
 of PROVIDENCE
  Magicians   Ex 8:16-19
 of TRUTH
  Disciples   Lk 24:50-51
 of VIRTUE
  Centurion   Lk 23:46-49

of ALIENATION
 of COMMUNITY
  Job   Job 19:13-19

of ANXIETY
 in BEHAVIOR
  Jesus   Mt 26:36-46;
                      Mk 14:32-42;
                      Lk 22:39-46
 in COMMITMENT
  Paul   Rom 9:1-5
 concerning PUNISHMENT
  Judahites   Jer 26:7-19
 as QUALITY OF LIFE
  David   Ps 55:1-3a;
                      3b-8
 through RATIONALIZATION
  Paul   2 Cor 12:19-21
 caused by SIN
  Paul   Rom 7:14-25

by AUTHORITY
 of ACCEPTANCE
  Centurion   Mt 8:5-13;
                      Lk 7:1-10
 of SUFFERING
  Paul   Phil 3:4-16

of **AUTHORITY**
  of **LEADERSHIP**
    David   2 Sam 5:6-16;
                  1 Chr 14:1-17
    Wisdom   Prov 8:1-21
  over **LIFE**
    Jesus   Jn 17:1-5

of **BEHAVIOR**
  revealing **ANXIETY**
    Jesus   Mt 26:36-46;
               Mk 14:32-42;
               Lk 22:39-46
  revealing **GRIEF**
    Jesus   Mt 26:36-46;
               Mk 14:32-42
  revealing **KILLING**
    Judas   Mt 27:3-10
  revealing **PARADOX**
    Paul   Rom 7:14-25
  revealing **REPENTANCE**
    Israelites   Ex 33:1-6
  revealing **SADNESS**
    Jesus   Mt 26:36-46;
               Mk 14:32-42
  revealing **SUFFERING**
    Paul   1 Thes 3:1-10

on **BELIEF**
  through **FAITH**
    Centurion   Lk 23:46-49
  through **GRACE**
    Paul   1 Tim 1:12-17
  through **SUFFERING**
    Paul   2 Tim 1:8-14

of **CAPTIVITY**
  caused by **SIN**
    Paul   Rom 7:14-25

of **COMMITMENT**
  through **FAITH**
    Paul   Gal 2:20-21

of **COMPULSION**
  of **EVIL**
    Eliphaz   Job 15:12-16
  to **SACRIFICE**
    Jesus   Mt 26:36-46;
               Mk 14:32-42;
               Lk 22:39-46

of **CONDEMNATION**
  as **JUDGMENT**
    Hypocrite   Mt 7:1-5;
               Lk 6:36-45

of **CONFRONTATION**
  with **FAITH**
    Jairus   Mk 5:21-24;
               Lk 8:40-56

of **CONVERSION**
  through **ACCEPTANCE**
    Gentiles   Acts 10:1-11:18
  through **REPENTANCE**
    Criminal   Lk 23:39-43
    Nebuchadnezzar Dan 4:34-35

of **DEATH**
    Jesus   Mt 26:36-46;

of **DEATH** (cont'd)
    Jesus   Mk 14:32-42;
               Lk 22:39-46
    Ungodly Men *Wis 5:1-14
  as **QUALITY OF LIFE**
    David   1 Chr 28:1-29:30
    Job   Job 13:28-14:6
    Moses   Ps 90:1-12
    Ungodly Men *Wis 1:16-2:5

of **DEFEAT**
  as **QUALITY OF LIFE**
    Job   Job 13:28-14:6

of **DESIRE**
  for **HUMILITY**
    Paul   2 Cor 12:19-21
  for **LIFE**
    Jesus   Mt 26:36-46;
               Mk 14:32-42
  for **OBEDIENCE**
    Paul   Rom 7:14-25
  for **WISDOM**
    Solomon   2 Chr 1:1-17

of **DESPAIR**
  as **QUALITY OF LIFE**
    Job   Job 19:13-19

of **DESTRUCTION**
  in **NEW AGE**
    Jesus   Lk 12:49-50
  caused by **SIN**
    Judahites   Jer 8:14-17

of **DIGNITY**
  as **VIRTUE**
    David   Ps 26:8-12

of **DISOBEDIENCE**
  to **LAW**
    Ezra   Ezra 9:6-15
    Nehemiah   Neh 1:5-11a
  through **SIN**
    Jonah   Jon 1:1-17

of **DOUBT**
  of **SALVATION**
    Moses   Ex 3:11-22

of **ELECTION**
  through **FAITH**
    Paul   1 Tim 1:12-17
  of **LEADERSHIP**
    Paul   1 Tim 1:12-17
  through **LOVE**
    Paul   1 Tim 1:12-17

of **ENEMY**
    Jesus   Mt 26:36-46;
               Mk 14:32-42

of **EQUALITY**
  with **EVIL**
    Solomon   2 Chr 5:1-7:10

of **EVIL**
    David   Ps 51:3-12
    Israelites   *Bar 1:15-21
    Judahites   Jer 26:7-19

of **EVIL**
　　Solomon　　　　　　2 Chr 5:1-7:10
　　Ungodly Men　　　　*Wis 5:1-14
　through **COMPULSION**
　　Eliphaz　　　　　　Job 15:12-16
　caused by **SIN**
　　David　　　　　　　Ps 51:3-12

of **FAITH**
　through **BELIEF**
　　Centurion　　　　　Lk 23:46-49
　in **COMMITMENT**
　　Paul　　　　　　　　Gal 2:20-21
　in **CONFRONTATION**
　　Jairus　　　　　　　Mk 5:21-24;
　　　　　　　　　　　　Lk 8:40-56
　in **ELECTION**
　　Paul　　　　　　　　1 Tim 1:12-17
　through **FIDELITY**
　　Paul　　　　　　　　2 Tim 4:6-8
　as **MOTIVATION**
　　Jesus　　　　　　　　Mt 26:36-46;
　　　　　　　　　　　　Mk 14:32-42;
　　　　　　　　　　　　Lk 22:39-46
　in **SALVATION**
　　Jesus　　　　　　　　Jn 17:1-5
　in **SECURITY**
　　Paul　　　　　　　　2 Tim 1:8-14
　as **VIRTUE**
　　Paul　　　　　　　　Phil 3:4-16

of **FIDELITY**
　in **FAITH**
　　Paul　　　　　　　　2 Tim 4:6-8
　in **LOVE**
　　Jesus　　　　　　　　Mt 26:36-46;
　　　　　　　　　　　　Mk 14:32-42;
　　　　　　　　　　　　Lk 22:39-46
　causing **SUFFERING**
　　Paul　　　　　　　　Col 1:24
　to **WILL**
　　Paul　　　　　　　　Rom 7:14-25

of in**FIDELITY**
　revealing **GUILT**
　　Peter　　　　　　　　Mt 26:69-75;
　　　　　　　　　　　　Mk 14:66-72;
　　　　　　　　　　　　Lk 22:54b-62
　causing **SADNESS**
　　Peter　　　　　　　　Mt 26:69-75;
　　　　　　　　　　　　Mk 14:66-72;
　　　　　　　　　　　　Lk 22:54b-62

of **FULFILLMENT**
　of **KNOWLEDGE**
　　Paul　　　　　　　　1 Cor 13:8-13

of **GIFT**
　of **LOVE**
　　Paul　　　　　　　　1 Cor 13:1-3

of **GOOD**
　　Paul　　　　　　　　Rom 7:14-25

of **GRACE**
　through **BELIEF**
　　Paul　　　　　　　　1 Tim 1:12-17
　as **VIRTUE**
　　Paul　　　　　　　　2 Cor 1:12-14

of **GRATITUDE**
　　Paul　　　　　　　　1 Tim 1:12-17

of **GRIEF**
　　Jesus　　　　　　　　Mt 26:36-46;
　　　　　　　　　　　　Mk 14:32-42
　as **QUALITY OF LIFE**
　　Naomi　　　　　　　Ruth 1:19-22

of **GUILT**
　overcome through **COMMITMENT**
　　Nehemiah　　　　　Neh 1:5-11a
　caused by in**FIDELITY**
　　Peter　　　　　　　　Mt 26:69-75;
　　　　　　　　　　　　Mk 14:66-72;
　　　　　　　　　　　　Lk 22:54b-62
　caused by **SIN**
　　Ezra　　　　　　　　Ezra 9:6-15
　　Joseph　　　　　　　Gen 42:18-25
　　Judas　　　　　　　　Mt 27:3-10
　　Pharaoh　　　　　　Ex 9:13-35;
　　　　　　　　　　　　10:1-20

of **HONESTY**
　in **LOVE**
　　Paul　　　　　　　　1 Cor 13:1-3
　through **WISDOM**
　　Wisdom　　　　　　Prov 8:1-21

of dis**HONESTY**
　in **TEMPTATION**
　　Eve　　　　　　　　Gen 3:9-13

of **HUMILITY**
　as **VIRTUE**
　　Jesus　　　　　　　　Mt 11:28-30

of **IGNORANCE**
　of **KNOWLEDGE**
　　Agur　　　　　　　　Prov 30:1-14

of **INNOCENCE**
　as **VIRTUE**
　　Job　　　　　　　　Job 32:1

of **JOY**
　as **QUALITY OF LIFE**
　　Apostles　　　　　　Acts 5:17-42
　　Paul　　　　　　　　Phil 4:10-20;
　　　　　　　　　　　　Col 1:24
　in **TRUTH**
　　Disciples　　　　　　Lk 24:50-51

of **JUDGMENT**
　as **CONDEMNATION**
　　Hypocrite　　　　　Mt 7:1-5;
　　　　　　　　　　　　Lk 6:36-45
　for **EVIL**
　　Judahites　　　　　　Jer 36:7-19
　for **FAMILY**
　　Jacob　　　　　　　　Gen 31:1-16
　for **GUILT**
　　Hypocrite　　　　　Mt 7:1-5;
　　　　　　　　　　　　Lk 6:36-45
　with **JUSTICE**
　　Judahites　　　　　　Jer 26:7-19

of **JUSTICE**
　in **JUDGMENT**
　　Judahites　　　　　　Jer 26:7-19

for inFIDELITY
    Daniel   Dan 9:4-19
    Hezekiah   2 Chr 32:1-33
    Judas   Mt 27:3-10

of STEWARDSHIP
    Jesus   Mt 26:36-46;
                        Mk 14:32-42;
                        Lk 22:39-46

of SUFFERING
    Paul   1 Thes 3:1-10
  by AUTHORITY
    Paul   Phil 3:4-16
  for BELIEF
    Paul   2 Tim 1:8-14
  through FIDELITY
    Paul   Col 1:24
  as QUALITY OF LIFE
    Baruch   Jer 45:1-5
    Eliphaz   Job 5:1-7
    Ezra   *2 Esd 7:62-74
    Job   Job 13:28-14:6
  in SALVATION
    Paul   2 Tim 2:8-13

of TEMPTATION
  through disHONESTY
    Eve   Gen 3:9-13

of TRUTH
    Disciples   Lk 24:50-51
    Paul   2 Cor 11:1-6

of VIRTUE
    Ungodly Men   *Wis 5:1-14
  in ACCEPTANCE
    Centurion   Lk 23:46-49
  in DIGNITY
    David   Ps 26:8-12
  in FAITH
    Paul   Phil 3:4-16
  in GRACE
    Paul   2 Cor 1:12-14
  in HUMILITY
    Jesus   Mt 11:28-30
  in INNOCENCE
    Job   Job 32:1

of WILL
  for FIDELITY
    Paul   Rom 7:14-25

of WISDOM
  in HONESTY
    Wisdom   Prov 8:1-21
  in KNOWLEDGE
    Preacher   Eccl 1:12-2:26
  in TRUTH
    Paul   2 Cor 11:1-6

of WITNESS
  to KNOWLEDGE
    John the Baptist Jn 3:31-36
    Leper   Mk 1:40-45

through AUTHORITY
  of DEITY
    Israelites   Ex 31:1-11
    Jesus   Jn 10:19-40
  by FOLLOWERs
    Jesus   Mt 10:1

to AUTHORITY
    David   1 Sam 16:14-23
    Hiram   1 Kgs 5:1-18;
                        2 Chr 2:1-4:22
    Job   Job 28:1-13
    Melchizedek   Heb 7:1-28
    Solomon   1 Kgs 4:7-19
  INSTRUCTION on
    Jesus   Mt 22:15-22;
                        Mk 12:13-17;
                        Lk 20:19-26
  by MESSIANIC FIGURE
    Jesus   Heb 7:1-28
  in MISSION
    Apostles   Mt 10:7-8
    Elders   1 Pet 5:1-5
    Paul   Tit 1:1-4
  in WORSHIP
    Satan   Rev 13:1-4

BEHAVIOR revealing
    Israelites   Ezra 8:31-36
    Shunammites   2 Kgs 4:8-37
  to DEITY
    Habakkuk   *Bel 1:31-39
  in ENVIRONMENT
    Joseph   Gen 43:16-34
  by FOLLOWER
    Paul   1 Cor 9:1-6
  INSTRUCTION on
    Isaac   Gen 27:1-40
    Jesus   Mt 5:38-42;
                        Lk 14:1-6
    John   3 Jn 1:3-8
    Paul   Phil 2:1-4;
                      Col 3:18-4:1;
                      1 Thes 5:1-11;
                      12-22;
                      Tit 3:12-15
  by MESSIANIC FIGURE
    Crowd   Mk 6:53-56
    Jesus   Jn 13:1-20
  in MISSION
    Paul   1 Thes 2:1-12

to BROTHERHOOD
  in ENVIRONMENT
    Levites   Judg 19:16-21
  by FOLLOWERs
    Paul   Col 4:10-14;
                      Philm 1:8-14
  INSTRUCTION on
    Author   Heb 3:12-19
    Jesus   Mt 23:5-12
    Paul   Rom 15:1-13;
                      1 Cor 10:23-11:1
                      16:5-12;
                      Gal 5:25-6:6;
                      7-10;
                      Eph 4:25-5:2;
                      1 Thes 5:25-28;
                      1 Tim 5:3-16

REVELATION on	
Isaiah	Is 65:1-25
in **WORSHIP**	
Israelites	Josh 24:16-24
ELECTION to	
Levites	Num 3:5-10;
	8:5-22;
	Deut 10:1-11;
	18:1-8
Moses	Num 4:1-20
by **DEITY**	
Aaron	Ex 4:10-16;
	Ps 105:26-36
God	Is 41:1-42:4
High Priest	Heb 5:1-10
Isaiah	Is 49:1-26
Israelites	Is 41:1-42:4;
	43:8-13
Jesus	Heb 5:1-10
Levites	1 Chr 15:1-16:43
Moses	Ps 105:26-36
Priests	Ex 28:1-5
to **ENVIRONMENT**	
Levites	Deut 18:1-8
of **FOLLOWERs**	
Jesus	Mk 3:13-19
in **MISSION**	
Believers	Eph 1:15-2:10
Jesus	Mt 15:21-28
PROPHECY of	
Elisha	1 Kgs 19:1-21
Jeremiah	Jer 1:4-10
REVELATION on	
Elisha	1 Kgs 19:1-21
Isaiah	Is 66:17-24
Israelites	Is 43:14-44:5;
	Jer 30:4-9
Jeremiah	Jer 1:13-16
Levites	Num 18:1-7;
	Ezek 44:10-14
Moses	Ex 28:40-43
Samuel	1 Sam 3:1-4:1a
as **TRADITION**	
Levites	Num 3:40-51
Merari	Num 4:29-33
in **WORSHIP**	
Aaron	Ex 29:1-9
to **ENVIRONMENT**	
by **AUTHORITY**	
Job	Job 28:1-13
BEHAVIOR revealing	
Joseph	Gen 43:16-34
through **BROTHERHOOD**	
Levites	Judg 19:16-21
COMMITMENT to	
Judah	Gen 44:1-34
by **COMMUNITY**	
Simon	Lk 23:26
COMPULSION of	
Solomon	1 Kgs 9:15-23
ELECTION of	
Levites	Deut 18:1-8
through **FIDELITY**	
Ruth	Ruth 2:1-23
as **PUNISHMENT**	
Gibeon	Josh 9:16-27
SECURITY through	
Ebedmelech	Jer 38:1-13

EQUALITY of	
INSTRUCTION on	
Paul	1 Cor 3:5-9
ETERNAL	
Melchizedek	Heb 7:1-28
to **DEITY**	
God	Ps 121:2-8
of **MESSIANIC FIGURE**	
Jesus	Heb 7:1-28
TRADITION of	
Israelites	Num 10:1-10
FIDELITY in	
Mordecai	Esth 6:1-5
Ruth	Ruth 2:1-23
to **DEITY**	
Believers	Ps 125:1-3
God	Hos 5:15-6:3
Isaiah	Is 63:7-64:12
Israelites	Josh 24:29-31
Job	Job 31:5-34
of **FOLLOWERs**	
Onesimus	Col 4:7-9
Philippians	Phil 4:10-20
Tychicus	Col 4:7-9
INSTRUCTION on	
Jesus	Lk 16:13
John	1 Jn 3:11-18
Moses	Deut 10:12-22
Paul	Eph 6:5-9;
	1 Tim 6:1-2b
in **MISSION**	
Paul	2 Cor 6:3-10
Servants	1 Tim 6:1-2b
Slaves	Tit 2:1-10
PROPHECY of	
Ezekiel	Ezek 16:44-52
in **WORSHIP**	
Israelites	Neh 10:39b
of **FOLLOWERs**	
AUTHORITY in	
Jesus	Mt 10:1
BEHAVIOR revealing	
Paul	1 Cor 9:1-6
in **BROTHERHOOD**	
Paul	Col 4:10-14;
	Philm 1:8-14
COMMITMENT to	
Titus	2 Cor 8:16-24
through **COMPULSION**	
Jesus	Jn 12:20-26
ELECTION to	
Jesus	Mk 3:13-19
FIDELITY in	
Onesimus	Col 4:7-9
Philippians	Phil 4:10-20
Tychicus	Col 4:7-9
through **FREEDOM**	
Paul	Gal 5:13-15
through **GIFT**	
Apostles	Eph 4:7-16
Evangelists	Eph 4:7-16
Holy Spirit	1 Cor 12:4-11
Pastors	Eph 4:7-16
Prophet	Eph 4:7-16
Teachers	Eph 4:7-16

through **PROVIDENCE** (cont'd)
Philip   Acts 8:26-40
through **RESURRECTION**
John   Rev 20:4-6
in **RITE**
Isaiah   Is 58:1-14
in **STEWARDSHIP**
Levites   Num 1:47-54

in **RITE**
by **FOLLOWER**
Joseph   Jn 19:17-42
INSTRUCTION on
David   1 Chr 23:1-26:32
REVELATION on
Isaiah   Is 58:1-14
TRADITION of
Priest   Lev 6:8-13;
                      21:1-22:33;
                      Ezek 44:15-31
in **WORSHIP**
Levites   1 Chr 6:31-48;
                      Neh 12:44-13:3

SALVATION through
INSTRUCTION on
James   Jas 2:14-26
Jesus   Lk 17:7-10;
                      19:1-10
in **MISSION**
Angels   Heb 1:5-14
Believers   Jude 1:21-23

SECURITY in
COVENANT of
Jesus   Heb 7:1-28
to **DEITY**
Believers   Ps 46:4-7
David   Ps 124:6-8
God   Ps 127:1-2;
                      Rev 7:9-17
Psalmist   Ps 121:2-8

SECURITY through
in **ENVIRONMENT**
Ebedmelech   Jer 38:1-13
REVELATION on
Isaiah   Is 58:1-14
Israelites   Is 49:1-26

SIGNS of
of **MESSIANIC FIGURE**
Jesus   Mt 11:2-6;
                      Lk 7:18-23
in **MISSION**
Believers   Acts 11:27-30
Disciples   Mk 6:7-13;
                      Lk 9:1-6
Isaiah   Is 61:1-11
Jesus   Mt 9:10-13;
                      Lk 5:29-32
REVELATION on
Levites   Num 1:47-54
TRADITION of
Abraham   Gen 14:17-20
Jacob   Gen 31:17-43

as **TRADITION**
ELECTION to
Levites   Num 3:40-51
Merari   Num 4:29-33

REVELATION on
John   Rev 7:1-8
                      8:1-6
Moses   Num 10:1-10
concerning **SIN**
INSTRUCTION on
Jesus   Lk 17:1-6

in **STEWARDSHIP**
Moses   Num 18:25-32
to **DEITY**
Samuel   1 Sam 2:11-26
by **FOLLOWER**
Joseph   Mt 27:57-61;
                      Mk 15:42-47;
                      Lk 23:50-53
Macedonians   2 Cor 8:1-6
Paul   2 Cor 1:3-7
INSTRUCTION on
Holy Spirit   Acts 8:26-40
Jesus   Mt 8:18-22;
                      10:40-42;
                      20:20-28;
                      Mk 10:35-45;
                      Lk 9:57-62;
                      10:29-37;
                      12:32-34;
                      14:12-14;
                      17:7-10;
                      19:11-27;
                      22:24-27;
                      24:44-49;
                      Jn 13:1-20
Paul   Acts 20:17-38;
                      Rom 12:14-21;
                      3:5-9;
                      4:1-5;
                      16:1-4;
                      2 Cor 8:7-15;
                      9:1-5
Peter   1 Pet 4:7-11
Solomon   2 Chr 2:1-4:22

TRADITION of
ETERNAL
Israelites   Num 10:1-10
as **QUALITY OF LIFE**
Priest   Lev 6:8-13
Priests   Lev 21:1-22:33;
                      Ezek 44:15-31
in **STEWARDSHIP**
Abraham   Gen 14:17-20
Jacob   Gen 31:17-43

to **TRUTH**
of **DEITY**
Jesus   Rom 15:1-13
by **FOLLOWER**s
Gaius   3 Jn 1:3-8
Philippians   Phil 1:3-11
Timothy   Phil 2:19-30
INSTRUCTION on
James   Jas 1:22-25
Jesus   Lk 17:1-6
Paul   Phil 1:12-30
in **MISSION**
Barnabas   Acts 14:19-28
Believers   Jas 1:27
Epaphroditus   Phil 2:19-30

in **WORSHIP**
  of **GIFT**
    Believers   1 Cor 14:26-33

SIGNS

ACCEPTANCE of
  by **FOLLOWERs**
    Believers   Acts 9:32-43
  INSTRUCTION on
    Paul   Phil 2:5-11
  from **MESSIANIC FIGURE**
    Jonah   Mt 16:1-4
    Nicodemus   Jn 3:1-21
  PROPHECY of
    Joseph   Gen 40:1-23
  REVELATION on
    Ezekiel   Ezek 17:1-10
    Jesus   Mt 17:1-8;
                  Mk 9:2-8;
                  Lk 9:28-36
    John   Rev 17:6b-18
    Jonah   Mt 12:38-42
  SCRIPTURES on
    Jonah   Lk 11:29-32

of **ACCEPTANCE**
    Rebekah   Gen 24:11-27
    Servant   Gen 24:11-27
  of **COVENANT**
    Abraham   Gen 21:22-34

of **ANGER**
  caused by **FALSE BELIEF**
    Babylonians   *Bel 1:28-30

of **ANXIETY**
  INSTRUCTION on
    John   Rev 12:10-12

BLASPHEMY as
  INSTRUCTION on
    Paul   2 Thes 2:3b-10;
                2 Tim 3:1-9
  PROPHECY of
    Jesus   Mt 24:9-14;
                15-22;
                23-28;
                Mk 13:14-23;
                Lk 21:7-19
  REVELATION on
    Daniel   Dan 8:9-12;
                13-14;
                9:24-27;
                12:5-13
    John   Rev 13:1-4;
                5-10
  in **WORSHIP**
    Antiochus   *1 Mc 1:54-61

of **BLASPHEMY**
  against **DEITY**
    Israelites   Neh 9:16-18

of **BLESSING**
  by **DEITY**
    David   Ps 86:14-17
    Obededom   1 Chr 13:1-14;

by **DEITY** (cont'd)
                2 Sam 6:1-23
  REVELATION on
    God   Mt 3:13-17;
                Mk 1:9-11
    Isaiah   Is 55:1-13
    Jesus   Lk 3:21-22

CAPTIVITY as
    Philistines   1 Sam 4:1b-22
  FALSE BELIEF concerning
    Prophets   Rev 19:17-21
  PROPHECY of
    Egyptian   Is 20:1-6
  REVELATION on
    Ezekiel   Ezek 12:1-16;
                17:1-10
    Israelites   Ezek 17:11-21;
                19:1-4;
                5-9
    Jeremiah   Jer 24:1-10
    John   Rev 13:5-10
    Zechariah   Zech 5:5-11

CHAOS as
  in the **ENVIRONMENT**
    Jesus   Mt 27:45-56;
                Lk 23:44-45
  PROPHECY of
    Isaiah   Is 24:18c-23
    Jesus   Mt 24:4-8;
                15-22;
                Mk 13:3-8;
                14-23;
                Lk 17:22-37;
                21:7-19;
                25-28
  REVELATION on
    John   Rev 6:12-17;
                8:12;
                16:17-21

COMPASSION as
  of **DEITY**
    Cain   Gen 4:1-16
  REVELATION on
    John   Rev 8:13
    Jonah   Jon 4:1-11

of **CONDEMNATION**
  INSTRUCTION on
    Jesus   Mk 8:11-13
  PROPHECY of
    Haggai   Hag 2:10-14
  REVELATION on
    Israelites   Hos 1:6-7
    John   Rev 17:6b-18
    Zechariah   Zech 5:1-4

DEATH as
    Elijah   2 Kgs 2:1-18
    Uzzah   1 Chr 13:1-14
  by **DEITY**
    Egyptians   Ex 12:29-32
    Uzzah   2 Sam 6:1-23
  through **FALSE BELIEF**
    Israelites   1 Sam 6:1-7:1
    Moses   Deut 12:32-13:18
  PROPHECY of
    Ezekiel   Ezek 24:15-24

by **DEITY** (cont'd)

Elijah	2 Kgs 1:1-18
Gideon	Judg 6:36-40
Moses	Ps 105:26-36
Philistines	1 Sam 5:1-12; 6:1-7:1
Samuel	1 Sam 12:1-25

in **ENVIRONMENT**

Apostles	Acts 5:11-16
Israelites	Num 21:4-9
Jesus	Lk 23:44-45
Moses	Ex 7:14-25; 8:1-15; 16-19; 9:8-12; 13-35; 10:1-20; 21-23; 11:1-10
Philip	Acts 8:4-13
Saints	Mt 27:45-56
Stephen	Acts 6:8-8:3

FALSE BELIEF in

Jesus	Lk 4:16-30

of **FOLLOWERs**

Apostles	Acts 2:42-47
Paul	2 Cor 12:11-13

INSTRUCTION on

God	Ex 4:1-9; 17; 7:14-25; 8:1-15; 16-19; 20-32; 9:1-7; 8-12; 13-35; 10:1-20; 21-23
Jesus	Mk 8:11-13
Moses	Num 16:25-35

by **MESSIANIC FIGURE**

Jesus	Mt 8:28-34; 9:32-34; 11:2-6; 14:13-21; 15:29-31; 32-39; 20:29-34; 21:18-22; Mk 5:1-20; 6:30-44; 8:1-10; 11:20-26; Lk 7:18-23; 8:26-39; 9:12-17; Jn 2:1-11; 4:43-54; 6:1-15

in **MISSION**

Barnabas	Acts 14:1-7
Paul	Acts 14:1-7

PROPHECY of

Isaiah	2 Kgs 20:1-11
Jeroboam	1 Kgs 13:1-34
Jesus	Jn 1:19-51
Micah	Mic 1:2-4; 7:7-20

REVELATION on

Angel	*2 Esd 6:7-28
Ezekiel	Ezek 2:8b-3:3; 8:1-4
Gideon	Judg 6:11-32
Israelites	Num 9:15-23; 17:1-13
Joel	Joel 2:30-32; 3:12-16a
John	Rev 13:11-18
Joshua	Josh 4:1-8
Moses	Ex 3:1-6
Zechariah	Zech 2:1-5

SELF-REALIZATION of

Jews	Acts 19:13-20

in **WORSHIP**

Elijah	1 Kgs 18:1-46
God	Lev 9:1-24

in **MISSION**
of **FULFILLMENT**

Israelites	*1 Esd 7:1-9

MIRACLE as

Barnabas	Acts 14:1-7
Paul	Acts 14:1-7

of **SACREDNESS**

Israelites	*1 Esd 7:1-9

of **VICTORY**

Jesus	Mt 11:28-30

of **OBEDIENCE**

Moses	Num 17:1-13

to **COVENANT**

Abraham	Gen 17:9-14
Moses	1 Cor 10:1-13

to **DEITY**

Abraham	Gen 17:23-27

INSTRUCTION on

God	Gen 17:9-14

REVELATION on

Ezekiel	Ezek 12:1-16; 33:1-9
Isaiah	Is 20:1-6

of **ONENESS**

Zechariah	Zech 11:4-14

REVELATION on

Ezekiel	Ezek 37:15-28

OPPRESSION as
PROPHECY of

Jesus	Mt 24:15-22; Mk 13:14-23; Lk 21:7-19; 20-24
Nineveh	Nah 2:11-13

REVELATION on

Ezekiel	Ezek 4:1-3; 24:25-27
Israelites	Ezek 19:10-14
John	Rev 16:12-16
Zechariah	Zech 1:18-21

of **OPPRESSION**
in **COVENANT**

Paul	Gal 4:21-26

ORDER as
PROPHECY of

Jesus	Mt 24:32-33;

of **SELFISHNESS** (cont'd)
    INSTRUCTION on
      Paul   2 Tim 3:1-9

SELF-REALIZATION of
    of **LEADERSHIP**
      Joseph   Gen 37:1-11
    of **MIRACLE**
      Jews   Acts 19:13-20

of **SERVICE**
    by **MESSIANIC FIGURE**
      Jesus   Mt 11:2-6;
                       Lk 7:18-23
    REVELATION on
      John   Rev 7:1-8;
                       8:1-6
      Moses   Num 10:1-10

of **SEX**
    REVELATION on
      Hosea   Hos 3:1-5

of **SHARING**
    by **MESSIANIC FIGURE**
      Jesus   Mt 14:13-21;
                       15:32-39;
                       Mk 6:30-44;
                       8:1-10;
                       Lk 9:12-17;
                       Jn 6:1-15

of **SUFFERING**
    by **DEITY**
      Philistines   1 Sam 5:1-12
    in **ENVIRONMENT**
      Philistines   1 Sam 6:1-7:1
    INSTRUCTION on
      Paul   2 Tim 3:1-9
    PROPHECY of
      Amos   Amos 1:1-2
      Jesus   Mt 24:4-8;
                       15-22;
                       Mk 13:3-8;
                       14-23;
                       Lk 17:22-37;
                       21:7-19
    REVELATION on
      Ezekiel   Ezek 4:4-8;
                       9-11;
                       12-15
      John   Rev 6:5-6;
                       9:1-12;
                       13:1-4;
                       15:1-16:1

of **TEMPTATION**
    PROPHECY of
      Jesus   Mt 24:23-28;
                       Mk 13:14-23

TRADITION of
    of **PURIFICATION**
      Israelites   Ex 30:17-21
    of **SACREDNESS**
      David   1 Chr 15:1-16:43
      Israelites   Ex 13:11-16
      Moses   Ex 4:24-26
    of **SACRIFICE**
      Israelites   Ex 13:3-10

of **VICTORY**
    INSTRUCTION on
      Elisha   2 Kgs 13:14-19
    in **MISSION**
      Jesus   Mt 11:28-30
    PROPHECY of
      Isaiah   Is 7:10-17
    REVELATION on
      Gideon   Judg 7:9-15
      John   Rev 6:1-2;
                       7:9-17;
                       10:1-11

VIOLENCE as
    PROPHECY of
      Jesus   Mt 24:1-3;
                       4-8;
                       Mk 13:3-8;
                       Lk 21:7-19
    REVELATION on
      Daniel   Dan 10:1
      Ezekiel   Ezek 5:1-4
      Israelites   Ezek 19:1-4;
                       5-9
      John   Rev 16:12-16;
                       17-21

of **WEALTH**
    in **ENVIRONMENT**
      Solomon   1 Kgs 7:40-47

of **WILL**
    REVELATION on
      Mordecai   *Esth 11:2-12

of **WISDOM**
    REVELATION on
      Daniel   Dan 2:24-45
      John   Rev 17:6b-18
      Zechariah   Zech 4:1-6a;
                       10b-14

as **WITNESS**
    to **COVENANT**
      Joshua   Josh 24:25-28

of **WITNESS**
    to **DEITY**
      Isaiah   Is 19:18-25
      Jesus   Jn 10:19-40;
                       Acts 2:14-36
    in **ENVIRONMENT**
      Israelites   Josh 22:9-34
    of **FOLLOWERs**
      Crowd   Jn 12:12-19
      Unbelievers 1 Cor 14:13-25
    INSTRUCTION on
      Jesus   Mt 11:2-6;
                       13:34-35;
                       Mk 4:33-34;
                       Lk 7:18-23
      Moses   Ex 16:31-36;
                       Deut 31:24-29
    by **MESSIANIC FIGURE**
      Jesus   Mt 11:2-6;
                       Lk 7:18-23
      John the Baptist Jn 1:19-51
    PROPHECY of
      Believers   1 Cor 14:13-25
      Ezekiel   Ezek 11:22-25
      Isaiah   Is 8:16-18

WITNESS to
REVELATION on
Daniel   Dan 4:19-27;
     5:18-25;
     7:1;
     8:1-2;
     10:2-9;
Ezekiel   Ezek 1:4-28
     4:1-3;
     10:1-22;
     24:25-27;
     40:1-5;
     6-16;
     17-19;
     20-27;
     28-37;
     38-43;
     44-47;
     48-49;
     41:1-4;
     5-11;
     12;
     13-15a;
     15b-26;
     42:1-10a;
     10b-12;
     13-14;
     15-20;
     43:13-17;
     47:1-12
Isaiah   Is 66:17-24
John   Rev 1:4-20;
     4:1-11;
     5:1-14;
Nebuchadnezzar   Dan 4:10-17

for WORSHIP (in sanctuary)
of SACRIFICE
Isarelites   *1 Esd 5:56-58
Jeroboam   1 Kgs 12:25-33
of SADNESS
Israelites   Ezra 3:12-13

in WORSHIP
of BLASPHEMY
Antiochus   *1 Mc 1:54-61
of FULFILLMENT
Solomon   1 Kgs 6:1-38
of GRACE
Naaman   2 Kgs 5:1-19
of JOY
Israelites   Ezra 3:12-13
of LOVE
Wise Men   Mt 2:1-12
MIRACLE as
Elijah   1 Kgs 18:1-46
God   Lev 9:1-24
of POLITICS
Jeroboam   1 Kgs 12:25-33

symbols for WORSHIP (in sanctuary)
SACREDNESS of
Israelites   Ex 25:10-22;
     23-30;
     31-40;
     26:1-14;
     15-30;
     31-37;
     27:1-8;
     9-19;

SACREDNESS of (cont'd)
Israelites   28:1-5;
     6-12;
     13-30;
     31-35;
     36-39;
     40-43;
     30:1-10;
     11-16;
     33:7-11;
     1 Kgs 8:1-13;
     *1 Esd 6:1-2
Moses   Ex 30:34-38
Solomon   1 Kgs 5:1-18;
     6:1-38

SIN

ACCEPTANCE of
by DEITY
Jesus   2 Cor 5:20-6:2

ALIENATION resulting from
Moses   Lev 7:11-21;
     22-27;
     Num 9:1-14;
     19:11-13

results in ALIENATION
from DEITY
Gentiles   Rom 1:24-32
God   Ps 34:15-22;
     37:23-40;
     Prov 15:1-33;
     Mic 7:7-20;
     Eph 5:3-14
Israelites   Ex 32:20-35;
     Deut 29:16-29;
     31:20-32:47
of FOLLOWER
Holy Spirit   Gal 5:16-21
Judas   Mt 26:14-16;
     Mk 14:10-11;
     Lk 22:3-6

INSTRUCTION on
Isaiah   Is 59:1-21
Jeremiah   Jer 5:20-25
Jesus   Mt 5:27-30;
     18:7-9;
     15-17;
     Mk 9:42-48
Paul   Rom 6:1-14;
     8:5-13;
     1 Cor 5:9-13;
     6:12-20;
     Gal 5:16-21;
     Eph 4:17-24;
     Col 2:16-23;
     3:5-17
Peter   1 Pet 2:21-25
Solomon   Prov 2:1-22;
     17:1-28

ALIENATION through
against MESSIANIC FIGURE
Crowd   Mt 27:33-44;
     Mk 15:21-32
Jesus   Heb 9:23-28
PROPHECY of

DEFEAT caused by	
Israelites	Josh 7:6-26
REVELATION on	
Zephaniah	Zeph 1:2-6
against **DEITY**	
ANXIETY concerning	
Psalmist	Ps 119:129-136;
	137-144
of **BLASPHEMY**	
Adversaries	Ps 74:3-9
Israelites	Amos 2:6-8
Mankind	Ps 10:3-11
causing **CHAOS**	
God	Is 48:1-22
causing **COMPASSION**	
Sirach	*Sir 18:1-14
causing **CONDEMNATION**	
Believer	Heb 10:19-31;
	1 Pet 3:8-12
God	Prov 3:1-35;
	6:16-19;
	12:1-28;
	14:1-35;
	Jn 3:31-36;
	1 Thes 4:1-12;
	2 Thes 2:11-12
Israelites	1 Sam 12:1-25;
	Neh 9:26-31;
	Ezek 16:15-34
Job	Job 19:1-6
Mankind	1 Sam 2:11-26;
	2 Sam 22:1-51;
	Ps 1:4-6;
	18:25-30
Zophar	Job 20:4-29
of **COVETOUSNESS**	
Levites	Num 16:3-11
resulting in **DEATH**	
Jesus	Rom 5:6-11
resulting in **DESTRUCTION**	
Bildad	Job 8:10-19
David	Ps 9:5-8;
	55:9-11;
	58:6-9;
	59:12-13b
Elihu	Job 34:21-28
God	Ps 37:12-22;
	23-40;
	73:13-20;
	94:20-23;
	145:13b-20;
	Prov 10:1-32
Mankind	Ps 1:4-6;
	9:17-20
Psalmist	Ps 92:5-11;
	104:31-35
Zimri	1 Kgs 16:8-14
through **DISOBEDIENCE**	
Eve	Gen 3:1-8
Israelites	Ps 106:6-12;
	*2 Esd 1:4-23
DOUBT as	
Ephraimites	Ps 78:9-20
Israelites	Ps 78:32-39
as **EVIL**	
Mankind	Ps 10:3-11
Sodomite	Gen 13:10-13
GOOD of	
Elihu	Job 35:5-8
forgiven through **GRACE**	
Abijam	1 Kgs 15:1-8
Asaph	Ps 79:5-13
David	Ps 25:1-7;
	16-21;
	32:1-2;
	3-7
God	Ps 65:1-4;
	103:6-13
	130:3-4
Hezekiah	Is 38:1-22
Israelites	Ps 78:32-39;
	*Bar 3:1-8
Joshua	Zech 3:1-10
Manasseh	*Mana 1:6-7;
	11-15
Psalmist	Ps 85:1-3
Sirach	*Sir 2:7-11;
	18:1-14
Solomon	1 Kgs 8:22-53;
	*Wis 11:21-12:2
causes **GRIEF**	
Ezra	*1 Esd 8:71-90
Israelites	*1 Esd 8:91-96
HATE of	
God	Ps 11:4-7;
	31:1-8;
	Prov 6:16-19;
	15:1-33;
	16:1-33;
	20:1-30
Mankind	Ps 5:4-7
Psalmist	Ps 119:97-104
IDOLATRY as	
Israelites	Ps 106:19-23
IGNORANCE concerning	
Mankind	Ps 14:4-6
INDIFFERENCE as	
Israelites	Neh 9:26-31;
	Ps 81:5c-16
causing **JEALOUSY**	
Israelites	Deut 31:30-32:47
Judahites	1 Kgs 14:21-24
JUSTICE in	
David	Ps 7:12-16
KILLING as	
Er	Gen 38:1-11
God	Prov 6:16-19
LOVE overcomes	
Jesus	Rom 5:6-11
through **MARRIAGE**	
Israelites	*1 Esd 8:91-96
through **OPPRESSION**	
Mankind	Ps 10:3-11
Psalmist	Ps 10:1-2
REJECTION of	
Believers	Heb 6:1-8;
	10:19-31
David	Ps 140:6-8
Elihu	Job 34:34-37
Gentiles	Rom 1:24-32
Israelites	Ps 78:56-66;
	Jer 2:1-13;
	6:27-30;
	Hos 10:1-8;
	13:4-6;
	*2 Esd 1:24-40
Mankind	Ps 14:1-3
Sinners	Jn 9:1-41
Sirach	*Sir 15:11-20

REPENTANCE of
David   Ps 7:12-16;
                         19:11-14;
                         51:1-2
Israelites   Num 14:39-45;
                         *Bar 2:27-35
Sirach   *Sir 17:15-32
REVENGE for
God   Ps 9:9-12;
                         Prov 20:1-30
Isaiah   Is 59:1-21;
                         63:1-6
REWARDs for
Zophar   Job 20:4-29
SACRIFICE as
God   Prov 15:1-33
causes **SUFFERING**
Solomon   2 Chr 5:1-7:10

reason for **DEITY's**
ANGER
God   Job 36:26-33;
                         Is 5:24b-30;
                         Rom 1:18;
                         Col 3:5-17
Isaiah   Is 63:7-64:12
Israelites   Num 11:31-35;
                         Deut 9:7-24;
                         29:16-29;
                         1 Kgs 16:8-14;
                         2 Kgs 17:7-23;
                         Ps 78:56-66
Judahites   Jer 44:1-14
Manasseh   2 Chr 33:1-25
Solomon   1 Kgs 11:1-13

causing **DESPAIR**
MEDITATION on
Jeremiah   Jer 8:18-9:1

causing **DESTRUCTION**
Asa   2 Chr 14:1-16:14
Jehu   2 Kgs 10:18-28
through **COVENANT**
Isaiah   Is 28:14-22
by **DEITY**
Bildad   Job 8:10-19
David   Ps 9:5-8;
                         55:9-11;
                         58:6-9;
                         59:12-13b
Elihu   Job 34:21-28
God   Ps 37:12-22;
                         23-40;
                         73:13-20;
                         94:20-23;
                         145:13b-20;
                         Prov 10:1-32
Mankind   Ps 1:4-6;
                         9:17-20
Psalmist   Ps 92:5-11;
                         104:31-35
Zimri   1 Kgs 16:8-14
through **FALSE BELIEF**
Israelites   Ezek 22:23-31
Moses   Deut 12:1-31;
                         20:10-18
Sinners   Jude 1:8-10;
                         11-13
INSTRUCTION on
Isaiah   Is 59:1-21

INSTRUCTION on (cont'd)
Jesus   Mt 7:24-27;
                         13:36-43;
                         47-50;
                         Lk 6:46-49
Paul   Rom 6:1-14;
                         Phil 3:17-21
Solomon   Prov 1:10-19;
                         11:1-31;
                         12:1-28;
                         13:1-25;
                         14:1-35
MEDITATION on
David   Ps 101:5-7;
                         8
by **MESSIANIC FIGURE**
Isaiah   Is 11:1-9
PROPHECY of
Eliezer   2 Chr 17:1-20:37
Isaiah   Is 1:27-31
Moses   Num 32:6-15
REVELATION on
Believers   Mal 3:13-4:3
Daniel   Dan 8:15-25
Isaiah   Is 66:17-24
SELF-REALIZATION of
Judahites   Jer 8:14-17

DESTRUCTION of
in **MISSION**
Jesus   1 Jn 3:4-10
in **WORSHIP**
Josiah   2 Kgs 23:24-25a

DISCIPLESHIP to
MISSION of
Jesus   Mt 9:10-13;
                         Mk 2:15-17;
                         Lk 5:29-32

DISOBEDIENCE as
Israelites   Num 14:39-45;
                         1 Sam 14:1-46;
                         Hos 4:1-3
Joab   2 Sam 18:1-19:8
Judahites   Jer 7:1-15
Saul   1 Sam 15:1-35
through **FALSE BELIEF**
Judahites   Amos 2:4-5
Satan   1 Jn 3:4-10
INSTRUCTION on
James   Jas 4:17
Jesus   Mt 15:15-20;
                         21:33-43;
                         Mk 7:1-23;
                         12:1-12;
                         Lk 20:9-18
Paul   Rom 8:5-13;
                         2 Thes 1:7b-10
PROPHECY of
Isaiah   Is 3:8-12
REVELATION on
Ezekiel   Ezek 12:1-16
Jehu   1 Kgs 15:33-16:7
SELF-REALIZATION of
Jonah   Jon 1:1-17
against **TRADITION**
Ezra   *2 Esd 3:1-36
Israelites   *Sir 48:15-16;
                         49:4-7;
                         *Bar 2:27-35

FALSE BELIEF causing (cont'd)
  of **DISOBEDIENCE**
    Judahites   Amos 2:4-5
    Satan   1 Jn 3:4-10
  of **DOUBT**
    James   Jas 1:5-8
  in **FAMILY**
    Satan   1 Jn 3:4-10
  of **GREED**
    Tyre   Ezek 26:1-6
  revealing **GUILT**
    Herod   Mk 6:17-29
    Lawyers   Lk 11:45-52
  HATE of
    Psalmist   Ps 119:113-120
  of **HERESY**
    Jezebel   Rev 2:18-29
    Pharisees   Mt 23:15
  of **IDOLATRY**
    Ephraimites   Hos 4:17-19;
        7:13-16;
        8:11-14;
        9:10-17;
        11:1-4;
        13:1-3
    Israelites   Num 25:1-5;
        2 Kgs 17:7-23;
        Neh 9:16-18;
        Jer 18:13-17;
        Ezek 16:15-34;
        20:9-26;
        23:36-49;
        Hos 2:2-8;
        4:4-15;
        8:4-7;
        10:1-8
    Jeremiah   *Jer 6:4-7;
        60-73
    Jezebel   Rev 2:18-29
    Judahites   Jer 7:29-8:3
    Moses   Num 33:50-56;
        Deut 12:32-13:18
    Prophets   Jer 23:13-15
    Solomon   *Wis 14:1-11
  IGNORANCE of
    Solomon   *Wis 15:7-19
  JOY in
    Ammonites   Ezek 25:1-7
  of **KILLING**
    Israelites   Ezek 22:23-31
  in **LEADERSHIP**
    Satan   1 Jn 3:4-10
  of **LUST**
    Israelites   Ezek 23:5-10;
        36-49
    Judahites   Ezek 23:11-21
    Peter   2 Pet 2:17-22
    Sinners   2 Pet 2:10b-16;
        3:3-7
  of **PRIDE**
    Israelites   Ezek 16:15-34
  of **REJECTION**
    Israelites   Hos 2:2-8
    Jeremiah   *Jer 6:8-40;
        45-59;
        60-73
    Paul   Phil 3:1-3;
        Tit 3:8-11
    Pharisees   Lk 7:24-30
  in **SACRIFICE**
    Israelites   2 Kgs 17:7-23

  in **SACRIFICE** (cont'd)
    Judahites   Jer 7:29-8:3
    Priests   Mal 1:6-2:9
  of **SELFISHNESS**
    James   Jas 5:1-6
    Lawyers   Lk 11:45-52
  in **SEX**
    Ephraimites   Hos 4:17-19;
        6:10-7:2
    Israelites   Ezek 16:15-34;
        23:5-10;
        Hos 4:4-15
    Judahites   Ezek 23:11-21
    Prophets   Jer 23:9-12
    Sinners   2 Pet 2:10b-16
  revealing **SUFFERING**
    People   Lk 13:1-5
  through **TEMPTATION**
    Satan   Mt 4:1-11;
        Lk 4:1-13
  WITNESS to
    James   Jas 5:1-6

through **FALSE BELIEF**
  causes **ANGER**
    God   Ex 32:7-14
    Moses   Ex 32:15-24
  causes **BLASPHEMY**
    Israelites   Ezek 16:15-34;
        20:9-26;
        22:23-31
    Prophets   Jer 23:9-12;
        13-15;
        2 Pet 2:1-3
  causes **CONDEMNATION**
    Isaiah   Is 1:21-23
    Paul   2 Tim 3:10-13;
        Tit 3:8-11
    Scribes   Mk 12:37b-40;
        Lk 20:45-57
  cause **DESTRUCTION**
    Israelites   Ezek 22:23-31
    Moses   Deut 12:1-31;
        20:10-18
    Sinners   Jude 1:8-10;
        11-13

in **FAMILY**
  through **FALSE BELIEF**
    Satan   1 Jn 3:4-10
  INSTRUCTION on
    Micah   Mic 7:1-6
    Sirach   *Sir 41:5-13

FEAR of
  INSTRUCTION on
    Solomon   *Wis 17:1-21
  of **FOLLOWERs**
  resulting **ALIENATION**
    Holy Spirit   Gal 5:16-21
    Judas   Mt 26:14-16;
        Mk 14:10-11;
        Lk 22:3-6
  COMPASSION for
    Paul   2 Cor 2:5-11
  GRACE for
    Woman   Lk 7:36-50
  LOVE overcomes
    Paul   2 Cor 2:5-11

SIN (cont'd)

HEALING of (cont'd)
Asa   2 Chr 14:1-16:14
INSTRUCTION on
Jesus   Jn 9:1-41

of **HERESY**
FALSE BELIEF causing
Jezebel   Rev 2:18-29
Pharisees   Mt 23:15
INSTRUCTION on
Jeremiah   Jer 5:30-31
Jesus   Mt 23:16-22
Pergamum   Rev 2:12-17

of **IDOLATRY**
Ahab   1 Kgs 16:29-34
Belshazzar   Dan 5:18-25
Israelites   Ps 106:28-31;
                   34-39
Jerusalemites   Mic 6:9-16
Judahites   1 Kgs 14:21-24
Moses   Lev 26:1-46
Nineveh   Nah 1:11;
                   14
Omri   1 Kgs 16:23-28
against **DEITY**
Israelites   Ps 106:19-23
in **ENVIRONMENT**
Israelites   Deut 9:7-24
FALSE BELIEF causing
Ephraimites   Hos 4:17-19;
                   7:13-16;
                   8:11-14;
                   9:10-17;
                   11:1-4;
                   13:1-3
Israelites   Num 25:1-5;
                   2 Kgs 17:7-23;
                   Neh 9:16-18;
                   Jer 18:13-17;
                   Ezek 16:15-34;
                   20:9-26;
                   23:36-49;
                   Hos 2:2-8;
                   4:4-15;
                   8:4-7;
                   10:1-8
Jeremiah   *Jer 6:4-7;
                   60-73
Jezebel   Rev 2:18-29
Judahites   Jer 7:29-8:3
Moses   Num 33:50-56;
                   Deut 12:32-13:18
Prophets   Jer 23:13-15
Solomon   *Wis 14:1-11
INSTRUCTION on
Jesus   Mt 23:16-22
Moses   Deut 6:4-19
Paul   Rom 1:19-23;
                   1 Cor 10:1-13
Solomon   *Wis 14:12-31;
                   15:7-19

PROPHECY of
Ahijah   1 Kgs 14:1-18
Jeremiah   Jer 5:1-14
REVELATION on
Ezekiel   Ezek 8:7-13;
                   14-15;
                   16-8;
                   22:1-16
Israelites   Jer 2:1-13;

REVELATION on (cont'd)
Israelites   20-29;
                   Ezek 20:27-29;
                   30-31
Jeremiah   Jer 1:13-16
Mankind   Rev 9:13-21
Moses   Ex 20:21-23
in **WORSHIP**
Ahaz   2 Chr 26:1-28:27
Amaziah   2 Chr 25:1-28
Amon   2 Chr 33:1-25
Babylonians   2 Kgs 17:24-41
Jeroboam   1 Kgs 12:25-33
Joash   2 Chr 24:1-27
Manasseh   2 Kgs 21:1-18;
                   2 Chr 33:1-25

IGNORANCE of
Jonathan   1 Sam 14:1-46
Moses   Lev 5:14-6:7;
                   Num 15:22-31
against **DEITY**
Mankind   Ps 14:4-6
FALSE BELIEF causing
Solomon   *Wis 15:7-19
INSTRUCTION on
Preacher   Eccl 5:1-7
Sirach   *Sir 19:20-24
Wisdom   Prov 1:20-33

INDIFFERENCE as
Edomites   Obad 1:10-14
Israelites   Hag 1:1-11
Zedekiah   2 Chr 36:1-23
against **DEITY**
Israelites   Neh 9:26-31;
                   Ps 81:5c-16
INSTRUCTION on
Jesus   Mt 12:43-45;
                   Lk 11:24-26

INSTRUCTION on
Jesus   Jn 15:18-25
Job   Job 21:7-13;
                   28-34
Paul   Gal 5:25-6:6;
                   2 Tim 2:20-26
resulting in **ALIENATION**
Isaiah   Is 59:1-21
Jeremiah   Jer 5:20-25
Jesus   Mt 5:27-30;
                   18:7-9;
                   15-17;
                   Mk 9:42-48
Paul   Rom 6:1-14;
                   8:5-13;
                   1 Cor 5:9-13;
                   6:12-20;
                   Gal 5:16-21;
                   Eph 4:17-24;
                   Col 2:16-23;
                   3:5-17
Peter   1 Pet 2:21-25
Solomon   Prov 2:1-22;
                   17:1-28
as **ANGER**
David   Ps 4:2-5
Paul   Eph 4:25-5:2
Sirach   *Sir 27:30-28:12
Solomon   Prov 22:22-23:14
                   29:1-27

of **PRIDE** (cont'd)
   Elihu   Job 35:9-12
   James   Jas 4:1-10;
                      13-16
   Jesus   Lk 18:9-14
   Moses   Deut 8:11-20
   Sirach   *Sir 3:17-31;
                      10:12-25
   Solomon   Prov 11:1-31;
                      21:1-31
of **REVENGE**
   Sirach   *Sir 27:30-28:12
causing **SACRIFICE**
   Israelites   *Bar 1:5-14
   Jesus   Mt 18:7-9;
                      Mk 9:42-48
   Sirach   *Sir 34:18-22
of **SELFISHNESS**
   Jesus   Mk 12:37b-40;
                      Lk 20:45-47
   Jude   Jude 1:14-16
in **SERVICE**
   Jesus   Lk 17:1-6
in **SEX**
   Agur   Prov 30:15-33
   Jesus   Jn 7:53-8:11
   Moses   Deut 22:13-30;
                      27:11-26
   Paul   1 Cor 5:1-5;
                      6:12-20;
                      Eph 5:3-14
   Preacher   Eccl 7:23-29
   Sirach   *Sir 23:16-27;
                      26:5-12
   Solomon   Prov 5:1-14;
                      6:20-7:27;
                      9:13-18;
                      23:15-24:22
causing **SUFFERING**
   Eliphaz   Job 15:17-35
   Hosea   Hos 14:9
   Paul   Rom 2:1-24
   Sirach   *Sir 40:1-11
in **TEMPERANCE**
   Jesus   Mk 9:42-48
of **TEMPTATION**
   Jesus   Mt 18:7-9;
                      Lk 17:1-6
   Paul   1 Cor 5:9-13;
                      8:7-13;
                      10:1-13;
                      Gal 5:16-21
of **VIOLENCE**
   Solomon   Prov 1:10-19
of **WEALTH**
   Sirach   *Sir 26:29-27:2;
                      29:1-7;
                      31:1-11
of **WILL**
   James   Jas 1:13-15
concerning **WISDOM**
   Solomon   *Wis 1:1-5

causing **JEALOUSY**
of **DEITY**
   Israelites   Deut 31:30-32:47
   Judahites   1 Kgs 14:21-24

of **JEALOUSY**
  INSTRUCTION on
    David   Ps 37:1-11

INSTRUCTION on (cont'd)
   Paul   Gal 5:25-6:6
   Solomon   Prov 3:1-35;
                      23:15-24:22

JOY in
  FALSE BELIEF causing
    Ammonites   Ezek 25:1-7

against **JUSTICE**
  in **ENVIRONMENT**
    Elders   *Susa 1:5-18

JUSTICE concerning
  by **DEITY**
    David   Ps 7:12-16

JUSTICE over
  INSTRUCTION on
    God   Ps 82:2-7
    Isaiah   Is 59:1-21
    Solomon   Prov 18:1-24
  MEDITATION on
    Preacher   Eccl 3:16-4:3

KILLING as
  against **DEITY**
    Er   Gen 38:1-11
    God   Prov 6:16-19

of **KILLING**
    Absalom   2 Sam 13:21-14:3
    Ammonites   Amos 1:13-15
    Jezebel   1 Kgs 18:1-46
    Manasseh   2 Kgs 21:1-18
    Moabites   Amos 2:1-3
    Priest   Hos 6:7-9
  in **ENVIRONMENT**
    Andronicus   *2 Mc 4:30-38
    Israelites   Hos 4:1-3
  FALSE BELIEF causing
    Israelites   Ezek 22:23-31
  INSTRUCTION on
    David   2 Sam 11:1-27
    Isaiah   Is 56:9-57:13
    Jesus   Mt 21:33-43;
                    Mk 12:1-12;
                    Lk 20:9-18
  REVELATION on
    Israelites   Ezek 22:1-16
    Mankind   Rev 9:13-21
  in **WORSHIP**
    Ahaz   2 Kgs 16:1-4

of **LEADERSHIP**
    Israelites   Mic 3:1-12
  in **ENVIRONMENT**
    Israelites   Ezek 34:1-10
  FALSE BELIEF causing
    Satan   1 Jn 3:4-10
  INSTRUCTION on
    Solomon   Prov 28:1-28
  PROPHECY of
    Isaiah   Is 9:8-10:4
    Jerusalemites Zeph 3:1-5

in **LIFE**
  INSTRUCTION on
    Paul   Rom 6:1-14
    Preacher   Eccl 7:1-22

REJECTION as	
against **MESSIANIC FIGURE**	
Crowd	Mt 27:33-44;
	Mk 15:21-32
Jesus	Jn 1:1-18
REJECTION of	
INSTRUCTION on	
Author	Heb 3:12-19;
	12:1-2
David	Ps 37:23-40
Father	Prov 4:10-19;
	20-27
God	Is 1:18-20
Isaiah	Is 59:1-21
James	Jas 1:19-21
Jeremiah	Jer 5:20-25
Jesus	Mt 12:22-32;
	21:33-43;
	Mk 12:1-12;
	Lk 20:9-18
John	1 Jn 2:12-17
Paul	1 Cor 15:29-34;
	2 Cor 6:14-7:1;
	2 Tim 2:14-19;
	20-26;
	3:1-9
Peter	1 Pet 4:1-6
Sirach	*Sir 7:1-36;
	9:11-12;
	12:1-7;
	8-18;
	18:27-33;
	19:4-12;
	21:1-7
Solomon	Prov 1:10-19;
	5:1-14;
	23:15-24:22
MEDITATION on	
David	Ps 26:4-6a;
	39:1-3;
	101:2c-4
Jeremiah	Jer 5:1-14
in **MISSION**	
Holy Spirit	Jn 16:5-11
PROPHECY of	
Isaiah	Is 2:6-11;
	3:8-12
Jerusalemites	Zeph 3:1-5
Jesus	Jn 6:60-71
REVELATION on	
Ezekiel	Ezek 12:1-16
Isaiah	Is 65:1-25
Israelites	Jer 3:1-5;
	Ezek 5:5-17;
	20:5-8
Jesus	Jn 1:1-18
of **REJECTION**	
Israelites	Hos 4:1-3
Joseph	Gen 39:1-23
Judahites	Jer 7:1-15
Mankind	Ps 112:10
Susanna	*Susa 1:19-27
against **DEITY**	
Believers	Heb 6:1-8;
	10:19-31
David	Ps 140:6-8
Elihu	Job 34:34-37
Gentiles	Rom 1:24-32

against **DEITY** (cont'd)	
Israelites	Ps 78:56-66;
	Jer 2:1-13;
	6:27-30;
	Hos 10:1-8;
	13:4-6;
	*2 Esd 1:24-40
Mankind	Ps 14:1-3
Sinners	Jn 9:1-41
Sirach	*Sir 15:11-20
FALSE BELIEF causing	
Israelites	Hos 2:2-8
Jeremiah	*Jer 6:8-40;
	45:59;
	60-73
Paul	Phil 3:1-3;
	Tit 3:8-11
Pharisees	Lk 7:24-30
REPENTANCE of	
Israelites	Deut 1:19-46;
	Judg 10:6-18
Saul	1 Sam 15:1-35
against **DEITY**	
David	Ps 7:12-16;
	19:11-14;
	51:1-2
Israelites	Num 14:39-45;
	*Bar 2:27-35
Sirach	*Sir 17:15-32
INSTRUCTION on	
Eli	1 Sam 2:11-26
Eliphaz	Job 22:21-30
Ezra	Ezra 10:7-15
God	Is 1:10-17
Isaiah	Is 28:14-22
Israelites	Is 31:4-9
Jesus	Lk 17:1-6;
	24:44-49
John	1 Jn 1:5-10
John the Baptist	Mk 1:2-8
Paul	Rom 6:1-14;
	1 Cor 15:29-34
Peter	Acts 3:1-26;
	1 Pet 4:1-6
Sirach	*Sir 34:23-26
Solomon	Prov 28:1-28
MEDITATION on	
David	Ps 38:17-22;
	41:4-10
MISSION of	
John the Baptist	Lk 3:1-6
PROPHECY of	
Isaiah	Is 17:7-8
REVELATION on	
Manasseh	2 Chr 33:1-25
Moses	Num 5:5-10
SELF-REALIZATION of	
Daniel	Dan 9:4-19
Hezekiah	2 Chr 32:1-33
Judas	Mt 27:3-10
in **WORSHIP**	
Israelites	Neh 9:1-5a
REVELATION on	
Joab	2 Sam 3:17-39
resulting in **ALIENATION**	
Israelites	Zeph 3:11-13
John	Rev 22:6-21
Moses	Num 19:14-22

SACRIFICE for (cont'd)
Israelites	8:31-36
Levites	2 Chr 29:1-36
Maccabeus	*2 Mc 12:38-45
Manasseh	2 Kgs 21:1-18; 2 Chr 33:1-25
Priest	Lev 15:1-33
Priests	Ezra 10:16-19
Saul	1 Sam 13:1-23

SEX as
Gentiles	*2 Mc 6:1-11

of false WORSHIP
resulting in ALIENATION
Benjaminites	Judg 21:1-7

causing ANGER
Nehemiah	Neh 13:4-9

causing DESTRUCTION
Josiah	2 Kgs 23:24-25a

SPIRIT

of AUTHORITY
of FOLLOWERs
Holy Spirit	Eph 3:14-19

INSTRUCTION on
Jesus	Jn 7:15-24

BEHAVIOR revealing
of DEITY
Ezra	*2 Esd 14:19-48

through FALSE BELIEF
Pharisees	Mt 16:5-12

PROPHECY of
Saul	1 Sam 19:18-24

in WORSHIP
Paul	Phil 3:1-3

COMMITMENT to
INSTRUCTION on
Paul	Rom 8:5-13

of CONVERSION
INSTRUCTION on
Paul	Rom 12:1-2

CREATION by
of DEITY
Mankind	Ps 104:27-30

SCRIPTURES on
Adam	1 Cor 15:42-50

of DEITY
BEHAVIOR revealing
Ezra	*2 Esd 14:19-48

CREATION by
Mankind	Ps 104:27-30

JUDGMENT through
Jesus	Rom 2:1-24; 1 Cor 4:1-5

KNOWLEDGE of
God	Prov 17:1-28
Jesus	Lk 10:21-22
Mankind	1 Sam 16:1-13; 1 Kgs 8:22-53; 1 Chr 28:1-29:30; 2 Chr 5:1-7:10

as MOTIVATION
Cyrus	*1 Esd 2:1-7
Daniel	*Susa 1:42-51
Israelites	Ex 35:30-36:7
Mankind	1 Sam 16:1-13
Zerubbabel	Zech 4:6b-10a

in NEW AGE
Believers	1 Cor 2:6-9

PRAYER for
Paul	2 Tim 4:19-22

PRESENCE of
Daniel	Dan 4:18
Eliphaz	Job 4:12-16
Ezekiel	Ezek 2:1-8a; 3:12-15; 22-27; 8:1-4; 11:1-13; 22-25; 43:1-5
God	Gen 1:1-2; 3:1-8; Ps 139:7-12
Holy Spirit	Tit 3:1-7
Isaiah	Is 32:15-20
Israelites	Ezek 37:1-14; 39:25-29; Hag 1:12-14
Jerusalemites	Zech 7:4-8:23
Joseph	Gen 41:1-57
Micah	Mic 3:1-12
Moses	Ex 17:1-7
Samson	Judg 13:24-25; 14:5-9
Saul	1 Sam 9:1-10:16

as QUALITY OF LIFE
God	2 Kgs 19:9b-37

SALVATION through
David	Ps 31:1-8

DESIRE for
Elisha	2 Kgs 2:1-18

of FALSE BELIEF
BEHAVIOR revealing
Pharisees	Mt 16:5-12

of FIDELITY
INSTRUCTION on
Jesus	Mk 12:28-34

of FOLLOWER
in AUTHORITY
Holy Spirit	Eph 3:14-19

as GIFT
Jesus	1 Cor 2:10-16

as QUALITY OF LIFE
Holy Spirit	Rom 12:9-13

FREEDOM of
INSTRUCTION on
Paul	Rom 8:1-4; Gal 4:1-3

GIFT of
for FOLLOWERs
Jesus	1 Cor 2:10-16

INSTRUCTION on
Paul	2 Tim 1:3-7

PROPHECY of
　Elders　　　　　　　　　Num 11:24b-30
　Holy Spirit　　　　　　　Joel 2:28-29

HONESTY related to
　INSTRUCTION on
　　Jesus　　　　　　　　　Mt 15:10-11;
　　　　　　　　　　　　　　Mk 7:1-23

INSTRUCTION on
　of **AUTHORITY**
　　Jesus　　　　　　　　　Jn 7:15-24
　of **CONVERSION**
　　Paul　　　　　　　　　　Rom 12:1-2
　of **FIDELITY**
　　Jesus　　　　　　　　　Mk 12:28-34
　as **GIFT**
　　Paul　　　　　　　　　　2 Tim 1:3-7
　revealing **HONESTY**
　　Jesus　　　　　　　　　Mt 15:10-11;
　　　　　　　　　　　　　　Mk 7:1-23
　concerning **JUDGMENT**
　　Jesus　　　　　　　　　Mt 15:15-20;
　　　　　　　　　　　　　　Mk 7:1-23
　concerning **KNOWLEDGE**
　　Jesus　　　　　　　　　Lk 8:16-18;
　　　　　　　　　　　　　　12:1-12;
　　　　　　　　　　　　　　Jn 14:25-26
　　Paul　　　　　　　　　　Rom 2:1-24;
　　　　　　　　　　　　　　1 Cor 4:1-5
　concerning **LAW**
　　Paul　　　　　　　　　　Rom 2:25-3:20
　in **NEW AGE**
　　Paul　　　　　　　　　　Rom 7:1-6;
　　　　　　　　　　　　　　8:5-13;
　　　　　　　　　　　　　　Eph 4:17-24
　in **PRAYER**
　　Paul　　　　　　　　　　1 Cor 14:13-25
　as **QUALITY OF LIFE**
　　Jesus　　　　　　　　　Mt 15:15-20;
　　　　　　　　　　　　　　Mk 7:1-23
　in **RESURRECTION**
　　Paul　　　　　　　　　　1 Cor 15:42-50
　in **SALVATION**
　　Paul　　　　　　　　　　1 Cor 5:1-5
　in **STEWARDSHIP**
　　Jesus　　　　　　　　　Mt 23:25-26
　in **TRUTH**
　　Jesus　　　　　　　　　Jn 14:15-17

JUDGMENT of
　by **DEITY**
　　Jesus　　　　　　　　　Rom 2:1-24;
　　　　　　　　　　　　　　1 Cor 4:1-5

JUDGMENT through
　INSTRUCTION on
　　Jesus　　　　　　　　　Mt 15:15-20;
　　　　　　　　　　　　　　Mk 7:1-23

concerning **KNOWLEDGE**
　INSTRUCTION on
　　Jesus　　　　　　　　　Lk 8:16-18;
　　　　　　　　　　　　　　12:1-12;
　　　　　　　　　　　　　　Jn 14:25-26
　　Paul　　　　　　　　　　Rom 2:1-24;
　　　　　　　　　　　　　　1 Cor 4:1-5
　of **MESSIANIC FIGURE**
　　Jesus　　　　　　　　　Jn 2:23-25

KNOWLEDGE of
　Zophar　　　　　　　　　Job 20:1-3
　by **DEITY**
　　God　　　　　　　　　　Prov 17:1-28
　　Jesus　　　　　　　　　Lk 10:21-22
　　Mankind　　　　　　　　1 Sam 16:1-13;
　　　　　　　　　　　　　　1 Kgs 8:22-53;
　　　　　　　　　　　　　　1 Chr 28:1-29:30;
　　　　　　　　　　　　　　2 Chr 5:1-7:10

concerning **LAW**
　INSTRUCTION on
　　Paul　　　　　　　　　　Rom 2:25-3:20

MEDITATION on
　as **QUALITY OF LIFE**
　　Asaph　　　　　　　　　Ps 77:1-10

of **MESSIANIC FIGURE**
　has **KNOWLEDGE**
　　Jesus　　　　　　　　　Jn 2:23-25

in **MISSION**
　as **QUALITY OF LIFE**
　　Jesus　　　　　　　　　Mt 11:28-30

MOTIVATION through
　of **DEITY**
　　Cyrus　　　　　　　　　*1 Esd 2:1-7
　　Daniel　　　　　　　　　*Susa 1:42-51
　　Israelites　　　　　　　Ex 35:30-36:7
　　Mankind　　　　　　　　1 Sam 16:1-13
　　Zerubbabel　　　　　　Zech 4:6b-10a

in **NEW AGE**
　of **DEITY**
　　Believers　　　　　　　1 Cor 2:6-9
　INSTRUCTION on
　　Paul　　　　　　　　　　Rom 7:1-6;
　　　　　　　　　　　　　　8:5-13;
　　　　　　　　　　　　　　Eph 4:17-24

in **PRAYER**
　　Paul　　　　　　　　　　2 Tim 4:19-22
　INSTRUCTION on
　　Paul　　　　　　　　　　1 Cor 14:13-25

PRESENCE of
　of **DEITY**
　　Daniel　　　　　　　　　Dan 4:18
　　Eliphaz　　　　　　　　Job 4:12-16
　　Ezekiel　　　　　　　　Ezek 2:1-8a;
　　　　　　　　　　　　　　3:12-15;
　　　　　　　　　　　　　　22-27;
　　　　　　　　　　　　　　8:1-4;
　　　　　　　　　　　　　　11:1-13;
　　　　　　　　　　　　　　22-25;
　　　　　　　　　　　　　　43:1-5
　　God　　　　　　　　　　Gen 1:1-2;
　　　　　　　　　　　　　　3:1-8;
　　　　　　　　　　　　　　Ps 139:7-12
　　Holy Spirit　　　　　　Tit 3:1-7
　　Isaiah　　　　　　　　　Is 32:15-20
　　Israelites　　　　　　　Ezek 37:1-14;
　　　　　　　　　　　　　　39:25-29;
　　　　　　　　　　　　　　Hag 1:12-14
　　Jerusalemites　　　　　Zech 7:4-23
　　Joseph　　　　　　　　Gen 41:1-57
　　Micah　　　　　　　　　Mic 3:1-12

of **DEITY** (cont'd)
Moses   Ex 17:1-7
Samson   Judg 13:24-25;
                                         14:5-9
Saul   1 Sam 9:1-10:16
INSTRUCTION on
Paul   Rom 8:5-13;
                                         1 Cor 3:10-17;
                                         6:12-20

REVELATION on
Holy Spirit   Joel 2:28-29

PROPHECY of
as **GIFT**
Elders   Num 11:24b-30
Holy Spirit   Joel 2:28-29
as **QUALITY OF LIFE**
Believers   1 Cor 14:26-33

through **PROVIDENCE**
REVELATION on
Israelites   Ezek 36:22-32

as **QUALITY OF LIFE**
of **DEITY**
God   2 Kgs 19:9b-37
of **FOLLOWERs**
Holy Spirit   Rom 12:9-13
INSTRUCTION on
Jesus   Mt 15:15-20;
                                         Mk 7:1-23

MEDITATION on
Asaph   Ps 77:1-10
in **MISSION**
Jesus   Mt 11:28-30
PROPHECY of
Believers   1 Cor 14:26-33

in **RESURRECTION**
INSTRUCTION on
Paul   1 Cor 15:42-50

REVELATION on
in **PRESENCE**
Holy Spirit   Joel 2:28-29
through **PROVIDENCE**
Israelites   Ezek 36:22-32

SALVATION of
INSTRUCTION on
Paul   1 Cor 5:1-5

SALVATION through
of **DEITY**
David   Ps 31:1-8

SCRIPTURES on
in **CREATION**
Adam   1 Cor 15:42-50

of **STEWARDSHIP**
INSTRUCTION on
Jesus   Mt 23:25-26

of **TRUTH**
INSTRUCTION on
Jesus   Jn 14:15-17
in **WORSHIP**
Believers   Jn 4:1-26
Jesus   Jn 4:1-26

in **WORSHIP**
BEHAVIOR revealing
Paul   Phil 3:1-3
of **TRUTH**
Believers   Jn 4:1-26
Jesus   Jn 4:1-26

STEALING

BEHAVIOR revealing
Isaiah   Is 61:1-11
in **ENVIRONMENT**
Danites   Judg 18:14-20
Micah   Judg 17:1-6

CONFRONTATION with
Jacob   Gen 31:17-43

FALSE BELIEF causing
through **disHONESTY**
Israelites   Ezek 22:23-31
KNOWLEDGE of
Lawyers   Lk 11:45-52
of **TRUTH**
Satan   Mt 13:18-23;
                                         Mk 4:10-20;
                                         Lk 8:11-15

through **disHONESTY**
Jacob   Gen 27:1-40
Moses   Lev 19:1-37
Rebekah   Gen 27:1-40
FALSE BELIEF causes
Israelites   Ezek 22:23-31
INSTRUCTION on
Moses   Deut 19:14;
                                         27:11-26

INSTRUCTION on
God   Ex 20:1-17
Jesus   Mt 19:16-22;
                                         Mk 10:17-22
Moses   Deut 5:1-21;
                                         23:15-25:19
Nathan   2 Sam 12:1-31
Paul   Rom 13:8-10
as **disHONESTY**
Moses   Deut 19:14;
                                         27:11-26
in **STEWARDSHIP**
John the Baptist   Lk 3:10-14

JUDGMENT on
by **MESSIANIC FIGURE**
Jesus   Mt 21:12-17;
                                         Mk 11:15-19;
                                         Lk 19:45-46

KNOWLEDGE of
through **FALSE BELIEF**
Lawyers   Lk 11:45-52

LAW concerning
Moses   Ex 21:33-22:17
INSTRUCTION on
God   Ex 20:1-17
Jesus   Mt 19:16-22;
                                         Mk 10:17-22

INSTRUCTION on (cont'd)
    Moses   Deut 5:1-21;
                         23:15-25:19
    Nathan   2 Sam 12:1-31
    Paul   Rom 13:8-10

PUNISHMENT for
    Moses   Ex 21:12-17

REVELATION on
  in RITE
    Israelites   Mal 3:6-12
  as SIN
    Joel   Joel 3:4-8
    Mankind   Rev 9:13-21

in RITE
  REVELATION on
    Israelites   Mal 3:6-12

as SIN
    Edomites   Obad 1:10-14
    Priest   Hos 6:7-9
  in ENVIRONMENT
    Israelites   Hos 4:1-3
    Menelaus   *2 Mc 4:30-38
  REVELATION on
    Joel   Joel 3:4-8
    Mankind   Rev 9:13-21

in STEWARDSHIP
  INSTRUCTION on
    John the Baptist Lk 3:10-14

of TRUTH
  FALSE BELIEF causing
    Satan   Mt 13:18-23;
                         Mk 4:10-20;
                         Lk 8:11-15

STEWARDSHIP

ACCEPTANCE of
    Moses   Lev 23:9-14
  by FOLLOWERs
    Apostles   Mt 10:26-39
  INSTRUCTION on
    Jesus   Mt 10:40-42;
                         21:33-43;
                         Mk 12:1-12;
                         Lk 15:11-32;
                         20:9-18

ANXIETY in
  of FOLLOWER
    Martha   Lk 10:38-42

BLESSING in
    Moses   Ex 39:32-43
  from DEITY
    David   Ps 41:1-3
  INSTRUCTION on
    Jesus   Mt 19:27-30;
                         Mk 10:28-31;
                         Lk 18:28-30
    Paul   Rom 12:14-21
  of MESSIANIC FIGURE
    Jesus   Mt 14:13-21;
                         Mk 6:30-44;

of MESSIANIC FIGURE (cont'd)
    Jesus   8:1-10;
                         Lk 9:12-17;
                         Jn 6:1-15
  REVELATION on
    Israelites   Ezek 44:15-31;
                         Mal 3:6-12

through CAPTIVITY
  in MISSION
    Paul   Philm 1:1-3

COMPASSION in
  of DEITY
    Solomon   Ps 72:8-14
  INSTRUCTION on
    Jesus   Lk 15:11-32
  in MISSION
    Isaiah   Is 61:1-11

CONDEMNATION in
  INSTRUCTION on
    Jesus   Mt 25:14-30

COURAGE in
  INSTRUCTION on
    Isaiah   Is 35:1-10

COVENANT of
  PIETY in
    Paul   Acts 18:18-23

COVETOUSNESS in
  INSTRUCTION on
    Paul   1 Tim 6:6-10

concerning DEATH
  PROPHECY of
    Isaiah   2 Kgs 20:1-11

DEFEAT in
  INSTRUCTION on
    Jesus   Mt 13:3b-9;
                         Lk 8:4-8

of DEITY
  BLESSING in
    David   Ps 41:1-3
  COMPASSION in
    Solomon   Ps 72:8-14
  GRACE through
    Macedonians   2 Cor 8:1-6
  HUMILITY in
    Paul   Eph 3:14-19
  PRAISE of
    Psalmist   Ps 116:12-19

DESTRUCTION for denial of
  PROPHECY of
    Isaiah   Is 60:1-22
    Israelites   Jer 51:1-64

DIGNITY in
  INSTRUCTION on
    Jesus   Lk 22:24-27
                         Mt 10:7-8;
                         26-39;
                         28:16-20;
                         Mk 4:21-25;
                         10:35-45;

INSTRUCTION on (cont'd)

Jesus	12:1-12; Lk 15:11-32; 18:28-30; 20:9-18
Paul	Rom 12:14-21

in **DISCIPLESHIP**

Jesus	Mt 10:7-8; 26-39; 28:16-20; Mk 4:21-25; 10:35-45; Lk 8:16-18; 14:25-27
John the Baptist	Lk 3:10-14
Paul	Tit 2:1-10

concerning **ENEMY**

Paul	Rom 12:14-21
Solomon	Prov 25:1-28

concerning **EVIL**

Paul	Rom 12:14-21

of **FAITH**

Jesus	Mt 24:42-44; Mk 13:28-37; Lk 8:16-18
Paul	2 Cor 9:1-5

toward **FAMILY**

Bishops	1 Tim 3:1-7
Deacons	1 Tim 3:8-13

of **FRIENDSHIP**

Jesus	Lk 10:29-37

of **GOOD**

Paul	Rom 14:1-23
Solomon	Prov 3:1-35

through **GRACE**

Jesus	Mk 10:28-31; Lk 18:28-30
Peter	1 Pet 4:7-11

involving **IDOLATRY**

Paul	1 Cor 8:1-3

of **LIFE**

John	1 Jn 3:11-18

through **LOVE**

Jesus	Mk 12:41-44; Lk 8:16-18; 10:29-37; 21:1-4; Jn 13:31-35; 21:15-23
Paul	2 Cor 8:7-15; 9:1-5; 6-11; 1 Tim 6:6-10

concerning **LUST**

Paul	1 Tim 6:6-10

concerning **OBEDIENCE**

Aaron	Ex 7:1-7
Israelites	Ex 39:1; 2-7; 8-21; 22-26; 27-31; 32-43
Jesus	Mt 19:16-22; Mk 10:17-22; Lk 12:41-46; 17:7-10; 18:18-27; 19:11-27
Moses	Ex 7:1-7; Deut 28:1-14

concerning **PIETY**

Jesus	Mt 6:2-4
Paul	1 Cor 16:1-4

concerning **POVERTY**

Jesus	Lk 14:12-14
Moses	Deut 15:1-11

of **SACRIFICE**

God	Ex 20:24-26
Jesus	Mt 20:20-28; Mk 10:35-45; 12:41-44; Lk 9:57-62; 12:32-34; 21:1-4
John the Baptist	Lk 3:10-14
Moses	Deut 16:16-17; 18:1-8; 26:1-11
Paul	Rom 12:1-2; 1 Cor 16:1-4; 2 Cor 9:6-11
Solomon	Prov 3:1-35

of **SERVICE**

Holy Spirit	Acts 8:26-40
Jesus	Mt 8:18-22; 10:40-42; 20:20-28; Mk 10:35-45; Lk 9:57-62; 10:29-37; 12:32-34; 14:12-14; 17:7-10; 19:11-27; 22:24-27; 24:44-49; Jn 13:1-20
Paul	Acts 20:17-38; Rom 12:14-21; 1 Cor 3:5-9; 4:1-5; 16:1-4; 2 Cor 8:7-15; 9:1-5; 12-15
Peter	1 Pet 4:7-11
Solomon	2 Chr 2:1-4:22

of **SHARING**

Jesus	Mt 6:2-4; 10:40-42; Mk 9:38-41; 12:41-44; Lk 10:29-37; 12:32-34; 14:12-14; 21:1-4; Jn 4:27-42
John the Baptist	Lk 3:10-14
Moses	Deut 14:22-29
Paul	Rom 12:14-21; 1 Cor 16:1-4; 2 Cor 8:7-15; 16-24; 9:6-11
Peter	1 Pet 4:7-11

of **SPIRIT**

Jesus	Mt 23:25-26

concerning **STEALING**

John the Baptist	Lk 3:10-14

of **VICTORY**

Jesus	Mt 13:3b-9;

REVELATION on
Aaron   21-24
SCRIPTURES on
Moses   1 Cor 9:7-14

SACREDNESS in
Aaron   Ex 29:42b-46
Israelites   Ex 36:8-19;
                               20-34;
                               35-38;
                               37:1-9;
                               17-24;
                               25-28;
                               29
Moses   Lev 24:1-4
of FOLLOWER
Holy Spirit   Rom 15:14-24
INSTRUCTION on
Ezra   Ezra 8:24-30
Israelites   Ex 37:10-16;
                               38:1-7;
                               8;
                               9-20;
                               21-31
Josiah   2 Kgs 22:3-20
Levites   Neh 8:9-12
Moses   Ex 35:4-29
REVELATION on
Moses   Ex 13:1-2;
                               Num 4:1-20;
                               21-28;
                               29-33

SCRIPTURES on
Luke   Lk 2:21-40
TRADITION of
Gershon   Num 4:21-28
in WORSHIP
Israelites   Ex 25:1-9;
                               27:20-21;
                               29:10-18;
                               30:17-21;
                               Neh 10:35-36

SACRIFICE in
David   Ps 54:6-7
Moses   Ex 22:21-31;
                               23:14-19;
                               Num 31:25-54
of FOLLOWER
Believers   Acts 2:42-47
Macedonians   2 Cor 8:1-6
of MISSION
Believers   Lk 10:1-16

of SACRIFICE
INSTRUCTION on
God   Ex 20:24-26
Jesus   Mt 20:20-28;
                               Mk 10:35-45;
                               12:41-44;
                               Lk 9:57-62;
                               12:32-34;
                               21:1-4
John the Baptist   Lk 3:10-14
Moses   Deut 16:16-17;
                               18:1-8;
                               26:1-11
Paul   Rom 12:1-2;
                               1 Cor 16:1-4;
                               2 Cor 9:6-11

INSTRUCTION on (cont'd)
Solomon   Prov 3:1-35
REVELATION on
Israelites   Ezek 46:11-15
Moses   Num 18:25-32
in WORSHIP
Israelites   Ex 30:11-16;
                               1 Chr 23:1-26:32;
                               Neh 10:37a;
                               37b-39a

SELFISHNESS in
in WORSHIP
Micah   Judg 17:7-13

SERVICE in
Moses   Num 18:25-32
Samuel   1 Sam 2:11-26
of FOLLOWER
Joseph   Mt 27:57-61;
                               Mk 15:42-47;
                               Lk 23:50-53
Macedonians   2 Cor 8:1-6
Paul   2 Cor 1:3-7
INSTRUCTION on
Holy Spirit   Acts 8:26-40
Jesus   Mt 8:18-22;
                               10:40-42;
                               20:20-28;
                               Mk 10:35-45;
                               Lk 9:57-62;
                               10:29-37;
                               12:32-34;
                               14:12-14;
                               17:7-10;
                               19:11-27;
                               22:24-27;
                               24:44-49;
                               Jn 13:1-20
Paul   Acts 20:17-38;
                               Rom 12:14-21;
                               1 Cor 3:5-9;
                               4:1-5;
                               16:1-4;
                               2 Cor 8:7-15;
                               9:1-5;
                               12-15
Peter   1 Pet 4:7-11
Solomon   2 Chr 2:1-4:22
of MISSION
Believers   Acts 11:27-30
Disciples   Mk 6:7-13;
                               Lk 9:1-6
Isaiah   Is 61:1-11
Jesus   Mt 9:10-13;
                               Lk 5:29-32
REVELATION on
Levites   Num 1:47-54
TRADITION of
Abraham   Gen 14:17-20
Jacob   Gen 31:17-43

SHARING in
Moses   Lev 25:35-38
Paul   Rom 15:25-33
of FOLLOWERs
Paul   1 Cor 9:7-14
INSTRUCTION on
Jesus   Mt 6:2-4;
                               10:40-42;

RECONCILIATION through
    Aaron   Num 16:36-50
SIGNS of
    Philistines   1 Sam 5:1-12
resulting from SIN
    Solomon   2 Chr 5:1-7:10

in ENVIRONMENT
    Israelites   *1 Mc 9:23-27
    Jesus   Mt 4:1-11;
                          Lk 4:1-13
    Samaritans   2 Kgs 6:24-31
    Tobit   *Tb 2:9-14
    CONFRONTATION with
        David   Ps 22:12-21
        Israelites   *Jdt 7:1-22
    as MOTIVATION
        Haman   *Esth 12:1-16
        Moses   Ex 2:11-15
    as PUNISHMENT
        Egyptians   Is 19:1-15
    as QUALITY OF LIFE
        Adam   Gen 3:14-19
        Eve   Gen 3:14-19
        Israel   Ex 5:15-21
        Paul   2 Cor 7:5-13a
        Serpent   Gen 3:14-19
    SIGNS of
        Philistines   1 Sam 6:1-7:1

for ETERNITY
    through FALSE BELIEF
        God   Rev 14:9-12
        Sinners   Rev 20:7-10

through FALSE BELIEF
    through FIDELITY
        Mankind   Ps 16:1-4
    MOTIVATION for
        Zechariah   Zech 10:1-2
    for SIN
        People   Lk 13:1-5

through FIDELITY
    Philadelphians Rev 3:7-13
    to DEITY
        Israelites   Ps 44:17-22
        Job   Job 2:1-3;
                        6:8-13
        Mother   *2 Mc 7:1-42
        Psalmist   Ps 119:65-72;
                        81-88;
                        105-112;
                        137-144

through FIDELITY
    of FOLLOWERs
        Author   Heb 10:32-39
    INSTRUCTION on
        Author   Heb 12:1-2;
                        3-11
        Believers   Rev 14:9-12
        Elihu   Job 36:16-25
        James   Jas 1:2-4
        Paul   2 Tim 2:1-7;
                        3:10-13;
                        4:1-5
        Peter   1 Pet 1:3-9

by MESSIANIC FIGURE
    Jesus   Heb 5:1-10
in MISSION
    Paul   2 Cor 4:7-12;
                        6:3-10
REVELATION on
    John   Rev 13:5-10;
                        11-18
SELF-REALIZATION of
    Paul   Col 1:24

through inFIDELITY
    FALSE BELIEF causing
        Mankind   Ps 16:1-4

of FOLLOWERs
    Apostles   1 Cor 4:6-13
    COMMITMENT to
        Paul   2 Cor 1:3-7
    caused by FIDELITY
        Author   Heb 10:32-39
    KNOWLEDGE of
        God   *2 Esd 16:51-78
    in PRESENCE
        Jesus   Heb 12:1-2
    PROVIDENCE through
        God   *Wis 16:15-29
    as PUNISHMENT
        Paul   Acts 14:19-28
    as QUALITY OF LIFE
        Jesus   1 Pet 2:21-25
        Peter   1 Pet 4:12-19;
                        5:6-11
    for TRUTH
        Paul   1 Cor 9:7-14

through disHONESTY
    of DEITY
        Jeremiah   Jer 20:7-18

INSTRUCTION on
    Holy Spirit   Acts 20:17-38
    Preacher   Eccl 11:9-12:7
    for BELIEF
        Paul   Phil 1:12-30
    in BROTHERHOOD
        Paul   2 Cor 2:5-11
    through FIDELITY
        Author   Heb 12:1-2;
                        3-11
        Believers   Rev 14:9-12
        Elihu   Job 36:16-25
        James   Jas 1:2-4
        Paul   2 Tim 2:1-7;
                        3:10-13;
                        4:1-5
        Peter   1 Pet 1:3-9
    as MOTIVATION
        Paul   2 Cor 1:23-2:4
    in NEW AGE
        Paul   Acts 14:19-28;
                      Rom 8:14-25;
                      2 Cor 4:16-18;
                      2 Thes 1:5-7a
    as PUNISHMENT
        Israelites   Is 50:1-11
        Jesus   Mt 13:47-50;
                      18:7-9;
                      Mk 9:42-48
        Moses   Deut 28:15-68

concerning **PROVIDENCE**

Isaiah	Is 17:1-6
Israelites	Is 14:1-23

as **PUNISHMENT**

Elijah	2 Chr 21:1-23:21
Ephraimites	Hos 9:10-17; 13:12-14
Habakkuk	Hab 2:6b-8
Haggai	Hag 1:1-11
Huldah	2 Chr 34:1-35:27
Isaiah	Is 8:19-22; 17:9-11; 24:1-12; 29:1-8
Jeremiah	Jer 4:19-22; 10:17-22; 14:1-6; 10-12; 21:1-10
Jesus	Lk 23:27-32
Moab	Is 15:1-16:14
Moabites	Jer 48:1-47
People	Zech 14:1-21
Prophets	Jer 23:9-12; 13-15
Zephaniah	Zeph 1:17-18

as **QUALITY OF LIFE**

Ephraimites	Hos 9:1-6
Isaiah	Is 33:7-16; 51:17-52:12
Jeremiah	Jer 4:30-31

in **SALVATION**

Jesus	Mt 24:9-14; Mk 13:9-13; Lk 21:7-19

caused by **SIN**

Isaiah	Is 52:13-53:12

PROVIDENCE concerning

DEITY's

Asaph	Ps 77:1-10
David	Ps 20:1-5; 31:1-8; 32:3-7; 34:4-10; 60:1-5
Elihu	Job 36:5-15; 16-25
Followers	Ps 80:4-7
God	Ps 107:33-38; 39-43; 140:12-13; 146:7c-9; 147:1-6
Israelites	Ps 78:32-39
Psalmist	Ps 88:3-9; 15-18; 119:49-56
Sirach	*Sir 35:12-20
Solomon	*Wis 16:1-14

of **FOLLOWER**

God	*Wis 16:15-29

PROPHECY of

Isaiah	Is 17:1-6
Israelites	Is 14:1-23

REVELATION on

Gog	Ezek 38:17-23

as **PUNISHMENT**

Gehazi	2 Kgs 5:20-27
Israelites	Ps 106:28-31

as **PUNISHMENT** (cont'd)

Judahites	Lam 4:1-22

by **DEITY**

Antiochus	*2 Mc 9:5-29
Azariah	2 Kgs 15:1-7
God	Rev 16:4-7
Israelites	Ex 32:30-35; Neh 9:26-31; Is 1:4-9
Job	Job 10:13-17; 19:7-12
Uzziah	2 Chr 26:1-28:27

in **ENVIRONMENT**

Egyptians	Is 19:1-15

of **FOLLOWER**

Paul	Acts 14:19-28

INSTRUCTION on

Israelites	Is 50:1-11
Jesus	Mt 13:47-50; 18:7-9; Mk 9:42-48
Moses	Deut 28:15-68

MEDITATION on

Jeremiah	Lam 2:1-22

PROPHECY of

Elijah	2 Chr 21:1-23:21
Ephraimites	Hos 9:10-17; 13:12-14
Habakkuk	Hab 2:6b-8
Haggai	Hag 1:1-11
Huldah	2 Chr 34:1-35:27
Isaiah	Is 8:19-22; 17:9-11; 24:1-12; 29:1-8
Jeremiah	Jer 4:19-22; 10:17-22; 14:1-6; 10-12; 21:1-10
Jesus	Lk 23:27-32
Moab	Is 15:1-16:14
Moabites	Jer 48:1-47
People	Zech 14:1-21
Prophets	Jer 23:9-12; 13-15
Zephaniah	Zeph 1:17-18

REVELATION on

Egyptians	Ezek 30:13-19
Ezekiel	Ezek 14:12-23
Isaiah	Is 65:1-25; 66:1-16
Israelites	Jer 2:14-19; 3:1-5; Ezek 4:16-17; 7:1-27; Amos 8:8-10; 11-14
Jeremiah	Jer 14:13-16; 15:1-4; 5-9; 25:15-29; 30:12-17
John	Rev 15:1-16:1; 2; 8-9; 10-11; 18:4-20; 20:11-15
Micah	Mic 6:9-16
Rulers	Zech 11:15-17

in **RESURRECTION** (cont'd)
Jesus	Lk 24:44-49

SECURITY in
Believers	Ps 33:13-19;
	145:13b-20;
	2 Pet 2:4-10a
David	Ps 22:22-26;
	27:4-6;
	32:3-7;
	35:17-18;
	38:17-22;
	40:1-3;
	54:6-7
Ezra	*2 Esd 7:1-18
God	Ps 91:1-13
Mankind	Ps 9:9-12;
	Rev 21:1-8

INSTRUCTION on
Servants	1 Pet 2:18-20
Solomon	Prov 6:1-5

PROPHECY of
Elisha	2 Kgs 8:1-6
Isaiah	Is 25:6-9

REVELATION on
God	*2 Esd 16:51-78
John	Rev 9:1-12

SELF-REALIZATION of
Paul	1 Thes 3:1-10

by **AUTHORITY**
Paul	Phil 3:4-16

for **BELIEF**
Paul	2 Tim 1:8-14

through **FIDELITY**
Paul	Col 1:24

as **QUALITY OF LIFE**
Baruch	Jer 45:1-5
Eliphaz	Job 5:1-7
Ezra	*2 Esd 7:62-74
Job	Job 13:28-14:6

for **SALVATION**
Paul	2 Tim 2:8-13

SIGNS of
attributed to **DEITY**
Philistines	1 Sam 5:1-12

in **ENVIRONMENT**
Philistines	1 Sam 6:1-7:1

INSTRUCTION on
Paul	2 Tim 3:1-9

PROPHECY of
Amos	Amos 1:1-2
Jesus	Mt 24:4-8;
	15-22;
	Mk 13:3-8;
	14-23;
	Lk 17:22-37;
	21:7-19

REVELATION on
Ezekiel	Ezek 4:4-8;
	9-11;
	12-15
John	Rev 6:5-6;
	9:1-12;
	13:1-4;
	15:1-16:1

caused by **SIN**
People	Ps 107:17-22
Solomon	2 Chr 5:1-7:10

FALSE BELIEF in
People	Lk 13:1-5

INSTRUCTION on
Eliphaz	Job 15:17-35
Hosea	Hos 14:9
Paul	Rom 2:1-24
Sirach	*Sir 40:1-11

MEDITATION on
David	Ps 38:3-10
Jeremiah	Lam 1:1-22

PROPHECY of
Isaiah	Is 52:13-53:12

TRADITION of
SALVATION through
Solomon	*Wis 18:20-25

for **TRUTH**
Thesssalonians	1 Thes 2:13-16

by **FOLLOWER**
Paul	1 Cor 9:7-14

INSTRUCTION on
Paul	2 Tim 1:8-14

VIRTUE in
INSTRUCTION on
Paul	Rom 5:1-5;
	1 Cor 6:1-8
Peter	1 Pet 3:13-17

TEMPERANCE

BEHAVIOR revealing
in **ENVIRONMENT**
Holofernes	*Jdt 12:1-20

INSTRUCTION on
James	Jas 3:1-12
Jesus	Mt 6:16-18
Lemuel	Prov 31:1-9
Paul	1 Cor 7:1-7;
	8-16;
	36-38;
	Col 2:16-23
Sirach	*Sir 19:1-3;
	37:27-31
Tobit	*Tb 4:1-21

of **MESSIANIC FIGURE**
Peter	Mt 16:21-28;
	Mk 8:31-33

of **COMPULSION**
INSTRUCTION on
Paul	Rom 14:1-23

CONFRONTATION with
INSTRUCTION on
Joshua	Josh 6:15-21

FALSE BELIEF concerning
reveals **disHONESTY**
Jesus	Lk 17:22-37

FIDELITY in
in **MISSION**
Men	Tit 2:1-10

TRADITION of
Judahites	Jer 35:6-17

of **FOLLOWER**

REVELATION on
Mary   Lk 1:26-38
in WORSHIP
Women   1 Tim 2:8-15

TEMPTATION

BEHAVIOR revealing
INSTRUCTION on
Jesus   Mk 4:1-11
Paul   1 Cor 7:8-16;
                        36-38
Solomon   Prov 23:15-24:22

in BROTHERHOOD
INSTRUCTION on
Paul   1 Cor 8:7-13

CONFRONTATION with
INSTRUCTION on
Solomon   Prov 6:20-7:27
of MESSIANIC FIGUREs
Satan   Mt 4:1-11;
                        Mk 1:12-13;
                        Lk 4:1-13

of DEITY
DESIRE for
Satan   Job 1:9-12;
                        2:4-6
RATIONALIZATION of
Satan   Mt 4:1-11;
                        Lk 4:1-13
Serpent   Gen 3:1-8

DESIRE for
Satan   Job 1:9-12;
                        2:4-6

DESIRE in
INSTRUCTION on
Paul   1 Tim 6:6-10

EQUALITY in
of FOLLOWERs
Jesus   Heb 4:14-16
through FALSE BELIEF
causes SIN
Satan   Mt 4:1-11;
                        Lk 4:1-13

FIDELITY through
Abraham   *Sir 44:19-21
INSTRUCTION on
Paul   1 Cor 7:1-7;
                        2 Cor 11:1-6;
                        Gal 5:7-12;
                        Col 2:6-15
Sirach   *Sir 2:1-6
Solomon   Prov 1:10-19

of FOLLOWER
EQUALITY in
Jesus   Heb 4:14-16

FREEDOM from
INSTRUCTION on
Paul   1 Cor 8:7-13

disHONESTY in
SELF-REALIZATION of
Eve   Gen 3:9-13

INSTRUCTION on
Jesus   Mt 4:1-11
Paul   1 Cor 6:12-20;
                        7:8-16;
                        36-38
Solomon   Prov 23:15-24:22
in BROTHERHOOD
Paul   1 Cor 8:7-13
in CONFRONTATION
Solomon   Prov 6:20-7:27
through DESIRE
Paul   1 Tim 6:6-10
to inFIDELITY
Paul   1 Cor 7:1-7;
                        2 Cor 11:1-6;
                        Gal 5:7-12;
                        Col 2:6-15
Sirach   *Sir 2:1-6
Solomon   Prov 1:10-19
as MOTIVATION
James   Jas 1:13-15
in PROVIDENCE
Paul   1 Cor 10:1-13
as QUALITY OF LIFE
Jesus   Mt 5:27-30
Solomon   Prov 25:1-28
concerning SECURITY
Paul   1 Tim 5:3-16
to SIN
Jesus   Mt 18:7-9;
                        Lk 17:1-16
Paul   1 Cor 5:9-13;
                        8:7-13;
                        10:1-13;
                        Gal 5:16-21

LAW concerning
Moses   Lev 19:1-37
INSTRUCTION on
Moses   Deut 27:11-26

of MESSIANIC FIGURE
through CONFRONTATION
Satan   Mt 4:1-11;
                        Mk 1:12-13;
                        Lk 4:1-13
RECONCILIATION through
Jesus   Heb 2:5-18

in MISSION
in STEWARDSHIP
Paul   2 Cor 6:3-10

as MOTIVATION
INSTRUCTION on
James   Jas 1:13-15

PRAYER concerning
INSTRUCTION on
Jesus   Mt 26:36-46;
                        Mk 14:32-42;
                        Lk 22:39-46

PROVIDENCEthrough
INSTRUCTION on
Paul   1 Cor 10:1-13

as **QUALITY OF LIFE**
  Holy Spirit   Gal 5:22-24
SALVATION through
  Women   1 Tim 2:8-15

as **GIFT**
  God   2 Tim 1:3-7

revealing dis**HONESTY**
  FALSE BELIEF concerning
    Jesus   Lk 17:22-37
  INSTRUCTION on
    James   Jas 3:1-12
    Jesus   Mt 6:16-18
    Lemuel   Prov 31:1-9
    Paul   1 Cor 7:1-7;
        8-16;
        36-38;
        Col 2:16-23
    Sirach   *Sir 19:1-3;
        37:27-31
    Tobit   *Tb 4:1-21
  of **COMPULSION**
    Paul   Rom 14:1-23
  in **CONFRONTATION**
    Joshua   Josh 6:15-21
  in **KNOWLEDGE**
    Peter   2 Pet 1:5-7
    Preacher   Eccl 12:12-14
    Sirach   *Sir 4:11-19
    Solomon   Prov 29:1-27
  in **PRAYER**
    Jesus   Lk 11:1-4
  as **QUALITY OF LIFE**
    Author   Heb 13:1-25
    Believers   Acts 15:6-29
    Bishops   1 Tim 3:1-7
    Deacons   1 Tim 3:8-13
    James   Jas 1:26
    Paul   1 Cor 7:25-35;
        8:7-13
    Solomon   Prov 26:1-28
    Women   1 Tim 3:8-13
  concerning **SIN**
    Jesus   Mk 9:42-48
  as **VIRTUE**
    Jesus   Mt 19:10-12
    Peter   1 Pet 2:11-12
    Sirach   *Sir 31:25-31

in **KNOWLEDGE**
  INSTRUCTION on
    Peter   2 Pet 1:5-7
    Preacher   Eccl 12:12-14
    Sirach   *Sir 4:11-19
    Solomon   Prov 29:1-27

LAW concerning
  INSTRUCTION on
    God   Lev 10:1-20
  REVELATION on
    Moses   Lev 11:1-47

MEDIATION concerning
  TRADITION on
    Israelites   Lev 3:1-17

in **MISSION**
  FIDELITY to
    Men   Tit 2:1-10

as **QUALITY OF LIFE**
  Bishop   Tit 1:5-8
  Paul   1 Cor 9:24-27

in **PRAYER**
  INSTRUCTION on
    Jesus   Lk 11:1-4

PROPHECY of
  in **RITE**
    Nazirites   Amos 2:9-12

as **QUALITY OF LIFE**
  of **FOLLOWER**s
    Holy Spirit   Gal 5:22-24
  INSTRUCTION on
    Author   Heb 13:1-25
    Believers   Acts 15:6-29
    Bishops   1 Tim 3:1-7
    Deacons   1 Tim 3:8-13
    James   Jas 1:26
    Paul   1 Cor 7:25-35;
        8:7-13
    Solomon   Prov 26:1-28
    Women   1 Tim 3:8-13
  in **MISSION**
    Bishop   Tit 1:5-8
    Paul   1 Cor 9:24-27
  REVELATION on
    Manoah   Judg 13:9-14
    Priests   Ezek 44:15-31

REVELATION on
  as **QUALITY OF LIFE**
    Manoah   Judg 13:9-14
    Priest   Ezek 44:15-31
  in **RITE**
    Nazirites   Judg 13:9-14
  as **VIRTUE**
    Mary   Lk 1:26-38

in **RITE**
    Nazirites   Num 6:1-21
  PROPHECY of
    Nazirites   Amos 2:9-12
  REVELATION on
    Nazirites   Judg 13:9-14

SALVATION through
  by **FOLLOWER**
    Women   1 Tim 2:8-15
  INSTRUCTION on
    Paul   1 Cor 6:9-11
  REVELATION on
    John   Rev 14:1-5

concerning **SIN**
  INSTRUCTION on
    Jesus   Mk 9:42-48

TRADITION of
  FIDELITY to
    Judahites   Jer 35:6-17
  MEDIATION concerning
    Israelites   Lev 3:1-17

VIRTUE in
  INSTRUCTION on
    Jesus   Mt 19:10-12
    Peter   1 Pet 2:11-12
    Sirach   *Sir 31:25-31

of **SACRIFICE** (cont'd)
  Israelites   29:36b-42a;
                    1 Sam 2:11-26;
                    Neh 10:34
  Josiah   *1 Esd 1:1-22
of **SERVICE**
  Priest   Lev 6:8-13;
                    21:1-22:33;
                    Ezek 44:15-31
of **VICTORY**
  Maccabeus   *2 Mc 15:28-36
of **SACREDNESS**
  in **AUTHORITY**
    John   *1 Mc 16:18-24
  of **BEHAVIOR**
    Jeremiah   *2 Mc 2:1-8
  in **CREATION**
    Esther   Esth 9:29-32
    God   Gen 2:1-4a;
                 Ex 20:1-17
    Israelites   Esth 9:16-19
    Mordecai   Esth 9:20-28
  of **ELECTION**
    Levites   Num 3:11-13
  ETERNAL
    Israelites   Ex 27:20-21
    Moses   Lev 23:26-32;
                 33-44;
                 24:1-4
  KNOWLEDGE of
    Nehemiah   *2 Mc 2:9-15
    Priests   *1 Esd 5:36-43
  of **LAW**
    Priest   Lev 21:1-22:33
  in **PROVIDENCE**
    Aaron   Ex 16:31-36
  of **RITE**
    Aaron   *Sir 45:6-22
    Israel   Gen 32:24-32
    Israelites   Ex 12:15-20;
                 37-42;
                 43-49;
                 13:11-16;
                 Ezra 3:3b-6
    Moses   Ex 4:24-26
    Priest   Lev 6:14-23
    Women   Lk 23:54-56
  in **STEWARDSHIP**
    Gershon   Num 4:21-28
of **SACRIFICE**
  ETERNAL
    Israelites   Lev 23:9-14;
                 Num 15:1-16
    Levites   Num 18:8-20
  in **RECONCILIATION**
    Aaron   Ex 30:1-10
    Priest   Lev 4:1-35;
                 7:1-10
  RITE as
    Israelites   Ex 12:21-28;
                 29:36b-42a;
                 1 Sam 2:11-26;
                 Neh 10:34
    Josiah   *1 Esd 1:1-22
  SIGNS of
    Israelites   Ex 13:3-10
  for **SIN**
    Eli   1 Sam 2:11-26
    Israelites   Lev 4:1-35
    Ruler   Lev 4:1-35

of **SALVATION**
  from **CAPTIVITY**
    Israelites   Deut 6:20-25
  from **ENEMY**
    Solomon   *Wis 18:1-4
  from **SUFFERING**
    Solomon   *Wis 18:20-25
  through **WISDOM**
    Solomon   *Wis 10:1-21;
                 11:1-20
of **SECURITY**
  from **CAPTIVITY**
    Egyptians   Gen 47:13-26
  REJECTION of
    Esau   Gen 25:27-34
  concerning **VICTORY**
    Mordecai   Esth 9:20-28
of **SERVICE**
  through **ELECTION**
    Levites   Num 3:40-51
    Merari   Num 4:29-33
  ETERNAL
    Israelites   Num 10:1-10
  as **QUALITY OF LIFE**
    Priest   Lev 21:1-22:33
  in **RECONCILIATION**
    Priest   Lev 16:29-34
  in **RITE**
    Priests   Lev 6:8-13;
                 21:1-22:33;
                 Ezek 44:15-31
  in **STEWARDSHIP**
    Abraham   Gen 14:17-20
    Jacob   Gen 31:17-43
of **SEX**
  as **MOTIVATION**
    Abimelech   Gen 20:1-18
  causing **SIN**
    Solomon   *Sir 47:12-22
of **SHARING**
  LAW on
    David   1 Sam 30:1-31
  in **STEWARDSHIP**
    Israelites   Lev 7:28-36
SIGNS of
  of **PURIFICATION**
    Israelites   Ex 30:17-21
  of **SACREDNESS**
    David   1 Chr 15:1-16:43
    Israelites   Ex 13:11-16
    Moses   Ex 4:24-26
  of **SACRIFICE**
    Israelites   Ex 13:3-10
of **SIN**
  caused by **DISOBEDIENCE**
    Ezra   *2 Esd 3:1-36
    Israelites   *Sir 48:15-16;
                 49:4-7;
                 *Bar 2:27-35

INSTRUCTION on
    Eliphaz   Job 15:1-6
    Jesus   Mt 23:29-33
    Paul   Gal 1:6-10;
                       2:11-14

COURAGE in
  INSTRUCTION on
    Paul   Phil 1:12-30

COVENANT of
  ACCEPTANCE of
    Jesus   2 Cor 3:12-18

concerning **DEATH**
  INSTRUCTION on
    Jesus   1 Pet 4:1-6

concerning **DEFEAT**
  INSTRUCTION on
    Jesus   Mk 4:1-9
  REVELATION on
    Daniel   Dan 8:9-12

of **DEITY**
    God   Ps 119:153-160
  ACCEPTANCE of
    David   Ps 17:1-2
    Jesus   Jn 7:15-24
    Nebuchadnezzar Dan 3:28-30
  DISCIPLESHIP to
    James   Jas 1:16-18
  FAITH in
    Unbelievers   2 Thes 2:11-12
  FULFILLMENT of
    Agur   Prov 30:1-14
  IGNORANCE concerning
    Unbelievers   2 Cor 4:1-6
  LOVE of
    Disciples   Lk 24:50-51;
                       Jn 8:21-59
  OBEDIENCE to
    John   1 Jn 1:5-10
  ONENESS in
    God   Eph 4:1-6
  PRAISE of
    Disciples   Lk 24:50-51
  REJECTION of
    God   Rom 1:18
    Judahites   Jer 7:21-28;
                       8:4-7
    Mankind   Rev 16:8-9;
                       10-11
  SERVICE to
    Jesus   Rom 15:1-13
  VICTORY revealing
    Elijah   1 Kgs 18:1-46
  WILL for
    David   Ps 86:11-13
  WISDOM in
    Elihu   Job 36:1-4
    God   Ps 19:7-10
  WITNESS to
    God   Is 45:14-25
    Israelites   Is 49:1-26
    Jeremiah   Jer 10:1-16
    Jesus   Jn 8:21-59
    John   1 Jn 1:5-10

DESTRUCTION of
  INSTRUCTION on
    Baruch   Jer 36:20-26

DIGNITY of
  INSTRUCTION on
    Jesus   Jn 18:28-19:16
  in **MISSION**
    Paul   2 Cor 12:14-18
    Titus   2 Cor 12:14-18

DISCIPLESHIP to
  in **DEITY**
    James   Jas 1:16-18
  INSTRUCTION on
    Jesus   Mt 5:1-2;
                       13:3b-9;
                       10-17;
                       18-23;
                       Mk 4:1-9;
                       10-20;
                       33-34;
                       Lk 8:1-3;
                       4-8;
                       9-10;
                       11-15;
                       9:10-11
  in **MISSION**
    Paul   Rom 1:1-7
    Saul   Acts 9:20-31

DISOBEDIENCE to
  through **FALSE BELIEF**
    Judahites   Jer 8:4-7
  INSTRUCTION on
    John the Baptist Jn 3:31-36
  PROPHECY of
    Johanan   Jer 43:4-7
    Judahites   Jer 25:1-7;
                       42:7-22
  REVELATION on
    Ezekiel   Ezek 33:30-33

DOUBT of
  caused by **FALSE BELIEF**
    Pharisees   Jn 7:32-36
  by **FOLLOWERs**
    Apostles   Acts 9:20-31
  INSTRUCTION on
    Jesus   Lk 22:66-71
  in **MESSIANIC FIGURE**
    Jews   Jn 8:21-59
    Nicodemus   Jn 3:1-21
    People   Jn 7:1-14
  PROPHECY of
    Jeremiah   Jer 38:1-13

ENEMY of
  of **FOLLOWERs**
    Israelites   Rom 11:25-32

FAITH in
  of **DEITY**
    Unbelievers   2 Thes 2:11-12
  by **FOLLOWERs**
    Believers   Jn 12:44-50;
                       Acts 5:11-16;
                       8:4-13
    People   Acts 17:1-9;
                       10-15;
                       16-34
  INSTRUCTION on
    Author   Heb 4:1-13
    Deacons   1 Tim 3:8-13
    Jesus   Mt 13:18-23;

INSTRUCTION on (cont'd)
  Elihu — Job 34:1-4
  Jesus — Lk 12:1-12

revealed by **LEADERSHIP**
  of **FOLLOWERs**
    Paul — 1 Cor 4:14-21
  in **MISSION**
    Paul — 1 Thes 2:1-12

concerning **LIFE**
  INSTRUCTION on
    Jesus — Jn 8:12-20;
      9:1-14;
      14:1-14
    Paul — 2 Cor 4:7-12

LIFE through
  of **MESSIANIC FIGURE**
    Jesus — Jn 4:1-26
  in **MISSION**
    Holy Spirit — 2 Cor 3:4-6
    Jesus — Eph 5:3-14

concerning **LOVE**
  INSTRUCTION on
    John — 1 Jn 2:7-11;
      12-17

LOVE of
  by **FOLLOWERs**
    Jesus — Eph 4:7-16
  in **MISSION**
    Believers — 1 Jn 3:11-18

LOVE through
  John — 2 Jn 1:1-3
  of **DEITY**
    Disciples — Lk 24:50-51;
      Jn 8:21-59

of **MESSIANIC FIGURE**
  ACCEPTANCE of
    Jesus — Jn 4:1-26
  DOUBT in
    Jews — Jn 8:21-59
    Nicodemus — Jn 3:1-21
    People — Jn 7:1-14
  FAITH in
    Disciples — Lk 24:50-51
    Jesus — Jn 4:1-26
  through **GRACE**
    Jesus — Jn 1:1-18
  IGNORANCE of
    Crowd — Mk 6:1-6
    Nicodemus — Jn 3:1-21
    People — Mt 13:53-58;
      Lk 4:16-30
    Rulers — 1 Cor 2:6-9
  LIFE through
    Jesus — Jn 4:1-26
  PRAISE of
    Holy Spirit — Jn 16:12-15
  REJECTION of
    Jews — Jn 8:21-59
    People — Jn 1:1-18
    Pharisees — Jn 8:12-20
  VICTORY through
    Jesus — Jn 1:1-18

WITNESS to
  Holy Spirit — 1 Cor 12:1-3
  Jesus — Mk 1:1
  John — Jn 19:17-42
  Peter — 2 Pet 1:16-19a

MISSION of
  ACCEPTANCE of
    Galatians — Gal 4:12-20
    Thessalonians — 1 Thes 1:2-10;
      2:13-16
  DIGNITY in
    Paul — 2 Cor 12:14-18
    Titus — 2 Cor 12:14-18
  DISCIPLESHIP to
    Paul — Rom 1:1-7
    Saul — Acts 9:20-31
  FAITH in
    John the Baptist — Jn 1:1-18
    Paul — 1 Cor 15:1-11;
      2 Cor 10:12-18;
      1 Tim 2:1-7
    Thessalonians — 1 Thes 2:13-16
  FULFILLMENT of
    Paul — 2 Tim 4:1-5
  GRACE in
    Paul — Rom 15:14-24;
      1 Cor 15:1-11
  HOPE in
    Paul — Tit 1:1-4
  HUMILITY in
    Paul — 1 Cor 2:1-5;
      9:15-23
  LEADERSHIP in
    Paul — 1 Thes 2:1-12
  LIFE through
    Holy Spirit — 2 Cor 3:4-6
    Jesus — Eph 5:3-14
  LOVE in
    Believers — 1 Jn 3:11-18
  OBEDIENCE to
    Disciples — Mk 6:7-13;
      Lk 9:1-6
    Paul — 2 Cor 13:5-10
  ONENESS in
    Paul — 1 Cor 1:13-17
  POVERTY in
    Jesus — Lk 4:16-30
  PRUDENCE in
    Paul — 1 Cor 1:13-17
  SELFISHNESS in
    Pharisees — Mt 23:15
  SERVICE in
    Barnabas — Acts 14:19-28
    Believers — Jas 1:27
    Epaphroditus — Phil 2:19-30
    John the Baptist — Jn 1:1-18
    Paul — Acts 14:19-28;
      2 Cor 4:1-6
    Timothy — 1 Thes 3:1-10
  WILL in
    Jesus — Mk 1:35-39;
      Lk 4:42-44
  WISDOM in
    Jesus — Lk 4:42-44
    Paul — Col 1:28-29
  WITNESS to
    Apostles — Acts 6:1-7;
      16:11-15
    Barnabas — Acts 14:1-7

WITNESS of (cont'd)
Believers	Acts 11:19-21
Bishop	Tit 1:9-16
Church	Eph 3:1-13;
	1 Tim 3:14-16
Disciples	Mk 6:7-13;
	Lk 9:1-6;
	Jn 17:6-19
Ezekiel	Ezek 3:16-21;
	22-27;
	38:1-2
Isaiah	Is 61:1-11
Jesus	Mt 9:35;
	Lk 4:42-44;
	Jn 4:27-42;
	18:28-19:16
Men	Tit 2:1-10
Paul	Acts 14:1-7;
	19-28;
	16:1-5;
	17:10-15;
	18:1-17;
	18-23;
	Rom 1:1-7;
	15:14-24;
	1 Cor 1:13-17;
	2:1-5;
	15:1-11;
	16:5-12;
	2 Cor 2:12-13;
	10:12-18;
	11:7-15;
	Eph 6:19-20;
	Col 1:25-27;
	1 Thes 2:1-12
Peter	2 Pet 1:12-15
Timothy	Acts 16:1-5;
	1 Tim 1:3-7

OBEDIENCE to
Balaam	Num 22:36-40

of DEITY
John	1 Jn 1:5-10

by FOLLOWERs
Believers	1 Pet 1:13-2:3
Corinthians	2 Cor 9:12-15
Disciples	Jn 8:21-59
John	1 Jn 3:19-24

INSTRUCTION on
Corinthians	2 Cor 7:13b-16
David	Ps 143:7-12
Jesus	Mt 13:3b-9;
	18-23;
	Mk 4:1-9;
	10-20;
	21-25;
	Lk 8:4-8;
	11-15;
	16-18;
	11:27-28;
	Jn 3:1-21;
	8:21-59;
	12:44-50
John	1 Jn 2:24-27
Paul	Rom 15:14-24;
	Phil 1:12-30;
	2 Tim 1:8-14
Peter	2 Pet 3:1-2

in MISSION
Disciples	Mk 6:7-13;
	Lk 9:1-6

in MISSION (cont'd)
Paul	2 Cor 13:5-10

PROPHECY of
Israelites	Deut 18:9-22
Jeremiah	Jer 26:7-19

REVELATION on
God	Rom 16:25-27
Jeremiah	Jer 23:23-32;
	26:1-6
Paul	Gal 1:18-2:10

through OLD AGE (maturity)
of FOLLOWERs
Jesus	Eph 4:7-16

INSTRUCTION on
Author	Heb 5:11-14;
	6:1-8
Peter	2 Pet 3:14-18a

ONENESS in
with DEITY
God	Eph 4:1-6

in MISSION
Paul	1 Cor 1:13-17

OPPRESSION of
INSTRUCTION on
Jesus	Mt 23:34-39

PARADOX in
INSTRUCTION on
Jesus	Mk 9:33-37;
	Jn 6:25-59

PATIENCE with
INSTRUCTION on
Paul	2 Tim 4:1-5

PEACE through
on FOLLOWERs
John	1 Jn 3:19-24

INSTRUCTION on
Jesus	Mk 9:49-50
Paul	Eph 6:10-18

REVELATION on
Disciples	Lk 9:28-36

PIETY of
INSTRUCTION on
Paul	1 Cor 5:6-8

POVERTY in
MISSION of
Jesus	Lk 4:16-30

PRAISE of
Disciples	Lk 24:50-51
Zerubbabel	*1 Esd 4:35-41

of MESSIANIC FIGURE
Holy Spirit	Jn 16:12-15

through WORSHIP
Nebuchadnezzar	Dan 3:28-30

PRIDE in
FALSE BELIEF concerning
Paul	1 Tim 6:2c-5

INSTRUCTION on
David	Ps 4:2-5

in WORSHIP
Pharisees	Mt 23:5-12

INSTRUCTION on (cont'd)
Paul   5:25-6:6;
                    2 Tim 2:1-7;
                    4:1-5

SPIRIT of
INSTRUCTION on
Jesus   Jn 14:15-17
in WORSHIP
Believers   Jn 4:1-26
Jesus   Jn 4:1-26

STEALING of
through FALSE BELIEF
Satan   Mt 13:18-23;
                    Mk 4:10-20;
                    Lk 8:11-15

SUFFERING for
Thessalonians   1 Thes 2:13-16
by FOLLOWER
Paul   1 Cor 9:7-14
INSTRUCTION on
Paul   2 Tim 1:8-14

VICTORY revealing
of DEITY
Elijah   1 Kgs 18:1-46
in ENVIRONMENT
Zerubbabel   *1 Esd 4:42-57
INSTRUCTION on
Jesus   Mk 4:1-9
of MESSIANIC FIGURE
Jesus   Jn 1:1-18
REVELATION on
God   Is 42:5-17;
                    Jn 1:1-18

WILL for
of DEITY
David   Ps 86:11-13
INSTRUCTION on
Jesus   Mk 4:10-20;
                    9:49-50
in MISSION
Jesus   Mk 1:35-39;
                    Lk 4:42-44

WISDOM in
of DEITY
Elihu   Job 36:1-4
God   Ps 19:7-10
for FOLLOWERs
Disciples   Mt 13:10-17;
                    51-52
John   1 Jn 2:18-23
INSTRUCTION on
Apollos   Acts 18:24-28
Jesus   Mt 6:19-24;
                    Mk 4:21-25;
                    Lk 8:16-18;
                    24:44-49
Job   Job 6:28-30
John   1 Jn 2:24-27;
                    5:13-21
Paul   Acts 20:17-38;
                    Rom 16:1-23;
                    1 Cor 1:18-25;
                    2 Cor 1:12-14;
                    Eph 5:3-14;
                    15-20;

INSTRUCTION on (cont'd)
Paul   Col 3:5-17
Preacher   Eccl 12:8-11
Sirach   *Sir 36:18-20
MISSION of
Jesus   Lk 4:42-44
Paul   Col 1:28-29
REVELATION on
Daniel   Dan 10:1
Holy Spirit   Eph 3:1-13
Paul   Rom 1:19-23;
                    Eph 3:1-13;
                    Phil 3:4-16
SELF-REALIZATION of
Paul   2 Cor 11:1-6

WITNESS to
Elihu   Job 32:15-22
Holy Spirit   1 Jn 5:8-12
of DEITY
God   Is 45:14-25
Israelites   Is 49:1-26
Jeremiah   Jer 10:1-16
Jesus   Jn 8:21-59
John   1 Jn 1:5-10
in ENVIRONMENT
Daniel   *Susa 1:52-59
by FOLLOWER
Barnabas   Acts 9:20-31
Holy Spirit   Rom 9:1-5;
                    1 Cor 2:10-16
Jesus   Jn 15:26-27
John   Jn 21:24-25
INSTRUCTION on
Apollos   Acts 18:24-28
Apostles   Acts 8:14-25
Barnabas   Acts 11:25-26
Baruch   Jer 36:8-10;
                    11-19
Holy Spirit   Jn 16:12-15
Israelites   Zech 7:4-8:23
Jesus   Mk 4:21-25;
                    26-29;
                    Lk 8:16-18;
                    9:57-62;
                    11:33-36;
                    Jn 5:19-47
John   1 Jn 1:1-4
Luke   Lk 1:1-4
Paul   Acts 13:14-52;
                    14:8-18;
                    19:1-12;
                    21:27-22:29;
                    26:1-32;
                    28:17-31;
                    1 Cor 11:23-26;
                    Gal 3:1-5;
                    Eph 4:25-5:2;
                    1 Tim 3:14-16;
                    4:6-10;
                    6:2c-5;
                    2 Tim 1:8-14;
                    2:1-7;
                    14-19;
                    4:1-5
Peter   Acts 10:1-11:18;
                    1 Pet 3:13-17;
                    5:12-14
Philip   Acts 8:4-13;
                    26-40
Saul   Acts 9:20-31

over **ENVIRONMENT** (cont'd)
Maccabeus	10-12;
	13-23;
	32-37;
	13:9-26
Macron	*2 Mc 10:14-23
Mattathias	*1 Mc 2:39-48
Nebuchadnezzar	*Jdt 1:1-2:20
Ptolemy	*1 Mc 11:1-19
Romans	*1 Mc 8:1-32
Shamgar	Judg 3:31
Simon	*1 Mc 11:54-74;
	12:24-34;
	13:42-53

INSTRUCTION on
Judith	*Jdt 14:1-5
Moses	Deut 7:1-5;
	21:10-14;
	28:1-14;
	31:1-8

by **MESSIANIC FIGURE**
Psalmist	Ps 2:7-9

PROPHECY of
Ahithophel	2 Sam 16:15-17:29
Babylonians	Jer 46:13-26
Balaam	Num 24:14-25
Deborah	Judg 4:6-9
Elisha	2 Kgs 3:1-27;
	13:14-19
Hezekiah	Is 38:1-22
Isaiah	Is 29:1-8
Israelites	Zech 9:13-17
Jerusalemites	Zech 14:1-21
Joshua	Josh 17:14-18
Samuel	1 Sam 15:1-35

REVELATION on
Babylonians	Ezek 32:1-16
Gideon	Judg 6:11-32
Isaiah	Is 54:1-17
Israel	Gen 32:24-32
Israelites	Judg 20:24-28;
	Ezek 39:1-16;
	Zeph 2:8-12
Jeremiah	Jer 1:17-19
John	Rev 12:10-12;
	13-17;
	15:1-16:1;
	17:6b-18;
	19:17-21
Joshua	Josh 8:1-29;
	10:1-15
Judahites	Is 7:1-9
Maccabeus	*2 Mc 15:11-19
Michael	Rev 12:7-9
Moses	Num 33:50-56
Nebuchadnezzar	Ezek 29:17-21

through **COVENANT**
PROMISE of
Moses	Ex 34:10-11

in the **CREATION**
REVELATION on
Isaiah	Is 54:1-17

by **DEITY**
through **PROVIDENCE**
Abijah	2 Chr 13:1-22
Asa	2 Chr 14:1-16:14
Believers	Ps 47:1-4;
	Eph 6:10-18

through **PROVIDENCE** (cont'd)
Cyrus	Is 44:24-45:13
David	2 Sam 8:1-18;
	22:1-51;
	1 Chr 18:1-20:8;
	Ps 9:1-4;
	18:16-19;
	46-50;
	20:6-9;
	21:8-13;
	22:1-5;
	27:1-3;
	4-6;
	35:9-10;
	59:16-17;
	61:4-5;
	89:19-37;
	110:5-7;
	124:1-5;
	144:9-11
Gideon	Judg 8:1-3
God	Ps 33:13-19;
	48:4-8;
	55:15-19;
	68:4-14;
	19-23;
	69:29-36;
	89:5-18;
	118:15-21;
	136:10-22;
	149:1-4;
	Prov 21:1-31
Hezekiah	2 Kgs 20:1-11
Isaiah	Is 59:1-21
Israelites	Ex 3:7-10;
	Num 21:33-35;
	Deut 1:19-46;
	2:26-3:11;
	12-22;
	9:1-6;
	12:1-31;
	31:1-8;
	Josh 11:16-23;
	Judg 4:10-16;
	7:16-22;
	1 Sam 19:1-10;
	1 Chr 15:1-16:43;
	Neh 4:13-23;
	Ps 44:1-3;
	4-8;
	105:7-15;
	23-25;
	106:6-12;
	Is 43:14-44:5
Jacob	Gen 46:1-7
Jephthah	Judg 11:29-33
Jeroboam	2 Kgs 14:23-29
Jesus	Rom 8:1-4;
	Col 2:6-15
Joshua	Num 14:8-9;
	Josh 23:1-16
Judah	Judg 1:1-21
Maccabeus	*1 Mc 4:1-35
Mankind	Ps 18:25-30
Paul	2 Tim 3:10-13
Psalmist	Ps 92:5-11;
	94:16-19
Uzziah	2 Chr 26:1-28:27

RECONCILIATION through
Isaiah	Is 63:1-6
Israelites	Nah 1:10, 12, 13;

in **RESURRECTION**
　Jesus　　　　　　Acts 2:14-36
SALVATION through
　Believers　　　　1 Jn 4:4-6
　David　　　　　　1 Sam 17:1-18:5;
　　　　　　　　　　Ps 54:6-7
　God　　　　　　Ps 3:7-8;
　　　　　　　　　　Mt 24:23-28;
　　　　　　　　　　Mk 13:14-23
　Isaiah　　　　　Is 63:1-6
　Israelites　　　Deut 33:1-29
　Jesus　　　　　1 Cor 15:51-58
　Judith　　　　　*Jdt 9:1-14
SECURITY in
　Believers　　　Ps 46:8-11

through **DEITY**
　BELIEF in
　　David　　　　Ps 56:6b-9;
　　　　　　　　　59:9-10
　　Jeremiah　　Jer 20:7-18
　　Jesus　　　　1 Jn 4:19-5:5
　in **CONFRONTATION**
　　David　　　　2 Sam 22:1-51;
　　　　　　　　　Ps 17:13-14;
　　　　　　　　　18:31-42;
　　　　　　　　　41:11-12
　　God　　　　　Ps 76:1-3;
　　　　　　　　　144:1-2
　　Israelites　　Neh 9:22-25
　　Jacob　　　　Hos 12:2-6
　　Judith　　　　*Jdt 16:1-17
　　Maccabeus　*1 Mc 3:10-26;
　　　　　　　　　*2 Mc 8:24-33;
　　　　　　　　　12:13-23;
　　　　　　　　　26-28;
　　　　　　　　　15:20-27
　　Psalmist　　Ps 118:10-14
　ELECTION of
　　Assyrians　　Is 10:5-16
　　Israelites　　Deut 4:15-31
　FIDELITY in
　　Believers　　Ps 149:5-9
　　Mattathias　*1 Mc 2:39-48
　FREEDOM in
　　Israelites　　2 Kgs 13:1-9
　IGNORANCE of
　　David　　　　Ps 17:3-5
　KNOWLEDGE of
　　Egyptians　　Ex 14:15-22
　in **NEW AGE**
　　Mankind　　Rev 21:1-8
　PRAYER for
　　David　　　　Ps 3:7-8;
　　　　　　　　　7:1-2;
　　　　　　　　　6-8;
　　　　　　　　　9:17-20;
　　　　　　　　　12:7-8;
　　　　　　　　　22:12-21;
　　　　　　　　　35:1-3;
　　　　　　　　　17-18;
　　　　　　　　　22-28;
　　　　　　　　　38:17-22;
　　　　　　　　　40:13-17;
　　　　　　　　　55:1-3a;
　　　　　　　　　59:1-5;
　　　　　　　　　60:1-5;
　　　　　　　　　9-12;
　　　　　　　　　68:1-3;
　　　　　　　　　69:1-3;
　　　　　　　　　4-12;

PRAYER for (cont'd)
　　　　　　　　　108:6-13;
　　　　　　　　　140:6-8;
　　　　　　　　　143:7-12
　Hezekiah　　　Is 37:8-20
　Isaiah　　　　Is 63:7-64:12
　Israelites　　Ps 25:22
　Job　　　　　Job 17:1-5
　Psalmist　　　Ps 43:1-5;
　　　　　　　　　71:1-21;
　　　　　　　　　80:1-3;
　　　　　　　　　14-19;
　　　　　　　　　118:22-27;
　　　　　　　　　120:1-2
PRESENCE of
　David　　　　2 Sam 7:1-29;
　　　　　　　　　1 Chr 17:1-27
　Israelites　　Deut 20:1-9;
　　　　　　　　　Jer 46:27-28;
　　　　　　　　　Zech 10:3-12
　Jephthah　　Judg 11:29-33
　Jeremiah　　Jer 1:4-10;
　　　　　　　　　17-19
　Samson　　　Judg 14:10-20;
　　　　　　　　　15:9-20
PROMISE of
　David　　　　Ps 110:1-4
　God　　　　　Ps 50:7-15
　Peter　　　　2 Pet 1:3-4
of **TRUTH**
　Elijah　　　　1 Kgs 18:1-46
VIRTUE of
　God　　　　　Ps 98:1-3

through **DEITY's**
　AUTHORITY
　　God　　　　Gen 18:9-15;
　　　　　　　　　Ps 24:7-10;
　　　　　　　　　48:9-14;
　　　　　　　　　60:6-8;
　　　　　　　　　76:4-6;
　　　　　　　　　Jer 32:16-25;
　　　　　　　　　Mt 19:23-26;
　　　　　　　　　Mk 10:23-27;
　　　　　　　　　Lk 1:26-38
　　Isaiah　　　Is 63:1-6
　　Jesus　　　Lk 18:18-27
　　Paul　　　　Phil 4:10-20

DESIRE for
　PROPHECY of
　　Zedekiah　Jer 21:1-10

ELECTION for
　by **DEITY**
　　Assyrians　Is 10:5-16
　　Israelites　Deut 4:15-31
　PROPHECY of
　　Israelites　Is 27:12-13
　　Jesus　　　Mt 24:29-31;
　　　　　　　　Mk 13:24-27

over **ENVIRONMENT**
　by **AUTHORITY**
　　Samson　　Judg 16:4-9;
　　　　　　　　10-12;
　　　　　　　　13-15;
　　　　　　　　23-31

　BELIEF in
　　Caleb　　　Num 13:26b-33
　　Danites　　Judg 18:7-10

through **KNOWLEDGE**
  Solomon   Prov 23:15-24:22
through **LAW**
  Jesus   Jn 12:44-50
in **NEW AGE**
  Ephesus   Rev 2:1-7
  Jesus   Mt 13:36-43;
                  19:27-30;
                  Mk 10:28-31;
                  Lk 13:18-19;
                  18:28-30
  Loadicea   Rev 3:14-22
  Paul   1 Cor 15:20-28;
                  Col 3:1-4
  Pergamum   Rev 2:12-17
  Philadelphians   Rev 3:7-13
  Sardis   Rev 3:1-6
  Smyrna   Rev 2:8-11
through **PROVIDENCE**
  Joshua   Josh 24:1-13
in **RESURRECTION**
  Paul   Rom 7:1-6
through **SALVATION**
  Paul   1 Thes 4:13-18
over **SIN**
  God   Gen 4:1-16
through **STEWARDSHIP**
  Jesus   Mt 13:3b-9;
                  Lk 8:4-8
through **TRUTH**
  Jesus   Mk 4:1-9

JUDGMENT in
  REVELATION on
    Daniel   Dan 7:17-27

KNOWLEDGE of
  through **DEITY**
    Egyptians   Ex 14:15-22
  of **FOLLOWER**
    Disciples   Jn 8:21-59
  MEDITATION on
    Paul   2 Tim 4:6-8
  REVELATION on
    Abraham   Gen 15:1-21
  TRADITIONS of
    Israelites   Josh 12:1-6;
                  7-24;
                  2 Sam 23:8-39;
                  1 Chr 11:1-12:40

through **KNOWLEDGE**
  INSTRUCTION on
    Solomon   Prov 23:15-24:22

through **LAW**
  INSTRUCTION on
    Jesus   Jn 12:44-50

through **MEDIATION**
  for **FOLLOWER**
    Jesus   Rom 8:28-39

of **MESSIANIC FIGURE**
  in **CONFRONTATION**
    Psalmist   Ps 2:7-9
  in **NEW AGE**
    Jesus   Jn 16:29-33
  PROMISE of
    Jesus   Jn 14:27-31
    Zechariah   Zech 9:1-12

SALVATION through
  Jesus   Heb 2:5-18

through **MESSIANIC FIGURE**
  AUTHORITY
    Jesus   Mt 8:28-34;
                  Mk 5:1-20;
                  Lk 8:26-39
  of **TRUTH**
    Jesus   Jn 1:1-18

in **MISSION**
  SIGNS of
    Jesus   Mt 11:28-30

as **MOTIVATION**
  in **ENVIRONMENT**
    Danites   Judg 18:11-13

in **NEW AGE**
  by **DEITY**
    Mankind   Rev 21:1-8
  INSTRUCTION on
    Ephesus   Rev 2:1-7
    Jesus   Mt 13:36-43;
                  19:27-30;
                  Mk 10:28-31;
                  Lk 13:18-19;
                  18:28-30
    Laodicea   Rev 3:14-22
    Paul   1 Cor 15:20-28;
                  Col 3:1-4
    Pergamum   Rev 2:12-17
    Philadelphians   Rev 3:7-13
    Sardis   Rev 3:1-6
    Smyrna   Rev 2:8-11
  through **MESSIANIC FIGURE**
    Jesus   Jn 16:29-33
  PROPHECY of
    Balaam   Num 23:27-24:13
    Isaiah   Is 9:1;
                  25:6-9;
                  51:17-52:12;
                  13:53:12
    Jesus   Mt 26:57-68;
                  Mk 14:53-65;
                  Lk 21:25-28
    Obadiah   Obad 1:17-21
  REVELATION on
    Daniel   Dan 17-27
    Isaiah   Is 60:1-22
    John   Rev 7:9-17;
                  12:10-12;
                  20:11-15
  PRAYER for
    through **DEITY**
    David   Ps 3:7-8;
                  7:1-2;
                  9:17-20;
                  12:7-8;
                  22:12-21;
                  35:1-3;
                  17-18;
                  22-28;
                  38:17-22;
                  40:13-17;
                  55:1-3a;
                  59:1-5;
                  60:1-5;
                  9-12;
                  68:1-3;

of **DEITY** (cont'd)

David	Ps 9:1-4; 18:16-19; 46-50; 20:6-9; 21:8-13; 22:1-5; 27:1-3; 4-6; 35:9-10; 59:16-17; 61:4-5; 89:19-37; 110:5-7; 124:1-5; 144:9-11
Gideon	Judg 8:1-3
God	Ps 33:13-19; 48:4-8; 55:15-19; 68:4-14; 19-23; 69:29-36; 89:5-18; 118:15-21; 136:10-22; 149:1-4; Prov 21:1-31
Hezekiah	2 Kgs 20:1-11
Isaiah	Is 59:1-21
Israelites	Ex 3:7-10; Num 21:33-35; Deut 1:19-46; 2:26-3:11; 12-22; 9:1-6; 12:1-31; 31:1-8; Josh 11:16-23; Judg 4:10-16; 7:16-22; 1 Sam 19:1-10; 1 Chr 15:1-16:43; Neh 4:13-23; Ps 44:1-3; 4-8; 105:7-15; 23-25; 106:6-12; Is 43:14-44:5
Jacob	Gen 46:1-7
Jephthah	Judg 11:29-33
Jeroboam	2 Kgs 14:23-29
Jesus	Rom 8:1-4; Col 2:6-15
Joshua	Num 14:8-9; Josh 23:1-16
Judah	Judg 1:1-21
Maccabeus	*1 Mc 4:1-35
Mankind	Ps 18:25-30
Paul	2 Tim 3:10-13
Psalmist	Ps 92:5-11; 94:16-19
Uzziah	2 Chr 26:1-28:27

in **ENVIRONMENT**

God	Ps 68:15-18
Joshua	Josh 10:28-43

INSTRUCTION on

Joshua	Josh 24:1-13

PROPHECY of

Ahab	1 Kgs 20:1-43

PROPHECY of (cont'd)

Amaziah	2 Chr 25:1-28
Ehud	Judg 3:26-30
Isaiah	2 Kgs 19:9b-37; Is 9-2-7; 11:10-16; 14:1-23; 26:1-6; 37:33-35; 40:12-31; 51:17-52:12
Jacobites	Mic 5:7-15
Jahaziel	2 Chr 17:1-20:37
Jerusalemites	Zech 12:1-13:6
Joshua	Josh 10:16-27
Judahites	Zech 12:1-13:6
Micah	Mic 4:9-5:6

REVELATION on

Babylonians	Ezek 30:6-9; 20-26
Cyrus	Is 44:24-45:13
David	1 Sam 23:1-13; 2 Sam 5:17-25; 1 Chr 14:1-17
Gideon	Judg 7:1-8
God	Is 41:1-42:4
Israelites	Is 45:14-25; 49:1-26; Zeph 3:14-20
Joshua	Josh 11:1-15; 13:1-7
Moses	Ex 14:15-22

RECONCILIATION through

of **DEITY**

Isaiah	Is 63:1-6
Israelites	Nah 1:10,12,13; 15-2:2

over **ENVIRONMENT**

Judith	*Jdt 13:11-20

PROPHECY of

Israelites	Nah 2:1-5

REVELATION on

Daniel	Dan 8:13-14

RESPECT through

REVELATION on

Israelites	Is 45:14-25

through **RESURRECTION**

by **DEITY**

Jesus	Acts 2:14-36

INSTRUCTION on

Paul	Rom 7:1-6

PROPHECY of

Jesus	Mt 16:21-28; 20:17-19; Lk 9:18-22; 18:31-34; Jn 2:12-22

REVELATION on

of **AUTHORITY**

Daniel	Dan 8:15-25
God	Is 41:1-42:4
John	Rev 13:5-10

in **CONFRONTATION**

Babylonians	Ezek 32:1-16
Gideon	Judg 6:11-32
Isaiah	Is 54:1-17

in CONFRONTATION (cont'd)

Israel	Gen 32:24-32
Israelites	Judg 20:24-28;
	Ezek 39:1-16;
	Zeph 2:8-12
Jeremiah	Jer 1:17-19
John	Rev 12:10-12;
	13-17;
	15:1-16:1;
	17:6b-18;
	19:17-21
Joshua	Josh 8:1-29;
	10:1-15
Judahites	Is 7:1-9
Maccabeus	*2 Mc 15:11-19
Michael	Rev 12:7-9
Moses	Num 33:50-56
Nebuchadnezzar	Ezek 29:17-21

in the CREATION

Isaiah	Is 54:1-17

for ETERNITY

Israelites	Is 45:14-25

through FIDELITY

John	Rev 14:13

in NEW AGE

Daniel	Dan 7:2-14;
	17-27
Isaiah	Is 60:1-22
John	Rev 7:9-17;
	12:10-12;
	20:11-15

through PROVIDENCE

Babylonians	Ezek 30:6-9;
	20-26
Cyrus	Is 44:24-45:13
David	1 Sam 23:1-13;
	2 Sam 5:17-25;
	1 Chr 14:1-17
Gideon	Judg 7:1-8
God	Is 41:1-42:4
Israelites	Is 45:14-25;
	49:1-26;
	Zeph 3:14-20
Joshua	Josh 11:1-15;
	13:1-7
Moses	Ex 14:15-22

in RECONCILIATION

Daniel	Dan 8:13-14

through RESPECT

Israelites	Is 45:14-25

through SALVATION

Daniel	Dan 12:1-4
Jeremiah	Jer 15:10-21
John	Rev 12:1-6
Judahites	Hos 1:6-7

of TRUTH

God	Is 42:5-17;
	Jn 1:1-18

as VIRTUE

Job	Job 40:6-14

RITE of

INSTRUCTION on

Deborah	Judg 5:10-11

as TRADITION

Maccabeus	*2 Mc 15:28-36

SALVATION through

Israelites	Ex 15:1-18

of DEITY

Believers	1 Jn 4:4-6

of DEITY (cont'd)

David	1 Sam 17:1-18:5;
	Ps 54:6-7
God	Ps 3:7-8;
	Mt 24:23-28;
	Mk 13:14-23
Isaiah	Is 63:1-6
Israelites	Deut 33:1-29
Jesus	1 Cor 15:51-58
Judith	*Jdt 9:1-14

over ENVIRONMENT

Othniel	Judg 3:7-11

INSTRUCTION on

Paul	1 Thes 4:13-18

of MESSIANIC FIGURE

Jesus	Heb 2:5-18

PROPHECY of

Isaiah	Is 11:10-16;
	51:17-52:12
Jesus	Mt 16:21-28;
	24:9-14;
	Mk 8:34-9:1;
	30-32;
	13:9-13;
	Lk 9:23-27;
	21:7-19

REVELATION on

Daniel	Dan 12:1-4
Jeremiah	Jer 15:10-21
John	Rev 12:1-6
Judahites	Hos 1:6-7

WORSHIP concerning

Miriam	Ex 15:19-21

SECURITY in

through DEITY

Believers	Ps 46:8-11

of FOLLOWERs

Jesus	2 Cor 2:14-17

PROPHECY of

Levite	Judg 18:1-6
Micah	Mic 4:9-5:6

REVELATION on

Gideon	Judg 7:9-15
Jeremiah	Jer 1:17-19

TRADITION of

Mordecai	Esth 9:20-28

SIGNS of

INSTRUCTION on

Elisha	2 Kgs 13:14-19

in MISSION

Jesus	Mt 11:28-30

PROPHECY of

Isaiah	Is 7:10-17

REVELATION on

Gideon	Judg 7:9-15
John	Rev 6:1-2;
	7:9-17;
	10:1-11

over **SIN**

INSTRUCTION on

God	Gen 4:1-16

through **STEWARDSHIP**

INSTRUCTION on

Jesus	Mt 13:3b-9;
	Lk 8:4-8

TRADITION of
   in **CONFRONTATION**
      David   *Sir 47:1-11
      Joshua   *Sir 46:1-10
      Samuel   *Sir 46:13-20
      Solomon   *Wis 10:1-21

of **TRUTH**
   through **DEITY**
      Elijah   1 Kgs 18:1-46
   over **ENVIRONMENT**
      Zerubbabel   *1 Esd 4:42-57
   INSTRUCTION on
      Jesus   Mk 4:1-9
   through **MESSIANIC FIGURE**
      Jesus   Jn 1:1-18
   REVELATION on
      God   Is 42:5-17;
                        Jn 1:1-18

VIRTUE in
   through **DEITY**
      God   Ps 98:1-3
   PROPHECY of
      Isaiah   Is 52:13-53:12
   REVELATION on
      Job   Job 40:6-14

WORSHIP in
   PRAYER for
      David   Ps 20:1-5
      Hezekiah   2 Chr 32:1-33
      Jacob   Gen 32:1-23
      Jesus   Jn 17:6-19
   for **SALVATION**
      Miriam   Ex 15:19-21

VIOLENCE

by **AUTHORITY**
   in the **ENVIRONMENT**
      Samson   Judg 16:1-3
   REVELATION on
      John   Rev 13:5-10

BEHAVIOR revealing
      Ephraimites   Hos 11:12-12:1
   in **ENVIRONMENT**
      Daniel   *Bel 1:28-30
      Levite   Judg 19:27-30
   INSTRUCTION on
      Preacher   Eccl 3:1-8

COMMITMENT to
      Mattathias   *1 Mc 2:39-48

CONFRONTATION with
      Abijam   1 Kgs 15:1-8
      Babylonians   Jer 52:4-27
      Chaldeans   Hab 1:5-11
      Gideon   Judg 8:10-12
      Habakkuk   Hab 1:2-4
      Israelites   Judg 3:26-30;
                        4:10-16;
                        1 Chr 10:1-14;
                        Esth 9:1-10
      Joshua   Josh 8:1-29
      Judahites   Jer 39:1-14
      Nebuchadnezzar Dan 1:1-7

CONFRONTATION with (cont'd)
      Satan   Rev 12:13-17
      Zedekiah   Jer 34:1-7
   of **DEITY**
      Nations   Zech 14:1-21
   in the **ENVIRONMENT**
      Abimelech   Judg 9:34-41;
                        42-45
      Caleb   Josh 15:13-19
      Danites   Judg 18:27-31
      Israelites   Judg 1:22-36;
                        Ex 17:8-16;
                        Num 21:21-32;
                        33-35;
                        31:7-12;
                        Deut 2:26-3:11;
                        Josh 10:1-15;
                        16-27;
                        11:1-15;
                        16-23;
                        Judg 3:12-14;
                        5:19-22;
                        7:23-25;
                        20:19-23;
                        24-28;
                        29-36
      Jephthah   Judg 11:29-33;
                        12:1-7
      Joshua   Josh 10:28-43
      Judah   Judg 1:1-21
      Maccabeus   *1 Mc 4:36-61
      Othniel   Judg 3:7-11
      Peter   Jn 18:1-11
      Psalmist   Ps 120:5-7
      Ptolemy   *1 Mc 11:1-19
      Samson   Judg 14:5-9
      Shamgar   Judg 3:31
   INSTRUCTION on
      Moses   Deut 20:1-9;
                        10-18;
                        19-20

by **MESSIANIC FIGURE**
      Demon   Mt 8:28-34;
                        Mk 5:1-20;
                        Lk 8:26-39

PROPHECY of
      Ammonites   Jer 49:1-6
      Babylonians   Jer 43:8-13;
                        50:1-46;
                        51:1-64
      Damascenes   Jer 49:23-27
      Edomites   Jer 49:7-22
      Egyptians   Jer 46:2-12;
                        13-26
      Ephraimites   Hos 7:13-16
      Gog   Ezek 38:10-13
      Hazorites   Jer 49:28-33
      Israelites   Deut 28:15-68;
                        Hos 10:9-15;
                        11:5-7;
                        Amos 6:12-14;
                        Nah 2:1-5
      Jeremiah   Jer 6:1-8;
                        21:1-10
      Jerusalemites Zech 12:1-13:6;
                        14:1-21
      Joel   Joel 1:2-20
      Judahites   Jer 25:8-14;
                        37:3-10
      Micah   Mic 4:9-5:6
      Moabites   Jer 48:1-47

of **FOLLOWER**s
    God — 1 Jn 3:4-10
  COURAGE as
    Mankind — Ps 112:5-9
  DISCIPLESHIP as
    Paul — 2 Thes 1:11-12
  FAITH as
    Abraham — Rom 3:31-4:25
  GOOD as
    Believers — Tit 2:11-15
    Noah — Gen 6:5-22
  OBEDIENCE as
    Noah — Gen 7:1-24
  REWARD for
    Mankind — Ps 112:5-9
  WILL as
    Paul — Philm 1:8-14
  WISDOM in
    Jesus — 1 Cor 1:26-31

in **FULFILLMENT**
  INSTRUCTION on
    Jesus — Mt 3:13-17; 5:3-12; 48; Lk 6:20-23
    Paul — 1 Tim 6:6-10
  of **MISSION**
    Holy Spirit — Jn 16:5-11

GOOD as
  of **DEITY**
    God — Ps 77:11-20; 86:1-7
    Job — Job 1:1
  of **FOLLOWER**s
    Believers — Tit 2:11-15
    Noah — Gen 6:5-22
  INSTRUCTION on
    Author — Heb 13:1-25
    Sirach — *Sir 5:1-6:1; 7:1-36; 18:15-18
  in **MISSION**
    Bishop — Tit 1:5-8

GRACE as
  of **COVENANT**
    Israelites — Hos 2:16-20
  of **DEITY**
    God — Ex 34:5b-9; Ps 86:1-7; 112:2-4; 116:1-11; 145:8-9
    James — Jas 3:13-18
  INSTRUCTION on
    Amos — Amos 5:14-15
    Zephaniah — Zeph 2:3
  SELF-REALIZATION of
    Paul — 2 Cor 1:12-14

GRATITUDE for
  of **DEITY**
    David — Ps 140:12-13
  MEDITATION on
    Isaiah — Is 61:1-11

concerning **GREED**
  INSTRUCTION on
    Sirach — *Sir 31:12-24

HOPE as
    Job — Job 4:1-6
  INSTRUCTION on
    Paul — Rom 8:14-25

HUMILITY as
    Moses — Num 12:3
  before **DEITY**
    David — Ps 143:1-2
  INSTRUCTION on
    Sirach — *Sir 3:17-31; 6:2-17; 7:1-36; 10:26-11:1; 2-9
    Solomon — Prov 12:1-28; 15:1-33; 16:1-33; 18:1-24; 22:1-16
    Women — 1 Pet 3:1-7
  SELF-REALIZATION of
    Jesus — Mt 11:28-30

INNOCENCE as
    David — Ps 35:11-16
  INSTRUCTION on
    Jesus — Mt 5:43-47
  SELF-REALIZATION of
    Job — Job 32:1

INSTRUCTION on
  concerning **ANGER**
    Sirach — *Sir 10:6-11
  in **COMPASSION**
    God — Ps 82:2-7; *Wis 12:19-22
    Sirach — *Sir 12:1-7
  in **COVENANT**
    Jesus — Mt 6:25-34
  concerning **DESTRUCTION**
    Isaiah — Is 56:9-57:13
  in **FAITH**
    Author — Heb 10:32-39
    Jesus — Mt 8:5-13; 25:1-13; Lk 7:1-10
    Paul — Rom 1:16-17; 3:31-4:25; 9:30-10:21; Gal 3:10-14; Eph 6:10-18; 1 Tim 6:11-16
    Peter — 2 Pet 1:5-7
  in **FEAR**
    Sirach — *Sir 10:12-25
  concerning **FULFILLMENT**
    Jesus — Mt 3:13-17; 5:3-12; 48; Lk 6:20-23
    Paul — 1 Tim 6:6-10
  as **GOOD**
    Author — Heb 13:1-25
    Sirach — *Sir 5:1-6:1; 7:1-36; 18:15-18
  as **GRACE**
    Amos — Amos 5:14-15
    Zephaniah — Zeph 2:3

concerning **GREED**
Sirach   *Sir 31:12-24
in **HOPE**
Paul   Rom 8:14-25
in **HUMILITY**
Sirach   *Sir 3:17-31;
6:2-17;
7:1-36;
10:26-11:1;
2-9
Solomon   Prov 12:1-28;
15:1-33;
16:1-33;
18:1-24;
22:1-16
Women   1 Pet 3:1-7
of **INNOCENCE**
Jesus   Mt 5:43-47
in **JOY**
Preacher   Eccl 7:1-22
Solomon   Prov 29:1-27
in **JUSTICE**
Bildad   Job 8:1-7
God   Is 56:1-8
Solomon   Prov 12:1-28;
21:1-31
in **LEADERSHIP**
Solomon   Prov 11:1-31
in **LIFE**
Solomon   Prov 10:1-32;
12:1-28;
15:1-33;
21:1-31
as **LOVE**
Paul   1 Cor 13:8-13
in **MARRIAGE**
Lemuel   Prov 31;10-31
Sirach   *Sir 7:1-36;
26:1-4;
13-18;
36:21-26;
40:18-27
Solomon   Prov 18:1-24
Women   1 Pet 3:1-7
in **OBEDIENCE**
Isaiah   Is 51:1-16
Peter   1 Pet 1:13-2:3
as **PATIENCE**
Peter   2 Pet 3:11-13
Preacher   Eccl 7:1-22
Sirach   *Sir 11:10-13
Solomon   Prov 16:1-33
of **PEACE**
Isaiah   Is 56:9-57:13
Sirach   *Sir 6:2-17
concerning **POVERTY**
Solomon   Prov 19:1-29
in **PRAISE**
Psalmist   Ps 99:6-9
Sirach   *Sir 26:13-18
Solomon   Prov 27:1-27
Wife   Prov 31:10-31
as **PRUDENCE**
Jesus   Mt 25:1-13
Paul   1 Cor 15:29-34
Sirach   *Sir 11:2-9
Solomon   Prov 12:1-28;
24:23-34
through **PURIFICATION**
Paul   2 Cor 6:14-7:1

INSTRUCTION on
of **SACREDNESS**
Paul   Rom 6:15-23
in **SERVICE**
God   Ps 82:2-7
Paul   Rom 6:1-14;
Tit 3:8-11
Wife   Prov 31:10-31
concerning **SEX**
Jesus   Mt 19:10-12
Sirach   *Sir 42:9-14
in **SUFFERING**
Paul   Rom 5:1-5;
1 Cor 6:1-8
Peter   1 Pet 3:13-17
in **TEMPERANCE**
Jesus   Mt 19:10-12
Peter   1 Pet 2:11-12
Sirach   *Sir 31:25-31
concerning **TEMPTATION**
Paul   1 Cor 6:12-20
concerning **WEALTH**
Sirach   *Sir 29:1-7;
8-13;
31:1-11;
40:18-27
Solomon   Prov 15:1-33
Wisdom   Prov 8:1-21
of **WILL**
James   Jas 1:2-4
Jesus   Mt 19:10-12
in **WISDOM**
Preacher   Eccl 7:1-22;
9:17-10:20
Solomon   Prov 2:1-22;
9:7-12;
10:1-32;
14:1-35;
16:1-33
Wife   Prov 31:10-31

JOY in
of **DEITY**
Believers   Ps 68:1-3
INSTRUCTION on
David   Ps 32:8-11
Preacher   Eccl 7:1-22
Solomon   Prov 29:1-27

JUSTICE as
Job   Job 2:14-20
of **DEITY**
God   Ps 89:5-18;
94:12-15;
97:1-5;
99:4-5;
145:13b-20;
Is 5:8-24a;
Jer 9:23-24;
11:18-12:6;
Dan 9:4-19;
Zeph 3:1-5
Psalmist   Ps 129:1-4
INSTRUCTION on
Bildad   Job 8:1-7
God   Is 56:1-8
Solomon   Prov 12:1-28;
21:1-31
PROPHECY of
Isaiah   Is 28:14-22

PROPHECY of (cont'd)
Jeremiah   Jer 22:1-9;
                        23:1-8
REVELATION on
Israelites   Ezek 45:1-9
Jeremiah   Jer 33:14-26

in LEADERSHIP
INSTRUCTION on
Solomon   Prov 11:1-31
PROPHECY of
Isaiah   Is 9:2-7;
                        32:1-8

LIFE of
before DEITY
Eliphaz   Job 4:17-21
INSTRUCTION on
Solomon   Prov 10:1-32;
                        12:1-28;
                        15:1-33;
                        21:1-31

REVELATION on
Ezekiel   Ezek 18:5-9;
                        14-20;
                        21-24;
                        25-29;
                        33:10-20

LOVE as
King   Ps 45:2-9
of DEITY
God   Ps 11:4-7;
                        33:4-9;
                        146:7c-9;
                        Prov 15:1-33

INSTRUCTION on
Paul   1 Cor 13:8-13

in MARRIAGE
INSTRUCTION on
Lemuel   Prov 31:10-31
Sirach   *Sir 7:1-36;
                        26:1-4;
                        13-18;
                        36:21-26;
                        40:18-27
Solomon   Prov 18:1-24
Women   1 Pet 3:1-7

of MESSIANIC FIGURE
DOUBT in
Pharisees   Mt 9:10-13;
                        Mk 2:15-17;
                        Lk 5:29-32
in SACRIFICE
Jesus   Heb 9:1-14
in SERVICE
Jesus   Heb 7:1-28

in MISSION
DIGNITY as
Men   Tit 2:1-10
FULFILLMENT through
Holy Spirit   Jn 16:5-11
GOOD as
Bishop   Tit 1:5-8

OBEDIENCE as
of FOLLOWER
Noah   Gen 7:1-24

INSTRUCTION on
Isaiah   Is 51:1-16
Peter   1 Pet 1:13-2:3
REVELATION on
Believers   Rev 19:6-10

in OPPRESSION
Habakkuk   Hab 1:12-17

PATIENCE as
of DEITY
God   Ex 34:5b-9
INSTRUCTION on
Peter   2 Pet 3:11-13
Preacher   Eccl 7:1-22
Sirach   *Sir 11:10-13
Solomon   Prov 16:1-33

PEACE as
of DEITY
James   Jas 3:13-18
Solomon   Ps 72:5-7
INSTRUCTION on
Isaiah   Is 56:9-57:13
Sirach   *Sir 6:2-17
REVELATION on
Isaiah   Is 60:1-22

in POVERTY
INSTRUCTION on
Solomon   Prov 19:1-29

in PRAISE
of DEITY
Psalmist   Ps 71:1-21;
                        111:2-4
INSTRUCTION on
Psalmist   Ps 99:6-9
Sirach   *Sir 26:13-18
Solomon   Prov 27:1-27
Wife   Prov 31:10-31
PROPHECY of
Isaiah   Is 61:1-11
in WORSHIP
David   Ps 145:4-7

PROPHECY of
in ACCEPTANCE
Isaiah   Is 52:13-53:12
as BLESSING
Isaiah   Is 3:8-12
in JUSTICE
Isaiah   Is 28:14-22
Jeremiah   Jer 22:1-9;
                        23:1-8
in LEADERSHIP
Isaiah   Is 9:2-7;
                        32:1-8
in PRAISE
Isaiah   Is 61:1-11
in REPENTANCE
Isaiah   Is 1:27-31
in VICTORY
Isaiah   Is 52:13-53:12

PRUDENCE as
INSTRUCTION on
Jesus   Mt 25:1-13
Paul   1 Cor 15:29-34
Sirach   *Sir 11:2-9
Solomon   Prov 12:1-28;
                        24:23-34

in **COMMUNITY**
Moses   Deut 21:15-17
through **FIDELITY**
Paul   1 Tim 6:17-19
through **disHONESTY**
Jezebel   1 Kgs 21:5-12
Nehemiah   Neh 5:6-13
Solomon   Prov 20:1-30;
                      21:1-31
in **NEW AGE**
Jesus   Mk 10:17-22;
                      23-27;
                      Lk 12:32-34;
                      18:18-27
through **PROVIDENCE**
Jesus   Lk 12:22-31
as **QUALITY OF LIFE**
James   Jas 1:9-11
Jesus   Mt 19:23-26;
                      Mk 10:23-27
Paul   1 Tim 6:17-19
Solomon   Prov 11:1-31;
                      13:1-25;
                      19:1-29;
                      28:1-28
concerning **SALVATION**
Jesus   Mt 19:16-22;
                      23-26;
                      Mk 10:23-27;
                      Lk 18:18-27
concerning **SIN**
Sirach   *Sir 26:29-27:2;
                      29:1-7;
                      31:1-11

JUDGMENT on
Shunammite   2 Kgs 8:1-6
INSTRUCTION on
Jesus   Lk 6:24-26;
                      16:14-15
REVELATION on
John   Rev 18:4-20

KNOWLEDGE of
Maiden   Sg 8:11-12
in **ENVIRONMENT**
Solomon   1 Kgs 7:1-12;
                      10:14-29
INSTRUCTION on
Moses   Num 13:17b-20
Solomon   *Wis 7:7-14

LAW concerning
INSTRUCTION on
Moses   Deut 15:1-11;
                      23:15-25:19
REVELATION on
Israelites   Ezek 45:10-12;
                      47:21-23
Moses   Lev 25:23-24
Prince   Ezek 46:16-18

of **MESSIANIC FIGURE**
CONFRONTATION with
Queen of Sheba   1 Kgs 10:1-13;
                      2 Chr 9:1-31
in **NEW AGE**
Man   Mt 19:16-22

as **MOTIVATION**

ENVIRONMENT
Ahaz   2 Kgs 16:5-9
Danites   Judg 18:11-13
Jacob   Gen 30:25-43
in **NEW AGE**
INSTRUCTION on
Jesus   Mk 10:17-22;
                      23-27;
                      Lk 12:32-34;
                      18:18-27
revealed by **MESSIANIC FIGURE**
Man   Mt 19:16-22
REVELATION on
John   Rev 21:18-21

PROMISE of
Young Man   Song 1:9-11
INSTRUCTION on
Artaxerxes   Ezra 7:20-24
Moses   Deut 28:1-14;
                      30:1-10
Nehemiah   Neh 5:6-13
PROPHECY of
Abraham   Gen 15:1-21
Isaiah   Is 60:1-22
REVELATION on
Isaiah   Is 54:1-17
Jeremiah   Jer 31:23-26
Moses   Num 11:14-24a;
                      Deut 1:6-8
Nebuchadnezzar   Ezek 29:17-21
WORSHIP
Israelites   *1 Esd 5:44-46

PROPHECY of
Isaiah   2 Kgs 20:12-21
Jeremiah   Jer 20:1-6
through **disHONESTY**
Jeremiah   Jer 17:11
as a **PROMISE**
Abraham   Gen 15:1-21
Isaiah   Is 60:1-22
through **PROVIDENCE**
Isaiah   Is 52:13-53:12
through **RECONCILIATION**
Jeremiah   Jer 32:26-44
Judahites   Zeph 2:4-7

through **PROVIDENCE**
Isaac   Gen 25:1-6
in **COVENANT**
Moses   Ex 34:12-28
of **DEITY**
Cyrus   Is 44:24-45:13
David   Ps 30:6-10
God   Ps 112:2-4;
                      Eccl 6:1-12;
                      1 Tim 6:17-19
Israelites   Ex 11:1-10;
                      12:33-36;
                      Deut 8:11-20;
                      17:14-20;
                      Josh 5:10-12;
                      2 Chr 17:1-20:37;
                      Neh 9:22-25;
                      Ps 105:37-42;
                      Hos 2:2-8
Job   Job 42:10-17

of **MESSIANIC FIGURE**
  BEHAVIOR revealing
    Jesus   Lk 2:41-52
  KNOWLEDGE of
    People   Jn 7:1-14
  PROVIDENCE through
    Jesus   Lk 22:14-23

in **MISSION**
  by **AUTHORITY**
    Paul   1 Cor 1:1-3
  of **TRUTH**
    Jesus   Mk 1:35-39;
                     Lk 4:42-44

MOTIVATION for
  MEDITATION on
    Centurion   Mt 8:5-13;
                     Lk 7:1-10

in **NEW AGE**
  of **DEITY**
    Believers   Lk 12:32-34
  INSTRUCTION on
    Jesus   Lk 14:15-24

PRAYER concerning
  of **DEITY**
    Jesus   Mt 26:36-46;
                     Mk 14:32-42;
                     22:39-46
  INSTRUCTION on
    Jesus   Lk 11:5-8
    Paul   Col 4:2-4

in **PRESENCE**
  in **ENVIRONMENT**
    God   Job 36:26-33
  REVELATION on
    Moses   Ex 3:11-22

PRESENCE of
  of **DEITY**
    Believers   Phil 2:12-18

PROMISE of
  of **DEITY**
    Solomon   1 Kgs 3:1-15
  REVELATION on
    Solomon   2 Chr 1:1-17

PROPHECY of
  in **SALVATION**
    Jesus   Mt 24:15-22;
                     Mk 13:14-23

PROVIDENCE through
  of **DEITY**
    God   Ps 135:5-7;
                 Mt 10:26-39
    James   Jas 1:16-18
    Job   Job 12:13-25
  in **ENVIRONMENT**
    God   Job 37:1-13
  of **MESSIANIC FIGURE**
    Jesus   Lk 22:14-23
  REVELATION on
    Jeremiah   Jer 18:1-12
  SCRIPTURES on
    God   Rom 9:14-29

in **PUNISHMENT**
  by **DEITY**
    Tyre   Is 23:1-14

as **QUALITY OF LIFE**
  of **DEITY**
    Isaiah   Is 52:13-53:12

RECONCILIATION through
  in **ENVIRONMENT**
    Levite   Judg 19:1-9

REVELATION on
  of **AUTHORITY**
    Daniel   Dan 11:21-45
  of **COMMUNITY**
    Ezra   *2 Esd 9:38-10:59
  in **CONFRONTATION**
    Balaam   Num 22:15-21
  in **ELECTION**
    Jesus   Jn 21:15-23
    Moses   Num 12:4-10
  in **PRESENCE**
    Moses   Ex 3:11-22
  in **PROVIDENCE**
    Jeremiah   Jer 18:1-12
  in **SALVATION**
    Israelites   Is 45:14-25
  in **STEWARDSHIP**
    Moses   Lev 23:33-44

SALVATION through
  of **DEITY**
    God   Ps 106:6-12;
                 Mt 18:12-14;
                 Rev 7:9-17
    Mankind   2 Pet 3:8-10
  PROPHECY of
    Jesus   Mt 24:15-22;
                 Mk 13:14-23
  REVELATION on
    Israelites   Is 45:14-25
  SCRIPTURES on
    God   Mt 21:33-43;
                 Mk 12:1-12;
                 Lk 20:9-18
    Israelites   Rom 9:14-29

SCRIPTURES on
  in **PROVIDENCE**
    God   Rom 9:14-29
  in **SALVATION**
    God   Mt 21:33-43;
                 Mk 12:1-12;
                 Lk 20:9-18
    Israelites   Rom 9:14-29

SECURITY in
  in **ENVIRONMENT**
    Boaz   Ruth 3:1-18

SELF-REALIZATION of
  FIDELITY to
    Paul   Rom 7:14-25

SIGNS of
  REVELATION on
    Mordecai   *Esth 11:2-12

concerning **SIN**

INSTRUCTION on	
James	Jas 1:13-15
in **STEWARDSHIP**	
of **FOLLOWER**s	
Macedonians	2 Cor 8:1-6
INSTRUCTION on	
Jesus	Mt 6:19-24;
	25:14-30;
	Lk 9:57-62
Paul	Rom 12:1-2;
	2 Cor 9:1-5;
	6-11
REVELATION on	
Moses	Lev 23:33-44
in **WORSHIP**	
Israelites	Ezra 3:3b-6
in **TRUTH**	
of **DEITY**	
David	Ps 86:11-13
INSTRUCTION on	
Jesus	Mk 4:10-20;
	9:49-50
MISSION of	
Jesus	Mk 1:35-39;
	Lk 4:42-44
VIRTUE in	
of **DEITY**	
Jesus	Mt 5:48
of **FOLLOWER**	
Paul	Philm 1:8-14
INSTRUCTION on	
James	Jas 1:2-4
Jesus	Mt 19:10-12
in **WORSHIP**	
STEWARDSHIP of	
Israelites	Ezra 3:3b-6

WISDOM

in **AUTHORITY**	
God	Eph 3:1-13
Jesus	Mt 21:23-27;
	Mk 11:27-33;
	Lk 20:1-8
Joshua	Deut 34:1-12
of **DEITY**	
Baruch	*Bar 3:24-37
Elihu	Job 36:5-15
God	Job 26:5-14;
	Ps 147:1-6;
	Prov 22:1-16
Job	Job 12:13-25
INSTRUCTION on	
Jesus	Mt 7:28-29
Preacher	Eccl 7:1-22;
	9:1-16
Sirach	*Sir 10:1-5
of **MESSIANIC FIGURE**	
Jesus	Mt 22:41-46;
	Mk 12:35-37a;
	Lk 20:41-44
PROPHECY of	
Holy Spirit	Jn 16:12-15
REVELATION on	
Holy Spirit	1 Cor 2:10-16

REVELATION on (cont'd)	
Isaiah	Is 55:1-13
Job	Job 38:4-7;
	16-18;
	19-21;
	22-24;
	25-30;
	31-38;
	39-41;
	39:1-4;
	5-8;
	13-18;
	26-30
SCRIPTURES on	
God	1 Cor 1:18-25
BEHAVIOR revealing	
INSTRUCTION on	
Agur	Prov 30:15-33
Daughters	Song 1:8
Jesus	Mt 5:31-32
Solomon	Prov 6:6-11
in **BROTHERHOOD**	
INSTRUCTION on	
Holy Spirit	Neh 9:19-21
COMPULSION of	
INSTRUCTION on	
Daniel	Dan 1:1-7
CONFRONTATION with	
Queen of Sheba	2 Chr 9:1-31;
	Mt 12:38-42;
	Lk 11:29-32
INSTRUCTION on	
Solomon	Prov 27:1-27
of **MESSIANIC FIGURE**	
Queen of Sheba	1 Kgs 10:1-13
in **MISSION**	
Apostles	Mt 10:16-22
in **CONVERSION**	
INSTRUCTION on	
Paul	2 Cor 3:12-18
in **COVENANT**	
of **LAW**	
Sirach	*Sir 24:1-34
in the **CREATION**	
by **DEITY**	
God	Ps 104:24-26;
	136:4-9;
	Prov 3:1-35;
	8:22-31;
	Jer 10:1-16;
	51:1-64
Job	Job 9:8-13
Sirach	*Sir 1:1-10;
	17:1-14
INSTRUCTION on	
Solomon	Prov 23:15-24:22
REVELATION on	
Job	Job 38:8-11
of **DEITY**	
AUTHORITY of	
Baruch	*Bar 3:24-37
Elihu	Job 36:5-15

CHOOL**

ATION** of
Solomon   2 Chr 1:1-17

ELECTION of
by **DEITY**
Sirach   *Sir 24:1-34

in **ENVIRONMENT**
concerning **AUTHORITY**
God   Eph 3:1-13
Jesus   Mt 21:23-27;
Mk 11:27-33;
Lk 20:1-8
Joshua   Deut 34:1-12
CONFRONTATION with
Queen of Sheba   Mt 12:38-42;
Lk 11:29-32
DESIRE for
Sirach   *Sir 51:13-30
KNOWLEDGE of
Job   Job 12:7-12
Solomon   1 Kgs 10:14-29
RESPECT for
Darius   *1 Esd 3:1-17

EQUALITY in
INSTRUCTION on
Job   Job 12:1-6;
13:1-12

ETERNAL
of **DEITY**
God   Ps 33:10-12
Sirach   *Sir 24:1-34

of **FIDELITY**
to **DEITY**
Ezra   *2 Esd 13:51-58
INSTRUCTION on
Baruch   *Bar 4:1-4
Father   Prov 4:1-9
Moses   Deut 4:1-14

of **FOLLOWERs**
as **GIFT**
Holy Spirit   1 Cor 2:10-16;
12:4-11
Unbelievers   1 Cor 14:13-25
in **JUDGMENT**
Paul   1 Cor 4:6-13;
6:1-8
KNOWLEDGE of
Holy Spirit   1 Cor 12:4-11
MEDIATION through
Holy Spirit   Rom 8:26-27
through **PROVIDENCE**
Holy Spirit   Mt 10:16-22;
Lk 12:1-12;
Jn 14:25-26;
1 Cor 2:1-5
through **TRUTH**
Disciples   Mt 13:10-17;
51-52
John   1 Jn 2:18-23
VIRTUE in
Jesus   1 Cor 1:26-31

GIFT of
Hiram   1 Kgs 7:13-14
from **DEITY**
Disciples   Acts 2:1-13

from **DEITY** (cont'd)
James   Jas 3:13-18
Solomon   *Wis 7:15-8:1;
8:2-21
for **FOLLOWERs**
Holy Spirit   1 Cor 2:10-16;
12:4-11
Unbelievers   1 Cor 14:13-25
INSTRUCTION on
Paul   1 Cor 2:6-9;
12:1-3;
14:1-12;
13-25

SELF—REALIZATION of
Wisdom   Prov 8:1-21

INSTRUCTION on
Daniel   Dan 1:1-7
Solomon   Prov 27:1-27
in **AUTHORITY**
Jesus   Mt 7:28-29
Preacher   Eccl 7:1-22;
9:1-16
Sirach   *Sir 10:1-5
of **BEHAVIOR**
Agur   Prov 20:15-33
Daughters   Song 1:8
Jesus   Mt 5:31-32
Solomon   Prov 6:6-11
in **BROTHERHOOD**
Holy Spirit   Neh 9:19-21
in **CONVERSION**
Paul   2 Cor 3:12-18
in the **CREATION**
Solomon   Prov 23:15-24:22
in **FIDELITY**
Baruch   *Bar 4:1-4
Father   Prov 4:1-9
Moses   Deut 4:1-14
as a **GIFT**
Paul   1 Cor 2:6-9;
12:1-3;
14:1-12;
13-25

in **JUDGMENT**
Jesus   Mt 11:16-19;
Lk 7:31-35;
Jn 7:15-24
Psalmist   Ps 119:65-72
Baruch   *Bar 3:9-14;
24-37;
4:1-4
Eliphaz   Job 15:7-11
God   Hos 6:4-6
Holy Spirit   Jn 14:25-26
Hosea   Hos 14:9
Jesus   Mt 7:24-27;
Lk 6:46-49
Job   Job 28:1-13;
14-22
Nebuchadnezzar   Dan 4:18;
Eccl 1:2-11;
7:1-22;
8:1-9;
10-17;
12:8-11
Psalmist   Ps 49:1-4
Sirach   *Sir 1:1-10;
11-20;
22-30;
3:17-31;

in **JUDGEMENT** (cont'd)

Sirach	4:11-19;
	5:1-6:1;
	18-37;
	8:1-19;
	9:14-18;
	10:26-11:1;
	14:20-27;
	15:1-10;
	18:27-33;
	19:20-24;
	20:1-8;
	9-17;
	18-23;
	24-31;
	21:8-28;
	22:16-18;
	24:1-34;
	25:3-6;
	7-11;
	27:8-15;
	32:14-24;
	33:4-6;
	16-23;
	34:8-12;
	37:7-26;
	38:24-34;
	39:1-11;
	40:18-27;
	41:14-23;
	50:27-29;
	51:13-30
Solomon	Prov 1:1;
	2-6;
	9:7-12;
	10:1-32;
	11:1-31;
	14:1-35;
	15:1-33;
	17:1-28;
	18:1-24;
	19:1-29;
	20:1-30;
	21:1-31;
	22:17-21;
	22-23:14;
	15-24:22;
	25:1-28;
	27:1-27;
	29:1-27;
	*Wis 1:1-5;
	6-11;
	6:1-11;
	12-25;
	7:7-14;
	15-8:1;
	2-21
Tobit	*Tb 4:1-21

in **LAW**

Baruch	*Bar 4:1-4
Jesus	Mt 4:21-26
Psalmist	Ps 119:25-32;
	57-64;
	65-72;
	121-128;
	129-136

in **NEW AGE**

Paul	1 Cor 2:6-9;
	2 Cor 3:7-11;
	2 Thes 2:3b-10

through **PROVIDENCE**

Jesus	Mk 4:10-20
Paul	2 Tim 2:1-7
Solomon	Prov 2:1-22

as **QUALITY OF LIFE**

Jesus	Mt 6:5-8
Paul	Rom 8:5-13;
	1 Cor 3:18-23
Preacher	Eccl 4:13-16
Solomon	Prov 13:1-25
Wisdom	Prov 8:32-36

through **RATIONALIZATION**

Jesus	Mk 12:13-17;
	Lk 20:19-26

in **RESURRECTION**

Jesus	Mt 22:23-33;
	Mk 12:18-27;
	Lk 20:27-40
Solomon	*Wis 8:2-21

in **SALVATION**

Paul	1 Cor 1:18-25
Solomon	Prov 11:1-31

concerning **SIN**

Solomon	*Wis 1:1-5

in **STEWARDSHIP**

Jesus	Lk 16:1-9;
	10-12

in **TRUTH**

Apollos	Acts 18:24-28
Jesus	Mt 6:19-24;
	Mk 4:21-25;
	Lk 8:16-18;
	24:44-49
Job	Job 6:28-30
John	1 Jn 2:24-27;
	13-21
Paul	Acts 20:17-38;
	Rom 16:1-23;
	1 Cor 1:18-25;
	2 Cor 1:12-14;
	Eph 5:3-14;
	15-20;
	Col 3:5-17
Preacher	Eccl 12:8-11

in **JUDGMENT**

Solomon	1 Kgs 3:16-28

of **DEITY**

Elihu	Job 34:21-28
God	Rom 11:33-36

of **FOLLOWER**

Paul	1 Cor 4:6-13;
	6:1-8

INSTRUCTION on

Jesus	Mt 11:16-19;
	Lk 7:31-35;
	Jn 7:15-24
Psalmist	Ps 119:65-72

PROPHECY of

Isaiah	Is 32:1-8

KNOWLEDGE of

Daniel	Dan 4:4-9
Ezra	Ezra 7:11-12
Solomon	1 Kgs 4:29-34

of **DEITY**

Asaph	Ps 73:13-20
Elihu	Job 34:21-28
Ezra	*2 Esd 14:19-48
God	Ps 19:4c-6;

to **BELIEF**
    by **FOLLOWER**s
        Jesus   1 Jn 5:8-12
        Samaritan   Jn 4:1-26;
                           27-42
    in **MESSIANIC FIGURE**
        Blind   Jn 9:1-41
        Crowd   Mt 21:1-11;
                           Mk 11:1-10;
                           Lk 19:28-38
        Disciples   Jn 2:1-11
        Peter   Mt 16:13-20
    in **MISSION**
        Paul   2 Cor 4:13-15
    SCRIPTURES on
        Jesus   Jn 20:30-31

of **BROTHERHOOD**
    to **DEITY**
        Holy Spirit   Rom 8:14-25
    in **MISSION**
        Holy Spirit   2 Cor 3:1-3

COMMITMENT through
    of **FOLLOWER**
        John   Acts 4:1-22
        Peter   Acts 4:1-22
    INSTRUCTION on
        Paul   2 Cor 5:11-13
    in **MISSION**
        Paul   Acts 19:21-22

to **COMMITMENT**
    to **DEITY**
        Israelites   Josh 24:16-24

to **COMMUNITY**
    REVELATION on
        Ezekiel   Ezek 40:1-5

COMPULSION to
    PROPHECY of
        God   Amos 3:3-8

CONFRONTATION with
    to **DEITY**
        Israelites   Num 14:11-24;
                           Deut 5:1-21
        Moses   Num 12:4-10;
                           Deut 34:1-12
    REVELATION on
        Angel   Judg 6:11-32;
                           13:2-7;
                           Lk 1:5-25
        Disciples   Lk 24:13-35
        Israelites   Deut 4:32-40;
                           Neh 9:12-15
        Jesus   Lk 24:13-35
        Job   Job 40:1-2
        Moses   Ex 20:21-23

to **CONVERSION**
    INSTRUCTION on
        Paul   Acts 26:1-32
    by **MESSIANIC FIGURE**
        Centurion   Mk 15:33-41

to **COVENANT**
    Isaiah   Is 59:1-21
    of **FREEDOM**
        God   Is 42:5-17

    of **LAW**
        Israelites   Jer 31:31-34
    of **NEW AGE**
        Paul   1 Cor 11:23-26
    of **PROVIDENCE**
        God   Ps 78:1-8
    of **RECONCILIATION**
        Holy Spirit   Heb 10:1-18
        Jacob   Gen 31:44-55
    through **SIGNS**
        Joshua   Josh 24:25-28

to the **CREATION**
    Angel   Judg 13:2-7
    God   Acts 14:8-18;
                     Rom 1:19-23
    by **DEITY**
        David   Ps 19:1-4b
        God   Ps 97:6-9
    SCRIPTURES on
        Jeremiah   Jer 36:1-7;
                           27-32

to **DEITY**
    by **BROTHERHOOD**
        Holy Spirit   Rom 8:14-25
    COMMITMENT to
        Israelites   Josh 24:16-24
    in **CONFRONTATION**
        Israelites   Num 14:11-24;
                           Deut 5:1-21
        Moses   Num 12:4-10;
                           Deut 34:1-12
    DESIRE for
        God   Hos 6:4-6

FIDELITY of
    David   Ps 40:6-10;
                   52:8-9
    Ethan   Ps 89:1-4
    Mary   Lk 1:39-56
    Moses   Heb 3:1-6a
    GIFT of
        Holy Spirit   Heb 2:1-4
    JUDGMENT of
        Aaron   Ex 28:13-30
    through **MEDIATION**
        Israelites   Mal 2:17-3:5
    PROMISE of
        Holy Spirit   Jn 15:26-27
    PROVIDENCE of
        David   Ps 145:4-7
        God   1 Jn 5:8-12
        Holy Spirit   Gal 4:4-7
        Israelites   Deut 10:12-22
        Jesus   Jn 3:31-36
        Mankind   Ps 64:7-10
        Paul   2 Tim 4:9-18
        Psalmist   Ps 66:13-20;
                         71:22-24
    RESPECT in
        Ezekiel   Ezek 44:4-5
    through **RITE**
        David   Ps 26:6b-7
    SIGNS of
        Isaiah   Is 19:18-25
        Jesus   Jn 10:19-40;
                           Acts 2:14-36
    VIRTUE in
        Mankind   Ezek 38:14-16
        Psalmist   Ps 71:22-24

DIETY's
    PRESENCE of
        Azariah   2 Chr 14:1-16:14
        Balaam   Num 23:27-24:13
        Barnabas   Acts 11:22-24
        David   2 Sam 23:1-7
        Holy Spirit   1 Jn 4:13-18
        Isaiah   Is 61:1-11
        Israelites   Num 14:10;
                         16:16-24
        Moses   Num 20:2-13
        Peter   Acts 4:1-22
        Prophets   Num 11:24b-30
        Zechariah   2 Chr 24:1-27

to DEITY's
    AUTHORITY
        David   Ps 9:9-12
        God   Deut 3:23-29;
                         Is 44:6-8;
                         21-23
        Jesus   Jn 8:21-59;
                         12:44-50
        Psalmist   Ps 71:1-21
    TRUTH
        God   Is 45:14-25
        Israelites   Is 49:1-26
        Jeremiah   Jer 10:1-16
        Jesus   Jn 8:21-59
        John   1 Jn 1:5-10

DESIRE for
    by DEITY
        God   Hos 6:4-6
    by MESSIANIC FIGURE
        Jesus   Lk 2:41-52

ELECTION to
    by DEITY
        Jesus   Mt 11:27
    in MISSION
        Barnabas   Acts 13:103
        Ezekiel   Ezek 3:4-9
        Gentiles   Gal 1:18-2:10
        Jesus   Jn 8:21-59
        John the Baptist Jn 1:1-18
        Paul   2 Cor 1:1-2
        Saul   Acts 13:1-3
    REVELATION on
        Ezekiel   Ezek 2:1-8a;
                         3:10-11;
                         16-21
        Isaiah   Is 6:1-13

in ENVIRONMENT
    to AUTHORITY
        God   Rom 1:19-23
    to CREATION
        God   Acts 14:8-18;
                         Rom 1:19-23
    to HONESTY
        Daniel   *Susa 1:42-51
        Elders   *Susa 1:28-41
    to KNOWLEDGE
        Israelites   Num 13:21-24;
                         25-26a
    to PROVIDENCE
        God   Acts 14:8-18
    to RESURRECTION
        Saints   Mt 27:45-56

    to SIGNS
        Israelites   Josh 22:9 34
    to SIN
        Elders   *Susa 1:28-41
    to TRUTH
        Daniel   *Susa 1:52-59

ETERNAL
    COVENANT of
        Isaiah   Is 59:1-21
    to DEITY
        God   Ps 135:13-14
        Israelites   Ps 48:9-14
    INSTRUCTION on
        Isaiah   Is 30:8-17
    SCRIPTURES on
        Isaiah   Is 40:1-11

to FALSE BELIEF
    reveals disHONESTY
        Ephraimites   Hos 11:12-12:1
    in JUDGMENT
        Author   Heb 10:19-31
    revealing RATIONALIZATION
        Micah   Mic 2:1-10
    revealing SIN
        James   Jas 5:1-6

to FIDELITY
    of DEITY
        David   Ps 40:6-10;
                         52:8-9
        Ethan   Ps 89:1-4
        Mary   Lk 1:29-56
        Moses   Heb 3:1-6a
    of FOLLOWERs
        Jesus   Jn 15:26-27
        Timothy   1 Cor 4:14-21
    INSTRUCTION on
        Isaiah   Is 48:1-22
        Paul   Phil 3:4-16;
                         2 Tim 3:10-13
    of MESSIANIC FIGURE
        Ezra   *2 Esd 2:42-48
    in MISSION
        Epaphras   Col 1:2-8

of FOLLOWERs
    to AUTHORITY
        God   Ps 145:10-13a
        Holy Spirit   1 Cor 2:1-5
        Jesus   Mt 10:1
    to BELIEF
        Jesus   1 Jn 5:8-12
        Samaritan   Jn 4:1-26;
                         27-42
    COMMITMENT to
        John   Acts 4:1-22
        Peter   Acts 4:1-22
    FIDELITY in
        Jesus   Jn 15:26-27
        Timothy   1 Cor 4:14-21
    as GIFT
        Holy Spirit   1 Cor 12:4-11
    KNOWLEDGE of
        Onesimus   Col 4:7-9
        Paul   2 Thes 3:17-18
        Tychicus   Col 4:7-9
    to NEW AGE
        Stephen   Acts 6:8-8:3

TRADITION of

Maccabeus	*2 Mc 2:19-32; 15:37-39

to LAW

COVENANT of

Israelites	Jer 31:31-34

of DEITY

God	Rom 3:21-30
Psalmist	Ps 119:9-16; 41-48

to MEDIATION

Joshua	Num 14:5-7

of DEITY

Israelites	Mal 2:17-3:5

of MESSIANIC FIGURE

Jesus	1 Tim 2:1-7

in MISSION

John the Baptist	Jn 3:22-30

against MESSIANIC FIGURE

JUDGMENT concerning

Jesus	Mt 27:11-26; Mk 15:1-5

by MESSIANIC FIGURE

DESIRE to

Jesus	Lk 2:41-52

of MESSIANIC FIGURE

to AUTHORITY

Peter	2 Pet 1:16-19a

to MESSIANIC FIGURE

because of BELIEF

Blind	Jn 9:1-41
Crowd	Mt 21:1-11; Mk 11:1-10; Lk 19:28-38
Disciples	Jn 2:1-11
Peter	Mt 16:13-20

through CONVERSION

Centurion	Mk 15:33-41

FREEDOM to

Isaiah	Is 61:1-11

through KNOWLEDGE

Peter	Mk 8:27-30; Lk 9:18-22
Shepherds	Lk 2:1-20

concerning MEDIATION

Jesus	1 Tim 2:1-7

RESPECT for

Centurion	Mt 27:45-56

RESURRECTION of

Jesus	Acts 1:1-5

SIGNS of

Jesus	Mt 11:2-6; Lk 7:18-23
John the Baptist	Jn 1:19-51

concerning TRUTH

Holy Spirit	1 Cor 12:1-3
Jesus	Mk 1:1
John	Jn 19:17-43
Peter	2 Pet 1:16-19a

in MISSION

to AUTHORITY

Israelites	Ps 106:6-12
Paul	2 Cor 2:14-17
Pharaoh	Ex 9:13-35;

to AUTHORITY (cont'd)

Pharaoh	Rom 9:14-29
Titus	Tit 2:11-15

to BELIEF

Paul	2 Cor 4:13-15

to BROTHERHOOD

Holy Spirit	2 Cor 3:1-3

COMMITMENT to

Paul	Acts 19:21-22

ELECTION of

Barnabas	Acts 13:1-3
Ezekiel	Ezek 3:4-9
Gentiles	Gal 1:18-2:10
Jesus	Jn 8:21-59
John the Baptist	Jn 1:1-18
Paul	2 Cor 1:1-2
Saul	Acts 13:1-3

FIDELITY in

Epaphras	Col 1:3-8

HONESTY in

Paul	2 Cor 2:14-17

JUDGMENT on

Ezekiel	Ezek 33:1-9

KNOWLEDGE of

Jeremiah	Jer 6:27-30
Paul	Acts 20:1-4; 5-16; 21:1-14; 15-26; Rom 15:25-33; Tit 1:1-4
Peter	2 Pet 1:12-15
Tychicus	Eph 6:21-22

MEDIATION through

John the Baptist	Jn 3:22-30

to NEW AGE

Jesus	Mt 9:35

RECONCILIATION through

Paul	Acts 26:1-32; 2 Cor 5:14-19; 20-62

SALVATION through

Isaiah	Is 49:1-26
Jesus	Mt 9:35

concerning SIN

Ezekiel	Ezek 3:16-21; 11:1-13; 33:1-9
Micah	Mic 3:1-12

STEWARDSHIP concerning

Apostles	Mt 10:5-6
Believers	Lk 10:1-16
Jesus	Mt 11:1

to TRUTH

Apostles	Acts 6:1-7; 16:11-15
Barnabas	Acts 14:1-7
Believers	Acts 11:19-21
Bishop	Tit 1:9-16
Church	Eph 3:1-13; 1 Tim 3:14-16
Disciples	Mk 6:7-13; Lk 9:1-6; Jn 17:6-19
Ezekiel	Ezek 3:16-21; 22-27; 38:1-2ħ
Isaiah	Is 61:1-11
Jesus	Mt 9:35; Lk 4:42-44; Jn 4:27-42;

REVELATION on
   Ezekiel   Ezek 3:22-27
   God   Heb 1:1-2a
   Isaiah   Is 66:1-6
   Paul   Acts 22:30-23:11

to PUNISHMENT
  of FOLLOWER
   Women   Lk 23:46-49
  PROPHECY of
   Amos   Amos 3:13-15

as QUALITY OF LIFE
  of FOLLOWERs
   Demetrius   3 Jn 1:12
  INSTRUCTION on
   Paul   Rom 2:1-24;
                     Phil 1:12-30
   Women   1 Pet 3:1-7

revealing RATIONALIZATION
  through FALSE BELIEF
   Micah   Mic 2:1-10

to RECONCILIATION
  COVENANT of
   Holy Spirit   Heb 10:1-18
   Jacob   Gen 31:44-55
  MISSION of
   Paul   Acts 26:1-32;
                     2 Cor 5:14-19;
                     20-6:2

RESPECT in
  to DEITY
   Ezekiel   Ezek 44:4-5
  of FOLLOWERs
   Mary   Mk 15:33-41
   Salome   Mk 15:33-41
  INSTRUCTION on
   Isaiah   Is 51:17-52:12
   Peter   1 Pet 2:11-12
  to MESSIANIC FIGURE
   Centurion   Mt 27:45-56
  REVELATION on
   Ezekiel   Ezek 43:1-5
  to RESURRECTION
   Disciples   Jn 21:1-14

to RESURRECTION
   Mary   Mt 28:1-8
  by DEITY
   Apostles   Acts 5:17-42
  in ENVIRONMENT
   Saints   Mt 27:45-56
  by FOLLOWERs
   Apostles   Acts 1:6-11
   Disciples   Jn 20:1-29
   Mary   Jn 20:1-29
   Matthias   Acts 1:12-36
   Thomas   Jn 20:1-29
  INSTRUCTION on
   Apostles   Acts 4:32-5:10
   Jesus   Mt 28:9-10
   Paul   Acts 22:30-23:11;
                     26:1-32;
                     1 Cor 15:1-11;
                     12-19;
                     20-28
   Peter   Acts 3:1-26

of MESSIANIC FIGURE
   Jesus   Acts 1:1-5
  REVELATION on
   Angel   Mt 28:1-8
   Disciples   Jn 21:1-14
   Mary   Mt 28:1-8

REVELATION on
   Believers   1 Cor 14:26-33
  to COMMUNITY
   Ezekiel   Ezek 40:1-5
  in CONFRONTATION
   Angel   Judg 6:11-32;
                     13:2-7;
                     Lk 1:5-25
   Disciples   Lk 24:13-35
   Israelites   Deut 4:32-40;
                     Neh 9:12-15
   Jesus   Lk 24:13-35
   Job   Job 40:1-2
   Moses   Ex 20:21-23
  to FREEDOM
   Apostles   Acts 5:17-42
  to JUDGMENT
   Isaiah   Is 66:17-24
   Israelites   Mal 2:17-3:5
   John   Rev 20:4-6
   Mankind   Ezek 39:17-24
  to KNOWLEDGE
   Amos   Amos 1:1-2
   God   Is 41:1-42:4
   Habakkuk   Hab 1:1
   Haggai   Hag 1:1-11
   Hosea   Hos 1:1
   Isaiah   Is 1:1
   Jeremiah   Jer 30:1-3;
                     46:1
   Joel   Joel 1:1
   Jonah   Jon 1:1-17;
                     3:1-10
   Malachi   Mal 1:1
   Micah   Mic 1:1
   Nahum   Nah 1:1-9
   Obadiah   Obad 1:1a
   Prophets   Num 12:4-10
   Zechariah   Zech 1:1-6;
                     4:6b-10a
   Zephaniah   Zeph 1:1
  to NEW AGE
   Daniel   Dan 10:10-21
   God   Is 42:5-17
   Jesus   Rev 22:6-21
   John   Rev 1:1-3;
                     10:1-11;
                     19:11-16;
                     22:6-21
  to PRESENCE
   Ezekiel   Ezek 1:1-3
   Heliodorus   *2 Mc 3:1-40
  to PROVIDENCE
   Ezekiel   Ezek 3:22-27
   God   Heb 1:1-2a
   Isaiah   Is 66:1-16
   Paul   Acts 22:30-23:11
  to RESPECT
   Ezekiel   Ezek 43:1-5
  to RESURRECTION
   Angel   Mt 28:1-8
   Disciples   Jn 21:1-14
   Mary   Mt 28:1-8

to **SIGNS**
  in **ENVIRONMENT**
    Israelites   Josh 22:9-34
  of **FOLLOWERs**
    Crowd   Jn 12:12-19
    Unbelievers   1 Cor 14:13-25
  INSTRUCTION on
    Jesus   Mt 11:2-6;
        13:34-35;
        Mk 4:33-34;
        Lk 7:18-23
    Moses   Ex 16:31-36;
        Deut 31:24-29
  of **MESSIANIC FIGURE**
    Jesus   Mt 11:2-6;
        Lk 7:18-23
    John the Baptist   Jn 1:19-51
  PROPHECY of
    Believers   1 Cor 14:13-25
    Ezekiel   Ezek 11:22-25
    Isaiah   Is 8:16-18
  REVELATION on
    Daniel   Dan 4:19-27;
        5:18-25;
        7:1;
        8:1-2;
        10:2-9
    Ezekiel   Ezek 1:4-28;
        4:1-3;
        10:1-22;
        24:25-27;
        40:1-5;
        6-16;
        17-19;
        20-27;
        28-37;
        38-43;
        44-47;
        48-49;
        41:1-4;
        5-11;
        12;
        13-15a;
        15b-26;
        42:1-10a;
        10b-12;
        13-14;
        15-20;
        43:13-17;
        47:1-12
    Isaiah   Is 66:17-24
    John   Rev 1:4-20;
        4:1-11;
        5:1-14
    Nebuchadnezzar   Dan 4:10-17

to **SIN**
  in **ENVIRONMENT**
    Elders   *Susa 1:28-41
  through **FALSE BELIEF**
    James   Jas 5:1-6
  INSTRUCTION on
    Isaiah   Is 59:1-21
    Paul   Tit 3:8-11
  in **MISSION**
    Ezekiel   Ezek 3:16-21;
        11:1-13;
        33:1-9
    Micah   Mic 3:1-12

REVELATION on
  Elders   Ezek 20:1-4
  Ezekiel   Ezek 16:1-7;
    22:1-16;
    23:36-49
  Isaiah   Is 58:1-14

STEWARDSHIP of
  of **FOLLOWER**
    Paul   1 Cor 1:1-3
  INSTRUCTION on
    Jesus   Lk 24:44-49
  in **MISSION**
    Apostles   Mt 10:5-6
    Believers   Lk 10:1-16
    Jesus   Mt 11:1
  PROPHECY of
    Jesus   Mk 8:34-9:1;
    Lk 9:23-27

to **TRADITION**
  KNOWLEDGE of
    Maccabeus   *2 Mc 2:19-32;
    15:37-39

to **TRUTH**
  Elihu   Job 32:15-22
  Holy Spirit   1 Jn 5:8-12
  of **DEITY**
    God   Is 45:14-25
    Israelites   Is 49:1-26
    Jeremiah   Jer 10:1-16
    Jesus   Jn 8:21-59
    John   1 Jn 1:5-10
  in **ENVIRONMENT**
    Daniel   *Susa 1:52-59
  by **FOLLOWER**
    Barnabas   Acts 9:20-31
    Holy Spirit   Rom 9:1-5;
    1 Cor 2:10-16
    Jesus   Jn 15:26-27
    John   Jn 21:24-25
  INSTRUCTION on
    Apollos   Acts 18:24-28
    Apostles   Acts 8:14-25
    Barnabas   Acts 11:25-26
    Baruch   Jer 36:8-10;
    11-19
    Holy Spirit   Jn 16:12-15
    Israelites   Zech 7:4-8:23
    Jesus   Mk 4:21-25;
        26-29;
        Lk 8:16-18;
        9:57-62;
        11:33-36;
        Jn 5:19-47
    John   1 Jn 1:1-4
    Luke   Lk 1:1-4
    Paul   Acts 13:14-52;
        14:8-18;
        19:1-12;
        21:27-22:29;
        26:1-32;
        28:17-31;
        1 Cor 11:23-26;
        Gal 3:1-5;
        Eph 4:25-5:2;
        1 Tim 3:14-16;
        4:6-10;
        6:2c-5;

revealing **HUMILITY**
    Women   1 Tim 2:8-15
revealing **OBEDIENCE**
    Ezra   *2 Esd 9:26-37
revealing **PEACE**
    Women   1 Cor 14:34-40
revealing **PRAISE**
    Angels   Lk 2:1-20
    Lepers   Lk 17:11-19
revealing **SACRIFICE**
    Jacob   Gen 31:44-55
revealing **SPIRIT**
    Paul   Phil 3:1-3
revealing **WEALTH**
    Cyrus   *1 Esd 2:8-15
    Israelites   *1 Esd 5:47-55
    Levites   *1 Esd 2:8-15

through **BELIEF**
    ACCEPTANCE of
        Mary   Mt 28:9-10

un**BELIEF** in
    causing **KILLING**
        John   Rev 13:11-18

BLASPHEMY in
        Antiochus   *2 Mc 5:11-27;
                              6:1-11
    through **disRESPECT**
        Judahites   Jer 7:29-8:3
    SIGNS of
        Antiochus   *1 Mc 1:54-61

BLESSING in
    of **COMMUNITY**
        Aaron   Lev 9:1-24
        Solomon   1 Kgs 8:54-61
    PRAYER for
        David   2 Sam 7:1-29;
                           21:1-14;
                           1 Chr 28:1-29:30;
                           Ps 20:1-5;
                           103:19-22
        Moses   Num 10:33-36
        David   Ps 26:8-12

COMMITMENT to house of
    through **PURIFICATION**
        Converts   Mt 3:1-12;
                          Mk 1:2-8
    SACREDNESS of
        Israelites   Neh 10:39b
    SACRIFICE in
        Hannah   1 Sam 1:1-28
        Israelites   Neh 10:32-33;
                          35-36
    through **WEALTH**
        Israelites   Neh 10:37a;
                          37b-39a

in **COMMUNITY**
    BLESSING in
        Aaron   Lev 9:1-24
        Solomon   1 Kgs 8:54-61
    SACREDNESS of
        Levites   Ezra 8:15-20

COMPASSION in
    PRAYER for
        Israelites   *Jdt 6:14-20
        Manasseh   *Mana 1:6-7
        Moses   Deut 3:23-29;
                           9:25-29

COMPULSION in
    to **IDOLATRY**
        John   Rev 13:11-18

CONDEMNATION of
    Josiah   2 Kgs 23:4-15
    as **JUDGMENT**
        Paul   1 Cor 11:17-22

CONFRONTATION in
    with **HUMILITY**
        Joshua   Josh 5:13-15
    with **SERVICE**
        God   Rev 22:1-5

COURAGE in
    PRAYER for
        Believers   Acts 4:23-31

CREATION in
    PRAISE of
        John   Rev 5:1-14
        Psalmist   Ps 136:4-9;
                           150:6

CREATION of house of
    DEFEAT of
        Israelites   Ezra 4:23-24
    FULFILLMENT of
        Israelites   Ezra 6:13-18
    SACREDNESS in
        Israelites   Ezra 3:1-3a;
                           7-9;
                           10-11;
                           5:1-2;
                           Hag 1:12-14
        Levites   2 Chr 34:1-35:27
    SERVICE in
        Jeroboam   1 Kgs 12:25-33

of **DEITY**
    through **PRAISE**
        Hilkaiah   *Susa 1:60-64

DESIRE for
    GRACE in
        Demons   Mk 5:1-20
        Nehemiah   Neh 1:5-11a

DESIRE to
    through **ACCEPTANCE**
        Wise Men   Mt 2:1-12
    PRUDENCE in
        Herod   Mt 2:1-12
    SERVICE in
        Israelites   Josh 24:16-24

DESTRUCTION in
    PROMISE of
        Nicanor   *2 Mc 14:31-33
    SIGNS of
        Alcimus   *1 Mc 9:54-57
        Israelites   2 Chr 30:1-31:21
        Josiah   2 Kgs 23:4-15;

SIGNS of (cont'd)
  Josiah   2 Chr 34:1-35:2
  Manasseh   2 Chr 33:1-25
of SIN
  Josiah   2 Kgs 23:24-25a

DIGNITY in
  Believers   1 Cor 11:27-34
  Women   1 Cor 14:34-40
through RESPECT
  Women   1 Cor 11:2-16

DISCIPLESHIP in
  PRAYER for
    Abraham   Gen 21:22-34
    Isaac   Gen 26:12-31
  RITE of
    Abraham   Gen 12:1-8;
                    13:2-9;
                    14-18
    Isaac   Gen 26:12-31

DISOBEDIENCE in house of
  LAW concerning
    Israelites   Neh 13:10-14
  in RITE
    Naphtali   *Tb 1:3-9
    Nicanor   *2 Mc 15:1-5
  caused by SIN
    Israelites   2 Kgs 14:1-4;
                    15:1-7
    Judahites   2 Kgs 11:21-12:3;
                    15:32-38

DOUBT in
  Disciples   Mt 28:16-20

ELECTION to
  SACREDNESS in
    Aaron   Ex 28:40-43
  SERVICE in
    Aaron   Ex 29:1-9
EQUALITY in
  ACCEPTANCE of
    Mankind   Is 66:17-24

ETERNAL
  PRAISE in
    God   Rev 4:1-11
  SACREDNESS in
    Jeremiah   Jer 17:12

FAITH in
  HONESTY of
    Author   Heb 10:19-31
  PRAYER for
    Jesus   Lk 22:31-32;
                    Jn 17:6-19;
                    20-26
    Paul   Eph 3:14-19;
                    6:23-24
by FAMILY
  through PRAYER
    Hannah   1 Sam 1:1-28
    Isaac   Gen 25:19-26
  brings RECONCILIATION
    Jews   *2 Mc 1:18-36;
                    2:16-18
  in RITE
    Job   Job 1:4-5

FIDELITY in
  of GOOD
    Sirach   *Sir 7:1-36
  of JUSTICE
    David   Ps 101:1-2b
  through OBEDIENCE
    Asa   1 Kgs 15:9-15
    Israelites   Josh 24:16-24
  PRAISE of
    David   Ps 22:22-26
    Psalmist   Ps 146:1-2
  through SACREDNESS
    Josiah   2 Kgs 23:21-23
    Simon   *Sir 50:1-21
  through SACRIFICE
    Widow   Lk 21:1-4
    Widows   Mk 12:41-44
  through SERVICE
    Israelites   Neh 10:39b

FULFILLMENT in
  DESIRE for
    David   Ps 28:1-5
    Ezra   *1 Esd 8:41-44
  PRAYER for
    Eli   1 Sam 1:1-28
    Ezra   Ezra 8:21-23;
                    Neh 9:9-11
    Samuel   1 Sam 7:2-17
  through PRESENCE
    David   Ps 132:1-5
  PROMISE of
    God   1 Kgs 8:14-21;
                 2 Chr 5:1-7:10
  SIGNS of
    Solomon   1 Kgs 6:1-38

GIFT in
  ORDER for
    Believers   1 Cor 14:26-33
  for SERVICE
    Believers   1 Cor 14:26-33
  for SHARING
    Believers   1 Cor 14:26-33

of GOOD
  FIDELITY in
    Sirach   *Sir 7:1-36

GRACE in
  DESIRE for
    Demons   Mk 5:1-20
    Nehemiah   Neh 1:5-11a
  MEDIATION through
    Priest   Num 15:22-31
  SIGNS of
    Naaman   2 Kgs 5:1-19

GRATITUDE in
  BEHAVIOR revealing
    Lepers   Lk 17:11-19
  for PROVIDENCE
    David   2 Sam 22:1-51
  for RESPECT
    David   1 Chr 15:1-16:43
    God   Rev 4:1-11;
                 7:9-17;
                 11:15-19
  RITE of
    Hezekiah   2 Chr 30:1-31:21
    Israelites   Ezra 3:10-11;

through **STEWARDSHIP**
  Widow   Lk 21:1-4
  Widows   Mk 12:41-44

MEDIATION in
  through **GRACE**
    Priest   Num 15:22-31
  for **LIFE**
    Jesus   Heb 10:19-31
  through **SACRIFICE**
    Priest   Lev 1:1-17;
                 2:1-16;
                 3:1-17;
                 4:1-35;
                 5:5-13;
                 14:6-7;
                 15:1-33
  for **SERVICE**
    David   Ps 20:1-5
    Levites   2 Chr 29:1-36

MIRACLE in
  BELIEF in
    Israelites   1 Kgs 18:1-46
  through **RITE**
    Jews   *2 Mc 1:18-36
    Solomon   2 Chr 5:1-7:10
  SIGNS of
    Elijah   1 Kgs 18:1-46
    God   Lev 9:1-24

MOTIVATION for
  ACCEPTANCE as
    Shepherds   Lk 2:1-20
  GRIEF as
    Job   Job 1:20-21

in **NEW AGE**
  SACREDNESS of
    God   Gen 4:25-26

OBEDIENCE in
  BEHAVIOR revealing
    Ezra   *2 Esd 9:26-37
  FIDELITY through
    Asa   1 Kgs 15:9-15
    Israelites   Josh 24:16-24
  LAW concerning
    Israelites   Neh 8:13-18;
                 10:34;
                 *1 Esd 7:1-9
    Josiah   *1 Esd 1:1-22
    Levites   Ezra 6:13-18;
                 Neh 12:24-26
  RITE of
    Levites   2 Chr 8:1-18
  STEWARDSHIP of
    Israelites   Ex 35:4-29

ONENESS in
  through **PRAYER**
    Disciples   Acts 1:12-26
    Jesus   Jn 17:6-19;
                 20-26

ORDER in
  CREATION of
    Ezra   *2 Esd 6:35-59
  for **GIFT**
    Believers   1 Cor 14:26-33

KNOWLEDGE of
  Women   1 Cor 14:34-40
  through **RITE**
    Israelites   Neh 12:31b-37;
                 38-42
    Levites   Neh 12:8-9
  through **STEWARDSHIP**
    Nehemiah   Neh 13:30-31

PARADOX in
  caused by **SIN**
    Babylonians   2 Kgs 17:24-41

PEACE in
  BEHAVIOR revealing
    Women   1 Cor 14:34-40
  PRAYER for
    Paul   Eph 6:23-24;
                 Phil 1:1-2
  RITE of
    Aaron   Lev 9:1-24
    Israelites   Josh 8:30-35
    Solomon   1 Kgs 9:25

PIETY in
  PRAYER revealing
    Abraham   Gen 12:1-8
    Jesus   Mk 6:45-52
  RESPECT through
    John   Rev 19:6-10
  RITE of
    High Priest   Heb 9:1-14
    Israelites   Josh 5:10-12;
                 Ezek 46:1-8
    Job   Job 1:4-5
    Mankind   Zech 14:1-21
    People   Jer 36:8-10
  SALVATION through
    Samartian   Jn 4:1-26

POLITICS in
  SIGNS of
    Jeroboam   1 Kgs 12:25-33

PRAISE in
  AUTHORITY
    David   Ps 24:7-10;
                 138:4-6
    Psalmist   Ps 150:2
  BEHAVIOR revealing
    Angels   Lk 2:1-20
    Lepers   Lk 17:11-19
  CREATION receives
    John   Rev 5:1-14
    Psalmist   Ps 136:4-9;
                 150:6
  of **DEITY**
    Hilkaiah   *Susa 1:60-64
  ETERNAL
    God   Rev 4:1-11
  FIDELITY receives
    David   Ps 22:22-26
    Psalmist   Ps 146:1-2
  because of **KNOWLEDGE**
    Crowd   Mt 15:29-31
  LAW receives
    Psalmist   Ps 119:1-8;
                 57-64
  through **PRAYER**
    Azariah   *Azar 1:28-68
    Believers   Acts 4:23-31

through **PRAYER** (cont'd)	
David	2 Sam 7:1-29;
	1 Chr 17:1-27;
	28:1-29:30;
	Ps 29:1-2;
	31:19-24;
	35:17-18;
	22-28;
	138:1-3
Ezra	Neh 9:6;
	*1 Esd 8:25-27;
	*2 Esd 13:51-58
Hannah	1 Sam 2:1-10
Israelites	*Jdt 13:11-20
Levites	Neh 9:5b
Manasseh	*Mana 1:1-5
Paul	Rom 16:25-27;
	2 Cor 2:14-17;
	Eph 3:20-21;
	Phil 4:10-20;
	1 Tim 6:11-16
Psalmist	Ps 42:1-5;
	6-11;
	43:1-5;
	119:105-112;
	135:19-21;
	146:10;
	150:1
Servant	Gen 24:11-27
Sirach	*Sir 50:22-24
Solomon	1 Kgs 8:22-53;
	*Wis 12:12-18;
	15:1-6
Tobiah	*Tb 8:1-21
Tobit	*Tb 13:1-18
Zerubbabel	*1 Esd 4:58-63
for **PROVIDENCE**	
David	1 Chr 15:1-16:43
revealing **RESPECT**	
God	Rev 4:1-11;
	7:9-17;
	11:15-19;
	15:1-16:1;
	19:1-5
John	Rev 5:1-14
Nebuchadnezzar	Dan 2:46-49
Paul	Rom 11:33-36
Psalmist	Ps 96:7-9
RITE of	
Believers	Acts 2:42-47
David	2 Sam 6:1-23;
	22:1-51;
	Ps 7:1-17;
	21:8-13;
	51:13-17;
	61:8;
	108:1-5;
	138:4-6
Deborah	Judg 5:2-5
Hannah	1 Sam 1:1-28
Hezekiah	2 Chr 30:1-31:21
Israelites	Ezra 3:10-11;
	*1 Esd 5:59-65
Jehoshaphat	2 Chr 17:1-20:37
Judith	*Jdt 15:8-13;
	16:1-17
Lame	Acts 3:1-26
Levites	2 Chr 29:1-36;
	Neh 12:24-26;
	44-13:3

RITE of (cont'd)	
Paul	Acts 16:25-40
Psalmist	Ps 92:1-4;
	104:31-35;
	111:1;
	118:22-27;
	146:1-2;
	150:3-5
Simon	*Sir 50:1-21
Solomon	2 Chr 5:1-7:10
of **TRUTH**	
Nebuchadnezzar	Dan 3:28-30
VIRTUE in	
David	Ps 145:4-7
PRAYER in	
for **BLESSING**	
David	2 Sam 7:1-29;
	21:1-14;
	1 Chr 28:1-29:30;
	Ps 20:1-5;
	103:19-22
Moses	Num 10:33-36
for **COMPASSION**	
Israelites	*Jdt 6:14-20
Manasseh	*Mana 1:6-7
Moses	Deut 3:23-29;
	9:25-29
for **COURAGE**	
Believers	Acts 4:23-31
for **DISCIPLESHIP**	
Abraham	Gen 21:22-34
Isaac	Gen 26:12-31
concerning **ENEMY**	
Esther	*Esth 14:1-19
Judith	*Jdt 9:1-14
Mordecai	*Esth 13:8-18
for **FAITH**	
Jesus	Lk 22:31-32;
	17:6-19;
	20-26
Paul	Eph 3:14-19;
	6:23-24
by **FAMILY**	
Hannah	1 Sam 1:1-28
Isaac	Gen 25:19-26
concerning **FEAR**	
David	1 Sam 23:1-13
Jacob	Gen 32:1-23
for **FULFILLMENT**	
Eli	1 Sam 1:1-28
Ezra	Ezra 8:21-23;
	Neh 9:9-11
Samuel	1 Sam 7:2-17
for **GOOD**	
Ezra	Neh 9:7-8
for **GRACE**	
Believers	Acts 4:23-31
David	2 Sam 12:1-31;
	24:1-25;
	1 Chr 21:1-22:1
Ezra	*1 Esd 8:71-90;
	*2 Esd 8:4-36
Hezekiah	2 Kgs 19:9b-37
Israelites	Num 21:4-9;
	Judg 4:1-3;
	6:1-6;
	7-10
Jehoshaphat	2 Chr 17:1-20:37
Manasseh	2 Chr 33:1-25;

for **GRACE** (cont'd)
Manasseh   *Mana 1:11-15
Moses   Ex 34:5b-9;
       Num 14:11-24;
       16:16-24;
       Deut 10:1-11
Paul   2 Cor 13:14;
       Eph 6:23-24;
       Phil 1:1-2;
       4:21-23

of **GRATITUDE**
David   1 Chr 17:1-27;
       Ps 7:17;
       138:1-3
Ezra   Ezra 7:27-28
Hannah   1 Sam 2:1-10
Paul   Eph 5:15-20;
       Phil 1:3-11

concerning **GRIEF**
Ezra   Ezra 10:1-6
Israelites   Judg 21:1-7
Moses   Ex 5:22-6:1
Nehemiah   Neh 1:1-4

concerning **GUILT**
Ezra   Ezra 9:6-15

for **JOY**
Jesus   Jn 17:6-19
Psalmist   Ps 84:1-2
Tobit   *Tb 11:7-19

concerning **LIFE**
Elijah   1 Kgs 17:1-24
Hezekiah   2 Kgs 20:1-11
Rebekah   Gen 25:19-26

concerning **LOVE**
Jesus   Jn 17:6-19;
       20-26
Paul   2 Cor 13:14;
       Eph 3:14-19;
       6:23-24

ONENESS in
Disciples   Acts 1:12-26
Jesus   Jn 17:6-19;
       20-26

for **PEACE**
Paul   Eph 6:23-24;
       Phil 1:1-2

PIETY in
Abraham   Gen 12:1-8
Jesus   Mk 6:45-52

revealing **PRAISE**
Azariah   *Azar 1:28-68
Believers   Acts 4:23-31
David   2 Sam 7:1-29;
       1 Chr 17:1-27;
       28:1-29:30;
       Ps 29:1-2;
       31:19-24;
       35:17-18;
       22-28;
       138:1-3
Ezra   Neh 9:6;
       *1 Esd 8:25-27;
       *2 Esd 13:51-58

RITE of
Ethiopian   Acts 8:26-40
Israelites   *1 Esd 7:10-15
Jews   *2 Mc 1:18-36
Levites   Ezra 6:19-22;
       Neh 12:30;
       44-13:3
Maccabeus   *1 Mc 4:36-61

RECONCILIATION through
for **FAMILY**
Jews   *2 Mc 1:18-36;
       2:16-18
for **LEADERSHIP**
Nehemiah   Neh 13:10-14
with **SACRIFICE**
Aaron   Lev 16:1-5;
       1 Chr 6:49-53
Moses   Lev 8:1-36
Noah   Gen 8:13-22
Priest   Lev 15:1-33;
       Num 15:22-31

REJECTION in
of **PRAYER**
Paul   2 Cor 12:1-10
as **PUNISHMENT**
God   Zech 14:1-21
through **disRESPECT**
John   Rev 22:6-21

for **REPENTANCE**
PRAYER in
Ezra   Ezra 9:6-15
Nehemiah   Neh 1:5-11a
of **SIN**
Israelites   Neh 9:1-5a

RESPECT in
ACCEPTANCE of
Believers   Heb 12:12-29
through **DIGNITY**
Women   1 Cor 11:2-16
FEAR revealing
David   1 Chr 15:1-16:43;
       Ps 5:8-10
revealing **GRATITUDE**
David   1 Chr 15:1-16:43
God   Rev 4:1-11;
       7:9-17;
       11:15-19
HUMILITY in
Women   1 Cor 11:2-16
for **JUSTICE**
God   Rev 15:1-16:1
through **PIETY**
John   Rev 19:6-10
PRAISE through
God   Rev 4:1-11;
       7:9-17;
       11:15-19;
       15:1-16:1;
       19:1-5
John   Rev 5:1-14
Nebuchadnezzar   Dan 2:46-49
Paul   Rom 11:33-36
Psalmist   Ps 96:7-9

disRESPECT in
through **BLASPHEMY**
Judahites   Jer 7:29-8:3
through **REJECTION**
John   Rev 22:6-21

RITE in
BLESSING through
David   Ps 26:8-12
DIGNITY in
Believers   1 Cor 11:27-34

as **PROMISE**
Psalmist   Ps 66:13-20
RECONCILIATION through
Aaron   Lev 16:1-5;
                              1 Chr 6:49-53
Moses   Lev 8:1-36
Noah   Gen 8:13-22
Priest   Lev 15:1-33;
                              Num 15:22-31
as **RITE**
Abel   Gen 4:1-16
Asa   2 Chr 14:1-16:14
Babylonians   2 Kgs 17:24-41
Balaam   Num 22:41-23:12;
                              27-24:13
Balak   Num 22:36-40
David   2 Sam 6:1-23;
                              24:1-25;
                              1 Chr 15:1-16:43;
                              21:1-22:1;
                              Ps 5:1-3
Gideon   Judg 6:11-32
Hannah   1 Sam 1:1-28
Hezekiah   2 Chr 30:1-31:21
Israelites   Num 7:1-89;
                              Judg 2:1-5;
                              20:24-28;
                              21:1-7;
                              1 Sam 6:1-7:1;
                              11:1-15;
                              Ezra 3:1-3a;
                              3b-6;
                              Neh 12:43;
                              *1 Esd 5:47-55;
                              7:1-9;
                              10-15;
                              *Jdt 16:18-20
Jethro   Ex 18:1-12
Jews   *2 Mc 1:18-36
Joash   2 Chr 24:1-27
Joshua   Josh 8:30-35
Josiah   2 Chr 34:1-35:27
Maccabeus   *1 Mc 4:36-61
Manoah   Judg 13:15-23
Moabite   2 Kgs 3:1-27
Moses   Ex 24:1-18;
                              40:1-33;
                              Num 28:1-2
Noah   Gen 8:13-22
Psalmist   Ps 96:7-9;
                              116:12-19
Samuel   1 Sam 7:2-17;
                              16:1-13
Solomon   1 Kgs 3:1-15;
                              8:1-13;
                              62-66;
                              9:25;
                              2 Chr 1:1-17;
                              2:1-4:22;
                              5:1-7:10;
                              8:1-18
SIGNS of
Israelites   *1 Esd 5:56-58
Jeroboam   1 Kgs 12:25-33
for **SIN**
Aaron   Lev 9:1-24
Ahaz   2 Kgs 16:1-4;
                              2 Chr 26:1-28:27
Author   Heb 10:1-18
Heliodorus   *2 Mc 3:1-40
High Priest   Heb 5:1-10

for **SIN** (cont'd)
Israelites   Ezra 6:13-18;
                              8:31-36
Levites   2 Chr 29:1-36
Maccabeus   *2 Mc 12:38-45
Manasseh   2 Kgs 21:1-18;
                              2 Chr 33:1-25
Priest   Lev 15:1-33
Priests   Ezra 10:16-19
Saul   1 Sam 13:1-23
through **STEWARDSHIP**
Israelites   Ex 30:11-16;
                              1 Chr 23:1-26:32;
                              Neh 10:37a;
                              37b-39a

VIRTUE in
Sirach   *Sir 35:1-11

SADNESS in
SIGNS of
Israelites   Ezra 3:12-13

for **SALVATION**
in **VICTORY**
Miriam   Ex 15:19-21

SALVATION through
JOY in
Women   Ex 15:19-21
PIETY in
Samaritan   Jn 4:1-26
SACREDNESS in
Isaiah   Is 27:12-13
Priests   *2 Mc 14:34-36

SECURITY in
from **VIOLENCE**
Ezra   *1 Esd 8:50-53
for **WEALTH**
Micah   Judg 17:7-13

SELFISHNESS in
through **STEWARDSHIP**
Micah   Judg 17:7-13

SERVICE in
Satan   Rev 13:1-4
DESIRE to
Israelites   Josh 24:16-24
ELECTION to
Aaron   Ex 29:1-9
FIDELITY in
Israelites   Neh 10:39b
GIFT of
Believers   1 Cor 14:26-33
KNOWLEDGE of
Levites   1 Chr 9:17-34;
                              Neh 12:24-26
MEDIATION through
David   Ps 20:1-5
Levites   2 Chr 29:1-36
as **RITE**
Levites   1 Chr 6:31-48;
                              Neh 12:44-13:3

SEX in sanctuary
PUNISHMENT for
Josiah   2 Kgs 23:4-15
as **SIN**
Gentiles   *2 Mc 6:1-11

SHARING in
   of **GIFT**
      Believers   1 Cor 14:26-33

SIGNS in
   of **BLASPHEMY**
      Antiochus   *1 Mc 1:54-61
   of **DESTRUCTION**
      Alcimus   *1 Mc 9:54-57
      Israelites   2 Chr 30:1-31:21
      Josiah   2 Kgs 23:4-15;
                            2 Chr 34:1-35:27
      Manasseh   2 Chr 33:1-25
   of **FULFILLMENT**
      Solomon   1 Kgs 6:1-38
   of **GRACE**
      Naaman   2 Kgs 5:1-19
   of **JOY**
      Israelites   Ezra 3:12-13
   of **LOVE**
      Wise Men   Mt 2:1-12
   of **MIRACLE**
      Elijah   1 Kgs 18:1-46
      God   Lev 9:1-24
   of **POLITICS**
      Jeroboam   1 Kgs 12:25-33
   of **SACREDNESS**
      Israelites   Ex 25:10-22;
                            23-30;
                            31-40;
                            26:1-14;
                            15-30;
                            31-37;
                            27:1-8;
                            9-19;
                            28:1-5;
                            6-12;
                            13-30;
                            31-35;
                            36-39;
                            40-43;
                            30:1-10;
                            11-16;
                            33:7-11;
                            1 Kgs 8:1-13;
                            *1 Esd 6:1-2
      Moses   Ex 30:34-38
      Solomon   1 Kgs 5:1-18;
                            6:1-38
   of **SACRIFICE**
      Israelites   *1 Esd 5:56-58
      Jeroboam   1 Kgs 12:25-33
   of **SADNESS**
      Israelites   Ezra 3:12-13

SIN in
   DISOBEDIENCE as
      Israelites   2 Kgs 14:1-4;
                            15:1-7
      Judahites   2 Kgs 11:21-12:3;
                            15:32-38
   IDOLATRY as
      Ahaz   2 Chr 26:1-28:27
      Amaziah   2 Chr 25:1-28
      Amon   2 Chr 33:1-25
      Babylonians   2 Kgs 17:24-41
      Jeroboam   1 Kgs 12:25-33
      Joash   2 Chr 24:1-27
      Manasseh   2 Kgs 21:1-18;
                            2 Chr 33:1-25

KILLING as
      Ahaz   2 Kgs 16:1-4
PARADOX in
      Babylonians   2 Kgs 17:24-41
PRIDE as
      Uzziah   2 Chr 26:1-28:27
REPENTANCE of
      Israelites   Neh 9:1-5a
   against **SACREDNESS**
      Jeroboam   1 Kgs 13:1-34
SACRIFICE for
      Aaron   Lev 9:1-24
      Ahaz   2 Kgs 16:1-4;
                          2 Chr 26:1-28:27
      Author   Heb 10:1-18
      Heliodorus   *2 Mc 3:1-40
      High Priest   Heb 5:1-10
      Israelites   Ezra 6:13-18;
                          8:31-36
      Levites   2 Chr 29:1-36
      Maccabeus   *2 Mc 12:38-45
      Manasseh   2 Kgs 21:1-18;
                          2 Chr 33:1-25
      Priest   Lev 15:1-33
      Priests   Ezra 10:16-19
      Saul   1 Sam 13:1-23
SEX as
      Gentiles   *2 Mc 6:1-11

of **SIN**
   DESTRUCTION of
      Josiah   2 Kgs 23:24-25a

in **SPIRIT**
   BEHAVIOR revealing
      Paul   Phil 3:1-3
   of **TRUTH**
      Believers   Jn 4:1-26
      Jesus   Jn 4:1-26

STEWARDSHIP of
   JOY in
      Israelites   1 Chr 28:1-29:30
      Levites   Neh 12:27-29
   LOVE in
      Widow   Lk 21:1-4
      Widows   Mk 12:41-44
   OBEDIENCE in
      Israelites   Ex 35:4-29
   ORDER in
      Nehemiah   Neh 13:30-31
   SACREDNESS in
      Israelites   Ex 25:1-9;
                          27:20-21;
                          29:10-18;
                          30:17-21;
                          Neh 10:35-36
   SACRIFICE in
      Israelites   Ex 30:11-16;
                          1 Chr 23:1-26:32;
                          Neh 10:37a;
                          37b-39a
   SELFISHNESS in
      Micah   Judg 17:7-13
   WEALTH through
      Israelites   Josh 6:22-27;
                          Ezra 2:68-70;
                          3:7-9;
                          Neh 10:31;
                          12:44-13:3;
                          1 Chr 28:1-29:30

WEALTH through (cont'd)
 Jacob — Gen 28:10-22
 People — Ezra 1:6
WILL in
 Israelites — Ezra 3:3b-6

TEMPERANCE in
VIRTUE in
 Women — 1 Tim 2:8-15

of **TRUTH**
 PRAISE through
  Nebuchadnezzar — Dan 3:28-30
 PRIDE in
  Pharisees — Mt 23:5-12
 SPIRIT of
  Believers — Jn 4:1-26
  Jesus — Jn 4:1-26

for **VICTORY**
 in **PRAYER**
  David — Ps 20:1-5
  Hezekiah — 2 Chr 32:1-33
  Jacob — Gen 32:1-23
  Jesus — Jn 17:6-19
 in **SALVATION**
  Miriam — Ex 15:19-21

VIRTUE in
 PRAISE of
  David — Ps 145:4-7
 of **SACRIFICE**
  Sirach — *Sir 35:1-11
 of **TEMPERANCE**
  Women — 1 Tim 2:8-15

WEALTH in
 BEHAVIOR revealing
  Cyrus — *1 Esd 2:8 15
  Israelites — *1 Esd 5:47-55
  Levites — *1 Esd 2:8-15
 COMMITMENT to
  Israelites — Neh 10:37a; 37b-39a
 PROMISE of
  Israelites — *1 Esd 5:44-46
 PROVIDENCE through
  Israelites — Deut 26:1-11
 SECURITY in
  Micah — Judg 17:7-13
 STEWARDSHIP of
  Israelites — Josh 6:22-27; Ezra 2:68-70; 3:7-9; Neh 10:31; 12:44-13:3; 1 Chr 28:1-29:30
  Jacob — Gen 28:10-22
  People — Ezra 1:6

WILL in
 STEWARDSHIP of
  Israelites — Ezra 3:3b-6

WISDOM in
 PRAYER for
  David — 2 Sam 5:17-25; 1 Chr 14:1-17
  Ezra — *2 Esd 3:1-36
  Manoah — Judg 13:8
  Paul — Eph 3:14-19

PRAYER for (cont'd)
 Solomon — *Wis 9:1-18
WITNESS in
 PRAYER for
  Paul — Rom 1:8-15

YOUTH

in **AUTHORITY**
 INSTRUCTION on
  Preacher — Eccl 9:17-10:20

BEHAVIOR concerning
 INSTRUCTION on
  Jesus — Mt 19:13-15; Mk 10:13-16
  Paul — Eph 6:1-4; Col 3:18-4:1
  Solomon — Prov 22:1-16

CONFRONTATION with
 INSTRUCTION on
  Jesus — Mk 9:42-48
  Paul — 2 Cor 6:11-13

FIDELITY of
 to **DEITY**
  God — Eccl 11:9-12:7

of **FOLLOWER**
 JUDGMENT on
  Corinthians — 1 Cor 3:1-4

INSTRUCTION on
 Jesus — Mt 19:13-15; Mk 10:13-16
 Paul — Eph 6:1-4; Col 3:18-4:1
 Solomon — Prov 22:1-16
 in **AUTHORITY**
  Preacher — Eccl 9:17-10:20
 in **NEW AGE**
  Jesus — Mt 19:13-15; Mk 10:13-16; Lk 18:15-17
 concerning **TRUTH**
  Author — Heb 5:11-14
  Paul — Eph 6:1-4

JUDGMENT on
 of **FOLLOWER**s
  Corinthians — 1 Cor 3:1-4
 INSTRUCTION on
  Paul — 1 Cor 3:1-4

KNOWLEDGE of
 INSTRUCTION on
  Paul — Gal 4:1-3

in **NEW AGE**
 INSTRUCTION on
  Jesus — Mt 19:13-15; Mk 10:13-16; Lk 18:15-17

PROVIDENCE for
    INSTRUCTION on
        Jesus   Mt 18:5-6;
                        Lk 9:46-48;
                        17:1-6

PUNISHMENT for
    INSTRUCTION on
        Solomon   Prov 22:22-23:14;
                        29:1-27

as **QUALITY OF LIFE**
        God   Is 40:12-31
    INSTRUCTION on
        Solomon   Prov 20:1-30

RESPECT for
    INSTRUCTION on
        Jesus   Mt 18:10
        Paul   1 Tim 4:11-16;
                        5:1-2

RESURRECTION through
    INSTRUCTION on
        Solomon   *Wis 4:10-20

SALVATION through
    INSTRUCTION on
        Jesus   Mt 19:13-15;
                        Mk 10:13-16

TRUTH through
    INSTRUCTION on
        Author   Heb 5:11-14
        Paul   Eph 6:1-4